20th International Conference on Spoken Language Translation (IWSLT 2023)

Toronto, Canada
13 - 14 July 2023

ISBN: 978-1-7138-8227-5

Printed from e-media with permission by:

Curran Associates, Inc.
57 Morehouse Lane
Red Hook, NY 12571

Some format issues inherent in the e-media version may also appear in this print version.

Printed with permission by Curran Associates, Inc. (2024)

Association for Computational Linguistics
209 N. Eighth Street
Stroudsburg, Pennsylvania 18360

Phone: 1-570-476-8006
Fax: 1-570-476-0860

acl@aclweb.org

Additional copies of this publication are available from:

Curran Associates, Inc.
57 Morehouse Lane
Red Hook, NY 12571 USA
Phone: 845-758-0400
Fax: 845-758-2633
Email: curran@proceedings.com
Web: www.proceedings.com

IWSLT 2023

The 20th International Conference on Spoken Language Translation

Proceedings of the Conference

July 13-14, 2023

The IWSLT 2023 organizers gratefully acknowledge the support from our sponsors: aiXplain, Apple, AppTek, and Translated.

Diamond

translated.

Gold

aiXplain

Silver

AppTek

Order copies of this and other ACL proceedings from:

Association for Computational Linguistics (ACL)
209 N. Eighth Street
Stroudsburg, PA 18360
USA
Tel: +1-570-476-8006
Fax: +1-570-476-0860
acl@aclweb.org

Introduction

The International Conference on Spoken Language Translation (IWSLT) is the premiere annual scientific conference for the study, development and evaluation of spoken language translation technology. Launched in 2004 and spun out from the C-STAR speech translation consortium before it (1992-2003), IWSLT is the main venue for scientific exchange on all topics related to speech-to-text translation, speech-to-speech translation, simultaneous and consecutive translation, speech dubbing, cross-lingual communication including all multimodal, emotional, paralinguistic, and stylistic aspects and their applications in the field. The conference organizes evaluations around challenge areas, and presents scientific papers and system descriptions. IWSLT is organized by the Special Interest Group on Spoken Language Translation (SIGSLT), which is supported by ACL, ISCA and ELRA.

This year, IWSLT featured nine shared tasks in spoken language translation: (i) simultaneous and (ii) offline translation, (iii) automatic subtitling and (iv) dubbing, (v) speech-to-speech translation, (vi) multilingual, (vii) dialect and (viii) low-resource speech translation, and (ix) formality control. Each shared task was coordinated by one or more chairs. The resulting evaluation campaigns attracted a total of 31 teams, from academia, research centers, and industry. System submissions resulted in system papers that will be presented at the conference. Following our call for papers, this year 51 submissions were received. In a blind review process, 8 research papers were selected out of 15 for oral presentation (57%) in addition to 37 system papers.

The program committee is excited about the quality of the accepted papers and expects lively discussion and exchange at the conference. The conference chairs and organizers would like to express their gratitude to everyone who contributed and supported IWSLT. In particular, we wish to thank our Diamond sponsors Apple and Translated, our Gold sponsor aiXplain, and our Silver sponsor AppTek. We thank the shared tasks chairs, organizers, and participants, the program committee members, as well as all the authors that went the extra mile to submit system and research papers to IWSLT, and make this year's conference a big success. We also wish to express our sincere gratitude to ACL for hosting our conference and for arranging the logistics and infrastructure that allow us to hold IWSLT 2023 as a hybrid conference.

Welcome to IWSLT 2023, welcome to Toronto!

Marine Carpuat, Program Chair
Marcello Federico and Alex Waibel, Conference Chairs

Organizing Committee

Conference Chairs

Marcello Federico, AWS AI Labs, USA
Alex Waibel, CMU, USA

Program Chair

Marine Carpuat, UMD, USA

Sponsorship Chair

Sebastian Stüker, Zoom, Germany

Evaluation Chairs

Jan Niehues, KIT, Germany

Website and Publication Chair

Elizabeth Salesky, JHU, USA

Publicity Chair

Atul Kr. Ohja, University of Galway, Ireland

Program Committee

Program Committee

Sweta Agrawal, University of Maryland, USA
Duygu Ataman, University of Zurich, Switzerland
Laurent Besacier, Naver Labs, France
Roldano Cattoni, FBK, Italy
Alexandra Chronopoulou, LMU Munich, Germany
Josep Maria Crego, Systran, France
Mattia Di Gangi, AppTek, Germany
Qianqian Dong, ByteDance AI Lab, China
Akiko Eriguchi, Microsoft, USA
Carlos Escolano, Universitat Politècnica de Catalunya, Spain
Markus Freitag, Google, USA
Hirofumi Inaguma, Meta AI, USA
Tom Ko, ByteDance AI Lab, China
Surafel Melaku Lakew, Amazon AI, USA
Yves Lepage, Waseda University, Japan
Xutai Ma, Meta AI, USA
Wolfgang Macherey, Google, USA
Prashant Mathur, AWS AI Labs, USA
Evgeny Matusov, AppTek, Germany
Kenton Murray, Johns Hopkins University, USA
Maria Nadejde, AWS AI Labs, USA
Matteo Negri, FBK, Italy
Xing Niu, AWS AI Labs, USA
Raghavendra Reddy Pappagari, Johns Hopkins University, USA
Juan Pino, Meta AI, USA
Elijah Rippeth, UMD, USA
Elizabeth Salesky, Johns Hopkins University, USA
Rico Sennrich, University of Zurich, Switzerland
Matthias Sperber, Apple, USA
Sebastian Stüker, Zoom, Germany
Katsuhito Sudoh, NAIST, Japan
Brian Thompson, AWS AI Labs, USA
Marco Turchi, Zoom, Germany
David Vilar, Google, Germany
Changhan Wang, Meta AI, USA
Krzystof Wolk, Polish-Japanese Academy of Information Technology, Poland

Table of Contents

Program

Thursday, July 13, 2023

08:30 - 09:10	*Welcome Remarks*
08:45 - 09:15	*Overview of the IWSLT 2023 Evaluation Campaign*
09:30 - 10:30	*Invited Talk*
10:30 - 11:00	*Coffee Break*
11:30 - 12:30	*Session 1 (Posters): System Papers*
12:30 - 14:00	*Lunch Break*
14:00 - 15:30	*Session 2 (Posters): System Papers*
15:30 - 16:00	*Coffee Break*
16:00 - 18:00	*Session 3 (Posters): Scientific Papers, including Findings of ACL*

Friday, July 14, 2023

09:00 - 10:30	*Session 4 (Oral): Scientific Papers*
10:30 - 11:00	*Coffee Break*
11:00 - 12:30	*Session 5 (Posters): System Papers*
12:30 - 14:00	*Lunch Break*
14:00 - 15:30	*Session 6 (Posters): System Papers*
15:30 - 16:00	*Coffee Break*
16:00 - 17:00	*Panel Discussion*
17:00 - 17:15	*Best Paper Awards*
17:15 - 17:30	*Closing Remarks*

FINDINGS OF THE IWSLT 2023 EVALUATION CAMPAIGN

Milind Agarwal[1] Sweta Agrawal[2] Antonios Anastasopoulos[1] Luisa Bentivogli[3] Ondřej Bojar[4] Claudia Borg[5] Marine Carpuat[2] Roldano Cattoni[3] Mauro Cettolo[3] Mingda Chen[6] William Chen[7] Khalid Choukri[8] Alexandra Chronopoulou[9] Anna Currey[10] Thierry Declerck[11] Qianqian Dong[12] Kevin Duh[13] Yannick Estève[14] Marcello Federico[10] Souhir Gahbiche[15] Barry Haddow[16] Benjamin Hsu[10] Phu Mon Htut[10] Hirofumi Inaguma[6] Dávid Javorský[4] John Judge[17] Yasumasa Kano[18] Tom Ko[12] Rishu Kumar[4] Pengwei Li[6] Xutai Ma[6] Prashant Mathur[10] Evgeny Matusov[19] Paul McNamee[13] John P. McCrae[20] Kenton Murray[13] Maria Nadejde[10] Satoshi Nakamura[18] Matteo Negri[3] Ha Nguyen[14] Jan Niehues[21] Xing Niu[10] Atul Kr. Ojha[20] John E. Ortega[22] Proyag Pal[16] Juan Pino[6] Lonneke van der Plas[23] Peter Polák[4] Elijah Rippeth[2] Elizabeth Salesky[13] Jiatong Shi[7] Matthias Sperber[24] Sebastian Stüker[25] Katsuhito Sudoh[18] Yun Tang[6] Brian Thompson[10] Kevin Tran[6] Marco Turchi[25] Alex Waibel[7] Mingxuan Wang[12] Shinji Watanabe[7] Rodolfo Zevallos[26]

[1]GMU [2]UMD [3]FBK [4]Charles U. [5]U. Malta [6]Meta [7]CMU [8]ELDA [9]LMU [10]AWS [11]DFKI [12]ByteDance [13]JHU [14]Avignon U. [15]Airbus [16]U. Edinburgh [18]NAIST [19]AppTek [20]U. Galway [21]KIT [22]Northeastern U. [23]IDIAP [24]Apple [25]Zoom [26]U. Pompeu Fabra

Abstract

This paper reports on the shared tasks organized by the 20th IWSLT Conference. The shared tasks address 9 scientific challenges in spoken language translation: simultaneous and offline translation, automatic subtitling and dubbing, speech-to-speech translation, multilingual, dialect and low-resource speech translation, and formality control. The shared tasks attracted a total of 38 submissions by 31 teams. The growing interest towards spoken language translation is also witnessed by the constantly increasing number of shared task organizers and contributors to the overview paper, almost evenly distributed across industry and academia.

1 Introduction

The International Conference on Spoken Language Translation (IWSLT) is the premier annual scientific conference for all aspects of spoken language translation (SLT). IWSLT is organized by the Special Interest Group on Spoken Language Translation (SIG-SLT), which is supported by ACL, ISCA and ELRA. Like in all previous editions (Akiba et al., 2004; Eck and Hori, 2005; Paul, 2006; Fordyce, 2007; Paul, 2008, 2009; Paul et al., 2010; Federico et al., 2011, 2012; Cettolo et al., 2013, 2014, 2015, 2016, 2017; Niehues et al., 2018, 2019; Ansari et al., 2020; Anastasopoulos et al., 2021, 2022b),this year's conference was preceded by an evaluation campaign featuring shared tasks addressing scientific challenges in SLT.

This paper reports on the 2023 IWSLT Evaluation Campaign, which offered the following 9 shared tasks:

- **Offline SLT**, with focus on speech-to-text translation of recorded conferences and interviews from English to German, Japanese and Chinese.

- **Simultaneous SLT**, focusing on speech-to-text translation of streamed audio of conferences and interviews from English to German, Japanese and Chinese.

- **Automatic Subtitling**, with focus on speech-to-subtitle translation of audio-visual documents from English to German and Spanish.

- **Multilingual SLT**, with focus on speech-to-text translation of recorded scientific talks from

Proceedings of the 20th International Conference on Spoken Language Translation (IWSLT 2023), pages 1–61
July 13-14, 2023

Team	Organization
ALEXA AI	Amazon Alexa AI, USA (Vishnu et al., 2023)
APPTEK	AppTek, Germany (Bahar et al., 2023)
BIGAI	Beijing Institute of General Artificial Intelligence, China (Xie, 2023)
BIT	Beijing Institute of Technology, China (Wang et al., 2023b)
BUT	Brno University of Technology, Czechia (Kesiraju et al., 2023)
CMU	Carnegie Mellon University, USA (Yan et al., 2023)
CUNI-KIT	Charles University, Czechia, and KIT, Germany (Polák et al., 2023)
FBK	Fondazione Bruno Kessler, Italy (Papi et al., 2023)
GMU	George Mason University, USA (Mbuya and Anastasopoulos, 2023)
HW-TSC	Huawei Translation Services Center, China (Li et al., 2023; Wang et al., 2023a) (Guo et al., 2023; Shang et al., 2023; Rao et al., 2023)
I2R	Institute for Infocomm Research, A*STAR, Singapore (Huzaifah et al., 2023)
JHU	Johns Hopkins University, USA (Hussein et al., 2023; Xinyuan et al., 2023)
KIT	Karlsruhe Institute of Technology, Germany (Liu et al., 2023)
KU	Kyoto University, Japan (Yang et al., 2023)
KU X UPSTAGE	Korea University X Upstage, South Korea (Wu et al., 2023; Lee et al., 2023)
MATESUB	Translated Srl, Italy (Perone, 2023)
MINETRANS	U. of Sci. and Techn. of China, Tancient AI Lab, State Key Lab. of Cognitive Intelligence (Du et al., 2023)
NAIST	Nara Institute of Science and Technology, Japan (Fukuda et al., 2023)
NAVER	NAVER Labs Europe, France (Gow-Smith et al., 2023)
NIUTRANS	NiuTrans, China (Han et al., 2023)
NPU-MSXF	Northwestern Polytechnical U., Nanjing U., MaShang Co., China (Song et al., 2023)
NEURODUB	NeuroDub, Armenia
NEMO	NVIDIA NeMo, USA(Hrinchuk et al., 2023)
ON-TRAC	ON-TRAC Consortium, France (Laurent et al., 2023)
QUESPA	Northeastern U, USA, U. de Pompeu Fabra, Spain, CMU, USA(Ortega et al., 2023)
UPC	Universitat Politècnica de Catalunya, Spain (Tsiamas et al., 2023)
SRI-B	Samsung R&D Institute Bangalore, India (Radhakrishnan et al., 2023)
UCSC	U. of California, Santa Cruz, USA (Vakharia et al., 2023)
UM-DFKI	U. of Malta, Malta, and DFKI, Germany (Williams et al., 2023)
USTC	U. of Science and Technology of China (Deng et al., 2023; Zhou et al., 2023)
XIAOMI	Xiaomi AI Lab, China (Huang et al., 2023)

Table 1: List of Participants

English into Arabic, Chinese, Dutch, French, German, Japanese, Farsi, Portuguese, Russian, and Turkish.

- **Speech-to-speech translation**, focusing on natural-speech to synthetic-speech translation of recorded utterances from English to Chinese.
- **Automatic Dubbing**, focusing on dubbing of short video clips from German to English.
- **Dialect SLT**, focusing on speech translation of recorded utterances from Tunisian Arabic to English.
- **Low-resource SLT**, focusing on speech translation of recorded utterances from Irish to English, Marathi to Hindi, Maltese to English, Pashto to French, Tamasheq to French, and Quechua to Spanish.
- **Formality Control for SLT**, focusing on formality/register control for spoken language translation from English to Korean, Vietnamese, EU Portuguese, and Russian.

The shared tasks attracted 38 submissions by 31 teams (see Table 1) representing both academic and industrial organizations. The following sections report on each shared task in detail, in particular: the goal and automatic metrics adopted for the task, the data used for training and testing data, the received submissions and the summary of results. Detailed results for some of the shared tasks are reported in a corresponding appendix.

2 Offline SLT

Offline speech translation is the task of translating audio speech in one language into text in a different target language, without any specific time or structural constraints (as, for instance, in the simultaneous, subtitling, and dubbing tasks). Under this general problem definition, the goal of the offline ST track (one of the speech tasks with the longest tradition at the IWSLT campaign) is to constantly challenge a technology in rapid evolution by gradually introducing novelty aspects that raise the difficulty bar.

2.1 Challenge

In continuity with last year, participants were given three sub-tasks corresponding to three language directions, namely English→German/Japanese/Chinese. Participation was allowed both with *cascade* architectures combining automatic speech recognition (ASR) and machine translation (MT) systems as core components, or by means of *end-to-end* approaches that directly translate the input speech without intermediate symbolic representations. Also this year, one of the main objectives was indeed to measure the performance difference between the two paradigms, a gap that recent research (Bentivogli et al., 2021) and IWSLT findings (Ansari et al., 2020; Anastasopoulos et al., 2021, 2022b) indicate as gradually decreasing.

The other main objective of this round was to assess the ability of SLT technology to deal with complex scenarios involving different types of input characterized by phenomena like spontaneous speech, noisy audio conditions and overlapping speakers. In light of this, the main novelty of the 2022 offline SLT task lies in a richer variety of speech data to be processed. To this aim, in addition to the classic TED talks test set, two novel test sets were released:

- **ACL presentations**, in which a single speaker is presenting on a stage. Although similar to the TED talks scenario, additional challenges posed by this test set include the presence of non-native speakers, different accents, variable recording quality, terminology, and controlled interactions with a second speaker.
- **Press conferences and interviews**, in which two persons interact on different topics. Inherent challenges, therefore, include the presence of spontaneous speech, non-native speakers, different accents, and controlled interaction with a second speaker.

All the test sets were used for evaluation in the English-German sub-task, while only TED Talks and ACL presentations were used to test the submissions to the English-Japanese and English-Chinese sub-tasks.

2.2 Data and Metrics

Training and development data. Participants were offered the possibility to submit systems built under three training data conditions:

1. **Constrained**: the allowed training data is limited to a medium-sized framework in order to keep the training time and resource requirements manageable. The complete list[1] of allowed training resources (speech, speech-to-text-parallel, text-parallel, text-monolingual) does not include any pre-trained language model.
2. **Constrained with large language models** (constrained^{+LLM}): in addition to all the constrained resources, a restricted selection[1] of large language models is allowed to give participants the possibility to leverage large language models and medium-sized resources.
3. **Unconstrained**: any resource, pre-trained language models included, can be used with the exception of evaluation sets. This setup is proposed to allow the participation of teams equipped with high computational power and effective in-house solutions built on additional resources.

The development data allowed under the constrained condition consist of the dev set from IWSLT 2010, as well as the test sets used for the 2010, 2013-2015 and 2018-2020 IWSLT campaigns. Besides this TED-derived material, additional development data were released to cover the two new scenarios included in this round of evaluation. For the ACL domain, 5 presentations from the ACL 2022 conference with translations and transcriptions were provided. Due to additional constraints, these references were generated by human post-editing of automatic transcriptions and translation. For the press conferences and interviews domain, 12 videos (total duration: 1h:3m) were selected from publicly available interviews from the Multimedia Centre of the European Parliament (EPTV)[2].

[1] See the IWSLT 2023 offline track web page: `https://iwslt.org/2023/offline`

[2] `https://multimedia.europarl.europa.eu`

Test data. Three new test sets were created for the three language directions. The new test sets include heterogeneous material drawn from each scenario. For the traditional TED scenario, a new set of 42 talks not included in the current public release of MuST-C was selected to build the en-de test set.[3] Starting from this material, the talks for which Japanese and Chinese translations are available were selected to build the en-zh and en-ja test sets (respectively, 38 and 37 talks). Similar to the 2021 and 2022 editions, we consider two different types of target-language references, namely:

- The original TED translations. Since these references come in the form of subtitles, they are subject to compression and omissions to adhere to the TED subtitling guidelines.[4] This makes them less literal compared to standard, unconstrained translations;
- Unconstrained translations. These references were created from scratch[5] by adhering to the usual translation guidelines. They are hence exact translations (i.e. literal and with proper punctuation).

For the ACL presentation scenario, paper presentations from ACL 2022 were transcribed and translated into the target languages. A detailed description of the data set can be found in Salesky et al. (2023). There are 5 presentations in each of the dev and test sets with a total duration 1h per split. Talks were selected to include diverse paper topics and speaker backgrounds. This test set is shared with the Multilingual task (§ 5).

For the press conferences and interviews scenario, the test set comprises 10 EPTV videos of variable duration (6m on average), amounting to a total of 1h:1m. The details of the new test sets are reported in Table 2.

Metrics. Systems were evaluated with respect to their capability to produce translations similar to the target-language references. The similarity was measured in terms of BLEU and COMET (Rei et al., 2020a) metrics. The submitted runs were ranked based on the BLEU calculated on the concatenation of the three test sets by using automatic resegmentation[6] of the hypotheses based on the reference translations. For the BLEU computed on the concatenation of the three test sets, the new unconstrained ones have been used for the TED data. As observed on IWSLT 2022 manual evaluation of simultaneous speech-to-text translation (Macháček et al., 2023), COMET is correlating with human judgments best and BLEU correlation is also satisfactory. Moreover, to meet the requests of last year's participants, a human evaluation was performed on the best-performing submission of each participant.

	Talks / Videos	Duration
English-German		
TED	42	3h:47m:53s
ACL	5	59m:22s
EPTV	10	1h:1m
English-Chinese		
TED	37	3h:2m:22s
ACL	5	59m:22s
English-Japanese		
TED	38	3h:19m:34s
ACL	5	59m:22s

Table 2: Statistics of the official test sets for the IWSLT 2023 offline speech translation task.

2.3 Submissions

This year, 10 teams participated in the offline task, submitting a total of 37 runs. Table 3 provides a breakdown of the participation in each sub-task showing, for each training data condition, the number of participants, the number of submitted runs and, for each training data condition (constrained, constrained^{+LLM}, unconstrained), the number of submitted runs obtained with cascade and direct systems.

- BIGAI (Xie, 2023) participated both with cascade and direct models for en-de, en-ja, and en-zh translations, which were trained under the constrained^{+LLM} condition. The cascade is the concatenation of an ASR model and an MT system. The ASR consists of the first 12 Transformer layers

[3] This set of 42 TED talks is also referred to as the "Common" test set (not to be confused with MuST-C "tst-COMMON") because it serves in both Offline and Simultaneous `https://iwslt.org/2023/simultaneous` tasks.

[4] `http://www.ted.com/participate/translate/subtitling-tips`

[5] We would like to thank Meta for providing us with this new set of references.

[6] Performed with mwerSegmenter - `https://www-i6.informatik.rwth-aachen.de/web/Software/mwerSegmenter.tar.gz`

<table>
<tr><th colspan="11">English-German</th></tr>
<tr><th>Participants</th><th>Runs</th><th colspan="3">Constrained</th><th colspan="3">Constrained^{+LLM}</th><th colspan="3">Unconstrained</th></tr>
<tr><td rowspan="2">6</td><td rowspan="2">16</td><td rowspan="2">2</td><td>Cascade</td><td>1</td><td rowspan="2">12</td><td>Cascade</td><td>1</td><td rowspan="2">2</td><td>Cascade</td><td>2</td></tr>
<tr><td>Direct</td><td>1</td><td>Direct</td><td>11</td><td>Direct</td><td>-</td></tr>
<tr><th colspan="11">English-Chinese</th></tr>
<tr><th>Participants</th><th>Runs</th><th colspan="3">Constrained</th><th colspan="3">Constrained^{+LLM}</th><th colspan="3">Unconstrained</th></tr>
<tr><td rowspan="2">7</td><td rowspan="2">16</td><td rowspan="2">5</td><td>Cascade</td><td>3</td><td rowspan="2">3</td><td>Cascade</td><td>1</td><td rowspan="2">8</td><td>Cascade</td><td>7</td></tr>
<tr><td>Direct</td><td>2</td><td>Direct</td><td>2</td><td>Direct</td><td>1</td></tr>
<tr><th colspan="11">English-Japanese</th></tr>
<tr><th>Participants</th><th>Runs</th><th colspan="3">Constrained</th><th colspan="3">Constrained^{+LLM}</th><th colspan="3">Unconstrained</th></tr>
<tr><td rowspan="2">3</td><td rowspan="2">5</td><td rowspan="2">2</td><td>Cascade</td><td>1</td><td rowspan="2">2</td><td>Cascade</td><td>1</td><td rowspan="2">1</td><td>Cascade</td><td>1</td></tr>
<tr><td>Direct</td><td>1</td><td>Direct</td><td>1</td><td>Direct</td><td>-</td></tr>
</table>

Table 3: Breakdown of the participation in each sub-task (English→German, English→Chinese, English→Japanese) of the IWSLT offline ST track. For each language direction, we report the number of participants, the number of submitted runs and, for each training data condition (constrained, constrained^{+LLM}, unconstrained), the number of submitted runs obtained with cascade and direct systems.

from wav2vec2-large-960h-lv60-self and an adapter model to compress the feature vectors. Transcripts are obtained through a CTC greedy decoding step. The MT is based on mbart-large-50-one-to-many-mmt. The direct model consists of two separate encoders for speech and text, followed by a shared decoder. The speech and text encoders are respectively based on the cascade ASR and MT encoders. An adapter model is introduced to connect the two encoders. The direct model combines the cross entropy loss for MT and the CTC loss for ASR, together with a hyperparameter to balance the weights between the two losses. The training procedure involves dedicated fine-tuning steps, data filtering and audio re-segmentation into shorter segments.

- I2R (Huzaifah et al., 2023) participated with a direct approach for en-de translation, which was trained under the constrained^{+LLM}condition. The model consists of two separate encoders for speech and text, followed by a shared encoder and a decoder. The speech encoder is initialised with WavLM large, while DeltaLM base is used to initialise the text encoder, the shared encoder and the decoder. To leverage both text and speech sources, the shared encoder is induced to learn a joint multimodal representation obtained through forced alignment of speech and text data. The resulting mixed speech-text representation is passed to the shared encoder initially pre-trained on text data only. A DeltaLM-based MT model incrementally trained on in-domain and out-of-domain data is used as a teacher during fine-tuning of the ST system. The ST model is built on a mix of ASR, ST and synthetic data. Additional techniques applied include on-the-fly audio augmentation to increase robustness to variable audio quality, domain tagging to condition the ST output to the different output styles of the test data, and ST model ensembling.

- HW-TSC (Li et al., 2023) participated with cascade systems for all language directions and in all three training data conditions. The ASR model used for the constrained training condition is the Conformer. For the constrained^{+LLM} condition, the encoder of wav2vec2 and the decoder of mBART50 are combined to fine-tune on all data an ASR model trained on MuST-C. Whisper (Radford et al., 2022), fine-tuned on MuST-C, is instead used for the unconstrained training condition. All models are built using audio inputs augmented with SpecAugment and CTC. The MT component is a Transformer-based model trained in a one-to-many multilingual fashion. It exploits data filtering and data augmentation techniques, combined with dropout regularization and domain adaptation methods, as well as solutions to increase robustness to ASR noise (through synthetic noise generation and data augmentation).

- MINETRANS (Du et al., 2023) participated with en-zh cascade systems trained under constrained and unconstrained conditions. The submitted runs are obtained with a pipeline of ASR, punctuation recognition, and MT components. The ASR is an RNN-Transducer. For the unconstrained condition, GigaSpeech is added to the training data allowed in the constrained setting. In both conditions, pre-processing and filtering techniques are applied to improve data quality, while SpecAugment is used for data augmentation. Before being passed to the MT component, the unpunctuated ASR output is processed by means of a BERT-based punctuation recognition model. For the MT component, two strategies are implemented. The first one relies on different Transformer-based models for supervised training. A base Transformer and an M2M_100 model are used for the constrained condition. A translation model trained on additional inhouse corpora is used for the unconstrained condition. The second strategy adopted for the MT component relies on a large language model (Chat-GPT) for prompt-guided translation.

- NIUTRANS (Han et al., 2023) participated with a direct en-zh system trained under the constrained condition. It consists of two separate encoders for speech and text with an adapter in between, followed by a decoder. The speech encoder is pre-trained with an ASR encoder, while the textual encoder and the decoder with pre-trained MT components. Different architectures with variable size were tested both for ASR (enhanced with CTC loss and inter-CTC loss to speed up convergence) and MT (used to generate pseudo-references so as to increase the size of the SLT data). The final system is an ensemble aiming at maximizing the diversity between models.

- NEURODUB[7] participated with a cascade en-de system trained under the unconstrained condition. It consists of a 4-staged process including the ASR, the punctuation module performing both sentence extraction and punctuation placement, the speaker- and gender distinction component, and the translation model. Every stage is trained on the crawled data from the web.

- NEMO (Hrinchuk et al., 2023) participated with direct systems for all language directions in the constrained training data condition. Pre-trained models and synthetic training data are exploited in different ways to cope with the scarcity of direct ST data. A Conformer-based ASR model trained on all allowed speech-to-text data is used to initialize the SLT encoder. A Transformer-based NMT model trained on all allowed parallel data and fine-tuned on TED talks is used to generate synthetic translation alternatives for all available speech-to-text and text-to-text data. A TTS model based on Fast Pitch (Łańcucki, 2021) and trained on the English transcripts of all TED-derived data is used to generate the synthetic speech version of English texts in the available text corpora. The submitted SLT systems are based on a Conformer-based encoder followed by a Transformer decoder trained on this mix of (gold and synthetic) speech-to-text and text-to-text data.

- XIAOMI (Huang et al., 2023) participated with a direct en-zh system trained under the constrained^{+LLM} condition. It consists of a speech encoder, a text encoder, and a text decoder, with all parameters initialized using the pre-trained HuBERT and mBART models. The speech encoder is composed of a feature extractor based on convolutional neural networks and a Transformer encoder. In addition to the cross-entropy loss, ASR, MT, and a contrastive loss, which tries to learn an encoder that produces similar representations for similar instances independently from the modalities, are added. Self-training is also used to leverage unlabelled data. In addition to the allowed datasets, a large set of pseudo references are generated translating the

[7]Unofficial participant, as no system paper is available.

transcripts of the ASR corpora. During training, a second fine-tuning is performed on MuST-C as in-domain data. The final system is an ensemble of the two best-performing models.

- UPC (Tsiamas et al., 2023) participated with a direct en-de system trained under the constrained^{+LLM} condition. It consists of a speech encoder, a textual encoder, and a text decoder. The speech encoder includes a semantic encoder to align speech and text encoder representations. The coupling modules include the CTC and Optimal Transport (OT) losses to the outputs of the acoustic and semantic encoders, and the addition of a second auxiliary OT loss for the inputs of the semantic encoder. The speech encoder is based on wav2vec 2.0, while the textual encoder uses mBART50. Knowledge distillation is used to generate additional data to fine-tune part of the SLT model architecture (the feature extractor, the acoustic encoder, and the CTC module are frozen during fine-tuning).

USTC (Zhou et al., 2023) participated with cascade and direct en-zh models trained under the unconstrained condition. For the ASR of the cascade, two approaches are implemented. The first one exploits a fusion models trained on the allowed data expanded with speed perturbation, oversampling, concatenation of adjacent voices and synthetic data generation via TTS. The second approach is based on Whisper large (Radford et al., 2022) and SHAS for audio segmentation. The MT component of the cascade system exploits an ensemble of Transformer-based models enhanced with knowledge distillation, domain adaptation and robust training strategies. For direct SLT, two approaches are implemented. The first one is an encoder-decoder initialized with the ASR and MT models of the cascade. The second approach is a Stacked Acoustic-and-Textual Encoding extension of SATE (Xu et al., 2021). The final submissions also include ensembles obtained by combining cascade and direct systems.

2.4 Results

Also this year, the submissions to the IWSLT Offline translation task were evaluated both with automatic metrics and through human evaluation. The results for each sub-task are shown in detail in the Appendix.

2.4.1 Automatic Evaluation

The results for each of the language pairs are shown in the tables in Appendix B.1. We present results for English-German (Table 14), English-Chinese (Table 16) and English-Japanese (Table 15). The evaluation was carried out in terms of BLEU (the primary metric, in continuity with previous years), and COMET. We report individual scores for the three (or two, as in the case of en-ja and en-zh) different test sets as well as metrics calculated on the concatenation of the different test sets. For each sub-task, systems are ranked based on the BLEU score computed on the concatenated test sets.

End-to-End vs Cascaded This year the cascaded systems performed in general better than the end-to-end systems. For English-to-German, for nearly all metrics, the cascaded systems are always ranked best. For English-to-Japanese, the results show a similar situation to English-to-German, with the cascade systems outperforming the end-to-end model. The supremacy of the cascade models is confirmed by all the metrics, with a clear gap in performance between the worst cascade and the best end-to-end models. For English-to-Chinese, the picture is not as clear. However, the only participant who submitted a primary system using the cascaded and one using the end-to-end paradigm (USTC), the cascaded performed better in all metrics.

Metrics For English-to-German, in general, the results of the BLEU metric correlate quite well with the scores of the COMET metric. Except for relatively small changes, e.g. the order is different for the different HW-TSC systems. One exception is the submissions by UPC and NeMo that are ranked differently in the two metrics. Therefore, a comparison to the human evaluation will be interesting. In the English-to-Japanese task, the scores of the HW-TSC systems are very close to each other and some swaps are visible between BLEU and COMET. However, the changes are only related to the HW-TSC systems and do not modify the overall evaluation of the systems. In the English-to-Chinese task, there are two situations where the metrics differ significantly. The ranking for USTC end-to-end compared to the HW-TSC systems is different with respect to COMET, which rewards the HW-TSC submissions. A similar situation is visible for NiuTrans and Xiaomi, where BLEU favors the NiuTrans translations, while COMET assigns higher scores, and ranking, to the Xiaomi submissions.

Data conditions For the different data conditions, the gains by using additional large language models or additional data are not clear. HW-TSC submitted three primary systems for each data condition and they all perform very similarly. However, for en-zh the unconstrained system by USTC was clearly the best and for en-de the best system except HW-TSC was also an unconstrained one. The additional benefit of the pre-trained models is even less clear. There is no clear picture that the systems with or without this technology perform better.

Domains One new aspect this year is the evaluation of the systems on three different test sets and domains. First of all, the absolute performance on the different domains is quite different. The systems perform clearly worse on the EPTV test sets. For the relationship between ACL and TED, the picture is not as clear. While the BLEU scores on ACL are higher, the COMET scores are lower. Only for English-to-Japanese, both metrics are higher on the ACL test set. One explanation could be that the references for the ACL talks are generated by post-editing an MT output. This could indicate that the post-edited references inflate the BLEU score, while the COMET score seems to be more robust to this phenomenon. When comparing the different systems, the tendency is for all cases the same. However, some perform slightly better in one condition. For example, the end-to-end system from USTC performs very well on TED compared to other systems but less well on ACL.

2.4.2 Human Evaluation

At the time of writing, human evaluation is still in progress. Its results will be reported at the conference and they will appear in the updated version of this paper in Appendix A.

3 Simultaneous SLT

Simultaneous speech translation means the system starts translating before the speaker finishes the sentence. The task is essential to enable people to communicate seamlessly across different backgrounds, in low-latency scenarios such as translation in international conferences or travel.

This year, the task included two tracks: speech-to-text and speech-to-speech, covering three language directions: English to German, Chinese and Japanese.

3.1 Challenge

There are two major updates compared with previous years:

- Removal of the text-to-text track. The task focuses on the real-world live-translation setting, where the speech is the input medium.
- Addition of a speech-to-speech track. Translation into synthetic speech has gained increasing attention within the research community, given its potential application to real-time conversations.

To simplify the shared task, a single latency constraint is introduced for each track: 2 seconds of Average Lagging for speech-to-text, and 2.5 seconds of starting offset for speech-to-speech. The participants can submit no more than one system per track / language direction, as long as the latency of the system is under the constraint. The latency of the system is qualified on the open MuST-C tst-COMMON test set (Di Gangi et al., 2019a).

The participants made submissions in a format of docker images, which were later run by organizers on the blind-test set in a controllable environment. An example of implementation was provided with the SimulEval toolkit (Ma et al., 2020a).

3.2 Data

The training data condition of the simultaneous task follows "constrained with large language models" setting in the Offline translation task, as described in Section 2.2

The test data has two parts:

Common TED talks. It's the the same as in the Offline task, as described in Section 2.2 .For English to German, Chinese and Japanese

Non-Native see Appendix A.1.1. For English to German.

3.3 Evaluation

Two attributes are evaluated in the simultaneous task: quality and latency.

For quality, we conducted both automatic and human evaluation. BLEU score (Papineni et al., 2002a) is used for automatic quality evaluation. For speech output, the BLEU score is computed on the transcripts from Whisper (Radford et al., 2022) ASR model. The ranking of the submission is based on the BLEU score on the Common blind test set. Furthermore, we conducted BLASER (Chen et al., 2022) evaluation on the speech output. We also conducted human evaluation on speech-to-text translation quality, including general human evaluation for all three language pairs, and task specific human evaluation on German and Japanese outputs.

For latency, we only conducted automatic evaluation. We report the following metrics for each speech-to-text systems.

- Average Lagging (AL; Ma et al., 2019, 2020b)
- Length Adaptive Average Lagging (LAAL; Polák et al., 2022; Papi et al., 2022)
- Average Token Delay (ATD; Kano et al., 2023)
- Average Proportion (AP; Cho and Esipova, 2016)
- Differentiable Average Lagging (DAL; Cherry and Foster, 2019)

We also measured the computation aware version of the latency metrics, as described by Ma et al. (2020b). However, due to the new synchronized SimulEval agent pipeline design, the actual computation aware latency can be smaller with carefully designed parallelism.

For speech-to-speech systems, we report start-offset and end-offset. The latency metrics will not be used for ranking.

3.4 Submissions

The simultaneous shared task received submissions from six teams, whereas all the teams participated in at least one language direction in speech-to-text translation. Among the teams, five teams entered the English-to-German track; four teams entered the English-to-Chinese track; three teams entered the English-to-Japanese track. Even though this year is our first time introducing the simultaneous speech-to-speech track, four teams out of six, submitted speech-to-speech systems.

- CMU(Yan et al., 2023) participated in both the speech-to-text and speech-to-speech tracks for English-German translation. Their speech-to-text model combined self-supervised speech representations, a Conformer encoder, and an mBART decoder. In addition to the cross-entropy attentional loss, the translation model was also trained with CTC objectives. They used machine translation pseudo labeling for data augmentation. Simultaneous decoding was achieved by chunking the speech signals and employing incremental beam search. For their speech-to-speech system, they incorporated a VITS-based text-to-speech model, which was trained separately.
- HW-TSC (Guo et al., 2023; Shang et al., 2023) participated in both the speech-to-text and speech-to-speech tracks for all three language directions. Their model was a cascaded system that combined an U2 ASR, a Transformer-based machine translation model, and a VITS-based text-to-speech model for speech-to-speech translation. The MT model was multilingual and offered translation in all three directions by conditioning on language embeddings. For data augmentation, they adopted data diversification and forward translation techniques. Their simultaneous decoding policy employed chunk-based incremental decoding with stable hypotheses detection. They also utilized additional TTS models for the speech-to-speech track.
- NAIST(Fukuda et al., 2023) participated in the speech-to-text translation direction for all three language directions and English-to-Japanese speech-to-speech translation. Their system consisted of a HuBERT encoder and an mBART decoder. They employed three techniques to improve translation quality: inter-connection to combine pre-trained representations, prefix alignment fine-tuning for simultaneous decoding, and local agreement

to find stable prefix hypotheses. They also utilized an additional Tacotron2-based TTS model for speech-to-speech translation with the wait-k decoding policy.

- FBK(Papi et al., 2023) participated in the English-to-German speech-to-text translation track, using an end-to-end Conformer-based speech-to-text model. Considering computational latency, their focus was on efficient usage of offline models. They employed three simultaneous policies, including local agreement, encoder-decoder attention, and EDATT v2, to achieve this.
- CUNI-KIT(Polák et al., 2023) participated in the English-to-German speech-to-text translation track. Their system utilized WavLM and mBART as the base framework. The key highlights of their system were in the decoding strategy and simultaneous policies. They applied empirical hypotheses filtering during decoding and adopted CTC to detect the completion of block inference.
- XIAOMI(Huang et al., 2023) participated in both the speech-to-text and speech-to-speech tracks for English-Chinese translation. Their end-to-end system utilized HuBERT and mBART with a wait-k decoding strategy and an Information-Transport-based architecture. They further enhanced their system by applying data filtering on long sentences and misaligned audio/text, data augmentation with pseudo labeling, and punctuation normalization. They also incorporated contrastive learning objectives.

3.5 Automatic Evaluation

We rank the system performance based on BLEU scores. The detailed results can be found in Appendix B.2.

3.5.1 Speech-to-Text

English-German On the Common test set, the ranking is HW-TSC, CUNI-KIT, FBK, NAIST, CMU, as shown in Table 17. Meanwhile, on the Non-Native test set, the ranking differs considerably. While HW-TSC performs best on Common test set, they end up second to last on Non-Native. The situation is reversed for NAIST and CMU who end up at the tail of Common scoring but reach the best scores on the Non-Native set. We attribute this to better robustness of NAIST and CMU towards the noise in Non-Native test set.

English-Chinese The ranking is HW-TSC, CUNI-KIT, XIAOMI, NAIST, as shown in Table 18.

English-Japanese The ranking is HW-TSC, CUNI-KIT, NAIST, as shown in Table 19.

3.5.2 Speech-to-Speech

Despite the great novelty and difficulty of speech-to-speech track, there are 5 submissions in total: 2 in German, 2 in Chinese and 1 in Japanese. The full results can be seen in table Table 20. For English-to-German, the ranking is CMU, HW-TSC. For English-to-Chinese, HW-TSC is the only participant. For English-to-Japanese, the ranking is HW-TSC, NAIST.

We also provide the BLASER scores, which directly predict the quality of translations based on speech embeddings. We note that since reference audios are not available in our datasets, we use text LASER (Heffernan et al., 2022) to embed reference text to compute the scores. While the BLASER scores indicate the same quality ranking for English to German as BLEU scores, on the Japanese output they are similar. It's possible that BLASER is adequately developed on Japanese outputs

3.6 Human Evaluation

In the Simultaneous task, speech-to-text track, English-German and English-Japanese were manually evaluated, each with a different scoring method.

3.6.1 English-German

For English-to-German, we used the same human evaluation method as last year, originally inspired by Javorský et al. (2022). We evaluated (1) the best system selected by BLEU score, and (2) transcription of human interpretation, the same as used in last year evaluation (more details can be found in Anastasopoulos et al. (2022a), Section 2.6.1).

Figure 1 plots automatic and manual evaluation in relation with each other. We confirm the generally good correlation with BLEU (Pearson .952 across the two test set parts), as observed by Macháček et al. (2023), although individual system results are rather interesting this year.

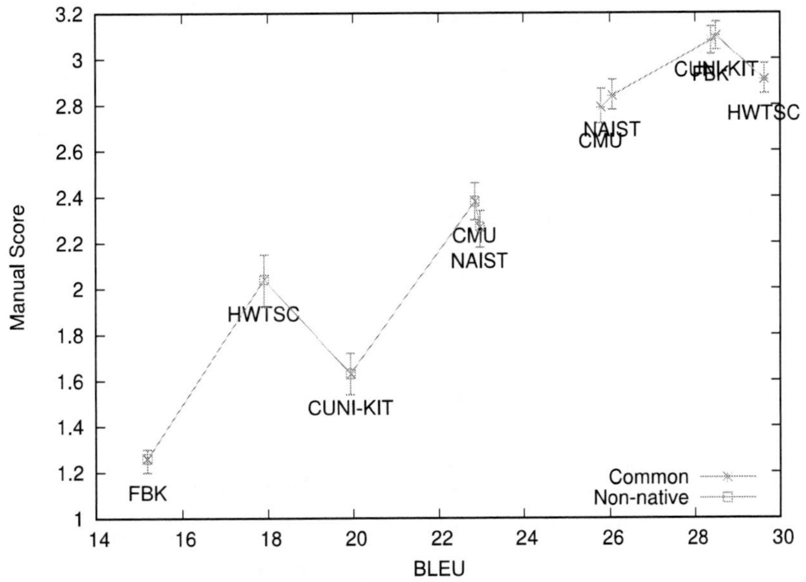

Figure 1: Manual and automatic evaluation of Simulatenous speech-to-text English-to-German translation on the Common (TED talks) and Non-Native test sets. The error bars were obtained by bootstrap resampling, see the caption of Table 22.

On the Common test set, HWTSC performed best in terms of BLEU but the manual scoring seems to prefer CUNI-KIT and FBK. CMU and NAIST are worst in BLEU but on par with HWTSC in terms of manual scores.

The situation is very different on the Non-Native test set: CMU and NAIST score best both in manual scores and in BLEU while CUNI-KIT and esp. FBK get much worse scores, again, both manual and automatic.

The Non-Native test set is substantially harder with respect to sound conditions, and the striking difference drop observed for both CUNI-KIT and FBK can be an indication of some form of overfitting towards the clean input of Common (TED talks).

Appendix A.1.1 presents details of the human evaluation and results are shown in Table 22.

3.6.2 English-Japanese

For English-to-Japanese, we also followed the methodology in the last year. We hired a professional interpreter for human evaluation using JTF Translation Quality Evaluation Guidelines (JTF, 2018) based on Multidimensional Quality Metrics (MQM; Lommel et al., 2014). We applied the error weighting by Freitag et al. (2021a). Appendix A.1.2 presents details of the human evaluation.

The human evaluation results are shown in Table 23. The error score almost correlates with BLEU against the additional reference, but the difference in the error scores was very small between HW-TSC and CUNI-KIT in spite of the 0.8 BLEU difference.

3.7 Final remarks

This year, we simplified the conditions by focusing solely on low-latency systems to reduce the burden of submission and evaluation. We also introduced the novel and challenging speech-to-speech track, and were happy to receive 5 submissions.

We note potential modifications for future editions:

- Providing further simplified submission format.
- Ranking with better designed metrics to address the overfitting towards BLEU scores.
- Aligning more with offline tasks on more test domains and evaluation metrics.

4 Automatic Subtitling

In recent years, the task of automatically creating subtitles for audiovisual content in another language has gained a lot of attention, as we have seen a surge in the amount of movies, series and user-generated videos which are being streamed and distributed all over the world.

For the first time, this year IWSLT proposed a specific track on automatic subtitling, where participants were asked to generate subtitles of audio-visual documents, belonging to different domains with increasing levels of complexity.

4.1 Challenge

The task of automatic subtitling is multi-faceted: starting from speech, not only the translation has to be generated, but it must be segmented into subtitles compliant with constraints that ensure high-quality user experience, like a proper reading speed, synchrony with the voices, the maximum number of subtitle lines and characters per line, etc. Most audio-visual companies define their own subtitling guidelines, which can differ slightly from each other. Participants were asked to generate subtitles according to some of the tips listed by TED, in particular:

- the maximum subtitle reading speed is 21 characters / second;
- lines cannot exceed 42 characters, white spaces included;
- never use more than two lines per subtitle.

It was expected that participants used only the audio track from the provided videos (dev and test sets), the video track being of low quality and provided primarily as a means to verify time synchronicity and other aspects of displaying subtitles on screen.

The subtitling track requires to automatically subtitle in German and/or Spanish audio-visual documents where the spoken language is always English, and which were collected from the following sources:

- TED talks from the MuST-Cinema[8] corpus;
- press interviews from the Multimedia Centre of the European Parliament (EPTV)[9];
- physical training videos offered by Peloton[10]
- TV series from ITV Studios.[11]

[8]https://ict.fbk.eu/must-cinema

[9]https://multimedia.europarl.europa.eu

[10]https://www.onepeloton.com

[11]https://www.itvstudios.com

domain	set	AV docs	hh: :mm	ref subtitles de	ref subtitles es
TED	dev	17	04:11	4906	4964
	test	14	01:22	1375	1422
EPTV	dev	12	01:03	960	909
	test	10	01:01	891	874
Peloton	dev	9	03:59	4508	4037
	test	8	02:43	2700	2661
ITV	dev	7	06:01	4489	4763
	test	7	05:08	4807	4897

Table 4: Statistics of the dev and test sets for the subtitling task.

4.2 Data and Metrics

Data. This track proposed two **training** conditions to participants: **constrained**, in which only a pre-defined list of resources is allowed, and **unconstrained**, without any data restrictions. The constrained setup allowed to use the same training data as in the Offline Speech Translation task (see Section 2.2 for the detailed list), with the obvious exclusion of the parallel resources not involving the English-{German, Spanish} pairs. In addition, two monolingual German and Spanish text corpora built on OpenSubtitles, enriched with subtitle breaks, document meta-info on genre and automatically predicted line breaks, have been released.

For each language and domain, a **development** set and a **test** set were released. Table 4 provides some information about these sets.

The evaluation was carried out from three perspectives, subtitle quality, translation quality and subtitle compliance, through the following automatic measures:

- Subtitle quality vs. reference subtitles:
  - **SubER**, primary metric, used also for ranking (Wilken et al., 2022)[12];
  - **Sigma** (Karakanta et al., 2022b)[13].
- Translation quality vs. reference translations:
  - **BLEU**[14] and **CHRF**[15] via sacreBLEU
  - **BLUERT** (Sellam et al., 2020)

[12]`https://github.com/apptek/SubER`

[13]`https://github.com/fyvo/EvalSubtitle`

[14]sacreBLEU signature: `nrefs:1|case:mixed||eff:no|tok:13a|smooth:exp|version:2.0.0`

[15]sacreBLEU signature: `nrefs:1|case:mixed||eff:yes|nc:6|nw:0|space:no|version:2.0.0`

Automatic subtitles are realigned to the reference subtitles using mwerSegmenter (Matusov et al., 2005a)[16] before running sacreBLEU and BLEURT.

- Subtitle compliance:[17]
  - rate of subtitles with reading speed higher than 21 char / sec (**CPS**);
  - rate of lines longer than 42 char (**CPL**);
  - rate of subtitles with more than two lines (white spaces included) (**LPB**).

4.3 Submissions

Three teams submitted automatically generated subtitles for the test sets of this task.

- APPTEK (Bahar et al., 2023) submitted runs in the constrained setup for both language pairs. The primary submissions came from a cascade architecture composed of the following modules: neural encoder-decoder ASR, followed by a neural Machine Translation model trained on the data allowed in the constrained track, with the source (English) side lowercased and normalized to resemble raw ASR output, as well as adapted to the IWSLT subtitling domains, followed by a subtitle line segmentation model (intelligent line segmentation by APPTEK). A contrastive run was generated for the en→de pair only by a direct speech translation system with CTC-based timestamp prediction, followed by the intelligent line segmentation model of APPTEK. The system was trained on the constrained allowed data plus forward translated synthetic data (translations of allowed ASR transcripts) and synthetic speech data for selected sentences from the allowed parallel data. For the en→de pair, APPTEK also submitted a run in the unconstrained setup, where a cascade architecture was employed consisting of: neural encoder-decoder CTC ASR, followed by a neural punctuation prediction model and inverse text normalization model, followed by an MT model adapted to the IWSLT domains (sentences similar in embedding similarity space to the development sets of the four domains TED, EPTV, ITV, Peloton), followed by a subtitle line segmentation model (intelligent line segmentation by APPTEK).

- FBK (Papi et al., 2023) submitted primary runs for the two language pairs, generated by a direct neural speech translation model, trained in the constrained setup, that works as follows: i) the audio is fed to a Subtitle Generator that produces the (un-timed) subtitle blocks; ii) the computed encoder representations are passed to a Source Timestamp Generator to obtain the caption blocks and their corresponding timestamps; iii) the subtitle timestamps are estimated by the Source-to-Target Timestamp Projector from the generated subtitles, captions, and source timestamps.

- MATESUB (Perone, 2023) submitted primary runs for the two language pairs, automatically generated by the back-end subtitling pipeline of MATESUB, its web-based tool that supports professionals in the creation of high-quality subtitles (https://matesub.com/). The MATESUB subtitling pipeline is based on a cascade architecture, composed of ASR, text segmenter and MT neural models, which allows covering any pair from about 60 languages and their variants, including the two language pairs of the task. Since MATESUB is a production software, its neural models are trained on more resources than those allowed for the constrained condition, therefore the submissions fall into the unconstrained setup.

4.4 Results

Scores of all runs as computed by automatic metrics are shown in Tables 24 and 25 in the Appendix. Averaged over the 4 domains, APPTEK achieved the lowest SubER scores with their primary submission for en→de in the constrained and unconstrained condition, with the overall best results for the latter. For en→es, MATESUB obtained the overall lowest SubER with their unconstrained system.

We observe that in terms of domain difficulty, the TV series (from ITV) pose the most challenges for automatic subtitling. This has to do with diverse acoustic conditions in which speech is found in movies and series - background music, noises,

[16] https://www-i6.informatik.rwth-aachen.de/web/Software/mwerSegmenter.tar.gz

[17] https://github.com/hlt-mt/FBK-fairseq/blob/master/examples/speech_to_text/scripts/subtitle_compliance.py

shouts, and cross-talk. All of this makes the task of recognizing speech quite challenging, which results in error accumulation in the downstream components. Unconstrained systems by APPTEK and MATESUB perform significantly better on this domain, which shows the importance of training on additional data that is more representative of real-life content.

The second-hardest domain are the fitness videos from Peloton. Here, despite a generally clear single-speaker audio with reduced background noise, the challenge is the MT: some of the fitness- and sports-specific terminology and slang pose significant challenges in translation to their German and Spanish equivalents.

Surprisingly, even the EPTV interviews pose significant challenges for subtitling, despite the fact that the topics discussed in the interviews are found in abundance in the allowed speech-to-text and text-to-text parallel data for the constrained condition (Europarl, Europarl-ST). Here, the issues such as spontaneous speech with many pauses, as well as speaker separation may have been cause of some of the errors.

The TED talks which have been the main domain for the IWSLT evaluations in the past years are the easiest to be automatically subtitled. Whereas the current level of subtitle quality for TED talks may require minimal human corrections or can even be shown unedited on the screen, for the other three domains the automatic subtitles will require significant post-editing. This shows the importance of running evaluations not only under very controlled conditions as in the case of TED talks, but on a variety of real-life content where multiple research challenges in speech translation are yet to be overcome.

This year's direct speech translation systems seem to be too weak to compete with the cascaded approaches. In particular, a full end-to-end approach like the one from FBK that directly generates subtitle boundaries is currently inferior in comparison with the systems that adopt a specific solution for segmenting the text (intelligent line segmentation by APPTEK and a neural text segmenter by MATESUB). Such specific solutions lead to almost perfect subtitle compliance. But even in terms of pure speech translation quality as measured e.g. with BLEU and BLEURT the cascaded systems currently provide better translations even under constrained training data conditions.

Regarding the automatic metrics used in the evaluation, we observed that the metric Sigma provides scores which are not consistent with the other measures: for example, German subtitles from MATESUB seem to be the worst as measured by Sigma, but this is unlikely based on the values of the other metrics. Yet the pure MT quality metrics also exhibit some discrepancies in how the performance of the same system on the four domains is ranked. This ranking sometimes differs depending on whether you choose BLEU, ChrF, or BLEURT as the "primary" metric. The two most striking cases are:

- the en→de APPTEK unconstrained primary submission, for which the BLEU score for the ITV test data was 14.43 and for Peloton 10.47, but the BLEURT scores were very similar: 0.4069 and 0.4028;
- the en→de FBK constrained primary system, for which the BLEU score was 7.73 on the Peloton part of the test data vs. 8.05 on the ITV part, but the BLEURT scores showed a better quality for Peloton translations: 0.3137 vs. 0.2255.

All of these discrepancies highlight the importance of human evaluation, which we have not conducted this time. One of the reasons for this is that in most prior research (Matusov et al., 2019; Karakanta et al., 2022a) the automatic subtitling quality is evaluated in post-editing scenarios, which are too expensive to be run on significant amounts of data as they require professional subtitle translators. On the other hand, as mentioned above, for 3 out of 4 domains the quality of the automatically generated subtitle translations is low, so that an evaluation of user experience when watching subtitles would be also challenging, especially if the users would have to assign evaluation scores to individual subtitles or sentences. With all of this in mind, we decided to postpone any human evaluation to the next edition of the subtitling track at IWSLT.

Overall, this first edition of the subtitling track emphasised the crucial role of the following components related to speech processing: noise reduction and/or speech separation, speaker diarization, and sentence segmentation. So far they have been underestimated in speech translation research. Current automatic solutions do not reach the level of quality that is necessary in subtitling. Therefore, we encourage further research into these areas, for which subtitle translation is a good test case.

5 Multilingual SLT

The NLP and speech communities are rapidly expanding with increasing focus on broader language coverage and multilinguality. However, despite the community's efforts on ASR and SLT, research is rarely focused on applying these efforts to the data within the scientific domain. It is clear from recent initiatives to caption technical presentations at NLP and speech conferences that transcription and translation in the technical domain is needed, desired, and remains a disproportionate challenge for current ASR and SLT models compared to standard datasets in these spaces. Motivated by the ACL 60-60 initiative[18] to translate the ACL Anthology to up to 60 languages for the 60th anniversary of ACL, which will be reported on at this year's ACL conference co-located with IWSLT, this year's Multilingual Task evaluates the ability of current models to translate technical presentations to a set of ten diverse target languages.

5.1 Challenge

Translating technical presentations combines several challenging conditions: domain-specific terminology, recording conditions varying from close-range microphones to laptop microphones with light background noise or feedback, diverse speaker demographics, and importantly unsegmented speech typically 10-60 minutes in duration. This task focuses on one-to-many translation from English to ten target languages. Providing English ASR was optional though encouraged. In-domain data is scarce, particularly parallel data, though all language pairs are covered by current publicly available corpora; further challenging for current domain adaptation techniques, monolingual data is typically available for the source language (English) only. We present two conditions: constrained (using only the out-of-domain data allowed and provided for other tasks this year) and unconstrained (allowing any additional data, included crawled, which may facilitate e.g., domain adaptation). To evaluate submissions, we use evaluation sets curated from presentations at ACL 2022 which were professionally transcribed and translated with the support of ACL and the 60-60 initiative as described in Salesky et al. (2023).

[18]https://www.2022.aclweb.org/dispecialinitiative

5.2 Data and Metrics

Data. We use the ACL 60-60 evaluation sets created by Salesky et al. (2023) to evaluate this challenge task. The data comes from ACL 2022 technical presentations and is originally spoken in English, and then transcribed and translated to ten target languages from the 60/60 initiative: Arabic, Mandarin Chinese, Dutch, French, German, Japanese, Farsi, Portuguese, Russian, and Turkish. The resulting dataset contains parallel speech, transcripts, and translation for ten language pairs, totaling approximately one hour for the development set and one hour for the evaluation set.

During the evaluation campaign, the only in-domain data provided is the development set. To simulate the realistic use case where recorded technical presentations would be accompanied by a research paper, in addition to the talk audio we provide the corresponding paper title and abstract, which are likely to contain a subset of relevant keywords and terminology and could be used by participants to bias or adapt their systems. Constrained training data follows the Offline task (see Sec. 2.2) with pretrained models and out-of-domain parallel speech and text provided for all 10 language pairs. The unconstrained setting allowed participants to potentially crawl additional in-domain data to assist with adaptation, as was done by one team (JHU). For the official rankings, we use the official evaluation set, which was held blind until after the evaluation campaign.

To mimic realistic test conditions where the audio for technical presentations would be provided as a single file, rather than gold-sentence-segmented, for both the development and evaluation sets we provided the full unsegmented wav files, as well as an automatically generated baseline segmentation using SHAS (Tsiamas et al., 2022) to get participants started. Two teams used the baseline segmentation, while one (JHU) used longer segments which improved the ASR quality of their particular pretrained model. To evaluate translation quality of system output using any input segmentation, we provided gold sentence-segmented transcripts and translations, which system output could be scored with as described below in 'Metrics.'

Metrics. Translation output was evaluated using multiple metrics for analysis: translation output using chrF (Popović, 2015a), BLEU (Papineni et al., 2002b) as computed by SACREBLEU (Post, 2018), and COMET (Rei et al., 2020b) and ASR output using WER. For BLEU we use the recommended language-specific tokenization in SACREBLEU for Chinese, Japanese, Korean, and the metric-default otherwise. Translation metrics were calculated with case and punctuation. WER was computed on lowercased text with punctuation removed. NFKC normalization was applied on submitted systems and references. All official scores were calculated using automatic resegmentation of the hypothesis based on the reference transcripts (ASR) or translations (SLT) by mwerSegmenter (Matusov et al., 2005b), using character-level segmentation for resegmentation for those languages which do not mark whitespace. The official task ranking is based on average chrF across all 10 translation language pairs.

5.3 Submissions

We received 11 submissions from 3 teams, as described below:

- BIT (Wang et al., 2023b) submitted a single constrained one-to-many multilingual model to cover all 10 language pairs, trained using a collection of multiple versions of the MuST-C dataset (Di Gangi et al., 2019b). They use English ASR pre-training with data augmentation from SpecAugment (Park et al., 2019), and multilingual translation finetuning for all language pairs together. The final model is an ensemble of multiple checkpoints. No adaptation to the technical domain is performed.

- JHU (Xinyuan et al., 2023) submitted two cascaded systems, one constrained and one unconstrained, combining multiple different pretrained speech and translation models, and comparing different domain adaptation techniques. Their unconstrained system uses an adapted Whisper (Radford et al., 2022) ASR model combined with NLLB (NLLB Team et al., 2022), M2M-100 (Fan et al., 2020), or mBART-50 (Tang et al., 2020) MT models depending on the language pair, while the constrained system uses wav2vec2.0 (Baevski et al., 2020a) and mBART-50 or M2M-100. They compare using talk abstracts to prompt Whisper to training in-domain language models on either the small amount of highly-relevant data in the talk abstract or larger LMs trained on significantly more data they scraped from the ACL Anthology and release with their paper. They see slight improvements over the provided SHAS (Tsiamas et al., 2022) segments using longer segments closer what Whisper observed in training. They show that prompting Whisper is *not* competitive with in-domain language models, and provide an analysis of technical term recall and other fine-grained details.

- KIT (Liu et al., 2023) submitted multiple constrained multilingual models, both end-to-end and cascaded, which combine several techniques to adapt to the technical domain given the absence of in-domain training data, using pretrained speech and translation models as initializations (WavLM: Chen et al. 2021, DeltaLM: Ma et al. 2021, mBART-50: Tang et al. 2020). These include kNN-MT to bias generated output to the technical domain; data diversification to enrich provided parallel data; adapters for lightweight finetuning to the language pairs for translation (though they note that this does not necessarily stack with data diversification); and for their cascaded model, adaptation of the ASR model to the target technical domain using n-gram re-weighting, noting that it is typically easier to adapt or add lexical constraints to models with separate LMs, as opposed to encoder-decoder models. Additional techniques (ensembling, updated ASR encoder/decoder settings, knowledge distillation, synthesized speech) are also used for further small improvements.

5.4 Results

All task results are shown in Appendix B.4. The official task ranking was determined by the average chrF across all 10 target languages after resegmentation to the reference translations.Table 26. Scores for all submissions by individual language pairs are shown in Table 28 (chrF), Table 29 (COMET), and Table 30 (BLEU).

Overall, the majority of approaches combined strong pretrained speech and translation models to do very well on the ACL 60-60 evaluation data. For this task, cascaded models performed consistently better than direct/end-to-end approaches; all of the top 6 submissions were cascades, and 4/5 of the lowest-performing systems were direct. Optional English ASR transcripts were submitted for 3 systems ($\text{JHU}_{unconstrained}$, $\text{KIT}_{primary}$, $\text{JHU}_{constrained}$), all of which were cascades; we see that WER aligns with speech translation performance in these cases. The only unconstrained model, from JHU, utilized larger pretrained models and crawled in-domain language modeling data for ASR to great success, and was the top system on all metrics (Table 26). The remaining submissions were all constrained (here meaning, used the white-listed training data and smaller pretrained models). The $KIT_{primary}$ system was the best performing constrained model. While BIT trained models from scratch on TED to reasonable performance on MuST-C, large pretrained models and domain adaptation were key for high performance on the technical in-domain test set. chrF and BLEU result in the same system rankings, while COMET favors the end-to-end models slightly more, though not affecting the top 3 systems ($\text{JHU}_{unconstrained}$, $\text{KIT}_{primary}$, $\text{KIT}_{constrastive1}$).

Domain adaptation techniques had consistent positive impact on system performance. The KIT team submitted constrained systems only and thus were limited to the dev bitext and talk abstracts for domain adaptation. Despite its small size (<500 sentences) they were able to generate consistent improvements of up to ~1chrF and ~ 1 BLEU using kNN-MT (*primary/contrastive1* vs *contrastive2*); with this method, extending the dev data to include the abstracts for the evaluation set talks (*primary* vs *contrastive1*) had neglible effect on all 3 metrics. The JHU submissions saw that decoding with interpolated in-domain language models outperformed knowledge distillation or prompting pretrained models with information for each talk in this case; small talk-specific LMs did provide slight improvements in WER, but significant improvements of 2-3 WER were gained by extending the limited highly relevant data from talk abstracts and the dev set to the larger domain-general data crawled from the 2021 ACL conference and workshop proceedings.

Without in-domain target-language monolingual data, conventional techniques for adaptation of end-to-end ST models did not apply (finetuning, backtranslation, ...). The data diversification applied by KIT via TTS 'backtranslation' (*contrastive5*, *contrastive7*) did not affect chrF or BLEU, but did provide small (0.5-0.6) improvements on COMET.

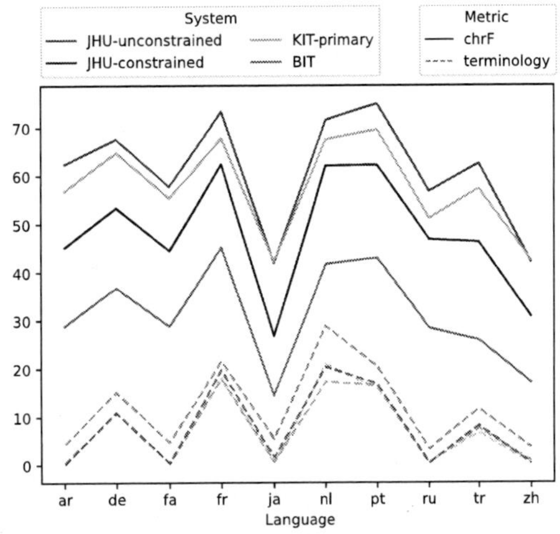

Figure 2: Official task metric performance (chrF) vs terminology recall for teams' primary submissions.

In addition to the overall evaluation set, we look at the recall of specific terminology annotated for the ACL evaluation sets. For the three submissions ($\text{JHU}_{unconstrained}$, $\text{KIT}_{primary}$, $\text{JHU}_{constrained}$) which provided supplementary ASR, we first investigate terminology recall and propagation between ASR and downstream ST. Recall that the overall WER of these systems was 16.9, 23.7, and 34.1, respectively. Of the 1107 labeled terminology words and phrases from the ACL 60-60 evaluation set annotations, 87.8% / 77.3% / 71.7% individual instances were correctly transcribed by these systems, respectively. Of these, 12.0% / 7.4% / 7.9% were then maintained and correctly translated to each target language respectively on average. We plot the official task metric (chrF) against terminology recall in Figure 2 for all primary submissions. We see that there were consistent differences across languages in how terminology was maintained, which generally but not fully corresponds to overall performance (ex: Dutch, Turkish). While the domain adaptation techniques used ensured strong *transcription* performance for the JHU and KIT submissions, this was not generally maintained for *translation* with a significant drop, converging with BIT which did not perform domain adaptation. Additional work is needed to ensure targeted lexical terms are correctly transcribed and translated, both in general as well as comparably across different languages.

While the JHU submissions finetuned to each target language individually, the KIT systems finetuned multilingually; no contrastive systems were submitted with which to ablate this point, but both teams' papers describe consistently worse performance finetuning multilingually rather than bilingually, which KIT was able to largely mitigate with language adapters in development in isolation but in their final submission on eval language adapters were consistently slightly worse (*contrastive4* 'with' vs *contrastive3* 'without.'). It remains to be seen the degree to which one-to-many models can benefit from multilingual training.

The Offline task additionally used the ACL 60-60 evaluation sets as part of their broader evaluation for 3 language pairs (en→ de, ja, zh), enabling a wider comparison across 25 total systems. We show the Multilingual task submissions compared to the Offline on these languages in Table 27. On these three language pairs, performance is generally higher than the remaining language pairs in the Multilingual task. We again consistently see stronger performance on this task from cascaded models, and unconstrained submissions or those with larger pretrained LLMs, though there are notable outliers such as the HW-TSC constrained model. The Offline submissions did not perform domain adaptation specifically to the technical ACL domain, but appear to be benefit from better domain-general performance in some cases, particularly for submissions targeting only Chinese. We note slight differences in system rankings between metrics (COMET and BLEU) and target languages, particularly for Japanese and Chinese targets, possibly highlighting the difference in metric tokenization for these pairs.

6 Speech-to-Speech Translation

Speech-to-speech translation (S2ST) involves translating audio in one language to audio in another language. In the offline setting, the translation system can assume that the entire input audio is available before beginning the translation process. This differs from streaming or simultaneous settings where the system only has access to partial input. The primary objective of this task is to encourage the advancement of automated methods for offline speech-to-speech translation.

6.1 Challenge

The participants were tasked with creating speech-to-speech translation systems that could translate from English to Chinese using various methods, such as a cascade system (ASR + MT + TTS or end-to-end speech-to-text translation + TTS), or an end-to-end / direct system. They were also allowed to use any techniques to enhance the performance of the system, apart from using unconstrained data.

6.2 Data and Metrics

Data. This task allowed the same training data from the Offline task on English-Chinese speech-to-text translation. More details are available in Sec. 2.2. In addition to the Offline task data, the following training data was allowed to help build English-Chinese speech-to-speech models and Chinese text-to-speech systems:

- **GigaS2S**, target synthetic speech for the Chinese target text of GigaST (Ye et al., 2023) that was generated with an in-house single-speaker TTS system;
- **aishell 3** (Shi et al., 2020), a multi-speaker Chinese TTS dataset.

It's noted that several datasets allowed for the Offline task such as Common Voice (Ardila et al., 2019) actually contain multi-speaker Chinese speech and text data that could help for this task.

Metrics. All systems were evaluated with both automatic and human evaluation metrics.

Automatic metrics. To automatically evaluate translation quality, the speech output was automatically transcribed with a Chinese ASR system[19] (Yao et al., 2021), and then **BLEU**[20] (Papineni et al., 2002a), **chrF**[21] (Popović, 2015b), **COMET**[22] (Rei et al., 2022) and **SEScore2**[23] (Xu et al., 2022) were computed between the generated transcript and the human-produced text reference. BLEU and chrF were computed using SacreBLEU

[19] `https://github.com/wenet-e2e/wenet/blob/main/docs/pretrained_models.en.md`

[20] sacreBLEU signature: `nrefs:1|case:mixed|eff:no|tok:zh|smooth:exp|version:2.3.1`

[21] sacreBLEU signature: `nrefs:1|case:mixed|eff:yes|nc:6|nw:0|space:no|version:2.3.1`

[22] `https://huggingface.co/Unbabel/wmt22-comet-da`

[23] `https://github.com/xu1998hz/SEScore2`

(Post, 2018). Furthermore, the output speech could be evaluated directly using BLASER (Chen et al., 2022). More information could be found at `stopes`[24] (Andrews et al., 2022).

Human evaluation. Output speech translations were evaluated with respect to translation quality and speech quality.

- **Translation quality:** Bilingual annotators were presented with the source audio, source transcript and the generated target audio, then gave scores on the translation quality between 1 and 5 (worst-to-best)). There were 4 annotators per sample and we retained the median score.
- **Output speech quality:** In addition to translation quality (capturing meaning), the quality of the speech output was also human-evaluated. The annotators were requested to give an overall score by considering three dimensions: naturalness (voice and pronunciation), clarity of speech (understandability), and sound quality (noise and other artifacts). Each sample was assessed by 4 annotators and scored on a scale of 1-5 (worst-to-best)), with a minimum score interval of 0.5.

The detailed guidelines for output speech quality evaluation were similar to last year (Anastasopoulos et al., 2022a).

6.3 Submissions

We received eight submissions from five teams. The MINETRANS team submitted four systems and each of the other teams submitted one system.

- HW-TSC (Wang et al., 2023a) submitted a cascaded system composed of an ensemble of Conformer and Transformer-based ASR models, a multilingual Transformer-based MT model and a diffusion-based TTS model. Their primary focus in their submission is to investigate the modeling ability of the diffusion model for TTS tasks in high-resource scenarios. The diffusion TTS model takes raw text as input and generates waveform by iteratively denoising on pure Gaussian noise. Based on the result, they conclude that the diffusion model outperforms normal TTS models and brings positive gain to the entire S2ST system.
- KU (Yang et al., 2023) submitted a cascade system composed of a speech-to-text translation (ST) model and a TTS model. Their ST model comprises a ST decoder and an ASR decoder. The two decoders can exchange information with each other with the interactive attention mechanism. For the TTS part, they use FastSpeech2 as the acoustic model and HiFi-GAN as the vocoder.
- NPU-MSXF (Song et al., 2023) submitted a cascaded system of separate ASR, MT, and TTS models. For ASR, they adopt ROVER-based model fusion and data augmentation strategies to improve the recognition accuracy and generalization ability. Then they use a three-stage fine-tuning process to adapt a pre-trained mBART50 model to translate the output of ASR model. The three-stage fine-tuning is based on Curriculum Learning and it involves three sets of data: (1) the original MT data, (2) the MT data in ASR transcription format and (3) the ASR outputs. For TTS, they leverage a two-stage framework, using network bottleneck features as a robust intermediate representation for speaker timbre and linguistic content disentanglement. Based on the two-stage framework, pre-trained speaker embedding is leveraged as a condition to transfer the speaker timbre in the source speech to the translated speech.
- XIAOMI (Huang et al., 2023) submitted a cascade system composed of a speech-to-text translation (ST) model and a TTS model. The ST model is the same as the one they submitted to the Offline SLT track. It is based on an encoder-decoder architecture from the pre-trained HuBERT and mBART models. For the TTS model, they use the Tacotron2 framework. It is first trained with AISHELL-3 dataset and then finetuned with GigaS2S dataset. Furthermore, they implement several popular techniques, such as data filtering, data augmentation, speech segmentation, and model ensemble, to improve the overall performance of the system.
- MINETRANS (Du et al., 2023) submitted three end-to-end S2ST systems (MINE-

[24] `https://github.com/facebookresearch/stopes/tree/main/demo/iwslt_blaser_eval`

TRANSE2E, including *primary*, *contrastive1*, and *contrastive2*), and a cascade S2ST system (MINETRANS_Cascade). Their end-to-end systems adopt the speech-to-unit translation (S2UT) framework. The end-to-end S2UT model comprises a speech encoder, a length adapter and an unit decoder. The S2UT model is trained to convert the source speech into units of target speech. A unit-based HiFi-GAN vocoder is finally applied to convert the units into waveform. Based on their results, they conclude that the widely used multi-task learning technique is not important for model convergence once large-scale labeled training data is available, which means that the mapping from source speech to target speech units can be learned directly and easily. Furthermore, they apply other techniques, such as consistency training, data augmentation, speech segmentation, and model ensemble to improve the overall performance of the system. Their cascade system consists of ASR, MT and TTS models. Their ASR and MT replicates those used for the Offline SLT submission. Their TTS model is a combination of FastSpeech2 and HiFi-GAN.

6.4 Results

Results as scored by automatic metrics are shown in Table 31 and human evaluation results are shown in Table 32 in the Appendix.

Overall results. According to the automatic metrics used in the evaluation, XIAOMI obtained the highest score in ASR-BLEU, ASR-chrF, ASR-COMET and ASR-SEScore2. NPU-MSXF obtained the second highest score, followed subsequently by HW-TSC, MINETRANS_E2E, KU and MINETRANS_Cascade. The BLEU, chrF, COMET and SEScore2 rankings were exactly the same. The scores for the test-expanded data were lower than those for the test-primary data, likely due to a domain mismatch with the training data. For human evaluation along the translation quality perspective, XIAOMI obtained the highest score, followed by NPU-MSXF, then HW-TSC and MINETRANS_E2E, then MINETRANS_Cascade, and finally KU. This ranking was mostly consistent with the automatic ranking, showing that automatic metrics were useful in evaluating the translation quality of systems. For human evaluation along the speech quality perspective, NPU-MSXF obtained the highest score, followed by HW-TSC, XIAOMI, MINETRANS_E2E, MINETRANS_Cascade and KU. With a equal weighting of translation quality and speech quality, NPU-MSXF obtained the highest overall score in human evaluation, followed by XIAOMI and the others.

S2ST approaches. This year, all systems but MINETRANS_E2E were cascaded systems, with three systems adopting an ASR + MT + TTS approach and two systems adopting an end-to-end S2T + TTS approach. This showed that cascade approach was still dominant in the community. Although MINETRANS_E2E performed better than MINETRANS_Cascade in all evaluation metrics, we could not draw conclusions on the comparison between cascade and end-to-end given the limited data points. Future challenges can encourage more direct or end-to-end submissions.

6.5 Conclusion

This is the second time that speech-to-speech translation (S2ST) is presented in one of the IWSLT tasks. S2ST is an important benchmark for general AI as other NLP tasks, e.g. dialogue system, question answering and summarization can also be implemented in speech-to-speech manner. Compared to the setting last year, the size of the training data set available to the participants is much larger. The BLEU scores obtained in this challenge is high in general, compared to MT and ST of the same language direction. Although not required by the task, NPU-MSXF is the only team that implemented speaker timbre transfer in their system. We plan to include evaluation metrics addressing this aspect in the next edition.

7 Dialect SLT

The Dialect Speech Translation shared task is a continuation of last year's task. We use the same training data as 2022 and evaluated systems on the 2022 evaluation set to measure progress; in addition, we added a new 2023 evaluation set as blind test. From the organizational perspective, we merged the call for shared task with the the Low-Resource tasks (Section 8) in order to encourage cross-submission of systems.

7.1 Challenge

Diglossic communities are common around the world. For example, Modern Standard Arabic (MSA) is used for formal spoken and written communication in most parts of the Arabic-speaking world, but local dialects such as Egyptian, Moroccan, and Tunisian are used in informal situations. Diglossia poses unique challenges to speech translation because local "low" dialects tend to be low-resource with little ASR and MT training data, and may not even have standardized writing, while resources from "high" dialects like MSA provides opportunities for transfer learning and multilingual modeling.

7.2 Data and Metrics

Participants were provided with the following datasets:

- (a) 160 hours of Tunisian conversational speech (8kHz), with manual transcripts
- (b) 200k lines of manual translations of the above Tunisian transcripts into English, making a three-way parallel data (i.e. aligned audio, transcript, translation) that supports end-to-end speech translation models
- (c) 1200 hours of Modern Standard Arabic (MSA) broadcast news with transcripts for ASR, available from MGB-2
- Approximately 42,000k lines of bitext in MSA-English for MT from OPUS (specifically: Opensubtitles, UN, QED, TED, GlobalVoices, News-Commentary).

In 2022, we constructed three conditions: The basic condition trains on (a) and (b), provided by the Linguistic Data Consortium (LDC); the dialect adaptation condition trains on (a), (b), (c), (d); the unconstrained condition can use any additional data and pre-trained models. In 2023, due to the coordinated organization with other Low-Resource Tasks this year, we renamed basic condition as **"constrained condition"**, and the other two conditions are merged as the **"unconstrained condition"**.

All train and test sets are time-segmented at the utterance level. Statistics are shown in Table 5. There are three test sets for evaluation with BLEU[25].

- **test1**: Participants are encouraged to use this for internal evaluation since references are provided. This is part of LDC2022E01 released to participants for training and development, obtained by applying the standard data split and preprocessing[26].
- **test2**: official evaluation for 2022, from LDC2022E02
- **test3**: official evaluation for 2023, from LDC2023E09

7.3 Submissions

We received submission from four teams:

- GMU (Mbuya and Anastasopoulos, 2023) participated in five language-pairs in the Low-Resource tasks as well as this task. They focused on investigating how different self-supervised speech models (Wav2vec 2.0, XLSR-53, and HuBERT) compare when initialized to an end-to-end (E2E) speech translation architecture.
- JHU (Hussein et al., 2023) submitted both cascaded and E2E systems, using transformer and branchformer architectures. They investigated the incorporation of pretrained text MT models, specifically mBART50 and distilled NLLB-200. Further, they explored different ways for system combination and handling of orthographic variation and channel mismatch.
- ON-TRAC (Laurent et al., 2023) participated in two language-pairs in the Low-Resource task as well as this task. For this task, they focused on using SAMU-XLS-R as the multilingual, multimodal pretrained speech encoder and mBART as the text decoder.
- USTC (Deng et al., 2023) proposed a method for synthesis of pseudo Tunisian-MSA-English paired data. For the cascaded system, they explored ASR with different feature extraction (VGG, GateCNN) and neural architectures (Conformer, Transformer). For E2E, they proposed using SATE and a hybrid SATE architecture to take advantage

[25] SacreBLEU signature for dialect speech translation task: `nrefs:1|case:lc|eff:no|tok:13a|smooth:exp|version:2.0.0`

[26] `https://github.com/kevinduh/iwslt22-dialect`

Dataset	Speech (#hours)	Text (#lines) Tunisian	MSA	English	Use
LDC2022E01 train	160	200k	-	200k	Constrained condition
LDC2022E01 dev	3	3833	-	3833	Constrained condition
LDC2022E01 test1	3	4204	-	4204	Participant's internal evaluation
LDC2022E02 test2	3	4288	-	4288	Evaluate progress from 2022
LDC2023E09 test3	3	4248	-	4248	Official evaluation for 2023
MGB2	1100	-	1.1M	-	Unconstrained condition
OPUS	-	-	42M	42M	Unconstrained condition
Any other data	-	-	-	-	Unconstrained condition

Table 5: Datasets for Dialect Shared Task.

of the pseudo Tunisian-MSA-English text data. Additionally, methods for adapting to ASR errors and system combination were examined.

7.4 Results

The full set of BLEU results on the English translations are available in Tables 33 and 34. We also evaluated the WER results for the ASR component of cascaded systems, in Table 35.

In general, there is an improvement compared to 2022. On test2, the best system in 2022 (achieved by the CMU team) obtained 20.8 BLEU; several systems this year improved upon that result, for example USTC's primary system achieved 23.6 BLEU and JHU's primary system achieved 21.2 BLEU. On the official evaluation on test3, the best system achieved 21.1 BLEU in the unconstrained condition and 18.1 BLEU in the constrained condition.

From the system descriptions, it appears the ingredients for strong systems include: (a) effective use of pretrained speech and text models, (b) system combination among both cascaded and E2E systems, and (c) synthetic data generation to increase the size of dialectal data.

We do not plan to continue this shared task next year. Instead, the plan is to make the data available from the LDC. We encourage researchers to continue exploring dialectal and diglossic phenomena in the future.

8 Low-resource SLT

The Low-resource Speech Translation shared task focuses on the problem of developing speech transcription and translation tools for low-resourced languages.

8.1 Challenge

This year, the task introduced speech translation of recorded utterances from Irish to English, Marathi to Hindi, Maltese to English, Pashto to French, Tamasheq to French, and Quechua to Spanish. The different language pairs vary by the amount of data available, but in general, they have in common the dearth of high-quality available resources, at least in comparison to other much higher-resourced settings.

8.2 Data and Metrics

We describe the data available for each language pair below. Table 6 provides an overview of the provided datasets.

Irish–English Irish (also known as Gaeilge) has around 170,000 L1 speakers and 1.85 million people (37% of the population) across the island (of Ireland) claim to be at least somewhat proficient with the language. In the Republic of Ireland, it is the national and first official language. It is also one of the official languages of the European Union (EU) and a recognized minority language in Northern Ireland with the ISO `ga` code.

The provided Irish audio data were compiled from Common Voice (Ardila et al., 2020a),[27] and Living-Audio-Dataset.[28] The compiled data were automatically translated into English and corrected by an Irish linguist. The Irish–English corpus consists of 11.55 hours of Irish speech data (see Table 6), translated into English texts.

Marathi–Hindi Marathi is an Indo-Aryan language which has the ISO code `mr`, and is domi-

[27] https://commonvoice.mozilla.org/en/datasets

[28] https://github.com/Idlak/Living-Audio-Dataset

Language Pairs		Train Set	Dev Set	Test Set	Additional Data
Irish–English	ga–eng	9.46	1.03	0.44	n/a
Marathi–Hindi	mr–hi	15.3	3.7	4.4	monolingual audio with transcriptions (ASR), monolingual text
Maltese–English	mlt–eng	2.5	-	1.35	monolingual audio with transcriptions (ASR), monolingual text
Pashto–French	pus–fra	61	2.5	2	n/a
Tamasheq–French	tmh–fra	17	-	-	untranscribed audio, data in other regional languages
Quechua–Spanish	que–spa	1.60	1.03	1.03	60 hours of monolingual audio with transcriptions (ASR) and MT data (not transcribed)

Table 6: Training, development and test data details (in hours) for the language pairs of the low-resource shared task.

nantly spoken in the state of Maharashtra in India. It is one of the 22 scheduled languages of India and the official language of Maharashtra and Goa. As per the 2011 Census of India, it has around 83 million speakers which covers 6.86% of the country's total population.[29] Marathi is the third most spoken language in India.

The provided Marathi–Hindi corpus consists of 22.33 hours of Marathi speech data (see Table 6) from the news domain, extracted from News On Air[30] and translated into Hindi texts.[31] The dataset was manually segmented and translated by Panlingua.[32] Additionally, the participants were directed that they may use monolingual Marathi audio data (with transcription) from Common Voice (Ardila et al., 2020a),[33] as well as the corpus provided by He et al. (2020)[34] and the Indian Language Corpora (Abraham et al., 2020).[35]

Maltese–English Maltese is a Semitic language, with about half a million native speakers, spoken in the official language of Malta and the EU. It is written in Latin script.

The provided data was divided into three parts. First, around 2.5 hours of audio with Maltese transcription and an English translation were released, along with about 7.5 hours of audio with only Maltese transcriptions. Last, the participants were directed to several monolingual Maltese textual resources. The provided datasets were taken from the MASRI corpus (Hernandez Mena et al., 2020).

Pashto–French Pashto is spoken by approximately forty to sixty million people in the world. It is particularly spoken by the Pashtun people in the south, east and southwest of Afghanistan (it is one of the two official languages), as well as in the north and northwest Pakistan but also in Iran, Tajikistan and India (Uttar Pradesh and Cashmere) and one of the two official languages of Afghanistan.

The corpus was totally provided by ELDA, and is available on the ELRA catalog: *TRAD Pashto Broadcast News Speech Corpus* (ELRA catalogue, 2016b) that consists of audio files and *TRAD Pashto-French Parallel corpus of transcribed Broadcast News Speech - Training data* (ELRA catalogue, 2016a) which are their transcriptions.

This dataset is a collection of about 108 hours of Broadcast News with transcriptions in Pashto and translations into French text. The dataset is built from collected recordings from 5 sources: Ashna TV, Azadi Radio, Deewa Radio, Mashaal Radio and Shamshad TV. Original training data contains 99 hours of speech in Pashto, which corresponds to 29,447 utterances translated into French. Training data corresponds to 61 hours of speech (Table 6).

Tamasheq–French Tamasheq is a variety of Tuareg, a Berber macro-language spoken by nomadic

[29]https://censusindia.gov.in/nada/index.php/catalog/42561
[30]https://newsonair.gov.in
[31]https://github.com/panlingua/iwslt2023_mr-hi
[32]http://panlingua.co.in/
[33]https://commonvoice.mozilla.org/en/datasets
[34]https://www.openslr.org/64/
[35]https://www.cse.iitb.ac.in/~pjyothi/indiccorpora/

tribes across North Africa in Algeria, Mali, Niger and Burkina Faso. It accounts for approximately 500,000 native speakers, being mostly spoken in Mali and Niger. This task is about translating spoken Tamasheq into written French. Almost 20 hours of spoken Tamasheq with French translation are freely provided by the organizers. A major challenge is that no Tamasheq transcription is provided, as Tamasheq is a traditionally oral language.

The provided corpus is a collection of radio recordings from Studio Kalangou[36] translated to French. It comprises 17 hours of clean speech in Tamasheq, translated into the French language. The organizers also provided a 19-hour version of this corpus, including 2 additional hours of data that was labeled by annotators as potentially noisy. Both versions of this dataset share the same validation and test sets. Boito et al. (2022a) provides a thorough description of this dataset.

In addition to the 17 hours of Tamasheq audio data aligned to French translations, and in light of recent work in self-supervised models for speech processing, we also provide participants with unlabeled raw audio data in the Tamasheq language, as well as in other 4 languages spoken from Niger: French (116 hours), Fulfulde (114 hours), Hausa (105 hours), Tamasheq (234 hours) and Zarma (100 hours). All this data comes from the radio broadcastings of Studio Kalangou and Studio Tamani.[37]

Note that this language pair is a continuation of last year's shared task. An additional separate test set was provided this year.

Quechua–Spanish Quechua is an indigenous language spoken by more than 8 million people in South America. It is mainly spoken in Peru, Ecuador, and Bolivia where the official high-resource language is Spanish. It is a highly inflective language based on its suffixes which agglutinate and are found to be similar to other languages like Finnish. The average number of morphemes per word (synthesis) is about two times larger than in English. English typically has around 1.5 morphemes per word and Quechua has about 3 morphemes per word.

There are two main regional divisions of Quechua known as Quechua I and Quechua II. This data set consists of two main types of Quechua spoken in Ayacucho, Peru (Quechua Chanka ISO: `quy`) and Cusco, Peru (Quechua Collao ISO: `quz`) which are both part of Quechua II and, thus, considered a "southern" languages. We label the data set with `que` - the ISO norm for Quechua II mixtures.

The constrained setting allowed a Quechua-Spanish speech translation dataset along with the additional parallel (text-only) data for machine translation compiled from previous work (Ortega et al., 2020). The audio files for training, validation, and test purposes consisted of excerpts of the Siminchik corpus (Cardenas et al., 2018) that were translated by native Quechua speakers. For the unconstrained setting, participants were directed to another larger data set from the Siminchik corpus which consisted of 60 hours of fully transcribed Quechua audio (monolingual).

8.2.1 Metrics

We use standard lowercase BLEU as well as charF++ to automatically score all submissions. Additional analyses for some language pairs are provided below.

Due to the exceptionally hard setting, which currently leads to generally less competent translation systems, we did not perform the human evaluation of the outputs.

8.3 Submissions

Below we discuss all submissions for all language pairs, given that there were several overlaps. A brief summary per language is below:

- Irish–English received four submissions from one team (GMU);
- Marathi–Hindi received submissions from four teams (ALEXA AI, BUT, GMU, and SRI-B);
- Maltese–English received five submissions from one team (UM-DFKI);
- Pashto–French received submissions from two teams (GMU, ON-TRAC);
- Tamasheq–French received submissions from four teams (ALEXA AI, GMU, NAVER, and ON-TRAC);
- Quechua-Spanish received three submissions (GMU, NAVER, and QUESPA).

[36] https://www.studiokalangou.org/
[37] https://www.studiotamani.org/

Below we discuss each team's submission in detail:

- ALEXA AI (Vishnu et al., 2023) submitted one primary and three contrastive systems, all of these are in the unconstrained condition (Table 44) for Tamasheq-French, and one primary and five contrastive systems on the unconstrained condition for Marathi–Hindi. For Marathi–Hindi, their systems relied on an end-to-end speech translation approach, using the wav2vec 2.0 base model finetuned on 960 hours of English speech (Baevski et al., 2020b) as encoder baseline and it was also finetuned on 94 hours of Marathi audio data. The team focused on evaluating three strategies including data augmentation, an ensemble model and post-processing techniques. For Tamasheq–French, they reuse the same end-to-end AST model proposed by the ON-TRAC Consortium in the last year's IWSLT edition (Boito et al., 2022b). This model consists of a speech encoder that is initialized by the wav2vec 2.0 (Baevski et al., 2020a) base model pre-trained on 243 hours of Tamasheq audio data released by the ON-TRAC Consortium [38]. The decoder of this model is a shallow stack of 2 transformer layers with 4 attention heads. A feed-forward layer is put in between the encoder and the decoder for matching the dimension of the encoder output and that of the decoder input. In this work, they focus on leveraging different data augmentation techniques including audio stretching, back translation, paraphrasing, and weighted loss. Another important endeavor of their work is experimenting with different post-processing approaches with LLMs, such as re-ranking, sentence correction, and token masking. Besides, they also ensemble AST models trained with different seeds and data augmentation methods, which is proven to improve the performance of their systems. Their primary system scores 9.30 BLEU on the 2023 test set.

- BUT (Kesiraju et al., 2023) submitted one primary and one contrastive system using the ESPnet (Inaguma et al., 2021) toolkit. The primary system was built with the end-to-end and bilingual ASR model while the contrastive was built with a cascade which uses various backbone models including ASR, the bilingual ASR, transformer-based seq2seq MT, LM for re-scoring and XLM.

- GMU (Mbuya and Anastasopoulos, 2023) focused on end-to-end speech translation systems. End-to-end (E2E) transformer-based encoder-decoder architecture (Vaswani et al., 2017) was used for primary constrained submission. For unconstrained submissions, they explored self-supervised pre-trained speech models and used wav2vec 2.0 (Baevski et al., 2020a) and HuBERT (Hsu et al., 2021) for the low resource task. They used wav2vec 2.0 - with removing the last three layers - for their primary submission. HuBERT was used for the contrastive1 submission - without removing any layer. For contrastive2, End-to-end with ASR (E2E-ASR) architecture uses the same architecture as the E2E. The difference is that a pre-trained ASR model was used to initialize its encoder.

- ON-TRAC (Laurent et al., 2023) participated in the Pashto–French (one primary and three contrastive systems, both for constrained and unconstrained settings) and Tamasheq–French (one primary and five contrastive systems, all of which are unconstrained (c.f. Table 44). For Pashto–French, the primary cascaded system is based on a convolutional model (Gehring et al., 2017) upgraded, while contrastive3 is based on small basic transformers. For Primary and contrastive1 systems, SAMU-XLS-R (Khurana et al., 2022) was used with pre-trained encoder with 100 and 53 languages. The two constrained contrastive E2E systems share the same encoder-decoder architecture using transformers (Vaswani et al., 2017). The difference lies in the use or not of a transformer language model trained from scratch on the provided dataset.

  All of their systems for Tamasheq–French are based on the same end-to-end encoder-decoder architecture. In this architecture, the encoder is initialized by a pre-

[38] https://huggingface.co/LIA-AvignonUniversity/IWSLT2022-tamasheq-only

trained semantic speech representation learning model named SAMU-XLS-R (Khurana et al., 2022), while the decoder is initialized with the decoder of the pre-trained mBART model. Their work heavily relies on different versions of the SAMU-XLS-R model, which are pre-trained on different combinations of multilingual corpora of 53, 60, and 100 languages. In addition, they leverage training data from higher resource corpora, such as CoVoST-2 (Wang et al., 2020a) and Europarl-ST (Iranzo-Sánchez et al., 2020), for training their end-to-end models. Their primary system, which scores 15.88 BLEU on the Tamasheq–French 2023 test set, was trained on the combination of (CoVoST-2, Europarl-ST and the IWSLT 2022's test set), with the encoder is initialized by the SAMU-XLS-R model trained on the data gathered from 100 languages.

- NAVER (Gow-Smith et al., 2023) submitted one primary and two contrastive systems to the Tamasheq–French track, as well as one primary and two contrastive systems for the unconstrained condition in the Quechua–Spanish track. In their work for the Tamasheq–French track, they concentrate on parameter-efficient training methods that can perform both ST and MT in a multilingual setting. In order to do so, they initialize their models with a pre-trained multilingual MT model (mBART (Liu et al., 2020) or NLLB (NLLB Team et al., 2022)), which is then fine-tuned on the ST task by inputting features extracted with a frozen pre-trained speech representation model (wav2vec 2.0 or HuBERT (Hsu et al., 2021)). The encoder of their translation model is slightly modified where they stack several modality-specific layers at the bottom. In addition, adapter layers are also inserted in between layers of the pre-trained MT model at both the encoder and decoder sides. While these new components get fine-tuned during the training process, the pre-trained components of the MT model are frozen. One of the appealing characteristics of their approach is that it allows the same model to do both speech-to-text and text-to-text translation (or transcription). Furthermore, their method maximizes knowledge transfer to improve low-resource performance. Their primary system, which is ensembled from 3 different runs on the combination of both ST and ASR data, scores 23.59 BLEU on the 2023 test set.

  For the Quechua–Spanish track, the overall architecture for their systems consists of first initializing a PLM which was then fine-tuned on the speech translation task by inputting features from a frozen pre-trained speech representation. Similar adaptations were done with an MT model to control domain and length mismatch issues. One of the interesting takeaways from their approaches is that their contrastive 2 system (1.3 billion parameters (NLLB Team et al., 2022)) outperformed their contrastive 1 system (3.3 billion parameters (NLLB Team et al., 2022)) despite it having less parameters. NAVER's primary submission was an ensemble approach that included the use of PLMs for both the ASR (Baevski et al., 2020a) and MT systems ((NLLB Team et al., 2022)) and included training on both Tamasheq and Quechua data. Their submissions to QUE–SPA did not include the use of mBART or HuBERT (Hsu et al., 2021) as was done for other language pairs that NLE submitted.

- QUESPA (Ortega et al., 2023) submitted to both conditions (constrained and unconstrained) a total of six systems including a primary, contrastive 1, and contrastive 2 for each condition. They also claim to have tried several other combinations but did not submit those systems. For the constrained condition, their primary system scored second best, slightly less than team GMU with a BLEU score of 1.25 and chrF2 of 25.35. They also scored third best for the constrained condition with 0.13 BLEU and 10.53 chrF2 using their contrastive 1 system. It is worthwhile to note that chrF2 was used by the organizers when BLEU scores were below five. For their constrained systems, a direct speech translation system was submitted similar to the GMU team's primary approach that used Fairseq (Wang et al., 2020b). QUESPA extracted mel-filter bank (MFB) features similar to the S2T approach in previous work Wang et al. (2020b). The main difference between QUESPA's submission and GMU's submissions was that the GMU team increased the number of decoder layers to 6 which resulted in a slightly better system for GMU. The other systems submitted for the constrained setting were cascade systems where ASR and MT were combined in a pipeline setting. Their contrastive 1 and 2 system submissions for the constrained task respectively used wav2letter++ (Pratap et al., 2019) and a conformer architecture similar to previous work (Gulati et al., 2020) along with an OpenNMT (Klein et al., 2017) translation system trained on the constrained ST and MT data. Both of those systems performed poorly scoring less than 1 BLEU. For the unconstrained condition, the three systems that were presented by QUESPA consisted of pipeline approaches of PLMs that were fine-tuned on the additional 60 hours of Siminchik audio data along with the constrained data. Their primary and contrastive 1 unconstrained ASR systems were trained using the 102-language FLEURS (Conneau et al., 2023) model and used the MT system that was based on NLLB (NLLB Team et al., 2022) which just so happens to include Quechua as one of its languages. Their contrastive 2 ASR system was based on wav2letter++ (Pratap et al., 2019) while their contrastive 2 MT system was identical to the MT systems used for their Primary and Contrastive 1 submissions.

- SRI-B (Radhakrishnan et al., 2023) submitted four systems. For Marathi–English, they submitted one primary and one contrastive system in the constrained setting and one primary and one contrastive system in the unconstrained setting. They used end-to-end speech translation networks comprising a conformer encoder and a transformer decoder for both constrained and unconstrained.

- UM-DFKI (Williams et al., 2023) submitted five systems. It included one primary and four contrastive systems in unconstrained settings. They used a pipeline approach for all of their submissions. For ASR, their system builds upon (Williams, 2022) on fine-tuning XLS-R based system. mBART-50 was used for fine-tuning the MT part of the pipeline.

8.4 Results

Irish–English As discussed earlier, only the GMU team participated in the GA–ENG translation track and submitted one primary system to constrained, one primary system to unconstrained and the rest of the two systems to contrastive on unconstrained conditions. The end-to-end and end-to-end with ASR models submitted primary constrained and contrastive2 unconstrained systems. Both the systems achieved 15.1 BLEU scores. They did not perform well in comparison to the wav2vec 2.0 and HuBERT models. The detail of the results of this track can be found in Table 36 and 37.

Marathi–Hindi The results of this translation track can be found in Table 38 and 39. Overall we see varying performances among the systems submitted to this track, with some performing much better on the test set. Out of the 16 submissions, the SRI-B team's primary system achieved the best result of 31.2 and 54.8 in BLEU and in charF++ respectively on the constrained condition while the BUT team's primary system achieved the best results of 39.6 in BLEU and 63.3 in charF++ on the unconstrained condition. In both constrained and unconstrained conditions, the GMU systems achieved the lowest results of 3.3 and 5.9 in BLEU and 16.8 and 20.3 in charF++ respectively.

Maltese–English The results of this translation track can be found in Table 42. UM-DFKI used contrastive approaches in training their ASR system. For their contrastive1 system, their fine-tuning consisted of using Maltese, Arabic, French and Italian corpora. Their contrastive2, contrastive3, and contrastive4 approaches respectively use a subset from Arabic, French and Italian ASR corpus along with Maltese data. The best result of 0.7 BLEU was achieved with their contrastive1 system.

Pashto–French The detailed results can be found in Table 41 and Table 40 of the Appendix. We rank the system performance based on test BLEU scores. The best score BLEU was achieved by ON-TRAC primary system (SAMU-XLS-R model trained on 100 languages). For the constrained condition, the cascaded approach based on convolutional models, gives the best performance.

Tamasheq-French The results of this translation track can be found in Table 43 and 44. Compared to the last year's edition, this year has witnessed a growing interest in this low-resource translation track in terms of both quantity and quality of submissions. Almost all submissions achieve relatively better results than the last year's best system (5.7 BLEU on test2022 (Boito et al., 2022b)). Furthermore, it is notable that cascaded systems are not favorable in this track while none of the submitted systems is of this kind.

This year, this language pair remains a challenging low-resource translation track. There is only one submission to the constrained condition from GMU with an end-to-end model scoring 0.48 BLEU on this year's test set. For this reason, all the participants are in favor of exploiting pre-trained models, hence being subject to the unconstrained condition. Among these pre-trained models, self-supervised learning (SSL) from speech models remains a popular choice for speech encoder initializing. Using a wav2vec2.0 model pre-trained on unlabelled Tamasheq data for initializing their speech encoder, GMU gains +7.55 BLEU score in comparison with their Transformer-based encoder-decoder model training from scratch (their primary constrained system). At the decoder side, pre-trained models such as mBART or NLLB are commonly leveraged for initializing the decoder of the end-to-end ST model. Besides, data augmentation and ensembling are also beneficial as shown by ALEXA AI when they consistently achieve ~ 9 BLEU in all of their settings.

Outstanding BLEU scores can be found in the work of the ON-TRAC team. An interesting pre-trained model named SAMU-XLS-R is shown to bring significant improvements. This is a multilingual multimodal semantic speech representation learning framework (Khurana et al., 2022) which fine-tunes the pre-trained speech transformer encoder XLS-R (Babu et al., 2021) using semantic supervision from the pre-trained multilingual semantic text encoder LaBSE (Feng et al., 2022). Exploiting this pre-trained model and training end-to-end ST models on the combinations of different ST corpora, they achieve more than 15 BLEU in all of their settings.

NAVER tops this translation track by a multilingual parameter-efficient training solution that allows them to leverage strong pre-trained speech and text models to maximize performance in low-resource languages. Being able to be trained on both ST and ASR data due to the multilingual nature, all of their submissions heavily outperform the second team ON-TRAC by considerable margins. Their primary system, which is ensembled from 3 different runs, uses NLLB1.3B as the pre-trained MT system, and wav2vec2.0 Niger-Mali [39] as the speech presentation extractor. After being trained on a combination of both ST corpora (Tamasheq-French, mTEDx fr-en, mTEDx es-fr, mTEDx es-en, mTEDx fr-es (Salesky et al., 2021)) and AST corpora (TED-LIUM v2 (Rousseau et al., 2014), mTEDx fr, mTEDx es), this system establishes an impressive state-of-the-art performance of the Tamasheq-French language pair, scoring 23.59 BLEU on the 2023 test set.

Quechua–Spanish The QUE–SPA results for all systems submitted to this low-resource translation track can be found in Table 45 and 46 of the appendix. To our knowledge, this first edition of the QUE–SPA language pair in the low-resource track of IWSLT has witnessed the best BLEU scores achieved by any known system in research for Quechua. The two best performing systems: 1.46 BLEU (constrained) and 15.70 (unconstrained) show that there is plenty of room to augment approaches presented here. Nonetheless, submissions from the three teams: GMU, NAVER, and QUESPA have shown that it is possible to use PLMs to create speech-translation systems with as little as 1.6 hours of parallel speech data. This is a notable characteristic of this task and surpasses previous work in the field.

We have found that the NLLB (NLLB Team et al., 2022) system's inclusion of Quechua in recent years has had a greater impact than expected for ease-of-use. Similarly, the use of Fairseq (Wang et al., 2020b) seems to be the preferred toolkit for creating direct S2T systems, cascaded or not. The QUE–SPA submissions for the unconstrained conditions preferred the use of a cascading system in a pipeline approach where pre-trained models were fine-tuned first for ASR and then for MT.

The constrained setting leaves much room for improvement. Nonetheless, GMU and QUESPA's near identical submissions have shown that the in-

[39] https://huggingface.co/LIA-AvignonUniversity/IWSLT2022-Niger-Mali

crease of 3 layers during decoding can be powerful and should be explored further. It would be worthwhile for the organizers of the QUE–SPA track to obtain more parallel data including translations for future iterations of this task.

The unconstrained setting clearly can benefit from an ensembling technique and training with multiple languages – in these submissions, the training of a model with an additional language like Tamasheq alongside Quechua does not seem to have a negative impact on performance. Although, it is hard to ascertain whether the slight performance gain of less than 1 BLEU point of the NLE team's submission compared to QUESPA's submission was due to the ensembling, freezing of the models, or the language addition.

As a final takeaway, the NLE team's submissions scored quite well under the unconstrained condition. It should be noted that for other language pairs NLE's high system performance was also due to the ensembling of systems that were executed using different initialization parameters on at least three unique runs. As an aside, small gains were achieved under the constrained condition when comparing the GMU submission to the QUESPA system due to the increase in decoding layers. QUESPA's inclusion of a language model on top of a state-of-the-art dataset (Fleurs) allowed them to achieve scores similar to NAVER's without additional tuning or ensembling. State-of-the-art performance was achieved by all three teams that submitted systems.

General Observations As in previous years, the low-resource shared task proved particularly challenging for the participants, but there are several encouraging signs that further reinforce the need for more research in the area.

First, more teams than ever participated in the shared task, showing a continued interest in the field. Second, we note that for the language pair that was repeated from last year (Tamasheq–French), almost all submissions outperformed last year's best submission, with an accuracy increase of more than 17 BLEU points in the unconstrained setting. Last, we highlight the breadth of different approaches employed by the participants, ranging from the use of finetuned pre-trained models to pre-training from scratch, to parameter efficient dine-tuning as well as cascaded pipeline systems, all of which seem to have benefits to offer, to a certain extent, to different language pairs.

Limitations As noted by some participants, the Irish–English and Maltese–English translation track data has limitations. For Irish–English, the speech translation systems can achieve very high BLEU scores on the test set if the built systems have used wav2vec 2.0 and/or the Irish ASR model which is trained on the Common Voice (Ardila et al., 2020b) dataset. Similarly, the GMU team has achieved high BLEU scores especially when they used wav2vec 2.0 and HuBERT models. We plan to continue this translation track next year by updating the test and training data to thoroughly investigate the data quality as well as the reason to obtain the high BLEU scores. For Maltese–English, some participants reported issues with the data quality, which we hope to resolve in future iterations of the shared task.

9 Formality Control for SLT

Different languages encode formality distinctions in different ways, including the use of honorifics, grammatical registers, verb agreement, pronouns, and lexical choices. While machine translation (MT) systems typically produce a single generic translation for each input segment, SLT requires adapting the translation output to be appropriate to the context of communication and target audience. This shared task thus challenges machine translation systems to generate translations of different formality levels.

9.1 Challenge

Task Given a source text, X in English, and a target formality level, $l \in \{F, IF\}$, the goal in formality-sensitive machine translation (Niu et al., 2017) is to generate a translation, Y, in the target language that accurately preserves the meaning of the source text and conforms to the desired formality level, l. The two formality levels typically considered are "F" for formal and "IF" for informal, resulting in two translations: Y_F and Y_{IF} respectively. For example, the formal and informal translations for the source text "Yeah Did your mom know you were throwing the party?" (originally informal) in Korean are shown in the table below:

This shared task builds on last year's offering, which evaluated systems' ability to control formality on the following translation tasks: translation from English (EN) into Korean (KO) and Vietnamese (VI) in the *supervised* setting, and from English (EN) into Portugal Portuguese (PT)

Source: Yeah Did your mom know you were throwing the party?

Korean Informal: 그, 어머님은 [F]네가[/F] 그 파티 연 거 [F]아셔[/F]?

Korean Formal: 그, 어머님은 [F]님이[/F] 그 파티 연 거 [F]아세요[/F]?

Table 7: Contrastive formal and informal translations into Korean. Grammatical formality markers are annotated with [F]text[/F].

and Russian (RU) in the *zero-shot setting*. Results showed that formality-control is challenging in zero-shot settings and for languages with many grammatical and lexical formality distinctions. This year's edition invited participants to advance research in effective methods for bridging the gap in formality control for zero-shot cases and for languages with rich grammatical and lexical formality distinctions.

9.2 Data and Metrics

Participants were provided with test data, as well as MT quality and formality control metrics. In addition, we provided training data, consisting of formal and informal translation of texts for the supervised language pairs (EN-KO, EN-VI).

9.2.1 Formality Annotated Dataset

We provide targeted datasets comprising source segments paired with two contrastive reference translations, one for each formality level (informal and formal) for two EN-VI, EN-KO in the *supervised* setting and EN-RU, EN-PT in the *zero-shot* setting (see Example 7)[40]. The sizes and properties of the released datasets for all the language pairs are listed in Table 8. Formal translations tend to be longer than informal texts for Vietnamese compared to other language pairs. The number of phrasal formality annotations ranges from 2 to 3.5 per segment, with Korean exhibiting a higher diversity between the formal and informal translations as indicated by the TER score.

9.2.2 Training Conditions

We allowed submissions under the constrained and unconstrained data settings described below:

[40]`https://github.com/amazon-science/contrastive-controlled-mt/tree/main/IWSLT2023`

Constrained (C) Participants were allowed to use the following resources: Textual MuST-C v1.2 (Di Gangi et al., 2019b), CCMatrix (Schwenk et al., 2021), OpenSubtitles (Lison and Tiedemann, 2016) and dataset in the constrained setting from the Formality Control track at IWSLT22 (Anastasopoulos et al., 2022a).

Unconstrained (U) Participants could use any publicly available datasets and resources: the use of pre-trained language models was also allowed. Additionally, using additionally automatically annotated bitext with formality labels was also allowed.

9.3 Formality Classifier

We release a multilingual classifier (MC) trained to predict the formality of a text for all the language pairs: EN-KO, EN-VI, EN-RU, and EN-PT. We finetune an `xlm-roberta-base` (Conneau et al., 2020) model on human-written formal and informal translations following the setup from Briakou et al. (2021). Our classifier achieves an accuracy of > 98% in detecting the formality of human-written translations for the four target languages (Table 10). Participants were allowed to use the classifier both for model development and for evaluation purposes as discussed below.

9.4 Automatic Metrics

We evaluate the submitted system outputs along the following two dimensions:

1. Overall translation quality, evaluated using SacreBLEU v2.0.0 (Papineni et al., 2002b; Post, 2018), and COMET (Rei et al., 2020b) on both the shared task-provided test sets based on topical chat (Gopalakrishnan et al., 2019) and on the FLORES devtest (NLLB Team et al., 2022; Goyal et al., 2022).

2. Formality control, evaluated using:
   - Matched-Accuracy (mACC), a reference-based corpus-level automatic metric that leverages phrase-level formality markers from the references to classify a system-generated hypothesis as formal, informal, or neutral (Nadejde et al., 2022).
   - Classifier-Accuracy (cACC), a reference-free metric that uses the multilingual formality classifier discussed above to label a system-generated hypothesis as formal or informal.

Language	Type	Size	Length			# Phrasal Annotations		TER(F, IF)
			Source	Formal	Informal	Formal	Informal	
EN-VI	Train	400	20.35	28.52	25.48	2.71	1.49	23.70
	Test	600	21.82	29.59	26.77	2.79	1.55	23.00
EN-KO	Train	400	20.00	13.41	13.40	3.35	3.35	24.52
	Test	600	21.22	13.56	13.55	3.51	3.51	25.32
EN-RU	Test	600	21.02	18.03	18.00	2.06	2.05	13.59
EN-PT	Test	600	21.36	20.22	20.27	1.93	1.93	10.46

Table 8: Formality Track Shared Task Data Statistics.

Participant	Settings	Classifier Use	Languages	Model type	Formality
UMD-baseline	U	✓	All	Multilingual	Exemplars
CoCoA-baseline	C	✗	EN-{VI, KO}	Bilingual	Side-constraint
AppTek	U	✗	EN-{PT, RU}	Bilingual	Side-constraint
HW-TSC	U+C	✓	All	Bilingual	Side-constraint
KUxUpStage	U	✓	All	Bilingual	N/A
UCSC	U	✗	EN-{VI, KO}	Multilingual	Style-Embedding

Table 9: Formality Track Submissions Summary. Most participants train bilingual systems but leverage a diverse set of formality encoding mechanisms for control.

Target Language	Accuracy
Korean	99.9%
Vietnamese	99.3%
Russian	99.9%
Portuguese	98.6%

Table 10: The multilingual classifier can identify the target formality for human written text across all languages with > 98% accuracy.

The final corpus-level score for each of the two metrics described above is the percentage of system outputs that matches the desired formality level. For example, the cAcc for the target formality, Formal (F), is given by, $c\text{Acc}(F) = \frac{1}{M}\sum_{i=1}^{M} \mathbb{1}[MC(Y) == F]$, where M is the number of system outputs.

9.5 Submissions

We provide methodology descriptions and a summary of the two baseline systems and four submissions received for the shared task below and in Table 9. Three out of six submissions made use of the formality classifier released for system development. We received two multilingual and four bilingual systems. We refer the reader to the system description papers for more details.

- CoCoA (baseline) uses a supervised method where a generic neural MT model is fine-tuned on labeled contrastive translation pairs (Nadejde et al., 2022). For the constrained, supervised setting, the generic neural MT model was trained on parallel data allowed for the constrained task and fine-tuned on formal and informal data released for the shared task. Following Nadejde et al. (2022), contrastive pairs were upsampled with a fixed upsampling factor of five for all language pairs.

- UMD (baseline) uses 16 few-shot target formality-specific exemplars to prompt XGLM-7.5B (Lin et al., 2021) to generate style-controlled translations. For the supervised setting, these examples are drawn from the official training data, whereas for the zero-shot setup, the examples from the Tatoeba corpus (Artetxe and Schwenk, 2019) are filtered and marked with target formality using the provided formality classifier.

- AppTek (Bahar et al., 2023) submitted outputs using their production quality translation systems that support formality-controlled translation generation for EN-PT and EN-

RU. These are Transformer-Big models trained on a large public dataset from the OPUS collection (Tiedemann, 2012), automatically marked with formality using a sequence of regular expressions. The formality level is encoded with a pseudo-token at the beginning of each training source sentence with one of 3 values: formal, informal, or no style.

- HW-TSC (Wang et al., 2023a) describes a system that uses a multi-stage pre-training strategy on task-provided data to train strong bilingual models. Using these bilingual models, they employ beam re-ranking on the outputs generated using the test source. The generated hypothesis are ranked using the formality classifier and phrasal annotations, iteratively fine-tuning the model on this data until test performance convergences. Initial formality control is enabled by a special token and re-affirmed through classifier output and annotations from training.

- KUxUPSTAGE (Lee et al., 2023) uses large-scale bilingual transformer-based MT systems trained on high-quality datasets and MBART for the supervised and zero-shot settings respectively. They generate a formality-controlled translation dataset for supervision in the zero-shot setting using GPT-4 and filter the generated source-translation pairs using the formality classifier. All bilingual models are then finetuned independently for the two target formality directions to generate formality-controlled outputs, resulting in #(Language-pairs) × 2 (Formal/Informal) models.

- UCSC (Vakharia et al., 2023) focused on using a single multilingual translation model for all the language pairs under the unconstrained setting. They finetune the pre-trained model, `mBART-large-50` (Tang et al., 2020), using the provided contrastive translations (§ 9.2.1) with an added *style embedding intervention* layer.

9.6 Results

Tables 47 and 48 in the Appendix show the main automatic evaluation results for the shared task.

Overall Results For the supervised language pairs in both constrained and unconstrained settings, most submitted systems were successfully able to control formality. The average `mAcc` scores ranged from 78-100. Controlling formality in Korean was found to be more challenging than translating with formality control in Vietnamese as reflected by the relatively lower `mAcc` scores which we believe to be due to the variation in formality expression of Korean honorific speech reflected in pretraining data.

HW-TSC consistently achieves the best scores across the board for all language pairs and both settings due to the use of transductive learning. Interestingly, the constrained submission by HW-TSC achieves better or competitive results compared to their unconstrained system suggesting that the use of a pre-trained language model or additional resources is not necessary to generate high-quality formality-controlled translations. Generally, the systems generate higher quality outputs in the formal setting relative to the informal setting for both supervised language pairs according to BLEU and COMET, which might be due to the bias of the dataset used during pre-training which is typically news and hence more formal.

In the zero-shot unconstrained setting, this formality bias is even more prominent. We observe a much wider distribution in the formality scores for English-Portuguese (`mAcc`: F 90-100, IF: 58-100), possibly due to the high ambiguity in the informal language and the confounding dialectal influence of Brazilian Portuguese dominant in the pre-training corpora, which is known to use formal register even in typically informal contexts (Costa-jussà et al., 2018). HW-TSC and APPTEK achieve the best translation quality for English-Portuguese and English-Russian respectively. The lowest scoring submission in both quality and formality control (UCSC) did not include any fine-tuning or adaptation of the base MBART model to the two zero-shot language pairs: English-Russian and English-Portuguese. This suggests that formality information is not transferred from the unrelated language pairs, EN-KO and EN-VI, and that some language-specific supervision is needed to mark grammatical formality appropriately in Russian and Portuguese.

How well do systems match the desired target formality? We show the distribution of the scores generated using the formality classifier for

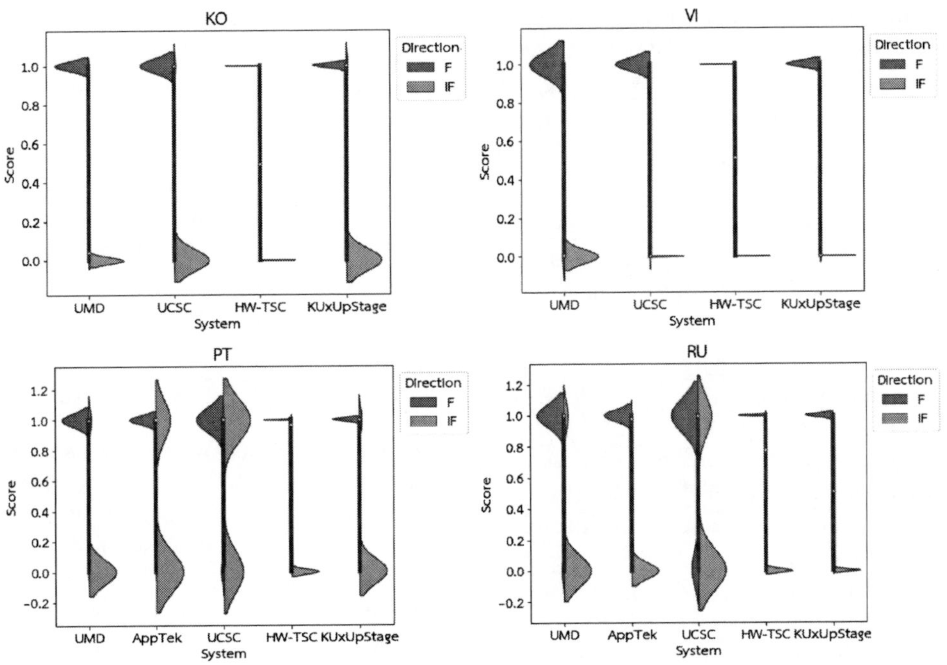

Figure 3: Formality Classifier Scores' Distribution on the submitted system outputs in the Unconstrained setting: HW-TSC can precisely match the target formality as depicted by the peaky distribution.

all the systems submitted to all language pairs under the unconstrained setting in Figure 3. For supervised language pairs, formal (blue) and informal (orange) output scores peak at 1.0 and 0.0 respectively. In the zero-shot setting, for both Portuguese (APPTEK, UCSC) and Russian (UCSC) translations, the informal outputs have a bimodal distribution, highlighting that these models generate many formal translations under informal control.

How contrastive are the generated translations? We show the Translation Edit Rate (TER) between the formal and informal outputs for all submitted systems across all language pairs in Figure 4. While the references are designed to be minimally contrastive, the formal and informal system outputs exhibit a much larger edit distance. HW-TSC has the lowest TER rate for all language pairs except English-Korean.

Discussion Overall, the shared task results show that finetuning a strong supervised general-purpose MT system with as low as 400 in-domain contrastive samples seems to be sufficient in generating high-quality contrastive formality-controlled translations. However, several avenues for improvement remain open. The languages that

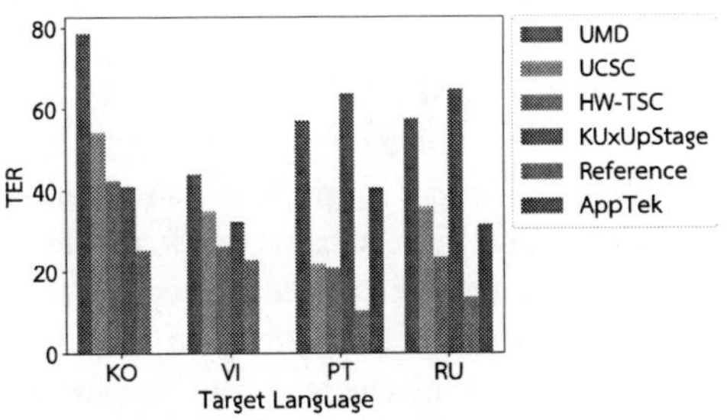

Figure 4: TER between the Formal (F) and Informal (IF) Outputs for all submitted systems across all language pairs.

exhibit an ambiguous or richer formality distinction either due to close dialectal variations (like Portuguese) or due to multiple levels of honorifics (like Korean and Japanese) still remain challenging. Unsupervised transfer of formality knowledge between related languages remains relatively unexplored (Sarti et al., 2023). Furthermore, this year's task only considered two levels of formality distinctions with minimal edits. It remains unclear whether the models are also capable of modeling multiple levels of formality potentially with minimal edits in the generated translations. Finally, no submissions have explored monolingual editing of translations as a potential solution for formality-controlled MT, despite the edit-focused nature of the contrastive translations. We recommend that future work on formality-controlled machine translation targets these challenges.

10 Automatic Dubbing

10.1 Challenge

This task focuses on automatic dubbing: translating the speech in a video into a new language such that the new speech is natural when overlayed on the original video (see Figure 5).

Participants were given German videos, along with their text transcripts, and were asked to produced dubbed videos where the German speech has been translated in to English speech.

Automatic dubbing is a very difficult/complex task (Brannon et al., 2023), and for this shared task we focus on the characteristic which is perhaps most characteristic of dubbing: isochrony. Isochrony refers to the property that the speech translation is time aligned with the original speaker's video. When the speaker's mouth is moving, a listener should hear speech; likewise, when their mouth isn't moving, a listener should not hear speech.

To make this task accessible for small academic teams with limited training resources, we make some simplifications: First, we assume the input speech has already been converted to text using an ASR system and the desired speech/pause times have been extracted from the input speech. Second, to alleviate the challenges of training a TTS model, the output is defined to be phonemes and their durations. These phonemes and durations are played through an open-source FastSpeech2 (Ren et al., 2022) text-to-speech model to produce the final speech.[41]

10.2 Data and Metrics

Official training and test data sets were provided[42] by the organizers. The training data was derived from CoVoST2 (Wang et al., 2021) and consists of:

1. Source (German) text
2. Desired target speech durations (e.g. 2.1s of speech, followed by a pause, followed by 1.3s of speech)
3. Target (English) phonemes and durations corresponding to a translation which adheres to the desired timing

The test data was produced by volunteers and consists of videos of native German speakers reading individual sentences from the German CoVoST-2 test set.[43] This test set was divided in to two subsets; *Subset 1* where there are no pauses in the speech and *Subset 2* where there is one or more pause in the speech. More details on this data are presented in (Chronopoulou et al., 2023).

10.3 Submissions

Despite high initial interest, we received only one submission, which was from the Huawei Translation Services Center (HW-TSC) (Rao et al., 2023). However, we had two systems (Chronopoulou et al., 2023; Pal et al., 2023) built for the task for which we had not yet performed human evaluation, so we still had enough systems for a interesting comparison.

- Interleaved (Baseline): Our first baseline and the basis for this shared task is from Chronopoulou et al. (2023). They propose to jointly model translations and speech timing, giving the model the freedom to change the translation to fit the timing, or and make scarifies in translation quality to meet timing constraints or relax timing constraints to improve translation quality. This is achieved by simply binning target phoneme durations and interleaving them with target phonemes during training and inference. To avoid teaching the model that speech durations should be prioritized over translation quality[44], noise with standard deviation 0.1 is added to the target phrase durations to simulate the source durations used at inference.

- Factored (Baseline): Pal et al. (2023) build on the first baseline by using target factors (García-Martínez et al., 2016), where alongside predicting phoneme sequences as the target, we also predict durations for each phoneme as a target factor. Additionally, they propose auxiliary counters, which are similar to target factors except the model is not

[41] https://github.com/mtresearcher/FastSpeech2

[42] https://github.com/amazon-science/iwslt-autodub-task/tree/main/data

[43] Each volunteer provided their consent to use this data for automatic dubbing task.

[44] Median speech overlap is just 0.731 in a large corpus of human dubs (Brannon et al., 2023)

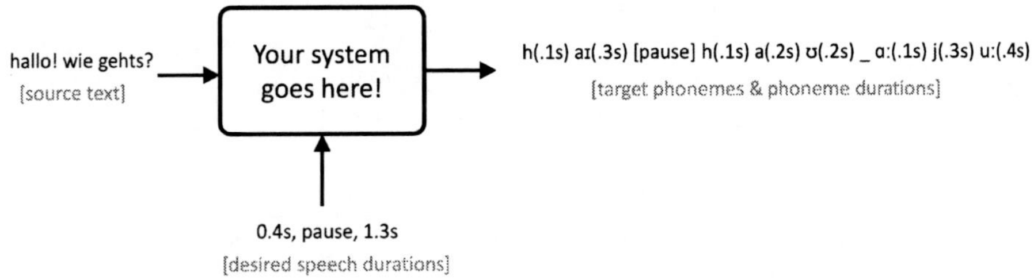

Figure 5: To illustrate, here's an example in which "hallo! wei gehts?" is translated to "hi! how are you?" such that the output will fit in the desired target speech durations of 0.4s and 1.3s, with a pause in between

trained to predict them. Instead, they providing additional information to the decoder consisting of (1) the total number of frames remaining, (2), the number of pauses remaining, and (3) the number of frames remaining in the current phrase. As in the first baseline, noise of standard deviation 0.1 is added to the target phrase durations during training to simulate source durations.

- Text2Phone (Baseline): As a sanity check, we added a third, non-isochronic baseline trained to take in German text and produce English phonemes, without any duration information. We train on the same data as the first two baselines, but exclude duration information from training and instead predict phoneme durations using the duration model from the FastSpeech2 model.

- HW-TSC: In contrast to our three baselines, (Rao et al., 2023) took a more traditional approach to dubbing and followed the prior works on verbosity control (Lakew et al., 2021, 2019) to first generate a set of translation candidates and later re-rank them. Their system consists of four parts: 1) voice activity detection followed by pause alignment, 2) generating a list of translation candidates, 3) phoneme duration prediction, followed by 4) re-ranking/scaling the candidates based on the durations (see Figure 6). With the last step in the pipeline, the top scored candidate is ensured to have the best speech overlap with the source speech amongst all candidate translations.

10.4 Evaluation & Metric

The dubbed English videos were judged by a mixture of native and non-native speakers, all of which were researchers in automatic dubbing. For each video in the the test set, one judge was shown the four system outputs in random order and asked to rate them from 1-6. The judges were not given a defined rubric or guidelines to follow but were asked to be consistent.

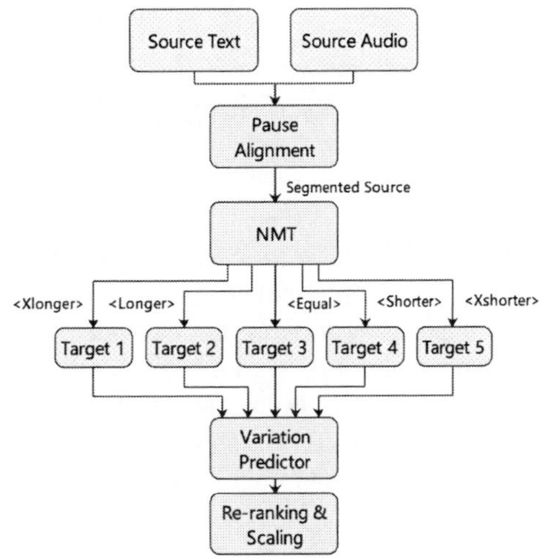

Figure 6: System diagram for HW-TSC dubbing system. Image from Rao et al. (2023).

As a metric we opted for mean opinion score (MOS) methodology where the scores for a system as judged by humans are averaged in one score.[45]

Feedback from the judges indicate that the baseline and submitted systems often produce poor translations (perhaps due to the small amount of training data used by each system), and the voice quality from the FastSpeech 2 model was far from perfect. However, they felt that having all systems share the same voice made it much easier to compare across dubbing systems.

When we looked at the distribution of scores per

[45]https://en.wikipedia.org/wiki/Mean_opinion_score

annotator (judge) level, the numbers showed that each annotator had a bias towards dubbing, some liked dubbing more than others which is intuitive but has not been studied before in the context of automatic dubbing. As shown in Table 11, it is clear that annotator A2 had a significantly higher preference for dubbing as compared to annotator A4 in terms of MOS.

Annotator	MOS↑	CI
A1	3.34	±0.16
A2	3.74	±0.19
A3	3.53	±0.13
A4	3.07	±0.15

Table 11: MOS (on a scale of 1-6) with confidence interval (CI) at 95% per annotator showing the biases towards general purpose dubbed content.

We also looked at MOS for the two different subsets to understand whether it was difficult for the submitted systems to dub the videos. As it turns out, *Subset 1* has an significantly higher MOS of 3.54 (± 0.11) compared to *Subset 2* with a MOS of 3.31 (± 0.11). This shows it is significantly more difficult for all systems to dub *Subset 2* than *Subset 1*.

10.5 Results

Results are shown in Table 12. All three dubbing systems outperform the non-isochronic Text2Phone baseline (Chronopoulou et al., 2023), as expected. The factored baseline improves over the interleaved baseline, consistent with the automatic metric results reported by Pal et al. (2023).

The HW-TSC system (Rao et al., 2023) outperforms all the baselines in terms of mean opinion score, making it the clear winner of the IWSLT 2023 dubbing shared task. Unfortunately, since HW-TSC system was unconstrained (it trains on additional bitext compared to the baselines) and uses fundamentally different approaches than the baselines, it is not possible to attribute it's performance to any single factor.

Lip-sync is an important feature of dubbing, it is important that the final generated audio is in sync with the lip movements of the on-screen speaker in the original video. As an analysis, we looked at Lip-Sync Error Distance (LSE-D) (Chung and Zisserman, 2016) following the evaluation methodology in Hu et al. (2021). LSE-D is not a perfect metric but it is an indication to

		MOS↑	
System	Constrained?	Mean	CI
Text2Phone	Yes	3.16	±0.19
Interleaved	Yes	3.33	±0.18
Factored	Yes	3.43	±0.19
HW-TSC	No	3.77	±0.19

Table 12: Mean opinion score for baselines 1) Text2Phone 2) Interleaved (Chronopoulou et al., 2023) 3) Factored (Pal et al., 2023) and 4) submitted system of HW-TSC (Rao et al., 2023).

	LSE-D↓	
System	Subset1	Subset2
Original	7.39	7.67
Text2Phone	11.64	13.31
Interleaved	11.71	12.35
Factored	11.73	12.48
HW-TSC	12.11	12.77

Table 13: Results of Lip-Sync Error Distance (LSE-D) via Syncnet pre-trained model (Chung and Zisserman, 2016). Lower the better.

the amount of Lip-Sync errors in the video. From Table 13, *Subset 1* consistently has a lower lip-sync error than *Subset 2* in all cases pointing that its difficult to generate lip-synced dubs for *Subset 2*. This result is also in line with the MOS scores we obtained for two subsets where the annotators preferred dubs for *Subset 1*. Secondly, original videos show significantly lower lip-sync error distance (12.x v/s 7.x) than dubbed videos showing that automatic dubbing research still has a long way to go to reach lip-sync quality in original videos.

Acknowledgements

Claudia Borg, Thierry Declerck, Rishu Kumar and John Judge acknowledge H2020 LT-Bridge Project (GA 952194). Rishu Kumar would also like to thank the EMLCT[46] programme. Atul Kr. Ojha and John P. McCrae would like to thank Science Foundation Ireland (SFI) under Grant Number SFI/12/RC/2289_ P2 Insight_2, and Panlingua Language Processing LLP for providing the Marathi-Hindi speech translation data and for their support. John Judge would also like to acknowledge the support of SFI under grant SFI/13/RC/2106_P2 ADPAT. Ondřej Bojar would like to acknowledge the grant 19-26934X

[46]https://mundus-web.coli.uni-saarland.de/

(NEUREM3) of the Czech Science Foundation. Antonios Anastasopoulos and Milind Agarwal are supported by the US National Science Foundation CCRI-Planning 2234895 award, as well as a National Endowment for the Humanities PR-276810-21 award.

References

Basil Abraham, Danish Goel, Divya Siddarth, Kalika Bali, Manu Chopra, Monojit Choudhury, Pratik Joshi, Preethi Jyoti, Sunayana Sitaram, and Vivek Seshadri. 2020. Crowdsourcing speech data for low-resource languages from low-income workers. In *Proceedings of the 12th Language Resources and Evaluation Conference*, pages 2819–2826.

Yasuhiro Akiba, Marcello Federico, Noriko Kando, Hiromi Nakaiwa, Michael Paul, and Jun'ichi Tsujii. 2004. Overview of the IWSLT04 Evaluation Campaign. In *Proceedings of the International Workshop on Spoken Language Translation*, pages 1–12, Kyoto, Japan.

Antonios Anastasopoulos, Loïc Barrault, Luisa Bentivogli, Marcely Zanon Boito, Ondřej Bojar, Roldano Cattoni, Anna Currey, Georgiana Dinu, Kevin Duh, Maha Elbayad, Clara Emmanuel, Yannick Estève, Marcello Federico, Christian Federmann, Souhir Gahbiche, Hongyu Gong, Roman Grundkiewicz, Barry Haddow, Benjamin Hsu, Dávid Javorský, Věra Kloudová, Surafel Lakew, Xutai Ma, Prashant Mathur, Paul McNamee, Kenton Murray, Maria Nădejde, Satoshi Nakamura, Matteo Negri, Jan Niehues, Xing Niu, John Ortega, Juan Pino, Elizabeth Salesky, Jiatong Shi, Matthias Sperber, Sebastian Stüker, Katsuhito Sudoh, Marco Turchi, Yogesh Virkar, Alexander Waibel, Changhan Wang, and Shinji Watanabe. 2022a. Findings of the IWSLT 2022 evaluation campaign. In *Proceedings of the 19th International Conference on Spoken Language Translation (IWSLT 2022)*, pages 98–157, Dublin, Ireland (in-person and online). Association for Computational Linguistics.

Antonios Anastasopoulos, Loïc Barrault, Luisa Bentivogli, Marcely Zanon Boito, Ondřej Bojar, Roldano Cattoni, Anna Currey, Georgiana Dinu, Kevin Duh, Maha Elbayad, Clara Emmanuel, Yannick Estève, Marcello Federico, Christian Federmann, Souhir Gahbiche, Hongyu Gong, Roman Grundkiewicz, Barry Haddow, Benjamin Hsu, Dávid Javorský, Věra Kloudová, Surafel Lakew, Xutai Ma, Prashant Mathur, Paul McNamee, Kenton Murray, Maria Nădejde, Satoshi Nakamura, Matteo Negri, Jan Niehues, Xing Niu, John Ortega, Juan Pino, Elizabeth Salesky, Jiatong Shi, Matthias Sperber, Sebastian Stüker, Katsuhito Sudoh, Marco Turchi, Yogesh Virkar, Alexander Waibel, Changhan Wang, and Shinji Watanabe. 2022b. Findings of the IWSLT 2022 Evaluation Campaign. In *Proceedings of the 19th International Conference on Spoken Language Translation (IWSLT 2022)*, pages 98–157, Dublin, Ireland (in-person and online). Association for Computational Linguistics.

Antonios Anastasopoulos, Ondřej Bojar, Jacob Bremerman, Roldano Cattoni, Maha Elbayad, Marcello Federico, Xutai Ma, Satoshi Nakamura, Matteo Negri, Jan Niehues, Juan Pino, Elizabeth Salesky, Sebastian Stüker, Katsuhito Sudoh, Marco Turchi, Alexander Waibel, Changhan Wang, and Matthew Wiesner. 2021. FINDINGS OF THE IWSLT 2021 EVALUATION CAMPAIGN. In *Proceedings of the 18th International Conference on Spoken Language Translation (IWSLT 2021)*, pages 1–29, Bangkok, Thailand (online). Association for Computational Linguistics.

Pierre Andrews, Guillaume Wenzek, Kevin Heffernan, Onur Çelebi, Anna Sun, Ammar Kamran, Yingzhe Guo, Alexandre Mourachko, Holger Schwenk, and Angela Fan. 2022. stopes-modular machine translation pipelines. In *Proceedings of the The 2022 Conference on Empirical Methods in Natural Language Processing: System Demonstrations*, pages 258–265.

Ebrahim Ansari, Amittai Axelrod, Nguyen Bach, Ondrej Bojar, Roldano Cattoni, Fahim Dalvi, Nadir Durrani, Marcello Federico, Christian Federmann, Jiatao Gu, Fei Huang, Kevin Knight, Xutai Ma, Ajay Nagesh, Matteo Negri, Jan Niehues, Juan Pino, Elizabeth Salesky, Xing Shi, Sebastian Stüker, Marco Turchi, and Changhan Wang. 2020. Findings of the IWSLT 2020 Evaluation Campaign. In *Proceedings of the 17th International Conference on Spoken Language Translation (IWSLT 2020)*, Seattle, USA.

Rosana Ardila, Megan Branson, Kelly Davis, Michael Henretty, Michael Kohler, Josh Meyer, Reuben Morais, Lindsay Saunders, Francis M Tyers, and Gregor Weber. 2019. Common voice: A massively-multilingual speech corpus. *arXiv preprint arXiv:1912.06670*.

Rosana Ardila, Megan Branson, Kelly Davis, Michael Henretty, Michael Kohler, Josh Meyer, Reuben Morais, Lindsay Saunders, Francis M Tyers, and Gregor Weber. 2020a. Common voice: A massively-multilingual speech corpus. In *LREC*.

Rosana Ardila, Megan Branson, Kelly Davis, Michael Kohler, Josh Meyer, Michael Henretty, Reuben Morais, Lindsay Saunders, Francis Tyers, and Gregor Weber. 2020b. Common voice: A massively-multilingual speech corpus. In *Proceedings of The 12th Language Resources and Evaluation Conference*, pages 4218–4222.

Mikel Artetxe and Holger Schwenk. 2019. Massively multilingual sentence embeddings for zero-shot cross-lingual transfer and beyond. *Transactions of the Association for Computational Linguistics*, 7:597–610.

Arun Babu, Changhan Wang, Andros Tjandra, Kushal Lakhotia, Qiantong Xu, Naman Goyal, Kritika

Singh, Patrick von Platen, Yatharth Saraf, Juan Pino, et al. 2021. XLS-R: Self-supervised cross-lingual speech representation learning at scale. *arXiv preprint arXiv:2111.09296*.

Alexei Baevski, Yuhao Zhou, Abdelrahman Mohamed, and Michael Auli. 2020a. wav2vec 2.0: A framework for self-supervised learning of speech representations. In *Advances in Neural Information Processing Systems*, volume 33, pages 12449–12460.

Alexei Baevski, Yuhao Zhou, Abdelrahman Mohamed, and Michael Auli. 2020b. wav2vec 2.0: A framework for self-supervised learning of speech representations. *Advances in Neural Information Processing Systems*, 33:12449–12460.

Parnia Bahar, Patrick Wilken, Javier Iranzo-Sánchez, Mattia Di Gangi, Evgeny Matusov, and Zoltán Tüske. 2023. Speech Translation with Style: AppTek's Submissions to the IWSLT Subtitling and Formality Tracks in 2023. In *Proceedings of the 20th International Conference on Spoken Language Translation (IWSLT)*.

Luisa Bentivogli, Mauro Cettolo, Marco Gaido, Alina Karakanta, Alberto Martinelli, and Marco Turchi Matteo Negri. 2021. Cascade versus Direct Speech Translation: Do the Differences Still Make a Difference? In *Proceedings of the 59th Annual Meeting of the Association for Computational Linguistics*, Bangkok, Thailand. Association for Computational Linguistics.

Marcely Zanon Boito, Fethi Bougares, Florentin Barbier, Souhir Gahbiche, Loïc Barrault, Mickael Rouvier, and Yannick Estéve. 2022a. Speech resources in the tamasheq language. *Language Resources and Evaluation Conference (LREC)*.

Marcely Zanon Boito, John Ortega, Hugo Riguidel, Antoine Laurent, Loïc Barrault, Fethi Bougares, Firas Chaabani, Ha Nguyen, Florentin Barbier, Souhir Gahbiche, and Yannick Estève. 2022b. ON-TRAC Consortium Systems for the IWSLT 2022 Dialect and Low-resource Speech Translation Tasks. In *Proceedings of the 19th International Conference on Spoken Language Translation (IWSLT)*.

William Brannon, Yogesh Virkar, and Brian Thompson. 2023. Dubbing in Practice: A Large Scale Study of Human Localization With Insights for Automatic Dubbing. *Transactions of the Association for Computational Linguistics*, 11:419–435.

Eleftheria Briakou, Sweta Agrawal, Joel Tetreault, and Marine Carpuat. 2021. Evaluating the evaluation metrics for style transfer: A case study in multilingual formality transfer. In *Proceedings of the 2021 Conference on Empirical Methods in Natural Language Processing*, pages 1321–1336, Online and Punta Cana, Dominican Republic. Association for Computational Linguistics.

Ronald Cardenas, Rodolfo Zevallos, Reynaldo Baquerizo, and Luis Camacho. 2018. Siminchik: A speech corpus for preservation of southern quechua. *ISI-NLP 2*, page 21.

Mauro Cettolo, Marcello Federico, Luisa Bentivogli, Jan Niehues, Sebastian Stüker, K. Sudoh, K. Yoshino, and Christian Federmann. 2017. Overview of the IWSLT 2017 Evaluation Campaign. In *Proceedings of the 14th International Workshop on Spoken Language Translation (IWSLT 2017)*, pages 2–14, Tokyo, Japan.

Mauro Cettolo, Jan Niehues, Sebastian Stüker, Luisa Bentivogli, Roldano Cattoni, and Marcello Federico. 2015. The IWSLT 2015 Evaluation Campaign. In *Proceedings of the 12th International Workshop on Spoken Language Translation (IWSLT 2015)*, Da Nang, Vietnam.

Mauro Cettolo, Jan Niehues, Sebastian Stüker, Luisa Bentivogli, and Marcello Federico. 2013. Report on the 10th IWSLT Evaluation Campaign. In *Proceedings of the Tenth International Workshop on Spoken Language Translation (IWSLT 2013)*, Heidelberg, Germany.

Mauro Cettolo, Jan Niehues, Sebastian Stüker, Luisa Bentivogli, and Marcello Federico. 2014. Report on the 11th IWSLT Evaluation Campaign, IWSLT 2014. In *Proceedings of the Eleventh International Workshop on Spoken Language Translation (IWSLT 2014)*, Lake Tahoe, USA.

Mauro Cettolo, Jan Niehues, Sebastian Stüker, Luisa Bentivogli, and Marcello Federico. 2016. The IWSLT 2016 Evaluation Campaign. In *Proceedings of the 13th International Workshop on Spoken Language Translation (IWSLT 2016)*, Seattle, USA.

Mingda Chen, Paul-Ambroise Duquenne, Pierre Andrews, Justine Kao, Alexandre Mourachko, Holger Schwenk, and Marta R. Costa-jussà. 2022. Blaser: A text-free speech-to-speech translation evaluation metric.

Sanyuan Chen, Chengyi Wang, Zhengyang Chen, Yu Wu, Shujie Liu, Zhuo Chen, Jinyu Li, Naoyuki Kanda, Takuya Yoshioka, Xiong Xiao, Jian Wu, Long Zhou, Shuo Ren, Yanmin Qian, Yao Qian, Micheal Zeng, and Furu Wei. 2021. Wavlm: Large-scale self-supervised pre-training for full stack speech processing. *IEEE Journal of Selected Topics in Signal Processing*, 16:1505–1518.

Colin Cherry and George Foster. 2019. Thinking slow about latency evaluation for simultaneous machine translation. *arXiv preprint arXiv:1906.00048*.

Kyunghyun Cho and Masha Esipova. 2016. Can neural machine translation do simultaneous translation? *arXiv preprint arXiv:1606.02012*.

Alexandra Chronopoulou, Brian Thompson, Prashant Mathur, Yogesh Virkar, Surafel M. Lakew, and Marcello Federico. 2023. Jointly Optimizing Translations and Speech Timing to Improve Isochrony in Automatic Dubbing. ArXiv:2302.12979.

J. S. Chung and A. Zisserman. 2016. Out of time: automated lip sync in the wild. In *Workshop on Multi-view Lip-reading, ACCV*.

Alexis Conneau, Kartikay Khandelwal, Naman Goyal, Vishrav Chaudhary, Guillaume Wenzek, Francisco Guzmán, Edouard Grave, Myle Ott, Luke Zettlemoyer, and Veselin Stoyanov. 2020. Unsupervised cross-lingual representation learning at scale. In *Proceedings of the 58th Annual Meeting of the Association for Computational Linguistics*, pages 8440–8451, Online. Association for Computational Linguistics.

Alexis Conneau, Min Ma, Simran Khanuja, Yu Zhang, Vera Axelrod, Siddharth Dalmia, Jason Riesa, Clara Rivera, and Ankur Bapna. 2023. Fleurs: Few-shot learning evaluation of universal representations of speech. In *2022 IEEE Spoken Language Technology Workshop (SLT)*, pages 798–805. IEEE.

Marta R. Costa-jussà, Marcos Zampieri, and Santanu Pal. 2018. A neural approach to language variety translation. In *Proceedings of the Fifth Workshop on NLP for Similar Languages, Varieties and Dialects (VarDial 2018)*, pages 275–282, Santa Fe, New Mexico, USA. Association for Computational Linguistics.

Pan Deng, Shihao Chen, Weitai Zhang, Jie Zhang, and Lirong Dai. 2023. The USTC's Dialect Speech Translation System for IWSLT 2023. In *Proceedings of the 20th International Conference on Spoken Language Translation (IWSLT)*.

Mattia A. Di Gangi, Roldano Cattoni, Luisa Bentivogli, Matteo Negri, and Marco Turchi. 2019a. MuST-C: a Multilingual Speech Translation Corpus. In *Proceedings of the 2019 Conference of the North American Chapter of the Association for Computational Linguistics: Human Language Technologies, Volume 1 (Long and Short Papers)*, pages 2012–2017, Minneapolis, Minnesota.

Mattia A. Di Gangi, Roldano Cattoni, Luisa Bentivogli, Matteo Negri, and Marco Turchi. 2019b. MuST-C: a Multilingual Speech Translation Corpus. In *Proceedings of the 2019 Conference of the North American Chapter of the Association for Computational Linguistics: Human Language Technologies, Volume 1 (Long and Short Papers)*, pages 2012–2017, Minneapolis, Minnesota. Association for Computational Linguistics.

Yichao Du, Guo Zhengsheng, Jinchuan Tian, Zhirui Zhang, Xing Wang, Jianwei Yu, Zhaopeng Tu, Tong Xu, and Enhong Chen. 2023. The MineTrans Systems for IWSLT 2023 Offline Speech Translation and Speech-to-Speech Translation Tasks. In *Proceedings of the 20th International Conference on Spoken Language Translation (IWSLT)*.

Matthias Eck and Chiori Hori. 2005. Overview of the IWSLT 2005 evaluation campaign. In *Proceedings of the International Workshop on Spoken Language Translation*, pages 1–22, Pittsburgh, PA.

ELRA catalogue. 2016a. Trad pashto broadcast news speech corpus. `https://catalogue.elra.info/en-us/repository/browse/ELRA-S0381/`. ISLRN: 918-508-885-913-7, ELRA ID: ELRA-S0381.

ELRA catalogue. 2016b. Trad pashto-french parallel corpus of transcribed broadcast news speech - training data. `http://catalog.elda.org/en-us/repository/browse/ELRA-W0093/`. ISLRN: 802-643-297-429-4, ELRA ID: ELRA-W0093.

Angela Fan, Shruti Bhosale, Holger Schwenk, Zhiyi Ma, Ahmed El-Kishky, Siddharth Goyal, Mandeep Baines, Onur Celebi, Guillaume Wenzek, Vishrav Chaudhary, Naman Goyal, Tom Birch, Vitaliy Liptchinsky, Sergey Edunov, Edouard Grave, Michael Auli, and Armand Joulin. 2020. Beyond english-centric multilingual machine translation.

Marcello Federico, Luisa Bentivogli, Michael Paul, and Sebastian Stüker. 2011. Overview of the IWSLT 2011 Evaluation Campaign. In *Proceedings of the International Workshop on Spoken Language Translation*, pages 11–27, San Francisco, USA.

Marcello Federico, Mauro Cettolo, Luisa Bentivogli, Michael Paul, and Sebastian Stüker. 2012. Overview of the IWSLT 2012 Evaluation Campaign. In *Proceedings of the International Workshop on Spoken Language Translation*, pages 11–27, Hong Kong, HK.

F. Feng, Y. Yang, D. Cer, N. Arivazhagan, and W. Wang. 2022. Language-agnostic BERT Sentence Embedding. In *Proceedings of the 60th ACL*.

Cameron Shaw Fordyce. 2007. Overview of the IWSLT 2007 evaluation campaign. In *Proceedings of the International Workshop on Spoken Language Translation*, pages 1–12, Trento, Italy.

Markus Freitag, George Foster, David Grangier, Viresh Ratnakar, Qijun Tan, and Wolfgang Macherey. 2021a. Experts, errors, and context: A large-scale study of human evaluation for machine translation. *Transactions of the Association for Computational Linguistics*, 9:1460–1474.

Markus Freitag, Ricardo Rei, Nitika Mathur, Chi-kiu Lo, Craig Stewart, George Foster, Alon Lavie, and Ondřej Bojar. 2021b. Results of the WMT21 metrics shared task: Evaluating metrics with expert-based human evaluations on TED and news domain. In *Proceedings of the Sixth Conference on Machine Translation*, pages 733–774, Online. Association for Computational Linguistics.

Ryo Fukuda, Yuta Nishikawa, Yasumasa Kano, Yuka Ko, Tomoya Yanagita, Kosuke Doi, Mana Makinae, Sakriani Sakti, Katsuhito Sudoh, and Satoshi Nakamura. 2023. NAIST Simultaneous Speech-to-speech Translation System for IWSLT 2023. In *Proceedings of the 20th International Conference on Spoken Language Translation (IWSLT)*.

Mercedes García-Martínez, Loïc Barrault, and Fethi Bougares. 2016. Factored neural machine translation architectures. In *Proceedings of the 13th International Conference on Spoken Language Translation*, Seattle, Washington D.C. International Workshop on Spoken Language Translation.

Jonas Gehring, Michael Auli, David Grangier, Denis Yarats, and Yann N. Dauphin. 2017. Convolutional sequence to sequence learning.

Karthik Gopalakrishnan, Behnam Hedayatnia, Qinlang Chen, Anna Gottardi, Sanjeev Kwatra, Anu Venkatesh, Raefer Gabriel, and Dilek Hakkani-Tür. 2019. Topical-Chat: Towards knowledge-grounded open-domain conversations. In *Proc. Interspeech 2019*, pages 1891–1895.

Edward Gow-Smith, Alexandre Berard, Marcely Zanon Boito, and Ioan Calapodescu. 2023. NAVER LABS Europe's Multilingual Speech Translation Systems for the IWSLT 2023 Low-Resource Track. In *Proceedings of the 20th International Conference on Spoken Language Translation (IWSLT)*.

Naman Goyal, Cynthia Gao, Vishrav Chaudhary, Peng-Jen Chen, Guillaume Wenzek, Da Ju, Sanjana Krishnan, Marc'Aurelio Ranzato, Francisco Guzmán, and Angela Fan. 2022. The Flores-101 evaluation benchmark for low-resource and multilingual machine translation. *Transactions of the Association for Computational Linguistics*, 10:522–538.

Anmol Gulati, James Qin, Chung-Cheng Chiu, Niki Parmar, Yu Zhang, Jiahui Yu, Wei Han, Shibo Wang, Zhengdong Zhang, Yonghui Wu, and Ruoming Pang. 2020. Conformer: Convolution-augmented transformer for speech recognition. *Interspeech*, pages 5036–5040.

Jiaxin Guo, Daimeng Wei, Zhanglin Wu, Zongyao Li, Zhiqiang Rao, Minghan Wang, Hengchao Shang, Xiaoyu Chen, Zhengzhe Yu, Shaojun Li, Yuhao Xie, Lizhi Lei, and Hao Yang. 2023. The HW-TSC's Simultaneous Speech-to-Text Translation system for IWSLT 2023 evaluation. In *Proceedings of the 20th International Conference on Spoken Language Translation (IWSLT)*.

Yuchen Han, Xiaoqian Liu, Hao Chen, Yuhao Zhang, Chen Xu, Tong Xiao, and Jingbo Zhu. 2023. The NiuTrans End-to-End Speech Translation System for IWSLT23 English-to-Chinese Offline Task. In *Proceedings of the 20th International Conference on Spoken Language Translation (IWSLT)*.

Fei He, Shan-Hui Cathy Chu, Oddur Kjartansson, Clara Rivera, Anna Katanova, Alexander Gutkin, Isin Demirsahin, Cibu Johny, Martin Jansche, Supheakmungkol Sarin, and Knot Pipatsrisawat. 2020. Open-source multi-speaker speech corpora for building Gujarati, Kannada, Malayalam, Marathi, Tamil and Telugu speech synthesis systems. In *Proceedings of the Twelfth Language Resources and Evaluation Conference*, pages 6494–6503, Marseille, France. European Language Resources Association.

Kevin Heffernan, Onur Çelebi, and Holger Schwenk. 2022. Bitext mining using distilled sentence representations for low-resource languages. In *Findings of the Association for Computational Linguistics: EMNLP 2022*, pages 2101–2112, Abu Dhabi, United Arab Emirates. Association for Computational Linguistics.

Carlos Daniel Hernandez Mena, Albert Gatt, Andrea DeMarco, Claudia Borg, Lonneke van der Plas, Amanda Muscat, and Ian Padovani. 2020. MASRI-HEADSET: A Maltese corpus for speech recognition. In *Proceedings of the Twelfth Language Resources and Evaluation Conference*, pages 6381–6388, Marseille, France. European Language Resources Association.

Oleksii Hrinchuk, Vladimir Bataev, Evelina Bakhturina, and Boris Ginsburg. 2023. NVIDIA NeMo Offline Speech Translation Systems for IWSLT 2023. In *Proceedings of the 20th International Conference on Spoken Language Translation (IWSLT)*.

Wei-Ning Hsu, Benjamin Bolte, Yao-Hung Hubert Tsai, Kushal Lakhotia, Ruslan Salakhutdinov, and Abdelrahman Mohamed. 2021. Hubert: Self-supervised speech representation learning by masked prediction of hidden units. *IEEE/ACM Trans. Audio, Speech and Lang. Proc.*, 29:3451–3460.

Chenxu Hu, Qiao Tian, Tingle Li, Wang Yuping, Yuxuan Wang, and Hang Zhao. 2021. Neural dubber: Dubbing for videos according to scripts. In *Thirty-Fifth Conference on Neural Information Processing Systems*.

Wuwei Huang, Mengge Liu, Xiang Li, Yanzhi Tian, Fengyu Yang, Wen Zhang, Jian Luan, Bin Wang, Yuhang Guo, and Jinsong Su. 2023. The Xiaomi AI Lab's Speech Translation Systems for IWSLT 2023 Offline Task, Simultaneous Task and Speech-to-Speech Task. In *Proceedings of the 20th International Conference on Spoken Language Translation (IWSLT)*.

Amir Hussein, Cihan Xiao, Neha Verma, Matthew Wiesner, Thomas Thebaud, and Sanjeev Khudanpur. 2023. JHU IWSLT 2023 Dialect Speech Translation System Description. In *Proceedings of the 20th International Conference on Spoken Language Translation (IWSLT)*.

Muhammad Huzaifah, Kye Min Tan, and Richeng Duan. 2023. I2R's End-to-End Speech Translation System for IWSLT 2023 Offline Shared Task. In *Proceedings of the 20th International Conference on Spoken Language Translation (IWSLT)*.

Hirofumi Inaguma, Brian Yan, Siddharth Dalmia, Pengcheng Guo, Jiatong Shi, Kevin Duh, and Shinji Watanabe. 2021. ESPnet-ST IWSLT 2021 Offline Speech Translation System. In *Proceedings of the 18th International Conference on Spoken Language Translation (IWSLT)*.

Javier Iranzo-Sánchez, Joan Albert Silvestre-Cerdà, Javier Jorge, Nahuel Roselló, Adrià Giménez, Albert Sanchis, Jorge Civera, and Alfons Juan. 2020. Europarl-st: A multilingual corpus for speech translation of parliamentary debates. In *Proc. of 45th Intl. Conf. on Acoustics, Speech, and Signal Processing (ICASSP 2020)*, pages 8229–8233, Barcelona (Spain).

Dávid Javorský, Dominik Macháček, and Ondřej Bojar. 2022. Continuous rating as reliable human evaluation of simultaneous speech translation. In *Proceedings of the Seventh Conference on Machine Translation (WMT)*, pages 154–164, Abu Dhabi, United Arab Emirates (Hybrid). Association for Computational Linguistics.

Japan Translation Federation JTF. 2018. JTF Translation Quality Evaluation Guidelines, 1st Edition (in Japanese).

Yasumasa Kano, Katsuhito Sudoh, and Satoshi Nakamura. 2023. Average Token Delay: A Latency Metric for Simultaneous Translation. In *Proceedings of Interspeech 2023*. To appear.

Alina Karakanta, Luisa Bentivogli, Mauro Cettolo, Matteo Negri, and Marco Turchi. 2022a. Post-editing in automatic subtitling: A subtitlers' perspective. In *Proceedings of the 23rd Annual Conference of the European Association for Machine Translation*, pages 261–270, Ghent, Belgium. European Association for Machine Translation.

Alina Karakanta, François Buet, Mauro Cettolo, and François Yvon. 2022b. Evaluating subtitle segmentation for end-to-end generation systems. In *Proceedings of the Thirteenth Language Resources and Evaluation Conference*, pages 3069–3078, Marseille, France. European Language Resources Association.

Santosh Kesiraju, Karel Beneš, Maksim Tikhonov, and Jan Černocký. 2023. BUT Systems for IWSLT 2023 Marathi - Hindi Low Resource Speech Translation Task. In *Proceedings of the 20th International Conference on Spoken Language Translation (IWSLT)*.

Sameer Khurana, Antoine Laurent, and James Glass. 2022. Samu-xlsr: Semantically-aligned multimodal utterance-level cross-lingual speech representation. *IEEE Journal of Selected Topics in Signal Processing*, pages 1–13.

Guillaume Klein, Yoon Kim, Yuntian Deng, Jean Senellart, and Alexander Rush. 2017. OpenNMT: Open-source toolkit for neural machine translation. In *Proceedings of ACL 2017, System Demonstrations*, pages 67–72, Vancouver, Canada. Association for Computational Linguistics.

Surafel M Lakew, Yogesh Virkar, Prashant Mathur, and Marcello Federico. 2021. Isometric mt: Neural machine translation for automatic dubbing. *arXiv preprint arXiv:2112.08682*.

Surafel Melaku Lakew, Mattia Di Gangi, and Marcello Federico. 2019. Controlling the output length of neural machine translation. In *Proc. IWSLT*.

Antoine Laurent, Souhir Gahbiche, Ha Nguyen, Haroun Elleuch, Fethi Bougares, Antoine Thiol, Hugo Riguidel, Salima Mdhaffar, Gaëlle Laperrière, Lucas Maison, Sameer Khurana, and Yannick Estève. 2023. ON-TRAC consortium systems for the IWSLT 2023 dialectal and low-resource speech translation tasks. In *Proceedings of the 20th International Conference on Spoken Language Translation (IWSLT)*.

Seugnjun Lee, Hyeonseok Moon, Chanjun Park, and Heuiseok Lim. 2023. Improving Formality-Sensitive Machine Translation using Data-Centric Approaches and Prompt Engineering. In *Proceedings of the 20th International Conference on Spoken Language Translation (IWSLT)*.

Zongyao Li, Zhanglin Wu, Zhiqiang Rao, Xie YuHao, Guo JiaXin, Daimeng Wei, Hengchao Shang, Wang Minghan, Xiaoyu Chen, Zhengzhe YU, Li ShaoJun, Lei LiZhi, and Hao Yang. 2023. HW-TSC at IWSLT2023: Break the Quality Ceiling of Offline Track via Pre-Training and Domain Adaptation. In *Proceedings of the 20th International Conference on Spoken Language Translation (IWSLT)*.

Xi Victoria Lin, Todor Mihaylov, Mikel Artetxe, Tianlu Wang, Shuohui Chen, Daniel Simig, Myle Ott, Naman Goyal, Shruti Bhosale, Jingfei Du, et al. 2021. Few-shot learning with multilingual language models. *arXiv preprint arXiv:2112.10668*.

Pierre Lison and Jörg Tiedemann. 2016. OpenSubtitles2016: Extracting large parallel corpora from movie and TV subtitles. In *Proceedings of the Tenth International Conference on Language Resources and Evaluation (LREC'16)*, pages 923–929, Portorož, Slovenia. European Language Resources Association (ELRA).

Danni Liu, Thai Binh Nguyen, Sai Koneru, Enes Yavuz Ugan, Ngoc-Quan Pham, Tuan Nam Nguyen, Tu Anh Dinh, Carlos Mullov, Alexander Waibel, and Jan Niehues. 2023. KIT's Multilingual Speech Translation System for IWSLT 2023. In *Proceedings of the 20th International Conference on Spoken Language Translation (IWSLT)*.

Yinhan Liu, Jiatao Gu, Naman Goyal, Xian Li, Sergey Edunov, Marjan Ghazvininejad, Mike Lewis, and Luke Zettlemoyer. 2020. Multilingual denoising pre-training for neural machine translation. *Transactions of the Association for Computational Linguistics*, 8:726–742.

Arle Lommel, Hans Uszkoreit, and Aljoscha Burchardt. 2014. Multidimensional Quality Metrics (MQM): A Framework for Declaring and DescribingTranslation Quality Metrics. *Revista Tradumàtica: tecnologies de la traducció*, 12:455–463.

Mingbo Ma, Liang Huang, Hao Xiong, Renjie Zheng, Kaibo Liu, Baigong Zheng, Chuanqiang Zhang, Zhongjun He, Hairong Liu, Xing Li, Hua Wu, and Haifeng Wang. 2019. STACL: Simultaneous translation with implicit anticipation and controllable latency using prefix-to-prefix framework. In *Proceedings of the 57th Annual Meeting of the Association for Computational Linguistics*, pages 3025–3036, Florence, Italy. Association for Computational Linguistics.

Shuming Ma, Li Dong, Shaohan Huang, Dongdong Zhang, Alexandre Muzio, Saksham Singhal, Hany Hassan Awadalla, Xia Song, and Furu Wei. 2021. DeltaLM: Encoder-decoder pre-training for language generation and translation by augmenting pretrained multilingual encoders. *arXiv*.

Xutai Ma, Mohammad Javad Dousti, Changhan Wang, Jiatao Gu, and Juan Pino. 2020a. SIMULEVAL: An evaluation toolkit for simultaneous translation. In *Proceedings of the 2020 Conference on Empirical Methods in Natural Language Processing: System Demonstrations*, pages 144–150, Online. Association for Computational Linguistics.

Xutai Ma, Juan Pino, and Philipp Koehn. 2020b. SimulMT to SimulST: Adapting simultaneous text translation to end-to-end simultaneous speech translation. In *Proceedings of the 1st Conference of the Asia-Pacific Chapter of the Association for Computational Linguistics and the 10th International Joint Conference on Natural Language Processing*, pages 582–587, Suzhou, China. Association for Computational Linguistics.

Dominik Macháček, Ondřej Bojar, and Raj Dabre. 2023. MT Metrics Correlate with Human Ratings of Simultaneous Speech Translation. In *Proceedings of the 20th International Conference on Spoken Language Translation (IWSLT)*.

Evgeny Matusov, Gregor Leusch, Oliver Bender, and Hermann Ney. 2005a. Evaluating machine translation output with automatic sentence segmentation. In *Proc. of the International Workshop on Spoken Language Translation (IWSLT)*, pages 138–144.

Evgeny Matusov, Gregor Leusch, Oliver Bender, and Hermann Ney. 2005b. Evaluating machine translation output with automatic sentence segmentation. In *Proceedings of the Second International Workshop on Spoken Language Translation*, Pittsburgh, Pennsylvania, USA.

Evgeny Matusov, Patrick Wilken, and Yota Georgakopoulou. 2019. Customizing neural machine translation for subtitling. In *Proceedings of the Fourth Conference on Machine Translation (Volume 1: Research Papers)*, pages 82–93, Florence, Italy. Association for Computational Linguistics.

Jonathan Mbuya and Antonios Anastasopoulos. 2023. GMU Systems for the IWSLT 2023 Dialect and Low-resource Speech Translation Tasks. In *Proceedings of the 20th International Conference on Spoken Language Translation (IWSLT)*.

Maria Nadejde, Anna Currey, Benjamin Hsu, Xing Niu, Marcello Federico, and Georgiana Dinu. 2022. CoCoA-MT: A dataset and benchmark for contrastive controlled MT with application to formality. In *Findings of the Association for Computational Linguistics: NAACL 2022*, pages 616–632, Seattle, United States. Association for Computational Linguistics.

J. Niehues, R. Cattoni, S. Stüker, M. Negri, M. Turchi, T. Ha, E. Salesky, R. Sanabria, L. Barrault, L. Specia, and M. Federico. 2019. The IWSLT 2019 Evaluation Campaign. In *Proceedings of the 16th International Workshop on Spoken Language Translation (IWSLT 2019)*, Hong Kong, China.

Jan Niehues, Roldano Cattoni, Sebastian Stüker, Mauro Cettolo, Marco Turchi, and Marcello Federico. 2018. The IWSLT 2018 Evaluation Campaign. In *Proceedings of the 15th International Workshop on Spoken Language Translation (IWSLT 2018)*, pages 2–6, Bruges, Belgium.

Xing Niu, Marianna Martindale, and Marine Carpuat. 2017. A study of style in machine translation: Controlling the formality of machine translation output. In *Proceedings of the 2017 Conference on Empirical Methods in Natural Language Processing*, pages 2814–2819, Copenhagen, Denmark. Association for Computational Linguistics.

NLLB Team, Marta R. Costa-jussà, James Cross, Onur Çelebi, Maha Elbayad, Kenneth Heafield, Kevin Heffernan, Elahe Kalbassi, Janice Lam, Daniel Licht, Jean Maillard, Anna Sun, Skyler Wang, Guillaume Wenzek, Al Youngblood, Bapi Akula, Loic Barrault, Gabriel Mejia-Gonzalez, Prangthip Hansanti, John Hoffman, Semarley Jarrett, Kaushik Ram Sadagopan, Dirk Rowe, Shannon Spruit, Chau Tran, Pierre Andrews, Necip Fazil Ayan, Shruti Bhosale, Sergey Edunov, Angela Fan, Cynthia Gao, Vedanuj Goswami, Francisco Guzmán, Philipp Koehn, Alexandre Mourachko, Christophe Ropers, Safiyyah Saleem, Holger Schwenk, and Jeff Wang. 2022. No language left behind: Scaling human-centered machine translation. *arXiv preprint*.

John E Ortega, Richard Castro Mamani, and Kyunghyun Cho. 2020. Neural machine translation with a polysynthetic low resource language. *Machine Translation*, 34(4):325–346.

John E. Ortega, Rodolfo Zevallos, and William Chen. 2023. QUESPA Submission for the IWSLT 2023 Dialect and Low-resource Speech Translation Tasks. In *Proceedings of the 20th International Conference on Spoken Language Translation (IWSLT)*.

Proyag Pal, Brian Thompson, Yogesh Virkar, Prashant Mathur, Alexandra Chronopoulou, and Marcello Federico. 2023. Improving isochronous machine translation with target factors and auxiliary counters.

Sara Papi, Marco Gaido, and Matteo Negri. 2023. Direct Models for Simultaneous Translation and Automatic Subtitling: FBK@IWSLT2023. In *Proceedings of the 20th International Conference on Spoken Language Translation (IWSLT)*.

Sara Papi, Marco Gaido, Matteo Negri, and Marco Turchi. 2022. Over-generation cannot be rewarded: Length-adaptive average lagging for simultaneous speech translation. In *Proceedings of the Third Workshop on Automatic Simultaneous Translation*, pages 12–17, Online. Association for Computational Linguistics.

Kishore Papineni, Salim Roukos, Todd Ward, and Wei-Jing Zhu. 2002a. Bleu: a method for automatic evaluation of machine translation. In *Proceedings of the 40th annual meeting on association for computational linguistics*. Association for Computational Linguistics.

Kishore Papineni, Salim Roukos, Todd Ward, and Wei-Jing Zhu. 2002b. Bleu: a method for automatic evaluation of machine translation. In *Proceedings of the 40th Annual Meeting of the Association for Computational Linguistics*, pages 311–318, Philadelphia, Pennsylvania, USA. Association for Computational Linguistics.

Daniel S. Park, William Chan, Yu Zhang, Chung-Cheng Chiu, Barret Zoph, Ekin D. Cubuk, and Quoc V. Le. 2019. SpecAugment: A Simple Data Augmentation Method for Automatic Speech Recognition. *Interspeech 2019*.

Michael Paul. 2006. Overview of the IWSLT 2006 Evaluation Campaign. In *Proceedings of the International Workshop on Spoken Language Translation*, pages 1–15, Kyoto, Japan.

Michael Paul. 2008. Overview of the IWSLT 2008 Evaluation Campaign. In *Proceedings of the International Workshop on Spoken Language Translation*, pages 1–17, Waikiki, Hawaii.

Michael Paul. 2009. Overview of the IWSLT 2009 Evaluation Campaign. In *Proceedings of the International Workshop on Spoken Language Translation*, pages 1–18, Tokyo, Japan.

Michael Paul, Marcello Federico, and Sebastian Stüker. 2010. Overview of the IWSLT 2010 Evaluation Campaign. In *Proceedings of the International Workshop on Spoken Language Translation*, pages 3–27, Paris, France.

Simone Perone. 2023. Matesub: the Translated Subtitling Tool at the IWSLT2023 Subtitling task. In *Proceedings of the 20th International Conference on Spoken Language Translation (IWSLT)*.

Peter Polák, Danni Liu, Ngoc-Quan Pham, Jan Niehues, Alexander Waibel, and Ondřej Bojar. 2023. Towards Efficient Simultaneous Speech Translation: CUNI-KIT System for Simultaneous Track at IWSLT 2023. In *Proceedings of the 20th International Conference on Spoken Language Translation (IWSLT)*.

Peter Polák, Ngoc-Quan Pham, Tuan Nam Nguyen, Danni Liu, Carlos Mullov, Jan Niehues, Ondřej Bojar, and Alexander Waibel. 2022. CUNI-KIT system for simultaneous speech translation task at IWSLT 2022. In *Proceedings of the 19th International Conference on Spoken Language Translation (IWSLT 2022)*, pages 277–285, Dublin, Ireland (in-person and online). Association for Computational Linguistics.

Maja Popović. 2015a. chrF: character n-gram F-score for automatic MT evaluation. In *Proceedings of the Tenth Workshop on Statistical Machine Translation*, pages 392–395, Lisbon, Portugal. Association for Computational Linguistics.

Maja Popović. 2015b. chrf: character n-gram f-score for automatic mt evaluation. In *Proceedings of the tenth workshop on statistical machine translation*, pages 392–395.

Matt Post. 2018. A call for clarity in reporting BLEU scores. In *Proceedings of the Third Conference on Machine Translation: Research Papers*, pages 186–191, Brussels, Belgium. Association for Computational Linguistics.

Vineel Pratap, Awni Hannun, Qiantong Xu, Jeff Cai, Jacob Kahn, Gabriel Synnaeve, Vitaliy Liptchinsky, and Ronan Collobert. 2019. Wav2letter++: A fast open-source speech recognition system. In *ICASSP 2019-2019 IEEE International Conference on Acoustics, Speech and Signal Processing (ICASSP)*, pages 6460–6464. IEEE.

Alec Radford, Jong Wook Kim, Tao Xu, Greg Brockman, Christine McLeavey, and Ilya Sutskever. 2022. Robust speech recognition via large-scale weak supervision.

Balaji Radhakrishnan, Saurabh Agrawal, Raj Prakash Gohil, Kiran Praveen, Advait Vinay Dhopeshwarkar, and Abhishek Pandey. 2023. SRI-B's systems for IWSLT 2023 Dialectal and Low-resource track: Marathi-Hindi Speech Translation. In *Proceedings of the 20th International Conference on Spoken Language Translation (IWSLT)*.

Zhiqiang Rao, Hengchao Shang, Jinlong Yang, Daimeng Wei, Zongyao Li, Lizhi Lei, and Hao Yang. 2023. Length-Aware NMT and Adaptive Duration for Automatic Dubbing. In *Proceedings of the 20th International Conference on Spoken Language Translation (IWSLT)*.

Ricardo Rei, José GC de Souza, Duarte Alves, Chrysoula Zerva, Ana C Farinha, Taisiya Glushkova, Alon Lavie, Luisa Coheur, and André FT Martins. 2022. Comet-22: Unbabel-ist 2022 submission for the metrics shared task. In *Proceedings of the Seventh Conference on Machine Translation (WMT)*, pages 578–585.

Ricardo Rei, Craig Stewart, Ana C Farinha, and Alon Lavie. 2020a. Comet: A neural framework for mt evaluation. *arXiv preprint arXiv:2009.09025*.

Ricardo Rei, Craig Stewart, Ana C Farinha, and Alon Lavie. 2020b. COMET: A neural framework for MT evaluation. In *Proceedings of the 2020 Conference on Empirical Methods in Natural Language Processing (EMNLP)*, pages 2685–2702, Online. Association for Computational Linguistics.

Yi Ren, Chenxu Hu, Xu Tan, Tao Qin, Sheng Zhao, Zhou Zhao, and Tie-Yan Liu. 2022. Fastspeech 2: Fast and high-quality end-to-end text to speech.

Anthony Rousseau, Paul Deléglise, and Yannick Esteve. 2014. Enhancing the ted-lium corpus with selected data for language modeling and more ted talks. In *LREC*.

Elizabeth Salesky, Kareem Darwish, Mohamed Al-Badrashiny, Mona Diab, and Jan Niehues. 2023. Evaluating Multilingual Speech Translation Under Realistic Conditions with Resegmentation and Terminology. In *Proceedings of the 20th International Conference on Spoken Language Translation (IWSLT 2023)*. Association for Computational Linguistics.

Elizabeth Salesky, Matthew Wiesner, Jacob Bremerman, Roldano Cattoni, Matteo Negri, Marco Turchi, Douglas W. Oard, and Matt Post. 2021. The Multilingual TEDx Corpus for Speech Recognition and Translation. In *Proc. Interspeech 2021*, pages 3655–3659.

Gabriele Sarti, Phu Mon Htut, Xing Niu, Benjamin Hsu, Anna Currey, Georgiana Dinu, and Maria Nadejde. 2023. RAMP: Retrieval and attribute-marking enhanced prompting for attribute-controlled translation.

Holger Schwenk, Guillaume Wenzek, Sergey Edunov, Edouard Grave, Armand Joulin, and Angela Fan. 2021. CCMatrix: Mining billions of high-quality parallel sentences on the web. In *Proceedings of the 59th Annual Meeting of the Association for Computational Linguistics and the 11th International Joint Conference on Natural Language Processing (Volume 1: Long Papers)*, pages 6490–6500, Online. Association for Computational Linguistics.

Thibault Sellam, Dipanjan Das, and Ankur Parikh. 2020. BLEURT: Learning robust metrics for text generation. In *Proceedings of the 58th Annual Meeting of the Association for Computational Linguistics*, pages 7881–7892, Online. Association for Computational Linguistics.

Hengchao Shang, Zhiqiang Rao, Zongyao Li, Zhanglin Wu, Jiaxin Guo, Minghan Wang, Daimeng Wei, Shaojun Li, Zhengzhe Yu, Xiaoyu Chen, Lizhi Lei, and Hao Yang. 2023. The HW-TSC's Simultaneous Speech-to-Speech Translation system for IWSLT 2023 evaluation. In *Proceedings of the 20th International Conference on Spoken Language Translation (IWSLT)*.

Yao Shi, Hui Bu, Xin Xu, Shaoji Zhang, and Ming Li. 2020. Aishell-3: A multi-speaker mandarin tts corpus and the baselines. *arXiv preprint arXiv:2010.11567*.

Kun Song, Yi Lei, Peikun Chen, Yiqing Cao, Kun Wei, Yongmao Zhang, Lei Xie, Ning Jiang, and Guoqing Zhao. 2023. The NPU-MSXF Speech-to-Speech Translation System for IWSLT 2023 Speech-to-Speech Translation Task. In *Proceedings of the 20th International Conference on Spoken Language Translation (IWSLT)*.

Yuqing Tang, Chau Tran, Xian Li, Peng-Jen Chen, Naman Goyal, Vishrav Chaudhary, Jiatao Gu, and Angela Fan. 2020. Multilingual translation with extensible multilingual pretraining and finetuning. *arXiv preprint arXiv:2008.00401*.

Jörg Tiedemann. 2012. Parallel data, tools and interfaces in OPUS. In *Proceedings of the Eighth International Conference on Language Resources and Evaluation (LREC'12)*, pages 2214–2218, Istanbul, Turkey. European Language Resources Association (ELRA).

Ioannis Tsiamas, Gerard I. Gállego, Jose Fonollosa, and Marta R. Costa-jussà. 2023. Speech Translation with Foundation Models and Optimal Transport: UPC at IWSLT23. In *Proceedings of the 20th International Conference on Spoken Language Translation (IWSLT)*.

Ioannis Tsiamas, Gerard I. Gállego, José A. R. Fonollosa, and Marta R. Costa-jussà. 2022. SHAS: Approaching optimal Segmentation for End-to-End Speech Translation. In *Proc. Interspeech 2022*, pages 106–110.

Priyesh Vakharia, Shree Vignesh S, Pranjali Basmatkar, and Ian Lane. 2023. Low-Resource Formality Controlled NMT Using Pre-trained LM. In *Proceedings of the 20th International Conference on Spoken Language Translation (IWSLT)*.

Ashish Vaswani, Noam Shazeer, Niki Parmar, Jakob Uszkoreit, Llion Jones, Aidan N Gomez, Łukasz Kaiser, and Illia Polosukhin. 2017. Attention is All You Need. In *Proceedings of NIPS 2017*.

Akshaya Vishnu, Kudlu Shanbhogue, Ran Xue, Soumya Saha, Daniel Zhang, and Ashwinkumar Ganesan. 2023. Amazon Alexa AI's Low-Resource Speech Translation System for IWSLT2023. In *Proceedings of the 20th International Conference on Spoken Language Translation (IWSLT)*.

Changhan Wang, Juan Pino, Anne Wu, and Jiatao Gu. 2020a. Covost: A diverse multilingual speech-to-text translation corpus. In *Proceedings of The 12th Language Resources and Evaluation Conference*, pages 4197–4203.

Changhan Wang, Yun Tang, Xutai Ma, Anne Wu, Dmytro Okhonko, and Juan Pino. 2020b. fairseq s2t: Fast speech-to-text modeling with fairseq. *arXiv preprint arXiv:2010.05171*.

Changhan Wang, Anne Wu, Jiatao Gu, and Juan Pino. 2021. CoVoST 2 and Massively Multilingual Speech Translation. In *Proc. Interspeech 2021*, pages 2247–2251.

Minghan Wang, Yinglu Li, Jiaxin Guo, Zongyao Li, Hengchao Shang, Daimeng Wei, Min Zhang, Shimin Tao, and Hao Yang. 2023a. The HW-TSC's Speech-to-Speech Translation System for IWSLT 2023. In *Proceedings of the 20th International Conference on Spoken Language Translation (IWSLT)*.

Zhipeng Wang, Yuhang Guo, and Shuoying Chen. 2023b. BIT's System for Multilingual Track. In *Proceedings of the 20th International Conference on Spoken Language Translation (IWSLT)*.

Patrick Wilken, Panayota Georgakopoulou, and Evgeny Matusov. 2022. SubER - a metric for automatic evaluation of subtitle quality. In *Proceedings of the 19th International Conference on Spoken Language Translation (IWSLT 2022)*, pages 1–10, Dublin, Ireland (in-person and online). Association for Computational Linguistics.

Aiden Williams. 2022. The applicability of Wav2Vec 2.0 for low-resource Maltese ASR. B.S. thesis, University of Malta.

Aiden Williams, Kurt Abela, Rishu Kumar, Martin Bär, Hannah Billinghurst, Kurt Micallef, Ahnaf Mozib Samin, Andrea DeMarco, Lonneke van der Plas, and Claudia Borg. 2023. UM-DFKI Maltese Speech Translation. In *Proceedings of the 20th International Conference on Spoken Language Translation (IWSLT)*.

Zhanglin Wu, Zongyao Li, Daimeng Wei, Hengchao Shang, Jiaxin Guo, Xiaoyu Chen, Zhiqiang Rao, Zhengzhe YU, Jinlong Yang, Shaojun Li, Yuhao Xie, Bin Wei, Jiawei Zheng, Ming Zhu, Lizhi Lei, Hao Yang, and Yanfei Jiang. 2023. Improving Neural Machine Translation Formality Control with Domain Adaptation and Reranking-based Transductive Learning. In *Proceedings of the 20th International Conference on Spoken Language Translation (IWSLT)*.

Zhihang Xie. 2023. The BIGAI Offline Speech Translation Systems for IWSLT 2023 Evaluation. In *Proceedings of the 20th International Conference on Spoken Language Translation (IWSLT)*.

Henry Li Xinyuan, Neha Verma, Bismarck Bamfo Odoom, Ujvala Pradeep, Matthew Wiesner, and Sanjeev Khudanpur. 2023. JHU IWSLT 2023 Multilingual Speech Translation System Description. In *Proceedings of the 20th International Conference on Spoken Language Translation (IWSLT)*.

Chen Xu, Bojie Hu, Yanyang Li, Yuhao Zhang, shen huang, Qi Ju, Tong Xiao, and Jingbo Zhu. 2021. Stacked acoustic-and-textual encoding: Integrating the pre-trained models into speech translation encoders.

Wenda Xu, Xian Qian, Mingxuan Wang, Lei Li, and William Yang Wang. 2022. Sescore2: Retrieval augmented pretraining for text generation evaluation. *arXiv preprint arXiv:2212.09305*.

Brian Yan, Jiatong Shi, Soumi Maiti, William Chen, Xinjian Li, Yifan Peng, Siddhant Arora, and Shinji Watanabe. 2023. CMU's IWSLT 2023 Simultaneous Speech Translation System. In *Proceedings of the 20th International Conference on Spoken Language Translation (IWSLT)*.

Zhengdong Yang, Shuichiro Shimizu, Sheng Li Wangjin Zhou, and Chenhui Chu. 2023. The Kyoto Speech-to-Speech Translation System for IWSLT 2023. In *Proceedings of the 20th International Conference on Spoken Language Translation (IWSLT)*.

Zhuoyuan Yao, Di Wu, Xiong Wang, Binbin Zhang, Fan Yu, Chao Yang, Zhendong Peng, Xiaoyu Chen, Lei Xie, and Xin Lei. 2021. Wenet: Production oriented streaming and non-streaming end-to-end speech recognition toolkit. *arXiv preprint arXiv:2102.01547*.

Rong Ye, Chengqi Zhao, Tom Ko, Chutong Meng, Tao Wang, Mingxuan Wang, and Jun Cao. 2023. Gigast: A 10,000-hour pseudo speech translation corpus. In *Interspeech 2023*.

Xinyuan Zhou, Jianwei Cui, Zhongyi Ye, Yichi Wang, Luzhen Xu, Hanyi Zhang, Weitai Zhang, and Lirong Dai. 2023. Submission of USTC's system for the IWSLT 2023 - Offline Speech Translation Track. In *Proceedings of the 20th International Conference on Spoken Language Translation (IWSLT)*.

Adrian Łańcucki. 2021. Fastpitch: Parallel text-to-speech with pitch prediction. In *ICASSP 2021 - 2021 IEEE International Conference on Acoustics, Speech and Signal Processing (ICASSP)*, pages 6588–6592, Toronto, Canada. IEEE.

Appendix A. Human Evaluation

A Human Evaluation

Human evaluation was carried out for the Simultaneous and Offline SLT shared tasks. At the time of writing, only the former evaluation has been completed which is reported here. The human evaluation of the Offline Task will be recounted during the conference and possibly in an update version of this report.

A.1 Simultaneous Speech Translation Task

Simultaneous Speech Translation Task ran two different types of manual evaluation: "continuous rating" for English-to-German and MQM for English-to-Japanese.

A.1.1 Human Evaluation for the English-to-German Simultaneous Task

We used a variant of "continuous rating" as presented by Javorský et al. (2022). The evaluation process and the guidelines presented to annotators were the same as during the last year evaluation (consult Section A.1.1 in Anastasopoulos et al. (2022a) for more details).

Time Shift for Better Simultaneity Last year, we reduced the delay by shifting the subtitles ahead in time to ease the memory overload of the evaluators. Since this year only a low latency regime was used, we left the subtitles intact for the system outputs. For interpreting, we used the same shift as last year.

Two Test Sets: Common and Non-Native The main part of the test set for the English-to-German task was the Common test set. The Common test set is a new instance (different from previous years) consisting of selected TED talks and it serves both in the Offline Speech Translation task as well as in the Simultaneous Translation task. Following the last year, we also added the Non-Native part that was created and is in use since IWSLT 2020 Non-Native Translation Task. The Non-Native part is described in Ansari et al. (2020) Appendix A.6.

We show the size of the corpus, as well as the amount of annotation collected in Table 21.

Processing of Collected Rankings Once the results are collected, they are processed as follows. We first inspect the timestamps on the ratings, and remove any ratings that have timestamps more than 20 seconds greater than the length of the audio. Because of the natural delay (even with the time-shift) and because the collection process is subject to network and computational constraints, there can be ratings that are timestamped greater than the audio length. If the difference is however too high, we judge it to be an annotation error. We also remove any annotated audio where there is fewer than one rating per 20 seconds, since the annotators were instructed to annotate every 5-10 seconds.

Obtaining Final Scores To calculate a score for each system, we average the ratings across each annotated audio,[47] then average across the multiple annotations for each audio to obtain a system score for that audio. Finally we average across all audios to obtain a score for each system. This type of averaging renders all input speeches equally important and it is not affected by the speech length.

We show the results in Table 22. We observe that all systems perform better on the Common part of the test set than on the Non-Native one. The difference in scores between the best and the worst system is not so significant: It makes only ~0.3. When examining the evaluation of Non-Native audios, we can see that best systems on the Common part are worst on Non-Native. Given that the quality of the recordings in the non-native part is low on average and the speakers are not native, we hypothesize that systems with worse performance on Common part are more robust. Such systems then achieve an increased performance given noisy inputs.

A.1.2 Human Evaluation for the English-to-Japanese Simultaneous Task

For the English-to-Japanese Simultaneous Translation Task, we conducted a human evaluation using a variant of Multidimensional Quality Metrics (MQM; Lommel et al., 2014). MQM has been used in recent MT evaluation studies (Freitag et al., 2021a) and WMT Metrics shared task (Freitag et al., 2021b). For the evaluation of Japanese translations, we used *JTF Translation Quality Evaluation Guidelines* (JTF,

[47]Note that the ratings could be also weighted with respect to the duration of time segments between the ratings but Macháček et al. (2023) documented on 2022 data that the difference is negligible.

2018), distributed by Japan Translation Federation (JTF). The guidelines are based on MQM but include some modifications in consideration of the property of the Japanese language.

We hired a Japanese-native professional interpreter as the evaluator, while the evaluator was a translator in the last year (Anastasopoulos et al., 2022a). The evaluator checked translation hypotheses along with their source speech transcripts and chose the corresponding error category and severity for each translation hypothesis using a spreadsheet. Here, we asked the evaluator to focus only on *Accuracy* and *Fluency* errors, because other types of errors in Terminology, Style, and Locale convention would not be so serious in the evaluation of simultaneous translation. Finally, we calculated the cumulative error score for each system based on the error weighting presented by Freitag et al. (2021a), where *Critical* and *Major* errors are not distinguished.

Appendix B. Automatic Evaluation Results and Details

B.1 Offline SLT

· Systems are ordered according to the BLEU score computed on the concatenation of the three test sets (Joint BLEU, third column).

· The "D" column indicates the data condition in which each submitted run was trained, namely: Constrained (C), constrained^{+LLM} (C^+), Unconstrained (U).

· For the BLEU scores computed on the TED test set, "Orig" and "New" respectively indicate the results computed on the original (subtitle-like) TED translations and the unconstrained (exact, more literal) translations as references.

· Direct systems are indicated by gray background.

· "*" indicates a late submission.

· "+" indicates an unofficial submission.

System	D	Joint		TED					ACL		EPTV	
		BLEU	COMET	BLEU			COMET		BLEU	COMET	BLEU	COMET
Ref				New	Orig	Both	New	Orig				
HW-TSC	C	32.4	0.8213	34.8	30.2	42.1	0.8327	0.8208	38.1	0.8090	16.7	0.3829
HW-TSC	U	32.3	0.8209	34.9	30.9	42.4	0.8331	0.8223	36.9	0.8073	16.9	0.3819
HW-TSC	C+	31.9	0.8210	34.4	30.6	41.9	0.8332	0.8230	37.2	0.8063	16.8	0.3823
NeuroDub+	U	30.4	0.8089	31.8	25.8	38.5	0.8205	0.8082	41.1	0.7956	15.4	0.3784
NEMo	C	28.5	0.7759	30.5	26.4	37.7	0.7977	0.7871	31.9	0.7171	15.6	0.3680
UPC	C+	27.9	0.7892	29.8	25.5	36.6	0.8098	0.7985	32.1	0.7473	15.6	0.3746
I2R	C+	22.4	0.7070	24.0	20.3	29.5	0.7248	0.7172	23.9	0.6841	13.3	0.3506
BIGAI*	C+	20.3	0.6945	22.3	19.3	27.4	0.7128	0.7055	19.6	0.6295	11.5	0.3555

Table 14: Official results of the automatic evaluation for the Offline Speech Translation Task, **English to German**.

System	D	Joint		TED					ACL	
		BLEU	COMET	BLEU			COMET		BLEU	COMET
Ref				New	Orig	Both	New	Orig		
HW-TSC	U	21.0	0.8177	18.8	22.6	29.1	0.8111	0.8029	30.7	0.8473
HW-TSC	C	20.9	0.8181	18.7	22.7	29.0	0.8123	0.8042	30.1	0.8443
HW-TSC	C+	20.9	0.8177	18.7	22.6	28.9	0.8114	0.8034	30.7	0.8463
NeMo	C	18.1	0.7741	16.5	20.4	25.6	0.7734	0.7666	24.9	0.7769
BIGAI*	C+	10.7	0.7122	10.7	13.2	16.8	0.7201	0.7228	10.4	0.6769

Table 15: Official results of the automatic evaluation for the Offline Speech Translation Task, **English to Japanese**.

System	D	Joint		TED					ACL	
		BLEU	COMET	BLEU			COMET		BLEU	COMET
Ref				New	Orig	Both	New	Orig		
USTC	U	54.7	0.8627	53.9	36.8	62.1	0.8648	0.7992	58.0	0.8535
USTC	U	52.8	0.8357	52.9	35.5	60.6	0.8439	0.7798	52.5	0.7999
HW-TSC	C	51.1	0.8499	50.6	34.5	57.8	0.8521	0.7876	53.0	0.8404
HW-TSC	C+	51.1	0.8494	50.6	34.5	57.9	0.8514	0.7870	53.0	0.8406
HW-TSC	U	51.0	0.8497	50.6	34.5	57.8	0.8519	0.7874	52.8	0.8401
NIUTRANS	C	49.4	0.8255	50.0	34.3	57.9	0.8376	0.7740	47.1	0.7733
XIAOMI	C+	47.1	0.8279	47.2	32.4	54.1	0.8375	0.7773	46.5	0.7866
NeMo	C	45.6	0.8032	46.5	31.8	53.8	0.8177	0.7575	41.8	0.7404
MINETRANS	U	45.0	0.7920	46.3	32.0	53.2	0.8134	0.7546	39.9	0.6997
BIGAI*	C+	31.9	0.7260	33.0	23.3	38.6	0.7428	0.7014	27.4	0.6534
MINETRANS	C	28.7	0.6371	27.7	18.6	32.2	0.6375	0.5976	31.8	0.6354

Table 16: Official results of the automatic evaluation for the Offline Speech Translation Task, **English to Chinese**.

B.2 Simultaneous SLT

Team	BLEU	LAAL	AL	AP	DAL	ATD
			Common			
HW-TSC	29.63	2.26 (3.93)	2.11 (3.86)	0.83 (1.59)	3.17 (8.99)	2.28 (6.77)
CUNI-KIT	28.51	2.35 (3.63)	2.24 (3.56)	0.79 (1.11)	2.88 (4.50)	2.26 (2.96)
FBK	28.38	2.25 (2.99)	2.09 (2.88)	0.84 (1.03)	2.70 (3.65)	2.15 (2.48)
NAIST	26.05	2.36 (3.30)	2.22 (3.21)	0.82 (1.07)	3.05 (4.45)	2.25 (3.06)
CMU	25.78	1.99 (3.39)	1.92 (3.33)	0.82 (1.31)	3.78 (6.56)	2.46 (4.63)
			Non-Native			
NAIST	22.96	2.43 (3.52)	1.95 (3.22)	0.845 (1.02)	3.37 (4.71)	3.13 (3.92)
CMU	22.84	2.47 (3.74)	2.36 (3.63)	0.798 (1.16)	4.54 (6.77)	3.77 (5.47)
CUNI-KIT	19.94	3.42 (5.00)	3.24 (4.87)	0.744 (1.04)	4.14 (5.87)	3.82 (4.84)
HW-TSC	17.91	3.57 (6.67)	3.44 (6.61)	0.705 (1.65)	4.39 (12.91)	4.04 (11.13)
FBK	15.19	4.10 (5.34)	3.94 (5.22)	0.89 (1.12)	4.53 (5.85)	3.76 (4.65)

Table 17: Simultaneous Speech-to-Text Translation, English to German. Except for AP, the latency is measured in seconds. Numbers in brackets are computation aware latency.

Team	BLEU	LAAL	AL	AP	DAL	ATD
HW-TSC	44.95	2.13 (3.80)	2.06 (3.76)	0.78 (1.48)	3.21 (8.66)	0.99 (5.31)
CUNI-KIT	44.16	2.13 (3.30)	2.06 (3.25)	0.77 (1.08)	2.78 (4.38)	0.89 (1.54)
XIAOMI	43.69	2.30 (3.03)	2.23 (2.98)	0.80 (1.08)	2.93 (4.08)	0.90 (1.47)
NAIST	36.80	2.00 (2.80)	1.88 (2.74)	0.76 (1.03)	2.66 (4.22)	0.77 (1.49)

Table 18: Simultaneous Speech-to-Text Translation, English to Chinese. Except for AP, the latency is measured in seconds. Numbers in brackets are computation aware latency.

Team	BLEU	LAAL	AL	AP	DAL	ATD
HW-TSC	16.63	2.60 (4.38)	2.56 (4.36)	0.71 (1.31)	3.62 (9.07)	0.83 (5.12)
CUNI-KIT	14.92	2.20 (3.55)	2.16 (3.53)	0.68 (1.06)	2.74 (5.17)	0.53 (1.50)
NAIST	14.66	2.52 (3.43)	2.45 (3.39)	0.75 (1.03)	3.24 (5.16)	0.60 (1.57)

Table 19: Simultaneous Speech-to-Text Translation, English to Japanese. Except for AP, the latency is measured in seconds. Numbers in brackets are computation aware latency.

Target Language	Team	ASR BLEU	BLASER	Start Offset	End Offset	ATD
German	CMU	22.62	0.122	2.37	5.21	4.22
	HW-TSC	19.74	-0.442	2.04	5.09	3.75
Japanese	HW-TSC	15.53	-1.70	2.37	3.48	3.56
	NAIST	10.19	-1.68	2.58	4.32	3.49
Chinese	HW-TSC	31.68	-0.696	1.92	3.12	3.23

Table 20: Simultaneous Speech-to-Speech from English Speech. The latency is measured in seconds. The BLEU scores are computed based on transcript from the default Whisper (Radford et al., 2022) ASR model for each language direction.

	Common	Non-native
Number of audios	42	43
Mean audio length (seconds)	400.3	208.8
Mean ratings per audio	65.6	36.5

Table 21: Human evaluation for the English-to-German task on two test sets: the Common one (used also in automatic scoring) and the Non-native one. We show the size of the test sets, and the number of ratings collected. On average, our annotators provide a quality judgement ever 6 seconds.

	Common	Non-native
CUNI-KIT	$3.10_{3.04\rightarrow3.16}$	$1.63_{1.54\rightarrow1.72}$
FBK	$3.08_{3.02\rightarrow3.14}$	$1.26_{1.20\rightarrow1.30}$
HWTSC	$2.91_{2.85\rightarrow2.98}$	$2.04_{1.92\rightarrow2.15}$
NAIST	$2.84_{2.78\rightarrow2.91}$	$2.27_{2.18\rightarrow2.34}$
CMU	$2.79_{2.72\rightarrow2.87}$	$2.38_{2.30\rightarrow2.46}$
Interpreter	–	$2.79_{2.71\rightarrow2.87}$

Table 22: Human evaluation results for English-to-German Simultaneous task on the 1–5 (worst-to-best) scale, with 95% confidence intervals. We calculate a mean score for each annotated audio file, then a mean across annotators (for each audio), then a mean across all audio files for each system. To compute confidence intervals, we take the scores for annotated audios, perform 10,000x bootstrap resampling, compute the mean score for each resample, then compute $[2.5, 97.5]$ percentiles across the resampled means.

Team	BLEU (on two talks)		Error score	Number of errors		
	TED ref.	Additional ref.		Critical	Major	Minor
HW-TSC	26.59	18.71	383	1	56	98
CUNI-KIT	24.21	17.95	384	0	56	104
NAIST	25.10	16.75	398	0	61	93
Baseline	7.69	6.27	1,074	3	205	34

Table 23: Human evaluation results on two talks (107 lines) in the English-to-Japanese Simultaneous speech-to-text translation task. Error weights are 5 for Critical and Major errors and 1 for Minor errors.

B.3 Automatic Subtitling

team	con-dition	system	domain	Subtitle quality		Translation quality			Subtitle compliance		
				SubER	Sigma	Bleu	ChrF	Bleurt	CPS	CPL	LPB
APPTEK	U	prmry	ALL	70.64	73.35	15.38	38.36	.4376	87.74	100.00	100.00
			ted	59.72	74.33	23.74	49.14	.5683	92.58	100.00	100.00
			eptv	73.98	67.09	15.81	45.21	.5229	86.65	100.00	100.00
			pltn	77.63	72.79	10.47	33.18	.4069	88.98	100.00	100.00
			itv	69.83	74.48	14.43	35.27	.4028	86.01	100.00	100.00
MATESUB	U	prmry	ALL	75.41	65.22	14.81	39.50	.4591	84.97	99.25	100.00
			ted	67.70	62.01	20.37	50.05	.5500	90.55	98.61	100.00
			eptv	87.04	57.73	12.08	43.59	.4705	88.59	99.20	100.00
			pltn	79.72	68.27	10.06	34.46	.4264	89.17	99.29	100.00
			itv	73.11	67.04	14.92	37.13	.4501	80.21	99.47	100.00
APPTEK	C	prmry	ALL	77.05	72.50	12.74	34.31	.3420	93.35	100.00	100.00
			ted	59.61	74.29	26.78	50.93	.5539	97.33	100.00	100.00
			eptv	76.25	68.49	14.43	42.37	.4604	95.76	100.00	100.00
			pltn	80.72	69.56	9.40	31.20	.3419	93.45	100.00	100.00
			itv	80.87	72.62	9.08	27.74	.2612	91.14	100.00	100.00
FBK	C	prmry	ALL	79.70	75.73	11.22	33.32	.3172	69.98	83.50	99.98
			ted	63.85	76.79	21.48	50.31	.5511	71.39	79.83	100.00
			eptv	79.76	69.04	13.20	42.69	.4722	74.95	82.08	99.91
			pltn	83.71	74.02	7.73	30.17	.3137	70.02	84.20	99.96
			itv	82.67	77.17	8.05	26.10	.2255	67.75	85.12	100.00
APPTEK	C	cntrstv	ALL	83.53	70.39	9.73	30.51	.2914	89.60	100.00	100.00
			ted	68.47	72.97	19.07	46.17	.4921	90.53	100.00	100.00
			eptv	81.69	66.36	11.46	39.25	.4150	94.57	100.00	100.00
			pltn	86.37	69.79	7.08	27.89	.2780	91.50	100.00	100.00
			itv	87.25	68.29	6.70	23.85	.2204	86.85	100.00	100.00

Table 24: Automatic evaluation results for the Subtitling Task: en→de. *C* and *U* stand for *constrained* and *unconstrained* training condition, respectively; *prmry* and *cntrstv* for *primary* and *contrastive* systems.

team	con-dition	system	domain	Subtitle quality		Translation quality			Subtitle compliance		
				SubER	Sigma	Bleu	ChrF	Bleurt	CPS	CPL	LPB
MATESUB	U	prmry	ALL	68.11	68.37	22.34	47.38	.5059	86.07	99.52	100.00
			ted	45.94	66.85	40.36	65.72	.7047	92.62	99.48	100.00
			eptv	74.47	59.59	21.06	54.11	.5728	90.15	99.44	100.00
			pltn	74.87	70.99	15.96	41.86	.4666	88.27	99.60	100.00
			itv	71.25	71.06	18.50	41.07	.4592	81.93	99.51	100.00
APPTEK	C	prmry	ALL	71.68	74.99	18.67	40.21	.3637	95.42	100.00	100.00
			ted	45.81	74.50	39.37	62.11	.6562	97.20	100.00	100.00
			eptv	66.60	73.31	23.57	51.94	.5379	96.27	100.00	100.00
			pltn	76.00	74.63	14.03	36.95	.3664	95.18	100.00	100.00
			itv	80.20	75.90	11.37	29.75	.2487	94.67	100.00	100.00
FBK	C	prmry	ALL	73.31	74.44	17.79	39.54	.3419	77.00	91.34	99.99
			ted	45.68	74.31	40.21	65.09	.6737	78.95	88.14	100.00
			eptv	68.47	69.63	23.92	52.19	.5490	79.81	88.05	100.00
			pltn	78.45	75.78	12.84	35.89	.3513	77.79	92.67	99.96
			itv	82.00	76.16	9.33	27.14	.2063	74.67	92.94	100.00

Table 25: Automatic evaluation results for the Subtitling Task: en→es. Legenda in Table 24.

B.4 Multilingual Speech Translation

Below we show the Multilingual task (§ 5) results and overall rankings, ordered according to the average chrF across all 10 target languages after resegmentation to the reference translations.

We also compare to the Offline submissions on the ACL 60-60 evaluation set on the 3 language pairs used for the Offline task.

Finally, we show the scores for each metric (chrF, COMET, BLEU) per language pair for all systems.

	System	Constrained?	chrF	COMET	BLEU	English WER
1	$\text{JHU}_{unconstrained}$		61.1	82.3	39.3	16.9
2	$\text{KIT}_{primary}$	✓ +LLM	57.5	77.0	34.9	23.7
3	$\text{KIT}_{contrastive1}$	✓ +LLM	57.5	76.8	34.8	—
4	$\text{KIT}_{contrastive2}$	✓ +LLM	56.4	76.5	34.0	—
5	$\text{KIT}_{contrastive4}$	✓ +LLM	56.2	76.4	33.7	—
6	$\text{KIT}_{contrastive3}$	✓ +LLM	55.9	76.3	33.5	—
7	$\text{KIT}_{contrastive5}$	✓ +LLM	54.5	76.7	31.7	—
8	$\text{KIT}_{contrastive7}$	✓ +LLM	53.9	76.6	31.1	—
9	$\text{KIT}_{contrastive6}$	✓ +LLM	53.7	75.9	30.9	—
10	$\text{JHU}_{constrained}$	✓ +LLM	48.1	65.3	24.5	34.1
11	$\text{BIT}_{primary}$	✓	31.0	51.7	11.7	—

Table 26: **Overall task ranking** with metrics averaged across **all ten** language pairs on the evaluation set. We show the official task metric (chrF) as well as the unofficial metrics (COMET, BLEU, and English WER). All metrics are calculated after resegmentation to reference transcripts and translations. Direct / end-to-end systems are highlighted in gray.

			de		ja		zh	
System	Task	Constrained?	COMET	BLEU	COMET	BLEU	COMET	BLEU
USTC	Off.						85.4 (1)	58.0 (1)
HW-TSC	Off.	✓	80.9 (2)	38.1 (3)	84.4 (3)	30.1 (7)	84.0 (2)	53.0 (2)
JHU	Mult.		81.3 (1)	41.2 (1)	84.7 (1)	33.9 (4)	82.0 (3)	46.5 (11)
HW-TSC	Off.		80.7 (3)	36.9 (6)	84.7 (1)	30.7 (6)	84.0 (2)	52.8 (3)
HW-TSC	Off.	✓ + LLM	80.6 (4)	37.2 (5)	84.6 (2)	30.7 (6)	84.0 (2)	53.0 (2)
NeuroDub	Off.		79.6 (5)	41.1 (2)				
USTC	Off.						80.0 (4)	52.5 (4)
KIT_{pr}	Mult.	✓ + LLM	74.9 (6)	37.5 (4)	82.0 (4)	35.7 (1)	79.3 (5)	49.4 (6)
KIT_{c1}	Mult.	✓ + LLM	74.6 (8)	36.5 (7)	82.0 (4)	35.2 (2)	79.3 (5)	49.7 (5)
KIT_{c2}	Mult.	✓ + LLM	74.3 (9)	36.5 (7)	81.6 (6)	34.0 (3)	78.6 (10)	49.4 (6)
KIT_{c3}	Mult.	✓ + LLM	74.7 (7)	36.1 (9)	81.4 (7)	33.3 (5)	78.4 (11)	48.6 (7)
KIT_{c4}	Mult.	✓ + LLM	74.2 (10)	36.4 (8)	81.7 (5)	33.9 (4)	78.4 (11)	48.2 (8)
KIT_{c5}	Mult.	✓ + LLM	74.9 (6)	33.8 (10)	80.3 (8)	27.3 (8)	79.1 (6)	46.7 (10)
UPC	Off.	✓ + LLM	74.7 (7)	32.1 (12)				
KIT_{c6}	Mult.	✓ + LLM	73.9 (11)	32.9 (11)	80.0 (9)	26.6 (9)	78.9 (7)	45.7 (13)
KIT_{c7}	Mult.	✓ + LLM	73.9 (11)	32.9 (11)	80.3 (8)	25.6 (10)	78.8 (8)	46.0 (12)
Xiaomi	Off.	✓ + LLM					78.7 (9)	46.5 (11)
NiuTrans	Off.	✓					77.3 (12)	47.1 (9)
NeMo	Off.	✓	71.7 (12)	31.9 (13)	77.7 (10)	24.9 (11)	74.0 (13)	41.8 (14)
I2R	Off.	✓ + LLM	68.4 (13)	23.9 (14)				
JHU	Mult.	✓ + LLM	59.0 (15)	23.7 (15)	69.3 (11)	18.9 (12)	67.9 (15)	37.4 (16)
MINE-Trans	Off.						70.0 (14)	39.9 (15)
BIGAI*	Off.	✓ + LLM	63.0 (14)	19.6 (16)	67.7 (12)	10.4 (13)	65.3 (16)	27.4 (18)
MINE-Trans	Off.	✓					63.5 (17)	31.8 (17)
BIT	Mult.	✓	47.2 (16)	11.1 (17)	56.2 (13)	8.0 (14)	55.7 (18)	19.8 (19)

Table 27: Submissions from all tracks on the ACL 60-60 evaluation sets on the **three** language pairs shared across tracks (En → De, Ja, Zh), ordered by average metric ranking. Direct / end-to-end systems are highlighted in gray.

Submission	ar	de	fa	fr	ja	nl	pt	ru	tr	zh	Avg.
JHU$_{unconstrained}$	62.4	67.6	57.8	73.4	42.0	71.6	75.0	56.8	62.5	42.2	61.1
KIT$_{primary}$	56.9	64.8	55.4	67.8	42.3	67.6	69.6	51.2	57.3	42.5	57.5
KIT$_{contrastive1}$	56.9	64.6	55.6	67.8	42.0	67.6	69.6	51.2	56.7	42.7	57.5
KIT$_{contrastive2}$	56.1	63.6	52.9	67.3	40.8	66.5	69.2	50.6	55.6	41.3	56.4
KIT$_{contrastive4}$	56.2	63.3	53.0	67.2	40.7	66.5	68.8	50.4	55.1	40.3	56.2
KIT$_{contrastive3}$	55.5	63.7	52.1	66.9	40.3	66.0	68.9	50.0	55.2	40.6	55.9
KIT$_{contrastive5}$	55.3	61.3	53.8	65.2	35.9	63.7	67.3	48.6	54.9	39.2	54.5
KIT$_{contrastive7}$	54.7	60.3	54.0	64.4	34.5	63.4	67.2	47.8	54.2	38.2	53.9
KIT$_{contrastive6}$	54.6	60.3	52.7	64.3	35.5	62.7	66.4	48.2	53.8	38.4	53.7
JHU$_{constrained}$	45.2	53.4	44.5	62.4	26.8	62.1	62.2	46.8	46.3	30.8	48.1
BIT	28.9	36.8	28.8	45.2	14.5	41.7	43.0	28.4	25.9	17.2	31.0

Table 28: chrF with resegmentation for each target language on the evaluation set, sorted by the system average. Direct / end-to-end systems are highlighted in gray.

Submission	ar	de	fa	fr	ja	nl	pt	ru	tr	zh	Avg.
JHU$_{unconstrained}$	82.7	81.3	80.6	81.4	84.7	84.1	84.9	78.9	82.5	82.0	82.3
KIT$_{primary}$	78.0	74.9	75.8	74.4	82.0	77.7	78.4	72.5	76.6	79.3	77.0
KIT$_{constrastive1}$	77.7	74.6	75.7	74.5	82.0	77.6	78.4	72.2	76.4	79.3	76.8
KIT$_{constrastive5}$	78.5	74.9	75.9	74.6	80.3	76.8	78.5	71.6	76.9	79.1	76.7
KIT$_{constrastive7}$	78.2	73.9	76.3	74.2	80.3	76.7	80.3	71.3	76.2	78.8	76.6
KIT$_{constrastive2}$	77.3	74.3	74.9	74.3	81.6	77.3	78.4	72.1	75.8	78.6	76.5
KIT$_{constrastive4}$	77.2	74.2	75.0	74.3	81.7	77.3	78.2	72.0	75.5	78.4	76.4
KIT$_{constrastive3}$	76.9	74.7	74.6	74.2	81.4	76.9	78.2	71.8	75.7	78.4	76.3
KIT$_{constrastive6}$	77.8	73.9	75.2	73.3	80.0	75.4	77.7	70.8	75.7	78.9	75.9
JHU$_{constrained}$	67.9	59.0	66.1	63.2	69.3	66.2	67.8	62.0	64.0	67.9	65.3
BIT	52.8	47.2	48.7	52.2	56.2	53.8	54.8	47.7	48.0	55.7	51.7

Table 29: COMET with resegmentation for each target language on the evaluation set, sorted by the system average. Direct / end-to-end systems are highlighted in gray.

	ar	de	fa	fr	ja	nl	pt	ru	tr	zh	Avg.
JHU$_{unconstrained}$	33.4	41.2	35.0	50.0	33.9	44.8	51.7	27.9	28.1	46.5	39.3
KIT$_{primary}$	25.9	37.5	29.8	41.3	35.7	40.4	44.3	22.4	21.8	49.4	34.9
KIT$_{constrastive1}$	25.6	37.5	30.1	41.1	35.2	40.6	44.5	22.6	21.3	49.7	34.8
KIT$_{constrastive2}$	24.7	36.5	28.0	42.4	34.0	38.8	43.8	21.9	20.6	49.4	34.0
KIT$_{constrastive4}$	24.4	36.4	28.4	42.1	33.9	38.9	43.0	21.6	20.3	48.2	33.7
KIT$_{constrastive3}$	24.0	36.1	27.6	41.9	33.3	38.2	43.6	21.5	20.1	48.6	33.5
KIT$_{constrastive5}$	23.7	33.8	28.7	39.6	27.3	35.9	40.7	19.6	20.6	46.7	31.7
KIT$_{constrastive7}$	23.4	32.9	28.6	38.8	25.6	36.0	40.9	19.1	20.1	46.0	31.1
KIT$_{constrastive6}$	23.0	32.9	28.3	38.9	26.6	35.0	39.7	19.7	19.1	45.7	30.9
JHU$_{constrained}$	15.0	23.7	21.9	33.1	18.9	31.3	33.2	17.2	12.8	37.4	24.5
BIT	5.7	11.1	7.4	19.7	8.0	16.3	18.6	6.3	4.1	19.8	11.7

Table 30: BLEU with resegmentation for each target language on the evaluation set, sorted by the system average. BLEU scores in grey are calculated using language-specific tokenization (ja) or at the character-level (zh); see §5.2 for specific tokenization details. Direct / end-to-end systems are highlighted in gray.

B.5 Speech-to-Speech Translation

System	Test-primary				Test-expanded				Overall			
Ref	BLEU	chrF	COMET	SEScore2	BLEU	chrF	COMET	SEScore2	BLEU	chrF	COMET	SEScore2
Cascade Systems												
XIAOMI	47.9	41.0	79.91	-12.27	34.5	29.2	79.07	-20.15	38.4	32.3	79.35	-17.48
NPU-MSXF	47.4	40.7	79.90	-12.21	34.0	28.5	78.68	-20.23	37.7	31.8	79.09	-17.52
HW-TSC	43.2	36.9	76.96	-14.23	32.4	27.7	76.43	-21.61	35.3	30.1	76.61	-19.12
KU	36.7	31.3	69.09	-17.07	25.0	21.7	67.94	-25.68	28.2	24.3	68.33	-22.77
MINETRANS_Cascade	33.9	28.6	67.49	-17.68	24.7	21.5	64.71	-26.34	27.2	23.4	65.65	-23.41
E2E Systems												
MINETRANS_E2E (contrastive2)	45.0	38.3	74.83	-13.62	31.1	26.4	73.28	-22.03	34.9	29.6	73.81	-19.18
MINETRANS_E2E (contrastive1)	44.5	38.0	74.14	-13.92	31.0	26.4	72.90	-22.20	34.8	29.5	73.32	-19.40
MINETRANS_E2E (primary)	44.4	38.0	74.40	-13.86	31.1	26.4	73.00	-22.12	34.7	29.5	73.47	-19.32

Table 31: Official results of the **automatic evaluation** for the English to Chinese Speech-to-Speech Translation Task.

System	Translation Quality Score	Speech Quality Score	Overall
Cascade Systems			
NPU-MSXF	3.70	3.98	3.84
XIAOMI	3.72	3.67	3.70
HW-TSC	3.58	3.75	3.67
MINETRANS_Cascade	3.16	3.26	3.21
KU	2.92	3.01	2.97
E2E Systems			
MINETRANS_E2E (contrastive2)	3.58	3.50	3.54

Table 32: Official results of the **human evaluation** for the English to Chinese Speech-to-Speech Translation Task.

B.6 Dialectal SLT

Tunisian Arabic→English (Unconstrained Condition)

		test2					test3				
Team	System	BLEU	bp	pr1	chrF	TER	BLEU	bp	pr1	chrF	TER
USTC	primary	23.6	1.0	52.7	46.7	64.6	21.1	1.0	49.0	43.8	69.0
USTC	contrastive1	22.8	1.0	51.7	45.7	65.7	20.2	1.0	47.7	42.9	70.7
JHU	contrastive5	21.6	.99	50.7	45.0	66.9	19.1	1.0	46.6	41.9	72.3
JHU	primary	21.2	1.0	50.0	44.8	67.7	18.7	1.0	46.0	41.9	73.1
JHU	contrastive4	20.7	1.0	49.3	44.2	68.4	18.3	1.0	45.5	41.3	73.7
JHU	contrastive3	19.9	.98	49.0	43.0	68.7	18.2	1.0	45.5	40.5	73.1
JHU	contrastive1	19.4	.99	48.2	42.4	69.8	17.1	1.0	44.3	39.7	74.9
JHU	contrastive2	18.7	.97	48.4	41.8	69.4	17.1	1.0	44.7	39.2	74.1
ON-TRAC	post-eval	18.2	1.0	45.9	42.7	73.8	16.3	1.0	41.6	40.3	79.6
GMU	contrastive1	15.0	1.0	41.4	38.4	78.2	13.4	1.0	37.2	36.1	83.9
GMU	contrastive2	14.1	1.0	40.1	37.5	79.8	12.9	1.0	36.6	35.4	84.7
GMU	primary	16.6	1.0	44.5	39.7	74.1	14.6	1.0	40.4	37.6	79.6
ON-TRAC	primary	7.0	1.0	27.3	36.4	86.9	6.2	1.0	24.2	34.3	92.0
2022 best:CMU		20.8	.93	53.1	44.3	64.5	-	-	-	-	-

Table 33: Automatic evaluation results for the Dialect Speech Translation task, Unconstrained Condition. Systems are ordered in terms of the official metric BLEU on test3. We also report brevity penalty (bp) and unigram precision (pr1) of BLEU, chrF, and TER.

Tunisian Arabic→English (Constrained Condition)

		test2					test3				
Team	System	BLEU	bp	pr1	chrF	TER	BLEU	bp	pr1	chrF	TER
USTC	primary	20.5	.99	49.9	43.6	67.6	18.1	1.0	45.7	40.8	73.1
JHU	primary	19.1	.94	50.5	42.4	67.2	17.6	.96	46.6	39.9	71.9
GMU	primary	5.0	1.0	20.3	21.9	102.2	4.5	1.0	18.4	20.7	105.5
2022 best:CMU		20.4	.94	52.2	43.8	65.4	-	-	-	-	-
baseline		11.1	.88	40.0	31.9	77.8	10.4	.90	36.6	29.9	81.4

Table 34: Automatic evaluation results for the Dialect Speech Translation task, Constrained Condition.

Tunisian Arabic ASR Automatic Evaluation Results

ASR System	test2 WER↓		test2 CER↓		test3 WER↓		test3 CER↓	
	Orig	Norm	Orig	Norm	Orig	Norm	Orig	Norm
JHU / constrained / primary	70.3	43.7	30.7	22.7	74.0	44.9	33.1	24.8
JHU / unconstrained / primary	69.3	40.6	29.0	20.7	72.9	41.6	31.5	22.9
USTC / constrained / primary	49.5	40.8	24.2	20.9	52.3	43.2	27.1	23.8
USTC / unconstrained / primary	47.4	39.3	23.1	20.0	49.2	40.5	25.2	22.1
2022best:ON-TRAC/unconstrained	65.7	41.5	28.1	21.1	-	-	-	-

Table 35: Word Error Rate (WER) and Character Error Rate (CER) of the ASR component of submitted cascaded systems on test2 and test3. The original version (Orig) matches the minimal text pre-processing provided by the organizer's data preparation scripts, and results in relatively high WER. As diagnosis, we ran additional Arabic-specific normalization (Norm) for e.g. Alif, Ya, Ta-Marbuta on the hypotheses and transcripts before computing WER/CER. We are grateful to Ahmed Ali for assistance on this.

B.7 Low-Resource SLT

Irish→English (Constrained Condition)

Team	System	BLEU	chrF2
GMU	primary	15.1	26.5

Table 36: Automatic evaluation results for the Irish to English task, Constrained Condition.

Irish→English (Unconstrained Condition)

Team	System	BLEU	chrF2
GMU	primary	68.5	74.5
GMU	contrastive1	77.4	81.6
GMU	contrastive2	15.1	26.5

Table 37: Automatic evaluation results for the Irish to English task, Unconstrained Condition.

Marathi→Hindi (Constrained Condition)

Team	System	BLEU	chrF2
GMU	primary	3.3	16.8
SRI-B	primary	31.2	54.8
SRI-B	contrastive	25.7	49.4

Table 38: Automatic evaluation results for the Marathi to Hindi task, Constrained Condition.

Marathi→Hindi (Unconstrained Condition)

Team	System	BLEU	chrF2
Alexa AI	primary	28.6	49.4
Alexa AI	contrastive1	25.6	46.3
Alexa AI	contrastive2	23	41.9
Alexa AI	contrastive3	28.4	49.1
Alexa AI	contrastive4	25.3	46.3
Alexa AI	contrastive5	19.6	39.9
BUT	primary	39.6	63.3
BUT	contrastive	28.6	54.4
GMU	primary	7.7	23.8
GMU	contrastive1	8.6	24.7
GMU	contrastive2	5.9	20.3
SRI-B	primary	32.4	55.5
SRI-B	contrastive	29.8	53.2

Table 39: Automatic evaluation results for the Marathi to Hindi task, Unconstrained Condition.

Pashto→French (Unconstrained Condition)

		BLEU	
Team	System	valid	test
ON-TRAC	primary	24.82	24.87
ON-TRAC	contrastive1	23.38	23.87
GMU	primary	11.99	16.87
GMU	contrastive1	11.27	15.24
ON-TRAC	contrastive2	12.26	15.18
ON-TRAC	contrastive3	12.16	15.07
GMU	contrastive2	9.72	13.32

Table 40: Automatic evaluation results for the Pashto to French task, Unconstrained Condition.

Pashto→French (Constrained Condition)

		BLEU	
Team	System	valid	test
ON-TRAC	primary	14.52	15.56
ON-TRAC	contrastive1	11.06	15.29
ON-TRAC	contrastive2	11.11	15.06
ON-TRAC	contrastive3	10.5	9.2
GMU	primary	2.66	5.92

Table 41: Automatic evaluation results for the Pashto to French task, Constrained Condition.

Maltese→English (Unconstrained Condition)

Team	System	BLEU
UM-DFKI	primary	0.6
UM-DFKI	contrastive1	0.7
UM-DFKI	contrastive2	0.4
UM-DFKI	contrastive3	0.3
UM-DFKI	contrastive4	0.4

Table 42: Automatic evaluation results for the Maltese to English task, Unconstrained Condition.

Tamasheq→French (Constrained Condition)

Team	System	BLEU	chrF2	TER
GMU	primary	0.48	19.57	106.23

Table 43: Automatic evaluation results for the Tamasheq to French task, Constrained Condition.

Tamasheq→French (Unconstrained Condition)

Team	System	BLEU	chrF2	TER
NAVER	primary	23.59	49.84	64.00
NAVER	contrastive1	21.31	48.15	66.41
NAVER	contrastive2	18.73	46.11	70.32
ON-TRAC	primary	15.88	43.88	73.85
ON-TRAC	contrastive1	16.35	44.22	74.26
ON-TRAC	contrastive2	15.46	43.59	75.30
ON-TRAC	contrastive3	15.49	43.74	75.07
ON-TRAC	contrastive4	16.25	44.11	74.26
ON-TRAC	contrastive5	15.54	43.91	75.08
Alexa AI	primary	9.30	32.29	81.25
Alexa AI	contrastive1	8.87	32.04	81.03
Alexa AI	contrastive2	9.50	33.67	80.85
Alexa AI	contrastive3	9.28	32.86	82.33
GMU	primary	8.03	33.03	87.81
GMU	contrastive1	1.30	23.63	96.72
GMU	contrastive2	2.10	24.33	94.58

Table 44: Automatic evaluation results for the Tamasheq to French task, Unconstrained Condition.

Quechua→Spanish (Constrained Condition)

Team	System	BLEU	chrF2
GMU	primary	1.46	21.46
QUESPA	primary	1.25	25.35
QUESPA	contrastive1	0.13	10.53
QUESPA	contrastive2	0.11	10.63

Table 45: Automatic evaluation results for the Quechua to Spanish task, Constrained Condition. ChrF2 scores were only taken into account for those systems that scored less than 5 points BLEU.

Quechua→Spanish (Unconstrained Condition)

Team	System	BLEU
GMU	primary	1.78
GMU	contrastive1	1.86
GMU	contrastive2	1.63
NAVER	primary	15.70
NAVER	contrastive1	13.17
NAVER	contrastive2	15.55
QUESPA	primary	15.36
QUESPA	contrastive1	15.27
QUESPA	contrastive2	10.75

Table 46: Automatic evaluation results for the Quechua to Spanish task, Unconstrained Condition. ChrF2 scores were only taken into account for those systems that scored less than 5 points BLEU.

B.8 Formality Control for SLT

	Model		EN-KO				EN-VI			
			BLEU	COMET	mAcc	cAcc	BLEU	COMET	mAcc	cAcc
CONSTRAINED	CoCoA (baseline)	F	11.1	0.5044	28.5	55	43.2	0.6189	99	99
		IF	11.1	0.5125	80.4	58	41.5	0.6021	98	99
	HW-TSC	F	**25.6**	**0.7512**	89	**100**	**51.3**	**0.7522**	**100**	**100**
		IF	**26.1**	**0.7367**	**100**	**100**	**49.8**	**0.7209**	**100**	**100**
UNCONSTRAINED	UMD (baseline)	F	4.9	0.2110	78	99	26.7	0.3629	96	95
		IF	4.9	0.1697	98	99	25.3	0.3452	97	98
	HW-TSC	F	25.4	**0.7347**	87	**100**	**48.2**	**0.7214**	**100**	**100**
		IF	26.2	**0.7218**	**100**	**100**	**48.3**	**0.7102**	**100**	**100**
	KUxUpStage	F	**26.6**	0.7269	87	**100**	47.0	0.6685	99	**100**
		IF	**27.1**	0.7145	98	95	45.6	0.6373	99	**100**
	UCSC	F	23.3	0.5210	86	98	44.6	0.6771	99	98
		IF	22.8	0.4724	98	96	43.5	0.6281	99	**100**

Table 47: Results for the Formality Track (Supervised Setting). Most systems perform well in this setting, though MT quality on formal (F) tends to be higher than informal (IF)

	Model		EN-PT				EN-RU			
			BLEU	COMET	mAcc	cAcc	BLEU	COMET	mAcc	cAcc
CONSTRAINED	HW-TSC	F	**47.4**	**0.7337**	**100**	**100**	**36.5**	**0.6472**	**100**	**100**
		IF	**47.9**	**0.7442**	**100**	**100**	**35.6**	**0.6442**	**100**	**100**
UNCONSTRAINED	UMD (baseline)	F	27.3	0.4477	96	98	21.3	0.3492	96	92
		IF	30.9	0.4161	93	91	21.0	0.3475	84	85
	AppTek	F	34.6	0.6089	99	99	**35.4**	**0.6165**	99	98
		IF	42.4	0.6776	64	65	**33.3**	**0.6026**	98	97
	HW-TSC	F	**45.4**	**0.7737**	**100**	**100**	33.7	0.5804	**100**	**100**
		IF	**49.1**	**0.7845**	**100**	**100**	32.4	0.5558	**100**	**100**
	KUxUpStage	F	31.0	0.5251	**100**	**100**	25.8	0.4446	**100**	**100**
		IF	19.9	0.2486	68	90	26.3	0.4181	**100**	**100**
	UCSC	F	26.6	0.4048	90	91	18.4	-0.1713	99	79
		IF	28.4	0.4252	58	42	14.9	-0.2766	52	67

Table 48: Results for the Formality Track (Zero-shot Setting). Appreciable differences in formality control exist between formal (F) and informal (IF), suggesting that formality bias exists in participant systems.

Evaluating Multilingual Speech Translation Under Realistic Conditions with Resegmentation and Terminology

Elizabeth Salesky[J] **Kareem Darwish**[A] **Mohamed Al-Badrashiny**[A]
Mona Diab[M] **Jan Niehues**[K]
[J]Johns Hopkins University [A]aiXplain [M]Meta AI [K]Karlsruhe Institute of Technology
esalesky@jhu.edu

Abstract

We present the ACL 60/60 evaluation sets for multilingual translation of ACL 2022 technical presentations into 10 target languages. This dataset enables further research into multilingual speech translation under realistic recording conditions with unsegmented audio and domain-specific terminology, applying NLP tools to text and speech in the technical domain, and evaluating and improving model robustness to diverse speaker demographics.

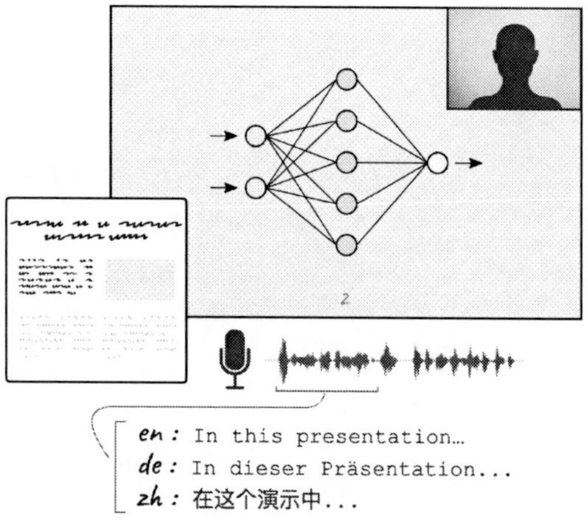

Figure 1: Multilingual translation of ACL presentations.

1 Introduction

The NLP and speech communities are rapidly expanding, which has motivated increased interest in multilingual scientific communication and accessibility. From the automatic captioning at NAACL 2019 provided by Microsoft to the current ACL 60-60 initiative[1] for the 60th anniversary of ACL at 2022, it is clear that transcription and translation in the technical domain is needed, desired, and still a disproportionate challenge for current models compared to standard datasets in these spaces.

Translating technical presentations presents challenging conditions, from domain-specific terminology and adaptation, to recordings often captured with a laptop microphone and light background noise, diverse speaker demographics as well as unsegmented speech typically 10-60 minutes in duration. We have curated evaluation sets from presentations at ACL 2022 which have been professionally transcribed and translated with the support of ACL and the 60-60 initiative. In this paper we describe the methodology to create this dataset, considerations and methods to evaluate speech translation models with it, and open challenges we believe this dataset may support research towards. We release all data and intermediate steps to support further research in this space.

We present the ACL 60/60 evaluation sets to enable greater development of tools by the field for the field. Specifically, we hope that this data enables further research into speech translation and other NLP applications in the technical domain with resegmentation and terminology, given a diverse speaker set and realistic recording conditions, with the goal of increased accessibility and multilinguality. Our dataset is publicly available through the ACL Anthology.[2]

2 Evaluation under realistic conditions

To evaluate transcription and translation under realistic conditions may require different metrics than with e.g. provided segmentation. Here we present the necessary metrics in order to discuss the dataset creation process.

2.1 Resegmentation

While most offline speech translation models are trained with provided segmentation, in an application setting segmentation is unlikely to be provided.

[1]https://www.2022.aclweb.org/dispecialinitiative

[2]https://aclanthology.org/2023.iwslt-1.2

Proceedings of the 20th International Conference on Spoken Language Translation (IWSLT 2023), pages 62–78
July 13-14, 2023 ©2023 Association for Computational Linguistics

Most models are typically unable to maintain output quality given audio of typical talk lengths (10+ minutes), necessitating the use of automatic segmentation methods. In order to evaluate output with variable segmentation, resegmentation to a fixed reference is necessary.

The standard tool within the field for many years has been mwerSegmenter (Matusov et al., 2005), which resegments model output to match a reference segmentation for downstream evaluation with various metrics. This is done by dynamically resegmenting the output using a given tokenization to minimize word error rate to the reference.[3] We use mwerSegmenter for all scores in this paper and suggest that resegmentation be the scoring standard for the ACL 60/60 dataset.

2.2 Evaluation metrics

We compare a variety of evaluation metrics to analyze both transcription and translation quality using the evaluation sets, as well as the results of intermediate steps in corpus creation such as post-editing.

For translation, we compare chrF (Popović, 2015) which is tokenization-agnostic and more appropriate for a wider array of target languages than BLEU; BLEU (Papineni et al., 2002) as computed by SACREBLEU (Post, 2018); and the model-based metric COMET (Rei et al., 2020), which often has higher correlation with human judgements (Mathur et al., 2020) though is limited by language coverage in pretrained models. For BLEU we use the suggested language-specific tokenizers in SACREBLEU for our non-space delimited target languages, Japanese (MeCab[4]) and Chinese (character-level).

To analyze both automatic and post-editing transcription quality, we use word error rate (WER). We note that we use case-sensitive and punctuation-sensitive WER here as these are both maintained in system output during dataset creation in order to be post-edited and translated. For downstream evaluation of ASR model quality using the final dataset, it may be desired to compute WER without case and without punctuation; if so, the scores would not be directly comparable to those presented here. We also use translation error rate (TER) (Snover et al., 2006) to assess the expected level of editing necessary to match the final reference quality.[5]

We caution against using any one translation metric in isolation, and suggest chrF and COMET as the standard evaluation metrics for this dataset.

3 Creating the ACL 60/60 evaluation sets

3.1 Languages

All data is originally spoken in English and then transcribed and translated to ten diverse languages from the 60/60 initiative for which publicly available speech translation corpora are available (see Table 5: §A.3): Arabic, Mandarin Chinese, Dutch, French, German, Japanese, Farsi, Portuguese, Russian, and Turkish. The resulting dataset contains three-way parallel (*speech, transcripts, translations*) one-to-many data for ten language pairs, and multi-way parallel text data for 100 language pairs.

3.2 Data selection

Data was selected from the ACL 2022 paper presentations for which precorded audio or video presentations were provided to the ACL Anthology. Talks were selected such that each of the two evaluation sets, development and evaluation, would have approximately one hour total duration. Oral presentations were advised to be up to 12 minutes per recording, resulting in 5 talks for each set with relatively balanced durations of $\sim$11.5 minutes each.

From the 324 available recordings, the final 10 were selected in order to balance speaker demographics, accents, and talk content, while lightly controlling for recording conditions. The majority of recordings were created using laptop microphones in quiet conditions, but background noise, microphone feedback, speech rate and/or volume in some cases affected understanding of the content. We selected talks with representative but minimal noise where conditions did not affect understanding of the content. We aimed for a gender balance representative of conference participation,[6] resulting in a 3:7 female:male speaker ratio. This is also a global field with a wide variety of native and non-native English accents, which remains a necessary challenge for speech models to address to mitigate performance biases (Sanabria et al., 2023; Feng et al., 2021; Koenecke et al., 2020; Tatman and Kasten, 2017). Talks were chosen and assigned to each set to maximize accent diversity, aiming for L1s from all continents with language families fre-

[3]We use word-level tokenization for all languages except Japanese and Chinese here, where we use character-level.

[4]`https://taku910.github.io/mecab/`

[5]We calculate TER with `--ter-normalized` and `--ter-asian-support` in SACREBLEU.

[6]Aggregate conference participation statistics provided by ACL 2022; see §A.2.

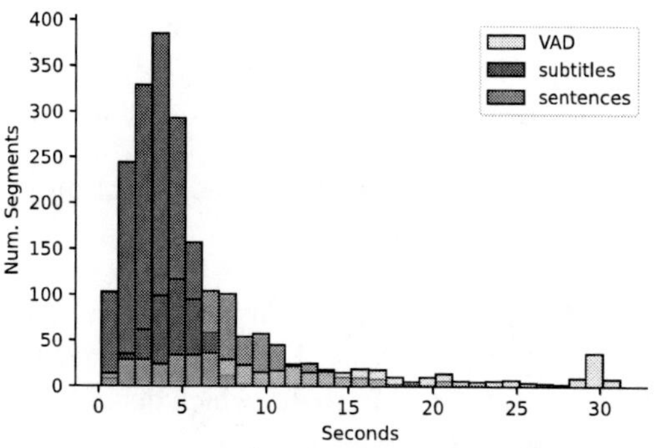

(a) Speech segment length distribution

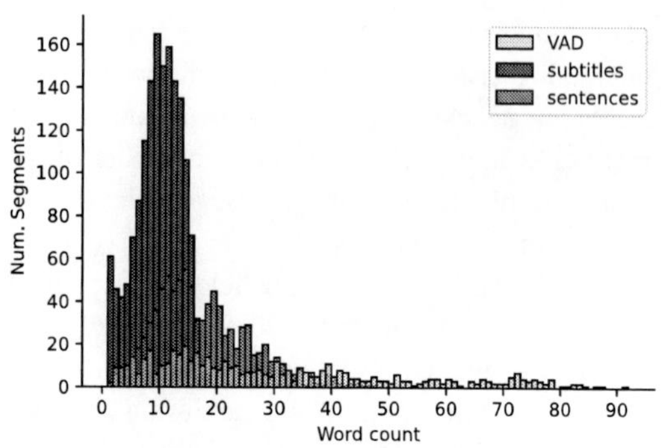

(b) Text segment length distribution

Figure 2: Distribution of English segment lengths via speech duration (seconds) and text length (word count) for each of three segmentations: VAD, subtitles, and sentences.

quently represented in the ACL community while balancing topic diversity and gender. We note native language and country where available. Talks were chosen to cover a diverse set of tracks and topics and therefore diverse technical vocabulary representative of the needs of the field. Where presentations were chosen within the same track, they covered different focuses and methodology, e.g. math word problems versus release note generation or few-shot adaptation for structured data. Metadata for all talks with exact durations and track and speaker annotations are shown in Table 3 in § A.1.

Holding out speakers and topics per set optimizes for overall system generalization but reduces the match between dev and eval sets; this e.g. reduces the benefit of finetuning on the dev set to maximize test set performance and overfitting the model or chosen hyperparameters to the dev set will adversely affect test set performance. However, high performance on both sets is more likely to indicate generalizable systems and representative performance beyond these data points than if the dev and eval data were more closely matched.

3.3 Automatic transcription

The first pass through the data used automatic segmentation and transcription to provide initial transcripts. We used the Azure API speech-to-text service,[7] which has the best cost and quality balance of currently available models. In addition to transcription, the service performs speaker diarization, with implicit voice activity detection (VAD), segmenting the initially ~11.5 minute audio files into segments of approximately 30 seconds or less based on pauses, speech, and non-speech phenomena. Figure 2 shows the resulting distribution of segment lengths. Evaluating these initial automatic transcripts against the final released version with resegmentation (§ 2.1), the automatic transcription yielded a WER of 15.4 and 22.4 for the development and evaluation sets, respectively.

[7] https://azure.microsoft.com/en-us/products/cognitive-services/speech-to-text

3.4 Human post-editing: Transcription

We contracted with aiXplain Inc. to professionally post-edit the ASR output. There was a three tier review process: an initial annotator post-edited per segment, followed by a quality assurance (QA) annotator who went through each full talk to ensure quality and consistency, and then finally 10-20% of the segments were randomly chosen for a final check. In addition to semantic content, annotators may theoretically also fix segmentation boundaries but in practice this rarely occurs. The annotators provided additional information about the speakers, namely gender (male, female) and age (child, young adult, adult, elderly). The annotators were also shown the video of the presentation to aid them ing recognizing technical terms, which may appear in the slides. Disfluencies were standardized such that false starts and repetitions were kept where there were perceivable pauses between them, and two hesitation spelling variations (*ah*, *um*) were used. The annotator guidelines and LabelStudio interface are shown in § A.4. After the professional post-editing pass, a domain expert verified and corrected the technical terms.

Post-editing analysis. ASR output is strongly monotonic with respect to the original speech, and accordingly most post-edits are for incorrectly tran-

REF:	we	find	a	BILSTM	**	CRF	model	using flare
HYP:	we	find	a	BIAS	TM	CRF	model	using flare
				S	D			

REF:	also	FASTTEXT	CHARACTER	EMBEDDINGS
HYP:	also	FASTTEX	KITCHEN	BEDDINGS
		S	S	S

REF:	multilingual	BERT	PERFORMS	better	than	BETO
HYP:	multilingual	BIRD	PERFORM	better	than	BETTER
		S	S			S

Figure 3: Sample ASR errors from dev using SCLITE. Corrections are emphasized with CASE.

scribed words, case, and punctuation. 93% of words were correctly transcribed by the initial ASR pass. Spurious punctuation and casing in the ASR output (ex 'Thank. You.') accounted for 43% of the errors captured by WER. Setting punctuation and case aside, in the professional post-editing pass, 60% of sentences had at least one correction made. The majority of post-edits were word-level substitutions for incorrectly transcribed words (62%). Dropped words were not common, with only 1.6% of words dropped by the ASR model and later inserted. Slightly more common (1.8%) were insertions due to words incorrectly transcribed as multiple tokens by the ASR system, and later corrected. Examples are shown in Figure 3.

Further corrections by a domain expert were made for 3% of words. While the majority were corrections to terminology requiring technical context (*'CONEL'* $\rightarrow$ *'CONLL'* or *'position or'* $\rightarrow$ *'positional'*), some fixes were for subtle number and tense changes in the ASR transcription possibly influenced by recording conditions or pronunciation.

Technical terms. The subset of technical terms appearing in the terminology lists created by the 60-60 initiative were automatically tagged on the source side (see Figure 4). These lists were not exhaustive but provide an initial keyword set to bootstrap identification and translation of technical terms and their evaluation, and which future work may find beneficial.

Technical terms comprised the majority of ASR errors. 86% of the tagged terminology were correctly transcribed the ASR model, 8% were corrected by the professional post-editors, and the remaining 6% were corrected by a domain expert.

3.5 Sentence segmentation

While it is common in speech corpora to segment based on voice activity detection or subtitle-like criteria, this may result in segments which are not parallel across languages (in the case of multilingual speech), which are too short to translate without additional context, or which are too long for effective system evaluation. For a multilingual dataset intended to be multi-way parallel and to be used for translation, it is critical to have consistent segmentation across all languages and for all segments to contain the necessary context to translate to the desired target languages.

And in fact, [automatically] [detecting] [lexical] borrowings ah has proven to be useful [for] [NLP] [downstream] [tasks] such as [parsing], [text]-to-[speech] synthesis or [machine translation].

Figure 4: Example of tagged terminology from dev. Terminology lists were not exhaustive; [text-to-speech] did not appear, leading [text] and [speech] to be tagged separately.

The VAD segments facilitated transcription, but resulted in a wide distribution of segment lengths, some just one to two words long, and others containing multiple sentences, potentially skewing downstream evaluation metrics and providing a mismatch to common training conditions. One option would be to subdivide the segments using subtitle guidelines,[8] where those segments which do not conform to particular length guidelines are realigned into smaller segments which is done using forced alignment. However, subtitle segments often contain partial sentences, which, particularly when including languages with different word orders or degrees of reordering from the source language (English), may place verbs across segment boundaries for some languages and not others. Sentences, then, may be a more appropriate unit for multi-way parallel segments. We resegmented the final post-edited English transcriptions into sentences manually to avoid noise from currently available tools. Examples of all three segmentations (VAD, subtitles, and sentences) are shown in Figure 12 in § A.8. To ensure the speech and text were correctly aligned given the final sentence segments, they were re-force aligned using WHISPER-TIMESTAMPED (Louradour, 2023), an extension of OpenAI's Whisper model (Radford et al., 2022) which uses DTW (Giorgino, 2009) to time align at the word level, and were manually rechecked by the annotators.

[8]Subtitle guidelines are shown in § A.7.

	Metric	*ar*	*de*	*fa*	*fr*	*ja*	*nl*	*pt*	*ru*	*tr*	*zh*
dev	chrF	75.3	72.8	54.9	80.0	56.9	82.7	82.3	59.3	69.0	60.5
	BLEU	54.1	48.3	25.3	63.0	50.7	63.6	65.9	30.5	39.1	65.9
	COMET	86.2	83.6	76.8	84.5	89.1	88.1	87.9	82.5	85.9	87.4
eval	chrF	77.2	71.7	56.3	83.7	53.6	86.6	84.8	65.3	77.0	62.7
	BLEU	55.4	48.5	27.1	68.3	47.3	71.5	68.7	39.4	51.6	67.9
	COMET	86.2	83.6	79.5	84.5	89.1	88.1	87.9	82.5	85.9	87.4

Table 1: Evaluating the initial commercial MT from ground-truth transcripts against the final released references. BLEU scores in grey are calculated using language-specific tokenization (*ja*) or at the character-level (*zh*); see § 2.2.

We compare the distribution of segment lengths for each of the three approaches (VAD, subtitles, and sentences) in terms of both duration (seconds) and number of words (English) in Figure 2. VAD results in the most uneven distribution, with segments ranging from <1 second to >30 seconds. Subtitles result in more uniform but distinctly shorter segments, with 58% containing less than 10 words and 19% shorter than two seconds, likely too short for some downstream tasks or metrics. Sentences result in less extreme segment lengths. Examples of each segmentation are shown in § A.8. The final data contains 468 sentences in the development set and 416 sentences in the evaluation set.

3.6 Machine translation

The first translation pass used publicly available bilingual MT models to translate the final sentence segments. We used the ModernMT API[9] for the 9 of 10 language pairs supported, and the Azure API[10] for English-Farsi. We evaluate the commercial machine translation output against the final released translation references (§ 3.7) using the metrics discussed in § 2.2, shown in Table 1.

Each metric suggests a different story about translation quality and the degree to which it is language-specific. While COMET suggests relatively consistent performance across languages, chrF and BLEU do not. chrF and BLEU suggest significantly worse performance for a subset of target languages, including all but one of the non-Latin script and non-Indo European languages. BLEU yields 1.7× greater variance than chrF. By all metrics, though, MT quality was consistent between the development and evaluation sets. We see in the next section that the amount of post-editing required to create the final references, however, is not necessarily indicated by these metrics.

3.7 Human post-editing: Translation

Post-editing has become the industry standard due its increased productivity, typically reducing processing time and cognitive load compared to direct translation, particularly for domain-specific texts (O'Brien, 2007; Groves and Schmidtke, 2009; Tatsumi, 2009; Plitt and Masselot, 2010).

We contracted with Translated to professionally post-edit the MT output. There was a two tier review process: an initial annotator who was a native speaker of the target language post-edited per segment, followed by a second to review the output and consistency of the first. Annotator guidelines and the post-editing interface are shown in § A.5.

Technical terms. Terminology was not handled separately during the MT step nor automatically tagged, given that the MT systems may omit or incorrectly translate technical terms. We did not use constrained decoding given the terminology lists translations as their validity could be context-dependent and some terms had multiple possible translations. Instead, translation post-editors were instructed to correct the translations of tagged terminology on the source if they were not maintained and then tag the appropriate target translations for each source tagged source span. Capitalized acronyms and terminology not on the lists and unknown to the translators was left in English.

Post-editing analysis. While the metrics in the previous section give a sense for the automatic translation quality, they do not necessarily reflect the effort required to post-edit the translations to final reference quality. Using TER to assess the degree of post-editing necessary, we see in Figure 5 that this varies by language. Most noticeably, we see that Farsi, Russian, Japanese as target languages required the highest amount of post-editing.

[9] `https://www.modernmt.com/api/`

[10] `https://azure.microsoft.com/en-us/products/cognitive-services/translator`

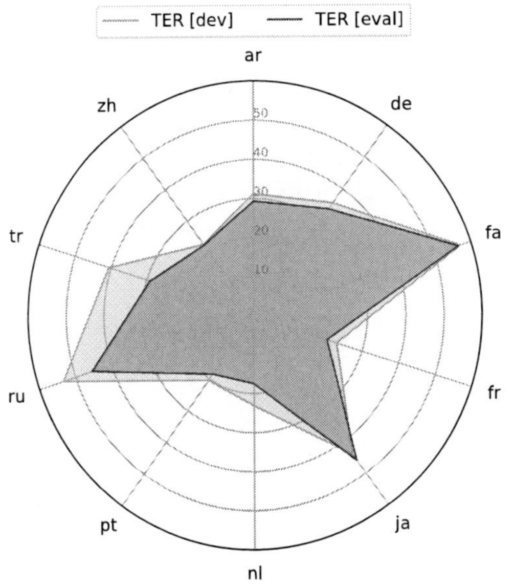

Figure 5: Estimated translation post-editing effort required per target language, as measured by TER.

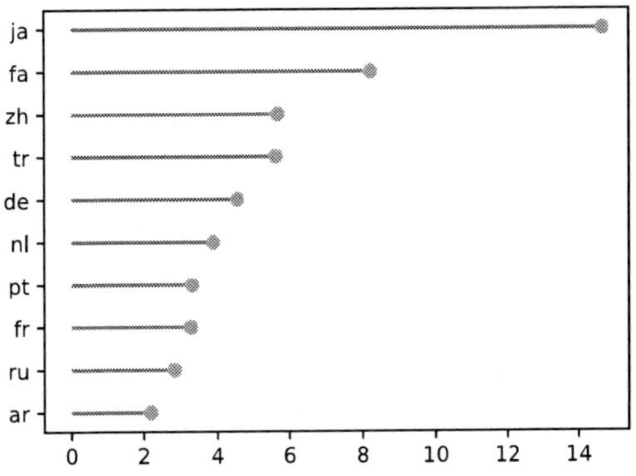

Figure 6: Degree of reordering done in MT post-editing.

For Farsi and Japanese, we see that this is predominantly due to reordering. Isolating reordering from semantic corrections by looking only at those tokens[11] which did not need to be corrected, we use Levenshtein distance to assess the degree of reordering from the MT output required. We observed a strong bias towards source language word order in the machine translation output, causing a greater degree of post-editing for languages with differing word orders. Figure 6 shows that reordering requirements are moderately correlated with overall post-editing effort for most languages ($\rho = 0.41$), while TER is only weakly suggested by COMET ($\rho = 0.29$) and is negatively correlated with chrF and BLEU (-0.63, -0.21 respectively).

For most target languages, there was no significant difference in post-editing effort between dev and test, but where there was a difference it was the dev talks that required additional editing, most noticeably for Turkish and Russian and to a lesser degree Dutch. Dividing the data into individual talks, which each vary in content within the technical domain, there was some variation in the quality of the first-pass MT (Figure 7). We found that which talks require similar levels of post-editing is moderately to strongly correlated across languages, suggesting this was due to topic rather than language, with the exception of Farsi and Japanese (Figure 8). This correlation does not appear to be influenced by language family and was not related to the proportion of tagged terminology per talk. For Russian and Turkish, a particular talk skewed overall dev TER, possibly due to a greater proportion of polysemous terms with domain-specific meaning in that area.

Terminology. Tagged terminology was more often correctly automatically transcribed than translated. Between 70-75% of the tagged spans were translated correctly by the initial MT model depending on the target language, as measured by an exact match with the final tagged post-edited span. The remaining 25-30% were manually corrected by the post-editors. In addition, 2-5% of words overall were left in English, predominantly made up of additional terminology and names.

4 Challenges to Address with ACL 60/60

4.1 Segmentation

Speech translation datasets customarily provide a segmentation for translation and evaluation, segmented either manually (e.g. CoVoST) or automatically (e.g. MuST-C). In realistic use cases, such segmentation is unavailable and long audio cannot be processed directly, resulting in mismatched conditions at inference time. There can be a noticeable performance gap between manual segmentation and automatic methods (Tsiamas et al., 2022).

We illustrate the impact of different speech segmentations on downstream transcription and translation quality by comparing manual sentence segmentation to the initial VAD segments as well as to SHAS (Tsiamas et al., 2022), using the top line commercial ASR and MT systems used during the

[11]Characters rather than words were used for this analysis for Japanese and Chinese.

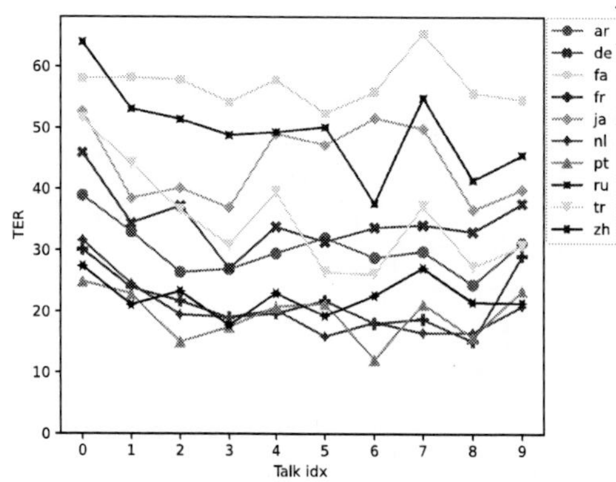

Figure 7: Range in TER by talk per language.

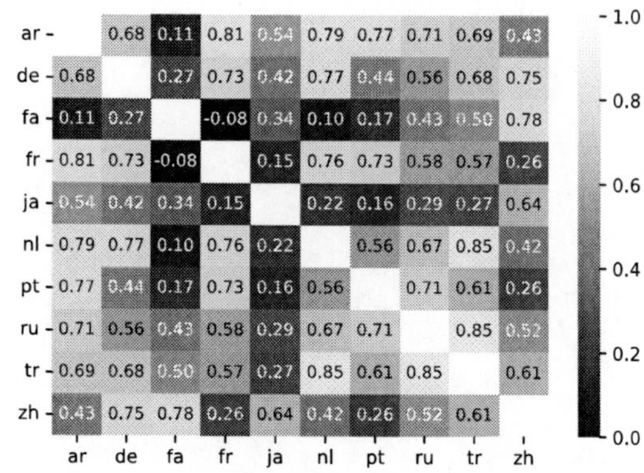

Figure 8: Correlation in TER across languages.

dataset creation pipeline. As seen in Table 2,[12] under certain circumstances automatic segmentation methods can perform as well as manual sentence segmentation, though this is not always the case and small resulting differences in ASR performance may cascade into larger performance gaps in downstream MT, meriting further research.

Variation due to segmentation also depends on model training conditions. Models are typically optimized for the segment lengths observed in training and/or may use additional internal segmentation. For example, when we compare the Whisper $_{\text{LARGE}}$ model (Radford et al., 2022) which is trained on longer segments, sentences are suboptimal compared to SHAS and VAD (0.1-0.9 WER), and when they are further segmented up to 4× by its internal VAD this cascades to disproportionately worse downstream MT performance (by up to 8 chrF) than with the Azure ASR.

	ASR		MT	
Segmentation	*dev*	*test*	*dev*	*test*
Manual sentences	15.2	21.4	69.4	71.5
Commercial VAD	15.4	22.4	62.0	59.6
SHAS	16.4	21.5	61.9	60.4

Table 2: Comparison between manual sentence segmentation and high quality automatic segmentation for ASR and cascaded ST in WER and avg. chrF, respectively.

Segmentation is an important open challenge, and we suggest that this dataset be used to evaluate segmentation by making the dataset standard scoring with resegmentation.

[12]chrF for individual languages is shown in Table 6.

4.2 Demographic fairness

The field is diverse and rapidly growing with a wide variety of speaker demographics and native and non-native English accents. As we train increasingly large and multilingual models it is important to evaluate their fairness to ensure any biases we may find decrease rather than increase over time, which we believe this dataset may help with.

The variety of speaker demographics in both the field and these evaluation sets remain disproportionately challenging to current ASR models. Looking at the average WER among talks of each gender, we see a margin of 10.5. 15% of dev sentences and 26% of eval sentences were misclassified as non-English languages when using the multilingual Whisper $_{\text{BASE}}$ model, showing a bias against varied pronunciations and L1s that it is necessary to address when pursuing multilingual modelling. WER is 23% better when the model is prompted to generate English only, however, there is still a further 16% gap to the English-only BASE model. Moving to the larger multilingual model, the discrepancy in performance with and without language prompting becomes 2.4× larger, though overall performance improves. At worst, the ΔWER between speakers is 62.2, and at best, 8.0, highlighting a significant discrepancy which needs to be improved.

Demographic fairness is an important issue which requires targeted research to address. We hope these evaluations sets may facilitate further research in this space, despite their small size.

4.3 Domain adaptation and terminology

Terminology. Constrained decoding of technical terms or domain-specific translations is an area of active research (Hu et al., 2019; Post and Vilar, 2018; Hokamp and Liu, 2017). The terminology lists were not exhaustive, containing just over 250 terms, but provide an initial keyword set to bootstrap identification and translation of technical terms in context and their evaluation, which future work may find beneficial.

We highlight the reduction in terminology recall between the strong ASR and MT systems used in the dataset creation pipeline below in Figure 9. It is clear that even commercial systems struggle with domain-specific terminology particularly without adaptation. While there are discrepancies across language pairs, terminology recall is strongly correlated with overall translation performance ($\rho = 0.8$) as measured by chrF.

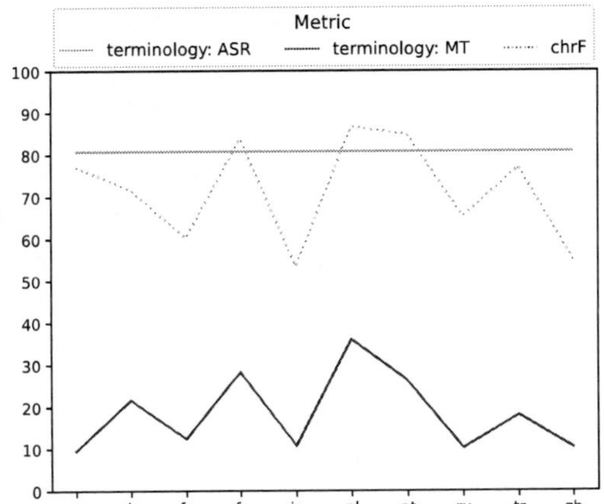

Figure 9: Terminology recall of ASR vs MT, with overall translation performance shown behind (chrF).

Lightweight domain adaptation. There are few publicly available datasets with technical content, and fewer translated. While it is possible to scrape in-domain material e.g. from the ACL Anthology, this would be in the source language (English) only rather than the target languages. While only having target-domain data in the source language is a realistic scenario, it is not the setting typically found in current research or approaches, and highlights the need for new methods for domain adaptation which can make use of this data. We additionally provide paper titles and abstracts, which are likely to contain both particularly important vocabulary and cue the talk topic. We hope this data may prove beneficial for lightweight methods to adapt to the technical domain or specific talk settings or to lexically constrain or prompt particular translations.

5 Related work

Previous work has studied data from the ACL Anthology for term mining and identification (Schumann and Martínez Alonso, 2018; Jin et al., 2013) and concept relation (Gábor et al., 2016) in the scientific domain.

Few speech translation datasets in the technical domain exist but those that do such as the QCRI Educational Corpus (Abdelali et al., 2014; Guzman et al., 2013) have primarily targeted educational lectures and videos. Additional datasets specifically for speech translation evaluation (Conneau et al., 2023) are primarily 'general domain.'

Significant previous work has studied various aspects of translation post-editing, including post-editing effort (Scarton et al., 2019), evaluating post-editing quality and reference bias (Bentivogli et al., 2018), bias from the initial MT quality and output patterns (Zouhar et al., 2021; Picinini and Ueffing, 2017), and the the efficacy of post-editing in highly technical domains (Pinnis et al., 2016) and resulting translation biases (Čulo and Nitzke, 2016).

The impact of automatic segmentation quality on various ST metrics has been evaluated in recent IWSLT shared tasks (Ansari et al., 2020; Anastasopoulos et al., 2021, 2022) and research (Tsiamas et al., 2022; Sen et al., 2022; Ansari et al., 2021) using other datasets (TED) with longer reference segmentations than ours. With longer sequences there is greater potential for variation, and past campaigns have observed larger differences between segmentations than seen here and even improvements over the provided segmentation. Significant additional work has been done in the simultaneous translation space, which we do not address here.

6 Conclusions

We introduced a new dataset to evaluate multilingual speech translation from English into ten target languages specifically in the technical NLP domain. We have discussed in detail the steps to create the corpus and the tools and considerations required. We have also provided a further view into evaluation methodology mimicking realistic conditions where segmentation is not provided. We hope that this dataset may be useful for the field to study the effectiveness of the tools we develop both for translation and additional applications in the technical domain in an increasingly multilingual space.

Limitations

While we have done our best to create high-quality evaluation data, there are limitations that should be kept in mind when using these datasets. It is known that creating translations by post-editing may bias data towards the output of the MT systems used for initial translations; however, many transcription and translation vendors now exclusively use post-editing rather than translation from scratch and so direct translation may not be an option in all cases. This could influence metrics toward similar MT systems. The presented evaluation sets are moderately sized compared to datasets in other domains with plentiful mined data, and may be best used in conjunction by reporting on both the development and evaluation sets for statistical significance. The evaluation sets also have a necessarily limited set of speakers which may not be fully representative. Systems which tune to the development set run the risk of over-fitting to specific speakers or content. We do not perform a comparison to human evaluation here, but refer interested readers to the IWSLT'23 evaluation campaign findings paper which runs this comparison for a variety of systems with the ACL 60/60 data (Agarwal et al., 2023).

Ethical Considerations

This dataset is constructed from a small set of speakers where each speaker may be the only representative of certain cross-sectional axes, and as such, even reporting aggregate metadata may break anonymity. While we do not distribute speaker annotations with the data some information is inherently recoverable due to the link to the Anthology. We nonetheless believe this data will be beneficial to the community in order to study language processing on technical data, and it is necessary to have a diverse evaluation set to provide a more realistic and representative measure for generalization. It is difficult and costly to construct datasets with human-edited transcripts and translations and this was the largest set possible to collect. Post-editors were compensated with professional wages.

Acknowledgements

We are very grateful to funding and support from ACL and the 60/60 initiative to create this dataset. We thank our annotators and the generous support of aiXplain and Translated. Elizabeth Salesky is supported by the Apple Scholars in AI/ML fellowship.

References

Ahmed Abdelali, Francisco Guzman, Hassan Sajjad, and Stephan Vogel. 2014. The AMARA corpus: Building parallel language resources for the educational domain. In *Proceedings of the Ninth International Conference on Language Resources and Evaluation (LREC'14)*, pages 1856–1862, Reykjavik, Iceland. European Language Resources Association (ELRA).

Milind Agarwal, Sweta Agrawal, Antonios Anastasopoulos, Ondřej Bojar, Claudia Borg, Marine Carpuat, Roldano Cattoni, Mauro Cettolo, Mingda Chen, William Chen, Khalid Choukri, Alexandra Chronopoulou, Anna Currey, Thierry Declerck, Qianqian Dong, Yannick Estéve, Kevin Duh, Marcello Federico, Souhir Gahbiche, Barry Haddow, Benjamin Hsu, Phu Mon Htut, Hirofumi Inaguma, Dávid Javorský, John Judge, Yasumasa Kano, Tom Ko, Rishu Kumar, Pengwei Li, Xutai Ma, Prashant Mathur, Evgeny Matusov, Paul McNamee, John P. McCrae, Kenton Murray, Maria Nadejde, Satoshi Nakamura, Matteo Negri, Ha Nguyen, Jan Niehues, Xing Niu, Atul Ojha Kr., John E. Ortega, Proyag Pal, Juan Pino, Lonneke van der Plas, Peter Polák, Elijah Rippeth, Elizabeth Salesky, Jiatong Shi, Matthias Sperber, Sebastian Stüker, Katsuhito Sudoh, Yun Tang, Brian Thompson, Kevin Tran, Marco Turchi, Alex Waibel, Mingxuan Wang, Shinji Watanabe, and Rodolfo Zevallos. 2023. Findings of the IWSLT 2023 Evaluation Campaign. In *Proceedings of the 20th International Conference on Spoken Language Translation (IWSLT 2023)*. Association for Computational Linguistics.

Antonios Anastasopoulos, Loïc Barrault, Luisa Bentivogli, Marcely Zanon Boito, Ondřej Bojar, Roldano Cattoni, Anna Currey, Georgiana Dinu, Kevin Duh, Maha Elbayad, Clara Emmanuel, Yannick Estève, Marcello Federico, Christian Federmann, Souhir Gahbiche, Hongyu Gong, Roman Grundkiewicz, Barry Haddow, Benjamin Hsu, Dávid Javorský, Věra Kloudová, Surafel Lakew, Xutai Ma, Prashant Mathur, Paul McNamee, Kenton Murray, Maria Nădejde, Satoshi Nakamura, Matteo Negri, Jan Niehues, Xing Niu, John Ortega, Juan Pino, Elizabeth Salesky, Jiatong Shi, Matthias Sperber, Sebastian Stüker, Katsuhito Sudoh, Marco Turchi, Yogesh Virkar, Alexander Waibel, Changhan Wang, and Shinji Watanabe. 2022. Findings of the IWSLT 2022 evaluation campaign. In *Proceedings of the 19th International Conference on Spoken Language Translation (IWSLT 2022)*, pages 98–157, Dublin, Ireland (in-person and online). Association for Computational Linguistics.

Antonios Anastasopoulos, Ondřej Bojar, Jacob Bremerman, Roldano Cattoni, Maha Elbayad, Marcello Federico, Xutai Ma, Satoshi Nakamura, Matteo Negri, Jan Niehues, Juan Pino, Elizabeth Salesky, Sebastian Stüker, Katsuhito Sudoh, Marco Turchi, Alexander Waibel, Changhan Wang, and Matthew Wiesner. 2021. FINDINGS OF THE IWSLT 2021 EVALUATION CAMPAIGN. In *Proceedings of the 18th*

International Conference on Spoken Language Translation (IWSLT 2021), pages 1–29, Bangkok, Thailand (online). Association for Computational Linguistics.

Ebrahim Ansari, Amittai Axelrod, Nguyen Bach, Ondřej Bojar, Roldano Cattoni, Fahim Dalvi, Nadir Durrani, Marcello Federico, Christian Federmann, Jiatao Gu, Fei Huang, Kevin Knight, Xutai Ma, Ajay Nagesh, Matteo Negri, Jan Niehues, Juan Pino, Elizabeth Salesky, Xing Shi, Sebastian Stüker, Marco Turchi, Alexander Waibel, and Changhan Wang. 2020. FINDINGS OF THE IWSLT 2020 EVALUATION CAMPAIGN. In *Proceedings of the 17th International Conference on Spoken Language Translation*, pages 1–34, Online. Association for Computational Linguistics.

Ebrahim Ansari, Ondřej Bojar, Barry Haddow, and Mohammad Mahmoudi. 2021. SLTEV: Comprehensive evaluation of spoken language translation. In *Proceedings of the 16th Conference of the European Chapter of the Association for Computational Linguistics: System Demonstrations*, pages 71–79, Online. Association for Computational Linguistics.

Luisa Bentivogli, Mauro Cettolo, Marcello Federico, and Christian Federmann. 2018. Machine translation human evaluation: an investigation of evaluation based on post-editing and its relation with direct assessment. In *Proceedings of the 15th International Conference on Spoken Language Translation*, pages 62–69, Brussels. International Conference on Spoken Language Translation.

Alexis Conneau, Min Ma, Simran Khanuja, Yu Zhang, Vera Axelrod, Siddharth Dalmia, Jason Riesa, Clara Rivera, and Ankur Bapna. 2023. Fleurs: Few-shot learning evaluation of universal representations of speech. In *2022 IEEE Spoken Language Technology Workshop (SLT)*, pages 798–805.

Oliver Čulo and Jean Nitzke. 2016. Patterns of terminological variation in post-editing and of cognate use in machine translation in contrast to human translation. In *Proceedings of the 19th Annual Conference of the European Association for Machine Translation*, pages 106–114.

Mattia A. Di Gangi, Roldano Cattoni, Luisa Bentivogli, Matteo Negri, and Marco Turchi. 2019. MuST-C: a Multilingual Speech Translation Corpus. In *Proceedings of the 2019 Conference of the North American Chapter of the Association for Computational Linguistics: Human Language Technologies, Volume 1 (Long and Short Papers)*, pages 2012–2017, Minneapolis, Minnesota. Association for Computational Linguistics.

Siyuan Feng, Olya Kudina, Bence Mark Halpern, and Odette Scharenborg. 2021. Quantifying bias in automatic speech recognition. *ArXiv*, abs/2103.15122.

Kata Gábor, Haïfa Zargayouna, Davide Buscaldi, Isabelle Tellier, and Thierry Charnois. 2016. Semantic annotation of the ACL Anthology corpus for the automatic analysis of scientific literature. In *Proceedings of the Tenth International Conference on Language Resources and Evaluation (LREC'16)*, pages 3694–3701, Portorož, Slovenia. European Language Resources Association (ELRA).

Toni Giorgino. 2009. Computing and visualizing dynamic time warping alignments in r: The dtw package. *Journal of Statistical Software*, 31(7).

Declan Groves and Dag Schmidtke. 2009. Identification and analysis of post-editing patterns for MT. In *Proceedings of Machine Translation Summit XII: Commercial MT User Program*, Ottawa, Canada.

Francisco Guzman, Hassan Sajjad, Stephan Vogel, and Ahmed Abdelali. 2013. The AMARA corpus: building resources for translating the web's educational content. In *Proceedings of the 10th International Workshop on Spoken Language Translation: Papers*, Heidelberg, Germany.

Chris Hokamp and Qun Liu. 2017. Lexically constrained decoding for sequence generation using grid beam search. In *Proceedings of the 55th Annual Meeting of the Association for Computational Linguistics (Volume 1: Long Papers)*, pages 1535–1546, Vancouver, Canada. Association for Computational Linguistics.

J. Edward Hu, Huda Khayrallah, Ryan Culkin, Patrick Xia, Tongfei Chen, Matt Post, and Benjamin Van Durme. 2019. Improved lexically constrained decoding for translation and monolingual rewriting. In *Proceedings of the 2019 Conference of the North American Chapter of the Association for Computational Linguistics: Human Language Technologies, Volume 1 (Long and Short Papers)*, pages 839–850, Minneapolis, Minnesota. Association for Computational Linguistics.

J. Iranzo-Sánchez, J. A. Silvestre-Cerdà, J. Jorge, N. Roselló, A. Giménez, A. Sanchis, J. Civera, and A. Juan. 2020. Europarl-st: A multilingual corpus for speech translation of parliamentary debates. In *ICASSP 2020 - 2020 IEEE International Conference on Acoustics, Speech and Signal Processing (ICASSP)*, pages 8229–8233.

Yiping Jin, Min-Yen Kan, Jun-Ping Ng, and Xiangnan He. 2013. Mining scientific terms and their definitions: A study of the ACL Anthology. In *Proceedings of the 2013 Conference on Empirical Methods in Natural Language Processing*, pages 780–790, Seattle, Washington, USA. Association for Computational Linguistics.

Allison Koenecke, Andrew Joo Hun Nam, Emily Lake, Joe Nudell, Minnie Quartey, Zion Mengesha, Connor Toups, John R. Rickford, Dan Jurafsky, and Sharad Goel. 2020. Racial disparities in automated speech recognition. *Proceedings of the National Academy of Sciences of the United States of America*, 117:7684 – 7689.

Jérôme Louradour. 2023. whisper-timestamped. https://github.com/linto-ai/whisper-timestamped.

Nitika Mathur, Johnny Wei, Markus Freitag, Qingsong Ma, and Ondřej Bojar. 2020. Results of the WMT20 metrics shared task. In *Proceedings of the Fifth Conference on Machine Translation*, pages 688–725, Online. Association for Computational Linguistics.

Evgeny Matusov, Gregor Leusch, Oliver Bender, and Hermann Ney. 2005. Evaluating machine translation output with automatic sentence segmentation. In *Proceedings of the Second International Workshop on Spoken Language Translation*, Pittsburgh, Pennsylvania, USA.

Sharon O'Brien. 2007. An empirical investigation of temporal and technical post-editing effort. *The Information Society*, 2:83–136.

Kishore Papineni, Salim Roukos, Todd Ward, and Wei-Jing Zhu. 2002. Bleu: a method for automatic evaluation of machine translation. In *Proceedings of the 40th Annual Meeting of the Association for Computational Linguistics*, pages 311–318, Philadelphia, Pennsylvania, USA. Association for Computational Linguistics.

Silvio Picinini and Nicola Ueffing. 2017. A detailed investigation of bias errors in post-editing of MT output. In *Proceedings of Machine Translation Summit XVI: Commercial MT Users and Translators Track*, pages 79–90, Nagoya Japan.

Marcis Pinnis, Rihards Kalnins, Raivis Skadins, and Inguna Skadina. 2016. What can we really learn from post-editing? In *Conferences of the Association for Machine Translation in the Americas: MT Users' Track*, pages 86–91, Austin, TX, USA. The Association for Machine Translation in the Americas.

Mirko Plitt and François Masselot. 2010. A productivity test of statistical machine translation post-editing in a typical localisation context. In *Prague Bulletin of Mathematical Linguistics*.

Maja Popović. 2015. chrF: character n-gram F-score for automatic MT evaluation. In *Proceedings of the Tenth Workshop on Statistical Machine Translation*, pages 392–395, Lisbon, Portugal. Association for Computational Linguistics.

Matt Post. 2018. A call for clarity in reporting BLEU scores. In *Proceedings of the Third Conference on Machine Translation: Research Papers*, pages 186–191, Brussels, Belgium. Association for Computational Linguistics.

Matt Post and David Vilar. 2018. Fast lexically constrained decoding with dynamic beam allocation for neural machine translation. In *Proceedings of the 2018 Conference of the North American Chapter of the Association for Computational Linguistics: Human Language Technologies, Volume 1 (Long Papers)*, pages 1314–1324, New Orleans, Louisiana. Association for Computational Linguistics.

Alec Radford, Jong Wook Kim, Tao Xu, Greg Brockman, Christine McLeavey, and Ilya Sutskever. 2022. Robust speech recognition via large-scale weak supervision. *arXiv preprint arXiv:2212.04356*.

Ricardo Rei, Craig Stewart, Ana C Farinha, and Alon Lavie. 2020. COMET: A neural framework for MT evaluation. In *Proceedings of the 2020 Conference on Empirical Methods in Natural Language Processing (EMNLP)*, pages 2685–2702, Online. Association for Computational Linguistics.

Ramon Sanabria, Nikolay Bogoychev, Nina Markl, Andrea Carmantini, Ondrej Klejch, and Peter Bell. 2023. The edinburgh international accents of english corpus: Towards the democratization of english asr.

Scarton Scarton, Mikel L. Forcada, Miquel Esplà-Gomis, and Lucia Specia. 2019. Estimating post-editing effort: a study on human judgements, task-based and reference-based metrics of MT quality. In *Proceedings of the 16th International Conference on Spoken Language Translation*, Hong Kong. Association for Computational Linguistics.

Anne-Kathrin Schumann and Héctor Martínez Alonso. 2018. Automatic annotation of semantic term types in the complete ACL Anthology reference corpus. In *Proceedings of the Eleventh International Conference on Language Resources and Evaluation (LREC 2018)*, Miyazaki, Japan. European Language Resources Association (ELRA).

Sukanta Sen, Ondřej Bojar, and Barry Haddow. 2022. Simultaneous translation for unsegmented input: A sliding window approach.

Matthew Snover, Bonnie Dorr, Rich Schwartz, Linnea Micciulla, and John Makhoul. 2006. A study of translation edit rate with targeted human annotation. In *Proceedings of the 7th Conference of the Association for Machine Translation in the Americas: Technical Papers*, pages 223–231, Cambridge, Massachusetts, USA. Association for Machine Translation in the Americas.

Rachael Tatman and Conner Kasten. 2017. Effects of talker dialect, gender & race on accuracy of bing speech and youtube automatic captions. In *Interspeech*.

Midori Tatsumi. 2009. Correlation between automatic evaluation metric scores, post-editing speed, and some other factors. In *Proceedings of Machine Translation Summit XII: Posters*, Ottawa, Canada.

Ioannis Tsiamas, Gerard I. Gállego, José A. R. Fonollosa, and Marta Ruiz Costa-jussà. 2022. Shas: Approaching optimal segmentation for end-to-end speech translation. In *Interspeech*.

Changhan Wang, Juan Pino, Anne Wu, and Jiatao Gu. 2020. CoVoST: A diverse multilingual speech-to-text translation corpus. In *Proceedings of the Twelfth Language Resources and Evaluation Conference*, pages 4197–4203, Marseille, France. European Language Resources Association.

Vilém Zouhar, Martin Popel, Ondřej Bojar, and Aleš Tamchyna. 2021. Neural machine translation quality and post-editing performance. In *Proceedings of the 2021 Conference on Empirical Methods in Natural Language Processing*, pages 10204–10214, Online and Punta Cana, Dominican Republic. Association for Computational Linguistics.

A Appendix

A.1 Additional Metadata for ACL 60/60 Evaluation Sets

Below we list the duration for talks in the evaluation sets, along with additional demographic metadata about the presenting author (speaker) and content (conference track). Conference tracks are taken from the ACL 2022 handbook. Gender annotations were checked with speakers' listed pronouns[13] and validated by speakers where available. For speaker demographics and accent we list L1 and native country where available, as well as country of affiliation as a rough proxy.

Gender	L1	Country	Affiliation	Time	Track
M	Kinyarwanda	Rwanda	USA	0:11:35	Theme: Language Diversity (Best Paper)
M	—	—	USA	0:11:35	Dialogue and Interactive Systems
F	Spanish	Spain	Spain	0:12:17	Resources and Evaluation
F	Marathi	India	USA	0:12:09	Question Answering
M	Polish	Poland	Poland	0:09:37	Machine Learning for NLP
				0:57:13	*Total development set duration*
M	Chinese	China	China	0:12:03	NLP Applications
M	—	Belgium	Netherlands	0:12:02	Resources and Evaluation
F	Romanian	Romania	Germany	0:09:22	Language Grounding, Speech and Multimodality
M	Japanese	Japan	Japan	0:14:02	NLP Applications
M	Hebrew	Israel	Israel	0:11:53	NLP Applications
				0:59:22	*Total evaluation set duration*

Table 3: Additional metadata for talks in the evaluation sets.

A.2 ACL 2022 Conference Participation Statistics

Aggregate statistics for self-identified gender as listed on conference registrations were provided by ACL.

Gender	#	%
Woman	909	28.7
Man	2164	68.3
Non-binary / Genderqueer / Third gender	14	<1
Genderfluid / Gender non-confirming	<10	<1
Prefer not to say	77	2.4
Specify your own	<10	<1
TOTAL	3170	100

Table 4: Aggregate statistics on gender of ACL 2022 conference participants.

[13]Though we note pronouns do not always indicate gender.

A.3 Publicly Available Corpora

Below are the current publicly available multi-way parallel speech translation corpora with English as the speech source. We note that for MuST-C not all target languages are available in all versions of the corpus as successive versions added additional language coverage. For full coverage v1.2 or above is required.

Corpus	Src	Tgt	
MuST-C (Di Gangi et al., 2019)	en	all (10)	ar, de, fa, fr, ja, nl, pt, ru, tr, zh
CoVoST (Wang et al., 2020)	en	all (10)	ar, de, fa, fr, ja, nl, pt, ru, tr, zh
Europarl-ST (Iranzo-Sánchez et al., 2020)	en	some (4)	de, fr, pt, tr

Table 5: Current publicly available aligned speech translation corpora covering the ACL 60/60 language pairs. Target languages are abbreviated using ISO 639-1 codes as follows – *Arabic: ar, German: de, Farsi: fa, French: fr, Japanese: ja, Dutch: nl, Portuguese: pt, Russian: ru, Turkish: tr, Mandarin Chinese: zh.*

A.4 Transcription Post-editing Guidelines and Interface

The following guidelines were used for transcription post-editing by aiXplain. The acceptance criterion was word accuracy >95%.

- Accuracy. Only type the words that are spoken in the audio file. Phrases or words you don't understand should NOT be omitted. Instead, they should be annotated using the label "#Unclear".
- Keep everything verbatim. Include every utterance and sound exactly as you hear. All filler words should be included (ex. #ah, #hmm). If the user corrects his/her self, all the utterances should be transcribed and corrected words need to preceded with a # mark (ex. She says #said that).
- Do not paraphrase. Do not correct the speaker's grammar nor rearrange words. Also, do not cut words that you think are off-topic or irrelevant. Any words not spoken should not be included. Type the actual words spoken. If the speaker makes a grammatical mistake, the transcript must reflect the mistake (ex. If the speaker says: "he were", it should be transcribed as is without correction).
- Repeat repeated words in the transcript. For example, if the user says: I I said, you must include both instances of I.
- Do not add additional information such as page numbers, job numbers, titles or your comments in your submission.
- Foreign words should be transliterated using Latin letters.
- All abbreviations need to be spelled out. For example, doctor should NOT be spelled as Dr. Similarly, percent should NOT be spelled as %.
- All numbers and special symbols (ex.: %, $, +, @, =, etc.), or combinations of both must be spelled out as words, and must match what the speaker says exactly.
- All proper names (ex. Google, NATO, Paris) should be transliterated in English.
- Proper punctuation needs to be placed in the text (ex. He, the boy, .). Please pay special attention and do not miss/omit these punctuation marks: , . ? ! :)(
- Personally identifiable information (like phone number, address, IDs) should be marked in the text as <PII></PII>. For example: My address is <PII>address</PII>
- Use double dashes "--" to indicate truncated words, attached whether at the beginning or the end of the word (ex. transfor–).

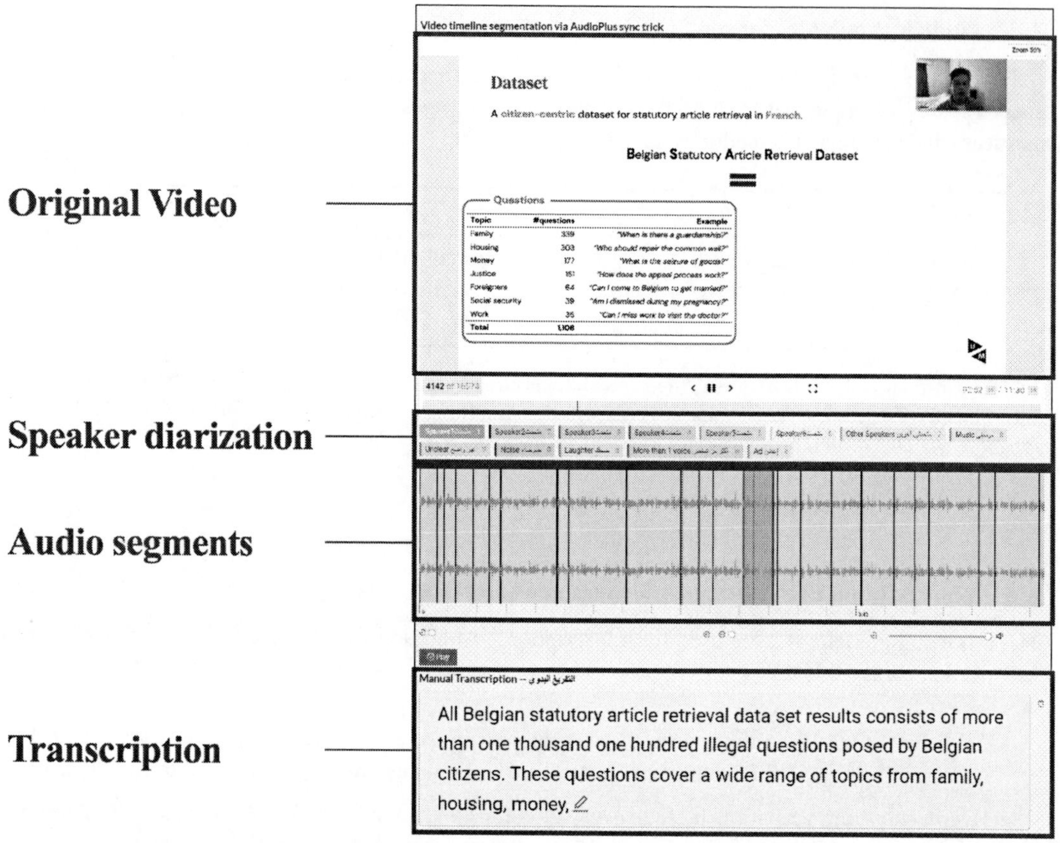

Figure 10: LabelStudio interface for transcription post-editing.

A.5 Translation Post-editing Instructions and Interface

The translation post-editing task was carried out in Matecat[14], an open-source CAT tool that allows annotators to collaborate and get suggestions from ModernMT in real-time. Matecat also offers an embedded glossary feature that ensures effective and consistent terminology management (as shown in the interface image in Figure 11 below, featuring Matecat glossary suggestions).

The following guidelines were used for translation post-editing:

- Any term found in the 60-60 terminologies list, should be translated using the translation in the terminologies list.
- Any abbreviation if not found in the terminologies list, should be kept it in the English form
- The terms in the terminologies list may contain one or more translation for each term separated by ':::'. The translator should pick the proper one based on the context
- If the translator thinks that none of the given translations for a specific term makes sense in the given context, the translators can use a better translation if they are very confident. If not very confident, keep the word in the English form

[14]https://site.matecat.com/

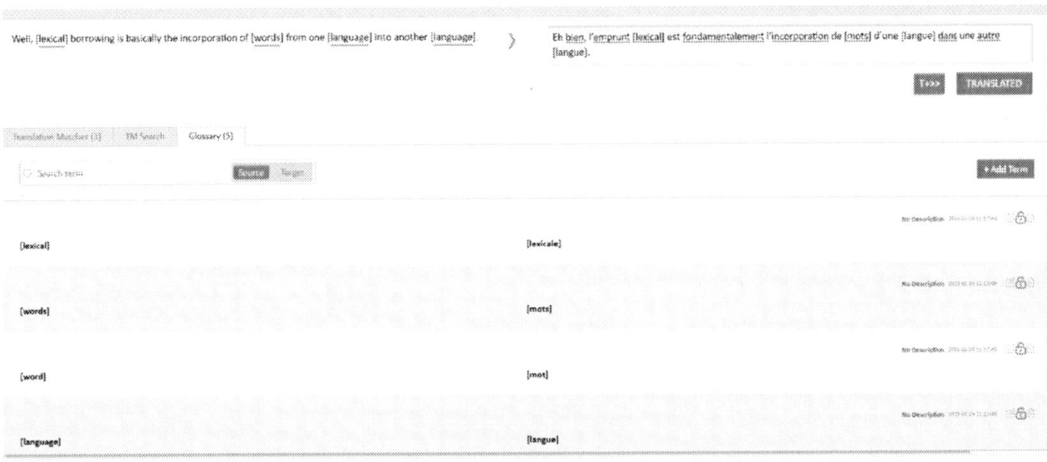

Figure 11: Matecat interface for translation post-editing.

A.6 Segmentation Comparison

Set	Segmentation	*ar*	*de*	*fa*	*fr*	*ja*	*nl*	*pt*	*ru*	*tr*	*zh*	Avg.
dev	Sentences	66.9	68.7	53.4	73.9	47.8	74.3	74.0	55.0	62.4	50.4	62.7
	Commercial VAD	66.6	68.5	52.7	74.1	46.2	73.6	73.7	53.9	60.6	49.8	62.0
	SHAS	66.5	68.6	52.8	73.7	46.9	73.8	73.5	54.3	59.9	49.7	62.0
eval	Sentences	64.0	66.1	51.3	69.0	43.9	71.0	71.9	55.8	63.8	46.0	60.3
	Commercial VAD	63.5	66.3	51.1	69.0	43.7	70.4	72.0	55.1	62.9	47.1	60.1
	SHAS	64.4	66.4	51.5	69.6	42.0	71.4	72.4	55.7	63.1	45.4	60.2

Table 6: Cascaded ST by language for different source speech segmentations, resegmented and scored with chrF.

A.7 Subtitle Guidelines

Subtitle guidelines following industry standards, see for example Netflix[15] and TED[16]:

- No one segment is allowed to be longer than 30 seconds.
- Each line can not be longer than 42 characters.
- A maximum of 2 lines of text can be shown on screen at once.
- The subtitle reading speed should kept to a maximum of $\sim$20 characters per second.[17]

If one of the segments created by the VAD does not adhere to the above guidelines, an English model is used to force alignment the long audio segment and its transcript to get the timestamp of each token, and then the segment is split into shorter subsegments. Note that these guidelines are automatically applied; the above means that if a VAD segment conforms to these guidelines it will not be resegmented, and subtitle segments may differ from manually created subtitles were semantic coherence may be prioritized over longer segments within these guidelines, or text may be lightly changed from what is spoken to optimize subtitle quality (here not allowed).

[15]https://partnerhelp.netflixstudios.com/hc/en-us/articles/217350977-English-Timed-Text-Style-Guide
[16]https://www.ted.com/participate/translate/subtitling-tips
[17]Varies by program audience, commonly between 17 and 21.

A.8 Segmentation Examples

Examples of each transcript segmentation approach discussed (VAD, subtitles, and sentences) for sample data from the development set. Examples were chosen to show segments from the longest and shortest VAD quartiles, and the resulting subtitles following subtitle guidelines from § A.7.

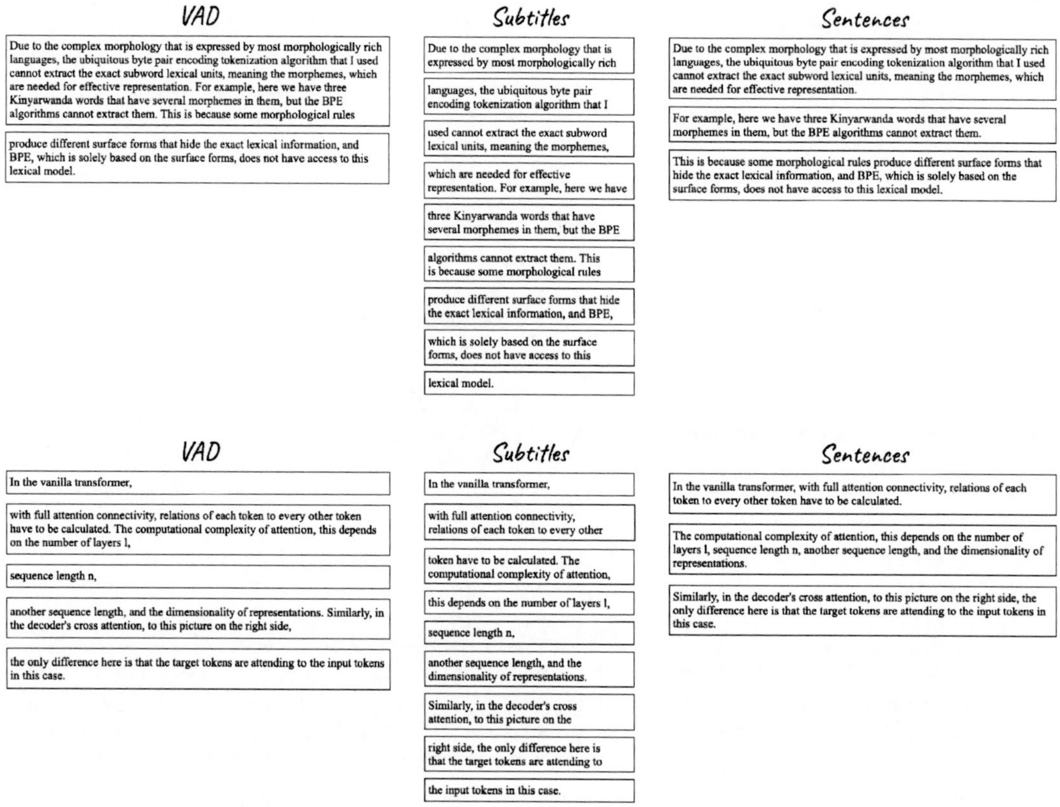

Figure 12: Examples of each discussed transcript segmentation approach for sample data from the development set.

The MINETRANS Systems for IWSLT 2023 Offline Speech Translation and Speech-to-Speech Translation Tasks

Yichao Du[♭‡], Zhengsheng Guo[♮], Jinchuan Tian[♮], Zhirui Zhang[♮], Xing Wang[♮], Jianwei Yu[♮], Zhaopeng Tu[♮], Tong Xu[♭‡] and Enhong Chen[♭‡]

[♭]University of Science and Technology of China [♮]Tencent AI Lab

[‡]State Key Laboratory of Cognitive Intelligence

[♭]duyichao@mail.ustc.edu.cn [♭]{tongxu, cheneh}@ustc.edu.cn [♮]zrustc11@gmail.com

[♮]{zhengshguo, tyriontian, tomasyu, brightxwang, zptu}@tencent.com

Abstract

This paper presents the MINETRANS English-to-Chinese speech translation systems developed for two challenge tracks of IWSLT 2023: Offline Speech Translation (S2T) and Speech-to-Speech Translation (S2ST). For the offline S2T track, MINETRANS employs a practical cascaded system consisting of automatic speech recognition (ASR) and machine translation (MT) modules to explore translation performance limits in both constrained and unconstrained settings. To this end, we investigate the effectiveness of multiple ASR architectures and two MT strategies, i.e., supervised in-domain fine-tuning and prompt-driven translation using ChatGPT. For the S2ST track, we propose a novel speech-to-unit translation (S2UT) framework to build an end-to-end system, which encodes the target speech as discrete units via our trained HuBERT and leverages the standard sequence-to-sequence model to learn the mapping between source speech and discrete units directly. We demonstrate that with a large-scale dataset, such as 10,000 hours of training data, this approach can well handle the mapping without any auxiliary recognition tasks (i.e., ASR and MT tasks). To the best of our knowledge, we are the first and only one to successfully train and submit the end-to-end S2ST model on this challenging track.

1 Introduction

In this paper, we describe the MINETRANS English-to-Chinese speech translation systems which participate in two challenge tracks of the IWSLT 2023 (Agarwal et al., 2023) evaluation campaign: Offline Speech Translation (S2T) and Speech-to-Speech Translation (S2ST).

The annual IWSLT evaluation campaign compares the models produced by different institutions on the task of automatically translating speech from one language to another. Traditional S2T/S2ST systems typically use a *cascade* approach (Ney, 1999; Sperber et al., 2017; Zhang et al., 2019; Wang et al., 2021b; Hrinchuk et al., 2022), which combines automatic speech recognition (ASR), machine translation (MT), and text-to-speech (TTS, for S2ST) components. Recent advances in *end-to-end* models (Liu et al., 2019; Jia et al., 2019; Lee et al., 2022; Du et al., 2021, 2022; Zhang et al., 2022b,a) that directly translate one language speech to another without intermediate symbolic representations, have shown great potential in overcoming the problems inherent in cascaded systems, such as error propagation and slow inference. Despite this, there is still a gap between the two approaches, as *end-to-end* models have much less supervised training data than sub-tasks, i.e., ASR, MT, and TTS. Last year's IWSLT offline S2T track (Anastasopoulos et al., 2022) confirmed this, with the best *end-to-end* model submission scoring 1.7 BLEU points lower than the top-ranked cascade system. This year's competition aims to answer the question of *whether cascade solutions remain dominant*, particularly in the S2ST track, where there has large-scale data for training.

In the offline S2T track, MINETRANS employs a practical cascaded system to explore the limits of translation performance in both constrained and unconstrained settings, in which the entire system consists of automatic speech recognition (ASR), and machine translation (MT) modules. We also investigate the effectiveness of multiple ASR architectures and explore two MT strategies: supervised in-domain fine-tuning (Wang et al., 2022) and prompt-driven translation using ChatGPT[1] (Jiao et al., 2023; He et al., 2023).

In the S2ST track, MINETRANS utilizes a speech-to-unit translation (S2UT) framework to construct an *end-to-end* system, which is similar to Lee et al. (2021a) but removes all auxiliary recognition tasks (i.e., ASR and MT tasks). This framework converts target speech into discrete units via our pre-trained HuBERT and then

[1] https://chat.openai.com

Proceedings of the 20th International Conference on Spoken Language Translation (IWSLT 2023), pages 79–88
July 13-14, 2023

leverages the standard sequence-to-sequence model to learn the mapping between source speech and discrete units directly. We found that with a large-scale dataset, such as 10,000 hours of training data, the previous multi-task learning technique (Jia; Lee et al., 2021a,b; Popuri et al., 2022; Dong et al., 2022) is not necessary for model convergence, and this approach can successfully handle the mapping between source speech and discrete units. We also explore various initialization strategies and several techniques to improve model performance, including (1) different self-supervised pre-trained speech encoders and pre-trained text-to-unit models, (2) data filtering and augmentation, consistency training, and model ensembles. To the best of our knowledge, we are the first and only one to successfully train and submit the end-to-end S2ST model on this challenging track. Our code is open-sourced at: `https://github.com/duyichao/MINETrans-IWSLT23`.

The remainder of this paper is organized as follows: Section 2 describes data preparation, including data statistics, data preprocessing, and data filtering. Section 3 describes our solution for the offline speech translation track. Section 4 describes our solution to the speech-to-speech track. In Section 5, we conclude this paper.

2 Data Preparation

2.1 Data Statistics

Table 1 lists statistics of the speech corpus we used for MINETRANS training, which can be divided into four categories: unlabeled speech, ASR, TTS and S2ST Corpus.

Unlabeled Speech. As shown in Table 1, we integrate source side speech from VoxPopuli (Wang et al., 2021a) and GigaSS[2] to build a large-scale unlabeled English speech corpus for self-supervised training of speech encoders Wav2vec2.0 (Baevski et al., 2020) and HuBert (Hsu et al., 2021), which are used for initializing the S2UT model in the S2ST track. Similarly, we also integrate target speech from GigaSS and AISHELL-3 (Shi et al., 2020) to train the Chinese HuBert, which is used for discretizing Chinese speech.

ASR Corpus. To train data-constrained English ASR models, we merge MuST-C (Gangi et al., 2019), Common Voice v11 (Ardila et al., 2019), Librispeech (Panayotov et al., 2015), and Europarl-ST (Iranzo-Sánchez et al., 2019), resulting in approximately 4500 hours of labeled ASR corpus, as shown in Table 1. For MuST-C and Europarl-ST, we collect source speech for all translation directions and de-duplicated them based on audio identifiers. In addition, GigaSpeech (Chen et al., 2021) is used to construct data-unconstrained ASR model, which includes 10k hours data covering various sources (audiobooks, podcasts, and stream media), speaking styles (reading and spontaneous), and topics (arts, science, sports, etc.). Of these corpus, we use MuST-C as the in-domain for the Offline track and the rest as the out-of-domain.

MT Corpus. To train data-constrained English-to-Chinese MT models, MuST-C v1&v2 are considered in-domain corpora, while OpenSubtitles2018 (Lison et al., 2018) and NewsCommentary[3] corpora are considered out-of-domain. Additionally, we utilize in-house corpora to train data-unconstrained MT models, although we cannot provide further details about it.

TTS Corpus. To ensure target speech timbre matching with the S2ST track, we consider the single-speaker GigaSS-S, a small subset of GigaSS, as in-domain and the multi-speaker AISHELL-3 (Shi et al., 2020) as out-of-domain. These corpora are used to train the TTS model and its corresponding vocoder.

S2ST Corpus. The full version of GigaSS is used to train our end-to-end S2UT model, which is an large-scale S2ST corpora derived from GigaSpeech (Chen et al., 2021) via MT and TTS. We also construct S2ST pseudo-data, the details of which will be presented in Section 4.1.2.

2.2 Data Pre-processing and Filtering

In general, a simple way to improve model performance is to provide them with better data. However, through a careful review of the data, we identified issues with the quality of the original data. To address this, we performed the following pre-processing and filtering:

- We convert all audio data to mono-channel 16kHz wav format. Since the sentences of spoken translation are generally short, we discarded sentences with text longer than 100 and speech frames longer than 3000. Then 80-dimensional

[2] `https://github.com/SpeechTranslation/GigaS2S`

[3] `https://opus.nlpl.eu/News-Commentary.php`

	Corpus	Utterances (k)	Duration (h)	S2T CST.	S2ST CST.
Unlabeled	VoxPopuli	22,905	28,708	✓	✓
ASR	MuST-C ASR v1&v2	342	617	✓	–
	Common Voice v11.0	1680	3,098	✓	–
	Librispeech	281	960	✓	–
	Europarl-ST	34	81	✓	–
	GigaSpeech	8,030	10,000	×	–
MT	NewsCommentary	32	–	✓	–
	OpenSubtitles	9,969	–	✓	–
	MuST-C v1&v2	543	–	✓	–
	In-house	–	–	×	–
TTS	AISHELL 3	88	85	–	✓
	GigaSS-S	210	244	–	✓
S2ST	GigaSS	7,635	9,000	–	✓
	CoVoST synthetic	288	288	–	✓
	MuST-C synthetic	358	587	–	✓

Table 1: Statistics of the training data. The "CST." indicates that a corpus is in the task constrained corpus list of corresponding S2T or S2ST. The "-" indicates this corpus is not available in that column.

log-mel filter banks acoustic features are extracted with a stepsize of 10ms and a window size of 25ms. The acoustic features are normalized by global channel mean and variance.

- We use a pre-trained ASR model on Librispeech to filter the audio with very poor quality, i.e., word error rate (WER) more than 75.
- Since the annotation format is not uniform across multiple datasets, we remove non-printing characters, speaker names, laughter, applause and other events. In addition, we also regularize punctuation marks.
- For the English-to-Chinese direction of MuST-C, we first merge the v1 and v2 versions and then remove duplicates based on audio identifiers.

3 Offline Speech Translation

3.1 Cascaded MINETRANS S2T System

3.1.1 Speech Recognition

A standard RNN-Transducer (Graves, 2012) model is used for speech recognition. It consists of an acoustic encoder, a prediction network and a joint network. The acoustic encoder contains 18 Conformer (Gulati et al., 2020) layers with the following dimensions: attention size is 512, feed-forward size is 2048, number of attention heads is 4, and convolutional kernels is 31. The prediction network is a standard 1-layer LSTM with a hidden size of 1024. The joint network is linear with a size of 512. The input acoustic features are 80-dim Fbank plus 3-dim pitch, which are down-sampled by a 2-layer CNN with a factor of 6 in the time-axis before being fed into the acoustic encoder. The overall parameter budget is 126M. During training, SpecAugment (Park et al., 2019) is consistently adopted for data augmentation. The training on both GigaSpeech and MuST-C datasets lasts for 50 epochs each, which consumes 32 Nvidia V100 GPUs. The Adam optimizer is adopted, with peak learning rate of 5e-3, warmup steps of 25k and inverse square root decay schedule(Vaswani et al., 2017a). Model weights from the last 10 epochs are averaged before decoding. The default decoding method described in Graves (2012) is adopted with a beam size of 10. External language models in any form are not adopted.

ASR Output Adaptation. In the realm of automatic speech recognition (ASR) and machine translation (MT), it is common for ASR output to lack punctuation, whereas MT models are sensitive to punctuation. To address this issue, we propose an ASR output adaptation method by incorporating a punctuation model between ASR and MT. Specifically, we adopt a BERT-based punctuation model that can automatically recover the original punctuation. The objective of this approach is to bridge the disparity between ASR and MT, leading to improved overall performance in speech translation tasks.

Speech Segmentation. Speech translation is a multi-faceted task that requires overcoming the challenges of bridging the gap between automatic speech recognition (ASR) and machine translation (MT) systems. To address these challenges, we employ several text augmentation techniques to improve the quality and accuracy of our training data. Specifically, we have utilized speech-based audio segmentation (SHAS (Tsiamas et al., 2022)) to identify and segment meaningful units of speech that can be accurately translated by the MT system.

3.1.2 Machine Translation

In our systems, we adopt four different types of translation strategies:

- **TRANSFORMER** is a system trained on the constrained data. We train the Transformer-base (Vaswani et al., 2017b) model on the constrained general data and finetune the model on the in-domain MuST-C data.
- **M2M-100**[4] (Fan et al., 2021) is a multilingual model trained for many-to-many multilingual translation. We employ the supervised in-domain fine-tuning strategy to finetune the M2M-100 1.2B-parameter model on the downstream MuST-C data.
- **CHATGPT** is a large language model product developed by OpenAI. Previous studies (Jiao et al., 2023; Wang et al., 2023) have demonstrated that ChatGPT is a good translator on high-resource languages. Therefore we utilize the proper translation prompts with ChatGPT to carry out the translation task.
- **IN-HOUSE MODEL** We fine-tune our in-house translation model (Huang et al., 2021) using the MuST-C data. Our in-house model is a Transformer-big (Vaswani et al., 2017b) model with a deep encoder (Dou et al., 2018).

Data Re-Annotation. We have identified two issues with the annotation of the English-to-Chinese translation direction in the MuST-C v2.0 test set[5]. Firstly, we have observed samples of incorrect literal translations. For example, for the parallel sentence pair, "I remember my first fire. ||| 记得我第一场火", we usually translate the English word "fire" into Chinese word "火灾 (huo zhai)" not "火 (huo)". Secondly, we have noticed inconsistencies in the punctuation annotation, as most Chinese translations lack proper full stop marks. To address these challenges, we have employed the services of a professional translator to accurately translate the English sentences. We will release the data, aiming to facilitate future research in the field.

Domain Augmentation. The MuST-C v2.0 training data contains considerable bilingual sentence pairs that are partially aligned. In the specific pair "Thank you so much Chris. ||| 非常谢谢，克里斯。的确非常荣幸", we are unable to locate the corresponding translation for the Chinese phrase "的确非常荣幸" in the English sentence. As Koehn and Knowles (2017); Wang et al. (2018) pointed out, data noise (partially aligned data) has been demonstrated to impact the performance of Neural Machine Translation (NMT). To address this issue, we employ a data rejuvenation strategy (Jiao et al., 2020). Specifically, we first finetune the model using the raw parallel data and then rejuvenate the low-quality bilingual samples to enhance the training data.

3.2 Experiment

The Cascaded MINETRANS S2T System we propose comprises an Automatic Speech Recognition (ASR) model and a machine translation (MT) model. In our evaluation, we assess the performance of each component separately. For the ASR system evaluation, we employ the Word Error Rate (WER) metric, while the BLEU score is utilized to evaluate the performance of our machine translation model.

The evaluation results obtained on the MuST-C dataset, with and without fine-tuning, are presented in Table 2. When the GigaSpeech ASR system is used without fine-tuning, we observe a WER of 10.0 on the MuST-C test set. However, when the system is fine-tuned using the MuST-C dataset, a significant improvement in performance is observed, resulting in a noticeable decrease in the error rate from WER of 10.0 to 5.8. This highlights the effectiveness of fine-tuning on the MuST-C dataset in enhancing the overall performance of our system.

[4] https://github.com/facebookresearch/fairseq/tree/main/exa\mples/m2m_100

[5] https://ict.fbk.eu/MuST-C/

System	Dev	Test
Gigaspeech	9.3	10.0
+ MuST-C Finetune	4.8	5.8

Table 2: ASR performance measured in terms of word error rates.

We evaluate various translation strategies using the MuST-C test set. The experimental results are presented in Table 2. In the constrained scenario, TRANSFORMER achieved a test BLEU score of 25.04, whereas M2M-100 attained a marginally higher score of 25.40. In the unconstrained setting, CHATGPT demonstrated superior performance with a BLEU score of 28.25, while IN-HOUSE MODEL obtained the highest BLEU score of 30.91. These results emphasize the significance of utilizing in-domain data for achieving optimal performance in spoken language translation.

System	Dev	tst-COMMON
TRANSFORMER	13.93	25.04
M2M-100	16.53	25.40
CHATGPT	—	28.25
IN-HOUSE MODEL	21.52	30.91

Table 3: Offline speech translation performance measured in terms of the BLEU score.

4 Speech-to-Speech Translation

4.1 End-to-End MINETRANS S2ST System

As shown in Figure 1, we construct an end-to-end S2UT (Lee et al., 2021a) model comprising a speech encoder, length adapter, and unit decoder. Following (Lee et al., 2021a), we encode target speech as discrete units via our trained Chinese HuBert and remove consecutive repetitive units to generate a reduced unit sequence. Unlike (Lee et al., 2021a), our S2UT model directly learns the mapping between source speech and discrete units without any auxiliary recognition tasks (i.e., ASR and MT tasks), which hyper-parameters are difficult to tune. Then we leverage a unit-based HiFi-GAN Vocoder to achieve unit-to-waveform conversion (Polyak et al., 2021). Next, we detail the efforts making in pre-training for model initialization, data augmentation, consistency training and model ensemble, which are used to improve the translation quality of our system.

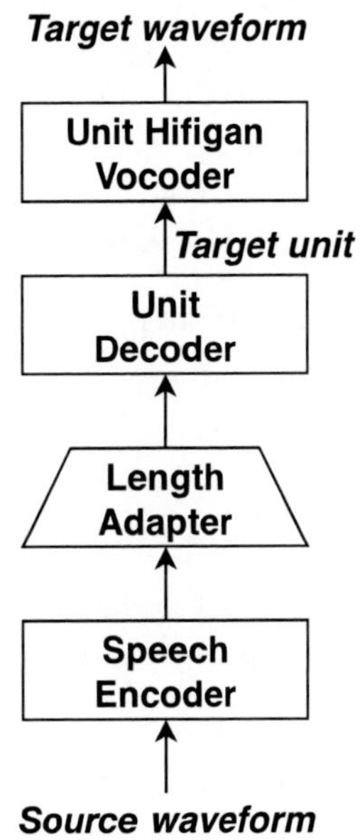

Figure 1: The overall architecture of the end-to-end S2ST system.

4.1.1 Pretrained Models

Previous experiences (Dong et al., 2022; Popuri et al., 2022) shown that better initialization can reduce learning difficulty, we explore pre-training of both the speech encoder and unit decoder.

Speech Encoder Pre-training. We use Wav2vec 2.0 (Baevski et al., 2020) and HuBert (Hsu et al., 2021), which are trained in a self-supervised manner, as speech encoders. Due to the data limitation of the S2ST track, we use the unlabeled speech described in Table 1 for training speech encoder:

- **Wav2vec 2.0** uses a multi layer convolution neural network to encode audio and then uses a transformer-based context encoder to construct a contextual representation. The model is trained by having a masked span of contrast loss on the input of the context encoder. In this paper, we modify Transformer as Conformer to obtain better performance.
- **HuBert** has the same model architecture as Wav2vec 2.0. However, its training process differs primarily in the use of cross-entropy and additionally in the construction of targets through a separate clustering process.

Unit Decoder Pre-training. We use the standard sequence-to-sequence model to model the Text-to-unit (T2U) task on GigaSS, and the decoder of this model will be used for the initialization of the unit decoder of S2UT. The T2U model contains 12 transformer layers for the encoder and coder, respectively. More specifically, we set the size of the self-attention layer, the feed-forward network, and the head to 1024, 4096, and 8, respectively.

4.1.2 Model Finetuning

We combine the pre-trained speech encoder and unit decoder, and adding a randomly initialized length adapter between the pre-trained modules. The length adapter consists of a one-dimensional convolutional layer with a stride of 2, which mitigates the length difference between the source audio and the reduced target unit, as well as the mismatch between representations.

Consistency Training. To further improve the consistency of our model, we employ the R-Drop algorithm (Liang et al., 2021) with a weight α set to 5. The R-Drop algorithm reduces inconsistencies predicted by the model between training and inference through dropout, thereby improving generalization. Specifically, it randomly drops out parts of the model during training, forcing it to learn more robust representations that are less sensitive to small changes in the input. For a more detailed description of the R-Drop algorithm and its implementation, please refer to the paper by (Liang et al., 2021).

4.1.3 Unit-based Vocoder

We utilize the unit-based HiFi-GAN (Polyak et al., 2021) vocoder to convert discrete units into waveform for the speech-to-unit model. Following the (Lee et al., 2021a) setup, we augment the vocoder with a duration prediction module for the reduced unit output, which consists of two 1D convolutional layers, each with ReLU activation, followed by layer normalization and a linear layer.

4.1.4 Ensemble

Model ensemble can reduce the inconsistency of the system to some extent, and we consider the ensemble of four variants of S2UT models:

- **W2V2-CONF-LARGE**: The speech encoder is initialized using Conformer-based Wav2vec 2.0 LARGE model. The unit decoder is initialized randomly.
- **W2V2-CONF-LARGE+T2U**: The speech encoder is initialized using Conformer-based Wav2vec 2.0 LARGE model. The unit decoder is initialized from the T2U model.
- **W2V2-TRANS-LARGE+T2U**: The speech encoder is initialized using Transformer-based Wav2vec 2.0 LARGE model. The unit decoder is initialized from the T2U model.
- **HUBERT-TRANS-LARGE+T2U**: The speech encoder is initialized using Transformer-based HuBert LARGE model. The unit decoder is initialized from the T2U model.

4.1.5 Data Augmentation

We utilize well trained Fastspeech2 (Ren et al., 2020) TTS models (see Section 4.2 for details) to generate speech for MuST-C and CoVoST Chinese texts to construct pseudo-corpora. These pseudo-corpora are used as training data together with the original labeled S2ST corpus.

4.2 Experiments

4.2.1 Implementation Details

All end-to-end S2UT models are implemented based on the FAIRSEQ[6] (Ott et al., 2019) toolkit. We use pre-trained Chinese HuBERT model and k-means model to encode Chinese target speech into a vocabulary of 250 units. The Chinese HuBERT and k-means models are learned from the TTS data in Table 1. The architectural details of the S2UT models are detailed in section 4.1.4. During training, we use the adam optimizer with a learning rate set to 5e-5 to update model parameters with 8K warm-up updates. The label smoothing and dropout ratios are set to 0.15 and 0.2, respectively. In practice, we train S2UT with 8 Nvidia Tesla A100 GPUs with 150K update steps. The batch size in each GPU is set to 1200K, and we accumulate the gradient for every 9 batches. For the first 5K steps of S2UT model training, we freeze the update of the speech encoder. The Unit HiFi-GAN Vocoder is trained using SPEECH-RESYNTHESISRES[7] toolkit for 500k steps. For FastSpeech2 and HiFi-GAN, we followed the paddlespeech AISHELL recipe[8] for training. During inference, we average the model parameters on the 30 best checkpoints based on the performance of the GigaSS dev set, and adopt beam search strategy with beam size of 10.

[6]https://github.com/facebookresearch/fairseq

[7]https://github.com/facebookresearch/speech-resynthesis

[8]https://github.com/PaddlePaddle/PaddleSpeech/tree/develop/examples/aishell3/tts3

ID	Model	BLEU	chrF
1	W2V2-CONF-LARGE	27.7	23.4
2	W2V2-CONF-LARGE+T2U	**27.8**	**23.7**
3	W2V2-TRANS-LARGE+T2U	25.2	22.3
4	HUBERT-TRANS-LARGE+T2U	26.2	23.2
5	HUBERT-TRANS-LARGE+T2U*	25.7	22.6
6	Ensemble(1, 2, 4)	**28.0**	**23.9**
7	Ensemble(2, 4, 5)	27.2	23.0

Table 4: ASR-BLEU and ASR-chrF on GigaSS validation set. '*' indicates adding the GigaST test set to the training data and fine-tuning it for one round.

4.2.2 Results

To evaluate the speech-to-speech translation system, we use a Chinese ASR system[9] trained on WenetSpeech (Zhang et al., 2021) to transcribe the speech output with the `ctc_greedy_serach` mode. Based on this, we report case-sensitive BLEU and chrF scores between the produced transcript and a textual human reference using sacreBLEU. The results on the GigaSS validation set is shown in Table 4. Comparing W2V2-CONF-LARGE+T2U and W2V2-TRANS-LARGE+T2U, using Conformer-based architecture pre-trained speech encoder for initialization has better performance. In addition, we find that adding the GigaST test set to training leads to a weak performance degradation on the validation set, possibly because the annotations of the test set are calibrated by humans and their style differs from that of the training data.

5 Conclusion

This paper presents the MINETRANS system for two challenge tracks of the IWSLT 2023: Offline Speech Translation (S2T) and Speech-to-Speech Translation (S2ST). For the S2T track, MINETRANS employs a cascaded system to investigate the limits of translation performance in both constrained and unconstrained settings. We explore two machine translation strategies: supervised in-domain fine-tuning and prompt-guided translation using a large language model. For the S2ST track, MINETRANS builds an end-to-end model based on the speech-to-unit (S2U) framework. To the best of our knowledge, we are the first and only team to successfully train and submit the end-to-end S2ST on this track. This model uses our trained HuBERT to encode the target speech as discrete units and leverages the standard sequence-to-sequence model to directly learn the mapping between source speech and discrete units without the need for auxiliary recognition tasks such as ASR and MT. We use several techniques to improve MINETRANS's performance, including speech encoder pre-training on large-scale data, data filtering, data augmentation, speech segmentation, consistency training, and model ensemble.

[9] `https://github.com/wenet-e2e/wenet/blob/main/docs/pretrained_models.en.md`

Acknowledgements

This work is supported by the grants from National Natural Science Foundation of China (No.62222213, U20A20229, 62072423), and the USTC Research Funds of the Double First-Class Initiative (No.YD2150002009). The authors would like to thank anonymous reviewers for their valuable comments. Zhirui Zhang and Tong Xu are the corresponding authors.

References

Milind Agarwal, Sweta Agrawal, Antonios Anastasopoulos, Ondřej Bojar, Claudia Borg, Marine Carpuat, Roldano Cattoni, Mauro Cettolo, Mingda Chen, William Chen, Khalid Choukri, Alexandra Chronopoulou, Anna Currey, Thierry Declerck, Qianqian Dong, Yannick Estève, Kevin Duh, Marcello Federico, Souhir Gahbiche, Barry Haddow, Benjamin Hsu, Phu Mon Htut, Hirofumi Inaguma, Dávid Javorský, John Judge, Yasumasa Kano, Tom Ko, Rishu Kumar, Pengwei Li, Xutail Ma, Prashant Mathur, Evgeny Matusov, Paul McNamee, John P. McCrae, Kenton Murray, Maria Nadejde, Satoshi Nakamura, Matteo Negri, Ha Nguyen, Jan Niehues, Xing Niu, Atul Ojha Kr., John E. Ortega, Proyag Pal, Juan Pino, Lonneke van der Plas, Peter Polák, Elijah Rippeth, Elizabeth Salesky, Jiatong Shi, Matthias Sperber, Sebastian Stüker, Katsuhito Sudoh, Yun Tang, Brian Thompson, Kevin Tran, Marco Turchi, Alex Waibel, Mingxuan Wang, Shinji Watanabe, and Rodolfo Zevallos. 2023. Findings of the IWSLT 2023 Evaluation Campaign. In *Proceedings of the 20th International Conference on Spoken Language Translation (IWSLT 2023)*. Association for Computational Linguistics.

Antonios Anastasopoulos, Loïc Barrault, Luisa Bentivogli, Marcely Zanon Boito, Ondrej Bojar, Roldano Cattoni, Anna Currey, Georgiana Dinu, Kevin Duh, Maha Elbayad, Clara Emmanuel, Y. Estève, Marcello Federico, Christian Federmann, Souhir Gahbiche, Hongyu Gong, Roman Grundkiewicz, Barry Haddow, B. Hsu, Dávid Javorský, Věra Kloudová, Surafel Melaku Lakew, Xutai Ma, Prashant Mathur,

Paul McNamee, Kenton Murray, Maria Nadejde, Satoshi Nakamura, Matteo Negri, Jan Niehues, Xing Niu, John E. Ortega, Juan Miguel Pino, Elizabeth Salesky, Jiatong Shi, Matthias Sperber, Sebastian Stüker, Katsuhito Sudoh, Marco Turchi, Yogesh Virkar, Alexander H. Waibel, Changhan Wang, and Shinji Watanabe. 2022. Findings of the iwslt 2022 evaluation campaign. In *IWSLT*.

Rosana Ardila, Megan Branson, Kelly Davis, Michael Henretty, Michael Kohler, Josh Meyer, Reuben Morais, Lindsay Saunders, Francis M. Tyers, and Gregor Weber. 2019. Common voice: A massively-multilingual speech corpus. In *International Conference on Language Resources and Evaluation*.

Alexei Baevski, Henry Zhou, Abdel rahman Mohamed, and Michael Auli. 2020. wav2vec 2.0: A framework for self-supervised learning of speech representations. *Advances in Neural Information Processing Systems*.

Guoguo Chen, Shuzhou Chai, Guan-Bo Wang, Jiayu Du, Weiqiang Zhang, Chao Weng, Dan Su, Daniel Povey, Jan Trmal, Junbo Zhang, Mingjie Jin, Sanjeev Khudanpur, Shinji Watanabe, Shuaijiang Zhao, Wei Zou, Xiangang Li, Xuchen Yao, Yongqing Wang, Yujun Wang, Zhao You, and Zhiyong Yan. 2021. Gigaspeech: An evolving, multi-domain asr corpus with 10, 000 hours of transcribed audio. *ArXiv*, abs/2106.06909.

Qianqian Dong, Fengpeng Yue, Tom Ko, Mingxuan Wang, Qibing Bai, and Yu Zhang. 2022. Leveraging pseudo-labeled data to improve direct speech-to-speech translation. In *Interspeech*.

Zi-Yi Dou, Zhaopeng Tu, Xing Wang, Shuming Shi, and Tong Zhang. 2018. Exploiting deep representations for neural machine translation. In *Proceedings of the 2018 Conference on Empirical Methods in Natural Language Processing*, pages 4253–4262.

Yichao Du, Weizhi Wang, Zhirui Zhang, Boxing Chen, Tong Xu, Jun Xie, and Enhong Chen. 2022. Non-parametric domain adaptation for end-to-end speech translation. In *Conference on Empirical Methods in Natural Language Processing*.

Yichao Du, Zhirui Zhang, Weizhi Wang, Boxing Chen, Jun Xie, and Tong Xu. 2021. Regularizing end-to-end speech translation with triangular decomposition agreement. In *AAAI Conference on Artificial Intelligence*.

Angela Fan, Shruti Bhosale, Holger Schwenk, Zhiyi Ma, Ahmed El-Kishky, Siddharth Goyal, Mandeep Baines, Onur Celebi, Guillaume Wenzek, Vishrav Chaudhary, et al. 2021. Beyond english-centric multilingual machine translation. *The Journal of Machine Learning Research*, 22(1):4839–4886.

Mattia Antonino Di Gangi, R. Cattoni, L. Bentivogli, Matteo Negri, and M. Turchi. 2019. Must-c: a multilingual speech translation corpus. In *NAACL*.

Alex Graves. 2012. Sequence transduction with recurrent neural networks. *arXiv preprint arXiv:1211.3711*.

Anmol Gulati, James Qin, Chung-Cheng Chiu, Niki Parmar, Yu Zhang, Jiahui Yu, Wei Han, Shibo Wang, Zhengdong Zhang, Yonghui Wu, and Ruoming Pang. 2020. Conformer: Convolution-augmented Transformer for Speech Recognition. In *Proc. Interspeech 2020*, pages 5036–5040.

Zhiwei He, Tian Liang, Wenxiang Jiao, Zhuosheng Zhang, Yujiu Yang, Rui Wang, Zhaopeng Tu, Shuming Shi, and Xing Wang. 2023. Exploring human-like translation strategy with large language models. *arXiv preprint arXiv:2305.04118*.

Oleksii Hrinchuk, Vahid Noroozi, Ashwinkumar Ganesan, Sarah Campbell, Sandeep Subramanian, Somshubra Majumdar, and Oleksii Kuchaiev. 2022. Nvidia nemo offline speech translation systems for iwslt 2022. In *IWSLT*.

Wei-Ning Hsu, Benjamin Bolte, Yao-Hung Hubert Tsai, Kushal Lakhotia, Ruslan Salakhutdinov, and Abdelrahman Mohamed. 2021. Hubert: Self-supervised speech representation learning by masked prediction of hidden units. *IEEE/ACM Transactions on Audio, Speech, and Language Processing*, 29:3451–3460.

Guoping Huang, Lemao Liu, Xing Wang, Longyue Wang, Huayang Li, Zhaopeng Tu, Chengyan Huang, and Shuming Shi. 2021. Transmart: A practical interactive machine translation system. *arXiv preprint arXiv:2105.13072*.

Javier Iranzo-Sánchez, Joan Albert Silvestre-Cerdà, Javier Jorge, Nahuel Roselló, Adrià Giménez, Alberto Sanchís, Jorge Civera Saiz, and Alfons Juan-Císcar. 2019. Europarl-st: A multilingual corpus for speech translation of parliamentary debates. *ICASSP 2020 - 2020 IEEE International Conference on Acoustics, Speech and Signal Processing (ICASSP)*, pages 8229–8233.

Ye Jia, Ron J Weiss, Fadi Biadsy, Wolfgang Macherey, Melvin Johnson, Zhifeng Chen, and Yonghui Wu. 2019. Direct speech-to-speech translation with a sequence-to-sequence model. *arXiv preprint arXiv:1904.06037*.

Wenxiang Jiao, Wenxuan Wang, Jen-tse Huang, Xing Wang, and Zhaopeng Tu. 2023. Is chatgpt a good translator? a preliminary study. *arXiv preprint arXiv:2301.08745*.

Wenxiang Jiao, Xing Wang, Shilin He, Irwin King, Michael Lyu, and Zhaopeng Tu. 2020. Data rejuvenation: Exploiting inactive training examples for neural machine translation. In *Proceedings of the 2020 Conference on Empirical Methods in Natural Language Processing (EMNLP)*, pages 2255–2266.

Philipp Koehn and Rebecca Knowles. 2017. Six challenges for neural machine translation. In *First Workshop on Neural Machine Translation*, pages 28–39. Association for Computational Linguistics.

Ann Lee, Peng-Jen Chen, Changhan Wang, Jiatao Gu, Xutai Ma, Adam Polyak, Yossi Adi, Qing He, Yun Tang, Juan Miguel Pino, and Wei-Ning Hsu. 2021a. Direct speech-to-speech translation with discrete units. In *Annual Meeting of the Association for Computational Linguistics*.

Ann Lee, Peng-Jen Chen, Changhan Wang, Jiatao Gu, Sravya Popuri, Xutai Ma, Adam Polyak, Yossi Adi, Qing He, Yun Tang, Juan Pino, and Wei-Ning Hsu. 2022. Direct speech-to-speech translation with discrete units. In *Proceedings of the 60th Annual Meeting of the Association for Computational Linguistics (Volume 1: Long Papers)*, pages 3327–3339, Dublin, Ireland. Association for Computational Linguistics.

Ann Lee, Hongyu Gong, Paul-Ambroise Duquenne, Holger Schwenk, Peng-Jen Chen, Changhan Wang, Sravya Popuri, Juan Miguel Pino, Jiatao Gu, and Wei-Ning Hsu. 2021b. Textless speech-to-speech translation on real data. *ArXiv*, abs/2112.08352.

Xiaobo Liang, Lijun Wu, Juntao Li, Yue Wang, Qi Meng, Tao Qin, Wei Chen, M. Zhang, and Tie-Yan Liu. 2021. R-drop: Regularized dropout for neural networks. *ArXiv*, abs/2106.14448.

Pierre Lison, Jörg Tiedemann, and Milen Kouylekov. 2018. Opensubtitles2018: Statistical rescoring of sentence alignments in large, noisy parallel corpora. In *International Conference on Language Resources and Evaluation*.

Yuchen Liu, Hao Xiong, Zhongjun He, Jiajun Zhang, Hua Wu, Haifeng Wang, and Chengqing Zong. 2019. End-to-end speech translation with knowledge distillation. In *INTERSPEECH*.

H. Ney. 1999. Speech translation: coupling of recognition and translation. *1999 IEEE International Conference on Acoustics, Speech, and Signal Processing. Proceedings. ICASSP99 (Cat. No.99CH36258)*, 1:517–520 vol.1.

Myle Ott, Sergey Edunov, Alexei Baevski, Angela Fan, S. Gross, Nathan Ng, David Grangier, and Michael Auli. 2019. fairseq: A fast, extensible toolkit for sequence modeling. In *NAACL*.

Vassil Panayotov, Guoguo Chen, Daniel Povey, and S. Khudanpur. 2015. Librispeech: An asr corpus based on public domain audio books. *2015 IEEE International Conference on Acoustics, Speech and Signal Processing (ICASSP)*, pages 5206–5210.

Daniel S. Park, William Chan, Yu Zhang, Chung-Cheng Chiu, Barret Zoph, Ekin D. Cubuk, and Quoc V. Le. 2019. Specaugment: A simple data augmentation method for automatic speech recognition. *Interspeech 2019*.

Adam Polyak, Yossi Adi, Jade Copet, Eugene Kharitonov, Kushal Lakhotia, Wei-Ning Hsu, Abdelrahman Mohamed, and Emmanuel Dupoux. 2021. Speech resynthesis from discrete disentangled self-supervised representations. *ArXiv*, abs/2104.00355.

Sravya Popuri, Peng-Jen Chen, Changhan Wang, Juan Miguel Pino, Yossi Adi, Jiatao Gu, Wei-Ning Hsu, and Ann Lee. 2022. Enhanced direct speech-to-speech translation using self-supervised pre-training and data augmentation. In *Interspeech*.

Yi Ren, Chenxu Hu, Xu Tan, Tao Qin, Sheng Zhao, Zhou Zhao, and Tie-Yan Liu. 2020. Fastspeech 2: Fast and high-quality end-to-end text to speech. *ArXiv*, abs/2006.04558.

Yao Shi, Hui Bu, Xin Xu, Shaojing Zhang, and Ming Li. 2020. Aishell-3: A multi-speaker mandarin tts corpus and the baselines. In *Interspeech*.

Matthias Sperber, Graham Neubig, J. Niehues, and A. Waibel. 2017. Neural lattice-to-sequence models for uncertain inputs. In *EMNLP*.

Ioannis Tsiamas, Gerard I Gállego, José AR Fonollosa, and Marta R Costa-jussà. 2022. Shas: Approaching optimal segmentation for end-to-end speech translation. *arXiv preprint arXiv:2202.04774*.

Ashish Vaswani, Noam Shazeer, Niki Parmar, Jakob Uszkoreit, Llion Jones, Aidan N Gomez, Łukasz Kaiser, and Illia Polosukhin. 2017a. Attention is all you need. *Advances in neural information processing systems*, 30.

Ashish Vaswani, Noam Shazeer, Niki Parmar, Jakob Uszkoreit, Llion Jones, Aidan N Gomez, Łukasz Kaiser, and Illia Polosukhin. 2017b. Attention is all you need. *Advances in neural information processing systems*, 30.

Changhan Wang, Morgane Rivière, Ann Lee, Anne Wu, Chaitanya Talnikar, Daniel Haziza, Mary Williamson, Juan Miguel Pino, and Emmanuel Dupoux. 2021a. Voxpopuli: A large-scale multilingual speech corpus for representation learning, semi-supervised learning and interpretation. In *Annual Meeting of the Association for Computational Linguistics*.

Longyue Wang, Chenyang Lyu, Tianbo Ji, Zhirui Zhang, Dian Yu, Shuming Shi, and Zhaopeng Tu. 2023. Document-level machine translation with large language models. *arXiv preprint arXiv:2304.02210*.

Minghan Wang, Yuxia Wang, Chang Su, Jiaxin Guo, Yingtao Zhang, Yujiao Liu, M. Zhang, Shimin Tao, Xingshan Zeng, Liangyou Li, Hao Yang, and Ying Qin. 2021b. The hw-tsc's offline speech translation system for iwslt 2022 evaluation. In *IWSLT*.

Wei Wang, Taro Watanabe, Macduff Hughes, Tetsuji Nakagawa, and Ciprian Chelba. 2018. Denoising neural machine translation training with trusted data and online data selection. In *Proceedings of the Third Conference on Machine Translation: Research Papers*, pages 133–143.

Wenxuan Wang, Wenxiang Jiao, Yongchang Hao, Xing Wang, Shuming Shi, Zhaopeng Tu, and Michael Lyu. 2022. Understanding and improving sequence-to-sequence pretraining for neural machine translation.

In *Proceedings of the 60th Annual Meeting of the Association for Computational Linguistics (Volume 1: Long Papers)*, pages 2591–2600.

Binbin Zhang, Hang Lv, Pengcheng Guo, Qijie Shao, Chao Yang, Lei Xie, Xin Xu, Hui Bu, Xiaoyu Chen, Chenchen Zeng, Di Wu, and Zhendong Peng. 2021. Wenetspeech: A 10000+ hours multi-domain mandarin corpus for speech recognition. *ICASSP 2022 - 2022 IEEE International Conference on Acoustics, Speech and Signal Processing (ICASSP)*, pages 6182–6186.

Peidong Zhang, Boxing Chen, Niyu Ge, and Kai Fan. 2019. Lattice transformer for speech translation. In *ACL*.

Weitai Zhang, Zhongyi Ye, Haitao Tang, Xiaoxi Li, Xinyuan Zhou, Jing Yang, Jianwei Cui, Dan Liu, Junhua Liu, and Lirong Dai. 2022a. The ustc-nelslip offline speech translation systems for iwslt 2022. In *IWSLT*.

Ziqiang Zhang, Junyi Ao, Shujie Liu, Furu Wei, and Jinyu Li. 2022b. The yitrans end-to-end speech translation system for iwslt 2022 offline shared task. *ArXiv*, abs/2206.05777.

Improving End-to-End Speech Translation by Imitation-Based Knowledge Distillation with Synthetic Transcripts

Rebekka Hubert*
Computational Linguistics
Heidelberg University, Germany
hubert@cl.uni-heidelberg.de

Artem Sokolov
Google Research
Berlin, Germany
artemsok@google.com

Stefan Riezler
Computational Linguistics & IWR
Heidelberg University, Germany
riezler@cl.uni-heidelberg.de

Abstract

End-to-end automatic speech translation (AST) relies on data that combines audio inputs with text translation outputs. Previous work used existing large parallel corpora of transcriptions and translations in a knowledge distillation (KD) setup to distill a neural machine translation (NMT) into an AST student model. While KD allows using larger pretrained models, the reliance of previous KD approaches on manual audio transcripts in the data pipeline restricts the applicability of this framework to AST. We present an imitation learning approach where a teacher NMT system corrects the errors of an AST student without relying on manual transcripts. We show that the NMT teacher can recover from errors in automatic transcriptions and is able to correct erroneous translations of the AST student, leading to improvements of about 4 BLEU points over the standard AST end-to-end baseline on the English-German CoVoST-2 and MuST-C datasets, respectively. Code and data are publicly available.[1]

1 Introduction

The success of data-hungry end-to-end automatic speech translation (AST) depends on large amounts of data that consist of speech inputs and corresponding translations. One way to overcome the data scarcity issue is a knowledge distillation (KD) setup where a neural machine translation (NMT) expert (also called oracle) is distilled into an AST student model (Liu et al., 2019; Gaido et al., 2020). The focus of our work is the question of whether the requirement of high-quality source language transcripts, as in previous applications of KD to AST, can be relaxed in order to enable a wider applicability of this setup to AST scenarios where no manual source transcripts are available. Examples for such scenarios are low-resource settings (e.g., for languages without written form for which mostly only audio-translation data are available), or settings where one of the main uses of source transcripts in AST — pre-training the AST encoder from an automatic speech recognition (ASR) system— is replaced by a large-scale pre-trained ASR system (which itself is trained on hundreds of thousands hours of speech, but the original training transcripts are not available (Radford et al., 2022; Zhang et al., 2022b)). Relaxing the dependence of pre-training AST encoders on manual transcripts has recently been studied by Zhang et al. (2022a). Our focus is instead to investigate the influence of manual versus synthetic transcripts as input to the student model in an imitation learning (IL) approach (Lin et al., 2020; Hormann and Sokolov, 2021), and to lift this scenario to AST. To our knowledge, this has not been attempted before. We present a proof-of-concept experiment where we train an ASR model on a few hundred hours of speech, but discard the manual transcripts in IL training, and show that this ASR model is sufficient to enable large NMT models to function as error-correcting oracle in an IL setup where the AST student model works on synthetic transcripts. Focusing on the IL scenario, we show that one of the key ingredients to make our framework perform on synthetic ASR transcripts is to give the AST student access to the oracle's full probability distribution instead of only the expert's optimal actions. Furthermore, when comparing two IL algorithms of different power — either correcting the student output in a single step, or repairing outputs till the end of the sequence — we find that, at least in the setup of a reference-agnostic NMT teacher, the single-step correction of student errors is sufficient.

One of the general reasons for the success of our setup may be a reduction of data complexity and an increase of variations of outputs, similar to applications of KD in NMT (Zhou et al., 2020).

*All work was done at Heidelberg University.

[1]https://github.com/HubReb/imitkd_ast/releases/tag/v1.1

Proceedings of the 20th International Conference on Spoken Language Translation (IWSLT 2023), pages 89–101
July 13-14, 2023

To investigate the special case of imitation-based KD on synthetic speech inputs, we provide a manual analysis of the NMT expert's behavior when faced with incorrect synthetic transcripts as input, or when having to correct a weak student's translation in the IL setting. We find that the NMT oracle can correct errors even if the source language input lacks semantically correct information, by utilizing its language modeling capability to correct the next-step token. This points to new uses of large pre-trained ASR and NMT models (besides initialization of encoder and decoder, respectively) as tools to improve non-cascading end-to-end AST.

2 Related Work

Imitation learning addresses a deficiency of sequence-to-sequence learning approaches, nicknamed *exposure bias* (Bengio et al., 2015; Ranzato et al., 2016), that manifests as the inference-time inability to recover from own errors, leading to disfluent or hallucinated translations (Wang and Sennrich, 2020). IL aims to replace the standard learning paradigm of teacher forcing (Williams and Zipser, 1989) (which decomposes sequence learning into independent per-step predictions, each conditioned on the golden truth context rather than the context the model would have produced on its own) by enriching the training data with examples of successful recovery from errors. We build upon two previous adaptations of IL to NMT (Lin et al., 2020; Hormann and Sokolov, 2021) and lift them to AST.

Knowledge distillation (Hinton et al., 2015) transfers the knowledge encoded in a large model, called teacher, to a far smaller student model by using the teacher to create soft labels and train the student model to minimize the cross-entropy to the teacher. KD has been successfully used for machine translation (Kim and Rush, 2016), speech recognition (Wong and Gales, 2016) and speech translation (Liu et al., 2019).

Synthetic speech translation training datasets have been used previously to train AST models: Pino et al. (2020) used an ASR-NMT model cascade to translate unlabeled speech data for augmentation. To obtain more machine translation (MT) training data, Jia et al. (2019); Pino et al. (2019) generated synthetic speech data with a text-to-speech model. Liu et al. (2019) applied KD between an NMT expert and an AST student with manual transcriptions as expert input to improve AST performance. Gaido et al. (2020) improved upon this by increasing the available training data by utilizing a MT model to translate the audio transcripts of ASR datasets into another language, yet they still use manual transcripts for distillation in the following finetuning phase.

Further attempts focused on improving AST models by utilizing MT data for multitask learning with speech and text data (Tang et al., 2021b,a; Bahar et al., 2019; Weiss et al., 2017; Anastasopoulos and Chiang, 2018), such as XSTNet (Ye et al., 2021) and FAT-MLM (Zheng et al., 2021).

A question orthogonal to ours, concerning the influence of pre-training encoder and/or decoder on source transcripts, has been investigated by Zhang et al. (2022a). They achieved competitive results without any pretraining via the introduction of parameterized distance penalty and neural acoustic feature modeling in combination with CTC regularization with translations as labels. Their question and solutions are orthogonal to ours and are likely to be yield independent benefits.

3 Imitation-based Knowledge Distillation

We view an auto-regressive NMT or AST system as a policy π that defines a conditional distribution over a vocabulary of target tokens $v \in V$ that is conditioned on the input x and the so far generated prefix $y_{<t}$: $\pi(v|y_{<t}; x)$. This policy is instantiated as the output of the softmax layer. When training with teacher-forcing, the cross-entropy (CE) loss $\ell(\cdot)$ is minimized under the *empirical* distribution of training data D: $\mathcal{L}_{\text{CE}}(\pi) = \mathbb{E}_{(y,x)\sim D}[\sum_{t=1}^{T} \ell(y_t, \pi)]$. To perform well at test time we are interested in the expected loss under the *learned* model distribution: $\mathcal{L}(\pi) = \mathbb{E}_{(y,x)\sim\pi}[\sum_{t=1}^{T} \ell(y_t, \pi)]$.

As shown by Ross et al. (2011), the discrepancy between $\mathcal{L}$ and $\mathcal{L}_{\text{CE}}$ accumulates quadratically with the sequence length T, which in practice could manifest itself as translation errors. They proposed the Dagger algorithm which has linear worst-case error accumulation. It, however, relies on the existence of an oracle policy π^* that, conditioned on the same input x and the partially generated π's prefix $y_{<t}$, can produce a single next-step correction to $y_{<t}$. Ross and Bagnell (2014) further proposed the AggreVaTe algorithm which relies on an even more powerful oracle that can produce a full continuation in the task-loss optimal fashion: For NMT, this means continuing the $y_{<t}$ in a way that maximizes BLEU, as done for example in Hormann and

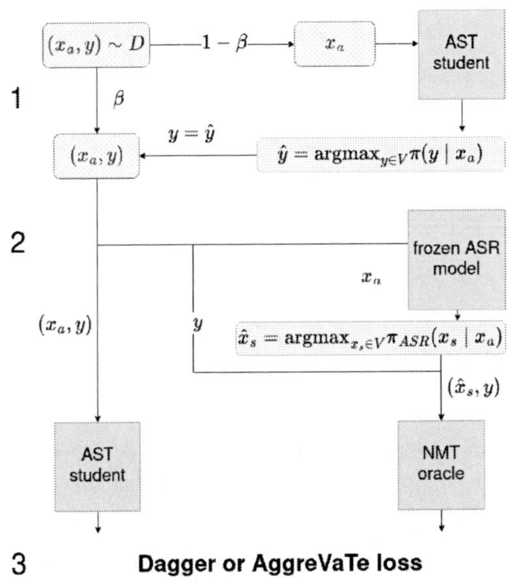

Figure 1: **Diagram of AST training with imitation learning and synthetic transcripts coming from ASR models**. (1) With probability $1-\beta$ the AST student creates a hypothesis $\hat{y}$ that replaces the reference translation y. (2) The ASR model generates the synthetic transcript $\hat{x}_s$ for the audio sample x_a to feed the NMT oracle as input. (3) Calculation of Dagger or AggreVaTe loss as shown in Algorithm 1.

Sokolov (2021).

IL for NMT We pretrain a large NMT model to serve as an oracle π^* that either simply predicts the next-step optimal output vocabulary token v_t^* given a source sentence x and any (potentially, erroneous) partial NMT student hypothesis $y_{<t}$ (Dagger):

$$v_t^* = \operatorname*{argmax}_{v \in V} \pi^*(v \mid y_{<t}; x), \quad (1)$$

or continues $y_{<t}$ till the end (AggreVaTe):

$$y_{>t}^* = \operatorname*{argmax}_{y_{>t}} \pi^*(y_{<t} + a_t + y_{\geq t} \mid y_{<t}; x), \quad (2)$$

where $y_{>t}$ is the continuation, a_t is an exploratory action, and the last argmax is implemented as beam search. The predicted v_t^* or $y_{>t}^*$ are viewed as one-step or multi-step corrections of the current policy, and the student is updated to increase the probability of the correction via the cross-entropy loss on triples (y_t, x, v_t^*) in case of Dagger, or to decrease a square loss between logit Q of the selected action a_t and the BLEU of the predicted suffix[2] from that action in case of AggreVaTe.

[2]We use the difference between the BLEU values of the full sequence and that of the prefix (Bahdanau et al., 2016).

Both algorithms proceed iteratively, where the newly generated set of triples form a provisional training data set D_i. Originally, Dagger and AggreVaTe train the student's π_i on the aggregated dataset $\cup_{j \leq i} D_j$ and use a probabilistic mixture for the current roll-out policy, which queries the oracle with probability β_i and the student otherwise. This setup guarantees that the prediction error scales at most linearly with time, unlike the quadratic scaling of the standard teacher forcing (Ross et al., 2011), which is standardly used in sequence-level KD. This makes Dagger and AggreVaTe promising candidates to improve over KD.

In our implementation, we follow Lin et al. (2020), who save memory via training on individual D_i in each iteration i, instead of training on the set union. They further speed up training by keeping the reference translation y with probability β_i, and otherwise generate a translation $\hat{y}$ of the source sentence x from the student policy (see Algorithm 1). For each t in the algorithm, AggreVaTe needs to generate an exploration token a_t and calculate the BLEU it would lead to, according to the oracle continuation starting off this action.

IL for AST Adapting Dagger and AggreVaTe to an AST student is relatively straightforward (see Figure 1): We feed the NMT oracle the source language transcript x_s of the audio data sample x_a that is also given to the AST student. We define an algorithm IKD (imitation knowledge distillation) that optimizes the cross-entropy of the student's policy w.r.t. the optimal expert prediction:

$$\mathcal{L}_{\text{IKD}}(\pi) = \mathbb{E}\left[-\sum_{t=1}^{T} \log \pi(v_t^* \mid y_{<t}; x_a)\right], \quad (3)$$

with v_t^* as in (1). Algorithm IKD$^+$ optimizes the cross-entropy w.r.t. the expert's policy:

$$\mathcal{L}_{\text{IKD}^+}(\pi) = \quad (4)$$
$$\mathbb{E}\left[-\sum_{v \in V} \pi^*(v \mid y_{<t}; x_s) \cdot \log \pi(v \mid y_{<t}; x_a)\right].$$

An important modification to these objectives that we propose in this work is to replace the gold source language transcripts x_s fed to the NMT oracle by synthetic transcripts generated by a pretrained ASR model. We call this algorithm SynthIKD, with a respective SynthIKD$^+$ variant.

Algorithm 1: Dagger/AggreVaTe for distillation in NMT; combined from (Lin et al., 2020) and (Hormann and Sokolov, 2021).

Data: Let D be original bi-text dataset, π^* the NMT oracle policy, I the total number of iterations, T the max sequence length, Q the final logits, and B the batch size.

Initialize π_1 arbitrarily.

for $i = 1 \ldots I$ **do**
- Initialize $D_i \leftarrow \emptyset$
- **for** $b = 1 \ldots B$ **do**
  - Sample an example $(x, y) \sim D$.
  - Sample uniformly $u \sim [0, 1]$
  - **if** $u > \beta_i$ **then**
    - Generate $\hat{y}$ from π_i given x.
    - Replace y with $\hat{y}$.
  - **if** *Dagger* **then**
    - **for** $t = 1 \ldots T$ **do**
      - Predict $v_t^* = \underset{v \in V}{\text{argmax}}\, \pi^*(v \mid y_{<t}; x)$
      - Append $(y_{<t}, x, v_t^*)$ to D_i
  - **else** `// AggreVaTe`
    - Sample uniformly $t \in \{1, .., T\}$.
    - Predict $a_t = \underset{v \in V}{\text{argmax}}\, \pi(v \mid y_{<t}; x)$
    - Predict $y_{>t}^* = \underset{y_{>t}}{\text{argmax}}\, \pi^*(y_{>t} \mid y_{<t} + a_t; x)$
    - Append $(y_{<t}, x, a_t, \text{BLEU}(y_{>t}^*))$ to D_i
- $\mathcal{L}_{\text{Dagger}} = \mathbb{E}_{D_i}\left[-\sum_{t=1}^{T} \log \pi_i(v_t^* \mid y_{<t}; x) \right]$
- $\mathcal{L}_{\text{AggreVaTe}} = \mathbb{E}_{D_i}\left[\sum_{t=1}^{T} \left(\sigma(Q(a_t \mid y_{<t}; x)) - \text{BLEU}(y_{>t}^*) \right)^2 \right]$
- Let $\pi_{i+1} = \pi_i - \alpha_i \cdot \frac{\partial \mathcal{L}}{\partial \pi_i}$.

Variant	Expert Input	Loss
Standard	-	CE
KD$^+$ (Liu et al., 2019)	gold	CE
SynthKD$^+$	synthetic	CE
IKD (Lin et al., 2020)	gold	$\mathcal{L}_{\text{IKD}}$
IKD$^+$ (Lin et al., 2020)	gold	$\mathcal{L}_{\text{IKD}^+}$
SynthIKD (ours)	synthetic	$\mathcal{L}_{\text{IKD}}$
SynthIKD$^+$ (ours)	synthetic	$\mathcal{L}_{\text{IKD}^+}$

Table 1: Summary of training variants: "Standard" denotes AST trained via cross-entropy (CE) on ground truth targets with a label smoothing. KD$^+$ denotes word-level knowledge distillation between the expert's and student's full output probability. IKD and IKD$^+$ denote imitation knowledge distillation where student model is corrected by the optimal expert action or the full expert policy (Lin et al., 2020), respectively. SynthIKD and SynthIKD$^+$ are our variants with synthetic transcripts. Expert Input indicates whether the NMT expert is given the original transcripts from the dataset or synthetic transcripts created by ASR. All IKD methods use the exponential decay schedule for β that (Lin et al., 2020) found to work best.

4 Experiments

We experiment with English-German AST on the CoVoST2 (Wang et al., 2021) (430 hours) and the MuST-C (Di Gangi et al., 2019) datasets (408 hours)[3]. As expert model, we use the Transformer from Facebook's submission to WMT19 (Ng et al., 2019), which is based on the Big Transformer architecture proposed by (Vaswani et al., 2017). Our sequence-to-sequence models for students are RNNs and Base Transformers. All models are based on the `fairseq` framework (Ott et al., 2019; Wang et al., 2020), but use different settings of meta-parameters and preprocessing than the default models. More details on models, meta-parameters and training settings are given in the Appendix A.

Our training setups are summarized in Table 1. We compare our trained student models with several baseline approaches: "Standard" denotes AST trained by teacher forcing on ground truth targets with a label smoothing (Szegedy et al., 2016) factor of 0.1. KD$^+$ (Liu et al., 2019) denotes word-level knowledge distillation between the expert's and student's full output probability. IKD and IKD$^+$ denote imitation knowledge distillation, where student model is corrected by the empirical distribution of the optimal expert actions or the full expert policy (Lin et al., 2020), respectively. SynthIKD and SynthIKD$^+$ are our variants with synthetic transcripts. We used the same same exponential decay schedule ($\beta = \frac{1}{T}$) used by (Lin et al., 2020) as early experiments showed that this performed best in our setup.

All AST models' encoders are initialized with the encoder of the corresponding ASR model, trained on the respective datasets with cross-entropy and the label-smoothing factor of 0.1. Because of the relatively small size of these datasets, our experiments should seen as proof-of-concept, showing that ASR models trained on a few hundred hours of audio provide synthetic transcripts of sufficient quality to enable imitation-based KD for AST. The standalone performance of our ASR models is listed in Table 2.

[3]We also experimented with a smaller Europarl-ST dataset and to save space we report results in Appendix B. Overall, they are similar to these on larger datasets.

Model	CoVoST2		MuST-C	
	dev	test	dev	test
RNN	26.68	33.94	23.42	24.44
Transformer	20.93	26.60	21.10	20.68

Table 2: WER↓ results for ASR models pretrained on CoVoST2 and MuST-C. These models are used to create the synthetic transcripts for respective experiments. Standard development and test splits were used for CoVoST2. For MuST-C, we tested on `tst-COMMON`.

4.1 Feasibility of Oracle Correction

The idea of using synthetic transcripts in place of gold transcripts has merit only if the NMT oracle's translations have higher quality than the translations the AST model generates. Therefore, we first verify if the NMT oracle is capable of completing an AST models' partial hypotheses $y_{<t}$ while improving quality at the same time.

We follow Lin et al. (2020) and let the AST models trained with label-smoothed CE on ground truth targets translate the audio input with greedy decoding up to a randomly chosen time step. Then, we feed the NMT expert the gold transcript as input and the partial translation as prefix, and let the oracle finish the translation with greedy decoding.

As Table 2 shows, the out-of-the-box ASR performance is relatively low (high WER), so errors in synthetic transcripts will be propagated through the NMT oracle. The question is whether the expert's continuation can be of higher quality than the student's own predictions despite the partially incorrect synthetic transcripts. In Table 3, lines 1 and 2 (or, 5 and 6) set the lower (end-to-end) and upper (cascade) bounds on the performance. We see that the NMT expert is able to complete the student hypotheses successfully (lines 3, 4 and 7, 8), bringing gains in both gold and synthetic setups, and reaching the upper bound (lines 3 vs. 2 and 7 vs. 6) for gold ones. Although the mistakes in the synthetic transcripts do result in lower BLEU scores (lines 4 and 8) they still improve over the AST student complete translations (lines 1 and 5).

4.2 Main Results

Table 4 shows the main results of applying Algorithm 1 for training an AST student with imitation-based knowledge distillation on CoVoST2 and MuST-C.

Dagger First we present results for the Dagger algorithm. In Table 4, for both CoVoST2 and MuST-C models, Dagger with the Transformer architecture outperforms all baselines[4], and matching full teacher distributions (the '+'-versions of losses) gives consistent gains. Distillation with RNNs, on the other hand, fails to improve BLEU scores over baselines, most likely due to their overall lower translation quality. This leads to the student hypotheses that are too far from the reference so that the expert's one-step corrections are not able to correct them.

The results show that Transformers and RNNs with synthetic transcripts show statistically insignificant differences in performance to the ones that are using gold transcripts. This is notable since the partially synthetic transcripts provided to the NMT oracle are often incorrect, yet do not result in a noticeable effect on the final student performance if used in the IL framework. A similar observation can be made when comparing the use of gold transcripts versus synthetic transcripts: Transformers on both datasets perform comparably and erroneous transcripts do not seem to harm the trained AST model.

AggreVaTe Finally, we evaluate the performance of AggreVaTe both with gold and synthetic transcripts. During training we targeted and evaluated with the non-decomposable BLEU metric (i.e. training with sentence-BLEU and evaluating with corpus-BLEU) as well as with the decomposable TER metric (Table 5). Following Hormann and Sokolov (2021) we warm-started AggreVaTe with differently trained standard or Dagger models, and trained with AggreVaTe objectives for up to 50 epochs with early stopping on respective development sets.

Surprisingly, we found that AggreVaTe does not bring additional benefits on top of Dagger despite the promise for a better matching between training and inference objectives. Also there is no significant difference between the results with the TER rewards objective and sentence-BLEU rewards on both CoVoST2 and MuST-C. We explain these results by the sufficiency of one-step corrections to correct a "derailed" student, with little benefit of continuing demonstration till the end of translation. The fact that Dagger turns out to reap all of the benefits from training with IL is good news in general, since running beam search during training (to get AggreVaTe's full continuations) is more expensive

[4] p-value < 0.005 using the paired approximate randomization test (Riezler and Maxwell, 2005)

Architecture	Hypotheses	#	Decoding Setup	Source Transcripts	dev-BLEU↑
RNN	full	1	AST	-	11.9
		2	ASR transcribes, NMT expert translates	-	21.8
	partial	3	AST starts, NMT expert completes	gold	21.9
		4	AST starts, NMT expert completes	synthetic	15.6
Transformer	full	5	AST	-	16.7
		6	ASR transcribes, NMT expert translates	-	25.4
	partial	7	AST starts, NMT expert completes	gold	25.4
		8	AST starts, NMT expert completes	synthetic	19.9

Table 3: Feasibility experiment: BLEU score on CoVoST2 development set of NMT expert's completion of AST model full or partial hypotheses with greedy decoding; *gold* denotes the usage of the dataset's source language transcripts as NMT inputs and *synthetic* denotes synthetic transcripts created by the respective ASR model.

Achitecture		Models	CoVoST2 dev	CoVoST2 test	MuST-C dev	MuST-C test
RNN	baseline	Standard	13.6	10.0	14.6	14.1
	baseline	KD$^+$	**14.6**	**11.1**	**17.9**	**17.2**
	baseline	IKD$^+$	13.1	10.1	15.7	14.9
	ours	SynthKD$^+$	14.1	10.6	16.9	15.9
	ours	SynthIKD$^+$	12.8	9.7	16.3	15.1
Transformer	baseline	Standard	18.4	14.2	19.5	19.4
	baseline	KD$^+$	21.3	17.7	17.7	22.2
	baseline	IKD$^+$	**21.8**	18.4	23.2	23.3
	ours	SynthKD$^+$	21.7	18.0	22.5	22.6
	ours	SynthIKD$^+$	**21.8**	**18.5**	**23.5**	**23.5**

Table 4: Main results: RNN and Transformer student models trained on expert inputs and loss variants of Table 1, using Dagger for IL. We used the `tst-COMMON` as the test set for MuST-C. (Synth)IKD is not included since its performance is worse than (Synth)KD$^+$. Transformers trained with IL outperform all baselines, while pure KD is the best for generally lower-quality RNN-based models. Synthetic transcripts do not harm performance for Transformer student models.

than greedily selecting one action (as does Dagger).

4.3 Quality of Synthetic Transcripts

In this section, we investigate explanations for the high performance of Dagger on synthetic transcripts: The first hypothesis is that synthetic transcripts are already "good enough" and per-step IL corrections add nothing on top. Second, the gains could be due to the known NMT "auto-correcting" ability and due to general robustness to the quality of the source (cf. the success of back-translation in NMT), and all benefits could be reached with KD alone. To test both hypotheses, we create new training datasets where we replace references with translated gold or synthetic transcripts by the same NMT expert with beam size 5. Evaluating on the unmodified references, we trained Transformer-based baselines and the IL model from Lin et al. (2020) on these two new corpora.

As Table 6 shows, Transformer KD$^+$ trained on translated gold transcripts outperforms its counterparts trained on translated synthetic transcripts, confirming errors in the synthetic transcripts. This refutes the first hypothesis.

Regarding the second hypothesis, we compare the KD$^+$ to IKD$^+$ from the synthetic translated part in Table 6. Were "auto-correction" sufficient we would see similar performance in both lines. This rejects the second hypothesis and suggests that IL adds value on top of general NMT robustness to inputs.

4.4 Qualitative Analysis

Here, we perform a human evaluation of successful IL corrections, aiming at an explanation of the performance of Dagger on synthetic transcripts.

We randomly sample 100 examples from the CoVoST2 training set on which the ASR Transformer has a non-zero sentence-wise word error rate, and compare the NMT expert's probability distributions over time for the given synthetic transcripts. From the WER histogram in Figure 2 we see that most of the sentences have a single-digit number of errors.

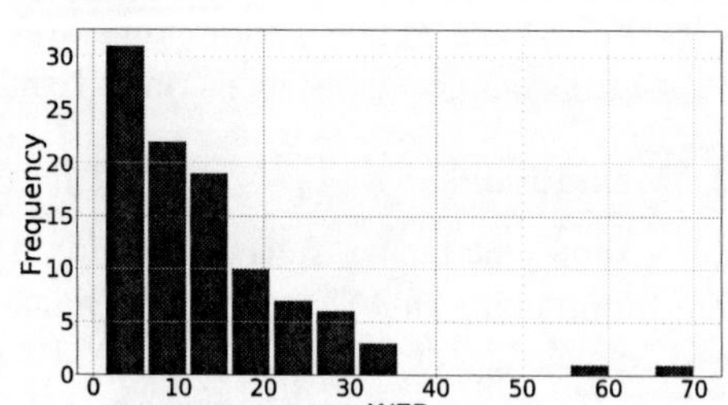

Figure 2: Histogram of sentence-wise WER of ASR Transformer on 100 samples from CoVoST2.

IL Algorithm	Model	Data	CoVoST2 BLEU↑ dev	CoVoST2 BLEU↑ test	CoVoST2 TER↓ dev	CoVoST2 TER↓ test	MuST-C BLEU↑ dev	MuST-C BLEU↑ test	MuST-C TER↓ dev	MuST-C TER↓ test
Dagger	Standard	gold	18.4	14.2	69.1	77.1	19.5	19.4	70.8	69.4
	IKD+	gold	21.8	18.4	63.7	70.0	23.2	23.3	67.4	65.6
	SynthIKD+	synth	21.8	**18.5**	63.6	69.8	**23.5**	23.5	67.2	65.6
	Warm-start Model	**Data**	**BLEU↑ dev**	**BLEU↑ test**	**TER↓ dev**	**TER↓ test**	**BLEU↑ dev**	**BLEU↑ test**	**TER↓ dev**	**TER↓ test**
	sentence-BLEU reward-to-go									
AggreVaTe	Standard	gold	18.7	14.6	68.2	76.0	19.9	19.9	70.2	68.1
	Standard	synth	18.7	14.6	68.2	75.9	20.0	19.7	70.1	68.7
	IKD+	gold	**22.1**	**18.5**	**63.1**	69.6	**23.5**	23.4	67.4	65.7
	SynthIKD+	synth	**22.1**	**18.5**	**63.1**	69.7	**23.5**	**23.6**	**67.0**	65.6
	TER reward-to-go									
	Standard	gold	18.7	14.7	67.8	75.4	20.0	19.9	70.0	68.5
	Standard	synth	18.7	14.6	67.9	75.6	19.9	19.6	69.8	68.4
	IKD+	gold	22.0	**18.5**	**63.1**	**69.4**	23.3	23.4	67.3	65.5
	SynthIKD+	synth	**22.1**	**18.5**	**63.1**	69.6	**23.5**	**23.6**	**67.0**	**65.3**

Table 5: Comparison of Dagger with warm-started AggreVaTe with a maximum of 50 epochs on CoVoST2 and MuST-C.

Training	CoVoST2 dev	CoVoST2 test	MuST-C dev	MuST-C test
training on translated gold transcripts				
Standard	18.1	14.9	20.0	20.0
KD+	21.3	17.6	23.4	23.1
IKD+	22.6	18.6	23.5	23.7
training on translated synthetic transcripts				
Standard	17.8	14.2	19.2	19.2
KD+	20.2	16.5	22.1	22.5
IKD+	21.0	17.4	23.0	23.1

Table 6: BLEU scores of Transformer models trained on the training set with original references replaced by translations of gold and synthetic transcripts in comparison to using the original training set (lower part of Table 4).

Error Type	Freq
omitted tokens	2
surface form error	17
contentual error, correct target in top-1	5
contentual error, correct target in top-8	12
critical error, expert predicts correctly due to prefix	32
critical error, expert does not predict correctly	32

Table 7: Error types in the synthetic transcripts created by the ASR model.

As WER cannot be used to differentiate between small but inconsequential (to the understanding of the sentence) errors and mistakes that change the meaning of the sentence, we further compare the generated transcript to the gold transcript *and* look at the top-8 output probabilities of the expert at each time step for each sample to classify each error in the synthetic transcripts. We further feed the sampled sentences to the NMT expert and find that in 36 out of 100 samples (all but the last two lines in Table 7), the expert is able to generate output probability distributions that favor the correct target token despite errors in the transcript. Although the expert can put large probability mass on the correct target token, whether it does so depends on the error type in the generated transcript. The expert is often able to deal with surface form errors, such as different spellings, punctuation errors and different word choice (17 occurrences). When the synthetic transcripts contain critical errors, e.g. partially hallucinated transcript, the expert is still able to produce the correct translation if the missing or wrong information can be still inferred from the prefix (32 occurrences).

Next, we verify that the decoder language modeling capability is what primarily drives the correction process. We do this by feeding parts of reference translations as prefix conditioned on erroneous synthetic transcripts. Consider the transcript "The king had taken possession of Glamis Castle and plywood." generated by the ASR model. Its gold transcript reads "plundered it" instead of "plywood". In Figure 3 we illustrate output probabilities that the expert generates in the last time-steps. Assume as in Figure 3a that the expert has been given the prefix "Der König hatte Glamis Castle in Besitz genommen und". According to the output probabilities, the next output symbol is the subword unit "Sperr" and would not be a proper

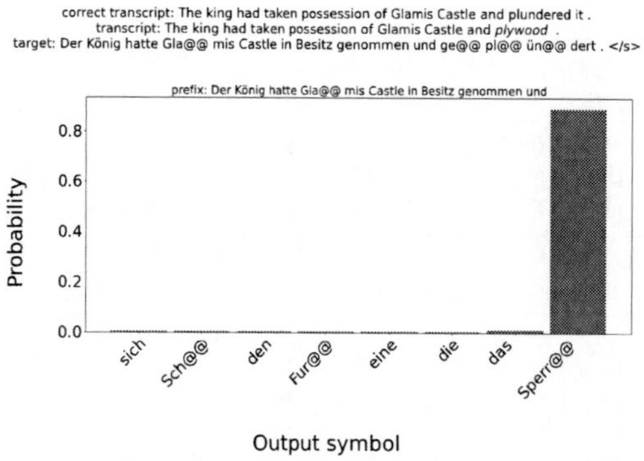

(a) with $y_{<t}$ = "Der König hatte Glamis Castle in Besitz genommen und "

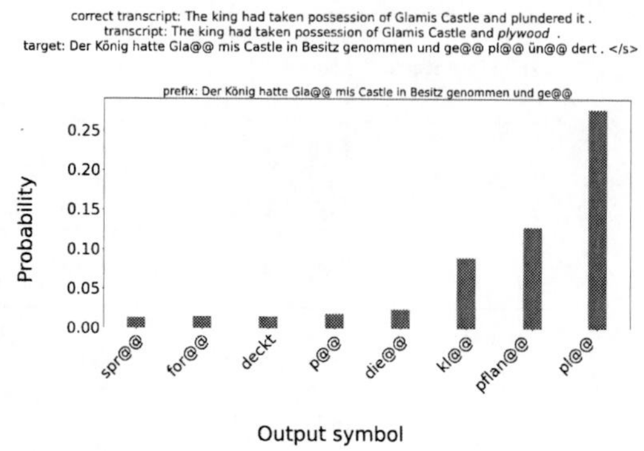

(b) with $y_{<t}$ = "Der König hatte Glamis Castle in Besitz genommen und ge"

Figure 3: NMT expert top-8 output probabilities when translating the incorrect synthetic transcript "The king had taken possession of Glamis Castle and plywood it."

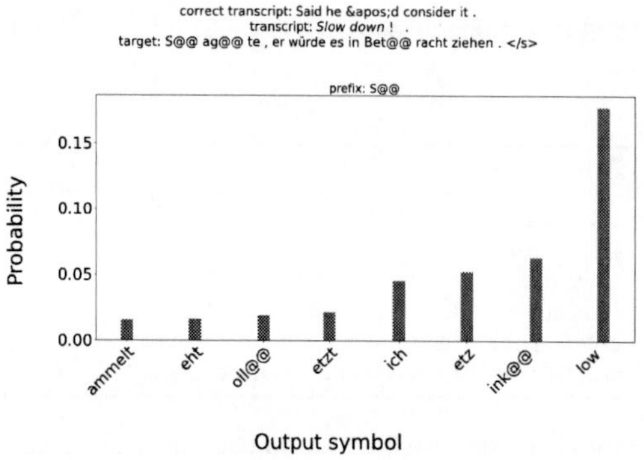

(a) with $y_{<t}$ = "S"

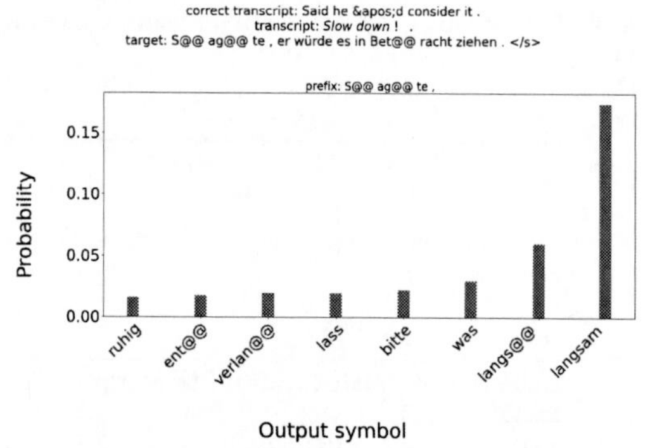

(b) with $y_{<t}$ = "Sagte , "

Figure 4: NMT expert top-8 output probabilities when translating the incorrect synthetic transcript "Slow down!"

correction. At the next timestep, however, the last symbol in the prefix is the subword unit "ge" and, as Figure 3b shows, the expert, being driven by its decoder language modeling capability, puts highest probabilities on subword units that are most likely to produce a fluent output (the correct one "pl@@", and less probable "pflan@@" and "kl@@" rather then paying attention to the (wrong) information in the synthetic transcripts.

Similar situations can be observed in samples with entirely wrong synthetic transcripts. In Figure 4, the expert has received the synthetic transcript "Slow down!" as input, which shares no meaning with the gold transcript "Said he'd consider it." As shown in Figure 4a, the expert assigns the highest probability to "@@low" if it is given the prefix "S" (as the expert has a shared vocabulary, it can complete the output this way), which turns the partial translation into an exact copy of the transcript. Again, the top-8 predictions do not share similar meaning with the transcript. After, in Figure 4b, the expert has received the prefix "Sagte,", it still attempts to complete $y_{<t}$ by generating output symbols that would turn y into a valid translation of this wrong transcript ("langsam" (slow), "ruhig" (quiet), "langs@@")) with the rest of options being mostly driven by language modeling rather then reproducing source semantics ("ent@@", "verlan@@").

Overall, with the SynthIKD$^+$ training, the expert induces smoothed output distributions and fluency on the student more than it enforces the student to predict one-hot labels produced by the expert as is done by sequence-level KD.

5 Conclusion

We showed that a pretrained NMT model can successfully be used as an oracle for an AST student, without requiring gold source language transcripts as in previous approaches to imitation learning for

AST. This widens the applicability of imitation learning approaches to datasets that do not contain manual transcripts or to pre-trained ASR models for which training transcripts are not available. Our qualitative analysis suggests an explanation of the fact that the NMT oracle is robust against mismatches between manual and synthetic transcripts by its large language model capabilities that allow it to continue the prefix solely based on its learned contextual knowledge.

6 Limitations

There are several limitations of this study. First, it is done on one language pair although we believe this should not qualitatively change the results. Second, only one set of standard model sizes was evaluated for AST student and NMT expert; we expect it be in line with reported findings for NMT (Ghorbani et al., 2021). Finally, while alluding to the potential of using large pre-trained ASR models instead of manual transcripts for IL-based AST, our current work must be seen as a proof-of-concept experiment where we train ASR models on a few hundred hours of audio, and discard the manual transcripts in IL training, showing the feasibility of our idea.

Acknowledgements

The authors acknowledge support by the state of Baden-Württemberg through bwHPC and the German Research Foundation (DFG) through grant INST 35/1597-1 FUGG.

References

Antonios Anastasopoulos and David Chiang. 2018. Tied multitask learning for neural speech translation. In *Proceedings of the 2018 Conference of the North American Chapter of the Association for Computational Linguistics: Human Language Technologies, Volume 1 (Long Papers)*, pages 82–91, New Orleans, Louisiana. Association for Computational Linguistics.

Parnia Bahar, Tobias Bieschke, and Hermann Ney. 2019. A comparative study on end-to-end speech to text translation. In *2019 IEEE Automatic Speech Recognition and Understanding Workshop (ASRU)*, pages 792–799.

Dzmitry Bahdanau, Philemon Brakel, Kelvin Xu, Anirudh Goyal, Ryan Lowe, Joelle Pineau, Aaron C. Courville, and Yoshua Bengio. 2016. An actor-critic algorithm for sequence prediction. *CoRR*, abs/1607.07086.

Samy Bengio, Oriol Vinyals, Navdeep Jaitly, and Noam Shazeer. 2015. Scheduled sampling for sequence prediction with recurrent neural networks. In *Advances in Neural Information Processing Systems*, volume 28. Curran Associates, Inc.

Alexandre Berard, Laurent Besacier, Ali Can Kocabiyikoglu, and Olivier Pietquin. 2018. End-to-end automatic speech translation of audiobooks. In *2018 IEEE International Conference on Acoustics, Speech and Signal Processing, ICASSP 2018, Calgary, AB, Canada, April 15-20, 2018*, pages 6224–6228. IEEE.

Mattia A. Di Gangi, Roldano Cattoni, Luisa Bentivogli, Matteo Negri, and Marco Turchi. 2019. MuST-C: a Multilingual Speech Translation Corpus. In *Proceedings of the 2019 Conference of the North American Chapter of the Association for Computational Linguistics: Human Language Technologies, Volume 1 (Long and Short Papers)*, pages 2012–2017, Minneapolis, Minnesota. Association for Computational Linguistics.

Marco Gaido, Mattia A. Di Gangi, Matteo Negri, and Marco Turchi. 2020. End-to-end speech-translation with knowledge distillation: FBK@IWSLT2020. In *Proceedings of the 17th International Conference on Spoken Language Translation*, pages 80–88, Online. Association for Computational Linguistics.

Behrooz Ghorbani, Orhan Firat, Markus Freitag, Ankur Bapna, Maxim Krikun, Xavier Garcia, Ciprian Chelba, and Colin Cherry. 2021. Scaling laws for neural machine translation. *CoRR*, abs/2109.07740.

Geoffrey Hinton, Oriol Vinyals, and Jeffrey Dean. 2015. Distilling the knowledge in a neural network. In *NIPS Deep Learning and Representation Learning Workshop*.

Luca Hormann and Artem Sokolov. 2021. Fixing exposure bias with imitation learning needs powerful oracles. *CoRR*, abs/2109.04114.

Javier Iranzo-Sánchez, Joan Albert Silvestre-Cerdà, Javier Jorge, Nahuel Roselló, Adrià Giménez, Albert Sanchis, Jorge Civera, and Alfons Juan. 2020. Europarl-st: A multilingual corpus for speech translation of parliamentary debates. In *ICASSP 2020 - 2020 IEEE International Conference on Acoustics, Speech and Signal Processing (ICASSP)*, pages 8229–8233.

Ye Jia, Melvin Johnson, Wolfgang Macherey, Ron J. Weiss, Yuan Cao, Chung-Cheng Chiu, Naveen Ari, Stella Laurenzo, and Yonghui Wu. 2019. Leveraging weakly supervised data to improve end-to-end speech-to-text translation. In *ICASSP 2019 - 2019 IEEE International Conference on Acoustics, Speech and Signal Processing (ICASSP)*, pages 7180–7184.

Yoon Kim and Alexander M. Rush. 2016. Sequence-level knowledge distillation. In *Proceedings of the 2016 Conference on Empirical Methods in Natural Language Processing*, pages 1317–1327, Austin, Texas. Association for Computational Linguistics.

Diederik P. Kingma and Jimmy Ba. 2015. Adam: A method for stochastic optimization. In *3rd International Conference on Learning Representations, ICLR 2015, San Diego, CA, USA, May 7-9, 2015, Conference Track Proceedings.*

Philipp Koehn, Hieu Hoang, Alexandra Birch, Chris Callison-Burch, Marcello Federico, Nicola Bertoldi, Brooke Cowan, Wade Shen, Christine Moran, Richard Zens, Chris Dyer, Ondřej Bojar, Alexandra Constantin, and Evan Herbst. 2007. Moses: Open source toolkit for statistical machine translation. In *Proceedings of the 45th Annual Meeting of the Association for Computational Linguistics Companion Volume Proceedings of the Demo and Poster Sessions*, pages 177–180, Prague, Czech Republic. Association for Computational Linguistics.

Alexander Lin, Jeremy Wohlwend, Howard Chen, and Tao Lei. 2020. Autoregressive knowledge distillation through imitation learning. In *Proceedings of the 2020 Conference on Empirical Methods in Natural Language Processing (EMNLP)*, pages 6121–6133, Online. Association for Computational Linguistics.

Yuchen Liu, Hao Xiong, Jiajun Zhang, Zhongjun He, Hua Wu, Haifeng Wang, and Chengqing Zong. 2019. End-to-End Speech Translation with Knowledge Distillation. In *Proc. Interspeech 2019*, pages 1128–1132.

Nathan Ng, Kyra Yee, Alexei Baevski, Myle Ott, Michael Auli, and Sergey Edunov. 2019. Facebook FAIR's WMT19 news translation task submission. In *Proceedings of the Fourth Conference on Machine Translation (Volume 2: Shared Task Papers, Day 1)*, pages 314–319, Florence, Italy. Association for Computational Linguistics.

Myle Ott, Sergey Edunov, Alexei Baevski, Angela Fan, Sam Gross, Nathan Ng, David Grangier, and Michael Auli. 2019. fairseq: A fast, extensible toolkit for sequence modeling. In *Proceedings of the 2019 Conference of the North American Chapter of the Association for Computational Linguistics (Demonstrations)*, pages 48–53, Minneapolis, Minnesota. Association for Computational Linguistics.

Kishore Papineni, Salim Roukos, Todd Ward, and Wei-Jing Zhu. 2002. Bleu: a method for automatic evaluation of machine translation. In *Proceedings of the 40th Annual Meeting of the Association for Computational Linguistics*, pages 311–318, Philadelphia, Pennsylvania, USA. Association for Computational Linguistics.

Juan Pino, Liezl Puzon, Jiatao Gu, Xutai Ma, Arya D. McCarthy, and Deepak Gopinath. 2019. Harnessing indirect training data for end-to-end automatic speech translation: Tricks of the trade. In *Proceedings of the 16th International Conference on Spoken Language Translation*, Hong Kong. Association for Computational Linguistics.

Juan Pino, Qiantong Xu, Xutai Ma, Mohammad Javad Dousti, and Yun Tang. 2020. Self-Training for End-to-End Speech Translation. In *Proc. Interspeech 2020*, pages 1476–1480.

Matt Post. 2018. A call for clarity in reporting BLEU scores. In *Proceedings of the Third Conference on Machine Translation: Research Papers*, pages 186–191, Brussels, Belgium. Association for Computational Linguistics.

Alec Radford, Jong Wook Kim, Tao Xu, Greg Brockman, Christine McLeavey, and Ilya Sutskever. 2022. Robust speech recognition via large-scale weak supervision. *CoRR*, abs/2212.04356.

Marc'Aurelio Ranzato, Sumit Chopra, Michael Auli, and Wojciech Zaremba. 2016. Sequence level training with recurrent neural networks. In *4th International Conference on Learning Representations, ICLR 2016, San Juan, Puerto Rico, May 2-4, 2016, Conference Track Proceedings.*

Stefan Riezler and John T. Maxwell. 2005. On some pitfalls in automatic evaluation and significance testing for MT. In *Proceedings of the ACL Workshop on Intrinsic and Extrinsic Evaluation Measures for Machine Translation and/or Summarization*, pages 57–64, Ann Arbor, Michigan. Association for Computational Linguistics.

Stéphane Ross and Andrew Bagnell. 2014. Reinforcement and imitation learning via interactive no-regret learning. *CoRR*, abs/1406.5979.

Stephane Ross, Geoffrey Gordon, and Drew Bagnell. 2011. A reduction of imitation learning and structured prediction to no-regret online learning. In *Proceedings of the Fourteenth International Conference on Artificial Intelligence and Statistics*, volume 15 of *Proceedings of Machine Learning Research*, pages 627–635, Fort Lauderdale, FL, USA. PMLR.

Rico Sennrich, Barry Haddow, and Alexandra Birch. 2016. Neural machine translation of rare words with subword units. In *Proceedings of the 54th Annual Meeting of the Association for Computational Linguistics (Volume 1: Long Papers)*, pages 1715–1725, Berlin, Germany. Association for Computational Linguistics.

Christian Szegedy, Vincent Vanhoucke, Sergey Ioffe, Jon Shlens, and Zbigniew Wojna. 2016. Rethinking the inception architecture for computer vision. In *2016 IEEE Conference on Computer Vision and Pattern Recognition (CVPR)*, pages 2818–2826.

Yun Tang, Juan Pino, Xian Li, Changhan Wang, and Dmitriy Genzel. 2021a. Improving speech translation by understanding and learning from the auxiliary text translation task. In *Proceedings of the 59th Annual Meeting of the Association for Computational Linguistics and the 11th International Joint Conference on Natural Language Processing (Volume 1: Long Papers)*, pages 4252–4261, Online. Association for Computational Linguistics.

Yun Tang, Juan Pino, Changhan Wang, Xutai Ma, and Dmitriy Genzel. 2021b. A general multi-task learning framework to leverage text data for speech to text tasks. In *ICASSP 2021 - 2021 IEEE International Conference on Acoustics, Speech and Signal Processing (ICASSP)*, pages 6209–6213.

Ashish Vaswani, Noam Shazeer, Niki Parmar, Jakob Uszkoreit, Llion Jones, Aidan N Gomez, Łukasz Kaiser, and Illia Polosukhin. 2017. Attention is all you need. *Advances in neural information processing systems*, 30.

Changhan Wang, Yun Tang, Xutai Ma, Anne Wu, Dmytro Okhonko, and Juan Pino. 2020. Fairseq S2T: Fast speech-to-text modeling with fairseq. In *Proceedings of the 1st Conference of the Asia-Pacific Chapter of the Association for Computational Linguistics and the 10th International Joint Conference on Natural Language Processing: System Demonstrations*, pages 33–39, Suzhou, China. Association for Computational Linguistics.

Changhan Wang, Anne Wu, Jiatao Gu, and Juan Pino. 2021. CoVoST 2 and Massively Multilingual Speech Translation. In *Interspeech*, pages 2247–2251.

Chaojun Wang and Rico Sennrich. 2020. On exposure bias, hallucination and domain shift in neural machine translation. In *ACL*.

Ron J. Weiss, Jan Chorowski, Navdeep Jaitly, Yonghui Wu, and Zhifeng Chen. 2017. Sequence-to-sequence models can directly translate foreign speech. In *Interspeech 2017, 18th Annual Conference of the International Speech Communication Association, Stockholm, Sweden, August 20-24, 2017*, pages 2625–2629. ISCA.

Ronald J. Williams and David Zipser. 1989. A learning algorithm for continually running fully recurrent neural networks. *Neural Computation*, 1(2):270–280.

Jeremy H.M. Wong and Mark J.F. Gales. 2016. Sequence Student-Teacher Training of Deep Neural Networks. In *Proc. Interspeech 2016*, pages 2761–2765.

Rong Ye, Mingxuan Wang, and Lei Li. 2021. End-to-end speech translation via cross-modal progressive training. In *Proc. of INTERSPEECH*.

Biao Zhang, Barry Haddow, and Rico Sennrich. 2022a. Revisiting end-to-end speech-to-text translation from scratch. In *International Conference on Machine Learning*, pages 26193–26205. PMLR.

Yu Zhang, Daniel S. Park, Wei Han, James Qin, Anmol Gulati, Joel Shor, Aren Jansen, Yuanzhong Xu, Yanping Huang, Shibo Wang, Zongwei Zhou, Bo Li, Min Ma, William Chan, Jiahui Yu, Yongqiang Wang, Liangliang Cao, Khe Chai Sim, Bhuvana Ramabhadran, Tara N. Sainath, Francoise Beaufays, Zhifeng Chen, Quoc V. Le, Chung-Cheng Chiu, Ruoming Pang, and Yonghui Wu. 2022b. BigSSL: Exploring the frontier of large-scale semi-supervised learning for automatic speech recognition. *IEEE Journal of Selected Topics in Signal Processing*, 16(6):1519–1532.

Renjie Zheng, Junkun Chen, Mingbo Ma, and Liang Huang. 2021. Fused acoustic and text encoding for multimodal bilingual pretraining and speech translation. In *International Conference on Machine Learning*, pages 12736–12746. PMLR.

Chunting Zhou, Jiatao Gu, and Graham Neubig. 2020. Understanding knowledge distillation in non-autoregressive machine translation. In *International Conference on Learning Representations (ICLR)*.

Model	BLEU↑ dev	test
original dataset		
Standard	13.8	14.4
KD^+	17.4	17.8
$SynthKD^+$	17.5	18.0
IKD^+	17.0	17.1
$SynthIKD^+$	17.0	17.0
translated gold training set		
Standard	15.3	15.3
KD^+	**18.2**	**18.4**
IKD	16.8	17.0
IKD+	17.1	17.5
synthetic translated training set		
Standard	14.7	15.3
KD^+	17.0	16.8
IKD	16.1	16.0
IKD+	16.3	16.6

Table A.1: Results on Europarl-ST

A Models, Meta-parameters, and Training Settings

We use the speech-to-text module of the `fairseq` framework (Ott et al., 2019; Wang et al., 2020) for all experiments and train both RNNs with convolutional layers for time dimension reduction as in Berard et al. (2018) and small Transformers as in Wang et al. (2020), which consist of a convolutional subsampler of two convolutional blocks, followed by 12 encoder layers and 6 decoder layers. The dimension of the self-attention layer is 256 and the number of attention heads is set to 4. For the NMT oracle, we use the trained Transformer model from the Facebook's submission to WMT19 (Ng et al., 2019) [5], which is based on the big Transformer (Vaswani et al., 2017) which has 6 encoder and decoder layers, 16 attention heads and the dimension of 1024, with a larger feed-forward layer size of 8192. This NMT oracle had been trained on all available WMT19 shared task en-de training data and on back-translated english and german portions of the News crawl dataset.

For all models we use Adam (Kingma and Ba, 2015) with gradient clipping at norm 10 and stop training if the development set loss has not improved for 10 epochs. For RNN architectures, we return the best model on the development set and for Transformers, we create each model by averaging over the last 10 checkpoints. For inference, a beam size of 5 was used and we report case-sensitive detokenized BLEU (Papineni et al., 2002) computed with sacreBLEU (Post, 2018). We tested for statistical significance with the paired approximate randomization test (Riezler and Maxwell, 2005).

For all experiments, we preprocess the datasets as follows: We extract log mel-scale filterbanks with a povey window, 80 bins, a pre-emphasis filter of 0.97, a frame length of 25 ms and a frame shift of 10 ms. We discard samples with less than five or more than 3000 frames and subtract the mean of the waveform from each frame and zero-pad the FFT input. For the text data, we normalize punctuation, remove non-printable characters, use the Moses tokenizer (Koehn et al., 2007) for tokenization and segment the text data into subword units with byte-pair encoding (Sennrich et al., 2016). We used a random seed of 1 for all experiments.

We list the final used and best performing hyperparameters in Table A.2. Parameters that do not differ between the training methods are not repeated in the table. We determine the batch size by defining a maximum number of input frames in the batch.

B Europarl-ST

We performed additional experiments on the Europarl-ST dataset (Iranzo-Sánchez et al., 2020) that provides 83 hours of speech training data. We train RNNs with a learning rate of 0.002 and a max-tokens size of 40,000 for a total of 80,000 updates. All other hyper-parameters are the same as listed for MuST-C in Table A.2. We only trained RNNs on the Europarl-ST dataset due to the small amount of available training data. We present the results in Table A.1.

Both improvements over standard training and by training on both the gold-translated and synthetic-translated translated training data correspond with the results presented in the main body of this work. Hence, the results presented here hold for relatively small datasets, too.

C Additional Example of NMT Expert Correction

Here we give another example of the NMT expert predicting the correct output token despite receiv-

[5] As the WMT19 submission consists of an ensemble of models, we use the `model1.pt` for our experiments.

Model	Hyperparameter	CoVoST2	MuST-C
RNN			
standard	learning rate	1e-3	1e-3
	max-tokens	60000	40000
	scheduler	fixed	fixed
	warmup-updates	20000	20000
	encoder freezing updates	10000	10000
	dropout	0.2	0.2
KD^+	learning rate	1e-3	2e-3
	max-tokens	50000	30000
	warmup-updates	25000	20000
	max-update	250000	250000
	encoder-freezing updates	20000	10000
	scheduler	inverse square root	inverse square root
Transformer			
ASR	learning rate	2e-3	1e-3
	max-tokens	50000	40000
	max-update	60000	100000
	scheduler	inverse square root	inverse square root
	warmup-updates	10000	10000
	dropout	0.15	0.1
AST			
standard	learning rate	2e-3	2e-3
	max-update	30000	100000
	encoder-freezing updates	1000	-
KD^+	max-tokens	50000	20000

Table A.2: list of hyperparameters that are dependent on model and dataset; we list only parameters which differ from the previous model's

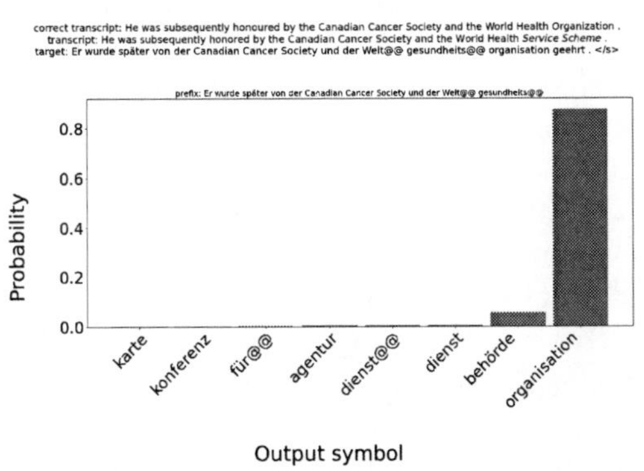

Figure C.1: NMT expert top-8 output probabilities with $y_{<t}$ = " Er wurde später von der Canadian Cancer Society und der Weltgesundheits".

ing a transcript with incomplete or false information.

Figure C.1 shows the expert's output probabilities in response to receiving factually false information in the transcript. The ASR model transcribed "World Health Organization" as "World Health Service Scheme", yet the expert produces a probability distribution that is skewed in favor of the correct proper name due to its learned context knowledge. Note that the probability of generating the correct output token "organisation" (organization) is above 0.8.

The USTC's Dialect Speech Translation System for IWSLT 2023

Pan Deng[1] **Shihao Chen**[1] **Weitai Zhang**[1,2] **Jie Zhang**[1] **Lirong Dai**[1]
[1]University of Science and Technology of China, Hefei, China
[2]iFlytek Research, Hefei, China
{pdeng, shchen16, zwt2021}@mail.ustc.edu.cn; {jzhang6, lrdai}@ustc.edu.cn

Abstract

This paper presents the USTC system for the IWSLT 2023 Dialectal and Low-resource shared task, which involves translation from Tunisian Arabic to English. We aim to investigate the mutual transfer between Tunisian Arabic and Modern Standard Arabic (MSA) to enhance the performance of speech translation (ST) by following standard pre-training and fine-tuning pipelines. We synthesize a substantial amount of pseudo Tunisian-English paired data using a multi-step pre-training approach. Integrating a Tunisian-MSA translation module into the end-to-end ST model enables the transfer from Tunisian to MSA and facilitates linguistic normalization of the dialect. To increase the robustness of the ST system, we optimize the model's ability to adapt to ASR errors and propose a model ensemble method. Results indicate that applying the dialect transfer method can increase the BLEU score of dialectal ST. It is shown that the optimal system ensembles both cascaded and end-to-end ST models, achieving BLEU improvements of 2.4 and 2.8 in test1 and test2 sets, respectively, compared to the best published system.

1 Introduction

In this paper, we present the USTC's submission to the Dialectal and Low-resource track of IWSLT 2023 Evaluation Campaign (Agarwal et al., 2023), aiming to translate Tunisian Arabic speech to English text. Modern Standard Arabic (MSA) is the official language of Arabic-spoken countries. However, Arabic dialects like Tunisian and Egyptian are prevalent in everyday communication, exhibiting a similar relation between Chinese and Cantonese. MSA benefits from an abundant supply of unlabeled speech and text data, as well as relatively adequate automatic speech recognition (ASR) and machine translation (MT) paired data. In contrast, dialectical forms of Arabic have much less paired data and more irregularities in both pronunciation and writing (Ben Abdallah et al., 2020).

This paper aims to explore the transfer between high-resource MSA and low-resource Tunisian dialects, as well as effective training and decoding strategies for speech translation (ST) tasks related to low-resource dialects. To facilitate **dialect transfer**, we introduce two approaches. Firstly, we pre-train a model using high-resource MSA data, which is then fine-tuned using low-resource Tunisian data. This approach involves transferring model parameters and can be used to train various models, e.g., ASR, MT, end-to-end ST. Secondly, we also develop two transformation models for explicit dialect transfer. On one hand, for the augmentation of MT data, we build an MT model that translates MSA into Tunisian, resulting in a vast amount of pseudo Tunisian-English paired data. On the other hand, the Tunisian-MSA MT encoder module is built and then integrated into the end-to-end ST model, which can implicitly normalize dialectal expressions. In addition, we also propose robust training and decoding strategies from two perspectives. To improve the robustness of the MT model against ASR errors, we fine-tune the MT model with the ASR output from the CTC (Graves et al., 2006) layer or the ASR decoder. The model ensemble method is exploited to decode multiple models synchronously, which is shown to be rather beneficial for the performance.

The rest of this paper is organized as follows. Section 2 describes data preparation (e.g., datasets, pre-processing). Section 3 presents the methods for training and decoding ASR, MT and ST models. Experimental setup and results are given in Section 4. Finally, Section 5 concludes this work.

2 Data Preparation

2.1 Datasets

In this year's shared task, there are two types of data conditions: constrained and unconstrained. In order to provide a fair comparison with last year's

Proceedings of the 20th International Conference on Spoken Language Translation (IWSLT 2023), pages 102–112
July 13-14, 2023 ©2023 Association for Computational Linguistics

Task	Dataset	Condition	Utterances	Hours
ASR	Tunisian	A	0.2M	160
	MGB2	B	1.1M	1100
	MGB2+Private data	C	3.4M	4600
ST	Tunisian	A	0.2M	160

Table 1: The summary of the Audio data.

	Dataset	Condition	Ta-En	MSA-En
Collected	Tunisian	A	0.2M	-
	OPUS	B	-	42M
	OPUS+Private data	C	-	61M
Filtered	Tunisian	A	0.2M	-
	OPUS	B	-	32M
	OPUS+Private data	C	-	47M

Table 2: The summary of the text data.

Translation direction	Training data	MT model
Tunisian-English	Ta-En	Ta2En
English-Tunisian	En-Ta	En2Ta
MSA-English	MSA-En	MSA2En
English-MSA	En-MSA	En2MSA
Tunisian-MSA	Ta-MSA	Ta2MSA
MSA-Tunisian	MSA-Ta	MSA2Ta
Tunisian-MSA-English	Ta-MSA-En	-

Table 3: Summary of abbreviations used in this paper.

results, we subdivided the unconstrained condition into the dialect adaption condition and the fully unconstrained condition. For convenience, we denote the constrained condition as **condition A**, the dialect adaption condition as **condition B**, and the fully unconstrained condition as **condition C**.

Table 1 summarizes statistics of the ASR and ST datasets. The Tunisian dataset[1] in condition A is Arabic dialect data. In addition to the MGB2 data (Ali et al., 2016) of condition B, we used additional private data mainly from MSA for ASR training in condition C. Table 2 summarizes the statistics of the MT datasets. The MT data for condition A are Tunisian-English (Ta-En) paired data, while for condition B/C, the MT data consist of MSA-English (MSA-En) paired data(Tiedemann and Thottingal, 2020). All MT data undergoes preprocessing, which includes cleaning and filtering. Table 3 summarizes the abbreviations for MT models and training data associated with the translation direction that are used in the sequel.

[1]The LDC Catalog ID of the Tunisian dataset for IWSLT is LDC2022E01.

2.2 Audio data pre-processing

As the audio data of condition B/C had a sampling rate of 16kHz, we upsampled the speech signal in the Tunisian dataset from 8kHz to 16kHz using the sox toolkit[2]. We extracted 40-dimensional log-mel filterbank features with a frame length of 25ms and a frame shift of 10ms, and then normalized these features with a zero mean and unit variance. We applied SpecAugment (Park et al., 2019) in the time dimension with mask parameters $(m_T, T) = (2, 70)$. Afterwards, we filtered out audio data that is longer than 3k frames. Further, we introduced speech perturbations at ratios of 0.9 and 1.1.

2.3 Text Processing & Filtering

We kept the MSA and Tunisian text data in their original form without any normalization such as removing diacritical marks or converting Alif/Ya/Ta-Marbuta symbols. We removed punctuations from MSA, Tunisian, and English text while we converted the English text to lowercase. Our data filtering process in condition B/C includes **Length Match** and **Inference Score**.

- **Length Match:** Text samples exceeding 250 words were dropped first. Next, we calculated the length ratio between the source and target language text. Text samples with length ratios exceeding 2 or below 0.4 were deemed to be length mismatching cases and were subsequently removed. As such, approximately 6M text data in condition B were eliminated.

- **Inference Score:** Initially, a basic MT model (scoring model) was trained on raw MSA-En data in condition B. Subsequently, the scoring model was used to infer the same MSA-En raw data, resulting in inference scores based on logarithmic posterior probabilities. Finally, MSA-En data associated with lower inference scores were removed, leading to another 4M text data being eliminated from condition B.

Table 2 summarizes the filtered data used for training. In total, 10M text data in condition B and 4M text data in condition C were removed.

3 Methods

3.1 Automatic Speech Recognition

We employed several ASR models with different structures in experiments, including the VGG-

[2]http://sox.sourceforge.net

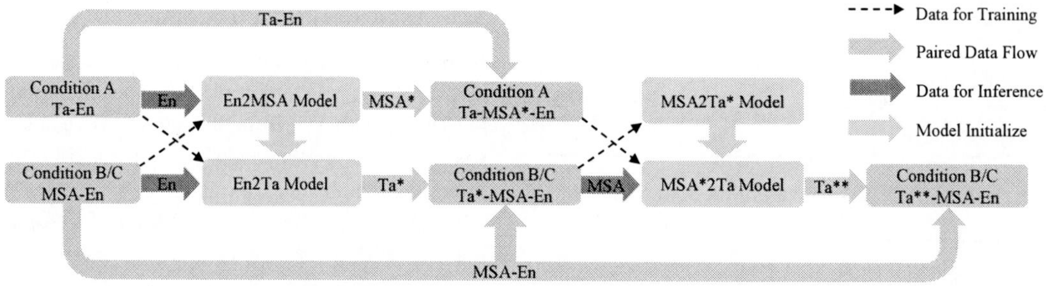

Figure 1: The data augmentation method for Tunisian-English Text, where * indicates the pseudo text.

Conformer model (Simonyan and Zisserman, 2014; Gulati et al., 2020), VGG-Transformer model (Vaswani et al., 2017) and GateCNN-Conformer model (Dauphin et al., 2017). These ASR models differ in their feature extractor modules (VGG, GateCNN) and acoustic modules (Conformer, Transformer). We chose diverse models with the expectation that increasing the variability of ASR models would improve the final ASR performance when using model ensemble methods. For dialect transfer in condition B/C, we pre-trained an ASR model using MSA data, which was then fine-tuned using the Tunisian data. Note that for condition A, we initially attempted to pre-train a phoneme recognition model for Tunisian but found it to be useless after fine-tuning the pre-trained model.

3.2 Data Augmentation for MT

We considered various data augmentation techniques for MT. To augment the Tunisian-English (Ta-En) dialect MT data, we used the back translation and forward translation (**BTFT**) method to create a synthetic parallel corpus that can be merged with the true bilingual data. To accomplish **dialect transfer** from MSA to Tunisian, we constructed a pivot MT model that converts MSA to Tunisian and produces abundant synthetic Ta-En data.

BTFT: Two MT models were first trained from Tunisian to English (Ta2En) and from English to Tunisian (En2Ta) using MT data of condition A. The Tunisian text and English text were then respectively fed to the corresponding MT models for inference, resulting in paired Tunisian to synthetic-English text and paired synthetic-Tunisian to English text. It is worth noting that the Ta2En model implements the forward translation approach similarly to the sequence-level knowledge distillation method (Kim and Rush, 2016), while the En2Ta model employs the backward translation (Sennrich et al., 2016a) approach. Ultimately, the obtained synthetic data and the original data were merged to form the BTFT dataset.

Dialect Transfer: In the IWSLT 2022 dialect ST track, (Yang et al., 2022) presented an effective Ta2En-bt-tune model that generates synthetic Tunisian-English data by converting MSA to pseudo-Tunisian with an MSA2Ta MT model. In Figure 1, we modified this approach by introducing a multi-step pre-training technique that improves the quality of pseudo-Tunisian and enhances downstream translation tasks. Our dialect transfer method is outlined as follows:

(1) Firstly, the En2MSA (English to MSA) model was pre-trained using condition B/C MT data and then fine-tuned using the MT data from condition A to create the En2Ta model.

(2) The En2MSA and En2Ta models were utilized separately with the English texts from condition A and condition B/C as inputs to generate paired Ta-MSA-En triple text data for condition A/B/C. The pseudo-text in condition A is the MSA* text, whereas the pseudo-text in condition B/C is the Tunisian* text (* representing pseudo-text). Notably, during this step, the pseudo-Tunisian* text derived from condition B/C is marked as the first iteration.

(3) Next, we trained an MSA2Ta (MSA to Tunisian) model, which serves as a pivot MT model. We pre-trained the model with the MSA-Ta* data of condition B/C and fine-tuned it using the MSA*-Ta data of condition A from step 2.

(4) Lastly, we input the MSA text of condition B/C to the MSA2Ta model for inference, generating the second iteration of the pseudo-Tunisian text (marked as pseudo-Tunisian**). We re-created the paired triple text data of Ta-MSA-En text by merging the pseudo-Tunisian** text with the primary MSA-English text from condition B/C.

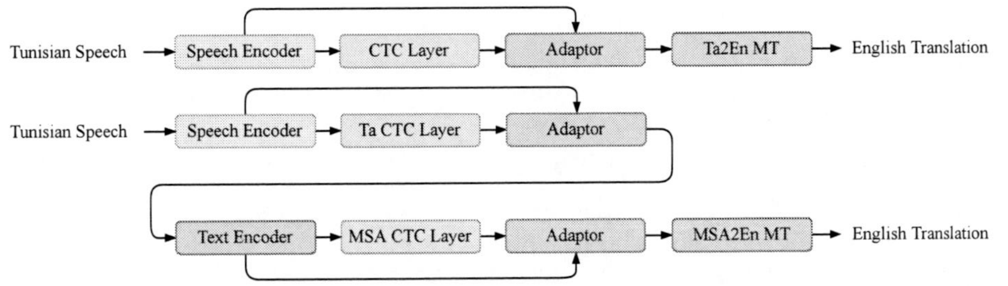

Figure 2: The top figure shows the SATE model (Xu et al., 2021), which implements a forward dialect transfer system from MSA to Tunisian through pre-training and fine-tuning techniques. The bottom part shows the Hybrid SATE model with a hierarchical text encoder, which can be used to reversely transfer from Tunisian to MSA.

3.3 End-to-end ST Model

The end-to-end ST approaches can mitigate issues of error propagation that often appears in low-resource scenarios. We developed an E2E ST system utilizing the SATE model (Xu et al., 2021) due to its effectiveness and simplicity for implementation, which is shown in Figure 2. In particular, we suggest two dialect transfer approaches for condition B/C, specifically the forward dialect transfer system from MSA to Tunisian and the reverse dialect transfer method from Tunisian to MSA.

3.3.1 Forward dialect transfer system

The forward dialect transfer system aims to transfer information from MSA to Tunisian by pre-training the ASR and MT models on the MSA dataset, respectively. These models are then fine-tuned using the Tunisian dataset to transfer from MSA to Tunisian. Note that the forward dialect transfer system is treated as a transfer of model parameters. In order to create an E2E ST system, we utilize the SATE model with pre-trained Tunisian ASR and MT models, followed by fine-tuning the SATE model with Tunisian ST dataset.

During training, the SATE model utilizes multi-task optimization, including the CTC loss of the source language $\mathcal{L}_{\text{CTC}}^{\text{Ta}}$, the cross-entropy loss for the target language $\mathcal{L}_{\text{CE}}^{\text{En}}$ and the knowledge distillation (KD) losses for both the source and target languages, i.e., $\mathcal{L}_{\text{KD}}^{\text{Ta}}$ and $\mathcal{L}_{\text{KD}}^{\text{En}}$. The overall loss function reads

$$\mathcal{L} = \lambda_1 \mathcal{L}_{\text{CTC}}^{\text{Ta}} + \lambda_2 \mathcal{L}_{\text{CE}}^{\text{En}} + \lambda_3 \mathcal{L}_{\text{KD}}^{\text{Ta}} + \lambda_4 \mathcal{L}_{\text{KD}}^{\text{En}}, \quad (1)$$

with four respective hyper weight parameters. The SATE model utilizes an adaptor to map speech features into the text feature space but suffers from inconsistent in-between sequence lengths. For this, we proposed a robust training method. Specifically, the Tunisian ASR model was first decoded by retaining both the repeated tokens and blank symbols of the CTC output. The resulting output was then combined with its corresponding English text to fine-tune the Ta2En MT model. The modified Ta2En MT model was well-suited to initialize the MT module of the SATE model.

3.3.2 Reverse dialect transfer system

It is a common issue that the Tunisian Arabic dialect is considered as being non-standardized at the linguistic level (Ben Abdallah et al., 2020). To address this, we proposed a reverse dialect transfer system that converts the Tunisian dialect to MSA, serving as a regularization of the dialect, which is illustrated in Figure 2. We modified the SATE model with a hierarchical text encoder (resulting in **Hybrid SATE**) to enable the reverse dialect transfer system. The proposed Hybrid SATE model primarily comprises a speech encoder, a Ta2MSA text encoder and an MSA2En MT module.

In order to initialize the model parameter for the Ta2MSA text encoder module in the Hybrid SATE model, we trained a Ta2MSA MT model. Based on the generated Ta-MSA* data in condition A and Ta**-MSA paired data in condition B/C from Section 3.2, we first pre-trained a Ta2MSA MT model with the Ta**-MSA data from condition B/C. Notably, the Ta2MSA MT model is equipped with a CTC layer on top of its encoder and is trained with an additional CTC loss for MSA. Then, we fine-tuned the model using the Ta-MSA* data from condition A. Finally, the encoder attached with a CTC layer of the Ta2MSA MT model was used to initialize the Ta2MSA text encoder.

The hybrid SATE model is optimized with an additional CTC loss for MSA, denoted as $\mathcal{L}_{\text{CTC}}^{\text{MSA}}$, resulting in the overall loss function

$$\begin{aligned}\mathcal{L} =& \lambda_1 \mathcal{L}_{\text{CTC}}^{\text{Ta}} + \lambda_2 \mathcal{L}_{\text{CE}}^{\text{En}} + \lambda_3 \mathcal{L}_{\text{KD}}^{\text{Ta}} + \lambda_4 \mathcal{L}_{\text{KD}}^{\text{En}} \\ &+ \lambda_5 \mathcal{L}_{\text{CTC}}^{\text{MSA}}. \end{aligned} \quad (2)$$

3.4 Model Ensemble Method

As training a single model can lead to implicit model bias, it is expected that a model ensemble decoding method can improve system robustness, especially in low-resource ST scenarios. We implemented synchronous decoding with multiple models and averaged the posterior probabilities predicted by each model at each time step. Consistent with single model decoding, the beam search decoding strategy was used with a beam size of 10. Subsequently, multiple models decoded the next tokens based on the same historical tokens. It should be noted that either E2E ST or MT models can be used for the model ensemble. Consequently, we can form ensembles of E2E ST and cascaded ST systems by using transcriptions from the ASR models as inputs for the MT models.

4 Experiments and results

4.1 Model Configurarions

ASR: For condition A, we employed the base model configurations, whereas the large model configurations were used for the experiments on condition B/C. Byte-Pair Encoding (BPE) (Sennrich et al., 2016b) subword segmentation with the Tunisian text was trained and the dictionary size was 1000. The detailed model configurations are given in Appendix A.

MT: We considered two encoder-decoder architectures for MT: the normal transformer model (Vaswani et al., 2017) and the macaron-like transformer model (Lu et al., 2019). The latter uses several FFN-attention-FFN layers instead of the attention-FFN layer used in the former. Our MT model has three variants based on the number of layers in the encoder and decoder and the type of model architecture: MT base, MT large, and MT macaron. For detailed model and dictionary sizes, please refer to Table 13 in Appendix A.

E2E ST: Since both the SATE and hybrid SATE models are initialized by pre-trained ASR and MT modules, the model parameters can be inferred straightforwardly from the aforementioned ASR and MT model settings.

4.2 Results

4.2.1 Automatic Speech Recognition

Table 4 shows the ASR performance in terms of word error rate (WER) of MSA. Among the three different model structures, the VGG-Conformer model achieves the best performance. It is clear that the performance can be further improved by using additional private data in condition C.

Model	B		C	
	dev	test	dev	test
VGG-Conformer	14.3	13.2	12.5	12
VGG-Transformer	16.6	15.5	14.2	13.3
GateCNN-Conformer	15.1	14.2	14.3	13.4

Table 4: The **WER** of the MSA MGB2 corpus.

Model	A		B		C	
	dev	test1	dev	test1	dev	test1
VGG-Conformer	48.5	55.4	45.4	53.2	42	49.7
VGG-Transformer	49.2	57	49	56.8	44.7	52.1
GateCNN-Conformer	46.6	53.4	47.2	53.7	46.1	53.3
Ensemble	**44.5**	**51.7**	**43.4**	**50.9**	**40.8**	**48.7**

Table 5: The **original WER** on Tunisian. Due to the non-standard orthography and grammar in Tunisian, the value of original WER is relatively higher than the normalized WER in Table 11.

The pre-trained MSA ASR models are fine-tuned using Tunisian data for dialect transfer in condition B/C. As shown in Table 5, the VGG-Conformer model continues to perform best among different single models in condition B/C, while the GateCNN-Conformer model performs best in condition A. We further ensemble the three single models mentioned above and get the final ASR model results for each condition[3]. This demonstrates that model ensemble can significantly improve the ASR performance, especially in condition A. Comparing the ASR results in condition B/C with that in condition A, we find that pre-training on high-resource MSA data can improve the ASR performance in low-resource Tunisian.

4.2.2 Cascaded Speech Translation

We will demonstrate the usage of the BTFT data via an ablation study on condition A. For condition B/C, we compare the quality of different versions of Ta-En pseudo data. Besides, we introduce two methods for robust training, called **constrained fine-tune** and **error adaptation fine-tune**.

BTFT and Constrained Fine-Tune Our baseline MT model of condition A is trained using the original Ta-En MT data. From Table 6, we see

[3]For model ensemble of condition B, the VGG Transformer and GateCNN-Conformer models are from condition A, and the VGG-Conformer model is from condition B.

Data & Method	MT		Cascaded ST	
	dev	test1	dev	test1
Baseline	26.3	23.0	19.4	16.7
BTFT data	28.2	24.0	20.3	17.1
+ Constrained FT	**28.5**	**24.3**	**20.6**	**17.3**

Table 6: The BLEU score of MT and cascaded MT experiments in condition A.

Model	Pretrain Model	MT BLEU	
		dev	test1
En2Ta	-	12.4	10.0
En2Ta	En2MSA	16.6	12.5
MSA2Ta*	-	8.3	6.8
MSA*2Ta	MSA2Ta*	12.1	9.6

Table 7: The BLEU score of different pivot MT models using Ta-MSA*-En triple text data of condition A.

that combining the training data with BTFT data brings a considerable performance gain for both MT and cascaded ST. The MT model trained by the BTFT data are further fine-tuned by the original true paired Ta-En data. In order to prevent excessive over-fitting while fine-tuning, we proposed a constrained fine-tune method, as depicted in Figure 3. Specifically, the student model is constrained by the teacher model using KL divergence loss to avoid catastrophic forgetting and over-fitting. In case of using the constrained fine-tune method, the MT training objective function is given by

$$\mathcal{L} = \mathcal{L}_{\mathrm{KL}} + \mathcal{L}_{\mathrm{CE}}. \quad (3)$$

Pseudo Ta-En paired data From Table 7, we see that the model initialized by a pre-trained model generates higher quality translations, i.e., higher quality pseudo-data. However, the performance comparison between the En2Ta model and the MSA*2Ta model may not be convincing since the input for the two models is different.

Comparing the performance of the Ta2En MT model is more appropriate to directly reveal the quality of the two versions of pseudo Ta-En data. In Table 8, it is clear that pre-training the MT model using Ta-En pseudo-data performs better than using MSA-En data. Moreover, the second version of Ta-En pseudo data outperforms the first when used for pre-training the Ta2En MT model. We believe that the MSA2Ta model is preferable for the En2Ta model due to the consistent use of MSA data during training and decoding. The En2Ta model employs English text from condition A for training, but uses

Model	MT		Cascaded ST	
	dev	test1	dev	test1
MSA2En-large	-	-	-	-
+ BTFT data FT	29.3	26.0	22.2	19.0
+ Constrained FT	30.1	26.2	22.5	19.2
Ta*2En-large	16.3	15.6	13.3	11.4
+ BTFT data FT	29.9	26.5	22.5	19.3
+ Constrained FT	30.4	26.6	22.8	19.5
Ta**2En-large	16.7	15.5	13.3	12.0
+ BTFT data FT	30.4	26.6	23.1	19.2
+ Constrained FT	**30.8**	**27.0**	**23.2**	**19.5**

Table 8: The BLEU score of the MT and the cascaded ST systems in condition C.

Model	MT		Cascaded ST	
	dev	test1	dev	test1
Condition A Best	28.5	24.3	20.6	17.3
+ Error Adapation FT	28.3	23.9	20.5	17.1
Condition C Best	30.8	27.0	23.2	19.5
+ Error Adapation FT	30.7	26.6	23.3	19.7

Table 9: The BLEU score of the MT and the cascaded ST systems in condition A/C when using error adaption fine-tune method.

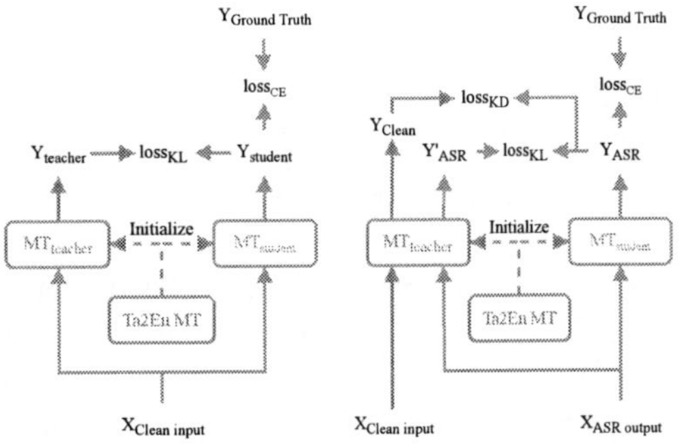

Figure 3: Left: Constrained Fine-tune, Right: Error Adaptation Fine-tune.

English text from condition B/C to generate pseudo-Tunisian text. In comparison, the MSA2Ta model consistently uses MSA data from condition B/C for both training and decoding.

Error Adaptation Fine-tune As shown in Figure 3, the error adaptation fine-tune method (Zhang et al., 2022) slightly adjusts the MT model to mitigate potential ASR prediction errors. This technique fine-tunes the Ta2En MT model using a combination of the ASR output text and the text from the target language. It is based on the constrained fine-tune method by incorporating true text from

Model		SATE			Hybrid-SATE	Ensemble
Speech encoder		Conformer		Transformer	Conformer	
MT module		MT	MT-Macaron	MT	MT	
A	dev	20.2	20.1	19.5	-	21.2
	test1	17.2	17.3	16.6	-	18.2
B	dev	22.0	22.0	20.9	22.0	23.4
	test1	19.0	19.1	18.0	18.9	20.3
C	dev	23.8	23.7	23.4	23.1	24.9
	test1	20.7	20.2	20.0	20.2	22.0

Table 10: The BLEU scores of our E2E ST in condition A/B/C, where the speech encoder and MT module represent the sub-modules, and MT and MT-Macaron represent MT large and MT macaron models, respectively.

the source language as soft-labels to enhance the training with the KD loss $\mathcal{L}_{\mathrm{KD}}$. The loss function for the error adaptation fine-tune method is given by

$$\mathcal{L} = 0.5\mathcal{L}_{\mathrm{KD}} + 0.5\mathcal{L}_{\mathrm{KL}} + \mathcal{L}_{\mathrm{CE}}. \quad (4)$$

From Table 9, we can observe that the error adaption fine-tune method enhances the performance of the cascaded ST system, albeit at a cost of MT performance decline. This reveals that this method is not effective in condition A but rather useful in condition B/C.

4.2.3 End-to-end Speech Translation

The SATE model can be instantiated in various structures by using different speech encoder and MT modules. Table 10 demonstrates that the conformer encoder outperforms the transformer encoder, showing an average improvement of 0.7 BLEU in condition A/B/C. For the different MT modules, the normal MT module is slightly better than the MT module in the macaroon form. Again, the results indicate model ensemble increases about 1.1 BLEU on the test1 set in condition A/B/C. The results of dialect transfer show an improvement for ST by 2.1 BLEU in condition B compared to condition A, and this is even greater in condition C, i.e., 3.8 BLEU. Additionally, the hybrid SATE model significantly improves the ST performance when used as a sub-model for model ensemble.

4.2.4 Model Ensemble

Table 11 presents the overall results of our ASR/MT/ST systems. The ASR results in terms of the normalized WER are derived from the model ensemble method in Table 5. It is worth noting that the ASR models are trained on original transcriptions but evaluated in a normalized form, which

#	data condition	A	B	C
	ASR	WER↓		
	JHU-IWSLT2022	44.8	43.8	44.5
A1	**ASR Ensemble**	43.0	42.9	40.6
	MT	BLEU↑		
	CMU-IWSLT2022	22.8	23.6	-
M1	MT base	23.8	26.5	26.5
M2	MT large	23.9	26.3	26.6
M3	MT macaron	23.8	26.6	26.9
M4	**MT Ensemble**	24.3	26.9	27.4
	Cascaded ST	BLEU↑		
	CMU-IWSLT2022	17.5	17.9	-
C1	A1 + M1	17.7	19.3	19.6
C2	A1 + M2	17.8	19.5	20.0
C3	A1 + M3	17.6	19.5	19.9
C4	**A1 + M4**	18.4	19.9	20.2
	E2E ST	BLEU↑		
	CMU-IWSLT2022 (Mix)	18.7	18.9	-
E1	Ensemble of SATE	18.2	20.0	21.3
E2	**Ensemble of SATE + Hybrid SATE**	-	20.3	22.0
	Cascaded and E2E ST	BLEU↑		
	CMU-IWSLT2022 (Ensemble)	19.2	19.5	-
E3	Ensemble of C4 + E1	19.0	20.5	21.4
E4	**Ensemble of C4 + E2**	-	20.8	21.9

Table 11: The overall results of our ASR/MT/ST systems on **test1** set. The hypothesis and reference are normalized before computing **normalized WER** in order to be consistent with last year's ASR system. We substituted the MT base model of condition C with the MT base model of condition B. JHU-IWSLT2022 and CMU-IWLST2022 are taken from (Yang et al., 2022) and (Yan et al., 2022), respectively.

may cause a performance drop. The ensemble of three single MT models achieves an average improvement of 0.4 BLEU in text translation and cascaded ST systems of condition A/B/C, compared to the best single model of each data condition. The results of the E2E ST systems are derived from Table 10. We find that the E2E ST system falls slightly behind the cascaded system in condition A but significantly surpasses it in condition B/C.

In the constrained condition, the primary system of our submission comprises an ensemble of cascaded and E2E ST models (see row **E3** of condition A). Additionally, for the unconstrained condition, we add the hybrid SATE model to the ensemble of cascaded and E2E ST models, which leads to a significant improvement of approximately 0.4 BLEU. Although the ensemble of cascaded and E2E ST system shows a 0.1 BLEU drop in condition C, it helps achieve the best performance in condition A/B. Therefore, the primary system of the submission for the unconstrained condition is in row **E4** of condition C. Moreover, we submit a contrastive system (i.e., row **E4** of condition B) to compare the performance without using private data.

5 Conclusion

This paper presents the methods and experimental results of the USTC team for the dialect ST (Tunisian Arabic to English) task in IWSLT 2023. The proposed forward and reverse dialect transfer methods, which were shown to be effective for augmenting text data and building hybrid SATE models. We utilized various model structures for implementing ASR, MT and ST tasks, and improved the robustness through model ensembling and error adaptation during training. The experiments showed a significant improvement in dialectal ST through the use of dialect transfer method. In unconstrained condition, our E2E ST system performs better than the cascaded ST system but is slightly less effective in constrained condition. Future studies might include the exploration of E2E ST models for unified modeling of multiple dialects (e.g., Tunisian, Egyptian) with MSA.

Acknowledgements

This work is supported by the National Natural Science Foundation of China (62101523), Hefei Municipal Natural Science Foundation (2022012) and USTC Research Funds of the Double First-Class Initiative (YD2100002008). We would like to thank Zhongyi Ye, Xinyuan Zhou and Ziqiang Zhang for valuable discussions and also thank Kevin Duh, Paul McNamee and Kenton Murray for organizing Tunisian Arabic to English track of the dialectal and low-resource speech translation shared task.

References

Milind Agarwal, Sweta Agrawal, Antonios Anastasopoulos, Ondřej Bojar, Claudia Borg, Marine Carpuat, Roldano Cattoni, Mauro Cettolo, Mingda Chen, William Chen, Khalid Choukri, Alexandra Chronopoulou, Anna Currey, Thierry Declerck, Qianqian Dong, Yannick Estève, Kevin Duh, Marcello Federico, Souhir Gahbiche, Barry Haddow, Benjamin Hsu, Phu Mon Htut, Hirofumi Inaguma, Dávid Javorský, John Judge, Yasumasa Kano, Tom Ko, Rishu Kumar, Pengwei Li, Xutail Ma, Prashant Mathur, Evgeny Matusov, Paul McNamee, John P. McCrae, Kenton Murray, Maria Nadejde, Satoshi Nakamura, Matteo Negri, Ha Nguyen, Jan Niehues, Xing Niu, Atul Ojha Kr., John E. Ortega, Proyag Pal, Juan Pino, Lonneke van der Plas, Peter Polák, Elijah Rippeth, Elizabeth Salesky, Jiatong Shi, Matthias Sperber, Sebastian Stüker, Katsuhito Sudoh, Yun Tang, Brian Thompson, Kevin Tran, Marco Turchi, Alex Waibel, Mingxuan Wang, Shinji Watanabe, and Rodolfo Zevallos. 2023. Findings of the IWSLT 2023 Evaluation Campaign. In *Proceedings of the 20th International Conference on Spoken Language Translation (IWSLT 2023)*. Association for Computational Linguistics.

Ahmed Ali, Peter Bell, James Glass, Yacine Messaoui, Hamdy Mubarak, Steve Renals, and Yifan Zhang. 2016. The mgb-2 challenge: Arabic multi-dialect broadcast media recognition. In *2016 IEEE Spoken Language Technology Workshop (SLT)*, pages 279–284. IEEE.

Najla Ben Abdallah, Saméh Kchaou, and Fethi Bougares. 2020. Text and speech-based Tunisian Arabic sub-dialects identification. In *Proceedings of the Twelfth Language Resources and Evaluation Conference*, pages 6405–6411, Marseille, France. European Language Resources Association.

Yann N Dauphin, Angela Fan, Michael Auli, and David Grangier. 2017. Language modeling with gated convolutional networks. In *International conference on machine learning*, pages 933–941. PMLR.

Alex Graves, Santiago Fernández, Faustino Gomez, and Jürgen Schmidhuber. 2006. Connectionist temporal classification: labelling unsegmented sequence data with recurrent neural networks. In *Proceedings of the 23rd international conference on Machine learning*, pages 369–376.

Anmol Gulati, James Qin, Chung-Cheng Chiu, Niki Parmar, Yu Zhang, Jiahui Yu, Wei Han, Shibo Wang, Zhengdong Zhang, Yonghui Wu, and Ruoming Pang. 2020. Conformer: Convolution-augmented Transformer for Speech Recognition. In *Proc. Interspeech 2020*, pages 5036–5040.

Hirofumi Inaguma, Shun Kiyono, Kevin Duh, Shigeki Karita, Nelson Yalta, Tomoki Hayashi, and Shinji Watanabe. 2020. ESPnet-ST: All-in-one speech translation toolkit. In *Proceedings of the 58th Annual Meeting of the Association for Computational Linguistics: System Demonstrations*, pages 302–311, Online. Association for Computational Linguistics.

Yoon Kim and Alexander M. Rush. 2016. Sequence-level knowledge distillation. In *Proceedings of the 2016 Conference on Empirical Methods in Natural Language Processing*, pages 1317–1327, Austin, Texas. Association for Computational Linguistics.

Yiping Lu, Zhuohan Li, Di He, Zhiqing Sun, Bin Dong, Tao Qin, Liwei Wang, and Tie-Yan Liu. 2019. Understanding and improving transformer from a multi-particle dynamic system point of view. *arXiv preprint arXiv:1906.02762*.

Myle Ott, Sergey Edunov, Alexei Baevski, Angela Fan, Sam Gross, Nathan Ng, David Grangier, and Michael Auli. 2019. fairseq: A fast, extensible toolkit for sequence modeling. *arXiv preprint arXiv:1904.01038*.

Daniel S. Park, William Chan, Yu Zhang, Chung-Cheng Chiu, Barret Zoph, Ekin D. Cubuk, and Quoc V. Le. 2019. SpecAugment: A Simple Data Augmentation Method for Automatic Speech Recognition. In *Proc. Interspeech 2019*, pages 2613–2617.

Matt Post. 2018. A call for clarity in reporting BLEU scores. In *Proceedings of the Third Conference on Machine Translation: Research Papers*, pages 186–191, Brussels, Belgium. Association for Computational Linguistics.

Rico Sennrich, Barry Haddow, and Alexandra Birch. 2016a. Improving neural machine translation models with monolingual data. In *Proceedings of the 54th Annual Meeting of the Association for Computational Linguistics (Volume 1: Long Papers)*, pages 86–96, Berlin, Germany. Association for Computational Linguistics.

Rico Sennrich, Barry Haddow, and Alexandra Birch. 2016b. Neural machine translation of rare words with subword units. In *Proceedings of the 54th Annual Meeting of the Association for Computational Linguistics (Volume 1: Long Papers)*, pages 1715–1725, Berlin, Germany. Association for Computational Linguistics.

Karen Simonyan and Andrew Zisserman. 2014. Very deep convolutional networks for large-scale image recognition. *arXiv preprint arXiv:1409.1556*.

Jörg Tiedemann and Santhosh Thottingal. 2020. OPUS-MT – building open translation services for the world. In *Proceedings of the 22nd Annual Conference of the European Association for Machine Translation*, pages 479–480, Lisboa, Portugal. European Association for Machine Translation.

Ashish Vaswani, Noam Shazeer, Niki Parmar, Jakob Uszkoreit, Llion Jones, Aidan N Gomez, Łukasz Kaiser, and Illia Polosukhin. 2017. Attention is all you need. *Advances in neural information processing systems*, 30.

Chen Xu, Bojie Hu, Yanyang Li, Yuhao Zhang, Shen Huang, Qi Ju, Tong Xiao, and Jingbo Zhu. 2021. Stacked acoustic-and-textual encoding: Integrating the pre-trained models into speech translation encoders. In *Proceedings of the 59th Annual Meeting of the Association for Computational Linguistics and the 11th International Joint Conference on Natural Language Processing (Volume 1: Long Papers)*, pages 2619–2630, Online. Association for Computational Linguistics.

Brian Yan, Patrick Fernandes, Siddharth Dalmia, Jiatong Shi, Yifan Peng, Dan Berrebbi, Xinyi Wang, Graham Neubig, and Shinji Watanabe. 2022. CMU's IWSLT 2022 dialect speech translation system. In *Proceedings of the 19th International Conference on Spoken Language Translation (IWSLT 2022)*, pages 298–307, Dublin, Ireland (in-person and online). Association for Computational Linguistics.

Jinyi Yang, Amir Hussein, Matthew Wiesner, and Sanjeev Khudanpur. 2022. JHU IWSLT 2022 dialect speech translation system description. In *Proceedings of the 19th International Conference on Spoken Language Translation (IWSLT 2022)*, pages 319–326, Dublin, Ireland (in-person and online). Association for Computational Linguistics.

Weitai Zhang, Zhongyi Ye, Haitao Tang, Xiaoxi Li, Xinyuan Zhou, Jing Yang, Jianwei Cui, Pan Deng, Mohan Shi, Yifan Song, Dan Liu, Junhua Liu, and Lirong Dai. 2022. The USTC-NELSLIP offline speech translation systems for IWSLT 2022. In *Proceedings of the 19th International Conference on Spoken Language Translation (IWSLT 2022)*, pages 198–207, Dublin, Ireland (in-person and online). Association for Computational Linguistics.

A Appendix. Model configurations

The detailed model configurations for ASR systems are as following:

- **Condition A:** The model configurations are almost identical to the ESPnet (Inaguma et al., 2020) baseline. There are 12-layer encoder and 6-layer decoder. The attention module of both the encoder and decoder comprises 256 hidden units and 4 attention heads. The size of the FFN module is 1024 for the encoder but 2048 for the decoder. We use two VGG blocks as the feature extractor for both the VGG-Conformer and the VGG-Transformer models. For the GateCNN-Conformer model, the feature extractor has a 6-layer GateCNN.

- **Condition B/C:** The model difference between the condition A and the condition B/C lies in the model size. For condition B/C, the attention module has 512 hidden units and 8 attention heads, and the size of FFN is 4096.

Condition	Training Stage	lr	Max-tokens	Warmup	Dropout rate	Training steps
A	Stage1: BTFT Pretrain	5e-4	12000	4000	0.3	120000
	Stage2: Constrained Fine-tune	-	4096	-	0.3	40000
B/C	Stage1: MSA-En Pretrain	1e-3	40000×8	4000	0.1	200000
	Stage2: Ta**-En Pretrain	5e-4	40000×8	None	0.1	20000
	Stage3: BTFT Fine-tune	4e-5	6144	4000	0.3	120000
	Stage4: Constrained Fine-tune	-	2048	-	0.3	80000
	Stage5: Error Adaptation Fine-tune	1e-5	4096	None	0.3	10000

Table 12: Hyper parameters in different stages ("-" means reuse from the former stage and "×" the GPU numbers).

Condition	A	B/C
Encoder dim	256	512
Encoder FFN dim	1024	2048
Encoder attn heads	4	8
Decoder dim	256	512
Decoder FFN dim	1024	2048
Decoder attn heads	4	8
Tunisian BPE units	1000	1000
MSA BPE units	-	32000
English BPE units	4000	32000

Table 13: The model sizes and dictionary sizes for MT training, where "attn" represents attention module.

#	A	B	C
test2		ASR WER↓	
IWSLT2022	43.8	42.9	41.5
A1	**40.8**	**40.5**	**39.3**
test2		ST BLEU↑	
IWSLT2022	20.4	20.8	18.7
E3	**20.5**	-	-
E4	-	**22.8**	**23.6**
test3		ASR WER↓	
A1	43.2	42.3	40.5
test3		ST BLEU↑	
E3	18.1	-	-
E4	-	20.2	21.1

Table 14: The overall results of our ASR/ST systems on **test2** set (IWSLT 2022 evaluation set) and **test3** set (IWSLT 2023 evaluation set).

For MT models, the 6-layer encoder and 6-layer decoder are used for both MT base and MT macaron models, but 12-layer encoder and 6-layer decoder for MT large model. The details of the MT system are summarized in Table13.

B Appendix. Training and Inference

ASR: We used the fairseq tool (Ott et al., 2019) for training and inference. During training, we used a dropout rate of 0.3, set the label-smoothing rate to 0.1 and used a CTC loss weight of 0.3. The max tokens and max sentences per batch were 32000 and 120, respectively. We used the inverse square learning rate schedule for training, with a learning rate of 1e-3 and warmup steps of 8000 for condition A. For condition B/C, we pre-trained with MSA ASR data and used a learning rate of 1e-3 and warmup steps of 30000. We used a learning rate of 2e-4 and warmup steps of 8000 while fine-tuning with in-domain Tunisian ASR data. The models were optimized through the Adam optimizer with $\beta_1 = 0.9, \beta_2 = 0.98$. During inference, we used an attention-based decoding strategy with a beam size of 10. We averaged the model parameters of 5 best model based on the WER on the dev set.

MT: The MT model training was also conducted using the fairseq toolkit. We conducted all training stages on the NVIDIA A40 GPU, varying the specific GPU number depending on the stage. Different training methods and hyper-parameters were used for optimal results depending on the condition, where we classified them into condition A and B/C. Specifically, we divided our training method into several stages, see Table 12. In Stage2 and Stage5 of condition B/C, the number of training steps is significantly lower than other stages. This was because the model had a tendency to overfit quickly during these stages; hence learning rate warmup method was not used during training. During inference, the beam size of decoding is 10. We used the official sacrebleu tool (Post, 2018) to calculate the normalized case-insensitive BLEU score. We averaged the model parameters of 5 best models based on the BLEU score on the dev set.

E2E ST: The hyper-parameters of the model training and inference are almost consistent with those used for ASR. The knowledge distillation weight (KD) for ASR is set to 0.2 but 0.3 for MT. The CTC loss weight for the speech encoder is set to 0.2 while it is 1.2 for the Ta2MSA text encoder of hybrid SATE. Note that the CTC loss weight for the Ta2MSA text encoder is much larger because translating Tunisian to MSA with pseudo Ta-MSA MT data is challenging.

C Appendix. Official Evaluation Results

The official evaluation results of our submitted systems on both test2 and test3 sets (both being blind tests) are summarized in Table 14. Our submissions outperformed last year's best performance in all data conditions (constrained and unconstrained) for both ASR and ST evaluations (e.g, see the results of test2 set).

KIT's Multilingual Speech Translation System for IWSLT 2023

Danni Liu, Thai Binh Nguyen, Sai Koneru, Enes Yavuz Ugan, Ngoc-Quan Pham, Tuan-Nam Nguyen, Tu Anh Dinh, Carlos Mullov, Alexander Waibel, Jan Niehues
Karlsruhe Institute of Technology
firstname.lastname@kit.edu

Abstract

Many existing speech translation benchmarks focus on native-English speech in high-quality recording conditions, which often do not match the conditions in real-life use-cases. In this paper, we describe our speech translation system for the multilingual track of IWSLT 2023, which focuses on the translation of scientific conference talks. The test condition features accented input speech and terminology-dense contents. The tasks requires translation into 10 languages of varying amounts of resources. In absence of training data from the target domain, we use a retrieval-based approach (kNN-MT) for effective adaptation (+0.8 BLEU for speech translation). We also use adapters to easily integrate incremental training data from data augmentation, and show that it matches the performance of re-training. We observe that cascaded systems are more easily adaptable towards specific target domains, due to their separate modules. Our cascaded speech system outperforms its end-to-end counterpart on scientific talk translation, although their performance remains similar on TED talks.

1 Introduction

This paper summarizes Karlsruhe Institute of Technology's speech translation system for the multilingual track of IWSLT 2023 (Agarwal et al., 2023). In this track, the task is to translate scientific talks in English into 10 languages: Arabic (ar), Chinese (zh), Dutch (nl), French (fr), German (de), Japanese (ja), Persian/Farsi (fa), Portuguese (pt), Russian (ru), Turkish (tr). The talks are from presentations in the 60th Annual Meeting of the Association for Computational Linguistics (ACL 2022).

Translating scientific talks presents several challenges. On the *source* side, most speakers are non-native, and the recording conditions often vary. This requires acoustic robustness to accents and noise. On the *target* side, domain-specific terminologies are frequently used, calling for accurate translation of these words that rarely occur in the training data. The styles of the talks, e.g. formality, also differ from other domains. As no training data from the same domain is provided, effective few-shot or zero-shot adaptation is crucial.

As the task focuses on *one-to-many* translation, it is also an interesting testbed for whether multilinguality improves speech translation quality. For text-to-text translation, the gain from multilinguality is mostly concentrated in *many-to-one* translation (Aharoni et al., 2019; Fan et al., 2021), i.e., multilinguality on the source side. In contrast, for *X-to-many* translation, it remains unclear whether incorporating *more target languages* improves translation quality.

In this system description paper, we present cascaded and end-to-end systems for the English-to-many speech translation task. We leverage pretrained models, including WavLM (Chen et al., 2022), mBART50 (Tang et al., 2020), and DeltaLM (Ma et al., 2021). The systems do not use additional data beyond the allowed corpora, and therefore fall under the *constrained* data condition.

For the cascaded system, to handle the unique style of scientific talks, we use kNN-MT (Khandelwal et al., 2021) to bias the output generation towards the target domain. Moreover, as no target monolingual data is provided, we use data diversification (Nguyen et al., 2020) to enrich the existing parallel data. We also use adapters (Rebuffi et al., 2017; Bapna and Firat, 2019) as a lightweight approach for incremental learning and language adaptation. For the ASR model, we improve over last year's performance by using a more recent audio encoder (Chen et al., 2022) and adding a dedicated decoder. To adapt the ASR system to the target domain, we use n-gram re-weighting and synthesized data for the target domain. For the end-to-end system, we use our machine translation model for knowledge distillation. We also ensemble models trained with and without synthesized speech data.

Proceedings of the 20th International Conference on Spoken Language Translation (IWSLT 2023), pages 113–122
July 13-14, 2023 ©2023 Association for Computational Linguistics

Our main findings are as follow:

- For cascaded ST systems, we can effectively adapt the model towards a target domain/style using kNN-MT (Khandelwal et al., 2021). A datastore as small as a few hundred sentence pairs was sufficient for achieving consistent gains (avg. +0.8 BLEU over 10 languages).
- Besides the common use-case of adding language-specific capacity, adapters (Bapna and Firat, 2019) is also an effective method when subsequently adding training data. Empirically, we show it matches the performance of re-training on all new data.
- For ASR, lexical constraints for domain adaptation are more easily integrated in CTC models. For encoder-decoder model, the control could be achieved by TTS-synthesized source speech, but it requires more careful tuning.

2 Data and Preprocessing

After describing the evaluation data (§2.1), we outline the training data and preprocessing steps for our automatic speech recognition (ASR; §2.2), machine translation (MT; §2.3), casing/punctuation restoration (§2.4), and speech translation (ST; §2.5) models.

2.1 Development and Test Data

In the multilingual track, the testing condition is scientific conference talks. Therefore, we primarily rely on the ACL development (dev) set for validation. It consists of English transcripts of the talks and translations into the 10 target languages. The systems are then evaluated on a blind test set. The dev and test sets consist of 5 talks each. The paper abstracts for all talks are available in English. The talks are pre-segmented. In all experiments, we use the given segmentation.

We also report performance on tst-COMMON of MuST-C (Di Gangi et al., 2019), tst2019 and tst2020 from previous years' evaluations (Anastasopoulos et al., 2021, 2022).

An overview of the development and test data is in Table 1.

Dev/Test set	Hours	# Utterances	Domain
ACL dev	1.0	468	ACL conference talks
tst-COMMON	4.9	2823	TED talks
tst2019	4.8	2279	TED talks
tst2020	4.1	1804	TED talks

Table 1: Overview of development and test data.

2.2 Speech Recognition Data

For the ASR training, we use Common Voice (Ardila et al., 2020), LibriSpeech (Panayotov et al., 2015), MuST-C v2 (Di Gangi et al., 2019), TED-LIUM v3 (Hernandez et al., 2018), and VoxPopuli (Wang et al., 2021). The data overview is in Table 2.

Corpus / Data Source	Hours	# Utterances
Common Voice	1667	1225k
LibriSpeech	963	281k
MuST-C v2	482	251k
TED-LIUM v3	452	268k
VoxPopuli	501	177k
TTS	7284	4.7M

Table 2: ASR data overview.

Synthesized Speech Data To adapt the ASR model to the ACL talks, we add synthesized speech created by a text-to-speech (TTS) model. Specifically, from the MT bitext English side (Table 3), we select sentences similar to the ACL domain based on similarity with the provided ACL dev bitext and abstracts. Inspired by data selection strategies for MT (Eck et al., 2005; Koneru et al., 2022), we use n-gram overlap as similarity metric. 4.7M sentences are selected and then synthesized to speech by a VITS (Kim et al., 2021) model trained on MuST-C. The synthesized data amount is shown in the last row of Table 2.

2.3 Machine Translation Data

The MT training data include the following text-to-text translation corpora: Europarl v7 and v10 (Koehn, 2005), NewsCommentary v16, OpenSubtitles v2018 (Lison and Tiedemann, 2016), Tatoeba (Tiedemann, 2012), and ELRC-CORDIS_News, JParaCrawl (Morishita et al., 2022) for Japanese, and TED2020 (Reimers and Gurevych, 2020) for German[1]. We also include the text translation part of the following ST corpora: MuST-C (Di Gangi et al., 2019), CoVoST v2 (Wang et al., 2020), and Europarl-ST (Iranzo-Sánchez et al., 2020). The aggregated data amount per language is summarized in the "Original" column of Table 3.

[1]This dataset has deplication with past evaluation sets: tst2019 tst2020 and tst-COMMON. The deplications were removed prior to training.

	Original	After Diversification	
Lang.	# sent. (M)	# sent. (M)	# tokens (M)
ar	26.0	65.2	865.0
zh	11.2	21.5	254.3
nl	33.1	82.1	1162.7
fr	38.9	91.6	1427.8
de	23.0	54.4	860.0
ja*	2.6	27.2	832.7
fa	5.8	11.3	162.1
pt	29.0	72.3	1024.3
ru	22.1	51.5	685.3
tr	36.7	89.7	1021.2
Total	228.4	566.8	8295.4

Table 3: MT data overview. *: For ja, the original data of 2.6M sentences did not include JParaCrawl, which was announced later as allowed data.

As preprocessing, we perform truecasing, deduplication, length ratio filtering, and histogram filtering using the statistics by Fan et al. (2021). Then we perform subword segmentation using Sentencepiece (Kudo and Richardson, 2018) based on the vocabulary of mBART50 (Tang et al., 2020).

Data Diversification Different from last years' shared tasks (Anastasopoulos et al., 2021, 2022), no monolingual (non-English) data is provided. This means conventional data augmentation techniques like backward translation are not directly applicable. On the other hand, forward translation from existing English monolingual data may introduce undesirable errors in the translation targets, especially on lower-resource languages. In this light, we use data diversification (Nguyen et al., 2020), a data augmentation method that enriches existing parallel data by forward and backward translating the training bitext. As the model has seen the parallel data in training, the synthetic translations are expected to have relatively high quality. Moreover, either the source or target side of the synthetic data is from the original bitext. The diversified data amount after deduplication is shown in Table 3. Here we perform one round of forward and backward translation, as Nguyen et al. (2020) have empirically shown further rounds do not lead to substantial gains.

2.4 Casing/Punctuation Restoration Data

The ASR outputs are lower-cased and unpunctuated, while the MT model expects cased and punctuated inputs. We randomly sample 1.5 million English sentences from the MT training data (Table 3), and remove the casing and punctuation marks as training source data. We then train a model to restore the casing and punctuation marks.

2.5 Speech Translation Data

The speech translation data are shown in Table 4. We additionally use our trained MT model to create forward translations based on the following transcript-only datasets: Common Voice, TEDLIUM, and VoxPopuli. The TTS data described in §2.2 is also used.

Lang.	Corpus / Data Source	Hours	# Utterances
ar	CoVoST	429	289k
	MuST-C	463	212k
	TTS	283	203k
zh	CoVoST	429	289k
	MuST-C	596	358k
	TTS	204	183k
nl	MuST-C	434	248k
	europarl-ST	75	32k
	TTS	1138	713k
fr	MuST-C	485	275k
	europarl-ST	76	32k
	TTS	1768	998k
de	CoVoST	429	289k
	MuST-C	440	269k
	europarl-ST	77	33k
	TTS	1891	779k
ja	CoVoST	429	289k
	MuST-C	541	329k
	TTS	73	56k
fa	CoVoST	429	289k
	MuST-C	347	182k
	TTS	89	88k
pt	MuST-C	377	206k
	europarl-ST	75	32k
	TTS	1678	639k
ru	MuST-C	482	265k
	TTS	331	331k
tr	CoVoST	429	289k
	MuST-C	446	236k
	TTS	428	511k
all	Common Voice	1488	948k
	TEDLIUM	453	268k
	VoxPopuli	502	177k

Table 4: ST data overview. The last section "all" indicates forward translated synthetic targets from transcript-only corpora, which are available for all 10 languages.

3 Cascaded System

For the cascaded system, we introduce our ASR (§3.1) and MT (§3.2) models.

3.1 Automatic Speech Recognition Module

Baseline Models The first baseline is our ASR model for last year's offline track (Pham et al., 2022). It is a Wav2vec 2.0 (Baevski et al., 2020) with LARGE configuration pretrained on 960 hours of Librispeech data. This year, after seeing initial favourable results compared to Wav2vec, we opt for WavLM (Chen et al., 2022) as audio encoder. We use the LARGE configuration with 24 layers. We use the mBART50 (Tang et al., 2020) decoder along with the WavLM encoder. As the ASR model only needs to transcribe English[2], we trim the mBART50 vocabulary from 256k down to 62k tokens by removing all non-alphabetic tokens.

In-Domain TTS Data We also use the synthesized TTS data. Compared to the same model without TTS data, the word error rate (WER) improves from 11.6% to 10.7% on ACL dev, but degrades from 8.4% to 9.0% on the TEDLIUM test set. There are two potential explanations: First, the noisy TTS speech may be helpful for handling the non-native utterances prominent in the ACL dev set. Second, the target side of the TTS data is more relevant to the ACL domain, as we selected them based on n-gram overlap with ACL data. This in turn improves ASR performance on the ACL dev set.

As shown in Table 5, compared to last year's submission, this year's ASR model achieves consistent gains across domains on ACL dev, tst-COMMON, and tst2020.

Model	ACL dev	tstCom.	tst2020
ASR 2022 (Pham et al., 2022)	12.5	5.4	5.6
WavLM + mBART50	10.7	3.9	4.8

Table 5: ASR results in WER(↓) in comparison to our submission last year (Pham et al., 2022) which used Wav2vec trained with CTC and a 5-gram LM. By using WavLM audio encoder and the mBART decoder, we achieve consistent gains across domains (ACL and TED, i.e., tst*).

Language Model (LM) Adaptation Aside from using TTS data, we also investigate other methods to adapt towards the ACL domain using the provided paper abstracts. On preliminary experiments with Connectionist Temporal Classification (CTC) + n-gram LM models, we integrate ACL abstract 5-grams statistics into the language models. As shown in the upper section of Table 6, this improves on ACL dev (WER 13.8% $\rightarrow$ 13.0%) while preserving the performance on TED talks (tst-COMMON WER stays at 7.6%).

[2]BART, the English-only predecessor of mBART, is not among the allowed pretrained models.

As our final system is an encoder-decoder model (WavLM + mBART50), adapting the LM alone is less straightforward. We create pseudo ASR training data with ACL data on the transcript side. Specifically, we use our TTS model to synthesize speech from the ACL dev and test abstracts. As the amount of ACL abstract data is very limited (less than 100 sentences in total), we heavily upsampled them, so that they consist of 60% of the training data. As shown in the lower section of Table 6, this leads to a minor improvement of WER for ACL dev. However, the gain does not carry over to ST performance when later cascading with our MT model. Therefore, our final ASR system did not use the abstracts. The lack of improvement could be related to the low amount of ACL abstract data, which requires heavy upsampling of the TTS data, and as a result hinders the ability of transcribing real speech.

The contrast between the two sets of experiments may be related to diminishing gains as WER improves, i.e., for the Wav2vec + CTC + LM model, gaining over a WER of 13.8% is easier than starting from a 10.7% WER. Another interpretation of the difference could be that adding specific constraints to "end-to-end" ASR models is more challenging than the counterparts with separate LMs.

Model	ACL dev	tst-COMMON
Wav2vec + CTC + 5-gram	13.8	7.6
+ ACL abstract 5-gram	13.0	7.6
WavLM + mBART50	10.7	3.9
+ ACL abstract TTS (upsampled)	10.5	4.3

Table 6: ASR adaptation results in WER(↓). On preliminary experiments with Wav2vec + CTC + LM models, we improve ASR performance on ACL dev by integrating n-gram statistics from the ACL abstracts. For the WavLM + mBART 50 model, adding synthesized audio-transcript data based ACL dev abstracts does not give consistent gain.

Casing/Punctuation Restoration We take a sequence-to-sequence approach to the casing and punctuation restoration problem. Specifically, we train a punctuation model initializing from DeltaLM-base (Ma et al., 2021) to restore the casing and punctuation information, using the training data described in §2.4.

3.2 Machine Translation Module

Baseline Model We start with the pretrained DeltaLM (Ma et al., 2021) with LARGE configura-

ID	ACL dev (en→X)											TED (en→de)	
	de	ja	zh	ar	nl	fr	fa	pt	ru	tr	Avg.	tst2019	tst2020
From ground-truth transcripts (**MT alone**)													
(1) base	39.8	44.2	47.4	30.4	45.7	48.9	23.6	51.1	19.5	22.9	37.4	29.5	32.9
(2) data divers. all	41.6	44.5	49.8	33.6	50.7	51.1	25.4	52.5	21.5	24.6	39.5	30.0	33.7
(3) (1) + data divers.; adapter	41.4	45.8	48.8	33.3	49.8	51.5	25.2	54.1	21.9	24.1	39.6	29.5	33.2
(4) ensemble (2) + (3)	41.7	46.1	49.6	33.7	50.8	52.1	25.9	54.3	23.1	24.8	40.2	30.4	33.7
(5) (4) + kNN-MT	43.7	47.3	49.8	35.4	52.3	52.8	27.2	55.3	23.9	27.1	41.5	30.4	33.4
From ASR outputs (**cascaded ST**)													
(1) base	34.3	38.2	41.6	25.3	36.6	39.9	19.1	40.7	16.7	18.9	31.1	26.5	28.0
(2) data divers. all	35.4	38.6	44.3	26.8	39.2	41.5	20.5	42.6	18.7	19.5	32.7	27.0	29.3
(3) (1) + data divers.; adapter	35.5	39.0	43.6	26.4	38.9	41.9	20.2	43.0	19.3	19.6	32.7	26.7	28.3
(4) ensemble (2) + (3)	36.1	39.8	44.4	26.9	39.8	42.3	20.7	43.5	19.2	19.7	33.2	26.9	28.7
(5) (4) + kNN-MT	36.8	40.2	44.6	28.2	40.8	42.0	21.8	44.5	19.7	21.1	34.0	26.9	28.5
End-to-end ST													
(6) WavLM + mBART50 decoder	31.7	29.2	40.7	25.0	36.7	40.5	19.5	43.0	16.9	18.5	30.2	27.0	29.3
(7) (6) + TTS	33.2	29.2	40.5	25.5	37.9	41.0	20.1	43.9	16.5	18.9	30.7	27.0	29.1
(8) ensemble (6) + (7)	34.0	29.9	41.7	25.5	38.2	42.0	20.2	44.4	18.3	20.2	31.4	27.3	29.6

Table 7: MT and ST results in BLEU(↑).

tion. The pretrained model has 24 and 12 encoder and decoder Transformer layers respectively. It uses postnorm layer normalization. It is a fully multilingual model where all parameters are shared across languages. The target language tokens are prepended to the source target sentences. We use temperature-based sampling (Arivazhagan et al., 2019) with $\tau = 5.0$ to counteract the data imbalance between languages. When training, we use a relatively large effective batch size of 128k as preliminary experiments with smaller batch sizes showed more instabilities in training. This might be a side effect of the postnorm layer normalization (Nguyen and Salazar, 2019). The results of the baseline are shown in Row (1) of Table 7, with an average score of 37.4 BLEU[3] on ACL dev.

Data Diversification As motivated in §2.3, we use data diversification as an alternative data augmentation method in absence of monolingual target data for backtranslation. As data diversification needs forward and backward translations on the training data, we additionally train a 10-to-English model to create the backward translations. Row (2) of Table 7 shows the results after data diversification on all languages pairs. On average, this data augmentation approach improves MT quality by 2.1 BLEU and (37.4 → 39.5), and ST quality by 1.6 BLEU (31.1 → 32.7).

[3]By default using `tok.13a` from sacreBLEU (Post, 2018), except for zh and ja where we use `tok.zh` and `tok.ja-mecab-0.996-IPA`.

Adapters for Incremental Data Retraining on the new training data after diversification (Row (2) of Table 7) is time-consuming and costly. To adapt the initial model (Row (1) of Table 7) rapidly towards to the augmented data, we use adapters (Bapna and Firat, 2019; Philip et al., 2020). In this case, the adapters are target-language-specific. The adapters are inserted after each encoder and decoder layer. We initialize from the trained baseline (Row (1) in Table 7), freeze trained parameters and update the adapters only. We use the efficient implementation from Baziotis et al. (2022). As shown in Row (3) of Table 7, only training the adapters on the new diversified training data performs on par with the re-training setup in Row (2) (39.6 on MT and 32.7 on ST on average for ACL dev). These results demonstrate that adapters are suitable for fast and effective incremental learning when additional training data emerges later.

To our surprise, adding adapters to the model trained with full data diversification (Row (2) from Table 7) does not bring further gain. A similar observation was reported by Pires et al. (2023), who opted for training the full network from scratch along with adapters instead. In our case, it therefore would be interesting to see the impact of training on data diversification with adapters from scratch.

Multilingual vs Bilingual To investigate the impact of interference from multiple target languages, in preliminary experiments, we also compare the multilingual and bilingual translation performance for selected language pairs. As shown in Table 8, compared to bilingual models, the multilingual model lags behind especially on higher-resource languages. Adding the adapters partly closes this gap. Note the score difference to main result table (Table 7) is because the preliminary experiments did not fully use diversified data for all languages.

Model	ACL dev			tst-COMMON		
	en-de	en-ru	en-fa	en-de	en-ru	en-fa
bilingual	41.0	20.0	24.2	34.3	22.7	16.0
multilingual	39.8	19.5	23.6	34.1	21.9	15.9
+ adapters	40.9	20.2	23.7	34.7	22.2	16.3

Table 8: Comparison of bilingual vs multilingual translation performance in BLEU (↑) on German (de), Russian (ru), Farsi (fa), which are high-, mid-, low-resource in the training data (Table 3). Multilingual system falls behind bilingual system, while adapters partly closes the gap. Note the score difference to main result table (Table 7) is because the experiments here did not fully use diversification.

Ensemble Although the models in Row (2) and (3) in Table 7 are trained on the same data and share the same base architecture, we expect their representations to be sufficiently different, as (3) additionally uses adapters. We therefore ensemble these two models. The results are in Row (4) of Table 7. On MT and ST, for ACL, ensembling shows an improvement of 0.6 and 0.5 BLEU respectively over the single models in Row (2) and (3). On TED, however, ensembling does not seem to impact the scores compared to the single models. One explanation is that the adapter model from Row (3) performs worse than its non-adapter counterpart (Row (2)) on TED, which limits the overall effectiveness of ensembling.

kNN-MT We also adapt the MT model to the target domain of scientific talks. A challenge is that we do not have sufficient training data to fully fine-tune the MT model towards the desired domain or style. In this case, we use kNN-MT (Khandelwal et al., 2021) to adapt the model at inference time. In kNN-MT, bitexts are passed through a trained MT model. For each target token, its decoder hidden state is stored in a datastore. At inference time, based on the current decoder hidden state, k candidate target tokens are retrieved from the datastore using a nearest neighbor lookup. The retrieved token distribution is then interpolated with the MT target distribution, which in turn generates the output tokens. Hyperparameters for kNN-MT include

Source (ASR output): ... in a zero shot evaluation setup, meaning that pre trained word embedding models are applied out of the box without any additional fine tuning **w/o kNN-MT** (Table 7 row (4)): ... in einer Null-Shot-Bewertungs-Setup (zero-shot evaluation setup), was bedeutet, dass vorgebildete (pre-educated) Wort-Einbettungsmodelle ohne zusätzliche Feinabstimmung direkt angewendet werden. **w/ kNN-MT** (Table 7 row (5)): ... in einer Null-Shot-Bewertung (zero-shot evaluation), was bedeutet, dass vortrainierte (pretrained) Wort-Einbettungsmodelle ohne zusätzliche Feinabstimmung direkt angewendet werden.
Source (ASR output): Hello. My name is Ramachandra, and I will present our paper. **w/o kNN-MT** (Table 7 row (4)): 你好 (Hello: addressing a single person),我叫拉玛钱德拉 我要发表 (publish)我们的论文 **w/ kNN-MT** (Table 7 row (5)): 大家好 (Hi all; addressing a group of audience),我叫拉玛钱德拉, 我要介绍 (introduce)我们的论文。

Table 9: Examples of kNN-MT improving translation quality for en→de (upper) and en→zh (lower). kNN-MT creates more accurate terminology translations ("pre trained" for en→de) and create more context-appropriate translation ("Hello" for en→zh).

the number of retrieved neighbors k, the temperature for smoothing the kNN distribution T, and the interpolation weight w.

In our experiments, we use systems (2) and (3) from Table 7 for creating the datastores. As different models' hidden states (which serve as keys in the datastore) also differ substantially, the datastore is MT-model-dependent. To use kNN-MT when ensembling systems (2) and (3), we therefore need two datastores for systems (2) and (3) respectively. The kNN-MT candidate tokens are interpolated with the output vocabulary distribtuion before the ensembling operation.

We use hyperparameters $k = 8$, $T = 50$, $w = 0.3$, after an initial search with $T \in [10, 50, 100], w \in [0.1, 0.3, 0.5]$. Our implementation mostly follows Zheng et al. (2021), which uses the FAISS toolkit (Johnson et al., 2019) for efficient kNN operations. Comparing the inference speed of system (4) and (5), with the same batch size of 64 sentences[4], using kNN-MT takes roughly 50% more time on a Nvidia Titan RTX GPU with 24GB memory.

Naively using all ACL dev bitext as datastore would lead the model to copying the oracle targets. To simulate the scenario on the blind test set, when

[4]System (5) requires more GPU memory than system (4). The latter would be able to use a larger batch size of 128 sentences.

translating the i-th talk, we use the other $j_{j \neq i} \in [n]$ talks' bitext as datastore, where n is the total number of talks.

As shown in Row (5) of Table 7, kNN-MT brings an additional gain of 1.3 BLEU on MT and 0.8 BLEU on ST. These results shows a datastore as small as hundreds of sentence pairs can be effectively used for inference-time domain adaptation.

Table 9 shows two examples of kNN-MT improving translation quality, apart from generic improvements in fluency and accuracy, in these examples kNN-MT also helps generate correct terminologies and context-appropriate greetings.

4 End-to-End System

For the end-to-end system, similar to our ASR model, after seeing initial favourable results of WavLM over Wav2vec, we choose WavLM as the audio encoder. Following last year's submission (Pham et al., 2022), we use the mBART50 decoder. The results are shown in Row (6) of Table 7. Contrasting Row (6) and (7) reveals that adding the TTS data does not substantially change ST performance. However, ensembling the two models trained with and without TTS data (Row (8)) improves over the single models (on average +0.7 for ACL, +0.4 for TED), despite them having the identical architecture.

Compared to the strongest cascaded system (Row (5)), the end-to-end system falls behind 2.6 BLEU on ACL dev. On TED, however, it appears to slightly outperform the cascaded system. One explanation is that the MT model of the cascaded system has not been separately adapted to TED texts (although parts of the full training data do cover TED data), which was shown essential in improving performance on TED test sets (Zhang et al., 2022; Pham et al., 2022). The end-to-end system, on the other hand, has seen a larger proportion of TED data in training (Table 4).

Similar to the previous year (Polák et al., 2022), we also adapt our end-to-end offline model for simultaneous track (Polák et al., 2023).

5 Conclusion

In this paper, we described our systems for the multilingual speech translation track of IWSLT 2023, which translates English speech into 10 target languages. To tackle the task of translating scientific conference talks, which feature non-native input speech and terminology-dense contents, our systems have several novelties. Lacking suitable training data for the target domain, we used kNN-MT for inference-time adaptation and showed an improvement of +0.8 BLEU for cascaded speech translation system. We also used adapters to integrate incremental data from augmentation, and achieved performance on-par with re-training on all data. In our experiments, we observed that cascaded systems are more easily adaptable towards desired target domains due to their separate modules. Our cascaded speech system outperforms its end-to-end counterpart on scientific talk translation, although their performance remains similar on TED talks. For future work, we are interested in the feasibility of applying the adaptation approaches shown effective on MT to end-to-end ST.

Acknowledgement We thank the anonymous reviewers for detailed and insightful feedback. Part of this work was performed on the HoreKa supercomputer funded by the Ministry of Science, Research and the Arts Baden-Württemberg and by the Federal Ministry of Education and Research of Germany. Part of this work was supported by the Federal Ministry of Education and Research of Germany under grant agreement 01EF1803B (RELATER).

References

Milind Agarwal, Sweta Agrawal, Antonios Anastasopoulos, Ondřej Bojar, Claudia Borg, Marine Carpuat, Roldano Cattoni, Mauro Cettolo, Mingda Chen, William Chen, Khalid Choukri, Alexandra Chronopoulou, Anna Currey, Thierry Declerck, Qianqian Dong, Yannick Estéve, Kevin Duh, Marcello Federico, Souhir Gahbiche, Barry Haddow, Benjamin Hsu, Phu Mon Htut, Hirofumi Inaguma, Dávid Javorský, John Judge, Yasumasa Kano, Tom Ko, Rishu Kumar, Pengwei Li, Xutai Ma, Prashant Mathur, Evgeny Matusov, Paul McNamee, John P. McCrae, Kenton Murray, Maria Nadejde, Satoshi Nakamura, Matteo Negri, Ha Nguyen, Jan Niehues, Xing Niu, Atul Ojha Kr., John E. Ortega, Proyag Pal, Juan Pino, Lonneke van der Plas, Peter Polák, Elijah Rippeth, Elizabeth Salesky, Jiatong Shi, Matthias Sperber, Sebastian Stüker, Katsuhito Sudoh, Yun Tang, Brian Thompson, Kevin Tran, Marco Turchi, Alex Waibel, Mingxuan Wang, Shinji Watanabe, and Rodolfo Zevallos. 2023. Findings of the IWSLT 2023 Evaluation Campaign. In *Proceedings of the 20th International Conference on Spoken Language Translation (IWSLT 2023)*. Association for Computational Linguistics.

Roee Aharoni, Melvin Johnson, and Orhan Firat. 2019. Massively multilingual neural machine translation. In *Proceedings of the 2019 Conference of the North*

American Chapter of the Association for Computational Linguistics: Human Language Technologies, Volume 1 (Long and Short Papers)*, pages 3874–3884, Minneapolis, Minnesota. Association for Computational Linguistics.

Antonios Anastasopoulos, Loïc Barrault, Luisa Bentivogli, Marcely Zanon Boito, Ondřej Bojar, Roldano Cattoni, Anna Currey, Georgiana Dinu, Kevin Duh, Maha Elbayad, Clara Emmanuel, Yannick Estève, Marcello Federico, Christian Federmann, Souhir Gahbiche, Hongyu Gong, Roman Grundkiewicz, Barry Haddow, Benjamin Hsu, Dávid Javorský, Věra Kloudová, Surafel Lakew, Xutai Ma, Prashant Mathur, Paul McNamee, Kenton Murray, Maria Nădejde, Satoshi Nakamura, Matteo Negri, Jan Niehues, Xing Niu, John Ortega, Juan Pino, Elizabeth Salesky, Jiatong Shi, Matthias Sperber, Sebastian Stüker, Katsuhito Sudoh, Marco Turchi, Yogesh Virkar, Alexander Waibel, Changhan Wang, and Shinji Watanabe. 2022. Findings of the IWSLT 2022 evaluation campaign. In *Proceedings of the 19th International Conference on Spoken Language Translation (IWSLT 2022)*, pages 98–157, Dublin, Ireland (in-person and online). Association for Computational Linguistics.

Antonios Anastasopoulos, Ondřej Bojar, Jacob Bremerman, Roldano Cattoni, Maha Elbayad, Marcello Federico, Xutai Ma, Satoshi Nakamura, Matteo Negri, Jan Niehues, Juan Pino, Elizabeth Salesky, Sebastian Stüker, Katsuhito Sudoh, Marco Turchi, Alexander Waibel, Changhan Wang, and Matthew Wiesner. 2021. FINDINGS OF THE IWSLT 2021 EVALUATION CAMPAIGN. In *Proceedings of the 18th International Conference on Spoken Language Translation (IWSLT 2021)*, pages 1–29, Bangkok, Thailand (online). Association for Computational Linguistics.

Rosana Ardila, Megan Branson, Kelly Davis, Michael Kohler, Josh Meyer, Michael Henretty, Reuben Morais, Lindsay Saunders, Francis M. Tyers, and Gregor Weber. 2020. Common voice: A massively-multilingual speech corpus. In *Proceedings of The 12th Language Resources and Evaluation Conference, LREC 2020, Marseille, France, May 11-16, 2020*, pages 4218–4222. European Language Resources Association.

Naveen Arivazhagan, Ankur Bapna, Orhan Firat, Dmitry Lepikhin, Melvin Johnson, Maxim Krikun, Mia Xu Chen, Yuan Cao, George F. Foster, Colin Cherry, Wolfgang Macherey, Zhifeng Chen, and Yonghui Wu. 2019. Massively multilingual neural machine translation in the wild: Findings and challenges. *CoRR*, abs/1907.05019.

Alexei Baevski, Yuhao Zhou, Abdelrahman Mohamed, and Michael Auli. 2020. wav2vec 2.0: A framework for self-supervised learning of speech representations. In *Advances in Neural Information Processing Systems 33: Annual Conference on Neural Information Processing Systems 2020, NeurIPS 2020, December 6-12, 2020, virtual.*

Ankur Bapna and Orhan Firat. 2019. Simple, scalable adaptation for neural machine translation. In *Proceedings of the 2019 Conference on Empirical Methods in Natural Language Processing and the 9th International Joint Conference on Natural Language Processing (EMNLP-IJCNLP)*, pages 1538–1548, Hong Kong, China. Association for Computational Linguistics.

Christos Baziotis, Mikel Artetxe, James Cross, and Shruti Bhosale. 2022. Multilingual machine translation with hyper-adapters. In *Proceedings of the 2022 Conference on Empirical Methods in Natural Language Processing*, pages 1170–1185, Abu Dhabi, United Arab Emirates. Association for Computational Linguistics.

Sanyuan Chen, Chengyi Wang, Zhengyang Chen, Yu Wu, Shujie Liu, Zhuo Chen, Jinyu Li, Naoyuki Kanda, Takuya Yoshioka, Xiong Xiao, Jian Wu, Long Zhou, Shuo Ren, Yanmin Qian, Yao Qian, Jian Wu, Michael Zeng, Xiangzhan Yu, and Furu Wei. 2022. Wavlm: Large-scale self-supervised pre-training for full stack speech processing. *IEEE J. Sel. Top. Signal Process.*, 16(6):1505–1518.

Mattia A. Di Gangi, Roldano Cattoni, Luisa Bentivogli, Matteo Negri, and Marco Turchi. 2019. MuST-C: a Multilingual Speech Translation Corpus. In *Proceedings of the 2019 Conference of the North American Chapter of the Association for Computational Linguistics: Human Language Technologies, Volume 1 (Long and Short Papers)*, pages 2012–2017, Minneapolis, Minnesota. Association for Computational Linguistics.

Matthias Eck, Stephan Vogel, and Alex Waibel. 2005. Low cost portability for statistical machine translation based on n-gram frequency and TF-IDF. In *Proceedings of the Second International Workshop on Spoken Language Translation*, Pittsburgh, Pennsylvania, USA.

Angela Fan, Shruti Bhosale, Holger Schwenk, Zhiyi Ma, Ahmed El-Kishky, Siddharth Goyal, Mandeep Baines, Onur Celebi, Guillaume Wenzek, Vishrav Chaudhary, Naman Goyal, Tom Birch, Vitaliy Liptchinsky, Sergey Edunov, Michael Auli, and Armand Joulin. 2021. Beyond english-centric multilingual machine translation. *The Journal of Machine Learning Research*, 22:107:1–107:48.

François Hernandez, Vincent Nguyen, Sahar Ghannay, Natalia A. Tomashenko, and Yannick Estève. 2018. TED-LIUM 3: Twice as much data and corpus repartition for experiments on speaker adaptation. In *Speech and Computer - 20th International Conference, SPECOM 2018, Leipzig, Germany, September 18-22, 2018, Proceedings*, volume 11096 of *Lecture Notes in Computer Science*, pages 198–208. Springer.

Javier Iranzo-Sánchez, Joan Albert Silvestre-Cerdà, Javier Jorge, Nahuel Roselló, Adrià Giménez, Albert Sanchís, Jorge Civera, and Alfons Juan. 2020.

Europarl-st: A multilingual corpus for speech translation of parliamentary debates. In *2020 IEEE International Conference on Acoustics, Speech and Signal Processing, ICASSP 2020, Barcelona, Spain, May 4-8, 2020*, pages 8229–8233. IEEE.

Jeff Johnson, Matthijs Douze, and Hervé Jégou. 2019. Billion-scale similarity search with GPUs. *IEEE Transactions on Big Data*, 7(3):535–547.

Urvashi Khandelwal, Angela Fan, Dan Jurafsky, Luke Zettlemoyer, and Mike Lewis. 2021. Nearest neighbor machine translation. In *9th International Conference on Learning Representations, ICLR 2021, Virtual Event, Austria, May 3-7, 2021*. OpenReview.net.

Jaehyeon Kim, Jungil Kong, and Juhee Son. 2021. Conditional variational autoencoder with adversarial learning for end-to-end text-to-speech. In *Proceedings of the 38th International Conference on Machine Learning, ICML 2021, 18-24 July 2021, Virtual Event*, volume 139 of *Proceedings of Machine Learning Research*, pages 5530–5540. PMLR.

Philipp Koehn. 2005. Europarl: A parallel corpus for statistical machine translation. In *Proceedings of Machine Translation Summit X: Papers*, pages 79–86, Phuket, Thailand.

Sai Koneru, Danni Liu, and Jan Niehues. 2022. Cost-effective training in low-resource neural machine translation. *CoRR*, abs/2201.05700.

Taku Kudo and John Richardson. 2018. SentencePiece: A simple and language independent subword tokenizer and detokenizer for neural text processing. In *Proceedings of the 2018 Conference on Empirical Methods in Natural Language Processing: System Demonstrations*, pages 66–71, Brussels, Belgium. Association for Computational Linguistics.

Pierre Lison and Jörg Tiedemann. 2016. OpenSubtitles2016: Extracting large parallel corpora from movie and TV subtitles. In *Proceedings of the Tenth International Conference on Language Resources and Evaluation (LREC'16)*, pages 923–929, Portorož, Slovenia. European Language Resources Association (ELRA).

Shuming Ma, Li Dong, Shaohan Huang, Dongdong Zhang, Alexandre Muzio, Saksham Singhal, Hany Hassan Awadalla, Xia Song, and Furu Wei. 2021. Deltalm: Encoder-decoder pre-training for language generation and translation by augmenting pretrained multilingual encoders. *CoRR*, abs/2106.13736.

Makoto Morishita, Katsuki Chousa, Jun Suzuki, and Masaaki Nagata. 2022. JParaCrawl v3.0: A large-scale English-Japanese parallel corpus. In *Proceedings of the Thirteenth Language Resources and Evaluation Conference*, pages 6704–6710, Marseille, France. European Language Resources Association.

Toan Q. Nguyen and Julian Salazar. 2019. Transformers without tears: Improving the normalization of self-attention. In *Proceedings of the 16th International Conference on Spoken Language Translation, IWSLT 2019, Hong Kong, November 2-3, 2019*. Association for Computational Linguistics.

Xuan-Phi Nguyen, Shafiq R. Joty, Kui Wu, and Ai Ti Aw. 2020. Data diversification: A simple strategy for neural machine translation. In *Advances in Neural Information Processing Systems 33: Annual Conference on Neural Information Processing Systems 2020, NeurIPS 2020, December 6-12, 2020, virtual.*

Vassil Panayotov, Guoguo Chen, Daniel Povey, and Sanjeev Khudanpur. 2015. Librispeech: An ASR corpus based on public domain audio books. In *2015 IEEE International Conference on Acoustics, Speech and Signal Processing, ICASSP 2015, South Brisbane, Queensland, Australia, April 19-24, 2015*, pages 5206–5210. IEEE.

Ngoc-Quan Pham, Tuan Nam Nguyen, Thai-Binh Nguyen, Danni Liu, Carlos Mullov, Jan Niehues, and Alexander Waibel. 2022. Effective combination of pretrained models - KIT@IWSLT2022. In *Proceedings of the 19th International Conference on Spoken Language Translation (IWSLT 2022)*, pages 190–197, Dublin, Ireland (in-person and online). Association for Computational Linguistics.

Jerin Philip, Alexandre Berard, Matthias Gallé, and Laurent Besacier. 2020. Monolingual adapters for zero-shot neural machine translation. In *Proceedings of the 2020 Conference on Empirical Methods in Natural Language Processing (EMNLP)*, pages 4465–4470, Online. Association for Computational Linguistics.

Telmo Pessoa Pires, Robin M. Schmidt, Yi-Hsiu Liao, and Stephan Peitz. 2023. Learning language-specific layers for multilingual machine translation. *CoRR*, abs/2305.02665.

Peter Polák, Danni Liu, Ngoc-Quan Pham, Jan Niehues, Alexander Waibel, and Ondřej Bojar. 2023. Towards efficient simultaneous speech translation: CUNI-KIT system for simultaneous track at IWSLT 2023. In *Proceedings of the 20th International Conference on Spoken Language Translation (IWSLT 2023)*, Toronto, Canada (in-person and online). Association for Computational Linguistics.

Peter Polák, Ngoc-Quan Pham, Tuan Nam Nguyen, Danni Liu, Carlos Mullov, Jan Niehues, Ondřej Bojar, and Alexander Waibel. 2022. CUNI-KIT system for simultaneous speech translation task at IWSLT 2022. In *Proceedings of the 19th International Conference on Spoken Language Translation (IWSLT 2022)*, pages 277–285, Dublin, Ireland (in-person and online). Association for Computational Linguistics.

Matt Post. 2018. A call for clarity in reporting BLEU scores. In *Proceedings of the Third Conference on*

Machine Translation: Research Papers, pages 186–191, Brussels, Belgium. Association for Computational Linguistics.

Sylvestre-Alvise Rebuffi, Hakan Bilen, and Andrea Vedaldi. 2017. Learning multiple visual domains with residual adapters. In *Advances in Neural Information Processing Systems 30: Annual Conference on Neural Information Processing Systems 2017, December 4-9, 2017, Long Beach, CA, USA*, pages 506–516.

Nils Reimers and Iryna Gurevych. 2020. Making monolingual sentence embeddings multilingual using knowledge distillation. In *Proceedings of the 2020 Conference on Empirical Methods in Natural Language Processing (EMNLP)*, pages 4512–4525, Online. Association for Computational Linguistics.

Yuqing Tang, Chau Tran, Xian Li, Peng-Jen Chen, Naman Goyal, Vishrav Chaudhary, Jiatao Gu, and Angela Fan. 2020. Multilingual translation with extensible multilingual pretraining and finetuning. *CoRR*, abs/2008.00401.

Jörg Tiedemann. 2012. Parallel data, tools and interfaces in OPUS. In *Proceedings of the Eighth International Conference on Language Resources and Evaluation (LREC'12)*, pages 2214–2218, Istanbul, Turkey. European Language Resources Association (ELRA).

Changhan Wang, Morgane Riviere, Ann Lee, Anne Wu, Chaitanya Talnikar, Daniel Haziza, Mary Williamson, Juan Pino, and Emmanuel Dupoux. 2021. VoxPopuli: A large-scale multilingual speech corpus for representation learning, semi-supervised learning and interpretation. In *Proceedings of the 59th Annual Meeting of the Association for Computational Linguistics and the 11th International Joint Conference on Natural Language Processing (Volume 1: Long Papers)*, pages 993–1003, Online. Association for Computational Linguistics.

Changhan Wang, Anne Wu, and Juan Miguel Pino. 2020. Covost 2: A massively multilingual speech-to-text translation corpus. *CoRR*, abs/2007.10310.

Weitai Zhang, Zhongyi Ye, Haitao Tang, Xiaoxi Li, Xinyuan Zhou, Jing Yang, Jianwei Cui, Pan Deng, Mohan Shi, Yifan Song, Dan Liu, Junhua Liu, and Lirong Dai. 2022. The USTC-NELSLIP offline speech translation systems for IWSLT 2022. In *Proceedings of the 19th International Conference on Spoken Language Translation (IWSLT 2022)*, pages 198–207, Dublin, Ireland (in-person and online). Association for Computational Linguistics.

Xin Zheng, Zhirui Zhang, Junliang Guo, Shujian Huang, Boxing Chen, Weihua Luo, and Jiajun Chen. 2021. Adaptive nearest neighbor machine translation. In *Proceedings of the 59th Annual Meeting of the Association for Computational Linguistics and the 11th International Joint Conference on Natural Language Processing (Volume 2: Short Papers)*, pages 368–374, Online. Association for Computational Linguistics.

The BIGAI Offline Speech Translation Systems for IWSLT 2023 Evaluation

Zhihang Xie
Beijing Institute of General Artificial Intelligence
zhihangxie@gmail.com

Abstract

This paper describes the BIGAI's submission to IWSLT 2023 Offline Speech Translation task on three language tracks from English to Chinese, German and Japanese. The end-to-end systems are built upon a Wav2Vec2 model for speech recognition and mBART50 models for machine translation. An adapter module is applied to bridge the speech module and the translation module. The CTC loss between speech features and source token sequence is incorporated during training. Experiments show that the systems can generate reasonable translations on three languages. The proposed models achieve BLEU scores of 22.3, 10.7 and 33.0 on tst2023 en→de, en→ja and en→zh TED datasets. It is found that the performance is decreased by a significant margin on complex scenarios like presentations and interviews.

1 Introduction

Speech translation aims to solve the problem of translating speech waveform in source language into written text in target language. Cascade systems decompose the problem into automatic speech recognition (ASR) to transcribe source speech into source text and machine translation (MT) to translate source text into target text (Wang et al., 2021b; Zhang et al., 2022a). It is clear that such architecture has the advantage of ensembling results from state-of-the-art (SOTA) ASR models and MT models and the disadvantages of accumulating subsystem errors and discarding paralinguistic features. Recent end-to-end speech translation (E2E ST) systems have shown the potential to outperform cascade systems (Hrinchuk et al., 2022; Shanbhogue et al., 2022). However, due to the lack of high-quality parallel training data, it is difficult to quantify the gap between the two categories.

Inspired by Zhang et al.'s (2022b) work, this submission explores various techniques to address problems in speech translation. 1) Perform fine-grained data filtering by calculating WERs for speech data and alignment scores for translation data. 2) Apply a straightforward split-and-merge method to split long audio clips into short segments. 3) Employ a three-stage training strategy to concatenate the finetuned speech module and the translation module. 4) Incorporate connectionist temporal classification (CTC) loss to leverage the divergence between speech features and source token sequences (Graves et al., 2006). Experiments are carried out to perform speech translation at sentence level and corpus level. The performance of the three PT36 models is finally evaluated on the tst2023 datasets with automatic metrics.

The rest of this paper is organized as follows. Section 2 describes how speech data and translation data are processed in the experiments. Section 3 explains how finetuned models are assembled to perform speech translation on all three languages. Section 4 illustrates experiment setups, results and analysis. Section 5 concludes the submission.

2 Data Processing

2.1 Speech Corpora

Under the constrained condition, there are five speech datasets used to train ASR models, namely LibriSpeech (Panayotov et al., 2015), Mozilla Common Voice v11.0 (Ardila et al., 2019), MuSTC (Cattoni et al., 2021), TEDLIUM v3 (Hernandez et al., 2018) and VoxPopuli (Wang et al., 2021a). Statistics on each dataset are shown as Table 1. Note that only the MuSTC datasets are used to train speech translation systems on the three language tracks, English-to-German (en→de), English-to-Japanese (en→ja) and English-to-Chinese (en→zh).

In general, all speech files are unified to single channel 16kHz format. During training, utterances shorter than 0.2s or longer than 20s are removed. An extra W2V model with 24 Transformer layers is finetuned on the LibriSpeech dataset and calculates WER scores by performing CTC greedy decoding

Proceedings of the 20th International Conference on Spoken Language Translation (IWSLT 2023), pages 123–129
July 13-14, 2023 ©2023 Association for Computational Linguistics

Table 1: Statistics on speech datasets

Dataset	Utterances	Hours
CommonVoice	948,736	1,503.28
LibriSpeech	281,241	961.05
MuSTC en→de v3	269,851	440.18
MuSTC en→ja v2	328,637	541.04
MuSTC en→zh v2	358,852	596.20
TEDLIUM	268,263	453.81
VoxPopuli	182,466	522.60
Total, loaded	2,638,046	5,018.17
Total, filtered	2,528,043	4,713.35

Table 2: Statistics on translation datasets

Dataset	en→de	en→ja	en→zh
MuSTC	0.269m	0.328m	0.358m
OpenSubtitles	22.512m	2.083m	11.203m
Commentaries	0.398m	0.002m	0.322m
Total	23.181m	2.414m	11.884m

at character level on the other speech datasets, so utterances with WER scores over 75% are discarded as well. As a result, the speech corpora contains nearly 2.53 million valid utterances with the total duration of 4,713.35 hours.

2.2 Translation Corpora

In addition to the MuSTC datasets, the OpenSubtitles v2018 (Lison et al., 2018) and the News Commentaries v16 (Farhad et al., 2021) datasets are added up to train MT models. Statistics on these translation datasets are described as Table 2. Since translation pairs do not perfectly match all the time, the translation quality is measured by the *fast-align*[1] toolkit in terms of the percentage of aligned words. Word sequences are obtained by splitting English texts and German texts using whitespaces and converting Chinese texts and Japanese texts into character sequences. Parallel training examples are filtered out if: 1) the source sentence contains more than 150 words; 2) the alignment score in either forward translation or backward translation is lower than a certain threshold.

3 Method

3.1 Pretrained Models

Two state-of-the-art models pretrained with self-supervised objectives are employed as base models for downstream tasks with labeled data, namely the *wav2vec2-large-960h-lv60-self*[2] model for speech recognition and the *mbart-large-50-one-to-many-mmt*[3] model for machine translation.

The W2V models (Baevski et al., 2020) are trained with contrastive learning to distinguish whether two transformations of convolution features result in similar latent representations. The first transformation is to learn high-level contextual speech representations through a sequence of Transformer layers (Vaswani et al., 2017). The second transformation is to create discrete targets for self-training by the quantization module. The best partial representations chosen from multiple codebooks with the Gumbel softmax (Jang et al., 2016) are concatenated and transformed to a quantized representation with a linear layer.

The mBART25 models (Liu et al., 2020) are Transformer-based encoder-decoder models that are pretrained on monolingual sentences from many languages and finetuned with parallel translation data on 25 languages. The pretraining objective is a denoising loss so that the model learns to reconstruct corrupted sentences to their original forms. The noise function randomly masks 35% of input sentences in consecutive spans and permutes sentence orders for document-level MT if multiple sentences are given. The mBART50 models (Tang et al., 2020) extend embedding layers with an extra set of 25 languages and are finetuned on translation task from English to the other 49 languages.

3.2 Finetuned Models

The two base models result in one ASR model, three MT models and three E2E ST models. Written texts in the four languages are tokenized into subword tokens in byte-pair encoding (BPE) using the SentencePiece toolkit (Kudo and Richardson, 2018). The tokenizer is inherited from the mBART50 model with a multilingual configuration by prepending language symbols and the total number of BPE tokens in the vocabulary is 250k.

For speech recognition, the finetuned model (ASR12) takes the first 12 Transformer layers from the base model. An adapter module (Li et al., 2020; Shanbhogue et al., 2022) compresses the feature vectors by a factor of eight, which consists of three one-dimensional convolution layers with a stride of two. A linear layer transforms the compressed representations into output probabilities.

[1] https://github.com/clab/fast_align

[2] facebook/wav2vec2-large-960h-lv60-self

[3] facebook/mbart-large-50-one-to-many-mmt

For end-to-end speech translation, the models have similar architecture as the PT36 models in Zhang et al.'s (2022b) work instead of the PT48 models to reduce computational complexity. Within a PT36 model, the speech module and the translation module are initialized with the ASR12 model and the MT24 model respectively. The adapter module that connects the two modules is not trained from random initialization, because it has been trained with the ASR12 model on the first stage. The training loss combines the cross entropy loss for machine translation and the CTC loss for speech recognition with a hyperparameter to balance the weights between the two losses.

3.3 Speech Resegmentation

Past years' systems (Anastasopoulos et al., 2021; Antonios et al., 2022) have proved that speech resegmentation has a great impact on the translation performance at corpus level. During evaluation, audio clips are splitted into segments with a simple two-stage strategy using the *WebRTCVAD*[4] toolkit. On the split stage, long audios are processed with three-level settings of aggressiveness modes increasing from 1 to 3 and frame sizes decreasing from 30ms to 10ms. In this way, most segments are no longer than a maximum duration dur_{max} and the outliers are further segmented into $\lfloor \frac{duration}{0.75 \times \theta} \rfloor$ chunks brutally. On the merge stage, consecutive segments are merged into final segments no shorter than a minimum duration dur_{min}.

4 Experiments

4.1 Settings

All the models are implemented with the SpeechBrain toolkit (Ravanelli et al., 2021). The total number of parameters in a PT36 model is about 794.0M, 183.2M in the speech module and 610.9M in the translation module. The feature extractor processes speech waveform with seven 512-channel convolution layers, in which kernel sizes and strides are [10,3,3,3,3,2,2] and [5,2,2,2,2,2,2]. There are 12 Transformer layers with 16 attention heads, model dimension of 1024 and inner dimension of 4096 in speech encoder, text encoder and decoder. The adapter module has three Conv1D layers with kernel sizes and strides being [3,3,3] and [2,2,2].

On the first stage, the ASR12 model is finetuned on the speech corpora using 16 NVIDIA A100 GPUs for 21 epochs with the batch size of 3 and

[4]https://github.com/wiseman/py-webrtcvad

Table 3: WER scores on test speech datasets

LibriSpeech	TEDLIUM	MuSTC
27.23	32.17	34.73

Table 4: BLEU scores on tst-COMMON datasets

Model	**en→de**	**en→ja**	**en→zh**
MT24	31.04	14.74	22.80
+ finetune	33.00	17.11	23.44
PT36	26.45	14.28	19.65

the update frequency of 8. The parameters in the Wav2Vec2 module and the linear layer are separately optimized by the Adam optimizer (Kingma and Ba, 2014). The learning rates are initialized with $1e^{-4}$ and $4e^{-4}$ with the annealing factors set to 0.9 and 0.8. The learning rates are updated based on the improvement of the training losses between the previous epoch and the current epoch. During training, speech waveform is perturbed with a random speed rate between 0.9 and 1.1 and speech features are augmented with the SpecAugment technique (Park et al., 2019).

On the second stage, three MT24 models are finetuned on the translation corpora with the batch size of 12 and the update frequency of 4. The en→de MT24 model is trained using 8 A100 GPUs for 2 epochs and the other two models are trained using 4 A100 GPUs for 6 epochs and 3 epochs. The model parameters are optimized with the Adam optimizer and the initial learning rates are set to $5e^{-5}$ with the annealing factor set to 0.9.

On the third stage, three PT36 models are finetuned on the corresponding MuSTC datasets, each of which is trained using 4 A100 GPUs for 10 epochs with the batch size of 12 and the update frequency of 4. The learning rates are initialized to $3e^{-5}$ for the W2V module and $5e^{-5}$ for the mBART module with the annealing factors set to 0.9. The loss weights are set to 0.1 for the ASR module and 0.9 for the MT module since the performance of the ASR module is not good enough.

4.2 Speech Recognition

Table 3 lists WER scores on test speech datasets, where 34.73% is the average WER score of the three MuSTC datasets. Obviously, the performance of the ASR12 model is much worse than that of other systems (Zhang et al., 2022b; Wang et al., 2021b) with WERs around 10%. Due to extremely large vocabulary size, the model requires a long

Table 5: Statistics on short segments in the tst2020 dataset with different dur_{min} and dur_{max} settings.

id	dur_{min}	dur_{max}	level1	level2	level3	brutal	split	merge
1	5	20	3,473	342	449	185	4,449	2,621
2	10	30	3,568	146	258	69	4,041	1,699
3	15	60	3,624	35	115	0	3,774	1,237
4	20	90	3,635	9	73	0	3,717	970

Table 6: BLEU scores on calculated on past years' IWSLT en→de test sets with hypotheses automatically resegmented by the *mwerSegmenter* toolkit (Ansari et al., 2021) based on source transcriptions and target translations.

id	dur_{min}	dur_{max}	2010	2013	2014	2018	2019	2020	Δ
1	5	20	21.44	27.37	25.87	12.41	18.95	20.14	21.03
2	10	30	23.79	30.33	28.53	16.29	21.22	22.60	+2.76
3	15	60	24.17	31.16	29.23	**18.38**	22.04	23.46	+3.71
4	20	90	**24.31**	**31.73**	**30.05**	17.98	**22.16**	**23.55**	**+3.93**

time to train. As a result, the model is still far from converge at the time of this submission.

4.3 Sentence-level Translation

The *tst-COMMON* datasets are used to evaluate the translation performance at sentence level and the BLEU scores are calculated by the *SacreBLEU*[5] toolkit, where Japanese texts are tokenized by the *Mecab*[6] morphological analyzer and Chinese texts are tokenized into characters. The BLEU scores on the three datasets are listed in Table 4.

For machine translation, compared with the base MT24 models, the performance of the fine-tuned MT24 models is improved by 1.96 (~6.3%), 2.37 (~16.1%) and 0.64 (~2.8%) BLEU scores on en→de, en→ja and en→zh translations. It indicates that adding out-of-domain corpora like OpenSubtitles and NewsCommentaries is able to boost the machine translation quality.

For speech translation, compared with the fine-tuned MT24 models, the performance of PT36 models is degraded by a large margin with 6.55 (~19.8%), 2.83 (~16.5%) and 3.79 (~16.2%) BLEU scores on en→de, en→ja and en→zh translations. Compared with the base MT24 models, the gaps are still relatively large with 4.59 (~14.8%), 0.46 (~3.1%) and 3.15 (~13.8%) BLEU scores.

4.4 Corpus-level Translation

The translation performance of en→de PT36 model is further evaluated on past years' test datasets with challenging scenarios. To keep consistency, all test audios are resegmented using the method described in Section 3.3. Statistics on short segments in the tst2020 dataset are shown as Table 5. It is noticed that the number of brutal segments is decreased to zero when dur_{min} is set to more than 15s.

Table 6 lists BLEU scores on past years' test datasets with different dur_{min} and dur_{max} settings. It is found that the performance is boosted as the segment duration gets longer, which means that more contextual information is provided to the model. When dur_{min} and dur_{max} are set to 20s and 90s, the best BLEU scores are achieved on most test datasets with an increment of 3.93 (~18.7%) mean BLEU score. Further investigation on long audio segments finds that avoiding brutal segmentation is another factor of such improvement. Comparing experiment 2 and experiment 3, the mean BLEU score is increased by 0.95 (~3.9%) points, when the number of brutal segments is decreased from 69 to 0. Comparing experiment 3 and experiment 4, the mean BLEU score is merely increased by 0.22 (~0.8%) points.

4.5 Submissions

The three PT36 models are finally evaluated on tst2023 datasets (Agarwal et al., 2023) with more challenging scenarios like presentations and interviews. Test audios are resegmented with dur_{min} and dur_{max} set to 20s and 90s. Official metrics are presented as Table 7 for en→de datasets, Table 8 for en→ja datasets and Table 9 for en→zh datasets.

Comparing the performance between in-domain TED datasets and out-of-domain ACL datasets, the BLEU scores are decreased by 2.7 (~12.1%), 0.3 (~2.8%) and 5.6 (~16.9%) points on en→de, en→ja and en→zh translations. Noticeably, the perfor-

[5]https://github.com/mjpost/sacrebleu

[6]https://github.com/taku910/mecab

Table 7: Official metrics on the tst2023 en→de subsets with hypotheses automatically resegmented by the *mwerSegmenter* toolkit (Ansari et al., 2021) based on source transcriptions and target translations.

TED							**ACL**			**Sub**		
Comet		BLEU			chrF		Comet	BLEU	chrF	Comet	BLEU	chrf
ref2	ref1	ref2	ref1	both	ref1	ref2						
0.7128	0.7055	22.3	19.3	27.4	0.49	0.50	0.6295	19.6	0.46	0.3555	11.5	0.45

Table 8: Official metrics on the tst2023 en→ja subsets.

TED					**ACL**	
Comet		BLEU			Comet	BLEU
ref2	ref1	ref2	ref1	both		
0.7201	0.7228	10.7	13.2	16.8	0.6769	10.4

mance is almost halved (~48.4%) with only 11.5 BLEU scores on the en→de Sub dataset. The results indicate that the proposed PT36 models have inadequate abilities of handling non-native speakers, different accents, spontaneous speech and controlled interaction with a second speaker.

5 Conclusion

In conclusion, this paper describes the end-to-end speech translation systems for IWSLT 2023 offline tasks. Built upon pretrained models, the systems are further trained on large amount of parallel data using the three-stage finetuning strategy. The PT36 model consists of an ASR12 module with an adapter module for ASR and an MT24 module for MT. The training loss sums up the CTC loss for ASR and the cross entropy loss for MT. Experiments demonstrate that the proposed methods have the potential to achieve a reasonable performance. However, due to limited resources, some modules has not well trained, which has a negative impact on subsequent tasks. Therefore, the end-to-end models still underperform SOTA systems.

References

Milind Agarwal, Sweta Agrawal, Antonios Anastasopoulos, Ondřej Bojar, Claudia Borg, Marine Carpuat, Roldano Cattoni, Mauro Cettolo, Mingda Chen, William Chen, Khalid Choukri, Alexandra Chronopoulou, Anna Currey, Thierry Declerck, Qianqian Dong, Yannick Estève, Kevin Duh, Marcello Federico, Souhir Gahbiche, Barry Haddow, Benjamin Hsu, Phu Mon Htut, Hirofumi Inaguma, Dávid Javorský, John Judge, Yasumasa Kano, Tom Ko, Rishu Kumar, Pengwei Li, Xutail Ma, Prashant Mathur, Evgeny Matusov, Paul McNamee, John P. McCrae, Kenton Murray, Maria Nadejde, Satoshi Nakamura, Matteo Negri, Ha Nguyen, Jan Niehues, Xing Niu, Atul Ojha Kr., John E. Ortega, Proyag Pal, Juan Pino, Lonneke van der Plas, Peter Polák, Elijah Rippeth, Elizabeth Salesky, Jiatong Shi, Matthias Sperber, Sebastian Stüker, Katsuhito Sudoh, Yun Tang, Brian Thompson, Kevin Tran, Marco Turchi, Alex Waibel, Mingxuan Wang, Shinji Watanabe, and Rodolfo Zevallos. 2023. Findings of the IWSLT 2023 Evaluation Campaign. In *Proceedings of the 20th International Conference on Spoken Language Translation (IWSLT 2023)*. Association for Computational Linguistics.

Antonios Anastasopoulos, Ondřej Bojar, Jacob Bremerman, Roldano Cattoni, Maha Elbayad, Marcello Federico, Xutai Ma, Satoshi Nakamura, Matteo Negri, Jan Niehues, Juan Pino, Elizabeth Salesky, Sebastian Stüker, Katsuhito Sudoh, Marco Turchi, Alexander Waibel, Changhan Wang, and Matthew Wiesner. 2021. Findings of the iwslt 2021 evaluation campaign. In *Proceedings of the 18th International Conference on Spoken Language Translation (IWSLT 2021)*, pages 1–29, Bangkok, Thailand (online). Association for Computational Linguistics.

Ebrahim Ansari, Ondřej Bojar, Barry Haddow, and Mohammad Mahmoudi. 2021. Sltev: Comprehensive evaluation of spoken language translation. In *Proceedings of the 16th Conference of the European Chapter of the Association for Computational Linguistics: System Demonstrations*, pages 71–79.

Anastasopoulos Antonios, Barrault Loc, Luisa Bentivogli, Marcely Zanon Boito, Bojar Ondřej, Roldano Cattoni, Currey Anna, Dinu Georgiana, Duh Kevin, Elbayad Maha, et al. 2022. Findings of the iwslt 2022 evaluation campaign. In *Proceedings of the 19th International Conference on Spoken Language Translation (IWSLT 2022)*, pages 98–157. Association for Computational Linguistics.

Rosana Ardila, Megan Branson, Kelly Davis, Michael Henretty, Michael Kohler, Josh Meyer, Reuben Morais, Lindsay Saunders, Francis M Tyers, and Gregor Weber. 2019. Common voice: A massively-multilingual speech corpus. *arXiv preprint arXiv:1912.06670.*

Table 9: Official metrics on the tst2023 en→zh subsets.

TED					ACL	
Comet		BLEU			Comet	BLEU
ref2	ref1	ref2	ref1	both		
0.7428	0.7014	33.0	23.3	38.6	0.6534	27.4

Alexei Baevski, Yuhao Zhou, Abdelrahman Mohamed, and Michael Auli. 2020. wav2vec 2.0: A framework for self-supervised learning of speech representations. *Advances in neural information processing systems*, 33:12449–12460.

Roldano Cattoni, Mattia Antonino Di Gangi, Luisa Bentivogli, Matteo Negri, and Marco Turchi. 2021. Must-c: A multilingual corpus for end-to-end speech translation. *Computer Speech & Language*, 66:101155.

Akhbardeh Farhad, Arkhangorodsky Arkady, Biesialska Magdalena, Bojar Ondřej, Chatterjee Rajen, Chaudhary Vishrav, Marta R Costa-jussa, España-Bonet Cristina, Fan Angela, Federmann Christian, et al. 2021. Findings of the 2021 conference on machine translation (wmt21). In *Proceedings of the Sixth Conference on Machine Translation*, pages 1–88. Association for Computational Linguistics.

Alex Graves, Santiago Fernández, Faustino Gomez, and Jürgen Schmidhuber. 2006. Connectionist temporal classification: labelling unsegmented sequence data with recurrent neural networks. In *Proceedings of the 23rd international conference on Machine learning*, pages 369–376.

François Hernandez, Vincent Nguyen, Sahar Ghannay, Natalia Tomashenko, and Yannick Esteve. 2018. Tedlium 3: Twice as much data and corpus repartition for experiments on speaker adaptation. In *Speech and Computer: 20th International Conference, SPECOM 2018, Leipzig, Germany, September 18–22, 2018, Proceedings 20*, pages 198–208. Springer.

Oleksii Hrinchuk, Vahid Noroozi, Ashwinkumar Ganesan, Sarah Campbell, Sandeep Subramanian, Somshubra Majumdar, and Oleksii Kuchaiev. 2022. Nvidia nemo offline speech translation systems for iwslt 2022. In *Proceedings of the 19th International Conference on Spoken Language Translation (IWSLT 2022)*, pages 225–231.

Eric Jang, Shixiang Gu, and Ben Poole. 2016. Categorical reparameterization with gumbel-softmax. *arXiv preprint arXiv:1611.01144*.

Diederik P Kingma and Jimmy Ba. 2014. Adam: A method for stochastic optimization. *arXiv preprint arXiv:1412.6980*.

Taku Kudo and John Richardson. 2018. Sentencepiece: A simple and language independent subword tokenizer and detokenizer for neural text processing. *arXiv preprint arXiv:1808.06226*.

Xian Li, Changhan Wang, Yun Tang, Chau Tran, Yuqing Tang, Juan Pino, Alexei Baevski, Alexis Conneau, and Michael Auli. 2020. Multilingual speech translation with efficient finetuning of pretrained models. *arXiv preprint arXiv:2010.12829*.

Pierre Lison, Jörg Tiedemann, and Milen Kouylekov. 2018. Opensubtitles2018: Statistical rescoring of sentence alignments in large, noisy parallel corpora. In *Proceedings of the 11th International Conference on Language Resources and Evaluation (LREC 2018)*. European Language Resources Association (ELRA).

Yinhan Liu, Jiatao Gu, Naman Goyal, Xian Li, Sergey Edunov, Marjan Ghazvininejad, Mike Lewis, and Luke Zettlemoyer. 2020. Multilingual denoising pre-training for neural machine translation. *Transactions of the Association for Computational Linguistics*, 8:726–742.

Vassil Panayotov, Guoguo Chen, Daniel Povey, and Sanjeev Khudanpur. 2015. Librispeech: an asr corpus based on public domain audio books. In *2015 IEEE international conference on acoustics, speech and signal processing (ICASSP)*, pages 5206–5210. IEEE.

Daniel S Park, William Chan, Yu Zhang, Chung-Cheng Chiu, Barret Zoph, Ekin D Cubuk, and Quoc V Le. 2019. Specaugment: A simple data augmentation method for automatic speech recognition. *arXiv preprint arXiv:1904.08779*.

Mirco Ravanelli, Titouan Parcollet, Peter Plantinga, Aku Rouhe, Samuele Cornell, Loren Lugosch, Cem Subakan, Nauman Dawalatabad, Abdelwahab Heba, Jianyuan Zhong, et al. 2021. Speechbrain: A general-purpose speech toolkit. *arXiv preprint arXiv:2106.04624*.

Akshaya Shanbhogue, Ran Xue, Ching Yun Chang, and Sarah Campbell. 2022. Amazon alexa ai's system for iwslt 2022 offline speech translation shared task. In *Proceedings of the 19th International Conference on Spoken Language Translation (IWSLT 2022)*, pages 169–176.

Yuqing Tang, Chau Tran, Xian Li, Peng-Jen Chen, Naman Goyal, Vishrav Chaudhary, Jiatao Gu, and Angela Fan. 2020. Multilingual translation with extensible multilingual pretraining and finetuning. *arXiv preprint arXiv:2008.00401*.

Ashish Vaswani, Noam Shazeer, Niki Parmar, Jakob Uszkoreit, Llion Jones, Aidan N Gomez, Łukasz

Kaiser, and Illia Polosukhin. 2017. Attention is all you need. *Advances in neural information processing systems*, 30.

Changhan Wang, Morgane Riviere, Ann Lee, Anne Wu, Chaitanya Talnikar, Daniel Haziza, Mary Williamson, Juan Pino, and Emmanuel Dupoux. 2021a. Voxpopuli: A large-scale multilingual speech corpus for representation learning, semi-supervised learning and interpretation. *arXiv preprint arXiv:2101.00390.*

Minghan Wang, Yuxia Wang, Chang Su, Jiaxin Guo, Yingtao Zhang, Yujia Liu, Min Zhang, Shimin Tao, Xingshan Zeng, Liangyou Li, et al. 2021b. The hw-tsc's offline speech translation systems for iwslt 2021 evaluation. *arXiv preprint arXiv:2108.03845.*

Weitai Zhang, Zhongyi Ye, Haitao Tang, Xiaoxi Li, Xinyuan Zhou, Jing Yang, Jianwei Cui, Pan Deng, Mohan Shi, Yifan Song, et al. 2022a. The ustc-nelslip offline speech translation systems for iwslt 2022. In *Proceedings of the 19th International Conference on Spoken Language Translation (IWSLT 2022)*, pages 198–207.

Ziqiang Zhang, Junyi Ao, Shujie Liu, Furu Wei, and Jinyu Li. 2022b. The yitrans end-to-end speech translation system for iwslt 2022 offline shared task. *arXiv preprint arXiv:2206.05777.*

Enhancing Video Translation Context with Object Labels

Jeremy Gwinnup[1,2], Tim Anderson[2], Brian Ore[2], Eric Hansen[2], Kevin Duh[1]
[1]Johns Hopkins University, [2]Air Force Research Laboratory
{jeremy.gwinnup.1, timothy,anderson.20, brian.ore.1, eric.hansen.5}@us.af.mil,
kevinduh@cs.jhu.edu

Abstract

We present a simple yet efficient method to enhance the quality of machine translation models trained on multimodal corpora by augmenting the training text with labels of detected objects in the corresponding video segments. We then test the effects of label augmentation in both baseline and two automatic speech recognition (ASR) conditions. In contrast with multimodal techniques that merge visual and textual features, our modular method is easy to implement and the results are more interpretable. Comparisons are made with Transformer translation architectures trained with baseline and augmented labels, showing improvements of up to +1.0 BLEU on the How2 dataset.

1 Introduction

Video streams are rich sources of content and the application of machine translation to videos present open research challenges. Specifically, we are interested in translating the speech content present in videos, using the visual modality as auxiliary input to improve translation quality. Intuitively, visual signals may help disambiguate under-specified words or correct speech recognition errors.

There has been much research in speech translation, which focuses on *speech* input, and multimodal machine translation, which focuses on *visual and textual* inputs; this work combines aspects of both areas. We assume a cascaded pipeline, where the speech in a video input is first passed to a speech recognition component, then the text transcripts together with the video frames are passed to a multimodal machine translation (MMT) system. Our contribution is a MMT system that augments text-based training data with labels obtained from a computer vision object detector (Fig. 1).

In contrast to more complex multimodal fusion techniques that combine vision and translation neural networks into end-to-end models, our modular approach is simple to implement, requiring no toolkit changes, and allows for easier interpretation of results.

On the How2 dataset (Sanabria et al., 2018), we experiment with using clean transcripts and automatic speech recognition transcripts of varying quality as input to our translation systems. This tests the effectiveness of our multimodal approach in noisy conditions, beneficial in real-world use cases. Results show gains of +0.4 to +1.0 BLEU on the How2 held-out test set.

src: And then you're going to stir it so have your stirrer available. PERSON CUP BOTTLE
tgt: E então você vai mexer, então tenha seu agitador disponível.

Figure 1: Demonstration of augmenting source data with detected object labels to provide additional context.

2 Object Class Label Augmentation

When considering the translation of instructional videos, the speaker's narration may use ambiguous language when describing the steps to the task as the viewer may be able to infer the intent through objects or actions in the scene. If MT systems are trained on the speaker's words and translations, these cues from the scene are not present. We proposed to address this omission by analyzing clips of the video and augmenting the text data with objects found in that clip.

Augmentation Process: To augment training data with object labels, an object recognition model

Proceedings of the 20th International Conference on Spoken Language Translation (IWSLT 2023), pages 130–137
July 13-14, 2023 ©2023 Association for Computational Linguistics

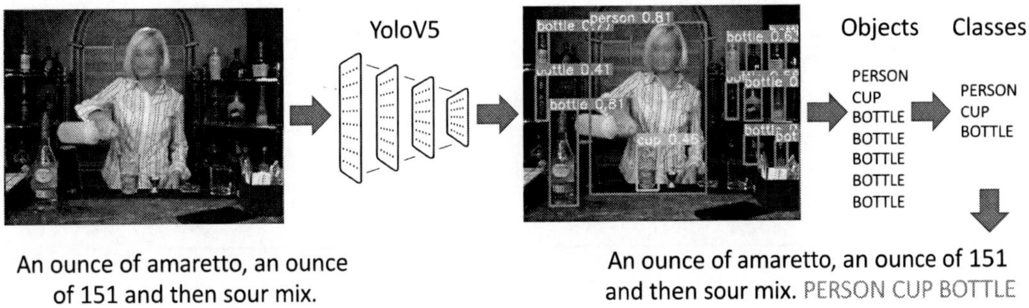

Figure 2: Illustration of the object label augmentation processing pipeline.

was applied to each of the videos in the training set in order to generate lists of objects present. To that end, we apply the YOLOv5[1] (Jocher et al., 2021) model (specifically `yolov5s`) to the 189k video clips corresponding to the utterances from the How2 training data. The object detection model can detect 80 types of objects as outlined in the COCO (Lin et al., 2015) dataset.

The detected labels for the time-slices in the video clip are collated and collapsed in order to keep final sentence length to a manageable size - we are interested in the presence of an object class versus how many times that class has occurred in the scene or the time slices in the video clip.

Once processed, the per-clip labels are appended to the source side of the training, dev and test sets as "context-markers". We do not apply these labels to the target side as we wish to generate coherent sentences in the target language. This processing pipeline is illustrated in Figure 2.

In particular, we note in the example in Figure 1 that the transcription discusses a stirrer but does not give context to what kind of stirrer: A laboratory sample stirrer, a paint stirrer, or in this case a stirrer to mix a drink. Using the object labels from the example, we see that the stirrer in this case refers to a drink - adding valuable context.

The augmented How2 corpus will be available for download at a future date.

Distribution of Augmentation Labels: When examining the counts of per-segment object class annotations in the training set (shown in Figure 3), we note that over 64% of the segments have between one and three object classes present, 13% have no detected object classes, and the remaining 23% have four or greater classes present with

[1]You Only Look Once

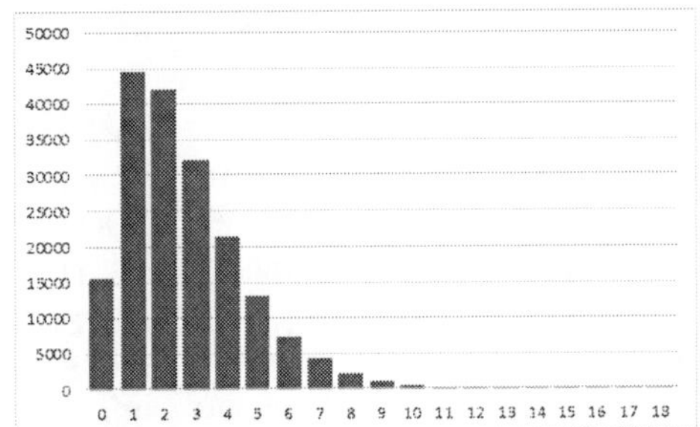

Figure 3: Training segments with N object classes detected.

higher class counts forming a long tail. Full class object counts are shown in Table 1.

Observing the most-detected class labels in training segments (shown in Figure 4), we see that PERSON is by far the most common object class with over 164k occurrences, while CUP and BOTTLE are the next most common with around 23.8k occurrences each. As How2 is comprised of instructional videos in which the authors are demonstrating how to perform a task, PERSON's high occurrence rate seems reasonable. The figure shows the top 15 object classes detected, the full list of detection counts is shown in Table 2.

While the above analyses focus on the training portion of the dataset, similar distributions are present in both the validation and test sets.

3 How2 Dataset

The How2 (Sanabria et al., 2018) dataset is a collection of instructional videos hosted on YouTube that are paired with spoken utterances, English subtitles and a set of crowdsourced Portuguese translations. Additional metadata such as video descriptions and summaries are also available. The dataset contains upwards of 2,000 hours of videos, but only a 300

Classes	Segments	Classes	Segments	Classes	Segments
0	15,544	6	7,508	12	143
1	44,496	7	4,300	13	79
2	41,950	8	2,259	14	42
3	32,077	9	1,166	15	14
4	21,428	10	626	16	7
5	13,011	11	293	17	3

Table 1: Video segments with n object classes present.

Class	Count	Class	Count	Class	Count
PERSON	164,605	MICROWAVE	4,298	TOILET	1,333
CUP	23,870	REFRIGERATOR	4,014	BROCCOLI	1,327
BOTTLE	23,809	CAKE	3,911	SURFBOARD	1,281
CHAIR	17,806	DONUT	3,729	HORSE	1,222
CELL_PHONE	17,016	DOG	3,496	BED	1,141
REMOTE	16,127	TOOTHBRUSH	2,839	BOAT	1,056
BOWL	13,524	SUITCASE	2,730	BACKPACK	1,034
POTTED_PLANT	13,045	APPLE	2,714	TRUCK	924
TV	11,455	BASEBALL_GLOVE	2,682	TRAFFIC_LIGHT	919
SPORTS_BALL	10,290	SPOON	2,636	ORANGE	841
TIE	9,971	HANDBAG	2,352	COW	794
LAPTOP	9,066	COUCH	2,316	SANDWICH	763
VASE	9,033	BASEBALL_BAT	2,293	FIRE_HYDRANT	722
BOOK	7,612	BIRD	2,292	TEDDY_BEAR	713
WINE_GLASS	7,229	BANANA	2,145	AIRPLANE	576
DINING_TABLE	6,315	PIZZA	2,103	BUS	516
TENNIS_RACKET	5,922	CAT	2,054	SKIS	456
KNIFE	5,355	CARROT	1,986	SNOWBOARD	387
CAR	5,198	BENCH	1,899	TRAIN	338
MOUSE	5,107	MOTORCYCLE	1,872	ELEPHANT	265
SINK	4,688	BICYCLE	1,856	STOP_SIGN	246
FRISBEE	4,675	HOT_DOG	1,652	PARKING_METER	218
OVEN	4,450	SCISSORS	1,529	SHEEP	215
CLOCK	4,382	FORK	1,480	BEAR	198
KEYBOARD	4,353	UMBRELLA	1,408	GIRAFFE	177
SKATEBOARD	4,304	KITE	1,384	ZEBRA	158

Table 2: Detected class counts for training segments.

hour subset contains the full set of annotations. This work focuses on that subset.

	Videos	Hours	Sentences
train	13,168	298.2	184,949
validation	150	3.2	2,022
test	175	3.7	2,305

Table 3: How2 300h subset statistics

This portion consists of 13,493 videos consisting of a total run-time of 305.1 hours from which 189,276 utterances are extracted. These videos and segments are then segregated into training, validation and test sets as shown in Table 3. These segments are then used to train systems in downstream tasks such as MT.

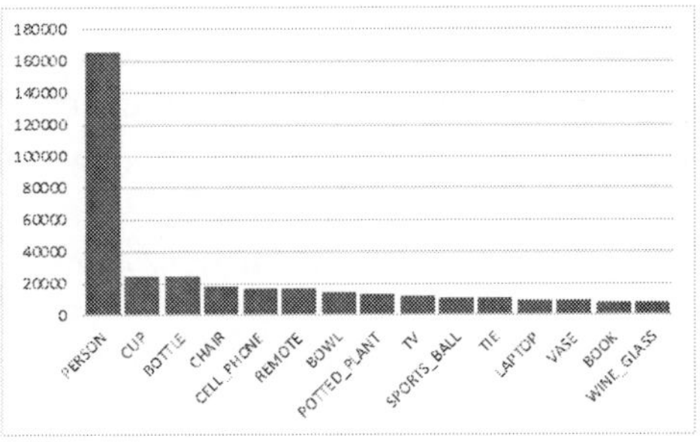

Figure 4: Top 15 classes present in training video snippets.

4 Experiments

To gauge the effectiveness of the label augmentation approach, we train baseline and object-label augmented systems in Marian (Junczys-Dowmunt et al., 2018) with a transformer-base (Vaswani et al., 2017) architecture. We also replicate the baseline and image feature augmented shallow recurrent neural network (RNN systems) described in (Sanabria et al., 2018) for comparison.

4.1 Training Hyperparameters

The Marian (Junczys-Dowmunt et al., 2018) systems trained for our experiments use transformer-base settings as described in Vaswani et al. (2017): 6-layer encoder, 6-layer decoder, 8 transformer heads, 2048 hidden units. These training sessions were performed on 2 NVidia Titan-X Pascal devices each with 12Gb GPU RAM, taking 6.5-7.5 hours per model.

4.2 Data preprocessing

In order to prepare the augmented data for use in training MT systems, we employ SentencePiece (Kudo and Richardson, 2018) unigram-model subword processing with a disjoint[2] vocabulary size of 32k. One important change we introduce is to preserve each of the COCO class labels as atomic tokens that are not broken apart. These labels are additionally in all caps to both disambiguate from natural occurrences of the label words and provide a convenient marker for diagnosis.

4.3 Pruning Over-represented Object Labels

As noted in Section 2, PERSON is by far the most represented object class label. We posit this prevalence may have a negative effect on performance. To investigate this hypothesis, we examine three methods to prune over-prevalent or under-represented object class labels: naïve dropping of the N most-represented labels, inverse document frequency (IDF) thresholding and normalized term frequency-inverse document frequency (TF-IDF) thresholding. For the first method, object labels are simply removed in the most common order - e.g. drop-3 removes the three most common classes: PERSON, CUP, and BOTTLE.

$$IDF_T = log_2 \frac{\text{Total Corpus Lines}}{\text{\# Lines with T present}} \quad (1)$$

Inverse document frequency thresholding (as calculated by Equation 1) removes labels that fall below a specified threshold compared to a precomputed table of IDF scores for each class, effectively removing the most represented labels.

Lastly, normalized TF-IDF thresholding does the same using the product of TF (calculated by the number of times an object label occurs in video time-slices[3]) and IDF scores normalized from 0 to 1 - this tries to bring a balance between most represented labels and more unique labels that may add a distinct contribution to a translation.

4.4 ASR-Degraded experiments

The How2 dataset is provided with reference speech transcription, but in realistic settings one may need to derive these automatically. Automatic speech recognition (ASR) errors may lead to additional ambiguity in the MT input, but hopefully can be recovered partially with image context. We build Kaldi (Povey et al., 2011) ASR systems to recognize the speech of the speakers in the How2 videos, then match the ASR output timings to those of the gold-standard utterances. These new utterances are used as the source side of the training corpus for both the baseline and object label augmented condition.

In a second experiment, we add 5 dB of background noise to the audio in the How2 videos using noise samples from the MUSAN corpus (Snyder et al., 2015). The same ASR system described above is then evaluated on the noisy audio to produce a second set of ASR hypotheses.

The English speech recognition system was trained using the Kaldi ASR toolkit. The acoustic models utilized 2400 hours of audio from Fisher

[2]Separate vocabularies for English and Portuguese.

[3]This is different than our use of object class occurrences in augmentation; the larger video-timeslice object count is needed for the TF-IDF calculation to work properly.

(Cieri et al., 2004–2005), TEDLIUM-v3 (Hernandez et al., 2018), and ATC (Godfrey, 1994); the language models (LM) were estimated on 1 billion words from Fisher, News-Crawl 2007-2017 (Kocmi et al., 2022), News-Discuss 2014-2017 (Kocmi et al., 2022), and TED. This system used Mel frequency cepstral coefficient (MFCC) features as input to a factorized time delay neural network (TDNN) with residual network style skip connections. Initial decoding was performed using a finite state transducer (FST) built from a bigram LM, and the resulting lattices were rescored with a RNN LM. The vocabulary included 100k words.

4.5 Results

Armed with an array of label pruning strategies, we run a series of experiments to determine the effectiveness of each method.

4.5.1 Marian Label Augmented Systems

Marian label augmentation and pruning results are shown in Table 4 reporting scores for BLEU (Papineni et al., 2002), chrF2 (Popović, 2015) and TER (Snover et al., 2006) as calculated by SacreBLEU (Post, 2018) and COMET (Rei et al., 2020) with the default `wmt20-comet-da` model.

We note that drop-3, tfidf at 0.20, and idf at 4.0 each yield a +0.9-1.0 gain in BLEU over baseline. We also report the number of labels pruned at each experimental threshold noting that drop and tfidf remove approximately 42-43% of object class labels at maximum performance, while idf removes a much larger 74.73%.

As we see from the results, each of the three label pruning methods yields improvements over both the text-only and non-pruned augmented systems. Using the `compare-mt` (Neubig et al., 2019) tool, we take a closer look at various characteristics of the translation hypotheses of each of these five systems to see if any trends emerge. Table 5 shows averaged sentence BLEU scores for hypotheses with outputs of varying lengths. The intuition is that these average scores will help determine if a given system or pruning strategy is better at certain output lengths.

From these averaged scores, we note that plain label augmentation tends to improve over baseline with hypothesis lengths between 30 and 60 tokens but performs worse when outside of those ranges. Of the three pruning strategies, drop 3 tends to bring the most improvement, especially with shorter hypotheses and idf 4.0 tends to help the longer sequences.

4.5.2 Nmtpytorch Baseline Experiments

For nmtpytorch baseline comparison systems, we note that maximum training sequence has an effect on system performance, most likely due to the shallow RNN architecture. Table 6 shows that using the default 120 max token limit from Sanabria et al. (2018) yields better performance (+0.9-1.1 BLEU) with both the visual perturbation and our label augmentation approach. These results show our approach yields a similar performance gain.

4.5.3 ASR Noise Experiments

For the ASR-based experiments shown in Table 7, we see improvements of +0.7 BLEU with both the clean and noisy Kaldi systems. We expect that the speech-recognition based systems would not perform as well as the gold-standard systems, but the use of object labels can help mitigate this loss in performance.

4.6 Analyzing Attention Outputs

We use Marian's ability to output soft attention weights to compare an augmented system against its baseline counterpart, as shown in Figure 5. For this example, line 221 of the test set, the baseline system scores a sentence-BLEU of 30.66 versus the augmented system's 61.32. We note the attention contributions of the object labels on the output tokens. Utilizing this feature as part of an unaltered MT toolkit allows for quick and easy analysis of the benefits of object label augmentation.

5 Related Work

Perhaps most closely related to our approach is ViTA (Gupta et al., 2021), which adds object labels extracted from images in an image captioning translation task. While the motivation of adding object labels are similar, there are important differences with our setup: 1) We work on video narration of an author's task demonstration where objects appear at different points in the clip, which differs significantly from static image captions. 2) Our work focuses on training MT systems from scratch as opposed to fine-tuning existing models.

For a broad survey of multimodal translation, refer to Sulubacak et al. (2020). Specifically for video translation on How2, Sanabria et al. (2018) investigates a MT system that adds a 2048-dimensional feature vector averaging features for every 16 frames to create a global feature vector for

System	BLEU	chrF2	TER	COMET	Dropped Labels
Marian baseline	57.9	75.0	29.6	0.6819	–
nmtpy baseline	56.2	74.2	30.7	0.6234	–
nmtpy visual	55.9	74.0	31.1	0.6090	–
drop 0	57.6	74.9	29.9	0.6732	0 (0%)
drop 1	58.6	75.4	28.9	0.6785	164,605 (33.55%)
drop 2	58.7	75.5	28.9	0.6840	188,475 (38.41%)
drop 3	**58.9**	**75.7**	**28.7**	**0.6907**	**212,284 (43.26%)**
drop 4	58.5	75.3	29.1	0.6766	230,090 (46.89%)
drop 5	58.5	75.2	29.3	0.6687	247,106 (50.36%)
tfidf 0.10	58.3	75.1	29.5	0.6778	162,762 (33.17%)
tfidf 0.20	**58.8**	75.4	**28.8**	**0.6817**	**205,938 (41.97%)**
tfidf 0.30	58.8	**75.5**	29.0	0.6812	398,643 (81.24%)
idf 3.0	58.4	75.2	29.2	0.6832	212,284 (43.26%)
idf 4.0	**58.9**	**75.5**	**29.0**	**0.6887**	**366,695 (74.73%)**
idf 5.0	58.5	75.4	29.0	0.6857	428,655 (87.36%)

Table 4: Marian system scores for How2 en–pt test set, measured in BLEU, chrF2, TER and COMET. There are 490,697 object class labels present in the entire augmented training corpus.

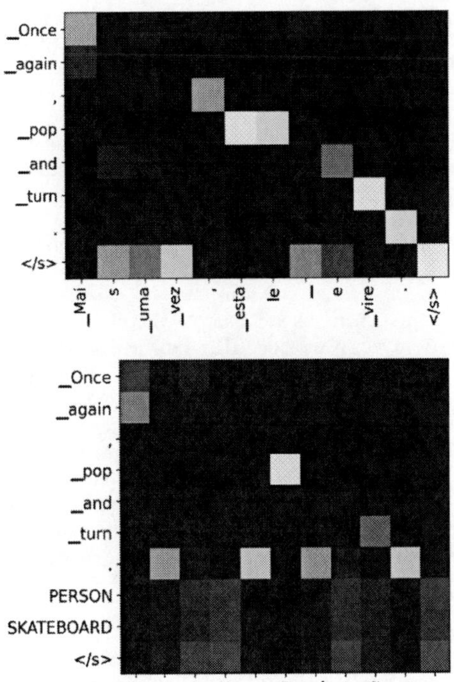

Figure 5: Attention grid for the same output sentence for Baseline (top, 30.66 sentence-BLEU) and Augmented (bottom, 61.32 sentence-BLEU) systems. We note the attention contributions of the augmented object labels.

length	base	aug	drop3	tfidf0.2	idf4.0
<10	52.7	51.8	**53.4**	52.8	53.1
[10,20)	57.6	57.1	**58.7**	58.3	57.8
[20,30)	53.7	53.6	54.8	**55.1**	55.2
[30,40)	53.1	54.1	55.4	54.9	**55.8**
[40,50)	52.4	52.0	52.9	52.6	**53.1**
[50,60)	48.3	49.3	**52.1**	49.8	48.8
>=60	46.6	44.6	45.5	47.3	**48.8**

Table 5: Averaged sentence BLEU scores for hypotheses in incremental length bins.

that entire video. This differs from our approach of creating labels solely for the objects in a clip directly corresponding to that text segment. Madhyastha et al. (2017) uses a similar approach as How2 on static imagery.

The Vatex (Wang et al., 2020) video description dataset includes a Video-guided Machine Translation (VMT) approach that utilizes an action detection model feeding a video encoder with temporal attention and a text source encoder with attention that both inform the target decoder, producing translated output from a unified network. The authors perform experiments in an video captioning setting, as opposed How2's task narration setting.

As part of the work in Calixto and Liu (2017), the authors project static image features into the

System	Max Tok	BLEU
nmtpy base	120	55.0
nmtpy vis	120	56.1
nmtpy aug	120	55.9
nmtpy base	250	56.2
nmtpy vis	250	55.9
nmtpy aug	250	55.7

Table 6: Max token length effect on BLEU for nmtpytorch baseline, visual perturbation and our label augmented systems.

System	BLEU	COMET
Kaldi clean base	52.0	0.556
Kaldi clean aug	52.7	0.583
Kaldi 5 dB noise base	50.8	0.459
Kaldi 5 dB noise aug	51.5	0.459

Table 7: Results for clean and noisy Kaldi systems for both baseline and augmented conditions.

word embedding space to produce image-based first and last words to influence word choice in their bidirectional RNN systems.

While there are a few examples of object detection as a separate task (including our work), Baltrusaitis et al. (2019) notes the rapid jump to joint representations as neural networks became popular tools for a variety of multimodal tasks, explaining the prevalence of work following that approach.

6 Future Work

Having proven our object label augmentation technique on How2, future work includes applying label augmentation to other datasets such as the VATEX (Wang et al., 2020) video description and VISA (Li et al., 2022) ambiguous subtitles datasets. Further research into the effects of ASR degraded speech and examining task-agnostic image-language models such as CLIP (Radford et al., 2021) for label augmentation may also be useful.

7 Conclusion

We present a straight-forward method to improve MT context quality by augmenting training data with objects detected in corresponding video clips. Using these augmented corpora, we realize gains of up to +1.0 BLEU over baselines without changes to the underlying MT toolkits used to build models. We additionally show improvements of up to +0.7 BLEU with object label augmentation when substituting ASR speech for gold standard inputs.

References

Tadas Baltrusaitis, Chaitanya Ahuja, and Louis-Philippe Morency. 2019. Multimodal machine learning: A survey and taxonomy. *IEEE Trans. Pattern Anal. Mach. Intell.*, 41(2):423–443.

Iacer Calixto and Qun Liu. 2017. Incorporating global visual features into attention-based neural machine translation. In *Proceedings of the 2017 Conference on Empirical Methods in Natural Language Processing*, pages 992–1003, Copenhagen, Denmark. Association for Computational Linguistics.

Christopher Cieri, David Graff, Owen Kimball, David Miller, and Kevin Walker. 2004–2005. Fisher English Training Part 1 and 2 Speech and Transcripts. Linguistic Data Consortium, Philadelphia.

John Godfrey. 1994. Air Traffic Control Complete. Linguistic Data Consortium, Philadelphia.

Kshitij Gupta, Devansh Gautam, and Radhika Mamidi. 2021. ViTA: Visual-linguistic translation by aligning object tags. In *Proceedings of the 8th Workshop on Asian Translation (WAT2021)*, pages 166–173, Online. Association for Computational Linguistics.

François Hernandez, Vincent Nguyen, Sahar Ghannay, Natalia Tomashenko, and Yannick Estève. 2018. TED-LIUM 3: Twice as much data and corpus repartition for experiments on speaker adaptation. In *Speech and Computer*, pages 198–208, Cham. Springer International Publishing.

Glenn Jocher, Alex Stoken, Ayush Chaurasia, Jirka Borovec, NanoCode012, TaoXie, Yonghye Kwon, Kalen Michael, Liu Changyu, Jiacong Fang, Abhiram V, Laughing, tkianai, yxNONG, Piotr Skalski, Adam Hogan, Jebastin Nadar, imyhxy, Lorenzo Mammana, AlexWang1900, Cristi Fati, Diego Montes, Jan Hajek, Laurentiu Diaconu, Mai Thanh Minh, Marc, albinxavi, fatih, oleg, and wanghaoyang0106. 2021. ultralytics/yolov5: v6.0 - YOLOv5n 'Nano' models, Roboflow integration, TensorFlow export, OpenCV DNN support.

Marcin Junczys-Dowmunt, Roman Grundkiewicz, Tomasz Dwojak, Hieu Hoang, Kenneth Heafield, Tom Neckermann, Frank Seide, Ulrich Germann, Alham Fikri Aji, Nikolay Bogoychev, André F. T. Martins, and Alexandra Birch. 2018. Marian: Fast

The views expressed are those of the authors and do not necessarily reflect the official policy or position of the Department of the Air Force, the Department of Defense, or the U.S. government. Distribution Statement A. Approved for public release: distribution is unlimited. Originator reference number RH-22-123269. Case number AFRL-2022-3098.

neural machine translation in C++. In *Proceedings of ACL 2018, System Demonstrations*, pages 116–121, Melbourne, Australia. Association for Computational Linguistics.

Tom Kocmi, Rachel Bawden, Ondřej Bojar, Anton Dvorkovich, Christian Federmann, Mark Fishel, Thamme Gowda, Yvette Graham, Roman Grundkiewicz, Barry Haddow, Rebecca Knowles, Philipp Koehn, Christof Monz, Makoto Morishita, Masaaki Nagata, Toshiaki Nakazawa, Michal Novák, Martin Popel, and Maja Popović. 2022. Findings of the 2022 conference on machine translation (WMT22). In *Proceedings of the Seventh Conference on Machine Translation (WMT)*, pages 1–45, Abu Dhabi, United Arab Emirates (Hybrid). Association for Computational Linguistics.

Taku Kudo and John Richardson. 2018. SentencePiece: A simple and language independent subword tokenizer and detokenizer for neural text processing. In *Proceedings of the 2018 Conference on Empirical Methods in Natural Language Processing: System Demonstrations*, pages 66–71, Brussels, Belgium. Association for Computational Linguistics.

Yihang Li, Shuichiro Shimizu, Weiqi Gu, Chenhui Chu, and Sadao Kurohashi. 2022. VISA: an ambiguous subtitles dataset for visual scene-aware machine translation. *CoRR*, abs/2201.08054.

Tsung-Yi Lin, Michael Maire, Serge Belongie, Lubomir Bourdev, Ross Girshick, James Hays, Pietro Perona, Deva Ramanan, C. Lawrence Zitnick, and Piotr Dollár. 2015. Microsoft coco: Common objects in context.

Pranava Swaroop Madhyastha, Josiah Wang, and Lucia Specia. 2017. Sheffield MultiMT: Using object posterior predictions for multimodal machine translation. In *Proceedings of the Second Conference on Machine Translation*, pages 470–476, Copenhagen, Denmark. Association for Computational Linguistics.

Graham Neubig, Zi-Yi Dou, Junjie Hu, Paul Michel, Danish Pruthi, Xinyi Wang, and John Wieting. 2019. compare-mt: A tool for holistic comparison of language generation systems. *CoRR*, abs/1903.07926.

Kishore Papineni, Salim Roukos, Todd Ward, and Wei-Jing Zhu. 2002. Bleu: a method for automatic evaluation of machine translation. In *Proceedings of the 40th Annual Meeting of the Association for Computational Linguistics*, pages 311–318, Philadelphia, Pennsylvania, USA. Association for Computational Linguistics.

Maja Popović. 2015. chrF: character n-gram F-score for automatic MT evaluation. In *Proceedings of the Tenth Workshop on Statistical Machine Translation*, pages 392–395, Lisbon, Portugal. Association for Computational Linguistics.

Matt Post. 2018. A call for clarity in reporting BLEU scores. In *Proceedings of the Third Conference on Machine Translation: Research Papers*, pages 186–191, Brussels, Belgium. Association for Computational Linguistics.

Daniel Povey, Arnab Ghoshal, Gilles Boulianne, Lukas Burget, Ondrej Glembek, Nagendra Goel, Mirko Hannemann, Petr Motlicek, Yanmin Qian, Petr Schwarz, Jan Silovsky, Georg Stemmer, and Karel Vesely. 2011. The kaldi speech recognition toolkit. In *IEEE 2011 Workshop on Automatic Speech Recognition and Understanding*. IEEE Signal Processing Society. IEEE Catalog No.: CFP11SRW-USB.

Alec Radford, Jong Wook Kim, Chris Hallacy, Aditya Ramesh, Gabriel Goh, Sandhini Agarwal, Girish Sastry, Amanda Askell, Pamela Mishkin, Jack Clark, Gretchen Krueger, and Ilya Sutskever. 2021. Learning transferable visual models from natural language supervision. In *Proceedings of the 38th International Conference on Machine Learning*, volume 139 of *Proceedings of Machine Learning Research*, pages 8748–8763. PMLR.

Ricardo Rei, Craig Stewart, Ana C Farinha, and Alon Lavie. 2020. COMET: A neural framework for MT evaluation. In *Proceedings of the 2020 Conference on Empirical Methods in Natural Language Processing (EMNLP)*, pages 2685–2702, Online. Association for Computational Linguistics.

Ramon Sanabria, Ozan Caglayan, Shruti Palaskar, Desmond Elliott, Loïc Barrault, Lucia Specia, and Florian Metze. 2018. How2: a large-scale dataset for multimodal language understanding. In *Proceedings of the Workshop on Visually Grounded Interaction and Language (ViGIL)*. NeurIPS.

Matthew Snover, Bonnie Dorr, Rich Schwartz, Linnea Micciulla, and John Makhoul. 2006. A study of translation edit rate with targeted human annotation. In *Proceedings of the 7th Conference of the Association for Machine Translation in the Americas: Technical Papers*, pages 223–231, Cambridge, Massachusetts, USA. Association for Machine Translation in the Americas.

David Snyder, Guoguo Chen, and Daniel Povey. 2015. MUSAN: A Music, Speech, and Noise Corpus. ArXiv:1510.08484v1.

Umut Sulubacak, Ozan Çağlayan, Stig-Arne Grönroos, Aku Rouhe, Desmond Elliott, Lucia Specia, and Jörg Tiedemann. 2020. Multimodal machine translation through visuals and speech. *Machine Translation*, 34.

Ashish Vaswani, Noam Shazeer, Niki Parmar, Jakob Uszkoreit, Llion Jones, Aidan N Gomez, Łukasz Kaiser, and Illia Polosukhin. 2017. Attention is all you need. In *Advances in Neural Information Processing Systems*, pages 6000–6010.

Xin Wang, Jiawei Wu, Junkun Chen, Lei Li, Yuan-Fang Wang, and William Yang Wang. 2020. Vatex: A large-scale, high-quality multilingual dataset for video-and-language research.

Length-Aware NMT and Adaptive Duration for Automatic Dubbing

Zhiqiang Rao, Hengchao Shang, Jinlong Yang, Daimeng Wei, Zongyao Li, Jiaxin Guo, Shaojun Li, Zhengzhe Yu, Zhanglin Wu, Yuhao Xie, Bin Wei, Jiawei Zheng, Lizhi Lei and Hao Yang
Huawei Translation Service Center, Beijing, China
{raozhiqiang,shanghengchao,yangjinlong7,weidaimeng,lizongyao, guojiaxin1,lishaojun18,yuzhengzhe,wuzhanglin2,xieyuhao2,weibin29, zhengjiawei15,leilizhi,yanghao30}@huawei.com

Abstract

This paper presents the submission of Huawei Translation Services Center for the IWSLT 2023 dubbing task in the unconstrained setting. The proposed solution consists of a Transformer-based machine translation model and a phoneme duration predictor. The Transformer is deep and multiple target-to-source length-ratio class labels are used to control target lengths. The variation predictor in FastSpeech2 is utilized to predict phoneme durations. To optimize the isochrony in dubbing, re-ranking and scaling are performed. The source audio duration is used as a reference to re-rank the translations of different length-ratio labels, and the one with minimum time deviation is preferred. Additionally, the phoneme duration outputs are scaled within a defined threshold to narrow the duration gap with the source audio.

1 Introduction

Automatic dubbing (AD) (Federico et al., 2020; Brannon et al., 2022; Chronopoulou et al., 2023) technology uses artificial intelligence (AI) to automatically generate dubbed audio for video content. Dubbing is the process of replacing the audio with a translation of the original audio in a different language. AI dubbing technology automates this process by using machine learning algorithms to translate the original audio and synthesize a new voice that sounds natural and resembles a human voice. The synthesized voice is then synchronized with the lip movements of the characters in the video to produce dubbed audio. This technology has the potential to significantly reduce the time and cost of creating dubbed audio and make it easier to reach a global audience by translating video content into multiple languages.

Recent advances in the field of automatic dubbing have contributed to the development of more efficient and cost-effective methods for producing localized content. Researchers have utilized various techniques and technologies, including machine translation (MT) (Lopez, 2008; Vaswani et al., 2017), speech synthesis (Wang et al., 2017b; Ren et al., 2022), and speech recognition (Gulati et al., 2020; Schneider et al., 2019), to improve the accuracy and quality of automatic dubbing systems.

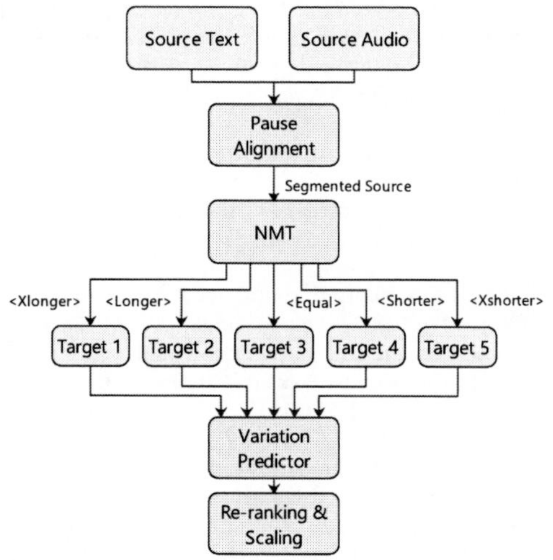

Figure 1: System pipeline.

Isometric machine translation (Lakew et al., 2022; Li et al., 2022) is a technique used in automatic dubbing where translations should match a given length to allow for synchronicity between source and target speech. For neural MT, generating translations of length close to the source length, while preserving quality is a challenging task. Controlling MT output length comes at a cost to translation quality, which is usually mitigated with a two-step approach of generating N-best hypotheses and then re-ranking based on length and quality.

Another area of research focuses on the synchronization of the dubbed audio with the original source audio. This is essential for ensuring that the dubbed audio matches the timing and intonation of the original speech. Researchers have developed various methods for achieving accurate synchro-

Proceedings of the 20th International Conference on Spoken Language Translation (IWSLT 2023), pages 138–143
July 13-14, 2023 ©2023 Association for Computational Linguistics

nization, including the use of phoneme duration predictors and machine learning algorithms to detect and align speech segments (Virkar et al., 2021; Effendi et al., 2022; Virkar et al., 2022).

One of the latest developments in automatic dubbing research is the use of deep neural networks for speech synthesis (Chronopoulou et al., 2023; Ren et al., 2022). These networks enable the creation of more naturalistic and expressive speech, improving the overall quality of the dubbed audio. In conclusion, recent research in automatic dubbing has shown significant progress and promise for the future of localized content production. By combining advanced machine learning techniques with speech synthesis, speech recognition, and sentiment analysis, researchers are developing more accurate, efficient, and cost-effective automatic dubbing systems.

The IWSLT 2023 (Agarwal et al., 2023) dubbing task focuses on isochrony in dubbing, which refers to the property that the speech translation is time aligned with the original speaker's video. The task assumes that the front Automatic Speech Recognition (ASR) output text and subsequent Text-to-Speech (TTS) models already exist, and the goal is to predict the phonemes and their durations. Our proposed solution involves using a Transformer-based (Vaswani et al., 2017) machine translation model and a phoneme duration predictor. A Deep Transformer (Wang et al., 2017a, 2019) model is utilized to handle multiple target-to-source length-ratio class labels, which are used to control target lengths. The phoneme duration predictor is based on the variation predictor used in FastSpeech2 (Ren et al., 2022). To optimize isochrony in dubbing, the solution utilizes re-ranking and scaling techniques. The translations generated by different length-ratio labels are re-ranked based on their time deviation from the source audio duration, with the minimum deviation one preferred. The phoneme duration outputs are also scaled within a predefined threshold to narrow the duration gap with the source audio. These techniques help to ensure that the translated speech is synchronized with the original speaker's video.

2 Data

The data provided in the constrained setting is derived from CoVoST2 (Wang et al., 2020) De-En data, consisting of German source text, English target text, speech durations, and English phonemes and durations (Brannon et al., 2022). We additionally apply WMT2014 De-En data for training the MT model. The amount of data for both sets is shown in Table 1.

Data	Size
CoVoST2	0.289M
WMT2014	4.5M

Table 1: The bilingual data sizes.

To achieve better training results of the MT model, we used some data pre-processing methods to clean the bilingual data, including removing duplicate sentences, using Moses (Koehn et al., 2007) to normalize punctuation, filtering out overly long sentences, using langid (Lui and Baldwin, 2011, 2012) to filter out sentences that do not match the desired language, and using fast-align (Dyer et al., 2013) to filter out unaligned sentence pairs.

3 System

The system consists of four parts: Pause Alignment, Machine Translation, Phoneme Duration Variation Predictor, and Re-ranking and Scaling. Figure 1 shows the system pipeline. The following describes the four parts in detail.

3.1 Pause Alignment

During inference, we use a Voice Activity Detector (VAD) (Team, 2021) to obtain speech segments and their durations from the source audio. The test data for the task already provides text segments separated by pauses. However, we found that the number of speech segments obtained by VAD sometimes does not match the number of text segments provided, resulting in incorrect matching of pause counts. This can cause significant discrepancy between the synthetic dubbing and the lip movements of the character in the video when the pause duration is long.

To address this issue, we first perform pause alignment between the source text and the source audio. We use the proportion of tokens in each text segment to the total number of tokens, and the proportion of duration of each speech segment to the total duration, to find the best alignment between the text and speech segments. When the number of text segments is less than the number of speech segments, we merge the audio segments to reduce the number of speech segments. The final speech segments that need to be retained are split at the following points:

$$i' = \arg\min_{j} \left| \frac{|s_{1..j}|}{S} - \frac{|t_{1..i}|}{T} \right| ; j \geq i$$

Where $|t_{1..i}|$ means total number of tokens from the first to the i-th text segment. $|s_{1..j}|$ means total duration from the first to the j-th speech segment. T and S represent the total number of tokens in the text and the total duration of the speech, respectively. i' is the i-th speech segmentation point after merging, corresponding to the i-th text segment.

Conversely, when the number of speech segments is less than the number of text segments, we merge the text segments. The final retained text segmentation points are:

$$j' = \arg\min_{i} \left| \frac{|t_{1..i}|}{T} - \frac{|s_{1..j}|}{S} \right| ; i \geq j$$

3.2 Machine Translation

We trained a Neural Machine Translation (NMT) model using Deep Transformer, which features pre-layer normalization, 25 encoder layers, and 6 decoder layers. Other structural parameters are consistent with the Transformer-Base model.

Following existing length control methods, we divided the bilingual data into 5 categories based on the target-to-source character length ratio (LR) for each sample (Lakew et al., 2022; Li et al., 2022). The labels were defined based on LR thresholds: $Xshorter < 0.8 < Shorter < 0.9 < Equal < 1.1 < Longer < 1.2 < Xlonger$. During training, we added a length tag <Xshorter/Shorter/Equal/Longer/Xlonger> at the beginning of each source sentence. In the inference process, text segments are sent to the translation model separately and the required tag is prepended at the beginning of each input segment.

3.3 Phoneme Duration Variation Predictor

As with FastSpeech2 (Ren et al., 2022), after using an open-source grapheme-to-phoneme tool (Park, 2019) to convert the NMT output translation sequence into a phoneme sequence, the pre-trained variation predictor module in FastSpeech2 was used to generate initial phoneme durations. The variation predictor takes the hidden sequence as input and predicts the variance of the mean squared error (MSE) loss for each phoneme's duration. It consists of a 2-layer 1D-convolutional network with ReLU activation, followed by layer-normalization and dropout layers, and an additional linear layer to project the hidden state into the output sequence. The final output is the length of each phoneme.

3.4 Re-ranking and Scaling

To select the best isochrony dubbing, we used source texts with 5 different tags prepended as inputs for the NMT model. After converting the output translations into phoneme durations using the phoneme duration variation predictor, we re-ranked them based on the source audio duration as reference, and selected the output with the least duration deviation.

Additionally, we used the ratio of the source audio duration to the total predicted phoneme duration as a reference, and scaled the predicted phoneme duration within a certain threshold to further optimize the synchronization between the synthesized dubbing and the source video.

$$s_j' = \arg\min_{s_{jk}'} (\left|s_{jk}'\right| - |s_j|); k \in [1, 5]$$

$$s_j' = s_j' \cdot Scale(\frac{|s_j|}{\left|s_j'\right|})$$

$$Scale(r) = \begin{cases} 1.1, & r > 1.1 \\ r, & 0.9 < r < 1.1 \\ 0.9, & r < 0.9 \end{cases}$$

Where $|s_j|$ is the total duration of source speech segment s_j, $\left|s_j'\right|$ is the total duration of generated dubbing segment s_j'. And $Scale()$ is a scaling function.

4 Experiments

We used SentencePiece (Kudo and Richardson, 2018) to process NMT bilingual text and obtain subword vocabularies, resulting in a German vocabulary of 29k and an English vocabulary of 25k. We trained a Transformer NMT model using fairseq (Ott et al., 2019), with an encoder of 25 layers, a decoder of 6 layers, 8 attention heads, embeddings of 512, and FFN embeddings of 2048. The model was optimized using Adam (Kingma and Ba, 2017) with an initial learning rate of 5e-4, and warmup steps of 4000. Dropout was set to 0.1. The model was trained on 8 GPUs, with a batch size of 2048 tokens and an update frequency of 4.

During the inference phase, an open-source VAD tool was used to process the source speech and obtain speech segments and durations for subsequent selection of NMT translated text lengths and adjusting the duration of synthetic dubbings. The NMT translated text was then converted to phoneme sequences using an open-source grapheme-to-phoneme tool, and the initial phoneme durations were predicted using a pre-trained variation predictor module in FastSpeech2.

As the main evaluation method for this task is manual evaluation, and our method allows for adjustment of phoneme duration prediction, We mainly experiment and compare BLEU (Papineni et al., 2002) under different strategies of machine translation. To measure the synchronicity between source and dubbed speech, we use speech overlap (SO) (Chronopoulou et al., 2023) metric. It should be noted that the metrics presented don't take into account speech naturalness, which is extremely important to people viewing dubs. (Brannon et al., 2022) showed that human dubbers produces natural speech even at the cost of isochrony. The experimental results on the two test sets of the task are shown in Table 2.

Strategy	subset1		subset2	
	BLEU	SO	BLEU	SO
Xlonger	24.8	0.71	22.0	0.49
Longer	28.0	0.82	26.1	0.70
Equal	37.4	0.83	32.4	0.83
Shorter	42.7	0.79	37.4	0.85
Xshorter	45.7	0.73	43.3	0.83
Re-ranking	31.2	0.92	33.8	0.93
Scaling	31.2	0.97	33.8	0.98
- w/o PA	31.6	0.89	34.7	0.87

Table 2: Experimental results of NMT.

We present the BLEU and SO results using five different LR tags, re-ranking and scaling strategies. The results of the two test sets have the same trend in BLEU, that is, the shorter the generated translation, the higher the BLEU value. Since subset2 has pause punctuation, it is more difficult to translate, so under the same LR tag at all levels, the BLEU value of subset2 will be lower than that of subset1. In terms of SO, both too long or too short translations will cause SO to decrease. The results of medium LR settings can achieve the highest SO value.

Too long translations will result in lower quality of machine translation, while short translations will result in insufficient duration for generating dubbing. After re-ranking, the translations can achieve more moderate results in translation quality and duration. Moreover, by setting appropriate scaling thresholds, scaling operation can further improve the isochrony without affecting BLEU.

We also compared the results without pause alignment, as shown in the last row of Table 2. The SO of both test sets decreased significantly, but the BLEU increased slightly. After analysis, the MT translation is more likely to mismatch with the shorter segment duration, so the shorter translation is selected during re-ranking. While our results show that the shorter the translation, the higher the BLEU.

5 Conclusion

This paper describes the submission of Huawei Translation Services Center for the IWSLT 2023 dubbing task under the unconstrained setting. Our solution consists of four parts: pause alignment, machine translation, phoneme duration variation predictor, re-ranking and scaling. Pause alignment is used to align source audio and source text to improve synchronization between synthetic dubbing and source video. The machine translation model is trained using the Deep Transformer structure. To control the output translation length, multiple target-to-source length-ratio tags are used to adjust the length. Pre-trained variation predictor in FastSpeech2 is used to predict phoneme durations. In order to optimize the isochrony in dubbing, the results of different lengths of the machine translation output are re-ranked and scaled. Using the source audio duration as a reference, the translations with different length ratios are re-ranked, and the output with the smallest time deviation is preferred. In addition, the phoneme duration output is scaled within a defined threshold, further narrowing the duration gap from the source audio. We compare the experimental results of different length-ratio strategies, and our method can achieve a balanced result in BLEU and speech overlap.

References

Milind Agarwal, Sweta Agrawal, Antonios Anastasopoulos, Ondřej Bojar, Claudia Borg, Marine Carpuat, Roldano Cattoni, Mauro Cettolo, Mingda

Chen, William Chen, Khalid Choukri, Alexandra Chronopoulou, Anna Currey, Thierry Declerck, Qianqian Dong, Yannick Estève, Kevin Duh, Marcello Federico, Souhir Gahbiche, Barry Haddow, Benjamin Hsu, Phu Mon Htut, Hirofumi Inaguma, John Javorský, Dávid and Judge, Yasumasa Kano, Tom Ko, Rishu Kumar, Pengwei Li, Xutail Ma, Prashant Mathur, Evgeny Matusov, Paul McNamee, John P. McCrae, Kenton Murray, Maria Nadejde, Satoshi Nakamura, Matteo Negri, Ha Nguyen, Jan Niehues, Xing Niu, Atul Ojha Kr., John E. Ortega, Proyag Pal, Juan Pino, Lonneke van der Plas, Peter Polák, Elijah Rippeth, Elizabeth Salesky, Jiatong Shi, Matthias Sperber, Ṡebastian Stüker, Katsuhito Sudoh, Yun Tang, Brian Thompson, Kevin Tran, Marco Turchi, Alex Waibel, Mingxuan Wang, Shinji Watanabe, and Rodolfo Zevallos. 2023. Findings of the IWSLT 2023 Evaluation Campaign. In *Proceedings of the 20th International Conference on Spoken Language Translation (IWSLT 2023)*. Association for Computational Linguistics.

William Brannon, Yogesh Virkar, and Brian Thompson. 2022. Dubbing in practice: A large scale study of human localization with insights for automatic dubbing.

Alexandra Chronopoulou, Brian Thompson, Prashant Mathur, Yogesh Virkar, Surafel M. Lakew, and Marcello Federico. 2023. Jointly optimizing translations and speech timing to improve isochrony in automatic dubbing.

Chris Dyer, Victor Chahuneau, and Noah A. Smith. 2013. A simple, fast, and effective reparameterization of IBM model 2. In *Proceedings of the 2013 Conference of the North American Chapter of the Association for Computational Linguistics: Human Language Technologies*, pages 644–648, Atlanta, Georgia. Association for Computational Linguistics.

Johanes Effendi, Yogesh Virkar, Roberto Barra-Chicote, and Marcello Federico. 2022. Duration modeling of neural tts for automatic dubbing. In *ICASSP 2022 - 2022 IEEE International Conference on Acoustics, Speech and Signal Processing (ICASSP)*, pages 8037–8041.

Marcello Federico, Robert Enyedi, Roberto Barra-Chicote, Ritwik Giri, Umut Isik, Arvindh Krishnaswamy, and Hassan Sawaf. 2020. From speech-to-speech translation to automatic dubbing. In *Proceedings of the 17th International Conference on Spoken Language Translation*, pages 257–264, Online. Association for Computational Linguistics.

Anmol Gulati, James Qin, Chung-Cheng Chiu, Niki Parmar, Yu Zhang, Jiahui Yu, Wei Han, Shibo Wang, Zhengdong Zhang, Yonghui Wu, and Ruoming Pang. 2020. Conformer: Convolution-augmented transformer for speech recognition.

Diederik P. Kingma and Jimmy Ba. 2017. Adam: A method for stochastic optimization.

Philipp Koehn, Hieu Hoang, Alexandra Birch, Chris Callison-Burch, Marcello Federico, Nicola Bertoldi, Brooke Cowan, Wade Shen, Christine Moran, Richard Zens, Chris Dyer, Ondřej Bojar, Alexandra Constantin, and Evan Herbst. 2007. Moses: Open source toolkit for statistical machine translation. In *Proceedings of the 45th Annual Meeting of the Association for Computational Linguistics Companion Volume Proceedings of the Demo and Poster Sessions*, pages 177–180, Prague, Czech Republic. Association for Computational Linguistics.

Taku Kudo and John Richardson. 2018. SentencePiece: A simple and language independent subword tokenizer and detokenizer for neural text processing. In *Proceedings of the 2018 Conference on Empirical Methods in Natural Language Processing: System Demonstrations*, pages 66–71, Brussels, Belgium. Association for Computational Linguistics.

Surafel M. Lakew, Yogesh Virkar, Prashant Mathur, and Marcello Federico. 2022. Isometric mt: Neural machine translation for automatic dubbing. In *ICASSP 2022 - 2022 IEEE International Conference on Acoustics, Speech and Signal Processing (ICASSP)*, pages 6242–6246.

Zongyao Li, Jiaxin Guo, Daimeng Wei, Hengchao Shang, Minghan Wang, Ting Zhu, Zhanglin Wu, Zhengzhe Yu, Xiaoyu Chen, Lizhi Lei, Hao Yang, and Ying Qin. 2022. HW-TSC's participation in the IWSLT 2022 isometric spoken language translation. In *Proceedings of the 19th International Conference on Spoken Language Translation (IWSLT 2022)*, pages 361–368, Dublin, Ireland (in-person and online). Association for Computational Linguistics.

Adam Lopez. 2008. Statistical machine translation. *ACM Comput. Surv.*, 40(3).

Marco Lui and Timothy Baldwin. 2011. Cross-domain feature selection for language identification. In *Proceedings of 5th International Joint Conference on Natural Language Processing*, pages 553–561, Chiang Mai, Thailand. Asian Federation of Natural Language Processing.

Marco Lui and Timothy Baldwin. 2012. langid.py: An off-the-shelf language identification tool. In *Proceedings of the ACL 2012 System Demonstrations*, pages 25–30, Jeju Island, Korea. Association for Computational Linguistics.

Myle Ott, Sergey Edunov, Alexei Baevski, Angela Fan, Sam Gross, Nathan Ng, David Grangier, and Michael Auli. 2019. fairseq: A fast, extensible toolkit for sequence modeling. In *Proceedings of the 2019 Conference of the North American Chapter of the Association for Computational Linguistics (Demonstrations)*, pages 48–53, Minneapolis, Minnesota. Association for Computational Linguistics.

Kishore Papineni, Salim Roukos, Todd Ward, and Wei-Jing Zhu. 2002. Bleu: a method for automatic evaluation of machine translation. In *Proceedings of the*

40th Annual Meeting of the Association for Computational Linguistics, pages 311–318, Philadelphia, Pennsylvania, USA. Association for Computational Linguistics.

Jongseok Park, Kyubyong Kim. 2019. g2pe. https://github.com/Kyubyong/g2p.

Yi Ren, Chenxu Hu, Xu Tan, Tao Qin, Sheng Zhao, Zhou Zhao, and Tie-Yan Liu. 2022. Fastspeech 2: Fast and high-quality end-to-end text to speech.

Steffen Schneider, Alexei Baevski, Ronan Collobert, and Michael Auli. 2019. wav2vec: Unsupervised pre-training for speech recognition.

Silero Team. 2021. Silero vad: pre-trained enterprise-grade voice activity detector (vad), number detector and language classifier. https://github.com/snakers4/silero-vad.

Ashish Vaswani, Noam Shazeer, Niki Parmar, Jakob Uszkoreit, Llion Jones, Aidan N Gomez, Ł ukasz Kaiser, and Illia Polosukhin. 2017. Attention is all you need. In *Advances in Neural Information Processing Systems*, volume 30. Curran Associates, Inc.

Yogesh Virkar, Marcello Federico, Robert Enyedi, and Roberto Barra-Chicote. 2021. Improvements to prosodic alignment for automatic dubbing. In *ICASSP 2021 - 2021 IEEE International Conference on Acoustics, Speech and Signal Processing (ICASSP)*, pages 7543–7574.

Yogesh Virkar, Marcello Federico, Robert Enyedi, and Roberto Barra-Chicote. 2022. Prosodic alignment for off-screen automatic dubbing.

Changhan Wang, Anne Wu, and Juan Pino. 2020. Covost 2 and massively multilingual speech-to-text translation.

Mingxuan Wang, Zhengdong Lu, Jie Zhou, and Qun Liu. 2017a. Deep neural machine translation with linear associative unit. In *Proceedings of the 55th Annual Meeting of the Association for Computational Linguistics (Volume 1: Long Papers)*, pages 136–145, Vancouver, Canada. Association for Computational Linguistics.

Qiang Wang, Bei Li, Tong Xiao, Jingbo Zhu, Changliang Li, Derek F. Wong, and Lidia S. Chao. 2019. Learning deep transformer models for machine translation. In *Proceedings of the 57th Annual Meeting of the Association for Computational Linguistics*, pages 1810–1822, Florence, Italy. Association for Computational Linguistics.

Yuxuan Wang, RJ Skerry-Ryan, Daisy Stanton, Yonghui Wu, Ron J. Weiss, Navdeep Jaitly, Zongheng Yang, Ying Xiao, Zhifeng Chen, Samy Bengio, Quoc Le, Yannis Agiomyrgiannakis, Rob Clark, and Rif A. Saurous. 2017b. Tacotron: Towards end-to-end speech synthesis.

NAVER LABS Europe's Multilingual Speech Translation Systems for the IWSLT 2023 Low-Resource Track

Edward Gow-Smith[1*] **Alexandre Bérard**[2†] **Marcely Zanon Boito**[2†] **Ioan Calapodescu**[2]

[1] University of Sheffield [2] NAVER LABS Europe

egow-smith1@sheffield.ac.uk first.last@naverlabs.com

Abstract

This paper presents NAVER LABS Europe's systems for Tamasheq-French and Quechua-Spanish speech translation in the IWSLT 2023 Low-Resource track. Our work attempts to maximize translation quality in low-resource settings using multilingual parameter-efficient solutions that leverage strong pre-trained models. Our primary submission for Tamasheq outperforms the previous state of the art by 7.5 BLEU points on the IWSLT 2022 test set, and achieves 23.6 BLEU on this year's test set, outperforming the second best participant by 7.7 points. For Quechua, we also rank first and achieve 17.7 BLEU, despite having only two hours of translation data. Finally, we show that our proposed multilingual architecture is also competitive for high-resource languages, outperforming the best unconstrained submission to the IWSLT 2021 Multilingual track, despite using much less training data and compute.

1 Introduction

The vast majority of speech pipelines are developed for *high-resource* languages, a small percentage of languages that have ample amounts of annotated data available (Joshi et al., 2020). However, the assessment of systems' performance based only on high-resource settings can be problematic, since it fails to reflect the real-world performance these approaches will have in diverse and smaller datasets. Moreover, as around half of the world's languages are considered to be not only *low-resource*, but also from oral tradition (i.e., without a written form), there is an urgent need for speech technology that can operate robustly in such *low-resource settings* (Bird, 2011). In this context, the *IWSLT conference*[1] proposes low-resource speech translation (ST) challenges that allow the speech community to realistically benchmark ST approaches using diverse and representative datasets. This paper describes NAVER LABS Europe's (NLE) submission to two of the language pairs from the IWSLT 2023 (Agarwal et al., 2023) Low-Resource Track: Tamasheq-French (*Taq-Fr*) and Quechua-Spanish (*Que-Es*).

Most successful approaches for tackling scenarios where ST data is scarce perform transfer learning across languages and modalities, leveraging multilingual pre-trained models for both speech and text (Anastasopoulos et al., 2022). However, due to the large number of parameters of current Transformer-based (Vaswani et al., 2017) approaches, training such systems is computationally expensive and not accessible to everyone. **NLE's submission focuses on a multilingual parameter-efficient training solution that allows us to leverage strong pre-trained speech and text models to maximize performance in low-resource languages.**

We present new SOTA results for the *Taq-Fr* pair (17 hours of training data) that represent a 57% BLEU increase compared to the results achieved by Khurana et al. (IWSLT 2022 post-evaluation).[2] This same system achieves 23.6 BLEU on the IWSLT 2023 test set, an improvement of 7.71 BLEU compared to the second best result submitted this year. We also present SOTA results in the unconstrained setting for the *Que-Es* pair (2 hours of training data), while maintaining most of the performance in the *Taq-Fr* pair. In addition, to showcase the usefulness of our parameter-efficient multilingual solution we evaluate it on the high-resource setting of the IWSLT 2021 Multilingual Task (Anastasopoulos et al., 2021). We find that our approach outperforms the best IWSLT 2021 submission (FAIR, Tang et al., 2021), despite training considerably fewer parameters (-64%), and using substantially

*Work done during an internship at NAVER LABS Europe.

†Equal contribution

[1] https://iwslt.org/

[2] https://www.clsp.jhu.edu/jsalt-2022-closing-presentations/

Proceedings of the 20th International Conference on Spoken Language Translation (IWSLT 2023), pages 144–158
July 13-14, 2023 ©2023 Association for Computational Linguistics

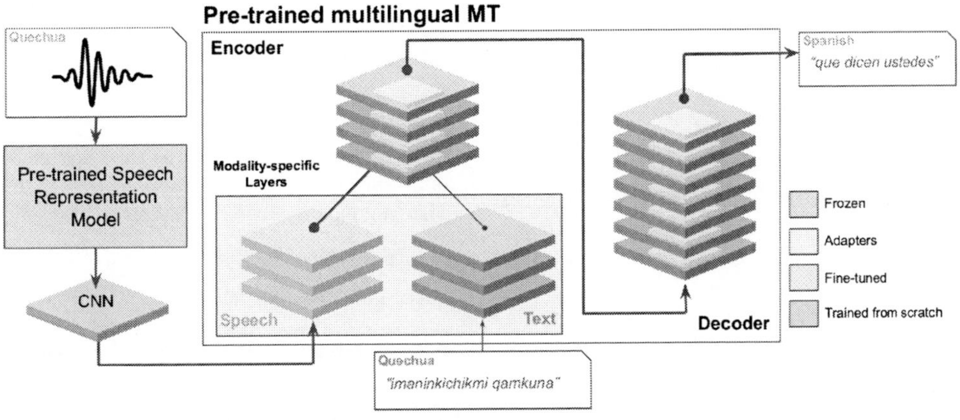

Figure 1: An illustration of our multilingual ST architecture as described in Section 2. The bold arrow path corresponds to the speech-to-text training path. At decoding time, we can choose between producing speech-to-text or text-to-text translations. Figure best seen in color.

less training data and compute.

This paper is organized as follows. We first describe the architecture and training settings of our multilingual ST systems in Section 2. We next list the resources we use in Section 3. Section 4 presents our results in both low and high-resource settings. Lastly, we highlight the zero-shot potential of our approach in Section 5 and present our concluding remarks in Section 6.

2 System Description

In this work we focus on a parameter-efficient training solution that allows us to input the features from a pre-trained speech representation model into a pre-trained multilingual MT model, producing translations from both speech and text in multilingual settings. This setting also allows us to leverage automatic speech recognition (ASR; i.e. speech-to-transcript) data. The general architecture is presented in Figure 1. The architecture is considered *parameter-efficient* because a small portion of its parameters are trained (bottom encoder layers and small adapters layers).

Architecture. We initialize our models with a pre-trained multilingual MT model, which we adapt to the ST task by inputting features extracted with a frozen pre-trained speech representation model. The MT model is also frozen, except for the bottom 2 or 3 encoder layers and small adapter modules (those introduced by Bapna and Firat (2019), with bottleneck dimension 64) added after each encoder and decoder layer. As we show in our results, the fine-tuned encoder layers are able to map the speech features into the representation space of the pre-trained MT model and the adapters can help with domain adaptation (and possibly help alleviate the length mismatch). At inference, this model can be used for MT with very little memory overhead: the convolutional layers and adapters are disabled, and the bottom encoder layers are swapped with those of the initial pre-trained model.

Training settings. We train on 4 V100 GPUs (80GB) for up to 200 000 updates, with a maximum batch size of 4 000 source features (or 80 seconds of audio) and accumulated gradients over two batches.[3] We sample language pairs with a temperature of 3.[4] We validate every 5 000 updates and perform early stopping on valid BLEU for the language pair(s) of interest, with a patience of 5, averaging model weights across the last 3 checkpoints.[5] We find best results using a single convolutional layer with stride 2, which downsamples the sequence of speech features by a factor of 2. The other hyperparameters are listed in Appendix Section A.1.

[3]This corresponds to a total of 32 000 features per update, or 640 seconds of audio. In practice, with padding, each update corresponds to approximately 80 utterances or 530 seconds of audio.

[4]$p_k = u_k^{1/3} / \sum u_i^{1/3}$ where u_k is the utterance count for language pair k.

[5]While all the configurations presented in this paper use checkpoint averaging, we later re-trained our contrastive submission for *Taq-Fr* and found virtually the same results without it.

Model	# params	Transformer layers	Feature dimension
Tamasheq (Boito et al., 2022b)	95M	12	768
Niger-Mali (Boito et al., 2022b)	95M	12	768
mHuBERT-Tamasheq	95M	12	768
XLSR-53 (Conneau et al., 2021)	317M	24	1024
XLS-R (Babu et al., 2022)	317M	24	1024

Table 1: Speech representation models. The top portion presents *Tamasheq-dedicated* models, while the bottom lists large *general purpose* multilingual models.

Task	Source	Target	hours:minutes	# utterances
ASR	Quechua	Quechua	51:39	8,301
ST	Quechua	Spanish	2:42	698
ST	Tamasheq	French	15:43	5,025

Table 2: Speech Translation (ST) and Speech Recognition (ASR) data provided by the organizers (train+valid). The ASR data is outside of the constrained setting.

3 Resources

3.1 Pre-trained Speech Representation Models

We experiment with different versions of two speech representation models: HuBERT (Hsu et al., 2021) and wav2vec 2.0 (Baevski et al., 2020). We do not fine-tune these models in any of our configurations, but instead use them as feature extractors (see Figure 1). Because of this, our models are sensitive to the layer we extract features from. Pasad et al. (2021) argue that, for wav2vec 2.0 models that are not fine-tuned on ASR, speech features from *middle* layers tend to have a higher abstraction from the speech signal, which is beneficial to downstream tasks. The results from Boito et al. (2022b) seem to confirm this observation holds for low-resource ST. To the best of our knowledge, there is no similar investigation for HuBERT models.[6]

Table 1 presents the speech representation models we experiment with. The *Tamasheq* model is a monolingual wav2vec 2.0 Base model trained on 243 h of Tamasheq speech. The *Niger-Mali* is a wav2vec 2.0 Base model trained on the same Tamasheq speech data plus 111 h of French, 109 h of Fulfulde, 100 h of Hausa, and 95 h of Zarma. This gives 658 h in total. The data for both models is sourced from the Niger-Mali audio collection (Boito et al., 2022a). The unreleased *mHuBERT-Tamasheq* model uses this same audio collection for training, while also including Common Voice (Ardila et al., 2020) data in four other languages (English, French, Arabic and Kabyle), resulting in 5 069 h of speech. *XLSR-53* (56k hours) and *XLS-R* (500k hours) are massively multilingual wav2vec 2.0 Large models covering 53 and 128 languages, respectively. Neither of these two multilingual models have seen Tamasheq or Quechua speech during training.[7]

3.2 Pre-trained Multilingual MT Models

To initialize our ST models, we first experimented with mBART for many-to-many translation (mBART50NN; Tang et al., 2020), but found the NLLB-200 models (Costa-jussà et al., 2022) to give better results. We experiment with the dense NLLB models of various sizes: the distilled 600M-parameter and 1.3B-parameter versions, and the 3.3B-parameter version. We end up using the larger versions in our submissions (1.3B and 3.3B). Note that NLLB covers 202 languages, including Tamsheq and Quechua, which is not the case for mBART. At the same model size, despite covering more languages, NLLB is also a stronger machine translation model overall than mBART. Also, unlike mBART, it is not English-centric.

Contrary to Tang et al. (2021), we keep the original mBART or NLLB vocabularies of size 250k and do not train any embeddings. Instead, like Berard et al. (2021), we find that it is possible to filter the vocabulary at test time to only cover the languages of interest, significantly reducing the memory footprint of the model with a minor reduction in performance.[8] We can also filter the vocabulary and embeddings before ST fine-tuning and achieve the same performance as with the full vocabulary without needing to train any embeddings. See Table 14 in Appendix for a comparison of these approaches. In order to study the zero-shot translation capabilities of our models (i.e., translating to languages and language pairs unseen at training), we do not apply vocabulary filtering to the configurations presented in the main paper.

[6]We hypothesize that layer selection is less important for HuBERT architectures due to the multi-iteration approach that increases signal abstraction at each iteration.

[7]Appendix Table 16 lists all models with links for downloading checkpoints, when available.

[8]With NLLB, 44k tokens are enough for a 100% coverage of the training data (mTEDx, TED-LIUM, Quechua, Tamasheq), or 35k when restricting to our *Taq-Fr* setting. This represents a reduction of more than 200M parameters.

Task	Source	Target	hours:minutes	# utterances
ASR	English	English	208:00	91,003
ASR	French	French	218:59	117,081
ASR	Spanish	Spanish	214:15	103,076
ST	French	English	57:39	31,207
ST	French	Spanish	42:14	21,862
ST	Spanish	English	79:37	37,168
ST	Spanish	French	9:34	4,568

Table 3: ASR and ST data in English, French and Spanish sourced from TED talks (unconstrained setting).

3.3 Datasets

We tackle the low-resource setting by building multilingual systems that utilize both ASR and ST data in the languages of interest (Tamasheq and Quechua), and in high-resource directions whose target language is of interest (French and Spanish). Note that we also include X→English data, as we initially planned to participate in the Irish-English task. Including more data in high-resource languages has several advantages. Firstly, it has a regularization effect that prevents us from immediately overfitting the low-resource training data. Secondly, this enables knowledge transfer from common target languages and from similarly-sounding source languages.[9] Thirdly, as we build multilingual ST systems by mapping the speech representation vectors into the same space as the multilingual MT model, our goal is to produce a model that is *as multilingual as possible*, not specializing in one specific language. Our results show that training on multiple languages at once achieves this effect, while also producing good zero-shot ST results.

Table 2 presents statistics for the datasets provided by the IWSLT 2023 organizers. The *Que-Es* dataset[10] is an unreleased dataset prepared for this year's challenge. It corresponds to a translated subset of the Quechua ASR data ("Siminchik") from Cardenas et al. (2018). The *Taq-Fr* dataset was introduced by Boito et al. (2022a). Table 3 presents statistics for the datasets in high-resource languages. English ASR data comes from TED-LIUMv2 (Rousseau et al., 2014), and the other data comes from mTEDx (Salesky et al., 2021). Appendix Table 15 lists the datasets used in each of our submissions. In Section 4.3, we also run experiments in the setting of the IWSLT 2021 Multilingual Task to measure how good our approach is on high-resource languages. The datasets used for this setting are presented in Appendix Table 10.

[9]Manual inspection revealed that audio from both datasets presents some degree of target language borrowing (e.g., Spanish words present in the Quechua speech, French words present in the Tamasheq speech).

[10]We are aware the dataset reference is *Que-Spa*. We chose to use the ISO 639-1 two letters abbreviation for Spanish for consistency with the other datasets used in this work.

		Taq-Fr IWSLT 2022	Taq-Fr IWSLT 2023	Que-Es IWSLT 2023
Taq-Fr	primary	**20.75**	**23.59**	✗
	contrastive 1	19.06	21.31	✗
	contrastive 2	18.58	18.73	**17.74**
Que-Es	primary	18.58	18.73	**17.74**
	contrastive 1	16.84	✗	15.67
	contrastive 2	16.21	✗	15.25

Table 4: Results on the official test sets for the IWSLT 2023 Low-Resource Task. We also show results on the IWSLT 2022 *Taq-Fr* test set. Note that all Quechua models are trained on Tamasheq data, but the reverse is not true (see Appendix Table 15). Lines 3 and 4 correspond to the same model.

4 Experiments and Results

All our submissions to the low-resource ST task are in the *unconstrained* setting, due to the use of pre-trained models, and from training on data in other languages. The datasets used in each submission are listed in Appendix Table 15. This section is organized as follows. We present our *Taq-Fr* results (4.1) with a detailed ablation study justifying our architectural choices. We then present our *Que-Es* results (4.2). Lastly, we evaluate and analyze our approach in a high-resource setting (4.3).

4.1 Tamasheq-French Results

We submit two systems that have *Taq-Fr* as the only low-resource language pair (**primary** and **contrastive 1**). Additionally, we take our primary submission for *Que-Es*, which has also been trained on *Taq-Fr*, and submit this as **contrastive 2**. The top portion of Table 4 gives the test BLEU scores, and the top portion of Appendix Table 11 presents the valid BLEU scores. Table 12 shows statistics (average and standard deviation) over multiple runs when applicable.

System description. The **contrastive 1** model uses as a speech feature extractor the *Niger-Mali* wav2vec 2.0 model (8th layer). It was initialized with NLLB 1.3B, whose bottom 3 encoder layers were finetuned. We took three runs of this setting with different random seeds and picked the best performing one on the validation set (in terms of

Taq-Fr BLEU) as our contrastive submission. We then ensembled the three runs as our **primary** submission. Finally, **constrastive 2** is the ensemble model used as primary submission to the *Que-Es* task, which covers both low-resource languages, and combines *XSL-R Large* with *NLLB 3.3B*.

Results. Our primary submission significantly outperforms the previous state of the art of 13.2 BLEU (+7.5 BLEU) on the IWSLT 2022 test set by Khurana et al. (2022).[11] It also ranks first in this year's edition, with +7.7 BLEU over the second best primary submission. Our contrastive submissions rank second and third (beating the second best primary submission by +5.4 and +2.8 BLEU).

4.1.1 Ablation Study

In Appendix Table 18 we compare our **contrastive 1** model (the non-ensembled version of our primary submission) with other architectures trained on the same data to validate our choice of hyperparameters.

Speech features. The wav2vec 2.0 models trained with Tamasheq (*Niger-Mali* and *Tamasheq*) largely outperform the well-known massively multilingual models (*XLSR-53* and *XLS-R*) on *Taq-Fr* (e.g. +2.5 BLEU *Tamasheq* compared to *XLS-R L*). These models are larger and trained on considerably more data, but do not include any Tamasheq speech. Similar to previous works (Pasad et al., 2021; Boito et al., 2022b), when extracting features from wav2vec 2.0 we find that the 8th layer gives better results than the 11th (penultimate) layer (+2.5 BLEU for *Niger-Mali*).

For HuBERT, on the contrary, features from the 11th layer give the best results (+0.2 BLEU compared to 8th layer). When using the *right layer*, we find that wav2vec 2.0 outperforms HuBERT (+2.7 BLEU *Niger-Mali* compared to *mHuBERT-Taq*).

Finally, *Niger-Mali* is as good on *Taq-Fr* as the *Tamasheq* wav2vec 2.0, but performs considerably better on *Fr-En* (+4.1 BLEU), probably because it was trained with French audio. The best *Fr-En* performance is achieved with *XLS-R L*. We find worse performance on *Fr-En* with *XLS-R XL* (-2.0 BLEU), but this may be due to layer selection.

Pre-trained MT model. The larger the model used for initialization, the better the performance (even more so for *Fr-En*). However, we find that the gain from using NLLB 3.3B over NLLB 1.3B is too small to justify the increase in model size and decoding latency (3 times slower). At the same model size, NLLB 600M performs considerably better than mBART (+1.7 BLEU on *Taq-Fr*, +3.6 BLEU on *Fr-En*).

Trained parameters. Fine-tuning too many encoder layers results in overfitting, which hurts *Taq-Fr* and *Fr-En* performance. On the other hand, fine-tuning just 1 or 2 layers instead of 3 does *not* result in a large BLEU drop. Similarly, adapter modules are not always needed. Disabling decoder adapters does not degrade *Taq-Fr* performance (+0.2 BLEU), but results in a slight drop in *Fr-En* performance (-0.9 BLEU), which could be attributed to a domain adaptation effect (to the mTEDx domain). Disabling encoder adapters has more impact on performance for *Taq-Fr* (-0.8 BLEU), with similar effect on performance for *Fr-En* (-1.0 BLEU). Section 4.3 shows that these adapters are important for domain adaptation.

Convolutions. The number of convolutional layers does not impact performance much (range of 1.1 BLEU on *Taq-Fr* and 3.2 BLEU on *Fr-En* for 0 to 3 layers), but it can have a large impact on decoding speed: each layer divides the input length by a factor of 2 resulting in a roughly 3.5× speed-up from 0 to 3 layers. Interestingly, even though it was trained on much shorter sequences, the MT model seems to adapt quite well to any input length, even without any convolutions – we achieve a better *Taq-Fr* result without any convolutions, but a worse *Fr-En* result.[12] However, models with fewer convolutional layers seem to converge faster (as shown in Appendix Figure 2).

Stacked layers. While our approach described in Section 2 fine-tunes some parameters of the pre-trained MT model, we can instead plug new Transformer layers at the bottom of the encoder, without changing any existing parameter. These "stacked layers" result in slightly larger models but are conceptually simpler, as they try to map the speech features into the same representation space as the input text embeddings of the MT model. Appendix Table 17 compares this architecture with the one used in our submission to the *Taq-Fr* task. We see

[11]Here we are referencing the model pre-trained using the Niger-Mali dataset that was presented at JSALT 2022: `https://www.clsp.jhu.edu/jsalt-2022-closing-presentations/`

[12]Without any convolution, the speech feature to target token ratio is **12:1**.

that it performs similarly well (sometimes better) and that it does not add any noticeable decoding latency. We can even reach the same *Taq-Fr* performance as our contrastive submission by just adding a single Transformer layer plus one convolution layer and small adapters (28M trained parameters in total). Finally, disabling all adapters only results in a small BLEU drop, suggesting that it is indeed possible to map the speech features into the text input space, with only one Transformer layer. This is surprising, considering that the input to this layer is 6 times as long as the target sequence on average.

4.2 Quechua-Spanish Results

The test and validation scores of our submissions to the *Que-Es* task are reported in the second half of Table 4 and 11, respectively. Because these models are also trained on *Taq-Fr* data, we additionally report their performance on that task.

System description. As we do not have a speech feature extractor specialized to Quechua speech, our **contrastive 1** submission uses a massively multilingual wav2vec 2.0 model: XLS-R Large (18th layer). Compared to our Tamasheq submission, it is also initialized with a larger MT model (NLLB 3.3B), which we found to perform better in this setting. The training settings are the same as for the Tamasheq models, except that we only fine-tune the bottom 2 encoder layers (instead of 3) and validate every 2 500 updates, since this larger model tends to converge faster. Another difference is that we train on both Tamasheq and Quechua data (in addition to the mTEDx and TED-LIUM data). Like in our Tamasheq submission, we train 3 models with different random seeds and ensemble them as our **primary** submission. Our **constrastive 2** submission uses a single model with the same training settings, but starts from a smaller pre-trained MT model (NLLB 1.3B).

Results. Our primary submission in the *Que-Es* task also ranked first, with 17.7 BLEU on the official test set. The full ranking results were not communicated in time to this camera-ready. They will be made available later through the conference findings paper (Agarwal et al., 2023).

Data contamination. We found shortly after our submission that all the audio files used in the official test and validation sets are also present in the ASR training data shared by the organizers for the unconstrained setting. This means that our *Que-Es* ST models are evaluated in an unrealistic setting, where they are tasked to translate Quechua utterances of which they already know the transcription into Quechua. For this reason, we filtered the ASR data to remove all audio files also present in the validation and test sets for *Que-Es*, and we re-trained models on this filtered data.[13] While our official submission results presented in Table 4 use the "contaminated" dataset for comparison with the other submissions, we think any future comparison to our work should be done with the updated results in Appendix Table 11. Note that similar care should be taken with the results of other participants.

4.3 Results and Analysis in a High-Resource Setting

The results of our ablation studies (Section 4.1.1) seem to indicate that our models are reasonably good on *Fr-En* translation, even though we do early stopping and tune our hyper-parameters based on *Taq-Fr* performance. Here, we further investigate the performance of our approach on high-resource ST by training models in the setting of the IWSLT 2021 Multilingual Task (Anastasopoulos et al., 2021). This task evaluates the performance of multilingual ST models in 4 *training directions*, for which in-domain training data is provided, and 3 *zero-shot directions*, for which no training data is provided.

We use *XLS-R Large* as the speech feature extractor, experiment with both *NLLB 1.3B* and *NLLB 3.3B* as the MT model, and perform early stopping based on the average validation BLEU across the 4 official training directions. We train our models on all the mTEDx language pairs that are not zero-shot, along with TED-LIUM (English ASR) and the Tamasheq and Quechua data (see Table 15). Note that the use of pre-trained models and English ASR means our models fall into the unconstrained setting.

Table 5 presents our results on this task, compared with the best unconstrained submission (FAIR; Tang et al., 2021).[14] We find that both our models outperform FAIR's ensemble submission in the training directions, even though they require substantially less compute and data to train, and they are not ensembled. In the zero-shot direc-

[13] In the updated version, we use NLLB 1.3B by default instead of NLLB 3.3B, like for *Taq-Fr*. Appendix Table 11 presents *uncontaminated* results.

[14] SacreBLEU signature (Post, 2018): `nrefs:1|case:mixed|eff:no|tok:13a|smooth:exp|version:2.1.0`

Model	Total params	Trained params	Training directions				Zero-shot directions		
			Es-En	Fr-En	Fr-Es	Pt-En	Pt-Es	It-En	It-Es
FAIR at IWSLT 2021	700M		40.4	36.4	34.4	29.0	34.4	28.4	34.6
(Tang et al., 2021)	3×700M (ensemble)		42.2	38.7	36.5	31.0	**38.2**	**29.4**	**37.3**
XLS-R + NLLB 1.3B	317M + 1.38B	70M	43.7	39.4	38.0	31.5	35.9	28.9	35.0
XLS-R + NLLB 3.3B	317M + 3.36B	115M	**44.0**	**39.9**	**38.3**	**33.1**	38.1	29.3	36.9
XLS-R + NLLB 1.3B, ASR + MT cascade			41.8	35.6	34.4	29.7	35.8	29.3	35.2

Table 5: Results on the IWSLT 2021 Multilingual task. We report BLEU scores on the IWSLT 2021 test sets. Our NLLB 1.3B and 3.3B models took respectively 34 and 46 h to train on 4 V100 GPUs, while FAIR's models each took 7 days to train on 8 V100 GPUs. Also note that FAIR's models were trained on much larger amounts of data, **including data for the "zero-shot" directions** (which, in their case is only zero-shot w.r.t the in-domain TED data).

Model	New params	Taq-Fr
Joint training	0	**21.06**
Adapters 64 (all)	6.4M	17.60
Adapters 256 (all)	15.9M	18.18
Adapters 256 (bottom)	1.6M	19.24
Conv + Adapters 256 (bottom)	2.5M	19.13

Table 6: BLEU scores on the *Taq-Fr* validation set, when training jointly with IWSLT 2021 and Tamasheq data; versus incremental (2-stage) training. The "New params" columns give the number of Tamasheq-specific parameters added.

tions, our NLLB 1.3B version performs worse than FAIR's ensemble, which is not surprising since they used training data for the zero-shot language directions (from other datasets), whilst we do not.[15] We find that using the larger NLLB 3.3B model for initialization considerably improves our zero-shot results.

4.3.1 Incremental Learning

A limitation of our approach for low-resource ST is that we need to know in advance (when training the multilingual ST model) the set of low-resource languages to cover. Here, we show that it is possible to add a new low-resource language into an existing model without re-training it, similar to what has been previously done by Berard (2021) for text-to-text MT. We train a model following the IWSLT 2021 setting presented above, but without any Tamasheq or Quechua data. Then, we attempt to adapt it to *Taq-Fr* using four different approaches: **1)** adding adapters of dimension 64 in the bottom layers and training all adapters (including in the decoder layers and top encoder layers); **2)** adding adapters of dimension 256 in the bottom layers and fine-tuning all adapters; **3)** adding adapters of dimension 256 in the bottom layers and training only those; **4)** adding adapters of dimension 256 in the bottom layers and training both those and the convolutional layer.

We keep the same training settings as before, except that: we train on *Taq-Fr* data only; we train only the parameters mentioned above; we validate more often (every 1 000 updates); and we disable checkpoint averaging. Table 6 shows the performance of these four incremental training methods, compared to training on the entire language set from scratch. Even though incremental training does not perform quite as well, it appears to be a viable option that can achieve decent results. Lastly, we highlight that our experiments were limited to these four incremental learning settings (without hyper-parameter search), and that better results may be obtained with other parameter-efficient adaptation methods, or with more regularization.

4.3.2 Multimodality and Domain Transfer

Since our systems are initialized with an MT model, of which just a few encoder layers are modified, it is straightforward to use our ST models for text-to-text translation: we just need to store both the MT and ST bottom layers and route tokens through the MT ones (see Figure 1). However, one question that remains is whether the ST adapters can be used for text-to-text decoding.

As an investigation of this, Appendix Table 19 measures the MT performance (NLLB 1.3B) on the IWSLT 2021 test sets (same domain as the mTEDx training data) with and without the ST adapters. Surprisingly, we see that not only can we use these adapters for both text and speech modalities, but they actually improve the MT scores (+2.7 BLEU on average), even though they were only trained with ST and ASR data. This suggests that the fine-tuned bottom layers are able to fully map the speech representations into the text represen-

[15] NLLB has been pretrained on these language pairs for MT, but we do not train on ST data for them.

Adapter Size	Encoder Adapters	Decoder Adapters	Taq-Fr BLEU	Taq-En BLEU	Taq-Ko BLEU	Taq-Fr chrF	Taq-En chrF	Taq-Ko chrF
64	✓	✓	19.1	**17.1**	12.6	44.2	40.8	18.2
128	✓	✓	19.2	16.7	9.6	**44.7**	40.3	14.5
64	✓	✗	**19.3**	16.8	14.6	44.4	**42.4**	21.5
✗	✗	✗	17.5	16.2	14.4	43.0	40.8	21.5
ST (contrastive 1) + MT (NLLB 1.3B) cascade			✗	15.0	**15.7**	✗	38.6	**22.2**

Table 7: BLEU and chrF results for *Taq-{Fr, En, Ko}* using **contrastive 1** and its variants (models trained without adapters or with larger adapters), on the IWSLT 2022 *Taq-Fr* test set or silver-standard Korean and English references obtained with MT. The last row is a cascade of speech translation followed by text translation (Taq→Fr→X).

tation space and that the adapters further improve performance by allowing domain adaptation of the MT model (which is hard to do at the very bottom layers). Note that the encoder adapters seem to be the most important ones, which is consistent with the findings of Cooper Stickland et al. (2021) that adapting the encoder is the most effective strategy for domain adaptation. Lastly, we highlight that adapting the MT model directly with MT data (mTEDx's transcriptions and translations) gives even better results (+4.6 BLEU on average), but this cross-modality domain transfer is an interesting by-product of our parameter-efficient approach.

5 Zero-Shot Capabilities

Throughout this paper we have argued that one advantage of the multilingual models we propose is their potential for zero-shot translation, a setting in which a system produces translation in an unseen language pair by leveraging its existing knowledge of both languages. In Section 4.3 we showed that our models are competitive with the best submission to IWSLT 2021 on the three zero-shot high-resource language pairs, despite the fact that these pairs were not truly zero-shot for that system. In this section, we further illustrate the zero-shot capabilities of our models by translating Tamasheq speech in two settings: **1)** target language seen during both MT pre-training and ST adaptation (English); **2)** target language only seen during MT pre-training (Korean).

Evaluation settings. To score BLEU and chrF[16] in the chosen target languages, we use a commercial translation service to translate the French side of the IWSLT 2022 test set to English and Korean. Note that this is only a *silver-standard* made of synthetic data, and thus the evaluation will inevitably be biased.[17] Our goal is solely to assess whether our systems have *some* zero-shot ST abilities. We evaluate our *Taq-Fr* **contrastive 1** system, and variants of this system with fewer or larger adapters. We compare with a *cascade* baseline, in which we first perform *Taq-Fr* ST, followed by *Fr-En* or *Fr-Ko* MT using the text-to-text path from Figure 1. In this setting, the adapters are disabled during MT.

Results. In Table 7, we measure the zero-shot translation capabilities of our approach on this silver-standard test set. We evaluate four models: our **contrastive 1** submission presented in Section 4.1, and variants of this model with increased adapter size, adapters only in the encoder, or no adapters. We compare against a cascade baseline that is not zero-shot, which consists in translating the Tamasheq speech into French text and then translating this text into English or Korean.

We observe that, in the case of English, which was seen during ST adaptation, adapters can be helpful (+2 BLEU over the cascade baseline). On the other hand, for Korean, unseen during ST adaptation, systems with adapters in the decoder (first two rows) perform worse, as they likely bring some degree of *language confusion*. Results are even worse with larger adapters, with over 40% of output sentences being in the wrong language. In this setting, the best results are achieved with only encoder adapters or no adapters at all (-1 BLEU compared to the baseline).

Appendix Table 13 measures the percentage of output sentences in the correct language and the percentage of Hangul versus Latin character in each system's outputs. We find that models with

[16]SacreBLEU signature: `nrefs:1|case:mixed|eff:no|tok:X|smooth:exp|version:2.3.1`, (En: `X=13a`, Ko: `X=ko-mecab-0.996/ko-0.9.2-KO`). chrF signature: `nrefs:1|case:mixed|eff:yes|nc:6|nw:0|space:no|version:2.3.1`

[17]For instance, we observe that these generated translations contain both the Korean transliteration in Hangul of named entities and the original version in the Latin script. This will likely penalize our produced translation during scoring.

Utterance id	Target	Content
2016-11-23_id_7	Ref	Chers auditeurs, rappelez-vous que vous écoutez **Studio Kalangou** en ce moment.
	Fr	Chers auditeurs, n'oubliez pas que vous êtes avec le **Studio Kalangou**.
	En	Well, listeners, don't forget that you are with **Studio Kalangou** right now.
	Ko	청취자 여러분, 지금 **Studio Kalangou**와 함께 있는 것을 잊지 마세요.
2016-06-27_id_5	Ref	Les examens du **BEPC** sont terminés et les corrections ont commencé hier après-midi dans la ville de Niamey.
	Fr	Les examens du **BEPC** sont terminés et sur toute l'étendue du territoire, les travaux de leur suivi ont débuté hier après-midi à Niamey.
	En	The **BEPC** exams are over and throughout the country, the monitoring activities started yesterday afternoon in Niamey.
	Ko	**BEPC** 시험은 끝났습니다. 전국에서 검사 작업은 어제 오후 Niamey에서 시작되었습니다.
2016-10-27_id_39	Ref	D'autres informations que nous apportons aujourd'hui concernent un projet appelé **aniamey.com** qui informe que l'État du Nigéria a refoulé des Nigériens, au nombre de 53, qui arrivent (), qui habitent dans la ville de Mina sur le territoire du Niger ou Neja.
	Fr	D'autres informations que nous apportons aujourd'hui concernent les informations apportées par un programme dénommé **Niamey Point Com** qui a apporté des informations selon lesquelles le Nigeria a accueilli 53 Nigériens qui habitent la ville de Mena qui se trouve sur le territoire du Niger ou le Niger.
	En	Today, we're going to talk about the information about a program called **Niamey Point Com**, which reports that Nigeria has brought back 53 Nigerians who live in the town of Mena in Niger.
	Ko	우리게임의 오늘 기사에서는 **Niamey Point Com**라는 프로그램으로 나이지리아가 미네에 거주하는 53명의 니그르인을 귀환시켰다는 소식이 있습니다.

Table 8: Some decoding examples for *Taq-Fr*, *Taq-En* and *Taq-Ko* language pairs, accompanied by the French reference (Ref). Utterance id corresponds to the suffix of the audio files in the IWSLT 2022 test set.

adapters in the decoder (first two rows) generate more Latin characters. Note that the ideal translation is not necessarily 100% Hangul, as it might sometimes be best to keep the foreign named entities in the Latin alphabet. Table 8 illustrates this with a few examples of translations from our **contrastive 1** system.

6 Conclusion

In this paper we presented our parameter-efficient multilingual systems as submissions to the IWSLT 2023 Low-Resource Task in the Tamasheq-French and Quechua-Spanish language pairs. The architecture we propose has several advantages: it is computationally and data efficient, it allows the same model to do both speech-to-text and text-to-text translation (or transcription), it maximizes knowledge transfer to improve low-resource performance, and it has good zero-shot translation capabilities. Our submissions reach a new state of the art performance, winning both speech translation challenges, especially for Tamasheq-French, where we outperform the previous state of the art by more than 7 BLEU points.

Future work will include a comprehensive evaluation of the ASR capabilities of our architecture, and the investigation of adapters inside the speech representation model. Moreover, when the speech representation model is frozen, a more in-depth analysis of the optimal layer is needed.

Acknowledgements

This work was partially funded by the European Horizon 2022 project UTTER (Unified Transcription and Translation for Extended Reality), under grant agreement No 101070631.

References

Milind Agarwal, Sweta Agrawal, Antonios Anastasopoulos, Ondřej Bojar, Claudia Borg, Marine Carpuat, Roldano Cattoni, Mauro Cettolo, Mingda Chen, William Chen, Khalid Choukri, Alexandra Chronopoulou, Anna Currey, Thierry Declerck, Qianqian Dong, Yannick Estève, Kevin Duh, Marcello Federico, Souhir Gahbiche, Barry Haddow, Benjamin Hsu, Phu Mon Htut, Hirofumi Inaguma, Dávid Javorský, John Judge, Yasumasa Kano, Tom Ko, Rishu Kumar, Pengwei Li, Xutail Ma, Prashant Mathur, Evgeny Matusov, Paul McNamee, John P. McCrae, Kenton Murray, Maria Nadejde, Satoshi Nakamura, Matteo Negri, Ha Nguyen, Jan Niehues, Xing Niu, Atul Ojha Kr., John E. Ortega, Proyag Pal, Juan Pino, Lonneke van der Plas, Peter Polák, Elijah Rippeth, Elizabeth Salesky, Jiatong Shi, Matthias Sperber, Sebastian Stüker, Katsuhito Sudoh, Yun Tang, Brian Thompson, Kevin Tran, Marco Turchi, Alex Waibel, Mingxuan Wang, Shinji Watanabe, and Rodolfo Zevallos. 2023. Findings of the IWSLT 2023 Evaluation Campaign. In *Proceedings of the 20th International Conference on Spoken Language Translation (IWSLT 2023)*. Association for Computational Linguistics.

Antonios Anastasopoulos, Loïc Barrault, Luisa Bentivogli, Marcely Zanon Boito, Ondřej Bojar, Roldano Cattoni, Anna Currey, Georgiana Dinu, Kevin Duh, Maha Elbayad, Clara Emmanuel, Yannick Estève, Marcello Federico, Christian Federmann, Souhir Gahbiche, Hongyu Gong, Roman Grundkiewicz, Barry Haddow, Benjamin Hsu, Dávid Javorský, Věra Kloudová, Surafel Lakew, Xutai Ma, Prashant Mathur, Paul McNamee, Kenton Murray, Maria Nădejde, Satoshi Nakamura, Matteo Negri, Jan Niehues, Xing Niu, John Ortega, Juan Pino, Elizabeth Salesky, Jiatong Shi, Matthias Sperber, Sebastian Stüker, Katsuhito Sudoh, Marco Turchi, Yogesh Virkar, Alexander Waibel, Changhan Wang, and Shinji Watanabe. 2022. Findings of the IWSLT 2022 evaluation campaign. In *Proceedings of the 19th International Conference on Spoken Language Translation (IWSLT 2022)*, pages 98–157, Dublin, Ireland (in-person and online). Association for Computational Linguistics.

Antonios Anastasopoulos, Ondřej Bojar, Jacob Bremerman, Roldano Cattoni, Maha Elbayad, Marcello Federico, Xutai Ma, Satoshi Nakamura, Matteo Negri, Jan Niehues, Juan Pino, Elizabeth Salesky, Sebastian Stüker, Katsuhito Sudoh, Marco Turchi, Alexander Waibel, Changhan Wang, and Matthew Wiesner. 2021. FINDINGS OF THE IWSLT 2021 EVALUATION CAMPAIGN. In *Proceedings of the 18th International Conference on Spoken Language Translation (IWSLT 2021)*, pages 1–29, Bangkok, Thailand (online). Association for Computational Linguistics.

Rosana Ardila, Megan Branson, Kelly Davis, Michael Kohler, Josh Meyer, Michael Henretty, Reuben Morais, Lindsay Saunders, Francis Tyers, and Gregor Weber. 2020. Common voice: A massively-multilingual speech corpus. In *Proceedings of the Twelfth Language Resources and Evaluation Conference*, pages 4218–4222, Marseille, France. European Language Resources Association.

Arun Babu, Changhan Wang, Andros Tjandra, Kushal Lakhotia, Qiantong Xu, Naman Goyal, Kritika Singh, Patrick von Platen, Yatharth Saraf, Juan Pino, Alexei Baevski, Alexis Conneau, and Michael Auli. 2022. XLS-R: Self-supervised Cross-lingual Speech Representation Learning at Scale. In *Proc. Interspeech 2022*, pages 2278–2282.

Alexei Baevski, Yuhao Zhou, Abdelrahman Mohamed, and Michael Auli. 2020. wav2vec 2.0: A framework for self-supervised learning of speech representations. *Advances in neural information processing systems*, 33:12449–12460.

Ankur Bapna and Orhan Firat. 2019. Simple, scalable adaptation for neural machine translation. In *Proceedings of the 2019 Conference on Empirical Methods in Natural Language Processing and the 9th International Joint Conference on Natural Language Processing (EMNLP-IJCNLP)*, pages 1538–1548, Hong Kong, China. Association for Computational Linguistics.

Alexandre Berard. 2021. Continual learning in multilingual NMT via language-specific embeddings. In *Proceedings of the Sixth Conference on Machine Translation*, pages 542–565, Online. Association for Computational Linguistics.

Alexandre Berard, Dain Lee, Stephane Clinchant, Kweonwoo Jung, and Vassilina Nikoulina. 2021. Efficient inference for multilingual neural machine translation. In *Proceedings of the 2021 Conference on Empirical Methods in Natural Language Processing*, pages 8563–8583, Online and Punta Cana, Dominican Republic. Association for Computational Linguistics.

Steven Bird. 2011. Bootstrapping the language archive: New prospects for natural language processing in preserving linguistic heritage. *Linguistic Issues in Language Technology*, 6(4).

Marcely Zanon Boito, Fethi Bougares, Florentin Barbier, Souhir Gahbiche, Loïc Barrault, Mickael Rouvier, and Yannick Estève. 2022a. Speech resources in the Tamasheq language. In *Proceedings of the Thirteenth Language Resources and Evaluation Conference*, pages 2066–2071, Marseille, France. European Language Resources Association.

Marcely Zanon Boito, John Ortega, Hugo Riguidel, Antoine Laurent, Loïc Barrault, Fethi Bougares, Firas Chaabani, Ha Nguyen, Florentin Barbier, Souhir Gahbiche, and Yannick Estève. 2022b. ON-TRAC consortium systems for the IWSLT 2022 dialect and low-resource speech translation tasks. In *Proceedings of the 19th International Conference on Spoken Language Translation (IWSLT 2022)*, pages 308–318, Dublin, Ireland (in-person and online). Association for Computational Linguistics.

Ronald Cardenas, Rodolfo Zevallos, Reynaldo Baquerizo, and Luis Camacho. 2018. Siminchik: A speech corpus for preservation of southern quechua. *ISI-NLP 2*, page 21.

Alexis Conneau, Alexei Baevski, Ronan Collobert, Abdelrahman Mohamed, and Michael Auli. 2021. Unsupervised Cross-Lingual Representation Learning for Speech Recognition. In *Proc. Interspeech 2021*, pages 2426–2430.

Asa Cooper Stickland, Alexandre Berard, and Vassilina Nikoulina. 2021. Multilingual domain adaptation for NMT: Decoupling language and domain information with adapters. In *Proceedings of the Sixth Conference on Machine Translation*, pages 578–598, Online. Association for Computational Linguistics.

Marta R Costa-jussà, James Cross, Onur Çelebi, Maha Elbayad, Kenneth Heafield, Kevin Heffernan, Elahe Kalbassi, Janice Lam, Daniel Licht, Jean Maillard, et al. 2022. No language left behind: Scaling human-centered machine translation. *arXiv preprint arXiv:2207.04672*.

Wei-Ning Hsu, Benjamin Bolte, Yao-Hung Hubert Tsai, Kushal Lakhotia, Ruslan Salakhutdinov, and Abdelrahman Mohamed. 2021. Hubert: Self-supervised speech representation learning by masked prediction of hidden units. *IEEE/ACM Transactions on Audio, Speech, and Language Processing*, 29:3451–3460.

Pratik Joshi, Sebastin Santy, Amar Budhiraja, Kalika Bali, and Monojit Choudhury. 2020. The state and fate of linguistic diversity and inclusion in the NLP world. In *Proceedings of the 58th Annual Meeting of the Association for Computational Linguistics*.

Sameer Khurana, Antoine Laurent, and James Glass. 2022. Samu-xlsr: Semantically-aligned multimodal utterance-level cross-lingual speech representation. *IEEE Journal of Selected Topics in Signal Processing*, 16(6):1493–1504.

Ankita Pasad, Ju-Chieh Chou, and Karen Livescu. 2021. Layer-wise analysis of a self-supervised speech representation model. In *2021 IEEE Automatic Speech Recognition and Understanding Workshop (ASRU)*, pages 914–921. IEEE.

Matt Post. 2018. A call for clarity in reporting BLEU scores. In *Proceedings of the Third Conference on Machine Translation: Research Papers*, pages 186–191, Brussels, Belgium. Association for Computational Linguistics.

Anthony Rousseau, Paul Deléglise, and Yannick Estève. 2014. Enhancing the TED-LIUM corpus with selected data for language modeling and more TED talks. In *Proceedings of the Ninth International Conference on Language Resources and Evaluation (LREC'14)*, pages 3935–3939, Reykjavik, Iceland. European Language Resources Association (ELRA).

Elizabeth Salesky, Matthew Wiesner, Jacob Bremerman, Roldano Cattoni, Matteo Negri, Marco Turchi, Douglas W. Oard, and Matt Post. 2021. Multilingual tedx corpus for speech recognition and translation. In *Proceedings of Interspeech*.

Yun Tang, Hongyu Gong, Xian Li, Changhan Wang, Juan Pino, Holger Schwenk, and Naman Goyal. 2021. FST: the FAIR speech translation system for the IWSLT21 multilingual shared task. In *Proceedings of the 18th International Conference on Spoken Language Translation (IWSLT 2021)*, pages 131–137, Bangkok, Thailand (online). Association for Computational Linguistics.

Yuqing Tang, Chau Tran, Xian Li, Peng-Jen Chen, Naman Goyal, Vishrav Chaudhary, Jiatao Gu, and Angela Fan. 2020. Multilingual translation with extensible multilingual pretraining and finetuning. *arXiv preprint arXiv:2008.00401*.

Ashish Vaswani, Noam Shazeer, Niki Parmar, Jakob Uszkoreit, Llion Jones, Aidan N Gomez, Łukasz Kaiser, and Illia Polosukhin. 2017. Attention is all you need. *Advances in neural information processing systems*, 30.

A Appendix

A.1 Hyperparameters

Hyper-parameter	Value
Batch size	4 000
Data-parallel GPUs	4
Update freq	2
Max learning rate	0.0005
Initial LR	10^{-7}
Schedule	inverse square root
Warmup steps	10 000
Adam betas	0.9, 0.999
Mixed precision	True
Label smoothing	0.2
Weight decay	0.0
Dropout	$0.3^{\dagger}$
Attention dropout	0.1
Gradient clipping	none
1D Convolutions	1
Conv channels	$80^{\star}$
Conv kernel size	5
Conv stride	2
Embed scaling factor	$\sqrt{1\,024}$
Positional encoding	sinusoidal$^{\alpha}$
Encoder layers	24
Decoder layers	24
Embed dim	$1\,024^{\ddagger}$
FFN dim	8 192
Activation	ReLU
Attention heads	16
Pre-norm	True
Adapter dim	64
Vocab size	250k
Lang-pair temperature	3
Heterogeneous batches	True
Valid freq	5 000
Checkpoint averaging	3
Patience	5
Early stopping metric	BLEU
Beam size	5

Table 9: Hyper-parameters used to train our models.
$\star$: a linear layer followed by a ReLU activation is trained to project the input features (of dimension 768 or 1 024) to the input dimension of the CNN (80).
$\dagger$: dropout is also applied to the source and target embeddings (after the convolutions and positional encoding) and FFN activations.
$\ddagger$: 2 048 when the pre-trained MT model is NLLB 3.3B.
α: learned positional embeddings in the decoder when the pre-trained model is mBART.

A.2 Additional Results

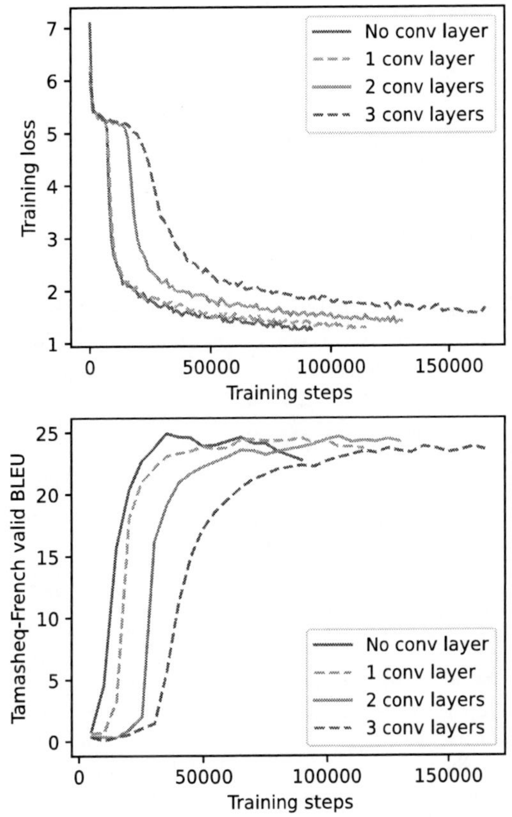

Figure 2: Training loss and *Taq-Fr* validation BLEU of variants of our *contrastive 1* model, that have 0 to 3 convolutional layers (1 by default).

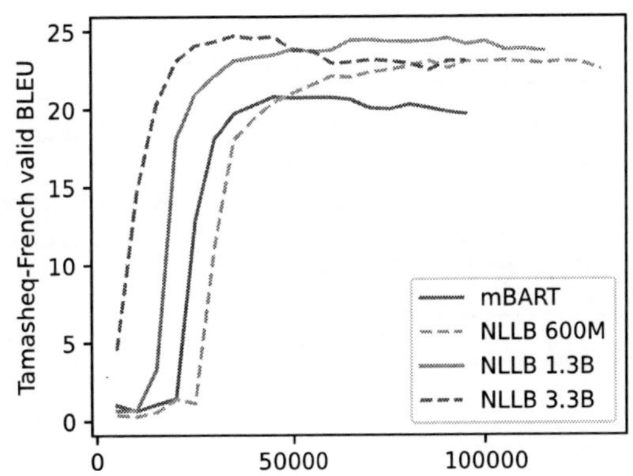

Figure 3: *Taq-Fr* validation BLEU of variants of our *contrastive 1* model that are initialized with various MT models (NLLB 1.3B by default).

Task	Source	Target	hours:minutes	# utterances
ASR	French	French	218:59	117,081
ASR	Italian	Italian	118:39	50,895
ASR	Portuguese	Portuguese	179:33	91,257
ASR	Spanish	Spanish	214:15	103,076
ST	French	English	57:39	31,207
ST	French	Spanish	42:14	21,862
ST	French	Portuguese	26:53	14,322
ST	Portuguese	English	63:13	31,868
ST	Spanish	French	9:34	4,568
ST	Spanish	English	79:37	37,168
ST	Spanish	Italian	11:50	5,616
ST	Spanish	Portuguese	47:01	22,012

Table 10: Statistics for all the mTEDx languages (train+valid) seen by our systems for the IWSLT 2021 evaluation setup described in Section 4.3.

		Taq-Fr valid	Que-Es valid	Que-Es test
Taq-Fr	**primary**	**26.13**	✗	✗
	contrastive 1	24.53	✗	✗
	contrastive 2	22.88	**20.29**	**17.74**
Que-Es	**primary**	22.88	**20.29**	**17.74**
	contrastive 1	20.81	19.03	15.67
	contrastive 2	21.31	16.78	15.25
Que-Es (updated)	**primary**	22.36	16.52	**15.70**
	contrastive 1	20.97	15.15	15.55
	contrastive 2	20.31	16.30	13.17

Table 11: Validation and test results on the IWSLT 2023 low-resource track. Lines 3 and 4 correspond to the same model. The "*Que-Es* (updated)" results correspond to new models trained on filtered Quechua ASR data, where we removed audio files that are also in the ST valid and test sets. In this updated version, **primary** and **contrastive 1** use NLLB 1.3B and **contrastive 2** uses NLLB 3.3B.

		Taq-Fr test	Que-Es valid
Taq-Fr	**contrastive 1**	19.13 ± 0.06	✗
	contrastive 2	16.89 ± 0.18	18.34 ± 0.59
Que-Es	**contrastive 1**	16.89 ± 0.18	18.34 ± 0.59
Que-Es (updated)	**contrastive 1**	16.51 ± 1.12	14.98 ± 0.16
	contrastive 2	16.56 ± 0.30	15.66 ± 0.60

Table 12: Statistics (BLEU average and standard deviation) for the submitted models which have 3 runs with different seeds. The *Taq-Fr* and *Que-Es* BLEU scores are respectively over the IWSLT 2022 test set and the IWSLT 2023 validation set.

Adapter Size	Encoder Adapters	Decoder Adapters	Taq-En Lang ID	Taq-Ko Lang ID	Hangul Percentage
64	✓	✓	100%	97%	88%
128	✓	✓	99%	84%	59%
64	✓	✗	100%	100%	95%
✗	✗	✗	100%	100%	96%
✗	✗	✗	100%	100%	93%

Table 13: Percentage of output sentences in the correct language according to the NLLB language ID (Costa-jussà et al., 2022). The last column shows the percentage of output characters that are in the Korean alphabet.

Train vocab	Inference vocab	Inference params	Taq-Fr BLEU	Fr-En BLEU	Speed
Full (256k)	Full (256k)	1.38B	19.1	**36.6**	12.5×
	Filtered (35k)	1.19B	18.9	35.8	**13.0×**
Filtered (35k)	Filtered (35k)	1.19B	**20.0**	35.5	**13.0×**

Table 14: Speech Translation performance on the IWSLT 2022 *Taq-Fr* and mTEDx *Fr-En* test sets of our contrastive *Taq-Fr* submission (non-ensemble version of our primary submission) with several vocabulary filtering strategies: no filtering (first row, corresponds to our submission); inference-time filtering (second row); or training-time filtering (third row). See Table 18 for an explanation of the "speed" column.

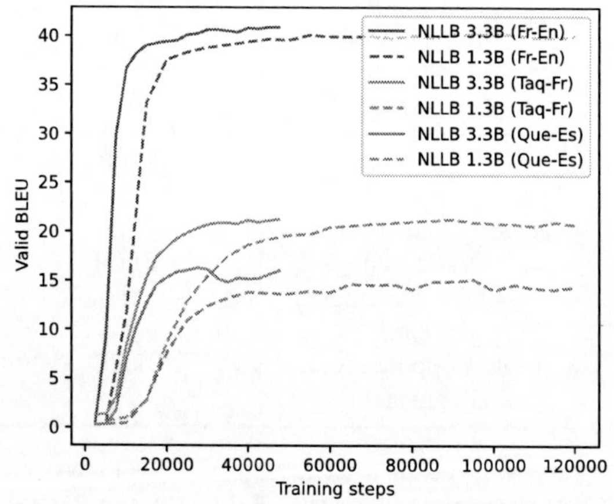

Figure 4: Validation BLEU by language direction (*Fr-En*, *Taq-Fr* and *Que-Es*) of a multilingual model (XLS-R + NLLB 1.3B) which includes both Tamasheq and Quechua (our *updated constrastive 1* submission).

Submission	IWSLT 2023			TED-LIUM v2	mTEDx ASR				mTEDx ST							
	Taq-Fr	Que-Es	Que-Que	En-En	Fr-Fr	Es-Es	It-It	Pt-Pt	Fr-En	Fr-Es	Es-Fr	Es-En	Fr-Pt	Pt-En	Es-It	Es-Pt
Taq-Fr primary	✓	✗	✗	✓	✓	✓	✗	✗	✓	✓	✓	✓	✗	✗	✗	✗
Taq-Fr contrastive 1	✓	✗	✗	✓	✓	✓	✗	✗	✓	✓	✓	✓	✗	✗	✗	✗
Taq-Fr contrastive 2	✓	✓	✓	✓	✓	✓	✗	✗	✓	✓	✓	✓	✗	✗	✗	✗
Que-Es primary	✓	✓	✓	✓	✓	✓	✗	✗	✓	✓	✓	✓	✗	✗	✗	✗
Que-Es contrastive 1	✓	✓	✓	✓	✓	✓	✗	✗	✓	✓	✓	✓	✗	✗	✗	✗
Que-Es contrastive 2	✓	✓	✓	✓	✓	✓	✗	✗	✓	✓	✓	✓	✗	✗	✗	✗
IWSLT 2021 setup	✓	✓	✓	✓	✓	✓	✓	✓	✓	✓	✓	✓	✓	✓	✓	✓

Table 15: Extensive list of datasets used for training (✓) each system presented in this paper.

Model	URL
mHuBERT-Tamasheq	Unavailable
Tamasheq	`https://huggingface.co/LIA-AvignonUniversity/IWSLT2022-tamasheq-only`
Niger-Mali	`https://huggingface.co/LIA-AvignonUniversity/IWSLT2022-Niger-Mali`
XLSR-53	`https://github.com/facebookresearch/fairseq/tree/main/examples/wav2vec`
XLS-R large and xlarge	`https://github.com/facebookresearch/fairseq/tree/main/examples/wav2vec/xlsr`

Table 16: Downloading sources for the speech representation models checkpoints used in our experiments.

Stacked layers	FT layers	Adapters	Total params	Trained params	Taq-Fr BLEU	Fr-En BLEU	Speed
1	0	enc+dec (64)	1.40B	28M	**19.2**	35.0	12.0×
1	0	none	1.39B	22M	17.9	33.8	12.2×
0	1	enc+dec (64)	1.38B	28M	18.2	35.1	12.0×
0	1	none	1.37B	22M	17.5	33.3	12.6×
2	0	enc+dec (64)	1.42B	49M	**19.2**	35.1	11.9×
2	0	none	1.41B	43M	18.4	35.0	12.5×
0	2	enc+dec (64)	1.38B	49M	19.0	36.2	12.0×
0	3	enc+dec (64)	<u>1.38B</u>	<u>70M</u>	<u>19.1</u>	<u>**36.6**</u>	<u>12.5×</u>

Table 17: Training stacked layers (i.e. adding and training new bottom encoder layers) versus fine-tuning the existing bottom layers; with or without adapters. The other hyper-parameters are identical to our constrastive submission (underlined scores).

Speech features	MT model	Conv. layers	FT layers	Adapters	Total params	Trained params	Taq-Fr BLEU	Fr-En BLEU	Speed
Tamasheq (layer 11)	NLLB 1.3B	1	3	enc+dec (64)	1.38B	70M	16.8	32.5	11.6×
Tamasheq (layer 8)					1.38B	70M	19.3	31.6	12.0×
mHuBERT-Taq (layer 11)					1.38B	70M	16.4	37.1	12.1×
mHuBERT-Taq (layer 8)					1.38B	70M	16.2	36.7	12.1×
Niger-Mali (layer 11)					1.38B	70M	16.6	34.6	11.8×
Niger-Mali (layer 8)					1.38B	70M	19.1	36.6	12.5×
XLSR-53 (layer 18)					1.38B	70M	15.9	38.0	12.4×
XLS-R L (layer 18)					1.38B	70M	16.8	**39.4**	12.7×
XLS-R XL (layer 46)					1.38B	70M	15.4	37.4	11.7×
Niger-Mali (layer 8)	mBART (600M)	1	3	enc+dec (64)	0.61B	41M	16.3	28.9	22.9×
	NLLB (600M)				0.62B	41M	18.0	32.5	24.2×
	NLLB (1.3B)				1.38B	70M	19.1	36.6	12.5×
	NLLB (3.3B)				3.36B	165M	19.3	37.3	4.5×
Niger-Mali (layer 8)	NLLB 1.3B	3	3	enc+dec (64)	1.38B	70M	18.5	33.4	**25.5×**
		2			1.38B	70M	19.4	35.4	19.5×
		1			1.38B	70M	19.1	36.6	12.5×
		0			1.38B	70M	**19.6**	34.4	7.1×
Niger-Mali (layer 8)	NLLB 1.3B	1	24	enc+dec (64)	1.37B	508M	16.7	30.7	11.9×
			4		1.38B	91M	19.6	36.8	12.3×
			3		1.38B	70M	19.1	36.6	12.5×
			2		1.38B	49M	19.0	36.2	12.0×
			1		1.38B	28M	18.2	35.1	12.0×
Niger-Mali (layer 8)	NLLB 1.3B	1	1	enc (64)	1.37B	25M	19.1	34.2	12.4×
				none	1.37B	**22M**	17.5	33.3	12.6×
			3	enc+dec (256)	1.40B	88M	18.8	35.8	12.2×
				enc+dec (128)	1.38B	76M	19.2	36.3	12.1×
				enc+dec (64)	1.38B	70M	19.1	36.6	12.5×
				enc (64)	1.37B	67M	19.3	35.7	12.7×
				none	1.37B	64M	18.3	35.6	13.1×

Table 18: Ablation study on *Taq-Fr* ST, with various speech feature extractors, pre-trained MT models used for initialization, and trained parameters. The total parameter counts do not include the parameters of the speech feature extractors. The BLEU scores reported are on the IWSLT 2022 *Taq-Fr* and mTEDx *Fr-En* test sets. The speed metric is relative to real time (i.e., seconds in the test set divided by seconds spent decoding) and does not include feature extraction time. It is obtained by decoding the *Taq-Fr* test set on a single T4 with a batch size of 10 utterances (averaged over 3 decoding runs). The underlined numbers all correspond to the same model, which is our first contrastive submission to the task (the non-ensemble version of our primary submission). All of these models are trained with the same data (see Table 15) and early stopping is done based on *Taq-Fr* valid BLEU scores. The numbers inside parentheses in the *Adapters* column correspond to the bottleneck dimension of the trained adapter modules. Adapters are not added in the encoder layers that are being fine-tuned. These models took between 15 and 47 h each to train on 4 V100 GPUs, with an average training time of 26 h.

Task	Model	Adapters	Training directions				Zero-shot directions		
			Es-En	Fr-En	Fr-Es	Pt-En	Pt-Es	It-En	It-Es
ST	NLLB 3.3B	enc+dec	44.0	**39.9**	38.3	**33.1**	38.1	29.3	36.9
ST	NLLB 1.3B	enc+dec	43.7	39.4	38.0	31.5	35.9	28.9	35.0
		none	36.7	35.0	31.7	23.8	30.5	25.2	31.3
		enc	41.4	38.3	36.0	30.8	36.2	26.2	35.1
		dec	39.1	38.2	33.1	26.9	31.9	27.9	32.9
MT	NLLB 3.3B	none	47.4	39.5	39.2	39.8	48.6	34.0	42.4
MT	NLLB 1.3B	none	47.9	38.9	39.6	39.8	48.5	33.8	41.9
		enc+dec	50.2	40.7	42.2	42.1	51.0	37.6	45.2
		enc	49.9	41.3	42.6	41.9	50.6	36.5	44.9
		dec	48.8	39.2	41.0	41.1	49.7	35.6	43.9
MT	NLLB 1.3B (DA)	enc+dec	**51.3**	**43.2**	**45.2**	**44.7**	**53.2**	**37.8**	**47.1**

Table 19: **Top half:** Speech translation BLEU scores on the IWSLT 2021 test sets, when deactivating encoder adapters, decoder adapters, or both in an ST model at inference time. The ST model is the same one as in Table 5, trained with encoder and decoder adapters. **Bottom half:** Text-to-text MT BLEU scores when using the ST adapters in the initial model and disabling the ST bottom layers and convolutions.

Direct Models for Simultaneous Translation and Automatic Subtitling: FBK@IWSLT2023

Sara Papi[◇,□], **Marco Gaido**[◇], **Matteo Negri**[◇]
[◇]Fondazione Bruno Kessler
[□]University of Trento
{spapi,mgaido,negri}@fbk.eu

Abstract

This paper describes the FBK's participation in the Simultaneous Translation and Automatic Subtitling tracks of the IWSLT 2023 Evaluation Campaign. Our submission focused on the use of direct architectures to perform both tasks: for the simultaneous one, we leveraged the knowledge already acquired by offline-trained models and directly applied a policy to obtain the real-time inference; for the subtitling one, we adapted the direct ST model to produce well-formed subtitles and exploited the same architecture to produce timestamps needed for the subtitle synchronization with audiovisual content. Our English-German SimulST system shows a reduced computational-aware latency compared to the one achieved by the top-ranked systems in the 2021 and 2022 rounds of the task, with gains of up to 3.5 BLEU. Our automatic subtitling system outperforms the only-existing solution based on a direct system by 3.7 and 1.7 SubER in English-German and English-Spanish respectively.

1 Introduction

In recent years, the advances in natural language processing and machine learning led to a surge of interest in developing speech translation (ST) systems that can translate speech from one language into text in another language without human intervention. Significant progress has been specially made toward end-to-end ST models (Bérard et al., 2016; Weiss et al., 2017) trained to directly translate speech without the intermediate steps of transcription (through automatic speech recognition - ASR) and translation (through machine translation - MT). Along with this growing interest in direct ST, also accompanied by a reduction of the performance gap with respect to cascaded architectures (Bentivogli et al., 2021), other trends have emerged thanks to deep learning advancements, which made it possible to deploy direct solutions to perform the task in real-time (i.e. to produce partial translations while continuing to process the input audio) or to automatically generate subtitles for audiovisual content (i.e. pieces of translated text which have to conform to specific spatiotemporal constraints and be synchronized with the video).

The International Workshop on Spoken Language Translation (IWSLT) is playing an important role in advancing the state-of-the-art in these fields by organizing a series of evaluation campaigns (Ansari et al., 2020; Anastasopoulos et al., 2021, 2022) focused on simultaneous speech translation (SimulST) and, this year for the first time, automatic subtitling. These campaigns provide a unique opportunity for researchers to compare their systems against others, share their findings, and identify areas for further improvement.

In this paper, we describe FBK's participation in the IWSLT 2023 Evaluation Campaigns (Agarwal et al., 2023) for simultaneous translation and automatic subtitling. Motivated by the promising results reported in previous works (Ren et al., 2020; Papi et al., 2022a), our approach is characterized by the use of direct ST models to address both tasks.

For the simultaneous speech-to-text translation (SimulST) task, we participated in the English→German track and leveraged an offline-trained direct model without performing any adaptation to the real-time scenario, as this has recently been shown not to be necessary to achieve competitive results (Papi et al., 2022b). For the automatic subtitling task, we participated in both the English→German and English→Spanish tracks by adapting a direct ST model to produce well-formed subtitles and exploiting the same architecture to produce the timestamps needed for their synchronization with audiovisual contents, as in (Papi et al., 2022a).

Our results demonstrate the effectiveness of our approach. In SimulST, the computational-aware latency of our models is lower compared to the winning systems of the last two rounds (2021, and

Proceedings of the 20th International Conference on Spoken Language Translation (IWSLT 2023), pages 159–168
July 13-14, 2023 ©2023 Association for Computational Linguistics

2022) of the IWSLT SimulST Evaluation Campaign, with gains up to 3.5 BLEU. In automatic subtitling, our systems improve the results reported in (Papi et al., 2022a) which, to the best of our knowledge, represents the only-existing solution based on a direct model. Specifically, on average among the various dev sets available for the task, we achieve 3.7 SubER on en-de and 1.7 SubER on en-es.

2 Applied Direct Models

For this year's submission, we applied the direct ST models to the two different scenarios of simultaneous translation and automatic subtitling.

2.1 Simultaneous Translation

Recent trends in SimulST consist of using offline-trained models for simultaneous inference (Papi et al., 2022b). There are several motivations for this choice: *i)* it avoids re-training or building specific architectures for SimulST, saving time and computational resources; *ii)* only one model has to be trained and maintained to perform both offline and simultaneous ST; and *iii)* there is no need to train several models, each specialized to support different latency regimes.

A key aspect of SimulST, also critical when approaching the task with offline models at inference time, is the so-called *decision policy*: the mechanism that is in charge of deciding whether to read more information or to emit a partial hypothesis. One of the first and most popular policies is the wait-k (Ma et al., 2019), initially introduced for simultaneous MT, and then applied to the speech scenario (Ma et al., 2020b; Chen et al., 2021; Zeng et al., 2021; Karakanta et al., 2021b). The wait-k, which prescribes waiting for an initial number of k words before starting to translate, is defined as a "fixed" policy (Zheng et al., 2020) because the decision is taken independently from the source input content. However, as the actual information contained in the input (e.g. in terms of ambiguity, completeness, and syntactic/semantic cohesion) is also important for the sake of good-quality incremental translations, several "adaptive" policies have been introduced, which instead adapt their decisions to the input content. Some adaptive policies require system re-training or the development of ad-hoc modules (Liu et al., 2021b; Chang and Lee, 2022; Zhang and Feng, 2022), while some others do not (Liu et al., 2020; Nguyen et al., 2021; Papi et al., 2022e). Since our objective is to avoid any modifications to the offline-trained model, we pointed our attention to the latter, more conservative category. Among these policies, we analyzed the three following alternatives:

- **Local Agreement (LA)** (Liu et al., 2020): this policy prescribes generating a partial hypothesis from scratch at every newly received audio segment, and emitting it (or only a part of it) if it coincides with one of those generated in the previous time step;
- **Encoder-Decoder Attention (EDATT)** (Papi et al., 2022e): it exploits the cross-attention scores modeling the audio-translation relation to decide whether to emit the words of a partial hypothesis or not. If, for the current word, the sum of the attention scores of the last λ received speech frames exceeds a certain threshold α (both λ and α are hyperparameters), the emission is delayed because the system needs more context to translate that word. Otherwise, the word is emitted and we proceed to the next word of the hypothesis;
- **ALIGNATT** (Papi et al., 2023b): as for EDATT, the cross-attention scores are leveraged to decide what to emit but, in this case, instead of summing the attention scores of the last speech frames, each word is uniquely assigned (or aligned) to the frame having the maximum attention score. If the aligned frame corresponds to one of the last f frames (f being a hyperparameter that controls the latency) the emission is stopped. Otherwise, we proceed to the next word.

2.2 Automatic Subtitling

So far, the adoption of direct ST architectures to address the automatic subtitling task has only been explored in (Papi et al., 2022a). As a matter of fact, all previous works on the topic (Piperidis et al., 2004; Melero et al., 2006; Matusov et al., 2019; Koponen et al., 2020; Bojar et al., 2021) rely on cascade architectures that usually involve an ASR component to transcribe the input speech, a subtitle segmenter that segments the transcripts into subtitles, a timestamp estimator that predicts the start and times of each subtitle, and an MT model that translates the subtitle transcripts.

Cascaded architectures, however, cannot access information contained in the speech, such as prosody, which related works proved to be an important source of information for the segmentation into subtitles (Öktem et al., 2019; Federico et al., 2020; Virkar et al., 2021; Tam et al., 2022). The importance of such information has been further verified in (Karakanta et al., 2020a), which proved that the direct ST models are better in subtitle segmentation compared to the cascade ones. Another study by Karakanta et al. 2021a, also pointed out the importance of consistency between captions (segmented transcripts) and subtitles (segmented translations), showing that the predicted caption content can also be useful for the translation. Specifically, the authors obtained significant improvements by using a Triangle Transformer-based architecture (Anastasopoulos and Chiang, 2018) composed of one encoder and two decoders: the first decoder is in charge of emitting the transcripts and the second one is in charge of emitting the translation by also attending to the output embeddings of the predicted transcript. Therefore, in our submission, based on the findings of the aforementioned work, we inspected the use of both a classic single encoder-single decoder architectures, as in (Papi et al., 2022a), and of the Triangle architecture for automatic subtitling.

3 Experimental Setup

3.1 Data

Simultaneous We developed a pure offline model trained on the same data used for our last year's (constrained) submission (Gaido et al., 2022b).

Subtitling We used the same data settings of (Papi et al., 2022a), for which we leverage the multimodal segmenter by Papi et al. (2022d) to segment into subtitles ST and machine-translated ASR corpora as per (Gaido et al., 2021b, 2022a).[1] No OpenSubtitles or text-only data were used to train our models.

3.2 Training Settings

All the models used for our participation were implemented using the newly released implementation of the Conformer architecture by Papi et al. (2023a)[2] based on Fairseq-ST (Wang et al., 2020). In their paper, the authors analyzed the most popular open-source libraries for speech recognition/translation and found at least one bug affecting all the existing Conformer implementations, therefore claiming the importance of testing code to avoid the propagation of unreliable findings masked by good results.

Simultaneous We tested a Conformer-based architecture (Gulati et al., 2020) with two configurations: 12 encoder layers and 16 encoder layers. The number of Transformer decoder layers is 6, we set 512 features for the attention layers and 2,048 hidden units for the feed-forward layers. We used 0.1 dropout for the feed-forward layers, attention layers, and convolutional modules. The kernel size was set to 31 for the point- and depth-wise convolutions. We trained with the Adam optimizer (Kingma and Ba, 2015) by setting $\beta_1 = 0.9$ and $\beta_2 = 0.98$, a weight decay of 0.001, the learning rate to 0.002 using the inverse square-root scheduler with 25,000 warm-up steps. Label smoothed cross-entropy loss (0.1 smoothing factor) was used together with the CTC loss (Graves et al., 2006) with weight 0.5. We experimented also by applying the CTC compression mechanism (Gaido et al., 2021a) to the source input to shrink its dimension and reduce RAM consumption. Utterance Cepstral Mean and Variance Normalization (CMVN) was applied during training. Also, we leveraged SpecAugment (Park et al., 2019) with frequency mask ($F = 27$, and $N = 2$), time mask ($N = 10$, $T = 300$, and $p = 0.05$), and no time warp. Both ST training and ASR pre-training were performed with the same settings. The target vocabulary is of size 16,000, and the source vocabulary is of size 10,000, and are both based on SentencePiece (Kudo and Richardson, 2018). We differentiate between original and machine-translated training data by pre-pending a tag (`nomt` and `mt`, respectively) to the target text as in all our last years' submissions (Gaido et al., 2020; Papi et al., 2021; Gaido et al., 2022b). The total batch size was set to 1,280,000 and was performed on 4 NVIDIA A40 GPUs with 40GB of RAM by setting the mini-batch update frequency to 8 and 40,000 maximum tokens. Maximum updates were set to 100,000.

[1] All the corpora used in (Papi et al., 2022a) are allowed ASR and ST training data for the Subtitling task (`https://iwslt.org/2023/subtitling#training-and-data-conditions`). Therefore, our submission has to be considered "Constrained".

[2] Code available at `https://github.com/hlt-mt/FBK-fairseq`

Automatic Subtitling Both the classic encoder-decoder architecture and the triangle architecture are composed of 12 layers of Conformer encoder and 6 layers of Transformer decoder (which is replicated twice in the triangle model). The dimension of the feed-forward layers is 2,048 and $d = 512$ in the attention. The kernel size of the point- and depth-wise convolutions in the convolutional modules is 31. The dropout was set to 0.1. CTC loss with compression is added with weight 0.5 to the cross entropy loss with label smoothing (0.1 of smoothing factor) and optimized with Adam ($\beta_1 = 0.9, \beta_2 = 0.98$). The source vocabulary is of size 8,000 and the target vocabulary of size 16,000 (`<eob>` and `<eol>` included); both are obtained by SentencePiece models. The ST pre-training was done by setting the learning rate to 0.002 with inverse square-root scheduler and 25,000 warm-up updates. The SubST fine-tuning was done by setting a constant learning rate of 0.001. A second fine-tuning was done with the same setting of (Papi et al., 2022a), but we restored the punctuation of the ASR datasets which do not contain any (i.e., the TEDLIUM corpus (Hernandez et al., 2018)) by using `bert-restore-punctuation`,[3] before machine-translating and segmenting the target texts into subtitles. We trained the standard architecture with 40,000 maximum tokens on 4 NVIDIA A100 GPUs with 40GB of RAM and we set the update frequency to 2. For the triangle architecture, we set maximum tokens to 20,000 to fit the architecture in memory and the update frequency to 4 to hold the same total batch size of 320,000 tokens. Maximum updates were set to 100,000 for both the pre-training and training phases.

3.3 Evaluation Settings

Simultaneous We exploit the SimulEval tool (Ma et al., 2020a). To be comparable with the previous years, all the results except this year's submission are shown for the SimulEval v1.0.2, which adopts BLEU (Post, 2018)[4] to measure translation quality and Average Lagging or AL (Ma et al., 2019) to measure latency. Instead, for this year's submission, we adopt the latest version of SimulEval (1.1.0) with BLEU measured with `sacrebleu` 2.3.0 and we also report Length-Adaptive Average Lagging or LAAL (Papi et al., 2022c) and Average Token Delay or ATD (Kano et al., 2022) as additional latency metrics. All the evaluations were run on a single NVIDIA K80 with 12GB of RAM, by applying global CMVN to audio input, whose features were estimated on the MuST-C v2 training set. Computational aware metrics ("_CA") refer to the single NVIDIA K80 setting and consider also the model computational time in the delay calculation.

Automatic Subtitling We adopt the following metrics: SubER-cased (henceforth, SubER) (Wilken et al., 2022) for overall subtitle quality, Sigma (Karakanta et al., 2022) for the subtitle segmentation quality, and BLEU[5] for translation quality. We also compute the conformity percentage of 42 characters per line (CPL) and 21 characters per second (CPS) or reading speed, as suggested on the track website.[6] We neglected the conformity computation of the subtitles with more than two lines since our model only produces subtitles with two lines or less, thus being always 100% conform. Conformity scores are computed by using the script released for the paper (Papi et al., 2022a).[7] Dev/test audios are segmented with SHAS (Tsiamas et al., 2022). No audio cleaning is applied.

4 Results

4.1 Simultaneous Translation

Since we directly employ an offline model for the simultaneous inference, we show in Table 1 the results of the offline ASR pre-training and ST training. Although the model with 12 encoder layers (row 0) obtains lower – hence better – WER compared to the 16 encoder-layers model (row 1), the highest – hence better – BLEU in ST is achieved by the bigger architecture. The performance is also slightly enhanced by adding the CTC compression (row 3) during training, which is particularly useful also for the SimulST scenario since it speeds up inference (of about 12/15%). Therefore, we select this model for the final submission. Compared to our last year's submission (row 5), our 16 encoder-layers model scores +0.4 BLEU even if, at this time, we have not fine-tuned it on the in-domain (TED talks) datasets. Our model also performs

[3] `https://huggingface.co/felflare/bert-restore-punctuation`

[4] case:mixed|eff:no|tok:13a|smooth:exp|version:1.5.1

[5] case:mixed|eff:no|tok:13a|smooth:exp|version:2.0.0

[6] `https://iwslt.org/2023/subtitling#automatic-evaluation`

[7] Script available at: `https://github.com/hlt-mt/FBK-fairseq/blob/master/examples/speech_to_text/scripts/subtitle_compliance.py`

better than the NAIST last year's system (+11.1 BLEU) while is worse (-1.0 BLEU) compared to the last year's SimulST task winner CUNI-KIT whose model, however, leveraged large pre-trained models such as wav2vec 2.0 and mBART50. Compared to last year's cascade model by UPV, we score -1.7 BLEU. This system, however, also outperformed the CUNI-KIT system by 0.7 BLEU points, indicating that a gap between direct and cascade architectures still exists.

id	Model	WER% (↓)	BLEU (↑)
1	12 encoder layers	**9.7**	31.6
2	16 encoder layers	9.9	**31.9**
3	+ CTC compress.	-	**32.1**
4	CUNI-KIT 2022†	-	33.1
5	FBK 2022	-	31.7
6	NAIST 2022‡	-	21.0
7	UPV 2022 (Cascade)*	9.5	33.8

Table 1: Offline results of our Conformer-based architectures on MuST-C v2 tst-COMMON together with the available results of the last year's SimulST competitors. †(Polák et al., 2022), ‡(Fukuda et al., 2022), *(Iranzo-Sánchez et al., 2022).

In Figure 1, we show the simultaneous results of the different policies mentioned in Section 2.1 applied to our offline model. The differences in terms of quality-latency trade-off between the LA and both EDATT and ALIGNATT are evident: the last ones outperform the former with an improvement peak of 1.5 BLEU at lower latency (approximately $1s$). Moreover, when the computationally aware AL is considered, EDATT and ALIGNATT are the only policies able to reach a latency $\leq 2s$. Regarding the comparison between EDATT and ALIGNATT, ALIGNATT can span a latency between 1 and $2.6s$ ideally (when unlimited computing resources are available), and between 1.8 and $3.7s$ computationally aware, while EDATT is limited to a latency of 1.4 to $2.5s$ ideally, and 2.3 to $3.6s$ computationally aware. We hence select ALIGNATT as it is able to reach a wider range of latency.

Lastly, we compare our policy with the two winning systems of the last two years (2021, and 2022). The 2021 winner (Liu et al., 2021a) was based on an architecture named Cross Attention Augmented Transducer (CAAT), which was specifically tailored for the SimulST task (Liu et al., 2021b) and still represents the state of the art in terms of low latency (considering ideal AL only). The 2022 winner (CUNI-KIT (Polák et al., 2022)) was based on the wav2vec 2.0 + mBART50 offline architecture

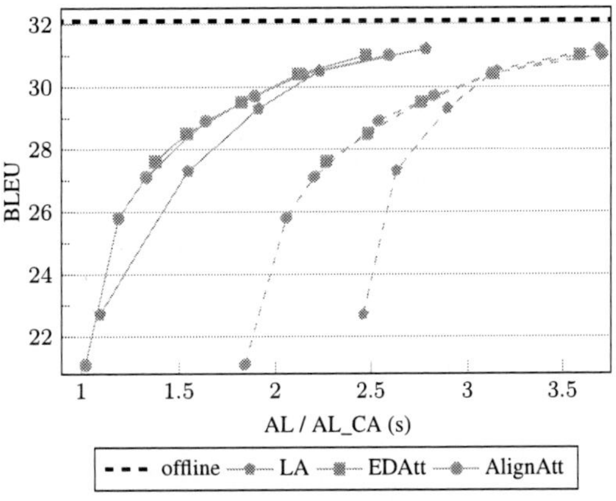

Figure 1: Comparison between the LA, EDATT, and ALIGNATT policies described in Section 2.1 on MuST-C v2 en→de tst-COMMON. Solid curves represent AL, dashed curves represent AL_CA.

reported in Table 1, row 4. They applied the LA policy, the same we analyze in Figure 1, to the aforementioned architecture for simultaneous inference. The comparison is reported in Figure 2. As we can see, there is a 1.0-2.0 BLEU difference between our approach and the IWSLT 2022 winner, which is expected since their offline system is superior compared to ours, as already observed in Table 1. Compared to the IWSLT 2021 winner, we observe a performance drop in our system with AL $\leq 1.5s$, while the situation is opposite with AL $> 1.5s$. However, when we look at the computationally aware metrics, the results completely change. Our system clearly outperforms the 2021 winner, with a maximum improvement of about 2 BLEU points. Moreover, our system is the only one able to reach a computational aware latency of $2s$ while, instead, the IWSLT 2022 winner curve starts only at around $3s$. Therefore, our system is significantly faster and, at around $3s$, we achieve a relative improvement of more than 3.5 BLEU compared to the IWSLT 2022 winner.

To sum up, when the computationally aware metric is considered, our approach outperforms the winners of both the 2021 and 2022 rounds of the SimulST task. In addition, in this year's round, the systems are evaluated with the threshold AL $= 2s$ and with the new version of SimulEval.[8] With respect to these settings, our submitted system scores 30.7 BLEU with AL $= 1.89s$ (LAAL $= 2.07s$, ATD $= 1.80s$).

[8]https://iwslt.org/2023/simultaneous#ranking

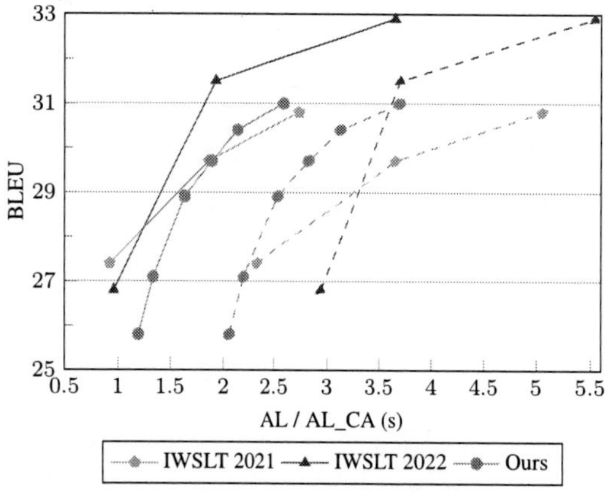

Figure 2: Comparison with the 2021 and 2022 winners of the SimulST Evaluation Campaigns MuST-C v2 en→{de, es} tst-COMMON. Solid curves represent AL, dashed curves represent AL_CA.

4.2 Automatic Subtitling

In Table 2, we show a comparison between the standard encoder-decoder and the Triangle architectures for automatic subtitling. The results are computed on MuST-Cinema (Karakanta et al., 2020b), the only existing corpus for SubST. Unfortunately, in contrast with the results achieved by (Karakanta et al., 2021a), we found that the standard architectures perform better on all the considered metrics. While the differences in terms of translation quality are not so big (0.8-9 BLEU drop in both languages), there is a huge gap in the quality of the segmentation into subtitles, with the standard model improving by 3.3 and 4.7 Sigma the scores obtained by the Triangle respectively on en-de and en-es. This is also reflected by a worse SubER score (the lower, the better) of the Triangle, exhibiting a performance drop of, respectively, 0.9 and 1.6 SubER for en-de and en-es compared to the standard architecture. Therefore, we can conclude that the generated captions seem not to help with subtitle generation. Rather, they negatively affect subtitle generation to the detriment of segmentation quality. For this reason, we decided to employ the standard encoder-decoder architecture for our participation in the automatic subtitling task.

In the following, we present the results of our model on the four dev sets released for the task,[9] namely: **MuST-Cinema or TED** containing TED talks videos, **EuroParlTV or EPTV** containing recordings related to the European Parliament activities, **Peloton** containing online fitness classes, and **ITV Studios or ITV** containing videos from a broad range of programming (drama, entertainment, factual). For both language pairs (en-de and en-es), Table 3 shows the results computed with SubER, which is the primary metric used for the task.[10] As we can see, the models fine-tuned on data with restored punctuation score the best results in both languages. Across the four dev sets, there is a 3.7 SubER improvement for en-de, and 1.7 for en-es. Moreover, coherently among languages, the TED talks scenario results in the easiest one for our model, as it is in-domain (e.g., MuST-Cinema, based on TED talks, was used to train the model). Conversely, the ITV scenario is the most difficult one since it contains TV series, which is a completely unseen domain for our model. Indeed, its data contain a larger amount of background music/noise, as well as dialogues with multiple speakers which are not present in our training data. In light of the results obtained by the fine-tuned models, we select them for our submission to the automatic subtitling task.

en-de					
Model	**SubER**	**BLEU**	**Sigma**	**CPL**	**CPS**
(Papi et al., 2022a)	**59.9**	**23.4**	**77.9**	**86.9**	**68.9**
Triangle	60.8	22.6	74.6	84.5	67.7
en-es					
Model	**SubER**	**BLEU**	**Sigma**	**CPL**	**CPS**
(Papi et al., 2022a)	**46.8**	**37.4**	**81.6**	**93.2**	**74.6**
Triangle	48.4	36.5	76.9	90.3	71.7

Table 2: Results of the direct ST models standard and Triangle architectures described in Section 2.2 on MuST-Cinema test set for en→{de, es}.

en-de					
Model	**TED**	**EPTV**	**Peloton**	**ITV**	**Avg**
(Papi et al., 2022a)	72.7	82.3	84.7	88.0	81.9
+ fine-tuning	**69.4**	**80.6**	**79.1**	**83.7**	**78.2**
en-es					
Model	**TED**	**EPTV**	**Peloton**	**ITV**	**Avg**
(Papi et al., 2022a)	54.8	75.3	82.3	84.1	74.1
+ fine-tuning	**52.5**	**73.7**	**80.3**	**82.2**	**72.4**

Table 3: SubER (↓) scores for en→{de, es} of the direct ST models on the four dev sets of the competition. "fine-tuning" represents the second fine-tuning on data with restored punctuation mentioned in Section 3.2.

[9] https://iwslt.org/2023/subtitling#development-and-evaluation-data

[10] https://iwslt.org/2023/subtitling#automatic-evaluation

5 Conclusions

We presented the FBK's systems built to participate in the IWSLT 2023 Evaluation Campaigns for simultaneous speech translation (en-de) and automatic subtitling (en-{de, es}). Our submissions are characterized by the use of direct speech translation models to address both tasks, without any further modification nor adaptation for the simultaneous task, and with a fine-tuning on subtitle-like translations for the automatic subtitling task. Our SimulST system achieves a lower computational-aware latency with up to 3.5 BLEU gain compared to the last two years' winners. Our automatic subtitling system achieves 3.7 and 1.7 SubER improvement on en-de and en-es respectively, compared to the only solution published in the literature based on a direct system.

Acknowledgements

This work has been supported by the project "AI@TN" funded by the Autonomous Province of Trento, Italy.

References

Milind Agarwal, Sweta Agrawal, Antonios Anastasopoulos, Ondřej Bojar, Claudia Borg, Marine Carpuat, Roldano Cattoni, Mauro Cettolo, Mingda Chen, William Chen, Khalid Choukri, Alexandra Chronopoulou, Anna Currey, Thierry Declerck, Qianqian Dong, Yannick Estève, Kevin Duh, Marcello Federico, Souhir Gahbiche, Barry Haddow, Benjamin Hsu, Phu Mon Htut, Hirofumi Inaguma, Dávid Javorský, John Judge, Yasumasa Kano, Tom Ko, Rishu Kumar, Pengwei Li, Xutail Ma, Prashant Mathur, Evgeny Matusov, Paul McNamee, John P. McCrae, Kenton Murray, Maria Nadejde, Satoshi Nakamura, Matteo Negri, Ha Nguyen, Jan Niehues, Xing Niu, Atul Ojha Kr., John E. Ortega, Proyag Pal, Juan Pino, Lonneke van der Plas, Peter Polák, Elijah Rippeth, Elizabeth Salesky, Jiatong Shi, Matthias Sperber, Sebastian Stüker, Katsuhito Sudoh, Yun Tang, Brian Thompson, Kevin Tran, Marco Turchi, Alex Waibel, Mingxuan Wang, Shinji Watanabe, and Rodolfo Zevallos. 2023. Findings of the IWSLT 2023 Evaluation Campaign. In *Proceedings of the 20th International Conference on Spoken Language Translation (IWSLT 2023)*.

Antonios Anastasopoulos, Loïc Barrault, Luisa Bentivogli, Marcely Zanon Boito, Ondřej Bojar, Roldano Cattoni, Anna Currey, Georgiana Dinu, Kevin Duh, Maha Elbayad, Clara Emmanuel, Yannick Estève, Marcello Federico, Christian Federmann, Souhir Gahbiche, Hongyu Gong, Roman Grundkiewicz, Barry Haddow, Benjamin Hsu, Dávid Javorský, Věra Kloudová, Surafel Lakew, Xutai Ma, Prashant Mathur, Paul McNamee, Kenton Murray, Maria Nădejde, Satoshi Nakamura, Matteo Negri, Jan Niehues, Xing Niu, John Ortega, Juan Pino, Elizabeth Salesky, Jiatong Shi, Matthias Sperber, Sebastian Stüker, Katsuhito Sudoh, Marco Turchi, Yogesh Virkar, Alexander Waibel, Changhan Wang, and Shinji Watanabe. 2022. Findings of the IWSLT 2022 evaluation campaign. In *Proceedings of the 19th International Conference on Spoken Language Translation (IWSLT 2022)*, pages 98–157, Dublin, Ireland (in-person and online).

Antonios Anastasopoulos, Ondřej Bojar, Jacob Bremerman, Roldano Cattoni, Maha Elbayad, Marcello Federico, Xutai Ma, Satoshi Nakamura, Matteo Negri, Jan Niehues, Juan Pino, Elizabeth Salesky, Sebastian Stüker, Katsuhito Sudoh, Marco Turchi, Alexander Waibel, Changhan Wang, and Matthew Wiesner. 2021. FINDINGS OF THE IWSLT 2021 EVALUATION CAMPAIGN. In *Proceedings of the 18th International Conference on Spoken Language Translation (IWSLT 2021)*, pages 1–29, Bangkok, Thailand (online).

Antonios Anastasopoulos and David Chiang. 2018. Tied multitask learning for neural speech translation. In *Proceedings of the 2018 Conference of the North American Chapter of the Association for Computational Linguistics: Human Language Technologies, Volume 1 (Long Papers)*, pages 82–91, New Orleans, Louisiana.

Ebrahim Ansari, Amittai Axelrod, Nguyen Bach, Ondřej Bojar, Roldano Cattoni, Fahim Dalvi, Nadir Durrani, Marcello Federico, Christian Federmann, Jiatao Gu, Fei Huang, Kevin Knight, Xutai Ma, Ajay Nagesh, Matteo Negri, Jan Niehues, Juan Pino, Elizabeth Salesky, Xing Shi, Sebastian Stüker, Marco Turchi, Alexander Waibel, and Changhan Wang. 2020. FINDINGS OF THE IWSLT 2020 EVALUATION CAMPAIGN. In *Proceedings of the 17th International Conference on Spoken Language Translation*, pages 1–34, Online.

Luisa Bentivogli, Mauro Cettolo, Marco Gaido, Alina Karakanta, Alberto Martinelli, Matteo Negri, and Marco Turchi. 2021. Cascade versus direct speech translation: Do the differences still make a difference? In *Proceedings of the 59th Annual Meeting of the Association for Computational Linguistics and the 11th International Joint Conference on Natural Language Processing (Volume 1: Long Papers)*, pages 2873–2887, Online.

Alexandre Bérard, Olivier Pietquin, Christophe Servan, and Laurent Besacier. 2016. Listen and Translate: A Proof of Concept for End-to-End Speech-to-Text Translation. In *NIPS Workshop on end-to-end learning for speech and audio processing*, Barcelona, Spain.

Ondřej Bojar, Dominik Macháček, Sangeet Sagar, Otakar Smrž, Jonáš Kratochvíl, Peter Polák, Ebrahim Ansari, Mohammad Mahmoudi, Rishu Kumar, Dario

Franceschini, Chiara Canton, Ivan Simonini, Thai-Son Nguyen, Felix Schneider, Sebastian Stüker, Alex Waibel, Barry Haddow, Rico Sennrich, and Philip Williams. 2021. ELITR multilingual live subtitling: Demo and strategy. In *Proceedings of the 16th Conference of the European Chapter of the Association for Computational Linguistics: System Demonstrations*, pages 271–277, Online.

Chih-Chiang Chang and Hung-Yi Lee. 2022. Exploring Continuous Integrate-and-Fire for Adaptive Simultaneous Speech Translation. In *Proc. Interspeech 2022*, pages 5175–5179.

Junkun Chen, Mingbo Ma, Renjie Zheng, and Liang Huang. 2021. Direct simultaneous speech-to-text translation assisted by synchronized streaming ASR. In *Findings of the Association for Computational Linguistics: ACL-IJCNLP 2021*, pages 4618–4624, Online.

Marcello Federico, Yogesh Virkar, Robert Enyedi, and Roberto Barra-Chicote. 2020. Evaluating and Optimizing Prosodic Alignment for Automatic Dubbing. In *Proc. Interspeech 2020*, pages 1481–1485.

Ryo Fukuda, Yuka Ko, Yasumasa Kano, Kosuke Doi, Hirotaka Tokuyama, Sakriani Sakti, Katsuhito Sudoh, and Satoshi Nakamura. 2022. NAIST simultaneous speech-to-text translation system for IWSLT 2022. In *Proceedings of the 19th International Conference on Spoken Language Translation (IWSLT 2022)*, pages 286–292, Dublin, Ireland (in-person and online).

Marco Gaido, Mauro Cettolo, Matteo Negri, and Marco Turchi. 2021a. CTC-based compression for direct speech translation. In *Proceedings of the 16th Conference of the European Chapter of the Association for Computational Linguistics: Main Volume*, pages 690–696, Online.

Marco Gaido, Mattia A. Di Gangi, Matteo Negri, and Marco Turchi. 2020. End-to-end speech-translation with knowledge distillation: FBK@IWSLT2020. In *Proceedings of the 17th International Conference on Spoken Language Translation*, pages 80–88, Online.

Marco Gaido, Mattia A. Di Gangi, Matteo Negri, and Marco Turchi. 2021b. On Knowledge Distillation for Direct Speech Translation . In *Proceedings of CLiC-IT 2020*, Online.

Marco Gaido, Matteo Negri, and Marco Turchi. 2022a. Direct speech-to-text translation models as students of text-to-text models. *Italian Journal of Computational Linguistics*.

Marco Gaido, Sara Papi, Dennis Fucci, Giuseppe Fiameni, Matteo Negri, and Marco Turchi. 2022b. Efficient yet competitive speech translation: FBK@IWSLT2022. In *Proceedings of the 19th International Conference on Spoken Language Translation (IWSLT 2022)*, pages 177–189, Dublin, Ireland (in-person and online).

Alex Graves, Santiago Fernández, Faustino J. Gomez, and Jürgen Schmidhuber. 2006. Connectionist Temporal Classification: Labelling Unsegmented Sequence Data with Recurrent Neural Networks. In *Proceedings of the 23rd international conference on Machine learning (ICML)*, pages 369–376, Pittsburgh, Pennsylvania.

Anmol Gulati, James Qin, Chung-Cheng Chiu, Niki Parmar, Yu Zhang, Jiahui Yu, Wei Han, Shibo Wang, Zhengdong Zhang, Yonghui Wu, and Ruoming Pang. 2020. Conformer: Convolution-augmented Transformer for Speech Recognition. In *Proc. Interspeech 2020*, pages 5036–5040.

François Hernandez, Vincent Nguyen, Sahar Ghannay, Natalia Tomashenko, and Yannick Estève. 2018. Tedlium 3: Twice as much data and corpus repartition for experiments on speaker adaptation. In *Speech and Computer*, pages 198–208, Cham. Springer International Publishing.

Javier Iranzo-Sánchez, Javier Jorge Cano, Alejandro Pérez-González-de Martos, Adrián Giménez Pastor, Gonçal Garcés Díaz-Munío, Pau Baquero-Arnal, Joan Albert Silvestre-Cerdà, Jorge Civera Saiz, Albert Sanchis, and Alfons Juan. 2022. MLLP-VRAIN UPV systems for the IWSLT 2022 simultaneous speech translation and speech-to-speech translation tasks. In *Proceedings of the 19th International Conference on Spoken Language Translation (IWSLT 2022)*, pages 255–264, Dublin, Ireland (in-person and online).

Yasumasa Kano, Katsuhito Sudoh, and Satoshi Nakamura. 2022. Average token delay: A latency metric for simultaneous translation. *arXiv preprint arXiv:2211.13173*.

Alina Karakanta, Franćois Buet, Mauro Cettolo, and Franćois Yvon. 2022. Evaluating Subtitle Segmentation for End-to-end Generation Systems. In *Proceedings of the 13th Language Resources and Evaluation Conference (LREC)*, pages 3069–3078, Marseilles, France.

Alina Karakanta, Marco Gaido, Matteo Negri, and Marco Turchi. 2021a. Between flexibility and consistency: Joint generation of captions and subtitles. In *Proceedings of the 18th International Conference on Spoken Language Translation (IWSLT 2021)*, pages 215–225, Bangkok, Thailand (online).

Alina Karakanta, Matteo Negri, and Marco Turchi. 2020a. Is 42 the answer to everything in subtitling-oriented speech translation? In *Proceedings of the 17th International Conference on Spoken Language Translation*, pages 209–219, Online.

Alina Karakanta, Matteo Negri, and Marco Turchi. 2020b. MuST-cinema: a speech-to-subtitles corpus. In *Proc. of the 12th Language Resources and Evaluation Conference*, pages 3727–3734, Marseille, France.

Alina Karakanta, Sara Papi, Matteo Negri, and Marco Turchi. 2021b. Simultaneous speech translation for live subtitling: from delay to display. In *Proceedings of the 1st Workshop on Automatic Spoken Language Translation in Real-World Settings (ASLTRW)*, pages 35–48, Virtual.

Diederik P. Kingma and Jimmy Ba. 2015. Adam: A method for stochastic optimization. In *3rd International Conference on Learning Representations, ICLR 2015, San Diego, CA, USA, May 7-9, 2015, Conference Track Proceedings*.

Maarit Koponen, Umut Sulubacak, Kaisa Vitikainen, and Jörg Tiedemann. 2020. MT for subtitling: User evaluation of post-editing productivity. In *Proceedings of the 22nd Annual Conference of the European Association for Machine Translation*, pages 115–124, Lisboa, Portugal.

Taku Kudo and John Richardson. 2018. SentencePiece: A simple and language independent subword tokenizer and detokenizer for neural text processing. In *Proceedings of the 2018 Conference on Empirical Methods in Natural Language Processing: System Demonstrations*, pages 66–71, Brussels, Belgium.

Dan Liu, Mengge Du, Xiaoxi Li, Yuchen Hu, and Lirong Dai. 2021a. The USTC-NELSLIP systems for simultaneous speech translation task at IWSLT 2021. In *Proceedings of the 18th International Conference on Spoken Language Translation (IWSLT 2021)*, pages 30–38, Bangkok, Thailand (online).

Dan Liu, Mengge Du, Xiaoxi Li, Ya Li, and Enhong Chen. 2021b. Cross attention augmented transducer networks for simultaneous translation. In *Proceedings of the 2021 Conference on Empirical Methods in Natural Language Processing*, pages 39–55, Online and Punta Cana, Dominican Republic.

Danni Liu, Gerasimos Spanakis, and Jan Niehues. 2020. Low-Latency Sequence-to-Sequence Speech Recognition and Translation by Partial Hypothesis Selection. In *Proc. Interspeech 2020*, pages 3620–3624.

Mingbo Ma, Liang Huang, Hao Xiong, Renjie Zheng, Kaibo Liu, Baigong Zheng, Chuanqiang Zhang, Zhongjun He, Hairong Liu, Xing Li, Hua Wu, and Haifeng Wang. 2019. STACL: Simultaneous translation with implicit anticipation and controllable latency using prefix-to-prefix framework. In *Proceedings of the 57th Annual Meeting of the Association for Computational Linguistics*, pages 3025–3036, Florence, Italy.

Xutai Ma, Mohammad Javad Dousti, Changhan Wang, Jiatao Gu, and Juan Pino. 2020a. SIMULEVAL: An evaluation toolkit for simultaneous translation. In *Proceedings of the 2020 Conference on Empirical Methods in Natural Language Processing: System Demonstrations*, pages 144–150, Online.

Xutai Ma, Juan Pino, and Philipp Koehn. 2020b. SimulMT to SimulST: Adapting simultaneous text translation to end-to-end simultaneous speech translation. In *Proceedings of the 1st Conference of the Asia-Pacific Chapter of the Association for Computational Linguistics and the 10th International Joint Conference on Natural Language Processing*, pages 582–587, Suzhou, China.

Evgeny Matusov, Patrick Wilken, and Yota Georgakopoulou. 2019. Customizing neural machine translation for subtitling. In *Proceedings of the Fourth Conference on Machine Translation (Volume 1: Research Papers)*, pages 82–93, Florence, Italy.

Maite Melero, Antoni Oliver, and Toni Badia. 2006. Automatic Multilingual Subtitling in the eTITLE Project. In *Proceedings of ASLIB Translating and the Computer 28*.

Ha Nguyen, Yannick Estève, and Laurent Besacier. 2021. An empirical study of end-to-end simultaneous speech translation decoding strategies. In *ICASSP 2021-2021 IEEE International Conference on Acoustics, Speech and Signal Processing (ICASSP)*, pages 7528–7532. IEEE.

Alp Öktem, Mireia Farrús, and Antonio Bonafonte. 2019. Prosodic phrase alignment for machine dubbing. *ArXiv*, abs/1908.07226.

Sara Papi, Marco Gaido, Alina Karakanta, Mauro Cettolo, Matteo Negri, and Marco Turchi. 2022a. Direct speech translation for automatic subtitling. *arXiv preprint arXiv:2209.13192*.

Sara Papi, Marco Gaido, Matteo Negri, and Andrea Pilzer. 2023a. Reproducibility is Nothing without Correctness: The Importance of Testing Code in NLP. *arXiv preprint arXiv:2303.16166*.

Sara Papi, Marco Gaido, Matteo Negri, and Marco Turchi. 2021. Dealing with training and test segmentation mismatch: FBK@IWSLT2021. In *Proceedings of the 18th International Conference on Spoken Language Translation (IWSLT 2021)*, pages 84–91, Bangkok, Thailand (online).

Sara Papi, Marco Gaido, Matteo Negri, and Marco Turchi. 2022b. Does simultaneous speech translation need simultaneous models? In *Findings of the Association for Computational Linguistics: EMNLP 2022*, pages 141–153, Abu Dhabi, United Arab Emirates.

Sara Papi, Marco Gaido, Matteo Negri, and Marco Turchi. 2022c. Over-generation cannot be rewarded: Length-adaptive average lagging for simultaneous speech translation. In *Proceedings of the Third Workshop on Automatic Simultaneous Translation*, pages 12–17, Online.

Sara Papi, Alina Karakanta, Matteo Negri, and Marco Turchi. 2022d. Dodging the data bottleneck: Automatic subtitling with automatically segmented ST corpora. In *Proceedings of the 2nd Conference of the Asia-Pacific Chapter of the Association for Computational Linguistics and the 12th International Joint*

Conference on Natural Language Processing (Volume 2: Short Papers), pages 480–487, Online only.

Sara Papi, Matteo Negri, and Marco Turchi. 2022e. Attention as a guide for simultaneous speech translation. *arXiv preprint arXiv:2212.07850*.

Sara Papi, Matteo Negri, and Marco Turchi. 2023b. Alignatt: Using attention-based audio-translation alignments as a guide for simultaneous speech translation. In *Proc. of Interspeech 2023*, Dublin, Ireland.

Daniel S. Park, William Chan, Yu Zhang, Chung-Cheng Chiu, Barret Zoph, Ekin D. Cubuk, and Quoc V. Le. 2019. SpecAugment: A Simple Data Augmentation Method for Automatic Speech Recognition. In *Proc. Interspeech 2019*, pages 2613–2617.

Stelios Piperidis, Iason Demiros, Prokopis Prokopidis, Peter Vanroose, Anja Hoethker, Walter Daelemans, Elsa Sklavounou, Manos Konstantinou, and Yannis Karavidas. 2004. Multimodal, multilingual resources in the subtitling process. In *Proceedings of the Fourth International Conference on Language Resources and Evaluation (LREC'04)*, Lisbon, Portugal.

Peter Polák, Ngoc-Quan Pham, Tuan Nam Nguyen, Danni Liu, Carlos Mullov, Jan Niehues, Ondřej Bojar, and Alexander Waibel. 2022. CUNI-KIT system for simultaneous speech translation task at IWSLT 2022. In *Proceedings of the 19th International Conference on Spoken Language Translation (IWSLT 2022)*, pages 277–285, Dublin, Ireland (in-person and online).

Matt Post. 2018. A call for clarity in reporting BLEU scores. In *Proceedings of the Third Conference on Machine Translation: Research Papers*, pages 186–191, Brussels, Belgium.

Yi Ren, Jinglin Liu, Xu Tan, Chen Zhang, Tao Qin, Zhou Zhao, and Tie-Yan Liu. 2020. SimulSpeech: End-to-end simultaneous speech to text translation. In *Proceedings of the 58th Annual Meeting of the Association for Computational Linguistics*, pages 3787–3796, Online.

Derek Tam, Surafel M. Lakew, Yogesh Virkar, Prashant Mathur, and Marcello Federico. 2022. Isochrony-Aware Neural Machine Translation for Automatic Dubbing. In *Proc. Interspeech 2022*, pages 1776–1780.

Ioannis Tsiamas, Gerard I. Gállego, José A. R. Fonollosa, and Marta R. Costa-jussà. 2022. SHAS: Approaching optimal Segmentation for End-to-End Speech Translation. In *Proc. Interspeech 2022*, pages 106–110.

Yogesh Virkar, Marcello Federico, Robert Enyedi, and Roberto Barra-Chicote. 2021. Improvements to prosodic alignment for automatic dubbing. In *ICASSP 2021 - 2021 IEEE International Conference on Acoustics, Speech and Signal Processing (ICASSP)*, pages 7543–7574.

Changhan Wang, Yun Tang, Xutai Ma, Anne Wu, Dmytro Okhonko, and Juan Pino. 2020. fairseq s2t: Fast speech-to-text modeling with fairseq. In *Proceedings of the 2020 Conference of the Asian Chapter of the Association for Computational Linguistics (AACL): System Demonstrations*.

Ron J. Weiss, Jan Chorowski, Navdeep Jaitly, Yonghui Wu, and Zhifeng Chen. 2017. Sequence-to-Sequence Models Can Directly Translate Foreign Speech. In *Proceedings of Interspeech 2017*, pages 2625–2629, Stockholm, Sweden.

Patrick Wilken, Panayota Georgakopoulou, and Evgeny Matusov. 2022. SubER - a metric for automatic evaluation of subtitle quality. In *Proceedings of the 19th International Conference on Spoken Language Translation (IWSLT 2022)*, pages 1–10, Dublin, Ireland (in-person and online).

Xingshan Zeng, Liangyou Li, and Qun Liu. 2021. RealTranS: End-to-end simultaneous speech translation with convolutional weighted-shrinking transformer. In *Findings of the Association for Computational Linguistics: ACL-IJCNLP 2021*, pages 2461–2474, Online.

Shaolei Zhang and Yang Feng. 2022. Information-transport-based policy for simultaneous translation. In *Proceedings of the 2022 Conference on Empirical Methods in Natural Language Processing*, pages 992–1013, Abu Dhabi, United Arab Emirates.

Baigong Zheng, Kaibo Liu, Renjie Zheng, Mingbo Ma, Hairong Liu, and Liang Huang. 2020. Simultaneous translation policies: From fixed to adaptive. In *Proceedings of the 58th Annual Meeting of the Association for Computational Linguistics*, pages 2847–2853, Online.

MT Metrics Correlate with Human Ratings of Simultaneous Speech Translation

Dominik Macháček[1] and **Ondřej Bojar**[1] and **Raj Dabre**[2]

Charles University, Faculty of Mathematics and Physics,
Institute of Formal and Applied Linguistics[1]

National Institute of Information and Communications Technology, Kyoto, Japan[2]
[1]{machacek,bojar}@ufal.mff.cuni.cz, [2]raj.dabre@nict.go.jp

Abstract

There have been several meta-evaluation studies on the correlation between human ratings and offline machine translation (MT) evaluation metrics such as BLEU, chrF2, BERTSCORE and COMET. These metrics have been used to evaluate simultaneous speech translation (SST) but their correlations with human ratings of SST, which has been recently collected as Continuous Ratings (CR), are unclear. In this paper, we leverage the evaluations of candidate systems submitted to the English-German SST task at IWSLT 2022 and conduct an extensive correlation analysis of CR and the aforementioned metrics. Our study reveals that the offline metrics are well correlated with CR and can be reliably used for evaluating machine translation in simultaneous mode, with some limitations on the test set size. We conclude that given the current quality levels of SST, these metrics can be used as proxies for CR, alleviating the need for large scale human evaluation. Additionally, we observe that correlations of the metrics with translation as a reference is significantly higher than with simultaneous interpreting, and thus we recommend the former for reliable evaluation.

1 Introduction

The current approach to evaluate simultaneous speech translation (SST, Cho and Esipova, 2016; Ma et al., 2019) systems that have text as the output modality is to use automatic metrics which are designed for offline text-to-text machine translation (MT), alongside other measures for latency and stability. Researchers tend to use offline metrics, such as BLEU (Papineni et al., 2002), chrF2 (Popović, 2017), BERTSCORE (Zhang et al., 2020), COMET (Rei et al., 2020) and others (Freitag et al., 2022) in SST despite no explicit evidence that they correlate with human ratings.

However, simultaneous speech-to-text translation has different characteristics compared to offline text-to-text MT. For example, when the users are following subtitles in real-time, they have limited time for reading and comprehension as they cannot fully control the reading pace by themselves. Therefore, they may be less sensitive to subtle grammar and factual flaws than while reading a text document without any time constraints. The human evaluation of SST should therefore reflect the simultaneity. The users may also prefer brevity and simplicity over verbatim word-for-word translation. Even if the reference is brief and simpler than the original, there may be lots of variants that the BLEU score and other MT metrics may not evaluate as correct.

Furthermore, SST and MT differ in their input modalities. MT sources are assumed to originate as texts, while the SST source is a speech given in a certain situation, accompanied by para-linguistic means and specific context knowledge shared by the speaker and listener. Transcribing speech to text for use in offline evaluation of SST may be limiting.

In this paper, we aim to determine the suitability of automatic metrics for evaluating SST. To this end, we analyze the results of the simultaneous speech translation task from English to German at IWSLT 2022 (Anastasopoulos et al., 2022), where we calculate the correlations between MT metrics and human judgements in simultaneous mode. There are five competing systems and human interpreting that are manually rated by bilingual judges in a simulated real-time event. Our studies show that BLEU does indeed correlate with human judgements of simultaneous translations under the same conditions as in offline text-to-text MT: on a sufficiently large number of sentences. Furthermore, chrF2, BERTSCORE and COMET exhibit similar but significantly larger correlations. To the best of our knowledge, we are the first to explicitly establish the correlation between automatic offline metrics with human SST ratings, indicating that they may be safely used in SST evaluation in

Proceedings of the 20th International Conference on Spoken Language Translation (IWSLT 2023), pages 169–179
July 13-14, 2023 ©2023 Association for Computational Linguistics

the currently achieved translation quality levels.

Additionally, we statistically compare the metrics with translation versus interpreting reference, and we recommend the most correlating one: translation reference and COMET metric, with BERTSCORE and chrF2 as fallback options.

We publish the code for analysis and visualisations that we created in this study.[1] It is available for further analysis and future work.

2 Related Work

We replicate the approach from text-to-text MT research (e.g. Papineni et al., 2002) that examined the correlation of MT metrics with human judgements. The strong correlation is used as the basis for taking the metrics as reliable. As far as we know, we are the first who apply this approach to SST evaluation in simultaneous mode.

In this paper, we analyze four metrics that represent the currently used or recommended (Freitag et al., 2022) types of MT metrics. BLEU and chrF2 are based on lexical overlap and are available for any language. BERTSCORE (Zhang et al., 2020) is based on embedding similarity of a pre-trained BERT language model. COMET (Rei et al., 2020) is a neural metric trained to estimate the style of human evaluation called Direct Assessment (Graham et al., 2015). COMET requires sentence-to-sentence aligned source, translation and reference in the form of texts, which may be unavailable in some SST use-cases; then, other metric types may be useful. Another fact is that BERTSCORE and COMET are available only for a limited set of languages.

3 Human Ratings in SST

As far as we know, the only publicly available collection of simultaneous (not offline) human evaluation of SST originates from IWSLT 2022 (Salesky et al., 2022) English-to-German Simultaneous Translation Task, which is described in "Findings" (Anastasopoulos et al., 2022, see highlights of it we discuss in Appendix A). The task focused on speech-to-text translation and was reduced to translation of individual sentences. The segmentation of the source audio to sentences was provided by organizers, and not by the systems themselves. The source sentence segmentation that was used in human evaluation was gold (oracle). It only approximates a realistic setup where the segmentation would be provided by an automatic system, e.g. Tsiamas et al. (2022), and may be partially incorrect and cause more translation errors compared to the gold segmentation.

The simultaneous mode in Simultaneous Translation Task means that the source is provided gradually, one audio chunk at a time. After receiving each chunk, the system decides to either wait for more source context, or produce target tokens. Once the target tokens are generated, they can not be rewritten.

The participating systems are submitted and studied in three latency regimes: low, medium and high. It means that the maximum Average Lagging (Ma et al., 2019) between the source and target on validation set must be 1, 2 or 4 seconds in a "computationally unaware" simulation where the time spent by computation, and not by waiting for context, is not counted. One system in low latency did not pass the latency constraints (see Findings, page 44, numbered 141), but it is manually evaluated regardless.

Computationally unaware latency was one of the main criteria in IWSLT 2022. It means that the participants did not need to focus on a low latency implementation, as it is more of a technical and hardware issue than a research task. However, the subtitle timing in manual evaluation was created in a way such that waiting for the first target token was dropped, and then it continued with computationally aware latency.

3.1 Continuous Rating (CR)

Continuous Rating (CR, Javorský et al., 2022; Macháček and Bojar, 2020) is a method for human assessment of SST quality in a simulated online event. An evaluator with knowledge of the source and target languages watches a video (or listens to an audio) document with subtitles created by the SST system which is being evaluated. The evaluator is asked to continuously rate the quality of the translation by pressing buttons with values 1 (the worst) to 4 (the best). Each evaluator can see every document only once, to ensure one-pass access to the documents, as in a realistic setup.

CR is analogous to Direct Assessment (Graham et al., 2015), which is a method of human text-to-text MT evaluation in which a bilingual evaluator expresses the MT quality by a number on a scale. It is natural that individual evaluators have different opinions, and thus it is a common practice to

[1] github.com/ufal/MT-metrics-in-SimST

have multiple evaluators evaluate the same outputs and then report the mean and standard deviation of evaluation scores, or the results of statistical significance tests that compare the pairs of candidate systems and show how confident the results are.

Javorský et al. (2022) showed that CR relates well to comprehension of foreign language documents by SST users. Using CR alleviates the need to evaluate comprehension by factual questionnaires that are difficult to prepare, collect and evaluate. Furthermore, Javorský et al. (2022) show that bilingual evaluators are reliable.

Criteria of CR In IWSLT 2022, the evaluators were instructed that the primary criterion in CR should be meaning preservation (or adequacy), and other aspects such as fluency should be secondary. The instructions do not mention readability due to output segmentation frequency or verbalizing non-linguistic sounds such as "laughter", despite the system candidates differ in these aspects.

3.2 Candidate Systems

Automatic SST systems There are 5 evaluated SST systems: FBK (Gaido et al., 2022), NAIST (Fukuda et al., 2022), UPV (Iranzo-Sánchez et al., 2022), HW-TSC (Wang et al., 2022), and CUNI-KIT (Polák et al., 2022).

Human Interpreting In order to compare the state-of-the-art SST with human reference, the organizers hired one expert human interpreter to simultaneously interpret all the test documents. Then, they employed annotators to transcribe the voice into texts. The annotators worked in offline mode. The transcripts were then formed as subtitles including the original interpreter's timing and were used in CR evaluation the same way as SST. However, human interpreters use their own segmentation to translation units so that they often do not translate one source sentence as one target sentence. There is no gold alignment of the translation sentences to interpreting chunks. The alignment has to be resolved before applying metrics to interpreting.

3.3 Evaluation Data

There are two subsets of evaluation data used in IWSLT22 En-De Simultaneous Translation task. The "Common" subset consists of TED talks of the native speakers.See the description in Findings on page 9 (numbered as 106). The "Non-Native" subset consists of mock business presentations of European high school students (Macháček et al., 2019), and of presentations by representatives of European supreme audit institutions. This subset is described in Findings on page 39 (numbered page 136). The duration statistics of audio documents in both test sets are in Findings in Table 17 on page 48 (numbered 145).

4 Correlation of CR and MT Metrics

In this section, we study the correlation of CR and MT metrics BLEU, chrF2, BERTSCORE and COMET. We measure it on the level of documents, and not on the test set level, increasing the number of observations for significance tests. There are 60 evaluated documents (17 in the Common subset and 43 in Non-Native) and 15 system candidates (5 systems, each in 3 latency regimes), which yields 900 data points.

We discovered that CUNI-KIT system outputs are tokenized, while the others are detokenized. Therefore, we first detokenized CUNI-KIT outputs. Then, we removed the final end of sequence token (</s>) from the outputs of all systems. Finally, we calculated BLEU and chrF2 using sacreBLEU (Post, 2018), BERTSCORE and COMET. See Appendix B for metric details and signatures.

In total, there are 1584 rating sessions of 900 candidate document translations. Each candidate document translation is rated either twice with different evaluators, once, or not at all. We aggregate the individual rating clicks in each rating session by plain average (CR definition in Appendix C) to get the CR scores. Then, we average the CR of the same documents and candidate translations, and we correlate it with MT metrics.

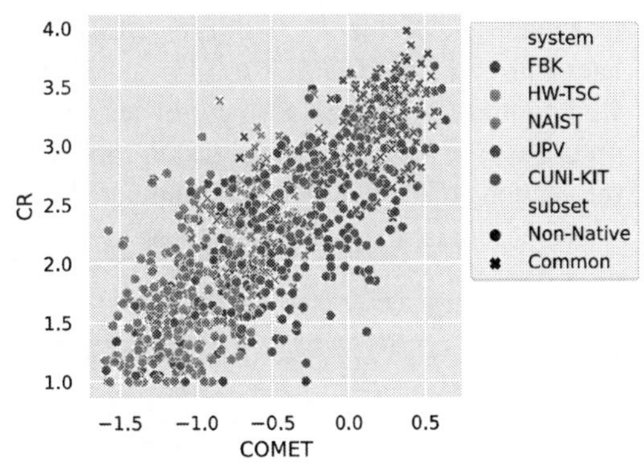

Figure 1: Averaged document CR vs COMET on both Common and Non-Native subsets.

subsets	num.	BLEU	chrF2	BERTS.	COMET
Averaged document ratings					
both	823	0.65	0.73	0.77	0.80
Common	228	*0.42*	0.63	0.68	0.76
Non-Native	595	0.70	0.70	0.73	0.75

subsets	num.	BLEU	chrF2	BERTS.	COMET
All document ratings					
both	1584	0.61	0.68	0.71	0.73
Common	441	*0.37*	*0.57*	0.60	0.68
Non-Native	1143	0.64	0.64	0.66	0.67

Table 1: Pearson correlation coefficients for CR vs MT metrics BLEU, chrF2, BERTSCORE and COMET for averaged document ratings by all 5 SST systems and 3 latency regimes (upper), and all ratings (lower). When the coefficient is less than 0.6 (in *italics*), the correlation is not considered as strong. Significance values are $p < 0.01$ in all cases, meaning strong confidence.

Correlation Results In Table 1, we report correlation coefficients with and without averaging, together with the number of observations. Figure 1 displays the relation between CR and COMET.

Pearson correlation is considered as strong if the coefficient is larger than 0.6 (Evans, 1996). The results show strong correlation (above 0.65) of CR with BLEU, chrF2, BERTSCORE and COMET at the document level on both test subsets. When we consider only one subset, the correlation is lower, but still strong for chrF2, BERTSCORE and COMET (0.63, 0.68 and 0.76, resp.). It is because the Common subset is generally translated better than Non-Native, so with only one subset, the points span a smaller part of the axes and contain a larger proportion of outliers.

The strong correlation is not the case of BLEU on the Common subset where the Pearson coefficient is 0.42. We assume it is because BLEU is designed for use on a larger test set, but we use it on short single documents. However, BLEU correlates with chrF2 and COMET (0.81 and 0.62 on the Common subset). BLEU also correlates with CR on the level of test sets, as reported in Findings in the caption of Table 18 (page 48, numbered 145).

We conclude that with the current overall levels of speech translation quality, BLEU, chrF2, BERTSCORE and COMET can be used for reliable assessment of human judgement of SST quality at least on the level of test sets. chrF2, BERTSCORE and COMET are reliable also at the document level.

Translation vs Interpreting Reference There is an open question whether SST should rather mimic offline translation, or simultaneous interpreting. As

metric	reference	alignment	corr.
COMET	TRANSL	SENT	0.80
COMET	TRANSL	SINGLESEQ	0.79
COMET	TRANSL+INTP	SINGLESEQ	0.79
BERTSCORE	TRANSL	SENT	0.77
BERTSCORE	TRANSL+INTP	SENT+MWER	0.77
COMET	INTP	SINGLESEQ	0.77
BERTSCORE	TRANSL+INTP	SINGLESEQ	0.76
BERTSCORE	TRANSL	SINGLESEQ	0.75
chrF2	TRANSL+INTP	SENT+MWER	0.73
BLEU	TRANSL+INTP	SINGLESEQ	0.73
chrF2	TRANSL	SENT	0.73
chrF2	TRANSL+INTP	SINGLESEQ	0.72
chrF2	TRANSL	SINGLESEQ	0.72
BLEU	TRANSL	SINGLESEQ	0.71
COMET	INTP	MWER	0.71
BERTSCORE	INTP	SINGLESEQ	0.69
BLEU	TRANSL+INTP	SENT+MWER	0.68
chrF2	INTP	SINGLESEQ	0.66
BLEU	TRANSL	SENT	0.65
chrF2	INTP	MWER	0.65
BLEU	INTP	SINGLESEQ	0.65
BERTSCORE	INTP	MWER	0.60
BLEU	INTP	MWER	0.58

Table 2: Pearson correlation of metric variants to averaged CR on both subsets, ordered from the most to the least correlating ones. Lines indicate "clusters of significance", i.e. boundaries between groups where all metric variants significantly differ from all in the other groups, with $p < 0.05$ for dashed line and $p < 0.1$ for dotted line. See the complete pair-wise comparison in Appendix D.

Macháček et al. (2021) discovered, translation may be more faithful, word-for-word, but also more complex to perceive by target audience. Simultaneous interpreting, on the other hand, tends to be brief and simpler than offline translation. However, it may be less fluent and less accurate. Therefore, we consider human translation (TRANSL) and transcript of simultaneous interpreting (INTP) as two possible references, and also test multi-reference metrics with both.

Since interpreting is not sentence-aligned to SST candidate translations, we consider two alignment methods: single sequence (SINGLESEQ), and mWERSegmenter (Matusov et al., 2005, MWER). SINGLESEQ method means that we concatenate all the sentences in the document to one single sequence, and then apply the metric on it, as if it was one sentence. mWERSegmenter is a tool for aligning translation candidates to reference, if their sentence segmentation differs. It finds the alignment with the minimum WER when comparing tokens in aligned segments. For translation, we also apply the default sentence alignment (SENT).

In Table 2, we report the correlations of metric,

reference and alignment variants and their significance, with more details in Appendix D.

4.1 Recommendations

Taking CR as the golden truth of human quality, we make the following recommendations of the most correlating metric, reference and sentence alignment method for SST evaluation.

Which metric? COMET, because it correlates significantly better with CR than BERTSCORE does. From the fall back options, chrF2 should be slightly preferred over BLEU.

Which reference? The metrics give significantly higher correlations with CR with translations than with interpreting as a reference. Difference between translation reference and two references (TRANSL+INTP) is insignificant. Therefore, we recommend translation as a reference for SST.

Which alignment method? With an unaligned reference, COMET and BERTSCORE correlate significantly more with SINGLESEQ than with MWER, probably because the neural metrics are trained on full, complete sentences, which are often split to multiple segments by mWERSegmenter. chrF2 correlates insignificantly better with MWER than with SINGLESEQ.

5 Conclusion

We found correlation of offline MT metrics to human judgements of simultaneous speech translation. The most correlating and thus preferred metric is COMET, followed by BERTSCORE and chrF2. We recommend text translation reference over interpreting, and single sequence alignment for neural, and mWERSegmenter for n-gram metrics.

6 Limitations

The data that we analyzed are limited to only one English-German language pair, 5 SST systems from IWSLT 2022, and three domains. All the systems were trained in the standard supervised fashion on parallel texts. They do not aim to mimic interpretation with shortening, summarization or redundancy reduction, and they do not use document context. The used MT metrics are good for evaluating individual sentence translations and that is an important, but not the only subtask of SST. We assume that some future systems created with a different approach may show divergence of CR and the offline MT metrics.

Furthermore, we used only one example of human interpreting. A precise in-depth study of human interpretations is needed to re-assess the recommendation of translation or interpreting as reference in SST.

Acknowledgements

We are thankful to Dávid Javorský and Peter Polák for their reviews.

This research was partially supported by the grants 19-26934X (NEUREM3) of the Czech Science Foundation, SVV project number 260 698, and 398120 of the Grant Agency of Charles University.

References

Antonios Anastasopoulos, Loïc Barrault, Luisa Bentivogli, Marcely Zanon Boito, Ondřej Bojar, Roldano Cattoni, Anna Currey, Georgiana Dinu, Kevin Duh, Maha Elbayad, Clara Emmanuel, Yannick Estève, Marcello Federico, Christian Federmann, Souhir Gahbiche, Hongyu Gong, Roman Grundkiewicz, Barry Haddow, Benjamin Hsu, Dávid Javorský, Věra Kloudová, Surafel Lakew, Xutai Ma, Prashant Mathur, Paul McNamee, Kenton Murray, Maria Nădejde, Satoshi Nakamura, Matteo Negri, Jan Niehues, Xing Niu, John Ortega, Juan Pino, Elizabeth Salesky, Jiatong Shi, Matthias Sperber, Sebastian Stüker, Katsuhito Sudoh, Marco Turchi, Yogesh Virkar, Alexander Waibel, Changhan Wang, and Shinji Watanabe. 2022. Findings of the IWSLT 2022 evaluation campaign. In *Proceedings of the 19th International Conference on Spoken Language Translation (IWSLT 2022)*, pages 98–157, Dublin, Ireland (in-person and online). Association for Computational Linguistics.

Kyunghyun Cho and Masha Esipova. 2016. Can neural machine translation do simultaneous translation? *CoRR*, abs/1606.02012.

James D. Evans. 1996. *Straightforward Statistics for the Behavioral Sciences*. Pacific Grove: Brooks/Cole Pub.

Markus Freitag, Ricardo Rei, Nitika Mathur, Chi-kiu Lo, Craig Stewart, Eleftherios Avramidis, Tom Kocmi, George Foster, Alon Lavie, and André F. T. Martins. 2022. Results of wmt22 metrics shared task: Stop using bleu – neural metrics are better and more robust. In *Proceedings of the Seventh Conference on Machine Translation*, pages 46–68, Abu Dhabi. Association for Computational Linguistics.

Ryo Fukuda, Yuka Ko, Yasumasa Kano, Kosuke Doi, Hirotaka Tokuyama, Sakriani Sakti, Katsuhito Sudoh, and Satoshi Nakamura. 2022. NAIST simultaneous speech-to-text translation system for IWSLT 2022. In *Proceedings of the 19th International Conference on*

Spoken Language Translation (IWSLT 2022), pages 286–292, Dublin, Ireland (in-person and online). Association for Computational Linguistics.

Marco Gaido, Sara Papi, Dennis Fucci, Giuseppe Fiameni, Matteo Negri, and Marco Turchi. 2022. Efficient yet competitive speech translation: FBK@IWSLT2022. In *Proceedings of the 19th International Conference on Spoken Language Translation (IWSLT 2022)*, pages 177–189, Dublin, Ireland (in-person and online). Association for Computational Linguistics.

Yvette Graham, Timothy Baldwin, and Nitika Mathur. 2015. Accurate evaluation of segment-level machine translation metrics. In *Proceedings of the 2015 Conference of the North American Chapter of the Association for Computational Linguistics: Human Language Technologies*, pages 1183–1191, Denver, Colorado. Association for Computational Linguistics.

Javier Iranzo-Sánchez, Javier Jorge Cano, Alejandro Pérez-González-de Martos, Adrián Giménez Pastor, Gonçal Garcés Díaz-Munío, Pau Baquero-Arnal, Joan Albert Silvestre-Cerdà, Jorge Civera Saiz, Albert Sanchis, and Alfons Juan. 2022. MLLP-VRAIN UPV systems for the IWSLT 2022 simultaneous speech translation and speech-to-speech translation tasks. In *Proceedings of the 19th International Conference on Spoken Language Translation (IWSLT 2022)*, pages 255–264, Dublin, Ireland (in-person and online). Association for Computational Linguistics.

Dávid Javorský, Dominik Macháček, and Ondřej Bojar. 2022. Continuous rating as reliable human evaluation of simultaneous speech translation. In *Proceedings of the Seventh Conference on Machine Translation*, pages 154–164, Abu Dhabi. Association for Computational Linguistics.

Mingbo Ma, Liang Huang, Hao Xiong, Renjie Zheng, Kaibo Liu, Baigong Zheng, Chuanqiang Zhang, Zhongjun He, Hairong Liu, Xing Li, Hua Wu, and Haifeng Wang. 2019. STACL: Simultaneous translation with implicit anticipation and controllable latency using prefix-to-prefix framework. In *Proceedings of the 57th Annual Meeting of the Association for Computational Linguistics*, pages 3025–3036, Florence, Italy. Association for Computational Linguistics.

Dominik Macháček and Ondřej Bojar. 2020. Presenting simultaneous translation in limited space. In *Proceedings of the 20th Conference Information Technologies - Applications and Theory (ITAT 2020), Hotel Tyrapol, Oravská Lesná, Slovakia, September 18-22, 2020*, volume 2718 of *CEUR Workshop Proceedings*, pages 34–39. CEUR-WS.org.

Dominik Macháček, Jonáš Kratochvíl, Tereza Vojtěchová, and Ondřej Bojar. 2019. A speech test set of practice business presentations with additional relevant texts. In *Statistical Language and Speech Processing*, pages 151–161, Cham. Springer International Publishing.

Dominik Macháček, Matúš Žilinec, and Ondřej Bojar. 2021. Lost in Interpreting: Speech Translation from Source or Interpreter? In *Proc. Interspeech 2021*, pages 2376–2380.

Evgeny Matusov, Gregor Leusch, Oliver Bender, and Hermann Ney. 2005. Evaluating machine translation output with automatic sentence segmentation. In *Proceedings of the Second International Workshop on Spoken Language Translation*, Pittsburgh, Pennsylvania, USA.

Kishore Papineni, Salim Roukos, Todd Ward, and Wei-Jing Zhu. 2002. Bleu: a method for automatic evaluation of machine translation. In *Proceedings of the 40th Annual Meeting of the Association for Computational Linguistics*, pages 311–318, Philadelphia, Pennsylvania, USA. Association for Computational Linguistics.

Peter Polák, Ngoc-Quan Pham, Tuan Nam Nguyen, Danni Liu, Carlos Mullov, Jan Niehues, Ondřej Bojar, and Alexander Waibel. 2022. CUNI-KIT system for simultaneous speech translation task at IWSLT 2022. In *Proceedings of the 19th International Conference on Spoken Language Translation (IWSLT 2022)*, pages 277–285, Dublin, Ireland (in-person and online). Association for Computational Linguistics.

Maja Popović. 2017. chrF++: words helping character n-grams. In *Proceedings of the Second Conference on Machine Translation*, pages 612–618, Copenhagen, Denmark. Association for Computational Linguistics.

Matt Post. 2018. A call for clarity in reporting BLEU scores. In *Proceedings of the Third Conference on Machine Translation: Research Papers*, pages 186–191, Brussels, Belgium. Association for Computational Linguistics.

Ricardo Rei, Craig Stewart, Ana C Farinha, and Alon Lavie. 2020. Unbabel's participation in the WMT20 metrics shared task. In *Proceedings of the Fifth Conference on Machine Translation*, pages 911–920, Online. Association for Computational Linguistics.

Elizabeth Salesky, Marcello Federico, and Marta Costa-jussà, editors. 2022. *Proceedings of the 19th International Conference on Spoken Language Translation (IWSLT 2022)*. Association for Computational Linguistics, Dublin, Ireland (in-person and online).

Ioannis Tsiamas, Gerard I. Gállego, José A. R. Fonollosa, and Marta R. Costa-jussà. 2022. SHAS: Approaching optimal Segmentation for End-to-End Speech Translation. In *Proc. Interspeech 2022*, pages 106–110.

Minghan Wang, Jiaxin Guo, Yinglu Li, Xiaosong Qiao, Yuxia Wang, Zongyao Li, Chang Su, Yimeng Chen, Min Zhang, Shimin Tao, Hao Yang, and Ying Qin. 2022. The HW-TSC's simultaneous speech translation system for IWSLT 2022 evaluation. In *Proceedings of the 19th International Conference on Spoken*

Language Translation (IWSLT 2022), pages 247–254, Dublin, Ireland (in-person and online). Association for Computational Linguistics.

Tianyi Zhang, Varsha Kishore, Felix Wu, Kilian Q. Weinberger, and Yoav Artzi. 2020. Bertscore: Evaluating text generation with bert. In *International Conference on Learning Representations*.

A Highlights of IWSLT22 Findings

The Findings of IWSLT22 (Anastasopoulos et al., 2022) are available in PDF. The most up-to-date version (version 2) is 61 pages long.[2] We highlight the relevant parts of Findings with page numbers in Table 3 so that we can refer to them easily.

Note that findings are a part of the conference proceedings (Salesky et al., 2022) as a chapter in a book. The order of findings pages in PDF does not match the page numbers at the footers.

Also note that in Section 2.4 on page 4 (in PDF, 101 in Proceedings), there is a description of MLLP-VRAIN which corresponds to the system denoted as UPV in all other tables and figures.

B Metric Signatures

BLEU and chrF2 SacreBLEU metric signature is case:mixed|eff:no|tok:13a|smooth:exp|version:2.3.1.

For BERTSCORE, we used F1 with signature bert-base-multilingual-cased_L9_no-idf_version=0.3.12(hug_trans=4.23.1)_fast-tokenizer.

We use COMET model `wmt20-comet-da` (Rei et al., 2020). For multi-reference COMET, we run the model separately with each reference and average the scores.

The standard way of using mWERSegmenter is to segment candidate translation according to reference. However, COMET requires aligned source as one of the inputs, and mWERSegmenter can not align it because it is in other language. For COMET INTP MWER variant, we therefore aligned interpreting to translation, which is already aligned to source. For the other metrics with INTP MWER, we aligned translation candidate to interpreting, which is the standard way.

C Aggregating Continuous Ratings

We revisited the processing of the individual collected clicks on the rating buttons into the aggregate score of Continuous Rating.

We found two definitions that can yield different results in certain situations: (1) The rating (as clicked by the evaluator) is valid at the instant time point when the evaluator clicked the rating button. The final score is the average of all clicks, each click has the equal weight. We denote this interpretation as CR.

(2) The rating is assigned to the time interval from the click time to the next click, or between the last click and the end of the document. The length of the interval is considered in averaging. The final score is the average of ratings weighted by interval lengths when the rating is valid. We denote this interpretation as CRi. [3]

To express them rigorously, let us have a document of duration T, and n ratings (r_i, t_i), where $i \in \{1, \ldots, n\}$ is an index, $r_i \in \{1, \ldots, 4\}$ is the rated value and $0 \leq t_1 < \cdots < t_n \leq T$ are times when the ratings were recorded.

Then, the definitions are as follows:

$$CR = \frac{1}{n} \sum_{i=1}^{n} r_i$$

$$CRi = \frac{1}{T - t_1} \Big(\sum_{i=1}^{n-1} (t_{i+1} - t_i) r_i + (T - t_n) r_n \Big)$$

If the judges press the rating buttons regularly, with a uniform frequency, then both definitions give equal scores. Otherwise, the CR and CRi may differ and may yield even opposite conclusions. For example, pressing "1" twelve times in one minute, then "4" and then waiting for one minute results in different scores: $CR = 1.2$, $CRi = 2$.

To examine the relationship between these definitions, we counted CR and CRi for each annotation of each document in the evaluation campaign. The results are in Figure 2 where we observe correlation between the two definitions. The Pearson correlation coefficient is 0.98, which indicates a very strong correlation.

Summary Based on the correlation score we observed, we conclude that both definitions are interchangeable, and any of them can be used in further analysis.

[2] `https://aclanthology.org/2022.iwslt-1.10v2.pdf`

[3] Other interpretations are also conceivable, for instance assuming that the rating applies to a certain time before the click and then till the next judgement.

marker	PDF page	numbered page	description
Section 2	3-5	100-102	Simultaneous Speech Translation Task
Figure 1	6	103	Quality-latency trade-off curves
Section 2.6.1	5	102	Description of human evaluation
Figure 5	8	105	Manual scores vs BLEU (plot)
Two Test Sets (paragraph)	39	136	Non-Native subset
Test data (paragraph)	9	106	Common (native) subset of test data
Automatic Evaluation Results	44	141	Latency and BLEU results (table)
A1.1 (appendix)	38-39	135-136	Details on human evaluation
Table 17	48	145	Test subsets duration
Table 18	48	145	Manual scores and BLEU (table)

Table 3: Relevant parts of IWSLT22 Findings (`https://aclanthology.org/2022.iwslt-1.10v2.pdf`) for En-De Simultaneous Speech Translation task and human evaluation.

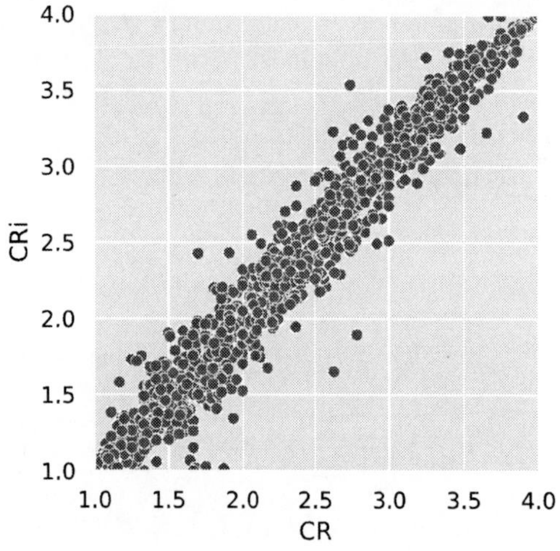

Figure 2: Relation between weighted interval averaging of continuous rating (CRi, y-axis) and average of all ratings (CR, x-axis) for each annotation of each document (blue data points).

D Pairwise Metrics Comparison

We test the statistical difference of correlations with Steiger's method.[4] The method takes into account the number of data points and the fact that all three compared variables correlate, which is the case of the MT metrics that are applied on the same texts. We use two-tailed test.

We applied the test on all pairs of metric variants. The results for both subsets are in Figure 3. Figure 4 displays results on the Common subset, and Figure 5 for the Non-Native subset. These results are analogous to those in Table 1 in Section 4. The correlation scores for the two subsets treated separately are lower and the differences along the diagonal are less significant. We explain it by the fact that in smaller data set, there is larger impact of noise.

[4] `https://github.com/psinger/CorrelationStats/`

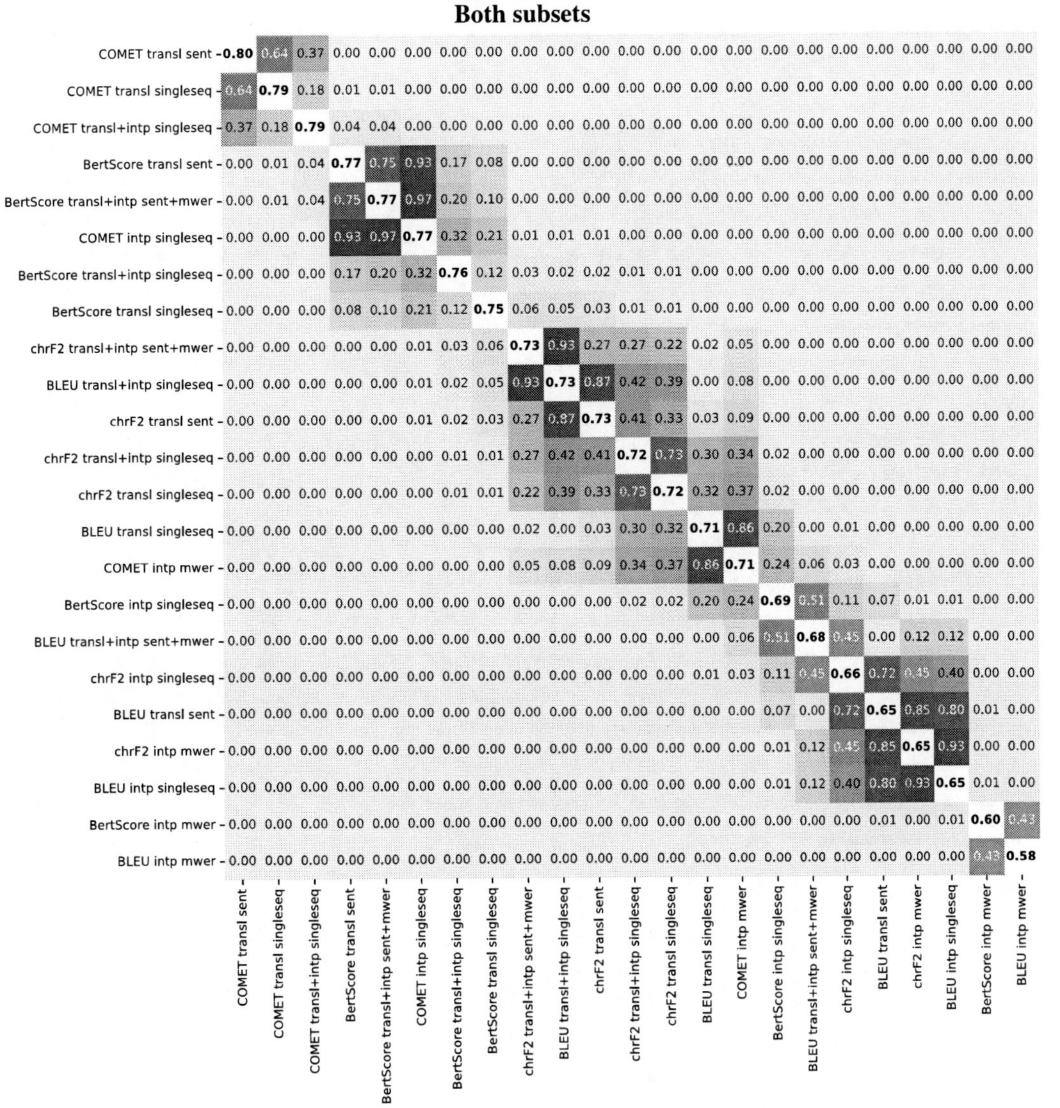

Figure 3: Results of significance test (p-values rounded to two decimal digits) for difference of correlations of the metrics variants to CR. The metrics variants are ordered by Pearson correlation to CR on both subsets from most correlating (top left) to least (bottom right). The bold numbers on the diagonal are the correlation coefficients to CR.

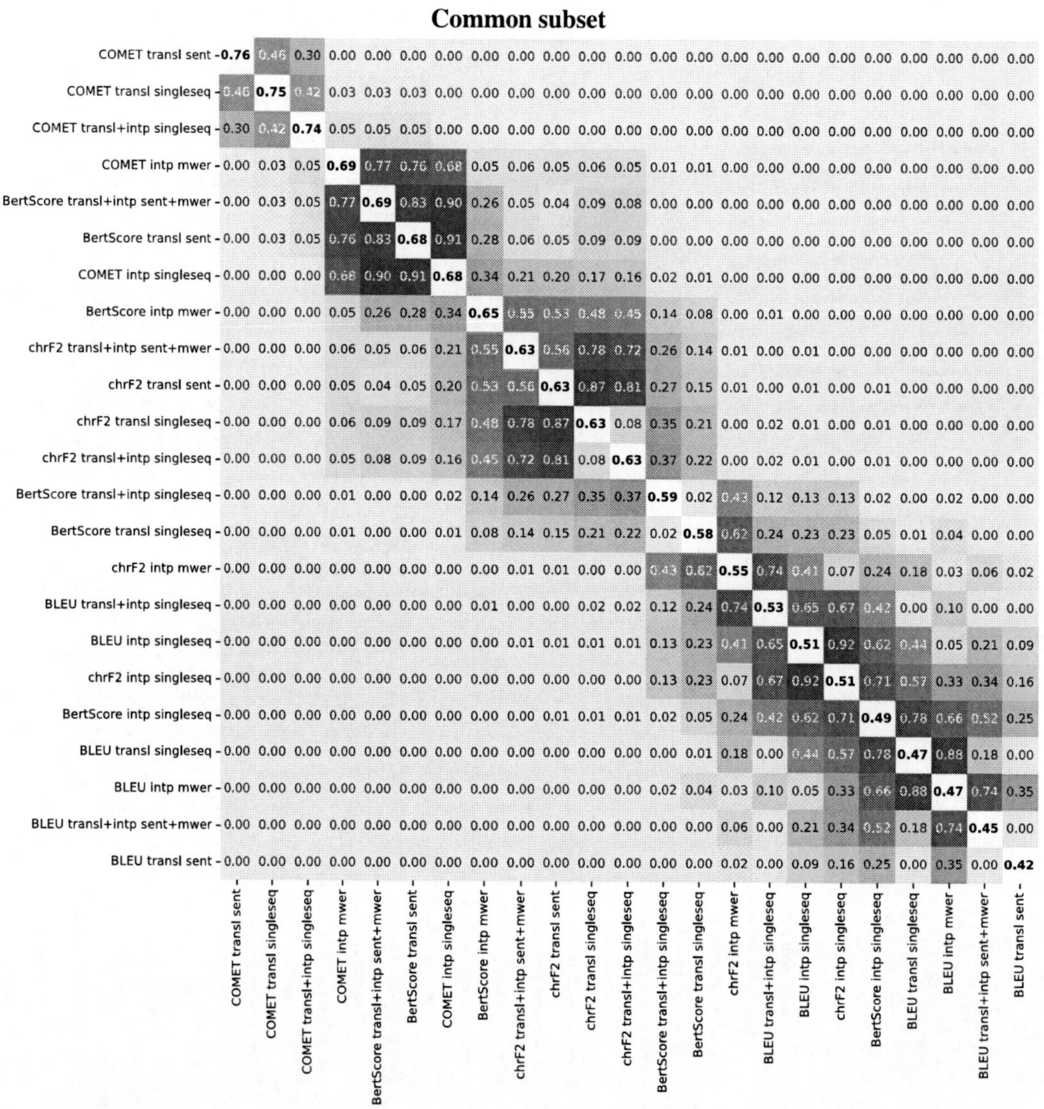

Figure 4: Results of significance test (p-values rounded to two decimal digits) for difference of correlations of the metrics variants to CR. The metrics variants are ordered by Pearson correlation to CR on the Common subset from most correlating (top left) to least (bottom right). The bold numbers on the diagonal are the correlation coefficients to CR.

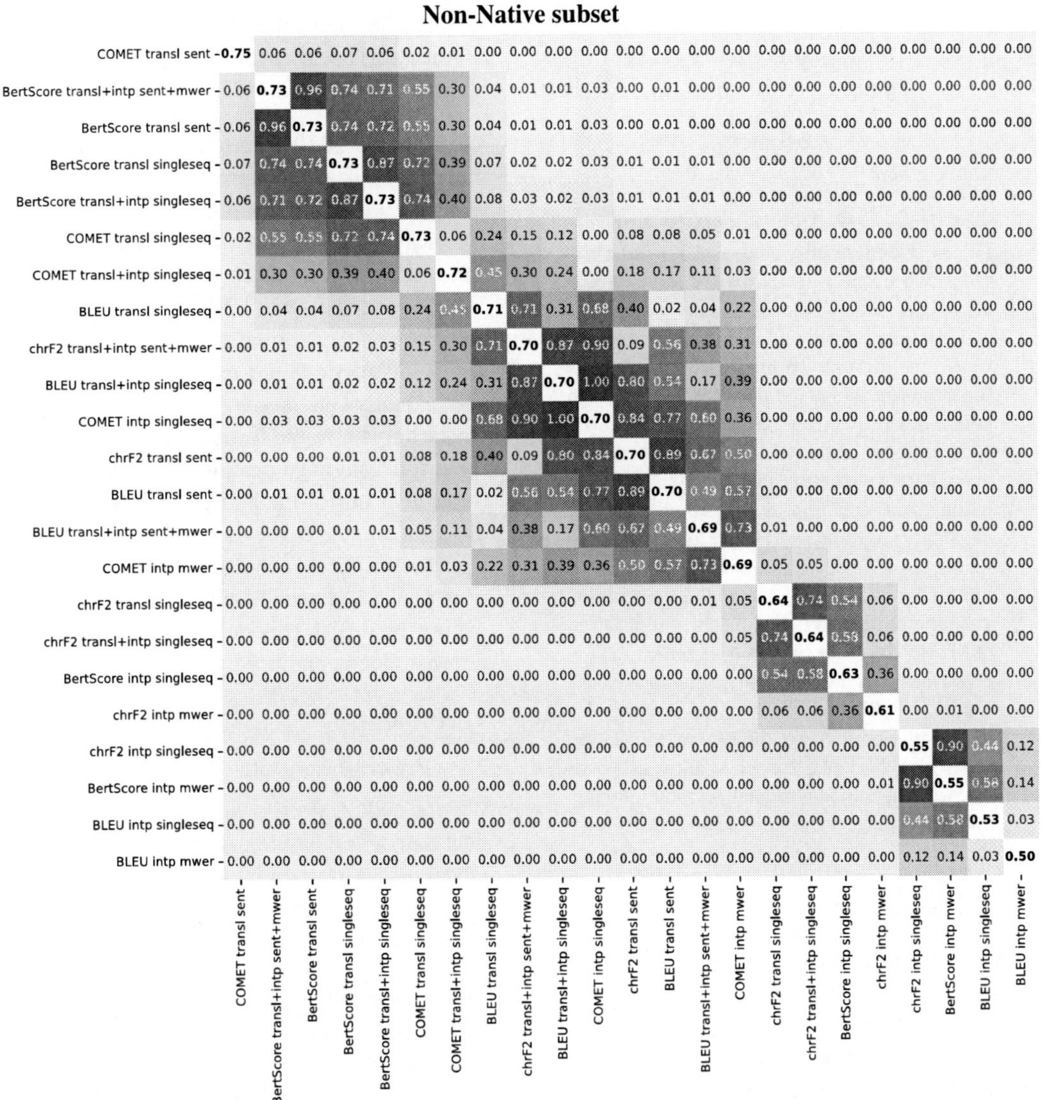

Figure 5: Results of significance test (p-values rounded to two decimal digits) for difference of correlations of the metrics variants to CR. The metrics variants are ordered by Pearson correlation to CR on the Non-Native subset from most correlating (top left) to least (bottom right). The bold numbers on the diagonal are the correlation coefficients to CR.

Improving Neural Machine Translation Formality Control with Domain Adaptation and Reranking-based Transductive Learning

Zhanglin Wu, Zongyao Li, Daimeng Wei, Hengchao Shang, Jiaxin Guo, Xiaoyu Chen, Zhiqiang Rao, Zhengzhe Yu, Jinlong Yang, Shaojun Li, Yuhao Xie, Bin Wei, Jiawei Zheng, Ming Zhu, Lizhi Lei, Hao Yang, Yanfei Jiang
Huawei Translation Service Center, Beijing, China
{wuzhanglin2,lizongyao,weidaimeng,shanghengchao,guojiaxin1,chenxiaoyu35, raozhiqiang,yuzhengzhe,yangjinlong7,lishaojun18,xieyuhao2,weibin29, zhengjiawei15,zhuming47,leilizhi,yanghao30,jiangyanfei}@huawei.com

Abstract

This paper presents Huawei Translation Service Center (HW-TSC)'s submission on the IWSLT 2023 formality control task, which provides two training scenarios: supervised and zero-shot, each containing two language pairs, and sets constrained and unconstrained conditions. We train the formality control models for these four language pairs under these two conditions respectively, and submit the corresponding translation results. Our efforts are divided into two fronts: enhancing general translation quality and improving formality control capability. According to the different requirements of the formality control task, we use a multi-stage pre-training method to train a bilingual or multilingual neural machine translation (NMT) model as the basic model, which can improve the general translation quality of the base model to a relatively high level. Then, under the premise of affecting the general translation quality of the basic model as little as possible, we adopt domain adaptation and reranking-based transductive learning methods to improve the formality control capability of the model.

1 Introduction

Machine translation (MT) (Lopez, 2008; Vaswani et al., 2017) models typically return one single translation for each input sentence. This means that when the input sentence is ambiguous, the MT model must choose a translation from among various valid options, without regard to the intended use case or target audience. Therefore, there is a need to control certain attributes (Schioppa et al., 2021) of the text generated in a target language such as politeness (Sennrich et al., 2016a; Feely et al., 2019) or formality (Niu et al., 2017, 2018; Viswanathan et al., 2020).

The lack of gold translation with alternate formality for supervised training and evaluation has lead researchers to rely on synthetic supervision training and manual evaluation in past work (Niu and Carpuat, 2020). Fortunately, the IWSLT formality control task now provides a new benchmark[1] (Nădejde et al., 2022; Agarwal et al., 2023) by contributing high-quality training datasets and test datasets for multiple language pairs.

This paper presents HW-TSC's submission on the IWSLT 2023 formality control task. How formality distinctions are expressed grammatically and lexically can vary widely by language. Thus, we participate in the formality control task of all these four language pairs to investigate a general formality control method that can be applied to different language pair. In addition, we also investigate the difference in formality control between constrained and unconstrained conditions by introducing the mBART model (Liu et al., 2020) under unconstrained condition.

2 Data

2.1 Pre-training Data

We use the CCMatrix[2] and OpenSubtitles[3] bilingual data given by the organizers to train a NMT model from scratch or fine-tune the mBART model as the general basic model. The bilingual data size of each language pair is shown in Table 1:

Language pair	CCMatrix	OpenSubtitles
EN-KO	19.4M	1.4M
EN-VI	50.1M	3.5M
EN-PT	173.7M	33.2M
EN-RU	139.9M	25.9M

Table 1: The bilingual data size of each language pair.

In order to achieve a better training effect, we also use some data pre-processing methods to clean bilingual data, such as: remove duplicate data, use

[1] https://github.com/amazon-science/contrastive-controlled-mt

[2] https://opus.nlpl.eu/CCMatrix.php

[3] https://opus.nlpl.eu/OpenSubtitles-v2018.php

Proceedings of the 20th International Conference on Spoken Language Translation (IWSLT 2023), pages 180–186
July 13-14, 2023

Moses[4] to normalize punctuation, filter extremely long sentences, use langid[5] (Lui and Baldwin, 2011, 2012) to filter sentences that do not meet the language requirements, use fast-align[6] (Dyer et al., 2013) to filter unaligned sentence pairs.

2.2 Formality-annotated Data

The formality-annotated data is provided by the organizers, and the data size of each language pair is shown in Table 2:

Setting	Language pair	Train	Test
Supervised	EN-KO	400	597
Supervised	EN-VI	400	598
Zero-shot	EN-PT	0	599
Zero-shot	EN-RU	0	600

Table 2: The formality-annotated data size of each language pair.

For supervised language pairs, we split the formality-annotated train data into a train set and a dev set with a ratio of 3:1, and use the formality-annotated train set and a small amount of bilingual data for formality control training, while for zero-shot language pairs, we use formality-annotated train set from the other two supervised language pairs for formality control training.

3 Model

3.1 Constrained Model

Transformer (Vaswani et al., 2017) is the state-of-the-art model in recent machine translation evaluations. There are two parts of research to improve this kind: the first part uses wide networks (eg: Transformer-Big (Vaswani et al., 2017)), and the other part uses deeper language representations (eg: Deep Transformer (Wang et al., 2019; Wu et al., 2022; Wei et al., 2022)). Under the constrained conditions, we combine these two improvements, adopt the Deep Transformer-Big model structure, and train a one-to-many multilingual NMT model (Johnson et al., 2017; Zhang et al., 2020) from scratch using bilingual data of four language pairs provided by the organizers. The main structure of Deep Transformer-Big is that it features pre-layer-normalization and 25-layer encoder, 6-layer decoder, 16-head self-attention, 1024-dimensional embedding and 4096-dimensional FFN embedding.

3.2 Unconstrained Model

Recently, multilingual denoising pre-training method (Liu et al., 2020; Tang et al., 2021) produces significant performance gains across a wide variety of machine translation tasks. As the earliest sequence-to-sequence model using multilingual denoising pre-training method, mBART (Liu et al., 2020) has also achieved good results in various machine translation-related tasks. Under unconstrained conditions, we use the mBART50 1n model[7] as the initial model of the unconstrained formality control task. The mBART50 1n model adopts Transformer structure, which features 12-layer encoder, 12-layer decoder, 16-head self-attention, 1024-dimensional embedding and 4096-dimensional FFN embedding, and an additional layer-normalization layer (Xu et al., 2019) on top of both the encoder and decoder.

4 Method

In our implementation, we first use a multi-stage pre-training method to train a general NMT model with relatively high translation quality. Then, we use domain adaptation method to fine-tune the NMT model so that the model can have basic formality control capability. Finally, we use the reranking-based transductive learning (RTL) method to further improve the formality control capability of the model.

4.1 Multi-stage Pre-training

There are four different types of formality control tasks, which are constrained supervised task, constrained zero-shot task, unconstrained supervised task, and unconstrained zero-shot task. For these four different tasks, we formulate different pre-training strategies and collectively refer to these strategies as multi-stage pre-training method.

Under the constrained condition, we adopt the Deep Transformer-Big model structure and use bilingual data of all four language pairs to train a one-to-many multilingual NMT model from scratch, which is used as the basic model for constrained zero-shot task. For constrained supervised task, we use the bilingual data of this task to further

[4]https://github.com/moses-smt/mosesdecoder

[5]https://github.com/saffsd/langid.py

[6]https://github.com/clab/fast_align

[7]https://dl.fbaipublicfiles.com/fairseq/models/mbart50/mbart50.ft.1n.tar.gz

pre-train the multilingual NMT model to obtain a bilingual NMT model as the basic model.

While under the unconstrained condition, we further pre-train the mBART50 1n model using bilingual data from all these four language pairs as the basic model for unconstrained zero-shot task. For unconstrained supervised task, we use the bilingual data of this task to further pre-train the pre-trained model, and use the final pre-trained bilingual model as the basic model.

4.2 Domain Adaptation for Formality Control

With the pre-trained basic model, we use domain adaptation method (Chu et al., 2017) to achieve basic formality control. First, we treat formal formality and informal formality as two special domains, and control the formality of the model's translation results using a tagging method (Chu et al., 2017; Nădejde et al., 2022), which attaches a formality-indicating tag to the source input. Then, in order to affect the general translation quality as little as possible, we use a mix fine-tuning method (Chu et al., 2017; Nădejde et al., 2022). Our specific implementation is to upsample the formality-annotated train set by 5 times, and mix it with the same amount of randomly sampled general bilingual data to fine-tune the pre-trained basic model.

As mentioned in Section 2.2, for the zero-shot task, due to the lack of formality-annotated data, we have to use the formality-annotated data of the two other supervised language pair, which is why we set the basic model of zero-shot task to a multilingual NMT model. After using domain adaptation method, the cross-lingual transfer learning capability of multilingual model can help zero-shot language pair achieve basic formality control.

4.3 Reranking-based Transductive Learning

After using domain adaptation method, we can enable the model to have the basic formality control capability. Inspired by the idea of transductive learning (Shi et al., 2018; Lee et al., 2021), we propose a RTL method, which can further improve the formality control capability of NMT model. Our method is mainly divided into two steps:

In the first step, we adopt beam search based decoding method (Sennrich et al., 2016b) for the formality control model, and then select the final translation result that meets the specified formality requirements from the top100 decoding results based on reranking idea (Dou et al., 2019). For supervised task, we use a reference-free formality classifier and the formality phrases from formality-annotated training data for reranking. The implementation details are shown in Algorithm 1. For zero-shot task, due to the lack of formality-annotated training data, we just use a reference-free formality classifier for reranking. Among them, the formality classifier under the constrained condition comes from self-training (Axelrod et al., 2011), while the formality classifier under the unconstrained condition comes from the organizer[8] (Briakou et al., 2021).

Algorithm 1: Reranking by reference-free formality classifier and formality phrases

Input: source sentence x, reference-free formality classifier C, formality control model M, formal and informal formality phrases $W_F = \{w_j^F\}_{j=1}^{|W_F|}$, $W_I = \{w_j^I\}_{j=1}^{|W_I|}$
Output: the formality translation y_F and y_I

translate x by M, the top 100 formality translations are respectively defined as: $D_F = \{y_i^F\}_{i=1}^{100}$, $D_I = \{y_i^I\}_{i=1}^{100}$
$y_F = y_0^F$
for y_i^F *in* D_F **do**
  $F_{flag} = False$
  for w_j^F *in* W_F **do**
    if w_j^F *in* y_i^F **then**
      $F_{flag} = True$
      break
    end
  end
  calculate the formality by C: C(y_i^F)
  if F_{flag} *and* $C(y_i^F)$*=="formal"* **then**
    $y_F = y_i^F$
    break
  end
end
pick y_I from D_I in a similar way to y_F
return y_F, y_I

In the second step, we add the source text of test set and the reranked formality translation results to the training data used for domain adaptation, and then use the adjusted training data to further fine-tune the formality control model.

We can also repeat the previous two steps until the formality control capability of the model on test set is no longer improved. We refer to this iterative

[8] https://github.com/amazon-science/contrastive-controlled-mt/releases/tag/classifier-v1.0.0

EN-VI	To Formal				To Informal				Flores	
	M-Acc	C-F	BLEU	COMET	M-Acc	C-F	BLEU	COMET	BLEU	COMET
AWS-baseline	99.40%	99.16%	43.2	0.6189	98.10%	98.49%	41.5	0.6021	-	-
Multilingual pre-training	10.86%	1.67%	25.6	0.2023	89.14%	98.33%	30.0	0.2873	42.3	0.6653
+ Bilingual pre-training	8.80%	3.01%	24.8	0.1782	91.20%	96.99%	28.9	0.2630	42.4	0.6706
+ Domain adaptation	98.17%	97.83%	49.1	0.7248	99.37%	99.83%	48.0	0.6952	41.3	0.6576
+ RTL	99.59%	**100.00%**	49.5	0.7296	99.38%	**100.00%**	48.1	0.7034	41.7	0.6614
+ Iterative RTL	**100.00%**	99.83%	**51.3**	**0.7522**	**100.00%**	**100.00%**	**49.8**	**0.7209**	**41.8**	**0.6730**
UMD-baseline	96.00%	99.67%	26.7	0.3629	96.00%	98.16%	25.3	0.3452	-	-
mBART50 1n	3.82%	1.51%	26.7	0.3516	96.18%	98.49%	31.0	0.4426	34.7	0.6040
+ Multilingual pre-training	9.44%	1.84%	25.4	0.2089	90.56%	98.16%	29.9	0.2975	42.2	0.6673
+ Bilingual pre-training	12.20%	2.51%	25.2	0.1579	87.80%	97.49%	29.4	0.2445	42.4	0.6698
+ Domain adaptation	99.02%	99.50%	47.8	0.7181	99.36%	**100.00%**	47.4	0.6930	43.2	0.6916
+ RTL	99.22%	**100.00%**	47.7	0.7190	99.16%	**100.00%**	47.8	0.7053	**43.4**	**0.7033**
+ Iterative RTL	**100.00%**	**100.00%**	**48.2**	**0.7214**	**100.00%**	**100.00%**	**48.3**	**0.7102**	**43.4**	0.6983

Table 3: The overall translation quality and formality control accuracy of EN-VI models.

EN-KO	To Formal				To Informal				Flores	
	M-Acc	C-F	BLEU	COMET	M-Acc	C-F	BLEU	COMET	BLEU	COMET
AWS-baseline	28.50%	54.61%	11.1	0.5044	80.40%	57.62%	11.1	0.5125	-	-
Multilingual pre-training	**100.00%**	69.85%	5.0	0.2408	0.00%	30.15%	4.5	0.2288	12.9	0.6497
+ Bilingual pre-training	**100.00%**	65.33%	5.5	0.2189	0.00%	34.67%	4.7	0.2105	13.8	0.6610
+ Domain adaptation	**100.00%**	97.49%	24.5	0.7234	**100.00%**	96.31%	25.1	0.7194	12.6	0.6528
+ RTL	**100.00%**	97.65%	**25.8**	0.7337	**100.00%**	98.51%	26.5	0.7337	13.0	**0.6828**
+ Iterative RTL	**100.00%**	**99.83%**	25.0	**0.7434**	**100.00%**	**99.66%**	**27.0**	**0.7495**	**13.2**	0.6729
UMD-baseline	78.30%	98.60%	4.9	0.2110	97.60%	99.50%	4.9	0.1697	-	-
mBART50 1n	**100.00%**	98.49%	4.1	0.4468	0.00%	1.51%	3.2	0.3670	9.5	0.5854
+ Multilingual pre-training	**100.00%**	65.66%	5.0	0.2501	0.00%	34.34%	4.3	0.2338	13.3	0.6605
+ Bilingual pre-training	**100.00%**	64.66%	5.2	0.2240	0.00%	35.34%	4.6	0.2114	14.2	0.6734
+ Domain adaptation	**100.00%**	99.33%	24.9	0.7297	**100.00%**	99.66%	25.5	0.7379	12.8	0.6666
+ RTL	**100.00%**	99.66%	**25.5**	**0.7393**	**100.00%**	**100.00%**	26.2	**0.7340**	13.8	0.6845
+ Iterative RTL	**100.00%**	**100.00%**	24.2	0.7254	**100.00%**	**100.00%**	**26.7**	0.7311	**14.0**	**0.6882**

Table 4: The overall translation quality and formality control accuracy of EN-KO models.

process as iterative RTL method.

5 Experiments

5.1 Training Details

We use the Pytorch-based Fairseq framework[9] (Ott et al., 2019) to pre-train or fine-tune NMT model, and use Adam optimizer (Kingma and Ba, 2014) with parameters $\beta 1$=0.9 and $\beta 2$=0.98. During the multi-stage pre-training phase, each model uses 8 GPUs for training, warmup steps is 4000, batch size is 4096, learning rate is 5×10^{-4}, label smoothing rate (Szegedy et al., 2016) is 0.1, and dropout is 0.1. In the domain adaptation and RTL phases, each model only uses 1 GPU for training without warm-up, batch size is 1024, learning rate is 3×10^{-5}, label smoothing rate is 0.1, and dropout is 0.3.

5.2 Evaluation Metrics

We evaluate the translation results of formality control model from the following two dimensions:

- We use SacreBLEU v2.0.0 [10] (Papineni et al., 2002; Post, 2018) and COMET (eamt22-cometinho-da)[11] (Rei et al., 2022) to evaluate the overall translation quality of formality control model on the official formality test sets and FLORES-200 devtest sets[12] (Goyal et al., 2022).
- We also use the reference-based corpus-level automatic metric Matched-Accuracy (M-Acc) and the reference-free automatic metric (C-F) that uses a multilingual formality classifier provided by the organizer to evaluate the formality control accuracy of the model on the official formality test sets, respectively.

5.3 Evaluation Results

Based on the above evaluation metrics, we evaluate the formality control models trained at different phases for each language pair under constrained and unconstrained conditions, and compare with constrained baseline (AWS-baseline) (Nădejde et al., 2022) and unconstrained baseline

[9]https://github.com/facebookresearch/fairseq

[10]https://github.com/mjpost/sacrebleu

[11]https://github.com/Unbabel/COMET

[12]https://github.com/facebookresearch/flores/tree/main/flores200

EN-RU	To Formal				To Informal				Flores	
	M-Acc	C-F	BLEU	COMET	M-Acc	C-F	BLEU	COMET	BLEU	COMET
Multilingual pre-training	99.27%	67.83%	29.7	0.4265	0.73%	32.17%	23.7	0.3869	32.2	0.7790
+ Domain adaptation	99.71%	90.67%	33.8	0.5977	85.49%	70.67%	31.2	0.5333	27.8	0.7040
+ RTL	99.74%	**100.00%**	34.5	0.6155	97.14%	**100.00%**	33.4	0.6019	**29.4**	**0.7261**
+ Iterative RTL	**100.00%**	**100.00%**	**36.5**	**0.6472**	**100.00%**	**100.00%**	**35.6**	**0.6442**	29.0	0.7153
UMD-baseline	96.20%	92.00%	22.0	0.3492	84.10%	85.17%	21.6	0.3475	-	-
mBART50 1n	**100.00%**	91.67%	25.6	0.2916	0.00%	8.33%	19.3	0.2351	25.0	0.5950
+ Multilingual pre-training	98.15%	67.00%	28.9	0.4263	1.85%	33.00%	23.1	0.3904	32.1	0.7638
+ Domain adaptation	99.49%	98.17%	31.8	0.5336	99.73%	**99.83%**	30.8	0.5214	30.7	0.7386
+ RTL	98.76%	**100.00%**	32.3	0.5575	99.73%	**99.83%**	31.6	0.5363	30.9	0.7417
+ Iterative RTL	**100.00%**	**100.00%**	**33.7**	**0.5804**	**100.00%**	**99.83%**	**32.4**	**0.5558**	**31.0**	**0.7521**

Table 5: The overall translation quality and formality control accuracy of EN-RU models.

EN-PT	To Formal				To Informal				Flores	
	M-Acc	C-F	BLEU	COMET	M-Acc	C-F	BLEU	COMET	BLEU	COMET
Multilingual pre-training	84.23%	77.46%	34.5	0.4750	15.77%	22.54%	31.4	0.4488	51.3	0.9047
+ Domain adaptation	**100.00%**	99.67%	43.0	0.6689	96.68%	96.49%	43.7	0.6689	45.0	0.7995
+ RTL	99.47%	**100.00%**	43.1	0.6769	92.76%	**100.00%**	44.1	0.6949	**45.3**	**0.7994**
+ Iterative RTL	**100.00%**	**100.00%**	**47.4**	**0.7337**	**100.00%**	**100.00%**	**47.9**	**0.7442**	44.9	0.7926
UMD-baseline	96.30%	97.66%	27.3	0.4477	93.20%	90.82%	30.9	0.4161	-	-
mBART50 1n	86.81%	91.32%	32.2	0.5011	13.19%	8.68%	31.5	0.4955	33.8	0.6767
+ Multilingual pre-training	82.19%	77.96%	34.1	0.4872	17.81%	22.04%	31.4	0.4598	49.8	0.8753
+ Domain adaptation	**100.00%**	99.83%	39.9	0.7070	98.29%	90.32%	45.1	0.7170	46.7	0.8302
+ RTL	**100.00%**	**100.00%**	39.9	0.7165	94.97%	99.33%	45.0	0.7341	48.0	**0.8457**
+ Iterative RTL	**100.00%**	**100.00%**	**45.4**	**0.7737**	**100.00%**	**99.66%**	**49.1**	**0.7845**	**48.1**	**0.8457**

Table 6: The overall translation quality and formality control accuracy of EN-PT models.

(UMD-baseline) (Lin et al., 2022) provided by the organizers.

5.3.1 EN-VI & EN-KO

The formality control task for EN-VI and EN-KO language pairs is supervised, and we adopt the same training methods on these two language pairs. Table 3 and Table 4 are the evaluation results of the models trained at different phases for these two language pairs. From the experimental results, the multi-stage pre-training method can improve the translation quality of the model on the FLORES-200 devtest sets, while domain adaptation and RTL methods are effective in improving formality control capability of the model. Besides, domain adaptation and RTL methods have relatively little impact on the general translation quality of the model on the FLORES-200 devtest sets. Finally, we submit the Iterative RTL model as primary system.

5.3.2 EN-RU & EN-PT

The formality control tasks for the EN-RU and EN-PT language pairs are zero-shot, and we only use one-stage pre-training on these two tasks. Table 5 and Table 6 are the evaluation results of the models trained in different phases for these two language pairs. The experimental results show that domain adaptation and RTL methods are still effective in improving the zero-shot formality control capability of multilingual model. Finally, we still submit the Iterative RTL model as primary system.

6 Conclusions

This paper presents HW-TSC's submission on the IWSLT 2023 formality control task, in which we participate in both constrained and unconstrained tasks for all four language pairs. For the formality control task, we use a multi-stage pre-training method to improve the general translation quality of the basic model. We also adopt domain adaptation and RTL methods to improve the model's formality control capability. Experimental results show that these methods we have adopted are extremely effective, but how to improve general translation quality more effectively and achieve formality control with less training resources is still worthy of further research.

References

Milind Agarwal, Sweta Agrawal, Antonios Anastasopoulos, Ondřej Bojar, Claudia Borg, Marine Carpuat, Roldano Cattoni, Mauro Cettolo, Mingda Chen, William Chen, Khalid Choukri, Alexandra Chronopoulou, Anna Currey, Thierry Declerck, Qianqian Dong, Yannick Estève, Kevin Duh, Marcello Federico, Souhir Gahbiche, Barry Haddow, Benjamin Hsu, Phu Mon Htut, Hirofumi Inaguma, Dávid Javorský, John Judge, Yasumasa Kano, Tom Ko, Rishu

Kumar, Pengwei Li, Xutail Ma, Prashant Mathur, Evgeny Matusov, Paul McNamee, John P. McCrae, Kenton Murray, Maria Nadejde, Satoshi Nakamura, Matteo Negri, Ha Nguyen, Jan Niehues, Xing Niu, Atul Ojha Kr., John E. Ortega, Proyag Pal, Juan Pino, Lonneke van der Plas, Peter Polák, Elijah Rippeth, Elizabeth Salesky, Jiatong Shi, Matthias Sperber, Sebastian Stüker, Katsuhito Sudoh, Yun Tang, Brian Thompson, Kevin Tran, Marco Turchi, Alex Waibel, Mingxuan Wang, Shinji Watanabe, and Rodolfo Zevallos. 2023. Findings of the IWSLT 2023 Evaluation Campaign. In *Proceedings of the 20th International Conference on Spoken Language Translation (IWSLT 2023)*. Association for Computational Linguistics.

Amittai Axelrod, Xiaodong He, and Jianfeng Gao. 2011. Domain adaptation via pseudo in-domain data selection. In *Proceedings of the 2011 conference on empirical methods in natural language processing*, pages 355–362.

Eleftheria Briakou, Sweta Agrawal, Joel Tetreault, and Marine Carpuat. 2021. Evaluating the evaluation metrics for style transfer: A case study in multilingual formality transfer. In *Proceedings of the 2021 Conference on Empirical Methods in Natural Language Processing*, pages 1321–1336.

Chenhui Chu, Raj Dabre, and Sadao Kurohashi. 2017. An empirical comparison of domain adaptation methods for neural machine translation. In *Proceedings of the 55th Annual Meeting of the Association for Computational Linguistics (Volume 2: Short Papers)*, pages 385–391.

Zi-Yi Dou, Xinyi Wang, Junjie Hu, and Graham Neubig. 2019. Domain differential adaptation for neural machine translation. *EMNLP-IJCNLP 2019*, page 59.

Chris Dyer, Victor Chahuneau, and Noah A Smith. 2013. A simple, fast, and effective reparameterization of ibm model 2. In *Proceedings of the 2013 Conference of the North American Chapter of the Association for Computational Linguistics: Human Language Technologies*, pages 644–648.

Weston Feely, Eva Hasler, and Adrià de Gispert. 2019. Controlling Japanese honorifics in English-to-Japanese neural machine translation. In *Proceedings of the 6th Workshop on Asian Translation*, pages 45–53, Hong Kong, China. Association for Computational Linguistics.

Naman Goyal, Cynthia Gao, Vishrav Chaudhary, Peng-Jen Chen, Guillaume Wenzek, Da Ju, Sanjana Krishnan, Marc'Aurelio Ranzato, Francisco Guzmán, and Angela Fan. 2022. The flores-101 evaluation benchmark for low-resource and multilingual machine translation. *Transactions of the Association for Computational Linguistics*, 10:522–538.

Melvin Johnson, Mike Schuster, Quoc V Le, Maxim Krikun, Yonghui Wu, Zhifeng Chen, Nikhil Thorat, Fernanda Viégas, Martin Wattenberg, Greg Corrado, et al. 2017. Google's multilingual neural machine translation system: Enabling zero-shot translation. *Transactions of the Association for Computational Linguistics*, 5:339–351.

Diederik P. Kingma and Jimmy Ba. 2014. Adam: A method for stochastic optimization. *CoRR*, abs/1412.6980.

Ann Lee, Michael Auli, and Marc'Aurelio Ranzato. 2021. Discriminative reranking for neural machine translation. In *Proceedings of the 59th Annual Meeting of the Association for Computational Linguistics and the 11th International Joint Conference on Natural Language Processing (Volume 1: Long Papers)*, pages 7250–7264.

Xi Victoria Lin, Todor Mihaylov, Mikel Artetxe, Tianlu Wang, Shuohui Chen, Daniel Simig, Myle Ott, Naman Goyal, Shruti Bhosale, Jingfei Du, Ramakanth Pasunuru, Sam Shleifer, Punit Singh Koura, Vishrav Chaudhary, Brian O'Horo, Jeff Wang, Luke Zettlemoyer, Zornitsa Kozareva, Mona Diab, Veselin Stoyanov, and Xian Li. 2022. Few-shot learning with multilingual generative language models. In *Proceedings of the 2022 Conference on Empirical Methods in Natural Language Processing*, pages 9019–9052, Abu Dhabi, United Arab Emirates. Association for Computational Linguistics.

Yinhan Liu, Jiatao Gu, Naman Goyal, Xian Li, Sergey Edunov, Marjan Ghazvininejad, Mike Lewis, and Luke Zettlemoyer. 2020. Multilingual denoising pre-training for neural machine translation. *Transactions of the Association for Computational Linguistics*, 8:726–742.

Adam Lopez. 2008. Statistical machine translation. *ACM Computing Surveys (CSUR)*, 40(3):1–49.

Marco Lui and Timothy Baldwin. 2011. Cross-domain feature selection for language identification. In *Proceedings of 5th International Joint Conference on Natural Language Processing*, pages 553–561, Chiang Mai, Thailand. Asian Federation of Natural Language Processing.

Marco Lui and Timothy Baldwin. 2012. langid.py: An off-the-shelf language identification tool. In *Proceedings of the ACL 2012 System Demonstrations*, pages 25–30, Jeju Island, Korea. Association for Computational Linguistics.

Xing Niu and Marine Carpuat. 2020. Controlling neural machine translation formality with synthetic supervision. In *Proceedings of the AAAI Conference on Artificial Intelligence*, pages 8568–8575.

Xing Niu, Marianna Martindale, and Marine Carpuat. 2017. A study of style in machine translation: Controlling the formality of machine translation output. In *Proceedings of the 2017 Conference on Empirical Methods in Natural Language Processing*, pages 2814–2819, Copenhagen, Denmark. Association for Computational Linguistics.

Xing Niu, Sudha Rao, and Marine Carpuat. 2018. Multi-task neural models for translating between styles within and across languages. In *Proceedings of the 27th International Conference on Computational Linguistics*, pages 1008–1021, Santa Fe, New Mexico, USA. Association for Computational Linguistics.

Maria Nădejde, Anna Currey, Benjamin Hsu, Xing Niu, Marcello Federico, and Georgiana Dinu. 2022. CoCoA-MT: A dataset and benchmark for Contrastive Controlled MT with application to formality. In *Findings of the Association for Computational Linguistics: NAACL 2022*, Seattle, USA. Association for Computational Linguistics.

Myle Ott, Sergey Edunov, Alexei Baevski, Angela Fan, Sam Gross, Nathan Ng, David Grangier, and Michael Auli. 2019. fairseq: A fast, extensible toolkit for sequence modeling. In *Proceedings of NAACL-HLT 2019: Demonstrations*.

Kishore Papineni, Salim Roukos, Todd Ward, and Wei-Jing Zhu. 2002. Bleu: a method for automatic evaluation of machine translation. In *Proceedings of the 40th annual meeting of the Association for Computational Linguistics*, pages 311–318.

Matt Post. 2018. A call for clarity in reporting BLEU scores. In *Proceedings of the Third Conference on Machine Translation: Research Papers*, pages 186–191, Belgium, Brussels. Association for Computational Linguistics.

Ricardo Rei, Ana C Farinha, José G.C. de Souza, Pedro G. Ramos, André F.T. Martins, Luisa Coheur, and Alon Lavie. 2022. Searching for COMETINHO: The little metric that could. In *Proceedings of the 23rd Annual Conference of the European Association for Machine Translation*, pages 61–70, Ghent, Belgium. European Association for Machine Translation.

Andrea Schioppa, David Vilar, Artem Sokolov, and Katja Filippova. 2021. Controlling machine translation for multiple attributes with additive interventions. In *Proceedings of the 2021 Conference on Empirical Methods in Natural Language Processing*, pages 6676–6696, Online and Punta Cana, Dominican Republic. Association for Computational Linguistics.

Rico Sennrich, Barry Haddow, and Alexandra Birch. 2016a. Controlling politeness in neural machine translation via side constraints. In *Proceedings of the 2016 Conference of the North American Chapter of the Association for Computational Linguistics: Human Language Technologies*, pages 35–40.

Rico Sennrich, Barry Haddow, and Alexandra Birch. 2016b. Improving neural machine translation models with monolingual data. In *Proceedings of the 54th Annual Meeting of the Association for Computational Linguistics (Volume 1: Long Papers)*, pages 86–96.

Weiwei Shi, Yihong Gong, Chris Ding, Zhiheng MaXiaoyu Tao, and Nanning Zheng. 2018. Transductive semi-supervised deep learning using min-max features. In *Proceedings of the European Conference on Computer Vision (ECCV)*, pages 299–315.

Christian Szegedy, Vincent Vanhoucke, Sergey Ioffe, Jon Shlens, and Zbigniew Wojna. 2016. Rethinking the inception architecture for computer vision. In *Proceedings of the IEEE conference on computer vision and pattern recognition*, pages 2818–2826.

Yuqing Tang, Chau Tran, Xian Li, Peng-Jen Chen, Naman Goyal, Vishrav Chaudhary, Jiatao Gu, and Angela Fan. 2021. Multilingual translation from denoising pre-training. In *Findings of the Association for Computational Linguistics: ACL-IJCNLP 2021*, pages 3450–3466.

Ashish Vaswani, Noam Shazeer, Niki Parmar, Jakob Uszkoreit, Llion Jones, Aidan N Gomez, Łukasz Kaiser, and Illia Polosukhin. 2017. Attention is all you need. *Advances in neural information processing systems*, 30.

Aditi Viswanathan, Varden Wang, and Antonina Kononova. 2020. Controlling formality and style of machine translation output using automl. In *Information Management and Big Data: 6th International Conference, SIMBig 2019, Lima, Peru, August 21–23, 2019, Proceedings 6*, pages 306–313. Springer.

Qiang Wang, Bei Li, Tong Xiao, Jingbo Zhu, Changliang Li, Derek F Wong, and Lidia S Chao. 2019. Learning deep transformer models for machine translation. In *Proceedings of the 57th Annual Meeting of the Association for Computational Linguistics*, pages 1810–1822.

Daimeng Wei, Zhiqiang Rao, Zhanglin Wu, Shaojun Li, Yuanchang Luo, Yuhao Xie, Xiaoyu Chen, Hengchao Shang, Zongyao Li, Zhengzhe Yu, et al. 2022. Hwtsc's submissions to the wmt 2022 general machine translation shared task. In *Proceedings of the Seventh Conference on Machine Translation, Online. Association for Computational Linguistics*.

Zhanglin Wu, Jinlong Yang, Zhiqiang Rao, Zhengzhe Yu, Daimeng Wei, Xiaoyu Chen, Zongyao Li, Hengchao Shang, Shaojun Li, Ming Zhu, et al. 2022. Hwtsc translation systems for the wmt22 biomedical translation task. In *Proceedings of the Seventh Conference on Machine Translation, Online. Association for Computational Linguistics*.

Jingjing Xu, Xu Sun, Zhiyuan Zhang, Guangxiang Zhao, and Junyang Lin. 2019. Understanding and improving layer normalization. *Advances in Neural Information Processing Systems*, 32.

Biao Zhang, Philip Williams, Ivan Titov, and Rico Sennrich. 2020. Improving massively multilingual neural machine translation and zero-shot translation. In *2020 Annual Conference of the Association for Computational Linguistics*, pages 1628–1639. Association for Computational Linguistics (ACL).

HW-TSC at IWSLT2023: Break the Quality Ceiling of Offline Track via Pre-Training and Domain Adaptation

Zongyao Li, Zhanglin Wu, Zhiqiang Rao, Xie YuHao, Guo JiaXin, Daimeng Wei, Hengchao Shang, Wang Minghan, Xiaoyu Chen Zhengzhe YU, Li ShaoJun, Lei LiZhi, Hao Yang
Huawei Translation Service Center, Beijing, China
{lizongyao,wuzhanglin2,raozhiqiang,xieyuhao2,guojiaxin1, weidaimeng,shanghengchao,wangminghan,chenxiaoyu35, yuzhengzhe,lishaojun18,leilizhi,yanghao30}@huawei.com

Abstract

This paper describes HW-TSC's submissions to the IWSLT 2023 Offline Speech Translation task, including speech translation of talks from English to German, English to Chinese and English to Japanese. We participated in all three tracks (Constrained training, Constrained with Large Language Models training, Unconstrained training), with using cascaded architectures models. We use data enhancement, pre-training models and other means to improve the quality of ASR, and use a variety of techniques including R-Drop, deep model, domain data selection, etc. to improve the quality of NMT. Compared with last year's best results, we have improved by 2.1 BLEU in the MuST-C English-German test set.

1 Introduction

The goal of the Offline Speech Translation Task is to examine automatic methods for translating audio speech in one language into text in the target language. In recent years, end-to-end system and cascade system are fundamental pipelines for speech translation tasks. Traditional cascade system is comprised of continuing parts, automatic speech recognition (ASR) is responsible for generating transcripts from audios and machine translation (MT) model aims at translating ASR outputs from source language into target language. ASR model like Conformer (Gulati et al., 2020) and S2T-Transformer (Synnaeve et al., 2019) are commonly used. MT models like Transformer (Vaswani et al., 2017) can be considered as a standard configuration. The End-to-end systems use a model to directly recognize speech into target text in another language.

The cascade system will cause some "missing information" due to the two encoding and decoding processes of ASR and MT. At the same time, the disadvantage of the end-to-end system is the lack of sufficient training data. However, with a fully trained cascade system, the accuracy of ASR and MT will reach a higher level. So from the results, the BLEU of the cascaded system will be higher than that of the end-to-end system. Currently in the industry, the mainstream speech translation system is still based on the cascade system. We use the cascade system for this task, mainly to further improve the performance of speech translation.

In this work, we carefully filter and preprocess the data, and adopt various enhancement techniques, such as pre-training model, data enhancement, domain adaptation, etc., to optimize the performance of ASR. We build machine translation systems with techniques like back translation (Edunov et al., 2018), domain adaptation and R-drop (Wu et al., 2021), which have been proved to be effective practices.

The main contribution of this paper can be summarized as follows:

1) According to the characteristics of three different tracks (constrained, constrained with large language models (LLM), and unconstrained), we use different strategies to optimize the results of ASR. After careful fine-tuning, the WER of the ASR system of the three tracks have achieved good performance.

2) Explored the multilingual machine translation model, and tried a variety of model enhancement strategies, and finally achieved good results on the MUST-C test set.

Section 2 focuses on our data processing strategies while section 3 describes the training techniques of ASR, including model architecture and training strategy, etc. Section 4 describes the training techniques of MT, and section 5 presents our experiment results.

Proceedings of the 20th International Conference on Spoken Language Translation (IWSLT 2023), pages 187–193
July 13-14, 2023 ©2023 Association for Computational Linguistics

Dataset	Duration(h)
LibriSpeech	960
MuST-C	590
CoVoST	1802
TEDLIUM3	453
Europarl	161
VoxPopuli	1270

Table 1: Data statistics of our ASR corpora.

2 Datasets and Preprocessing

2.1 ASR Data

There are six different datasets used in the training of our ASR models, such as MuST-C V2 (Cattoni et al., 2021), LibriSpeech (Panayotov et al., 2015), TED-LIUM 3 (Hernandez et al., 2018), CoVoST 2(Wang et al., 2020), VoxPopuli (Wang et al., 2021), Europarl-ST (Iranzo-Sánchez et al., 2020), as described in Table 1. We use the exactly same data processing strategy to train our ASR models following the configuration of (Wang et al., 2022). We extend one data augmentation method (Zhang et al., 2022): adjacent voices are concatenated to generate longer training speeches. Tsiamas et al. (2022) propose Supervised Hybrid Audio Segmentation (SHAS), a method that can effectively learn the optimal segmentation from any manually segmented speech corpus. For test set, we use SHAS to split long audios into shorter segments.

2.2 MT Data

We used all provided data, including text-parallel and speech-to-text-parallel, text-monolingual data, and use the exactly same data processing strategy to process our MT data following (Wei et al., 2021). Data sizes before and after cleaning are listed in Table 2.

3 ASR Model

3.1 Constrained training

In this track, we trained the constrained ASR model using the Conformer (Gulati et al., 2020) and U2 (Zhang et al., 2020b) model architectures. The first model is standard auto-regressive ASR models built upon the Transformer architecture. The last one is a unified model that can perform both streaming and non-streaming ASR, supported by the dynamic chunking training strategy. The model configurations are as follows:

1) **Conformer**: The encoder is composed of 2 layers of VGG and 16 layers of Conformer, and the decoder is composed of 6 layers of Transformer. The embedding size is 1024, and the hidden size of FFN is 4096, and the attention head is 16.

2) **U2**: Two convolution subsampling layers with kernel size 3*3 and stride 2 are used in the front of the encoder. We use 12 Conformer layers for the encoder and 6 Transformer layers for the decoder. The embedding size is 1024, and the hidden size of FFN is 4096, and the attention head is 16.

During the training of ASR models, we set the batch size to the maximum of 20,000 frames per-card. Inverse sqrt is used for lr scheduling with warm-up steps set to 10,000 and peak lr set as 5e-4. Adam is used as the optimizer. All ASR models are trained on 8 A100 GPUs for 100 epochs. Parameters for last 5 epochs are averaged. Audio features are normalized with utterance-level CMVN for Conformer, and with global CMVN for U2. All audio inputs are augmented with spectral augmentation (Park et al., 2019), and Connectionist Temporal Classification (CTC) is added to make models converge better.

3.2 Constrained with Large Language Models training

Large Language Models (LLM) is currently the mainstream method in the field of artificial intelligence. In ASR, the pre-training model has been proved to be an effective means to improve the quality, especially the models such as wav2vec (Schneider et al., 2019) and Hubert (Hsu et al., 2021) have been proposed in recent years. Li et al. (2020) combine the encoder of wav2vec2 (Baevski et al., 2020) and the decoder of mBART50 (Tang et al., 2020) to fine-tune an end2end model. We also adopt a similar strategy, but combine the encoder of wav2vec2 and the decoder of mBART50 to fine-tune an ASR model (w2v2-mBART). Due to the modality mismatch between pre-training and fine-tuning, in order to better train cross-attention, we freeze the self-attention of the encoder and decoder. We first use all the constrained data for fine-tuning, and only use the MUST-C data after 30 epochs of training.

3.3 Unconstrained training

Whisper (Radford et al., 2022) is an automatic speech recognition (ASR) system trained on 680,000 hours of multilingual and multitask supervised data collected from the web. It show that

language pairs	Raw Data	Filter Data	LaBSE Filter Data	Domain Selection
En2De	19.8M	14.5M	5.8M	0.4M
En2Zh	8.1M	5.5M	2.2M	0.4M
En2Ja	16.4M	14.1M	5.6M	0.4M

Table 2: Bilingual data sizes before and after filtering used in tasks.

the use of such a large and diverse dataset leads to improved robustness to accents, background noise and technical language. The Whisper architecture is a simple end-to-end approach, implemented as an encoder-decoder Transformer. Even though it enables transcription in multiple languages, we only use its speech recognition feature, transcribing audio files to English text. In this task, we use it as a pre-trained model, and use the MUST-C dataset for fine-tuning to improve its performance in specific domains. We trained for 2 epochs with a small learning rate of 10e-6.

4 Neural Machine Translation

4.1 Model architecture

Transformer is the state-of-the-art model in recent machine translation evaluations. There are two parts of research to improve this kind: the first part uses wide networks (eg: Transformer-Big), and the other part uses deeper language representations (eg: Deep Transformer (Wang et al., 2017, 2019a)). Under the constrained conditions, we combine these two improvements, adopt the Deep Transformer-Big model structure, and train a one-to-many multilingual NMT model (Johnson et al., 2017; Zhang et al., 2020a) from scratch using bilingual data of three language pairs (En2De, En2Zh, En2Ja) provided by the organizers. The main structure of Deep Transformer-Big is that it features pre-layer-normalization and 25-layer encoder, 6-layer decoder, 16-head self-attention, 1024-dimensional embedding and 4096-dimensional FFN embedding.

We trained the constrained model using all the provided data, and trained the unconstrained model with the WMT data. But after domain adaptation, the performance of the two is similar. Therefore, in this task, we only use the constrained MT model.

4.2 Multi-stage Pre-training

In order to get a better model effect, we optimize the model in several stages. First, we use the data of all three language pairs to train a one-to-many multilingual model, and add tags (<ja>, <zh>, <de>) at the beginning of the source sentence respectively. Second, use LaBSE (Feng et al., 2020) to filter the bilingual data, and use the filtered data for incremental training. In Table 2, there are the number of filtered data for each languages. Then, for the three languages, the backward models are trained separately, and the monolingual datas are used for backward translation (BT). Finally, we combine backward translation and forward translation (FT) for iterative joint training (Zhang et al., 2018). After the above several stages, a base model with better performance is obtained, which can be used for further optimization.

4.3 R-Drop

Dropout-like method (Srivastava et al., 2014; Gao et al., 2022) is a powerful and widely used technique for regularizing deep neural networks. Though it can help improve training effectiveness, the randomness introduced by dropouts may lead to inconsistencies between training and inference. R-Drop (Wu et al., 2021) forces the output distributions of different sub models generated by dropout be consistent with each other. Therefore, we use R-Drop training strategy to augment the base model for each track and reduce inconsistencies between training and inference.

4.4 Domain Adaptation

Since the quality of the translation model is easily affected by the domain, we try to select domain-related data to incrementally train the model. We adopted the domain adaptation strategy by (Wang et al., 2019b). The strategy uses a small amount of in-domain data to tune the base model, and then leverages the differences between the tuned model and the base to score bilingual data. The score is calculated based on formula 1.

$$score = \frac{logP(y|x;\theta_{in}) - logP(y|x;\theta_{base})}{|y|} \quad (1)$$

Where θ_{base} denotes the base model; θ_{in} denotes the model after fine-tuning on a small amount of in-domain data, and |y| denotes the length of the sentence. Higher score means higher quality.

System	En2De	En2Ja	En2Zh
Constrained	37.28	20.26	28.91
Constrained with LLM	37.96	20.29	28.91
Unconstrained	38.71	20.34	28.93

Table 3: The BLEU of speech translation on tst-COM.

System	tst-COM	tst2018	tst2019	tst2020	avg
Conformer	5.3	9.3	6.7	8.9	7.6
U2	6.1	9.8	6.6	8.7	7.8
w2v2-mBART	4.9	9.3	6.9	8.9	7.5
Whisper	4.5	11.0	5.4	6.6	6.8
Whisper fine-tuning	4.3	8.5	6.3	7.9	6.8

Table 4: The experimental results of ASR. We present WER performance of tst-COM, tst2018, tst2019 and tst2020.

System	En2De	En2Ja	En2Zh
One2Many	36.22	15.43	29.05
+ LaBSE bitext	37.58	15.48	29.48
+ Domain adaptation	41.55	17.08	29.27
+ Iter FTBT	43.03	17.86	29.82
+ Dev fine-tuning	43.66	20.88	30.48

Table 5: The BLEU of MT using tst-COM golden transcription.

System	En2De	En2Ja	En2Zh
One2Many	31.54	14.08	26.69
+ LaBSE bitext	32.65	13.88	27.14
+ Domain adaptation	35.96	15.4	27.15
+ Iter FTBT	36.38	15.81	27.98
+ Dev fine-tuning	37.83	18.6	28.86
+ Robustness	38.71	20.34	28.93

Table 6: The BLEU of MT using tst-COM transcription by the Whisper fine-tuning model.

In this task, we use TED and MUST-C data as in-domain data. We score all the training bilingual data through Equation 1, and filter out 80% - 90% of the data according to the score distribution. We use the remaining 0.4M in-domain data to continue training on the previous model.

4.5 Robustness to ASR Noise

We use two methods to improve the robustness of the system to ASR output noise.

Synthetic Noise Generation. We refer to the method proposed in Guo et al. (2022) to synthesize part of the noise data to enhance the robustness of the model.

ASR Transcript Data. Because some triplet data are provided in this task, including $audio$, $source$ and $target$. We use the trained ASR to transcribe the audio file to get $source'$, and finally get the MT training data like $(source', target)$. The $source'$ transcribed by ASR may have some errors, but when used in MT, it will increase the robustness of the MT encoder.

When using the data generated above, we refer to the tagged BT method (Caswell et al., 2019), and add a special token at the beginning of the source sentence.

5 Experiments and Results

We use the open-source fairseq (Ott et al., 2019) for training, word error rate (WER) to evaluate the ASR models and report case-sensitive SacreBLEU (Post, 2018) scores for machine translation. We evaluated our system on the test sets of MuST-C tst-COMMON (tst-COM).

Table 3 is our results on three languages for three tracks (Constrained, Constrained with LLM, Unconstrained). After a series of optimizations, although the ASR results of the three systems are somewhat different, the BLEU of all systems are very close. Since there is no testset for iwslt2022, we only compared with last year's teams on tst-COM. Compared with last year's best results (Zhang et al., 2022), we have improved by 2.1 BLEU in the MuST-C En2De test set; in En2Zh and En2Ja, we have achieved close to last year's best results.

We analyze the main reasons for the similar results of the three systems: 1. The three systems use the same MT, and our MT system has the ability to correct wrong input after the robustness is enhanced. 2. Using the same data to finetuning the three ASR systems, the WER are relatively close.

5.1 Automatic Speech Recognition

We compare the results of different model architectures, the overall experimental results about ASR is described in Table 4. We evaluated our system on the test sets of tst-COM, IWSLT tst2018/tst2019/tst2020 respectively. For long audio in the test set, we use SHAS for segmentation. We calculate the WER after the reference and hypothesis are lowercased and the punctuation is removed.

In Table 4, all ASR systems achieve good performance, and the results are relatively close. Conformer and U2 are trained using constrained data. w2v2-mBART is obtained through fine-tuning using pre-trained models, which are constrained. Whisper is the result of transcribing long audio without segmentation using the native whisper medium model. Whisper fine-tuning is obtained after fine-tuning on MuST-C dataset, with using the Whisper medium model. The WER of Conformer and U2 is relatively close. In submitting the results of constrained track, we use Conformer as the final ASR system. The experimental results show that pre-trained models exhibit their advantages, w2v2-mBART can achieve better results than just training with constrained data. Whisper itself has a very good performance in the general domain, and after fine-tuning, it has even better results in the specific domain. However, it is very difficult to perform finetuning on whisper and improve the performance of all domains. WER performance on tst2019 and tst2020 has deteriorated.

5.2 Neural Machine Translation

We evaluate the performance of the MT model in detail on the MUST-C test set. Table 5 shows the performance results of each optimization strategy using golden as the source; Table 6 uses the transcription generated by Whisper fine-tuning model as the source. The results show that there is a gap in BLEU between golden and transcription of ASR, which is mainly due to errors (punctuation, capitalization, vocabulary, etc.) in transcription of ASR. On the En2De test set, this gap is particularly wide.

One2Many is a multilingual model trained using the R-drop strategy, and has achieved relatively good performance on the test set. LaBSE can bring a little improvement to the model, and domain adaptation can bring a huge improvement to the model, which proves the effectiveness of our strategy. Iterative joint training with FT and BT (Iter FTBT) is also an effective mean to improve quality. After dev fine-tuning, the results are already very competitive. With improving the robustness of the system to ASR output, our BLEU in En2De, En2Zh, and En2Ja are 38.71, 20.34, and 28.93, respectively.

6 Conclusion

This paper presents our offline speech translation systems in the IWSLT 2023 evaluation. We explored different strategies in the pipeline of building the cascade system. In the data preprocessing, we adopt efficient cleansing approaches to build the training set collected from different data sources. We tried various ASR training strategies and achieved good performance. For the MT system, we have used various methods such as multilingual machine translation, R-drop, domain adaptation, and enhanced robustness. Finally, compared with last year's best results, we have improved by 2.1 BLEU in the MuST-C English-German test set.

References

Alexei Baevski, Yuhao Zhou, Abdelrahman Mohamed, and Michael Auli. 2020. wav2vec 2.0: A framework for self-supervised learning of speech representations. *Advances in neural information processing systems*, 33:12449–12460.

Isaac Caswell, Ciprian Chelba, and David Grangier. 2019. Tagged back-translation. *arXiv preprint arXiv:1906.06442*.

Roldano Cattoni, Mattia Antonino Di Gangi, Luisa Bentivogli, Matteo Negri, and Marco Turchi. 2021. Must-c: A multilingual corpus for end-to-end speech translation. *Computer Speech & Language*, 66:101155.

Sergey Edunov, Myle Ott, Michael Auli, and David Grangier. 2018. Understanding back-translation at scale. *arXiv preprint arXiv:1808.09381*.

Fangxiaoyu Feng, Yinfei Yang, Daniel Cer, Naveen Arivazhagan, and Wei Wang. 2020. Language-agnostic bert sentence embedding. *arXiv preprint arXiv:2007.01852*.

Pengzhi Gao, Zhongjun He, Hua Wu, and Haifeng Wang. 2022. Bi-simcut: A simple strategy for boosting neural machine translation. *arXiv preprint arXiv:2206.02368*.

Anmol Gulati, James Qin, Chung-Cheng Chiu, Niki Parmar, Yu Zhang, Jiahui Yu, Wei Han, Shibo Wang, Zhengdong Zhang, Yonghui Wu, et al.

2020. Conformer: Convolution-augmented transformer for speech recognition. *arXiv preprint arXiv:2005.08100*.

Bao Guo, Mengge Liu, Wen Zhang, Hexuan Chen, Chang Mu, Xiang Li, Jianwei Cui, Bin Wang, and Yuhang Guo. 2022. The xiaomi text-to-text simultaneous speech translation system for iwslt 2022. In *Proceedings of the 19th International Conference on Spoken Language Translation (IWSLT 2022)*, pages 216–224.

François Hernandez, Vincent Nguyen, Sahar Ghannay, Natalia Tomashenko, and Yannick Esteve. 2018. Tedlium 3: Twice as much data and corpus repartition for experiments on speaker adaptation. In *Speech and Computer: 20th International Conference, SPECOM 2018, Leipzig, Germany, September 18–22, 2018, Proceedings 20*, pages 198–208. Springer.

Wei-Ning Hsu, Benjamin Bolte, Yao-Hung Hubert Tsai, Kushal Lakhotia, Ruslan Salakhutdinov, and Abdelrahman Mohamed. 2021. Hubert: Self-supervised speech representation learning by masked prediction of hidden units. *IEEE/ACM Transactions on Audio, Speech, and Language Processing*, 29:3451–3460.

Javier Iranzo-Sánchez, Joan Albert Silvestre-Cerda, Javier Jorge, Nahuel Roselló, Adria Giménez, Albert Sanchis, Jorge Civera, and Alfons Juan. 2020. Europarl-st: A multilingual corpus for speech translation of parliamentary debates. In *ICASSP 2020-2020 IEEE International Conference on Acoustics, Speech and Signal Processing (ICASSP)*, pages 8229–8233. IEEE.

Melvin Johnson, Mike Schuster, Quoc V Le, Maxim Krikun, Yonghui Wu, Zhifeng Chen, Nikhil Thorat, Fernanda Viégas, Martin Wattenberg, Greg Corrado, et al. 2017. Google's multilingual neural machine translation system: Enabling zero-shot translation. *Transactions of the Association for Computational Linguistics*, 5:339–351.

Xian Li, Changhan Wang, Yun Tang, Chau Tran, Yuqing Tang, Juan Pino, Alexei Baevski, Alexis Conneau, and Michael Auli. 2020. Multilingual speech translation with efficient finetuning of pretrained models. *arXiv preprint arXiv:2010.12829*.

Myle Ott, Sergey Edunov, Alexei Baevski, Angela Fan, Sam Gross, Nathan Ng, David Grangier, and Michael Auli. 2019. fairseq: A fast, extensible toolkit for sequence modeling. *arXiv preprint arXiv:1904.01038*.

Vassil Panayotov, Guoguo Chen, Daniel Povey, and Sanjeev Khudanpur. 2015. Librispeech: an asr corpus based on public domain audio books. In *2015 IEEE international conference on acoustics, speech and signal processing (ICASSP)*, pages 5206–5210. IEEE.

Daniel S Park, William Chan, Yu Zhang, Chung-Cheng Chiu, Barret Zoph, Ekin D Cubuk, and Quoc V Le. 2019. Specaugment: A simple data augmentation method for automatic speech recognition. *arXiv preprint arXiv:1904.08779*.

Matt Post. 2018. A call for clarity in reporting bleu scores. *arXiv preprint arXiv:1804.08771*.

Alec Radford, Jong Wook Kim, Tao Xu, Greg Brockman, Christine McLeavey, and Ilya Sutskever. 2022. Robust speech recognition via large-scale weak supervision. *arXiv preprint arXiv:2212.04356*.

Steffen Schneider, Alexei Baevski, Ronan Collobert, and Michael Auli. 2019. wav2vec: Unsupervised pre-training for speech recognition. *arXiv preprint arXiv:1904.05862*.

Nitish Srivastava, Geoffrey Hinton, Alex Krizhevsky, Ilya Sutskever, and Ruslan Salakhutdinov. 2014. Dropout: a simple way to prevent neural networks from overfitting. *The journal of machine learning research*, 15(1):1929–1958.

Gabriel Synnaeve, Qiantong Xu, Jacob Kahn, Tatiana Likhomanenko, Edouard Grave, Vineel Pratap, Anuroop Sriram, Vitaliy Liptchinsky, and Ronan Collobert. 2019. End-to-end asr: from supervised to semi-supervised learning with modern architectures. *arXiv preprint arXiv:1911.08460*.

Yuqing Tang, Chau Tran, Xian Li, Peng-Jen Chen, Naman Goyal, Vishrav Chaudhary, Jiatao Gu, and Angela Fan. 2020. Multilingual translation with extensible multilingual pretraining and finetuning. *arXiv preprint arXiv:2008.00401*.

Ioannis Tsiamas, Gerard I Gállego, José AR Fonollosa, and Marta R Costa-jussà. 2022. Shas: Approaching optimal segmentation for end-to-end speech translation. *arXiv preprint arXiv:2202.04774*.

Ashish Vaswani, Noam Shazeer, Niki Parmar, Jakob Uszkoreit, Llion Jones, Aidan N Gomez, Łukasz Kaiser, and Illia Polosukhin. 2017. Attention is all you need. *Advances in neural information processing systems*, 30.

Changhan Wang, Morgane Riviere, Ann Lee, Anne Wu, Chaitanya Talnikar, Daniel Haziza, Mary Williamson, Juan Pino, and Emmanuel Dupoux. 2021. Voxpopuli: A large-scale multilingual speech corpus for representation learning, semi-supervised learning and interpretation. *arXiv preprint arXiv:2101.00390*.

Changhan Wang, Anne Wu, and Juan Pino. 2020. Covost 2 and massively multilingual speech-to-text translation. *arXiv preprint arXiv:2007.10310*.

Minghan Wang, Jiaxin Guo, Yinglu Li, Xiaosong Qiao, Yuxia Wang, Zongyao Li, Chang Su, Yimeng Chen, Min Zhang, Shimin Tao, et al. 2022. The hw-tsc's simultaneous speech translation system for iwslt 2022 evaluation. In *Proceedings of the 19th International Conference on Spoken Language Translation (IWSLT 2022)*, pages 247–254.

Mingxuan Wang, Zhengdong Lu, Jie Zhou, and Qun Liu. 2017. Deep neural machine translation with linear associative unit. *arXiv preprint arXiv:1705.00861*.

Qiang Wang, Bei Li, Tong Xiao, Jingbo Zhu, Changliang Li, Derek F Wong, and Lidia S Chao. 2019a. Learning deep transformer models for machine translation. *arXiv preprint arXiv:1906.01787*.

Wei Wang, Isaac Caswell, and Ciprian Chelba. 2019b. Dynamically composing domain-data selection with clean-data selection by" co-curricular learning" for neural machine translation. *arXiv preprint arXiv:1906.01130*.

Daimeng Wei, Zongyao Li, Zhanglin Wu, Zhengzhe Yu, Xiaoyu Chen, Hengchao Shang, Jiaxin Guo, Minghan Wang, Lizhi Lei, Min Zhang, Hao Yang, and Ying Qin. 2021. HW-TSC's participation in the WMT 2021 news translation shared task. In *Proceedings of the Sixth Conference on Machine Translation*, pages 225–231, Online. Association for Computational Linguistics.

Lijun Wu, Juntao Li, Yue Wang, Qi Meng, Tao Qin, Wei Chen, Min Zhang, Tie-Yan Liu, et al. 2021. R-drop: Regularized dropout for neural networks. *Advances in Neural Information Processing Systems*, 34:10890–10905.

Biao Zhang, Philip Williams, Ivan Titov, and Rico Sennrich. 2020a. Improving massively multilingual neural machine translation and zero-shot translation. *arXiv preprint arXiv:2004.11867*.

Binbin Zhang, Di Wu, Zhuoyuan Yao, Xiong Wang, Fan Yu, Chao Yang, Liyong Guo, Yaguang Hu, Lei Xie, and Xin Lei. 2020b. Unified streaming and non-streaming two-pass end-to-end model for speech recognition. *arXiv preprint arXiv:2012.05481*.

Weitai Zhang, Zhongyi Ye, Haitao Tang, Xiaoxi Li, Xinyuan Zhou, Jing Yang, Jianwei Cui, Pan Deng, Mohan Shi, Yifan Song, et al. 2022. The ustc-nelslip offline speech translation systems for iwslt 2022. In *Proceedings of the 19th International Conference on Spoken Language Translation (IWSLT 2022)*, pages 198–207.

Zhirui Zhang, Shujie Liu, Mu Li, Ming Zhou, and Enhong Chen. 2018. Joint training for neural machine translation models with monolingual data. In *Proceedings of the AAAI Conference on Artificial Intelligence*, volume 32.

The USTC's Offline Speech Translation Systems for IWSLT 2023

Xinyuan Zhou[2], Jianwei Cui[1], Zhongyi Ye[2], Yichi Wang[1], Luzhen Xu[1], Hanyi Zhang[2], Weitai Zhang[1,2], Lirong Dai[1]

[1]University of Science and Technology of China, Hefei, China

[2]iFlytek Research, Hefei, China

{jwcui,wangyichi,lzxu,zwt2021}@mail.ustc.edu.cn

lrdai@ustc.edu.cn

{xyzhou15,zyye7,hyzhang56}@iflytek.com

Abstract

This paper describes the submissions of the research group USTC-NELSLIP to the 2023 IWSLT Offline Speech Translation competition, which involves translating spoken English into written Chinese. We utilize both cascaded models and end-to-end models for this task. To improve the performance of the cascaded models, we introduce Whisper to reduce errors in the intermediate source language text, achieving a significant improvement in ASR recognition performance. For end-to-end models, we propose Stacked Acoustic-and-Textual Encoding extension (SATE-ex), which feeds the output of the acoustic decoder into the textual decoder for information fusion and to prevent error propagation. Additionally, we improve the performance of the end-to-end system in translating speech by combining the SATE-ex model with the encoder-decoder model through ensembling.

1 Introduction

This paper describes the submission for the IWSLT 2023 Offline Speech Translation task (Agarwal et al., 2023) by National Engineering Laboratory for Speech and Language Information Processing (NELSLIP) at the University of Science and Technology of China.

Speech translation (ST) solutions include cascaded and end-to-end approaches. The cascaded approach combines Automatic Speech Recognition (ASR) and Machine Translation (MT) systems. The ASR system recognizes the source speech as intermediate text in the source language, and the MT system translates the intermediate text into text in the target language. While the end-to-end approach directly translates the source speech into text in target language, without using source language text as an intermediate representation. Compared with cascaded approaches, the end-to-end paradigm can overcome higher architectural complexity and error propagation (Duong et al., 2016). The Stacked Acoustic-and-Textual Encoding (SATE) (Xu et al., 2021) method combines the acoustic and textual encoders using an adapter module to approach the performance levels of cascaded solutions. Furthermore, ST can be improved using large-scale and cross-modal pretraining methods (Radford et al., 2022; Zhang et al., 2022b) such as Whisper (Radford et al., 2022), which leverages large-scale weak supervision, and SpeechUT (Zhang et al., 2022b), which optimizes the alignment of speech and text modalities by hidden units.

In this study, we employ a cascaded approach wherein the ASR system is built using the pre-trained Whisper (Radford et al., 2022) to ensure the recognition performance of speech to source language text. Furthermore, the MT systems in the cascaded setup are created using diverse techniques like back translation (Sennrich et al., 2016a), self-training (Kim and Rush, 2016; Liu et al., 2019), domain adaptation and model ensemble.

In end-to-end condition, we implement two types of architectures, including encoder-decoder (Le et al., 2021) and Stacked Acoustic-and-Textual Encoding extension (SATE-ex). For the encoder-decoder, we use the corresponding components of ASR models to initialize the encoder, and the corresponding components of MT models to initialize the decoder. For SATE-ex, we utilize the textual decoder to receive the output features of the acoustic decoder to assist in generating the target language text, achieving information complementarity of different ASR decoding hidden states, and preventing intermediate error propagation. Additionally, we employ adaptation training, along with the adaptation module and multi-teacher knowledge distillation of Stacked Acoustic-and-Textual Encoding (SATE) (Xu et al., 2021) to bridge the gap between pre-training and fine-tuning. Our approach included the utilization of augmentation strategies commonly used in cascaded systems, like speech synthesis (Casanova et al., 2022) and gen-

Proceedings of the 20th International Conference on Spoken Language Translation (IWSLT 2023), pages 194–201
July 13-14, 2023 ©2023 Association for Computational Linguistics

Corpus	Duration (h)	Sample Scale
Librispeech	960	1
Europarl	161	1
MuST-C (v1)	399	3
MuST-C (v2)	449	3
TED-LIUM3	452	3
CoVoST2	1985	1
VoxPopuli	1270	1

Table 1: The used speech recognition datasets.

Data	Duration (h)
Raw data	8276
+ concat	16000
+ oversampling	32000
+ TTS	56000

Table 2: Augmented training data for ASR.

erating as much semi-supervised data as possible to enhance the model's performance. Furthermore, we try to achieve further performance optimization with ensemble of cascaded and end-to-end models.

2 Data Preprocessing

2.1 Speech Recognition

The speech recognition datasets utilized in our experiments are listed in Table 1, including Librispeech, MuST-C (v1, v2), TED Lium3, Europarl, VoxPopuli, and CoVoST. We first extracted 40-dimensional log-mel filter bank features computed with a 25ms window size and a 10ms window shift. And then, a baseline ASR model, which is used to filter training samples with WER > 40%, is trained. Moreover, to generate sufficient speech recognition corpora, we applied speed perturbation and over-sampling techniques on the TED/MuST-C corpus (Liu et al., 2021). As a result, we generated nearly 8k hours of speech data.

To improve our training data, we applied two more data augmentation techniques. Firstly, we combined adjacent voices to produce longer training utterances. Secondly, we trained a model using Glow-TTS (Casanova et al., 2021) on MuST-C datasets and generated 24,000 hours of audio features by using sentences from EN→DE text translation corpora. The resulting training data for ASR is summarized in Table 2.

	Parallel	Monolingual
EN-ZH	50M	50M

Table 3: Training data for text MT.

2.2 Text Translation

We participate in translating English to Chinese. Both the bilingual data as well as the monolingual data are used for training. To ensure optimal training data quality, we apply several filters including language identification. We remove sentences longer than 250 tokens and those with a source/target length ratio exceeding 3. Additionally, we train a baseline machine translation model to filter out sentences with poor translation quality.

To tokenize the text, we utilize LTP4.0[1] (Wanxiang et al., 2020) for Chinese and Moses for English. The subwords are generated via Byte Pair Encoding (BPE) (Sennrich et al., 2016b) with 30,000 merge operations for each language direction. Table 3 summarizes the detailed statistics on the parallel and monolingual data used for training our systems.

EN→ZH For EN→ZH task, we utilize nearly 50 million sentence pairs collected from CCMT Corpus, News Commentary, ParaCrawl, Wiki Titles, UN Parallel Corpus, WikiMatrix, Wikititles, MuST-C, and CoVoST2, to train our MT models. In addition, we randomly extract 50 million monolingual Chinese sentences from News crawl and Common Crawl for back-translation purposes to augment our training data.

2.3 Speech Translation

Table 4 outlines the speech translation datasets used in our experiments. MuST-C and CoVoST2 are available for speech translation.

To augment our data, we implemented two additional methods. Firstly, we utilized a text translation model to generate the corresponding target language text from the transcriptions of the speech recognition datasets. The generated text was then added to our speech translation dataset along with its corresponding speech, referred to as KD Corpus in Table 4. This process is similar to sentence knowledge distillation. Secondly, we applied the trained Glow-TTS model to produce audio features from randomly selected sentence pairs in EN→ZH text translation corpora. The resulting filter bank features and their corresponding target language

[1] https://github.com/HIT-SCIR/ltp

	Corpus	Duration (h)	Sample Scale
EN-ZH	MuST-C	593	2
	CovoST2	1092	2
	KD	16000	2
	TTS	27000	1

Table 4: Speech Translation Corpora.

text are utilized to enhance our speech translation dataset, referred to as TTS Corpus in Table 4.

3 Cascaded Speech Translation

3.1 Automatic Speech Recognition

We implement ASR model in cascaded condition via Supervised Hybrid Audio Segmentation (SHAS) and Whisper.

Supervised Hybrid Audio Segmentation. Supervised Hybrid Audio Segmentation (SHAS) (Tsiamas et al., 2022) is used to split long audio into short segments with quality comparable to manual segmentation. Hence, we use SHAS as a Voice Activity Detection (VAD) in the ASR system, as well as a speech segmentation tool in the Speech Translation system. This way, the output of the ASR system can be directly fed into the text translation component.

Whisper. We incorporated the pre-trained Whisper (Radford et al., 2022) as the ASR model of the cascaded system to reduce errors in the intermediate source language text.

Whisper scales weakly supervised speech-to-text tasks to 680,000 hours of labeled audio data and expands the pre-training scope from English-only speech recognition to multilingual and multitask. In comparison with the previous unsupervised pre-training approach (Baevski et al., 2020), Whisper not only improves the quality of the audio encoder, but also trains a pre-trained decoder with high equivalency, enhancing usefulness and robustness. Results demonstrate that the pre-trained Whisper model can be well transferred to different or even zero-shot datasets without any dataset-specific fine-tuning.

We used the large version of the pre-trained whisper model, which contains 32 layers and a total of 1550M parameters.

3.2 Neural Machine Translation

We adopted the same strategy as last year's (Zhang et al., 2022a) and built machine translation models based on the Transformer (Vaswani et al., 2017) implemented in the Fairseq (Ott et al., 2019) toolkit. Each single model was executed on 16 NVIDIA V100 GPUs. Our experiments utilized several crucial technologies including Back Translation, Sentence-level Knowledge Distillation, Domain Adaptation, Robust MT Training, and Ensembling.

Back Translation. The utilization of Back-Translation (Sennrich et al., 2016a) is a proficient technique for enhancing translation accuracy. This method generates synthetic sentence pairs by translating target-side monolingual data. It has gained significant popularity in both academic research and commercial applications. We train NMT models with bilingual data, and translate Chinese sentences to English.

Knowledge Distillation. Sentence-level Knowledge Distillation (Kim and Rush, 2016), also known as Self-training, is an effective method for enhancing performance. We expand our training dataset by leveraging a trained NMT model to translate English sentences into Chinese. This approach has proven to be highly beneficial in improving model accuracy.

Domain Adapatation. Due to the critical importance of high-quality, domain-specific translation (Saunders, 2022), we fine-tune the NMT model by using a mix of in-domain data (such as MuST-C, TED-LIUM3, etc.) and out-of-domain data. Additionally, the labelled English sentences from the speech recognition training data is also utilized as augmented in-domain self-training data by translating them.

We adopt a Denoise-based approach (Wang et al., 2018) to assess and select data for domain-specific MT and use it to denoise NMT training. The technique of denoising addresses data quality issues and reduces the adverse effects of noise on MT training, particularly NMT training.

Robust MT Training. To enhance the robustness of the MT model to ASR errors in cascaded ST, the ASR output adaptive training approach (Zhang et al., 2022a) is introduced. The English transcripts of all speech translation datasets are inputted into a trained ASR model to generate text in source side, which is then paired with the transcription text in target side. We improve the robustness of the MT model through three methods: 1) fine-tuning the MT model with synthetic data; 2) incorporating KL loss during fine-tuning to prevent over-fitting; and 3) distilling the model using clean source text and

ASR output.

Ensemble. For each target language, we trained 4 variants based on the large Transformer configuration, and the final model is an ensemble of these 4 models.

- E15D6-v1: 15 layers for the encoder and 6 layers for the docoder. The embedding size is 1024. FFN size is 8192 and attention head is 16. All available corpora including bilingual, BT and FT are used.
- E15D6-v2: 15 layers for the encoder, 10% training data are randomly dropped.
- E18D6: 18 layers for the encoder and 10-30% training data with low machine translation scores are dropped.
- Macaron: A version with macaron architecture (Lu et al., 2019) based on data of E18D6. 36 layers for the encoder and FFN size is 2048.

3.3 End-to-End Speech Translation

In the end-to-end condition, we ensemble the encoder-decoder and the Stacked Acoustic-and-Textual Encoding extension (SATE-ex) models described in Section 3.4.

Encoder-Decoder. The encoder-decoder-based end-to-end ST model processes the speech in the source language by its encoder and generates text in the target language by its decoder. The encoder and decoder are initialized using the corresponding parts of the cascade ASR and MT models. As regards model architecture, we investigate 4 variants in end-to-end ST.

- VGG-C: The encoder of VGG-C is initialized by the ASR VGG-Conformer architecture, which consists of 2 layers of VGG and 12 layers of Conformer. And the ASR VGG-Conformer is trained using the data in Section 2.1. The decoder of VGG-C is 6 layers of Transformer with embedding size of 1024, attention head of 16 and FFN size of 8192.
- VGG-C-init: The encoder is VGG-Conformer, initialized by ASR VGG-Conformer architecture. The decoder is 6 layers of Transformer, initialized by NMT E15D6-v2 variant.
- VGG-T: The encoder of VGG-T is initialized by the ASR VGG-Transformer architecture, which consists of 2 layers of VGG and 16 layers of Transformer. The decoder of VGG-T is 6 layers of Transformer with embedding size of 1024, attention head of 16 and FFN size of 8192.
- VGG-T-init: The VGG-Transformer encoder is initialized by the ASR VGG-Transformer architecture. The decoder is 6 layers of Transformer, initialized by NMT E15D6-v2 variant.

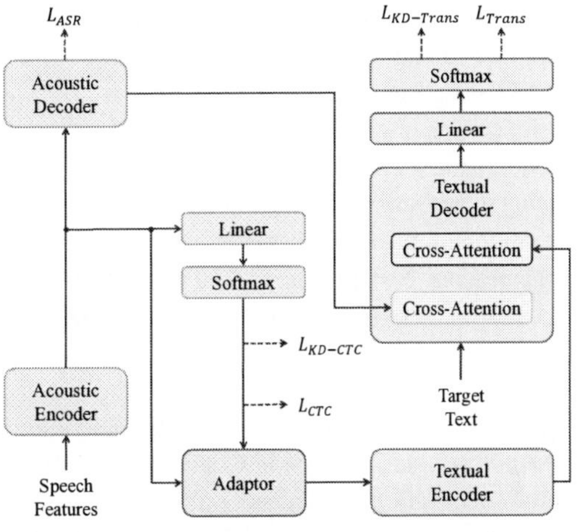

Figure 1: The architecture of Stacked Acoustic-and-Textual Encoding extension (SATE-ex).

3.4 Stacked Acoustic-and-Textual Encoding Extension

To further improve the performance of end-to-end ST, we propose Stacked Acoustic-and-Textual Encoding extension (SATE-ex) based on SATE (Xu et al., 2021).

SATE. The MT encoder captures the long-distance dependency structure, while ASR encoder focuses on local dependencies in the input sequence. Thus, the encoder-decoder model initialized with the ASR encoder and the MT decoder may have inconsistent on intermediate representations.

SATE stacks two encoders, an acoustic encoder and a textual encoder. The acoustic encoder processes the acoustic input, while the textual encoder generates global attention representations for translation. Moreover, an adapter is designed after the acoustic encoder, which maps the acoustic representation to the latent space of the textual encoder while retaining acoustic information. By doing so, SATE can maintain consistency in representation across different pre-trained components. Besides, the multi-teacher knowledge distillation has been developed to preserve pre-training knowledge during fine-tuning (Hinton et al., 2015).

SATE-ex. Figure 1 shows the SATE-ex architecture, comprising the acoustic encoder, acoustic decoder, textual encoder, and textual decoder components. Theses components are initialized with their corresponding components in cascade ASR and MT models. Notably, the textual decoder in SATE-ex has a Cross-Attention module (highlighted in yellow) that processes the acoustic decoder's output. By doing so, this approach fuses the last layer decoding hidden states of the ASR decoder into the textual decoder, alongside Connectionist Temporal Classification (CTC) decoding hidden states of ASR that are injected through adaptor and textual encoder. Similar to (Zhang et al., 2020), this idea facilitates to fuse and complement different decoding strategies, which can improve inner recognition accuracy, reduce the propagation of intermediate representation errors, and thereby enhance translation performance.

The loss function of SATE-ex, similar to SATE (Xu et al., 2021), computes CTC loss L_{CTC}, ASR loss L_{ASR}, and translation loss L_{Trans}. Additionally, the losses L_{KD-CTC} and $L_{KD-Trans}$ of multi-teacher knowledge distillation are used to preserve pre-trained knowledge during fine-tuning.

Adaptation Training. To further eliminate the intermediate representation mismatch in pre-trained ASR and MT, before end-to-end training, we adopt adaptation training to fine-tune the MT part of SATE-ex (including the textual encoder and textual decoder). Specifically, we first generate greedy CTC decoding without removing duplicates and blanks through the acoustic encoder. Then, we pair these CTC decoding with text in target language to fine-tune the textual encoder and textual decoder. Please note that the textual decoder here does not contain the Cross-Attention module (highlighted in yellow) in Figure 1.

4 Experiments

Our experimental results are presented in Table 5 and Table 6. All experiments are performed using the Fairseq (Ott et al., 2019) toolkit. We report case-sensitive SacreBLEU scores (Post, 2018) for speech translation. The performance of the systems is evaluated on MuST-C-v2 tst-COMMON (tst-COM) and Development set (Dev). Additionally, we set two values for the parameters of SHAS $(min, max, threshold)$, namely $(1, 18, 0.5)$ and $(5, 54, 0.1)$. We also provide the results of MT as reference (System #1-5).

System	tst2018	tst2019	tst2020	tst2022	tst-COM
ASR*	95.59	97.55	95.71	96.67	98.04
Whisper	95.75	98.34	97.17	97.86	97.01

Table 5: The recognition accuracy of the ASR fusion model and pre-trained Whisper. ASR* indicates the ASR fusion model.

4.1 Automatic Speech Recognition

We evaluate the recognition performance of ASR fusion model and pre-trained Whisper. The ASR fusion model comprises three model structures, each trained with and without Text-to-Speech (TTS) data, resulting in a total of six ASR models. These models are fused to obtain the final ASR* model. The three ASR structures are presented below.

- VGG-Conformer: 2 layers of VGG and 12 layers of Conformer in encoder, 6 layers of Transformer in decoder.
- VGG-Transformer: 2 layers of VGG and 16 layers of Transformer in encoder, 6 layers of Transformer in decoder.
- GateCNN-Transformer: 6 layers of GateCNN and 12 layers of Conformer in encoder, 6 layers of Transformer in decoder.

The recognition results of the ASR fusion model and pre-trained Whisper are presented in Table 5. The results indicate that Whisper has a superior recognition performance compared to the ASR fusion model, with an average improvement of 0.51%. However, the ASR fusion model outperforms Whisper slightly on the tst-COM dataset, which could be due to the ASR fusion model upsampling, making its data distribution closer to tst-COM.

4.2 Cascaded Systems

We construct two cascaded systems, one consisting of six-model fusion ASR and six-model fusion MT (System #6), and the other consisting of Whisper and six-model fusion MT (System #7).

For ASR in System #6, we employ the ASR fusion model described in Section 4.1. For MT in System #6, we train the four MT models described in Section 3.2. E18D6 and Macaron are both saved with two different checkpoints, resulting in six MT models that are fused to obtain MT*.

#	System	Official Segment		SHAS (1, 18, 0.5)		SHAS (5, 54, 0.1)	
		Dev	tst-COM	Dev	tst-COM	Dev	tst-COM
	MT						
1	E15D6-v1	27.23	30.19	-	-	-	-
2	E15D6-v2	27.14	29.95	-	-	-	-
3	E18D6	27.53	30.48	-	-	-	-
4	Macaron	27.48	30.71	-	-	-	-
5	ensemble (1-4)	27.81	31.03	-	-	-	-
	Cascaded						
6	ASR*+MT*	26.40	29.83	26.05	29.69	26.45	29.62
7	Whisper+MT*	26.72	29.42	27.00	29.55	26.82	29.03
	End-to-End						
8	SATE-ex-T (w/ TTS)	24.78	28.17	24.43	27.43	23.30	26.49
9	SATE-ex-T (w/o TTS)	25.27	28.00	25.19	27.81	24.37	27.39
10	SATE-ex-M (w/ TTS)	24.52	28.18	23.61	26.62	22.08	24.67
11	SATE-ex-M (w/o TTS)	24.18	27.26	23.96	27.51	20.91	25.66
12	VGG-C-init	24.62	28.74	24.61	28.50	24.12	28.06
13	VGG-T-init	24.59	28.28	24.51	27.84	23.89	27.59
14	VGG-C	24.75	28.68	24.70	28.35	24.29	27.65
15	VGG-T	24.72	28.42	24.60	27.93	24.09	27.77
16	ensemble (8-11)	25.85	29.00	25.50	28.45	24.22	27.54
17	ensemble (12-15)	25.53	28.86	25.54	28.68	25.36	28.68
18	ensemble (8-15)	26.42	29.29	26.22	29.11	25.92	28.92
	Ensemble of cascaded and e2e						
19	ensemble (6, 18)	26.85	29.46	26.65	29.19	26.28	29.41
20	ensemble (7, 18)	27.09	29.53	26.82	29.35	26.62	29.45

Table 6: The BLEU scores of machine translation (MT), cascaded, end-to-end, and ensemble systems. * indicates fusion models. The parameter of SHAS is $(min, max, threshold)$.

System #7 uses the large version of Whisper[3] as ASR, while the MT* is consistent with System #6. As shown, on Dev set, using Whisper to reduce errors in the source language text has improved the performance of ST. However, on tst-COM, the cascade model with ASR* performs better, presumably due to the closer match between the data distribution of ASR* and that of tst-COM.

4.3 End-to-End Systems

In the end-to-end setting, we adopt the encoder-decoder and SATE-ex architectures. Systems #12-15 are built based on the encoder-decoder, with specific parameters referred to Section 3.3. Systems #8-11 adopt the SATE-ex architecture. SATE-ex-T uses the VGG-Conformer ASR model in Section 4.2 to initialize the acoustic encoder and decoder, and the E18D6 MT model in Section 3.2 to initialize the textual encoder and decoder. SATE-ex-M uses the Macaron MT model in Section 3.2 to initialize the textual encoder and decoder.

It can be seen that the results of ensemble SATE-ex (System #16) outperform those of ensemble encoder-decoder (System #17). However, the performance of a single SATE-ex model is slightly worse than that of a single encoder-decoder model, which we attribute to the lack of fine-tuning for the single SATE-ex model. In future work, we will discuss SATE-ex in detail.

4.4 Ensemble Systems

We ensemble the two cascade models (Systems #6 and #7) and the end-to-end model (System #18) separately. The results are shown in Systems #19 and #20 in Table 6. It can be seen that the ensemble

[3]https://github.com/openai/whisper

systems achieves excellent performance.

4.5 System Description

Our system is primarily based on the full dataset allowed by IWSLT 2022, supplemented with Whisper large and SHAS for audio segmentation, which is trained on MUSTC. We have trained six ASR models and six MT models based on the IWSLT 2022 training data for model fusion. Additionally, we have trained four end-to-end ST models and four SATE-ex end-to-end ST models for end-to-end model fusion.

For the end-to-end system, we use a fusion of the above-mentioned eight end-to-end models. For the cascaded systems, we build two cascades: one with ASR based on Whisper and the other with ASR based on six-model fusion. The MT side used six-model fusion for both cascades. The submitted systems are based on these two cascades, each combined with the eight-model fusion end-to-end system.

The system structure and SHAS parameter $(min, max, threshold)$ settings of the five submitted systems are shown below.

- Primary Cascade: System #7 with SHAS parameters set to $(5, 54, 0.1)$.
- Contrastive1: System #20 with SHAS parameters set to $(1, 18, 0.5)$.
- Contrastive2: System #19 with SHAS parameters set to $(1, 18, 0.5)$.
- Contrastive3: System #6 with SHAS parameters set to $(5, 54, 0.1)$.
- Primary e2e: System #18 with SHAS parameters set to $(1, 18, 0.5)$.

5 Conclusion

This paper summarizes the results on the IWSLT 2023 Offline Speech Translation task. We employ various model architectures and data augmentation techniques to build speech translation systems in cascaded and end-to-end settings. The experimental results demonstrate the effectiveness of strategies such as pre-trained Whisper models, adaptation training, and the Stacked Acoustic-and-Textual Encoding extension (SATE-ex). In future work, we will further investigate SATE-ex and explore multimodal representation learning in speech translation.

References

Milind Agarwal, Sweta Agrawal, Antonios Anastasopoulos, Ondřej Bojar, Claudia Borg, Marine Carpuat, Roldano Cattoni, Mauro Cettolo, Mingda Chen, William Chen, Khalid Choukri, Alexandra Chronopoulou, Anna Currey, Thierry Declerck, Qianqian Dong, Yannick Estève, Kevin Duh, Marcello Federico, Souhir Gahbiche, Barry Haddow, Benjamin Hsu, Phu Mon Htut, Hirofumi Inaguma, Dávid Javorský, John Judge, Yasumasa Kano, Tom Ko, Rishu Kumar, Pengwei Li, Xutail Ma, Prashant Mathur, Evgeny Matusov, Paul McNamee, John P. McCrae, Kenton Murray, Maria Nadejde, Satoshi Nakamura, Matteo Negri, Ha Nguyen, Jan Niehues, Xing Niu, Atul Ojha Kr., John E. Ortega, Proyag Pal, Juan Pino, Lonneke van der Plas, Peter Polák, Elijah Rippeth, Elizabeth Salesky, Jiatong Shi, Matthias Sperber, Sebastian Stüker, Katsuhito Sudoh, Yun Tang, Brian Thompson, Kevin Tran, Marco Turchi, Alex Waibel, Mingxuan Wang, Shinji Watanabe, and Rodolfo Zevallos. 2023. Findings of the IWSLT 2023 Evaluation Campaign. In *Proceedings of the 20th International Conference on Spoken Language Translation (IWSLT 2023)*. Association for Computational Linguistics.

Alexei Baevski, Yuhao Zhou, Abdelrahman Mohamed, and Michael Auli. 2020. wav2vec 2.0: A framework for self-supervised learning of speech representations. *Advances in neural information processing systems*, 33:12449–12460.

Edresson Casanova, Christopher Shulby, Eren Gölge, Nicolas Michael Müller, Frederico Santos de Oliveira, Arnaldo Candido Jr., Anderson da Silva Soares, Sandra Maria Aluisio, and Moacir Antonelli Ponti. 2021. SC-GlowTTS: An Efficient Zero-Shot Multi-Speaker Text-To-Speech Model. In *Proc. Interspeech 2021*, pages 3645–3649.

Edresson Casanova, Christopher Shulby, Alexander Korolev, Arnaldo Candido Junior, Anderson da Silva Soares, Sandra Aluísio, and Moacir Antonelli Ponti. 2022. Asr data augmentation using cross-lingual multi-speaker tts and cross-lingual voice conversion. *arXiv preprint arXiv:2204.00618*.

Long Duong, Antonios Anastasopoulos, David Chiang, Steven Bird, and Trevor Cohn. 2016. An attentional model for speech translation without transcription. In *Proceedings of the 2016 Conference of the North American Chapter of the Association for Computational Linguistics: Human Language Technologies*, pages 949–959, San Diego, California. Association for Computational Linguistics.

Geoffrey Hinton, Oriol Vinyals, and Jeff Dean. 2015. Distilling the knowledge in a neural network. *arXiv preprint arXiv:1503.02531*.

Yoon Kim and Alexander M Rush. 2016. Sequence-level knowledge distillation. In *Proceedings of the 2016 Conference on Empirical Methods in Natural Language Processing*, pages 1317–1327.

Hang Le, Florentin Barbier, Ha Nguyen, Natalia Tomashenko, Salima Mdhaffar, Souhir Gabiche Gahbiche, Benjamin Lecouteux, Didier Schwab, and Yannick Estève. 2021. ON-TRAC' systems for the IWSLT 2021 low-resource speech translation and multilingual speech translation shared tasks. In *Proceedings of the 18th International Conference on Spoken Language Translation (IWSLT 2021)*, pages 169–174, Bangkok, Thailand (online). Association for Computational Linguistics.

Dan Liu, Mengge Du, Xiaoxi Li, Yuchen Hu, and Lirong Dai. 2021. The USTC-NELSLIP systems for simultaneous speech translation task at IWSLT 2021. In *Proceedings of the 18th International Conference on Spoken Language Translation (IWSLT 2021)*, pages 30–38, Bangkok, Thailand (online). Association for Computational Linguistics.

Yuchen Liu, Hao Xiong, Jiajun Zhang, Zhongjun He, Hua Wu, Haifeng Wang, and Chengqing Zong. 2019. End-to-end speech translation with knowledge distillation. *Proc. Interspeech 2019*, pages 1128–1132.

Yiping Lu, Zhuohan Li, Di He, Zhiqing Sun, Bin Dong, Tao Qin, Liwei Wang, and Tie-Yan Liu. 2019. Understanding and improving transformer from a multiparticle dynamic system point of view. *arXiv preprint arXiv:1906.02762*.

Myle Ott, Sergey Edunov, Alexei Baevski, Angela Fan, Sam Gross, Nathan Ng, David Grangier, and Michael Auli. 2019. fairseq: A fast, extensible toolkit for sequence modeling. In *Proceedings of the 2019 Conference of the North American Chapter of the Association for Computational Linguistics (Demonstrations)*, pages 48–53, Minneapolis, Minnesota. Association for Computational Linguistics.

Matt Post. 2018. A call for clarity in reporting BLEU scores. In *Proceedings of the Third Conference on Machine Translation: Research Papers*, pages 186–191, Brussels, Belgium. Association for Computational Linguistics.

Alec Radford, Jong Wook Kim, Tao Xu, Greg Brockman, Christine McLeavey, and Ilya Sutskever. 2022. Robust speech recognition via large-scale weak supervision. *arXiv preprint arXiv:2212.04356*.

Danielle Saunders. 2022. Domain adaptation and multidomain adaptation for neural machine translation: A survey. *Journal of Artificial Intelligence Research*, 75:351–424.

Rico Sennrich, Barry Haddow, and Alexandra Birch. 2016a. Improving neural machine translation models with monolingual data. In *Proceedings of the 54th Annual Meeting of the Association for Computational Linguistics (Volume 1: Long Papers)*, pages 86–96, Berlin, Germany. Association for Computational Linguistics.

Rico Sennrich, Barry Haddow, and Alexandra Birch. 2016b. Neural machine translation of rare words with subword units. In *Proceedings of the 54th Annual Meeting of the Association for Computational Linguistics (Volume 1: Long Papers)*, pages 1715–1725, Berlin, Germany. Association for Computational Linguistics.

Ioannis Tsiamas, Gerard I Gállego, José AR Fonollosa, and Marta R Costa-jussà. 2022. Shas: Approaching optimal segmentation for end-to-end speech translation. *arXiv preprint arXiv:2202.04774*.

Ashish Vaswani, Noam Shazeer, Niki Parmar, Jakob Uszkoreit, Llion Jones, Aidan N Gomez, Łukasz Kaiser, and Illia Polosukhin. 2017. Attention is all you need. *Advances in neural information processing systems*, 30.

Wei Wang, Taro Watanabe, Macduff Hughes, Tetsuji Nakagawa, and Ciprian Chelba. 2018. Denoising neural machine translation training with trusted data and online data selection. In *Proceedings of the Third Conference on Machine Translation: Research Papers*, pages 133–143, Brussels, Belgium. Association for Computational Linguistics.

Che Wanxiang, Feng Yunlong, Qin Libo, and Liu Ting. 2020. N-ltp: A open-source neural chinese language technology platform with pretrained models. *arXiv preprint*.

Chen Xu, Bojie Hu, Yanyang Li, Yuhao Zhang, Shen Huang, Qi Ju, Tong Xiao, and Jingbo Zhu. 2021. Stacked acoustic-and-textual encoding: Integrating the pre-trained models into speech translation encoders. In *Proceedings of the 59th Annual Meeting of the Association for Computational Linguistics and the 11th International Joint Conference on Natural Language Processing (Volume 1: Long Papers)*, pages 2619–2630.

Binbin Zhang, Di Wu, Zhuoyuan Yao, Xiong Wang, Fan Yu, Chao Yang, Liyong Guo, Yaguang Hu, Lei Xie, and Xin Lei. 2020. Unified streaming and non-streaming two-pass end-to-end model for speech recognition. *arXiv preprint arXiv:2012.05481*.

Weitai Zhang, Zhongyi Ye, Haitao Tang, Xiaoxi Li, Xinyuan Zhou, Jing Yang, Jianwei Cui, Pan Deng, Mohan Shi, Yifan Song, et al. 2022a. The ustc-nelslip offline speech translation systems for iwslt 2022. In *Proceedings of the 19th International Conference on Spoken Language Translation (IWSLT 2022)*, pages 198–207.

Ziqiang Zhang, Long Zhou, Junyi Ao, Shujie Liu, Lirong Dai, Jinyu Li, and Furu Wei. 2022b. Speechut: Bridging speech and text with hidden-unit for encoder-decoder based speech-text pre-training. *arXiv preprint arXiv:2210.03730*.

I2R's End-to-End Speech Translation System for IWSLT 2023 Offline Shared Task

Muhammad Huzaifah, Kye Min Tan, Richeng Duan
Institute for Infocomm Research, Agency for Science, Technology and Research, Singapore

Abstract

This paper describes I2R's submission to the offline speech translation track for IWSLT 2023. We focus on an end-to-end approach for translation from English audio to German text, one of the three available language directions in this year's edition. The I2R system leverages on pretrained models that have been exposed to large-scale audio and text data for our base model. We introduce several stages of additional pretraining followed by fine-tuning to adapt the system for the downstream speech translation task. The strategy is supplemented by other techniques such as data augmentation, domain tagging, knowledge distillation, and model ensemble, among others. We evaluate the system on several publicly available test sets for comparison.

1 Introduction

Historically, speech translation (ST) has involved combining automatic speech recognition (ASR) and machine translation (MT) systems in a cascade. The ASR system would transcribe speech signals into text in the source language, and the MT system would then translate this text into the target language. However, recent developments in deep learning have made it possible to use an end-to-end speech translation model (Bérard et al., 2016; Weiss et al., 2017), which directly translates speech in the source language into text in the target language, without relying on intermediate symbolic representations. This approach offers the advantages of lower latency and avoids error propagation. While cascaded models initially outperformed end-to-end models, recent results from IWSLT campaigns (Le et al., 2020; Bentivogli et al., 2021; Anastasopoulos et al., 2022) have shown that the performance of end-to-end models is now approaching that of cascaded solutions.

Large pretrained models (Lewis et al., 2020; Conneau et al., 2021; Raffel et al., 2020) have become a prevalent basis for speech and language processing work (Ma et al., 2021; Chen et al., 2022a). Through the utilization of pretrained models and subsequent finetuning using a small amount of labeled data, many tasks have exhibited significant improvements in performance (Baevski et al., 2020; Hsu et al., 2021; Guillaume et al., 2022; Navarro et al., 2022), some even reaching state-of-the-art results.

In this work, we describe our end-to-end system for the Offline Speech Translation Task at IWSLT 2023 (Agarwal et al., 2023) in the English-German (En-De) language direction. The current year's task not only includes the traditional TED talk evaluation set translated from English to German, but also introduces two additional test sets consisting of ACL presentations, press conferences and interviews (EMPAC), which are more complex and challenging. Furthermore, this year's constrained data track allows less data than previous years. Our team enhances the end-to-end ST system within the context of the pretrain-finetune paradigm. We introduce several pretraining stages before finetuning for the downstream ST task. Furthermore, we implemented dynamic audio augmentation methods to account for differences in audio recording quality. We boost the system's robustness by ensembling multiple individual models and use domain tagging to direct the model towards specific output styles. Here, we evaluate our system against various standard public test sets for both speech translation and text machine translation.

2 Methodology

In this section, we introduce the model architecture of our system, and describe some of the methods we incorporated into the design and training process.

Proceedings of the 20th International Conference on Spoken Language Translation (IWSLT 2023), pages 202–210
July 13-14, 2023

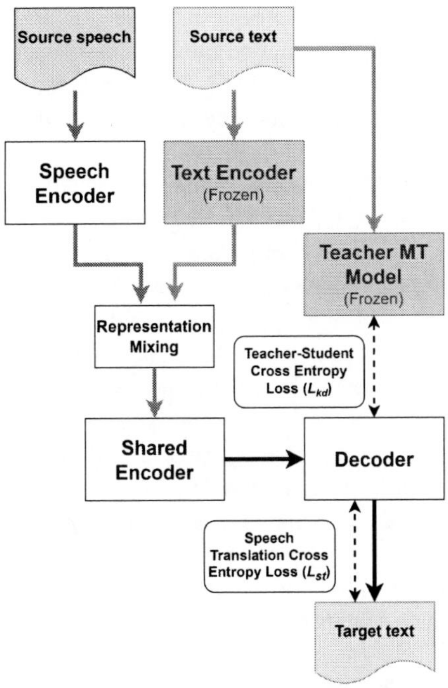

Figure 1: Our end-to-end ST model architecture

2.1 Model

As shown in Fig 1, our end-to-end ST model uses two separate encoders for speech and text, followed by a shared encoder and decoder. As the shared encoder is pretrained on text inputs while the final system has to work with speech inputs, we try to bring speech and text into a shared representation space by devising a training task using mixed speech and text inputs, described in Section 2.2.

Due to limited computational resources, we make use of the allowed pretrained models in the constrained track. The speech encoder is initialized from the WavLM (Chen et al., 2022a) large checkpoint which was pretrained on Libri-Light, GigaSpeech and VoxPopuli data in a self-supervised fashion. WavLM was selected as it includes more data relevant to this year's test set, and showed better performance in our preliminary experiments compared to similar models like HuBERT. DeltaLM base (Ma et al., 2021) was used to initialize the text encoder, shared encoder and decoder sections. Prior to the final ST training, the DeltaLM model was first finetuned on text-to-text MT (described in Section 3.2). The text encoder includes the text and positional embedding layers of DeltaLM and is frozen in the final finetuning stage. The shared encoder encompasses the transformer layers of the DeltaLM encoder.

Given that ST data is commonly provided as a triplet of source speech, source text transcription and target text translations, we leverage both text and speech sources in our proposed architecture. Aside from the audio waveforms processed through the speech encoder, we take as input upsampled tokenized source text by repeating subword tokens according to a pre-calculated ratio given by an alignment system. For data with paired speech and text inputs, we mix representations from the two input encoders through random swapping. Otherwise, unimodal data is processed by their respective encoders and the mixing step is skipped, such as the case during speech-only ST inference. We also recognise that the flexible nature of the architecture allows the use of ASR and MT data as unimodal inputs to further expand the training data and train a multilingual model. However, due to time and computational constraints, this was not explored in this submission and is left as future work.

2.2 Representation Mixing

Recent work in unified representation learning of speech and text (Liu et al., 2020; Zhang et al., 2022; Chen et al., 2022b; Fang et al., 2022; Sainath et al., 2023) try to leverage abundant text data to supplement speech-based models. We similarly encourage our model to learn a joint multimodal representation by bringing speech and text inputs into a shared representation space.

To handle the large difference in sequence lengths of audio and text, systems from the literature often upsample text using a trained duration model or a resampling scheme. Here, we utilize offline forced alignment and upsampling to align the speech and text data. Specifically, a pretrained ASR model is used to first force align text transcripts to audio, returning an upsampling ratio between a particular subword and its corresponding speech segment. Each subword token is then repeated up to this ratio before being fed to the text encoder such that the final encoded subword is of the same length as its speech counterpart. The alignment and resampling procedure is described in detail in Section 3.1.

As the shared encoder was pretrained only on text, we hypothesize that the model may better adapt to the downstream speech task by using a mixed speech-text representation compared to training on pure speech inputs. When finetuning the ST model on data with both source speech and text, we feed both the audio and upsampled text tokens into the respective speech and text encoders, then mix the resultant embeddings at the individual subword token level using a fixed probability. In practice, a swapping mask is created before upsampling, with text embeddings being replaced with speech embeddings according to a swapping ratio α, where $0 < \alpha < 1$. The tokens and swap mask are upsampled together and passed into the model so that sequences of identical upsampled tokens can be replaced with speech embeddings during the representation mixing step.

2.3 Knowledge Distillation

To fully utilize the larger amounts of text-only MT data allowed in the challenge, we train a separate MT model using DeltaLM large. This larger model is then frozen and used as a teacher during fine-tuning of the ST model via negative log-likelihood minimization between the hypotheses generated by both the models, similar to the knowledge distillation method proposed in Tang et al. (2021).

Our overall loss function therefore consists of cross entropy loss between the ground truth and hypothesis produced by the ST system (L_{st}) and negative log-likelihood loss between the teacher and student model hypotheses (L_{kd}), weighted by γ and β respectively: $L = \gamma L_{st} + \beta L_{kd}$

3 Experimental Setup

3.1 Data Preparation

Training data was compiled in accordance to constrained conditions. They can be divided into text and audio-based categories which were used to train the initial MT model and final ST model respectively.

Text data Parallel En-De lines were gathered from both MT and ST datasets, seen in Table 1. These were split into in-domain and out-of-domain based on whether the text was derived from TED-like sources. The in-domain sources include a combination of MuST-C v1, v2 and v3 (Cattoni et al., 2021), ST TED (Niehues et al., 2018), and TED 2020 (Reimers and Gurevych, 2020), whereas the out-of-domain sources mostly comprised of OpenSubtitles (Lison and Tiedemann, 2016) and Europarl (Koehn, 2005), but also include CoVoST v2 (Wang et al., 2021b), ELRC-CORDIS News, Europarl-ST (Iranzo-Sánchez et al., 2020), News-Commentary (Tiedemann, 2012) and Tatoeba. A common pre-processing pipeline was applied to the text data, namely removing any tags and control codes, normalizing bullet points, simplifying punctuation by removing repeats (with the exception of '...') and normalizing whitespace characters. Sentence pairs where source and target differed by more than three times in length were then removed given that they were likely to be misaligned. Finally, the remaining sentences were deduplicated. The out-of-domain data was further filtered using Language-agnostic BERT Sentence Embedding (LaBSE) (Feng et al., 2022). Specifically, we removed sentence pairs with sentence representations lower than 0.5 cosine similarity. We opted not to use any backtranslation data for training since the provided monolingual dataset was found to largely overlap with OpenSubtitles. The final dataset contained 850,003 in-domain and 13,083,335 out-of-domain sentence pairs.

Dataset	Lines
in-domain	
MuST-C v1/v2/v3	391K
ST TED corpus	170K
TED2020 v1	288K
out-of-domain	
CoVoST v2	300K
ELRC-CORDIS News v1	111K
Europarl v10	1.7M
Europarl-ST v1.1	69K
NewsCommentary v16	380K
OpenSubtitles v2018 apptek	10.1M
Tatoeba v1	288K
Total	13.9M

Table 1: Breakdown of text training data. For ST datasets only transcription and translation pairs were used.

Audio data Audio data sources include both ASR and ST corpora, listed in Table 2. ASR data consist of Commonvoice (Ardila et al., 2020), Librispeech (Panayotov et al., 2015), TED LIUM (Rousseau et al., 2012), and Vox Populi (Wang et al., 2021a), whereas the ST data include CoVoST (Wang et al., 2021b), Europarl-ST (Iranzo-Sánchez et al., 2020), MuSTC v3 (Cattoni et al., 2021) and ST TED (Niehues et al., 2018). Speech was first converted to mono channel and resampled to 16kHz if required before being saved in FLAC format. Only utterances between 800 to 480,000 samples (i.e. 0.05-30s) were kept and utilized for

Dataset	Utterances	Hours
ASR data		
Commonvoice v11.0	949K	2320
Librispeech v12	281K	960
TED LIUM v3	268K	453
Vox Populi	177K	543
ST data		
CoVoST v2	289K	364
Europarl-ST v1.1	68K	89
MuST-C v3	265K	273
ST TED corpus	169K	252
Total	2.47M	5254

Table 2: Breakdown of available audio training data

training. The provided segmentation was used for all speech training data.

To increase the amount of available ST data, we generated additional translations from ASR transcription data using our trained MT model. These synthetic speech-text pairs were used as part of the ST dataset during the finetuning phase.

Forced alignment and upsampling To prepare text inputs for mixing with speech inputs, we preprocessed the text by upsampling and aligning it to its corresponding speech features using a pretrained HuBERT ASR model. First, we normalized the transcripts from ASR and ST datasets by deleting non-verbal fillers and converting numbers into their corresponding words. Characters not found among the HuBERT labels were then removed after tokenizing the text. Next, we obtained an alignment between the subword tokens and parallel speech using a pretrained HuBERT large model (Hsu et al., 2021) and, following those alignments, duplicated the input tokens to match the lengths of the speech representation produced by the speech encoder. The frequency of the upsampled text tokens is 50 Hz (equivalent to 16 kHz input audio downsampled 320 times by the WavLM feature extractor).

Audio segmentation As segmentation information was not provided in this year's evaluation data, we used the pretrained Supervised Hybrid Audio Segmentation (SHAS) model (Tsiamas et al., 2022) to perform voice activity detection and segmentation on the input audio from the IWSLT test sets. SHAS has been evaluated on MuST-C and mTEDx and shows results approaching manual segmentation.

3.2 Training configuration

On-the-fly audio augmentation To make our model more robust against the bigger variances in recording quality of the evaluation data introduced this year, we implemented an on-the-fly augmentation pipeline for input audio via the Audiomentations library. In addition to initial utterence cepstral mean and variance normalization (CMVN), we apply gain, seven-band parametric equalization, gaussian noise, time stretch, pitch shift and a lowpass filter, where each augmentation independently has a 20% chance of being utilized. During inference only CMVN is used.

Machine translation We finetuned several configurations of DeltaLM base and large for En-De machine translation. DeltaLM base has 12 encoder and six decoder layers, with an embedding dimension of 768 and 12 attention heads per transformer layer. In contrast, DeltaLM large contains 24 encoder and 12 decoder layers, an embedding dimension of 1024 and 16 attention heads per layer.

We used a two phase approach to finetuning. In the first phase, we directly initialized the MT model with DeltaLM pretrained weights and trained on all available MT data. We then continued finetuning only on in-domain data after checkpoint averaging the best five checkpoints from the first phase in terms of BLEU on the validation set that comprised of IWSLT test sets from 2015, 2018, 2019 and 2020, plus MuST-C v3 tst-COMMON split. We also tried progressive finetuning (Li et al., 2020) during the second phase for the DeltaLM base configuration where the depth of the encoder was increased to 16 with four extra randomly initialized layers.

All models were implemented with the Fairseq library. Models were trained with Adam optimization, an inverse square root learning rate (LR) schedule and a peak LR of 1e-4 for the first phase and 1e-5 for the second phase. Label smoothing of 0.1 was also used. Training was carried out on four NVIDIA V100 GPUs. We employ subword tokenization for all text inputs using a Sentencepiece model inherited from the original DeltaLM, with a vocabulary size of 250,000.

Speech translation finetuning As described in section 2.1, the end-to-end speech translation model consists of separate speech encoder and text embedding input layers, followed by a shared encoder and decoder. The speech encoder is initialized with a pretrained WavLM large model that contains a seven layer convolutional feature extractor followed by 24 transformer layers. We initialize the text embeddings, shared encoder and decoder layers with the DeltaLM base model previously finetuned for MT. The input text embeddings are frozen throughout the ST finetuning. Meanwhile, the teacher text model was instead initialized with the finetuned DeltaLM large configuration.

Domain tagging has been shown in previous MT (Britz et al., 2017) and ST (Li et al., 2022) work to be effective for domain discrimination and to condition the model towards certain output styles. Given the distinct TED-style outputs of the evaluation data, we introduce '*<indomain>*' and '*<outdomain>*' tags as prefix tokens during decoding to help the model better distinguish the data distribution and style of the in-domain data from the other parts of the dataset.

Similar to the approach employed during MT training, we initially trained the end-to-end ST model on all available ST data, including those synthesized from ASR data. Adam optimization with inverse square root LR schedule and peak LR of 1e-5 was used. A swapping ratio of 0.8 was used during training but 1.0 (i.e. pure speech representation) was used for inference and testing. In the second phase we continued finetuning two separate models with different data splits, while swapping ratio was kept at 1.0. To target the usual TED evaluation data, we trained one with only MuST-C and ST-TED data, while the other also included CoVoST and Europarl to help deal with the more diverse speech patterns found in the ACL and EMPAC parts of the evaluation data (given that no direct development data was provided). We weight the ST loss and knowledge distillation loss with $\gamma = 1$ and $\beta = 0.1$ respectively. Training was carried out on four NVIDIA V100 GPUs for both phases.

4 Results and Analysis

We present our experimental results and analyses in this section.

4.1 Effect of audio augmentations and pretrained speech encoder

As a preliminary experiment, we tested whether the input audio augmentations have a tangible impact on downstream applications. We finetuned a pretrained WavLM large model together with a six layer transformer decoder for ASR using MuST-C v2 data, with and without input augmentations (Table 3). Furthermore, we trained a HuBERT large model in the same setup to contrast between different pretrained speech encoders.

Model	WER
HuBERT large without augmentation	7.59
WavLM large without augmentation	5.86
WavLM large with augmentation	5.56

Table 3: ASR results on MuST-C v2 tst-COMMON.

As observed, the audio augmentations were found to be beneficial, leading to a reduction of WER by 0.3. We found WavLM large together with augmentations to perform the best overall and so was adopted for the rest of the experiments.

4.2 Machine translation results

The results of the MT systems for En-De are shown in Table 4, separated into the full-domain training phase and the in-domain training phase. Performance was evaluated using cased BLEU with default `SacreBLEU` options (13a tokenization).

It was evident that the continuous finetuning with in-domain data improves performance on similar datasets such as past year IWSLT evaluation data or MuST-C. While the DeltaLM large models achieved the best results, the base variants were not far behind and generally performed within 1 BLEU score of the former. However, we found no added benefit to the progressively finetuned models. It may be the case that the extra representative power of the expanded encoder layers were not beneficial at the relatively small scale of the in-domain data, which was less than 1 million sentence pairs. Some training runs produced better scores by checkpoint averaging the best five checkpoints. Nevertheless, the improvement was not consistent throughout all test sets.

An ensemble of model variants 6 and 9 further improved the BLEU scores on the test sets. We utilize the ensemble model to generate translations from ASR transcriptions to supplement the available ST data. The best checkpoint for DeltaLM base (model 5) and DeltaLM large (model 9) were subsequently used to initialize the end-to-end ST model and teacher text model respectively for the final finetuning.

	Model	BLEU			
		tst2020	tst2019	MuST-C v3	MuST-C v2
	full-domain				
1	base (best)	31.76	28.81	33.11	33.77
2	base (avg 5)	32.86	29.43	34.05	34.67
3	large (best)	31.82	29.01	33.20	34.21
4	large (avg 5)	32.52	29.54	33.65	34.68
	in-domain				
5	base (best)	33.64	30.67	35.29	35.99
6	base (avg 5)	33.73	30.64	35.26	36.11
7	base-progressive (best)	33.40	30.51	34.25	34.83
8	base-progressive (avg 5)	33.26	30.48	34.37	35.09
9	large (best)	**34.44**	**31.47**	35.60	36.26
10	large (avg 5)	34.32	31.42	**35.89**	**36.48**
	Ensemble (6 + 9)	**34.91**	**31.77**	**36.14**	**36.93**

Table 4: MT results on various test sets.

	Model	BLEU				
		tst2020	tst2019	MuST-C v3	MuST-C v2	CoVoST v2
	in-domain					
1	base (best)	**25.70**	**22.68**	**30.29**	**30.56**	27.92
2	base (avg 5)	24.81	22.25	29.98	30.29	28.11
	extended-domain					
3	base (best)	22.80	21.17	29.33	29.50	28.63
4	base (avg 3)	23.21	21.20	29.61	29.95	**29.30**
	Ensemble (1 + 2 + 4)	24.99	22.64	29.99	30.35	29.13

Table 5: ST results on various test sets.

4.3 Speech translation results

Results from our end-to-end ST systems for English speech to German text are provided in Table 5. As mentioned in section 3.2, we trained two models during the second ST finetuning phase, which are labelled here as 'in-domain', targeting more TED-like inputs, and 'extended-domain' for other input domains. As reference segmentation information was not provided for IWSLT-tst2019 and IWSLT-tst2020 test sets, we used SHAS to segment the audio. The translation hypotheses were then compared to the references provided by using the `SLT.KIT` evaluation script listed on the challenge website, that uses the mwerSegmenter resegmentation tool and the BLEU calculation script from the `Moses` toolkit. The provided segmentation and `SacreBLEU` were utilized for the other test sets.

Comparing CoVoST against the rest of the test sets reveals that the in-domain and extended-domain models show better results in their respective domain specializations, as was intended. We unexpectedly get poor results on IWSLT-tst2019 and IWSLT-tst2020 relative to last year's best performing entries, which may point to a weakness in the current training procedure, a domain mismatch since training was more aligned to MuST-C, or compounded errors due to resegmentation. We plan to investigate the reasons more precisely in future papers. The ensemble model of variants 1, 2 and 4 shows balanced performance across both domains, and we submit this as our primary submission, with variants 1 and 4 as our contrastive systems.

5 Conclusion

In this paper we outline our proposed end-to-end system that incorporates pretrained models trained on large-scale audio and text data to enhance the ST performance. The system underwent several stages of additional pretraining followed by finetuning for the downstream speech translation task. We explored several techniques including audio augmentation, domain tagging, knowledge distillation and model ensemble to improve the system's performance. We utilize both speech and text inputs, and propose a mixing procedure to unify representations from both modalities to not only increase the amount of available training data but also better adapt the model to downstream speech tasks. We plan to carry out more experiments to further explore the effect of modality mixing and improve the performance of such models for speech-to-text tasks.

Acknowledgements

This work was supported by the A*STAR Computational Resource Centre through the use of its high performance computing facilities.

References

Milind Agarwal, Sweta Agrawal, Antonios Anastasopoulos, Ondřej Bojar, Claudia Borg, Marine Carpuat, Roldano Cattoni, Mauro Cettolo, Mingda Chen, William Chen, Khalid Choukri, Alexandra Chronopoulou, Anna Currey, Thierry Declerck, Qianqian Dong, Yannick Estève, Kevin Duh, Marcello Federico, Souhir Gahbiche, Barry Haddow, Benjamin Hsu, Phu Mon Htut, Hirofumi Inaguma, Dávid Javorský, John Judge, Yasumasa Kano, Tom Ko, Rishu Kumar, Pengwei Li, Xutail Ma, Prashant Mathur, Evgeny Matusov, Paul McNamee, John P. McCrae, Kenton Murray, Maria Nadejde, Satoshi Nakamura, Matteo Negri, Ha Nguyen, Jan Niehues, Xing Niu, Atul Ojha Kr., John E. Ortega, Proyag Pal, Juan Pino, Lonneke van der Plas, Peter Polák, Elijah Rippeth, Elizabeth Salesky, Jiatong Shi, Matthias Sperber, Sebastian Stüker, Katsuhito Sudoh, Yun Tang, Brian Thompson, Kevin Tran, Marco Turchi, Alex Waibel, Mingxuan Wang, Shinji Watanabe, and Rodolfo Zevallos. 2023. Findings of the IWSLT 2023 Evaluation Campaign. In *Proceedings of the 20th International Conference on Spoken Language Translation (IWSLT 2023)*. Association for Computational Linguistics.

Antonios Anastasopoulos, Loïc Barrault, Luisa Bentivogli, Marcely Zanon Boito, Ondrej Bojar, Roldano Cattoni, Anna Currey, Georgiana Dinu, Kevin Duh, Maha Elbayad, Clara Emmanuel, Y. Estève, Marcello Federico, Christian Federmann, Souhir Gahbiche, Hongyu Gong, Roman Grundkiewicz, Barry Haddow, B. Hsu, Dávid Javorský, Věra Kloudová, Surafel Melaku Lakew, Xutai Ma, Prashant Mathur, Paul McNamee, Kenton Murray, Maria Nadejde, Satoshi Nakamura, Matteo Negri, Jan Niehues, Xing Niu, John E. Ortega, Juan Miguel Pino, Elizabeth Salesky, Jiatong Shi, Matthias Sperber, Sebastian Stüker, Katsuhito Sudoh, Marco Turchi, Yogesh Virkar, Alexander H. Waibel, Changhan Wang, and Shinji Watanabe. 2022. Findings of the IWSLT 2022 evaluation campaign. In *International Workshop on Spoken Language Translation (IWSLT 2022)*, pages 98–157. Association for Computational Linguistics.

Rosana Ardila, Megan Branson, Kelly Davis, Michael Kohler, Josh Meyer, Michael Henretty, Reuben Morais, Lindsay Saunders, Francis Tyers, and Gregor Weber. 2020. Common voice: A massively-multilingual speech corpus. In *Proceedings of the Twelfth Language Resources and Evaluation Conference*, pages 4218–4222, Marseille, France. European Language Resources Association.

Alexei Baevski, Yuhao Zhou, Abdelrahman Mohamed, and Michael Auli. 2020. wav2vec 2.0: A framework for self-supervised learning of speech representations. *Advances in Neural Information Processing Systems*, 33:12449–12460.

Luisa Bentivogli, Mauro Cettolo, Marco Gaido, Alina Karakanta, Alberto Martinelli, Matteo Negri, and Marco Turchi. 2021. Cascade versus direct speech translation: Do the differences still make a difference? In *Proceedings of the 59th Annual Meeting of the Association for Computational Linguistics and the 11th International Joint Conference on Natural Language Processing (Volume 1: Long Papers)*, pages 2873–2887. Association for Computational Linguistics.

Alexandre Bérard, Olivier Pietquin, Laurent Besacier, and Christophe Servan. 2016. Listen and translate: A proof of concept for end-to-end speech-to-text translation. In *NIPS Workshop on end-to-end learning and speech and audio precessing*, Barcelona, Spain.

Denny Britz, Quoc Le, and Reid Pryzant. 2017. Effective domain mixing for neural machine translation. In *Proceedings of the Second Conference on Machine Translation*, pages 118–126, Copenhagen, Denmark. Association for Computational Linguistics.

Roldano Cattoni, Mattia Antonino Di Gangi, Luisa Bentivogli, Matteo Negri, and Marco Turchi. 2021. MuST-C: A multilingual corpus for end-to-end speech translation. *Computer Speech & Language*, 66:101155.

Sanyuan Chen, Chengyi Wang, Zhengyang Chen, Yu Wu, Shujie Liu, Zhuo Chen, Jinyu Li, Naoyuki Kanda, Takuya Yoshioka, Xiong Xiao, Jian Wu, Long Zhou, Shuo Ren, Yanmin Qian, Yao Qian, Jian Wu, Michael Zeng, Xiangzhan Yu, and Furu Wei. 2022a. WavLM: Large-scale self-supervised pre-training for full stack speech processing. *IEEE Journal of Selected Topics in Signal Processing*, 16(6):1505–1518.

Zhehuai Chen, Yu Zhang, Andrew Rosenberg, Bhuvana Ramabhadran, Pedro J. Moreno, Ankur Bapna, and Heiga Zen. 2022b. MAESTRO: Matched speech text representations through modality matching. In *Interspeech*, pages 4093–4097.

Alexis Conneau, Alexei Baevski, Ronan Collobert, Abdelrahman Mohamed, and Michael Auli. 2021. Unsupervised Cross-Lingual Representation Learning for Speech Recognition. In *Interspeech*, pages 2426–2430.

Qingkai Fang, Rong Ye, Lei Li, Yang Feng, and Mingxuan Wang. 2022. STEMM: Self-learning with speech-text manifold mixup for speech translation. In *Proceedings of the 60th Annual Meeting of the Association for Computational Linguistics (Volume 1: Long Papers)*, pages 7050–7062, Dublin, Ireland. Association for Computational Linguistics.

Fangxiaoyu Feng, Yinfei Yang, Daniel Cer, Naveen Arivazhagan, and Wei Wang. 2022. Language-agnostic BERT sentence embedding. In *Proceedings of the 60th Annual Meeting of the Association for Computational Linguistics (Volume 1: Long Papers)*, pages 878–891, Dublin, Ireland. Association for Computational Linguistics.

Séverine Guillaume, Guillaume Wisniewski, Cécile Macaire, Guillaume Jacques, Alexis Michaud, Benjamin Galliot, Maximin Coavoux, Solange Rossato, Minh-Châu Nguyên, and Maxime Fily. 2022. Fine-tuning pre-trained models for automatic speech recognition, experiments on a fieldwork corpus of japhug (trans-himalayan family). In *Proceedings of the Fifth Workshop on the Use of Computational Methods in the Study of Endangered Languages*, pages 170–178, Dublin, Ireland. Association for Computational Linguistics.

Wei-Ning Hsu, Yao-Hung Hubert Tsai, Benjamin Bolte, Ruslan Salakhutdinov, and Abdelrahman Mohamed. 2021. HuBERT: How much can a bad teacher benefit ASR pre-training? In *2021 IEEE International Conference on Acoustics, Speech and Signal Processing (ICASSP)*, pages 6533–6537.

Javier Iranzo-Sánchez, Joan Albert Silvestre-Cerdà, Javier Jorge, Nahuel Roselló, Adrià Giménez, Albert Sanchis, Jorge Civera, and Alfons Juan. 2020. Europarl-ST: A multilingual corpus for speech translation of parliamentary debates. In *2020 IEEE International Conference on Acoustics, Speech and Signal Processing (ICASSP)*, pages 8229–8233.

Philipp Koehn. 2005. Europarl: A parallel corpus for statistical machine translation. In *Proceedings of Machine Translation Summit X: Papers*, pages 79–86, Phuket, Thailand.

Hang Le, Juan Pino, Changhan Wang, Jiatao Gu, Didier Schwab, and Laurent Besacier. 2020. Dual-decoder transformer for joint automatic speech recognition and multilingual speech translation. In *28th International Conference on Computational Linguistics*, pages 3520–3533, Barcelona, Spain.

Mike Lewis, Yinhan Liu, Naman Goyal, Marjan Ghazvininejad, Abdelrahman Mohamed, Omer Levy, Veselin Stoyanov, and Luke Zettlemoyer. 2020. BART: Denoising sequence-to-sequence pre-training for natural language generation, translation, and comprehension. In *Proceedings of the 58th Annual Meeting of the Association for Computational Linguistics*, pages 7871–7880, Online. Association for Computational Linguistics.

Bei Li, Ziyang Wang, Hui Liu, Yufan Jiang, Quan Du, Tong Xiao, Huizhen Wang, and Jingbo Zhu. 2020. Shallow-to-deep training for neural machine translation. In *Proceedings of the 2020 Conference on Empirical Methods in Natural Language Processing (EMNLP)*, pages 995–1005, Online. Association for Computational Linguistics.

Yinglu Li, Minghan Wang, Jiaxin Guo, Xiaosong Qiao, Yuxia Wang, Daimeng Wei, Chang Su, Yimeng Chen, Min Zhang, Shimin Tao, Hao Yang, and Ying Qin. 2022. The HW-TSC's offline speech translation system for IWSLT 2022 evaluation. In *Proceedings of the 19th International Conference on Spoken Language Translation (IWSLT 2022)*, pages 239–246, Dublin, Ireland (in-person and online). Association for Computational Linguistics.

Pierre Lison and Jörg Tiedemann. 2016. OpenSubtitles2016: Extracting large parallel corpora from movie and TV subtitles. In *Proceedings of the Tenth International Conference on Language Resources and Evaluation (LREC'16)*, pages 923–929, Portorož, Slovenia. European Language Resources Association (ELRA).

Yuchen Liu, Junnan Zhu, Jiajun Zhang, and Chengqing Zong. 2020. Bridging the modality gap for speech-to-text translation. *arXiv preprint arXiv:2010.14920.*

Shuming Ma, Li Dong, Shaohan Huang, Dongdong Zhang, Alexandre Muzio, Saksham Singhal, Hany Hassan Awadalla, Xia Song, and Furu Wei. 2021. DeltaLM: Encoder-decoder pre-training for language generation and translation by augmenting pretrained multilingual encoders.

David Fraile Navarro, Mark Dras, and Shlomo Berkovsky. 2022. Few-shot fine-tuning SOTA summarization models for medical dialogues. In *Proceedings of the 2022 Conference of the North American Chapter of the Association for Computational Linguistics: Human Language Technologies: Student Research Workshop*, pages 254–266, Hybrid: Seattle, Washington + Online. Association for Computational Linguistics.

Jan Niehues, Rolando Cattoni, Sebastian Stüker, Mauro Cettolo, Marco Turchi, and Marcello Federico. 2018. The IWSLT 2018 evaluation campaign. In *Proceedings of the 15th International Conference on Spoken Language Translation*, pages 2–6, Brussels. International Conference on Spoken Language Translation.

Vassil Panayotov, Guoguo Chen, Daniel Povey, and Sanjeev Khudanpur. 2015. Librispeech: An asr corpus based on public domain audio books. In *2015 IEEE International Conference on Acoustics, Speech and Signal Processing (ICASSP)*, pages 5206–5210.

Colin Raffel, Noam Shazeer, Adam Roberts, Katherine Lee, Sharan Narang, Michael Matena, Yanqi

Zhou, Wei Li, and Peter J. Liu. 2020. Exploring the limits of transfer learning with a unified text-to-text transformer. *Journal of Machine Learning Research*, 21(1).

Nils Reimers and Iryna Gurevych. 2020. Making monolingual sentence embeddings multilingual using knowledge distillation. In *Proceedings of the 2020 Conference on Empirical Methods in Natural Language Processing*. Association for Computational Linguistics.

Anthony Rousseau, Paul Deléglise, and Yannick Estève. 2012. TED-LIUM: an automatic speech recognition dedicated corpus. In *Proceedings of the Eighth International Conference on Language Resources and Evaluation (LREC'12)*, pages 125–129, Istanbul, Turkey. European Language Resources Association (ELRA).

Tara N Sainath, Rohit Prabhavalkar, Ankur Bapna, Yu Zhang, Zhouyuan Huo, Zhehuai Chen, Bo Li, Weiran Wang, and Trevor Strohman. 2023. JOIST: A joint speech and text streaming model for asr. In *2022 IEEE Spoken Language Technology Workshop (SLT)*, pages 52–59. IEEE.

Yun Tang, Juan Pino, Xian Li, Changhan Wang, and Dmitriy Genzel. 2021. Improving speech translation by understanding and learning from the auxiliary text translation task. In *Proceedings of the 59th Annual Meeting of the Association for Computational Linguistics and the 11th International Joint Conference on Natural Language Processing (Volume 1: Long Papers)*, pages 4252–4261, Online. Association for Computational Linguistics.

Jörg Tiedemann. 2012. Parallel data, tools and interfaces in OPUS. In *Proceedings of the Eight International Conference on Language Resources and Evaluation (LREC'12)*, Istanbul, Turkey. European Language Resources Association (ELRA).

Ioannis Tsiamas, Gerard I. Gállego, Carlos Escolano, José Fonollosa, and Marta R. Costa-jussà. 2022. Pretrained speech encoders and efficient fine-tuning methods for speech translation: UPC at IWSLT 2022. In *Proceedings of the 19th International Conference on Spoken Language Translation (IWSLT 2022)*, pages 265–276, Dublin, Ireland (in-person and online). Association for Computational Linguistics.

Changhan Wang, Morgane Riviere, Ann Lee, Anne Wu, Chaitanya Talnikar, Daniel Haziza, Mary Williamson, Juan Pino, and Emmanuel Dupoux. 2021a. VoxPopuli: A large-scale multilingual speech corpus for representation learning, semi-supervised learning and interpretation. In *Proceedings of the 59th Annual Meeting of the Association for Computational Linguistics and the 11th International Joint Conference on Natural Language Processing (Volume 1: Long Papers)*, pages 993–1003, Online. Association for Computational Linguistics.

Changhan Wang, Anne Wu, Jiatao Gu, and Juan Pino. 2021b. CoVoST 2 and Massively Multilingual Speech Translation. In *Interspeech*, pages 2247–2251.

Ron J. Weiss, Jan Chorowski, Navdeep Jaitly, Yonghui Wu, and Zhifeng Chen. 2017. Sequence-to-Sequence Models Can Directly Translate Foreign Speech. In *Interspeech*, pages 2625–2629.

Ziqiang Zhang, Sanyuan Chen, Long Zhou, Yu Wu, Shuo Ren, Shujie Liu, Zhuoyuan Yao, Xun Gong, Lirong Dai, Jinyu Li, and Furu Wei. 2022. SpeechLM: Enhanced speech pre-training with unpaired textual data. *arXiv preprint arXiv:2209.15329*.

The NiuTrans End-to-End Speech Translation System for IWSLT23 English-to-Chinese Offline Task

Yuchen Han[1]*, Xiaoqian Liu[1]*, Hao Chen[1], Yuhao Zhang[1], Chen Xu[1], Tong Xiao[1,2], Jingbo Zhu[1,2]

[1]School of Computer Science and Engineering, Northeastern University, Shenyang, China

[2]NiuTrans Research, Shenyang, China

{hanyuchen114,yoohao.zhang}@gmail.com,methanechen@126.com

{liuxiaoqian0319,xuchennlp}@outlook.com

{xiaotong,zhujingbo}@mail.neu.edu.cn

Abstract

This paper describes the NiuTrans end-to-end speech translation system submitted for the IWSLT 2023 English-to-Chinese offline task. Our speech translation models are composed of pre-trained ASR and MT models under the stacked acoustic and textual encoding framework. Several pre-trained models with diverse architectures and input representations (e.g., log Mel-filterbank and waveform) were utilized. We proposed an iterative data augmentation method to iteratively improve the performance of the MT models and generate the pseudo ST data through MT systems. We then trained ST models with different structures and data settings to enhance ensemble performance. Experimental results demonstrate that our NiuTrans system achieved a BLEU score of 29.22 on the MuST-C En-Zh tst-COMMON set, outperforming the previous year's submission by 0.12 BLEU despite using less MT training data.

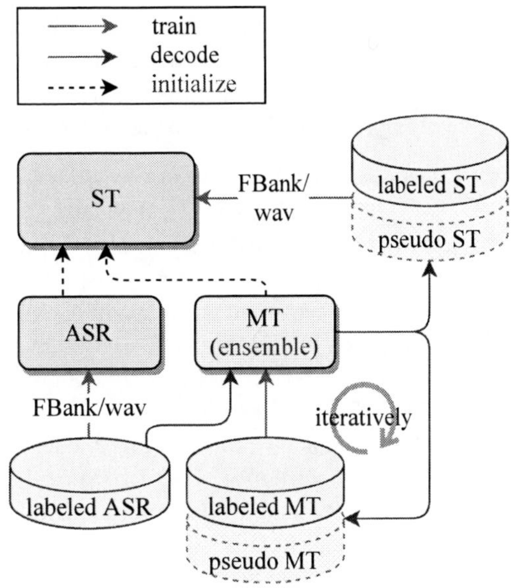

Figure 1: Overview of our system.

1 Introduction

End-to-end speech translation (E2E ST) directly translate speech in the source language into text in the target language without generating an intermediate representation, which has gained significant attention in recent years due to several advantages over cascade methods, including low latency and the ability to avoid error propagation (Berard et al., 2016; Weiss et al., 2017). In this paper, we describe our NiuTrans E2E ST system that participated in the IWSLT23 English-to-Chinese offline track, the overview of our system is shown in Fig 1.

To improve the performance of our system, we aim to maximize the diversity of our ensemble of E2E ST models. Our E2E ST models are based on the stacked acoustic and textual encoding (SATE) method (Xu et al., 2021a), which is a framework to make the best of pre-trained automatic speech recognition (ASR) and machine translation (MT) components. Using this framework, we explore multiple architectures of pre-trained ASR and MT models with varying numbers of parameters and input representations such as FBank features or waveform data.

Pseudo data is a crucial component of E2E ST, often generated by ensemble MT systems (Gaido et al., 2020). This year, we focused more on the performance of MT models and developed an Iterative Data Augmentation method to leverage text data from all corpora, improving the MT models and enabling the generation of multiple pseudo data. We then used these multiple pseudo data to train diverse E2E ST models for optimal performance. Our best ST ensemble system includes models with different input representations, architectures, and training corpora, achieving a BLEU score of 29.22 on the MuST-C En-Zh tst-COMMON set.

The remainder of the paper is organized as follows: Section 2 describes the data processing, data

*Authors contributed equally.

Proceedings of the 20th International Conference on Spoken Language Translation (IWSLT 2023), pages 211–218
July 13-14, 2023 ©2023 Association for Computational Linguistics

augmentation and speech segmentation. Section 3 outlines the construction of the vocabulary and structures of our ASR, MT and ST models. The experimental settings and final results are presented in Section 4. Finally, Section 5 concludes the submission.

2 Data

2.1 Data Processing

Our system was built under the "constrained" training condition. The training data can be divided into three categories: ASR, MT, and ST corpora. We used the NiuTrans toolkit (Xiao et al., 2012) to segment English and Chinese text in all corpora.

ASR corpora. We followed the previous work (Xu et al., 2021b) and standardized all audio samples to a single channel and a sample rate of 16,000 Hz. For the Common Voice corpus, we selected only the cleaner parts according to the CoVoST v2 En-Zh corpus. In the MuST-C v1 En-De corpus, we removed repetitive items by comparing the MuST-C v2 En-Zh transcriptions. We used the Librispeech corpus to train the ASR model and scored the Common Voice, TED LIUM, and ST TED corpus. Data with a WER greater than 0.75 were removed, and frames with lengths less than 5 or greater than 3000 were filtered. In addition, utterances with more than 400 characters were removed.

MT corpora. Following the methodology of (Zhang et al., 2020), we cleaned the parallel texts of the OpenSubtitle corpus and used fast-align to score all sentences. We averaged the scores by the sentence length and filtered out sentences with scores below -6.0. In the News Commentary v16 corpus, we used langid (Lui and Baldwin, 2012) to filter out sentences with incorrect language identification results. In the Tatoeba corpus, we converted 90% of the sentences from traditional Chinese to simplified Chinese using OpenCC[1].

ST corpora. For the MuST-C v2 En-Zh and CoVoST v2 En-zh corpus, we only filtered frames by length, similar to the ASR corpora. For the pseudo ST data, we removed sentences containing repeated n-gram words (n is 2 to 4) more than four times. Additionally, sentences with length ratios outside the range of 0.25 to 4 and those with incorrect language identification results were filtered out.

[1]https://github.com/BYVoid/OpenCC

Task	Corpus	Sentence	Hour
ASR	LibriSpeech	0.28	960
	Europarl-ST	0.03	77
	TED LIUM	0.26	448
	ST TED	0.16	235
	VoxPopuil	0.17	478
	MuST-C V1 En-De	0.07	138
	MuST-C V2 En-Zh	0.36	572
	CoVoST v2 En-Zh	0.28	416
	Total	1.61	3324
MT	News Commentary	0.31	-
	OpenSubtitle	8.62	-
	MuST-C V2 En-Zh	0.36	-
	CoVoST V2 En-Zh	0.28	-
	Tatoeba	0.05	-
	Total	9.62	-
ST	MuST-C En-Zh	0.36	572
	CoVoST V2 En-Zh	0.28	416
	Total	0.64	988

Table 1: Details about the size of all labeled corpora. The unit of sentence is million (M).

Task	Corpus	Sentence	Hour
MT	ASR corpora+MT	1.38	-
ST	ASR corpora+MT	1.61	3323
	Audio+ASR+MT	1.4e-2	3

Table 2: Details about the size of all pseudo corpora.

2.2 Data Augmentation

We only used SpecAugment (Bahar et al., 2019) and not used speed perturb for ASR data augmentation, because speed perturb requires more training resources but has the limited improvement. It is also worth noting that we did not use back translation technology in either MT or E2E ST, as there was no target-side monolingual data available.

The MT model or ensemble MT systems represent the upper limit for E2E ST. Translating the transcript in the ASR corpus into the target language using MT models is a simpler and more effective way to augment the ST corpus than generating source speech features from the source texts in the MT corpus using TTS models. Based on this, we propose an **I**terative **D**ata **A**ugmentation (IDA) method, which aims to use text data from all corpora to improve the performance of MT models and generate high-quality ST corpus iteratively, as illustrated in Algorithm 1.

We also discovered incomplete transcriptions in

a few sentences from the TED LIUM, ST-TED, and voxpupil corpus. Therefore, we generated pseudo transcriptions using the ASR model and then translated them using the best MT ensemble systems.

Algorithm 1: IDA

Input: $D_{ASR} = \{(s_{asr}, x_{asr})\}$,$D_{MT} = \{(x_{mt}, y_{mt})\}$
Output: $D^*_{ST_{aug}} = \{(s_{asr}, x_{asr}, y^{'}_{asr})\}$

$D^*_{MT} \leftarrow D_{MT}$;
$s^* \leftarrow 0$;
for $i \leftarrow 1$ **to** MAXITER **do**
  $M_1, M_2, \cdots, M_n \leftarrow \text{train}(D^*_{MT})$;
  $E^i \leftarrow \text{ensemble}(M_1, M_2, \cdots, M_n)$;
  $s^i \leftarrow \text{score}(E^i)$;
  if $i \neq 1$ *and* $s^i <= s^*$ **then**
    break;
  else
    $y^{'}_{asr} \leftarrow \text{decode}(E^i, x_{asr})$;
    $D^i_{MT_{aug}} \leftarrow \{(x_{asr}, y^{'}_{asr})\}$;
    $D^i_{ST_{aug}} \leftarrow \{(s_{asr}, x_{asr}, y^{'}_{asr})\}$;
    $D^*_{MT} \leftarrow D_{MT} \cup D^i_{MT_{aug}}$;
    $s^* \leftarrow s^i$;
return $D^*_{ST_{aug}}$;

2.3 Speech Segmentation

To avoid the significant performance drop due to the mismatch between the training and inference data, we adopted Supervised Hybrid Audio Segmentation (SHAS) (Tsiamas et al., 2022) to split long audios in the test sets. However, we did not fine-tune our models on the resegmented data, according the findings in Gaido et al. (2022).

3 Model Architecture

We explored the performances of different ASR, MT, and ST architectures and found that using larger models is more conducive to performance improvement in all three tasks.

3.1 Vocabulary

We adopted a unified vocabulary for all tasks, trained by the SentencePiece (Kudo and Richardson, 2018) model (SPM) from the MT corpora. To incorporate more subwords from the TED domain, we up-sampled the MuST-C corpus by 10x [2] in the training corpora for the SPM. The vocabulary size for English and Chinese is 10k and 44k, respectively.

3.2 ASR Models

Inspired by Zhang et al. (2022a), we used three ASR encoders with different architectures and input representations to achieve better ensemble performance.

- Transformer-HuBERT (TH): This encoder consists of 7 layers of 512-channel-CNN with strides [5,2,2,2,2,2,2] and 12 layers of Transformer (Vaswani et al., 2017). The hidden size, ffn size, and number of heads are 768, 3072, and 8, respectively. This architecture takes waveform data as input.

- Conformer-PDS-Medium (CPM): This encoder consists of 18 layers of Conformer (Gulati et al., 2020) with progressive downsampling (PDS) methods (Xu et al., 2023). The hidden size, ffn size, and number of heads are 512, 2048, and 8, respectively. This architecture takes log Mel-filterbank features as input.

- Conformer-PDS-Deep (CPD): This encoder is the same as the Conformer-PDS-Medium, but with the number of layers adjusted from 18 to 24.

Due to limited computational resources, we pretrained the Transformer-HuBERT only on the Librispeech corpus using the method outlined in Hsu et al. (2021). The Conformer-PDS-Medium/Deep architectures were trained on all ASR corpora, and we employed an additional decoder with 6 layers to utilize the Cross Entropy loss. We also adopted CTC loss (Graves et al., 2006) and inter-CTC loss (Lee and Watanabe, 2021) to accelerate the convergence.

3.3 MT Models

While deep models have shown success in translation tasks, we observed that wider architectures with more parameters generally yield superior performance (Shan et al., 2022). As such, we selected the DLCL Transformer (Wang et al., 2019) and the ODE Transformer (Li et al., 2022) for the deep and wide models, respectively.

[2] Specifically, we created 10 copies of the MuST-C corpus and combined them with additional MT data.

- DLCL: This model consists of 30 layers of Transformer encoder and 6 layers of Transformer decoder with dynamic linear combination of layers and relative position encoding (Shaw et al., 2018) methods. The hidden size, ffn size, and number of heads are 512, 2048, and 8, respectively.
- ODE: This model consists of 12 layers of Transformer encoder and 6 layers of Transformer decoder with an ordinary differential equation-inspired method, which has been proven to be efficient in parameters. The hidden size, ffn size, and number of heads are 1024, 4096, and 16, respectively.
- ODE-Deep: This model is the same as ODE but with the number of encoder layers adjusted from 12 to 18.

Since the transcript in the ASR corpora lacks punctuation and is in lower-case, we lowered-cased and removed punctuation from the source text of the MT corpora for consistency before training the MT models. While this operation may have a negative impact on MT performance, we have demonstrated its usefulness for data augmentation and the final ST performance in Section 4.3.

3.4 ST Models

We utilized the SATE method to enhance the usage of pre-trained ASR and MT models for the ST task. Specifically, we decoupled the ST encoder into an acoustic encoder and a textual encoder, with an adapter in between. The pre-trained ASR encoder was used to initialize the acoustic encoder, while the pre-trained MT model was used to initialize the textual encoder and decoder. To optimize performance with limited memory, we successively attempted multiple structures, ranging from small to large, as presented in Table 3. The models with TH-DLCL structure were trained using the techniques outlined in Zhang et al. (2022b).

Structure	ASR	MT	Params.
TH-DLCL	TH	DLCL	251M
CPM-DLCL	CPM	DLCL	289M
CPM-ODE	CPM	ODE	444M
CPD-ODE	CPD	ODE	472M

Table 3: The ST structures initialized with different ASR and MT models under the SATE framework.

Model	dev	tst-M	test-clean	test-other
CPM	5.01	4.17	2.81	6.51
CPD	4.76	4.25	2.86	6.10

Table 4: WER scores on the dev, tst-COMMON (tst-M), and test sets of Librispeech.

4 Experiments

4.1 Experimental settings

All experiments were implemented using the Fairseq toolkit (Ott et al., 2019). We trained all models using pre-norm and utilized dropout with a ratio ranging from 0.1 to 0.3 and label smoothing with 0.1 to prevent overfitting. Training was stopped early when the indicators on the dev set did not improve for 5 consecutive times. During decoding, we averaged the best 5 or 10 models in the dev set in all tasks. For single models, we set the beam size and length penalty to 5 and 1.0, respectively, while for ensemble systems we used different values adapted from our test sets. The MT and ST models were evaluated using SacreBLEU (Post, 2018), while the ASR models were evaluated using WER. All the models were trained on 8 NVIDIA 3090 or 8 TITAN RTX GPUs.

4.2 ASR

Table 4 presents the ASR results. We observed that the deeper model performed better in confronting noise test sets (dev set of MuST-C and test-other), but it also overfitted in some test sets (tst-COMMON and test-clean). We did not calculate the WER of Transformer-HuBERT because it was only pre-trained as a feature extractor and was not fine-tuned for speech recognition tasks.

4.3 MT and IDA

Table 5 shows the MT and IDA results on the test sets of MuST-C and CoVoST. We found that pre-training on all the MT corpora and fine-tuning on the in-domain corpora can improve performance. Fine-tuning on both MuST-C and CoVoST together is better than only on MuST-C corpus (ODE1 vs. ODE2). It is worth noting that fine-tuning not only improves the performance of in-domain test sets, but also enhances the performance on out-domain test sets, such as the test set of WMT21-news (not included in this paper for simplicity).

We found that both DLCL and ODE models outperformed our baseline, which was a Transformer-Base model with fewer parameters. Additionally,

Model	Pre-train		Fine-tune	
	tst-M	tst-C	tst-M	tst-C
Baseline$^{\diamond\dagger}$	28.20	50.98	28.96	50.18
-	-	-	26.25	46.27
Baseline†	26.99	49.12	28.04	49.49
DLCL1	27.68	50.66	28.62	54.12
ODE1†	28.28	51.67	28.56	51.09
ODE2	-	-	29.03	55.28
ODE3	28.17	50.98	29.06	54.41
E^1: ensemble (above four)			**29.61**	**56.20**
DLCL2	29.12	53.95	29.46	55.24
ODE4	29.27	54.31	29.56	55.47
ODE-Deep1	29.39	54.21	29.36	55.47
ODE-Deep2	29.44	54.28	29.47	55.71
E^2: ensemble (above four)			**30.02**	**57.18**

Table 5: BLEU scores on the tst-COMMON (tst-M) and the test set of CoVoST (tst-C). All data are in lower case. Models marked with $^{\diamond}$ indicate that the punctuation of the source text in corpora for pre-training, fine-tuning and testing was kept. The † means that only the MuST-C corpus was used in fine-tuning.

ID	Model	Data	tst-M	tst-C
1	Baseline	M	23.09	-
2	TH-DLCL2	P^2	27.50	41.94
3	CPM-DLCL1	P^1	28.37	44.20
4	CPM-DLCL2	P^1	28.44	45.58
5	CPM-DLCL2	P^2	28.57	45.98
6	CPM-ODE4	P^1	28.72	46.76
7	CPM-ODE4	P^2	29.00	47.15
8	CPD-ODE4	P^1	28.79	47.18
9	CPD-ODE4	P^2	29.01	47.65
10	ensemble (7,9)		29.07	48.67
11	ensemble (2,7,9)		29.11	48.88
12	ensemble (2,7,8,9)		29.16	48.98
13	+adjusted beam/alpha		**29.22**	**49.27**

Table 6: BLEU scores on the tst-COMMON (tst-M) and the test set of CoVoST (tst-C). M refers to the MuST-C corpus, C refers to the CoVoST corpus, and P^i refers to $M\&C\&D^i_{ST_{aug}}$. The models with different parameters are separated by the dotted line.

we demonstrated that although models trained on the corpora with punctuation perform better on test sets including punctuation (28.96 vs. 28.04), they do not perform as well on test sets without punctuation (26.25 vs. 28.04), which is more consistent with the situation of the ASR transcript.

Since each round of iteration in IDA requires retraining multiple MT models, we set the MAX-ITER parameter in IDA to 2 to balance computing resources and model performance. We observed that models trained during the second iteration outperformed those trained during the first iteration. During the second iteration, we found that further increasing the number of parameters resulted in limited improvement (ODE4 vs. ODE-Deep1/2). Additionally, iterative training resulted in a considerable improvement in ensemble systems (from 29.61 to 30.02). Finally, we employed the ensemble systems E^1 and E^2 to generate the pseudo data $D^1_{ST_{aug}}$ and $D^2_{ST_{aug}}$ for ST, respectively.

4.4 ST and Ensemble

Table 6 displays the ST results on the test sets of MuST-C and CoVoST. In contrast to MT, we did not use in-domain fine-tuning, as we found in the pre-experiments that it did not improve performance and may even have caused some damage.

Experiments 1-9 demonstrated that increasing the number of parameters, initializing with better pre-trained models, and training with higher-quality pseudo ST corpora were all effective ways for enhancing the performance of the ST model. These modifications resulted in a significant improvement over the baseline model, which has 32M parameters and was trained solely on the MuST-C dataset.

In the ensemble stage, we aimed to maximize the diversity between models. To achieve this, we selected models with different input representations, architectures, and training corpora. Finally, by expanding the beam size and adjusting the length penalty (alpha), we achieved a BLEU score of 29.22 on tst-COMMON sets, which represents a 0.12 BLEU improvement over our optimal result from the previous year, despite using less MT training data than last year (Agarwal et al., 2023).

5 Conclusion

This paper presented our submission to the IWSLT23 English-to-Chinese offline speech translation task. Our system aimed to find the optimal ensemble system under the "constrained" training condition. To achieve this goal, we explored different input representations, model architectures, and proposed an IDA method to utilize all available texts to improve the MT systems and generate multiple pseudo ST data. Our final system achieved a BLEU score of 29.22 on the MuST-C En-Zh tst-COMMON set, and the results on the IWSLT 23 test sets are shown in Table 7.

System	TED					ACL	
	Comet		BLEU			Comet	BLEU
Ref	2	1	2	1	both		
NiuTrans	0.8376	0.7740	50.0	34.3	57.9	0.7733	47.1

Table 7: Scores on the IWSLT23 test sets.

Acknowledgement

The authors would like to thank anonymous reviewers for their insightful comments. This work was supported in part by the National Science Foundation of China (No. 62276056), the National Key R&D Program of China, the China HTRD Center Project (No. 2020AAA0107904), the Natural Science Foundation of Liaoning Province of China (2022-KF-16-01), the Yunnan Provincial Major Science and Technology Special Plan Projects (No. 202103AA080015), the Fundamental Research Funds for the Central Universities (Nos. N2216016, N2216001, and N2216002), and the Program of Introducing Talents of Discipline to Universities, Plan 111 (No. B16009).

References

Milind Agarwal, Sweta Agrawal, Antonios Anastasopoulos, Ondřej Bojar, Claudia Borg, Marine Carpuat, Roldano Cattoni, Mauro Cettolo, Mingda Chen, William Chen, Khalid Choukri, Alexandra Chronopoulou, Anna Currey, Thierry Declerck, Qianqian Dong, Yannick Estève, Kevin Duh, Marcello Federico, Souhir Gahbiche, Barry Haddow, Benjamin Hsu, Phu Mon Htut, Hirofumi Inaguma, Dávid Javorský, John Judge, Yasumasa Kano, Tom Ko, Rishu Kumar, Pengwei Li, Xutail Ma, Prashant Mathur, Evgeny Matusov, Paul McNamee, John P. McCrae, Kenton Murray, Maria Nadejde, Satoshi Nakamura, Matteo Negri, Ha Nguyen, Jan Niehues, Xing Niu, Atul Ojha Kr., John E. Ortega, Proyag Pal, Juan Pino, Lonneke van der Plas, Peter Polák, Elijah Rippeth, Elizabeth Salesky, Jiatong Shi, Matthias Sperber, Sebastian Stüker, Katsuhito Sudoh, Yun Tang, Brian Thompson, Kevin Tran, Marco Turchi, Alex Waibel, Mingxuan Wang, Shinji Watanabe, and Rodolfo Zevallos. 2023. Findings of the IWSLT 2023 Evaluation Campaign. In *Proceedings of the 20th International Conference on Spoken Language Translation (IWSLT 2023)*. Association for Computational Linguistics.

Parnia Bahar, Albert Zeyer, Ralf Schlüter, and Hermann Ney. 2019. On using specaugment for end-to-end speech translation. In *Proceedings of the 16th International Conference on Spoken Language Translation, IWSLT 2019, Hong Kong, November 2-3, 2019*. Association for Computational Linguistics.

Alexandre Berard, Olivier Pietquin, Christophe Servan, and Laurent Besacier. 2016. Listen and translate: A proof of concept for end-to-end speech-to-text translation. *CoRR*, abs/1612.01744.

Marco Gaido, Mattia Antonino Di Gangi, Matteo Negri, and Marco Turchi. 2020. End-to-end speech-translation with knowledge distillation: Fbk@iwslt2020. In *Proceedings of the 17th International Conference on Spoken Language Translation, IWSLT 2020, Online, July 9 - 10, 2020*, pages 80–88. Association for Computational Linguistics.

Marco Gaido, Sara Papi, Dennis Fucci, Giuseppe Fiameni, Matteo Negri, and Marco Turchi. 2022. Efficient yet competitive speech translation: Fbk@iwslt2022. In *Proceedings of the 19th International Conference on Spoken Language Translation, IWSLT@ACL 2022, Dublin, Ireland (in-person and online), May 26-27, 2022*, pages 177–189. Association for Computational Linguistics.

Alex Graves, Santiago Fernández, Faustino J. Gomez, and Jürgen Schmidhuber. 2006. Connectionist temporal classification: labelling unsegmented sequence data with recurrent neural networks. In *Machine Learning, Proceedings of the Twenty-Third International Conference (ICML 2006), Pittsburgh, Pennsylvania, USA, June 25-29, 2006*, volume 148 of *ACM International Conference Proceeding Series*, pages 369–376. ACM.

Anmol Gulati, James Qin, Chung-Cheng Chiu, Niki Parmar, Yu Zhang, Jiahui Yu, Wei Han, Shibo Wang, Zhengdong Zhang, Yonghui Wu, and Ruoming Pang. 2020. Conformer: Convolution-augmented transformer for speech recognition. In *Interspeech 2020, 21st Annual Conference of the International Speech Communication Association, Virtual Event, Shanghai, China, 25-29 October 2020*, pages 5036–5040. ISCA.

Wei-Ning Hsu, Benjamin Bolte, Yao-Hung Hubert Tsai, Kushal Lakhotia, Ruslan Salakhutdinov, and Abdelrahman Mohamed. 2021. Hubert: Self-supervised speech representation learning by masked prediction of hidden units. *IEEE ACM Trans. Audio Speech Lang. Process.*, 29:3451–3460.

Taku Kudo and John Richardson. 2018. Sentencepiece: A simple and language independent subword tokenizer and detokenizer for neural text processing. In *Proceedings of the 2018 Conference on Empirical Methods in Natural Language Processing, EMNLP 2018: System Demonstrations, Brussels, Belgium, October 31 - November 4, 2018*, pages 66–71. Association for Computational Linguistics.

Jaesong Lee and Shinji Watanabe. 2021. Intermediate loss regularization for ctc-based speech recognition. In *IEEE International Conference on Acoustics, Speech and Signal Processing, ICASSP 2021, Toronto, ON, Canada, June 6-11, 2021*, pages 6224–6228. IEEE.

Bei Li, Quan Du, Tao Zhou, Yi Jing, Shuhan Zhou, Xin Zeng, Tong Xiao, Jingbo Zhu, Xuebo Liu, and Min

Zhang. 2022. ODE transformer: An ordinary differential equation-inspired model for sequence generation. In *Proceedings of the 60th Annual Meeting of the Association for Computational Linguistics (Volume 1: Long Papers), ACL 2022, Dublin, Ireland, May 22-27, 2022*, pages 8335–8351. Association for Computational Linguistics.

Marco Lui and Timothy Baldwin. 2012. langid.py: An off-the-shelf language identification tool. In *The 50th Annual Meeting of the Association for Computational Linguistics, Proceedings of the System Demonstrations, July 10, 2012, Jeju Island, Korea*, pages 25–30. The Association for Computer Linguistics.

Myle Ott, Sergey Edunov, Alexei Baevski, Angela Fan, Sam Gross, Nathan Ng, David Grangier, and Michael Auli. 2019. fairseq: A fast, extensible toolkit for sequence modeling. In *Proceedings of the 2019 Conference of the North American Chapter of the Association for Computational Linguistics: Human Language Technologies, NAACL-HLT 2019, Minneapolis, MN, USA, June 2-7, 2019, Demonstrations*, pages 48–53. Association for Computational Linguistics.

Matt Post. 2018. A call for clarity in reporting BLEU scores. In *Proceedings of the Third Conference on Machine Translation: Research Papers, WMT 2018, Belgium, Brussels, October 31 - November 1, 2018*, pages 186–191. Association for Computational Linguistics.

Weiqiao Shan, Zhiquan Cao, Yuchen Han, Siming Wu, Yimin Hu, Jie Wang, Yi Zhang, Hou Baoyu, Hang Cao, Chenghao Gao, Xiaowen Liu, Tong Xiao, Anxiang Ma, and Jingbo Zhu. 2022. The niutrans machine translation systems for WMT22. In *Proceedings of the Seventh Conference on Machine Translation, WMT 2022, Abu Dhabi, United Arab Emirates (Hybrid), December 7-8, 2022*, pages 366–374. Association for Computational Linguistics.

Peter Shaw, Jakob Uszkoreit, and Ashish Vaswani. 2018. Self-attention with relative position representations. In *Proceedings of the 2018 Conference of the North American Chapter of the Association for Computational Linguistics: Human Language Technologies, NAACL-HLT, New Orleans, Louisiana, USA, June 1-6, 2018, Volume 2 (Short Papers)*, pages 464–468. Association for Computational Linguistics.

Ioannis Tsiamas, Gerard I. Gállego, José A. R. Fonollosa, and Marta R. Costa-jussà. 2022. SHAS: approaching optimal segmentation for end-to-end speech translation. In *Interspeech 2022, 23rd Annual Conference of the International Speech Communication Association, Incheon, Korea, 18-22 September 2022*, pages 106–110. ISCA.

Ashish Vaswani, Noam Shazeer, Niki Parmar, Jakob Uszkoreit, Llion Jones, Aidan N. Gomez, Lukasz Kaiser, and Illia Polosukhin. 2017. Attention is all you need. In *Advances in Neural Information Processing Systems 30: Annual Conference on Neural Information Processing Systems 2017, December 4-9, 2017, Long Beach, CA, USA*, pages 5998–6008.

Qiang Wang, Bei Li, Tong Xiao, Jingbo Zhu, Changliang Li, Derek F. Wong, and Lidia S. Chao. 2019. Learning deep transformer models for machine translation. In *Proceedings of the 57th Conference of the Association for Computational Linguistics, ACL 2019, Florence, Italy, July 28- August 2, 2019, Volume 1: Long Papers*, pages 1810–1822. Association for Computational Linguistics.

Ron J. Weiss, Jan Chorowski, Navdeep Jaitly, Yonghui Wu, and Zhifeng Chen. 2017. Sequence-to-sequence models can directly translate foreign speech. In *Interspeech 2017, 18th Annual Conference of the International Speech Communication Association, Stockholm, Sweden, August 20-24, 2017*, pages 2625–2629. ISCA.

Tong Xiao, Jingbo Zhu, Hao Zhang, and Qiang Li. 2012. Niutrans: An open source toolkit for phrase-based and syntax-based machine translation. In *The 50th Annual Meeting of the Association for Computational Linguistics, Proceedings of the System Demonstrations, July 10, 2012, Jeju Island, Korea*, pages 19–24. The Association for Computer Linguistics.

Chen Xu, Bojie Hu, Yanyang Li, Yuhao Zhang, Shen Huang, Qi Ju, Tong Xiao, and Jingbo Zhu. 2021a. Stacked acoustic-and-textual encoding: Integrating the pre-trained models into speech translation encoders. In *Proceedings of the 59th Annual Meeting of the Association for Computational Linguistics and the 11th International Joint Conference on Natural Language Processing, ACL/IJCNLP 2021, (Volume 1: Long Papers), Virtual Event, August 1-6, 2021*, pages 2619–2630. Association for Computational Linguistics.

Chen Xu, Xiaoqian Liu, Xiaowen Liu, Laohu Wang, Canan Huang, Tong Xiao, and Jingbo Zhu. 2021b. The niutrans end-to-end speech translation system for IWSLT 2021 offline task. In *Proceedings of the 18th International Conference on Spoken Language Translation, IWSLT 2021, Bangkok, Thailand (online), August 5-6, 2021*, pages 92–99. Association for Computational Linguistics.

Chen Xu, Yuhao Zhang, Chengbo Jiao, Xiaoqian Liu, Chi Hu, Xin Zeng, Tong Xiao, Anxiang Ma, Huizhen Wang, and Jingbo Zhu. 2023. Bridging the granularity gap for acoustic modeling. In *Findings of the Association for Computational Linguistics: ACL 2023*. Association for Computational Linguistics.

Yuhao Zhang, Canan Huang, Chen Xu, Xiaoqian Liu, Bei Li, Anxiang Ma, Tong Xiao, and Jingbo Zhu. 2022a. The niutrans's submission to the IWSLT22 english-to-chinese offline speech translation task. In *Proceedings of the 19th International Conference on Spoken Language Translation, IWSLT@ACL 2022, Dublin, Ireland (in-person and online), May 26-27, 2022*, pages 232–238. Association for Computational Linguistics.

Yuhao Zhang, Ziyang Wang, Runzhe Cao, Binghao Wei, Weiqiao Shan, Shuhan Zhou, Abudurexiti Reheman,

Tao Zhou, Xin Zeng, Laohu Wang, Yongyu Mu, Jingnan Zhang, Xiaoqian Liu, Xuanjun Zhou, Yinqiao Li, Bei Li, Tong Xiao, and Jingbo Zhu. 2020. The niutrans machine translation systems for WMT20. In *Proceedings of the Fifth Conference on Machine Translation, WMT@EMNLP 2020, Online, November 19-20, 2020*, pages 338–345. Association for Computational Linguistics.

Yuhao Zhang, Chen Xu, Bojie Hu, Chunliang Zhang, Tong Xiao, and Jingbo Zhu. 2022b. Improving end-to-end speech translation by leveraging auxiliary speech and text data. *CoRR*, abs/2212.01778.

ON-TRAC consortium systems for the IWSLT 2023 dialectal and low-resource speech translation tasks

Antoine Laurent[1], **Souhir Gahbiche**[5], **Ha Nguyen**[2], **Haroun Elleuch**[4], **Fethi Bougares**[4], **Antoine Thiol**[5], **Hugo Riguidel**[1,3], **Salima Mdhaffar**[2], **Gaëlle Laperrière**[2], **Lucas Maison**[2], **Sameer Khurana**[6], **Yannick Estève**[2]

[1]LIUM - Le Mans University, France, [2]LIA - Avignon University, France, [3]Systran - France, [4]ELYADATA - Tunis, Tunisia, [5]Airbus - France, [6]MIT Computer Science and Artificial Intelligence Laboratory, Cambridge, MA, USA

Abstract

This paper describes the ON-TRAC consortium speech translation systems developed for IWSLT 2023 evaluation campaign. Overall, we participated in three speech translation tracks featured in the low-resource and dialect speech translation shared tasks, namely; i) spoken Tamasheq to written French, ii) spoken Pashto to written French, and iii) spoken Tunisian to written English. All our primary submissions are based on the end-to-end speech-to-text neural architecture using a pre-trained SAMU-XLSR model as a speech encoder and an mbart model as a decoder. The SAMU-XLSR model is built from the XLS-R 128 in order to generate language agnostic sentence-level embeddings. This building is driven by the LaBSE model trained on a multilingual text dataset. This architecture allows us to improve the input speech representations and achieve significant improvements compared to conventional end-to-end speech translation systems.

1 Introduction

IWSLT is a unique opportunity that allows each year the assessment of progress made in the area of Spoken Language Translation (SLT). This assessment is made possible throughout the organisation of an evaluation campaign including various shared tasks that address specific scientific challenges of the SLT domain. In addition to the well-established shared tasks, IWSLT organisers introduce new tasks to address the many challenges settings related to SLT area like data scarcity, multilingualism, time and computation constraints, etc.

In this context, the IWSLT 2023 proposes two interesting shared tasks: low-resource and dialect speech translation (ST). The former aims to assess the exploitability of current translation systems in data scarcity settings. The latter focuses on the assessment of the systems' capabilities in *noisy* settings: different dialects are mixed in a single dataset of spontaneous speech. For the low-resource task, several language pairs were proposed this year. In this paper, we focus on Tamasheq-French, Tunisian Arabic-English and Pashto-French.

This paper reports the ON-TRAC consortium submissions for the aforementioned tasks. The ON-TRAC Consortium is composed of researchers from three academic laboratories, LIUM (Le Mans University - France), LIA (Avignon University - France), MIT (Cambridge - USA) together with three industrial partners: Airbus France, ELYADATA and Systran. Our systems for the dialect task focus on both cascaded and end-to-end approaches for ST. For the low-resource task, we focus on the leveraging of models based on self-supervised learning (SSL), and on the training of ST models with joint automatic speech recognition (ASR), machine translation (MT) and ST losses.

This paper is organized as follows. Section 2 presents the related work. Section 3 is dedicated to detail our primary systems encoder-decoder approach. The experiments with the Tunisian Arabic-English dataset for low-resource and dialect ST tasks are presented in Section 4. Results for the Tamasheq-French and Pashto-French tracks are presented in Section 5 and 6 respectively. Section 7 concludes the paper and discusses future work.

2 Related work

Before the introduction of *direct* or *end-to-end* ST models (Berard et al., 2016; Weiss et al., 2017), the ST task was approached as a *cascaded* problem: the speech is transcribed using an ASR model, and the transcriptions are used to train a classic MT model. The limitations of this approach include the need for extensive transcriptions of the speech signal, and the error propagation between ASR and MT modules. In comparison to that, end-to-end ST models offer a simpler encoder-decoder architecture, removing the need for intermediate representations of the speech signal. Although at first, cas-

Proceedings of the 20th International Conference on Spoken Language Translation (IWSLT 2023), pages 219–226
July 13-14, 2023 ©2023 Association for Computational Linguistics

caded models were superior in performance compared to end-to-end models, results from recent IWSLT campaigns illustrate how end-to-end models have been closing this gap (Ansari et al., 2020; Bentivogli et al., 2021; Anastasopoulos et al., 2021, 2022). Moreover, the joint optimization of ASR, MT and ST losses in end-to-end ST models was shown to increase overall performance (Le et al., 2020; Sperber et al., 2020).

Furthermore, SSL models for speech processing are now a popular foundation blocks in speech pipelines (Schneider et al., 2019; Hsu et al., 2021; Baevski et al., 2019, 2020). These models are large trainable networks with millions, or even billions (Babu et al., 2021b), of parameters that are trained on unlabeled audio data only. The goal of training these models is providing a powerful and reusable abstraction block, which is able to process raw audio in a given language or in multilingual settings (Conneau et al., 2020; Babu et al., 2021b), producing a richer audio representation for the downstream tasks to train with, compared to surface features such as MFCCs or filterbanks. Recent work found considerable performance gains and/or state-of-the-art performance by including these blocks in their target tasks, and more importantly, the final models can be trained with a smaller amount of labeled data, increasing the *accessibility* of current approaches for speech processing (Kawakami et al., 2020; Schneider et al., 2019; Hsu et al., 2021; Baevski et al., 2019, 2020).[1] Recent work found considerable performance gains and/or state-of-the-art performance by including these blocks in downstream tasks. Most of them focused on ASR (Kawakami et al., 2020; Schneider et al., 2019; Hsu et al., 2021; Baevski et al., 2019, 2020), but recent speech benchmarks (Evain et al., 2021b,a; Yang et al., 2021) cover tasks such as ST, spoken language understanding, emotion recognition from speech and more.

3 Primary systems encoder-decoder architecture

3.1 SAMU-XLS-R (`SAMU−XLS−R`)

`SAMU−XLS−R` is a multilingual multimodal semantic speech representation learning framework where the speech transformer encoder `XLS−R` (Babu et al., 2021a) is fine-tuned using semantic supervision from the pre-trained multilingual semantic text encoder `LaBSE` (Feng et al., 2022). The training and modeling details can be found in the original paper (Khurana et al., 2022). In this work, we use the same training framework but train the model using transcribed speech collected from approximately 100 spoken languages from several datasets such as CommonVoice-v10 (Ardila et al., 2020a), Multilingual Speech (MLS) (Pratap et al., 2020), Babel, IndicSuperb (Javed et al., 2022), Shrutilipi (Bhogale et al., 2023), Voxpopuli (Wang et al., 2021), MGB-2 Arabic (Ali et al., 2019) and Wenetspeech (Zhang et al., 2022).

3.2 Translation model

We use the standard encoder-decoder architecture for our translation model. We initialize the encoder using the pre-trained `SAMU−XLS−R`. Following (Li et al., 2020), the decoder is initialized with the decoder of a pre-trained text-to-text translation model, namely `MBART`[2]. The encoder-decoder model is trained using corpora that consist of tuples $(\mathbf{a}_{1:S}, \mathbf{y}_{1:L})$, where $\mathbf{y}_{1:L}$ is the text translation sequence of the speech sequence $\mathbf{a}_{1:S}$.

To maintain the pre-trained `SAMU−XLS−R` values of the speech encoder, we leave its parameters unchanged. However, we introduce task-specific parameters in the form of adapters (Houlsby et al., 2019), consisting of a bottleneck Feed-Forward layer, which are added after the Multi-Headed Self-Attention and fully-connected blocks in each transformer layer. While most parameters of the decoder remain fixed from pre-training, we fine-tune the Layer Normalization and Encoder-Decoder Cross-Attention blocks based on (Li et al., 2020).

4 Tunisian Arabic-English track

In this section, we present our experiments for translating Tunisian Arabic to English in the context of the dialect and low-resource tasks from IWSLT 2023. Section 4.1 describes the data used in our experiments. Results on the ST task are presented in Section 4.3.

4.1 Data

The training and development data conditions are identical to IWSLT 2022 edition. It consisted of two types of datasets: (1) 383h of manually transcribed conversational speech and (2) 160h, subpart of it, augmented with their English translations to form a three-way parallel corpus (audio, transcript,

[1] Recent benchmarks for SSL models can be found in Evain et al. (2021b,a); Yang et al. (2021); Conneau et al. (2022).

[2] Text-to-text translation model: MBART

translation). This dataset is made available by LDC under reference LDC2022E01. The goal of this track is to train speech translation systems under two training conditions: constrained, in which only the provided dataset resources are allowed, and unconstrained where participants may use any public or private resources.

4.2 End-to-end ST

We used the end-to-end translation model presented in section 3.2. The model was trained directly on the Tunisian to English task (no pre-training of the encoder-decoder model), using SAMU−XLS−R trained on 100 languages. We used adapters (Houlsby et al., 2019) inside the encoder to keep the semantic information while fine-tuning.

4.3 Results

Table 1 presents our ST results for the Tunisian to English Dialectal and Low-resource track. Our primary system obtained a BLEU of 20.7 on our validation set. As shown in the tables, the official evaluation scores appear to be low compared to the good result obtained on the validation set. We suspect that our test submission was not conform to the evaluation specifications. We speculate that this difference between validation and test scores is due to the fact we did not remove the punctuation nor the disfluencies tokens from the case-sensitive translation we submitted, while the evaluation is made lowercase and no punctuation. We mistakenly expected this normalization step to be applied by the organizers instead of the participant. We were able to ask the organizers to evaluate our normalized output after the evaluation period. The results are reported in Table 1. Test2 refers to the IWSLT 2022 evaluation campaign test, and test3 refers to the one of IWSLT 2023. This normalization before the training of our translation model is expected to further improve our results because we believe that the post-deadline fix more accurately reflects our system's true performance.

System	Description	valid	test2	test3
primary	SAMU−XLS−R 100	20.7	9.6	8.8
post-deadline fix	SAMU−XLS−R 100	20.7	18.2	16.3

Table 1: Results for Tunisian Arabic to English translation systems in terms of %BLEU for low-resource (LR)track.

5 Tamasheq-French Experiments

In this section we present our experiments for the Tamasheq-French dataset in the context of the low-resource ST track.

5.1 Data

This dataset, recently introduced in Boito et al. (2022), contains 14 h of speech in the Tamasheq language for the training split which corresponds to 4,444 utterances translated to French. The development set contains 581 utterances (a little bit less than 2 h of speech), the 2022 test set contains 804 utterances (approximatively 2 h of speech). The 2023 test set contains 374 utterances (approximatively 1 h of speech). Additional audio data was also made available through the *Niger-Mali audio collection*: 224 h in Tamasheq and 417 h in geographically close languages (French from Niger, Fulfulde, Hausa, and Zarma).[3] For all this data, the speech style is radio broadcasting, and the dataset presents no transcription.

5.2 Models

For the Tamasheq to French task, we performed several experiments. First of all, we did the same experiment that was done for Pashto-French and Tunisian-English tasks. We used the end-to-end translation model presented in section 3.2, directly trained on the Tamasheq→French task. Directly means that we used SAMU−XLS−R-xx (xx corresponds to the number of languages in the training set, equals to 53, 60 and 100) to initialise the encoder and performed the training of the encoder-decoder model using the Tamasheq→French training set.

We used the CoVoST-2 (Wang et al., 2020) $\mathcal{X}\rightarrow$EN speech-translation dataset in which we translated the EN text into French (using Mbart Many-to-Many). Additionally, we exploited the Europarl benchmark, which comprises 72 translation tasks (denoted as $\mathcal{X}\rightarrow\mathcal{Y}$), with the source language set ($\mathcal{X}$) consisting of nine languages: FR, DE, ES, IT, PL, PT, RO, NL, and EN. The target language set ($\mathcal{Y}$) is equivalent to the source language set. For the specific training data distribution of each of the 72 translation tasks, refer to (Iranzo-Sánchez et al., 2019).

We trained a translation model using CoVost-2 X→FR,EN and Europarl X→FR, namely models

[3] https://demo-lia.univ-avignon.fr/studios-tamani-kalangou/

System	Description	valid	test 2023
primary	samu100l[cv2_xx→(en,fr)+europarl_xx→fr] + test22	21.39	16.00
contrastive1	samu100l[cv2_xx→(en,fr)+europarl_xx→fr]	**21.41**	**16.52**
contrastive2	samu60l[cv2_xx→(en,fr)+europarl_xx→fr] + test22	20.80	15.84
contrastive3	samu60l[cv2_xx→(en,fr)+europarl_xx→fr]	20.66	15.35
contrastive4	samu100l continue training + test22	21.39	16.30
contrastive5	samu100l continue training	20.78	15.60
baseline	best system from IWSLT2022	8.34	5.70

Table 2: Results of the Tamasheq-French ST systems in terms of BLEU score.

samu60l[cv2_xx→(en,fr)+europarl_xx→fr] and samu100l[cv2_xx→(en,fr)+europarl_xx→fr]). We also translated the French translation of the Tamasheq speech into Spanish, Portuguese and English (still using MBart Many to Many).

Using the pre-trained models, we trained a translation model from Tamasheq to French, Spanish, English and Portugese. We added the 2022 test set inside the training corpus for the Primary model.

Moreover, we used the last checkpoint of the `SAMU−XLS−R` training (100 languages) and pushed further the training using the `LaBSE` embeddings of the translations of the Tamasheq into French, Spanish, English and Portuguese. Then using the specialized Tamasheq `SAMU−XLS−R`, we trained a Tamasheq to French, Spanish, English, Portuguese model.

5.3 Results

Table 2 presents our ST results for the Tamasheq to French task. Our first contrastive model performed better than the Primary model (16.52 for the contrastive model compare to 16.00 for the primary model). This was unexpected because the 2022 test set was added inside the training corpus for the Primary model and not in the contrastive one. The constrative4 and contrastive5 performances (in which we push the training of the `SAMU−XLS−R`-100 model further) are very close to the primary and contrastive1 (16.30 BLEU vs 16.52 BLEU).

We did not use the 224 hours of unlabelled data. We could probably get better results by using pseudo-labelling using our best model and then using the translation for the training of the translation model. Another direction could be the use of another decoder like the recently proposed NLLB model (Costa-jussà et al., 2022).

6 Pashto-French Experiments

In this section, we present our experiments for the first edition of translating Pashto speech to French in the context of the low-resource ST track for IWSLT 2023.

6.1 Data

The Pashto-French dataset used in our experiments was provided by ELDA. This dataset is available in the ELRA catalog, *TRAD Pashto Broadcast News Speech Corpus* (ELRA catalogue, 2016b) concern audio files and *TRAD Pashto-French Parallel corpus of transcribed Broadcast News Speech - Training data* (ELRA catalogue, 2016a) are their transcriptions.

This dataset is a collection of about 108 hours of Broadcast News with transcriptions in Pashto and translations in French text. Dataset is build from collected recordings from 5 sources: Ashna TV, Azadi Radio, Deewa Radio, Mashaal Radio and Shamshad TV. Training data contains 99h of speech in Pashto, which corresponds to 29,447 utterances translated into French.

We participated for Pashto to French task for both types of submissions: constrained and unconstrained conditions. For constrained conditions, systems are trained only on the dataset provided by the organizers, while for unconstrained conditions, systems can be trained with any resource, including pre-trained models.

We investigate two types of ST architectures: end-to-end architectures 6.2, and pipeline 6.3 models.

6.2 Pipeline models

For the cascaded approach, i.e. the task of using an ASR model followed by a MT model, we focused on Wav2Vec2.0 (Baevski et al., 2020) as a Speech-to-Text system. The architecture used is Wav2Vec2-

XLSR-53 (Conneau et al., 2020), a large version of Wav2Vec2 pre-trained on the multilingual dataset Common-Voice (Ardila et al., 2020b). Once adding a language modeling head on top of the model for fine-tuning on the Pashto dataset, we observed a score of less than 20% of WER and a good modeling of the reference language since the difference of the scores for translating written Pashto to written French when using either the reference or the generated Pashto text, was always less than 0.5 of BLEU. For the MT system, we tested multiple approaches using auto regressive Sequence-2-Sequence models.

We mainly focused on transformers encoder-decoder systems from small basic transformers (contrastive3 in Table 3) to large pre-trained multilingual text-to-text transformers such as T5 (Raffel et al., 2020) and mT5 (multilingual T5). For primary cascaded system, models are based on a convolutional model (fconv) (Gehring et al., 2017) upgraded (fconv-up). We reduced the depth and the width of both the encoder and decoder to adapt the size of our fconv model to our dataset. Our fconv-up model achieves 14.52 of BLEU on valid set and 15.56 on the test set, while fconv would give 13 of BLEU. Compared to the cascaded baseline system, based on small basic transformers (contrastive3), fconv-up cascaded system outperforms by 6 BLEU points.

Experiments have been carried out in order to extract the encoder of the fine-tuned W2V and use the latent representation of the audio to train an auto-regressive decoder and thus to skip the Speech-to-Text part, but without any success.

6.3 End-to-end models

We used the end-to-end translation model presented in section 3.2. The model was trained directly on the Pashto to French task (no pre-training of the encoder-decoder model), using SAMU−XLS−R trained on 53 and 100 languages. We used adapters (Houlsby et al., 2019) inside the encoder to keep the semantic information while fine-tuning.

Two constrained contrastive end-to-end systems were submitted for this task. Both share the same encoder-decoder architecture using transformers (Vaswani et al., 2017). The system encoder is the encoder from a Whisper small (768) (Radford et al., 2022) pre-trained model. The decoder has a dimension of 512 using 8 heads and 6 layers. It is not pre-trained. A feed forward network projection layer is used between the encoder and decoder to connect both modules. The difference between both systems lies in the use of a transformer language model trained from scratch on the provided dataset.

Both of these systems were also trained on additional Pashto data and submitted as contrastive unconstrained systems 2 and 3. The language model was not trained on the additional data.

6.4 Results

Results for constrained and unconstrained conditions are presented in Table 3 and Table 4 respectively.

System	Description	Constrained valid	Constrained test
primary	Pipeline, fconv-up	14.52	15.56
contrastive1	E2E, without LM	11.06	15.29
contrastive2	E2E, with LM	11.11	15.06
contrastive3	Pipeline	10.5	9.2

Table 3: Results for Constrained Pashto-to-French ST systems in terms of %BLEU score.

As for constrained setting, we noted that a pipeline of two E2E ASR and NMT system gives better results compared to using one speech translation E2E system. Although the usage of a LM improves the E2E ST further, we were not able to exceed the pipeline of the two E2E systems (ASR+NMT).

System	Description	Unconstrained valid	Unconstrained test
primary	SAMU_XLSR 100l	24.82	24.87
contrastive1	SAMU_XLSR 53l	23.38	23.87
contrastive2	E2E, without LM	12.26	15.18
contrastive3	E2E, with LM	12.16	15.07

Table 4: Results for Unconstrained Pashto-to-French ST systems in terms of %BLEU score.

When we switch to the unconstrained setting, we see a significant improvement demonstrated by a dramatic increases of the BLEU score with the SAMU−XLS−R system. SAMU−XLS−R obtained a BLEU of 24.87 on the test set when trained starting from a pretrained encoder with 100 languages (SAMU−XLS−R-100) and a full BLEU point less (23.87) when we start from a 53 languages encoder (SAMU−XLS−R-53).

7 Conclusion

This paper presents results obtained on three tasks from the IWSLT 2023 Dialectal and Low-resource ST track, namely Tunisian to English, Tamasheq to French and Pashto to French. Given an unconstrained condition, our submission relies heavily on the semantic speech representation learning framework SAMU-XLS-R that greatly improves results compared to the other submitted end-to-end ST models by leveraging multilingual data from other languages. These data can thus come from high resource languages and help to alleviate the low-resource setting difficulty. We indeed observe slightly improved results when using a SAMU-XLS-R model trained on more languages (Tamasheq to French : 15.35 BLEU when using 60 languages, 16.52 BLEU when using 100 languages). We believe results could be further improved by using the unlabelled data available for the Tunisian to English and the Tamasheq to French tasks, and by investigating other decoders in our encoder-decoder framework.

Acknowledgements

This work was partially funded by the following projects: French Research Agency (ANR) ON-TRAC project under contract number ANR-18-CE23-0021, European Commission SELMA project under grant number 957017, European Union's Horizon 2020 ESPERANTO research and innovation programme under the Marie Skłodowska-Curie grant agreement No 101007666 and the DGA RAPID COMMUTE project. This work was partially performed using HPC resources from GENCI–IDRIS, grants AD011012527. The Pashto-French data was totally provided by ELRA. We acknowledge ELRA catalogue (http://catalog.elra.info) TRAD Pashto-French Parallel corpus of transcribed Broadcast News Speech - Training data, ISLRN: 802-643-297-429-4, ELRA ID: ELRA-W0093, TRAD Pashto Broadcast News Speech Corpus, ISLRN: 918-508-885-913-7, ELRA ID: ELRA-S0381.

References

Ahmed Ali, Peter Bell, James Glass, Yacine Messaoui, Hamdy Mubarak, Steve Renals, and Yifan Zhang. 2019. The mgb-2 challenge: Arabic multi-dialect broadcast media recognition.

Antonios Anastasopoulos, Loïc Barrault, Luisa Bentivogli, Marcely Zanon Boito, Ondřej Bojar, Roldano Cattoni, Anna Currey, Georgiana Dinu, Kevin Duh, Maha Elbayad, Yannick Estève, Marcello Federico, Christian Federmann, Souhir Gahbiche, Hongyu Gong, Roman Grundkiewicz, Barry Haddow, Benjamin Hsu, Dávid Javorský, Věra Kloudová, Surafel M. Lakew, Xutai Ma, Prashant Mathur, Paul McNamee, Kenton Murray, Maria Nădejde, Satoshi Nakamura, Matteo Negri, Jan Niehues, Xing Niu, John Ortega, Juan Pino, Elizabeth Salesky, Jiatong Shi, Sebastian Stüker, Katsuhito Sudoh, Marco Turchi, Yogesh Virkar, Alex Waibel, Changhan Wang, and Shinji Watanabe. 2022. FINDINGS OF THE IWSLT 2022 EVALUATION CAMPAIGN. In *Proceedings of the 19th International Conference on Spoken Language Translation (IWSLT 2022)*, Dublin, Ireland. Association for Computational Linguistics.

Antonios Anastasopoulos, Ondřej Bojar, Jacob Bremerman, Roldano Cattoni, Maha Elbayad, Marcello Federico, Xutai Ma, Satoshi Nakamura, Matteo Negri, Jan Niehues, Juan Pino, Elizabeth Salesky, Sebastian Stüker, Katsuhito Sudoh, Marco Turchi, Alexander Waibel, Changhan Wang, and Matthew Wiesner. 2021. FINDINGS OF THE IWSLT 2021 EVALUATION CAMPAIGN. In *Proceedings of the 18th International Conference on Spoken Language Translation (IWSLT 2021)*, pages 1–29, Bangkok, Thailand (online). Association for Computational Linguistics.

Ebrahim Ansari, Amittai Axelrod, Nguyen Bach, Ondřej Bojar, Roldano Cattoni, Fahim Dalvi, Nadir Durrani, Marcello Federico, Christian Federmann, Jiatao Gu, et al. 2020. Findings of the iwslt 2020 evaluation campaign. In *Proceedings of the 17th International Conference on Spoken Language Translation*, pages 1–34.

Rosana Ardila, Megan Branson, Kelly Davis, Michael Henretty, Michael Kohler, Josh Meyer, Reuben Morais, Lindsay Saunders, Francis M. Tyers, and Gregor Weber. 2020a. Common Voice: A massively-multilingual speech corpus. *arXiv:1912.06670*.

Rosana Ardila, Megan Branson, Kelly Davis, Michael Henretty, Michael Kohler, Josh Meyer, Reuben Morais, Lindsay Saunders, Francis M. Tyers, and Gregor Weber. 2020b. Common voice: A massively-multilingual speech corpus.

Arun Babu, Changhan Wang, Andros Tjandra, Kushal Lakhotia, Qiantong Xu, Naman Goyal, Kritika Singh, Patrick von Platen, Yatharth Saraf, Juan Pino, Alexei Baevski, Alexis Conneau, and Michael Auli. 2021a. Xls-r: Self-supervised cross-lingual speech representation learning at scale. *arXiv:2111.09296*.

Arun Babu, Changhan Wang, Andros Tjandra, Kushal Lakhotia, Qiantong Xu, Naman Goyal, Kritika Singh, Patrick von Platen, Yatharth Saraf, Juan Pino, et al. 2021b. Xls-r: Self-supervised cross-lingual speech representation learning at scale. *arXiv preprint arXiv:2111.09296*.

Alexei Baevski, Michael Auli, and Abdelrahman Mohamed. 2019. Effectiveness of self-supervised pretraining for speech recognition. *arXiv preprint arXiv:1911.03912*.

Alexei Baevski, Yuhao Zhou, Abdelrahman Mohamed, and Michael Auli. 2020. wav2vec 2.0: A framework for self-supervised learning of speech representations. *Advances in Neural Information Processing Systems*, 33:12449–12460.

Luisa Bentivogli, Mauro Cettolo, Marco Gaido, Alina Karakanta, Alberto Martinelli, Matteo Negri, and Marco Turchi. 2021. Cascade versus direct speech translation: Do the differences still make a difference? *CoRR*, abs/2106.01045.

Alexandre Berard, Olivier Pietquin, Christophe Servan, and Laurent Besacier. 2016. Listen and translate: A proof of concept for end-to-end speech-to-text translation. *CoRR*, abs/1612.01744.

Kaushal Bhogale, Abhigyan Raman, Tahir Javed, Sumanth Doddapaneni, Anoop Kunchukuttan, Pratyush Kumar, and Mitesh M Khapra. 2023. Effectiveness of mining audio and text pairs from public data for improving asr systems for low-resource languages. In *ICASSP 2023-2023 IEEE International Conference on Acoustics, Speech and Signal Processing (ICASSP)*, pages 1–5. IEEE.

Marcely Zanon Boito, Fethi Bougares, Florentin Barbier, Souhir Gahbiche, Loïc Barrault, Mickael Rouvier, and Yannick Estéve. 2022. Speech resources in the tamasheq language. *Language Resources and Evaluation Conference (LREC)*.

Alexis Conneau, Alexei Baevski, Ronan Collobert, Abdelrahman Mohamed, and Michael Auli. 2020. Unsupervised cross-lingual representation learning for speech recognition. *arXiv preprint arXiv:2006.13979*.

Alexis Conneau, Ankur Bapna, Yu Zhang, Min Ma, Patrick von Platen, Anton Lozhkov, Colin Cherry, Ye Jia, Clara Rivera, Mihir Kale, et al. 2022. Xtreme-s: Evaluating cross-lingual speech representations. *arXiv preprint arXiv:2203.10752*.

Marta R Costa-jussà, James Cross, Onur Çelebi, Maha Elbayad, Kenneth Heafield, Kevin Heffernan, Elahe Kalbassi, Janice Lam, Daniel Licht, Jean Maillard, et al. 2022. No language left behind: Scaling human-centered machine translation. *arXiv preprint arXiv:2207.04672*.

ELRA catalogue. 2016a. Trad pashto broadcast news speech corpus. `https://catalogue.elra.info/en-us/repository/browse/ELRA-S0381/`. ISLRN: 918-508-885-913-7, ELRA ID: ELRA-S0381.

ELRA catalogue. 2016b. Trad pashto-french parallel corpus of transcribed broadcast news speech - training data. `http://catalog.elda.org/en-us/repository/browse/ELRA-W0093/`. ISLRN: 802-643-297-429-4, ELRA ID: ELRA-W0093.

Solène Evain, Ha Nguyen, Hang Le, Marcely Zanon Boito, Salima Mdhaffar, Sina Alisamir, Ziyi Tong, Natalia Tomashenko, Marco Dinarelli, Titouan Parcollet, et al. 2021a. Task agnostic and task specific self-supervised learning from speech with *LeBenchmark*. In *Thirty-fifth Conference on Neural Information Processing Systems Datasets and Benchmarks Track (Round 2)*.

Solène Evain, Ha Nguyen, Hang Le, Marcely Zanon Boito, Salima Mdhaffar, Sina Alisamir, Ziyi Tong, Natalia Tomashenko, Marco Dinarelli, Titouan Parcollet, Alexandre Allauzen, Yannick Estève, Benjamin Lecouteux, François Portet, Solange Rossato, Fabien Ringeval, Didier Schwab, and Laurent Besacier. 2021b. *LeBenchmark*: A Reproducible Framework for Assessing Self-Supervised Representation Learning from Speech. In *Interspeech*, pages 1439–1443.

F. Feng, Y. Yang, D. Cer, N. Arivazhagan, and W. Wang. 2022. Language-agnostic BERT Sentence Embedding. In *Proceedings of the 60th ACL*.

Jonas Gehring, Michael Auli, David Grangier, Denis Yarats, and Yann N. Dauphin. 2017. Convolutional sequence to sequence learning.

Neil Houlsby, Andrei Giurgiu, Stanislaw Jastrzebski, Bruna Morrone, Quentin de Laroussilhe, Andrea Gesmundo, Mona Attariyan, and Sylvain Gelly. 2019. Parameter-efficient transfer learning for nlp. In *Proc. ICML*.

Wei-Ning Hsu, Benjamin Bolte, Yao-Hung Hubert Tsai, Kushal Lakhotia, Ruslan Salakhutdinov, and Abdelrahman Mohamed. 2021. Hubert: Self-supervised speech representation learning by masked prediction of hidden units. *IEEE/ACM Transactions on Audio, Speech, and Language Processing*, 29:3451–3460.

Javier Iranzo-Sánchez, Joan Albert Silvestre-Cerdà, Javier Jorge, Nahuel Roselló, Adrià Giménez, Albert Sanchis, Jorge Civera, and Alfons Juan. 2019. Europarl-st: A multilingual corpus for speech translation of parliamentary debates. *arXiv:1911.03167*.

Tahir Javed, Kaushal Santosh Bhogale, Abhigyan Raman, Anoop Kunchukuttan, Pratyush Kumar, and Mitesh M Khapra. 2022. Indicsuperb: A speech processing universal performance benchmark for indian languages. *arXiv preprint arXiv:2208.11761*.

Kazuya Kawakami, Luyu Wang, Chris Dyer, Phil Blunsom, and Aaron van den Oord. 2020. Learning robust and multilingual speech representations. In *Findings of the Association for Computational Linguistics: EMNLP 2020*, pages 1182–1192, Online. Association for Computational Linguistics.

Sameer Khurana, Antoine Laurent, and James Glass. 2022. Samu-xlsr: Semantically-aligned multimodal utterance-level cross-lingual speech representation. *IEEE Journal of Selected Topics in Signal Processing*, pages 1–13.

Hang Le, Juan Pino, Changhan Wang, Jiatao Gu, Didier Schwab, and Laurent Besacier. 2020. Dual-decoder transformer for joint automatic speech recognition and multilingual speech translation. *arXiv preprint arXiv:2011.00747.*

Xian Li, Changhan Wang, Yun Tang, Chau Tran, Yuqing Tang, Juan Pino, Alexei Baevski, Alexis Conneau, and Michael Auli. 2020. Multilingual speech translation with efficient finetuning of pretrained models. *arXiv:2010.12829.*

Vineel Pratap, Qiantong Xu, Anuroop Sriram, Gabriel Synnaeve, and Ronan Collobert. 2020. Mls: A large-scale multilingual dataset for speech research. *arXiv:2012.03411.*

Alec Radford, Jong Wook Kim, Tao Xu, Greg Brockman, Christine McLeavey, and Ilya Sutskever. 2022. Robust speech recognition via large-scale weak supervision.

Colin Raffel, Noam Shazeer, Adam Roberts, Katherine Lee, Sharan Narang, Michael Matena, Yanqi Zhou, Wei Li, and Peter J. Liu. 2020. Exploring the limits of transfer learning with a unified text-to-text transformer.

Steffen Schneider, Alexei Baevski, Ronan Collobert, and Michael Auli. 2019. wav2vec: Unsupervised pre-training for speech recognition. *arXiv preprint arXiv:1904.05862.*

Matthias Sperber, Hendra Setiawan, Christian Gollan, Udhyakumar Nallasamy, and Matthias Paulik. 2020. Consistent transcription and translation of speech. *Transactions of the Association for Computational Linguistics*, 8:695–709.

Ashish Vaswani, Noam Shazeer, Niki Parmar, Jakob Uszkoreit, Llion Jones, Aidan N Gomez, Łukasz Kaiser, and Illia Polosukhin. 2017. Attention is all you need. *Advances in neural information processing systems*, 30.

Changhan Wang, Juan Pino, Anne Wu, and Jiatao Gu. 2020. Covost: A diverse multilingual speech-to-text translation corpus. *arXiv:2002.01320.*

Changhan Wang, Morgane Riviere, Ann Lee, Anne Wu, Chaitanya Talnikar, Daniel Haziza, Mary Williamson, Juan Pino, and Emmanuel Dupoux. 2021. VoxPopuli: A large-scale multilingual speech corpus for representation learning, semi-supervised learning and interpretation. In *Proceedings of the 59th Annual Meeting of the Association for Computational Linguistics and the 11th International Joint Conference on Natural Language Processing (Volume 1: Long Papers)*, pages 993–1003, Online. Association for Computational Linguistics.

Ron J. Weiss, Jan Chorowski, Navdeep Jaitly, Yonghui Wu, and Zhifeng Chen. 2017. Sequence-to-Sequence Models Can Directly Translate Foreign Speech. In *Proc. Interspeech 2017*, pages 2625–2629.

Shu-wen Yang, Po-Han Chi, Yung-Sung Chuang, Cheng-I Jeff Lai, Kushal Lakhotia, Yist Y. Lin, Andy T. Liu, Jiatong Shi, Xuankai Chang, Guan-Ting Lin, Tzu-Hsien Huang, Wei-Cheng Tseng, Ko tik Lee, Da-Rong Liu, Zili Huang, Shuyan Dong, Shang-Wen Li, Shinji Watanabe, Abdelrahman Mohamed, and Hung yi Lee. 2021. SUPERB: Speech Processing Universal PERformance Benchmark. In *Interspeech*, pages 1194–1198.

Binbin Zhang, Hang Lv, Pengcheng Guo, Qijie Shao, Chao Yang, Lei Xie, Xin Xu, Hui Bu, Xiaoyu Chen, Chenchen Zeng, et al. 2022. Wenetspeech: A 10000+ hours multi-domain mandarin corpus for speech recognition. In *ICASSP 2022-2022 IEEE International Conference on Acoustics, Speech and Signal Processing (ICASSP)*, pages 6182–6186. IEEE.

BUT Systems for IWSLT 2023 Marathi - Hindi Low Resource Speech Translation Task

Santosh Kesiraju, Karel Beneš, Maksim Tikhonov and **Jan Černocký**
Speech@FIT, Brno University of Technology, Czechia
{kesiraju,ibenes,cernocky}@fit.vutbr.cz,
xtikho00@stud.fit.vutbr.cz

Abstract

This paper describes the systems submitted for Marathi to Hindi low-resource speech translation task. Our primary submission is based on an end-to-end direct speech translation system, whereas the contrastive one is a cascaded system. The backbone of both the systems is a Hindi-Marathi bilingual ASR system trained on 2790 hours of imperfect transcribed speech. The end-to-end speech translation system was directly initialized from the ASR, and then fine-tuned for direct speech translation with an auxiliary CTC loss for translation. The MT model for the cascaded system is initialized from a cross-lingual language model, which was then fine-tuned using 1.6 M parallel sentences. All our systems were trained from scratch on publicly available datasets. In the end, we use a language model to re-score the n-best hypotheses. Our primary submission achieved 30.5 and 39.6 BLEU whereas the contrastive system obtained 21.7 and 28.6 BLEU on official dev and test sets respectively. The paper also presents the analysis on several experiments that were conducted and outlines the strategies for improving speech translation in low-resource scenarios.

1 Introduction

A typical end-to-end (E2E) speech translation model is trained with the help of data triplets $(\boldsymbol{x}, \boldsymbol{y}, \boldsymbol{z})$, i.e., the speech signal $(\boldsymbol{x})$ in source language, along with its transcription $(\boldsymbol{y})$, and, text translation $(\boldsymbol{z})$ in target language. In usual low-resource scenarios, the transcriptions in source language are unavailable and moreover the speech signal and the translation pairs $(\boldsymbol{x}, \boldsymbol{z})$ are also limited, which is the case for the IWSLT 2023 Marathi to Hindi low-resource speech translation task (Agarwal et al., 2023). In such cases, one can rely on transfer learning, where models trained on relatively large amounts of data (possibly on a related task such as automatic speech recognition) are transferred (adapted) to the target task/scenario (such as speech translation) using little amounts of labelled data (Bansal et al., 2019). To be specific, we train automatic speech recognition (ASR) systems on relatively large amount of transcribed speech data (2790 hours), and transfer the model for speech translation task by fine-tuning it on relatively small amount (16 hours) of IWSLT Marathi-Hindi training data.

This paper describes the systems submitted for the aforementioned task. While building the systems, we mainly focused on end-to-end systems, which resulted in our primary submission. We have also put some efforts in building a cascade pipeline that was submitted as a contrastive system. Both the systems come under the unconstrained category, i.e., we relied on external, publicly available data to train models. These models, which we refer to as *back-bone models*, mainly comprise automatic speech recognition (ASR), machine translation (MT) and language models (LM).

The Section 2 describes the various datasets used for training the back-bone models, and Section 3 presents the details of each individual back-bone models (ASR, MT, LM), followed by description of transfer learning for actual speech translation systems in Section 4. The Section 5 gives the results and analysis, quantifying the effect of various factors on the target translation task. Finally, we conclude in Section 6 and discuss directions for future works.

2 Datasets for training

Here we describe the details and present the statistics of various datasets used for training the back-bone models. These datasets come under various categories, i.e., paired speech data for training ASR, parallel text data for training MT and monolingual data for training LMs. All the data we considered for training covers only Hindi and Marathi languages. Both these share the same Devanagari script (unicode block) but there a few set of charac-

Proceedings of the 20th International Conference on Spoken Language Translation (IWSLT 2023), pages 227–234
July 13-14, 2023 ©2023 Association for Computational Linguistics

ters that are mutually exclusive.

2.1 Paired speech data

The paired speech data for Marathi and Hindi are collected from various publicly available datasets as listed below:

- **GramVaani (GV)**[1] comprises telephone quality speech in Hindi (hi). The dataset was used for Interspeech 2022 special session (Bhanushali et al., 2022; Patel and Scharenborg, 2022). We considered only the 100 hour labelled split of the dataset.
- **Indian Language Corpora (ILC)** (Abraham et al., 2020)[2] is crowdsourced speech data along with transcriptions in Marathi language. The dataset is collected from 36 participants with various socio-economic backgrounds and dialects.
- **Mozilla Common Voice v12 (MCV)** (Ardila et al., 2020) is a crowdsource collection of paired speech data across various languages. We took the validated versions of Hindi (hi) and Marathi (mr) from this corpus.
- **MUCS** (Diwan et al., 2021)[3] is multilingual and code-switched corpus for training ASR systems in 6 different Indian languages. The dataset was introduced in Interspeech 2021 as part of a special session focusing on ASR for Indian languages. We considered Hindi and Marathi data from this corpus. Although MUCS contains about 100 hours of transcribed speech for both Marathi and Hindi, the lexical content is not diverse, i.e., the same utterances were spoken by various speakers.
- **Multi-speaker speech corpora (MSSC)** (He et al., 2020)[4] is a collection of clean speech data with transcriptions intended for building text-to-speech synthesis systems for various Indian languages. We considered only the Marathi split from this corpus.
- **Shrutilipi (SL)**[5] is collected from public archives and contains about 6400 hours of radio broadcast news in various Indian languages. The corresponding transcriptions were obtained with the help of OCR and other heuristics (Bhogale et al., 2022). This corpus is the bigger chunk of the data we used for training, but the transcriptions obtained are not accurate. A manual inspection revealed some erroneous alignments at the beginning and end of the utterances. By setting a threshold (≥ 85) on the provided alignment score, we filtered Hindi (hi) and Marathi (mr) data from this corpus. We believe the domain of this data is closer to IWSLT 2023 speech translation data.

The statistics of each of the above datasets is presented in Table 1. This data was used to train mono and bilingual ASR systems that are described later in Section 3.1. All the speech data was upsampled to 16 kHz. Using Kaldi toolkit (Povey et al., 2011) 80 dimensional filter banks and 3-dimensional pitch features are extracted for every 25 ms of speech frame sliding with 10 ms.

2.2 Monolingual and parallel text data

We prepared monolingual data for both Hindi and Marathi. We pooled data from transcribed speech (Table 1), Samanantar (Ramesh et al., 2022), Indic2Indic, IIIT-H CVIT (Siripragada et al., 2020) corpus, resulting in 9 M sentences (217 M tokens) for Hindi and 4M sentences for Marathi[6].

The parallel text was taken only from Indic2Indic split from Samanantar (Ramesh et al., 2022), whose statistics are given in Table 2. We retained punctuation in all the text.

2.3 Speech translation data

The official speech translation data for Marathi - Hindi involves around 16 hours of training split, i.e., Marathi speech and its translations in Hindi. There are no transcriptions for the Marathi speech. Table 3 presents the statistics of the provided speech translation data. We used speed perturbation (0.9, 1.0, 1.1) to augment the speech translation data. The effect of such augmentation on the final translation performance is discussed later in Section 5.

[1] https://sites.google.com/view/gramvaaniasrchallenge/

[2] https://www.cse.iitb.ac.in/~pjyothi/indiccorpora/

[3] https://navana-tech.github.io/MUCS2021/data.html

[4] https://www.openslr.org/64/

[5] https://ai4bharat.org/shrutilipi

[6] Due to a bug in data preparation, only Shrutilipi text data 400 K (8.2 M tokens) out of 4 M sentences were used to train Marathi LM.

Dataset	Language	Duration in hours (number of utterances) Training		Dev		Test	
GV	hi	97.9	(37,152)	4.9	(1885)	2.8	(1032)
ILC	mr	109.2	(92,471)	-	-	-	-
MCV	hi	5.3	(4481)	2.8	(2179)	4.1	(2962)
	mr	12.0	(7321)	3.0	(1678)	3.2	(1827)
MUCS	hi	95.1	(99,925)	5.6	(3843)	-	-
	mr	93.8	(79,432)	5.0	(4675)	-	-
MSSC	mr	3.0	(1569)	-	-	-	-
SL	hi	1478.6	(764,237)	-	-	-	-
	mr	894.8	(466,203)	-	-	-	-
Total	hi	1676.8	(898,369)	13.3	(7895)	6.9	(3994)
	mr	1112.8	(638,159)	8.0	(6353)	3.2	(1827)

Table 1: Statistics of the data used for training ASR systems. The dev and test splits are only used for internal evaluation of the ASR systems.

Number of utterance pairs Training	Dev	Test
1634551	2000	2000

Table 2: Number of parallel utterance (sentence) pairs between Marathi-Hindi that are used for training XLM and MT models.

3 Back-bone models

Here, we describe the architecture and training details of various backbone models.

3.1 ASR

The ASR model is a transformer based seq2seq model. The speech features are passed through 2 layers of convolution, followed by 12 layers of transformer encoder blocks and 6 layer of transformer decoder blocks, with $d_{\text{model}} = \{256, 512\}$[7], heads $= 4$, $d_{\text{ff}} = 2048$. The dropout was set to 0.1. The model is trained with a batch size of 128 for 100 epochs using Adam optimizer (Kingma and Ba, 2015), and warm up scheduler with a peak learning rate of 0.0005. The training is done with joint CTC and attention objective (Karita et al., 2019), where the CTC is applied at the end of encoder layer and the attention acts at the output of autoregressive decoder (teacher-forcing).

$$\mathcal{L}_{\text{asr}} = \alpha\, \mathcal{L}_{\text{ctc}}(\boldsymbol{x}, \boldsymbol{y}) + (1-\alpha)\mathcal{L}_{\text{att}}(\boldsymbol{x}, \boldsymbol{y}). \quad (1)$$

In case of bilingual ASR, the CTC layer, input and output layers of the decoder are specific to each language, i.e., the (sub-)word embeddings are *not* shared across languages. Such a design ensures that only target language tokens are decoded, irrespective of the phonetic similarity with other languages in the model. The ASR models were trained using ESPnet toolkit (Watanabe et al., 2018). The performance of various mono and bilingual ASR systems is discussed later in Section 5.

3.2 XLM

The architecture of pre-training masked-language model is based on cross-lingual language model (XLM) (Lample and Conneau, 2019)[8]. More specifically, we use translation language modelling objective along with masked language modelling to train the transformer based encoder. Here, we use BPE-based sub-word vocabulary that is obtained jointly for both languages. The model has 6 transformer blocks with 512 embedding dimension, 8 attention heads, dropout of 0.1 for both attention and feed-forward layers. The model is trained for a maximum of 1000 epochs using Adam optimizer with a learning rate of 0.0001.

[7] Smaller models use $d_{\text{model}} = 256$, where as bigger models use $d_{\text{model}} = 512$.

[8] `https://github.com/facebookresearch/XLM`

Duration in hours (# utterances)		
Training	Dev	Test
15.9 (7990)	3.7 (2103)	4.4 (2164)

Table 3: Statistics of Marathi-Hindi IWSLT2023 speech translation data.

3.3 MT

The MT model is a transformer based seq2seq model initialized from XLM. Both the encoder and decoder parameters are initialized from XLM encoder, except for the cross-attention parameters in the decoder that are randomly initialized. The model is then fine-tuned on the same 1.6 M parallel sentences with a batch size of 64 and a maximum of 1000 epochs. The model achieved **23.0** and **22.6** BLEU scores on the internal valid and test sets (Table 2) respectively.

3.4 LM for re-scoring

For Hindi, we used an LSTM of three layers of 4096 units each, with no dropout. The model was trained on 217 M sub-word tokens obtained by tokenizing the monolingual Hindi corpus into a 10k Unigram vocabulary (Kudo, 2018). The model achieved validation perplexity of 46. Thereafter, we have fine-tuned it on text data from Shrutilipi (SL) data for 500 steps.

For Marathi, we used an LSTM of 2 layers per 2048 units, again with no dropout. This model also utilized a 10k Unigram vocabulary and was trained on 8.2 M tokens. This model achieved validation perplexity of 120.

4 Speech translation systems

Here, we briefly describe both the end-to-end and cascade systems.

4.1 End-to-end

The E2E models are initialized from pre-trained ASR models. We use both the encoder and decoder from the ASR, as it provides a better initialization since the representations from the encoder are readily compatible with the decoder (Bansal et al., 2019). The model is then trained for direct speech translation, with the auxiliary CTC objective also for translation (Zhang et al., 2022; Yan et al., 2023; Kesiraju et al., 2023).

$$\mathcal{L}_{\text{st}} = \lambda\, \mathcal{L}_{\text{ctc}}(\boldsymbol{x}, \boldsymbol{z}) + (1-\lambda)\mathcal{L}_{\text{att}}(\boldsymbol{x}, \boldsymbol{z}) \quad (2)$$

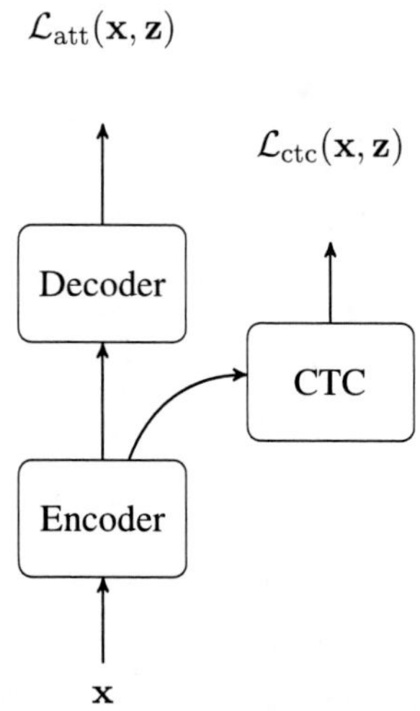

Figure 1: End-to-end framework for speech translation. $\mathbf{x}$ is the input speech (features), $\mathbf{z}$ is the target text translation.

The effect of various initializations and their influence on downstream speech translation is discussed later in Section 5.

The E2E speech translation was also trained using ESPnet toolkit. Our changes to the original toolkit, along with the training recipes, are available online[9].

A beam search based joint decoding (Karita et al., 2019) that relies on the weighted average of log-likelihoods from both the CTC and transformer decoder modules is used, that produces the most likely hypotheses according to

$$\hat{\mathbf{z}} = \arg\max_{\mathbf{z}} \beta \log p_{\text{ctc}}(\mathbf{z} \mid \mathbf{x}) + (1-\beta) \log p_{\text{att}}(\mathbf{z} \mid \mathbf{x}) \quad (3)$$

We found $\lambda = \{0.1, 0.3\}$, $\beta = \{0.1, 0.3\}$ suitable for joint training and decoding respectively.

4.2 Cascade systems

For the cascade speech translation systems, we first decode n-best hypotheses from ASR model and obtain 1-best from Marathi LM rescorer. These are then passed directly to the MT system, which gives us n-best translation hypotheses in target language Hindi. These are then re-scored by Hindi LM to give us 1-best translation hypotheses.

[9] `https://github.com/BUTSpeechFIT/espnet/tree/main/egs2/iwslt23_low_resource/st1`

Model name	Training data (hrs)	Model type	Sub-word vocab per language	Dev WER mr	Dev WER hi	Test WER mr	Test WER hi
H1	198†	Mono (hi)	1000	-	30.7	-	35.9
H2	1676	Mono (hi)	8000	-	24.7	-	28.4
M1	218†	Mono (mr)	1000	14.3	-	42.4	-
M2	1112	Mono (mr)	8000	19.0	-	36.0	-
B1	416†	Bilingual (mr, hi)	1000	11.1	31.5	31.9	35.1
B2	2789	Bilingual (mr, hi)	8000	16.0	24.2	23.7	26.9

Table 4: Word-error-rates (WER) of various mono and bilingual ASR systems, trained on various amounts of data. † implies that the training data contains everything from Table 1 except Shrutilipi (SL).

A further fine-tuning of the MT system using 1-best hypotheses from Marathi to Hindi IWSLT training set did not improve the results. Due to time constraints, we did not try various strategies (Bentivogli et al., 2021) or hyperparameter tuning for the cascade systems.

4.3 Re-scoring n-best hypotheses

We have utilized the language models to re-score up to 100-best hypotheses in both languages. Using BrnoLM[10], we have introduced the language model scores. Here, we have tuned the two hyperparameters: The weight of the LM score (additive to 1.0 weight of the acoustic system) and an insertion bonus, added for each token of the hypothesis, in the LM tokenization. For the E2E system, we have achieved optimal results with LM weight 1.2 and insertion bonus 5.5. For the Marathi ASR in the cascade system, optimal setting was 0.3 and 3.5. For the translation system in the cascade, we did not achieve any improvement by re-scoring the output with the Hindi LM.

5 Results and analysis

Here, we present the performance of various backbone models, along with analysis showing the effectiveness of various factors such as initializations, data augmentation, auxiliary objectives and joint decoding.

5.1 Performance of ASR systems

From the Table 4 we can see that the bilingual models perform (B1, B2) better than the monolingual parts (H1, M1, H2, M2). Here, H1, M1 and B1 are smaller models with $d_{\text{model}} = 256$, whereas H2, M2 and B2 are bigger ones with $d_{\text{model}} = 512$. All the ASR models were trained with joint CTC and attention loss, where the CTC weight of 0.3 was found to be optimal. The same weight was used during joint decoding. Since we retained the original punctuation in the text, the WER is slightly affected.

5.2 Performance of ST

Here we present the results of speech translation systems based on end-to-end architecture. As shown in Table 5, all the ST models were initialized either from mono or bilingual ASR systems and fine-tuned using the speech translation data (with or without data augmentation). While most of these systems can be considered direct end-to-end; using an external LM for re-scoring the n-best makes an exception. Using a Marathi monolingual ASR model would be sub optimal because the internal language model represented in the decoder of the ASR would not be suitable for generating linguistically acceptable text sequences in Hindi.

Fig. 2 shows the effect of CTC weight during joint training and decoding. We can see that 0.3 is the optimal weight both for training and decoding. Since, we have a separate vocabulary for both the languages, the posterior probabilities from CTC during joint decoding will only correspond to the tokens from the target language Hindi. This is important, since both the languages come from same family with high phonetic similarity, and use same Devanagari script, the non auto regressive CTC decoder does not accidentally provide higher scores for tokens from source language Marathi. The latter scenario can happen when using a joint-sub word vocabulary for both the languages.

Sacrebleu library (Post, 2018) was used to com-

[10]https://github.com/BUTSpeechFIT/BrnoLM

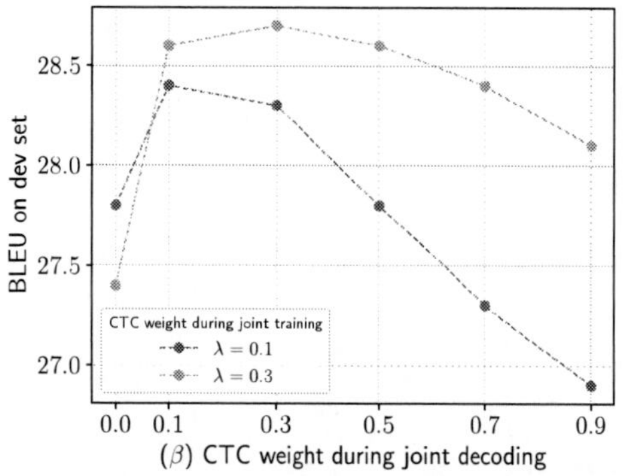

Figure 2: Effect of hyperparameters in joint training and decoding for direct speech translation. The model is initialized from B2 and trained on augmented training data.

pute BLEU[11] and CHRF2[12] scores in the dev sets.

From the Table 5, we can see that independent improvements come from using bilingual ASR trained on more data, data augmentation (speed perturbation) and LM re-scoring. In case of cascade system, the LM re-scoring did not improve the results. We believe this is because the Marathi LM was trained on much fewer amounts of data (400K sentences). We plan to rerun these experiments in the near future.

Finally, our primary submission was based on B2 + ST fine-tuning with data augmentation + LM re-scoring which obtained **39.6** BLEU and **63.3** CHRF2 scores on official test set. Our contrastive system was based on B2 + MT + LM re-scoring which obtained **28.6** BLEU and **54.4** CHRF2 scores.

A manual inspection of the translation outputs revealed that several mismatches occurred where there are ambiguous numerals, i.e., some numbers were written using digits while the others were spelled out verbatim. There are also cases where both notations were mixed. We believe, further text normalization of both reference and hypothesis could give us a better picture of the evaluation scores.

[11] nrefs:1 | case:mixed | eff:no | tok:13a | smooth:exp | version:2.3.1

[12] nrefs:1 | case:mixed | eff:yes | nc:6 | nw:0 | space:no | version:2.3.1

ST Model initialization	Speed perturb	Dev set BLEU	Dev set CHRF2
H1	✗	16.3	45.0
H2	✓	24.9	51.0
B1	✗	17.4	46.2
B1	✓	20.1	48.2
B2	✓	28.7	54.4
B2 + LM rescore	✓	30.6	55.9
Cascade	-	21.7	48.2

Table 5: Speech translation results on Marathi - Hindi dev set. All the ST models are fine-tuned on training data from Table 3.

6 Conclusions

In this paper, we presented the systems submitted to the IWSLT 2023 Marathi Hindi low resource track. Our main efforts were along the end-to-end direct speech translation system, initialized from a bilingual ASR. The model was jointly trained with CTC and attention objective directly for translation. The joint decoding provided additional benefits. These strategies combined with speed perturbation for data augmentation and re-scoring the n-best hypotheses using external LM provided further significant improvements. We also submitted a cascade system which uses the same bilingual ASR as the backbone, followed by an MT system. Both systems performed competitively, while the one based on end-to-end provided superior results in terms of BLEU. It is yet to be investigated, if the large pre-trained MT systems would close the gap between cascade and end-to-end systems.

Acknowledgements

The work was supported by Czech National Science Foundation (GACR) project NEUREM3 No. 19-26934X, Czech Ministry of Education, Youth and Sports project no. LTAIN19087 "Multi-linguality in speech technologies" and Horizon 2020 Marie Skłodowska-Curie grant ESPERANTO, No. 101007666. Computing on IT4I supercomputer was supported by the Czech Ministry of Education, Youth and Sports through the e-INFRA CZ (ID:90254). We thank the reviewers for their constructive feedback.

References

Basil Abraham, Danish Goel, Divya Siddarth, Kalika Bali, Manu Chopra, Monojit Choudhury, Pratik Joshi, Preethi Jyoti, Sunayana Sitaram, and Vivek Seshadri. 2020. Crowdsourcing speech data for low-resource languages from low-income workers. In *Proceedings of the Twelfth Language Resources and Evaluation Conference*, pages 2819–2826, Marseille, France. European Language Resources Association.

Milind Agarwal, Sweta Agrawal, Antonios Anastasopoulos, Ondřej Bojar, Claudia Borg, Marine Carpuat, Roldano Cattoni, Mauro Cettolo, Mingda Chen, William Chen, Khalid Choukri, Alexandra Chronopoulou, Anna Currey, Thierry Declerck, Qianqian Dong, Yannick Estève, Kevin Duh, Marcello Federico, Souhir Gahbiche, Barry Haddow, Benjamin Hsu, Phu Mon Htut, Hirofumi Inaguma, Dávid Javorský, John Judge, Yasumasa Kano, Tom Ko, Rishu Kumar, Pengwei Li, Xutail Ma, Prashant Mathur, Evgeny Matusov, Paul McNamee, John P. McCrae, Kenton Murray, Maria Nadejde, Satoshi Nakamura, Matteo Negri, Ha Nguyen, Jan Niehues, Xing Niu, Atul Ojha Kr., John E. Ortega, Proyag Pal, Juan Pino, Lonneke van der Plas, Peter Polák, Elijah Rippeth, Elizabeth Salesky, Jiatong Shi, Matthias Sperber, Sebastian Stüker, Katsuhito Sudoh, Yun Tang, Brian Thompson, Kevin Tran, Marco Turchi, Alex Waibel, Mingxuan Wang, Shinji Watanabe, and Rodolfo Zevallos. 2023. Findings of the IWSLT 2023 Evaluation Campaign. In *Proceedings of the 20th International Conference on Spoken Language Translation (IWSLT 2023)*. Association for Computational Linguistics.

Rosana Ardila, Megan Branson, Kelly Davis, Michael Kohler, Josh Meyer, Michael Henretty, Reuben Morais, Lindsay Saunders, Francis Tyers, and Gregor Weber. 2020. Common voice: A massively-multilingual speech corpus. In *Proceedings of the 12th Language Resources and Evaluation Conference*, pages 4218–4222, Marseille, France. European Language Resources Association.

Sameer Bansal, Herman Kamper, Karen Livescu, Adam Lopez, and Sharon Goldwater. 2019. Pre-training on high-resource speech recognition improves low-resource speech-to-text translation. In *Proceedings of the 2019 Conference of the North American Chapter of the Association for Computational Linguistics: Human Language Technologies, Volume 1 (Long and Short Papers)*, pages 58–68, Minneapolis, Minnesota. Association for Computational Linguistics.

Luisa Bentivogli, Mauro Cettolo, Marco Gaido, Alina Karakanta, Alberto Martinelli, Matteo Negri, and Marco Turchi. 2021. Cascade versus direct speech translation: Do the differences still make a difference? In *Proceedings of the 59th Annual Meeting of the Association for Computational Linguistics and the 11th International Joint Conference on Natural Language Processing (Volume 1: Long Papers)*, pages 2873–2887, Online. Association for Computational Linguistics.

Anish Bhanushali, Grant Bridgman, Deekshitha G, Prasanta Ghosh, Pratik Kumar, Saurabh Kumar, Adithya Raj Kolladath, Nithya Ravi, Aaditeshwar Seth, Ashish Seth, Abhayjeet Singh, Vrunda Sukhadia, Umesh S, Sathvik Udupa, and Lodagala V. S. V. Durga Prasad. 2022. Gram Vaani ASR Challenge on spontaneous telephone speech recordings in regional variations of Hindi. In *Proc. Interspeech 2022*, pages 3548–3552.

Kaushal Santosh Bhogale, Abhigyan Raman, Tahir Javed, Sumanth Doddapaneni, Anoop Kunchukuttan, Pratyush Kumar, and Mitesh M. Khapra. 2022. Effectiveness of mining audio and text pairs from public data for improving asr systems for low-resource languages.

Anuj Diwan, Rakesh Vaideeswaran, Sanket Shah, Ankita Singh, Srinivasa Raghavan, Shreya Khare, Vinit Unni, Saurabh Vyas, Akash Rajpuria, Chiranjeevi Yarra, Ashish Mittal, Prasanta Kumar Ghosh, Preethi Jyothi, Kalika Bali, Vivek Seshadri, Sunayana Sitaram, Samarth Bharadwaj, Jai Nanavati, Raoul Nanavati, and Karthik Sankaranarayanan. 2021. MUCS 2021: Multilingual and Code-Switching ASR Challenges for Low Resource Indian Languages. In *Proc. Interspeech 2021*, pages 2446–2450.

Fei He, Shan-Hui Cathy Chu, Oddur Kjartansson, Clara Rivera, Anna Katanova, Alexander Gutkin, Isin Demirsahin, Cibu Johny, Martin Jansche, Supheakmungkol Sarin, and Knot Pipatsrisawat. 2020. Open-source multi-speaker speech corpora for building Gujarati, Kannada, Malayalam, Marathi, Tamil and Telugu speech synthesis systems. In *Proceedings of the 12th Language Resources and Evaluation Conference*, pages 6494–6503, Marseille, France. European Language Resources Association.

Shigeki Karita, Nelson Enrique Yalta Soplin, Shinji Watanabe, Marc Delcroix, Atsunori Ogawa, and Tomohiro Nakatani. 2019. Improving Transformer-Based End-to-End Speech Recognition with Connectionist Temporal Classification and Language Model Integration. In *Proc. of Interspeech*, pages 1408–1412.

Santosh Kesiraju, Marek Sarvaš, Tomáš Pavliček, Cécile Macaire, and Alejandro Ciuba. 2023. Strategies for improving low resource speech to text translation relying on pre-trained asr models.

Diederik P. Kingma and Jimmy Ba. 2015. Adam: A method for stochastic optimization. In *3rd International Conference on Learning Representations, ICLR 2015, San Diego, CA, USA, May 7-9, 2015, Conference Track Proceedings*.

Taku Kudo. 2018. Subword regularization: Improving neural network translation models with multiple subword candidates. In *Proceedings of the 56th Annual Meeting of the Association for Computational Linguistics (Volume 1: Long Papers)*, pages 66–75, Melbourne, Australia. Association for Computational Linguistics.

Guillaume Lample and Alexis Conneau. 2019. Cross-lingual language model pretraining. *CoRR*, abs/1901.07291.

Tanvina Patel and Odette Scharenborg. 2022. Using cross-model learnings for the Gram Vaani ASR Challenge 2022. In *Proc. Interspeech 2022*, pages 4880–4884.

Matt Post. 2018. A call for clarity in reporting BLEU scores. In *Proceedings of the Third Conference on Machine Translation: Research Papers*, pages 186–191, Brussels, Belgium. Association for Computational Linguistics.

Daniel Povey, Arnab Ghoshal, Gilles Boulianne, Lukáš Burget, Ondřej Glembek, K. Nagendra Goel, Mirko Hannemann, Petr Motlíček, Yanmin Qian, Petr Schwarz, Jan Silovský, Georg Stemmer, and Karel Veselý. 2011. The kaldi speech recognition toolkit. In *Proceedings of ASRU 2011*, pages 1–4. IEEE Signal Processing Society.

Gowtham Ramesh, Sumanth Doddapaneni, Aravinth Bheemaraj, Mayank Jobanputra, Raghavan AK, Ajitesh Sharma, Sujit Sahoo, Harshita Diddee, Mahalakshmi J, Divyanshu Kakwani, Navneet Kumar, Aswin Pradeep, Srihari Nagaraj, Kumar Deepak, Vivek Raghavan, Anoop Kunchukuttan, Pratyush Kumar, and Mitesh Shantadevi Khapra. 2022. Samanantar: The largest publicly available parallel corpora collection for 11 indic languages. *Transactions of the Association for Computational Linguistics*, 10:145–162.

Shashank Siripragada, Jerin Philip, Vinay P. Namboodiri, and C V Jawahar. 2020. A multilingual parallel corpora collection effort for Indian languages. In *Proceedings of the 12th Language Resources and Evaluation Conference*, pages 3743–3751, Marseille, France. European Language Resources Association.

Shinji Watanabe, Takaaki Hori, Shigeki Karita, Tomoki Hayashi, Jiro Nishitoba, Yuya Unno, Nelson Enrique Yalta Soplin, Jahn Heymann, Matthew Wiesner, Nanxin Chen, Adithya Renduchintala, and Tsubasa Ochiai. 2018. ESPnet: End-to-end speech processing toolkit. In *Proceedings of Interspeech*, pages 2207–2211.

Brian Yan, Siddharth Dalmia, Yosuke Higuchi, Graham Neubig, Florian Metze, Alan W Black, and Shinji Watanabe. 2023. CTC alignments improve autoregressive translation. In *Proceedings of the 17th Conference of the European Chapter of the Association for Computational Linguistics*, pages 1623–1639, Dubrovnik, Croatia. Association for Computational Linguistics.

Biao Zhang, Barry Haddow, and Rico Sennrich. 2022. Revisiting End-to-End Speech-to-Text Translation From Scratch. In *International Conference on Machine Learning*, volume 162 of *Proc. of Machine Learning Research*, pages 26193–26205. PMLR.

CMU's IWSLT 2023 Simultaneous Speech Translation System

Brian Yan*[1] Jiatong Shi*[1] Soumi Maiti[1] William Chen[1]
Xinjian Li[1] Yifan Peng[2] Siddhant Arora[1] Shinji Watanabe[1,3]
[1]Language Technologies Institute, Carnegie Mellon University, USA
[2]Electrical and Computer Engineering, Carnegie Mellon University, USA
[3]Human Language Technology Center of Excellence, Johns Hopkins University, USA
{byan, jiatongs}@cs.cmu.edu

Abstract

This paper describes CMU's submission to the IWSLT 2023 simultaneous speech translation shared task for translating English speech to both German text and speech in a streaming fashion. We first build offline speech-to-text (ST) models using the joint CTC/attention framework. These models also use WavLM front-end features and mBART decoder initialization. We adapt our offline ST models for simultaneous speech-to-text translation (SST) by 1) incrementally encoding chunks of input speech, re-computing encoder states for each new chunk and 2) incrementally decoding output text, pruning beam search hypotheses to 1-best after processing each chunk. We then build text-to-speech (TTS) models using the VITS framework and achieve simultaneous speech-to-speech translation (SS2ST) by cascading our SST and TTS models.

1 Introduction

In this paper, we present CMU's English to German simultaneous speech translation systems. Our IWSLT 2023 (Agarwal et al., 2023) shared task submission consists of both simultaneous speech-to-text (SST) and simultaneous speech-to-speech (SS2ST) systems. Our general strategy is to first build large-scale offline speech translation (ST) models which leverage unpaired speech data, ASR data, and ST data. We then adapt these offline models for simultaneous inference. Finally, we use a text-to-speech model to achieve SS2ST in a cascaded manner.

In particular, our system consists of:

1. Offline ST using joint CTC/attention with self-supervised speech/text representations (§3.1)
2. Offline-to-online adaptation via chunk-based encoding and incremental beam search (§3.2)
3. Simultaneous S2ST by feeding incremental text outputs to a text-to-speech model (§3.3)

2 Task Description

The IWSLT 2023 simultaneous speech translation track[1] is a shared task for streaming speech-to-text and speech-to-speech translation of TED talks. This track mandates that systems do not perform re-translation, meaning that the streaming outputs cannot be edited after the system receives more input audio. Systems are required to meet a particular latency regime: SST systems must have <2 seconds average lagging (AL) and SS2ST systems must have <2.5 seconds start offset (SO) (Ma et al., 2020).

Of the allowed training data, we selected a subset of in-domain data to train our ASR and ST models: for ASR we use TEDLIUM v1 and v2 (Zhou et al., 2020) and for ST we used MuST-C v2 (Di Gangi et al., 2019). We also use a set of cross-domain data to train our MT and TTS models due to the lack of in-domain data: for MT we use Europarl, NewsCommentary, OpenSubtitles, TED2020, Tatoeba, and ELRC-CORDIS News (Tiedemann et al., 2020). For TTS we use CommonVoice (Ardila et al., 2020). The following section describes how each of the ASR, ST, MT, and TTS components fit together in our ultimate systems.

3 System Description

3.1 Offline Speech Translation (ST)

As shown in Figure 1, our offline ST models are based on the joint CTC/attention framework (Watanabe et al., 2017; Yan et al., 2023a). Compared to a purely attention-based approach, joint CTC/attention has been shown to reduce the soft-alignment burden, provide a positive ensembling effect, and improve the robustness of end-detection during inference (Yan et al., 2023a).

To leverage unpaired speech data, we use first use WavLM representations (Chen et al., 2022) as

[1]https://iwslt.org/2023/simultaneous

Proceedings of the 20th International Conference on Spoken Language Translation (IWSLT 2023), pages 235–240
July 13-14, 2023

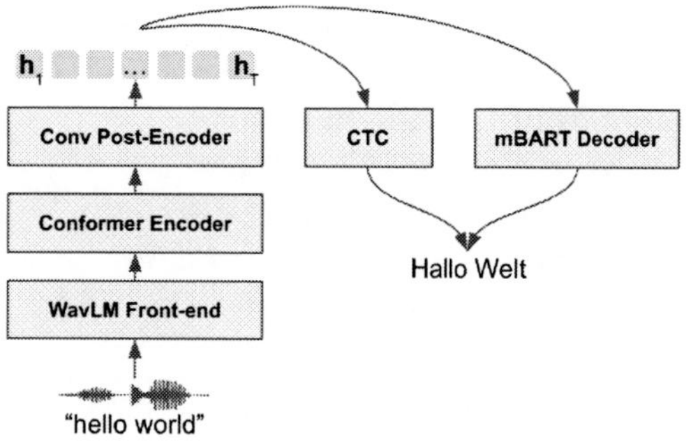

Figure 1: Offline ST model architecture based on the joint CTC/attention framework with a WavLM front-end and mBART decoder.

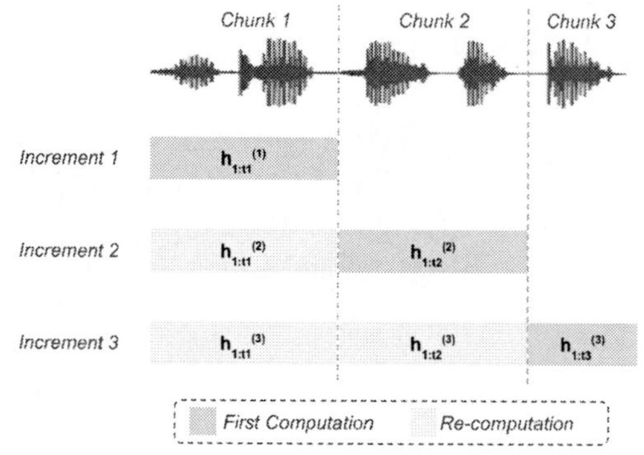

Figure 2: Incremental encoding strategy which processes chunks of input speech by re-computing representations corresponding to earlier chunks.

front-end features to train ASR models. In these models, a pre-encoder module (Chang et al., 2021) applies feature dimension down-sampling and a learned weighted combination of WavLM layers before feeding to a Conformer encoder (Gulati et al., 2020). The pre-encoder and encoder modules from ASR are then used to initialize our ST models.

To leverage unpaired text data, we use the mBART decoder (Tang et al., 2020) as an initialization for our ST models. Following (Li et al., 2020), we freeze all feed-forward layers during fine-tuning and use a post-encoder down-sampling layer to reduce the computational load.

We fine-tune our ST models using the following interpolated loss function: $\mathcal{L} = \lambda_1 \mathcal{L}_{\text{ASR\_CE}} + \lambda_2 \mathcal{L}_{\text{ASR\_CTC}} + \lambda_3 \mathcal{L}_{\text{ST\_CE}} + \lambda_4 \mathcal{L}_{\text{ST\_CTC}}$. Here, the cross-entropy (CE) losses are used to train attentional decoders. Note that in Figure 1, we omit the ASR attentional decoder and CTC components as these function as training regularizations and do not factor into the inference proceedure. We perform fine-tuning on in-domain data consisting primarily of MuST-C (Di Gangi et al., 2019).

To leverage additional in-domain data, we apply MT pseudolabeling to TEDLIUM ASR data (Zhou et al., 2020). We also use the same MT model to apple sequence-level knowledge distillation to the MuST-C data. The MT model is a pre-trained DeltaLM-large (Ma et al., 2021) fine-tuned on the corpora listed in Section 2. The pseudo-labels and distilled sequences were then translated from English to German using a beam size of 10.

3.2 Simultaneous Speech Translation (SST)

We adapt our offline ST model for streaming inference by using a chunk-based processing of input speech. As shown in Figure 2, our scheme uses a fixed duration (e.g. 2 seconds) to compute front-end and encoder representations on chunks of input speech. With each new chunk, we re-compute front-end and encoder representations using the incrementally longer input speech.

To produce incremental translation outputs, we apply several modifications to the offline joint CTC/attention beam search. As shown in Algorithm 1, we run beam search for each chunk of input. Unless we know that the current chunk is the final chunk, we perform end-detection using the

Algorithm 1 Beam search step with rewinding of unreliable hypotheses on non-final chunks and incremental pruning upon end-detection.

```
procedure BEAMSTEP(hyps, prevHyps, isFinal)
    newHyps = {}; endDetected = False
    for y_{1:l-1} ∈ prtHs do
        attnCnds = top-k(P_Attn(y_l|X, y_{1:l-1}), k = p)
        for c ∈ attnCnds do
            y_{1:l} = y_{1:l-1} ⊕ c
            α_CTC = CTCScore(y_{1:l}, X_{1:T})
            α_Attn = AttnScore(y_{1:l}, X_{1:T})
            β = LengthPen(y_{1:l})
            P_Beam(y_{1:l}|X) = α_CTC + α_Attn + β
            newHyps[y_{1:l}] = P_Beam(·)
            if (!isFinal) and (c is <eos> or repeat) then
                endDetected = True
                newHyps = prevHyps                ▷ rewind
            else if l is max L then
                endDetected = True
            end if
        end for
    end for
    if endDetected then                  ▷ incremental pruning
        newHyps = top-k(P_Beam(·), k = 1)
    else                                 ▷ standard pruning
        newHyps = top-k(P_Beam(·), k = b)
    end if
    return newHyps, endDetected
end procedure
```

Model	Quality	Latency	
Offline Speech Translation (ST)	BLEU ↑	-	
Multi-Decoder CTC/Attn (Yan et al., 2023b)	30.1	-	-
WavLM-mBART CTC/Attn (Ours)	32.5	-	-
Simul Speech Translation (SST)	BLEU ↑	AL ↓	LAAL ↓
Time-Sync Blockwise CTC/Attn (Yan et al., 2023b)	26.6	1.93	1.98
WavLM-mBART CTC/Attn (Ours)	30.4	1.92	1.99
Simul Speech-to-Speech Translation (SS2T)	ASR-BLEU ↑	SO ↓	EO ↓
WavLM-mBART CTC/Attn + VITS (Ours)	26.7	2.33	5.67

Table 1: Results of our English to German ST/SST/SS2ST models on MuST-C-v2 tst-COMMON.

heuristics introduced by (Tsunoo et al., 2021). If any of the hypotheses in our beam propose a next candidate which is the special end-of-sequence token or a token which already appeared in the hypothesis, then this strategy determines that the outputs have likely covered all of the available input. At this point, the current hypotheses should be considered unreliable and thus the algorithm rewinds hypotheses to the previous step.

After the end has been detected within the current chunk, we prune the beam to the 1-best hypothesis and select this as our incremental output – this pruning step is necessary to avoid re-translation. When the next input chunk is received, beam search continues from this 1-best hypothesis.

3.3 Simultaneous Speech-to-Speech Translation (S2ST)

Simultaneous S2ST model is created by feeding incremental text outputs to a German text-to-speech model. We use end-to-end TTS model VITS (Kim et al., 2021) and train a single speaker German TTS model using CommonVoice dataset(Ardila et al., 2020). VITS consists of text-encoder, flow based stochastic duration predictor from text, variational auto-encoder for learning latent feature from audio and generator-discriminator based decoder for generating speech from latent feature. We use character as input to the TTS model.

We select a suitable speaker from CommonVoice German dataset and train single speaker TTS. As CommonVoice may contain many noisy utterances which can hurt performance of TTS, we use data-selection for high-quality subset. The data selection process involves identifying the speaker who has the highest number of utterances with high speech quality. To determine the speech quality, we use speech enhancement metric DNSMOS (Reddy et al., 2021) which provides an estimation of the speech quality. We evaluate the speech quality for the top five speakers with the largest number of utterances. To establish the high-quality subset, we set a threshold of 4.0 for selecting sentences that meet the desired quality level. Based on this criterion, we choose the second speaker, who has approximately 12 hours of high-quality data.

Finally, we combine our trained German TTS model with SST module during inference. We feed incremental translation text outputs to TTS and synthesize translated speech.

4 Experimental Setup

Our models were developed using the ESPnet-ST-v2 toolkit (Yan et al., 2023b). Our ST/SST model uses WavLM-large as a front-end (Chen et al., 2022). A linear pre-encoder down-samples from 1024 to 80 feature dim. Our encoder is a 12 layer Conformer with 1024 attention dim, 8 attention heads, and 2048 linear dim (Gulati et al., 2020). A convolutional post-encoder then down-samples along the length dimension by a factor of 2. Our decoder follows the mBART architecture and we initialize using the mBART-large-50-many-to-many model (Tang et al., 2020). Our ST CTC branch uses the same 250k vocabulary as the mBART decoder to enable joint decoding. Our TTS model consists of 6 transformer encoder layers for text-encoder, 4 normalizing flow layers for duration predictor, 16 residual dilated convolutional blocks as posterior encoder and multi-period HiFiGan (Kong et al., 2020) style decoder. We train VITS model for 400 epochs with AdamW (Loshchilov and Hutter, 2019) optimizer.

During inference, we use a chunk size of 2 seconds for SST and 2.5 seconds for SS2ST. For both SST and SS2ST we use beam size 5, CTC weight 0.2, and no length penalty/bonus. To account for incremental outputs which end in a prefix of a word rather than a whole word, we delay outputs for scoring by 1 token. There are two exceptions to this token delay: if the last token is a valid German word or a punctuation, then we do not delay.

We evaluate translation quality using BLEU score (Papineni et al., 2002) for ST/SST and ASR-BLEU score for SS2ST. ST/SST references are case-sensitive and punctuated while SS2ST references are case-insensitive and un-punctuated. The ASR model used for ASR-BLEU is Whisper-small (Radford et al., 2022). We evaluate translation latency for SST using average lagging (AL) (Ma et al., 2020) and length-adaptive average lagging (LAAL) (Papi et al., 2022). We evaluate translation latency for SS2ST using start (SO) and end-offset (EO) (Ma et al., 2020).

5 Results

Table 1 shows the quality and latency of our SST and SS2ST models as measured on En-De tst-COMMON. We also show the ST performance of our model for reference. As a baseline, we compare to the IWSLT-scale ST and SST systems developed in Yan et al. (2023b) – our systems show improved quality, primarily due to the use of WavLM and mBART self-supervised representations.

From ST to SST, we observe a 6% quality degradation. Note that the average duration of tst-COMMON utterances is around 5 seconds, meaning the corresponding latency gain is 60%. From SST to SS2ST, we observe a 12% quality degradation. Note that both the TTS model and the Whisper ASR model powering the ASR-BLEU metric contribute to this gap.

6 Conclusion

We describe our English to German simultaneous speech-to-text and speech-to-speech translation systems for the IWSLT 2023 shared task. We start by building large-scale offline speech-to-text systems which leverage self-supervised speech and text representations. We then adapt these offline models for online inference, enabling simultaneous speech-to-text translation. Finally, we feed streaming text outputs to a down-stream TTS model, enabling simultaneous speech-to-speech translation.

Acknowledgements

Brian Yan and Shinji Watanabe are supported by the Human Language Technology Center of Excellence. This work used the Extreme Science and Engineering Discovery Environment (XSEDE) (Towns et al., 2014), which is supported by National Science Foundation grant number ACI-1548562; specifically, the Bridges system (Nystrom et al., 2015), as part of project cis210027p, which is supported by NSF award number ACI-1445606, at the Pittsburgh Supercomputing Center. This work also used GPUs donated by the NVIDIA Corporation.

References

Milind Agarwal, Sweta Agrawal, Antonios Anastasopoulos, Ondřej Bojar, Claudia Borg, Marine Carpuat, Roldano Cattoni, Mauro Cettolo, Mingda Chen, William Chen, Khalid Choukri, Alexandra Chronopoulou, Anna Currey, Thierry Declerck, Qianqian Dong, Yannick Estève, Kevin Duh, Marcello Federico, Souhir Gahbiche, Barry Haddow, Benjamin Hsu, Phu Mon Htut, Hirofumi Inaguma, Dávid Javorský, John Judge, Yasumasa Kano, Tom Ko, Rishu Kumar, Pengwei Li, Xutail Ma, Prashant Mathur, Evgeny Matusov, Paul McNamee, John P. McCrae, Kenton Murray, Maria Nadejde, Satoshi Nakamura, Matteo Negri, Ha Nguyen, Jan Niehues, Xing Niu, Atul Ojha Kr., John E. Ortega, Proyag Pal, Juan Pino, Lonneke van der Plas, Peter Polák, Elijah Rippeth, Elizabeth Salesky, Jiatong Shi, Matthias Sperber, Sebastian Stüker, Katsuhito Sudoh, Yun Tang, Brian Thompson, Kevin Tran, Marco Turchi, Alex Waibel, Mingxuan Wang, Shinji Watanabe, and Rodolfo Zevallos. 2023. Findings of the IWSLT 2023 Evaluation Campaign. In *Proceedings of the 20th International Conference on Spoken Language Translation (IWSLT 2023)*. Association for Computational Linguistics.

Rosana Ardila, Megan Branson, Kelly Davis, Michael Kohler, Josh Meyer, Michael Henretty, Reuben Morais, Lindsay Saunders, Francis Tyers, and Gregor Weber. 2020. Common voice: A massively-multilingual speech corpus. In *Proceedings of the Twelfth Language Resources and Evaluation Conference*, pages 4218–4222, Marseille, France. European Language Resources Association.

Xuankai Chang, Takashi Maekaku, Pengcheng Guo, Jing Shi, Yen-Ju Lu, Aswin Shanmugam Subramanian, Tianzi Wang, Shu-wen Yang, Yu Tsao, Hung-yi Lee, et al. 2021. An exploration of self-supervised pretrained representations for end-to-end speech recognition. In *2021 IEEE Automatic Speech Recognition and Understanding Workshop (ASRU)*, pages 228–235. IEEE.

Sanyuan Chen, Chengyi Wang, Zhengyang Chen, Yu Wu, Shujie Liu, Zhuo Chen, Jinyu Li, Naoyuki

Kanda, Takuya Yoshioka, Xiong Xiao, et al. 2022. Wavlm: Large-scale self-supervised pre-training for full stack speech processing. *IEEE Journal of Selected Topics in Signal Processing*, 16(6):1505–1518.

Mattia A. Di Gangi, Roldano Cattoni, Luisa Bentivogli, Matteo Negri, and Marco Turchi. 2019. MuST-C: a Multilingual Speech Translation Corpus. In *Proceedings of the 2019 Conference of the North American Chapter of the Association for Computational Linguistics: Human Language Technologies, Volume 1 (Long and Short Papers)*, pages 2012–2017, Minneapolis, Minnesota. Association for Computational Linguistics.

Anmol Gulati, James Qin, Chung-Cheng Chiu, Niki Parmar, Yu Zhang, Jiahui Yu, Wei Han, Shibo Wang, Zhengdong Zhang, Yonghui Wu, and Ruoming Pang. 2020. Conformer: Convolution-augmented Transformer for speech recognition. In *Proceedings of Interspeech*, pages 5036–5040.

Jaehyeon Kim, Jungil Kong, and Juhee Son. 2021. Conditional variational autoencoder with adversarial learning for end-to-end text-to-speech. In *International Conference on Machine Learning*. PMLR.

Jungil Kong, Jaehyeon Kim, and Jaekyoung Bae. 2020. Hifi-gan: Generative adversarial networks for efficient and high fidelity speech synthesis. volume 33, pages 17022–17033.

Xian Li, Changhan Wang, Yun Tang, Chau Tran, Yuqing Tang, Juan Pino, Alexei Baevski, Alexis Conneau, and Michael Auli. 2020. Multilingual speech translation with efficient finetuning of pretrained models. *arXiv preprint arXiv:2010.12829*.

Ilya Loshchilov and Frank Hutter. 2019. Decoupled weight decay regularization. In *International Conference on Learning Representations*.

Shuming Ma, Li Dong, Shaohan Huang, Dongdong Zhang, Alexandre Muzio, Saksham Singhal, Hany Hassan Awadalla, Xia Song, and Furu Wei. 2021. DeltaLM: Encoder-decoder pre-training for language generation and translation by augmenting pretrained multilingual encoders.

Xutai Ma, Mohammad Javad Dousti, Changhan Wang, Jiatao Gu, and Juan Pino. 2020. Simuleval: An evaluation toolkit for simultaneous translation. In *Proceedings of the EMNLP*.

Nicholas A Nystrom, Michael J Levine, Ralph Z Roskies, and J Ray Scott. 2015. Bridges: a uniquely flexible hpc resource for new communities and data analytics. In *Proceedings of the 2015 XSEDE Conference: Scientific Advancements Enabled by Enhanced Cyberinfrastructure*, pages 1–8.

Sara Papi, Marco Gaido, Matteo Negri, and Marco Turchi. 2022. Over-generation cannot be rewarded: Length-adaptive average lagging for simultaneous speech translation. In *Proceedings of the Third Workshop on Automatic Simultaneous Translation*, pages 12–17.

Kishore Papineni, Salim Roukos, Todd Ward, and Wei-Jing Zhu. 2002. Bleu: a method for automatic evaluation of machine translation. In *Proceedings of the 40th Annual Meeting of the Association for Computational Linguistics*, pages 311–318, Philadelphia, Pennsylvania, USA. Association for Computational Linguistics.

Alec Radford, Jong Wook Kim, Tao Xu, Greg Brockman, Christine McLeavey, and Ilya Sutskever. 2022. Robust speech recognition via large-scale weak supervision. *arXiv preprint arXiv:2212.04356*.

Chandan KA Reddy, Vishak Gopal, and Ross Cutler. 2021. Dnsmos: A non-intrusive perceptual objective speech quality metric to evaluate noise suppressors. In *IEEE International Conference on Acoustics, Speech and Signal Processing (ICASSP)*, pages 6493–6497. IEEE.

Yuqing Tang, Chau Tran, Xian Li, Peng-Jen Chen, Naman Goyal, Vishrav Chaudhary, Jiatao Gu, and Angela Fan. 2020. Multilingual translation with extensible multilingual pretraining and finetuning.

Jörg Tiedemann, Santhosh Thottingal, et al. 2020. Opus-mt–building open translation services for the world. In *Proceedings of the 22nd Annual Conference of the European Association for Machine Translation*. European Association for Machine Translation.

J. Towns, T. Cockerill, M. Dahan, I. Foster, K. Gaither, A. Grimshaw, V. Hazlewood, S. Lathrop, D. Lifka, G. D. Peterson, R. Roskies, J. R. Scott, and N. Wilkins-Diehr. 2014. Xsede: Accelerating scientific discovery. *Computing in Science & Engineering*, 16(5):62–74.

Emiru Tsunoo, Yosuke Kashiwagi, and Shinji Watanabe. 2021. Streaming transformer asr with blockwise synchronous beam search. In *2021 IEEE Spoken Language Technology Workshop (SLT)*, pages 22–29. IEEE.

Shinji Watanabe, Takaaki Hori, Suyoun Kim, John R Hershey, and Tomoki Hayashi. 2017. Hybrid ctc/attention architecture for end-to-end speech recognition. *IEEE Journal of Selected Topics in Signal Processing*, 11(8):1240–1253.

Brian Yan, Siddharth Dalmia, Yosuke Higuchi, Graham Neubig, Florian Metze, Alan W Black, and Shinji Watanabe. 2023a. CTC alignments improve autoregressive translation. In *Proceedings of the 17th Conference of the European Chapter of the Association for Computational Linguistics*, pages 1615–1631, Dubrovnik, Croatia. Association for Computational Linguistics.

Brian Yan, Jiatong Shi, Yun Tang, Hirofumi Inaguma, Yifan Peng, Siddharth Dalmia, Peter Polák, Patrick Fernandes, Dan Berrebbi, Tomoki Hayashi, et al. 2023b. Espnet-st-v2: Multipurpose spoken language translation toolkit. *arXiv preprint arXiv:2304.04596*.

Wei Zhou, Wilfried Michel, Kazuki Irie, Markus Kitza, Ralf Schlüter, and Hermann Ney. 2020. The rwth asr system for ted-lium release 2: Improving hybrid hmm with specaugment. In *ICASSP 2020-2020 IEEE International Conference on Acoustics, Speech and Signal Processing (ICASSP)*, pages 7839–7843. IEEE.

Improving Low Resource Speech Translation with Data Augmentation and Ensemble Strategies

Akshaya Vishnu Kudlu Shanbhogue **Ran Xue*** **Soumya Saha***
Daniel Yue Zhang* **Ashwinkumar Ganesan***
Amazon Alexa AI
{ashanbho,ranxue,soumyasa,dyz,gashwink}@amazon.com

Abstract

This paper describes the speech translation system submitted as part of the IWSLT 2023 shared task on low resource speech translation. The low resource task aids in building models for language pairs where the training corpus is limited. In this paper, we focus on two language pairs, namely, Tamasheq-French (Tmh→Fra) and Marathi-Hindi (Mr→Hi) and implement a speech translation system that is *unconstrained*. We evaluate three strategies in our system: (a) Data augmentation where we perform different operations on audio as well as text samples, (b) an ensemble model that integrates a set of models trained using a combination of augmentation strategies, and (c) post-processing techniques where we explore the use of large language models (LLMs) to improve the quality of sentences that are generated. Experiments show how data augmentation can relatively improve the BLEU score by 5.2% over the baseline system for Tmh→Fra while an ensemble model further improves performance by 17% for Tmh→Fra and 23% for Mr→Hi task.

1 Introduction

Speech translation (ST) systems have multiple applications. They can be utilized in a wide range of scenarios such as closed captioning in different languages while watching videos or even as a real-time assistant that translates speeches to live audiences. One persistent challenge for speech translation systems continues to be performing translations for low resource language pairs.[1] The IWSLT 2023 (Agarwal et al., 2023) shared task for low resource speech translation targets 8 language pairs that include Tunisian Arabic (Aeg) to English (En), Irish (Ga) to English (En), Marathi (Mr) to Hindi (Hi), Maltese (Mlt) to English (En), Pashto (Pus) to French (Fr), Tamasheq (Tmh) to French (Fr), and Quechua (Que) to Spanish (Es). This paper outlines a low resource speech translation system (from the Amazon Alexa AI team) for 2 language pairs, namely, Tamasheq-French (**Tmh→Fra**) and Marathi-Hindi (**Mr→Hi**).

Depending on the type of output that is generated the end-to-end speech translation task has two formats: (a) Speech-to-text (S2T), and (b) Speech-to-Speech (S2S). There are two types of ST systems. The first is a cascaded system where speech recognition and language translation are decoupled.[2] The second is an end-to-end (E2E) model that combines both audio processing and language translation. We design and evaluate an E2E model in this paper.

In the past, various approaches have been proposed to build E2E low resource speech translation models. Bansal et al. (2018) designs an initial system that is an encoder-decoder architecture that integrates a convolutional neural network (CNN) and recurrent neural network (RNN). Stoian et al. (2020) try to improve ST models for low resource languages by pretraininig the model on automated speech recognition (ASR) task. Cheng et al. (2021) propose a new learning framework called AlloST that trains a transformer architecture with language-independent phonemes. Mi et al. (2022) improves translation performance by expanding the training corpus through generation of synthetic translation examples, where the target sequences are replaced with diverse paraphrases. In IWSLT 2022 (Anastasopoulos et al., 2022), Boito et al. (2022b) utilized a wav2vec encoder and trained an E2E ST model where source audios are directly translated to the target language.[3]

In this paper, we extend the previous work with the following contributions:

- We train and assess a speech translation model

* These authors contributed equally to this work.

[1] https://iwslt.org/2023/low-resource

[2] For the S2S version, speech generation is separate too.

[3] They contributed towards the low resource speech translation task for Tmh→Fra.

Proceedings of the 20th International Conference on Spoken Language Translation (IWSLT 2023), pages 241–250
July 13-14, 2023 ©2023 Association for Computational Linguistics

for Tmh→Fra with audio stretching (Yang et al., 2021).

- The baseline model for Tmh→Fra is trained with a back-translation corpus generated using the NLLB-200 machine translation model (Team et al., 2022).
- For Tmh→Fra, we build a separate training corpus of paraphrases and show that model performance improves when trained on this dataset (Bhavsar et al., 2022).
- We show how a weighted cross entropy loss further improves the performance of the Tmh→Fra translation model. The model trained with this loss, additional data generated using paraphrases and audio stretching is shown to perform 5.2% better than the baseline.
- An ensemble of models trained on the above strategies shows the best performance, with BLEU score that is 17.2% higher than the average BLEU score of the individual models within the ensemble.
- In case of Mr→ Hi, our best independent ensemble model shows a 23% improvement over the average BLEU score of the individual models within the ensemble.

Apart from these contributions, we also explore post-processing techniques with large language models (LLMs), focusing on re-ranking generated translations (Kannan et al., 2018), correcting the grammar of translations and masking tokens so that the LLM can complete the translate sentence. These methods though, did not yield any noticeable improvement.

The paper is organized as follows: Section 2 describes our speech translation system, 3.1 has details about the datasets for various language pairs, 3.2 contains analysis of our experimental results and we finally conclude in 4.

2 Speech Translation System

2.1 Baseline Model

Our base model for Tmh→Fra ST task is an end-to-end speech translation system which employs an encoder-decoder architecture (Vaswani et al., 2017). We initialize the audio feature extractor and the 6-layer transformer encoder from a pretrained wav2vec 2.0 base model (Baevski et al., 2020). We reuse the wav2vec 2.0 model pretrained on 243 hours of Tamasheq audio data released by ON-TRAC Consortium Systems (Boito et al., 2022b). During initialization, the last 6 layers of the pre-trained wav2vec 2.0 model are discarded. We use a shallow decoder which consists 2 transformer layers with 4 attention heads. Between encoder and decoder, we use one feed-forward layer to match the dimension of encoder output and decoder input.

During training, the model directly performs speech to text translation task without generating intermediate source language text. The training loss is the cross entropy loss between ground truth and hypothesis with label smoothing of 0.1. Each experiment is trained for 200 epochs and check-points are selected based on best validation BLEU.

For Marathi-Hindi speech-to-text (ST) model, we chose a Wav2Vec 2.0 base model finetuned on 960 h of English speech (Baevski et al., 2020) as the encoder baseline. We also used the same encoder model finetuned on 94 hours of Marathi audio data (Chadha et al., 2022) in our experiments. For these models, the last 6 layers of the pretrained models were discarded, while the decoder architecture and other hyperparameters were kept same as the Tmh→Fra models [4]. For audio encoder, we also experimented with Wav2vec 2.0 XLS-R 0.3B model (Babu et al., 2021) and another XLS-R 0.3B model specifically finetuned on Marathi audio (Bhattacharjee, 2022). Because the XLS-R base model was trained on audio from a range of Indian languages including Marathi and Hindi, we chose to incorporate XLS-R in our experimentation. For the XLS-R based models, we utilized the first 12 out of 24 encoder layers to initialize the encoder followed by a linear projection layer to transform the output features of 1024 dimensions to the desired decoder dimensionality of 256. We trained all Marathi-Hindi ST models for 300 epochs and we chose the best checkpoint based on validation BLEU score.

2.2 Data Augmentation

2.2.1 Audio Stretching

We apply audio stretching directly on wav form data using torchaudio library (Yang et al., 2021).[5] For each audio sample, we alter the speed of the audio with a rate uniformly sampled from $[0.8, 1.2]$ with a probability of 0.8 while maintaining the audio sample rate.

[4] Detailed hyperparameters used can be found in A.1.
[5] https://github.com/pytorch/audio

2.2.2 Back-Translation

We use the NLLB-200 machine translation model to generate variations of target text in French (Team et al., 2022). The original French data is first translated into English, and then translated back into French. For French to English translation, only 1 best prediction is used. For English to French translation, we take the top 5 results with a beam size of 5.

We also try to generate synthetic transcription of the Tamasheq audio by translating French text into Tamasheq. However, we notice that the translation quality is unstable and decide to not use it for the experiment.

2.2.3 Paraphrasing

We use a French paraphrase model (Bhavsar, 2022), which is a fine tuned version of mBART model (Liu et al., 2020), to generate variations of target text in French. We take the top 5 paraphrases using beam search with a beam size of 5.

2.2.4 Weighted Loss

As the quality of synthetically generated sentences varies, we apply a sentence level weight to the corresponding sample's cross entropy loss during training.

$$l = \sum_{i}^{N} w_i * CE(y_i, \hat{y}_i) \quad (1)$$

where N is the size of the corpus, y_i, $\hat{y}_i$, w_i are ground truth, prediction, and loss weight for sample i respectively . For back-translation data, the weights are directly taken from the prediction score of NLLB-200. For paraphrasing data, we calculate the perplexity of each generated paraphrase and then take the exponential of the perplexity as the weight. For original training data (clean and full), weight are set to 1.

2.3 Ensemble Model

Ensemble decoding (Liu et al., 2018; Zhang and Ao, 2022) is a method of combining probability values generated by multiple models while decoding the next token. We provide equal-weight to N different ensemble models as shown in 2.

$$logP(y_t|x, y_{1...t-1}) = \frac{1}{N}\sum_{i}^{N} logP_{\theta_i}(y_t|x, y_{1...t-1}) \quad (2)$$

Where, y_t denotes the decoded token at time t, x denotes the input and θ_i denotes the ith model in the ensemble.

We apply the following ensemble decoding strategies:

- Independent ensemble: we ensemble checkpoints having the highest BLEU scores on the validation set, on N training runs. The N different models have the same architecture, but initialized with different seed values.
- Data-augmented ensemble: we ensemble checkpoints having the highest BLEU scores on the validation set, on N training runs. The N different models have the same architecture, but trained on different data augmentation strategies.

We additionally attempt a checkpoint ensemble, where N different checkpoints having the highest validation BLEU within the same training run are ensembled. Since we notice marginal improvements with checkpoint ensemble, we decide to not explore checkpoint ensemble in depth for our experiments.

2.4 Post Processing with LLMs

We further explore a set of post processing strategies by leveraging large language models (LLM) to 1) rerank the top-k generated samples; 2) correct grammar of the output; and 3) guess the missing tokens of the sentence. The strategy is based on the observation that translation outputs from the validation set often carry incomplete sentences and broken grammar. We found that LLMs are good fit to address this problem as they have brought promising improvements in sentence re-ranking, and rewriting tasks (Liu et al., 2023). We summarize our proposed strategies as follows:

2.4.1 Re-ranking

The reranking approach takes the top 5 results from the best-performing candidate, and rerank these outputs with language models. We first explore performing shallow fusion (Kannan et al., 2018) with language model (GPT2-Fr).[6] Additionally, we leverage a LLM (French finetuned-Alpaca 7B [7]) to guess the most probable sentence that is from a radio broadcast news with the prompt:

quelle phrase est plus susceptible d'apparaître dans un journal télévisé

[6] https://github.com/aquadzn/gpt2-french

[7] https://github.com/bofenghuang/vigogne

2.4.2 Sentence Correction

The sentence correction approach rewrites the whole output prediction by correcting the grammatical and spelling errors. We use two LLMs for this tasks - aforementioned Alpaca model and Bloom 7B with the following prompt: [8]

> *Corrigez la faute de frappe et la grammaire de la phrase sans changer la structure*

2.4.3 Token Masking

The token masking approach first masks the translation output with <blank> tokens for out-of-vocabulary (OOV) tokens. For example the predicted output "...Les questions sont [pi];." is replaced with " <blank> Les questions sont <blank>." where [pi] is a common token we observed in the prediction output that does not carry meaning. We then apply the following prompt to let the LLMs to complete the sentence:

> *complétez la phrase en remplaçant les jetons <blank>*

3 Experiments

3.1 Datasets

3.1.1 Tamasheq-French Corpus

The dataset used for our training, validation, and testing is obtained from Boito et al. (2022a), which is shared as a part of IWSLT 2023 shared task. It consists of a parallel corpus of radio recordings in Tamasheq language predominantly from male speakers. The dataset includes approximately 18 hours of speech divided in training, validation and test sets along with its French translation. We refer to this data as "clean". Additionally, there is approximately 2 hours of possible noisy training data from the same source, which we include in our experiments along with the clean data. We refer to this combined 20 hour dataset as "full" data. The statistics of the dataset are in Table 2.

Data Split	Hours	# Utterances
train clean	13.6	4,444
train full	15.5	4,886
valid	1.7	581
test2022	2	804
test2023	1	374

Table 2: **Data statistics for tmh→fra corpus.** *Hours* shows the number of hours of audio samples available while *# Utterances* is the associated number of utterances.

[8] https://huggingface.co/bigscience/bloom-7b1

3.1.2 Marathi-Hindi Corpus

For Marathi-Hindi we use the data from Panlingua (2023) containing approximately 25 hours of speech. The audio recordings are sourced from the news domain. The statistics of the dataset is shown in Table 3.

Data Split	Hours	# Utterances
train	16	7,990
valid	3.7	2,103
test	4.5	2,164

Table 3: **Data statistics for mr→hi corpus.** *Hours* shows the number of hours of audio samples available while *# Utterances* is the associated number of utterances.

3.2 Experimental Results

In this section, we compare the effects of data augmentation, ensembling and post-processing strategies on the tmh→fra task on test 2022 dataset. We additionally compare results on the mr→hi task on the validation dataset.

3.2.1 Impact of Data Augmentation

Table 1 shows the effect of various data augmentation strategies used. We find that using full-audio dataset performs better than using just the clean-audio data. Also, adding audio stretching alone does not improve model performance.

Adding synthetically generated back-translation data shows mixed results. We hypothesize that this is due to cascading errors while performing back-translation. However, adding paraphrases data performs slightly better than baseline. We find that using a weighted loss while using synthetically generated translation data is beneficial.

3.2.2 Performance of Ensemble Model

Table 6 shows the summary of the effect of different ensembling strategies. For complete results, refer to table 12. We find that the performance of the ensemble model increases with the increase in number of models present in the ensemble. We also find that the data-augmented ensemble works better than independent ensemble. Additionally, data-augmented ensembling using paraphrase data performs better than data-augmented ensembling using back-translation data.

3.2.3 Impact of Post-processing Methods

Table 4 summarizes the experimental results for the post-editing strategies. We make the following observations. First, sentence correction strategy

#	Data	Data Augmentation	Vocab size	Loss	Test2022 BLEU
cb	clean	baseline	1k	baseline	8.85
fb	full	baseline	1k	baseline	9.25
ft	full	back-translation	3k	baseline	8.84
ftw	full	back-translation	3k	weighted	9.45
fta	full	back-translation + audio stretching	3k	baseline	9.01
ftaw	full	back-translation + audio stretching	3k	weighted	**9.71**
fp	full	paraphrase	3k	baseline	**9.70**
fpw	full	paraphrase	3k	weighted	**9.73**
fpa	full	paraphrase + audio stretching	3k	baseline	9.47
fpaw	full	paraphrase + audio stretching	3k	weighted	9.53

Table 1: **Impact of Data Augmentation on tmh→fra models.** The table shows the BLEU scores for different strategies in comparison to the baseline trained on *clean* and *full* dataset. *Back-Translation + audio stretching* and *Paraphrase* dataset augmentation improve the BLEU score. *Back-Translation* alone can improve model performance when combined with a weighted loss.

Approach	Model	Test2022 BLEU
Baseline	Ensembled Wav2Vec2	11.26
Reranking	Shallow-Fusion-based (GPT2-French)	11.24
	Instruct-based (Stanford Alpaca 7B)	10.78
Token Masking	Stanford Alpaca 7B	11.20
	Bloom 6.7B	10.84
Sentence Correction	Stanford Alpaca 7B	8.70
	Bloom 6.7B	8.54
Translation + Reranking	Stanford Alpaca 7B	3.45
	Bloom 6.7B	3.58

Table 4: **Impact of Post Processing on tmh→fra corpus.** The post-processing steps outlined are applied to an *Ensembled Wav2Vec2* model. The post-processing with a LLM does not provide any additional benefit.

Reranking	*Instruct*: quelle phrase est plus susceptible d'apparaître dans un journal télévisé *Input*: top k hypothesis *Output*: best hypothesis picked by LLM
Token Masking	*Instruct*: complétez la phrase en remplaçant les jetons <blank>? *Input*: Donc, on dirait que l'organisation de l'UENA, elle est <blank> *Output*: Donc, on dirait que l'organisation de l'UENA, elle est **un organisme de bienfaits**
Sentence Correction	*Instruct*: Corrigez la faute de frappe et la grammaire de la phrase sans changer la structure *Input*: Les a été libérés et ceux qui sont rentrés. *Output*: Ils ont été libéré et ceux rentrant.

Table 5: **Prompt Designs.** Example LLM Prompts for Post Processing tmh→fra corpus.

Ensemble Models (Refer Table 1)	Ensemble Type	Test2022 BLEU
cb-ensemble	Independent	10.32
fb-ensemble	Independent	10.79
ft+ftw+fta+ftaw	Data Augmented Back-translation	10.95
fp+fpw+fpa+fpaw	Data Augmented Paraphrase	**11.26**

Number of models	Avg Test BLEU
4	**10.83**
3	10.60
2	10.23
1 (No Ensemble)	9.24

Table 6: **Impact of Ensembling tmh→fra ST models.** Ensembling models trained with different seeds increases the BLEU score. Increasing the number of models in ensemble also increases performance.

leads to significant performance degradation compared to the ensemble baseline. We attribute this observation to the fact that the pretrained LLMs lacks context-specific data of the Tamasheq corpus. For example, when asked to correct the output sentence, LLMs tend to re-frame the phrases related to more generic topics like sports or events.

Second, we find reranking and token masking strategies both lead to slight degradation compared to the baseline. This is due to the fact that both approaches make less aggressive changes to the original output. In general, we find LLMs do not perform well when the predicted text deviates too much from the ground truth.

Finally, we perform the same set of the strategies but using translated English output from the original French translation. We present the best performing candidates (Translation+Reranking in Table 4). We find that this strategy caused the worst performance degradation due to error propagation

#	Model	Vocab size	Validation BLEU
mwb	wav2vec2-base-960h	1k	11.41
mwbm1k	wav2vec2-base-marathi	1k	**13.19**
mwbm3k	wav2vec2-base-marathi	3k	11.85
mwx	wav2vec2-xls-r-300m	1k	**15.94**
mwxm	wav2vec2-xls-r-300m-marathi	1k	10.76

Table 7: **Model performance on mr→hi task.** Average BLEU scores are shown for the models which we trained with multiple seeds. Move to XLS-R model as encoder improved BLEU by 40% over baseline. Complete results in Table 13

Ensemble Models (Refer Table 7)	Validation BLEU
mwbm1k-ensemble	**16.17**
mwbm3k-ensemble	13.80
mwx-ensemble	**19.63**

Table 8: **Impact of Ensembling mr→hi models.** Consistent with experiments from tmh→fra, an independent ensemble model built from different seeds improves BLEU score.

Ensemble Models (Refer Table 1)	Ensemble Type	Test2023 BLEU
cb-ensemble	Independent	9.28
fb-ensemble	Independent	**9.50**
ft+ftw+fta+ftaw	Data Augmented Back-translation	8.87
fp+fpw+fpa+fpaw	Data Augmented Paraphrase	9.30

Table 9: **Test 2023 results for tmh→fra ST models.**

Models	Test2023 BLEU
mwbm1k-ensemble	25.60
mwbm3k-ensemble	23.00
mwx-ensemble	**28.60**

Table 10: **Test 2023 results for mr→hi ST models.**

caused by fra→eng→fra translation.

3.2.4 Marathi-Hindi

We present the BLEU scores of various models we have trained on the validation dataset. From Table 7 we can see that our *wav2vec2-base-marathi* model outperforms the baseline *wav2vec2-base-960h* model by 16% in terms of BLEU score. We also notice increasing vocabulary size of the tokenizer leads to worse performance. It could be attributed to the fact that the size of the data is not adequate for the model to properly train with the provided hyperparameters. The *wav2vec2-xls-r-300m* model outperforms baseline *wav2vec2-base-960h* model by 40%. We notice that the Marathi finetuned version of the same model performs worse than our baseline.

We perform independent ensemble decoding on the models with the same architecture and hyperparameters but trained with different seeds. The results are shown in Table 8. Refer Table 14 for full results. We notice that ensemble decoding improves the BLEU score of the best model by 23% compared to the average BLEU score of the individual models used in the ensemble.

3.3 Test 2023 results

Results for the different models on Test 2023 dataset for Tmh→Fra are present in Table 9 and Mr→Hi results are present in Table 10.

4 Conclusion

In this paper, we explore multiple types of strategies to improve speech translation for two language pairs: Tamasheq-French (Tmh→Fra) and Marathi-Hindi (Mr→Hi). We show expanding the training dataset with paraphrases of translated sentences as well as an ensemble model (of trained ST models with different seeds and data augmentation methods), improves performance over the baseline model for (Tmh→Fra). Similarly, an ensemble model for Marathi-Hindi (Mr→Hi) has a higher BLEU score in comparison to the baseline architecture. We also explore the use of large language models and find that post-processing using them did not show any noticeable improvement.

References

Milind Agarwal, Sweta Agrawal, Antonios Anastasopoulos, Ondřej Bojar, Claudia Borg, Marine Carpuat, Roldano Cattoni, Mauro Cettolo, Mingda Chen, William Chen, Khalid Choukri, Alexandra Chronopoulou, Anna Currey, Thierry Declerck, Qianqian Dong, Yannick Estève, Kevin Duh, Marcello Federico, Souhir Gahbiche, Barry Haddow, Benjamin Hsu, Phu Mon Htut, Hirofumi Inaguma, Dávid Javorský, John Judge, Yasumasa Kano, Tom Ko, Rishu Kumar, Pengwei Li, Xutail Ma, Prashant Mathur, Evgeny Matusov, Paul McNamee, John P. McCrae, Kenton Murray, Maria Nadejde, Satoshi Nakamura, Matteo Negri, Ha Nguyen, Jan Niehues, Xing Niu, Atul Ojha Kr., John E. Ortega, Proyag Pal, Juan Pino, Lonneke van der Plas, Peter Polák, Elijah Rippeth, Elizabeth Salesky, Jiatong Shi, Matthias Sperber, Sebastian Stüker, Katsuhito Sudoh, Yun Tang, Brian Thompson, Kevin Tran, Marco Turchi, Alex Waibel, Mingxuan Wang, Shinji Watanabe, and Rodolfo Zevallos. 2023. Findings of the IWSLT 2023 Evaluation Campaign. In *Proceedings of the 20th International Conference on Spoken Language Translation (IWSLT 2023)*. Association for Computational Linguistics.

Antonios Anastasopoulos, Loic Barrault, Luisa Bentivogli, Marcely Zanon Boito, Ondrej Bojar, Roldano Cattoni, Anna Currey, Georgiana Dinu, Kevin Duh, Maha Elbayad, Clara Emmanuel, Yannick Esteve, Marcello Federico, Christian Federmann, Souhir Gahbiche, Hongyu Gong, Roman Grundkiewicz, Barry Haddow, Benjamin Hsu, David Javorsky, Vera Kloudova, Surafel Melaku Lakew, Xutai Ma, Prashant Mathur, Paul McNamee, Kenton Murray, Maria Nădejde, Satoshi Nakamura, Matteo Negri, Jan Niehues, Xing Niu, John Ortega, Juan Pino, Elizabeth Salesky, Jiatong Shi, Matthias Sperber, Sebastian Stuker, Katsuhito Sudoh, Marco Turchi, Yogesh Virkar, Alex Waibel, Changhan Wang, and Shinji Watanabe. 2022. Findings of the iwslt 2022 evaluation campaign. In *IWSLT 2022*.

Arun Babu, Changhan Wang, Andros Tjandra, Kushal Lakhotia, Qiantong Xu, Naman Goyal, Kritika Singh, Patrick von Platen, Yatharth Saraf, Juan Pino, Alexei Baevski, Alexis Conneau, and Michael Auli. 2021. Xls-r: Self-supervised cross-lingual speech representation learning at scale.

Alexei Baevski, Henry Zhou, Abdelrahman Mohamed, and Michael Auli. 2020. wav2vec 2.0: A framework for self-supervised learning of speech representations.

Sameer Bansal, Herman Kamper, Karen Livescu, Adam Lopez, and Sharon Goldwater. 2018. Low-resource speech-to-text translation. *arXiv preprint arXiv:1803.09164*.

Joydeep Bhattacharjee. 2022. Xls-r marathi pre-trained model. `https://huggingface.co/infinitejoy/wav2vec2-large-xls-r-300m-marathi-cv8`. Accessed: 2023-04-15.

Nidhir Bhavsar. 2022. French paraphrase model. `https://huggingface.co/enimai/mbart-large-50-paraphrase-finetuned-for-fr`. Accessed: 2023-04-12.

Nidhir Bhavsar, Rishikesh Devanathan, Aakash Bhatnagar, Muskaan Singh, Petr Motlicek, and Tirthankar Ghosal. 2022. Team innovators at SemEval-2022 for task 8: Multi-task training with hyperpartisan and semantic relation for multi-lingual news article similarity. In *Proceedings of the 16th International Workshop on Semantic Evaluation (SemEval-2022)*, pages 1163–1170, Seattle, United States. Association for Computational Linguistics.

Marcely Zanon Boito, Fethi Bougares, Florentin Barbier, Souhir Gahbiche, Loïc Barrault, Mickael Rouvier, and Yannick Estéve. 2022a. Speech resources in the tamasheq language. *Language Resources and Evaluation Conference (LREC)*.

Marcely Zanon Boito, John Ortega, Hugo Riguidel, Antoine Laurent, Loïc Barrault, Fethi Bougares, Firas Chaabani, Ha Nguyen, Florentin Barbier, Souhir Gahbiche, et al. 2022b. On-trac consortium systems for the iwslt 2022 dialect and low-resource speech translation tasks. *IWSLT*.

Harveen Singh Chadha, Anirudh Gupta, Priyanshi Shah, Neeraj Chhimwal, Ankur Dhuriya, Rishabh Gaur, and Vivek Raghavan. 2022. Vakyansh: Asr toolkit for low resource indic languages.

Yao-Fei Cheng, Hung-Shin Lee, and Hsin-Min Wang. 2021. Allost: Low-resource speech translation without source transcription. *arXiv preprint arXiv:2105.00171*.

Anjuli Kannan, Yonghui Wu, Patrick Nguyen, Tara N Sainath, Zhijeng Chen, and Rohit Prabhavalkar. 2018. An analysis of incorporating an external language model into a sequence-to-sequence model. In *2018 IEEE International Conference on Acoustics, Speech and Signal Processing (ICASSP)*, pages 1–5828. IEEE.

Pengfei Liu, Weizhe Yuan, Jinlan Fu, Zhengbao Jiang, Hiroaki Hayashi, and Graham Neubig. 2023. Pre-train, prompt, and predict: A systematic survey of prompting methods in natural language processing. *ACM Computing Surveys*, 55(9):1–35.

Yinhan Liu, Jiatao Gu, Naman Goyal, Xian Li, Sergey Edunov, Marjan Ghazvininejad, Mike Lewis, and Luke Zettlemoyer. 2020. Multilingual denoising pre-training for neural machine translation. *Transactions of the Association for Computational Linguistics*, 8:726–742.

Yuchen Liu, Long Zhou, Yining Wang, Yang Zhao, Jiajun Zhang, and Chengqing Zong. 2018. A comparable study on model averaging, ensembling and reranking in nmt. In *Natural Language Processing and Chinese Computing*.

Ilya Loshchilov and Frank Hutter. 2019. Decoupled weight decay regularization.

Chenggang Mi, Lei Xie, and Yanning Zhang. 2022. Improving data augmentation for low resource speech-to-text translation with diverse paraphrasing. *Neural Networks*, 148:194–205.

Language Processing LLP Panlingua. 2023. Dataset for marathi-hindi speech translation shared task@iwslt-2023. Contributor/©holder: Panlingua Languague Processing LLP, India and Insight Centre for Data Analytics, Data Science Institue, University of Galway, Ireland.

Mihaela C Stoian, Sameer Bansal, and Sharon Goldwater. 2020. Analyzing asr pretraining for low-resource speech-to-text translation. In *ICASSP 2020-2020 IEEE International Conference on Acoustics, Speech and Signal Processing (ICASSP)*, pages 7909–7913. IEEE.

NLLB Team, Marta R. Costa-jussà, James Cross, Onur Çelebi, Maha Elbayad, Kenneth Heafield, Kevin Heffernan, Elahe Kalbassi, Janice Lam, Daniel Licht, Jean Maillard, Anna Sun, Skyler Wang, Guillaume Wenzek, Al Youngblood, Bapi Akula, Loic Barrault, Gabriel Mejia Gonzalez, Prangthip Hansanti, John Hoffman, Semarley Jarrett, Kaushik Ram Sadagopan, Dirk Rowe, Shannon Spruit, Chau Tran, Pierre Andrews, Necip Fazil Ayan, Shruti Bhosale, Sergey Edunov, Angela Fan, Cynthia Gao, Vedanuj Goswami, Francisco Guzmán, Philipp Koehn, Alexandre Mourachko, Christophe Ropers, Safiyyah Saleem, Holger Schwenk, and Jeff Wang. 2022. No language left behind: Scaling human-centered machine translation.

Ashish Vaswani, Noam Shazeer, Niki Parmar, Jakob Uszkoreit, Llion Jones, Aidan N. Gomez, Lukasz Kaiser, and Illia Polosukhin. 2017. Attention is all you need.

Yao-Yuan Yang, Moto Hira, Zhaoheng Ni, Anjali Chourdia, Artyom Astafurov, Caroline Chen, Ching-Feng Yeh, Christian Puhrsch, David Pollack, Dmitriy Genzel, Donny Greenberg, Edward Z. Yang, Jason Lian, Jay Mahadeokar, Jeff Hwang, Ji Chen, Peter Goldsborough, Prabhat Roy, Sean Narenthiran, Shinji Watanabe, Soumith Chintala, Vincent Quenneville-Bélair, and Yangyang Shi. 2021. Torchaudio: Building blocks for audio and speech processing. *arXiv preprint arXiv:2110.15018*.

Ziqiang Zhang and Junyi Ao. 2022. The YiTrans speech translation system for IWSLT 2022 offline shared task. In *Proceedings of the 19th International Conference on Spoken Language Translation (IWSLT 2022)*, pages 158–168, Dublin, Ireland (in-person and online). Association for Computational Linguistics.

A Appendix

A.1 Hyperparameters and Computing Resource

- encoder
  - n layers: 6
  - hidden dim: 1024 for mr-hi xls-r model, 768 for tmh-fra model and other mr-hi model
  - n head: 12
  - activation: gelu
- decoder
  - n layers: 2
  - hidden dim: 256
  - n head: 4
  - activation: gelu
- training
  - optimizer: AdamW (Loshchilov and Hutter, 2019)
  - lr: $1e-3$
  - encoder lr: $1e-5$
  - label smoothing: 0.1
  - batch size: 4
- computing resource: AWS g5.12xlarge instance (4x NVIDIA A10G Tensor Core GPUs)

A.2 Full Results

#	Data	Data Augmentation	Vocab size	Loss	Seed	Test2022 BLEU
cb1	clean	baseline	1k	baseline	v1	8.98
cb2	clean	baseline	1k	baseline	v2	8.91
cb3	clean	baseline	1k	baseline	v3	8.82
cb4	clean	baseline	1k	baseline	v4	8.69
fb1	full	baseline	1k	baseline	v1	9.53
fb2	full	baseline	1k	baseline	v2	9.10
fb3	full	baseline	1k	baseline	v3	9.21
fb4	full	baseline	1k	baseline	v4	9.17

Table 11: Results of different seed experiments on tmh→fra models.

Data	Data Augmentation	Models in Ensemble (Refer to Table 1)	Test BLEU
clean	baseline	cb1+cb2+cb3+cb4	10.32
clean	baseline	cb1+cb2+cb3	10.22
clean	baseline	cb1+cb2+cb4	9.97
clean	baseline	cb1+cb3+cb4	10.17
clean	baseline	cb2+cb3+cb4	10.14
clean	baseline	cb1+cb2	9.79
clean	baseline	cb1+cb3	9.76
clean	baseline	cb1+cb4	9.86
clean	baseline	cb2+cb3	9.93
clean	baseline	cb2+cb4	10.17
clean	baseline	cb3+cb4	9.67
full	baseline	fb1+fb2+fb3+fb4	10.79
full	baseline	fb1+fb2+fb3	10.52
full	baseline	fb1+fb2+fb4	10.69
full	baseline	fb1+fb3+fb4	10.58
full	baseline	fb2+fb3+fb4	10.42
full	baseline	fb1+fb2	10.00
full	baseline	fb1+fb3	10.16
full	baseline	fb1+fb4	10.22
full	baseline	fb2+fb3	10.08
full	baseline	fb2+fb4	9.98
full	baseline	fb3+fb4	10.06
full	back-translation	ft+ftw+fta+ftaw	10.95
full	back-translation	ft+ftw+fta	10.49
full	back-translation	ft+ftw+ftaw	10.75
full	back-translation	ft+fta+ftaw	10.93
full	back-translation	ftw+fta+ftaw	11.26
full	back-translation	ft+ftw	10.08
full	back-translation	ft+fta	9.82
full	back-translation	ft+ftaw	10.49
full	back-translation	ftw+fta	10.4
full	back-translation	ftw+ftaw	10.72
full	back-translation	fta+ftaw	10.78
full	paraphrase	fp+fpw+fpa+fpaw	11.26
full	paraphrase	fp+fpw+fpa	10.78
full	paraphrase	fp+fpw+fpaw	10.91
full	paraphrase	fp+fpa+fpaw	10.77
full	paraphrase	fpw+fpa+fpaw	11.95
full	paraphrase	fp+fpw	10.40
full	paraphrase	fp+fpa	10.62
full	paraphrase	fp+fpaw	10.76
full	paraphrase	fpw+fpa	10.60
full	paraphrase	fpw+fpaw	10.61
full	paraphrase	fpa+fpaw	10.44

Table 12: Impact of Ensembling tmh→fra models (complete).

#	Model	Vocab size	Seed	Validation BLEU
mwbm1k1	wav2vec2-base-marathi	1k	v1	13.19
mwbm1k2	wav2vec2-base-marathi	1k	v2	13.15
mwbm1k3	wav2vec2-base-marathi	1k	v3	**13.39**
mwbm1k4	wav2vec2-base-marathi	1k	v4	13.01
mwbm3k1	wav2vec2-base-marathi	3k	v1	11.63
mwbm3k2	wav2vec2-base-marathi	3k	v2	11.71
mwbm3k3	wav2vec2-base-marathi	3k	v3	11.80
mwbm3k4	wav2vec2-base-marathi	3k	v4	12.26
mwx1	wav2vec2-xls-r-300m	1k	v1	**16.31**
mwx2	wav2vec2-xls-r-300m	1k	v2	15.35
mwx3	wav2vec2-xls-r-300m	1k	v4	16.09
mwx4	wav2vec2-xls-r-300m	1k	v4	16.00

Table 13: Results of different seed experiments on mr→hi models.

Model	Ensemble Models (Refer Table 13)	Validation BLEU
wav2vec2-base-marathi	mwbm1k1+mwbm1k2+mwbm1k3+mwbm1k4	**16.17**
wav2vec2-base-marathi	mwbm1k1+mwbm1k2+mwbm1k3	16.15
wav2vec2-base-marathi	mwbm1k1+mwbm1k2+mwbm1k4	15.85
wav2vec2-base-marathi	mwbm1k1+mwbm1k3+mwbm1k4	15.89
wav2vec2-base-marathi	mwbm1k2+mwbm1k3+mwbm1k4	15.70
wav2vec2-base-marathi	mwbm1k1+mwbm1k2	15.23
wav2vec2-base-marathi	mwbm1k1+mwbm1k3	15.38
wav2vec2-base-marathi	mwbm1k1+mwbm1k4	14.96
wav2vec2-base-marathi	mwbm1k2+mwbm1k3	15.22
wav2vec2-base-marathi	mwbm1k2+mwbm1k4	14.95
wav2vec2-base-marathi	mwbm1k3+mwbm1k4	15.03
wav2vec2-base-marathi	mwbm3k1+mwbm3k2+mwbm3k3+mwbm3k4	13.80
wav2vec2-xls-r-300m	mwx1+mwx2+mwx3+mwx4	**19.63**
wav2vec2-xls-r-300m	mwx1+mwx2+mwx3	19.27
wav2vec2-xls-r-300m	mwx1+mwx2+mwx4	19.00
wav2vec2-xls-r-300m	mwx1+mwx3+mwx4	19.60
wav2vec2-xls-r-300m	mwx2+mwx3+mwx4	19.20
wav2vec2-xls-r-300m	mwx1+mwx2	17.89
wav2vec2-xls-r-300m	mwx1+mwx3	18.66
wav2vec2-xls-r-300m	mwx1+mwx4	18.35
wav2vec2-xls-r-300m	mwx2+mwx3	18.20
wav2vec2-xls-r-300m	mwx2+mwx4	17.79
wav2vec2-xls-r-300m	mwx3+mwx4	18.59

Table 14: Impact of Ensembling mr→hi models (complete).

Speech Translation with Style: AppTek's Submissions to the IWSLT Subtitling and Formality Tracks in 2023

Parnia Bahar,* Patrick Wilken,* Javier Iranzo-Sánchez, Mattia di Gangi, Evgeny Matusov, Zoltán Tüske
Applications Technology (AppTek), Aachen, Germany
{pbahar,pwilken,jiranzo,mdigangi,ematusov,ztuske}@apptek.com

Abstract

AppTek participated in the subtitling and formality tracks of the IWSLT 2023 evaluation. This paper describes the details of our subtitling pipeline - speech segmentation, speech recognition, punctuation prediction and inverse text normalization, text machine translation and direct speech-to-text translation, intelligent line segmentation - and how we make use of the provided subtitling-specific data in training and fine-tuning. The evaluation results show that our final submissions are competitive, in particular outperforming the submissions by other participants by 5% absolute as measured by the SubER subtitle quality metric. For the formality track, we participated with our En-Ru and En-Pt production models, which support formality control via prefix tokens. Except for informal Portuguese, we achieved near perfect formality level accuracy while at the same time offering high general translation quality.

1 Introduction

This paper presents AppTek's submissions to the subtitling and formality tracks of the IWSLT 2023 evaluation campaign. In the subtitling track, we participate in constrained and unconstrained conditions and in both language pairs English-to-German (En-De) and English-to-Spanish (En-Es). In the formality track, we participate in the zero-shot unconstrained condition for English-to-Portuguese (En-Pt) and English-to-Russian (En-Ru).

This paper is organized as follows: Section 2 briefly describes our data preparation. Section 3 presents AppTek's pipeline for subtitle translation. Its different components, namely audio segmentation, speech translation (ST), automatic speech recognition (ASR), machine translation (MT) models, and our subtitle segmentation algorithm are described in Sections 3.1-3.5. Section 3.6 contains experiments and an analysis of our subtitling systems. Section 4 presents AppTek's approach to formality-controlled machine translation. Finally, Section 4.1 shows the results of our formality track submission.

2 Data Preparation

2.1 Text Data

We use all of the allowed "speech-to-text parallel" and "text-parallel" data, including Europarl, Europarl-ST, News Commentary, CORDIS News, Tatoeba, TED2020, IWSLT TED, MuST-C v3, CoVoST v2, and OpenSubtitles[1]. We apply common parallel data filtering steps based on language identification, sentence length ratios between source and target sentences and additional heuristics. After filtering, we obtain 13.5M sentence pairs with 152M running words (counted on the English side) for En-De and 16.5M sentence pairs with 183M words for En-Es.

Next, we clone this data and process the En side of the clone with our text normalization tool NEWTN. It implements elaborate regular expressions to convert numbers, dates, monetary amounts, and other entities with digits into their spoken form. It is also used to remove punctuation and word case information. After training on such source data, our MT systems are able to directly translate from raw ASR output that lacks punctuation and casing into properly formatted written target language text.

For the parallel corpora which have document labels, we also create a version in which we concatenate two subsequent sentences from the same document using a separator symbol. Our past experience shows that adding such data is beneficial even if we do not add the context of the previous sentence at inference time.

Finally, for each language pair, we extract about 4M words of bilingual phrases (based on unsupervised word alignment) as additional training "sen-

*equal contribution

[1]The filtered version provided by the track organizers.

Proceedings of the 20th International Conference on Spoken Language Translation (IWSLT 2023), pages 251–260
July 13-14, 2023 ©2023 Association for Computational Linguistics

tence" pairs to make sure that the MT system can cope well with incomplete sentences or too fine-grained automatic sentence segmentation.

2.2 Speech Data

We use all the allowed datasets marked as "speech" and "speech-to-text parallel", including Europarl-ST, How2, MuST-C, TED-LIUM, LibriSpeech, Mozilla Common Voice, VoxPopuli, CoVoST, and IWSLT TED. After removing very short (< 0.1s) and long (> 120s) segments, we obtain about 3590 hours of speech with transcripts. From each dataset, we only take the train sets, where applicable. The English text is processed to be lower-cased, punctuation-free using NEWTN, and split into 10k byte-pair-encoding (BPE) tokens (Sennrich et al., 2016).

2.3 Direct Speech Translation Data

All data marked as "speech-to-text parallel", i.e. Europarl-ST, MuST-C, CoVoST, and IWSLT TED – except MuST-Cinema – is utilized for direct speech translation. It results in a total of approximately 1220 hours of speech with transcripts and corresponding translations after only keeping segments between 0.1 and 120 seconds. As for our data processing, on the English text, we carried out the same scheme as for speech data, while following almost the same German data processing scheme as described in Section 2.1. plus tokenization using the Moses toolkit (Koehn et al., 2007). Then 10k and 20k BPEs are used on the English and German texts, respectively. The dev set for the direct model is chosen to be the concatenation of IWSLT dev2010, MuST-C, Europal-ST, and CoVoST dev sets, resulting in a large dev set of 33 hours.

2.3.1 Synthetic Data

To leverage more training data for our direct model, we translate the English transcripts of the allowed "speech" data (Jia et al., 2019) using our constrained machine translation model described in Section 3.4 with output length control "short" (Wilken and Matusov, 2022). Combining the real ST data with the synthetic data, we obtain about 4100 hours of translated-speech parallel utterances.

3 Subtitle Translation

3.1 Audio Segmentation

We use the SHAS method (Tsiamas et al., 2022) for audio segmentation. SHAS scores every audio frame with a binary classifier (speech/no-speech), followed by a probabilistic divide-and-conquer (*pDAC*) algorithm that iteratively splits audio at the positions with the lowest probability of the speech class. For the unconstrained condition, we use the English segmentation model published by the authors of SHAS, which is an XLS-R 300M model (Babu et al., 2022) fine-tuned for the frame classification task on the MuST-C train set. For the constrained condition, we train our own frame classifier with Wav2Vec2 (Baevski et al., 2020), pre-trained on LibriSpeech, followed by fine-tuning for the frame classification task using MuST-C.

A hyper-parameter search was conducted to find the number of layers (constrained model), as well as the inference parameters (max. segment length and *pDAC* threshold) that optimize the performance of the downstream speech translation pipeline. We found that the *pDAC* threshold, which is the minimum probability required to keep a frame, has significant effects on the translation quality, and that the optimal value can vary depending on the task and acoustic conditions.

3.2 Direct Speech Translation

3.2.1 Attention Encoder-Decoder

We train an attention-based model (Bahdanau et al., 2015) composed of a Conformer encoder (Gulati et al., 2020) and a Transformer decoder (Vaswani et al., 2017). The encoder consists of 12 layers with a size of 512, a feed-forward size of 2048, and 8 heads, whereas the decoder has 6 layers with the same hidden size and number of heads. For fast yet stable convergence, we apply a layer-wise network construction scheme (Zeyer et al., 2018, 2019). Specifically, we start with 2 layers of halved hidden dimensions in both encoder and decoder (18M parameters) and linearly scale the model depth and width to full size (125M parameters) in the first 5 sub-epochs where each sub-epoch is one-twentieth of the whole training data. Also, L2-norm regularization and dropout are scaled up from 0 to 0.0001 and 0.1 respectively. Label smoothing is enabled only afterwards. We apply Adam (Kingma and Ba, 2015) with an initial learning rate of 0.0005 and dynamic learning scheduling based on dev set loss.

Audio log mel 80-dimensional features are extracted every 10ms. The first layer of Conformer is composed of 2 convolution layers with strides of 3 and 2 over time giving a reduction factor of 6. We use SpecAugment (Park et al., 2019; Bahar et al., 2019b) and speed perturbation in a random interval of $[0.9, 1.1]$ as data augmentation. In order to train a single direct speech translation model that also supports time alignment between source label sequence and time frames, we add the source CTC loss (Graves et al., 2006; Kim et al., 2017; Bahar et al., 2019a) on top of the encoder in training.

We also add a second shallow 1-layer Transformer decoder (with 14M parameters) in order to generate better source transcripts for time alignment. Given this network with a shared speech encoder and two independent decoders, multi-task learning is employed to train all model parameters jointly. The final objective function is computed as a sum of the 3 losses (source CTC, source enc-dec, and target enc-dec).

3.2.2 Forced Alignment

CTC relies on Viterbi alignment to obtain the best path going through the source token at position n at time frame t. It is therefore possible to obtain word timings from CTC which can be used for subtitle generation. To do so, we first generate the source transcripts using the source decoder of the network and then use them to run forced-alignment on the CTC output. The model's alignments are on BPE-level, we therefore combine the timings of all subwords belonging to a word to obtain the final word-level timestamps.

We experimented with this approach and were able to generate accurate timestamps appropriate for creating subtitles in the source language. However, as we decide against using the source template approach for the constrained systems (see Section 3.5), only the timings of the first and last word in a segment are used for the target subtitles of the constrained submission. We plan to explore how to make better use of the CTC timings from this model in future experiments. In particular, we plan to add silence modeling to obtain information about pauses within speech segments, which can then be reflected in the subtitle timings.

3.3 Automatic Speech Recognition

Constrained We train a Conformer-Transformer model for the constrained task mainly following Section 3.2.1 using 3590 hours of speech. Layer-wise network construction, SpecAugment, and CTC loss are applied. Since the model is not trained for multiple tasks (no additional decoder is added), it has better performance in terms of WER compared to the source decoder part of the ST model. The final checkpoint achieves a WER of 9.6% on the concatenated dev set of 33h.

Unconstrained We train an attention-based encoder-decoder model to run ASR decoding and also a CTC model which is used to generate word timings by force-aligning the audio with the decoded hypotheses. Here, the CTC model uses an explicit word boundary `<space>` symbol between words. It serves as `silence` modeling. Both models are trained on the same training set of 15K hours of speech mixing publicly available data with a commercial license and in-house data.

The 185M-parameter attention-based model uses a 31-layer Conformer encoder of hidden size 384; 8 heads with 64 dimensions per head; Macaron-style (Lu et al., 2019) feed-forward layers with size 2048; convolutional layers with 1024 channels and kernel size 31. The decoder is a single-headed attention-based model (Tüske et al., 2020), and consists of 4 stacked projected long short-term memory (pLSTM) recurrent layers with layer size 2048 (Hochreiter and Schmidhuber, 1997; Sak et al., 2014). The first two LSTMs operate on the embedding of the label sequence only. The other two decoder LSTM layers also process the acoustic information extracted by the encoder using a single-head, additive, location-aware cross-attention. The decoder predicts 1K BPE units. Decoding is done using an external neural LM consisting of 4 stacked LSTM layers of size 3072 with the same output vocabulary as the ASR models. The 273M-parameter language model is trained on 2.4B running words segmented to BPE units. The language model data are selected from a wide range of various domains, e.g. books, movies, news, reviews, Wikipedia, talks, etc. ASR transcription is obtained after decoding with beam search limited to 16 hypotheses without any vocabulary constraints. The CTC model uses the same encoder structure as the attention-based model.

3.4 Machine Translation

3.4.1 Unconstrained Condition

For the unconstrained subtitling pipeline we use AppTek's production MT systems which have been trained on large amounts of parallel data, mostly from the OPUS collection (Tiedemann, 2012). Both En-De and En-Es systems are Transformer *Big* systems that support additional API parameters which can in particular control the genre (e.g. patents, news articles, dialogs) and length (automatic, short, long, etc.). The control is implemented via pseudo-tokens in the beginning of the source or target sentence (Matusov et al., 2020).

For the IWSLT experiments, we set the genre to "dialogs" because it reflects best the spoken spontaneous style in the dev 2023 data. When not mentioned otherwise, we set the length to "short". This yields more condensed translations, similar to how human subtitlers would translate to comply with a given reading speed limit.

3.4.2 Constrained Condition

For the constrained condition we use the parallel training data prepared as described in Section 2.1. As the dev data for learning rate control, we use the Europarl-ST and MuST-C dev sets.

Our MT model is a variant of the Transformer *Big* model (Vaswani et al., 2017) with additional encoder layers and using relative positional encoding (Shaw et al., 2018). We use a batch size of 800 words, but the effective batch size is increased by accumulating gradients over 8 batches. We add the same length control feature as for the unconstrained system by classifying the training data into 5 bins of target-to-source length ratios and adding the class label as a target-side prefix token.

We apply SentencePiece (Kudo and Richardson, 2018) segmentation with a vocabulary size of 10K for En and 20K for De/Es and use a translation factor to predict the casing of the target words (Wilken and Matusov, 2019). Our MT models have been trained for 100 sub-epochs with 1M lines in each; thus, all of the prepared data has been observed in training 1-3 times. For each sub-epoch, we select sentence pairs proportionally to the following distribution and then randomly mix them:

20% Europarl and Europarl-ST data
20% TED data (MuST-C, IWSLT, TED2020)
20% OpenSubtitles (other)
10% News (Commentary+CORDIS), Tatoeba, CoVoST
15% Concatenated neighboring sentence pairs[2]
5% OpenSubtitles (documentaries)
5% OpenSubtitles (sports)
5% Bilingual phrases

3.4.3 Length ROVER

For all final submissions, we optimize the length control of MT by using a length ROVER (Wilken and Matusov, 2022). For each segment we create 3 translations: without forcing the target-side length token, forcing length bin 2 ("short"), and forcing length bin 1 ("extra short"). From those translations we select the first – given the order above – that provides a translation with a target-to-source character ratio of less than 1.1. This is motivated by the fact that translations need to be fitted into the source subtitle template (Section 3.5.1). We note that the reading speed compliance of our submission could have been increased even further by exploiting timing information to select the MT length variants.

[2] See Section 2.1.

System	MuST-C	TED	EPTV	ITV	Peloton
English-to-German					
unconstrained	33.7	27.1	19.0	30.6	23.9
+ fine-tuning	35.0	27.7	20.3	31.0	24.4
constrained	32.3	34.2	18.4	27.2	20.3
+ fine-tuning	32.9	–	19.0	28.1	21.5
English-to-Spanish					
baseline	37.2	46.1	34.1	24.5	23.6
+ fine-tuning	38.2	46.4	34.8	25.5	24.7

Table 1: BLEU scores in % for text-only MT fine-tuning experiments on the MuST-C tst-COMMON set and on the AppTek's aligned subsets of the 2023 subtitling track dev data.

3.4.4 Fine-tuning Experiments

For our fine-tuning experiments, we first select "in-domain" training data in terms of similarity to the seed data – the dev 2023 set – from the real parallel data, as well as the synthetic data described in Section 2.3.1. The selection is done by clustering distributed sentence representations in the embedding space, and then keeping sentence pairs from the clusters which correspond to the seed data clusters. This is done considering both source and target seed data sentences, but independently, so that no sentence-level alignment of seed data is necessary. For details on this data selection method, please refer to our 2020 submission to the offline speech translation track (Bahar et al., 2020). With this method, we create two versions of the in-domain data: one using all 4 parts of the dev 2023 set as seed data (in-domain A: En-De: 1.9M lines, 27M En words; En-Es: 1.7M lines, 25M words), and one, for En-De only, using just ITV and Peloton dev 2023 parts as seed data (in-domain B: 1.5M lines, 20M words).

We then use the dev 2023 set as a dev set in fine-tuning of the MT model for learning rate control. Since the dev 2023 data is not aligned at sentence-level, but is available as (in part) independently created subtitle files, we had to sentence-align it. To do so, we first extracted full sentences from the English subtitles based on sentence-final punctuation marks, translated these sentences with the (constrained) baseline MT, and then resegmented the target side into sentences that match the source sentences using Levenshtein alignment as implemented by the SUBER tool (Wilken et al., 2022). The source-target segments obtained this way are kept in the final dev set only if the BERT F-score (Zhang et al., 2019) for a given pair is > 0.5 for TED, EPTV, and Peloton sets and > 0.55 for the ITV set. With this method, the obtained dev set contains 7645 sentence-like units with 27.7K words for TED, 2.3K for EPTV, 20.7K for Peloton, and 13.9K for ITV.

We perform fine-tuning for up to 20 sub-epochs ranging in size from 100K to 400K sentence pairs using a small learning rate between 10^{-06} and 10^{-05}, and select the best configuration for each of the four dev 2023 domains.

The fine-tuning results are shown in Table 1. Despite the fact that no real in-domain data, not even the dev 2023 set, is used as training data in fine-tuning we are able to improve MT quality in terms of BLEU scores (Papineni et al., 2002; Post, 2018), as well as BERT and other scores skipped due to space constraints. The improvements are more pronounced for the constrained system, but the absolute scores are generally better with the unconstrained setup[3]. However, since the TED talk and Europarl domains are covered well in the data allowed for the constrained condition, the difference between our unconstrained and constrained system for the TED and EPTV domains is small. It is worth noting that for ITV and Peloton domains we could only improve MT quality by fine-tuning on the in-domain B set that did not include any TED-related data, and also not using any TED or EPTV dev data for learning rate control.

3.5 Subtitle Creation

3.5.1 Source Template Approach

To create subtitle files from translation hypotheses, the text has to be segmented into blocks with start/end time information. One challenge is to transfer timings extracted from the source speech to the target subtitles. An approach to generate timings that is also used in human subtitling workflows (Georgakopoulou, 2019), is to first create subtitles in the source language – a so-called subtitle template – and to keep the same subtitle blocks during translation. This creates a nice viewing experience, since subtitles appear on the screen only during the actual speech. However, the source template constraints might be sub-optimal in terms of target language reading speed.

We use the source template approach for the unconstrained submission. To create subtitles in the original language of the videos (English), we start with a timed word list provided by the ASR system. We train a 3-layer bidirectional LSTM model (hidden size 256, embedding dim 128) to jointly add basic punctuation marks (. , ! ?) and casing information to the word list. As training data, we use 14M English sentences from the Gigaword and OpenSubtitles corpora. The model operates on full words and has two softmax output layers, one with the four punctuation tokens and "no punctuation" as target classes (to be added after the word), the other one with lower-cased, capitalized, all-upper, and mixed-cased classes as targets.

In addition, we train an inverse text normalization model to convert spoken forms of numbers, dates, currencies, etc. into the proper written form. This model is a Transformer *Big* trained on data where the source data is processed using our text normalization tool NEWTN, see Section 2.1. Applying it to the transcriptions helps MT to produce proper digits also on the target side. This has a slight positive effect on automatic scores (0.8% SUBER for Peloton, only up to 0.4% for the other domains), but mainly helps subjectively perceived quality and also reduces the number of characters.

The resulting timed, punctuated, and cased word list is split into sentences using punctuation (. ! ?) and pauses between words longer than 3 seconds. Those are fed into a subtitle segmentation algorithm similar to the one described in (Matusov et al., 2019). Its core component is an LSTM segmentation model that is trained on English OpenSubtitles XML data, which includes subtitle block boundary information[4], to estimate the probability of a subtitle break after each word of a given input sentence. Within a beam search framework, this model is combined with hard subtitling constraints such as the character limit per line to create valid subtitles. Here, we adjust it for the creation of subtitles from timed words by including minimum and maximum subtitle duration as constraints, and not forcing any predefined number of subtitles.

After segmentation, we use the start time of the

[3]The BLEU score of the constrained system on the En-De TED part is higher because, as we found out shortly before submission, some of the dev 2023 TED talks were part of the allowed TED2020 training corpus. Hence, further fine-tuning did not help for this system on this set. The unconstrained system had not been trained on this corpus.

[4]https://opus.nlpl.eu/download.php?f=OpenSubtitles/v2018/xml/en.zip

first word and the end time of the last word in each subtitle block as the subtitle start and end time. The subtitle template defined this way is then translated using the fine-tuned MT system described in Section 3.4.4, employing the length ROVER (Section 3.4.3) to avoid long translations that do not fit the template. Sentences as defined above are used as translation units, note that they may span several subtitle blocks. To insert the translations back into the template, we again apply the subtitle segmentation algorithm, this time with the exact settings as in (Matusov et al., 2019).

3.5.2 Template-Free Approach

By definition, the source template approach is not desirable for direct speech translation without intermediate source text representation. Also, the constrained condition does not include English OpenSubtitles data with subtitle breaks. We hence fall back to a simpler subtitle creation approach for our constrained direct and cascade systems. We use the segments provided by the audio segmenter as translation units. For the cascade system, we translate the transcription of each segment with the fine-tuned constrained MT, also using the length ROVER (Section 3.4.3). End-of-line and end-of-block tokens are inserted into the translated text of each segment using the subtitle segmentation algorithm configured similarly to the case of template creation in the previous section but without duration-based constraints. Timestamps for the additional subtitle block boundaries are then created by linearly interpolating the audio segment timings according to character count ratios. Assuming the translation of an audio segment with start time T_{start} and end time T_{end} is split into N blocks with $c_1, ..., c_N$ characters, respectively, the start time of block n is set to $T_{\text{start}} + (T_{\text{end}} - T_{\text{start}}) \cdot \frac{\sum_{n'=1}^{n-1} c_{n'}}{\sum_{n'=1}^{N} c_{n'}}$. This method leads to reasonable timings in most cases but can create temporary time shifts between speech and subtitles inside long audio segments.

3.5.3 Subtitle Post-Processing

To all subtitles, we apply a final post-processing that splits rare cases of subtitles with more than 2 lines (same segmentation method as for template-free approach) and shifts subtitle end times to later in time if needed to comply with the maximum reading speed of 21 characters per second. The latter is only possible if there is a large enough gap after a given subtitle and will therefore not guarantee low enough reading speed in all cases.

system	TED	EPTV	Peloton	ITV
SHAS 0.31	21.1	14.9	12.1	15.6
SHAS 0.50	22.4	14.9	11.6	13.9
SHAS 0.71	20.8	14.6	10.8	10.7
ASR Segm.	19.8	14.8	11.3	13.5

Table 2: Impact of different segmentation schemes on the translation quality (BLEU in %).

3.6 Results

We first decide which audio segmentation to use based on dev set results using our final ASR and MT unconstrained systems. We set different *pDAC* thresholds for the unconstrained SHAS (0.31, 0.50, and 0.71) and compare them with an in-house segmenter optimized for ASR. The results in Table 2 show that a low threshold of 0.31 leads to better translations overall. There is however variation depending on the domain: it is 1.3 BLEU points worse than SHAS 0.50 on TED, but as good or up to 1.7 BLEU points better in all other domains. Results for ITV are highly sensitive to the threshold. We attribute this to the fact that in TV series speech is often mixed with music and other sounds and a lower threshold is required not to miss speech segments. Given these results, we use SHAS 0.31 as our segmenter for unconstrained experiments. For the constrained experiments, we use SHAS 0.31 everywhere except on TED with SHAS 0.50.

Table 3 compares the performance of the final constrained cascade (separate ASR + MT) and direct En-De subtitling systems as well as the unconstrained cascade system. All metrics are computed using the SubER tool[5] (Wilken et al., 2022) directly on subtitle files. To calculate the BLEU and CHRF (Popović, 2015) metrics, it performs an alignment of hypothesis to reference sentences similar to (Matusov et al., 2005). On all metrics, the constrained cascade system outperforms our direct model. We observe imperfections in the direct model's output such as repetitions. This can be partially attributed to the fact that it has been trained jointly for 3 tasks leading to sub-optimal optimization for the final translation process. The lack of length control of our direct ST model is another reason for the gap between the two constrained systems. For the cascade systems, we find length control via the length ROVER to be crucial, giving consistent improvements of 4 to 5% points in SubER compared to no length control at all. As seen in Table 3, the unconstrained system out-

[5]https://github.com/apptek/SubER

system	constr.	SUBER (↓)	BLEU	CHRF
TED				
cascade	yes	63.0	26.0	53.9
direct	yes	75.9	17.1	47.6
cascade	no	64.3	22.1	51.0
EPTV				
cascade	yes	78.7	13.5	45.2
direct	yes	85.1	10.9	42.6
cascade	no	75.8	14.8	44.1
Peloton				
cascade	yes	87.6	9.9	32.0
direct	yes	86.1	6.8	26.9
cascade	no	71.9	11.6	34.3
ITV				
cascade	yes	83.6	8.5	26.1
direct	yes	90.9	5.7	21.0
cascade	no	71.4	14.8	35.2

Table 3: En-De subtitle translation results in % (constrained and unconstrained setting) on the dev2023 sets.

Domain	SUBER (↓)	BLEU (↑)	CHRF (↑)
TED	48.8	37.8	61.8
EPTV	70.2	20.4	50.6
Peloton	79.0	12.2	36.2
ITV	82.1	9.2	26.8

Table 4: Subtitle translation results in % on the dev2023 sets for En-Es via the constrained cascade system.

performs both constrained systems except on the TED set. This is due to a data overlap, some TED talks present in the dev set have also been part of the constrained training data. To analyze the impact of the source template approach we re-create the subtitles of the unconstrained system using the template-free approach. We find that this deteriorates the SUBER scores for TED, Peloton and ITV by 0.7, 3.6 and 3.8% points, respectively, while actually giving better results for EPTV by 0.7%. In general, the results in Table 3 show a higher automatic subtitling quality for the TED domain, which represents the case of well recorded and prepared speech, but also show the need to focus research on harder conditions such as interviews and TV series. Table 4 contains the scores we are able to achieve for En-Es under constrained conditions. Also here, acceptable subtitle quality can only be reached for TED and EPTV content, but not for the more challenging Peloton and ITV content.

4 Formality Control

AppTek's production systems support formality or, as we call it, style control for selected language pairs (Matusov et al., 2020). This year, we decided to test these systems in the unconstrained condition of the IWSLT formality track for En-Pt and En-to-Ru. Each of these two systems is trained in a Transformer Big setup (Vaswani et al., 2017). The formality level is encoded with a pseudo-token in the beginning of each training source sentence with one of 3 values: formal, informal, no style. The system is trained on large public data from the OPUS collection (Tiedemann, 2012) that has been partitioned into the 3 style classes as follows.

First, we write a sequence of regular expressions for the target language (in this case, European Pt and Ru) which try to match sentences containing formal or informal features. Thus, for Russian, we try to match either the formal or informal second-person pronoun that corresponds to English "you", including their possessive forms. For Portuguese, we additionally match the forms of most common verbs which agree with the corresponding pronoun. The regex list for Russian is given in Table 5[6].

Each list of regular expressions uses standard regex syntax and makes either case-sensitive or insensitive matches. For each sentence pair from the parallel data, the regex list is processed from top to bottom. As soon as a match in the target sentence is found, the FORMAL or INFORMAL label is assigned to the sentence pair. The sentence pair is labeled with NO_STYLE if there is no match.

If document information is available and at least 5% of the document sentence pairs are labeled as formal/informal according to the regex rules (with no sentences labeled with the opposite class), then all of the sentence pairs in the document are assigned the corresponding label. Such data is useful to model stylistic traits which are not limited to the choice of second-person pronouns. Note that document annotations are available for some of the IWSLT data, including TED talks, OpenSubtitles (each subtitle file corresponds to a document), individual sessions of European Parliament, etc.

We further smooth the three style classes to ensure that e.g., sentences containing second-person pronouns can be translated well even when no style is specified at inference time. To this end, 5 to 8% of sentence pairs which had been assigned to one of the 3 style classes as described above are randomly re-assigned to one of the other two classes.

For En-Ru, the training data that had been partitioned into style classes in this way included about

[6]We released the En-Pt and En-Ru lists of regular expressions as part of our evaluation submission.

```
INFORMAL IGNORECASE \b(ты|теб[яе]|тобой|тво[йеёяю]|твоей|твоего|твоему|твоим|тво[ёе]м)\b
FORMAL   IGNORECASE \b(вы|вами?|ваш[ае]?|вашей|вашего|вашему?|вашу|вас|вашим)\b
```

Table 5: The regular expressions used to partition En-Ru training data into formal, informal, and (in case of no match) "no style" classes.

language pair / requested style		BLEU [%]	COMET	M-Acc [%]
En-Pt	formal	34.6	0.6089	99
	informal	42.4	0.6776	64
En-Ru	formal	35.4	0.6165	99
	informal	33.3	0.6026	98

Table 6: Automatic evaluation results for AppTek's submission to the formality track of IWSLT 2023.

40M sentence pairs. At the time this model was trained in early 2022, the larger CCMatrix corpus (Schwenk et al., 2021) was not included. For En-Pt, we did use a filtered version of CCMatrix in training, so that the total number of parallel sentence pairs was 140M. The filtering of CCMatrix and other large crawled data included removing sentence pairs with low cross-lingual sentence embedding similarity as given by the LABSE scores (Feng et al., 2022). All of our parallel training data is also filtered based on sentence-level language identification scores and other heuristics.

When training the Transformer Big model, we balanced the contribution of formal, informal, and "no style" data by adding them in equal proportions (number of lines) to each sub-epoch.

4.1 Results

We did not perform any experiments, but just set the API parameter `style=formal` or `style=informal` and translated the evaluation data with the AppTek's production systems, trained as described above. The results in terms of automatic error metrics, as reported by the track organizers, are summarized in Table 6.

Among the 5 participants of the unconstrained condition, we obtain the best results for En-Ru in terms of BLEU and COMET (Rei et al., 2020), while producing the correct formality level for more than 98% of the sentences. The second-best competitor system obtains formality accuracy of 100%, but scores 1.7% absolute lower in BLEU for the formal and 0.9% BLEU absolute for the informal class.

For En-Pt, our system scores second in terms of automatic MT quality metrics and correctly produced the formal style for 99% of the sentences in the evaluation data. However, when the informal style was requested, our system could generate it in only 64% of the cases. We attribute this low score to the imperfect regular expressions we defined for informal Portuguese pronouns and corresponding verb forms, since some of them are ambiguous. However, we find it difficult to explain that e.g. the BLEU score of AppTek's "informal" MT output with respect to the informal reference is almost 8% absolute higher than for our "formal" output with respect to the formal reference. This may indicate that the human reference translation also has not always followed the requested style, the informal one in particular.

5 Conclusion

We described AppTek's submissions to the subtitling and formality tracks of the IWSLT 2023.

For the subtitling track, we obtained good results, outperforming the other two evaluation participants either with our constrained or unconstrained cascaded approach on all 4 domains. Part of this success is due to our subtitle creation process, in which we employ AppTek's intelligent line segmentation models. However, the results varied by domain, with the domain of movie subtitles posing the most challenges for ASR, and the domain of fitness-related videos (Peloton) being hardest for MT. Yet our biggest overall challenge, especially for the direct (end-to-end) submission was speech segmentation and creating sentence-like units, on real ITV movies in particular, in which there is music, background noise, and multiple speakers. In the future, we plan to improve this component of our speech translation technology. We also plan to include length control in our direct models which showed to be an important factor for those applications with time constraints.

Our formality track participation was a one-shot attempt at a zero-shot task that showed the competitiveness of the formality control that we have implemented in AppTek's production systems. However, our approach currently requires the creation of manual regular expression rules for partitioning the parallel training data into formality classes, and the participation in the IWSLT evaluation revealed some weaknesses of this approach for one of the involved target languages. In the future, we plan to further improve our approach, reducing or eliminating the need for writing rules.

References

Arun Babu, Changhan Wang, Andros Tjandra, Kushal Lakhotia, Qiantong Xu, Naman Goyal, Kritika Singh, Patrick von Platen, Yatharth Saraf, Juan Pino, Alexei Baevski, Alexis Conneau, and Michael Auli. 2022. XLS-R: Self-supervised Cross-lingual Speech Representation Learning at Scale. In *Proc. Interspeech 2022*, pages 2278–2282.

Alexei Baevski, Yuhao Zhou, Abdelrahman Mohamed, and Michael Auli. 2020. wav2vec 2.0: A framework for self-supervised learning of speech representations. In *Advances in Neural Information Processing Systems 33: Annual Conference on Neural Information Processing Systems 2020, NeurIPS 2020, December 6-12, 2020, virtual.*

Parnia Bahar, Tobias Bieschke, and Hermann Ney. 2019a. A comparative study on end-to-end speech to text translation. In *IEEE Automatic Speech Recognition and Understanding Workshop (ASRU)*, pages 792–799, Sentosa, Singapore.

Parnia Bahar, Patrick Wilken, Tamer Alkhouli, Andreas Guta, Pavel Golik, Evgeny Matusov, and Christian Herold. 2020. Start-before-end and end-to-end: Neural speech translation by apptek and rwth aachen university. In *Proceedings of the 17th International Conference on Spoken Language Translation*, pages 44–54.

Parnia Bahar, Albert Zeyer, Ralf Schlüter, and Hermann Ney. 2019b. On using specaugment for end-to-end speech translation. In *International Workshop on Spoken Language Translation (IWSLT)*.

Dzmitry Bahdanau, Kyunghyun Cho, and Yoshua Bengio. 2015. Neural machine translation by jointly learning to align and translate. In *Proceedings of the International Conference on Learning Representations (ICLR)*.

Fangxiaoyu Feng, Yinfei Yang, Daniel Cer, Naveen Arivazhagan, and Wei Wang. 2022. Language-agnostic BERT sentence embedding. In *Proceedings of the 60th Annual Meeting of the Association for Computational Linguistics (Volume 1: Long Papers)*, pages 878–891, Dublin, Ireland. Association for Computational Linguistics.

Panayota Georgakopoulou. 2019. Template files:: The holy grail of subtitling. *Journal of Audiovisual Translation*, 2(2):137–160.

Alex Graves, Santiago Fernández, Faustino J. Gomez, and Jürgen Schmidhuber. 2006. Connectionist temporal classification: Labelling unsegmented sequence data with recurrent neural networks. In *International Conference on Machine Learning (ICML)*, volume 148, pages 369–376, Pittsburgh, PA, USA.

Anmol Gulati, James Qin, Chung-Cheng Chiu, Niki Parmar, Yu Zhang, Jiahui Yu, Wei Han, Shibo Wang, Zhengdong Zhang, Yonghui Wu, et al. 2020. Conformer: Convolution-augmented transformer for speech recognition. *21th Annual Conference of the International Speech Communication Association (INTERSPEECH)*, pages 5036–5040.

Sepp Hochreiter and Jürgen Schmidhuber. 1997. Long short-term memory. *Neural computation*, 9(8):1735–1780.

Ye Jia, Melvin Johnson, Wolfgang Macherey, Ron J. Weiss, Yuan Cao, Chung-Cheng Chiu, Naveen Ari, Stella Laurenzo, and Yonghui Wu. 2019. Leveraging weakly supervised data to improve end-to-end speech-to-text translation. In *IEEE International Conference on Acoustics, Speech and Signal Processing, ICASSP 2019, Brighton, United Kingdom, May 12-17, 2019*, pages 7180–7184. IEEE.

Suyoun Kim, Takaaki Hori, and Shinji Watanabe. 2017. Joint ctc-attention based end-to-end speech recognition using multi-task learning. In *Proc. Int. Conf. on Acoustics, Speech, and Signal Processing*, pages 4835–4839, New Orleans, LA, USA.

Diederik P. Kingma and Jimmy Ba. 2015. Adam: A method for stochastic optimization. In *3rd International Conference on Learning Representations, ICLR 2015, San Diego, CA, USA, May 7-9, 2015, Conference Track Proceedings*.

Philipp Koehn, Hieu Hoang, Alexandra Birch, Chris Callison-Burch, Marcello Federico, Nicola Bertoldi, Brooke Cowan, Wade Shen, Christine Moran, Richard Zens, Chris Dyer, Ondrej Bojar, Alexandra Constantin, and Evan Herbst. 2007. Moses: Open source toolkit for statistical machine translation. In *ACL 2007, Proceedings of the 45th Annual Meeting of the Association for Computational Linguistics, June 23-30, 2007, Prague, Czech Republic*.

Taku Kudo and John Richardson. 2018. Sentencepiece: A simple and language independent subword tokenizer and detokenizer for neural text processing. In *Proceedings of the 2018 Conference on Empirical Methods in Natural Language Processing: System Demonstrations*, pages 66–71.

Yiping Lu, Zhuohan Li, Di He, Zhiqing Sun, Bin Dong, Tao Qin, Liwei Wang, and Tie-yan Liu. 2019. Understanding and improving transformer from a multi-particle dynamic system point of view. In *ICLR 2020 Workshop on Integration of Deep Neural Models and Differential Equations*.

Evgeny Matusov, Gregor Leusch, Oliver Bender, and Hermann Ney. 2005. Evaluating machine translation output with automatic sentence segmentation. In *International Workshop on Spoken Language Translation*, pages 148–154, Pittsburgh, PA, USA.

Evgeny Matusov, Patrick Wilken, and Yota Georgakopoulou. 2019. Customizing neural machine translation for subtitling. In *Proceedings of the Fourth Conference on Machine Translation (Volume 1: Research Papers)*, pages 82–93, Florence, Italy. Association for Computational Linguistics.

Evgeny Matusov, Patrick Wilken, and Christian Herold. 2020. Flexible customization of a single neural machine translation system with multi-dimensional metadata inputs. In *Proceedings of the 14th Conference of the Association for Machine Translation in the Americas (Volume 2: User Track)*, pages 204–216, Virtual. Association for Machine Translation in the Americas.

Kishore Papineni, Salim Roukos, Todd Ward, and Wei-Jing Zhu. 2002. Bleu: a method for automatic evaluation of machine translation. In *Proceedings of the 40th Annual Meeting of the Association for Computational Linguistics*, pages 311–318, Philadelphia, Pennsylvania, USA. Association for Computational Linguistics.

Daniel S Park, William Chan, Yu Zhang, Chung-Cheng Chiu, Barret Zoph, Ekin D Cubuk, and Quoc V Le. 2019. SpecAugment: A simple data augmentation method for automatic speech recognition.

Maja Popović. 2015. chrF: character n-gram F-score for automatic MT evaluation. In *Proceedings of the Tenth Workshop on Statistical Machine Translation*, pages 392–395, Lisbon, Portugal. Association for Computational Linguistics.

Matt Post. 2018. A call for clarity in reporting BLEU scores. In *Proceedings of the Third Conference on Machine Translation: Research Papers*, pages 186–191, Brussels, Belgium. Association for Computational Linguistics.

Ricardo Rei, Craig Stewart, Ana C Farinha, and Alon Lavie. 2020. COMET: A neural framework for MT evaluation. In *Proceedings of the 2020 Conference on Empirical Methods in Natural Language Processing (EMNLP)*, pages 2685–2702, Online. Association for Computational Linguistics.

Haşim Sak, Andrew W. Senior, and Françoise Beaufays. 2014. Long short-term memory based recurrent neural network architectures for large vocabulary speech recognition. *arXiv preprint arXiv:1402.1128*.

Holger Schwenk, Guillaume Wenzek, Sergey Edunov, Edouard Grave, Armand Joulin, and Angela Fan. 2021. CCMatrix: Mining billions of high-quality parallel sentences on the web. In *Proceedings of the 59th Annual Meeting of the Association for Computational Linguistics and the 11th International Joint Conference on Natural Language Processing (Volume 1: Long Papers)*, pages 6490–6500, Online. Association for Computational Linguistics.

Rico Sennrich, Barry Haddow, and Alexandra Birch. 2016. Neural machine translation of rare words with subword units. In *Proceedings of the 54th Annual Meeting of the Association for Computational Linguistics, ACL 2016, August 7-12, 2016, Berlin, Germany, Volume 1: Long Papers*.

Peter Shaw, Jakob Uszkoreit, and Ashish Vaswani. 2018. Self-attention with relative position representations. In *Proceedings of the 2018 Conference of the North American Chapter of the Association for Computational Linguistics: Human Language Technologies, Volume 2 (Short Papers)*, pages 464–468.

Jörg Tiedemann. 2012. Parallel data, tools and interfaces in OPUS. In *Proceedings of the Eighth International Conference on Language Resources and Evaluation (LREC'12)*, pages 2214–2218, Istanbul, Turkey. European Language Resources Association (ELRA).

Ioannis Tsiamas, Gerard I. Gállego, José A. R. Fonollosa, and Marta R. Costa-jussà. 2022. SHAS: Approaching optimal Segmentation for End-to-End Speech Translation. In *Proc. Interspeech 2022*, pages 106–110.

Zoltán Tüske, George Saon, Kartik Audhkhasi, and Brian Kingsbury. 2020. Single headed attention based sequence-to-sequence model for state-of-the-art results on Switchboard. In *Interspeech*, pages 551–555, Shanghai, China.

Ashish Vaswani, Noam Shazeer, Niki Parmar, Jakob Uszkoreit, Llion Jones, Aidan N Gomez, Łukasz Kaiser, and Illia Polosukhin. 2017. Attention is all you need. In *Advances in Neural Information Processing Systems*, pages 5998–6008.

Patrick Wilken, Panayota Georgakopoulou, and Evgeny Matusov. 2022. SubER - a metric for automatic evaluation of subtitle quality. In *Proceedings of the 19th International Conference on Spoken Language Translation (IWSLT 2022)*, pages 1–10, Dublin, Ireland (in-person and online). Association for Computational Linguistics.

Patrick Wilken and Evgeny Matusov. 2019. Novel applications of factored neural machine translation. *arXiv preprint arXiv:1910.03912*.

Patrick Wilken and Evgeny Matusov. 2022. AppTek's submission to the IWSLT 2022 isometric spoken language translation task. In *Proceedings of the 19th International Conference on Spoken Language Translation (IWSLT 2022)*, pages 369–378, Dublin, Ireland (in-person and online). Association for Computational Linguistics.

Albert Zeyer, Parnia Bahar, Kazuki Irie, Ralf Schlüter, and Hermann Ney. 2019. A comparison of transformer and lstm encoder decoder models for asr. In *IEEE Automatic Speech Recognition and Understanding Workshop*, pages 8–15, Sentosa, Singapore.

Albert Zeyer, Kazuki Irie, Ralf Schlüter, and Hermann Ney. 2018. Improved training of end-to-end attention models for speech recognition. In *19th Annual Conf. Interspeech, Hyderabad, India, 2-6 Sep.*, pages 7–11.

Tianyi Zhang, Varsha Kishore, Felix Wu, Kilian Q Weinberger, and Yoav Artzi. 2019. Bertscore: Evaluating text generation with bert. *arXiv preprint arXiv:1904.09675*.

QUESPA Submission for the IWSLT 2023 Dialect and Low-resource Speech Translation Tasks

John E. Ortega[1], **Rodolfo Zevallos**[2], **and William Chen**[3]
[1]Northeastern University, USA, [2]Universitat de Pompeu Fabra, Spain
[3]Carnegie Mellon University, USA
contact email: j.ortega@northeastern.edu

Abstract

This article describes the QUESPA team speech translation (ST) submissions for the Quechua to Spanish (QUE–SPA) track featured in the Evaluation Campaign of IWSLT 2023: low-resource and dialect speech translation. Two main submission types were supported in the campaign: *constrained* and *unconstrained*. We submitted six total systems of which our best (primary) constrained system consisted of an ST model based on the Fairseq S2T framework where the audio representations were created using log mel-scale filter banks as features and the translations were performed using a transformer. The best (primary) unconstrained system used a pipeline approach which combined automatic speech recognition (ASR) with machine translation (MT). The ASR transcriptions for the best unconstrained system were computed using a pre-trained XLS-R–based model along with a fine-tuned language model. Transcriptions were translated using a MT system based on a fine-tuned, pre-trained language model (PLM). The four other submissions are presented in this article (2 constrained and 2 unconstrained) for comparison because they consist of various architectures. Our results show that direct ST (ASR and MT combined together) can be more effective than a PLM in a low-resource (constrained) setting for Quechua to Spanish. On the other hand, we show that fine-tuning of any type on both the ASR and MT system is worthwhile, resulting in nearly 16 BLEU for the unconstrained task.

1 Introduction

Low-resource machine translation (LRMT) can be considered a difficult task due to the low amount of parallel data on hand. (Haddow et al., 2022) By adding the task of automatic speech recognition (ASR), complexity can be even more difficult. Findings from the previous year's IWSLT 2022 (Antonios et al., 2022) have shown that for low-resource language pairs like Tamasheq–French, it is difficult to achieve more than 5 BLEU (Papineni et al., 2002) score points for the combined task of speech translation (ST), even in a unconstrained setting.

This year, the IWSLT 2023 (Agarwal et al., 2023) evaluation campaign for low-resource and dialect speech translation has included Tamasheq–French along with several other language pairs. One of the newly introduced language pairs is Quechua–Spanish deemed **QUE–SPA** by the organizers. Quechua is an indigenous language spoken in the Andes mountainous region in South America. It is spoken by millions of native speakers mostly from Peru, Ecuador and Bolivia. In those regions, the high-resource language is Spanish. Quechua displays many unique morphological properties of which high inflection and poly-synthetic are the two most commonly known. It is worthwhile to note that previous work (Ortega and Pillaipakkamnatt, 2018; Ortega et al., 2020) has been somewhat successful in identifying the inflectional properties of Quechua such as agglutination where another high-resource language, namely Finnish, can aid for translation purposes achieving nearly 20 BLEU on religious-based (text-only) tasks.

Since this is the first year that QUE–SPA has been included in the IWSLT 2023 campaign, we feel that it is important to set a proper baseline. The aim of our submission was to increase the viability of the use of a Quechua–Spanish ST system and we thus attempted several approaches that included the use of pipelines (cascade) approaches along with joint ASR + MT. We report on the six system submissions as a final takeaway for this article; however, we also compare other approaches that performed worse (1 BLEU or less). Our team is called **QUESPA** and consists of a consortium that spans across three universities: Northeastern University (USA), Universitat de Pompeu Fabra (Spain), and Carnegie Mellon University (USA). Our objective is to help to solve the LRMT prob-

Proceedings of the 20th International Conference on Spoken Language Translation (IWSLT 2023), pages 261–268
July 13-14, 2023 ©2023 Association for Computational Linguistics

lem for Quechua with the intention of at some point releasing an ST system to the Quechua community where we have strategic partners located in areas of Peru where Quechua is mostly spoken. The authors of this article have participated in several other events and written literature that includes native Quechua annotations for natural language processing (NLP) systems including MT and more.

This article reports the QUESPA consortium submissions for the IWSLT 2023 dialect and low-resource tasks. We focus only on the low-resource task despite the mention of two dialects *Quechua I and II*. Our focus is on creating the optimum models we can for the *constrained* task and leveraging pre-trained models for the *unconstrained* task further described in Section 3.

The rest of this article is organized as follows. Section 2 presents the related work. The experiments for QUE–SPA low-resource track are presented in Section 3. Section 4 provides results from the six submitted systems and concludes this work.

2 Related work

In this section, we first cover work directly related to the ASR and MT tasks of QUE–SPA done in the past. Then, we introduce related work on ST models in general to provide an idea of what work is current in the field.

Quechua to Spanish MT approaches have become more abundant in the past few years. When it comes to ASR–>MT, or ST approaches, there are few attempts officially recorded. In this section, we list previous work in chronological order to better explain the MT approaches attempted. First, Rios (2015) provided an advanced linguistic Quechua toolkit that used finite state transducers (FSTs) to translate from Spanish to Quechua. Her work laid the foundation for future work and helped to promote the digitization of the Quechua language. After that, Ortega and Pillaipakkamnatt (2018) and Cardenas et al. (2018) introduced several new findings that included the ASR corpus used in the IWSLT 2023 task for both unconstrained and constrained purposes. Not long after, Ortega et al. (2020) introduced the first known attempt of a neural MT system that included several annotators along with the state-of-the-art techniques in subsegmentation such as byte-pair encoding (BPE) (Sennrich et al., 2015). Their work was then extended by others (Chen and Fazio, 2021) more recently to achieve 23 BLEU on religious-based text, the highest performing QUE–SPA for its time.

None of the approaches before Chen and Fazio (2021) work included the use of pre-trained language models (PLMs) for low-resource languages. However, the introduction of zero-shot models occurred at the low-resource machine translation workshop in 2020 (Ojha et al., 2020) and not long after in 2021 at the Americas NLP workshop (Mager et al., 2021). The Americas NLP 2021 workshop included the use of QUE–SPA, albeit for MT only achieving scores of 5.39 BLEU through the use of a multi-lingual model trained on 10 other indigenous languages. Their work did not include zero-shot task approaches as introduced by Ebrahimi et al. (2022) where fine-tuning was performed on a pre-trained XLM-R (Conneau et al., 2020) model that achieved impressive results (40–55 BLEU). More recent work (Weller-Di Marco and Fraser; Costa-jussà et al., 2022) did not surpass those results for MT of QUE–SPA.

To our knowledge only one competition/shared task has attempted to process QUE–SPA for speech translation purposes – Americas NLP 2022[1]. However, the findings for the task have not beeen published as of the writing of this article. Their competition used corpora similar to IWSLT 2023 but lacks MT data as a separate (constrained) resource. They also do not introduce the concept of constrained or unconstrained tasks as was done at IWSLT 2023.

Apart from those tasks that directly use the QUE–SPA language pair, several mainstream techniques are currently being used as alternatives to supervised (from scratch) training. For example, one of the most common approaches for both ST and MT approaches tend to use a transformer in some capacity along with a PLM. One such model that uses a multi-lingual low-resource corpus called Flores (Guzmán et al., 2019) is Facebook's NLLB (no language left behind) approach (NLLB Team et al., 2022). Their approach uses self-supervised learning (SSL) from previous innovation (Pino et al., 2020) for multi-lingual approaches that combines ASR with MT in a ST task alone and is made available through Fairseq (Wang et al., 2020). In our work, our primary systems use Fairseq and Facebook's PLMs with sentence embeddings based on previous work (Artetxe and Schwenk, 2019) and the M2M (multi-to-multi) model (Fan et al., 2021) consisting of 1.2 Billion parameters. This

[1]https://github.com/AmericasNLP/americasnlp2022

enables zero-shot cross-lingual transfer for many low-resource languages, including Quechua.

We provide reference to previous work that includes either a *direct* or *end-to-end* ST models (Berard et al., 2016; Weiss et al., 2017). More traditional approaches typically use a *cascade* approach which first transcribes using an ASR model and then translates using a MT model. While recent work (Bentivogli et al., 2021; Anastasopoulos et al., 2021; Antonios et al., 2022) has shown that the direct ST approaches are worthy, traditional approaches work well for low-resource situations too. In our system submissions, all of our systems with exception of the primary constrained used the cascade approach.

3 Quechua-Spanish

In this section we present our experiments for the QUE–SPA dataset provided in the low-resource ST track at IWSLT 2023. This is the first time that this dataset has been officially introduced in its current state which contains 1 hour and 40 minutes of *constrained* speech audio along with its corresponding translations and nearly 60 hours of ASR data (with transcriptions) from the Siminichik (Cardenas et al., 2018) corpus. AmericasNLP 2022's task used a smaller part of the dataset but the data was not presented or compiled with the same offering and, as of this writing, have not published their results. This dataset aggregates the QUE–SPA MT corpus from previous neural MT work (Ortega et al., 2020). The audio and corresponding transcriptions along with their translations are mostly made of of radio broadcasting, similar to the work from Boito et al. (2022) which contains 17 hours of speech in the Tamasheq language.

We present the six submissions for both the *constrained* and *unconstrained* as follows:

1. a primary constrained system that uses a direct ST approach;

2. a contrastive 1 constrained system consisting of a wav2letter (Pratap et al., 2019) ASR system and a neural MT system created from scratch;

3. a contrastive 2 constrained system consisting of a conformer-based (Gulati et al., 2020) ASR system and a neural MT system created from scratch;

4. a primary unconstrained system consisting of a multi-lingual PLM ASR model, a Quechua recurrent neural-network language model, and a fine-tuned neural MT system based on a PLM;

5. a contrastive 1 unconstrained system consisting of a multi-lingual PLM ASR model and a fine-tuned neural MT system based on a PLM;

6. a contrastive 2 unconstrained system consisting of a wav2letter ASR system and a fine-tuned neural MT system based on a PLM.

We present the experimental settings and results for all systems starting off with constrained systems in Section 3.1 and continuing with the unconstrained systems in Section 3.2. We then describe the other less successful approaches in Section 3.3. Finally, we offer results and discussion in Section 4.

3.1 Constrained Setting

The IWSLT 2023 constrained setting for QUE–SPA consists of two main datasets. First, the speech translation dataset consists of 1 hour and 40 minutes divided into 573 training files, 125 validation files, and 125 test files where each file is a .wav file with a corresponding transcription and human-validated translation from Simanchik (Cardenas et al., 2018). Secondly, there is a MT data set combined by previous work (Ortega et al., 2020) which consists of 100 daily magazine article sentences and 51140 sentences which are of religious context in nature.

3.1.1 Primary System

The Primary System consists of a direct ST approach. Since the constrained setting does not allow for external data, we used only the data provided. We use the Fairseq (Ott et al., 2019) toolkit to perform direct ST using the 573 training files, a total of 1.6 hours of audio. The system extracts log mel-filter bank (MFB) features and is based on the S2T approach by (Wang et al., 2020). We generate a 1k unigram vocabulary for the Spanish text using SentencePiece (Kudo and Richardson, 2018), with no pre-tokenization. Our model consists of a convolutional feature extractor and transformer encoder-decoder (Vaswani et al., 2017) with 6 encoder layers and 3 decoder layers. Error is measured using cross entropy and optimization is done using Adam. Our model was run for 500 epochs with a learning rate of .0002.

3.1.2 Contrastive 1 System

The Contrastive 1 System is a cascade system where first ASR is performed to produce transcriptions that are translated using a separate MT system. For the ASR system, we used the wav2letter++ (Pratap et al., 2019) model. The wav2letter++ model consists of a RNN with 30M parameters (2 spatial convolution layers, 5 bidirectional LSTM layers, and 2 linear layers) and a CNN with 100M parameters (18 temporal convolution layers and 1 linear layer). We use the convolutional gated linear unit (GLU) (Dauphin et al., 2017) architecture proposed in the recipe wav2letter (WSJ) (Collobert et al., 2016). Our experiments using wav2letter++ took 134 epochs to train, using Stochastic Gradient Descent (SGD) with Nesterov momentum and a minibatch of 8 utterances. The initial learning rate was set to 0.006 for faster convergence, and it was annealed with a constant factor of 3.6 after each epoch, with momentum set to 0. The model was optimized using the Auto Segmentation Criterion (ASG) (Collobert et al., 2016). During development, the ASR system WER was 72.15 on the validation set. The MT system was created from scratch using the OpenNMT framework (Klein et al., 2020) with the MT data provided for the constrained task along with the ASR training data. More specifically, the MT system's encoder and decoder are based on a transformer (Vaswani et al., 2017) (encode/decode) architecture of 6 layers. Hidden layer and vectors sizes were 512. Dropout was set to 0.1. Optimization was done using the Adam optimizer. Tokenization was done using SentencePiece (Kudo and Richardson, 2018). Both source and target vocabularies were 50k. Initial BLEU score on the validation set was 21.13.

3.1.3 Contrastive 2 System

Similar to the Contrastive 1 System, the Contrastive 2 system is a cascade approach. The ASR system, however, is distinct. It is derived using MFB features similar to previous work Berrebbi et al. (2022). It uses a conformer instead of the transformer encoder like Gulati et al. (2020). Training was performed using a hybrid CTC/attention loss (Watanabe et al., 2017). The model was optimized using Adam (Kingma and Ba, 2015) and a Noam learning rate scheduler (Vaswani et al., 2017) with 4000 warmup steps. The MT system is identical to the OpenNMT MT system mentioned for the Contrastive 1 submisison covered in Section 3.1.2.

3.2 Unconstrained Setting

For the unconstrained setting in IWSLT 2023, an additional 60 hours of speech data with their corresponding transcriptions was made available by the organizers. This allowed for greater mono-lingual fine-tuning of the ASR data. Additionally, for both the ASR and MT components of all three of our submitted unconstrained systems, PLMs were used along with fine-tuning. The three submissions were cascade systems.

3.2.1 Primary System

The Primary System for the unconstrained setting consists of two systems, the ASR and the MT system. Both systems are fine-tuned. First, the ASR system is multi-lingual model pre-trained on the 102-language FLEURS (Conneau et al., 2023) dataset. The model consists of a conformer (Gulati et al., 2020) encoder and transformer decoder and is trained using hybrid CTC/attention loss (Watanabe et al., 2017) and hierarchical language identification conditioning (Chen et al., 2023). The model inputs are encoded representations extracted from a pre-trained XLS-R 128 model (Babu et al., 2021) with its weights frozen, augmented with SpecAug (Park et al., 2019) and speech perturbation (Ko et al., 2015). In order to jointly decode, we also trained an RNN language model. The RNN consists of 2 layers with a hidden size of 650, trained using SGD with a flat learning rate of 0.1. The word-error rate on the validation set was 15. For the MT system, we use the Fairseq (Ott et al., 2019) tool kit for translation. The Flores 101 model was used (Guzmán et al., 2019) as the PLM and is based on a transformer (Vaswani et al., 2017) architecture used at WMT 2021[2] by Facebook. Fine-tuning was performed using the training ASR+MT data from the *constrained* task as was used for training in the Constrained Contrastive 1 task in Section 3.1.2.

3.2.2 Contrastive 1 System

The Constrastive 1 system is nearly identical to the Primary System for the unconstrained setting. The MT system is identical to that of the Primary System submission for the unconstrained setting. For the ASR system, a FLEURS approach is used identical to the unconstrained Primary System in Section 3.2.1. The only difference is that this Unconstrained Contrastive 1 system does not use a language model.

[2] https://www.statmt.org/wmt21/large-scale-multilingual-translation-task.html

3.2.3 Contrastive 2 System

The Contrastive 2 System is also a cascade (ASR+MT) system. The MT system is identical to that of the Primary System submission for the unconstrained setting. The ASR system architecture is identical to the Constrained Contrastive 1 System in Section 3.1.2, but with other hyperparameters. In this experiment took 243 epochs to train, using Stochastic Gradient Descent (SGD) with Nesterov momentum and a minibatch of 16 utterances. The initial learning rate was set to 0.002 for faster convergence, and it was annealed with a constant factor of 1.2 after each epoch, with momentum set to 0. In this system, we add the additional 60 hours of monolingual transcribed speech data from the *unconstrained* setting mentioned in the IWSLT 2023 low-resource task in addition to the 1.6 hours provided for the *constrained* setting.

3.3 Other Approaches

As noted in Section 2, there have been other successful approaches worth visiting. While we could not exhaustively attempt to use all of those approaches, we did focus on several that are worth noting.

For ASR approaches, we focused on experimenting with different model architectures. This included using different encoders (transformer, conformer) and decoders (auto-regressive Transformer, CTC-only). Regardless, all of the ASR systems achieved at best 100 WER in the constrained setting, limiting the effectiveness of any cascaded approach. In the unconstrained setting, we also looked at different ways to incorporate pre-training. For example, we tried directly fine-tuning a pre-trained XLS-R model (Babu et al., 2021; Baevski et al., 2020) instead of using extracted layer-wise features from a frozen model. These approaches were somewhat more successful by achieving up to 20.4 WER on the validation set; however, the top three systems reported performed better with ASR.

For MT approaches, several attempts were made to experiment with other systems. For example, the OpenNMT (Klein et al., 2020) toolkit now offers PLMs that include the Flores 101 (Guzmán et al., 2019) dataset. However, since Quechua was not included in the language list, the performance was extremely low on the validation set (0.06 BLEU). The Hugging Face version of the Flores 200 dataset was also tested and resulted in 23.5 on its own data. However, when testing on the validation set, the score was of 6.27 BLEU. The Flores 200 model is made available as the NLLB task on Fairseq, however, we experienced several conflicts with the machine infrastructure causing complexity with the Stopes tokenization that prevented us from moving forward.

For direct ST approaches, we also were unsuccessful using w2v feature encoding without major modification. Overall, the cascade approaches seemed to work better for this task and, thus, we made a decision to use those instead. The results for the *constrained* task, nonetheless, show that the direct s2t approach worked well using MFB features.

4 Results and Discussion

Team **QUESPA** BLEU and CHRF Scores			
Constrained			
System	**Description**	**BLEU**	**CHRF**
primary	mfb+s2t	1.25	25.35
contrastive 1	w2vl+onmt	0.13	10.53
contrastive 2	conformer+onmt	0.11	10.63
Unconstrained			
System	**Description**	**BLEU**	**CHRF**
primary	fleurs+lm+floresmt	15.36	47.89
contrastive 1	fleurs+floresmt	15.27	47.74
contrastive 2	w2vl+floresmt	10.75	42.89

Table 1: Team QUESPA results for the Quechua to Spanish low-resource task at IWSLT 2023.

Results are presented in Table 1. For the constrained task, we were unable to create a system that would be viable for deployment. Notwithstanding, we believe that the primary submission which used MFB features along with the default Fairseq S2T recipe could be used to further research in the field. Other systems, based on w2vletter (Pratap et al., 2019) and a conformer (Gulati et al., 2020) resulted in a near zero BLEU score and are probably only valid as proof of the non-functional status of the two systems when performing ASR on the QUE–SPA language pair. It is clear that with 1.6 hours of data for training, few constrained systems will perform better than 5 BLEU, as seen in previous IWSLT tasks.

For the unconstrained setting, our findings have shown that for both the ASR and MT models, the use of a PLM with fine-tuning is necessary. We were unable to create a system from scratch that would perform as well as those presented in previ-

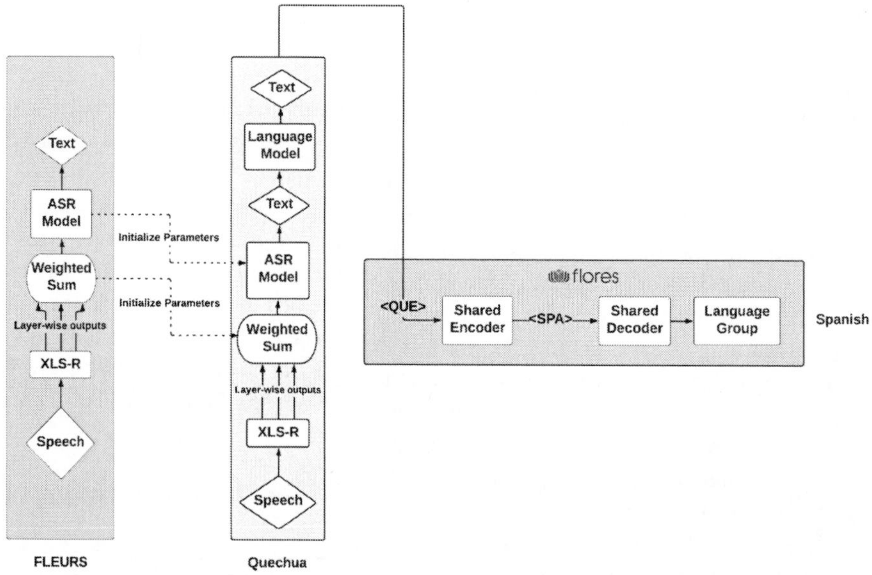

Figure 1: The best-performing *unconstrained* speech translation pipeline.

ous tasks. The combination of a language model and the FLEURS PLM for ASR along with the FLORES 101 PLM for MT constitutes our best performing system overall as shown in Figure 1. The language model slightly helped for the Primary system by a gain of nearly 0.10 points in BLEU. The other unconstrained system based on w2vletter (Pratap et al., 2019) performed much better than the constrained version making it worthwhile to explore for future iterations since it doesn't require other languages.

5 Conclusion

Concluding, we have experimented with several options for both the constrained and unconstrained settings. This constitutes the first time that experiments have been put together along with the other team submissions for the Quechua to Spanish task. We believe that the performance achieved here can serve as baselines for more sophisticated approaches. Additionally, it came to our attention that data splits provided by the organizers can be adjusted to better fit the data. There are multiple speakers in several of the audio files, we did not take advantage of this and hope to address it in the future. Also for the future, we believe that more work could be done using direct ST systems with fine-tuning. We did not follow that path in this work but feel it would be advantageous.

References

Milind Agarwal, Sweta Agrawal, Antonios Anastasopoulos, Ondřej Bojar, Claudia Borg, Marine Carpuat, Roldano Cattoni, Mauro Cettolo, Mingda Chen, William Chen, Khalid Choukri, Alexandra Chronopoulou, Anna Currey, Thierry Declerck, Qianqian Dong, Yannick Estève, Kevin Duh, Marcello Federico, Souhir Gahbiche, Barry Haddow, Benjamin Hsu, Phu Mon Htut, Hirofumi Inaguma, Dávid Javorský, John Judge, Yasumasa Kano, Tom Ko, Rishu Kumar, Pengwei Li, Xutail Ma, Prashant Mathur, Evgeny Matusov, Paul McNamee, John P. McCrae, Kenton Murray, Maria Nadejde, Satoshi Nakamura, Matteo Negri, Ha Nguyen, Jan Niehues, Xing Niu, Atul Ojha Kr., John E. Ortega, Proyag Pal, Juan Pino, Lonneke van der Plas, Peter Polák, Elijah Rippeth, Elizabeth Salesky, Jiatong Shi, Matthias Sperber, Sebastian Stüker, Katsuhito Sudoh, Yun Tang, Brian Thompson, Kevin Tran, Marco Turchi, Alex Waibel, Mingxuan Wang, Shinji Watanabe, and Rodolfo Zevallos. 2023. Findings of the IWSLT 2023 Evaluation Campaign. In *Proceedings of the 20th International Conference on Spoken Language Translation (IWSLT 2023)*. Association for Computational Linguistics.

Antonios Anastasopoulos, Ondřej Bojar, Jacob Bremerman, Roldano Cattoni, Maha Elbayad, Marcello Federico, Xutai Ma, Satoshi Nakamura, Matteo Negri, Jan Niehues, Juan Pino, Elizabeth Salesky, Sebastian Stüker, Katsuhito Sudoh, Marco Turchi, Alexander Waibel, Changhan Wang, and Matthew Wiesner. 2021. FINDINGS OF THE IWSLT 2021 EVALUATION CAMPAIGN. In *Proceedings of the 18th International Conference on Spoken Language Translation (IWSLT 2021)*, pages 1–29, Bangkok, Thailand (online). Association for Computational Linguistics.

Anastasopoulos Antonios, Barrault Loc, Luisa Bentivogli, Marcely Zanon Boito, Bojar Ondřej, Roldano Cattoni, Currey Anna, Dinu Georgiana, Duh Kevin, Elbayad Maha, et al. 2022. Findings of the iwslt 2022 evaluation campaign. In *Proceedings of the 19th International Conference on Spoken Language Translation (IWSLT 2022)*, pages 98–157. Association for Computational Linguistics.

Mikel Artetxe and Holger Schwenk. 2019. Massively multilingual sentence embeddings for zero-shot cross-lingual transfer and beyond. *Transactions of the Association for Computational Linguistics*, 7:597–610.

Arun Babu, Changhan Wang, Andros Tjandra, Kushal Lakhotia, Qiantong Xu, Naman Goyal, Kritika Singh, Patrick von Platen, Yatharth Saraf, Juan Pino, et al. 2021. Xls-r: Self-supervised cross-lingual speech representation learning at scale. *arXiv preprint arXiv:2111.09296*.

Alexei Baevski, Yuhao Zhou, Abdelrahman Mohamed, and Michael Auli. 2020. wav2vec 2.0: A framework for self-supervised learning of speech representations. *Advances in Neural Information Processing Systems*, 33:12449–12460.

Luisa Bentivogli, Mauro Cettolo, Marco Gaido, Alina Karakanta, Alberto Martinelli, Matteo Negri, and Marco Turchi. 2021. Cascade versus direct speech translation: Do the differences still make a difference? *CoRR*, abs/2106.01045.

Alexandre Berard, Olivier Pietquin, Christophe Servan, and Laurent Besacier. 2016. Listen and translate: A proof of concept for end-to-end speech-to-text translation. *CoRR*, abs/1612.01744.

Dan Berrebbi, Jiatong Shi, Brian Yan, Osbel López-Francisco, Jonathan Amith, and Shinji Watanabe. 2022. Combining Spectral and Self-Supervised Features for Low Resource Speech Recognition and Translation. In *Proc. Interspeech 2022*, pages 3533–3537.

Marcely Zanon Boito, Fethi Bougares, Florentin Barbier, Souhir Gahbiche, Loïc Barrault, Mickael Rouvier, and Yannick Estéve. 2022. Speech resources in the tamasheq language. *Language Resources and Evaluation Conference (LREC)*.

Ronald Cardenas, Rodolfo Zevallos, Reynaldo Baquerizo, and Luis Camacho. 2018. Siminchik: A speech corpus for preservation of southern quechua. *ISI-NLP 2*, page 21.

William Chen and Brett Fazio. 2021. Morphologically-guided segmentation for translation of agglutinative low-resource languages. *Proceedings of Machine Translation Summit XVIII*.

William Chen, Brian Yan, Jiatong Shi, Yifan Peng, Soumi Maiti, and Shinji Watanabe. 2023. Improving massively multilingual asr with auxiliary CTC objectives. *arXiv preprint arXiv:2302.12829*.

Ronan Collobert, Christian Puhrsch, and Gabriel Synnaeve. 2016. Wav2letter: an end-to-end convnet-based speech recognition system. *arXiv preprint arXiv:1609.03193*.

Alexis Conneau, Alexei Baevski, Ronan Collobert, Abdelrahman Mohamed, and Michael Auli. 2020. Unsupervised cross-lingual representation learning for speech recognition. *arXiv preprint arXiv:2006.13979*.

Alexis Conneau, Min Ma, Simran Khanuja, Yu Zhang, Vera Axelrod, Siddharth Dalmia, Jason Riesa, Clara Rivera, and Ankur Bapna. 2023. Fleurs: Few-shot learning evaluation of universal representations of speech. In *2022 IEEE Spoken Language Technology Workshop (SLT)*, pages 798–805.

Marta R Costa-jussà, James Cross, Onur Çelebi, Maha Elbayad, Kenneth Heafield, Kevin Heffernan, Elahe Kalbassi, Janice Lam, Daniel Licht, Jean Maillard, et al. 2022. No language left behind: Scaling human-centered machine translation. *arXiv preprint arXiv:2207.04672*.

Yann N Dauphin, Angela Fan, Michael Auli, and David Grangier. 2017. Language modeling with gated convolutional networks. In *International conference on machine learning*, pages 933–941. PMLR.

Abteen Ebrahimi, Manuel Mager, Arturo Oncevay, Vishrav Chaudhary, Luis Chiruzzo, Angela Fan, John Ortega, Ricardo Ramos, Annette Rios Gonzales, Ivan Meza-Ruiz, et al. 2022. Americasnli: Evaluating zero-shot natural language understanding of pretrained multilingual models in truly low-resource languages. In *Proceedings of the 60th Annual Meeting of the Association for Computational Linguistics (Volume 1: Long Papers)*, pages 6279–6299.

Angela Fan, Shruti Bhosale, Holger Schwenk, Zhiyi Ma, Ahmed El-Kishky, Siddharth Goyal, Mandeep Baines, Onur Celebi, Guillaume Wenzek, Vishrav Chaudhary, et al. 2021. Beyond english-centric multilingual machine translation. *The Journal of Machine Learning Research*, 22(1):4839–4886.

Anmol Gulati, James Qin, Chung-Cheng Chiu, Niki Parmar, Yu Zhang, Jiahui Yu, Wei Han, Shibo Wang, Zhengdong Zhang, Yonghui Wu, and Ruoming Pang. 2020. Conformer: Convolution-augmented Transformer for Speech Recognition. In *Proc. Interspeech 2020*, pages 5036–5040.

Francisco Guzmán, Peng-Jen Chen, Myle Ott, Juan Pino, Guillaume Lample, Philipp Koehn, Vishrav Chaudhary, and Marc'Aurelio Ranzato. 2019. The flores evaluation datasets for low-resource machine translation: Nepali–english and sinhala–english. In *Proceedings of the 2019 Conference on Empirical Methods in Natural Language Processing and the 9th International Joint Conference on Natural Language Processing (EMNLP-IJCNLP)*, pages 6098–6111.

Barry Haddow, Rachel Bawden, Antonio Valerio Miceli Barone, Jindřich Helcl, and Alexandra Birch. 2022. Survey of low-resource machine translation. *Computational Linguistics*, 48(3):673–732.

Diederik P. Kingma and Jimmy Ba. 2015. Adam: A method for stochastic optimization. In *ICLR 2015, Conference Track Proceedings*.

Guillaume Klein, François Hernandez, Vincent Nguyen, and Jean Senellart. 2020. The opennmt neural machine translation toolkit: 2020 edition. In *Proceedings of the 14th Conference of the Association for Machine Translation in the Americas (Volume 1: Research Track)*, pages 102–109.

Tom Ko, Vijayaditya Peddinti, Daniel Povey, and Sanjeev Khudanpur. 2015. Audio augmentation for speech recognition. In *Proc. Interspeech 2015*, pages 3586–3589.

Taku Kudo and John Richardson. 2018. Sentencepiece: A simple and language independent subword tokenizer and detokenizer for neural text processing. *arXiv preprint arXiv:1808.06226*.

Manuel Mager, Arturo Oncevay, Abteen Ebrahimi, John Ortega■, Annette Riosψ, Angela Fan, Ximena Gutierrez-Vasquesψ, Luis Chiruzzo, Gustavo A Giménez-Lugo, Ricardo Ramosη, et al. 2021. Findings of the americasnlp 2021 shared task on open machine translation for indigenous languages of the americas. *NAACL-HLT 2021*, page 202.

NLLB Team, Marta R. Costa-jussà, James Cross, Onur Çelebi, Maha Elbayad, Kenneth Heafield, Kevin Heffernan, Elahe Kalbassi, Janice Lam, Daniel Licht, Jean Maillard, Anna Sun, Skyler Wang, Guillaume Wenzek, Al Youngblood, Bapi Akula, Loic Barrault, Gabriel Mejia-Gonzalez, Prangthip Hansanti, John Hoffman, Semarley Jarrett, Kaushik Ram Sadagopan, Dirk Rowe, Shannon Spruit, Chau Tran, Pierre Andrews, Necip Fazil Ayan, Shruti Bhosale, Sergey Edunov, Angela Fan, Cynthia Gao, Vedanuj Goswami, Francisco Guzmán, Philipp Koehn, Alexandre Mourachko, Christophe Ropers, Safiyyah Saleem, Holger Schwenk, and Jeff Wang. 2022. No language left behind: Scaling human-centered machine translation.

Atul Kr Ojha, Valentin Malykh, Alina Karakanta, and Chao-Hong Liu. 2020. Findings of the loresmt 2020 shared task on zero-shot for low-resource languages. In *Proceedings of the 3rd Workshop on Technologies for MT of Low Resource Languages*, pages 33–37.

John E Ortega, Richard Castro Mamani, and Kyunghyun Cho. 2020. Neural machine translation with a polysynthetic low resource language. *Machine Translation*, 34(4):325–346.

John E Ortega and Krishnan Pillaipakkamnatt. 2018. Using morphemes from agglutinative languages like quechua and finnish to aid in low-resource translation. *Technologies for MT of Low Resource Languages (LoResMT 2018)*, page 1.

Myle Ott, Sergey Edunov, Alexei Baevski, Angela Fan, Sam Gross, Nathan Ng, David Grangier, and Michael Auli. 2019. fairseq: A fast, extensible toolkit for sequence modeling. In *NAACL (Demonstrations)*, pages 48–53, Minneapolis, Minnesota. Association for Computational Linguistics.

Kishore Papineni, Salim Roukos, Todd Ward, and Wei-Jing Zhu. 2002. Bleu: a method for automatic evaluation of machine translation. In *Proceedings of the 40th annual meeting of the Association for Computational Linguistics*, pages 311–318.

Daniel S Park, William Chan, Yu Zhang, Chung-Cheng Chiu, Barret Zoph, Ekin D Cubuk, and Quoc V Le. 2019. Specaugment: A simple data augmentation method for automatic speech recognition. *arXiv preprint arXiv:1904.08779*.

Juan Pino, Qiantong Xu, Xutai Ma, Mohammad Javad Dousti, and Yun Tang. 2020. Self-training for end-to-end speech translation.

Vineel Pratap, Awni Y. Hannun, Qiantong Xu, Jeff Cai, Jacob Kahn, Gabriel Synnaeve, Vitaliy Liptchinsky, and Ronan Collobert. 2019. Wav2letter++: A fast open-source speech recognition system. *IEEE International Conference on Acoustics, Speech and Signal Processing (ICASSP)*, pages 6460–6464.

Annette Rios. 2015. *A basic language technology toolkit for Quechua*. Ph.D. thesis, University of Zurich.

Rico Sennrich, Barry Haddow, and Alexandra Birch. 2015. Neural machine translation of rare words with subword units. *arXiv preprint arXiv:1508.07909*.

Ashish Vaswani, Noam Shazeer, Niki Parmar, Jakob Uszkoreit, Llion Jones, Aidan N Gomez, Łukasz Kaiser, and Illia Polosukhin. 2017. Attention is all you need. *Advances in neural information processing systems*, 30.

Changhan Wang, Yun Tang, Xutai Ma, Anne Wu, Dmytro Okhonko, and Juan Pino. 2020. fairseq s2t: Fast speech-to-text modeling with fairseq. *arXiv preprint arXiv:2010.05171*.

Shinji Watanabe, Takaaki Hori, Suyoun Kim, John R. Hershey, and Tomoki Hayashi. 2017. Hybrid CTC/attention architecture for end-to-end speech recognition. *IEEE Journal of Selected Topics in Signal Processing*, 11(8):1240–1253.

Ron J. Weiss, Jan Chorowski, Navdeep Jaitly, Yonghui Wu, and Zhifeng Chen. 2017. Sequence-to-Sequence Models Can Directly Translate Foreign Speech. In *Proc. Interspeech 2017*, pages 2625–2629.

Marion Weller-Di Marco and Alexander Fraser. Findings of the wmt 2022 shared tasks in unsupervised mt and very low resource supervised mt.

GMU Systems for the IWSLT 2023 Dialect and Low-resource Speech Translation Tasks

Jonathan Kabala Mbuya
George Mason University
jmbuya@gmu.edu

Antonios Anastasopoulos
George Mason University
antonis@gmu.edu

Abstract

This paper describes the GMU Systems for the IWSLT 2023 Dialect and Low-resource Speech Translation Tasks. We submitted systems for five low-resource tasks and the dialectal task. In this work, we explored self-supervised pre-trained speech models and finetuned them on speech translation downstream tasks. We use the Wav2vec 2.0, XLSR-53, and Hubert as self-supervised models. Unlike Hubert, Wav2vec 2.0 and XLSR-53 achieve the best results when we remove the top three layers. Our results show that Wav2vec 2.0 and Hubert perform similarly with their relative best configuration. In addition, we found that Wav2vec 2.0 pre-trained on audio data of the same language as the source language of a speech translation model achieves better results. For the low-resource setting, the best results are achieved using either the Wav2vec 2.0 or Hubert models, while XLSR-53 achieves the best results for the dialectal transfer task. We find that XLSR-53 does not perform well for low-resource tasks. Using Wav2vec 2.0, we report close to 2 BLEU point improvements on the test set for the Tamasheq-French compared to the baseline system at the IWSLT 2022.

1 Introduction

Recently, speech-to-text translation (S2T) has received a lot of focus in the community where neural, end-to-end approaches outperform traditional statistical approaches (Weiss et al., 2017). Recent neural approaches to S2T have shown superior performance on this task (Fang et al., 2022; Tang et al., 2022). Despite the success of neural approaches to S2T, data scarcity is one of the significant challenges, given that neural networks require hundreds to thousands of hours of labeled data to train a good speech translation model (Sperber and Paulik, 2020). This makes developing such S2T models challenging, especially for low-resource languages.

The IWSLT 2023 Low-resource and dialectal shared tasks (Agarwal et al., 2023) give the possibilities for researchers to find innovative ways to develop speech translation systems for languages with limited data. Unlike previous years, this year noticed an addition of more low-resource languages language pairs (up to 6) in addition to a dialect language pair.

This paper describes the GMU submissions to the low-resource and dialectal tasks. Our systems use self-supervised pre-trained speech models to improve speech translation models' performance in general, particularly for low-resource languages. Self-supervised pre-training is possible because unlabeled data (i.e., audio or text) can be obtained easier compared to labeled data. Previous research has addressed using self-supervised speech models for speech translation (Wu et al., 2020; Nguyen et al., 2020; Popuri et al., 2022). However, these prior work did not consider exploring the impact of different layers of these self-supervised models to maximize the performance of S2T models.

In this paper, we consider three self-supervised speech models: Wav2vec 2.0 (Baevski et al., 2020), XLSR (Conneau et al., 2020) and Hubert (Hsu et al., 2021). Following the discussion by Pasad et al. (2022), we experimented to study the impact of removing the top n layers of these models for the speech translation task. By removing the last three layers of the Wav2vec 2.0 model, we achieve more than 2 BLEU improvement (8.03) on the blind test set for the Tamasheq-French pair compared to the best system submitted to the IWSLT 2022 low-resource shared task (Anastasopoulos et al., 2022; Zanon Boito et al., 2022). Similarly, using a pre-trained XLSR-53, we achieved a BLEU score of 16.3 on the Tunisian Arabic-to-English language pair without using the transcripts.

2 Task Descriptions

We are concerned with developing speech translation models in low-resource and dialectal tracks. Each track poses distinct challenges. The low-

Proceedings of the 20th International Conference on Spoken Language Translation (IWSLT 2023), pages 269–276
July 13-14, 2023

Language Pairs	Language Code	Train Set Hours	Shared Task
Irish to English (Agarwal et al., 2023)	ga-eng	11	Low-resource
Marathi to Hindi (Agarwal et al., 2023)	mr-hi	15.3	Low-resource
Pashto to French (ELRA)	pus-fra	61	Low-resource
Tamasheq to French (Boito et al., 2022)	tmh-fra	17	Low-resource
Quechua to Spanish	que-spa	1.6	Low-resource
Tunisian Arabic to English	aeb-eng	160	Dialectal

Table 1: Language pair details used in our experiments.

resource setting has limited training data, while the dialectal one lacks standard orthography and formal grammar. Both shared tasks allowed the submission of models trained under constrained and unconstrained conditions. In the constrained condition, models are only trained on data provided by the organizers. In contrast, models in the unconstrained condition can be trained on any available resources, including pre-trained models.

2.1 Data

Six low-resource languages were made available, and one dialectal. However, due to data quality issues (see Section 5) we do not report results on the Maltese to English task. Table 1 shows the data details for each language pair. The organizers shared additional data for specific languages, including data for automatic speech recognition (ASR) and machine translation (MT). However, our approach used the data described in table 1. The exception is for Tamasheq-French, where we used the provided 234 hours of unlabeled Tamasheq audio to pre-train a self-supervised speech model.

For the unconstrained condition, we used data from MUST-C[1] (Di Gangi et al., 2019) to train an ASR model for which we used its encoder to initialize the speech translation training. We used publicly available pre-trained self-supersized models (Wav2vec 2.0 (Baevski et al., 2020), XLSR-53 (Conneau et al., 2020), and Hubert (Hsu et al., 2021)). The Wav2vec 2.0 and Hubert checkpoints we used were trained on the Librispeech 960hr English-only data (Panayotov et al., 2015), while XLSR-53 was trained on 53 different languages (Conneau et al., 2020). No source language of all language pairs appears in any self-supervised models except Tamasheq-French, where we pre-trained the Wav2vec 2.0 model we used for Tamasheq-French was pre-trained on Tamasheq audio-only data. Though Tunisian Arabic is not part of the XLSR-53, the XLSR-53 contains Arabic data that may be related to Tunisian Arabic.

[1]English to French only

3 Proposed Methods

Our methods consist of three different architectures. The first is an end-to-end based transformer-based architecture (E2E) trained on only provided data. The second architecture, which we name E2E-ASR, is the same as the first, except that we initialize the encoder with an ASR encoder. The third architecture uses self-supervised speech models as an encoder and a transformer-based decoder. We used three different self-supervised models, Wav2vec 2.0, XLSR-53, and Hubert, and refer to these architectures as W2V-E2E, XLSR-E2E, and Hubert-E2E respectively.

We used the Fairseq ST (Wang et al., 2020) framework for all our experiments and modified this framework to accommodate our new custom model architectures.

3.1 End-to-end and End-to-end with ASR

For End-to-end (E2E) architecture, we used a transformer-based encoder-decoder architecture (Vaswani et al., 2017) (`st_tranformer_s`) as implemented in the Fairseq S2T framework (Wang et al., 2020). The E2E architecture consists of a 6-block transformer encoder and a 6-block transformer decoder and is optimized using the cross-entropy loss with label smoothing. We used this model architecture to train the model for the primary constrained category (**primary-constrained**).

The End-to-end with ASR (E2E-ASR) architecture, similar to (Stoian et al., 2019) and (Bansal et al., 2019), uses the same architecture as the E2E. The difference is that we use a pre-trained ASR model to initialize its encoder. We used a transformer-based architecture identical to the one for E2E to train the ASR on the English data of the English-French Must-C dataset (Di Gangi et al., 2019). We chose this architecture for the ASR model to facilitate the transfer of the ASR encoder weights to initialize the E2E-ASR encoder. The decoder of the E2E-ASR was randomly initialized and did not use the ASR decoder because it was trained on a different language with a different vocabulary. We used this model architecture to train the model for the second contrastive unconstrained category (**contrastive2-unconstrained**).

3.2 Self-Supervised Approaches

The self-supervised approach uses self-supervised speech models as acoustic encoders with a transformer-based decoder. The use of these self-supervised models is motivated by the scarcity of data in the low-resource setting. However, we found these models useful even for the dialectal task. The self-supervised architecture is illustrated in figure 1.

We used three different self-supervised models, Wav2vec 2.0, XLSR-53, and Hubert, which correspond to the respective architectures W2V-E2E, XLSR-E2E, and Hubert-E2E. These models consist of a feature encoder and a context network. The feature encoder has seven temporal convolution blocks, and the context network consists of several transformer blocks. The Wav2vec 2.0 and Hubert models used in our experiments have 12 transformer blocks, whereas the XLSR-53 has 24.[2]

We use these self-supervised models as encoders following the traditional encoder-decoder model architecture. The decoder consists of a transformer network with six layers preceded by a linear layer.

3.2.1 Using Wav2vec 2.0 and XLSR-53

Instead of using all the layers of the context network for the Wav2vec 2.0 and XLSR-53 models, we explored the impact of removing the top n most layers. The exploration of removing the top layers was inspired by Pasad et al. (2022), who analyzed self-supervised speech models and measures the acoustic, phonetic, and word-level properties encoded in individual layers of the context network. For Wav2vec 2.0 and XLSR, the analyses show that the initial and the final layers are more similar to the inputs than the intermediate layers. Instead of re-initializing the top n layers and then fine-tuning these models on a downstream task as done in Pasad et al. (2022), we explored the idea of removing these layers and then fine-tuning the modified model on a downstream task. Through a series of experiments, we found that removing the last three layers for the Wav2vec 2.0 and XLSR-53 models yields the highest BLEU score.

We found the Wav2vec 2.0 helpful for the low-resource languages, while the XLSR-53 was more beneficial for the dialectal language. Therefore, we used the Wav2vec 2.0 for the primary unconstrained category (**primary unconstrained**) for the low-resource task. The XLSR-53 was used as the primary unconstrained category (**primary unconstrained**) for the dialectal transfer task.

The Wav2vec 2.0 we used for all the low-resource languages (except Tamasheq-French) was trained on the English raw audio of the Librispeech 960hr data (Panayotov et al., 2015). However, due to the availability of Tamasheq raw audio, we also trained a Wav2vec 2.0 model on Tamasheq raw audio that used this model on the Tamasheq to French language pair. The XLSR-53 model we used was trained on 53 raw audio data from 53 different languages.

3.2.2 Using Hubert

Unlike Wav2vec 2.0 and XSLR-53, we did not remove any layers for the Hubert model. We rather fine-tuned the out-of-the-box pre-trained Hubert model on the English raw audio data of Librispeech 960hr. As discussed by (Pasad et al., 2022), Hubert does not follow the autoencoder pattern, given that the higher layers appear to encode more phonetic and word information. The choice of not removing top layers for the Hubert model was also corroborated through our empirical experiments, where we achieved the highest BLEU score for the Hubert model when we did not remove any top layers.

We used the Hubert model for the first contrastive constrained category (**contrastivel unconstrained**) for the low-resource and dialectal tasks.

3.3 Data

The input to architectures E2E and E2E-ASR consist of 80-channel log-mel filterbank features computed on a 25 ms window with a 10 ms shift. We used raw audio as input for all the architectures using self-supervised models. For the translation text, we use the byte pair encoding (BPE) (Sennrich et al., 2016) algorithm with the sentencepiece toolkit from the Fairseq ST framework (Wang et al.,

[2]We refer the reader to the following papers (Baevski et al., 2020), (Conneau et al., 2020) and (Hsu et al., 2021) for more details on these models.

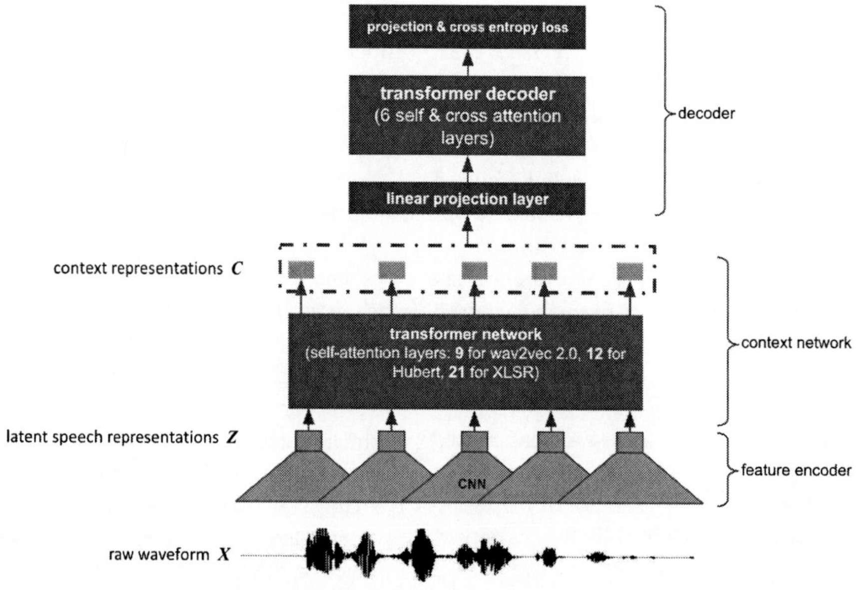

Figure 1: Self-supervised model architecture. This is an end-to-end architecture that uses self-supervised speech models as the encoder. The encoder is one of the Wav2vec 2.0, XLSR, or Hubert models. We removed the top 3 layers of the Wav2vec 2.0 and XLSR models.

Language Pairs	Vocab. Size
Irish-English	1000
Marathi-Hindi	1000
Pashto-French	3000
Tamasheq-French	1000
Quechua Spanish	400
Tunisian Arabic-English	8000

Table 2: BPE vocabulary for each language.

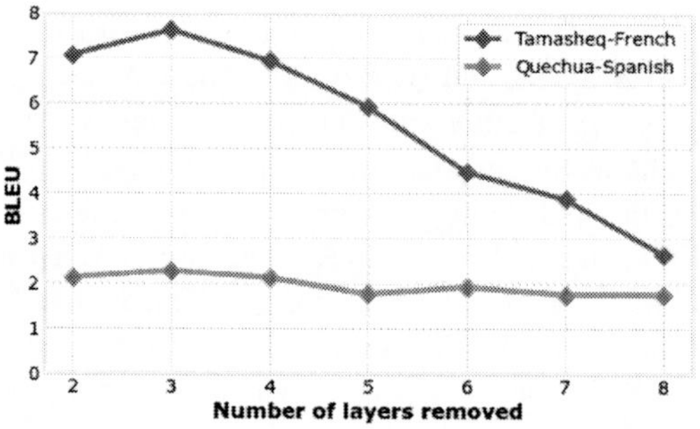

Figure 2: BLEU score on the test set for Tamasheq-French (tmh-fra) and Quechua-Spanish [3](que-spa) after removing top n number of layers of the Wav2vec 2.0. These results are run using the W2V-E2E architecture. For both Tamasheq-French and Quechua-Spanish, the best BLEU is achieved after removing the top 3 layers.

2020) to create vocabularies for all the target languages. We chose the vocabulary size based on the amount of text data we had for each language. Table 2 shows the BPE vocabulary size we used for each language pair. Though we used the training data size as a heuristic for choosing these BPE vocabulary sizes, we empirically tested a few configurations. We kept the sizes that gave the best BLEU score.

4 Results and Analyses

Table 3 shows results for all the systems we submitted. Our primary system reports the best results for the unconstrained setting where we used the *W2V-E2E* and *XLSR-E2E* architectures for the low-resource and dialectal tasks, respectively.

We explored the impact of removing the top n layers for the Wav2vec 2.0 model used in the *W2V-E2E* architecture. As illustrated in figure 2, the highest BLEU was achieved by removing the top three layers of the Wav2vec 2.0 model. We, therefore, used the same heuristic for the XLSR-53 model, given that it has the same architecture as the Wav2vec 2.0 model.

[3]The results for Quechua to Spanish are different from those in Table 3 because they were run after the evaluation period.

Language	System	Task	Architecture	dev/valid	test1	test2	test3
ga-eng	primary constr.	LR	E2E	-	-	15.1	-
	primary unconstr.		W2V-E2E	-	-	66.5	-
	contrastive1 unconstr.		Hubert-E2E	-	-	**77.4**	-
	contrastive2 unconstr.		E2E-ASR	-	-	15.1	-
mr-hi	primary constr.	LR	E2E	0.77	-	3.3	-
	primary unconstr.		W2V-E2E	4.76	-	7.7	-
	contrastive1 unconstr.		Hubert-E2E	**5.78**	-	**8.6**	-
	contrastive2 unconstr.		E2E-ASR	4.07	-	5.9	-
pus-fra	primary constr.	LR	E2E	2.66	-	5.92	-
	primary unconstr.		W2V-E2E	**11.99**	-	**16.87**	-
	contrastive1 unconstr.		Hubert-E2E	11.27	-	15.24	-
	contrastive2 unconstr.		E2E-ASR	9.72	-	13.32	-
tmh-fra	primary constr.	LR	E2E	1.24	1.0	0.48	-
	primary unconstr.		W2V-E2E	**12.07**	**7.63**	**8.03**	-
	contrastive1 unconstr.		Hubert-E2E	4.79	2.77	1.3	-
	contrastive2 unconstr.		E2E-ASR	5.24	3.77	2.1	-
que-spa	primary constr.	LR	E2E	1.46	-	1.46	-
	primary unconstr.		W2V-E2E	1.2	-	1.78	-
	contrastive1 unconstr.		Hubert-E2E	**1.84**	-	**1.86**	-
	contrastive2 unconstr.		E2E-ASR	1.63	-	1.63	-
aeb-eng	primary constr.	DT	E2E	11.49	8.94	5.0	4.5
	primary unconstr.		XLSR-E2E	**19.35**	**16.31**	**16.6**	**14.6**
	contrastive1 unconstr.		Hubert-E2E	17.69	14.52	15.0	13.4
	contrastive2 unconstr.		W2V-E2E	16.7	14.4	14.1	12.9

Table 3: BLEU score for all the submitted systems. LR and DT indicate low-resource and dialectal transfer, respectively. dev/valid refers to the validation or development sets we used during training. test1 refers to the test set we used during training (some language pairs did not have this set). test2 refers to the blind test set. Some language pairs (i.e., aeb-eng) had an additional blind test set called test3. The "-" character indicates that we do not have BLEU results for that category. We did not report the dev/valid results for the Irish to English (ga-eng) task due to the data quality issue discussed in section 5.

4.1 Low-Resource Task

For the low-resource shared task, the highest BLEU is obtained on average by the architecture that uses the Wav2vec 2.0 model (W2V-E2E). However, the Hubert (Hubert-E2E) architecture yields competitive BLEU compared to the W2V-E2E architecture. In fact, for Marathi-Hindi and Quechua-Spanish language pairs, the highest BLEU is achieved by using the Hubert model. Based on our experiments, we think both the Hubert and the Wav2vec 2.0 models may have similar performance though each model may require different configurations. In the future, we hope to have a detailed analysis of the conditions under which one model performs better than the other. Table 3 shows the BLEU results for the low-resource task.

The *W2V-E2E* architecture achieves a relatively high BLEU score compared to *Hubert-E2E* for Tamasheq-French. This behavior is explained by the fact that the Wav2vec 2.0 models used for Tamasheq-French were pre-trained on 234 hours of Tamasheq audio, while the Hubert was pre-trained on 960 hours of English data from the Librispeech dataset. Therefore, pre-training a self-supervised model on audio data from the same source language helps improve the model's performance on a downstream task.

Interestingly, pre-training on audio data from a different language than the source language for the speech translation task still yields improvement compared to starting with random weights. While Bansal et al. (2019) reported this behavior for ASR pre-training, we still see the same pattern for self-supervised pre-training.

Particularly for Tamasheq-French, which had a baseline BLEU score of 5.7 for the best IWSLT 2022 system (Anastasopoulos et al., 2022), we nevertheless improved upon the baseline by more than 2 BLEU on the blind test set.

4.2 Dialectal Task

Unlike the low-resource task, the highest BLEU for the dialectal task was achieved by using the XLSR-53 model (*XLSR-E2E*). Therefore, we used this architecture for our primary unconstrained setting. Table 3 shows the results for Tunisian Arabic-English.

For this task, Wav2vec 2.0 and Hubert had comparable BLEU scores. However, surprisingly, they did not perform as well as XLSR-53. This finding was counterintuitive given that the XLSR-53 model did not perform as well as the Wav2vec 2.0 or Hubert on all the low-resource languages. The XLSR-53 model was also reported to have poor performance by Zanon Boito et al. (2022) on a low-resource language. Based on our experiments, we think that the poor performance of the XLSR-53 model for the low-resource task was related to its size. We speculate that the XLSR-53 model size may fail to adapt while fine-tuning it on little data. However, fine-tuning it on a lot of data, like the case of Tunisian-Arabic-English, may yield overall improvement.

It is also possible that the best performance of the XLSR-53 model on the Tunisian Arabic-English data is because it was trained on more languages. It will be interesting to investigate the impact of the model size and multilinguality for self-supervised pre-trained speech models to improve the performance of speech translation downstream tasks. In addition, we think there may be room to study further the speech representation of the XLSR-53 model across layers so that they can be better adapted in low-resource settings.

5 Data Quality Issues

The low-resource shared tasks of the IWSLT 2023 consists of six tasks, each task corresponding to one language pair. As we worked on these shared tasks, we noticed issues with the data of two tasks: Maltese to English and Irish to English.

The Maltese to English data had a number of issues that made it hard to work with. For instance, the metadata of about 1001 out of 1698 samples mentioned zero or less than zero duration for audio samples (`start_time >= end_time`) while the aligned utterances had several words in most cases. Therefore, we were not able to align most audio data with their utterances.

The Irish to English data had an issue with the development set. Initially, the samples in the development were also present in the training set. However, the organizer later fixed this issue by updating the development set data. However, no matter how we trained our models, we never achieved more than 1 BLEU score on the updated development set. After troubleshooting our model on the training data, we were confident that we should have gotten a BLEU score that was well above 1. We proceeded with submitting our system for this task. However, we are very suspicious of the high BLEU score reported on the blind test, as shown in Table 3, as it suggests that there's an overlap between training and test sets.

6 Conclusion

In this paper, we presented the GMU Systems for the IWSLT 2023 Dialect and Low-resource Speech Translation Tasks. Our approach mainly focused on using self-supervised pre-trained speech models to improve the performance of speech translation on downstream tasks. The self-supervised pre-trained speech models used in this paper are the Wav2vec 2.0, XLSR-53, and Hubert. We showed that the Wav2vec 2.0 and the Hubert model have comparable results in low resource and dialectal transfer tasks. However, the Wav2vec 2.0 performs well when we remove the top three layers, while the Hubert model has no such requirements.

Our experiments showed that the XLSR-53 model performs poorly in the low-resource setting compared to the Wav2vec 2.0 and Hubert models. However, in the dialectal task, the XLSR-53 model outperforms the Wav2vec 2.0 and Hubert models.

In the future, we plan to conduct an in-depth analysis to understand the advantages and limitations of these self-supervised pre-trained speech models while fine-tuning them on downstream speech translation tasks.

Acknowledgements

We are thankful to the organizers of the IWSLT 2023 low resource and dialectal shared tasks. This work was generously supported by NSF grant

IIS-2125466 and by a Meta Sponsored Research Award. We are also thankful to the Office of Research Computing at George Mason University (https://orc.gmu.edu), funded in part by grants from the National Science Foundation (Awards Number 1625039 and 2018631), for the computing resources we used to train our models.

References

Milind Agarwal, Sweta Agrawal, Antonios Anastasopoulos, Ondřej Bojar, Claudia Borg, Marine Carpuat, Roldano Cattoni, Mauro Cettolo, Mingda Chen, William Chen, Khalid Choukri, Alexandra Chronopoulou, Anna Currey, Thierry Declerck, Qianqian Dong, Yannick Estève, Kevin Duh, Marcello Federico, Souhir Gahbiche, Barry Haddow, Benjamin Hsu, Phu Mon Htut, Hirofumi Inaguma, Dávid Javorský, John Judge, Yasumasa Kano, Tom Ko, Rishu Kumar, Pengwei Li, Xutail Ma, Prashant Mathur, Evgeny Matusov, Paul McNamee, John P. McCrae, Kenton Murray, Maria Nadejde, Satoshi Nakamura, Matteo Negri, Ha Nguyen, Jan Niehues, Xing Niu, Atul Ojha Kr., John E. Ortega, Proyag Pal, Juan Pino, Lonneke van der Plas, Peter Polák, Elijah Rippeth, Elizabeth Salesky, Jiatong Shi, Matthias Sperber, Sebastian Stüker, Katsuhito Sudoh, Yun Tang, Brian Thompson, Kevin Tran, Marco Turchi, Alex Waibel, Mingxuan Wang, Shinji Watanabe, and Rodolfo Zevallos. 2023. Findings of the IWSLT 2023 Evaluation Campaign. In *Proceedings of the 20th International Conference on Spoken Language Translation (IWSLT 2023)*. Association for Computational Linguistics.

Antonios Anastasopoulos, Loïc Barrault, Luisa Bentivogli, Marcely Zanon Boito, Ondřej Bojar, Roldano Cattoni, Anna Currey, Georgiana Dinu, Kevin Duh, Maha Elbayad, Clara Emmanuel, Yannick Estève, Marcello Federico, Christian Federmann, Souhir Gahbiche, Hongyu Gong, Roman Grundkiewicz, Barry Haddow, Benjamin Hsu, Dávid Javorský, Věra Kloudová, Surafel Lakew, Xutai Ma, Prashant Mathur, Paul McNamee, Kenton Murray, Maria Nădejde, Satoshi Nakamura, Matteo Negri, Jan Niehues, Xing Niu, John Ortega, Juan Pino, Elizabeth Salesky, Jiatong Shi, Matthias Sperber, Sebastian Stüker, Katsuhito Sudoh, Marco Turchi, Yogesh Virkar, Alexander Waibel, Changhan Wang, and Shinji Watanabe. 2022. Findings of the IWSLT 2022 evaluation campaign. In *Proceedings of the 19th International Conference on Spoken Language Translation (IWSLT 2022)*, pages 98–157, Dublin, Ireland (in-person and online). Association for Computational Linguistics.

Alexei Baevski, Henry Zhou, Abdel rahman Mohamed, and Michael Auli. 2020. wav2vec 2.0: A framework for self-supervised learning of speech representations. *ArXiv*, abs/2006.11477.

Sameer Bansal, Herman Kamper, Karen Livescu, Adam Lopez, and Sharon Goldwater. 2019. Pre-training on high-resource speech recognition improves low-resource speech-to-text translation. In *Proceedings of the 2019 Conference of the North American Chapter of the Association for Computational Linguistics: Human Language Technologies, Volume 1 (Long and Short Papers)*, pages 58–68, Minneapolis, Minnesota. Association for Computational Linguistics.

Marcely Zanon Boito, Fethi Bougares, Florentin Barbier, Souhir Gahbiche, Loïc Barrault, Mickael Rouvier, and Y. Estève. 2022. Speech resources in the tamasheq language. In *International Conference on Language Resources and Evaluation.*

Alexis Conneau, Alexei Baevski, Ronan Collobert, Abdel rahman Mohamed, and Michael Auli. 2020. Unsupervised cross-lingual representation learning for speech recognition. In *Interspeech.*

Mattia A. Di Gangi, Roldano Cattoni, Luisa Bentivogli, Matteo Negri, and Marco Turchi. 2019. MuST-C: a Multilingual Speech Translation Corpus. In *Proceedings of the 2019 Conference of the North American Chapter of the Association for Computational Linguistics: Human Language Technologies, Volume 1 (Long and Short Papers)*, pages 2012–2017, Minneapolis, Minnesota. Association for Computational Linguistics.

ELRA. Elra catalogue (http://catalog.elra.info), trad pashto-french parallel corpus of transcribed broadcast news speech - training data, islrn: 802-643-297-429-4, elra id: Elra-w0093, trad pashto broadcast news speech corpus, islrn: 918-508-885-913-7, elra id: Elra-s0381.

Qingkai Fang, Rong Ye, Lei Li, Yang Feng, and Mingxuan Wang. 2022. STEMM: Self-learning with speech-text manifold mixup for speech translation. In *Proceedings of the 60th Annual Meeting of the Association for Computational Linguistics (Volume 1: Long Papers)*, pages 7050–7062, Dublin, Ireland. Association for Computational Linguistics.

Wei-Ning Hsu, Benjamin Bolte, Yao-Hung Hubert Tsai, Kushal Lakhotia, Ruslan Salakhutdinov, and Abdelrahman Mohamed. 2021. Hubert: Self-supervised speech representation learning by masked prediction of hidden units. *IEEE/ACM Transactions on Audio, Speech, and Language Processing*, 29:3451–3460.

Ha Nguyen, Fethi Bougares, Natalia Tomashenko, Yannick Estève, and laurent besacier. 2020. Investigating self-supervised pre-training for end-to-end speech translation. In *ICML 2020 Workshop on Self-supervision in Audio and Speech.*

Vassil Panayotov, Guoguo Chen, Daniel Povey, and Sanjeev Khudanpur. 2015. Librispeech: An asr corpus based on public domain audio books. *2015 IEEE International Conference on Acoustics, Speech and Signal Processing (ICASSP)*, pages 5206–5210.

Ankita Pasad, Bowen Shi, and Karen Livescu. 2022. Comparative layer-wise analysis of self-supervised speech models. *ArXiv*, abs/2211.03929.

Sravya Popuri, Peng-Jen Chen, Changhan Wang, Juan Miguel Pino, Yossi Adi, Jiatao Gu, Wei-Ning Hsu, and Ann Lee. 2022. Enhanced direct speech-to-speech translation using self-supervised pre-training and data augmentation. In *Interspeech*.

Rico Sennrich, Barry Haddow, and Alexandra Birch. 2016. Neural machine translation of rare words with subword units. In *Proceedings of the 54th Annual Meeting of the Association for Computational Linguistics (Volume 1: Long Papers)*, pages 1715–1725, Berlin, Germany. Association for Computational Linguistics.

Matthias Sperber and Matthias Paulik. 2020. Speech translation and the end-to-end promise: Taking stock of where we are. In *Annual Meeting of the Association for Computational Linguistics*.

Mihaela Stoian, Sameer Bansal, and Sharon Goldwater. 2019. Analyzing asr pretraining for low-resource speech-to-text translation. *ICASSP 2020 - 2020 IEEE International Conference on Acoustics, Speech and Signal Processing (ICASSP)*, pages 7909–7913.

Yun Tang, Hongyu Gong, Ning Dong, Changhan Wang, Wei-Ning Hsu, Jiatao Gu, Alexei Baevski, Xian Li, Abdelrahman Mohamed, Michael Auli, and Juan Pino. 2022. Unified speech-text pre-training for speech translation and recognition. In *Proceedings of the 60th Annual Meeting of the Association for Computational Linguistics (Volume 1: Long Papers)*, pages 1488–1499, Dublin, Ireland. Association for Computational Linguistics.

Ashish Vaswani, Noam M. Shazeer, Niki Parmar, Jakob Uszkoreit, Llion Jones, Aidan N. Gomez, Lukasz Kaiser, and Illia Polosukhin. 2017. Attention is all you need. *ArXiv*, abs/1706.03762.

Changhan Wang, Yun Tang, Xutai Ma, Anne Wu, Dmytro Okhonko, and Juan Miguel Pino. 2020. Fairseq s2t: Fast speech-to-text modeling with fairseq. In *AACL*.

Ron J. Weiss, Jan Chorowski, Navdeep Jaitly, Yonghui Wu, and Z. Chen. 2017. Sequence-to-sequence models can directly translate foreign speech. In *Interspeech*.

Anne Wu, Changhan Wang, Juan Miguel Pino, and Jiatao Gu. 2020. Self-supervised representations improve end-to-end speech translation. *ArXiv*, abs/2006.12124.

Marcely Zanon Boito, John Ortega, Hugo Riguidel, Antoine Laurent, Loïc Barrault, Fethi Bougares, Firas Chaabani, Ha Nguyen, Florentin Barbier, Souhir Gahbiche, and Yannick Estève. 2022. ON-TRAC consortium systems for the IWSLT 2022 dialect and low-resource speech translation tasks. In *Proceedings of the 19th International Conference on Spoken Language Translation (IWSLT 2022)*, pages 308–318, Dublin, Ireland (in-person and online). Association for Computational Linguistics.

The HW-TSC's Speech-to-Speech Translation System for IWSLT 2023

Minghan Wang, Yinglu Li, Jiaxin Guo, Zongyao Li, Hengchao Shang, Daimeng Wei, Chang Su, Min Zhang, Shimin Tao, Hao Yang
[1]Huawei Translation Services Center, Beijing, China
{wangminghan,liyinglu,guojiaxin1,lizongyao,shanghengchao, weidaimeng,suchang8,zhangmin186,taoshimin,yanghao30}@huawei.com

Abstract

This paper describes our work on the IWSLT2023 Speech-to-Speech task. Our proposed cascaded system consists of an ensemble of Conformer and S2T-Transformer-based ASR models, a Transformer-based MT model, and a Diffusion-based TTS model. Our primary focus in this competition was to investigate the modeling ability of the Diffusion model for TTS tasks in high-resource scenarios and the role of TTS in the overall S2S task. To this end, we proposed DTS, an end-to-end diffusion-based TTS model that takes raw text as input and generates waveform by iteratively denoising on pure Gaussian noise. Compared to previous TTS models, the speech generated by DTS is more natural and performs better in code-switching scenarios. As the training process is end-to-end, it is relatively straightforward. Our experiments demonstrate that DTS outperforms other TTS models on the GigaS2S benchmark, and also brings positive gain for the entire S2S system.

1 Introduction

Compared to previous iterations of the IWSLT-S2S task (Anastasopoulos et al., 2022; Guo et al., 2022), this year's task (Agarwal et al., 2023) is distinct, particularly in terms of data. The official training dataset provided is GigaS2S (Chen et al., 2021; Ye et al., 2022), which is substantially larger than previous S2S datasets, with a data size of 10,000 hours. Although the target text and speech are generated by MT and TTS systems, their quality is relatively high, making them suitable for initiating research on end-to-end S2S or TTS models in high-resource scenarios.

Our strategy is similar to that of last year (Guo et al., 2022), where we used a cascaded S2S system, but our research focus has shifted. In last year's work, we primarily studied the role of ASR and MT in the S2S system and attempted to optimize the context consistency of translation results. In this year's competition, we shifted our research focus to the TTS component. Therefore, we directly used the ASR and MT systems in our offline ST track (Wang et al., 2022a,b). Additionally, we no longer considered the issue of context consistency during inference.

Given the unprecedented success of the Diffusion Model (Ho et al., 2020; Rombach et al., 2022) in image generation over the past few years, we sought to explore its potential in speech synthesis. Thus, we proposed an end-to-end Diffusion TTS (DTS) model. Unlike previous TTS models, such as FastSpeech2 (Ren et al., 2021), which use phonemes as input and use a duration predictor to determine the duration and generate mel-spectrograms, DTS uses raw text as input, predicts the total audio length, and generates the waveform by iteratively denoising the output.

The structure of this paper is as follows: We first introduce the dataset used in this task, followed by a brief introduction to the ASR and MT models used. Then, we provide a detailed description of our proposed DTS model. Finally, we showcase the performance of each model on the GigaS2S dataset.

2 Method

2.1 Dataset

To train the ASR model, we combined five datasets and added corresponding domain tags to enable the model to generate speech in the desired style (Wang et al., 2022b). For the MT model, we aggregated all available en-de, en-zh, and en-ja translation data allowed for constrained offline tasks and added language tags to train a multilingual model. Finally, for the TTS model, we utilized the Chinese text and speech pairs from GigaS2S (Ye et al., 2022).

2.2 ASR

We trained our ASR models using a combination of five datasets: MuST-C V2, LibriSpeech, TED-

Proceedings of the 20th International Conference on Spoken Language Translation (IWSLT 2023), pages 277–282
July 13-14, 2023

Dataset	Number of Utterance	Duration(hrs)
LibriSpeech	281,241	960.85
MuST-C	340,421	590.67
IWSLT	170,229	254.41
CoVoST	1362,422	1802.52
TEDLIUM3	268,214	453.42

Table 1: Data statistics of our ASR corpora

LIUM 3, CoVoST, and IWSLT. Table 1 provides statistics for these datasets. Our model uses an 80-dimensional filterbank feature, with input samples restricted to a frame size between 50 to 3000 and a token limit of 150 to ensure that the Transformer model's encoder and decoder can process sequences of limited size.

To identify outliers, we calculated the speech speed of each sample based on the transcript length and frame size. We excluded samples with speeds outside the range of $\mu(\tau) \pm 4 \times \sigma(\tau)$, where $\tau = \frac{\text{\# frames}}{\text{\# tokens}}$.

We utilized an ensemble of two models to improve ASR performance: Conformer (Gulati et al., 2020) and S2TTransformer (Synnaeve et al., 2019). The encoder of Conformer incorporates a macaron structure at each layer based on the S2TTransformer's encoder to enhance speech encoding capability. Our ensemble method involves averaging the probabilities output by both decoders at each decoding step during beam-search. To control the model's generation style, we added prefix tags corresponding to the COVOST dataset for inference, making the model's inference style closer to GigaS2S transcripts.

2.3 MT

For MT, we utilized the multilingual Transformer model that we developed for the offline track, training it on en-zh, en-de, and en-ja datasets. To ensure high-quality pairs, we first cleaned and removed duplicates from the data, then filtered it using LaBSE (Feng et al., 2022) to select domain-specific data. During training, we employed R-Drop (Liang et al., 2021) for additional regularization. Our Transformer (Vaswani et al., 2017) model consisted of a 25-layer encoder and a 6-layer decoder with a dimension of 1024 and an FFN dimension of 4096.

2.4 TTS

2.4.1 Modeling

The Denoising Diffusion Model (DDM) (Ho et al., 2020) models a continuous process of iteratively denoising Gaussian noise to restore the original sample. The model consists of two processes: the forward process of adding noise and the reverse process of denoising. These continuous processes are assumed to have Markovian properties and can be decomposed into T conditional distributions through a Markov chain, with x_0 representing the original data (raw waveform in the TTS task) and x_T representing pure noise.

In the forward process of DDM, $q(x_{1:T}|x_0, c)$ is decomposed into a Markov process of T steps and conditioned on the input text c:

$$q(x_{1:T}|x_0, c) = \prod_{t=1}^{T} q(x_t|x_{t-1}) \quad (1)$$

$$q(x_t|x_{t-1}, c) = \mathcal{N}(x_t; \sqrt{1-\beta_t}x_{t-1}, \beta_t \mathbf{I}). \quad (2)$$

The sampling of x_t given x_{t-1} can be expressed as:

$$x_t = \sqrt{1-\beta_t}x_{t-1} + \sqrt{\beta_t}\epsilon, \quad (3)$$

where $\epsilon \in \mathcal{N}(0, \mathbf{I})$, and $\beta_t \in [0, 1]$ is a noise scheduler related to t. Therefore, each step of the forward process is adding a certain amount of Gaussian noise to the previously corrupted speech x_{t-1}. Finally, x_0 ultimately evolves into white noise that follows a Gaussian distribution. An important characteristic of the forward process is that $x_t \sim q(x_t|x_0, c)$ for any t has a closed form:

$$q(x_t|x_0, c) = \mathcal{N}(x_t; \sqrt{\bar{\alpha}_t}x_0, (1-\bar{\alpha}_t)\mathbf{I}\} \quad (4)$$

$\alpha_t = 1 - \beta_t$, and $\bar{\alpha}_t = \prod_{s=1}^{t} \alpha_s$, so we can efficiently obtain x_t for any t from x_0 during training.

In the reverse process, the denoising process is similar to the forward process, and is also described as a T-step Markov process:

$$p_\theta(x_{0:T}, c) = p(x_T) \prod_{t=1}^{T} p_\theta(x_{t-1}|x_t) \quad (5)$$

$$p_\theta(x_{t-1}|x_t, c) = \mathcal{N}(x_{t-1}; \mu_\theta(x_t, t, c), \sigma_t^2 \mathbf{I}), \quad (6)$$

where the μ_θ can be learned by neural networks and $\sigma_t^2 = 1 - \alpha_t$.

The training objective of the Diffusion Model is to maximize the log-likelihood of $p(x_0|c)$, which is intractable, so optimization on the variational bound is used instead. (Ho et al., 2020) further simplify it to an unweighted version of L2 regression loss with respect to $\hat{\epsilon}$ and added noise ϵ. In our work, we predict the x_0 with the model instead of the noise:

$$L(\theta) = \mathbb{E}_{t,x_0,\epsilon}\left[||\hat{x}_\theta(x_t, t, c) - x_0||\right] \quad (7)$$

Here, t is uniformly sampled from the interval $[0, T]$.

During inference, the model iteratively samples x_{t-1} from x_t:

$$x_{t-1} = \frac{1}{\sqrt{\alpha_t}}\left(x_t - \frac{1-\alpha_t}{\sqrt{1-\bar{\alpha}_t}}\epsilon_\theta(x_t, t, c) + \sigma_t \mathbf{z}\right) \quad (8)$$

$$\epsilon_\theta = \frac{1}{\sqrt{1-\bar{\alpha}_t}}\left(x_t - \sqrt{\bar{\alpha}_t}\hat{x}_\theta(x_t, t, c)\right) \quad (9)$$

where $\sigma_t = \sqrt{1-\alpha_t}$ and $\mathbf{z} \sim \mathcal{N}(0, \mathbf{I})$. In our experiments, to allow for flexible determination of the maximum step T, we choose to use a continuous t ranging from 0 to 1. During training, t is uniformly sampled, and we use the cosine noise scheduler (Nichol and Dhariwal, 2021).

In addition to modeling the denoising process, DTS also needs to predict the length of the target audio in advance, as DTS is essentially a non-autoregressive (NAR) model. However, unlike previous TTS models that predict the duration of each phoneme, we directly model the total number of frames in the target audio, which is more convenient. Specifically, we use the text representation after average pooling, denoted as $\mathbf{h}_c$, as the input to the classifier ϕ to predict the length distribution. Then, we calculate the cross-entropy loss with the frame number N_{x_0} of x_0.

$$L_{\text{length}} = CE(\phi(\mathbf{h}_c; \theta), N_{x_0}) \quad (10)$$

2.4.2 Model Architecture

The DTS model is essentially a parameterized denoising function $\hat{x}(x_t, t, c)$ which takes x_t, t as input, conditions on c, and predicts the x_0 for the sampling of x_{t-1}. The model makes some modifications on top of the Transformer model to make it more suitable for speech synthesis. As shown in Figure 1, the main modifications are as follows:

- On top of the Encoder, we add a two-layer FFN network to predict the length of the target audio.

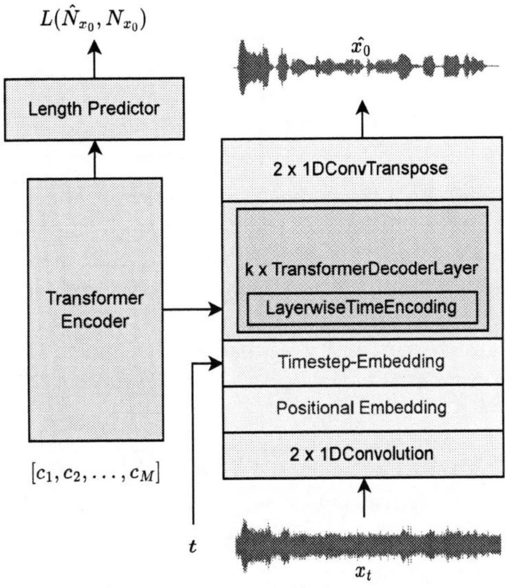

Figure 1: The architecture of DTS model, which takes $C = [c_1, ..., c_M]$ as the encoder input to predict the frame length N. For the decoder, it takes x_t and t as input, conditions on C to predict x_0 for the sampling of x_{t-1} according to Eq 8 and 9.

- In the input part of the Decoder, we use two 1D convolutions with a proper setting of kernel size, stride, and padding, so the sequence length before and after convolution remains unchanged.

- As the Diffusion model depends on the time step t, we additionally introduce a Timestep Embedding, and use the same implementation as (Ho et al., 2020).

- To make the time step encoding more comprehensive, we add Layerwise time encoding at each layer and added to the encoded hidden states from the last layer.

- In the output part of the decoder, we add 2 1D deconvolutions to restore the hidden state back to the waveform. We use deconvolution because we found that using only linear projection leads to a lack of dependency between the generated waveform and the previous waveform, resulting in noticeable jitter, which can be significantly eliminated by using deconvolution.

Model	WER-all-punct	WER-all	WER-code-switch	WER-zh
FastSpeech 2	13.18	10.75	15.70	8.37
DTS-Mel	13.32	10.28	15.66	7.69
DTS-Wave	**12.68**	**9.82**	**15.33**	**7.17**

Table 2: This table shows the performance of our TTS models on the GigaS2S dev set, using ground truth transcripts as input. We compare our models against FastSpeech 2 (Ren et al., 2021), which serves as the baseline. Additionally, we present a DTS model trained to predict mel-spectrograms (DTS-Mel) for comparison with DTS for waveform (DTS-Wave). The table reports the word error rate (WER) for the entire set with punctuation (WER-all-punct), WER for all samples without punctuation (WER-all), WER for code-switch samples without punctuation (WER-code-switch), and WER for Chinese-only samples without punctuation (WER-zh). The results indicate that DTS-Wave outperforms the other models, achieving the lowest WER values in all categories.

Model	WER	WER-no-punct
S2TTransformer	22.67	18.15
Conformer	22.42	17.80
Ensemble	21.57	16.92

Table 3: The performance of our two independent ASR models and the ensemble of them with or without punctuation.

Model Input	BLEU	ChrF
ASR output	29.0	25.4
Ground Truth	30.7	27.3

Table 4: The performance of our MT models with ground truth input and asr outputs as the input.

3 Experiment

3.1 Experimental Setup

For the ASR and MT parts of our S2S system, we directly used the same setting as in the Offline track. For the TTS part, we trained the model on the GigaS2S dataset for 360k steps, with a maximum learning rate of 1e-4, warmup of 20000 steps, and a batch size of 32 samples per GPU. The maximum and minimum audio lengths were restricted to 25 seconds and 0.5 seconds, respectively. The model has 12 layers in the encoder and 16 layers in the decoder, with a hidden dimension of 512 and an FFN dimension of 2048. DTS can directly generate waveforms, but since audio waveforms are usually long, we pre-segment them into equally sized non-overlapping frames. In this way, the model learns to generate the waveform frame by frame, and we only need to flatten these frames to get the final output. In our experiments, we used a frame length of 1200 and a sampling rate of 24000. When inference, we set the sampling step to 100. In addition to the raw waveform, DTS can also learn to generate mel-spectrogram, simply by changing wave frames to spectrogram frames. This is also evaluated in our experiment.

Model	BLEU	ChrF
FastSpeech2	21.8	22.7
DTS-Mel	22.3	23.1
DTS-Wave	22.7	23.4

Table 5: The overall cascade performance evaluated by BLEU and ChrF.

3.2 Experimental Results

In the experiments, we tested the performance of each module in our S2S system separately. In addition to testing with the cascaded results as input, we also conducted independent tests with ground truth input. For the three modules, we mainly used the dev set of GigaS2S for evaluation. In terms of evaluation metrics, for ASR and MT, we used WER, BLEU and ChrF, respectively. For TTS, we used a Whisper-medium (Radford et al., 2022) model to transcribe the TTS-generated audio back into the text for automatic evaluation and calculated WER.

ASR Results We evaluated the results of two ASR models trained on the same corpus separately, as well as the ensemble version. As shown in Table 3, the ensemble results were slightly better.

MT Results In the evaluation of MT, we considered two scenarios: using ground truth transcripts as input and using the output of the previous ASR module as input. The experimental results showed that the robustness of MT was relatively good, even if there were errors in the ASR output, the difference in BLEU score was not significant as shown in Table 4.

TTS Results In the TTS experiments, because the development set of GigaS2S contains code-switching samples, we evaluated not only the WER of the entire set but also separately evaluated the cases without the code-switching. As for the models, we chose FastSpeech 2 as the baseline. In addition, we trained an additional DTS based on mel-spectrogram for comparison with the waveform-based DTS. Both FS2 and DTS-mel used the Griffin-lim vocoder. As shown in Table 2, DTS-Wave outperformed the other two models, especially on Chinese monolingual data.

Full Pipeline Results In addition to testing each module separately, we also tested the final metrics of the entire pipeline. We compared the difference between the speech generated by the three TTS models with the MT results as input by computing the BLEU and ChrF with the ground truth translation. Table 5 shows that there is a difference that existed, but it is not significant. Therefore, we can conclude that the quality of the speech generated by TTS does affect the final performance of S2S system in terms of automatic evaluation, but the impact is still limited.

4 Conclusion

In this paper, we present the system we developed for the IWSLT2023 speech-to-speech competition. The system includes relatively simple and effective ASR and MT modules, as well as a TTS module proposed by us based on the Diffusion Model. In the experiments, we demonstrate that the denoising diffusion process can effectively learn end-to-end TTS task, simplifying both training and inference. However, its generation speed is relatively slow. In our future work, we will continue to optimize its quality and generation efficiency, and further explore the application of diffusion in end-to-end S2S tasks.

References

Milind Agarwal, Sweta Agrawal, Antonios Anastasopoulos, Claudia Borg, Marine Carpuat, Roldano Cattoni, Mauro Cettolo, William Chen, Khalid Choukri, Alexandra Chronopoulou, Thierry Declerck, Qianqian Dong, Yannick Estève, Kevin Duh, Marcello Federico, Souhir Gahbiche, Benjamin Hsu, John Judge, Tom Ko, Rishu Kumar, Xutail Ma, Prashant Mathur, Evgeny Matusov, Paul McNamee, John P. McCrae, Kenton Murray, Matteo Negri, Jan Niehues, Xing Niu, Atul Ojha Kr., John E. Ortega, Proyag Pal, Juan Pino, Lonneke van der Plas, Elijah Rippeth, Elizabeth Salesky, Matthias Sperber, Sebastian Stüker, Katsuhito Sudoh, Brian Thompson, Marco Turchi, Alex Waibel, Mingxuan Wang, and Rodolfo Zevallos. 2023. Findings of the IWSLT 2023 Evaluation Campaign. In *Proceedings of the 20th International Conference on Spoken Language Translation (IWSLT 2023)*. Association for Computational Linguistics.

Antonios Anastasopoulos, Loïc Barrault, Luisa Bentivogli, Marcely Zanon Boito, Ondrej Bojar, Roldano Cattoni, Anna Currey, Georgiana Dinu, Kevin Duh, Maha Elbayad, Clara Emmanuel, Yannick Estève, Marcello Federico, Christian Federmann, Souhir Gahbiche, Hongyu Gong, Roman Grundkiewicz, Barry Haddow, Benjamin Hsu, Dávid Javorský, Vera Kloudová, Surafel Melaku Lakew, Xutai Ma, Prashant Mathur, Paul McNamee, Kenton Murray, Maria Nadejde, Satoshi Nakamura, Matteo Negri, Jan Niehues, Xing Niu, John Ortega, Juan Miguel Pino, Elizabeth Salesky, Jiatong Shi, Matthias Sperber, Sebastian Stüker, Katsuhito Sudoh, Marco Turchi, Yogesh Virkar, Alexander Waibel, Changhan Wang, and Shinji Watanabe. 2022. Findings of the IWSLT 2022 evaluation campaign. In *Proceedings of the 19th International Conference on Spoken Language Translation, IWSLT@ACL 2022, Dublin, Ireland (in-person and online), May 26-27, 2022*, pages 98–157. Association for Computational Linguistics.

Guoguo Chen, Shuzhou Chai, Guan-Bo Wang, Jiayu Du, Wei-Qiang Zhang, Chao Weng, Dan Su, Daniel Povey, Jan Trmal, Junbo Zhang, Mingjie Jin, Sanjeev Khudanpur, Shinji Watanabe, Shuaijiang Zhao, Wei Zou, Xiangang Li, Xuchen Yao, Yongqing Wang, Zhao You, and Zhiyong Yan. 2021. Gigaspeech: An evolving, multi-domain ASR corpus with 10, 000 hours of transcribed audio. In *Interspeech 2021, 22nd Annual Conference of the International Speech Communication Association, Brno, Czechia, 30 August - 3 September 2021*, pages 3670–3674. ISCA.

Fangxiaoyu Feng, Yinfei Yang, Daniel Cer, Naveen Arivazhagan, and Wei Wang. 2022. Language-agnostic BERT sentence embedding. In *Proceedings of the 60th Annual Meeting of the Association for Computational Linguistics (Volume 1: Long Papers), ACL 2022, Dublin, Ireland, May 22-27, 2022*, pages 878–891. Association for Computational Linguistics.

Anmol Gulati, James Qin, Chung-Cheng Chiu, Niki Parmar, Yu Zhang, Jiahui Yu, Wei Han, Shibo Wang, Zhengdong Zhang, Yonghui Wu, and Ruoming Pang. 2020. Conformer: Convolution-augmented transformer for speech recognition. In *Interspeech 2020, 21st Annual Conference of the International Speech Communication Association, Virtual Event, Shanghai, China, 25-29 October 2020*, pages 5036–5040. ISCA.

Jiaxin Guo, Yinglu Li, Minghan Wang, Xiaosong Qiao, Yuxia Wang, Hengchao Shang, Chang Su, Yimeng Chen, Min Zhang, Shimin Tao, Hao Yang, and Ying

Qin. 2022. The hw-tsc's speech to speech translation system for IWSLT 2022 evaluation. In *Proceedings of the 19th International Conference on Spoken Language Translation, IWSLT@ACL 2022, Dublin, Ireland (in-person and online), May 26-27, 2022*, pages 293–297. Association for Computational Linguistics.

Jonathan Ho, Ajay Jain, and Pieter Abbeel. 2020. Denoising diffusion probabilistic models. In *Advances in Neural Information Processing Systems 33: Annual Conference on Neural Information Processing Systems 2020, NeurIPS 2020, December 6-12, 2020, virtual*.

Xiaobo Liang, Lijun Wu, Juntao Li, Yue Wang, Qi Meng, Tao Qin, Wei Chen, Min Zhang, and Tie-Yan Liu. 2021. R-drop: Regularized dropout for neural networks. In *Advances in Neural Information Processing Systems 34: Annual Conference on Neural Information Processing Systems 2021, NeurIPS 2021, December 6-14, 2021, virtual*, pages 10890–10905.

Alexander Quinn Nichol and Prafulla Dhariwal. 2021. Improved denoising diffusion probabilistic models. In *Proceedings of the 38th International Conference on Machine Learning, ICML 2021, 18-24 July 2021, Virtual Event*, volume 139 of *Proceedings of Machine Learning Research*, pages 8162–8171. PMLR.

Alec Radford, Jong Wook Kim, Tao Xu, Greg Brockman, Christine McLeavey, and Ilya Sutskever. 2022. Robust speech recognition via large-scale weak supervision. *CoRR*, abs/2212.04356.

Yi Ren, Chenxu Hu, Xu Tan, Tao Qin, Sheng Zhao, Zhou Zhao, and Tie-Yan Liu. 2021. Fastspeech 2: Fast and high-quality end-to-end text to speech. In *9th International Conference on Learning Representations, ICLR 2021, Virtual Event, Austria, May 3-7, 2021*. OpenReview.net.

Robin Rombach, Andreas Blattmann, Dominik Lorenz, Patrick Esser, and Björn Ommer. 2022. High-resolution image synthesis with latent diffusion models. In *IEEE/CVF Conference on Computer Vision and Pattern Recognition, CVPR 2022, New Orleans, LA, USA, June 18-24, 2022*, pages 10674–10685. IEEE.

Gabriel Synnaeve, Qiantong Xu, Jacob Kahn, Edouard Grave, Tatiana Likhomanenko, Vineel Pratap, Anuroop Sriram, Vitaliy Liptchinsky, and Ronan Collobert. 2019. End-to-end ASR: from supervised to semi-supervised learning with modern architectures. *CoRR*, abs/1911.08460.

Ashish Vaswani, Noam Shazeer, Niki Parmar, Jakob Uszkoreit, Llion Jones, Aidan N. Gomez, Lukasz Kaiser, and Illia Polosukhin. 2017. Attention is all you need. In *Advances in Neural Information Processing Systems 30: Annual Conference on Neural Information Processing Systems 2017, December 4-9, 2017, Long Beach, CA, USA*, pages 5998–6008.

Minghan Wang, Jiaxin Guo, Yinglu Li, Xiaosong Qiao, Yuxia Wang, Zongyao Li, Chang Su, Yimeng Chen, Min Zhang, Shimin Tao, Hao Yang, and Ying Qin. 2022a. The hw-tsc's simultaneous speech translation system for IWSLT 2022 evaluation. In *Proceedings of the 19th International Conference on Spoken Language Translation, IWSLT@ACL 2022, Dublin, Ireland (in-person and online), May 26-27, 2022*, pages 247–254. Association for Computational Linguistics.

Minghan Wang, Jiaxin Guo, Xiaosong Qiao, Yuxia Wang, Daimeng Wei, Chang Su, Yimeng Chen, Min Zhang, Shimin Tao, Hao Yang, and Ying Qin. 2022b. The hw-tsc's offline speech translation system for IWSLT 2022 evaluation. In *Proceedings of the 19th International Conference on Spoken Language Translation, IWSLT@ACL 2022, Dublin, Ireland (in-person and online), May 26-27, 2022*, pages 239–246. Association for Computational Linguistics.

Rong Ye, Chengqi Zhao, Tom Ko, Chutong Meng, Tao Wang, Mingxuan Wang, and Jun Cao. 2022. Gigast: A 10, 000-hour pseudo speech translation corpus. *CoRR*, abs/2204.03939.

JHU IWSLT 2023 Dialect Speech Translation System Description

Amir Hussein[†] **Cihan Xiao**[†] **Neha Verma**[†] **Thomas Thebaud**[†]
Matthew Wiesner[‡] **Sanjeev Khudanpur**[†‡]
[†]Center for Language and Speech Processing, and
[‡] Human Language Technology Center of Excellence,
Johns Hopkins University
{ahussei6, cxiao7, nverma7, tthebau1, wiesner, khudanpur}@jhu.edu

Abstract

This paper presents JHU's submissions to the IWSLT 2023 dialectal and low-resource track of Tunisian Arabic to English speech translation. The Tunisian dialect lacks formal orthography and abundant training data, making it challenging to develop effective speech translation (ST) systems. To address these challenges, we explore the integration of large pretrained machine translation (MT) models, such as mBART and NLLB-200 in both end-to-end (E2E) and cascaded speech translation (ST) systems. We also improve the performance of automatic speech recognition (ASR) through the use of pseudo-labeling data augmentation and channel matching on telephone data. Finally, we combine our E2E and cascaded ST systems with Minimum Bayes-Risk decoding. Our combined system achieves a BLEU score of 21.6 and 19.1 on test2 and test3, respectively.

1 Introduction

The performance of machine translation systems is closely tied to the amount of available training data. Regional dialects, which are less prevalent and primarily spoken languages, pose a challenge for these systems due to the scarcity of digital data, the absence of standard orthography, and prevalence of non-standard grammar. The IWSLT 2023 dialect and low-resource track focuses these challenges.

In this paper we present the JHU Tunisian Arabic to English speech translation systems submitted to the IWSLT 2023 dialectal and low-resource track (Agarwal et al., 2023). Arabic and its dialects form a *dialect continuum* anchored by Modern Standard Arabic (MSA) (Badawi et al., 2013). While MSA is the language of *formal* and *written* communication, most native Arabic speakers colloquially use local *dialects*, which often lack a standardized written form. In many North African Arabic dialects, including Tunisian, there is a significant code-switching with and borrowing from several *contact languages*: Berber and Romance languages like French, Spanish and Italian.

Recent successes in machine translation (MT) of text for low-resource languages or non-standard dialects have entailed the use of large pretrained models such as mBART (Liu et al., 2020a) and NLLB (NLLB Team et al., 2022). These models have demonstrated state-of-the-art performance via transfer learning from higher-resource languages, particularly through related languages. However, there is a lack of understanding regarding how to effectively integrate these models with speech recognition systems to develop speech translation systems. To fill this gap we investigate dialect transfer by integrating large pretrained models with speech recognition models in end-to-end (E2E) and cascaded speech translation (ST) systems. The key components of our system are:

- Dialectal transfer from large pre-trained models to improve translation in both E2E and Cascaded ST settings (§3.1,§3.2).
- Improved ASR of dialectal speech by reducing orthographic variation in training transcripts, and by channel matching (§3.1.1).
- System combination with Minimum Bayes-Risk decoding based on the COMET similarity metric (§3.3).

Our system outperforms the best previous approaches (Yang et al., 2022; Yan et al., 2022) for both ASR (WER) and ST (BLEU). We also found that integrating pre-trained MT models into end-to-end ST systems did not improve performance.

2 Dialect Speech Translation Task

The dialect speech translation task permitted submissions using models trained under two data conditions, (A) constrained and (B) unconstrained. For

Proceedings of the 20th International Conference on Spoken Language Translation (IWSLT 2023), pages 283–290
July 13-14, 2023

Condition	ASR	MT
(A) Basic	166 hours of manually transcribed Tunisian telephone speech	212K lines of manual English translation of the Tunisian transcripts
(B) Unconstrained	1200 hours of Modern Standard Arabic broadcast speech (MGB-2) (Ali et al., 2016). 250 hours of Levantine Arabic telephone conversations (LDC2006S29[1], LDC2006T07[2])	Any other English, Arabic dialects, or multilingual models beyond English and Arabic

Table 1: Data used for constrained and unconstrained conditions.

brevity, we will refer to these conditions as (A) and (B) respectively.

2.1 Data description

The data we used for the conditions (A) and (B) are listed in Table 1, and sizes of the training, development-testing and test partitions are listed in Table 2. The development and test sets for Tunisian data are provided by the organizers of IWLST 2023. The data is 3-way parallel: Tunisian Arabic transcripts and English translations are available for each Tunisian Arabic audio utterance. We use the development set for model comparison and hyper-parameter tuning, and the test1 set for evaluating our ST systems. Finally, the task organizers provided blind evaluation (test2, test3) sets for final comparison of submissions.

	ASR (hours)	MT (lines)
train (condition A)	160	~202k
train (condition B)	1200+160+250	-
dev	3.0	3833
test1	3.3	4204
test2	3.6	4288
test3	3.5	4284

Table 2: Details for train, dev and test1 sets for constrained condition (A) and unconstrained condition (B).

3 Methods

In this section we describe our cascaded (§3.1), and end-to-end (E2E) (§3.2) speech translation systems as well as our strategy for combining both approaches (§3.3).

3.1 Cascaded ASR-MT

3.1.1 Automatic Speech Recognition

To train ASR models for E2E and cascaded systems, we use the ESPnet (Watanabe et al., 2018) toolkit. Our ASR architecture uses a Branchformer encoder (Peng et al., 2022), a Transformer decoder (Vaswani et al., 2017) and follows the hybrid CTC/attention (Watanabe et al., 2017) approach. Each Branchformer encoder block consists of two branches that work in parallel. One branch uses self-attention to capture long-range dependencies while the other branch uses a multi-layer perceptron with convolutional gating (Sakuma et al., 2021) to capture local dependencies. To mitigate orthographic variations (or inconsistencies) in the ASR transcripts, we augment the training data during the fine-tuning stage by reusing the audio training samples paired with their *ASR transcripts*, which tend to be orthographically more consistent. We refer to this approach as *pseudo-labeling*.

[1]https://catalog.ldc.upenn.edu/LDC2006S29
[2]https://catalog.ldc.upenn.edu/LDC2006T07

Condition (A). We train the ASR model described previously using the constrained Tunisian Arabic audio and transcripts.

Condition (B). The ASR Branchformer in this condition is pretrained on our MGB-2 standard Arabic data (Ali et al., 2016) and then fine-tuned on the provided Tunisian Arabic data. The MGB-2 MSA data differ from the Tunisian data in channel, and dialect. Since the Tunisian data are telephone conversations sampled at 8kHz, we downsample the MGB-2 speech from 16kHz to 8kHz, which we previously found was more effective than upsampling the telephone conversations to 16kHz (Yang et al., 2022). We also added additional telephone speech from the Levantine Arabic dialect (Maamouri et al., 2006). Note that Levantine Arabic is very different from Tunisian, and the hope here is to benefit from matched genre and channel conditions, not dialect.

We did not explicitly attempt to reduce the dialect mismatch. However, we mitigated some of the spurious orthographic variations in transcripts of dialectal speech by using pseudo-labels for training instead of of the manual transcripts, as noted above, in the final fine-tuning step.

3.1.2 Machine Translation

Condition (A). We train an MT model on Tunisian Arabic transcripts paired with their English translations. The MT architecture is similar to §3.1.1 model architecture, and uses a Branchformer encoder and Transformer decoder.

Condition (B). We experiment with two main pre-trained models: mBART and NLLB-200. In the first setting, we use the mBART25 model, which was shown to be slightly better for MSA versus the newer mBART50 model (Liu et al., 2020a; Tang et al., 2020). mBART25 also contains French, Turkish, Italian, and Spanish, all of which contribute loanwords to Tunisian (Zribi et al., 2014). Although these loanwords are transcribed in the Arabic script in our data, there is prior evidence that multilingual language models can benefit from cross-lingual transfer even between different scripts of the same language (Pires et al., 2019).

For NLLB-200, we use the distilled 1.3 billion parameter version of the model, due to space constraints. This model is a dense Transformer distilled from the original NLLB-200 model, which is a 54 billion parameter Mixture-of-Experts model that can translate into and out-of 200 different languages. We note that this model supports Tunisian Arabic, the aforementioned contact languages, MSA, as well as other closely related Maghrebi dialects (Moroccan, Egyptian, Maltese). The breadth of language coverage seen during the training of NLLB-200 makes this model an attractive choice for a dialect speech translation task.

We fine-tune these models on the provided $\sim$ 200K lines of Tunisian Arabic-English data. The source side is normalized as described in Section 4. We preprocess all data with the provided pre-trained `sentencepiece` vocabularies released with the models with no pre-tokenization. Results on MT systems are included in Table 8.

3.2 End-to-End Speech Translation

For the constrained condition we adopt the hierarchical multi-decoder architecture proposed by (Yan et al., 2022).

Condition (A). The system consists of a multi-task learning approach, which combines ASR and MT sub-nets into one differentiable E2E system where the hidden representation of the speech decoder is fed as input to the MT encoder. Additionally, the authors proposed using a hierarchical MT encoder with an auxiliary connectionist temporal classification (CTC) loss on top of the speech encoder. The MT decoder performs cross-attention over both the speech encoder and MT encoder representations. The ASR module is initialized with a Branchformer trained on the Tunisian data. In this part, we explore the effect of text normalization on the E2E-ST system and pre-trained MT initialization.

Condition (B). For the unconstrained condition, we propose a novel E2E-ST system that incorporates the combination of a pretrained ASR module and a pretrained MT module. Specifically, we combine the Branchformer ASR module described in Section 3.1, with mBART (Liu et al., 2020b), which was fine-tuned on Tunisian data. We modify the ESPnet ST recipe to incorporate the mBART model trained by the fairseq (Ott et al., 2019) framework. The architecture of the model is shown in Figure 1. In contrast to the modified Hierarchical Multi-Decoder architecture for Condition (A), to fully exploit the effect of MT pretraining, we removed the speech attention from the MT decoder that attends to the hierarchical encoder's hidden representations.

Specifically, the ASR encoder module in the proposed architecture takes in a sequence of audio features $x_1, x_2, \cdots, x_T$ and generates a sequence of hidden representations with length N, optimized with respect to the ASR CTC objective. The ASR decoder takes in the ASR encoder's hidden representations and autoregressively produces a sequence of logits with length L trained by the label-smoothing loss. The hierarchical speech encoder module is trained directly by the ST CTC loss for generating auxiliary frame-level labels in the target language to aid the ST decoding process. The primary innovation of the proposed system lies in the fully-connected layer that maps the ASR decoder's output hidden representations to some representations that resemble mBART's encoder's embedding layer's outputs, making the full system differentiable. The ST encoder subsequently encodes the input representations and feeds them into its decoder. The ST decoder, slightly different from the vanilla mBART decoder, optionally runs hybrid/joint CTC decoding at inference time, with the ST-CTC auxiliary labels and the autoregressively generated ST outputs with target length M, i.e. $y_1^{ST}, y_2^{ST}, \cdots, y_M^{ST}$.

3.3 System Combination

We perform a system combination across 5 of our systems: best constrained end-to-end system, best unconstrained end-to-end system, best cascaded system, and 2 additional cascaded systems (Fernandes et al., 2022). The two additional systems use the ASR produced by our end-to-end systems,

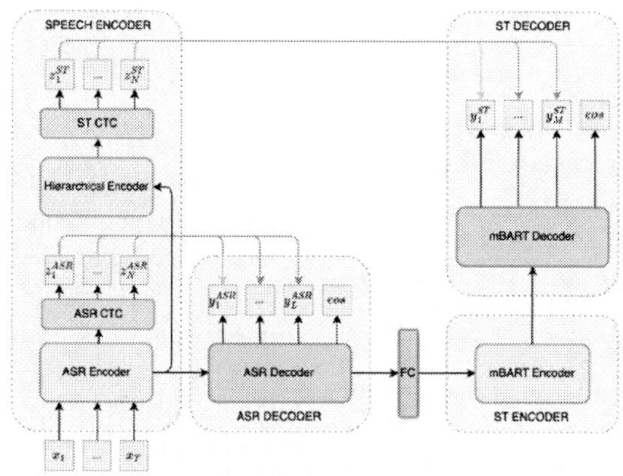

Figure 1: E2E model architecture with mBART MT module. The fully-connected (FC) layer applies a linear transformation to the ASR decoder's final hidden representation, which is then used to replace mBART's encoder's embedding layer's output.

and the same NLLB-200 MT component as in our best cascaded system. In Table 6, the 5 combined systems are referred to as A3, B1, B3, B4, and B5, in order.

3.3.1 Minimum Bayes Risk

We applied Minimum Bayes Risk decoding (Kumar and Byrne, 2004) to combine the hypotheses produced by five systems. For a given speech utterance x_i, and for a given system $s^j_{\theta_j}$ ($j \in \mathcal{S}$ and θ_j the set of parameters used by the jth trained system), we can define the translation hypothesis as $y^j_i = f^j_{\theta_j}(x_i)$ and p^j_i be the probability that the hypothesis y^j_i would be outputted. We use this probability as a self-confidence score. Let $\mathcal{L}$ be similarity metric used to compare two hypothesis, outputting a scalar that rises if the two hypothesis are more similar. Then, for a given speech utterance x_i, and for a given set of systems $\mathcal{S}$, we define the best output as the one minimizing the distance with others while having the highest confidence:

$$y^{mbr}_i = \max_{y^j_i} \sum_{j \in \mathcal{F}} p^j_i \sum_{k \in \mathcal{F}} \mathcal{L}(y^j_i, y^k_i) \quad (1)$$

3.3.2 Variations of MBR

Baseline MBR For our first combination, we compute the outputs according to the MBR using the BLEU score of sacrebleu (Post, 2018a) as the $\mathcal{L}$ similarity metric and the posterior probabilities p^j_i used are the log-likelihood ratios given by the end-to-end systems and the MT systems.

Unscored MBR For our second combination, we use the same technique but with a constant $p^j_i = 1$ for every system, as a simplified version of the Generalized MBR (Duh et al., 2011).

COMET-MBR For our third combination, we utilized the `comet-mbr` framework, which employs the COMET score between the source and hypothesis as the similarity metric ($\mathcal{L}$), using same equation (1), without the use of posterior probabilities (Fernandes et al., 2022). We used `wmt20-comet-da` for MBR scoring (Rei et al., 2020). Despite Tunisian Arabic not being a COMET-supported language, we observed an improvement compared to our single best system, suggesting that this approach may extend to dialects of languages covered by COMET.

4 Experiments

In this section, we describe our experiments on the ASR, MT, and ST tasks. In order to reduce the orthographic variation in the Tunisian speech transcription we performed additional text normalization similar to (Yang et al., 2022) which showed significant improvements on ASR, MT and ST tasks. The normalization is performed on both Tunisian and MSA transcripts and includes removing diacritics and single character words, and Alif/Ya/Ta-Marbuta normalization (see (Yang et al., 2022) for more details).

4.1 ASR

First we augment the raw audio segments by applying speed perturbation with three speed factors of 0.9, 1.0 and 1.1 (Ko et al., 2015). Then we transform the augmented audio to a sequence of 83-dimensional feature frames for the E2E model;

80-dimensional log-mel filterbank coefficients with 3 pitch features (Ghahremani et al., 2014). We normalize the features by the mean and the standard deviation calculated on the entire training set. In addition, we augment the features with specaugment approach (Park et al., 2019), with mask parameters $(mT, mF, T, F) = (5, 2, 27, 0.05)$ and bi-cubic time-warping. The E2E Branchformer-based ASR model was trained using Adam optimizer for 50 epochs with dropout-rate 0.001, warmup-steps of 25000 for condition (A) and 40000 for condition (B). The BPE vocabulary size is 500 for condition (A) and 2000 for condition (B). Table 3 summarizes the best set of parameters that were found for the Branchformer architecture. We note here that the Branchformer has 28.28 M parameters, which is approximately one-fourth the number of parameters in the Conformer (Yang et al., 2022), which is 116.15 M.

Att heads	CNN	Enc layers	Dec layers	d^k	FF
4	31	12	6	256	2048

Table 3: Values of condition (A) and (B) hyperparameters CNN: refers to CNN module kernel, Att: attention, Enc: encoder, Dec: decoder, and FF: fully connected layer

MGB2-tune: the pretrained model on MGB-2 is fine-tuned on Tunisian data from condition (A) by updating all model parameters with 1/10 of the learning rate that was used during the training similar to (Hussein et al., 2021). In addition, we examine the effect of adding ASR outputs to the ground truth source during finetuning (**pseudo labeling**) and adding additional telephone data (**Tel**). The ASR results are summarized in Table 4 and compared to the state-of-the-art conformer results from (Yang et al., 2022). The MD refers to the hierarchical multi-decoder ST architecture adopted from (Yan et al., 2022), and MD-ASR refers to the ASR sub-module of the ST. It can be observed that the Branchformer provides slightly better results compared to the previous best conformer with similar size on both conditions (A) and (B). In addition, it can be also seen that pseudo labeling provides 2% relative improvement. We found that there is a high inconsistency between different transcribers since there is no standard orthography in Tunisian dialect. By incorporating the ASR predictions in this way, we aim to provide the model with more examples of the Tunisian dialect and help it better generalize to variations in the spoken language. To confirm this hypothesis we take a closer look at the most frequent top four substitutions shown in Table 5. The words are transliterated using Buckwalter transliteration (BW)[3] to make it readable for non-Arabic speakers. It can be seen that the ASR substitutions are present in both hypothesis and as correct reference which indicates that the assumption of reference inconsistency holds true. Finally, channel matching using more telephone data provides an additional 2.5% relative improvement.

		dev	test1	test2	test3
ASR-ID	Model	WER (↓)			
A1	Conformer (Yang et al., 2022)	40.8	44.8	43.8	-
A2	Branchformer	**40.1**	**44.5**	-	-
B1	MGB2-tune (Yang et al., 2022)	38.8	43.8	42.8	-
B2	MGB2-tune Branchformer	38.3	43.1	-	-
B3	+ Pseudo	37.5	42.6	-	-
B4	+ Tel	**36.5**	**41.7**	**40.6**	**41.6**
B5	E2E-MD-ASR	40.6	45.1	43.7	44.9
B6	E2E-mBART-ASR	37.7	43.2	41.5	42.6

Table 4: WER (%) of ASR models on dev, test1, test2 and test3 sets. A* and B* IDs are the ASR models developed under condition (A) and condition (B) respectively. B5 refers to the ASR submodule of the MD-ASR system under the constrained condition and B6 refers to the ASR sub-module of the E2E-mBART system both described in Section 3.2.

BW (REF / HYP)	Arabic	English Translation
69: Ayh / Ay	اي / ايه	yes
61: Ay / Ayh	ايه / اي	yes
18: Akhw / khw	اكهو / كهو	it's
17: khw / Akhw	كهو / اكهو	it's
8: gdwA / gdwh	غدوه / غدوا	tomorrow
7: gdwh / gdwA	غدوا / غدوه	tomorrow

Table 5: Top 6 substitutions with inconsistencies for ASR system transliterated using Buckwalter (BW). The number of times each error occurs is followed by the word in the reference and the corresponding hypothesis.

4.2 MT

We train the MT models as described in Section 3.1.2. For condition (A) the MT system parameters are shown in Table 7. In this condition, our MT system is finetuned on the training Tunisian data where the source data is mixed with ASR outputs, in order to be more robust to noisy source data. We use 5000 Byte-pair encoding (BPE) units shared between Tunisian Arabic and English. We train

[3] https://en.wikipedia.org/wiki/Buckwalter_transliteration

		Pretrained		dev	test1	test2	test3
ST-ID	Type	ASR	MT	BLEU (↑)	BLEU (↑)	BLEU (↑)	BLEU (↑)
A1	Cascade	A2	A3	18.9	15.6	-	-
A2	E2E-MD (Yan et al., 2022)	A2	-	20.6	17.1	-	-
A3	E2E-MD+norm	A2	-	**20.7**	**17.5**	19.1	17.6
B1	E2E-mBART	B4	B2	20.7	17.5	17.5	17.1
B2	Cascade-mBART	B4	B2	20.9	17.9	-	-
B3	Cascade-Base-NLLB200	B4	B3	**22.2**	**19.2**	**21.2**	**18.7**
B4	Cascade-B5-ASR-NLLB200	B5	B3	21.1	18.3	19.9	18.2
B5	Cascade-B6-ASR-NLLB200	B6	B3	22.2	18.8	20.7	18.3
B6	MBR with scores	-	-	21.7	18.8	18.7	17.1
B7	MBR no scores	-	-	22.7	19.6	20.6	18.8
B8	`comet-mbr`	-	-	**22.7**	**19.6**	**21.6**	**19.1**

Table 6: Results of cascaded, E2E, and combined systems measured by BLEU score on the dev, test1, test2 and test3. E2E-MD is the hierarchical multi-decoder described in (§3.2). Norm indicates the use of text normalization (§4) which is used with all systems except A2. The pretrained indicates the use of pretrained ASR and MT systems from Tables(8,4). A* and B* IDs are the models developed under condition (A) and condition (B) respectively

	layers	embed-dim	FF-embed	att-heads
Encoder	6	256	1024	4
Decoder	6	256	2048	4

Table 7: Values of constrained MT system parameters Enc: encoder, Dec: decoder, and FF: feed-forward

			dev	test1
MT-ID	Model Type	Model Size	BLEU (↑)	BLEU (↑)
A1	Transformer (Yang et al., 2022)		24.5	21.5
A2	Transformer Espnet	13.63 M	23.5	19.9
A3	Branchformer Espnet	16.81 M	25.0	21.4
B1	Transformer (Yang et al., 2022)		29.0	25.0
B2	mBART	610M	29.2	24.6
B3	NLLB-200	1.3B	**30.5**	**26.4**

Table 8: BLEU scores of various MT models using the gold reference transcripts. A* and B* IDs are the MT models developed under condition (A) and condition (B) respectively.

with the Adam optimizer; the maximum learning rate is 3e-03, attained after 20000 warm-up steps, and then decayed according to an inverse square root scheduler; we use dropout probability of 0.3; the model is trained for 200 epochs. For condition (B), for both NLLB-200 and mBART25, we finetune our model for up to 80000 updates and use loss to select our best model checkpoint. We use `sacrebleu` to compute the case-insensitive BLEU scores for all evaluation sets (Papineni et al., 2002; Post, 2018b) as shown in Table 8. The comparative analysis of our Espnet MT transformer with the best MT models reported in previous works based on Fairseq transformer (Yang et al., 2022) reveals a noticeable performance lag of up to -1.6 in absolute BLEU. However, incorporating the Branchformer module yields similar performance to the best Fairseq model. Finally finetuning NLLB-200 MT achieves the best results in the unconstrained category with 30.5 and 26.4 BLEU scores.

4.3 ST

Table 6 presents the results of our submitted cascaded and E2E ST systems. The pretrained column refers to the pretrained ASR and MT systems from Tables (4, 8). B1 denotes the end-to-end ST with B4 ASR and B2 mBART under the unconstrained condition, as described in Section 3.2. The E2E-MD is a hierarchical multi-decoder architecture described in Section 3.2, where the MT component is trained from scratch. The cascaded ST systems, Cascade-Base-NLLB200, Cascade-B5-ASR-NLLB200 and Cascade-B6-ASR-NLLB200, utilize the best MT model (NLLB200 B3) and ASR submodules including branchformer (B4), branchformer finetuned in E2E-MD setup (B5) and branchformer finetuned in with mBART setup (B6) respectively from Table 4.

It can be seen that the E2E-multidecoder architecture outperforms the cascaded system in the constrained condition, with a significant improvement of up to +1.7 in absolute BLEU. Text normalization provides additional boost of +0.4 in absolute BLEU. On the other hand for the unconstrained system, we observe that the cascaded system B2 outperforms the E2E B1 by up to 0.4 in absolute BLEU that utilizes identical submodules. The reason for this performance difference may be attributed to the inability of the input linear layer that was added to the MT encoder in the E2E setup (B1) to adjust the length of the ASR output to match the length of the mBART encoder's tokenization. This length discrepancy may lead to a loss of crucial information during the integration of the two modules, ultimately resulting in a degradation of overall performance. Further analysis is required to confirm this hypothesis and to identify potential solutions to address this issue. The highest performance of single ST system is obtained using Cascade-NLLB200-1.3B with BLEU of 21.2 and 18.7 on test2 and test3 respectively. Finally, we combine A3, B1, B3, B4 and B5 with `comet-mbr` which achieves the highest BLEU scores of 21.6 and 19.1 on test2 and test3 respectively.

5 Conclusion

In this paper, we have presented our submission for the IWSLT 2023 dialect speech translation task. We compared end-to-end to cascaded systems under constrained and unconstrained conditions. We found that an E2E-ST system outperformed the cascaded system under the constrained condition, while the cascaded models significantly outperformed the E2E-ST systems under the unconstrained condition. We provided a new E2E-ST baseline combining large pretrained MT with ASR under the unconstrained condition. Finally, we demonstrated that pseudo-labeling and channel matching provided significant improvements for the ASR and hence improved cascaded ST systems. In future work we plan to explore more effective ways of integrating the large pretrained MT models into E2E ST systems.

Acknowledgements

This work was partially supported by NSF CCRI Grant No 2120435. In addition, we thank the Qatar Computing Research Institute, Doha, for providing some of the computational resources that made this work possible.

References

Milind Agarwal, Sweta Agrawal, Antonios Anastasopoulos, Ondřej Bojar, Claudia Borg, Marine Carpuat, Roldano Cattoni, Mauro Cettolo, Mingda Chen, William Chen, Khalid Choukri, Alexandra Chronopoulou, Anna Currey, Thierry Declerck, Qianqian Dong, Yannick Estève, Kevin Duh, Marcello Federico, Souhir Gahbiche, Barry Haddow, Benjamin Hsu, Phu Mon Htut, Hirofumi Inaguma, Dávid Javorský, John Judge, Yasumasa Kano, Tom Ko, Rishu Kumar, Pengwei Li, Xutail Ma, Prashant Mathur, Evgeny Matusov, Paul McNamee, John P. McCrae, Kenton Murray, Maria Nadejde, Satoshi Nakamura, Matteo Negri, Ha Nguyen, Jan Niehues, Xing Niu, Atul Ojha Kr., John E. Ortega, Proyag Pal, Juan Pino, Lonneke van der Plas, Peter Polák, Elijah Rippeth, Elizabeth Salesky, Jiatong Shi, Matthias Sperber, Sebastian Stüker, Katsuhito Sudoh, Yun Tang, Brian Thompson, Kevin Tran, Marco Turchi, Alex Waibel, Mingxuan Wang, Shinji Watanabe, and Rodolfo Zevallos. 2023. Findings of the IWSLT 2023 Evaluation Campaign. In *Proceedings of the 20th International Conference on Spoken Language Translation (IWSLT 2023)*. Association for Computational Linguistics.

Ahmed M. Ali, Peter Bell, James R. Glass, Yacine Messaoui, Hamdy Mubarak, Steve Renals, and Yifan Zhang. 2016. The mgb-2 challenge: Arabic multi-dialect broadcast media recognition. *2016 IEEE Spoken Language Technology Workshop (SLT)*, pages 279–284.

El Said Badawi, Michael Carter, and Adrian Gully. 2013. *Modern written Arabic: A comprehensive grammar*. Routledge.

Kevin Duh, Katsuhito Sudoh, Xianchao Wu, Hajime Tsukada, and Masaaki Nagata. 2011. Generalized minimum bayes risk system combination. In *Proceedings of 5th International Joint Conference on Natural Language Processing*, pages 1356–1360.

Patrick Fernandes, António Farinhas, Ricardo Rei, José De Souza, Perez Ogayo, Graham Neubig, and Andre Martins. 2022. Quality-aware decoding for neural machine translation. In *Proceedings of the 2022 Conference of the North American Chapter of the Association for Computational Linguistics: Human Language Technologies*, pages 1396–1412, Seattle, United States. Association for Computational Linguistics.

Pegah Ghahremani, Bagher BabaAli, Daniel Povey, Korbinian Riedhammer, Jan Trmal, and Sanjeev Khudanpur. 2014. A pitch extraction algorithm tuned for automatic speech recognition. In *IEEE international conference on acoustics, speech and signal processing (ICASSP)*, pages 2494–2498. IEEE.

Amir Hussein, Shammur Chowdhury, and Ahmed Ali. 2021. Kari: Kanari/qcri's end-to-end systems for the interspeech 2021 indian languages code-switching challenge. *arXiv preprint arXiv:2106.05885*.

Tom Ko, Vijayaditya Peddinti, Daniel Povey, and Sanjeev Khudanpur. 2015. Audio augmentation for speech recognition. In *Sixteenth Annual Conference of the International Speech Communication Association*.

Shankar Kumar and Bill Byrne. 2004. Minimum bayes-risk decoding for statistical machine translation. In *Proceedings of the Human Language Technology Conference of the North American Chapter of the Association for Computational Linguistics: HLT-NAACL 2004*, pages 169–176.

Yinhan Liu, Jiatao Gu, Naman Goyal, Xian Li, Sergey Edunov, Marjan Ghazvininejad, Mike Lewis, and Luke Zettlemoyer. 2020a. Multilingual denoising pre-training for neural machine translation. *Transactions of the Association for Computational Linguistics*, 8:726–742.

Yinhan Liu, Jiatao Gu, Naman Goyal, Xian Li, Sergey Edunov, Marjan Ghazvininejad, Mike Lewis, and Luke Zettlemoyer. 2020b. Multilingual denoising pre-training for neural machine translation.

Mohamed Maamouri et al. 2006. Levantine arabic qt training data set 5, speech ldc2006s29. Web Download.

NLLB Team, Marta R. Costa-jussà, James Cross, Onur Çelebi, Maha Elbayad, Kenneth Heafield, Kevin Heffernan, Elahe Kalbassi, Janice Lam, Daniel Licht, Jean Maillard, Anna Sun, Skyler Wang, Guillaume Wenzek, Al Youngblood, Bapi Akula, Loic Barrault, Gabriel Mejia-Gonzalez, Prangthip Hansanti, John Hoffman, Semarley Jarrett, Kaushik Ram Sadagopan, Dirk Rowe, Shannon Spruit, Chau Tran, Pierre Andrews, Necip Fazil Ayan, Shruti Bhosale, Sergey Edunov, Angela Fan, Cynthia Gao, Vedanuj Goswami, Francisco Guzmán, Philipp Koehn, Alexandre Mourachko, Christophe Ropers, Safiyyah Saleem, Holger Schwenk, and Jeff Wang. 2022. No language left behind: Scaling human-centered machine translation.

Myle Ott, Sergey Edunov, Alexei Baevski, Angela Fan, Sam Gross, Nathan Ng, David Grangier, and Michael Auli. 2019. fairseq: A fast, extensible toolkit for sequence modeling. In *Proceedings of NAACL-HLT 2019: Demonstrations*.

Kishore Papineni, Salim Roukos, Todd Ward, and Wei-Jing Zhu. 2002. Bleu: a method for automatic evaluation of machine translation. In *Proceedings of the 40th Annual Meeting of the Association for Computational Linguistics*, pages 311–318, Philadelphia, Pennsylvania, USA. Association for Computational Linguistics.

Daniel S Park, William Chan, Yu Zhang, Chung-Cheng Chiu, Barret Zoph, Ekin D Cubuk, and Quoc V Le. 2019. Specaugment: A simple data augmentation method for automatic speech recognition. *Proc. Interspeech*, pages 2613–2617.

Yifan Peng, Siddharth Dalmia, Ian Lane, and Shinji Watanabe. 2022. Branchformer: Parallel mlp-attention architectures to capture local and global context for speech recognition and understanding. In *International Conference on Machine Learning*, pages 17627–17643. PMLR.

Telmo Pires, Eva Schlinger, and Dan Garrette. 2019. How multilingual is multilingual BERT? In *Proceedings of the 57th Annual Meeting of the Association for Computational Linguistics*, pages 4996–5001, Florence, Italy. Association for Computational Linguistics.

Matt Post. 2018a. A call for clarity in reporting BLEU scores. In *Proceedings of the Third Conference on Machine Translation: Research Papers*, pages 186–191, Belgium, Brussels. Association for Computational Linguistics.

Matt Post. 2018b. A call for clarity in reporting BLEU scores. In *Proceedings of the Third Conference on Machine Translation: Research Papers*, pages 186–191, Brussels, Belgium. Association for Computational Linguistics.

Ricardo Rei, Craig Stewart, Ana C Farinha, and Alon Lavie. 2020. Comet: A neural framework for mt evaluation. *arXiv preprint arXiv:2009.09025*.

Jin Sakuma, Tatsuya Komatsu, and Robin Scheibler. 2021. Mlp-based architecture with variable length input for automatic speech recognition.

Yuqing Tang, Chau Tran, Xian Li, Peng-Jen Chen, Naman Goyal, Vishrav Chaudhary, Jiatao Gu, and Angela Fan. 2020. Multilingual translation with extensible multilingual pretraining and finetuning. *arXiv preprint arXiv:2008.00401*.

A. Vaswani, N. Shazeer, N. Parmar, J. Uszkoreit, L. Jones, A. Gomez, u. Kaiser, and I. Polosukhin. 2017. Attention is all you need. In *Advances in neural information processing systems*, pages 5998–6008.

Shinji Watanabe, Takaaki Hori, Shigeki Karita, Tomoki Hayashi, Jiro Nishitoba, Yuya Unno, Nelson Yalta, Jahn Heymann, Matthew Wiesner, Nanxin Chen, Adithya Renduchintala, and Tsubasa Ochiai. 2018. Espnet: End-to-end speech processing toolkit. *ArXiv*, abs/1804.00015.

Shinji Watanabe, Takaaki Hori, Suyoun Kim, John R. Hershey, and Tomoki Hayashi. 2017. Hybrid ctc/attention architecture for end-to-end speech recognition. *IEEE Journal of Selected Topics in Signal Processing*, 11:1240–1253.

Brian Yan, Patrick Fernandes, Siddharth Dalmia, Jiatong Shi, Yifan Peng, Dan Berrebbi, Xinyi Wang, Graham Neubig, and Shinji Watanabe. 2022. CMU's IWSLT 2022 dialect speech translation system. In *Proceedings of the 19th International Conference on Spoken Language Translation (IWSLT 2022)*, pages 298–307, Dublin, Ireland (in-person and online). Association for Computational Linguistics.

Jinyi Yang, Amir Hussein, Matthew Wiesner, and Sanjeev Khudanpur. 2022. Jhu iwslt 2022 dialect speech translation system description. In *Proceedings of the 19th International Conference on Spoken Language Translation (IWSLT 2022)*, pages 319–326.

Inès Zribi, Rahma Boujelbane, Abir Masmoudi, Mariem Ellouze, Lamia Belguith, and Nizar Habash. 2014. A conventional orthography for Tunisian Arabic. In *Proceedings of the Ninth International Conference on Language Resources and Evaluation (LREC'14)*, pages 2355–2361, Reykjavik, Iceland. European Language Resources Association (ELRA).

Learning Nearest Neighbour Informed Latent Word Embeddings to Improve Zero-Shot Machine Translation

Nishant Kambhatla **Logan Born** **Anoop Sarkar**
School of Computing Science, Simon Fraser University
8888 University Drive, Burnaby BC, Canada
{nkambhat, loborn, anoop}@sfu.ca

Abstract

Multilingual neural translation models exploit cross-lingual transfer to perform zero-shot translation between unseen language pairs. Past efforts to improve cross-lingual transfer have focused on aligning contextual *sentence*-level representations. This paper introduces three novel contributions to allow exploiting nearest neighbours at the *token* level during training, including: (i) an efficient, gradient-friendly way to share representations between neighboring tokens; (ii) an attentional semantic layer which extracts latent features from shared embeddings; and (iii) an agreement loss to harmonize predictions across different sentence representations. Experiments on two multilingual datasets demonstrate consistent gains in zero shot translation over strong baselines.

1 Introduction

Many-to-many multilingual neural translation models (Firat et al., 2016; Johnson et al., 2017; Khandelwal et al., 2020; Fan et al., 2022) share a single representation space across multiple language pairs, which enables them to perform *zero-shot* translations between unseen pairs (Ha et al., 2017; Chen et al., 2022; Wu et al., 2022). Prior work on zero-shot translation has focused on aligning *contextual*, *sentence*-level representations from multiple languages (Ji et al., 2020; Pan et al., 2021a), to make these more 'universal' or language-agnostic (Gu et al., 2018; Gu and Feng, 2022). *Non*-contextual, *token*-level representations offer another space in which this kind of alignment could be pursued, but this space has not been thoroughly explored in prior work. Even lexicon-based methods (Conneau et al., 2020; Reid and Artetxe, 2022), which exploit token-level anchors from multilingual dictionaries (Duan et al., 2020), still use these to align representations at the sentence level.

In this work, we explore a novel technique for sharing information across languages at the *token* level, which exploits nearest neighbours (NNs) to aggregate information from subwords across multiple languages. When analysing embedding spaces, many authors speak in terms of "neighborhoods" or "subspaces" which group together tokens from a particular semantic field or other natural class. These neighborhoods form implicitly as a model learns similarities between embedded words or subwords. We propose to make this neighborhood structure *explicit* by forcing a model to consider a token's neighbors when learning its embedding. Specifically, we dynamically perturb a translation model's token embeddings at training time by averaging them with their nearest neighbors; thus a token like *soccer* may end up mixed together with related tokens such as *football*, *fußball*, or *futbol* from potentially distinct languages (Figure 1). This encourages the model to organize its subword embeddings in such a way that nearby tokens convey similar information to one another. We hypothesize that this process will produce a more structured embedding space which will in turn enable more fluent outputs. This process only uses the model's embedding layer, and does not require any offline dictionaries or additional data.

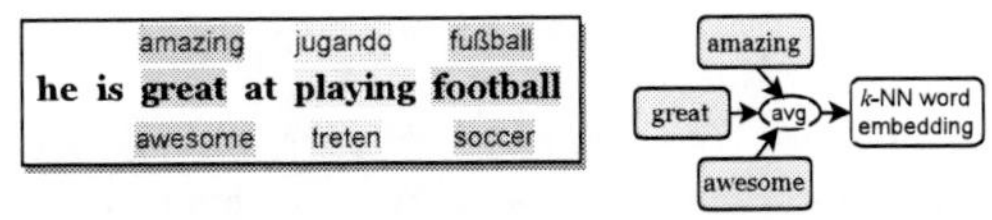

Figure 1: NN-informed embeddings average representations from nearby subwords in the embedding space.

Our experiments and ablations show that this simple technique significantly increases the effectiveness of translation models on the IWSLT17 and TED59 massively multilingual datasets. Concretely, our contributions include: (i) an efficient, gradient-friendly, soft representation-mixing technique which exploits token-level neighbors without changing the Transformer architecture; (ii) an attentional semantic layer which extracts features from

Proceedings of the 20th International Conference on Spoken Language Translation (IWSLT 2023), pages 291–301

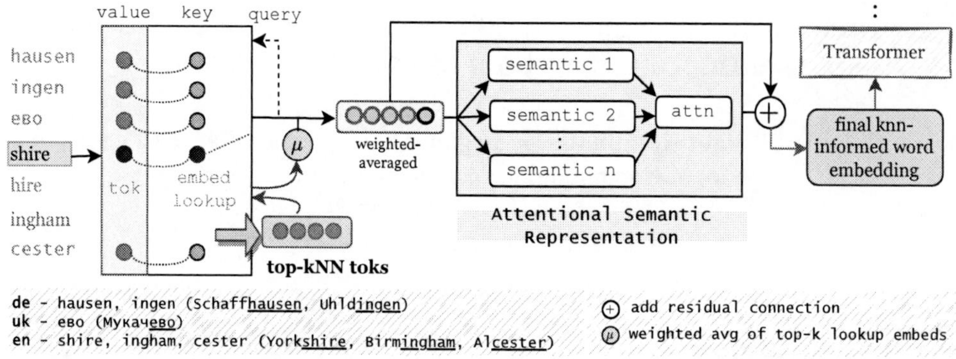

Figure 2: A NN-informed embedding for an arbitrary subword `shire` is produced by averaging across nearby subwords from various languages, and combining with a semantic representation extracted from this average.

mixed representations to give neighbour-informed latent word embeddings, and which is a drop-in replacement for a conventional embedding layer; and (iii) an agreement loss which harmonizes predictions with and without neighbor-informed embeddings.

2 Translation with Nearest Neighbour Augmented Embeddings

We describe our model for *nearest-neighbour informed token level embeddings* (Figure 2) of subwords from multiple source languages.

Nearest Neighbor Retrieval Let $\mathcal{L}_{emb}$ be a word embedding layer that performs a lookup $\text{EMB}(\cdot)$ using weights $\mathcal{W}_{emb} \in \mathbb{R}^{|\mathcal{V}| \times D}$, where $\mathcal{V}$ is a joint subword vocabulary over all languages and D is a fixed embedding dimension. Given the embedding $q = \text{EMB}(w) \in \mathbb{R}^{1 \times D}$ of a subword w, we wish to find q's nearest neighbour n (or neighbors $n_1, ..., n_k$) using maximum inner product search (MIPS) over the weight matrix $\mathcal{W}_{emb}$:

$$\begin{aligned} n &= \arg\min_{x \subset \mathcal{W}_{emb}} ||q - x||_2^2 \\ &= \arg\min_{x \subset \mathcal{W}_{emb}} (||x||_2^2 - 2q^T x) \end{aligned} \tag{1}$$

Approximate solutions to (1) can be efficiently computed on-the-fly using anisotropic vector quantization (Guo et al., 2020).[1]

Given the approximate nearest neighbors (ANNs) $n_1, ..., n_k$ of subword w, we compute a weighted average over these tokens' embeddings with a weighting term λ:

$$\text{EMB}_\mu(w) = \lambda \frac{1}{k} \sum_{i=1}^{k} (\text{EMB}(n_i)) + (1 - \lambda)\text{EMB}(w) \tag{2}$$

$\text{EMB}_\mu(\cdot)$ is computed directly from $\mathcal{W}_{emb}$, which ensures that our technique remains gradient-friendly[2] and does not need a separate warm-up step. Previous NN-based proposals for translation (Khandelwal et al., 2020) and language modeling (Khandelwal et al., 2019) have only explored NNs of contextualized representations, strictly for generation, and using neighbors from an offline *frozen datastore* of pretrained candidates. Their method proved effective for MT domain adaptation, rather than zero-shot translation which is the focus of this work. The ability to propagate gradients to a subword's neighbors during training is novel and unique compared to previous NN-based techniques.

Attentional Semantic Representation To extract contextually-salient information from $\text{EMB}_\mu(w)$, which combines information from many subwords in potentially disparate languages, we use a shared semantic embedding inspired by Gu et al. 2018; Wang et al. 2018 that shows a similar effect as topical modelling.

We introduce $\mathcal{W}_{sem} \in \mathbb{R}^{\mathcal{N} \times D}$, where each of the $\mathcal{N}$ rows is taken to be a language-agnostic semantic representation. $\mathcal{W}_{sem}$ is shared across all languages. We use attention (Luong et al., 2015) to compute a latent embedding $\text{EMB}_{latent}(w)$ using

[1]Exact and approximate solutions yield similar results, but approximation gives significant gains in training speed.

[2]In Section 3.3 we introduce a caching heuristic which is not gradient-friendly; however, this is simply an implementation detail to speed up training, and the gradient-friendly presentation in this section achieves equivalent performance.

	De - It		De - Nl		De - Ro		It - Nl		It - Ro		Nl - Ro		zero	sup.
	←	→	←	→	←	→	←	→	←	→	←	→		
Base M2M	15.64	15.28	18.46	18.14	14.42	14.98	18.16	18.79	17.91	20.14	15.81	16.41	17.01	**30.62**
SRA (2019)	16.44	16.45	18.44	19.15	15.07	15.83	**19.30**	19.10	18.52	21.52	16.83	17.66	17.85	30.41
SF (2019)	16.34	15.77	18.37	18.16	14.74	15.25	18.6	19.18	18.54	21.64	16.09	16.94	17.46	30.50
LV (2021)	16.82	15.81	18.74	18.64	15.12	**16.32**	18.92	19.29	18.70	22.13	16.21	18.22	17.91	30.51
CL (2021b)	17.31	16.21	19.70	**19.57**	15.32	16.25	18.90	20.09	19.07	**22.44**	17.14	17.99	18.33	30.29
DP (2021)	16.62	15.64	19.64	18.78	15.07	15.96	19.01	**20.15**	18.67	21.56	16.46	18.18	17.97	30.49
Ours	**17.41**	**16.89**	**19.71**	**19.21**	**15.60**	16.22	**19.30**	20.10	**19.60**	21.88	**17.25**	**18.40**	**18.47**	**30.62**

Table 1: BLEU on IWSLT17 test set (mean of 3 runs). `Zero` and `sup.` are average zero-shot and supervised results.

the averaged embedding $\text{EMB}_{\mu}(w)$ as query:

$$\text{EMB}_{latent}(w) = \text{Softmax}(\text{EMB}_{\mu}(w).\mathcal{W}_{sem}^{T})\mathcal{W}_{sem} \quad (3)$$

A residual connection from $\text{EMB}_{\mu}(w)$ gives the final NN-informed word embedding:

$$\text{EMB}_{knn}(w) = \text{EMB}_{latent}(w) + \text{EMB}_{\mu}(w) \quad (4)$$

$\text{EMB}_{knn}(w)$ is a drop-in replacement for a conventional word embedding $\text{EMB}(w)$.

Modelling Prediction Consistency Given a source sentence represented using conventional word embeddings and using NN-informed embeddings, following Kambhatla et al. (2022b) we model the loss with respect to target sentence y_i as:

$$\begin{aligned}\mathcal{L}^i = \; & \underbrace{\alpha_1 \mathcal{L}^i_{NLL}(p_\Theta(y_i|x_i))}_{\text{source x-entropy}} \\ + \; & \underbrace{\alpha_2 \mathcal{L}^i_{NLL}(p_\Theta(y_i|\,kNN(x_i)))}_{k\text{-NN embeds. source x-entropy}} \\ + \; & \underbrace{\beta \mathcal{L}^i_{dist}(\,p_\Theta(y_i|x_i),\; p_\Theta(y_i|kNN(x_i)))}_{\text{agreement loss}}\end{aligned} \quad (5)$$

where $k\text{NN}(x_i)$ denotes the set of k-nearest neighbors to token x_i. This loss combines three terms: the first two are conventional negative log-likelihoods, while the third is an *agreement loss* measuring pairwise symmetric KL divergence between the output distributions for x_i and $kNN(x_i)$. This agreement-loss term performs *co-regularization* by allowing explicit interactions between source sentences with and without NN-informed embeddings.

3 Experiments

3.1 Datasets

We conduct experiments on 2 multilingual datasets, each with BPE (Sennrich et al., 2016) vocabulary size of 32k subwords:

IWSLT17 (Cettolo et al., 2012) is an English-centric dataset[3] totalling 1.8M parallel sentences. It has 8 supervised directions to and from German, Italian, Dutch and Romanian, each with about 220,000 parallel sentences, and 12 zero-shot directions. We use the official validation and test sets.

Ted59 (Qi et al., 2018) is a massively multilingual English-centric dataset[4] with 116 translation directions totalling 10.8M parallel sentences. The imbalanced data—from 0.25M to just 2000 parallel samples for some language pairs—makes it ideal to study the effects of our method. Following (Aharoni et al., 2019; Raganato et al., 2021) we evaluate on 16 supervised pairs and 4 zero-shot (Arabic ↔ French, Ukranian ↔ Russian).

3.2 Baselines and Related Work

We compare against methods for encoder manifold alignment. These include strong baselines such as sentence representation alignment (SRA; Arivazhagan et al. 2019), softmax forcing (SF; Pham et al. 2019), the contrastive multilingual model (CL; Pan et al. 2021b), multilingual Transformer with disentagled positional embedding (DP; Liu et al. 2021), and latent variable based denoising (LV; Wang et al. 2021), along with the vanilla many-to-many zero-shot model (M2M). On TED59, we compare against CL and 3 explicit multilingual alignment techniques proposed by Raganato et al. (2021): word-alignment, language tag alignment, and the union of the two. We also implement and compare against Raganato et al.'s (2021) sparse 1.5`entmax` cross-attention variant.

3.3 Model and Implementation Details

All models use the configuration in Vaswani et al. 2017 using the `fairseq` toolkit (Ott et al., 2019). See reproducibility details in Appendix A.

[3] `https://wit3.fbk.eu/2017-01`

[4] `github.com/neulab/word-embeddings-for-nmt`

	Θ	En→X	X→En	Zero-Shot	Acc_O
Aharoni et al. – 106 langs	473M	20.11	29.97	9.17	-
Aharoni et al. – 59 langs	93M	19.54	28.03	-	-
Transformer M2M reimp.	93M	18.98	27.22	7.12	74.10
Constrastive (2021b)	93M	19.09	27.29	8.16	73.90
Ours	77M	19.01	27.11	**10.03**	**95.81**
Raganato et al. (2021)					
ZS + 1.5`entmax` (ibid.)	93M	18.90	27.21	10.02	87.81
↳ Word Align (ibid.)	93M	18.99	27.58	8.38	73.12
↳ LangID Align (ibid.)	93M	18.98	27.48	6.35	65.01
↳ Word + LangID Align	93M	19.06	27.37	11.94	97.25
Ours + 1.5`entmax`	77M	18.94	27.42	**12.11**	**98.90**

Table 2: Average BLEU scores on the TED59 dataset. Our model produces zero-shot translations in the correct output language with high accuracy (Acc_O).

We use ScANN (Guo et al., 2020) for efficient ANN search [5] with $k = 3$. To increase training speeds, we cache each subword's ANNs for 400 iterations before recomputing them. We only (peridocally) cache subword IDs: the embedding $\text{EMB}_\mu(\cdot)$ is always computed directly from $\mathcal{W}_{emb}$. We set $\lambda = 0.5, \alpha_1, \alpha_2 = 1$, and $\beta = 5$. The *attentional latent semantic representation* layer has 512 dim (same as the embedding layer) and a size $\mathcal{N}$ of 1000 for IWSLT17 (smaller dataset) and 5000 for TED59 (larger dataset). We did not tune this hyperparameter and chose the values based on the size of the datasets. For evaluation, we report `sacreBLEU` (Post, 2018).

3.4 Results

Main Results. Tables 1 and 2 show our main results. On IWSLT17, our latent k-NN embedding model outperforms several strong baselines, including sentence-representation alignment and contrastive learning, by an average of 0.62 and 0.11 BLEU respectively across the 12 zero-shot pairs. Compared to the baseline many-to-many model, our method yields a 1.5 BLEU gain on average. Our method is able to improve zero-shot performance without deteriorating supervised performance.

On the TED59 dataset, we follow Raganato et al. (2021) in comparing against two multilingual model variants: the standard Transformer, and the Transformer with sparse `entmax` instead of standard softmax cross-attention. Our approach gains ~3 BLEU points against the baseline, and 2 BLEU against the stronger contrastive model. Further, our model consistently outperforms strong, explicitly alignment-based methods.

Target-language Accuracy. To supplement the evaluation, we provide the accuracy score for target language identification[6] in zero-shot scenarios, called Acc_O. While the classical many-to-many NMT models (Johnson et al., 2017; Aharoni et al., 2019) enable zero-shot translations, several studies have shown that these models fail to reliably generalize to unseen language pairs, ending up with an *off-target* translation issue (Zhang et al., 2020). The model ignores the language label and the wrong target language is produced as a result. We observe significant improvements in target language accuracy, up to nearly 99% (absolute).

4 Analysis

Ablation Study. Table 3 reports ablations on the IWSLT17 test set. We find that kNN embeddings alone yield improvements over the baseline many-to-many model. By contrast, absent the other parts of our model, the attentional semantic layer *deteriorates* model performance. Only in combination with the agreement loss do we observe a benefit from this component.

Embedding Analysis. Figure 3 visualizes subword representations from models trained on IWSLT17. Each subword is colored according to the language in which it is most frequent. The overall layout of the two spaces is similar, although the

[5] We use asymmetric hashing with 2-dimensional blocks and a quantization threshold of 0.2, and re-order the top 100 ANN candidates.

[6] We utilize FastText (Joulin et al., 2017) as a language identification tool to compare the translation language with the reference target language and keep count of the number of matches.

ID	Component	dev.2010	test.2010
1	many-to-many (zero-shot)	15.95	18.46
2	① + attn. semantic repr.	15.43	17.83
3	① + kNN embeds	17.11	19.69
4	② + kNN embeds	16.60	19.08
5	③ + agreement loss	17.99	20.91
6	④ + agreement loss	**18.31**	**21.01**

Table 3: Effect of different components of our model on the IWSLT17 datasets. We report sacreBLEU scores on the two official validation sets with beam size 1.

baseline model (left) exhibits a clear ring-shaped gap dividing the embeddings into two groups. With ANN embeddings (right), this gap is eliminated and the layout of the embeddings appears more homogeneous. Quantitatively, the average distance from a subword to its neighbors exhibits a smaller variance in the ANN model than in the baseline, which further supports the reading that ANN training creates a more homogeneous representation space in which subwords are more uniformly distributed.

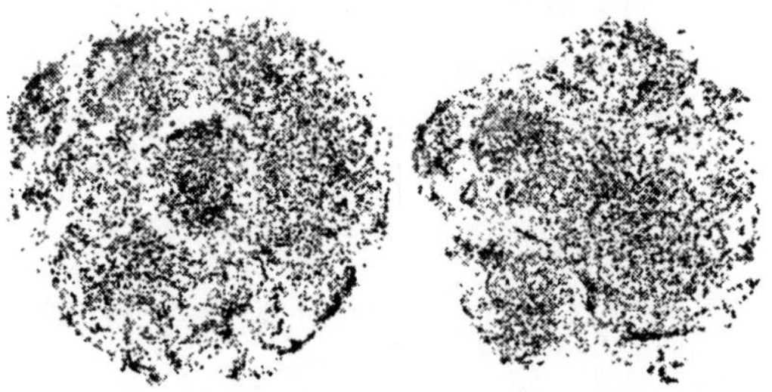

Figure 3: t-SNE visualization of subword embeddings from IWSLT17 models trained without (left) and with (right) ANN embeddings. Points are colored according to the language where the corresponding subword is most frequent. ANN embeddings decrease the separation between some monolingual subspaces, and remove others entirely.

Table 4 shows nearest neighbors for a random sample of subwords (additional examples in Table 5 in Appendix B). With ANN training, a subword's nearest neighbors are generally its synonyms (e.g. `_wonderful`, `_large` `_tremendous`, and `_big` as neighbors to `_great`) or derived forms (e.g. `_încep`, `_începem`, `_început`, `_începe` beside `_înceap`). In the baseline, it is more likely to find neighbors with no apparent relation, such as `_erzählen` 'tell' and `_stemmen` 'hoist' or 'accomplish' beside `_America`. This suggests that ANN embeddings help a model to better organize its subword embedding space into coherent, semantically-related subspaces.

We quantify this trend by labeling each subword according to the language in which it is most frequently attested. In the baseline model, we find that on average only 2.7 of a subword's 6 nearest neighbors come from the same language as that subword. This average rises to 3.6 in the ANN model, demonstrating that ANN training significantly increases the number of same-language neighbors on average.

In the ANN model, a few rare subwords ($\surd$, ž, ĉ) are disproportionately common among the nearest neighbors of many other subwords. We speculate that these tokens may act as pivots for information to flow between their many neighbours. Their high centrality means that these tokens provide avenues for information to flow between a large number of subwords, even those which never occur in sentences together. Because these tokens are rare, there is also very little penalty for the model to "corrupt" their representations with information from neighboring subwords.

5 Other Related Work

A vast body of work addresses zero-shot translation. Most methods focus on producing language-agnostic encoder outputs (Pham et al., 2019). Wei et al. (2021) introduce multilingual contrastive learning, while Yang et al. (2021) adopt auxiliary target language prediction. To enable the input tokens to be positioned without constraints, Liu et al. (2021) eliminate the residual connections within a middle layer of the encoder. Yang et al. (2022); Gu and Feng (2022) employ optimal transport to improve contextual cross-alignments, in contrast to our method which performs *soft*, non-contextual alignment between subwords in the continuously-updating embedding space. Other methods extend the training data using monolingual data (Al-Shedivat and Parikh, 2019) to pretrain the decoder (Gu et al., 2019), and random-online backtranslation (Zhang et al., 2020). Lin et al. (2021); Reid and Artetxe (2022) use dictionary based alignments to produce pseudo-cross-lingual sentences. Other approaches that enhance token level representations include multiple subword segmentations (Wu et al., 2020; Kambhatla et al., 2022a), enciphered source text (Kambhatla et al., 2022b) and stroke sequence modelling (Wang et al., 2022). While all these techniques rely on multilingual training paradigm for machine translation, they either rely on external data and use explicit augmentations. We do not

Subword	**Nearest Neighbors (Baseline)**						**Nearest Neighbors (Ours)**					
_great	_gesproken	_schaffen	ppy	ită	_prosper	_senior	_wonderful	_large	_tremendous	_big	_great	√
_înceapă	_popolare	_condotto	_mişcă	_bekijken	_crească	_creeze	_gepubliceerd	_încep	_începem	_început	_începe	muovono
_America	tate	_erzählen	_stemmen	dine	_facultate	_chestiune	_USA	_Asia	_Africa	_American	_America	ć
_play	_lavori	eranno	_tenuto	_bekijken	-	möglichkeiten	play	_playing	_Play	_played	_play	√
_football	_pesci	bon	_surf	_betrachten	_Hintergrund	möglichkeiten	_weather	_baseball	ball	_montagna	_biodiversità	_football
ing	ificazione	izăm	amento	tung	erende	ende	ling	ting	ung	ž	ingen	ing
_fish	_petrec	schen	_Sachen	_feed	_chestii	möglichkeiten	fisch	_pesce	_pesca	_Fisch	_fish	√

Table 4: Approximate nearest neighbors for a sample of subwords, computed with (right) and without (left) ANN training.

use any external data or explicit alignments and our model can be trained end-to-end like a regular multilingual model.

6 Conclusion

We described a novel approach to harness nearest neighbors at the token level and learn *nearest-neighbour informed word embeddings* for every word in a source language for many-to-many multilingual translation. Our experiments show that this simple yet effective approach results in consistently better zero-shot translations across multiple multilingual datasets. Additionally, our model produces translations in the right target language with high accuracy. Our analysis shows that our model learns to organize subwords into semantically-related neighborhoods, and reduces the separation between monolingual subspaces in the embedding space.

Limitations

While our method is effective in zero-shot settings, we find that it has limited implications in supervised settings. This is because improving zero-shot translation presents a tug-of-war between language-agnostic and language-specific representations, each of which has a distinct effect on the model. Another major downside is reduced training speed relative to the baseline many-to-many model. We note that this is an artifact of the agreement loss (KLDiv.) which entails two forward-passes for each update. Finally, in the present work, we compute k-NNs for every source word in a sentence. Although this has yielded strong results, we would like to explore a more explainable setting where k-NNs can be applied to specific source words. We leave such explorations to future work.

Acknowledgements

We would like to thank the anonymous reviewers for their helpful comments. The research was partially supported by the Natural Sciences and Engineering Research Council of Canada grants NSERC RGPIN-2018-06437 and RGPAS-2018-522574 and a Department of National Defence (DND) and NSERC grant DGDND-2018-00025 to the third author, and by an NSERC award CGSD3-547773-2020 to the second author.

References

Roee Aharoni, Melvin Johnson, and Orhan Firat. 2019. Massively multilingual neural machine translation. In *Proceedings of the 2019 Conference of the North American Chapter of the Association for Computational Linguistics: Human Language Technologies, Volume 1 (Long and Short Papers)*, pages 3874–3884, Minneapolis, Minnesota. Association for Computational Linguistics.

Maruan Al-Shedivat and Ankur Parikh. 2019. Consistency by agreement in zero-shot neural machine translation. In *Proceedings of the 2019 Conference of the North American Chapter of the Association for Computational Linguistics: Human Language Technologies, Volume 1 (Long and Short Papers)*, pages 1184–1197, Minneapolis, Minnesota. Association for Computational Linguistics.

Naveen Arivazhagan, Ankur Bapna, Orhan Firat, Roee Aharoni, Melvin Johnson, and Wolfgang Macherey. 2019. The missing ingredient in zero-shot neural machine translation. *arXiv preprint arXiv:1903.07091*.

Mauro Cettolo, Christian Girardi, and Marcello Federico. 2012. Wit3: Web inventory of transcribed and translated talks. In *Proceedings of the 16th Annual conference of the European Association for Machine Translation*, pages 261–268.

Guanhua Chen, Shuming Ma, Yun Chen, Dongdong Zhang, Jia Pan, Wenping Wang, and Furu Wei. 2022. Towards making the most of cross-lingual transfer for zero-shot neural machine translation. In *Proceedings of the 60th Annual Meeting of the Association for Computational Linguistics (Volume 1: Long Papers)*, pages 142–157, Dublin, Ireland. Association for Computational Linguistics.

Alexis Conneau, Shijie Wu, Haoran Li, Luke Zettlemoyer, and Veselin Stoyanov. 2020. Emerging cross-lingual structure in pretrained language models. In *Proceedings of the 58th Annual Meeting of the Association for Computational Linguistics*, pages 6022–6034, Online. Association for Computational Linguistics.

Xiangyu Duan, Baijun Ji, Hao Jia, Min Tan, Min Zhang, Boxing Chen, Weihua Luo, and Yue Zhang. 2020. Bilingual dictionary based neural machine translation without using parallel sentences. In *Proceedings of the 58th Annual Meeting of the Association for Computational Linguistics*, pages 1570–1579, Online. Association for Computational Linguistics.

Angela Fan, Shruti Bhosale, Holger Schwenk, Zhiyi Ma, Ahmed El-Kishky, Siddharth Goyal, Mandeep Baines, Onur Celebi, Guillaume Wenzek, Vishrav Chaudhary, Naman Goyal, Tom Birch, Vitaliy Liptchinsky, Sergey Edunov, Edouard Grave, Michael Auli, and Armand Joulin. 2022. Beyond english-centric multilingual machine translation. *J. Mach. Learn. Res.*, 22(1).

Orhan Firat, Kyunghyun Cho, and Yoshua Bengio. 2016. Multi-way, multilingual neural machine translation with a shared attention mechanism. In *Proceedings of the 2016 Conference of the North American Chapter of the Association for Computational Linguistics: Human Language Technologies*, pages 866–875, San Diego, California. Association for Computational Linguistics.

Jiatao Gu, Hany Hassan, Jacob Devlin, and Victor O.K. Li. 2018. Universal neural machine translation for extremely low resource languages. In *Proceedings of the 2018 Conference of the North American Chapter of the Association for Computational Linguistics: Human Language Technologies, Volume 1 (Long Papers)*, pages 344–354, New Orleans, Louisiana. Association for Computational Linguistics.

Jiatao Gu, Yong Wang, Kyunghyun Cho, and Victor O.K. Li. 2019. Improved zero-shot neural machine translation via ignoring spurious correlations. In *Proceedings of the 57th Annual Meeting of the Association for Computational Linguistics*, pages 1258–1268, Florence, Italy. Association for Computational Linguistics.

Shuhao Gu and Yang Feng. 2022. Improving zero-shot multilingual translation with universal representations and cross-mappings. In *Proceedings of the EMNLP 2022 Long Findings*.

Ruiqi Guo, Philip Sun, Erik Lindgren, Quan Geng, David Simcha, Felix Chern, and Sanjiv Kumar. 2020. Accelerating large-scale inference with anisotropic vector quantization. In *International Conference on Machine Learning*, pages 3887–3896. PMLR.

Thanh-Le Ha, Jan Niehues, and Alexander Waibel. 2017. Effective strategies in zero-shot neural machine translation. In *Proceedings of the 14th International Conference on Spoken Language Translation*, pages 105–112, Tokyo, Japan. International Workshop on Spoken Language Translation.

Baijun Ji, Zhirui Zhang, Xiangyu Duan, Min Zhang, Boxing Chen, and Weihua Luo. 2020. Cross-lingual pre-training based transfer for zero-shot neural machine translation. In *Proceedings of the AAAI conference on artificial intelligence*, volume 34, pages 115–122.

Melvin Johnson, Mike Schuster, Quoc V. Le, Maxim Krikun, Yonghui Wu, Zhifeng Chen, Nikhil Thorat, Fernanda Viégas, Martin Wattenberg, Greg Corrado, Macduff Hughes, and Jeffrey Dean. 2017. Google's multilingual neural machine translation system: Enabling zero-shot translation. *Transactions of the Association for Computational Linguistics*, 5:339–351.

Armand Joulin, Edouard Grave, Piotr Bojanowski, and Tomas Mikolov. 2017. Bag of tricks for efficient text classification. In *Proceedings of the 15th Conference of the European Chapter of the Association for Computational Linguistics: Volume 2, Short Papers*, pages 427–431, Valencia, Spain. Association for Computational Linguistics.

Nishant Kambhatla, Logan Born, and Anoop Sarkar. 2022a. Auxiliary subword segmentations as related languages for low resource multilingual translation. In *Proceedings of the 23rd Annual Conference of the European Association for Machine Translation*, pages 131–140, Ghent, Belgium. European Association for Machine Translation.

Nishant Kambhatla, Logan Born, and Anoop Sarkar. 2022b. CipherDAug: Ciphertext based data augmentation for neural machine translation. In *Proceedings of the 60th Annual Meeting of the Association for Computational Linguistics (Volume 1: Long Papers)*, pages 201–218, Dublin, Ireland. Association for Computational Linguistics.

Urvashi Khandelwal, Angela Fan, Dan Jurafsky, Luke Zettlemoyer, and Mike Lewis. 2020. Nearest neighbor machine translation. In *International Conference on Learning Representations*.

Urvashi Khandelwal, Omer Levy, Dan Jurafsky, Luke Zettlemoyer, and Mike Lewis. 2019. Generalization through memorization: Nearest neighbor language models. In *International Conference on Learning Representations*.

Yusen Lin, Jiayong Lin, Shuaicheng Zhang, and Haoying Dai. 2021. Bilingual dictionary-based language model pretraining for neural machine translation.

Danni Liu, Jan Niehues, James Cross, Francisco Guzmán, and Xian Li. 2021. Improving zero-shot translation by disentangling positional information. In *Proceedings of the 59th Annual Meeting of the Association for Computational Linguistics and the 11th International Joint Conference on Natural Language Processing (Volume 1: Long Papers)*, pages 1259–1273, Online. Association for Computational Linguistics.

Thang Luong, Hieu Pham, and Christopher D. Manning. 2015. Effective approaches to attention-based neural machine translation. In *Proceedings of the 2015 Conference on Empirical Methods in Natural Language*

Processing, pages 1412–1421, Lisbon, Portugal. Association for Computational Linguistics.

Myle Ott, Sergey Edunov, Alexei Baevski, Angela Fan, Sam Gross, Nathan Ng, David Grangier, and Michael Auli. 2019. fairseq: A fast, extensible toolkit for sequence modeling. In *Proceedings of the 2019 Conference of the North American Chapter of the Association for Computational Linguistics (Demonstrations)*, pages 48–53, Minneapolis, Minnesota. Association for Computational Linguistics.

Xiao Pan, Mingxuan Wang, Liwei Wu, and Lei Li. 2021a. Contrastive learning for many-to-many multilingual neural machine translation. In *Proceedings of ACL 2021*.

Xiao Pan, Mingxuan Wang, Liwei Wu, and Lei Li. 2021b. Contrastive learning for many-to-many multilingual neural machine translation. In *Proceedings of the 59th Annual Meeting of the Association for Computational Linguistics and the 11th International Joint Conference on Natural Language Processing (Volume 1: Long Papers)*, pages 244–258, Online. Association for Computational Linguistics.

Kishore Papineni, Salim Roukos, Todd Ward, and Wei-Jing Zhu. 2002. Bleu: a method for automatic evaluation of machine translation. In *Proceedings of the 40th Annual Meeting of the Association for Computational Linguistics*, pages 311–318, Philadelphia, Pennsylvania, USA. Association for Computational Linguistics.

Ngoc-Quan Pham, Jan Niehues, Thanh-Le Ha, and Alex Waibel. 2019. Improving zero-shot translation with language-independent constraints. In *Proceedings of the Fourth Conference on Machine Translation (Volume 1: Research Papers)*, pages 13–23.

Matt Post. 2018. A call for clarity in reporting BLEU scores. In *Proceedings of the Third Conference on Machine Translation: Research Papers*, pages 186–191, Belgium, Brussels. Association for Computational Linguistics.

Ye Qi, Devendra Sachan, Matthieu Felix, Sarguna Padmanabhan, and Graham Neubig. 2018. When and why are pre-trained word embeddings useful for neural machine translation? In *Proceedings of the 2018 Conference of the North American Chapter of the Association for Computational Linguistics: Human Language Technologies, Volume 2 (Short Papers)*, pages 529–535, New Orleans, Louisiana. Association for Computational Linguistics.

Alessandro Raganato, Raúl Vázquez, Mathias Creutz, and Jörg Tiedemann. 2021. An empirical investigation of word alignment supervision for zero-shot multilingual neural machine translation. In *Proceedings of the 2021 Conference on Empirical Methods in Natural Language Processing*, pages 8449–8456, Online and Punta Cana, Dominican Republic. Association for Computational Linguistics.

Machel Reid and Mikel Artetxe. 2022. PARADISE: Exploiting parallel data for multilingual sequence-to-sequence pretraining. In *Proceedings of the 2022 Conference of the North American Chapter of the Association for Computational Linguistics: Human Language Technologies*, pages 800–810, Seattle, United States. Association for Computational Linguistics.

Rico Sennrich, Barry Haddow, and Alexandra Birch. 2016. Neural machine translation of rare words with subword units. In *Proceedings of the 54th Annual Meeting of the Association for Computational Linguistics (Volume 1: Long Papers)*, pages 1715–1725, Berlin, Germany. Association for Computational Linguistics.

Ashish Vaswani, Noam Shazeer, Niki Parmar, Jakob Uszkoreit, Llion Jones, Aidan N Gomez, Łukasz Kaiser, and Illia Polosukhin. 2017. Attention is all you need. *Advances in neural information processing systems*, 30.

Weizhi Wang, Zhirui Zhang, Yichao Du, Boxing Chen, Jun Xie, and Weihua Luo. 2021. Rethinking zero-shot neural machine translation: From a perspective of latent variables. In *Findings of the Association for Computational Linguistics: EMNLP 2021*, pages 4321–4327, Punta Cana, Dominican Republic. Association for Computational Linguistics.

Xinyi Wang, Hieu Pham, Philip Arthur, and Graham Neubig. 2018. Multilingual neural machine translation with soft decoupled encoding. In *International Conference on Learning Representations*.

Zhijun Wang, Xuebo Liu, and Min Zhang. 2022. Breaking the representation bottleneck of Chinese characters: Neural machine translation with stroke sequence modeling. In *Proceedings of the 2022 Conference on Empirical Methods in Natural Language Processing*, pages 6473–6484, Abu Dhabi, United Arab Emirates. Association for Computational Linguistics.

Xiangpeng Wei, Rongxiang Weng, Yue Hu, Luxi Xing, Heng Yu, and Weihua Luo. 2021. On learning universal representations across languages. In *International Conference on Learning Representations*.

Lijun Wu, Shufang Xie, Yingce Xia, Yang Fan, Jian-Huang Lai, Tao Qin, and Tieyan Liu. 2020. Sequence generation with mixed representations. In *Proceedings of the 37th International Conference on Machine Learning*, volume 119 of *Proceedings of Machine Learning Research*, pages 10388–10398. PMLR.

Shijie Wu, Benjamin Van Durme, and Mark Dredze. 2022. Zero-shot cross-lingual transfer is under-specified optimization. In *Proceedings of the 7th Workshop on Representation Learning for NLP*, pages 236–248, Dublin, Ireland. Association for Computational Linguistics.

Yilin Yang, Akiko Eriguchi, Alexandre Muzio, Prasad Tadepalli, Stefan Lee, and Hany Hassan. 2021. Improving multilingual translation by representation and gradient regularization. In *Proceedings of the 2021 Conference on Empirical Methods in Natural Language Processing*, pages 7266–7279, Online and Punta Cana, Dominican Republic. Association for Computational Linguistics.

Zhe Yang, Qingkai Fang, and Yang Feng. 2022. Low-resource neural machine translation with cross-modal alignment. pages arXiv–2210.

Biao Zhang, Philip Williams, Ivan Titov, and Rico Sennrich. 2020. Improving massively multilingual neural machine translation and zero-shot translation. In *Proceedings of the 58th Annual Meeting of the Association for Computational Linguistics*, pages 1628–1639, Online. Association for Computational Linguistics.

A Reproducibility Details

A.1 Data

IWSLT17 (Cettolo et al., 2012) is an English-centric dataset[7] totalling 1.8M parallel sentences. It has 8 supervised directions to and from German, Italian, Dutch and Romanian, each with about 220,000 parallel sentences, and 12 zero-shot directions. We use the official validation and test sets.

Ted59 (Qi et al., 2018) is a massively multilingual English-centric dataset[8] with 116 translation directions totalling 10.8M parallel sentences. The imbalanced data—from 0.25M to just 2000 parallel samples for some language pairs—makes it ideal to study the effects of our method. Following (Aharoni et al., 2019; Raganato et al., 2021) we evaluate on 16 supervised pairs (Azerbaijani, Belarusian, Galician, Slovak, Arabic, German, Hebrew, and Italian to and from English) and 4 zero-shot (Arabic $\leftrightarrow$ French, Ukranian $\leftrightarrow$ Russian). Note that of these languages, Azerbaijani, Belarusian, Galician, and Slovak are low resource with only 5.9k, 4.5k, 10k and 61.5k paralle samples to/from English.

All settings and baselines use `sentencepiece`[9] for subword tokenization using byte-pair encodings (BPEs; Sennrich et al. 2016) with 32000 merge operations.

A.2 Model and Hyperparameters

All models follow the basic configuration of Vaswani et al. (2017), using the `fairseq` toolkit (Ott et al., 2019) in PyTorch. This includes 6 layers of encoder and eecoder each with 512 dim and 2048 feed-forward dimension. The 512 dim word embedding layer has a vocabulary size of 32000. All word-embeddings in the model (encoder, decoder input/output) are shared, although the latent embedding layer alone is specific to encoder only. This implies that any updates to the actual embedding layer because of k-NN tokens also impacts the decoder.

The *attentional latent semantic representation* layer has 512 dim (same as the embedding layer) and a size $\mathcal{N}$ of 1000 for IWSLT17 (smaller dataset) and 5000 for TED59 (larger dataset). We did not tune this hyperparameter and chose the values based on the size of the datasets. This implies that this layer adds 0.5M trainable parameters to the IWSLT17 model and 2.5M parameters to the TED59 model. However, note that the total trainable parameters are still much lower than that of the baselines – this because our models have shared embedding layers.

We use the Adam optimizer with inverse square root learning scheduling and 6k warm steps, $lr = 0.0007$ and dropout of 0.3 (IWSLT17), or 10k warmup steps, $lr = 0.005$ and dropout of 0.2 (TED59). The batch size is 4096 tokens for each of four A100 GPUs.

We use ScANN (Guo et al., 2020) for efficient ANN search[10] with $k = 3$. To increase training speeds, we cache each subword's ANNs for 400 iterations before recomputing them. We only (peridocally) cache subword IDs: the embedding $\text{EMB}_\mu(\cdot)$ is always computed directly from $\mathcal{W}_{emb}$. The value of λ is set to 0.5 (Equation 1). We follow Kambhatla et al. (2022b) to set the values of α_1, α_2 to 1, and β to 5 (Equation 5).

Evaluation. For evaluation, all translations are generated with beam size 5. We report case-sensitive BLEU scores (Papineni et al., 2002) using `sacreBLEU`[11] (Post, 2018). We report detokenized BLEU for IWSLT17 and tokenized BLEU for TED59 for fair comparison with prior work (Aharoni et al., 2019; Raganato et al., 2021).

B Nearest Neighbor Examples

See Table 5.

[7] `https://wit3.fbk.eu/2017-01`

[8] `github.com/neulab/word-embeddings-for-nmt`

[9] `https://github.com/google/sentencepiece`

[10] `https://github.com/google-research/google-research/tree/master/scann`. We use asymmetric hashing with 2-dimensional blocks and a quantization threshold of 0.2, and re-order the top 100 ANN candidates.

[11] case:mixed|eff:no|tok:13a|smooth:exp|version:2.3.1

Subword	Nearest Neighbors (Baseline)						Nearest Neighbors (Ours)					
_Fisch	_findet	œ	_chestii	_Netz	fisch	möglichkeiten	erei	fisch	_pesca	_fish	_Fisch	ž
schaft	hood	erung	ungen	gaat	_gehabt	schaft	würdig	lichkeit	ship	nisse	äglich	schaft
the	tje	ped	own	asta	by	_solamente	tech	ther	th	by	the	√
_the	isce	izăm	_erzählen	"&	_gehabt	oara	_your	_their	_our	_the	ć	ž
_Music	mat	_cartoon	hood	_connessione	zia	_şcoala	_musica	_music	ž	_Music	dine	ć
_picior	_sfârşit	_plaatje	_mesaj	_teren	_avion	_gehabt	_corpul	_braț	_pagină	_picior	ž	√
ern	eien	iere	eren	erung	_tenuto	_gehabt	uren	ungen	ert	eren	stern	ern
_începă	_popolare	_condotto	_mişcă	_bekijken	_crească	_creeze	_gepubliceerd	_încep	_începem	_început	_începe	muovono
_democrația	analisi	_înțelege	_popolare	izăm	_şcoala	_deshalb	_terorism	muovono	_democratic	dine	_biodiversità	ć
_pure	rische	_giovane	_appena	_tare	\u0e22	_avesse	_semplicemente	_unique	_tragic	_complete	_sole	_pure
_genomic	_finanzia	Â	_popolare	_răspândi	_genomen	möglichkeiten	_electronic	_genome	_robotic	ž	_genetic	_genomic
_Abbiamo	_perciò	_gehabt	_spunem	_condotto	izăm	_avesse	abbiamo	mmo	iamo	_Abbiamo	_abbiamo	ć
izări	amento	isieren	ierung	izzazione	_răspândi	izare	izare	ităţi	aţie	izări	muovono	nelli
_negative	_altele	azioni	iere	_bune	_enormous	oase	_illegal	_alternative	_evil	_positive	_negativ	_negative
_take	_solamente	_gemacht	_spinge	_accompagna	_preso	_tenuto	_takes	_taken	_taking	_took	ć	_take
_muziek	_percorso	_besef	_onderwijs	_erzählen	_vreugde	oara	_music	muovono	_Musik	_musica	_muziek	ć
_Karte	_Bibliothek	_lavori	strategie	_chestii	_cifre	kaart	_Weise	_Sprache	_carta	_montagna	kjes	_Karte
_funcționa	_mişcă	_munci	matig	_realiza	_funcție	_funcționa	_funcționează	_funcționează	_funziona	_funcționa	_funcționa	ć
_național	_popolare	iere	_bază	_condotto	_esențial	_politic	juist	_rural	äglich	_National	_național	_national
_America	tate	_erzählen	_stemmen	dine	_facultate	_chestiune	_USA	_Asia	_Africa	_American	_America	ć

Table 5: Approximate nearest-neighbors for a sample of subwords, computed with (right) and without (left) ANN training.

JHU IWSLT 2023 Multilingual Speech Translation System Description

Henry Li Xinyuan[1*] **Neha Verma**[1*] **Bismarck Bamfo Odoom**[1] **Ujvala Pradeep**[1]
Matthew Wiesner[2] **Sanjeev Khudanpur**[1,2]
[1]Center for Language and Speech Processing, and
[2] Human Language Technology Center of Excellence,
Johns Hopkins University
{xli257, nverma7, bodoom1, upradee1, wiesner, khudanpur}@jhu.edu

Abstract

We describe the Johns Hopkins ACL 60-60 Speech Translation systems submitted to the IWSLT 2023 Multilingual track, where we were tasked to translate ACL presentations from English into 10 languages. We developed cascaded speech translation systems for both the constrained and unconstrained subtracks. Our systems make use of pre-trained models as well as domain-specific corpora for this highly technical evaluation-only task. We find that the specific technical domain which ACL presentations fall into presents a unique challenge for both ASR and MT, and we present an error analysis and an ACL-specific corpus we produced to enable further work in this area.

1 Introduction

In this work, we describe the 2023 JHU 60-60 Multilingual speech translation track submissions and their development (Agarwal et al., 2023; Salesky et al., 2023). This multilingual task involved the translation of ACL conference oral presentations, given in English, into 10 different target languages. High quality translation systems that can assist in translating highly technical and scientific information helps in the dissemination of knowledge to more people, which in turn can help make our field more inclusive and accessible.

We briefly describe the task in Section 2. In Section 3 we describe the collection and preparation of in-domain ACL data to improve ASR and MT performance by addressing the domain-specificity of the task. We then describe our systems in Section 4, including their motivation and design in context of this shared task. Technical details of our experiments are in 5. We present our results and a discussion of our contributions in Section 6.

* Authors contributed equally

2 The Speech Translation of Talks Task

In 2022, the ACL began the 60-60 initiative, a diversity and inclusion initiative to translate the ACL Anthology into 60 languages for its 60th anniversary. The initiative provided evaluation data for the IWSLT 2023 *multilingual track* on *speech translation of talks* from English into 10 major languages.

It was further split into *constrained* and *unconstrained* subtracks. The constrained subtrack allowed the use of only certain datasets and pre-trained models, whereas the unconstrained subtrack had no such restrictions. We submitted systems to both subtracks and describe them in Section 4.

2.1 Evaluation Data

The ACL 60-60 development data provided to participants is composed of the audio of 5 talks, their transcripts, and multi-parallel translations into 10 languages. Each talk is about 12 minutes in length – a total of about an hour of English speech for the entire set. Additionally, participants are provided with the text abstract of each talk taken from the corresponding paper.

The nature of these data presents a few major challenges for speech translation. The ACL is a global community of researchers from many different countries who speak in a variety of accents, which can pose a challenge to even modern day speech recognition systems. Additionally, the content of these talks is highly technical and contains terms and acronyms that are specific to the field. Sentence-level translations of the talks are provided along with unsegmented audio of the full ~12 minute talk. An audio segmentation produced with the SHAS baseline segmentation method (Tsiamas et al., 2022) is also provided.

3 In-domain Data

Utilizing additional in-domain data has been shown to be helpful in improving the performance and

Proceedings of the 20th International Conference on Spoken Language Translation (IWSLT 2023), pages 302–310
July 13-14, 2023

robustness of translation systems. In light of this, we scraped talks and papers from the proceedings and workshops of ACL 2021.

3.1 Data Collection

About 65% of the papers accepted in ACL 2021 have video presentations recorded and uploaded on the ACL website. We scraped 1847 papers and 1193 talks from the proceedings and workshops. The format of the papers and talks are pdf and mp4 respectively. We extract the text from the papers using `pypdf`.[1] The talks are split into 30-second chunks, converted into FLAC format, and resampled to 16KHz. This amounts to about 155 hours of speech and about 200K lines of text. We plan to release the data under a CC BY 4.0 license[2] (same as the license for the ACL talks).

3.2 Data Filtering

To make the corpora (including ACL papers before 2022) useful, we first denoised the data and made it similar to ASR text outputs. A comprehensive list of the filters we applied to the data includes:

- Removing any information past the References section.
- Removing links ("https..").
- Reforming broken words since the text was in a two column format.
- Removing any information before the Abstract section.
- Removing any non alpha-numeric or punctuation characters.
- Removing any lines that start with or that have too many numbers (to account for tables with data).
- Removing any lines with less that 10 characters (number obtained from averaging minimum character length of each sentence in dev data).
- Removing any lines larger than 297 characters (number obtained through a similar process as above).
- Reformatting the data such that it has one sentence per line.

[1] `https://github.com/py-pdf/pypdf`

[2] `https://github.com/IWSLT-23/60_60_data/tree/main/acl_data`

These constraints were applied in order to mimic the text-normalization of the dev data so that these scraped ACL data could be incorporated into our model's source language side.

4 Systems

In this section, we separately describe our unconstrained and constrained submissions. Since we built cascaded models, we describe the automatic speech recognition (ASR) and machine translation (MT) components of each system.

4.1 Unconstrained Subtrack

4.1.1 Automatic Speech Recognition

An important characteristic of ACL presentations is the wide array of accents represented, which reflects the diverse background of NLP researchers. Accent-robust speech recognition continues to present a challenge to the community (Tadimeti et al., 2022; Riviere et al., 2021; Radford et al., 2022).

One model that demonstrated a degree of robustness to accented speech, is Whisper (Radford et al., 2022), an ASR model trained on 680,000 hours of web-crawled data. Its performance on the accented splits of the VoxPopuli (Wang et al., 2021), while significantly worse than non-accented English, was comparable (without an external language model) to methods designed for accent robustness (with a strong language model) (Riviere et al., 2021). This robustness to accented speech, as well as its overall strong performance on English ASR makes it well-suited for the accent-diverse ACL presentations.

The domain specificity and technical terms of ACL presentations may still prove difficult for a strong ASR model like Whisper. We therefore condition the decoder towards key technical vocabulary and named entities by prompting Whisper with the corresponding abstracts when decoding each presentation.

Additionally, we test the effect of using the pre-segmented audio files (with oracle segmentation provided by the IWSLT 60-60 challenge organizers) versus using longer speech segments for Whisper decoding. We find that decoding the full talk at once results in a lower WER than decoding segment-by-segment. For Whisper-large, the best performing model, this difference is 0.6 WER. Longer form inputs more closely match the training segments of Whisper, which were in 30 second segments (Radford et al., 2022).

4.1.2 Audio Segmentation

Since we found that decoding using unsegmented audio outperformed decoding using the predefined segments, we segment our ASR text output in order to perform sentence-level machine translation. We choose to perform sentence-level machine translation rather than incorporating more document context because our final systems make use of many large pre-trained multilingual models that are trained at a sentence level rather than a document level.

Because we require sentence-level segments from our ASR outputs, we use the state-of-the-art `ersatz` neural sentence segmenter. `ersatz` has been shown to be more robust to technical terms including acronyms and irregular punctuation, which is particularly helpful in the ACL domain (Wicks and Post, 2021).

4.1.3 Machine Translation

We test several pre-trained MT systems on our data. Specifically, we test NLLB-200 (NLLB Team et al., 2022), mBART50 (Tang et al., 2020), and M2M100 (Fan et al., 2021). All 10 of our target languages are supported by these models.

The original NLLB-200 model is a 54 billion parameter Mixture-of-Experts model that translates to and from 200 languages. It is trained on a large amount of mined parallel, back-translated, and monolingual data. We use the 3.3B parameter version of NLLB-200, which is a dense Transformer model that is trained via online distillation of the original model, but still supports all of the original 200 languages.

mBART50 is the second iteration of the multilingual BART model, which is a dense transformer architecture trained on multilingual text using a denoising task. The authors of mBART50 also release a checkpoint of mBART50 that is fine-tuned on the one-to-many translation task, which we will refer to as mBART50-1toN. In this case, English is the source, and all 50 covered languages are the targets.

Finally, M2M100 is another transformer-based model that is trained directly on the MT task. It translates to and from 100 languages, and is a previous iteration of the initiative that produced NLLB-200. However, we still test both models because sometimes adding additional language pairs to a model can lead to the reduced performance of some language pairs (Aharoni et al., 2019; Arivazhagan et al., 2019). We use the 1.2B parameter version of M2M100 in our experiments.

4.1.4 Domain-Specific Data

Using the 2021 ACL data described in Section 3, we attempted to perform sequence knowledge distillation (SeqKD) (Kim and Rush, 2016). Because we only had additional source-side monolingual data, SeqKD could give us pseudo-target labels in order to retrain our best model on these outputs.

Although NLLB-200-3.3B is our best model for many of our language pairs, we fine-tune NLLB-200-1.3B instead due to computational constraints. While benchmarking these models, however, there is only a marginal improvement in using the larger model over the smaller (average +0.6 chrF). For en-ja, however, we continue to use mBART50-1toN.

Despite the large amount of in-domain source language data we made available, we did not see much benefit from it ourselves, specifically for data augmentation via SeqKD. We speculate that the data may be too noisy in spite of filtering, and that its best use may be as *source context* during inference, rather than for *training data augmentation*.

4.2 Constrained Subtrack

4.2.1 Automatic Speech Recognition

We leveraged the pre-trained wav2vec 2.0 model (Baevski et al., 2020) for the constrained ST task. Wav2vec 2.0 was trained in a self-supervised fashion and requires fine-tuning on an annotated corpus in order to be used for the ASR task, with the domain-similarity between the choice of the fine-tuning corpus and the evaluation data being crucial for ASR performance. The most commonly used wav2vec 2.0 model is fine-tuned with a CTC objective on Librispeech, a corpus made of audiobooks that is considered to have a considerable domain mismatch compared to the ACL 60-60 data. Since the development split of the ACL 60-60 data alone is insufficient for wav2vec 2.0 fine-tuning, we instead performed a two-stage fine tuning with TED-LIUM 3 (Hernandez et al., 2018) being used in the first stage and the ACL 60-60 development data used in the second.

Our approach to tackling the content domain mismatch between the training data and ACL presentations is to perform ASR decoding with the help of an content-domain matching language model. What it means in practice is that we rescore the per-frame output trellis with a content-domain matching language model, which in turn was created by interpolating a general language model (trained from all the available English corpora in the constrained challenge) and a domain-specific language model (trained with transcripts from the ACL 60-60 development data). In order to bias our model towards named entities mentioned in each specific presentation, we train a separate language model for each presentation by re-interpolating the above-mentioned language model with one trained with the corresponding paper abstract.

4.2.2 Machine Translation

In the constrained setting, we use mBART50-1toN and M2M100 as our base models. We additionally test fine-tuning these models on MuST-C data, which we hypothesized to be closely related to the ACL talk data, domain-wise (Di Gangi et al., 2019). This data is comprised of professionally translated English TED talks, which matches the presentation domain as well as some of the technical nature of the ACL talks, although to a lesser degree.

We fine-tune both mBART and M2M100 using the MuST-C transcripts and translations available in all 10 language pairs. We use data from both v1.2 (v1.0 is contained in v1.2) and v2.0 depending on language pair availability. A summary of this data is provided in Table 1. For mBART, we additionally test multilingual fine-tuning where we fine-tune on all the language pairs simultaneously, rather than fine-tuning on a single language pair bitext (Tang et al., 2020).

lang. pair	MuST-C release	# lines
en-ar	v1.2	212085
en-de	v1.0	229703
en-fa	v1.2	181772
en-fr	v1.0	275085
en-ja	v2.0	328639
en-nl	v1.0	248328
en-pt	v1.0	206155
en-ru	v1.0	265477
en-tr	v1.2	236338
en-zh	v1.2	184801

Table 1: Dataset statistics and source of MuST-C bitext across the 10 task language pairs.

5 Experimental Setup

In this section, we provide technical details of our experiments and our evaluation practices.

5.1 ASR Experiments

5.1.1 Prompting Whisper

In the unconstrained setting, we evaluate Whisper on both the segmented and unsegmented audio files. We simulate LM biasing by using the "prompt" interface provided by Whisper.

5.1.2 Decoding with an Interpolated Language Model

In the constrained setting, we build a domain-adapted language model as follows: first we combine transcripts from a number of ASR corpora that are available in the constrained challenge, namely Librispeech, VoxPopuli, Common Voice (Ardila et al., 2020), and TED-LIUM 3, to train a flexible 6-gram general bpe-level language model for English. We proceed to interpolate the general English language model with one trained on the development split transcripts from the ACL 60-60 challenge, allowing the model to gain exposure to technical terms within the NLP field. Finally, during decoding, we further interpolate the previously obtained language model with a low-order language model trained from the paper abstract corresponding to the current presentation, biasing our model towards technical terms and named entities that are likely to appear in the presentation.

We used KenLM (Heafield, 2011) to train and integrate our language models. The interpolation weights for each step were estimated using a leave-one-out strategy on the development split, minimising the perplexity on the held-out transcript and averaging the interpolation weights.

5.1.3 Decoding with a Language Model Trained on Additional ACL Anthology data

We use the text scraped from the proceedings and workshops of ACL 2021 to train a 6-gram domain-matching language model for decoding. Without interpolation or additional data, this gives a WER of 18.9 and a technical term recall of 0.47 using Wav2Vec2-TED-LIUM 3 as the acoustic model. We observe that using data from a similar domain improves performance even though the data are relatively noisy.

5.1.4 Evaluation

We compare ASR performance, as measured by Word Error Rate (WER), across the different systems that we built. Specifically, we compute WER on depunctuated lowercase transcripts. Since we

Acoustic Model	Language Model	WER	Tech. Term Recall
Whisper-medium.en	-	8.1	0.861
Whisper-medium.en	abstract prompting	8.7	0.865
Whisper-large	-	6.8	0.854
Whisper-large	abstract prompting	6.9	0.852
Whisper-large	abstract and conclusion prompting	6.7	0.863
Whisper-large	abstract, conclusion and intro prompting	6.6	0.851
Whisper-large	abstract, conclusion, intro & author name prompting	6.4	0.854
Wav2Vec2-960h librispeech	librispeech-4gram	25.1	0.306
Wav2Vec2-960h librispeech	interpolated LM	24.3	0.370
Wav2Vec2-960h librispeech	inter. LM + dev transcripts	24.1	0.382
Wav2Vec2-960h librispeech	inter. LM + dev + abstract	23.7	0.392
Wav2Vec2-960h librispeech	inter. LM + dev + abstract + ACL anthology	20.7	0.462
HUBERT-960h librispeech	librispeech-4gram	22.0	0.390
HUBERT-960h librispeech	interpolated LM	21.7	0.386
HUBERT-960h librispeech	inter. LM + dev transcripts	20.4	0.421
HUBERT-960h librispeech	inter. LM + dev + abstract	20.4	0.498
HUBERT-960h librispeech	inter. LM + dev + abstract + ACL anthology	18.5	0.473
Wav2Vec2-TED-LIUM 3	librispeech-4gram	20.9	0.383
Wav2Vec2-TED-LIUM 3	interpolated LM	19.5	0.422
Wav2Vec2-TED-LIUM 3	inter. LM + dev transcripts	18.9	0.436
Wav2Vec2-TED-LIUM 3	inter. LM + dev + abstract	14.2	0.626
Wav2Vec2-TED-LIUM 3	inter. LM + dev + abstract + ACL anthology	16.7	0.505
Wav2Vec2-TED-LIUM 3	ACL anthology only	18.9	0.470

Table 2: ASR results. WER is measured against depunctuated, all lower-case reference text.

either perform ASR on unsegmented talks (unconstrainted), or on the SHAS-segmented audio (constrained), we use `mwerSegmenter` to align our outputs to the gold transcripts (Matusov et al., 2005).

Because we are interested in the effect of using domain-specific text to improve ASR on technical terms, we compute the recall of NLP-specific technical words in our output. We obtain these technical terms by asking domain experts to flag all technical terms in the development set reference transcript.

5.2 MT Experiments

5.2.1 MuST-C fine-tuning

For bilingual fine-tuning on mBART50 and M2M100, we train for 40K updates, and use loss to select the best checkpoint. For multilingual fine-tuning on mBART50-1toN, we train for 100K updates, and use temperature sampling of the mixed datset using $T = 1.5$. We use loss to select the best checkpoint. For all experiments, we use an effective batch size of 2048 tokens.

5.2.2 Evaluation

For all experiments, we report BLEU and chrF scores as reported by `sacrebleu` (Post, 2018). For Japanese and Chinese, we use the appropriate tokenizers provided by `sacrebleu` (`ja-mecab` and `zh`, respectively).

For evaluating translations of ASR outputs, either segmented using `ersatz` or pre-segmented using the provided SHAS-segmented wav files, we use the `mwerSegmenter` to resegment the translations based on the references. For all languages except Japanese and Chinese, we use detokenized text as input to resegmentation. However, for Japanese and Chinese, we first use whitespace tokenization as input to `mwerSegmenter`, and then detokenize for scoring, which is retokenized according to the `sacrebleu` package.

6 Results

6.1 ASR Results

For the Whisper-based systems, we focus on the effects of prompting; for the constrained systems, we contrast different families of pre-trained ASR models fine-tuned on different ASR corpora; finally, we assess the efficacy of incorporating an in-domain language model during decoding. The full list of results is shown in Table 2.

Contrary to what we expected, prompting Whisper with the corresponding paper abstracts not only had little impact on the ASR WER, but also failed

	mBART50-1toN		M2M100		NLLB-200	
language pair	BLEU	chrF	BLEU	chrF	BLEU	chrF
en-ar	22.6	52.9	16.2	46.3	37.6	**65.4**
en-de	37.4	66.0	39.7	66.8	42.9	**69.6**
en-fa	17.2	49.6	20.4	49.5	27.4	**57.3**
en-fr	46.4	70.4	54.5	74.6	55.9	**76.2**
en-ja	37.5	**45.9**	35.2	43.8	25.7	36.3
en-nl	41.0	69.0	50.9	75.3	51.5	**76.1**
en-pt	44.3	69.7	57.6	77.4	61.6	**79.0**
en-ru	22.2	52.0	24.3	54.3	27.4	**57.2**
en-tr	15.5	50.7	22.3	56.5	28.6	**62.8**
en-zh	43.8	38.8	45.7	**40.7**	42.2	38.5

Table 3: Unconstrained MT results on the development set using oracle transcripts as input. Both chrF and BLEU scores are computed using the mWER Segmenter and sacrebleu. BLEU scores for ja and zh are computed using the ja-mecab and zh tokenizers in sacrebleu, respectively. We bold our best chrF scores as it is the main metric of the task.

	mBART50-1toN		+MuST-C (indiv)		+MuST-C (multi)		M2M-100		+MuST-C (indiv)	
lang pair	BLEU	chrF	BLEU	chrF	BLEU	chrF	BLEU	chrF	BLEU	chrF
en-ar	22.6	52.9	24.7	**55.9**	19.6	51.0	16.2	46.3	24.0	55.7
en-de	37.4	66.0	35.6	63.7	36.8	64.5	39.7	**66.8**	34.7	62.8
en-fa	17.2	49.6	28.9	**56.0**	26.3	52.4	20.4	49.5	17.9	54.4
en-fr	46.4	70.4	48.0	70.9	46.7	70.1	54.5	**74.6**	49.0	71.1
en-ja	37.5	**45.9**	24.0	35.7	24.9	37.0	35.2	43.8	21.0	32.3
en-nl	41.0	69.0	43.3	70.1	38.5	67.1	50.9	**75.3**	42.1	69.0
en-pt	44.3	69.7	48.2	71.4	42.8	68.5	57.6	**77.4**	50.0	72.3
en-ru	22.2	52.0	21.0	50.4	19.5	47.9	24.3	**54.3**	22.1	50.7
en-tr	15.5	50.7	18.9	53.3	15.6	50.8	22.3	**56.5**	21.4	56.0
en-zh	43.8	38.8	45.3	40.6	31.5	39.2	45.7	**40.7**	42.8	37.5

Table 4: Constrained MT results on the development set using oracle transcripts as input. Both chrF and BLEU scores are computed using the mWER Segmenter and sacrebleu. BLEU scores for ja and zh are computed using the ja-mecab and zh tokenizers in sacrebleu, respectively. We bold our best chrF scores as it is the main metric of the task.

to improve the recall of technical terms of the ASR system. Further increasing the length and relevance of the prompts provided to whisper, such as adding the conclusion and part of the introduction section of each paper corresponding to the ACL presentation in question, had marginal impact on both of the above-mentioned metrics. A more detailed look at the mechanism and behaviour of Whisper prompting could help to understand this observation.

On the constrained side, the incorporation of the interpolated LM during ASR decoding had a significant impact on the performance of our ASR systems, regardless of the upstream acoustic model. As expected, increasing the quality of the out-of-domain language model (from Librispeech-4gram to Interpolated LM) resulted in WER improvements while not necessarily helping technical term recall; by contrast, while LMs that better fit the domain may not necessarily help WER, they bring substantial gains in technical term recall.

The language model that best fits our domain, namely the model that interpolates the LMs trained from every ASR corpus in addition to the development transcripts, from the current paper abstract, and from the crawled ACL anthology, provided substantial improvement on both WER and technical term recall for the weaker acoustic models (Wav2Vec2 fine-tuned on Librispeech) but not on

	Constrained			Unconstrained		
language	MT system	BLEU	chrF	MT system	BLEU	chrF
en-ar	mBART50-1toN+MuST-C	15.3	45.6	NLLB-200-3.3B	33.7	62.5
en-de	M2M100	24.3	55.2	NLLB-200-3.3B	39.6	67.8
en-fa	mBART50-1toN+MuST-C	14.8	42.0	NLLB-200-3.3B	24.5	54.3
en-fr	M2M100	33.3	61.9	NLLB-200-3.3B	49.3	72.5
en-ja	mBART50-1toN	21.9	29.9	mBART50-1toN	34.8	43.1
en-nl	M2M100	30.6	62.5	NLLB-200-3.3B	45.7	72.4
en-pt	M2M100	34.9	63.4	NLLB-200-3.3B	54.7	75.6
en-ru	M2M100	15.0	45.1	NLLB-200-3.3B	24.8	54.4
en-tr	M2M100	11.9	43.5	NLLB-200-3.3B	24.7	58.8
en-zh	M2M100	32.2	26.6	M2M100	37.7	33.5

Table 5: Final speech translation results for both our constrained and unconstrained systems on the development set. Both chrF and BLEU scores are computed using the mWER Segmenter and `sacrebleu`. BLEU scores for ja and zh are computed using the ja-mecab and zh tokenizers in `sacrebleu`, respectively. We used output from our strongest ASR system, Whisper-large with abstract prompting, as the input to our translation system.

the stronger acoustic models.

6.2 MT results

We detail the results of testing pre-trained MT models as described in Section 4 on the oracle transcripts in Table 3. This table reflects experiments we performed for the unconstrained setting. We find that for almost all language pairs, NLLB-200-3.3B has the best performance, except for en-ja and en-zh, which perform best with mBART and M2M100, respectively.

We summarize our fine-tuning results in Table 4. This table reflects experiments we performed for the constrained setting. We find that in general, the additional data can provide a boost over mBART50-1toN, but not for M2M100. Additionally, we find that despite positive results in Tang et al. (2020), multilingual fine-tuning does not outperform bilingual fine-tuning in this setting. For a majority of pairs, M2M100 without fine-tuning is the best system, but for en-ar and en-fa, mBART50-1toN with fine-tuning is the best system, and similar to the unconstrained system, mBART50-1toN without fine-tuning is the best system for en-ja.

6.3 ST Results

Final results for both our constrained and unconstrained systems are summarized in Table 5. We translate the transcripts from our best ASR systems using the best language-pair specific MT systems. In the unconstrained case, the average reduction in chrF from using ASR outputs versus oracle transcripts is -5.7 chrF. In the constrained case, this value is -12.8 chrF. The small reduction in the unconstrained system indicates that our cascaded approach of two strong components is a viable option for ST in this setting. However, our constrained system could likely benefit from techniques that help reduce the error propagation from ASR, like mixing ASR outputs with gold source sentences during MT training, or joint training of ASR and MT components.

7 Conclusion

We present a constrained and unconstrained system for the IWSLT 2023 Multilingual speech translation task. We address some of the major challenges of this dataset with our design choices: ASR robust to speaker accents, adaptation to match the domain specificity, and ASR prompting to incorporate context in this academic talk-level translation task. We additionally release a supplemental ACL audio and text corpus to encourage further work in high quality speech translation of ACL content.

References

Milind Agarwal, Sweta Agrawal, Antonios Anastasopoulos, Ondřej Bojar, Claudia Borg, Marine Carpuat, Roldano Cattoni, Mauro Cettolo, Mingda Chen, William Chen, Khalid Choukri, Alexandra Chronopoulou, Anna Currey, Thierry Declerck, Qianqian Dong, Yannick Estève, Kevin Duh, Marcello Federico, Souhir Gahbiche, Barry Haddow, Benjamin Hsu, Phu Mon Htut, Hirofumi Inaguma, Dávid Javorský, John Judge, Yasumasa Kano, Tom Ko, Rishu Kumar, Pengwei Li, Xutai Ma, Prashant Mathur, Evgeny Matusov, Paul McNamee, John P. McCrae, Kenton Murray, Maria Nadejde, Satoshi Nakamura, Matteo Negri, Ha Nguyen, Jan Niehues, Xing Niu, Atul Ojha Kr., John E. Ortega, Proyag Pal, Juan Pino, Lonneke van der Plas, Peter Polák, Elijah Rippeth, Elizabeth Salesky, Jiatong Shi, Matthias Sperber, Sebastian Stüker, Katsuhito Sudoh, Yun Tang, Brian Thompson, Kevin Tran, Marco Turchi, Alex Waibel, Mingxuan Wang, Shinji Watanabe, and Rodolfo Zevallos. 2023. Findings of the IWSLT 2023 Evaluation Campaign. In *Proceedings of the 20th International Conference on Spoken Language Translation (IWSLT 2023)*. Association for Computational Linguistics.

Roee Aharoni, Melvin Johnson, and Orhan Firat. 2019. Massively multilingual neural machine translation. In *Proceedings of the 2019 Conference of the North American Chapter of the Association for Computational Linguistics: Human Language Technologies, Volume 1 (Long and Short Papers)*, pages 3874–3884, Minneapolis, Minnesota. Association for Computational Linguistics.

Rosana Ardila, Megan Branson, Kelly Davis, Michael Kohler, Josh Meyer, Michael Henretty, Reuben Morais, Lindsay Saunders, Francis Tyers, and Gregor Weber. 2020. Common voice: A massively-multilingual speech corpus. In *Proceedings of the Twelfth Language Resources and Evaluation Conference*, pages 4218–4222, Marseille, France. European Language Resources Association.

Naveen Arivazhagan, Ankur Bapna, Orhan Firat, Dmitry Lepikhin, Melvin Johnson, Maxim Krikun, Mia Xu Chen, Yuan Cao, George Foster, Colin Cherry, et al. 2019. Massively multilingual neural machine translation in the wild: Findings and challenges. *arXiv preprint arXiv:1907.05019*.

Alexei Baevski, Yuhao Zhou, Abdelrahman Mohamed, and Michael Auli. 2020. wav2vec 2.0: A framework for self-supervised learning of speech representations. In *Advances in Neural Information Processing Systems*, volume 33, pages 12449–12460. Curran Associates, Inc.

Mattia A. Di Gangi, Roldano Cattoni, Luisa Bentivogli, Matteo Negri, and Marco Turchi. 2019. MuST-C: a Multilingual Speech Translation Corpus. In *Proceedings of the 2019 Conference of the North American Chapter of the Association for Computational Linguistics: Human Language Technologies, Volume 1 (Long and Short Papers)*, pages 2012–2017, Minneapolis, Minnesota. Association for Computational Linguistics.

Angela Fan, Shruti Bhosale, Holger Schwenk, Zhiyi Ma, Ahmed El-Kishky, Siddharth Goyal, Mandeep Baines, Onur Celebi, Guillaume Wenzek, Vishrav Chaudhary, et al. 2021. Beyond english-centric multilingual machine translation. *The Journal of Machine Learning Research*, 22(1):4839–4886.

Kenneth Heafield. 2011. KenLM: Faster and smaller language model queries. In *Proceedings of the Sixth Workshop on Statistical Machine Translation*, pages 187–197, Edinburgh, Scotland. Association for Computational Linguistics.

François Hernandez, Vincent Nguyen, Sahar Ghannay, Natalia A. Tomashenko, and Yannick Estève. 2018. TED-LIUM 3: twice as much data and corpus repartition for experiments on speaker adaptation. *CoRR*, abs/1805.04699.

Yoon Kim and Alexander M. Rush. 2016. Sequence-level knowledge distillation. In *Proceedings of the 2016 Conference on Empirical Methods in Natural Language Processing*, pages 1317–1327, Austin, Texas. Association for Computational Linguistics.

Evgeny Matusov, Gregor Leusch, Oliver Bender, and Hermann Ney. 2005. Evaluating machine translation output with automatic sentence segmentation. In *Proceedings of the Second International Workshop on Spoken Language Translation*, Pittsburgh, Pennsylvania, USA.

NLLB Team, Marta R. Costa-jussà, James Cross, Onur Çelebi, Maha Elbayad, Kenneth Heafield, Kevin Heffernan, Elahe Kalbassi, Janice Lam, Daniel Licht, Jean Maillard, Anna Sun, Skyler Wang, Guillaume Wenzek, Al Youngblood, Bapi Akula, Loic Barrault, Gabriel Mejia-Gonzalez, Prangthip Hansanti, John Hoffman, Semarley Jarrett, Kaushik Ram Sadagopan, Dirk Rowe, Shannon Spruit, Chau Tran, Pierre Andrews, Necip Fazil Ayan, Shruti Bhosale, Sergey Edunov, Angela Fan, Cynthia Gao, Vedanuj Goswami, Francisco Guzmán, Philipp Koehn, Alexandre Mourachko, Christophe Ropers, Safiyyah Saleem, Holger Schwenk, and Jeff Wang. 2022. No language left behind: Scaling human-centered machine translation.

Matt Post. 2018. A call for clarity in reporting BLEU scores. In *Proceedings of the Third Conference on Machine Translation: Research Papers*, pages 186–191, Brussels, Belgium. Association for Computational Linguistics.

Alec Radford, Jong Wook Kim, Tao Xu, Greg Brockman, Christine McLeavey, and Ilya Sutskever. 2022. Robust speech recognition via large-scale weak supervision. *arXiv preprint arXiv:2212.04356*.

Morgane Riviere, Jade Copet, and Gabriel Synnaeve. 2021. Asr4real: An extended benchmark for speech models. *arXiv preprint arXiv:2110.08583*.

Elizabeth Salesky, Kareem Darwish, Mohamed Al-Badrashiny, Mona Diab, and Jan Niehues. 2023. Evaluating Multilingual Speech Translation Under Realistic Conditions with Resegmentation and Terminology. In *Proceedings of the 20th International Conference on Spoken Language Translation (IWSLT 2023)*. Association for Computational Linguistics.

Divya Tadimeti, Kallirroi Georgila, and David Traum. 2022. Evaluation of off-the-shelf speech recognizers on different accents in a dialogue domain. In *Proceedings of the Thirteenth Language Resources and Evaluation Conference*, pages 6001–6008, Marseille, France. European Language Resources Association.

Yuqing Tang, Chau Tran, Xian Li, Peng-Jen Chen, Naman Goyal, Vishrav Chaudhary, Jiatao Gu, and Angela Fan. 2020. Multilingual translation with extensible multilingual pretraining and finetuning. *arXiv preprint arXiv:2008.00401*.

Ioannis Tsiamas, Gerard I. Gállego, José A. R. Fonollosa, and Marta R. Costa-jussà. 2022. SHAS: Approaching optimal Segmentation for End-to-End Speech Translation. In *Proc. Interspeech 2022*, pages 106–110.

Changhan Wang, Morgane Riviere, Ann Lee, Anne Wu, Chaitanya Talnikar, Daniel Haziza, Mary Williamson, Juan Pino, and Emmanuel Dupoux. 2021. VoxPopuli: A large-scale multilingual speech corpus for representation learning, semi-supervised learning and interpretation. In *Proceedings of the 59th Annual Meeting of the Association for Computational Linguistics and the 11th International Joint Conference on Natural Language Processing (Volume 1: Long Papers)*, pages 993–1003, Online. Association for Computational Linguistics.

Rachel Wicks and Matt Post. 2021. A unified approach to sentence segmentation of punctuated text in many languages. In *Proceedings of the 59th Annual Meeting of the Association for Computational Linguistics and the 11th International Joint Conference on Natural Language Processing (Volume 1: Long Papers)*, pages 3995–4007, Online. Association for Computational Linguistics.

The NPU-MSXF Speech-to-Speech Translation System for IWSLT 2023 Speech-to-Speech Translation Task

Kun Song[1]**, Yi Lei**[1]**, Peikun Chen**[1]**, Yiqing Cao**[2]**, Kun Wei**[1]**, Yongmao Zhang**[1]**,**
Lei Xie[1*]**, Ning Jiang**[3]**, Guoqing Zhao**[3]
[1]Audio, Speech and Language Processing Group (ASLP@NPU),
School of Computer Science, Northwestern Polytechnical University, China
[2]Department of Computer Science and Technology, Nanjing University, China
[3]MaShang Consumer Finance Co., Ltd, China

Abstract

This paper describes the NPU-MSXF system for the IWSLT 2023 speech-to-speech translation (S2ST) task which aims to translate from English speech of multi-source to Chinese speech. The system is built in a cascaded manner consisting of automatic speech recognition (ASR), machine translation (MT), and text-to-speech (TTS). We make tremendous efforts to handle the challenging multi-source input. Specifically, to improve the robustness to multi-source speech input, we adopt various data augmentation strategies and a ROVER-based score fusion on multiple ASR model outputs. To better handle the noisy ASR transcripts, we introduce a three-stage fine-tuning strategy to improve translation accuracy. Finally, we build a TTS model with high naturalness and sound quality, which leverages a two-stage framework, using network bottleneck features as a robust intermediate representation for speaker timbre and linguistic content disentanglement. Based on the two-stage framework, pre-trained speaker embedding is leveraged as a condition to transfer the speaker timbre in the source English speech to the translated Chinese speech. Experimental results show that our system has high translation accuracy, speech naturalness, sound quality, and speaker similarity. Moreover, it shows good robustness to multi-source data.

1 Introduction

In this paper, we describe NPU-MSXF team's cascaded speech-to-speech translation (S2ST) system submitted to the speech-to-speech (S2S) track[1] of the IWSLT 2023 evaluation campaign. The S2S track aims to build an offline system that realizes speech-to-speech translation from English to Chinese. Particularly, the track allows the use of large-scale data, including the data provided in this track as well as all training data from the offline track[2] on speech-to-text translation task. Challengingly, the test set contains multi-source speech data, covering a variety of acoustic conditions and speaking styles, designed to examine the robustness of the S2ST system. Moreover, speaker identities conveyed in the diverse multi-source speech test data are unseen during training, which is called *zero-shot S2ST* and better meets the demands of real-world applications.

Current mainstream S2ST models usually include *cascaded* and *end-to-end* systems. Cascaded S2ST systems, widely used in the speech-to-speech translation task (Nakamura et al., 2006), usually contain three modules, i.e. automatic speech recognition (ASR), machine translation (MT), and text-to-speech (TTS). Meanwhile, end-to-end (E2E) S2ST systems (Jia et al., 2019; Lee et al., 2022) have recently come to the stage by integrating the above modules into a unified model for directly synthesizing target language speech translated from the source language. E2E S2ST systems can effectively simplify the overall pipeline and alleviate possible error propagation. Cascaded S2ST systems may also alleviate the error propagation problem by leveraging the ASR outputs for MT model fine-tuning. Meanwhile, thanks to the individual training process of sub-modules, cascaded systems can make better use of large-scale text and speech data, which can significantly promote the performance of each module.

In this paper, we build a cascaded S2ST system aiming at English-to-Chinese speech translation with preserving the speaker timbre of the source English speech. The proposed system consists of Conformer-based (Gulati et al., 2020) ASR models, a pretrain-finetune schema-based MT model (Radford et al., 2018), and a VITS-based TTS model (Kim et al., 2021). For ASR, model fusion and data augmentation strategies are adopted to improve the recognition accuracy and generalization ability of ASR with multi-source input.

*Lei Xie is the corresponding author.

[1]https://iwslt.org/2023/s2s

[2]https://iwslt.org/2023/offline

Proceedings of the 20th International Conference on Spoken Language Translation (IWSLT 2023), pages 311–320
July 13-14, 2023 ©2023 Association for Computational Linguistics

For MT, we use a three-stage fine-tuning process to adapt the translation model to better facilitate the output of ASR. Meanwhile, back translation and multi-fold verification strategies are adopted. Our TTS module is composed of a text-to-BN stage and a BN-to-speech stage, where speaker-independent neural bottleneck (BN) features are utilized as an intermediate representation bridging the two stages. Specifically, the BN-to-speech module, conditioned on speaker embedding extracted from the source speech, is to synthesize target language speech with preserving the speaker timbre. Combined with a pre-trained speaker encoder to provide speaker embeddings, the TTS model can be generalized to unseen speakers, who are not involved in the training process. Experimental results demonstrate the proposed S2ST system achieves good speech intelligibility, naturalness, sound quality, and speaker similarity.

2 Automatic Speech Recognition

Our ASR module employs multiple models for score fusion in the inference. Moreover, data augmentation is adopted during training to handle noisy multi-source speech.

2.1 Model Structure

Our system employs both Conformer (Gulati et al., 2020) and E-Branchformer models (Kim et al., 2023) in our ASR module to address the diversity of the test set. Conformer sequentially combines convolution, self-attention, and feed-forward layers. The self-attention module serves to capture global contextual information from the input speech, while the convolution layer focuses on extracting local correlations. This model has demonstrated remarkable performance in ASR tasks with the ability to capture local and global information from input speech signals. E-Branchformer uses dedicated branches of convolution and self-attention based on the Conformer and applies efficient merging methods, in addition to stacking point-wise modules. E-Branchformer achieves state-of-the-art results in ASR.

2.2 Data Augmentation

Considering the diversity of the testing data, we leverage a variety of data augmentation strategies to expand the training data of our ASR system, including the following aspects.

- **Speed Perturbation**: We notice that the testing set contains spontaneous speech such as conversations with various speaking speeds. So speed perturbation is adopted to improve the generalization ability of the proposed model. Speed perturbation is the process of changing the speed of an audio signal while preserving other information (including pitch) in the audio. We perturb the audio speech with a speed factor of 0.9, 1.0, and 1.1 to all the training data. Here speed factor refers to the ratio compared to the original speed of speech.
- **Pitch Shifting**: Pitch shifting can effectively vary the speaker identities to increase data diversity. Specifically, we use SoX[3] audio manipulation tool to perturb the pitch in the range [-40, 40].
- **Noise Augmentation**: There are many cases with heavy background noise in the test set, including interfering speakers and music. However, the data set provided by the organizer is much cleaner than the test set, which makes it necessary to augment the training data by adding noises to improve the recognition performance. Since there is no noise set available, we create a noise set from the data provided. A statistical VAD (Sohn et al., 1999) is used to cut the non-vocal and vocal segments from the data and the non-vocal segments with energy beyond a threshold comprise our noise set. We add the noise segments to the speech utterances with a signal-to-noise ratio ranging from 0 to 15 dB.
- **Audio Codec**: Considering the test data come from multiple sources, we further adopt audio codec augmentation to the training data. Specifically, we use the FFmpeg[4] tool to convert the original audio to Opus format at [48, 96, 256] Kbps.
- **Spectrum Augmentation**: To prevent the ASR model from over-fitting, we apply the SpecAugment method (Park et al., 2019) to the input features during every mini-batch training. SpecAugment includes time warping, frequency channel masking, and time step masking, and we utilize all of these techniques during training.

2.3 Model Fusion

Since a single ASR model may overfit to a specific optimization direction during training, it cannot guarantee good recognition accuracy for the

[3]https://sox.sourceforge.net/
[4]https://ffmpeg.org/

speech of various data distributions. To let the ASR model generalize better to the multi-source input, we adopt a model fusion strategy. Specifically, we train the Conformer and E-branchformer models introduced in Section 2.1 using the combination of the original and the augmented data. Each testing utterance is then transcribed by these different models, resulting in multiple outputs. Finally, ROVER (Fiscus, 1997) is adopted to align and vote with equal weights on the multiple outputs, resulting in the final ASR output.

2.4 ASR Output Post-processing

Given that the spontaneous speech in the test set contains frequent filler words such as "Uh" and "you know", it is necessary to address their impact on subsequent MT accuracy and TTS systems that rely on the ASR output. To mitigate this issue, we use a simple rule-based post-processing step to detect and eliminate these expressions from the ASR output. By doing so, we improve the accuracy of the downstream modules.

3 Machine Translation

For the MT module, we first use a pre-trained language model as a basis for initialization and then employ various methods to further enhance translation accuracy.

3.1 Pre-trained Language Model

As pre-trained language models are considered part of the training data in the offline track and can be used in the S2ST track, we use the pre-trained mBART50 model for initializing our MT module. mBART50 (Liu et al., 2020) is a multilingual BART (Lewis et al., 2020) model with 12 layers of encoder and decoder, which we believe will provide a solid basis for improving translation accuracy.

3.2 Three-stage Fine-tuning based on Curriculum Learning

We perform fine-tuning on the pre-trained model to match the English-to-Chinese (En2Zh) translation task. There are substantial differences between the ASR outputs and the texts of MT data. First, ASR prediction results inevitably contain errors. Second, ASR outputs are normalized text without punctuation. Therefore, directly fine-tuning the pre-trained model with the MT data will cause a mismatch problem with the ASR output during inference. On the other hand, fine-tuning the model with the ASR outputs will cause difficulty in model coverage because of the difference between the ASR outputs and the MT data. Therefore, based on Curriculum Learning (Bengio et al., 2009), we adopt a three-stage fine-tuning strategy to mitigate such a mismatch.

- **Fine-tuning using the MT data**: First, we use all the MT data to fine-tune the pre-trained model to improve the accuracy of the model in the En2Zh translation task.
- **Fine-tuning using the MT data in ASR transcription format**: Second, we convert the English text in the MT data into the ASR transcription format. Then, we fine-tune the MT model using the converted data, which is closer to the actual text than the ASR recognition output. This approach can enhance the stability of the fine-tuning process, minimize the impact of ASR recognition issues on the translation model, and improve the model's ability to learn punctuation, thereby enhancing its robustness.
- **Fine-tuning using the ASR outputs**: Third, we leverage *GigaSpeech* (Chen et al., 2021) to address the mismatch problem between the ASR outputs and the MT data. Specifically, we use the ASR module to transcribe the *GigaSpeech* training set and replace the corresponding transcriptions in *GigaST* (Ye et al., 2022) with the ASR transcriptions for translation model fine-tuning. This enables the MT model to adapt to ASR errors.

3.3 Back Translation

Following (Akhbardeh et al., 2021), we adopt the back translation method to enhance the data and improve the robustness and generalization of the model. First, we train a Zh2En MT model to translate Chinese to English, using the same method employed for the En2Zh MT module. Next, we generate the corresponding English translations for the Chinese text of the translation data. Finally, we combine the back translation parallel corpus pairs with the real parallel pairs and train the MT model.

3.4 Cross-validation

We use 5-fold cross-validation (Ojala and Garriga, 2010) to improve the robustness of translation and reduce over-fitting. Firstly, we randomly divide the data into five equal parts and train five models on different datasets by using one of them as the validation set each time and combining the remaining four as the training set. After that, we integrate the predicted probability distributions from these five

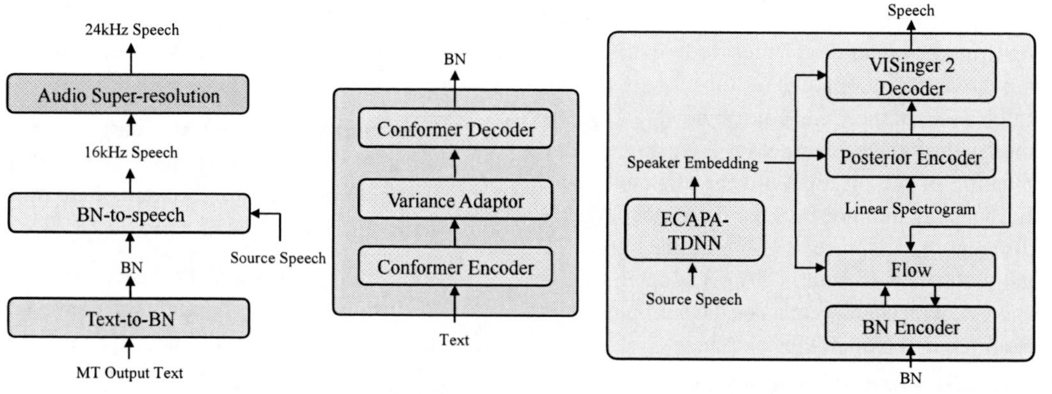

(a) pipeline (b) Text-to-BN (c) BN-to-speech

Figure 1: Architecture of our text-to-speech module.

models to obtain the final predicted probability distribution for the next word during token generation for predicting the translation results.

4 Text-to-speech

4.1 Overview

Figure 1 (a) shows the pipeline of the text-to-speech module in the proposed S2ST system. The TTS module is built on a BN-based two-stage architecture, which consists of a text-to-BN and a BN-to-speech procedure. The text-to-BN stage tends to generate BN features from the Chinese text translated by the MT module. The BN-to-speech stage produces 16KHz Chinese speech from the BN feature, conditioning on the speaker embedding of source speech. Given the translated Chinese speech which preserves the speaker timbre in the source English speech, an audio super-resolution model is further leveraged to convert the synthesized speech from 16KHz to 24KHz for higher speech fidelity.

Building on the two-stage framework AdaVITS (Song et al., 2022a), we employ bottleneck (BN) features as the intermediate representations in the two-stage TTS module. BN features, extracted from a multi-condition trained noise-robust ASR system, mainly represent the speaker-independent linguistic content. So BN can effectively *disentangle* the speaker timbre and the linguistic content information. In the text-to-BN stage, high-quality TTS data is adopted in the training phase to model the speaker-independent BN features with prosody information. In the BN-to-speech stage, both high-quality TTS data and low-quality ASR data should be involved during training to sufficiently model the speech of various speaker identities. Extracted from speech, BN features contain the duration and prosody information, which eliminates the need for text transcripts and prosody modeling. Instead, the BN-to-speech stage focuses on time-invariant information modeling, such as speaker timbre.

As the goal of this work is to conduct zero-shot English-to-Chinese speech translation, we concentrate on the method to transfer the unseen speaker timbre of the source English speech to the synthesized Chinese speech through voice cloning (Chen et al., 2019). To capture new speaker timbre during inference, the TTS module requires to model abundant various speakers during training, which relies on large-scale high-quality TTS data. Unfortunately, we are limited in the high-quality TTS data we can use in this task and must rely on additional data such as ASR to model the speaker timbre. However, this data is not suitable for TTS model training because the labels are inconsistent with TTS, and the prosody of the speakers is not as good as high-quality TTS data.

Furthermore, we incorporate ASR data into the BN-to-speech training procedure by re-sampling all the training speech to 16kHz, which can not reach high-quality audio. Therefore, we utilize audio super-resolution techniques to upsample the synthesized 16KHz audio and convert it into higher sampling rate audio.

4.2 Text-to-BN

Our text-to-BN stage network in TTS is based on DelightfulTTS (Liu et al., 2021), which employs a Conformer-based encoder, decoder, and a variance adapter for modeling duration and prosody. The model extends phoneme-level linguistic features to frame-level to guarantee the clarity and naturalness of speech in our system.

4.3 BN-to-speech

We build the BN-to-speech model based on VITS (Kim et al., 2021), which is a mainstream end-to-end TTS model. VITS generates speech waveforms directly from the input textual information, rather than a conventional pipeline of using the combination of an acoustic model and a neural vocoder.

The network of the BN-to-speech stage consists of a BN encoder, posterior encoder, decoder, flow, and speaker encoder. The monotonic alignment search (MAS) from the original VITS is removed since BN features contain the duration information. For achieving zero-shot voice cloning, an ECAPA-TDNN (Desplanques et al., 2020) speaker encoder is pre-trained to provide the speaker embedding as the condition of the synthesized speech. To avoid periodic signal prediction errors in the original HiFiGAN-based (Kong et al., 2020) decoder in VITS, which induces sound quality degradation, we follow VISinger2 (Zhang et al., 2022) to adopt a decoder with the sine excitation signals. Since The VISinger2 decoder requires pitch information as input, we utilize a pitch predictor with a multi-layer Conv1D that predicts the speaker-dependent pitch from BN and speaker embedding. With the desired speaker embedding and corresponding BN features, the BN-to-speech module produces Chinese speech in the target timbre.

4.4 Audio Super-resolution

Following (Liu et al., 2021), we use an upsampling network based vocoder to achieve audio super-resolution (16kHz→24kHz). During training, the 16KHz mel-spectrogram is used as the condition to predict the 24KHz audio in the audio super-resolution model. Specifically, we adopt the *AISHELL-3* (Shi et al., 2021) dataset, composing the paired 16KHz and 24KHz speech data for model training. During inference, the high-quality 24kHz speech is produced for the mel-spectrogram of the 16KHz speech generated by the BN-to-speech model. Here DSPGAN (Song et al., 2022b) is adopted as our audio super-resolution model, which is a universal vocoder that ensures robustness and good sound quality without periodic signal errors.

5 Data Preparation

5.1 Datasets

Following the constraint of data usage, the training dataset for the S2ST system is illustrated in Table 1.

[5]https://github.com/SpeechTranslation/GigaS2S

5.1.1 ASR Data

For the English ASR module in our proposed system, we use *GigaSpeech*, *LibriSpeech*, *TED-LIUM v2&v3* as training data. For the ASR system used to extract BN features in TTS, we use text-to-speech data in *AISHELL-3* and Chinese speech in *GigaS2S*, along with the corresponding Chinese text in *GigaST*, as the training set. Since the test set's MT output text is a mix of Chinese and English, including names of people and places, the TTS module needs to support both languages. Therefore, we also add the aforementioned English data to the training set.

5.1.2 MT Data

We use the text-parallel data including *News Commentary* and *OpenSubtitles2018* as MT training set. Moreover, we also add the Chinese texts in *GigaST* and the English texts in *GigaSpeech* corresponding to the Chinese texts in *GigaST* to the training set.

5.1.3 TTS Data

We use *AISHELL-3* as training data in Text-to-BN and audio super-resolution. For the pre-trained speaker encoder, we adopt *LibriSpeech*, which contains 1166 speakers, as the training data.For the BN-to-speech model, in addition to using *AISHELL-3* which has 218 speakers, we also use *LibriSpeech* to meet the data amount and speaker number requirements of zero-shot TTS.

5.2 Data Pre-processing

5.2.1 ASR Data

To prepare the ASR data, we pre-process all transcripts to remove audio-related tags. Next, we map the text to the corresponding byte-pair encoding (BPE) unit and count the number of BPE units in the ASR dictionary, which totals 5,000 units. For audio processing, we use a frame shift of 10ms and a frame length of 25ms and normalize all audio to 16KHz.

5.2.2 MT Data

For the MT data, we use the same tokenizer as mBART50 to perform sub-word segmentation for English and Chinese texts and to organize them into a format for neural network training. By doing so, we can maximize the benefits of initializing our translation model with mBART50 pre-trained model parameters. The mBART tokenizer mentioned above is a Unigram tokenizer. A Unigram model is a type of language model that considers each token to be independent of the tokens before it. What's more, the tokenizer has a total of 250,054 word segmentations, supports word segmentation processing for English, Chinese, and

Table 1: Datasets used in our proposed system.

Datasets	Utterances	Hours
English Labeled Speech Data		
GigaSpeech (Chen et al., 2021)	8,315K	10,000
LibriSpeech (Panayotov et al., 2015)	281K	961
TED-LIUM v2 (Rousseau et al., 2012)&v3 (Hernandez et al., 2018)	361K	661
CommonVoice (Ardila et al., 2020)	1,225K	1,668
Text-parallel Data		
News Commentary (Chen et al., 2021)	322K	-
OpenSubtitles2018 (Lison et al., 2018)	10M	-
ST Data		
GigaST (Ye et al., 2022)	7,651K	9,781
S2S Data		
GigaS2S[5]	7,626K	-
Chinese TTS Data		
AISHELL-3 (Shi et al., 2021)	88K	85

other languages, and uses special tokens like <s>, </s>, and <unk>.

5.2.3 TTS Data

For *AISHELL-3*, we downsample it to 16KHz and 24KHz respectively as the TTS modeling target and the audio super-resolution modeling target. All other data is down-sampled to 16KHz. All data in TTS adopts 12.5ms frame shift and 50ms frame length.

Speech Enhancement. Given the presence of substantial background noise in the test set, the discriminative power of speaker embeddings is significantly reduced, thereby impeding the performance of the TTS module. Furthermore, the ASR data incorporated during the training of the BN-to-speech model is also subject to background noise. Therefore, we employ a single-channel wiener filtering method (Lim and Oppenheim, 1979) to remove such noise from these data. Please note that we do not perform speech enhancement on the test set in the ASR module, because there is a mismatch between the denoised audio and which is used in ASR training, and denoising will reduce the speech recognition accuracy.

5.2.4 Evaluation Data

For all evaluations, we use the English-Chinese (En-Zh) development data divided by the organizer from *GigaSpeech*, *GigaST* and *GigaS2S*, including 5,715 parallel En-Zh audio segments, and their corresponding En-Zh texts. It is worth noting that the development data for evaluations has been removed from the training dataset.

6 Experiments

6.1 Experimental Setup

All the models in our system are trained on 8 A100 GPUs and optimized with Adam (Kingma and Ba, 2015).

ASR Module. All ASR models are implemented in ESPnet[6]. Both Conformer and E-Branchformer models employ an encoder with 17 layers and a feature dimension of 512, with 8 heads in the self-attention mechanism and an intermediate hidden dimension of 2048 for the FFN. In addition, we employ a 6-layer Transformer decoder with the same feature hidden dimension as the encoder. The E-Branchformer model uses a cgMLP with an intermediate hidden dimension of 3072. The total number of parameters for the Conformer and E-Branchformer model in Section 2.1 is 147.8M and 148.9M respectively. We train the models with batch size 32 sentences per GPU for 40 epochs, and set the learning rate to 0.0015, the warm-up step to 25K.

For data augmentation, we conduct speed perturbation, pitch shifting, and audio codec on the original recordings. Spectrum augmentation and

[6] `https://github.com/espnet/espnet`

noise augmentation are used for on-the-fly model training.

MT Module. All MT models are implemented in HuggingFace[7]. Using MT data, we fine-tune the mBART-50 large model, which has 611M parameters, with a batch size of 32 sentences per GPU for 20 epochs. The learning rate is set to 3e-5 and warmed up for the first 10% of updates and linearly decayed for the following updates. For fine-tuning using the MT data in ASR transcription format and the ASR outputs, we also fine-tune the model with batch size 32 sentences per GPU for 5 epochs and set the learning rate to 3e-5, which is warmed up for the first 5% of updates and linearly decayed for the following updates.

TTS Module. We complete our system based on VITS official code[8]. The text-to-BN follows the configuration of DelightfulTTS and has about 64M parameters. To extract the duration required for text-to-BN, we train a Kaldi[9] model using *AISHELL-3*. The ASR system used for extracting BN is the Chinese-English ASR model mentioned in Section 5.1.1. For BN-to-speech, we use a 6-layer FFT as the BN encoder and follow the other configuration in VIsinger2 with about 45M parameters in total. The pitch predictor has 4 layers of Conv1D with 256 channels. Pitch is extracted by Visinger2 decoder and DSPGAN from Harvest (Morise, 2017) with Stonemask. To predict pitch in DSPGAN, we use the method described in Section 4.3. Up-sampling factors in DSPGAN is set as [5, 5, 4, 3] and other configuration of DSPGAN-mm is preserved for audio super-resolution. The DSPGAN model has about 9M parameters in total. We train all the above models with a batch size of 64 sentences per GPU for 1M steps and set the learning rate to 2e-4. For the pre-trained speaker encoder, we follow the model configuration and training setup of ECAPA-TDNN (C=1024) with 14.7M parameters.

6.2 Evaluation Models

Baseline. To evaluate the effectiveness of the proposed cascaded S2ST system, we adopt the original cascaded S2ST system as a baseline, including an E-Branchformer ASR model, a mBART50 MT model fine-tuned using the MT data, and an end-to-end TTS model based on VITS trained with *AISHELL-3*.

Proposed system & Ablation Study. We further conduct ablation studies to evaluate each component in the proposed system. Specifically, the ablation studies are designed to verify the effectiveness of model fusion and data augmentation in ASR, three-stage fine-tuning, back translation, cross-verification in MT, two-stage training with BN, pre-trained speaker embedding, and audio super-resolution in TTS.

6.3 Results & Analysis

We conduct experiments on the effectiveness of each sub-module and the performance of our proposed cascaded S2ST system.

6.3.1 ASR Module

We calculate the word error rate (WER) of each ASR module to evaluate the English speech recognition accuracy. As shown in Table 2, the WER of the proposed system has a significant drop compared with the baseline, which indicates that the proposed system greatly improves the recognition accuracy. Moreover, the results of the ablation study demonstrate the effectiveness of both model fusion and data augmentation in improving speech recognition accuracy.

Table 2: The WER results of each ASR module.

Model	WER (%)
Baseline	13.53
Proposed system	10.25
w/o model fusion	11.95
w/o data augmentation	12.40

6.3.2 MT Module

We evaluate our MT module in terms of the BLEU score, which measures the n-gram overlap between the predicted output and the reference sentence.

Table 3: The BLEU results of each MT module.

Model	BLEU
Baseline	28.1
Proposed system	33.4
w/o three-stage fine-tuning	28.7
w/o back translation	30.8
w/o cross-validation	31.0

As shown in Table 4, the proposed system with three-stage fine-tuning achieves a significantly bet-

[7]https://github.com/huggingface/transformers

[8]https://github.com/jaywalnut310/vits

[9]https://github.com/kaldi-asr/kaldi

Table 4: Experimental results of TTS in terms of MOS and WER. BN means using two-stage training with BN and pre-trained spkr. embed. means using pre-trained speaker embedding.

Model	Clarity in CER (%)	Naturalness (MOS)	Sound Quality (MOS)	Speaker Similarity (MOS)
Baseline	7.14	3.38±0.05	3.81±0.04	2.12±0.06
Proposed system	6.12	3.70±0.06	3.86±0.06	3.72±0.06
w/o BN	7.12	3.40±0.04	3.81±0.05	3.10±0.07
w/o Pre-trained spkr. embd.	-	-	4.05±0.05	2.22±0.06
w/o Audio super-resolution	-	-	3.64±0.04	-
Recording	4.53	4.01±0.04	3.89±0.03	4.35±0.05

ter BLEU score than the baseline, demonstrating the effectiveness of curriculum learning in our scenario. Furthermore, by incorporating back translation and cross-validation, the translation performance can be further improved.

6.3.3 TTS Module

We calculate the character error rate (CER) to evaluate the clarity of speech for each TTS module. The ASR system used for calculating CER is the Chinese-English ASR model mentioned in Section 5.1.1. Additionally, we conduct mean opinion score (MOS) tests with ten listeners rating each sample on a scale of 1 (worst) to 5 (best) to evaluate naturalness, sound quality, and speaker similarity.

In the ablation study without pre-trained speaker embedding, speaker ID is to control the speaker timbre of the synthesized speech. To eliminate the influence of ASR and MT results on TTS evaluation, we use the Chinese text in the evaluation data and its corresponding English source speech as the reference of speaker timbre as the test set for TTS evaluation.

As shown in Table 3, our proposed system has achieved significant improvement in naturalness, sound quality, speaker similarity, and clarity of speech compared with the baseline. Interestingly, the system without pre-trained speaker embedding has better sound quality than both the proposed system and recording. We conjecture the reason is that the pre-trained speaker embedding greatly influences the sound quality in the zero-shot TTS setup. Therefore, the quality of the synthesized 24KHz audio is superior to the 16KHz recording, which can be demonstrated by the 3.64 MOS score of the system without audio super-resolution. Meanwhile, the speaker similarity MOS score is very low due to the lack of generalization ability to unseen speakers. Without using the BN-based two-stage model, the system decreases performance on all indicators, which shows the effectiveness of BN as an intermediate representation in our experimental scenario.

6.3.4 System Evaluation

Finally, we calculate the ASR-BLEU score for the baseline and the proposed system to evaluate the speech-to-speech translation performance. Specifically, we use the ASR system to transcribe the Chinese speech generated by TTS, and then compute the BLEU scores of the ASR-decoded text with respect to the reference English translations. The ASR system for transcribing Chinese speech is the same as that in Section 6.2.3.

Table 5: The ASR-BLEU results of each system.

Model	ASR-BLEU
Baseline	27.5
Proposed system	32.2

As shown in Table 5, our proposed system achieves a higher ASR-BLEU score than the baseline, which indicates that our proposed system has good speech-to-speech translation accuracy.

7 Conclusion

This paper describes the NPU-MSXF speech-to-speech translation system, which we develop for the IWSLT 2023 speech-to-speech translation task. Our system is built as a cascaded system that includes ASR, MT, and TTS modules. To ensure good performance with multi-source data, we improved each module using various techniques such as model fusion and data augmentation in the ASR, three-stage fine-tuning, back translation, and cross-validation in the MT, and two-stage training, pre-trained speaker embedding, and audio super-resolution in the TTS. Through extensive experiments, we demonstrate that our system achieves high translation accuracy, naturalness, sound quality, and speaker similarity with multi-source input.

References

Farhad Akhbardeh, Arkady Arkhangorodsky, Magdalena Biesialska, Ondrej Bojar, Rajen Chatterjee, Vishrav Chaudhary, Marta R. Costa-jussà, Cristina España-Bonet, Angela Fan, Christian Federmann, Markus Freitag, Yvette Graham, Roman Grundkiewicz, Barry Haddow, Leonie Harter, Kenneth Heafield, Christopher Homan, Matthias Huck, Kwabena Amponsah-Kaakyire, Jungo Kasai, Daniel Khashabi, Kevin Knight, Tom Kocmi, Philipp Koehn, Nicholas Lourie, Christof Monz, Makoto Morishita, Masaaki Nagata, Ajay Nagesh, Toshiaki Nakazawa, Matteo Negri, Santanu Pal, Allahsera Auguste Tapo, Marco Turchi, Valentin Vydrin, and Marcos Zampieri. 2021. Findings of the 2021 conference on machine translation (WMT21). In *Proceedings of the Sixth Conference on Machine Translation, WMT@EMNLP 2021, Online Event, November 10-11, 2021*, pages 1–88. Association for Computational Linguistics.

Rosana Ardila, Megan Branson, Kelly Davis, Michael Kohler, Josh Meyer, Michael Henretty, Reuben Morais, Lindsay Saunders, Francis M. Tyers, and Gregor Weber. 2020. Common voice: A massively-multilingual speech corpus. In *Proceedings of The 12th Language Resources and Evaluation Conference, LREC 2020, Marseille, France, May 11-16, 2020*, pages 4218–4222. European Language Resources Association.

Yoshua Bengio, Jérôme Louradour, Ronan Collobert, and Jason Weston. 2009. Curriculum learning. In *Proceedings of the 26th Annual International Conference on Machine Learning, ICML 2009, Montreal, Quebec, Canada, June 14-18, 2009*, volume 382 of *ACM International Conference Proceeding Series*, pages 41–48. ACM.

Guoguo Chen, Shuzhou Chai, Guan-Bo Wang, Jiayu Du, Wei-Qiang Zhang, Chao Weng, Dan Su, Daniel Povey, Jan Trmal, Junbo Zhang, Mingjie Jin, Sanjeev Khudanpur, Shinji Watanabe, Shuaijiang Zhao, Wei Zou, Xiangang Li, Xuchen Yao, Yongqing Wang, Zhao You, and Zhiyong Yan. 2021. Gigaspeech: An evolving, multi-domain ASR corpus with 10, 000 hours of transcribed audio. In *Interspeech 2021, 22nd Annual Conference of the International Speech Communication Association, Brno, Czechia, 30 August - 3 September 2021*, pages 3670–3674. ISCA.

Yutian Chen, Yannis M. Assael, Brendan Shillingford, David Budden, Scott E. Reed, Heiga Zen, Quan Wang, Luis C. Cobo, Andrew Trask, Ben Laurie, Çaglar Gülçehre, Aäron van den Oord, Oriol Vinyals, and Nando de Freitas. 2019. Sample efficient adaptive text-to-speech. In *7th International Conference on Learning Representations, ICLR 2019, New Orleans, LA, USA, May 6-9, 2019*. OpenReview.net.

Brecht Desplanques, Jenthe Thienpondt, and Kris Demuynck. 2020. ECAPA-TDNN: emphasized channel attention, propagation and aggregation in TDNN based speaker verification. In *Interspeech 2020, 21st Annual Conference of the International Speech Communication Association, Virtual Event, Shanghai, China, 25-29 October 2020*, pages 3830–3834. ISCA.

Jonathan G Fiscus. 1997. A post-processing system to yield reduced word error rates: Recognizer output voting error reduction (ROVER). In *1997 IEEE Workshop on Automatic Speech Recognition and Understanding Proceedings*, pages 347–354. IEEE.

Anmol Gulati, James Qin, Chung-Cheng Chiu, Niki Parmar, Yu Zhang, Jiahui Yu, Wei Han, Shibo Wang, Zhengdong Zhang, Yonghui Wu, and Ruoming Pang. 2020. Conformer: Convolution-augmented transformer for speech recognition. In *Interspeech 2020, 21st Annual Conference of the International Speech Communication Association, Virtual Event, Shanghai, China, 25-29 October 2020*, pages 5036–5040. ISCA.

François Hernandez, Vincent Nguyen, Sahar Ghannay, Natalia A. Tomashenko, and Yannick Estève. 2018. TED-LIUM 3: Twice as much data and corpus repartition for experiments on speaker adaptation. In *Speech and Computer - 20th International Conference, SPECOM 2018, Leipzig, Germany, September 18-22, 2018, Proceedings*, volume 11096 of *Lecture Notes in Computer Science*, pages 198–208. Springer.

Ye Jia, Ron J. Weiss, Fadi Biadsy, Wolfgang Macherey, Melvin Johnson, Zhifeng Chen, and Yonghui Wu. 2019. Direct speech-to-speech translation with a sequence-to-sequence model. In *Interspeech 2019, 20th Annual Conference of the International Speech Communication Association*, pages 1123–1127. ISCA.

Jaehyeon Kim, Jungil Kong, and Juhee Son. 2021. Conditional variational autoencoder with adversarial learning for end-to-end text-to-speech. In *Proceedings of the 38th International Conference on Machine Learning, ICML 2021, 18-24 July 2021, Virtual Event*, volume 139 of *Proceedings of Machine Learning Research*, pages 5530–5540. PMLR.

Kwangyoun Kim, Felix Wu, Yifan Peng, Jing Pan, Prashant Sridhar, Kyu J Han, and Shinji Watanabe. 2023. E-branchformer: Branchformer with enhanced merging for speech recognition. In *2022 IEEE Spoken Language Technology Workshop (SLT)*, pages 84–91. IEEE.

Diederik P. Kingma and Jimmy Ba. 2015. Adam: A method for stochastic optimization. In *3rd International Conference on Learning Representations, ICLR 2015, San Diego, CA, USA, May 7-9, 2015, Conference Track Proceedings*.

Jungil Kong, Jaehyeon Kim, and Jaekyoung Bae. 2020. HiFi-GAN: Generative adversarial networks for efficient and high fidelity speech synthesis. In *Advances in Neural Information Processing Systems 33: Annual Conference on Neural Information Processing Systems 2020, NeurIPS 2020, December 6-12, 2020, virtual*.

Ann Lee, Peng-Jen Chen, Changhan Wang, Jiatao Gu, Sravya Popuri, Xutai Ma, Adam Polyak, Yossi Adi, Qing He, Yun Tang, Juan Pino, and Wei-Ning Hsu. 2022. Direct speech-to-speech translation with discrete units. In *Proceedings of the 60th Annual Meeting of the Association for Computational Linguistics (Volume 1: Long Papers), ACL 2022*, pages 3327–3339. Association for Computational Linguistics.

Mike Lewis, Yinhan Liu, Naman Goyal, Marjan Ghazvininejad, Abdelrahman Mohamed, Omer Levy, Veselin Stoyanov, and Luke Zettlemoyer. 2020. BART: denoising sequence-to-sequence pre-training for natural language generation, translation, and comprehension. In *Proceedings of the 58th Annual Meeting of the Association for Computational Linguistics, ACL 2020, Online, July 5-10, 2020*, pages 7871–7880. Association for Computational Linguistics.

Jae Soo Lim and Alan V Oppenheim. 1979. Enhancement and bandwidth compression of noisy speech. *Proceedings of the IEEE*, 67(12):1586–1604.

Pierre Lison, Jörg Tiedemann, and Milen Kouylekov. 2018. Opensubtitles2018: Statistical rescoring of sentence alignments in large, noisy parallel corpora. In *Proceedings of the Eleventh International Conference on Language Resources and Evaluation, LREC 2018, Miyazaki, Japan, May 7-12, 2018*. European Language Resources Association (ELRA).

Yanqing Liu, Zhihang Xu, Gang Wang, Kuan Chen, Bohan Li, Xu Tan, Jinzhu Li, Lei He, and Sheng Zhao. 2021. DelightfulTTS: The microsoft speech synthesis system for blizzard challenge 2021. *CoRR*, abs/2110.12612.

Yinhan Liu, Jiatao Gu, Naman Goyal, Xian Li, Sergey Edunov, Marjan Ghazvininejad, Mike Lewis, and Luke Zettlemoyer. 2020. Multilingual denoising pretraining for neural machine translation. *Trans. Assoc. Comput. Linguistics*, 8:726–742.

Masanori Morise. 2017. Harvest: A high-performance fundamental frequency estimator from speech signals. In *Interspeech 2017, 18th Annual Conference of the International Speech Communication Association*, pages 2321–2325. ISCA.

Satoshi Nakamura, Konstantin Markov, Hiromi Nakaiwa, Gen-ichiro Kikui, Hisashi Kawai, Takatoshi Jitsuhiro, Jinsong Zhang, Hirofumi Yamamoto, Eiichiro Sumita, and Seiichi Yamamoto. 2006. The ATR multilingual speech-to-speech translation system. *IEEE Trans. Speech Audio Process.*, 14(2):365–376.

Markus Ojala and Gemma C. Garriga. 2010. Permutation tests for studying classifier performance. *J. Mach. Learn. Res.*, 11:1833–1863.

Vassil Panayotov, Guoguo Chen, Daniel Povey, and Sanjeev Khudanpur. 2015. Librispeech: An ASR corpus based on public domain audio books. In *2015 IEEE International Conference on Acoustics, Speech and Signal Processing, ICASSP 2015, South Brisbane, Queensland, Australia, April 19-24, 2015*, pages 5206–5210. IEEE.

Daniel S. Park, William Chan, Yu Zhang, Chung-Cheng Chiu, Barret Zoph, Ekin D. Cubuk, and Quoc V. Le. 2019. Specaugment: A simple data augmentation method for automatic speech recognition. In *Interspeech 2019, 20th Annual Conference of the International Speech Communication Association, Graz, Austria, 15-19 September 2019*, pages 2613–2617. ISCA.

Alec Radford, Karthik Narasimhan, Tim Salimans, Ilya Sutskever, et al. 2018. Improving language understanding by generative pre-training.

Anthony Rousseau, Paul Deléglise, and Yannick Estève. 2012. TED-LIUM: an automatic speech recognition dedicated corpus. In *Proceedings of the Eighth International Conference on Language Resources and Evaluation, LREC 2012, Istanbul, Turkey, May 23-25, 2012*, pages 125–129. European Language Resources Association (ELRA).

Yao Shi, Hui Bu, Xin Xu, Shaoji Zhang, and Ming Li. 2021. AISHELL-3: A multi-speaker mandarin TTS corpus. In *Interspeech 2021, 22nd Annual Conference of the International Speech Communication Association, Brno, Czechia, 30 August - 3 September 2021*, pages 2756–2760. ISCA.

Jongseo Sohn, Nam Soo Kim, and Wonyong Sung. 1999. A statistical model-based voice activity detection. *IEEE Signal Process. Lett.*, 6(1):1–3.

Kun Song, Heyang Xue, Xinsheng Wang, Jian Cong, Yongmao Zhang, Lei Xie, Bing Yang, Xiong Zhang, and Dan Su. 2022a. AdaVITS: Tiny VITS for low computing resource speaker adaptation. In *13th International Symposium on Chinese Spoken Language Processing, ISCSLP 2022, Singapore, December 11-14, 2022*, pages 319–323. IEEE.

Kun Song, Yongmao Zhang, Yi Lei, Jian Cong, Hanzhao Li, Lei Xie, Gang He, and Jinfeng Bai. 2022b. DSPGAN: a gan-based universal vocoder for high-fidelity TTS by time-frequency domain supervision from DSP. *CoRR*, abs/2211.01087.

Rong Ye, Chengqi Zhao, Tom Ko, Chutong Meng, Tao Wang, Mingxuan Wang, and Jun Cao. 2022. GigaST: A 10, 000-hour pseudo speech translation corpus. *CoRR*, abs/2204.03939.

Yongmao Zhang, Heyang Xue, Hanzhao Li, Lei Xie, Tingwei Guo, Ruixiong Zhang, and Caixia Gong. 2022. Visinger 2: High-fidelity end-to-end singing voice synthesis enhanced by digital signal processing synthesizer. *CoRR*, abs/2211.02903.

Low-Resource Formality Controlled NMT Using Pre-trained LM

Priyesh Vakharia and **Shree Vignesh S** and **Pranjali Basmatkar**
Department of Computer Science
University of California, Santa Cruz
{pvakhari, ss64293, pbasmatk}@ucsc.edu

Abstract

This paper describes the UCSC's submission to the shared task on formality control for spoken language translation at IWSLT 2023. For this task, we explored the use of "additive style intervention" using a pre-trained multilingual translation model, namely mBART. Compared to prior approaches where a single style-vector was added to all tokens in the encoder output, we explored an alternative approach in which we learn a unique style-vector for each input token. We believe this approach, which we call "style embedding intervention," is better suited for formality control as it can potentially learn which specific input tokens to modify during decoding. While the proposed approach obtained similar performance to "additive style intervention" for the supervised English-to-Vietnamese task, it performed significantly better for English-to-Korean, in which it achieved an average matched accuracy of 90.6 compared to 85.2 for the baseline. When we constrained the model further to only perform style intervention on the <bos> (beginning of sentence) token, the average matched accuracy improved further to 92.0, indicating that the model could learn to control the formality of the translation output based solely on the embedding of the <bos> token.

1 Introduction

In the past decade, neural machine translation has made remarkable strides, achieving translation quality that is increasingly comparable to human-level performance across various languages. However, despite these advancements, the field of controllable machine translation remains relatively under-explored. One crucial aspect of translation variation is formality, which manifests through grammatical registers, adapting the language to suit specific target audiences. Unfortunately, current neural machine translation (NMT) systems lack the capability to comprehend and adhere to grammatical registers, specifically concerning formality. Consequently, this limitation can result in inaccuracies in selecting the appropriate level of formality, potentially leading to translations that may be deemed inappropriate in specific contexts. Recognizing the significance of formality control, we aim to build a formality-controlled machine translation system to foster smooth and reliable conversations and enhance communication across languages and cultures, facilitating more nuanced and effective linguistic exchanges.

Formality-controlled Neural Machine Translation is the IWSLT 2023 task (Nădejde et al., 2022) under the Formality track. The goal of the task is to achieve formality controlled machine translation for the English-Vietnamese (En-Vi), English-Korean (En-Ko) in a supervised setting and English-Portuguese (En-Pt) and English-Russian (En-Ru) in a zero-shot setting as detailed in (Agarwal et al., 2023). We provide an example of formal and informal translations of an English sentence into Vietnamese in Figure 1. The formal and informal tokens are in bold.

2 Related Works

Machine translation (MT) research has primarily focused on preserving the meaning between languages. However, it is widely recognized that maintaining the intended level of formality in communication is a crucial aspect of the problem (Hovy, 1987) (Hovy, 1987). This field of research was named formality-sensitive machine translation (FSMT) (Niu et al., 2017), where the target formality level is considered in addition to the source segment in determining the translated text. Further, several studies have attempted to regulate formality in MT through side constraints to control politeness, or formality (Sennrich et al., 2016); (Feely et al., 2019); (Schioppa et al., 2021a). Other studies have tried to address this with custom models trained on data with consistent formality (Viswanathan et al., 2020). Most prior research

Proceedings of the 20th International Conference on Spoken Language Translation (IWSLT 2023), pages 321–329
July 13-14, 2023

English: Awesome, and now I just need your billing address, that is associated with the card.
Formal: Tuyệt vời [F]ạ[/F], giờ tôi chỉ cần địa chỉ thanh toán của [F]quý vị[/F], địa chỉ đó được liên kết với thẻ [F]ạ[/F].
Informal: Tuyệt vời, giờ tôi chỉ cần địa chỉ thanh toán của [F]bạn[/F], địa chỉ đó được liên kết với thẻ.

Figure 1: Contrastive Data Sample

has been tailored to individual languages and has labeled large amounts of data using word lists or morphological analyzers.

3 Approach

3.1 Overview

The task of formality-controlled generation can be viewed as a seq2seq machine translation task. More formally, given an input sequence x, we design a model that does the following:

$$\hat{y} = \arg\max_{y \in Y} p(y|x, l_s, l_t, f; \theta) \tag{1}$$

Where,
x is the input sequence,
l_s is the source language,
l_t is the target language,
f is the formality,
$\hat{y}$ is the formality controlled translation

We propose a single model that produces an output, given input *x*, and formality setting *f*. Despite being part of the unconstrained task, our proposed approach does not mine or develop any formality annotated data for training and just uses a pre-trained checkpoint of mBART.

3.2 Design

We looked at previous works incorporating contrasting styles Rippeth et al., 2022, and Schioppa et al., 2021b as motivation for our approach. For controlling styles, the aforementioned works use an additive intervention approach. This approach entails adding a *single style intervention vector V* to the pre-trained encoder output *Z*. The same vector *V* is added to all the tokens of the encoder outputs, thereby changing the encoder outputs uniformly.

We modify the above approach to allow for more flexibility while learning. Instead of a single intervention vector *V*, we propose a unique vector V_i for every token *i* in the input space. In short, we repurpose an Embedding layer as a style intervening layer between the encoder and the decoder. This design resulted from our original question: will allowing more flexibility in the encoder enable it to identify which tokens require stylization, thus making it more interpretable. The hypothesis that originated from this question was: by giving each token its own intervention vector V_i, the model will learn each intervention vector V_i differently based on whether the token at that time step has a contrasting translation that is dependent on the formality setting. In short, we let the model learn different V_i*'s* for each token. If true, this will provide some interpretability on which tokens the model recognizes as having a formality marker and translates them differently in formal and informal settings. This approach is visualized in Figure 2. Since our approach uses an embedding layer for style intervention, we call our approach *'style embedding intervention.'*

We learn the style embedding layer only in the formal setting and use a zero vector in the informal setting. In other words, the style embedding intervention is performed only in the formal setting, and encoder outputs are not perturbed in the informal setting. We do not have separate Embedding layers to learn each formality style, simply because, it would be difficult to switch between layers during batched training. Looking at (Schioppa et al., 2021b), the combination of a style vector and a zero vector for contrasting styles was sufficient to learn the style.

4 Experimental Apparatus

4.1 Dataset

The IWSLT formality shared task provided a formality annotated dataset (Nadejde et al., 2022). This dataset comprises source segments paired with two contrastive reference translations, one for each

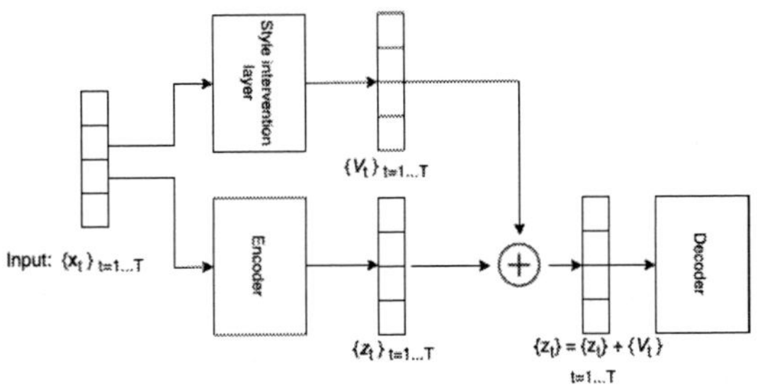

Figure 2: Approach

formality level (informal and formal) for two language pairs: EN-KO, VI in the supervised setting and two language pairs: EN-PT, RU in the zero-shot setting. The data statistics can be seen in Table 1. We use a random split of 0.2 to construct the validation dataset during model development.

4.2 Training Setup

For all our modeling experiments, we use mbart-large-50-one-to-many-mmt, a fine-tuned checkpoint of mBART-large-50 (Liu et al., 2020). This model, introduced by (Tang et al., 2020), is a fine-tuned mBART model which can translate English to 49 languages, including the languages we are interested in: KO, VI, PT, and RU.

For our baseline, we perform zero-shot inference on the mBART model for the four language pairs. The results are shown in tables 3 - 6.

Based on the findings of (Nakkiran et al., 2019) and (Galke and Scherp, 2022) we fixed our loss function to be 'cross entropy with logits' and optimizer to AdamW (Loshchilov and Hutter, 2017). We use the default learning rate of 10^{-3}, standard weight decay of 10^{-2} and set β_1, β_2 and ϵ to 0.9, 0.998 and 10^{-8} respectively.

To effectively train the transformer-based mBART model, we used a learning rate scheduler - a linear schedule with a warm-up, as introduced by (Vaswani et al., 2017). This creates a schedule with a learning rate that decreases linearly from the initial learning rate to 0 after a warm-up period. The warm-up period is set to 10% of the total training steps, during which the learning rate increases linearly from 0 to the initial learning rate set in the optimizer. All the other hyper-parameters are left at their defaults.

We trained our models using one NVIDIA A100 GPU with 80GB memory. To fit our model in this GPU we used a batch size of 16 and a max sequence length of 128. We trained for 15 epochs with an early stopping callback set at 3.

We have implemented all the models in PyTorch (Paszke et al., 2019) leveraging Huggingface (Wolf et al., 2019) transformers and evaluate libraries.

4.3 Evaluation

To assess the performance of the models, we use four metrics to evaluate the two main underlying tasks - translation quality and formality control.

For evaluating the translation quality, we use the following two metrics:

- **Bilingual Understudy Evaluation (BLEU) score**: BLEU score (Papineni et al., 2002) calculates the similarity between a machine translation output and a reference translation using n-gram precision. We use SacreBLEU 2.0 (Post, 2018) implementation for reporting our scores.
- **Cross-lingual Optimized Metric for Evaluation of Translation (COMET) score**: COMET score (Rei et al., 2020) calculates the similarity between a machine translation output and a reference translation using token or sentence embeddings. We use COMET wmt22-comet-da (Rei et al., 2022) model for reporting our scores.

For evaluating the formality control, we use the following two metrics:

- **Matched-Accuracy (M-Acc)**: A reference-based corpus-level automatic metric that leverages phrase-level formality markers from the references to classify a system-generated translation as either formal or informal. This metric was provided by the IWSLT Formality shared task organizers.
- **Reference-free Matched-Accuracy (RF-M-Acc)**: A reference-free variant of M-Acc that uses a multilingual formality classifier, based on xlm-roberta-base, fine-tuned on human-written formal and informal text, to label a system-generated hypothesis as formal or informal. This metric was provided by the IWSLT Formality shared task organizers.

In addition to this, we evaluate our generic translation quality on FLORES-200 (Goyal et al., 2022) for all language pairs under supervised and zero-shot settings. We use the devtest set of FLORES-200 and compute the BLEU and COMET scores.

Language pair	Training Data points	Testing Data points
EN-KO	400	600
EN-VI	400	600
EN-PT	0	600
EN-RU	0	600

Table 1: Data description

	Formal		Informal	
	BLEU	Matched Acc	BLEU	Matched Acc
Rippeth et al., 2022	38.3	98.4	38.3	82.7
Style embedding intervention	38	99.2	37.4	98

Table 2: Grounding our model for EN-ES data

5 Grounding results and observations

Along with the validation splits, we ground our approach by comparing our results with the 2022 formality track submission Rippeth et al., 2022. We compare our results on one language pair i.e. English-Spanish. The comparison is shown in Table 2.

As seen in Table 2, the BLEU scores between our approach - “style embedding intervention” - and the approach in Rippeth et al., 2022 - "additive style intervention" - are similar but our approach makes significant gains in Matched Accuracy, especially in the informal setting indicating improved formality control.

5.1 Style embedding layer analysis

In this section, we analyze the style embedding layer and compare the analysis with the original hypothesis - giving each token its own intervention vector V_i, the model will learn each vector differently based on whether the token at that time step has a contrasting translation that is dependent on the formality setting. Due to the unique nature of our training setup - learning zero vector in the informal setting - for our hypothesis testing, we compare the encoder vectors with and without the style embedding intervention. For this purpose, we use the dot product similarity. At each time step, we compute the dot product similarity between the encoder output before style intervention and the output after style intervention. This is equivalent to comparing the encoder outputs in the formal and the informal setting. The similarity scores are visualized in Figure 3. For a closer look, Table 8 displays the similarity scores.

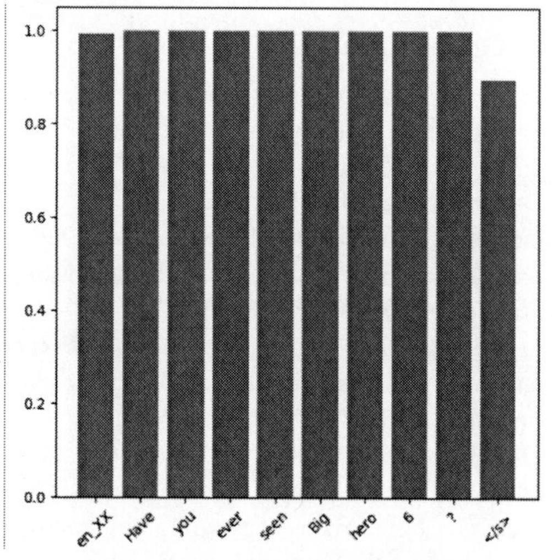

Figure 3: Similarity scores for hypothesis analysis.

As seen from the token representation similarity scores, the model does not seem to learn new information in tokens that have a contrasting setting-dependent translation - the tokens’ similarity scores are very near 1. Instead, it uses the </s>’s representation to store the style ’signal’, by creating a style vector that makes the </s>’s representation $\sim$11% different between formality settings.

Another interesting observation is the extremely slight dissimilarity produced at the beginning of the sentence or ’en_xx’ token. Did the model learn the same style information in $\sim$1% of information space in the ’en_xx’ token compared to the $\sim$11% of information space in the ’</s>’ token? To an-

Models	EN-VI				EN-KO			
	BLEU	COMET	%M-Acc	%C-F	BLEU	COMET	%M-Acc	%C-F
Baseline 1	26.7	0.3629	96	0.95	4.9	0.2110	78	0.99
Baseline 2	26.1	0.829	3	0.006	3.9	0.8445	66.7	0.979
Model 1	44.8	0.8467	99	0.989	22.2	0.8246	74.1	0.9815
Model 2	44.2	0.8702	98.6	0.9782	22.5	0.831	82.9	0.9765
Model 3	44.6	0.874	99	0.9849	23.3	0.836	85.7	0.9832
Model 4	44.3	0.8462	99.2	0.9849	23.2	0.8287	75.3	0.9815

Baseline 1: UMD-baseline
Baseline 2: Zero-Shot mBart
Model 1: single vector intervention with train-dev split of 0.1
Model 2: style embedding intervention
Model 3: bos style intervention - **Primary Submission**
Model 4: single vector intervention with train-dev split of 0.2

Table 3: Results on the official test split in the ***formal supervised*** setting for language pairs ***EN-VI*** and ***EN-KO***.

Models	EN-PT				EN-RU			
	BLEU	COMET	%M-Acc	%C-F	BLEU	COMET	%M-Acc	%C-F
Baseline 1	27.3	0.4477	96.3	0.9766	22.0	0.3492	96.20	0.92
Baseline 2	33	0.8445	54.9	0.8447	24.9	0.7604	99.4	0.9116
Model 1	27.2	0.7686	84.6	0.918	23.8	0.737	97.6	0.865
Model 2	26.6	0.7895	81.5	0.8748	18.5	0.6837	99.2	0.76
Model 3	26.6	0.7889	89.9	0.9082	18.4	0.6664	98.8	0.79
Model 4	28.2	0.7726	80.5	0.9348	24.3	0.7373	97.9	0.858

Baseline 1: UMD-baseline
Baseline 2: Zero-Shot mBart
Model 1: single vector intervention with train-dev split of 0.1
Model 2: style embedding intervention
Model 3: bos style intervention - **Primary Submission**
Model 4: single vector intervention with train-dev split of 0.2

Table 4: Results on the official test split in the ***formal unsupervised*** setting for language pairs ***EN-PT*** and ***EN-RU***.

swer this question, we added another modification to our approach - we masked out the intervention vectors for all tokens except the 'en_xx' token.

For naming purposes, we call this approach '*bos style intervention*' respectively.

6 Official Results

Along with the approach from Rippeth et al., 2022 taken as a baseline and an adapted version of it, we submit the results of our approach and of the '*bos style intervention*' approach. We analyse the performance of our models under the supervised setting and the zero-shot setting. We also generate results on the FLORES-200 test split.

6.1 Supervised Setting

We trained our models multi-lingually on EN-VI and EN-KO for the supervised setting. In the formal setting, we obtain a BLEU score of 44.6 for EN-VI and 23.3 for EN-KO on the official test split. In the informal setting, we obtain a BLEU score of 43.5 for EN-VI and 22.8 for EN-KO. Tables 3 and 5 have detailed results of all our models. Our primary model - '*bos style intervention*' - outperforms the UMD baseline significantly for both languages with around 20 BLEU increase and more than double the COMET score. This answers our hypothesis that the model can learn the formality style in the small $\sim$1% information space at the beginning of the sentence in 'en_xx' token. Moreover, we obtain higher scores on the metrics M-Acc% & C-F% that compute the degree of formality/informality induced.

Qualitative analysis of the translations, especially for KO, revealed that code-switching was a major issue. For example, some translations have

Models	EN-VI				EN-KO			
	BLEU	COMET	%M-Acc	%C-F	BLEU	COMET	%M-Acc	%C-F
Baseline 1	25.3	0.3452	96	0.9816	4.9	0.1697	97.6	0.995
Baseline 2	31.9	0.8352	97	0.9933	3.2	0.8311	33.3	0.020
Model 1	43.3	0.8238	98.7	0.9949	22.1	0.8115	96.3	0.889
Model 2	43.6	0.8514	98.9	0.9949	23.0	0.8256	98.3	0.9514
Model 3	43.5	0.8504	98.9	1	22.8	0.8257	98.3	0.9581
Model 4	42.5	0.8232	98.3	0.9765	22.6	0.8162	96.4	0.9028

Baseline 1: UMD-baseline
Baseline 2: Zero-Shot mBart
Model 1: single vector intervention with train-dev split of 0.1
Model 2: style embedding intervention
Model 3: bos style intervention - **Primary Submission**
Model 4: single vector intervention with train-dev split of 0.2

Table 5: Results on the official test split in the ***informal supervised*** setting for language pairs ***EN-VI*** and ***EN-KO***.

Models	EN-PT				EN-RU			
	BLEU	COMET	%M-Acc	%C-F	BLEU	COMET	%M-Acc	%C-F
Baseline 1	30.9	0.4161	93.2	0.9082	21.6	0.3475	84.1	0.8417
Baseline 2	33.2	0.8229	45.1	0.1552	18.8	0.7489	0.6	0.0883
Model 1	28.2	0.7606	55.6	0.378	18.8	0.7109	47.7	0.556
Model 2	28.7	0.7821	58.8	0.5092	18.6	0.6544	45.1	0.6
Model 3	28.4	0.7853	58	0.419	14.9	0.6365	51.6	0.6683
Model 4	28.8	0.7673	57	0.3305	20	0.7102	46.9	0.55

Baseline 1: UMD-baseline
Baseline 2: Zero-Shot mBart
Model 1: single vector intervention with train-dev split of 0.1
Model 2: style embedding intervention
Model 3: bos style intervention - **Primary Submission**
Model 4: single vector intervention with train-dev split of 0.2

Table 6: Results on the official test split in the ***informal unsupervised*** setting for language pairs ***EN-PT*** and ***EN-RU***.

Models	EN-VI		EN-KO		EN-PT		EN-RU	
	BLEU	COMET	BLEU	COMET	BLEU	COMET	BLEU	COMET
Model 1	29.8	0.8169	5.5	0.773	30.6	0.8082	21.4	0.794
Model 2	27.8	0.8205	4.6	0.758	30.8	0.8258	19.3	0.7686
Model 3	27.9	0.8225	4.5	0.7586	30.4	0.8264	19.1	0.7543
Model 4	30.3	0.8186	5.6	0.7752	30.9	0.814	21.5	0.7935

Model 1: single vector intervention with train-dev split of 0.1
Model 2: style embedding intervention
Model 3: bos style intervention - **Primary Submission**
Model 4: single vector intervention with train-dev split of 0.2

Table 7: Results on ***Flores-200*** test split for language pairs ***EN-VI*** & ***EN-KO*** in supervised setting and for language pairs ***EN-PT*** & ***EN-RU*** in unsupervised setting.

entire phrases or latter parts of sentences in English as shown in Figure 4.

6.2 Zero-shot Setting

We evaluate the above multi-lingually trained model on RU and PT in a zero-shot setting. In the formal setting, we obtain a BLEU score of 26.6 for

Token	Similarity Score
en_xx	0.99037
Have	0.99928
you	0.99914
ever	0.99935
seen	0.99916
Big	0.99916
hero	0.99919
6	0.99920
?	0.99910
</s>	0.89028

Table 8: Similarity scores for hypothesis analysis.

Source(EN) : Okay, I got you. Sorry about that.
Gold Translation(KO) : 네, 이해했어요. 죄송해요.
Predicted translation(KO) : 좋아요, 당신을 잡았어요. Sorry about that.

Figure 4: Similarity scores for hypothesis analysis.

EN-PT and 18.4 for EN-RU on the official test split. In the informal setting, we obtain a BLEU score of 28.4 for EN-PT and 14.9 for EN-RU. Tables 4 and 6 have detailed results of all our models. We observe that our model does not transfer the style knowledge very well. In both cases, the model is often biased toward formal translations. Moreover, our models have a slightly degraded performance in the translation quality than UMD baseline model. This cements our earlier observation that style knowledge transfer is incomplete. Qualitative analysis of the translations revealed that the zero-shot language translations also suffer from code-switching.

6.3 Testing on FLORES-200 dataset

In addition to evaluating formality, we assess the translation quality of our models by evaluating on the FLORES-200 test split. The results can be seen in Table 7.

7 Conclusion

In this paper, we presented and explored "style embedding intervention," a new approach for low-resource formality control in spoken language translation. By assigning unique style vectors to each input token, the proposed approach shows promising results in understanding and controlling the nuances of formal and informal style translation. It outperforms previous "additive style intervention" methods, specifically for the English-to-Korean translation task, resulting in an average matched accuracy improvement from 85.2 to 90.6. Further, on analysis of our "style embedding intervention" model, we find that most of the style information is learnt in the <bos> token. Constraining style addition to the <bos> token - "bos style intervention" - further improved our averaged matched accuracy from 90.6 to 92.

We also observed that in a zero-shot setting, the formality control doesn't seem to transfer well, and the model leans towards biases learnt during pre-training rather than the transferred style interventions. This is more pronounced for En-Ru translations where the model is more biased towards the formal style, with a matched accuracy of 98.8, than the informal style, with a matched accuracy of 51.6.

Future works focused on alleviating the style biases of pre-trained models might be necessary to ensure style transfer works equally well in a zero-shot setting.

We hope our work on translation models with interpretable formality control can serve as a base for other future works on interpretable models, especially in low-resource settings.

Code used for our implementation can be accessed at `https://github.com/Priyesh1202/IWSTL-2023-Formality`.

8 Acknowledgements

We thank Prof. Lane, Prof. Rao and Brendan King from UC Santa Cruz for their constant guidance and support.

References

Milind Agarwal, Sweta Agrawal, Antonios Anastasopoulos, Claudia Borg, Marine Carpuat, Roldano Cattoni, Mauro Cettolo, William Chen, Khalid Choukri, Alexandra Chronopoulou, Thierry Declerck, Qianqian Dong, Yannick Estève, Kevin Duh, Marcello Federico, Souhir Gahbiche, Benjamin Hsu, John Judge, Tom Ko, Rishu Kumar, Xutail Ma, Prashant Mathur, Evgeny Matusov, Paul McNamee, John P. McCrae, Kenton Murray, Matteo Negri, Jan Niehues, Xing Niu, Atul Ojha Kr., John E. Ortega, Proyag Pal, Juan Pino, Lonneke van der Plas, Elijah Rippeth, Elizabeth Salesky, Matthias Sperber, Sebastian Stüker, Katsuhito Sudoh, Brian Thompson, Marco Turchi, Alex Waibel, Mingxuan Wang, and Rodolfo Zevallos. 2023. Findings of the IWSLT 2023 Evaluation Campaign. In *Proceedings of the 20th International Conference on Spoken Language Translation (IWSLT 2023)*. Association for Computational Linguistics.

Weston Feely, Eva Hasler, and Adrià de Gispert. 2019. Controlling japanese honorifics in english-to-japanese neural machine translation. In *Proceedings of the 6th Workshop on Asian Translation*, pages 45–53.

Lukas Galke and Ansgar Scherp. 2022. Bag-of-words vs. graph vs. sequence in text classification: Questioning the necessity of text-graphs and the surprising strength of a wide MLP. In *Proceedings of the 60th Annual Meeting of the Association for Computational Linguistics (Volume 1: Long Papers)*, pages 4038–4051, Dublin, Ireland. Association for Computational Linguistics.

Naman Goyal, Cynthia Gao, Vishrav Chaudhary, Peng-Jen Chen, Guillaume Wenzek, Da Ju, Sanjana Krishnan, Marc'Aurelio Ranzato, Francisco Guzmán, and Angela Fan. 2022. The Flores-101 evaluation benchmark for low-resource and multilingual machine translation. *Transactions of the Association for Computational Linguistics*, 10:522–538.

Eduard Hovy. 1987. Generating natural language under pragmatic constraints. *Journal of Pragmatics*, 11(6):689–719.

Yinhan Liu, Jiatao Gu, Naman Goyal, Xian Li, Sergey Edunov, Marjan Ghazvininejad, Mike Lewis, and Luke Zettlemoyer. 2020. Multilingual denoising pre-training for neural machine translation.

Ilya Loshchilov and Frank Hutter. 2017. Fixing weight decay regularization in adam. *CoRR*, abs/1711.05101.

Maria Nădejde, Anna Currey, Benjamin Hsu, Xing Niu, Marcello Federico, and Georgiana Dinu. 2022. Cocoa-mt: A dataset and benchmark for contrastive controlled mt with application to formality. *arXiv preprint arXiv:2205.04022*.

Maria Nadejde, Anna Currey, Benjamin Hsu, Xing Niu, Marcello Federico, and Georgiana Dinu. 2022. CoCoA-MT: A dataset and benchmark for contrastive controlled MT with application to formality. In *Findings of the Association for Computational Linguistics: NAACL 2022*, pages 616–632, Seattle, United States. Association for Computational Linguistics.

Preetum Nakkiran, Gal Kaplun, Yamini Bansal, Tristan Yang, Boaz Barak, and Ilya Sutskever. 2019. Deep double descent: Where bigger models and more data hurt. *CoRR*, abs/1912.02292.

Xing Niu, Marianna Martindale, and Marine Carpuat. 2017. A study of style in machine translation: Controlling the formality of machine translation output. In *Proceedings of the 2017 Conference on Empirical Methods in Natural Language Processing*, pages 2814–2819.

Kishore Papineni, Salim Roukos, Todd Ward, and Wei-Jing Zhu. 2002. Bleu: a method for automatic evaluation of machine translation. In *Proceedings of the 40th Annual Meeting of the Association for Computational Linguistics*, pages 311–318, Philadelphia, Pennsylvania, USA. Association for Computational Linguistics.

Adam Paszke, Sam Gross, Francisco Massa, Adam Lerer, James Bradbury, Gregory Chanan, Trevor Killeen, Zeming Lin, Natalia Gimelshein, Luca Antiga, Alban Desmaison, Andreas Köpf, Edward Z. Yang, Zach DeVito, Martin Raison, Alykhan Tejani, Sasank Chilamkurthy, Benoit Steiner, Lu Fang, Junjie Bai, and Soumith Chintala. 2019. Pytorch: An imperative style, high-performance deep learning library. *CoRR*, abs/1912.01703.

Matt Post. 2018. A call for clarity in reporting BLEU scores. In *Proceedings of the Third Conference on Machine Translation: Research Papers*, pages 186–191, Brussels, Belgium. Association for Computational Linguistics.

Ricardo Rei, José G. C. de Souza, Duarte Alves, Chrysoula Zerva, Ana C Farinha, Taisiya Glushkova, Alon Lavie, Luisa Coheur, and André F. T. Martins. 2022. COMET-22: Unbabel-IST 2022 submission for the metrics shared task. In *Proceedings of the Seventh Conference on Machine Translation (WMT)*, pages 578–585, Abu Dhabi, United Arab Emirates (Hybrid). Association for Computational Linguistics.

Ricardo Rei, Craig Stewart, Ana C Farinha, and Alon Lavie. 2020. COMET: A neural framework for MT evaluation. In *Proceedings of the 2020 Conference on Empirical Methods in Natural Language Processing (EMNLP)*, pages 2685–2702, Online. Association for Computational Linguistics.

Elijah Rippeth, Sweta Agrawal, and Marine Carpuat. 2022. Controlling translation formality using pre-trained multilingual language models. In *Proceedings of the 19th International Conference on Spoken Language Translation (IWSLT 2022)*, pages 327–340, Dublin, Ireland (in-person and online). Association for Computational Linguistics.

Andrea Schioppa, David Vilar, Artem Sokolov, and Katja Filippova. 2021a. Controlling machine translation for multiple attributes with additive interventions. In *Proceedings of the 2021 Conference on Empirical Methods in Natural Language Processing*, pages 6676–6696.

Andrea Schioppa, David Vilar, Artem Sokolov, and Katja Filippova. 2021b. Controlling machine translation for multiple attributes with additive interventions. In *Proceedings of the 2021 Conference on Empirical Methods in Natural Language Processing*, pages 6676–6696, Online and Punta Cana, Dominican Republic. Association for Computational Linguistics.

Rico Sennrich, Barry Haddow, and Alexandra Birch. 2016. Controlling politeness in neural machine translation via side constraints. In *Proceedings of the 2016 Conference of the North American Chapter of the Association for Computational Linguistics: Human Language Technologies*, pages 35–40.

Yuqing Tang, Chau Tran, Xian Li, Peng-Jen Chen, Naman Goyal, Vishrav Chaudhary, Jiatao Gu, and Angela Fan. 2020. Multilingual translation with extensible multilingual pretraining and finetuning. *CoRR*, abs/2008.00401.

Ashish Vaswani, Noam Shazeer, Niki Parmar, Jakob Uszkoreit, Llion Jones, Aidan N. Gomez, Lukasz Kaiser, and Illia Polosukhin. 2017. Attention is all you need.

Aditi Viswanathan, Varden Wang, and Antonina Kononova. 2020. Controlling formality and style of machine translation output using automl. In *Information Management and Big Data: 6th International Conference, SIMBig 2019, Lima, Peru, August 21–23, 2019, Proceedings 6*, pages 306–313. Springer.

Thomas Wolf, Lysandre Debut, Victor Sanh, Julien Chaumond, Clement Delangue, Anthony Moi, Pierric Cistac, Tim Rault, Rémi Louf, Morgan Funtowicz, and Jamie Brew. 2019. Huggingface's transformers: State-of-the-art natural language processing. *CoRR*, abs/1910.03771.

NAIST Simultaneous Speech Translation System for IWSLT 2023

Ryo Fukuda[†] **Yuta Nishikawa**[†] **Yasumasa Kano**[†] **Yuka Ko**[†]
Tomoya Yanagita[†] **Kosuke Doi**[†] **Mana Makinae**[†]
Sakriani Sakti[‡†] **Katsuhito Sudoh**[†] **Satoshi Nakamura**[†]
[†]Nara Institute of Science and Technology, Japan
[‡]Japan Advanced Institute of Science and Technology, Japan
fukuda.ryo.fo3@is.naist.jp

Abstract

This paper describes NAIST's submission to the IWSLT 2023 Simultaneous Speech Translation task: English-to-{German, Japanese, Chinese} speech-to-text translation and English-to-Japanese speech-to-speech translation. Our speech-to-text system uses an end-to-end multilingual speech translation model based on large-scale pre-trained speech and text models. We add Inter-connections into the model to incorporate the outputs from intermediate layers of the pre-trained speech model and augment prefix-to-prefix text data using Bilingual Prefix Alignment to enhance the simultaneity of the offline speech translation model. Our speech-to-speech system employs an incremental text-to-speech module that consists of a Japanese pronunciation estimation model, an acoustic model, and a neural vocoder.

1 Introduction

This paper presents NAIST's simultaneous speech translation (SimulST) systems for the IWSLT 2023 English-to-{German, Japanese, Chinese} speech-to-text track and the English-to-Japanese speech-to-speech track (Agarwal et al., 2023).

Many previous studies on end-to-end SimulST have focused on training methodologies and architectures specialized for the simultaneous scenario. However, such a specialized system setup for SimulST is not trivial and increases the difficulty of the system development and the computational complexity. One recent approach to SimulST systems is to use an offline speech translation (ST) model for prefix-to-prefix translation required in SimulST. In last year's IWSLT Evaluation Campaign (Anastasopoulos et al., 2022), Polák et al. (2022) demonstrated superior results using such multilingual offline ST models. In our last year's systems (Fukuda et al., 2022), we used an offline model fine-tuned for SimulST with data augmentation based on Bilingual Prefix Alignment (Kano et al., 2022).

In this year, we use an end-to-end multilingual offline ST model based on large-scale pretrained speech and text models for the speech-to-text track, following Polák et al. (2022). We used Hidden-Unit BERT (HuBERT) (Hsu et al., 2021) as the speech encoder fine-tuned using English automatic speech recognition (ASR) data and mBART50 (Tang et al., 2020) as the text decoder fine-tuned using a multilingual machine translation data. We prepare the multilingual ST model in the following steps:

1. Initialize the model with the parameters of HuBERT and mBART50 models and add Inter-connections between the intermediate layer of the speech encoder and the text decoder.
2. Train the model using multilingual ST corpora.
3. Fine-tune the model using bilingual prefix pairs in English-to-{German, Japanese, Chinese} extracted using Bilingual Prefix Alignment.

We use a SimulST policy called *local agreement* (Liu et al., 2020) that finds the longest common prefixes among successive decoding steps. For the English-to-Japanese speech-to-speech track, we developed a cascade of the SimulST above and an incremental text-to-speech module using a pronunciation estimation model, an acoustic model, and a neural vocoder.

2 System Architecture

Figure 1 illustrates an overview of our system architecture. The following subsections explain our methodologies: Inter-connection in 2.1 and Bilingual Prefix Alignment in 2.2, the local agreement in 2.3, and the incremental text-to-speech in 2.4.

Proceedings of the 20th International Conference on Spoken Language Translation (IWSLT 2023), pages 330–340

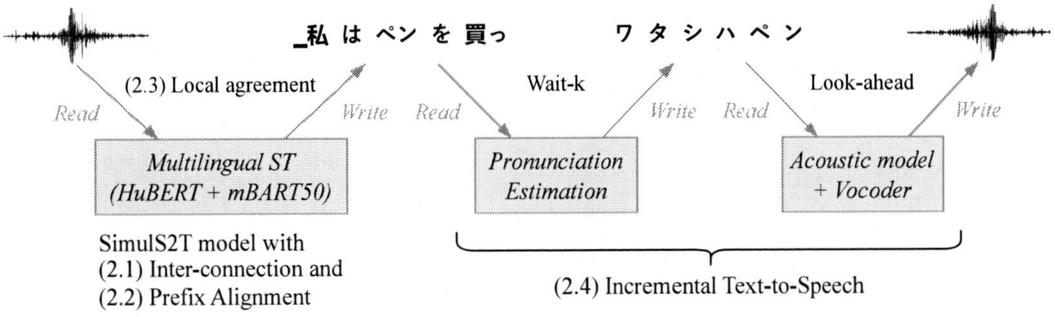

Figure 1: Block diagram of SimulS2S.

2.1 Inter-connection

Intermediate layers of a speech SSL (Self-Supervised Learning) model contain useful information for downstream tasks (Pasad et al., 2021). However, the simple addition of connections from the intermediate layers of the speech encoder to the text decoder does not always work well. We use a weighted integration of the encoder's intermediate layers, called *Inter-connection* (Nishikawa and Nakamura, 2023), where the output tensors from the intermediate layers are aggregated with the weights. The weights are additional learnable parameters optimized through the training. We also apply layer normalization after the weighted aggregation to stabilize the training.

2.2 Prefix Alignment

In simultaneous translation, the model translates a prefix of the entire input to the corresponding output prefix. The prefix translation using a full-sentence model often suffers from so-called *over-translation* (or *hallucination*) due to the lack of training examples in the prefix-to-prefix scenarios. To mitigate this problem, we leverage the training corpus using Bilingual Prefix Alignment (Kano et al., 2022) for data augmentation for prefix-to-prefix pairs to fine-tune the SimulST model.

2.3 Local Agreement

Liu et al. (2020) proposed Local agreement to find a stable prefix translation hypothesis in the prefix-to-prefix translation based on chunk-wise inputs with the fixed length. It verifies the stability of the hypothesis at step t using the hypothesis at step $t + 1$ by taking the agreeing prefix (i.e., the longest common prefix) of them. This is based on an idea that the agreeing prefix translation outputs with growing input prefixes should be reliable. Polák et al. (2022) generalized this idea using agreement among the prefixes at n consecutive steps (LA-n) and demonstrated that $n = 2$ works well on SimulST. According to their finding, we use LA-2 as a SimulST policy and adjust the input chunk length (in milliseconds) to control the quality-latency trade-offs.

2.4 Incremental Text-to-Speech

Our English-to-Japanese speech-to-speech simultaneous translation system uses the aforementioned SimulST system with incremental Japanese text-to-speech (TTS). The incremental TTS consists of three modules: a pronunciation estimation, an acoustic model, and a neural vocoder. The pronunciation estimation predicts the pronunciations of SimulST outputs, the acoustic model predicts acoustic features from the pronunciations, and the neural vocoder synthesizes speech from the acoustic features.

We use the wait-k approach (Ma et al., 2019) for the incremental pronunciation estimation, taking a subword sequence as the input and predicting pronunciation symbols in Japanese katakana phonograms and a couple of special characters representing accents as the output. To control the output length, we extend the wait-k policy by allowing the decoder to output an arbitrary length of symbols; The decoder stops its *write* steps when the largest weight of its cross attention goes over the last two tokens in the input prefix. This also works as a lookahead mechanism for pronunciation estimation. We use Tacotron2 (Shen et al., 2018) for the acoustic modeling and Parallel WaveGAN (Yamamoto et al., 2020) as the neural vocoder in the prefix-to-prefix manner (Ma et al., 2020a).

Table 1: Training data measured in hours.

Dataset	En-De	En-Ja	En-Zh
MuST-C v1	408h		
MuST-C v2	436h	526h	545h
Europarl-ST	83h		
CoVoST-2	413h	413h	413h
TED-LIUM	415h		
Total	1,755h	939h	958h

Table 2: Comparison of the removed ratios resulting from data filtering with maximum ratios of 4,800, 4,000, and 3,200.

	Removed Ratio (%)		
Filter (max ratio)	En-De	En-Ja	En-Zh
No filtering	0.0	0.0	0.0
4,800	37.8	59.4	59.7
4,000	53.9	72.5	74.1
3,200	78.0	87.9	89.4

3 System Setup

3.1 Data

We used MuST-C v2.0 (Di Gangi et al., 2019) and CoVoST-2 (Wang et al., 2020) for all language pairs: English-to-German (En-De), English-to-Japanese (En-Ja), and English-to-Chinese (En-Zh). We also used MuST-C v1.0, Europarl-ST (Iranzo-Sánchez et al., 2020), and TED-LIUM (Rousseau et al., 2012) for English-to-German. We included the development and test portions of CoVoST-2 and Europarl-ST in our training data. The overall statistics for these corpora are shown in Table 1. For evaluation, we used the tst-COMMON portion of MuST-C v2.0. All the text data in the corpora were tokenized using a multilingual SentencePiece tokenizer with a vocabulary of 250,000 subwords, distributed with mBART50 pre-trained model.

3.2 Data Filtering

We conducted a data filtering on the prefix translation pairs obtained through the Bilingual Prefix Alignment, following our IWSLT 2022 system (Fukuda et al., 2022). We compared three cut-off ratios of the number of samples in the input speech to the number of tokens in the output: 4,800, 4,000, and 3,200. Table 2 shows the percentage of data that was removed following the application of filters. We also applied the same filtering to the development data.

3.3 Simultaneous Speech-to-Text System

We deveoped an end-to-end speech-to-text model initialized with two pre-trained models for its speech encoder and text decoder. The speech encoder was initialized with HuBERT-Large, which consists of a feature extractor trained on 60 K hours of unlabeled speech data Libri-Light (Kahn et al., 2020) and Transformer encoder layers. The feature extractor has seven convolutional layers with a kernel size of (10, 3, 3, 3, 3, 2, 2), a stride of (5, 2, 2, 2, 2, 2, 2), and 512 channels. The number of the Transformer encoder layers is 24. The text decoder was initialized with the decoder of mBART50 (Tang et al., 2020). The decoder consists of twelve Transformer layers, and an embedding layer and linear projection weights are shared, with a size of 250,000. The size of each Transformer and feed-forward layer is 1,024 and 4,096, respectively, the number of attention heads is 16, the activation function is ReLU, and the layer normalization is applied before the attention operations. The encoder and decoder are also connected via Inter-connection (2.1) and a length adapter (Tsiamas et al., 2022). The length adapter is a 3-layer convolutional network with 1,024 channels, the stride of 2, and the activation function of a Gated Linear Unit (GLU).

Speech input is given as waveforms with a 16-kHz sampling rate, normalized to zero mean and unit variance. During training, each source audio was augmented (Kharitonov et al., 2020) before normalization, with a probability of 0.8. We trained multilingual models on all the data listed in Table 1 with a maximum source length of 400,000 frames and a target length of 1,024 tokens. We applied gradient accumulation and data-parallel computations to achieve a batch size of approximately 32 million tokens. We used Adam with $\beta_1 = 0.99$, $\beta_2 = 0.98$, and a base learning rate of 2.5×10^{-4}. The learning rate was controlled by a tri-stage scheduler with phases of 0.15, 0.15, and 0.70 for warm-up, hold, and decay, respectively, while the initial and final learning rate had a scale of 0.01 compared to base. We used sentence averaging and gradient clipping of 20. We applied a dropout probability of 0.1 and used time masking for 10-length spans with a probability of 0.2, and channel masking for 20-length spans with a probability of 0.1 in the encoder feature extractor's output. The loss was the cross-entropy loss with a label smoothing with 20% probability mass.

The offline SimulST model was fine-tuned, and then checkpoint averaging was performed. In the checkpoint averaging, the model checkpoints were saved every 1,000 training steps, and the averaged parameter values among the five-best models in the loss on the development data were taken for the final model. Subsequently, one epoch of fine-tuning was performed on the training data-only prefix alignment pairs in MuST-C v2. We reduced the learning rate to 2.5×10^{-5} during the fine-tuning using translation pairs obtained using Bilingual Prefix Alignment.

As a SimulST policy, the local agreement with $n = 2$ (LA-2) was used. The chunk size was varied from 200 ms to 1000 ms to adjust the quality-latency trade-off. A beam search of beam size five was used to generate hypotheses for input chunks.

3.4 Simulaneous Speech-to-Speech System

Here, we describe the detailed setup of the incremental TTS. Pronunciation symbols were obtained from the text using Open Jtalk[1]. We used the Balanced Corpus of Contemporary Written Japanese (BCCWJ; Maekawa, 2008) for training the pronunciation estimation model. The training, development, and test data were approximately 1.4 M, 10 K, and 10 K sentences, respectively. We also used the training portion of MuST-C as additional training data. We used an LSTM-based attentional encoder-decoder model for the pronunciation estimation model. Its encoder and decoder were implemented with two-layer uni-directional LSTM, and the cross-attention was based on the dot product. The optimizer was Adam with the learning rate of 1e-3 and hyperparameters of $\beta_1 = 0.9$ and $\beta_2 = 0.999$. The batch size was 256 in the number of sentences.

JSUT corpus (Sonobe et al., 2017) was used for training Tacotron2 and Parallel WaveGAN. The numbers of sentences in the training, development, and test data were 7,196, 250, and 250, respectively. Speech is downsampled from 48 kHz to 16 kHz, and 80 dimensional Mel spectrum was used as the acoustic features. The size of the Fourier transform, frameshift length, window length, and window function are 2,048, 10 ms, 50 ms, and Hann window, respectively. We replaced bi-directional LSTM with uni-directional LSTM in Tacotron2 and attention mechanism to the forward attention with the transit agent (Zhang et al., 2018) for incremental processing. Guided Attention Loss (Tachibana et al., 2018) was used as an additional Loss function. The input size of Tactoron2 is 89, and the optimizer was Adam with the learning rate of 1e-3 and the hyperparameters of $\beta_1 = 0.9$ and $\beta_2 = 0.999$ and $\epsilon = 1e - 6$. The batch size was 32 in the number of sentences. Experimental conditions for Parallel WaveGan are the same as in the original paper, except for the parameters related to acoustic features and speech.

The pronunciation estimation used the wait-3 policy. The incremental TTS has a couple of look-ahead parameters, indicating the length to control the quality-latency trade-off. We tune these parameters to keep the quality of synthesized speech within the latency threshold requirement (2.5 seconds).

3.5 Evaluation

We evaluated our systems using SimulEval (Ma et al., 2020b) toolkit[2]. For the SimulST systems, translation quality was evaluated by BLEU using sacreBLEU[3]. Translation latency was evaluated using the following metrics:

- Average Lagging (Ma et al., 2019)
- Length Adaptive Average Lagging (Papi et al., 2022)
- Average Token Delay (Kano et al., 2023)
- Average Proportion (Cho and Esipova, 2016)
- Differentiable Average Lagging (Cherry and Foster, 2019)

For the SimulS2S system, translation quality was evaluated by BLEU after transcribing the output speech with Whisper (Radford et al., 2022) (WHISPER_ASR_BLEU). Translation latency was evaluated with ATD and the time offset of the start and end of the translation.

AL is a latency metric commonly used for text-to-text and speech-to-text simultaneous translation. However, AL focuses on when the translation starts but does not consider enough when the translation for each input chunk finishes. Since the speech segments are generated sequentially in

[1] https://open-jtalk.sourceforge.net

[2] https://github.com/facebookresearch/SimulEval

[3] https://github.com/mjpost/sacrebleu

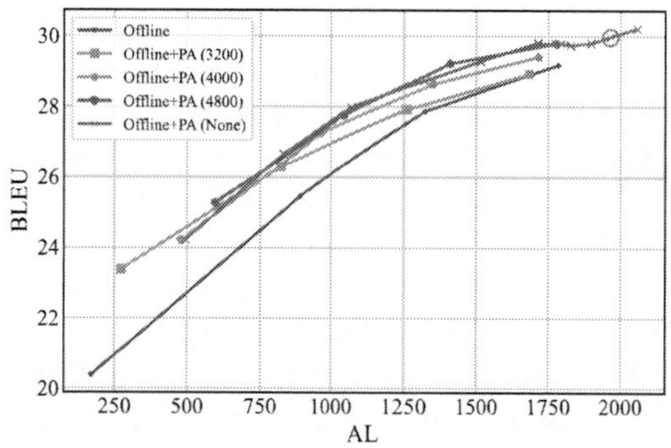

Figure 2: BLEU and AL results of the offline model and the models fine-tuned with prefix alignment on En-De. The parentheses indicate the max ratio of prefix pair filtering. Circled dots indicate our sumitted SimulS2t system.

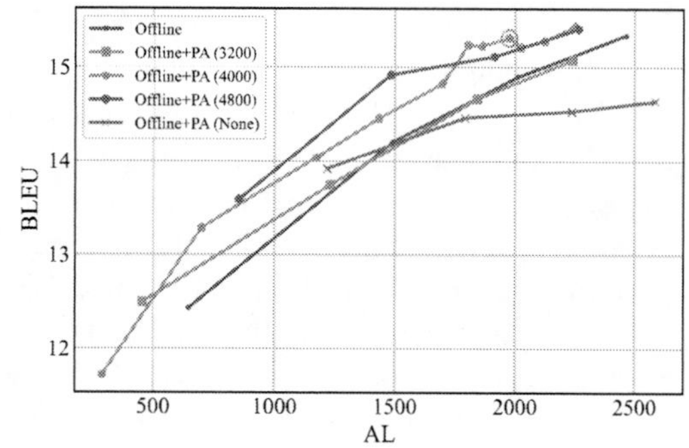

Figure 3: BLEU and AL results of the offline model and the models fine-tuned with prefix alignment on En-Ja.

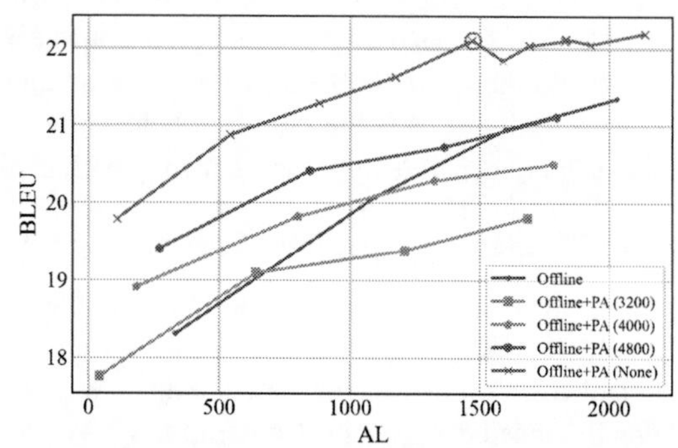

Figure 4: BLEU and AL results of the offline model and the models fine-tuned with prefix alignment on En-Zh.

a speech-to-speech translation scenario, the translation output will be delayed if its preceding translation outputs are delayed and occupy the speech output channel. Thus, AL is not appropriate to evaluate the latency of speech-to-speech simultaneous translation, so we use ATD which includes the delays caused by the outputs in the latency calculation. ATD calculates the delay by having the average time difference between the source token and its corresponding target token. In the setting of SimulEval, assuming one word requires 300 ms to speak, the input and output speech are segmented into the size of 300 ms regarding the segments as the tokens when calculating ATD.

4 Experimental Results

4.1 Submitted Speech-to-Text System

For each language direction, we selected one submission with the settings satisfying the task requirement, $AL \leq 2$ sec. Table 3 shows the scores of the submitted Speech-to-Text systems. The results of all chunk settings for the models used in the submitted systems are shown in Appendix A. The following sections discuss the effectiveness of each of the techniques we used.

4.2 Prefix Alignment

Figures 2 to 4 show quality-latency trade-offs on En-De, En-Ja, and En-Zh tst-COMMON, respectively. For En-De and En-Ja, the quality and latency were roughly proportional in the range of $AL \leq 2000$, while the quality improvement saturated at around $AL = 1,500$ for En-Zh. The fine-tuned model with Bilingual Prefix Alignment outperformed the baseline offline model for all language pairs. In En-Ja, the best results were obtained when prefix pair filtering was applied with the maximum ratio of 4,000, similar to Fukuda et al. (2022). It suggests the importance of the filtering to reduce unbalanced data pairs consisting of long source speech and short target text in language pairs with the large word order differnce. On the other hand, the prefix pair filtering did not work well for the other language directions.

4.3 Inter-connection

We analyzed the effectiveness of Inter-connection through an ablation study on the connection methods and the checkpoint averaging. The results are shown in Table 4.

The results show that checkpoint averaging improved BLEU for the En-Ja and En-Zh and that Inter-connection worked for En-De and En-Ja. This could be attributed to differences in the speech features required for speech translation.

Language pair	chunk size	BLEU	LAAL	AL	AP	DAL	ATD
En-De	950 ms	29.975	2172.927	1964.329	0.846	2856.738	1893.749
En-Ja	840 ms	15.316	2290.716	1973.586	0.892	2889.950	547.752
En-Zh	700 ms	22.105	1906.995	1471.287	0.821	2436.948	667.780

Table 3: Results of the submitted speech-to-text systems on the MuST-C v2 tst-COMMON.

Model	En-De	En-Ja	En-Zh	Ave.
Simple Connection	30.49	15.28	24.50	23.42
Simple Connection + Ckpt Ave.	30.47	15.71	**25.01**	23.73
Inter-connection	30.49	15.53	24.23	23.42
Inter-connection + Ckpt Ave.	**30.89**	**15.89**	24.75	**23.84**

Table 4: BLEU scores for models without and with checkpoint averaging for simple and Inter-connection were evaluated with MuST-C v2 tst-COMMON.

In the multilingual model, the weights required for each language pair are different because the weights of the weighted sum in Inter-connection are shared. In the case of En-Zh, there was larger difference in the weights than in En-De and En-Ja, and sharing weights leads to decrease the performance.

4.4 Computation-aware Latency

We also evaluated models with computation-aware Average Lagging (AL_CA). AL_CA is a variant of AL that adds the actual elapsed time $elapsed_i$ to the delay d_i of i-th target token y_i:

$$d_i = \sum_{k=1}^{j} (T_k + elapsed_i) \tag{1}$$

where T_k is the duration of the k-th input speech segment and j is the position of the input segment already read when generating y_i. The elapsed time $elapsed_i$ is measured as the time from the start of the translation to the output of target token y_i.

The evaluation was conducted using an NVIDIA GeForce RTX 2080 Ti. Figure 5 shows the result. Unlike the non-computation-aware latency metrics, the fixed-size segmentation worked better than the local agreement in the quality-latency trade-off. The local agreement often discards the latter part of the prefix translation due to the disagreement with the next prefix translation, while such a trackback does not happen in the fixed segmentation scenario. Therefore, the local agreement needs to predict more tokens every time and increases the decoding time. This result suggests another trade-off between quality improvement with a sophisticated segmentation strategy and latency reduction with a fixed strategy.

ASR_BLEU	StartOffset	EndOffset	ATD
9.873	2495.01	4134.752	3278.809

Table 5: Results of the submitted SimulS2S system on the MuST-C v2 tst-COMMON.

4.5 Submitted SimulS2S System

Table 5 shows the scores of the SimulS2S system. Compared to the BLEU results with the SimulS2T systems with similar chunk size settings, the SimulS2S system resulted in much worse ASR_BLEU in nearly five points due to the quality of the synthesized speech and possible ASR errors. Figure 6 shows the quality-latency trade-offs of SimulS2S, with ASR_BLEU stagnating around 10.5 points. In addition, the output of the submitted SimulS2S system had a character error rate of 28.3% relative to the output of the SimulS2T system with the same chunk size. These results indicate that there is a significant room for improvement both in the TTS and ASR.

5 Conclusions

In this paper, we described our SimulST systems for the IWSLT 2023 Simultaneous Speech Translation task. Experimental results demonstrated the effectivenesses of Inter-connection and Bilingual Prefix Alignment. The speech-to-speech system is still challenging but showed promising performance by a simple cascade of speech-to-text SimulST and incremental TTS.

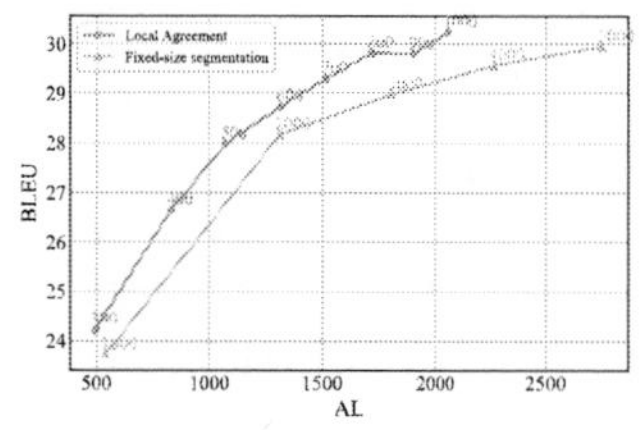

(a) BLEU and AL in En-De.

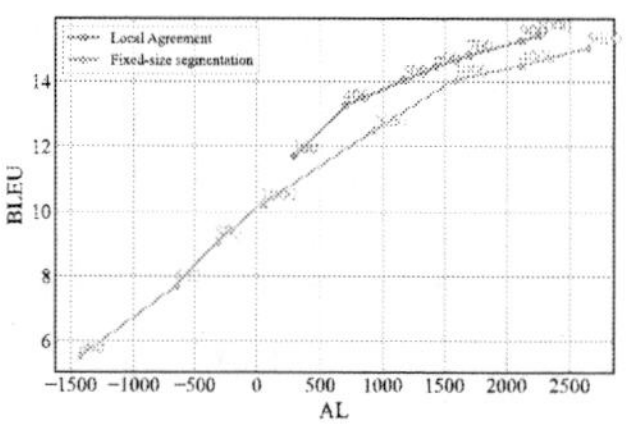

(b) BLEU and AL in En-Ja.

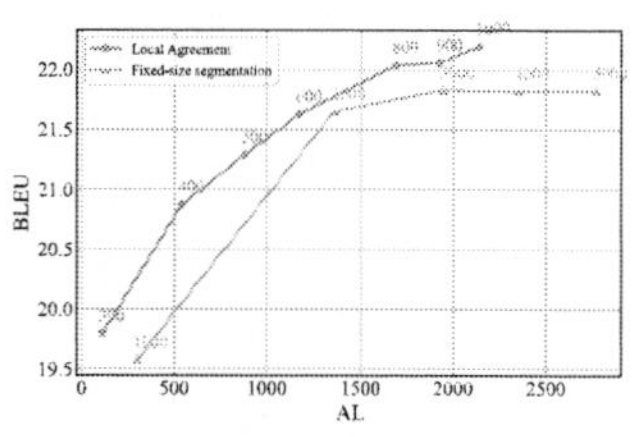

(c) BLEU and AL in En-Zh.

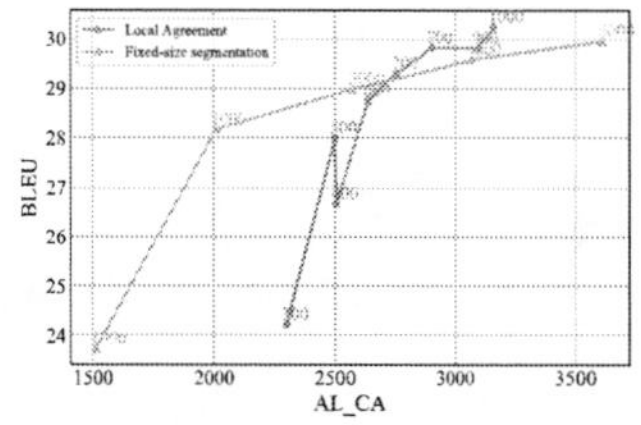

(d) BLEU and AL_CA in En-De.

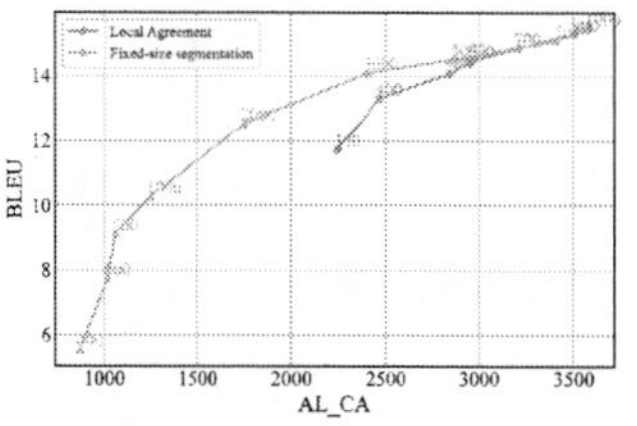

(e) BLEU and AL_CA in En-Ja.

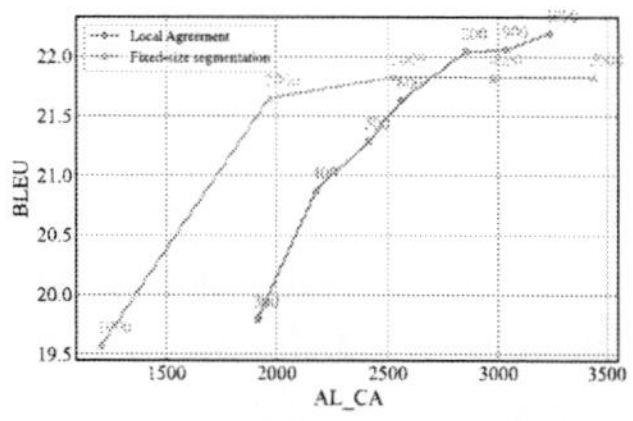

(f) BLEU and AL_CA in En-Zh.

Figure 5: Comparison of the local agreement with $n = 2$ and fixed-size segmentation policies.

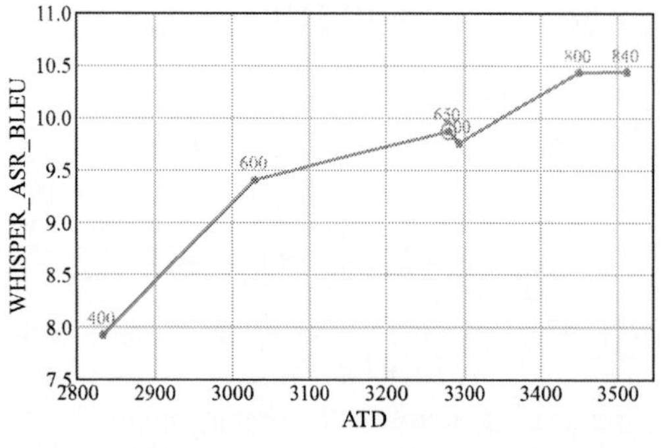

Figure 6: WHISPER_ASR_BLEU and ATD results of the SimulS2S systems on En-Ja. The numbers above the marks indicates chunk size. Circled dots indicate our sumitted system.

Acknowledgements

Part of this work was supported by JSPS KAKENHI Grant Number JP21H05054.

References

Milind Agarwal, Sweta Agrawal, Antonios Anastasopoulos, Ondřej Bojar, Claudia Borg, Marine Carpuat, Roldano Cattoni, Mauro Cettolo, Mingda Chen, William Chen, Khalid Choukri, Alexandra Chronopoulou, Anna Currey, Thierry Declerck, Qianqian Dong, Yannick Estève, Kevin Duh, Marcello Federico, Souhir Gahbiche, Barry Haddow, Benjamin Hsu, Phu Mon Htut, Hirofumi Inaguma, Dávid Javorský, John Judge, Yasumasa Kano, Tom Ko, Rishu Kumar, Pengwei Li, Xutail Ma, Prashant Mathur, Evgeny Matusov, Paul McNamee, John P. McCrae, Kenton Murray, Maria Nadejde, Satoshi Nakamura, Matteo Negri, Ha Nguyen, Jan Niehues, Xing Niu, Atul Ojha Kr., John E. Ortega, Proyag Pal, Juan Pino, Lonneke van der Plas, Peter Polák, Elijah Rippeth, Elizabeth Salesky, Jiatong Shi, Matthias Sperber, Sebastian Stüker, Katsuhito Sudoh, Yun Tang, Brian Thompson, Kevin Tran, Marco Turchi, Alex Waibel, Mingxuan Wang, Shinji Watanabe, and Rodolfo Zevallos. 2023. Findings of the IWSLT 2023 Evaluation Campaign. In *Proceedings of the 20th International Conference on Spoken Language Translation (IWSLT 2023)*. Association for Computational Linguistics.

Antonios Anastasopoulos, Loïc Barrault, Luisa Bentivogli, Marcely Zanon Boito, Ondřej Bojar, Roldano Cattoni, Anna Currey, Georgiana Dinu, Kevin Duh, Maha Elbayad, Clara Emmanuel, Yannick Estève, Marcello Federico, Christian Federmann, Souhir Gahbiche, Hongyu Gong, Roman Grundkiewicz, Barry Haddow, Benjamin Hsu, Dávid Javorský, Věra Kloudová, Surafel Lakew, Xutai Ma, Prashant Mathur, Paul McNamee, Kenton Murray, Maria Nădejde, Satoshi Nakamura, Matteo Negri, Jan Niehues, Xing Niu, John Ortega, Juan Pino, Elizabeth Salesky, Jiatong Shi, Matthias Sperber, Sebastian Stüker, Katsuhito Sudoh, Marco

Turchi, Yogesh Virkar, Alexander Waibel, Changhan Wang, and Shinji Watanabe. 2022. Findings of the IWSLT 2022 evaluation campaign. In *Proceedings of the 19th International Conference on Spoken Language Translation (IWSLT 2022)*, pages 98–157, Dublin, Ireland (in-person and online). Association for Computational Linguistics.

Colin Cherry and George Foster. 2019. Thinking slow about latency evaluation for simultaneous machine translation. *arXiv preprint arXiv:1906.00048*.

Kyunghyun Cho and Masha Esipova. 2016. Can neural machine translation do simultaneous translation? *arXiv preprint arXiv:1606.02012*.

Mattia A. Di Gangi, Roldano Cattoni, Luisa Bentivogli, Matteo Negri, and Marco Turchi. 2019. MuST-C: a Multilingual Speech Translation Corpus. In *Proceedings of the 2019 Conference of the North American Chapter of the Association for Computational Linguistics: Human Language Technologies, Volume 1 (Long and Short Papers)*, pages 2012–2017, Minneapolis, Minnesota. Association for Computational Linguistics.

Ryo Fukuda, Yuka Ko, Yasumasa Kano, Kosuke Doi, Hirotaka Tokuyama, Sakriani Sakti, Katsuhito Sudoh, and Satoshi Nakamura. 2022. NAIST simultaneous speech-to-text translation system for IWSLT 2022. In *Proceedings of the 19th International Conference on Spoken Language Translation (IWSLT 2022)*, pages 286–292, Dublin, Ireland (in-person and online). Association for Computational Linguistics.

Wei-Ning Hsu, Benjamin Bolte, Yao-Hung Hubert Tsai, Kushal Lakhotia, Ruslan Salakhutdinov, and Abdelrahman Mohamed. 2021. Hubert: Self-supervised speech representation learning by masked prediction of hidden units.

Javier Iranzo-Sánchez, Joan Albert Silvestre-Cerdà, Javier Jorge, Nahuel Roselló, Adrià Giménez, Albert Sanchis, Jorge Civera, and Alfons Juan. 2020. Europarl-st: A multilingual corpus for speech translation of parliamentary debates. In *ICASSP 2020 - 2020 IEEE International Conference on Acoustics, Speech and Signal Processing (ICASSP)*, pages 8229–8233.

J. Kahn, M. Rivière, W. Zheng, E. Kharitonov, Q. Xu, P. E. Mazaré, J. Karadayi, V. Liptchinsky, R. Collobert, C. Fuegen, T. Likhomanenko, G. Synnaeve, A. Joulin, A. Mohamed, and E. Dupoux. 2020. Libri-light: A benchmark for asr with limited or no supervision. In *ICASSP 2020 - 2020 IEEE International Conference on Acoustics, Speech and Signal Processing (ICASSP)*, pages 7669–7673. `https://github.com/facebookresearch/libri-light`.

Yasumasa Kano, Katsuhito Sudoh, and Satoshi Nakamura. 2022. Simultaneous neural machine translation with prefix alignment. In *Proceedings of the 19th International Conference on Spoken Language Translation (IWSLT 2022)*, pages 22–31, Dublin, Ireland (in-person and online). Association for Computational Linguistics.

Yasumasa Kano, Katsuhito Sudoh, and Satoshi Nakamura. 2023. Average token delay: A latency metric for simultaneous translation. In *Proc, Interspeech 2023*. To appear.

Eugene Kharitonov, Morgane Rivière, Gabriel Synnaeve, Lior Wolf, Pierre-Emmanuel Mazaré, Matthijs Douze, and Emmanuel Dupoux. 2020. Data augmenting contrastive learning of speech representations in the time domain. *arXiv preprint arXiv:2007.00991*.

Danni Liu, Gerasimos Spanakis, and Jan Niehues. 2020. Low-Latency Sequence-to-Sequence Speech Recognition and Translation by Partial Hypothesis Selection. In *Proc. Interspeech 2020*, pages 3620–3624.

Mingbo Ma, Liang Huang, Hao Xiong, Renjie Zheng, Kaibo Liu, Baigong Zheng, Chuanqiang Zhang, Zhongjun He, Hairong Liu, Xing Li, Hua Wu, and Haifeng Wang. 2019. STACL: Simultaneous translation with implicit anticipation and controllable latency using prefix-to-prefix framework. In *Proceedings of the 57th Annual Meeting of the Association for Computational Linguistics*, pages 3025–3036, Florence, Italy. Association for Computational Linguistics.

Mingbo Ma, Baigong Zheng, Kaibo Liu, Renjie Zheng, Hairong Liu, Kainan Peng, Kenneth Church, and Liang Huang. 2020a. Incremental text-to-speech synthesis with prefix-to-prefix framework. In *Findings of the Association for Computational Linguistics: EMNLP 2020*, pages 3886–3896, Online. Association for Computational Linguistics.

Xutai Ma, Mohammad Javad Dousti, Changhan Wang, Jiatao Gu, and Juan Pino. 2020b. SIMULEVAL: An evaluation toolkit for simultaneous translation. In *Proceedings of the 2020 Conference on Empirical Methods in Natural Language Processing: System Demonstrations*, pages 144–150, Online. Association for Computational Linguistics.

Kikuo Maekawa. 2008. Balanced Corpus of Contemporary Written Japanese. In *Proceedings of the 6th Workshop on Asian Language Resources*.

Yuta Nishikawa and Satoshi Nakamura. 2023. Interconnection: Effective connection between pre-trained encoder and decoder for speech translation. In *Proc, Interspeech 2023*. To appear.

Sara Papi, Marco Gaido, Matteo Negri, and Marco Turchi. 2022. Over-generation cannot be rewarded: Length-adaptive average lagging for simultaneous speech translation. In *Proceedings of the Third Workshop on Automatic Simultaneous Translation*, pages 12–17, Online. Association for Computational Linguistics.

Ankita Pasad, Ju-Chieh Chou, and Karen Livescu. 2021. Layer-wise analysis of a self-supervised speech representation model. *2021 IEEE Automatic Speech Recognition and Understanding Workshop (ASRU)*, pages 914–921.

Peter Polák, Ngoc-Quan Pham, Tuan Nam Nguyen, Danni Liu, Carlos Mullov, Jan Niehues, Ondřej Bojar, and Alexander Waibel. 2022. CUNI-KIT system for simultaneous speech translation task at IWSLT 2022. In *Proceedings of the 19th International Conference on Spoken Language Translation (IWSLT 2022)*, pages 277–285, Dublin, Ireland (in-person and online). Association for Computational Linguistics.

Alec Radford, Jong Wook Kim, Tao Xu, Greg Brockman, Christine McLeavey, and Ilya Sutskever. 2022. Robust speech recognition via large-scale weak supervision. *arXiv preprint arXiv:2212.04356*.

Anthony Rousseau, Paul Deléglise, and Y. Estève. 2012. Ted-lium: an automatic speech recognition dedicated corpus. In *International Conference on Language Resources and Evaluation*.

Jonathan Shen, Ruoming Pang, Ron J. Weiss, Mike Schuster, Navdeep Jaitly, Zongheng Yang, Zhifeng Chen, Yu Zhang, Yuxuan Wang, Rj Skerrv-Ryan, Rif A. Saurous, Yannis Agiomvrgiannakis, and Yonghui Wu. 2018. Natural tts synthesis by conditioning wavenet on mel spectrogram predictions. In *2018 IEEE International Conference on Acoustics, Speech and Signal Processing (ICASSP)*, pages 4779–4783.

Ryosuke Sonobe, Shinnosuke Takamichi, and Hiroshi Saruwatari. 2017. Jsut corpus: free large-scale japanese speech corpus for end-to-end speech synthesis. *arXiv preprint arXiv:1711.00354*.

Hideyuki Tachibana, Katsuya Uenoyama, and Shunsuke Aihara. 2018. Efficiently trainable text-to-speech system based on deep convolutional networks with guided attention. In *2018 IEEE International Conference on Acoustics, Speech and Signal Processing (ICASSP)*, pages 4784–4788.

Yuqing Tang, Chau Tran, Xian Li, Peng-Jen Chen, Naman Goyal, Vishrav Chaudhary, Jiatao Gu, and Angela Fan. 2020. Multilingual translation with extensible multilingual pretraining and finetuning.

Ioannis Tsiamas, Gerard I. Gállego, Carlos Escolano, José Fonollosa, and Marta R. Costa-jussà. 2022. Pretrained speech encoders and efficient fine-tuning methods for speech translation: UPC at IWSLT 2022. In *Proceedings of the 19th International Conference on Spoken Language Translation (IWSLT 2022)*, pages 265–276, Dublin, Ireland (in-person and online). Association for Computational Linguistics.

Changhan Wang, Juan Pino, Anne Wu, and Jiatao Gu. 2020. CoVoST: A diverse multilingual speech-to-text translation corpus. In *Proceedings of the 12th Language Resources and Evaluation Conference*, pages 4197–4203, Marseille, France. European Language Resources Association.

Ryuichi Yamamoto, Eunwoo Song, and Jae-Min Kim. 2020. Parallel wavegan: A fast waveform generation model based on generative adversarial networks with multi-resolution spectrogram. In *ICASSP 2020 - 2020 IEEE International Conference on Acoustics, Speech and Signal Processing (ICASSP)*, pages 6199–6203.

Jing-Xuan Zhang, Zhen-Hua Ling, and Li-Rong Dai. 2018. Forward attention in sequence- to-sequence acoustic modeling for speech synthesis. In *2018 IEEE International Conference on Acoustics, Speech and Signal Processing (ICASSP)*, pages 4789–4793.

A Appendix

Tables 6, 7, and 8 show the results for all chunk size settings for the En-De, En-Ja, and En-Zh models used in the submitted system, respectively.

chunk size	BLEU	LAAL	AL	AP	DAL	ATD
300	24.217	947.509	495.162	0.732	1465.822	814.368
400	26.657	1189.696	829.689	0.753	1738.568	1180.684
500	27.986	1416.459	1071.682	0.774	1992.596	1375.404
600	28.739	1618.746	1318.715	0.791	2232.175	1367.612
700	29.298	1797.061	1515.356	0.811	2432.087	1608.334
800	29.809	1956.321	1714.173	0.826	2617.073	1720.705
820	29.78	2011.518	1772.404	0.827	2672.554	1765.76
840	29.792	2022.322	1790.452	0.832	2680.218	1741.386
860	29.746	2054.923	1825.194	0.834	2726.204	1740.656
900	29.805	2115.625	1895.961	0.841	2783.033	1711.2
950	29.975	2172.927	1964.329	0.846	2856.738	1893.749
1000	30.234	2255.583	2057.579	0.852	2938.408	1884.775

Table 6: Results of the **Offline+PA (None)** model on the MuST-C v2 tst-COMMON En-De.

chunk size	BLEU	LAAL	AL	AP	DAL	ATD
300	11.714	1096.676	288.185	0.807	1643.59	181.268
400	13.284	1377.647	697.522	0.827	1949.44	260.12
500	14.04	1642.289	1171.154	0.845	2246.513	343.565
600	14.458	1858.317	1433.278	0.866	2463.025	386.054
700	14.828	2064.974	1695.339	0.877	2672.509	471.012
800	15.235	2224.392	1803.111	0.895	2831.076	519.566
820	15.232	2256.386	1862.014	0.892	2865.29	537.516
840	15.316	2290.716	1973.586	0.892	2889.95	547.752
860	15.214	2341.734	2023.29	0.896	2946.322	557.76
900	15.281	2389.836	2121.337	0.898	3010.863	563.603
1000	15.439	2528.8	2247.036	0.907	3126.384	630.97

Table 7: Results of the **Offline+PA (4000)** model on the MuST-C v2 tst-COMMON En-Ja.

chunk size	BLEU	LAAL	AL	AP	DAL	ATD
300	19.794	1011.202	109.706	0.755	1411.409	206.106
400	20.874	1283.497	540.576	0.774	1718.894	370.356
500	21.291	1522.251	881.957	0.796	1984.268	474.854
600	21.628	1714.688	1173.412	0.811	2216.213	499.254
700	22.105	1906.995	1471.287	0.821	2436.948	667.78
750	21.844	1994.88	1587.405	0.83	2526.013	672.637
800	22.041	2071.358	1689.633	0.831	2621.874	738.394
840	22.101	2126.632	1826.245	0.829	2689.418	761.502
860	22.125	2167.874	1829.369	0.836	2728.565	760.173
900	22.057	2211.844	1927.426	0.838	2779.555	749.444
1000	22.196	2383.854	2137.905	0.851	2946.303	882.875

Table 8: Results of the **Offline+PA (None)** model on the MuST-C v2 tst-COMMON En-Zh.

Language Model Based Target Token Importance Rescaling for Simultaneous Neural Machine Translation

Aditi Jain* IIT Delhi mt6190739@iitd.ac.in

Nishant Kambhatla* School of Computing Science Simon Fraser University nkambhat@sfu.ca

Anoop Sarkar School of Computing Science Simon Fraser University anoop@sfu.ca

Abstract

The decoder in simultaneous neural machine translation receives limited information from the source while having to balance the opposing requirements of latency versus translation quality. In this paper, we use an auxiliary target-side language model to augment the training of the decoder model. Under this notion of target adaptive training, generating rare or difficult tokens is rewarded which improves the translation quality while reducing latency. The predictions made by a language model in the decoder are combined with the traditional cross entropy loss which frees up the focus on the source side context. Our experimental results over multiple language pairs show that compared to previous state of the art methods in simultaneous translation, we can use an augmented target side context to improve BLEU scores significantly. We show improvements over the state of the art in the low latency range with lower average lagging values (faster output). [1]

1 Introduction

Simultaneous Machine Translation (SiMT; Grissom II et al. (2014); Cho and Esipova (2016)) is a special case of neural machine translation (NMT; Vaswani et al. (2017)) that aims to produce real time-translations in the target language from a streaming input in the source language. The cornerstone of this task, as well as a key challenge, is the trade-off between the translation quality and the latency in producing the translations. This balance is ensured by a fixed (Ma et al., 2019; Elbayad et al., 2020) or adaptive (Arivazhagan et al., 2019; Ma et al., 2020; Zhang and Feng, 2022b) read/write policy that determines whether to wait for the next source token (a READ action) or to generate a translation (a WRITE action). Adaptive policies dynamically predict the action based on the current source and target contexts (Zheng et al., 2020). Although adaptive policies achieve a better latency/BLEU trade-off, they often fail to account for the varying importance of different tokens when deciding a READ/WRITE action.

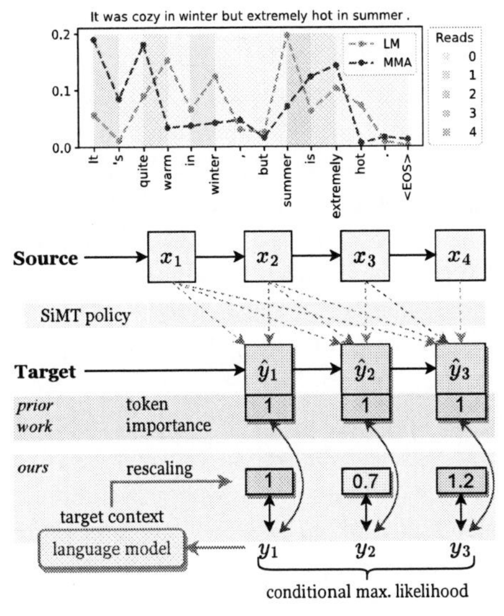

Figure 1: Prior work on simultaneous MT weighs every target token equally. **Top**: Normalized negative log-likelihood (nll) scores of each generated in-context target token as scored by the baseline SiMT along with the number of reads preceding a target token, and a target language model (LM). As the translations are imperfect, the LM shows disagreement by following an opposite nll trend compared to the translation model. **Bottom**: Our method rescales the importance of each target token using the target context during training.

In Figure 1 (top), there is a negative correlation between the normalized negative log likelihoods of output tokens as measured by MMA (a SiMT model with an adaptive policy; Ma et al. 2020) versus a left-to-right language model (LM). This reflects a translation which the SiMT model is confident about, but which the LM regards as poor English (possibly due to the semantic mismatch

[1] github.com/sfu-natlang/target_rescale_siMT

*Equal contribution. Listing order is random. Work performed while AJ was visiting SFU Natlang Lab.

Proceedings of the 20th International Conference on Spoken Language Translation (IWSLT 2023), pages 341–356
July 13-14, 2023 ©2023 Association for Computational Linguistics

evident in "*warm in winter*"). Since a simultaneous policy can only access partial source context, its outputs are likely to reflect imperfect guesses such as these, particularly when translating in real-time between language pairs with different word orderings (Subject-Object-Verb) and very long compounds. As a result, training objectives which treat all translated tokens with equal importance are sub-optimal.

In the context of translation, content words are generally considered more informative than function words (Chen et al., 2020). This is because content words carry the main semantic and lexical meaning of a sentence, while function words provide grammatical context and help to convey the syntactic structure of a sentence. Similarly, high-frequency words that are easier for the translation model to generate may sometimes carry less information than the desirable low-frequency (rare) words that the model struggles to generate (Chen et al., 2017). To this end, Zhang et al. (2022b) proposed to leverage conditional mutual information (MI) to estimate the weight-coefficients between the source and target to reweigh the importance of each target token. However, such an approach hasn't been explored to address simultaneous or streaming MT to the best of our knowledge, and the lack of a complete source context makes the adaptation of this method to SiMT non-trivial. To improve simultaneous MT, Alinejad et al. (2018) proposed a prediction mechanism on the source side to get future information and aid the lack of information on target-side for translation. Instead of directly predicting a source token, Zhang and Feng (2022a) predict its aligned future-position for a given target token to guide its policy. On the other hand, Zhang and Feng (2022b) and Zhang et al. (2022a) explored policies that assign varying importance to source/target tokens based on their level of information, with more informative tokens having a greater influence on the model.

In this paper, we propose a technique to alleviate this problem in SiMT using an information theoretic approach and an adaptive training paradigm. Inspired by the recent work in using pointwise mutual information for guiding the decoder in full-sentence (non-simultaneous) translation (Lee et al., 2022), we differentiate the importance of various target tokens by their dependence on the source sentence. As shown in Figure 1 (bottom), to guide our simultaneous translation model, we incorporate a language model that provides an additional signal indicating the importance of each target token or sentence. This *target-context aware estimation* leverages the relative probabilities of the translation model and language model to guide the generation process by explicitly re-weighting the training loss of each target token in the translation. Experiments show the strength of our simple method, outperforming several strong baselines in terms of both latency and BLEU scores. We perform exhaustive analysis to show that our model performs particularly well on translating low frequency words and longer sentences.

2 Background

Target adaptive training (Lin et al., 2017) in NMT addresses the token imbalance problem (Gu et al., 2020). While a translation model is conventionally trained with conditional maximum likelihood estimation or cross-entropy:

$$\mathcal{L}_{\mathrm{CE}}(\mathbf{x},\mathbf{y}) = -\sum_{j=1}^{N} \log p\left(y_j \mid \mathbf{y}_{<j}, \mathbf{x}\right) \quad (1)$$

adaptive training rescales this objective by assigning static or dynamic weights to further guide the translation model:

$$\mathcal{L}_{\mathrm{adapt}}(\mathbf{x},\mathbf{y}) = -\sum_{j=1}^{N} w_j \log p\left(y_j \mid \mathbf{y}_{<j}, \mathbf{x}\right) \quad (2)$$

Frequency based approaches (Gu et al., 2020; Xu et al., 2021) to assign these weights are promising but maintaining a frequency count can be an expensive overhead and would not be directly transferable to a simultaneous setting. More recently, Zhang et al. (2022b) proposed to leverage pointwise mutual information (MI) to estimate the weight-coefficients between the source $\mathbf{x}$ and target $\mathbf{y}$ as :

$$\mathrm{MI}(\mathbf{x},\mathbf{y}) = \log\left(\frac{p(\mathbf{x},\mathbf{y})}{p(\mathbf{x}).p(\mathbf{y})}\right) \quad (3)$$

which can reflect the importance of target tokens for translation models.

Monotonic Infinite-Lookback Attention Arivazhagan et al. (2019) models a Bernoulli variable to make the READ or WRITE decision at every time step, while processing the input sequence incrementally. Ma et al. (2020) present monotonic multihead attention to extend this policy to the multihead attention of transformers. For each encoder state in MMA, every head in the cross-attention of each decoder layer produces a probability $p_{i,j}$ that dictates if it should write target token y_j while having read till the source token x_i, or wait for more inputs. This is computed using the softmax energy:

$$\text{energy}_{i,j} = \left(\frac{m_j W^K \left(s_{i-1} W^Q \right)^T}{\sqrt{d_k}} \right)_{i,j} \quad (4)$$
$$p_{i,j} = \text{Sigmoid}\left(\text{energy}_{i,j}\right)$$

where m signifies the encoder states, W the input projection matrix for query Q and key K, and d_k is the dimension of the attention head. The probability $p_{i,j}$ is then used to parameterize the Bernoulli random variable:

$$b_{i,j} \sim \text{Bernoulli}\left(p_{i,j}\right) \quad (5)$$

If $b_{i,j} = 1$ then the model performs a WRITE action on y_j based on previous source tokens, otherwise it performs a READ.

Our method is based on MMA and we use it as our main simultaneous policy. To mitigate the negative impact of outlier heads[2] on the read/write path, we have made slight modifications to MMA to ensure more stable performance. Instead of allowing the heads in each decoder layer to independently determine the READ/WRITE action, we now share the READ/WRITE action between the decoder layers. This adjustment helps to avoid outlier heads that could potentially disrupt the system performance and stability (Indurthi et al., 2022).

3 Approach

3.1 Target-context Aware Information Quotient

Inspired by Lee et al. (2022), we leverage the point-wise mutual information (MI) between each target token and its source context under the condition of previous target context. For a target token y_j and the streaming source context $\mathbf{x} \leq i$, factoring in the partially constructed target prefix $\mathbf{y} < j$ gives the *target information quotient* (TIQ) is calculated as:

$$\begin{aligned} \text{TIQ}\left(y_j\right) &= \log\left(\frac{p\left(y_j, \mathbf{x}_{\leq i} \mid \mathbf{y}_{<j}\right)}{p\left(y_j \mid \mathbf{y}_{<j}\right) \cdot p\left(\mathbf{x}_{\leq i} \mid \mathbf{y}_{<j}\right)}\right) \\ &= \log\left(\frac{p\left(y_j \mid \mathbf{x}_{\leq i}, \mathbf{y}_{<j}\right) \cdot p\left(\mathbf{x}_{\leq i} \mid \mathbf{y}_{<j}\right)}{p\left(y_j \mid \mathbf{y}_{<j}\right) \cdot p\left(\mathbf{x}_{\leq i} \mid \mathbf{y}_{<j}\right)}\right) \\ &= \log\left(\frac{p\left(y_j \mid \mathbf{x}_{\leq i}, \mathbf{y}_{<j}\right)}{p\left(y_j \mid \mathbf{y}_{<j}\right)}\right) \\ &= \log\left(\frac{p_{\text{SiMT}}\left(y_j\right)}{p_{\text{LM}}\left(y_j\right)}\right) \end{aligned} \quad (6)$$

where $p_{\text{SiMT}}(.)$ is the simultaneous translation model probability and $p_{\text{LM}}(.)$ is the auxiliary target-side language model of the same size as the translation decoder. By decomposing the conditional joint distribution, this can be formalized as the log quotient of the streaming translation model probability and target language model probability. This captures the information of a target token conditioned on the target context and uses it to rescale the loss, thereby making the model pay more attention to more "informative" words.

To incorporate weights into the adaptive training objective (equation 2), two separate weights are used:

Token-level weight is used to determine weights of loss from each target token y_j and streaming source context, conditioned on the obtained partial translation at the current timestep. We use a token TIQ measure and normalise it to reduce variance:

$$\text{TIQ}_{\text{tok}} = \left(\text{TIQ}(y_j) - \mu^{tok}\right) / \sigma^{tok} \quad (7)$$

where μ^{tok}, and σ^{tok} are the mean and standard deviation of $\text{TIQ}(y_j)$ respectively, for every sentence.

Sentence-level weight on the other hand, is token-level TIQ is aggregated and averaged over the target sentence length $|\mathbf{y}|$:

$$\text{TIQ}_{\text{sen}} = \left(\frac{1}{|y|}\sum_{j=1}^{|y|} \text{TIQ}(y_j) - \mu^{sen}\right) / \sigma^{sen} \quad (8)$$

where μ^{sen}, and σ^{sen} are the mean and standard deviation of $\text{TIQ}(y_j)$ respectively, over a batch.

The final rescaling factor to assign weights in equation 2 is calculated as:

$$w_j = \left(\lambda_{\text{tok}} \text{TIQ}_{\text{tok}} + 1\right) \cdot \left(\lambda_{\text{sen}} \text{TIQ}_{\text{sen}} + 1\right) \quad (9)$$

The rescaling allows the model to learn the source side information for a particular target token y_j, while also factoring in the target context so far.

[2] In MMA, every head in the transformer multihead attention independently decides its read/write action and has access to all previous encoder states. The write action only takes place when the slowest head has arrived to a write decision.

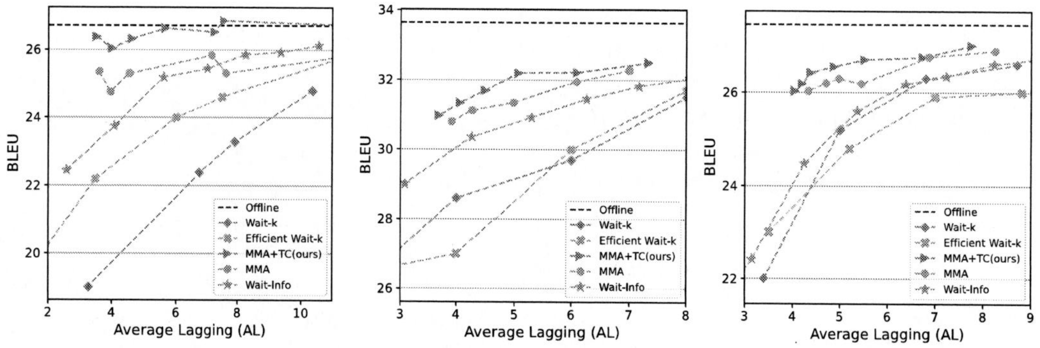

(a) Vi→En (b) De→En (c) En→De

Figure 2: Results on IWSLT15 Vi → En (a), and IWSLT14 En⇔De (b,c)

Given that information (from source) is constrained in the nature of this task, this additional signal of the target context acts as reinforcement for translation. The likelihood score from the LM should serve to strengthen the predictive capability of the decoder. Frequent words would have a higher LM score and therefore a smaller weight w_j. On the other hand, rare words would be scored lower by the LM, and thus have a higher rescaling weight w_j, allowing the model to focus on them more.

3.2 Final Training Objective with Adaptive Weights and Latency Constraints

In MMA models, following Ma et al. (2020), we use the weighted average of differentiable lagging metric $\mathcal{C}$ (Arivazhagan et al., 2019) over all the attentions heads as the weighted average latency L_{avg} constraint[3].

The MMA model uses both these loss terms in its final loss, with the hyperparameters λ_{avg} and λ_{var} respectively. Combining the latency average loss and the target-context aware information quotient, the final training objective for our model is:

$$\mathcal{L}_{\text{MMA+TC}} = L_{\text{adapt}}(\text{TIQ}) + \lambda_{\text{avg}} L_{\text{avg}} \quad (10)$$

where L_{adapt} is adaptive cross-entropy loss from equation 2 with TIQ (equation 9) as its rescaling-weight, and λ_{avg} is a hyperparameter to control the latency constraint.

[3]Early experiments with other policies such as GMA and Wait-info showed the approach to be ineffective. The explicit latency loss in MMA is crucial for the working of target adaptive training for simultaneous MT.

4 Experiments

4.1 Data

IWSLT'15 English ↔ Vietnamese (133K pairs) with TED tst2012 (1553 pairs) as validation set and TED tst2013 (1268 pairs) as test set. The vocabulary sizes of English and Vietnamese are 17K and 7.7K respectively.

IWSLT'14 English ↔ German (160K pairs) with validation set and test set of 7283 and 6750 pairs respectively. The vocabulary size of German is 13.5K and 9.98K for English.

4.2 Baselines and Model Settings

The following are the **main baselines** we compare our method against:

Offline Transformer (Vaswani et al., 2017) model for full-sentence translation.

Wait-k policy (Ma et al., 2019) which is a fixed-policy that reads k source tokens initially, and then alternates between reading and writing.

Efficient Wait-k (Elbayad et al., 2020) uses multiple k's to train a Wait-k model and relieves the constraint of test k being equal to train k.

Monotonic Multihead Attention (MMA; Ma et al. (2020)) extends infinite lookback attention (Arivazhagan et al., 2019) to all the Transformer heads.

Wait-Info (Zhang et al., 2022a) quantifies source and target token info to decide R/W action.

We also juxtapose our method against several **other baselines** on the En → Vi direction:

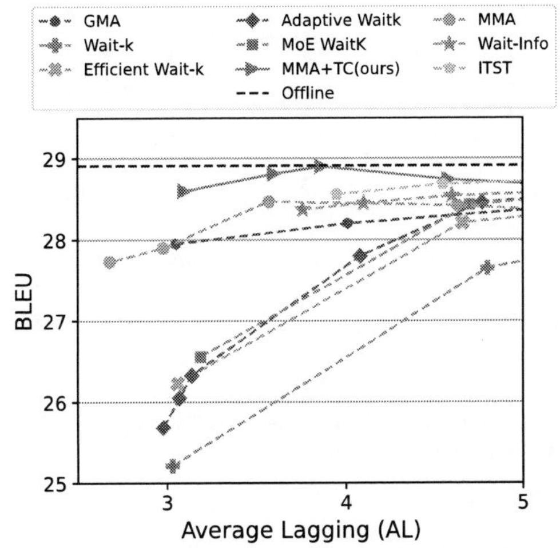

Figure 3: Performance of several methods on the En→Vi dataset in the *low latency* (AL<5) window.

Gaussian Multihead Attention (GMA; Zhang and Feng (2022a)) that predicts the aligned source position for a target token and rescales attention with a gaussian distribution centred at this position.

ITST (Zhang and Feng, 2022b) finds the optimal information transport between source and target.

Adaptive Wait-k(Zheng et al., 2020) dynamically chooses an optimal k in the wait-k policy at every step.

MoE Wait-k (Zhang and Feng, 2021b) uses attention heads as experts trained with different k with the wait-k policy.

MMA+TC (ours) is the proposed MMA model with target context aware adaptive training objective. We use an auxiliary target-side LM decoder of the same configuration as the MT decoder. Note that the LM is only used during training and discarded at test time. We do not use extra data.

The implementation of our method is based on `fairseq` (Ott et al., 2019). Following MMA, we use `transformer` (Vaswani et al., 2017) with 6 encoder and decoder layers and 4 monotonic attention heads for the IWSLT datasets En↔Vi, De↔En. All baselines are trained with same configurations and are trained with 16k tokens. Our auxiliary language model follows the decoder settings in the model.

4.3 Evaluation

We evaluate using BLEU (Papineni et al., 2002) for translation quality and Average Lagging (AL) (Ma et al., 2019) for latency. AL denotes the lagging behind the ideal policy (Wait-0). Other metrics used are Average Proportion (AP) (Cho and Esipova, 2016) and Differentiable Average Lagging (DAL) (Arivazhagan et al., 2019). Given a read/write policy g_i, AL is :

$$\mathrm{AL} = \frac{1}{\tau}\sum_{i=1}^{\tau} \mathrm{g}_i - \frac{i-1}{|y|/|x|} \tag{11}$$

where $\tau = \mathrm{argmax}_i\,(g_i = |x|)$, $|x|$ and $|y|$ are source sentence and target sentence lengths respectively.

5 Results

Figure 2 shows the comparison of BLEU vs. Latency (in terms of Average Lagging) of our method against previous methods on the IWSLT'15 Vi → En and IWSLT'14 En ↔ De directions. For Vi → En, we observe a significant improvement in the BLEU scores at the same latencies, compared to the baselines. We also reach the offline translation quality in low AL on this dataset. In the En → De, De → En directions too, there is a boost in the translation quality, more noticeably for lower latencies. The plots show that our method boosts translation quality in the earlier latencies and the effect of reweighing is more pronounced in these regions, where the source context is more limited. In higher latency regions, when the source information window increases, the other baselines start to reach our BLEU score in the English-German directions.

In Figure 3, we compare against several state-of-the-art methods on the En → Vi. Our method gets better translation quality compared all others, in the *low-latency* zone, matching the offline score at 3.86 AL. We show the BLEU vs. AL plot in a low latency range to compare performance in the more challenging area of this task, the low latency points.

6 Analysis

6.1 Token-level vs. Sentence-Level Weight

Ablation Study The two hyperparameters in our method are Sentence-Level Weight and Token-Level Weight, which determine the sentence and token-level effect of rescaling with LM. In Fig. 5

Token Order (Descending)	Avg. Freq.	Ref (%)	MMA (%)	MMA+ TC (%)
[0, 10%)	1385	85.56	87.63	87.21
[10, 30%)	56	6.89	6.48	6.34
[30, 50%)	20	2.19	1.75	**1.95**
[50, 70%)	11	1.30	0.70	**0.86**
[70, 100%]	6	0.95	0.26	**0.31**

Table 1: Avg. frequency on the training set and the proportion of tokens of different frequencies in the test set and the translations generated by the baseline and our model.

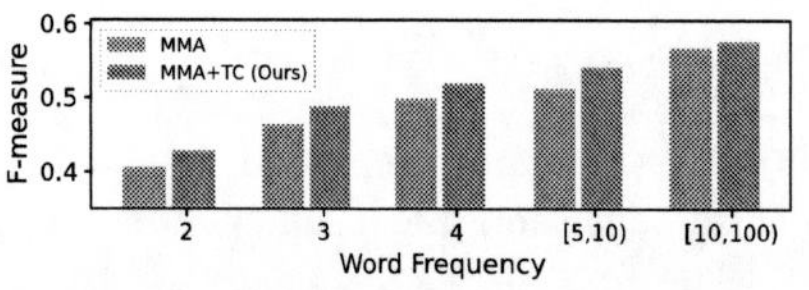

Figure 4: F-measure between model outputs and reference tokens for the low-frequency words, bucketed by frequency of the reference token.

we report the BLEU scores with different hyperparameter settings on Vi-En. (AL across the table are similar as experiments are done with the same λ). We set the values of these hyperparameters to 0.2 in all our experiments.

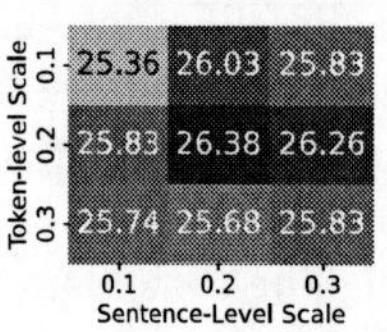

Figure 5: MMA+TC with different combinations for tok-level scale (λ_{tok}) and sent-level scale (λ_{sen}) values.

6.2 Effect on Low-frequency Words

With reweighing loss using the Language Model likelihood, we aim to reduce the effect of frequency imbalance in the corpus on training. We compare our translations against MMA on rare and frequent words. In addition to an overall BLEU improvement, we also see an improvement in the F-measure of rare words. As shown in Figure 4, our method does better on extremely rare words (freq ≤ 10). Table 1 shows that while the baseline overfits to the most frequent words, our method captures rare words, from the bottom two frequency bins (50-70% and 70-100%), better. The results show that our method makes the model train better on rare words and remedy the effect of token imbalance.

POS	Ref	MMA (%)	+TC (%)	MSE (↓)
ADJ	1497	82.1	**83.5**	0.18 | **0.16**
ADV	1323	83.5	**87.6**	0.20 | **0.12**
INTJ	74	**98.6**	94.6	**0.01** | 0.04
NOUN	4187	90.5	**93.4**	0.09 | **0.06**
PROPN	1315	99.4	99.4	- | -
VERB	3226	94.0	**95.7**	0.06 | **0.04**

Table 2: Our method generates more content words than the baseline MMA. Columns 2 and 3 show the percentage of the reference content words recovered in MMA and MMA+TC (in blue) respectively. The last column shows normalized mean squared error (MSE) of the recovered content words wrt reference. Lower MSE values are better.

Content word occurrences. Zhang et al. (2022a) show that focusing on the right content words in the target is crucial to getting the necessary target information in a subcutaneous translation setting. Following Moradi et al. (2019) we inspect the content words generated by our model using spacy to get POS tags over the translations. As evident from Table 2, our model recovers more content words in the translations wrt the reference.

6.3 Effect on Translation Length

Following the rationale of Lakew et al. (2019) in NMT and Zhang and Feng (2022d) in simultaneous translation, we inspect the translation quality of our model on varying target sentence lengths in Figure 8 and observe that our method shows a big improvement in BLEU on the longer sentences. Our method prevents the model from over-producing words (as seen in the top figure in Figure 8). We hypothesize that this is because the model does not generate as many words (and overuse them) from the most frequent word bin (see Table 1, top 10% bin) as MMA. Our target sentence lengths are consistently less than MMA's and are closer to the ground truth sentence lengths (as shown in the bin 0, Fig. 8 (top)).

6.4 Effect on Translation Paths

Attention Heatmaps and READ/WRITE Sequences. Figure 6 compares attention heatmaps from MMA and MMA+TC (our method) on the Vi $\rightarrow$ En direction. As evident, our method performs READ actions in smaller intervals between predicting consecutive WRITE actions.

Consider the READ/WRITE actions generated by MMA and MMA+TC for the given source sen-

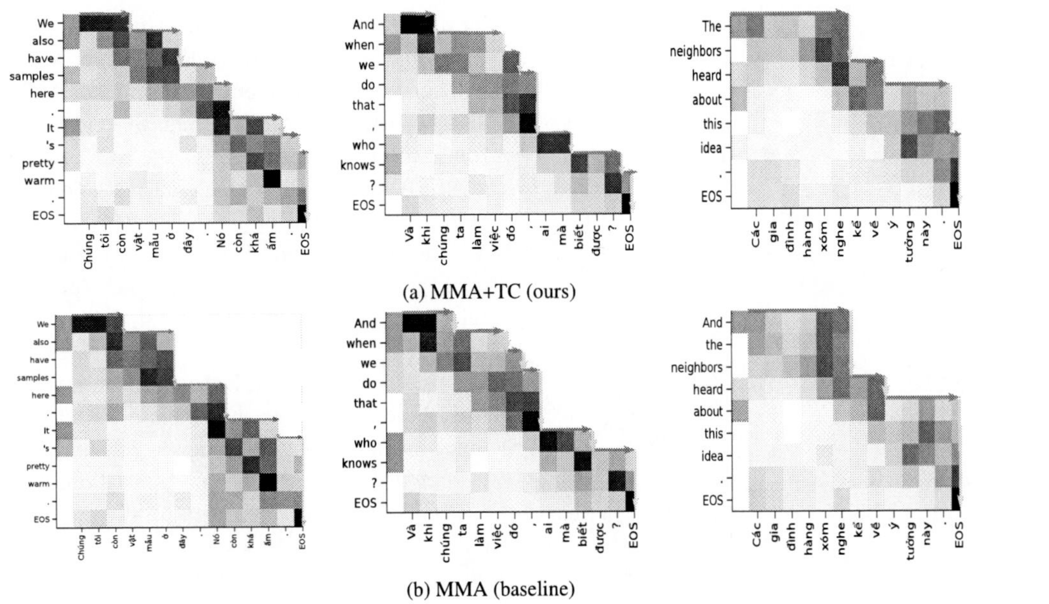

(a) MMA+TC (ours)

(b) MMA (baseline)

Figure 6: Attention heatmap comparison on the Vi → En direction. The Read-Write policy is drawn with red and green arrows respectively. The pink column at the start denotes the source tokens read to produce the target token on the left (darker implies more source words read, and white denotes 0 reads between consecutive target tokens)

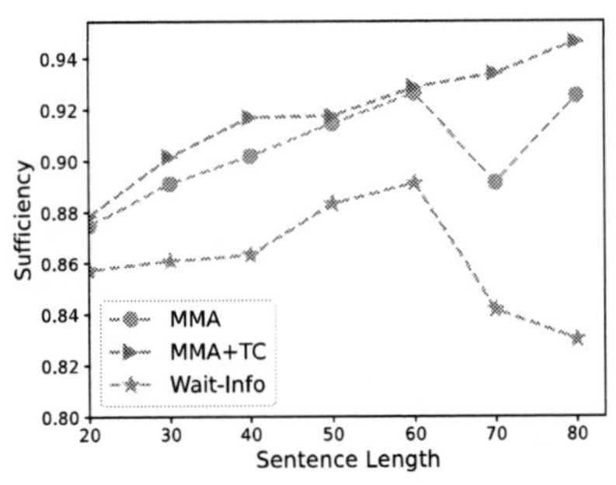

Figure 7: Sufficiency as a function of target length. All models produce translation with an AL of 4.

tence are:

Src: Chúng tôi còn vt mu đây . Nó còn khá m .

MMA: RRR W RRR WWW RRR WW RRR W RR WWWWW

Ours: RRR W RRR WW RR W R WW RRR W R W R WWWW

In this example, MMA reads more than required for a write in certain places. It shows that at a similar lag, our model gets a higher probability of a WRITE action, compared to MMA, after having read the same number of source words.

***Sufficiency* of the READ actions.** Zhang and Feng (2022c) introduce a metric of sufficiency A^{Suf} in Read/Write paths with the notion that too many but not all necessary READs would result in high latency while few but not sufficient READ actions would exclude needed information and could cause poor translation quality. When the ground truth aligned source position of the jth target word is denoted by a_j, and the number of source words read when writing target j^{th} word is denoted by r_j:

$$\mathrm{A}^{Suf} = \frac{1}{|y|}\sum_{j=1}^{|y|} \mathbb{1}_{a_j \leq r_j} \tag{12}$$

We compare our method against MMA and Wait-Info on AL=4 with the sufficiency metric. Using equation(12) across sentences of varying lengths, we evaluate the read-write paths of each model, against reference alignments from Eflomal (Östling and Tiedemann, 2016)[4]. In Figure 7, we can see a clearly increasing and higher score on sufficiency as compared to the baselines - Wait-Info and MMA. This signifies that our target-context augmented training helps the model read sufficient source tokens required for producing a translation, while maintaining the same latency as others, showing that the model learns and correctly gauges the information it requires to translate a target token, and

[4]We use the Eflomal library to get alignment priors from IWSLT'15 Vi-En train set, and use them to generate alignments for the test set. `https://github.com/robertostling/eflomal`

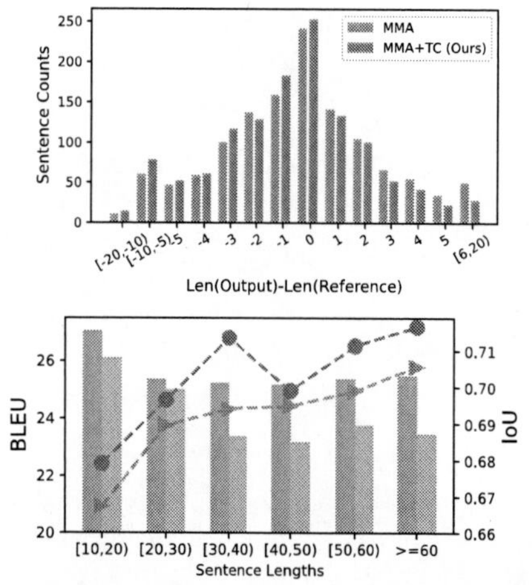

Figure 8: **Top**: Length difference compared to ref. **Bottom**: Sentence BLEU bucketed by target length (shown in bars), and the ratio of aligned READ actions for each bucket (IoU scores, Eqn. 13) shown with lines.

makes READ actions accordingly.

Ratio of Aligned READ actions. We compare MMA and our Read-Write policy against the reference source-target alignments by computing the overlap between the hard alignments and the translation path for all output translations :

$$IoU_{a,r} = \sum_{i=1} \left(\frac{intersection(a_i, r_i)}{union(a_i, r_i)} \right) \quad (13)$$

where a_i is the reference alignment matrix for the ith sentence, made by setting all aligned source positions to 1 and r_i is the upper triangular matrix set to 1 using reads from the policy.[5] The IoU scores for our policy and for MMA are shown in Figure 8 (bottom) with varying sentence lengths. Our policy shows a stronger adherence to the source-target monotonic alignment path.

7 Related Work

Simultaneous Translation. Fixed Policy methods (Ma et al., 2019; Elbayad et al., 2020) follow the fixed rule of waiting for the first k source tokens before generating a target token, and alternate thereafter. Adaptive Wait-k (Zheng et al., 2020) dynamically chooses the best k at every step. Han et al. (2020) applied meta learning in wait-k. Zhang and Feng (2021b) use each attention head as an expert of wait-k policy whereas Zhang and Feng (2021a) introduce a character level wait-k policy. But fixed policy methods aren't feasible for complex inputs and cannot adapt to them. Full-sentence MT has also been leveraged to augment the policy with future information (Zhang et al., 2020; Alinejad et al., 2021). But using such oracle or gold (Zheng et al., 2019; Arthur et al., 2021) READ/WRITE actions does not optimize policy with translation quality. Alinejad et al. (2018) proposes providing future-information on the source side using prediction. Grissom II et al. (2014) predict unseen verbs and uses reinforcement learning to learn when to trust these predictions and when to wait for more input. In contrast, we leverage target side context to strengthen the simultaneous translations.

Zhang and Feng (2022c) train two models on either language directions and make their policies converge. Wilken et al. (2020) propose external ground-truth alignments to train the policy. Papi et al. (2023) use cross attention scores to guide policy. Infinite-lookback (Arivazhagan et al., 2019) and chunkwise (Chiu* and Raffel*, 2018) attention propose to use a soft monotonic attention over previous encoder states. We use a variant of the policy proposed by Ma et al. (2020) that adapts monotonic attention to the multihead architecture of the Transformer. GMA (Zhang and Feng, 2022a) predicts the aligned source position of the current target token and rescales attention based on it. But these methods treat all words equally during training whereas our method improves upon MMA via adaptive training.

Some recent work explores capturing and quantifying *information* from the source tokens and use it to model READ/WRITE actions (Zhang et al., 2022a; Zhang and Feng, 2022b). But these works do not use the target context in their information. Unlike their quantization method, we present a simple scoring by using an auxiliary target-side LM.

Adaptive Training for MT. Target adaptive objectives have been explored by (Lin et al., 2017) which uses probability of a class to scale, but actually only scale down high frequency classes; (Jiang et al., 2019) which directly uses normalized frequency count but have high variance. (Gu et al., 2020) use a chi-square and an exponential distribution function with frequency. However these use only static word frequency. BMI (Xu et al., 2021) attempt to capture mutual information between each source and target token. CBMI (Zhang et al., 2022b) incorporate target context as well, in

[5]We choose this metric to show the extent to which the policy follows the source-target alignments. In an ideal setting, $IoU = 1$.

mutual information. However, these adaptive methods are not directly transferable to the streaming nature of our task.

8 Conclusion

We have presented a simple technique for rescaling target-token importance in simultaneous translation using an information theoretic approach and an adaptive training paradigm. We differentiate the importance of various target tokens by their dependence on the source sentence. To guide our simultaneous translation model, we incorporate a target-side language model that provides an additional signal indicating the importance of each target token or sentence under the condition of the previous target context. Our model shows strong performance on several datasets and outperforms several state-of-the-art techniques in the low latency range (AL<5). Further analysis shows that our technique is better able to translate long sentences and those with rare words. We also showed that the translation path (read/write action sequence) has a stronger correlation to the source-target alignment.

Limitations and Future Work

Since our auxiliary target-side LM decoder is spawned with the same configuration as the MT decoder, this significantly adds to the model size at training time. This makes it difficult to scale/slower to train with translation models of large size. While this problem can be easily mitigated by using a GPU of larger memory, we would like to explore more efficient ways of incorporating the target context which we leave for future work. Secondly, even though our method gives a significant boost to translation quality in the early latencies, it relies on the MMA (Ma et al., 2020) policy that has some limitations in terms of latency because of a suboptimal decision making using multiple heads (Indurthi et al., 2022). While our policy shows improvement, it could be further optimized, for instance, in following reference alignments more closely which would have a positive effect on latency. Finally, using additional monolingual data is also a viable direction for future work to strengthen the language model used in the approach.

Acknowledgements

We would like to thank the anonymous reviewers for their helpful comments. We would also like to thank Logan Born for the numerous discussions that helped shape this paper and Dr. Angel Chang for lending us the GPU resources. The research was partially supported by the Natural Sciences and Engineering Research Council of Canada grants NSERC RGPIN-2018-06437 and RGPAS-2018-522574 and a Department of National Defence (DND) and NSERC grant DGDND-2018-00025 to the third author.

References

Ashkan Alinejad, Hassan S. Shavarani, and Anoop Sarkar. 2021. Translation-based supervision for policy generation in simultaneous neural machine translation. In *Proceedings of the 2021 Conference on Empirical Methods in Natural Language Processing*, pages 1734–1744, Online and Punta Cana, Dominican Republic. Association for Computational Linguistics.

Ashkan Alinejad, Maryam Siahbani, and Anoop Sarkar. 2018. Prediction improves simultaneous neural machine translation. In *Proceedings of the 2018 Conference on Empirical Methods in Natural Language Processing*, pages 3022–3027, Brussels, Belgium. Association for Computational Linguistics.

Naveen Arivazhagan, Colin Cherry, Wolfgang Macherey, Chung-Cheng Chiu, Semih Yavuz, Ruoming Pang, Wei Li, and Colin Raffel. 2019. Monotonic infinite lookback attention for simultaneous machine translation. In *Proceedings of the 57th Annual Meeting of the Association for Computational Linguistics*, pages 1313–1323, Florence, Italy. Association for Computational Linguistics.

Philip Arthur, Trevor Cohn, and Gholamreza Haffari. 2021. Learning coupled policies for simultaneous machine translation using imitation learning. In *Proceedings of the 16th Conference of the European Chapter of the Association for Computational Linguistics: Main Volume*, pages 2709–2719, Online. Association for Computational Linguistics.

Kehai Chen, Rui Wang, Masao Utiyama, and Eiichiro Sumita. 2020. Content word aware neural machine translation. In *Proceedings of the 58th Annual Meeting of the Association for Computational Linguistics*, pages 358–364, Online. Association for Computational Linguistics.

Kehai Chen, Rui Wang, Masao Utiyama, Eiichiro Sumita, and Tiejun Zhao. 2017. Context-aware smoothing for neural machine translation. In *Proceedings of the Eighth International Joint Conference on Natural Language Processing (Volume 1: Long Papers)*, pages 11–20, Taipei, Taiwan. Asian Federation of Natural Language Processing.

Chung-Cheng Chiu* and Colin Raffel*. 2018. Monotonic chunkwise attention. In *International Conference on Learning Representations*.

Kyunghyun Cho and Masha Esipova. 2016. Can neural machine translation do simultaneous translation?

Maha Elbayad, Laurent Besacier, and Jakob Verbeek. 2020. Efficient Wait-k Models for Simultaneous Machine Translation. In *Proc. Interspeech 2020*, pages 1461–1465.

Alvin Grissom II, He He, Jordan Boyd-Graber, John Morgan, and Hal Daumé III. 2014. Don't until the final verb wait: Reinforcement learning for simultaneous machine translation. In *Proceedings of the 2014 Conference on Empirical Methods in Natural Language Processing (EMNLP)*, pages 1342–1352, Doha, Qatar. Association for Computational Linguistics.

Shuhao Gu, Jinchao Zhang, Fandong Meng, Yang Feng, Wanying Xie, Jie Zhou, and Dong Yu. 2020. Token-level adaptive training for neural machine translation. In *Proceedings of the 2020 Conference on Empirical Methods in Natural Language Processing (EMNLP)*, pages 1035–1046, Online. Association for Computational Linguistics.

Hou Jeung Han, Mohd Abbas Zaidi, Sathish Reddy Indurthi, Nikhil Kumar Lakumarapu, Beomseok Lee, and Sangha Kim. 2020. End-to-end simultaneous translation system for IWSLT2020 using modality agnostic meta-learning. In *Proceedings of the 17th International Conference on Spoken Language Translation*, pages 62–68, Online. Association for Computational Linguistics.

Sathish Reddy Indurthi, Mohd Abbas Zaidi, Beomseok Lee, Nikhil Kumar Lakumarapu, and Sangha Kim. 2022. Infusing future information into monotonic attention through language models.

Shaojie Jiang, Pengjie Ren, Christof Monz, and Maarten de Rijke. 2019. Improving neural response diversity with frequency-aware cross-entropy loss. New York, NY, USA. Association for Computing Machinery.

Surafel Melaku Lakew, Mattia Di Gangi, and Marcello Federico. 2019. Controlling the output length of neural machine translation. In *Proceedings of the 16th International Conference on Spoken Language Translation*, Hong Kong. Association for Computational Linguistics.

Youngwon Lee, Changmin Lee, Hojin Lee, and Seung-won Hwang. 2022. Normalizing mutual information for robust adaptive training for translation. In *Proceedings of the 2022 Conference on Empirical Methods in Natural Language Processing*, pages 8008–8015, Abu Dhabi, United Arab Emirates. Association for Computational Linguistics.

Tsung-Yi Lin, Priya Goyal, Ross Girshick, Kaiming He, and Piotr Dollár. 2017. Focal loss for dense object detection. In *Proceedings of the IEEE international conference on computer vision*, pages 2980–2988.

Mingbo Ma, Liang Huang, Hao Xiong, Renjie Zheng, Kaibo Liu, Baigong Zheng, Chuanqiang Zhang, Zhongjun He, Hairong Liu, Xing Li, Hua Wu, and Haifeng Wang. 2019. STACL: Simultaneous translation with implicit anticipation and controllable latency using prefix-to-prefix framework. In *Proceedings of the 57th Annual Meeting of the Association for Computational Linguistics*, pages 3025–3036, Florence, Italy. Association for Computational Linguistics.

Xutai Ma, Juan Miguel Pino, James Cross, Liezl Puzon, and Jiatao Gu. 2020. Monotonic multihead attention. In *International Conference on Learning Representations*.

Pooya Moradi, Nishant Kambhatla, and Anoop Sarkar. 2019. Interrogating the explanatory power of attention in neural machine translation. In *Proceedings of the 3rd Workshop on Neural Generation and Translation*, pages 221–230, Hong Kong. Association for Computational Linguistics.

Robert Östling and Jörg Tiedemann. 2016. Efficient word alignment with Markov Chain Monte Carlo. *Prague Bulletin of Mathematical Linguistics*, 106:125–146.

Myle Ott, Sergey Edunov, Alexei Baevski, Angela Fan, Sam Gross, Nathan Ng, David Grangier, and Michael Auli. 2019. fairseq: A fast, extensible toolkit for sequence modeling. In *Proceedings of NAACL-HLT 2019: Demonstrations*.

Sara Papi, Marco Turchi, and Matteo Negri. 2023. Alignatt: Using attention-based audio-translation alignments as a guide for simultaneous speech translation.

Kishore Papineni, Salim Roukos, Todd Ward, and Wei-Jing Zhu. 2002. Bleu: A method for automatic evaluation of machine translation. In *Proceedings of the 40th Annual Meeting on Association for Computational Linguistics*, ACL '02, page 311–318, USA. Association for Computational Linguistics.

Ashish Vaswani, Noam Shazeer, Niki Parmar, Jakob Uszkoreit, Llion Jones, Aidan N Gomez, Ł ukasz Kaiser, and Illia Polosukhin. 2017. Attention is all you need. In *Advances in Neural Information Processing Systems*, volume 30. Curran Associates, Inc.

Patrick Wilken, Tamer Alkhouli, Evgeny Matusov, and Pavel Golik. 2020. Neural simultaneous speech translation using alignment-based chunking. In *Proceedings of the 17th International Conference on Spoken Language Translation*, pages 237–246, Online. Association for Computational Linguistics.

Yangyifan Xu, Yijin Liu, Fandong Meng, Jiajun Zhang, Jinan Xu, and Jie Zhou. 2021. Bilingual mutual information based adaptive training for neural machine translation. In *Proceedings of the 59th Annual Meeting of the Association for Computational Linguistics and the 11th International Joint Conference on Natural Language Processing (Volume 2: Short Papers)*, pages 511–516, Online. Association for Computational Linguistics.

Shaolei Zhang and Yang Feng. 2021a. ICT's system for AutoSimTrans 2021: Robust char-level simultaneous translation. In *Proceedings of the Second Workshop on Automatic Simultaneous Translation*, pages 1–11, Online. Association for Computational Linguistics.

Shaolei Zhang and Yang Feng. 2021b. Universal simultaneous machine translation with mixture-of-experts wait-k policy. In *Proceedings of the 2021 Conference on Empirical Methods in Natural Language Processing*, pages 7306–7317, Online and Punta Cana, Dominican Republic. Association for Computational Linguistics.

Shaolei Zhang and Yang Feng. 2022a. Gaussian multihead attention for simultaneous machine translation. In *Findings of the Association for Computational Linguistics: ACL 2022*, pages 3019–3030, Dublin, Ireland. Association for Computational Linguistics.

Shaolei Zhang and Yang Feng. 2022b. Information-transport-based policy for simultaneous translation. In *Proceedings of the 2022 Conference on Empirical Methods in Natural Language Processing*, pages 992–1013, Abu Dhabi, United Arab Emirates. Association for Computational Linguistics.

Shaolei Zhang and Yang Feng. 2022c. Modeling dual read/write paths for simultaneous machine translation. In *Proceedings of the 60th Annual Meeting of the Association for Computational Linguistics (Volume 1: Long Papers)*, pages 2461–2477, Dublin, Ireland. Association for Computational Linguistics.

Shaolei Zhang and Yang Feng. 2022d. Reducing position bias in simultaneous machine translation with length-aware framework. In *Proceedings of the 60th Annual Meeting of the Association for Computational Linguistics (Volume 1: Long Papers)*, pages 6775–6788, Dublin, Ireland. Association for Computational Linguistics.

Shaolei Zhang, Yang Feng, and Liangyou Li. 2020. Future-guided incremental transformer for simultaneous translation. In *AAAI Conference on Artificial Intelligence*.

Shaolei Zhang, Shoutao Guo, and Yang Feng. 2022a. Wait-info policy: Balancing source and target at information level for simultaneous machine translation. In *Findings of the Association for Computational Linguistics: EMNLP 2022*, pages 2249–2263, Abu Dhabi, United Arab Emirates. Association for Computational Linguistics.

Songming Zhang, Yijin Liu, Fandong Meng, Yufeng Chen, Jinan Xu, Jian Liu, and Jie Zhou. 2022b. Conditional bilingual mutual information based adaptive training for neural machine translation. In *Proceedings of the 60th Annual Meeting of the Association for Computational Linguistics (Volume 1: Long Papers)*, pages 2377–2389, Dublin, Ireland. Association for Computational Linguistics.

Baigong Zheng, Kaibo Liu, Renjie Zheng, Mingbo Ma, Hairong Liu, and Liang Huang. 2020. Simultaneous translation policies: From fixed to adaptive. In *Proceedings of the 58th Annual Meeting of the Association for Computational Linguistics*, pages 2847–2853, Online. Association for Computational Linguistics.

Baigong Zheng, Renjie Zheng, Mingbo Ma, and Liang Huang. 2019. Simpler and faster learning of adaptive policies for simultaneous translation. In *Proceedings of the 2019 Conference on Empirical Methods in Natural Language Processing and the 9th International Joint Conference on Natural Language Processing (EMNLP-IJCNLP)*, pages 1349–1354, Hong Kong, China. Association for Computational Linguistics.

A Hyperparameters

Hyperparameter	IWSLT'15 En ↔ Vi IWSLT'14 De ↔ En
encoder layers	6
encoder attention heads	4
encoder embed dim	512
encoder ffn embed dim	1024
decoder layers	6
decoder attention heads	4
decoder embed dim	512
decoder ffn embed dim	1024
dropout	0.3
optimizer	adam
adam-β	(0.9,0.98)
clip-norm	0
lr	5e-4
lr scheduler	inverse sqrt
warmup-updates	4000
warmup-init-lr	1e-7
weight decay	0.0001
label-smoothing	0.1
max tokens	16000

Table 3: Hyperparameters used in our experiments

All models were trained on 2 x Titan RTX with 24 GB memory each. An entire training run finishes within 2.5 hours with fp32 completing about 40 epochs.

B Detailed Results

IWSLT15 En-Vi Transformer-Small					
Full-sentence MT		AP	AL	DAL	BLEU
		1.00	22.08	22.08	28.91
MMA	λ	AP	AL	DAL	BLEU
	0.4	0.58	2.68	3.46	27.73
	0.3	0.59	2.98	3.81	27.90
	0.2	0.63	3.57	4.44	28.47
	0.1	0.67	4.63	5.65	28.42
	0.04	0.70	5.44	6.57	28.33
	0.02	0.76	7.09	8.29	28.28
Wait-K	k	AP	AL	DAL	BLEU
	1	0.63	3.03	3.54	25.21
	3	0.71	4.80	5.42	27.65
	5	0.78	6.46	7.06	28.34
	7	0.83	8.21	8.79	28.60
	9	0.88	9.92	10.51	28.69
Efficient Wait-K	k	AP	AL	DAL	BLEU
	1	0.63	3.06	3.61	26.23
	3	0.71	4.66	5.20	28.21
	5	0.78	6.38	6.94	28.56
	7	1.96	8.13	8.69	28.62
	9	0.87	9.80	10.34	28.52
Wait-Info	$\mathcal{K}$	AP	AL	DAL	BLEU
	1	0.67	3.76	4.33	28.37
	2	0.69	4.10	4.71	28.45
	3	0.71	4.60	5.28	28.54
	4	0.74	5.28	5.97	28.59
	5	0.77	6.01	6.71	28.70
	6	0.80	6.80	7.51	28.78
	7	0.82	7.61	8.33	28.80
	8	0.84	8.39	9.11	28.82
MMA+TC	λ	AP	AL	DAL	BLEU
	0.55	0.66	3.1	5.12	28.6
	0.5	0.67	3.60	5.78	28.81
	0.3	0.68	3.86	6.12	28.9
	0.2	0.71	4.58	7.22	28.74
	0.1	0.74	5.34	8.18	28.65
	0.01	0.89	9.89	14.37	28.67

Table 4: Experiments on IWSLT15 English $\rightarrow$ Vietnamese

IWSLT15 Vi - En Transformer-Small					
Full-sentence MT (Offline)		AP	AL	DAL	BLEU
		1.00	27.56	27.56	26.11
MMA	λ	AP	AL	DAL	BLEU
	0.4	0.63	3.60	6.96	25.36
	0.3	0.64	3.95	7.59	24.75
	0.2	0.67	4.54	9.09	25.33
	0.1	0.75	7.14	11.60	25.84
	0.05	0.77	7.61	15.70	25.31
	0.01	0.88	13.63	23.95	26.11
Wait-K	k	AP	AL	DAL	BLEU
	1	0.42	-2.89	1.62	7.57
	3	0.53	-0.18	3.24	14.66
	5	0.61	1.49	5.08	17.44
	7	0.67	3.28	7.05	19.02
	9	0.76	6.75	8.96	22.39
	11	0.80	7.91	10.71	23.28
	13	0.84	10.37	12.36	24.80
Wait-Info	$\mathcal{K}$	AP	AL	DAL	BLEU
	4	0.62	2.58	5.06	22.45
	5	0.67	4.08	6.27	23.75
	6	0.72	5.61	7.72	25.19
	7	0.76	7.01	9.19	25.45
	8	0.79	8.26	10.66	25.86
	9	0.82	9.37	11.98	25.93
	10	0.84	10.56	13.30	26.13
MMA+TC	λ	AP	AL	DAL	BLEU
	0.4	0.63	3.51	5.902	26.38
	0.3	0.65	4.01	6.558	26.04
	0.2	0.67	4.62	7.527	26.32
	0.1	0.71	5.67	9.212	26.63
	0.05	0.76	7.23	10.579	26.52
	0.04	0.77	7.55	11.76	26.85
	0.01	0.89	13.31	18.627	26.67

Table 5: Experiments on IWSLT15 Vietnamese → English

IWSLT15 De-En Transformer-Small					
Full-sentence MT		AP	AL	DAL	BLEU
(Offline)		1.00	22.97	22.97	33.64
	λ	AP	AL	DAL	BLEU
	0.4	0.67	3.91	6.36	30.8
MMA	0.3	0.69	4.27	6.84	31.12
	0.2	0.72	4.97	7.82	31.34
	0.1	0.77	6.08	9.47	31.95
	$\mathcal{K}$	AP	AL	DAL	BLEU
	1	0.57	1.32	2.53	26.26
	2	0.59	1.97	3.17	27.39
	3	0.64	3.08	4.35	29.01
Wait-Info	4	0.69	4.27	5.61	30.36
	5	0.739	5.30	6.84	30.92
	6	0.77	6.26	8.03	31.45
	7	0.80	7.17	9.09	31.82
	8	0.82	8.06	9.94	32.05
	k		AL		BLEU
	3		1.8		26
Wait-K	5		4		28.6
	7		6		29.7
	9		8		31.5
	k		AL		BLEU
	3		2		26.4
Efficient Wait-K	5		4		27
	7		6		30
	9		8		31.7
	λ	AP	AL	DAL	BLEU
	0.5	0.66	3.68	5.92	30.97
	0.4	0.68	4.06	6.51	31.33
MMA+TC	0.3	0.70	4.49	7.12	31.69
	0.2	0.73	5.06	7.93	32.2
	0.1	0.77	6.10	9.54	32.22

Table 6: Experiments on IWSLT14 German $\rightarrow$ English

IWSLT15 En-De Transformer-Small					
Full-sentence MT		AP	AL	DAL	BLEU
(Offline)		1.00	22.21	22.21	27.46
	λ	AP	AL	DAL	BLEU
	0.5	0.69	4.32	6.42	26.03
	0.4	0.71	4.70	6.95	26.20
MMA	0.3	0.72	4.97	7.28	26.30
	0.2	0.74	5.44	7.96	26.19
	0.1	0.79	6.86	9.72	26.77
	0.05	0.84	8.25	11.42	26.91
	K	AP	AL	DAL	BLEU
	1	0.61	2.62	3.09	21.75
	2	0.63	3.15	3.89	22.42
	3	0.68	4.24	5.30	24.48
Wait-Info	4	0.73	5.36	6.77	25.60
	5	0.77	6.38	8.09	26.18
	6	0.80	7.23	9.18	26.35
	7	0.83	8.23	10.35	26.61
	8	0.86	9.25	11.46	26.74
	k		AL		BLEU
	3		3.41		22.00
Wait-K	5		5.00		25.21
	7		6.83		26.32
	9		8.72		26.61
	k		AL		BLEU
	3		3.51		23.01
Efficient Wait-K	5		5.27		24.80
	7		7.03		25.93
	9		8.81		26.11
	λ	AP	AL	DAL	BLEU
	0.6	0.68	4.04	6.07	26.03
	0.5	0.69	4.19	6.25	26.19
MMA+TC	0.4	0.69	4.38	6.52	26.43
	0.3	0.71	4.87	7.14	26.56
	0.2	0.74	5.51	8.09	26.71
	0.1	0.79	6.74	9.80	26.76
	0.06	0.82	7.75	10.94	27.01

Table 7: Experiments on IWSLT14 English $\rightarrow$ German

Kyoto Speech-to-Speech Translation System for IWSLT 2023

Zhengdong Yang[1] **Shuichiro Shimizu**[1] **Zhou Wangjin**[1] **Sheng Li**[2] **Chenhui Chu**[1]
Kyoto University[1] National Institute of Information and Communications Technology[2]
{zd-yang, sshimizu, chu}@nlp.ist.i.kyoto-u.ac.jp
zhou@sap.ist.i.kyoto-u.ac.jp
sheng.li@nict.go.jp

Abstract

This paper describes the Kyoto speech-to-speech translation system for IWSLT 2023. Our system is a combination of speech-to-text translation and text-to-speech synthesis. For the speech-to-text translation model, we used the dual-decoder Transformer model. For the text-to-speech synthesis model, we took a cascade approach of an acoustic model and a vocoder.

1 Introduction

This paper describes the Kyoto speech-to-speech translation system for IWSLT 2023 (Agarwal et al., 2023). Our system is a combination of speech-to-text translation and text-to-speech synthesis. For speech-to-text translation model, we used dual-decoder Transformer model following Le et al. (2020). For text-to-speech synthesis model, we took cascade approach of an acoustic model and a vocoder. We used FastSpeech 2 (Ren et al., 2021) as the acoustic model and HiFi-GAN (Kong et al., 2020) as the vocoder.

2 System Description

The speech-to-speech translation system is a combination of speech-to-text translation and text-to-speech synthesis.

2.1 Speech-to-Text Translation

We adopt the end-to-end speech-to-text translation architecture. The speech-to-text translation model is based on dual-decoder Transfomer (Le et al., 2020).

As shown in Figure 1, the model is a Transformer-based model, comprising two decoders - one for speech-to-text translation (ST) and the other for automatic speech recognition (ASR). The task of ASR and ST can be defined as follows:

- For ASR, the input sequence $\boldsymbol{s} = [s_1, ..., s_{T_s}]$ is a sequence of speech features. The output sequence $\boldsymbol{x} = [x_1, ..., x_{T_x}]$ is the corresponding transcription, where T_x indicates the length of the transcription.
- For ST, the input sequence $\boldsymbol{s} = [s_1, ..., s_{T_s}]$ is the same with ASR and the output sequence $\boldsymbol{y} = [y_1, ..., y_{T_y}]$ is the corresponding translation in target language, where T_y indicates the length of the translation.

The model performs the multi-task learning of ASR and ST and the output distributions can be written as

$$D_{asr\text{-}st} = p(\boldsymbol{x}, \boldsymbol{y}|\boldsymbol{s}) = \prod_{t=0}^{max(T_x,T_y)} p(x_t, y_t|\boldsymbol{x}_{<t}, \boldsymbol{y}_{<t}, \boldsymbol{s}) \quad (1)$$

The training objective is a weighted sum of cross-entropy losses for both tasks:

$$L_{asr\text{-}st} = \alpha L_{asr} + (1 - \alpha) L_{st} \quad (2)$$

Different decoders can exchange information with each other with the interactive attention mechanism, which refers to replacing attention sub-layers in the standard Transformer decoder with interactive attention sub-layers (Liu et al., 2020). In our models, the replaced sub-layers are the encoder-decoder attention sub-layers.

As illustrated in the lower part of Figure 1, an interactive attention sub-layer consists of one main attention sub-layer and a cross-attention sub-layers. The main attention sub-layer is the same as the replaced attention sub-layer. The cross-attention sub-layers receive query $\boldsymbol{Q}$ from the same decoder A and receive key $\boldsymbol{K}$ and value $\boldsymbol{V}$ from another decoder B. We adopt the parallel variation of dual-decoder Transformers where $\boldsymbol{K}$ and $\boldsymbol{V}$ are hidden states from the same layer in decoder B.

The final output is obtained by merging the output of the primary attention sub-layer $\boldsymbol{H}_{main}$ with

Proceedings of the 20th International Conference on Spoken Language Translation (IWSLT 2023), pages 357–362
July 13-14, 2023

the output of the cross attention sub-layer $\boldsymbol{H}_{cross}$. We adopt linear interpolation as the merging function. Therefore the output representations of the interactive attention sub-layers are

$$\boldsymbol{H}_{dual} = \boldsymbol{H}_{main} + \lambda \boldsymbol{H}_{cross} \quad (3)$$

where λ is a learnable parameter.

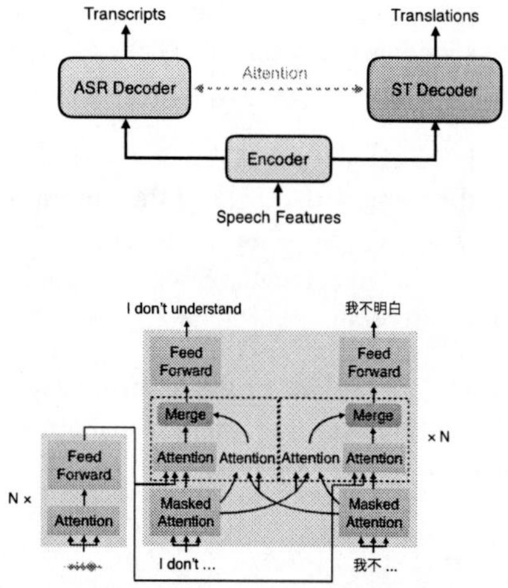

Figure 1: General architecture of dual-decoder Transformer (upper) and interactive attention mechanism (lower). Interactive attention sub-layers are marked with dotted boxes. They merge the outputs of the main attention sub-layers (red boxes) and cross-attention sub-layers (yellow boxes).

2.2 Text-to-Speech Synthesis

We adopted the approach to cascade an acoustic model and a vocoder. We used FastSpeech 2 (Ren et al., 2021) as the acoustic model and HiFi-GAN (Kong et al., 2020) as the vocoder. FastSpeech 2 adopts Transformer-based architecture for the encoder and the Mel-spectrogram decoder, and the variance adapter between them predicts the duration, pitch, and energy of the audio. HiFi-GAN employs generative adversarial networks to generate waveforms from Mel-spectrograms. It is composed of one generator and two discriminators, a multi-period discriminator, and a multi-scale discriminator. We used the PaddleSpeech toolkit (Zhang et al., 2022a) and the pretrained models provided by Zhang et al. (2022a) to generate waveforms.

Dataset	Sentence Embedding Model Used for Filtering	Total Length (Hours)
MuST-C	None	600.2
GigaST	None	9873.2
GigaST	LASER	919.1
GigaST	Sentence Transformers	601.1

Table 1: The size of the datasets and the filtered versions used for training the ST system.

3 Experiments

3.1 Speech-to-Text Translation

3.1.1 Datasets

To train our ST system, we utilized two distinct datasets: MuST-C (Di Gangi et al., 2019) v2 with Chinese translations, and GigaST (Ye et al., 2022) which is the original dataset that was used to construct the GigaS2S dataset provided by the organizers.

Both datasets offer unique advantages. While GigaST is in the same domain as the development and test data, MuST-C is not. In addition, GigaST is considerably larger than MuST-C. However, it is worth noting that the translations in GigaST were generated by a machine translation system and may not be of the same quality as those in MuST-C, which were translated by human. As a result, determining which dataset is more likely to yield better results requires further experimentation.

To shorten the training time and improve performance, we filtered the extremely large GigaST dataset to select utterances with better translation quality. As the translations in GigaST are machine-generated and there are no reference translations available, we evaluated the translation quality using the cosine similarity of sentence embeddings from the source and target sentences. We tested two different models for generating the embeddings: LASER[1] and "paraphrase-xlm-r-multilingual-v1" from Sentence Transformers[2] (simply referred to as "Sentence Transformers" subsequently). The resulting similarity distributions are shown in Figure 2. We selected the top 10% of the data based on similarity scores (data that is on the right-hand side of the red line). Table 1 shows the sizes of MuST-C and GigaST before and after filtering.

[1]https://github.com/facebookresearch/LASER
[2]https://github.com/UKPLab/sentence-transformers/tree/master/examples/training/paraphrases

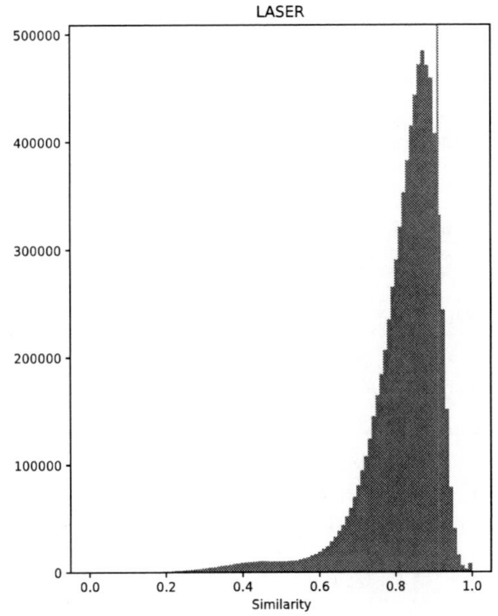

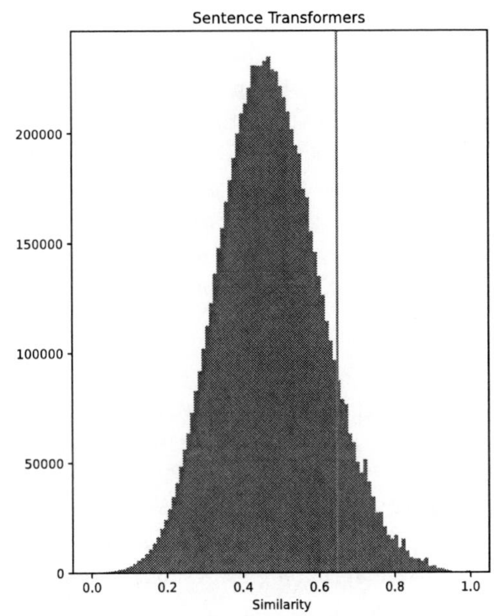

Figure 2: Histograms of cosine similarity between source and target sentence embedding based on LASER and Sentence Transformers. The red line marks the 90th percentile.

3.1.2 Training and Decoding

English sentences were normalized and tokenized using the Moses tokenizer (Koehn et al., 2007), and punctuations were stripped. Chinese sentences were tokenized using jieba.[3] English and Chinese tokens were further split into subwords using the BPE method (Sennrich et al., 2016) with a joint vocabulary of 16,000 subwords.

We used Kaldi (Ravanelli et al., 2019) to extract 83-dimensional features normalized by the mean and standard deviation computed on the training set. We removed utterances with more than 6,000 frames or more than 400 characters and used speed perturbation (Inaguma et al., 2020) with factors of 0.9, 1.0, and 1.1 for data augmentation.

Our implementation was based on the ESPnet-ST toolkit (Inaguma et al., 2020). We used the same architecture for all the ST models with a 12-layer encoder and 8-layer decoders. The coefficient α in the loss function (Equation 2) was set to 0.3 in all the experiments. We used the Adam optimizer (Kingma and Ba, 2015) and Noam learning rate schedule (Vaswani et al., 2017) with 25,000 warm-up steps and a maximum learning rate of $2.5e-3$. We used a batch size of 48 per GPU and trained models on a single machine with 4 Tesla V100 GPUs. The models were trained for 25 epochs. We kept checkpoints after each epoch and averaged the five best models on the development set based on prediction accuracy. For decoding, the beam size was set to 5 for ST and 1 for ASR.

3.1.3 Results

We conducted experiments to investigate the impact of using different datasets for training the system. The results are presented in Table 2. Additionally, we evaluated the performance of the system when using different sentence embedding models for data filtering. Our findings reveal that LASER produces better results compared to Sentence Transformers. Notably, after filtering the data using LASER, the total number of hours of audio is higher compared to that obtained using Sentence Transformers. Given this observation, it might be more appropriate to perform filtering based on the length of the audio rather than the number of utterances.

Our experiments also revealed that training the model with GigaST alone yielded better results compared to using only the MuST-C dataset. Fur-

[3]https://github.com/fxsjy/jieba

Training Data	BLEU
MuST-C	9.71
GigaST (LASER)	**13.96**
GigaST (Sentence Transformers)	11.57
MuST-C → GigaST (LASER)	13.52
GigaST (LASER) → MuST-C	13.30

Table 2: Experimental results on training with different datasets. "→" indicates training with the dataset on the left and use the best checkpoint to initiate the training with the dataset on the right.

thermore, we evaluated an approach in which we trained the model with one dataset and use the best checkpoint to initiate the training with the other dataset. However, we observed that this approach did not yield any improvement compared to training the model with GigaST alone.

Based on these findings, we adopted the translation generated by the ST system trained solely on GigaST filtered based on LASER for our submission.

3.2 Text-to-Speech Synthesis

We used pretrained models provided by Zhang et al. (2022a) trained on the AISHELL-3 dataset (Shi et al., 2021). The PaddleSpeech toolkit provides several models trained with the AISHELL-3 dataset, including FastSpeech 2 and HiFi-GAN. We used the best-performing model combination in terms of MOS reported in (Zhang et al., 2022a). For other configurations, such as grapheme-to-phoneme conversion, we followed Zhang et al. (2022a).

The generated audio files have one channel, a sample width of 16 bit, and a frame rate of $24,000$. Because the predictions of speech-to-text translation sometimes contained English words that were preprocessed to empty strings by the grapheme-to-phoneme conversion, some (less than 1 % of the test set) audio files could not be generated.

4 Conclusion

In this paper, we described our system, which is a combination of speech-to-text translation and text-to-speech synthesis. For speech-to-text translation, we trained the Dual-decoder Transformer model with the GigaST dataset filtered based on the similarity of multilingual sentence embeddings. For the text-to-speech synthesis model, we took a cascade approach of an acoustic model and a vocoder and used a combination of FastSpeech 2 and HiFi-GAN. In the future, we will try to perform multi-level pretraining based on transforming SpeechUT (Zhang et al., 2022b) with phonemes as unit. We will also try to use Encodec-based speech synthesis method similar to VALL-EX (Zhang et al., 2023) to increase the accurate representation of emotions and vocal patterns.

References

Milind Agarwal, Sweta Agrawal, Antonios Anastasopoulos, Ondřej Bojar, Claudia Borg, Marine Carpuat, Roldano Cattoni, Mauro Cettolo, Mingda Chen, William Chen, Khalid Choukri, Alexandra Chronopoulou, Anna Currey, Thierry Declerck, Qianqian Dong, Yannick Estève, Kevin Duh, Marcello Federico, Souhir Gahbiche, Barry Haddow, Benjamin Hsu, Phu Mon Htut, Hirofumi Inaguma, Dávid Javorský, John Judge, Yasumasa Kano, Tom Ko, Rishu Kumar, Pengwei Li, Xutail Ma, Prashant Mathur, Evgeny Matusov, Paul McNamee, John P. McCrae, Kenton Murray, Maria Nadejde, Satoshi Nakamura, Matteo Negri, Ha Nguyen, Jan Niehues, Xing Niu, Atul Ojha Kr., John E. Ortega, Proyag Pal, Juan Pino, Lonneke van der Plas, Peter Polák, Elijah Rippeth, Elizabeth Salesky, Jiatong Shi, Matthias Sperber, Sebastian Stüker, Katsuhito Sudoh, Yun Tang, Brian Thompson, Kevin Tran, Marco Turchi, Alex Waibel, Mingxuan Wang, Shinji Watanabe, and Rodolfo Zevallos. 2023. Findings of the IWSLT 2023 Evaluation Campaign. In *Proceedings of the 20th International Conference on Spoken Language Translation (IWSLT 2023)*. Association for Computational Linguistics.

Mattia A. Di Gangi, Roldano Cattoni, Luisa Bentivogli, Matteo Negri, and Marco Turchi. 2019. MuST-C: a Multilingual Speech Translation Corpus. In *Proceedings of the 2019 Conference of the North American Chapter of the Association for Computational Linguistics: Human Language Technologies, Volume 1 (Long and Short Papers)*, pages 2012–2017, Minneapolis, Minnesota. Association for Computational Linguistics.

Hirofumi Inaguma, Shun Kiyono, Kevin Duh, Shigeki Karita, Nelson Yalta, Tomoki Hayashi, and Shinji Watanabe. 2020. Espnet-st: All-in-one speech translation toolkit. In *Proceedings of the 58th Annual Meeting of the Association for*

Computational Linguistics: System Demonstrations, ACL 2020, pages 302–311. Association for Computational Linguistics.

Diederik P. Kingma and Jimmy Ba. 2015. Adam: A method for stochastic optimization. In *3rd International Conference on Learning Representations, ICLR 2015, Conference Track Proceedings*.

Philipp Koehn, Hieu Hoang, Alexandra Birch, Chris Callison-Burch, Marcello Federico, Nicola Bertoldi, Brooke Cowan, Wade Shen, Christine Moran, Richard Zens, Chris Dyer, Ondrej Bojar, Alexandra Constantin, and Evan Herbst. 2007. Moses: Open source toolkit for statistical machine translation. In *ACL 2007, Proceedings of the 45th Annual Meeting of the Association for Computational Linguistics*. The Association for Computational Linguistics.

Jungil Kong, Jaehyeon Kim, and Jaekyoung Bae. 2020. HiFi-GAN: Generative Adversarial Networks for Efficient and High Fidelity Speech Synthesis. In *Proceedings of the 34th International Conference on Neural Information Processing Systems*, NIPS'20, Red Hook, NY, USA. Curran Associates Inc.

Hang Le, Juan Pino, Changhan Wang, Jiatao Gu, Didier Schwab, and Laurent Besacier. 2020. Dual-decoder transformer for joint automatic speech recognition and multilingual speech translation. In *Proceedings of the 28th International Conference on Computational Linguistics*, pages 3520–3533, Barcelona, Spain (Online). International Committee on Computational Linguistics.

Yuchen Liu, Jiajun Zhang, Hao Xiong, Long Zhou, Zhongjun He, Hua Wu, Haifeng Wang, and Chengqing Zong. 2020. Synchronous speech recognition and speech-to-text translation with interactive decoding. In *The Thirty-Fourth AAAI Conference on Artificial Intelligence, AAAI 2020, The Thirty-Second Innovative Applications of Artificial Intelligence Conference, IAAI 2020, The Tenth AAAI Symposium on Educational Advances in Artificial Intelligence, EAAI 2020*, pages 8417–8424. AAAI Press.

Mirco Ravanelli, Titouan Parcollet, and Yoshua Bengio. 2019. The pytorch-kaldi speech recognition toolkit. In *IEEE International Conference on Acoustics, Speech and Signal Processing, ICASSP 2019, Brighton, United Kingdom, May 12-17, 2019*, pages 6465–6469. IEEE.

Yi Ren, Chenxu Hu, Xu Tan, Tao Qin, Sheng Zhao, Zhou Zhao, and Tie-Yan Liu. 2021. FastSpeech 2: Fast and High-Quality End-to-End Text to Speech. In *International Conference on Learning Representations*.

Rico Sennrich, Barry Haddow, and Alexandra Birch. 2016. Neural machine translation of rare words with subword units. In *Proceedings of the 54th Annual Meeting of the Association for Computational Linguistics, ACL 2016, Volume 1: Long Papers*. The Association for Computer Linguistics.

Yao Shi, Hui Bu, Xin Xu, Shaoji Zhang, and Ming Li. 2021. AISHELL-3: A Multi-Speaker Mandarin TTS Corpus. In *Proc. Interspeech 2021*, pages 2756–2760.

Ashish Vaswani, Noam Shazeer, Niki Parmar, Jakob Uszkoreit, Llion Jones, Aidan N. Gomez, Lukasz Kaiser, and Illia Polosukhin. 2017. Attention is all you need. In *Advances in Neural Information Processing Systems 30: Annual Conference on Neural Information Processing Systems 2017*, pages 5998–6008.

Rong Ye, Chengqi Zhao, Tom Ko, Chutong Meng, Tao Wang, Mingxuan Wang, and Jun Cao. 2022. GigaST: A 10,000-hour Pseudo Speech Translation Corpus.

Hui Zhang, Tian Yuan, Junkun Chen, Xintong Li, Renjie Zheng, Yuxin Huang, Xiaojie Chen, Enlei Gong, Zeyu Chen, Xiaoguang Hu, Dianhai Yu, Yanjun Ma, and Liang Huang. 2022a. PaddleSpeech: An easy-to-use all-in-one speech toolkit. In *Proceedings of the 2022 Conference of the North American Chapter of the Association for Computational Linguistics: Human Language Technologies: System Demonstrations*, pages 114–123, Hybrid: Seattle, Washington + Online. Association for Computational Linguistics.

Ziqiang Zhang, Long Zhou, Junyi Ao, Shujie Liu, Lirong Dai, Jinyu Li, and Furu Wei. 2022b. Speechut: Bridging speech and text with hidden-unit for encoder-decoder based speech-text pre-training. *arXiv preprint arXiv:2210.03730*.

Ziqiang Zhang, Long Zhou, Chengyi Wang, Sanyuan Chen, Yu Wu, Shujie Liu, Zhuo Chen, Yanqing Liu, Huaming Wang, Jinyu Li, et al. 2023. Speak foreign languages with your own voice: Cross-lingual neural codec language modeling. *arXiv preprint arXiv:2303.03926*.

Tagged End-to-End Simultaneous Speech Translation Training using Simultaneous Interpretation Data

Yuka Ko Ryo Fukuda Yuta Nishikawa Yasumasa Kano
Katsuhito Sudoh Satoshi Nakamura
Nara Institute of Science and Technology
ko.yuka.kp2@is.naist.jp

Abstract

Simultaneous speech translation (SimulST) translates partial speech inputs incrementally. Although the monotonic correspondence between input and output is preferable for smaller latency, it is not the case for distant language pairs such as English and Japanese. A prospective approach to this problem is to mimic simultaneous interpretation (SI) using SI data to train a SimulST model. However, the size of such SI data is limited, so the SI data should be used together with ordinary bilingual data whose translations are given in offline. In this paper, we propose an effective way to train a SimulST model using mixed data of SI and offline. The proposed method trains a single model using the mixed data with style tags that tell the model to generate SI- or offline-style outputs. Experiment results show improvements of BLEURT in different latency ranges, and our analyses revealed the proposed model generates SI-style outputs more than the baseline.

1 Introduction

Simultaneous speech translation (SimulST) is a technique to translate speech incrementally without waiting for the end of a sentence. Since SimulST should work in small latency against the input speech, monotonic translation following the word order of the source language is preferable. However, making translation monotonic is not trivial especially for distant language pairs with different word orders, such as English and Japanese. Most recent SimulST studies still use parallel corpora only with offline translations and potentially have the limitation to work in a monotonic way.

A prospective approach to this problem is to use SI data to train a SimulST model for mimicking simultaneous interpretation (SI). There are several SI data resources developed so far for English-Japanese (Toyama et al., 2004; Shimizu et al., 2013; Doi et al., 2021). Despite these efforts, SI data are still very small compared to bilingual data based on offline translations. Using such scarce SI data to fine-tune an offline translation model causes overfitting on the small SI data. Training a model using mixed data of offline and SI data is another option to mitigate the problem of data scarcity, but the simple data mixture causes confusion between the output styles of offline translation and SI.

In this paper, we propose a method to train a SimulST model using mixed data of SI and offline translation with style tags to tell the model to generate SI- or offline-style output selectively. It has the advantage of sharing two different styles in a single model and generating SI-style outputs by putting the SI-style tag in the decoding, which are leveraged by offline translation data. Experiment results using MuST-C and small SI data showed improvements of BLEURT by the proposed method over the baselines in different latency ranges. Further analyses revealed that the proposed model generates more appropriate SI-style outputs than baselines.

2 Related Work

There have been many studies on simultaneous translation for text and speech in decades (Fügen et al., 2007; Oda et al., 2014; Dalvi et al., 2018). Most recent approaches are based on deep neural networks and have evolved with the technologies of neural machine translation (NMT) (Gu et al., 2017) and neural speech recognition (ASR) (Rao et al., 2017). An important advantage of the neural SimulST methods (Ma et al., 2020b; Ren et al., 2020) is their end-to-end modeling of the whole process, which improves the efficiency compared to a cascade approach. Such an end-to-end SimulST model is trained using speech translation corpora such as MuST-C (Di Gangi et al., 2019), but these corpora are usually based on offline translation due to the lack of large-scale SI data.

For the English-Japanese language pair, there

Proceedings of the 20th International Conference on Spoken Language Translation (IWSLT 2023), pages 363–375
July 13-14, 2023

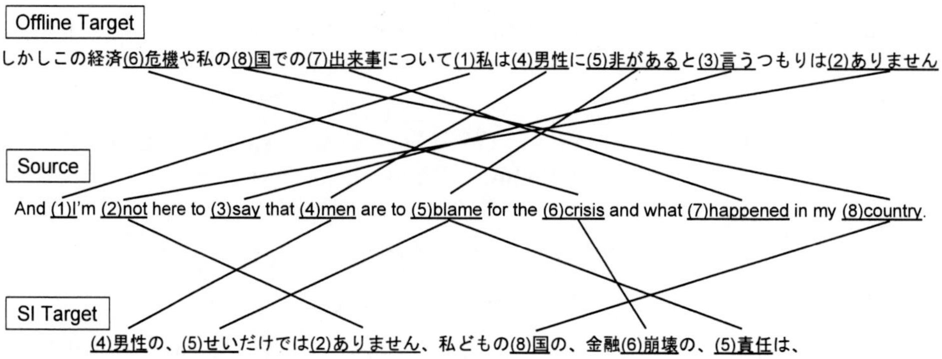

Figure 1: Example of English-to-Japanese offline translation and SI.

have been some attempts for the development of SI corpora (Toyama et al., 2004; Shimizu et al., 2013; Doi et al., 2021). However, the amount of such SI corpora is still very limited compared to offline translations. We tackle this problem by using a larger-scale offline translation corpus. This condition can be seen as domain adaptation from resource-rich offline translation to resource-poor simultaneous translation. In a typical domain adaptation scenario, an out-of-domain model is fine-tuned using in-domain data (Luong and Manning, 2015; Sennrich et al., 2016), but it tends to overfit to the small in-domain data (Chu et al., 2017). As another adaptation approach, tag-based NMT works to control the politeness of translations (Sennrich et al., 2016) and to enable zero-shot multilingual NMT (Johnson et al., 2017). This tag-based approach has been extended to multi-domain fine-tuning (Kobus et al., 2017) and mixed fine-tuning (Chu et al., 2017). These studies fine-tune NMT models using mixed data of in-domain and out-of-domain corpora. Tagged Back-Translation (Caswell et al., 2019) is an application of the tag-based approach to well-known back-translation-based data augmentation. It distinguishes source language sentences from parallel corpora and those obtained from back-translation to handle possible back-translation noise in the training of an NMT model. Our work is motivated by these tag-based methods and tackles the scarcity of SI data.

3 Differences between Offline Translation and Simultaneous Interpretation

There is a large style difference between SI and offline translation. Figure 1 shows an example of offline translation and SI transcript in Japanese for a given English source sentence. The solid lines in the figure represent word correspondences. In this figure, we can find:

- Most English content words are translated into Japanese in the offline translation, while some are missing in the SI transcript.
- The SI tries to translate the former half of the input earlier than the latter half with some unnaturalness, while the offline translation keeps naturalness in Japanese with long-distance reordering from the input English.

These points suggest important differences between offline translation and SI; SI focuses on the simultaneity of the interpretation to deliver the contents as early as possible and to maintain the interpreter's working memory. The word order difference between English and Japanese poses a serious difficulty in SI, as mentioned in the literature (Mizuno, 2017). Thus, it is important to use SI data to train a SimulST model to improve its simultaneity.

4 Proposed Method

Although training a SimulST model using SI data is necessary, we suffer from data scarcity in practice. We propose a method to use a relatively large offline translation corpus to mitigate for the SI data scarcity for training a SimulMT model. Following the tag-based NMT studies, we put a style tag at the beginning of the target string in training and predict a specified tag forcibly at the first step in inference. In this work, we use two tags: `<si>` for SI and `<off>` for offline translation.

Suppose we have an SI transcript: 私は、買った。ペンを、 for an English input: *I bought a*

	Offline		SI	
	#segm.	#En words	#segm.	#En words
train	328,639	5,714,360	65,008	1,120,245
dev	1,369	23,059	165	2,804
test	2,841	46,144	511	8,104

Table 1: Data sizes of offline data and SI data in the number of aligned segments.

pen. as a training example. We put the SI-style tag at the beginning of the SI transcript as follows:

<si>私は、買った。ペンを、

This string is tokenized into subwords[1]:

_<␣si␣>␣私 は␣、 ␣買 っ␣た␣。 ␣ペ ン␣を␣、

Here, we assume we have a pre-trained sequence-to-sequence model such as mBART (Liu et al., 2020b; Tang et al., 2021) as a basis of the SimulST model, as described later in the next section. The aforementioned style tags may not be included in the subword vocabulary of the pre-trained model and are tokenized further like "_<␣si␣>", but it works in practice.

5 Experimental Setup

5.1 Dataset

We used MuST-C (Di Gangi et al., 2019) v2 English-Japanese data as our offline speech translation corpus. We also prepared development and test sets from our in-house Japanese SI recordings on TED Talks that are not included in the training sets above. As for the SI data for training, we used NAIT-SIC-Aligned (Zhao et al., 2023). This SI data is constructed by applying heuristic sentence alignment to extract parallel sentence pairs using the latest version of NAIST-SIC[2] (Doi et al., 2021). From NAIST-SIC-Aligned, we selected INTRA, AUTO-DEV and AUTO-TEST as train, dev and test data, respectively. For all the SI sets, we aligned the English text segments with the corresponding audio tracks in MuST-C using an English forced-aligner Gentle[3]. Here, we excluded segments not aligned with the source speech from the aligned dataset. Table 1 shows the size of the offline and SI data.

[1]"_" is the meta-character representing white spaces in an original string by SentencePiece (Kudo and Richardson, 2018), and "␣" represents a white space in a tokenized string.

[2]https://dsc-nlp.naist.jp/data/NAIST-SIC/2022

[3]https://github.com/lowerquality/gentle

5.2 Simultaneous Speech Translation

We used our SimulST implementation based on `fairseq` (Ott et al., 2019). It followed the system architecture of the best-scored system in the IWSLT 2022 evaluation campaign (Polák et al., 2022), which used an offline ST model in the online simultaneous decoding based on Local Agreement (LA) (Liu et al., 2020a)[4].

5.2.1 Offline ST Model

We built the initial offline ST model by connecting two pre-trained models. Firstly, we used HuBERT Large as the encoder, which consists of a feature extractor trained on 60k hours of unlabeled speech data Libri-Light (Kahn et al., 2020) and a transformer encoder layer. The feature extractor is a 7-layer convolutional layer with a kernel size of (10,3,3,3,3,2,2), a stride of (5,2,2,2,2,2,2), and 512 channels, while the transformer encoder layer consists of 24 layers. Next, we used the decoder portion of mBART50, an encoder-decoder model pre-trained with 50 language pairs, as the decoder. The decoder consists of 12 layers of transformer decoders, and the embedding layer and linear projection weights are shared, with a size of 250,000. The dimension of each layer of the transformer encoder and decoder is 1024, the dimension of the feed forward network is 4096, the number of multi-heads is 16, the activation function is the ReLU function, and the normalization method is pre-layer normalization (Baevski and Auli, 2019). These two models are connected by an Inter-connection (Nishikawa and Nakamura, 2023) that weights each transformer layer of the encoder and integrates the output tensors of each layer in a weighted sum, and a length adapter (Tsiamas et al., 2022). The length adapter is a 3-layer convolutional network with 1024 channels, the stride of 2, and the activation function of GELU.

The inputs are waveforms with a 16-kHz sampling rate that are normalized to zero mean and unit variance. During training, each source audio is augmented (Kharitonov et al., 2020) with a probability of 0.8. We train the model on MuST-C (Di Gangi et al., 2019), CoVoST-2 (Wang et al., 2020), Europarl-ST (Iranzo-Sánchez et al., 2020), and TED-LIUM (Rousseau et al., 2012). We use gradient accumulation and data parallelism to achieve a batch size of approximately 32 million

[4]We also tried wait-k (Ma et al., 2019), but LA worked better than wait-k in our pilot test.

tokens. We use Adam with $\beta_1 = 0.99$, $\beta_2 = 0.98$, and a base learning rate of 2.5×10^{-4}. The learning rate is controlled by a tri-stage scheduler with phases of 0.15, 0.15, and 0.70 for warm-up, hold, and decay, respectively, while the initial and final learning rate has a scale of 0.01 compared to base. We use sentence averaging and gradient clipping of 20. We apply a dropout of 0.1 before every non-frozen layer and use time masking for 10-length spans with a probability of 0.2, and channel masking for 20-length spans with a probability of 0.1 in the encoder feature extractor's output. The loss is the cross-entropy loss with label smoothing of 0.2. We call this trained model *base* model.

The *base* model was fine-tuned using the offline training and development sets (Table 1). During fine-tuning, we set the learning rate of 2.5×10^{-5}, saved models in every 1,000 updates, and adopted checkpoint averaging over five-best checkpoints according to the loss on the development set. We call this fine-tuned model *base+O* model. About those *base* and *base+O* models, we use the NAIST IWSLT 2023 Simultaneous speech-to-speech model for the Simultaneous Speech Translation task (Fukuda et al., 2023). We further fine-tune the *base+O* model using the SI data in the same manner to derive *base+O+S* model. Here, following (Tsiamas et al., 2022), to avoid overfitting the small SI data, the parameters of the following components were kept fixed: the feature extractor and feedforward layers of the encoder and the embedding, self-attention, and feedforward layers of the decoder.

5.2.2 Fine-tuning using Prefix Alignment

For further fine-tuning toward SimulST, we extracted prefix-to-prefix translation pairs from the available training sets using Prefix Alignment (PA) (Kano et al., 2022). PA uses an offline translation model to find prefix-to-prefix translation pairs that can be obtained as intermediate translation results using a given offline translation model. Finally, we fine-tuned the *base+O* model using the prefix pairs.

5.2.3 Compared Methods

We compared the following conditions on the final fine-tuning data:

Offline FT Fine-tuned using the prefix pairs from the offline data (baseline in offline).

(BLEURT)	SI	Offline
Offline FT	0.386	0.518
SI FT	0.359	0.347
Mixed FT	0.393	0.483
Mixed FT + Style	**0.445**	**0.522**
Mixed FT + Style + Up	0.443	0.516

Table 2: BLEURT in full-sentence offline ST on SI and offline test sets.

(BLEU)	SI	Offline
Offline FT	7.8	**16.0**
SI FT	10.9	6.3
Mixed FT	9.4	13.3
Mixed FT + Style	10.3	15.4
Mixed FT + Style + Up	**12.2**	14.2

Table 3: BLEU in full-sentence offline ST on SI and offline test sets.

SI FT Fine-tuned using the prefix pairs from the SI data (baseline in SI).

Mixed FT Fine-tuned using prefix pairs from both of the offline and SI data (baseline in mixed).

Mixed FT + Style Fine-tuned using prefix pairs from both of the offline and SI data with the style tags (proposed method).

Mixed FT + Style + Up The SI portions were up-sampled in **Mixed FT + Style** to balance the data size between the offline and SI data (proposed method).

Here, the prefix pairs from the offline data were obtained using *base+O* model, and those from the SI data were obtained using the *base+O+S* model. The hyperparameter settings for the fine-tuning were the same as that for the *base+O* model.

5.3 Evaluation Metrics

We evaluated the SimulST systems using SimulEval[5] (Ma et al., 2020a). The unit length of speech segments was set to {200, 400, 600, 800, 1,000} milliseconds[6]. For the SimulST systems, translation quality was evaluated in BLEURT (Sellam et al., 2020) and BLEU (Papineni et al., 2002)[7].

[5]`https://github.com/facebookresearch/SimulEval`

[6]We also evaluated SI FT on the SI test set with 120 and 160 ms speech segments to investigate its performance in low latency ranges.

[7]BLEU was calculated using SacreBLEU (Post, 2018).

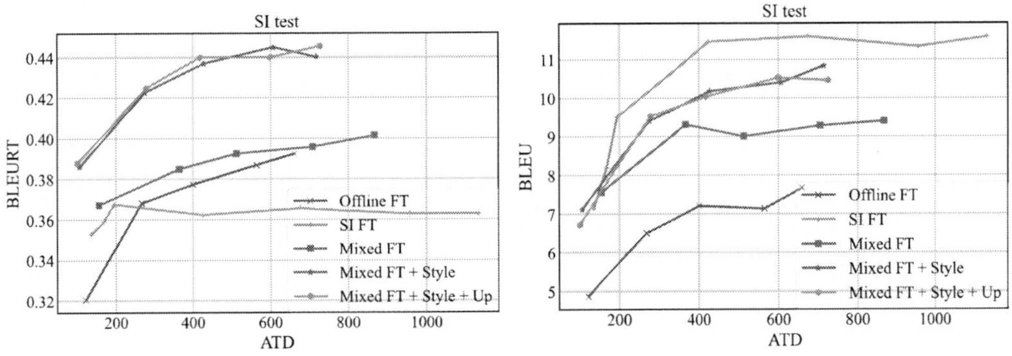

(a) BLEURT (b) BLEU

Figure 2: SimulST latency (ATD) – quality results on SI test set.

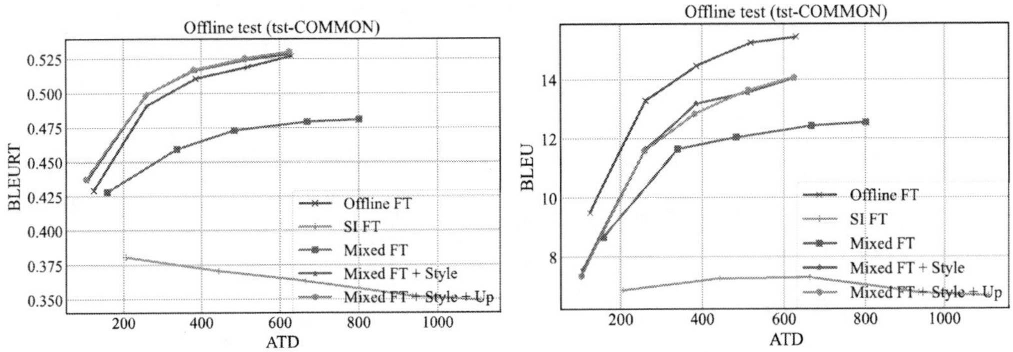

(a) BLEURT (b) BLEU

Figure 3: SimulST latency (ATD) – quality results on offline test set.

The latency in SimulST was evaluated in Average Token Delay (ATD) (Kano et al., 2023) implemented in SimulEval. Even though Average Lagging (AL) (Ma et al., 2019) is the most popular latency metric, it sometimes resulted in negative values, as suggested by Kano et al. (2023). Thus, we present the results using ATD and include the AL results in Appendix A.

6 Results

6.1 Offline Translation Results

Tables 2 and 3 show the offline translation results in BLEURT and BLEU for the SI and offline test sets. These results show that our proposed Mixed FT + Style and Mixed FT + Style + Up surpassed baselines in BLEURT for SI test. On the offline test set (MuST-C tst-COMMON), the performance of the proposed models was almost the same as Offline FT. This suggests that our proposed method leads to outputs semantically close to SI references than the baseline. Contrary, the SI FT baseline surpassed the Mixed FT + Style in BLEU. The result shows that the upsampling worked for BLEU improvement for the SI test set in the offline translation condition.

6.2 Simultaneous Translation Results

Figure 2 shows SimulST results in BLEURT and BLEU for the SI test set. In Figure 2a, the proposed method with the style tags showed clearly better BLEURT results than the baselines. The upsampling did not bring clear differences, the same as findings on the offline translation results shown in Table 2. In contrast, Figure 2b shows SI FT worked the best in almost all latency ranges, while the proposed method outperformed the other two baselines (Offline and Mixed).

Figure 3 shows SimulST results for the offline test set. They reflect the difference in reference translations between the SI and offline test sets. The Offline FT baseline worked well in BLEURT and outperformed the proposed method in BLEU. The other baselines resulted in worse BLEURT and BLEU scores than the proposed method.

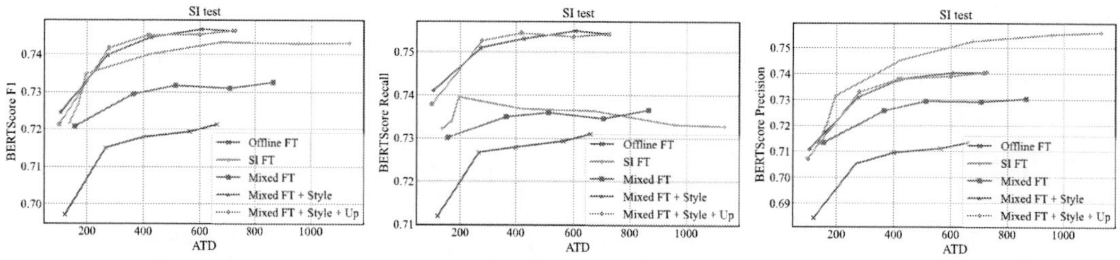

(a) BERTScore F1 (b) BERTScore Recall (c) BERTScore Precision

Figure 4: SimulST latency (ATD) – quality (BERTScore) results on SI test set.

These results suggest the proposed method conveys the information given in source language speech better than the baselines.

7 Discussions

The results shown in Figures 2, 3 demonstrated the advantage of the proposed method in BLEURT, but not in BLEU. In this section, we discuss the results in detail to reveal which model works the best from the viewpoint of SimulST.

7.1 BERTScore Details

Figure 4 shows the detailed results in F1, recall, and precision by BERTScore (Zhang et al., 2020) for the SI test set. The proposed method worked the best in BERTScore recall, and the recall curves look similar to BLEURT curves shown in Figure 2a. On the other hand, the SI FT baseline worked the best in BERTScore precision, and the precision curves look very similar to the BLEU curves shown in Figure 2b. We conducted further analyses below to investigate the mixed results in different quality metrics.

7.2 Length Differences

First, we focus on the length differences between translation outputs and references. Figure 5 shows the length ratios of translation results and their references. The proposed method resulted in longer outputs than the baselines, and the SI FT baseline preferred shorter output than the others and references. From the viewpoint of the precision of the translation results, outputs longer than their references are unfavorable. Figure 6 shows the histogram of length differences between SI FT and Mixed FT + Style. They showed different distributions; this suggests that SI FT suffered from under-translation, and the proposed method suffered from over-translation.

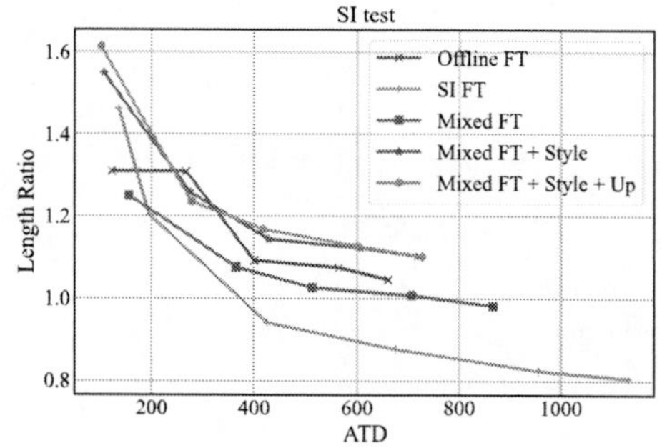

Figure 5: Length ratio results on SI test set.

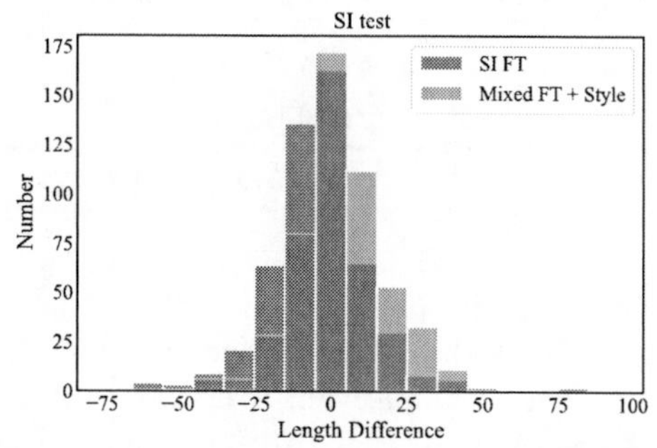

Figure 6: The length differences between hypotheses and references in SI FT and Mixed FT + Style (speech segment size is 600ms) on SI test set.

Table 4 shows the translation examples by SI FT and Mixed FT + Style. Here, SI FT generates very short outputs compared with Mixed FT + Style; BLEU is not always good due to the brevity penalty, but SI FT would have an advantage in BERTScore precision.

7.3 Non-speech Sound Events and Repetitions

Next, we investigated the over-translation suggested in the analyses above.

We observed serious repetitions by the proposed method, such as (拍手) (拍手) ..., which means (Applause). This kind of non-speech sound events (applause and laughter) are found many times in

Source	TEMPT was one of the foremost graffiti artists in the 80s. There's no hospital that can say "No." Anybody who's paralyzed now has access to actually draw or communicate using only their eyes.
SI FT (Baseline)	テンプトは、グラフィティアーティストの (*TEMPT was, graffiti artists'*) 病院は、(*a hospital*) 麻痺した人達は、 (*paralyzed people*)
Mixed FT + Style (Proposed)	テンプトは、グラフィティアーティストの一人です。(*TEMPT is one of graffiti artists.*) 病院では「いいえ」は言えません。(*In a hospital, we cannot say "No."*) 麻痺した人なら誰でも、絵を描いたり、会話をすることができます。 (*Anybody who is paralyzed can draw a picture and have a talk.*)
SI reference	八十年代の素晴らしいグラフィックアーティストでした。 (*(He) was a great graphic artist in the 80s.*) 病院も、ノーとは言えない。(*There's no hospital that can say "No."*) 麻痺してる人達は、これを全員使うことが出来るようになっています。 (*Everybody who is paralyzed can use this.*)
Offline reference	80年代を代表するグラフィティ・アーティストでした 病院もダメと言えません 全身麻痺の人誰もが目だけで絵を描いたりコミュニケーションできます

Table 4: Example sentences in SI FT and Mixed FT + Style (speech segment size: 600ms) on SI test set.

TED Talks, but they are not translated by interpreters and excluded from the SI data. According to this assumption, we tried to eliminate typical repetitions as follows and to conduct the evaluation after that.

- Removing tokens if they are surrounded by "()" and "<>". (if the tokens include parts of "(拍手)" like "拍手)" or "(", they were also excluded.)

- Stopping the generating output when at least one kind of 3-gram appeared at least 3 times in the steps until reaching the end of the sentence.

We applied this repetition removal on the results by Mixed FT + Style and SI + Style; they are labeled as Mixed FT + Style + Rmrep and SI FT + Rmrep, respectively. Figure 7 shows BLEU and length ratio results before and after the repetition removal. BLEU increased consistently on the proposed method while almost no changes were observed on the SI FT baseline except for one sample at ATD=200. This suggests the existence of many repetitions in the translation results by the proposed method. We also investigated BLEURT and BERTScore, as shown in Figure 8. The repetition removal made almost no changes in BLEURT, probably due to the semantic-oriented evaluation strategy of BLEURT. BERTScore Precision and F1 of the proposed method increased in the middle latency ranges, while they decreased almost consistently for the SI FT baseline. These findings suggest an over-translation problem with the proposed method, but it made little impact on semantic-oriented automatic evaluation results.

8 Conclusion

In this paper, we proposed an effective method to train a SimulST model using mixed data of SI- and offline-style translations with style tags to tell the model to generate outputs in either style, motivated by the tag-based approach to domain adaptation. Experiment results on English-to-Japanese SimulST demonstrated the advantage of the proposed method in BLEURT and BERTScore recall despite the inferior performance in BLEU and BERTScore precision due to over-translations and repetitions. Future work includes an extension to other language pairs and further verification via human evaluation.

9 Limitation

The scores reported in the SI test were lower than those in the offline test. Reporting results on other SI data would support seeing the effectiveness of our method. To our knowledge, this is the first work to use SI data as speech translation data. There are no other language pairs SI data than English-Japanese pairs those source speech and target text aligned.

Acknowledgement

Part of this work was supported by JSPS KAKENHI Grant Number JP21H05054 and JST SPRING Grant Number JPMJSP2140.

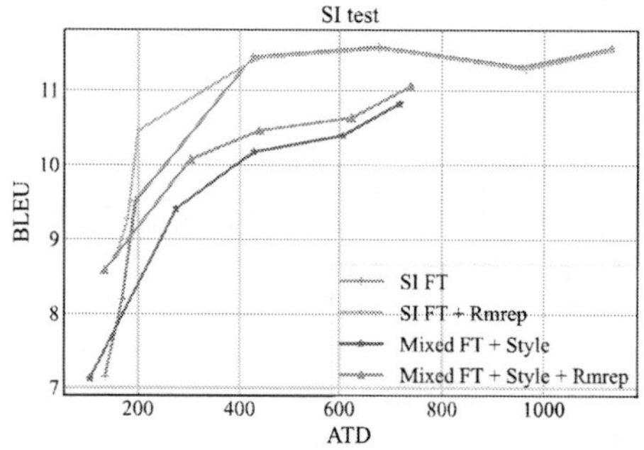

(a) BLEU

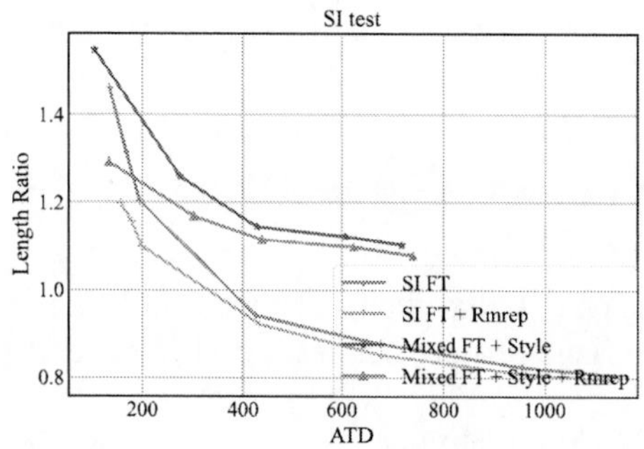

(b) Length ratio

Figure 7: Results with repetition removal (Rmrep) in BLEU and length ratio against ATD on SI test set.

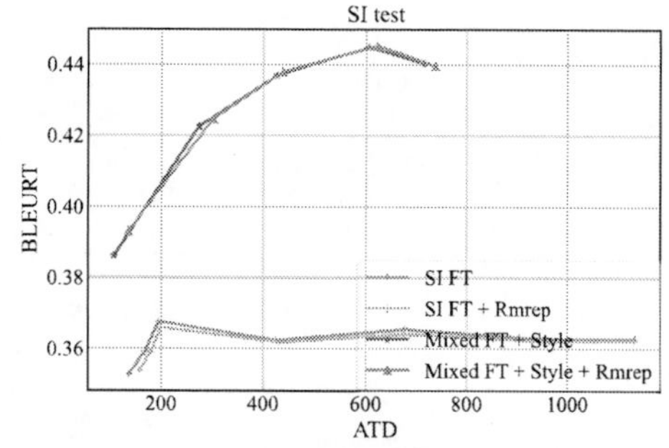

(a) BLEURT

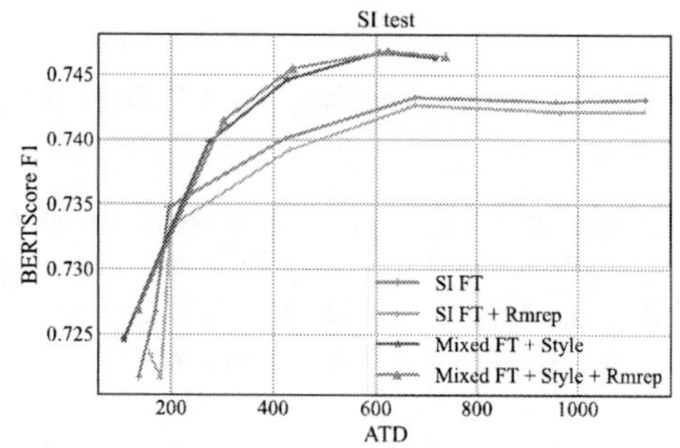

(b) BERTScore-F1

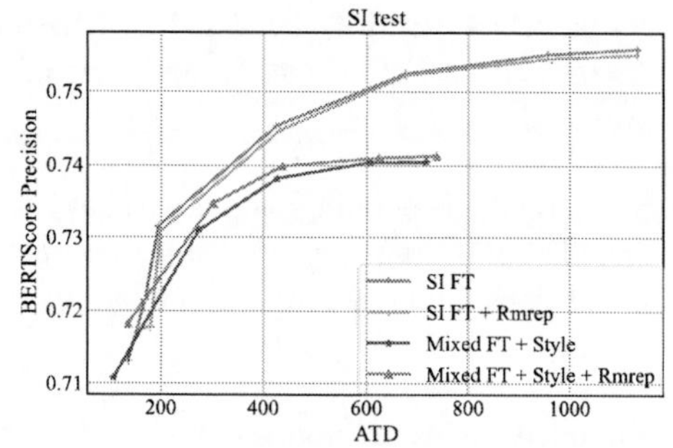

(c) BERTScore-Precision

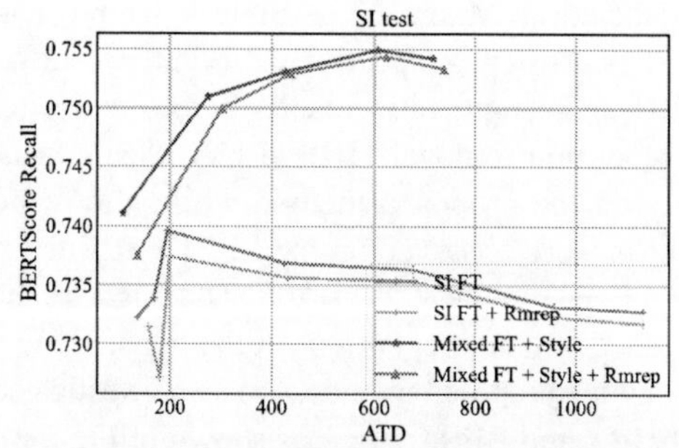

(d) BERTScore-Recall

Figure 8: Results with repetition removal (Rmrep) in BLEURT and BERTScore F1, precision and recall against ATD on SI test set.

References

Alexei Baevski and Michael Auli. 2019. Adaptive Input Representations for Neural Language Modeling. In *7th International Conference on Learning Representations, ICLR 2019, New Orleans, LA, USA, May 6-9, 2019*. OpenReview.net.

Isaac Caswell, Ciprian Chelba, and David Grangier. 2019. Tagged back-translation. In *Proceedings of the Fourth Conference on Machine Translation (Volume 1: Research Papers)*, pages 53–63, Florence, Italy. Association for Computational Linguistics.

Chenhui Chu, Raj Dabre, and Sadao Kurohashi. 2017. An empirical comparison of domain adaptation methods for neural machine translation. In *Proceedings of the 55th Annual Meeting of the Association for Computational Linguistics (Volume 2: Short Papers)*, pages 385–391, Vancouver, Canada. Association for Computational Linguistics.

Fahim Dalvi, Nadir Durrani, Hassan Sajjad, and Stephan Vogel. 2018. Incremental decoding and training methods for simultaneous translation in neural machine translation. In *Proceedings of the 2018 Conference of the North American Chapter of the Association for Computational Linguistics: Human Language Technologies, Volume 2 (Short Papers)*, pages 493–499, New Orleans, Louisiana. Association for Computational Linguistics.

Mattia A. Di Gangi, Roldano Cattoni, Luisa Bentivogli, Matteo Negri, and Marco Turchi. 2019. MuST-C: a Multilingual Speech Translation Corpus. In *Proceedings of the 2019 Conference of the North American Chapter of the Association for Computational Linguistics: Human Language Technologies, Volume 1 (Long and Short Papers)*, pages 2012–2017, Minneapolis, Minnesota. Association for Computational Linguistics.

Kosuke Doi, Katsuhito Sudoh, and Satoshi Nakamura. 2021. Large-scale English-Japanese simultaneous interpretation corpus: Construction and analyses with sentence-aligned data. In *Proceedings of the 18th International Conference on Spoken Language Translation (IWSLT 2021)*, pages 226–235, Bangkok, Thailand (online). Association for Computational Linguistics.

Christian Fügen, Alex Waibel, and Muntsin Kolss. 2007. Simultaneous translation of lectures and speeches. *Machine translation*, 21:209–252.

Ryo Fukuda, Yuta Nishikawa, Yasumasa Kano, Yuka Ko, Tomoya Yanagita, Kosuke Doi, Mana Makinae, Katsuhito Sudoh, Sakriani Sakti, and Satoshi Nakamura. 2023. NAIST Simultaneous Speech Translation System for IWSLT 2023. In *Proceedings of the 20th International Conference on Spoken Language Translation (IWSLT2023)*. To appear.

Jiatao Gu, Graham Neubig, Kyunghyun Cho, and Victor O.K. Li. 2017. Learning to translate in real-time with neural machine translation. In *Proceedings of the 15th Conference of the European Chapter of the Association for Computational Linguistics: Volume 1, Long Papers*, pages 1053–1062, Valencia, Spain. Association for Computational Linguistics.

Javier Iranzo-Sánchez, Joan Albert Silvestre-Cerdà, Javier Jorge, Nahuel Roselló, Adrià Giménez, Albert Sanchis, Jorge Civera, and Alfons Juan. 2020. Europarl-ST: A Multilingual Corpus for Speech Translation of Parliamentary Debates. In *ICASSP 2020 - 2020 IEEE International Conference on Acoustics, Speech and Signal Processing (ICASSP)*, pages 8229–8233.

Melvin Johnson, Mike Schuster, Quoc V. Le, Maxim Krikun, Yonghui Wu, Zhifeng Chen, Nikhil Thorat, Fernanda Viégas, Martin Wattenberg, Greg Corrado, Macduff Hughes, and Jeffrey Dean. 2017. Google's multilingual neural machine translation system: Enabling zero-shot translation. *Transactions of the Association for Computational Linguistics*, 5:339–351.

J. Kahn, M. Rivière, W. Zheng, E. Kharitonov, Q. Xu, P. E. Mazaré, J. Karadayi, V. Liptchinsky, R. Collobert, C. Fuegen, T. Likhomanenko, G. Synnaeve, A. Joulin, A. Mohamed, and E. Dupoux. 2020. Libri-Light: A Benchmark for ASR with Limited or No Supervision. In *ICASSP 2020 - 2020 IEEE International Conference on Acoustics, Speech and Signal Processing (ICASSP)*, pages 7669–7673. `https://github.com/facebookresearch/libri-light`.

Yasumasa Kano, Katsuhito Sudoh, and Satoshi Nakamura. 2022. Simultaneous neural machine translation with prefix alignment. In *Proceedings of the 19th International Conference on Spoken Language Translation (IWSLT 2022)*, pages 22–31, Dublin, Ireland (in-person and online). Association for Computational Linguistics.

Yasumasa Kano, Katsuhito Sudoh, and Satoshi Nakamura. 2023. Average Token Delay: A Latency Metric for Simultaneous Translation. In *Proceedings of Interspeech 2023*. To appear.

Eugene Kharitonov, Morgane Rivière, Gabriel Synnaeve, Lior Wolf, Pierre-Emmanuel Mazaré, Matthijs Douze, and Emmanuel Dupoux. 2020. Data Augmenting Contrastive Learning of Speech Representations in the Time Domain. *arXiv preprint arXiv:2007.00991*.

Catherine Kobus, Josep Crego, and Jean Senellart. 2017. Domain control for neural machine translation. In *Proceedings of the International Conference Recent Advances in Natural Language Processing, RANLP 2017*, pages 372–378, Varna, Bulgaria. INCOMA Ltd.

Taku Kudo and John Richardson. 2018. SentencePiece: A simple and language independent subword tokenizer and detokenizer for neural text processing. In *Proceedings of the 2018 Conference on Empirical Methods in Natural Language Processing: System Demonstrations*, pages 66–71, Brussels, Belgium. Association for Computational Linguistics.

Danni Liu, Gerasimos Spanakis, and Jan Niehues. 2020a. Low-Latency Sequence-to-Sequence Speech Recognition and Translation by Partial Hypothesis Selection. In *Proc. Interspeech 2020*, pages 3620–3624.

Yinhan Liu, Jiatao Gu, Naman Goyal, Xian Li, Sergey Edunov, Marjan Ghazvininejad, Mike Lewis, and Luke Zettlemoyer. 2020b. Multilingual denoising pre-training for neural machine translation. *Transactions of the Association for Computational Linguistics*, 8:726–742.

Minh-Thang Luong and Christopher Manning. 2015. Stanford neural machine translation systems for spoken language domains. In *Proceedings of the 12th International Workshop on Spoken Language Translation: Evaluation Campaign*, pages 76–79, Da Nang, Vietnam.

Mingbo Ma, Liang Huang, Hao Xiong, Renjie Zheng, Kaibo Liu, Baigong Zheng, Chuanqiang Zhang, Zhongjun He, Hairong Liu, Xing Li, Hua Wu, and Haifeng Wang. 2019. STACL: Simultaneous translation with implicit anticipation and controllable latency using prefix-to-prefix framework. In *Proceedings of the 57th Annual Meeting of the Association for Computational Linguistics*, pages 3025–3036, Florence, Italy. Association for Computational Linguistics.

Xutai Ma, Mohammad Javad Dousti, Changhan Wang, Jiatao Gu, and Juan Pino. 2020a. SIMULEVAL: An evaluation toolkit for simultaneous translation. In *Proceedings of the 2020 Conference on Empirical Methods in Natural Language Processing: System Demonstrations*, pages 144–150, Online. Association for Computational Linguistics.

Xutai Ma, Juan Pino, and Philipp Koehn. 2020b. SimulMT to SimulST: Adapting simultaneous text translation to end-to-end simultaneous speech translation. In *Proceedings of the 1st Conference of the Asia-Pacific Chapter of the Association for Computational Linguistics and the 10th International Joint Conference on Natural Language Processing*, pages 582–587, Suzhou, China. Association for Computational Linguistics.

Akira Mizuno. 2017. Simultaneous interpreting and cognitive constraints. *Bull. Coll. Lit*, 58:1–28.

Yuta Nishikawa and Satoshi Nakamura. 2023. Inter-connection: Effective Connection between Pre-trained Encoder and Decoder for Speech Translation. In *Proceedings of Interspeech 2023*. To appear.

Yusuke Oda, Graham Neubig, Sakriani Sakti, Tomoki Toda, and Satoshi Nakamura. 2014. Optimizing segmentation strategies for simultaneous speech translation. In *Proceedings of the 52nd Annual Meeting of the Association for Computational Linguistics (Volume 2: Short Papers)*, pages 551–556.

Myle Ott, Sergey Edunov, Alexei Baevski, Angela Fan, Sam Gross, Nathan Ng, David Grangier, and Michael Auli. 2019. fairseq: A fast, extensible toolkit for sequence modeling. In *Proceedings of the 2019 Conference of the North American Chapter of the Association for Computational Linguistics (Demonstrations)*, pages 48–53, Minneapolis, Minnesota. Association for Computational Linguistics.

Kishore Papineni, Salim Roukos, Todd Ward, and Wei-Jing Zhu. 2002. Bleu: a method for automatic evaluation of machine translation. In *Proceedings of the 40th Annual Meeting of the Association for Computational Linguistics*, pages 311–318, Philadelphia, Pennsylvania, USA. Association for Computational Linguistics.

Peter Polák, Ngoc-Quan Pham, Tuan Nam Nguyen, Danni Liu, Carlos Mullov, Jan Niehues, Ondřej Bojar, and Alexander Waibel. 2022. CUNI-KIT system for simultaneous speech translation task at IWSLT 2022. In *Proceedings of the 19th International Conference on Spoken Language Translation (IWSLT 2022)*, pages 277–285, Dublin, Ireland (in-person and online). Association for Computational Linguistics.

Matt Post. 2018. A call for clarity in reporting BLEU scores. In *Proceedings of the Third Conference on Machine Translation: Research Papers*, pages 186–191, Brussels, Belgium. Association for Computational Linguistics.

Kanishka Rao, Haşim Sak, and Rohit Prabhavalkar. 2017. Exploring architectures, data and units for streaming end-to-end speech recognition with rnn-transducer. In *2017 IEEE Automatic Speech Recognition and Understanding Workshop (ASRU)*, pages 193–199. IEEE.

Yi Ren, Jinglin Liu, Xu Tan, Chen Zhang, Tao Qin, Zhou Zhao, and Tie-Yan Liu. 2020. SimulSpeech: End-to-end simultaneous speech to text translation. In *Proceedings of the 58th Annual Meeting of the Association for Computational Linguistics*, pages 3787–3796, Online. Association for Computational Linguistics.

Anthony Rousseau, Paul Deléglise, and Y. Estève. 2012. TED-LIUM: an Automatic Speech Recognition dedicated corpus. In *International Conference on Language Resources and Evaluation*.

Thibault Sellam, Dipanjan Das, and Ankur Parikh. 2020. BLEURT: Learning robust metrics for text generation. In *Proceedings of the 58th Annual Meeting of the Association for Computational Linguistics*, pages 7881–7892, Online. Association for Computational Linguistics.

Rico Sennrich, Barry Haddow, and Alexandra Birch. 2016. Controlling politeness in neural machine translation via side constraints. In *Proceedings of the 2016 Conference of the North American Chapter of the Association for Computational Linguistics: Human Language Technologies*, pages 35–40, San Diego, California. Association for Computational Linguistics.

Hiroaki Shimizu, Graham Neubig, Sakriani Sakti, Tomoki Toda, and Satoshi Nakamura. 2013. Constructing a speech translation system using simultaneous interpretation data. In *Proceedings of IWSLT*.

Yuqing Tang, Chau Tran, Xian Li, Peng-Jen Chen, Naman Goyal, Vishrav Chaudhary, Jiatao Gu, and Angela Fan. 2021. Multilingual translation from denoising pre-training. In *Findings of the Association for Computational Linguistics: ACL-IJCNLP 2021*, pages 3450–3466.

Hitomi Toyama, Shigeki Matsubara, Koichiro Ryu, Nobuo Kawaguchi, and Yasuyoshi Inagaki. 2004. CIAIR Simultaneous Interpretation Corpus. In *Proceedings of Oriental COCOSDA*.

Ioannis Tsiamas, Gerard I. Gállego, Carlos Escolano, José Fonollosa, and Marta R. Costa-jussà. 2022. Pretrained speech encoders and efficient fine-tuning methods for speech translation: UPC at IWSLT 2022. In *Proceedings of the 19th International Conference on Spoken Language Translation (IWSLT 2022)*, pages 265–276, Dublin, Ireland (in-person and online). Association for Computational Linguistics.

Changhan Wang, Juan Pino, Anne Wu, and Jiatao Gu. 2020. CoVoST: A diverse multilingual speech-to-text translation corpus. In *Proceedings of the Twelfth Language Resources and Evaluation Conference*, pages

4197–4203, Marseille, France. European Language Resources Association.

Tianyi Zhang, Varsha Kishore, Felix Wu, Kilian Q. Weinberger, and Yoav Artzi. 2020. BERTScore: Evaluating Text Generation with BERT. In *8th International Conference on Learning Representations, ICLR 2020, Addis Ababa, Ethiopia, April 26-30, 2020*. OpenReview.net.

Jinming Zhao, Yuka Ko, Ryo Fukuda, Katsuhito Sudoh, Satoshi Nakamura, et al. 2023. NAIST-SIC-Aligned: Automatically-Aligned English-Japanese Simultaneous Interpretation Corpus. *arXiv preprint arXiv:2304.11766*.

A Evaluation Results in AL.

Figure 9 shows the main results in BLEURT and BLEU in SI test in AL. Figure 10 shows the main results in BLEURT and BLEU in offline test in AL. Those results trends are almost the same as the trends in main results in Figure 2, 3.

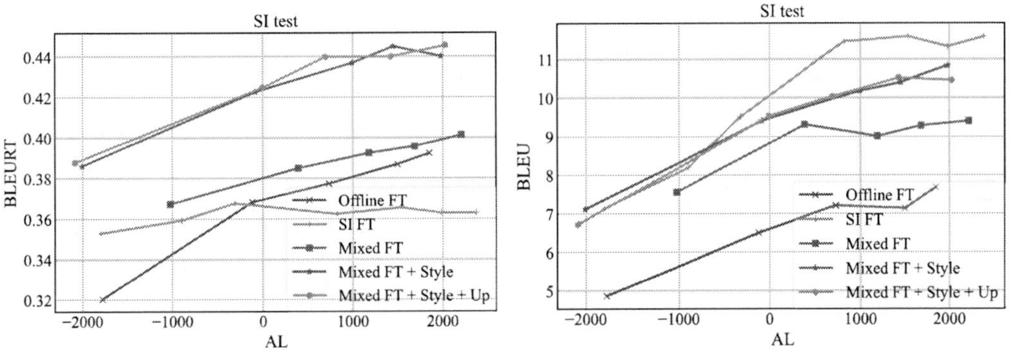

(a) BLEURT

(b) BLEU

Figure 9: SimulST latency (AL) – quality results on SI test set.

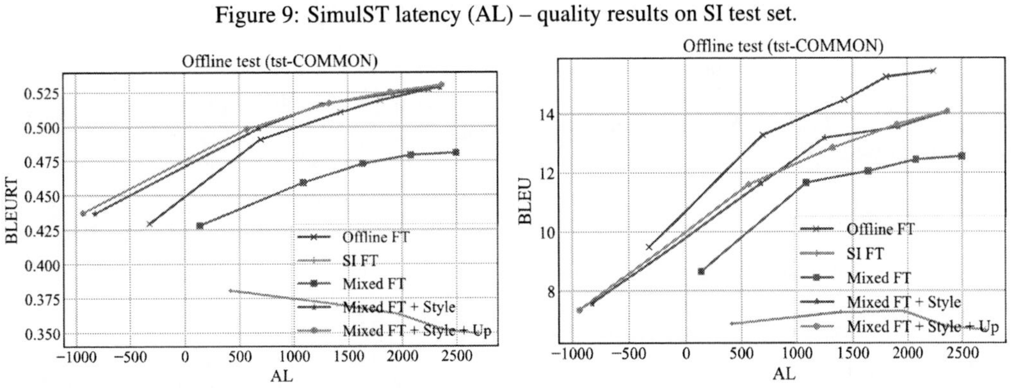

(a) BLEURT

(b) BLEU

Figure 10: SimulST latency (AL) – quality results on offline test set.

The HW-TSC's Simultaneous Speech-to-Text Translation system for IWSLT 2023 evaluation

Jiaxin GUO, Daimeng Wei, Zhanglin Wu, Zongyao Li, Zhiqiang Rao, Minghan Wang,

Hengchao Shang, Xiaoyu Chen, Zhengzhe Yu, Shaojun Li, Yuhao Xie, Lizhi Lei, Hao Yang

{guojiaxin1, weidaimeng, wuzhanglin2, lizongyao, raozhiqiang, wangminghan, shanghengchao, chenxiaoyu35, yuzhengzhe, lishaojun18, xieyuhao2, leilizhi, yanghao30}@huawei.com

Abstract

In this paper, we present our submission to the IWSLT 2023 (Agarwal et al., 2023) Simultaneous Speech-to-Text Translation competition. Our participation involves three language directions: English-German, English-Chinese, and English-Japanese. Our proposed solution is a cascaded incremental decoding system that comprises an ASR model and an MT model. The ASR model is based on the U2++ architecture and can handle both streaming and offline speech scenarios with ease. Meanwhile, the MT model adopts the Deep-Transformer architecture. To improve performance, we explore methods to generate a confident partial target text output that guides the next MT incremental decoding process. In our experiments, we demonstrate that our simultaneous strategies achieve low latency while maintaining a loss of no more than 2 BLEU points when compared to offline systems.

1 Introduction

This paper describes the HW-TSC's submission to the Simultaneous Speech-to-Text Translation (SimulS2T) task at IWSLT 2023 (Agarwal et al., 2023).

From a systems architecture perspective, current research on simultaneous speech-to-text translation (SimulS2T) can be categorized into two forms: cascade and end-to-end. Cascade systems typically consist of a streaming Automatic Speech Recognition (ASR) module and a streaming text-to-text machine translation (MT) module, with the possibility of incorporating additional correction modules. While integrating these modules can be complex, training each module with sufficient data resources can prove to be worthwhile. Alternatively, an end-to-end approach is also an option for SimulS2T, where translations can be directly generated from a unified model with speech inputs. However, it is important to note that bilingual speech translation datasets, which are necessary for end-to-end models, are still scarce resources.

The current efforts in simultaneous speech-to-text translation (SimulS2T) concentrate on developing dedicated models that are tailored to this specific task. However, this approach has certain drawbacks, such as the requirement of an additional model, which typically involves a more challenging training and inference process, as well as heightened computational demands and the possibility of decreased performance when utilized in an offline environment.

Our approach for this study involves utilizing a sturdy offline ASR model and a robust offline MT model as the foundation for our system. By modifying the onlinization approach of (Polák et al., 2022) and introducing an enhanced technique that can be seamlessly integrated into the cascade system, we are able to demonstrate that our simultaneous system can perform at the similar level as the offline models under strict latency restrictions without any adjustments to the original models. Furthermore, our system even surpasses previous higher latency IWSLT systems.

Our contribution is as follows:

- We have revised the approach of onlinization adopted by (Polák et al., 2022) and put forward an enhanced technique that can be easily integrated into the cascade system.
- Our findings show that the pre-training plus fine-tuning paradigm yields significant improvements in both ASR and MT.
- Our research highlights that enhancing the offline MT model has a direct positive impact on the online cascade system as well.

2 Related Work

Simultaneous speech-to-text translation can be achieved through either a cascaded system or an

Proceedings of the 20th International Conference on Spoken Language Translation (IWSLT 2023), pages 376–382
July 13-14, 2023 ©2023 Association for Computational Linguistics

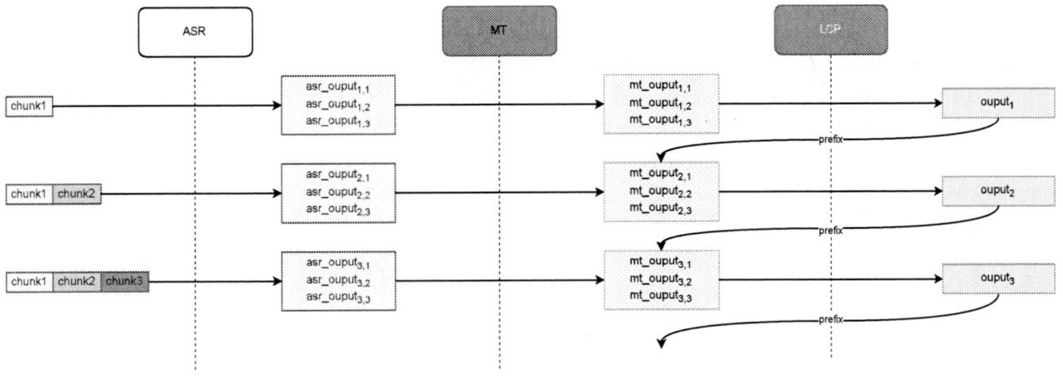

Figure 1: An overview of hw-tsc's s2t framework.

end-to-end model, both of which can be (hybrid) in nature. While cascaded systems currently offer the highest quality in offline speech translation, end-to-end speech translation provides a better trade-off between quality and latency (Guo et al., 2022; Wang et al., 2022a,b).

End-to-end speech translation systems incorporate various techniques to enable simultaneous translation. For example, (Ma et al., 2019) implements a wait-k model and utilizes meta-learning to address data scarcity, while (Zhang et al., 2022b) employs a wait-info model that incorporates information entropy from both the original text and the translation into the model. Additionally, (Liu et al., 2020) utilizes a unidirectional encoder with monotonic cross-attention to constrain dependence on future context.

In addition, some research has focused on detecting stable hypotheses. For instance, (Liu et al., 2020) proposed the Hold-n strategy, which identifies the best hypothesis in the beam and removes the last n tokens from it. Similarly, (Liu et al., 2020) introduced the LA-n strategy, which identifies the matching prefixes of two consecutive chunks. Additionally, like the LA-n strategy, (Nguyen et al., 2021) developed the SP-n strategy, which identifies the longest common prefix among all items in the beam of a chunk. Our work directly addresses this issue.

3 Methods

Figure 1 illustrates our framework.

3.1 ASR

In our cascade system, we have incorporated the U2 (Wu et al., 2021) as the ASR module. This framework has the flexibility to be implemented on standard Transformer or Conformer architectures and can perform both streaming and non-streaming ASR. One of the major advantages of U2 over other offline autoregressive ASR models is its ability to support streaming through dynamic chunk training and decoding with a CTC decoder on top of the encoder. Additionally, U2 includes a standard autoregressive attention decoder and can be jointly trained with the CTC decoder to improve training stability. The dynamic chunk training method involves applying a causal mask with varying chunk sizes at the self-attention layer within the encoder. This allows the hidden representation to condition on some look-ahead contexts within the chunk, similar to the self-attention of an autoregressive decoder.

U2 offers four different decoding strategies: "ctc_greedy_search", "ctc_beam_search", "attention_decoding", and "attention_rescoring". The CTC decoder, with argmax decoding, guarantees that the tokens decoded in previous chunks are unaltered, leading to a smooth streaming experience. The attention decoder generates output token by token and also has the ability to re-score CTC generated texts using prefix beam search in the event of multiple candidate proposals.

After building on our findings from last year, we have discovered that U2 offers stability and robustness in predicting audio without real utterances. This improvement is due to the model's training strategy, specifically the use of dynamic chunk training. In our current work, we have further improved the performance of the model by breaking the chunk-based attention approach and employing the "attention_rescoring" decoding strategy.

3.2 MT

Our cascade system includes the Transformer (Vaswani et al., 2017) as the MT module, which has become a prevalent method for machine translation (Guo et al., 2021) in recent years. The Transformer has achieved impressive results, even with a primitive architecture that requires minimal modification. To improve the offline MT model performance, we utilize multiple training strategies (Wei et al., 2021).

Multilingual Translation (Johnson et al., 2017) has proposed a simple solution for translating multiple languages using a single neural machine translation model with no need to alter the model architecture. The proposed technique involves inserting an artificial token at the start of the input sentence to specify the target language. Furthermore, all languages use the same vocabulary, eliminating the need to add additional parameters. In this study, En-De/ZH/JA data was combined and jointly trained, demonstrating that a multilingual model can significantly enhance translation performance.

Data diversification Data diversification (Nguyen et al., 2020) is an effective strategy to improve the performance of NMT. This technique involves utilizing predictions from multiple forward and backward models and then combining the results with raw data to train the final NMT model. Unlike other methods such as knowledge distillation and dual learning, data diversification does not require additional monolingual data and can be used with any type of NMT model. Additionally, this strategy is more efficient and exhibits a strong correlation with model integration.

Forward translation Forward translation (Wu et al., 2019) refers to using monolingual data in the source language to generate synthetic data through beam search decoding. This synthetic data is then added to the training data in order to increase its size. While forward translation alone may not yield optimal results, when combined with a back translation strategy, it can enhance performance more effectively than back translation alone. In this work, we use only the forward model to create synthetic data and add the data to the original parallel corpora.

Domain Fine-tuning Previous studies have shown that fine-tuning a model with in-domain data can significantly enhance its performance. We hypothesize that there are domain-like distinctions between ASR-generated results and actual text. To further improve the performance, we use the generation from a well-trained ASR model to replace source-side text in the training corpus data. This fine-tuning approach enables us to achieve further improvements in the MT model.

3.3 Onlinization

Incremental Decoding Translation tasks may require reordering or additional information that is not apparent until the end of the source utterance, depending on the language pair. In offline settings, processing the entire utterance at once produces the highest-quality results. However, this approach also leads to significant latency in online mode. One possible solution to reduce latency is to divide the source utterance into smaller parts and translate each one separately.

To perform incremental inference, we divide the input utterance into chunks of a fixed size and decode each chunk as it arrives. Once a chunk has been selected, its predictions are then committed to and no longer modified to avoid visual distractions from constantly changing hypotheses. The decoding of the next chunk is dependent on the predictions that have been committed to. In practice, decoding for new chunks can proceed from a previously buffered decoder state or begin after forced decoding with the tokens that have been committed to. In either case, the source-target attention can span all available chunks, as opposed to only the current chunk.

Stable Hypothesis Detection Our approach is based on prior research in (Polák et al., 2022), and we have implemented stable hypothesis detection to minimize the potential for errors resulting from incomplete input. Their methods, such as LA-n (Liu et al., 2020) and SP-n (Nguyen et al., 2021), are designed for use in end-to-end systems that search for a shared prefix among the hypotheses generated from different chunk inputs. In contrast, our approach operates within a cascaded system that processes the same chunk input.

We can denote the MT and ASR generating functions as G and F respectively. Let $F_{i,n}^{C}$ represent the i output generated by the ASR function for a c-chunk input with a beam size of n. Then the final common prefix for the c-chunk input can be expressed as $prefix^{c}$, which is determined as follows:

Model	Language Pair	Lantency	BLEU	AL	AP	DAL
IWSLT22 Best System	EN-DE	Low	26.82	0.96	0.77	2.07
		Medium	31.47	1.93	0.86	2.96
		High	32.87	3.66	0.96	4.45
Our System	EN-DE	-	**33.54**	**1.88**	0.83	2.84
IWSLT22 Best System	EN-JA	Low	16.92	2.46	0.9	3.22
		Medium	16.94	3.77	0.97	4.29
		High	16.91	4.13	0.98	4.53
Our System	EN-JA	-	**17.89**	**1.98**	0.83	2.89
IWSLT22 Best System	EN-ZH	Low	25.87	1.99	0.87	3.35
		Medium	26.21	2.97	0.94	4.16
		High	26.46	3.97	0.98	4.62
Our System	EN-ZH	-	**27.23**	**1.98**	0.83	2.89

Table 1: Final systems results

$$prefix^c = LCP(G(F_{1,n}^c), ..., G(F_{n,n}^c)) \quad (1)$$

where $LCP(\cdot)$ is longest common prefix of the arguments.

4 Experiments Setup

4.1 ASR

Model We extract 80-dimensional Mel-Filter bank features from audio files to create the ASR training corpus. For tokenization of ASR texts, we utilize Sentencepiece with a learned vocabulary of up to 20,000 sub-tokens. The ASR model is configured as follows: $n_{encoder\ layers}$ = 12, $n_{decoder\ layers}$ = 8, n_{heads} = 8, d_{hidden} = 512, d_{FFN} = 2048. We implement all models using wenet (Zhang et al., 2022a).

Dataset To train the ASR module, we utilized four datasets: LibriSpeech V12, MuST-C V2 (Gangi et al., 2019), TEDLIUM V3, and CoVoST V2. LibriSpeech consists of audio book recordings with case-insensitive text lacking punctuation. MuST-C, a multilingual dataset recorded from TED talks, was used solely for the English data in the ASR task. TEDLIUM is a large-scale speech recognition dataset containing TED talk audio recordings along with text transcriptions. CoVoST is also a multilingual speech translation dataset based on Common Voice, with open-domain content. Unlike LibriSpeech, both MuST-C and CoVoST have case-sensitive text and punctuation.

Training During the training of the ASR model, we set the batch size to a maximum of 40,000 frames per card. We use inverse square root for lr scheduling, with warm-up steps set to 10,000 and peak lr set at $5e-4$. Adam is utilized as the optimizer. The model is trained on 4 V100 GPUs for 50 epochs, and the parameters for the last 4 epochs are averaged. To improve accuracy, all audio inputs are augmented with spectral augmentation and normalized with utterance cepstral mean and variance normalization.

4.2 MT

Model For our experiments using the MT model, we utilize the Transformer deep model architecture. The configuration of the MT model is as follows: $n_{encoder\ layers}$ = 25, $n_{decoder\ layers}$ = 6, n_{heads} = 16, d_{hidden} = 1024, d_{FFN} = 4096, $pre\_ln = True$.

Dataset To train the MT model, we collected all available parallel corpora from the official websites and selected data that was similar to the MuST-C domain. We first trained a multilingual MT baseline model on all data from three language directions. Then, we incrementally trained the baseline model based on data from each language direction.

Training We utilize the open-source Fairseq (Ott et al., 2019) for training, with the following main parameters: each model is trained using 8 GPUs, with a batch size of 2048, a parameter update frequency of 32, and a learning rate of $5e-4$. Additionally, a label smoothing value of 0.1 was used, with 4000 warmup steps and a dropout of 0.1. The

Adam optimizer is also employed, with $\beta1 = 0.9$ and $\beta2 = 0.98$. During the inference phase, a beam size of 8 is used. The length penalties are set to 1.0.

5 Results

From Table 1, we can see that the our systems work well on various language pairs. And our systems even beat the best IWSLT 22 systems under higher latency.

Language Pair	Model	BLEU
En-DE	Offline	35.23
-	Simul	33.54
En-JA	Offline	19.45
-	Simul	17.89
En-ZH	Offline	27.93
-	Simul	27.23

Table 2: Comparison to offline system

Previous research has shown that the quality of simultaneous translation can now match or even surpass that of offline systems. However, in our current study, we first established a new baseline for the offline system. Furthermore, we found that there is still a difference of 1-2 BLEU between simultaneous translation and offline translation, see Table 2.

5.1 Ablation Study on different ASR decoding strategies

Language Pair	Decoding strategies	BLEU
En-DE	ctc_beam_search	32.88
En-JA	ctc_beam_search	16.56
En-ZH	ctc_beam_search	26.47
En-DE	attention_rescoring	33.54
En-JA	attention_rescoring	17.89
En-ZH	attention_rescoring	27.23

Table 3: Ablation Study on different ASR decoding strategies

The decoding strategy of "attention_rescoring" involves using a decoder to re-rank the results based on the decoding output of "ctc_beam_search". As a result, "attention_rescoring" can obtain better ASR results. Table 3 demonstrates that a better ASR decoding strategy can lead to overall better quality results for the system.

5.2 Ablation Study on MT training strategies

Training strategies	BLEU
Baseline	33.54
- Domain Fine-tuning	27.87
- Forward Translation	25.49
- Multiligual Translation	23.76

Table 4: Ablation Study on MT training strategies for EN-DE direction

In the field of machine translation, Domain Fine-tuning, Forward Translation, and Multiligual Translation are frequently employed methods to enhance translation quality. It is evident from Table 4 that these training strategies can effectively improve the overall quality of the system.

6 Conclusion

In this paper, we report on our work in the IWSLT 2023 simultaneous speech-to-text translation evaluation. We propose an onlinization strategy that can be applied to cascaded systems and demonstrate its effectiveness in three language directions. Our approach is simple and efficient, with ASR and MT modules that can be optimized independently. Our cascade simultaneous system achieves results that are comparable to offline systems. In the future, we plan to further explore the direction of end-to-end systems.

References

Milind Agarwal, Sweta Agrawal, Antonios Anastasopoulos, Ondřej Bojar, Claudia Borg, Marine Carpuat, Roldano Cattoni, Mauro Cettolo, Mingda Chen, William Chen, Khalid Choukri, Alexandra Chronopoulou, Anna Currey, Thierry Declerck, Qianqian Dong, Yannick Estève, Kevin Duh, Marcello Federico, Souhir Gahbiche, Barry Haddow, Benjamin Hsu, Phu Mon Htut, Hirofumi Inaguma, Dávid Javorský, John Judge, Yasumasa Kano, Tom Ko, Rishu Kumar, Pengwei Li, Xutail Ma, Prashant Mathur, Evgeny Matusov, Paul McNamee, John P. McCrae, Kenton Murray, Maria Nadejde, Satoshi Nakamura, Matteo Negri, Ha Nguyen, Jan Niehues, Xing Niu, Atul Ojha Kr., John E. Ortega, Proyag Pal, Juan Pino, Lonneke van der Plas, Peter Polák, Elijah Rippeth, Elizabeth Salesky, Jiatong Shi, Matthias Sperber, Sebastian Stüker, Katsuhito Sudoh, Yun Tang, Brian Thompson, Kevin Tran, Marco Turchi, Alex Waibel, Mingxuan Wang, Shinji Watanabe, and Rodolfo Zevallos. 2023. Findings of the IWSLT 2023 Evaluation Campaign. In Proceedings of the 20th International Conference on Spoken Language

Translation (IWSLT 2023). Association for Computational Linguistics.

Mattia Antonino Di Gangi, Roldano Cattoni, Luisa Bentivogli, Matteo Negri, and Marco Turchi. 2019. Must-c: a multilingual speech translation corpus. In Proceedings of the 2019 Conference of the North American Chapter of the Association for Computational Linguistics: Human Language Technologies, NAACL-HLT 2019, Minneapolis, MN, USA, June 2-7, 2019, Volume 1 (Long and Short Papers), pages 2012–2017. Association for Computational Linguistics.

Jiaxin Guo, Yinglu Li, Minghan Wang, Xiaosong Qiao, Yuxia Wang, Hengchao Shang, Chang Su, Yimeng Chen, Min Zhang, Shimin Tao, Hao Yang, and Ying Qin. 2022. The hw-tsc's speech to speech translation system for IWSLT 2022 evaluation. In Proceedings of the 19th International Conference on Spoken Language Translation, IWSLT@ACL 2022, Dublin, Ireland (in-person and online), May 26-27, 2022, pages 293–297. Association for Computational Linguistics.

Jiaxin Guo, Minghan Wang, Daimeng Wei, Hengchao Shang, Yuxia Wang, Zongyao Li, Zhengzhe Yu, Zhanglin Wu, Yimeng Chen, Chang Su, Min Zhang, Lizhi Lei, Shimin Tao, and Hao Yang. 2021. Self-distillation mixup training for non-autoregressive neural machine translation. CoRR, abs/2112.11640.

Melvin Johnson, Mike Schuster, Quoc V. Le, Maxim Krikun, Yonghui Wu, Zhifeng Chen, Nikhil Thorat, Fernanda B. Viégas, Martin Wattenberg, Greg Corrado, Macduff Hughes, and Jeffrey Dean. 2017. Google's multilingual neural machine translation system: Enabling zero-shot translation. Trans. Assoc. Comput. Linguistics, 5:339–351.

Danni Liu, Gerasimos Spanakis, and Jan Niehues. 2020. Low-latency sequence-to-sequence speech recognition and translation by partial hypothesis selection. In Interspeech 2020, 21st Annual Conference of the International Speech Communication Association, Virtual Event, Shanghai, China, 25-29 October 2020, pages 3620–3624. ISCA.

Mingbo Ma, Liang Huang, Hao Xiong, Renjie Zheng, Kaibo Liu, Baigong Zheng, Chuanqiang Zhang, Zhongjun He, Hairong Liu, Xing Li, Hua Wu, and Haifeng Wang. 2019. STACL: simultaneous translation with implicit anticipation and controllable latency using prefix-to-prefix framework. In Proceedings of the 57th Conference of the Association for Computational Linguistics, ACL 2019, Florence, Italy, July 28- August 2, 2019, Volume 1: Long Papers, pages 3025–3036. Association for Computational Linguistics.

Thai-Son Nguyen, Sebastian Stüker, and Alex Waibel. 2021. Super-human performance in online low-latency recognition of conversational speech. In Interspeech 2021, 22nd Annual Conference of the International Speech Communication Association, Brno, Czechia, 30 August - 3 September 2021, pages 1762–1766. ISCA.

Xuan-Phi Nguyen, Shafiq R. Joty, Kui Wu, and Ai Ti Aw. 2020. Data diversification: A simple strategy for neural machine translation. In Advances in Neural Information Processing Systems 33: Annual Conference on Neural Information Processing Systems 2020, NeurIPS 2020, December 6-12, 2020, virtual.

Myle Ott, Sergey Edunov, Alexei Baevski, Angela Fan, Sam Gross, Nathan Ng, David Grangier, and Michael Auli. 2019. fairseq: A fast, extensible toolkit for sequence modeling. CoRR, abs/1904.01038.

Peter Polák, Ngoc-Quan Pham, Tuan-Nam Nguyen, Danni Liu, Carlos Mullov, Jan Niehues, Ondrej Bojar, and Alexander Waibel. 2022. CUNI-KIT system for simultaneous speech translation task at IWSLT 2022. In Proceedings of the 19th International Conference on Spoken Language Translation, IWSLT@ACL 2022, Dublin, Ireland (in-person and online), May 26-27, 2022, pages 277–285. Association for Computational Linguistics.

Ashish Vaswani, Noam Shazeer, Niki Parmar, Jakob Uszkoreit, Llion Jones, Aidan N. Gomez, Lukasz Kaiser, and Illia Polosukhin. 2017. Attention is all you need. In Advances in Neural Information Processing Systems 30: Annual Conference on Neural Information Processing Systems 2017, December 4-9, 2017, Long Beach, CA, USA, pages 5998–6008.

Minghan Wang, Jiaxin Guo, Yinglu Li, Xiaosong Qiao, Yuxia Wang, Zongyao Li, Chang Su, Yimeng Chen, Min Zhang, Shimin Tao, Hao Yang, and Ying Qin. 2022a. The hw-tsc's simultaneous speech translation system for IWSLT 2022 evaluation. In Proceedings of the 19th International Conference on Spoken Language Translation, IWSLT@ACL 2022, Dublin, Ireland (in-person and online), May 26-27, 2022, pages 247–254. Association for Computational Linguistics.

Minghan Wang, Jiaxin Guo, Xiaosong Qiao, Yuxia Wang, Daimeng Wei, Chang Su, Yimeng Chen, Min Zhang, Shimin Tao, Hao Yang, and Ying Qin. 2022b. The hw-tsc's offline speech translation system for IWSLT 2022 evaluation. In Proceedings of the 19th International Conference on Spoken Language Translation, IWSLT@ACL 2022, Dublin, Ireland (in-person and online), May 26-27, 2022, pages 239–246. Association for Computational Linguistics.

Daimeng Wei, Zongyao Li, Zhanglin Wu, Zhengzhe Yu, Xiaoyu Chen, Hengchao Shang, Jiaxin Guo, Minghan Wang, Lizhi Lei, Min Zhang, Hao Yang, and Ying Qin. 2021. Hw-tsc's participation in the WMT 2021 news translation shared task. In Proceedings of the Sixth Conference on Machine Translation, WMT@EMNLP 2021, Online Event, November 10-11, 2021, pages 225–231. Association for Computational Linguistics.

Di Wu, Binbin Zhang, Chao Yang, Zhendong Peng, Wenjing Xia, Xiaoyu Chen, and Xin Lei. 2021. U2++: unified two-pass bidirectional end-to-end model for speech recognition. CoRR, abs/2106.05642.

Lijun Wu, Yiren Wang, Yingce Xia, Tao Qin, Jianhuang Lai, and Tie-Yan Liu. 2019. Exploiting monolingual data at scale for neural machine translation. In Proceedings of the 2019 Conference on Empirical Methods in Natural Language Processing and the 9th International Joint Conference on Natural Language Processing, EMNLP-IJCNLP 2019, Hong Kong, China, November 3-7, 2019, pages 4205–4215. Association for Computational Linguistics.

Binbin Zhang, Di Wu, Zhendong Peng, Xingchen Song, Zhuoyuan Yao, Hang Lv, Lei Xie, Chao Yang, Fuping Pan, and Jianwei Niu. 2022a. Wenet 2.0: More productive end-to-end speech recognition toolkit. In Interspeech 2022, 23rd Annual Conference of the International Speech Communication Association, Incheon, Korea, 18-22 September 2022, pages 1661–1665. ISCA.

Shaolei Zhang, Shoutao Guo, and Yang Feng. 2022b. Wait-info policy: Balancing source and target at information level for simultaneous machine translation. In Findings of the Association for Computational Linguistics: EMNLP 2022, Abu Dhabi, United Arab Emirates, December 7-11, 2022, pages 2249–2263. Association for Computational Linguistics.

The HW-TSC's Simultaneous Speech-to-Speech Translation system for IWSLT 2023 evaluation

Hengchao Shang, Zhiqiang Rao, Zongyao Li, Jiaxin GUO, Zhanglin Wu, Minghan Wang,

Daimeng Wei, Shaojun Li, Zhengzhe Yu, Xiaoyu Chen, Lizhi Lei, Hao Yang

{shanghengchao, raozhiqiang, lizongyao, guojiaxin1, wuzhanglin2, wangminghan, weidaimeng, lishaojun18, yuzhengzhe, chenxiaoyu35, leilizhi, yanghao30}@huawei.com

Abstract

In this paper, we present our submission to the IWSLT 2023 (Agarwal et al., 2023) Simultaneous Speech-to-Speech Translation competition. Our participation involves three language directions: English-German, English-Chinese, and English-Japanese. Our solution is a cascaded incremental decoding system, consisting of an ASR model, an MT model, and a TTS model. By adopting the strategies used in the Speech-to-Text track, we have managed to generate a more confident target text for each audio segment input, which can guide the next MT incremental decoding process. Additionally, we have integrated the TTS model to seamlessly reproduce audio files from the translation hypothesis. To enhance the effectiveness of our experiment, we have utilized a range of methods to reduce error conditions in the TTS input text and improve the smoothness of the TTS output audio.

1 Introduction

This paper describes the HW-TSC's submission to the Simultaneous Speech-to-Speech Translation (SimulS2S) task at IWSLT 2023 (Agarwal et al., 2023).

Simultaneous speech-to-speech translation (SimulS2S) is currently being researched using Cascade systems. These systems typically involve a streaming Automatic Speech Recognition (ASR) module, a streaming Text-to-Text machine translation (MT) module, and an offline Text-to-Speech(TTS) module, with the option of incorporating additional correction modules. Although integrating these modules can be complex, training each module with sufficient data resources can prove to be worthwhile.

Our study adopts a comprehensive approach that utilizes several key components to build a strong system. We incorporate a formidable offline ASR model, a robust offline MT model, and a pre-trained TTS model as the foundation for our system. Moreover, we introduce a refined onlinization technique based on the approach developed by (Polák et al., 2022), which seamlessly integrates into the cascade system.

Offline TTS models often produce a blank sound at the end of a sentence. As a result, when generating audio results in the simultaneous interpreting mode, it can lead to blank tones between clips, causing the final audio to lack smoothness. To address this issue, we have developed several strategies aimed at mitigating this problem in our work.

2 Related Methods

2.1 ASR

In our cascade system, we have incorporated the U2 (Wu et al., 2021) as the ASR module. This framework has the flexibility to be implemented on standard Transformer or Conformer architectures and can perform both streaming and non-streaming ASR. One of the major advantages of U2 over other offline autoregressive ASR models is its ability to support streaming through dynamic chunk training and decoding with a CTC decoder on top of the encoder. Additionally, U2 includes a standard autoregressive attention decoder and can be jointly trained with the CTC decoder to improve training stability. The dynamic chunk training method involves applying a causal mask with varying chunk sizes at the self-attention layer within the encoder. This allows the hidden representation to condition on some look-ahead contexts within the chunk, similar to the self-attention of an autoregressive decoder.

U2 offers multiple decoding strategies. In this work, we use "attention_rescoring" decoding strategy, which is to use the attention decoder re-score CTC generated texts using prefix beam search in the event of multiple candidate proposals.

Proceedings of the 20th International Conference on Spoken Language Translation (IWSLT 2023), pages 383–388
July 13-14, 2023

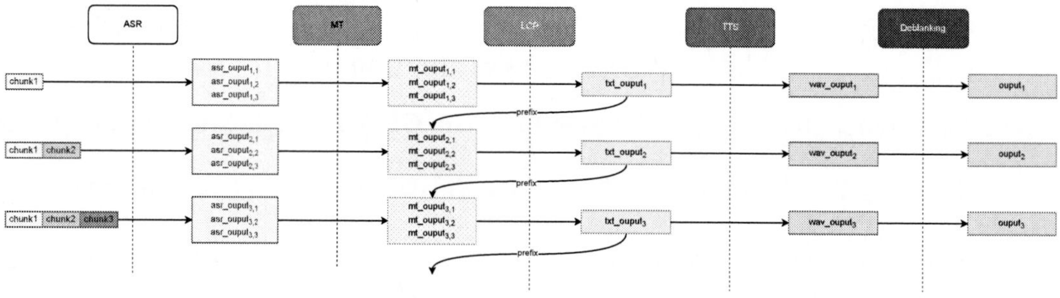

Figure 1: An overview of hw-tsc's s2s framework.

2.2 MT

Our cascade system includes the Transformer (Vaswani et al., 2017) as the MT module, which has become a prevalent method for machine translation (Wei et al., 2021; Guo et al., 2021) in recent years. The Transformer has achieved impressive results, even with a primitive architecture that requires minimal modification.

In this work, we use multiple training strategies to improve the offline MT model performance. First, we train a multilingual model for three directions En-De/ZH/JA. Multilingual Translation (Johnson et al., 2017) has proposed a simple solution to enhance translation performance for translating multiple languages using a single neural machine translation model with no need to alter the model architecture. Second, we use Forward translation (Wu et al., 2019) to generate synthetic data through beam search decoding. The we add the data to the original parallel corpora and re-train the MT model. Finally, we use the generation from a well-trained ASR model to replace source-side text in the training corpus data and fine-tune the MT model to reduce the domain gap.

2.3 TTS

In a cascaded speech-to-speech translation system, the TTS module plays a critical role in rendering high-quality speech output from translated text. To this end, we utilize the state-of-the-art VITS (Kim et al., 2021) model, which is pretrained on massive amounts of data and incorporates advanced techniques such as variational inference augmented with normalizing flows and adversarial training. This model has been shown to produce speech output that is more natural and fluent compared to traditional TTS models.

The inference process involves providing the VITS model with the generated text, after which the model generates the raw audio waveform. This process is highly efficient and requires no additional input from the user. By leveraging the VITS model, we are able to streamline the TTS module and deliver high-quality speech output in a fraction of the time traditionally required by other systems. This results in a more seamless and intuitive user experience, enabling our system to be used by a wider range of individuals and applications.

3 Framework

Figure 1 illustrates our framework.

3.1 Onlinization

The primary method for onlinizing an offline model and transforming it into a simul model is Incremental Decoding. Depending on the language pair, translation tasks may require reordering or additional information that is not apparent until the end of the source utterance. In offline settings, processing the entire utterance at once usually produces the highest-quality results, but this approach can result in significant latency in online mode. One possible solution to reduce latency is to divide the source utterance into smaller parts and translate each part separately. This approach helps to reduce the time required for processing while still maintaining translation quality. By using incremental decoding in conjunction with smaller processing units, we can significantly improve the speed and efficiency of the translation process, making it ideal for online settings where speed is of the essence.

To perform incremental inference, we divide the input utterance into chunks of a fixed size and decode each chunk as it arrives. Once a chunk has been selected, its predictions are then committed to and no longer modified to avoid visual distractions from constantly changing hypotheses. The decoding of the next chunk is dependent on the predictions that have been committed to. In practice, decoding for new chunks can proceed from a previously buffered decoder state or begin after forced decoding with the tokens that have been committed to. In either case, the source-target attention can span all available chunks, as opposed to only the current chunk.

3.2 Stable Hypothesis Detection

Our approach is based on prior research in (Polák et al., 2022), and we have implemented stable hypothesis detection to minimize the potential for errors resulting from incomplete input. In previous research, some methods focused on detecting stable hypotheses using strategies such as the Hold-n strategy proposed by (Liu et al., 2020), which identifies the best hypothesis in the beam and removes the last n tokens from it. Similarly, (Liu et al., 2020) introduced the LA-n strategy, which identifies the matching prefixes of two consecutive chunks. In addition, (Nguyen et al., 2021) developed the SP-n strategy, which identifies the longest common prefix among all items in the beam of a chunk.

However, these methods were designed for end-to-end systems that search for a shared prefix among the hypotheses generated from different chunk inputs. Our approach, on the other hand, operates within a cascaded system that processes the same chunk input. As such, we have adapted these strategies to better fit our context, resulting in a more effective approach for stable hypothesis detection. By using our approach, we are able to achieve higher accuracy and stability in our system, thereby improving its overall performance.

We can denote the MT and ASR generating functions as G and F respectively. Let $F_{i,n}^{C}$ represent the i output generated by the ASR function for a c-chunk input with a beam size of n. Then the final common prefix for the c-chunk input can be expressed as $prefix^c$, which is determined as follows:

$$prefix^c = LCP(G(F_{1,n}^c), ..., G(F_{n,n}^c)) \quad (1)$$

where $LCP(\cdot)$ is longest common prefix of the arguments.

3.3 Deblanking

Our team conducted a manual evaluation of the audio output generated by TTS and identified two issues. The first scenario involved the TTS model producing unusual waveforms for previously unseen tokens. The second scenario involved TTS generating blank sounds to indicate pauses within the audio fragments. To address these issues, we implemented two strategies which we have collectively named Deblanking.

Unknown Filtering In the Chinese and Japanese language directions, we initially remove tokens that are not included in the vocabulary, such as infrequent punctuation marks and words. For Chinese in particular, we must convert Arabic numerals into textual numerals.

Context-Aware Pause Detection When analyzing the waveform generated by TTS, we evaluate whether or not the original text indicates a pause. If the text does not indicate a pause, we eliminate the final prolonged silence that produces the waveform. Additionally, to ensure speech coherence, we've reserved at least 160 frames of blank audio.

4 Experiments

4.1 Dataset

To train the ASR module, we utilized four datasets: LibriSpeech V12, MuST-C V2 (Gangi et al., 2019), TEDLIUM V3, and CoVoST V2. LibriSpeech consists of audio book recordings with case-insensitive text lacking punctuation. MuST-C, a multilingual dataset recorded from TED talks, was used solely for the English data in the ASR task. TEDLIUM is a large-scale speech recognition dataset containing TED talk audio recordings along with text transcriptions. CoVoST is also a multilingual speech translation dataset based on Common Voice, with open-domain content. Unlike LibriSpeech, both MuST-C and CoVoST have case-sensitive text and punctuation.

To train the MT model, we collected all available parallel corpora from the official websites and selected data that was similar to the MuST-C domain. We first trained a multilingual MT baseline model on all data from three language directions. Then, we incrementally trained the baseline model based on data from each language direction.

4.2 Model

ASR We extract 80-dimensional Mel-Filter bank features from audio files to create the ASR training corpus. For tokenization of ASR texts, we utilize Sentencepiece with a learned vocabulary of up to

Model	Language Pair	BLEU/Whisper_ASR_BLEU	StartOffset	EndOffset	ATD
	EN-DE	33.54			
Our S2T System	EN-JA	17.89			
	EN-ZH	27.23			
Our System	EN-DE	10.45	1.04	2.73	1.97
Our System	EN-JA	14.53	1.59	2.96	2.76
Our System	EN-ZH	20.19	1.77	2.98	2.93

Table 1: Final systems results

20,000 sub-tokens. The ASR model is configured as follows: $n_{encoder\ layers} = 12$, $n_{decoder\ layers} = 8$, $n_{heads} = 8$, $d_{hidden} = 512$, $d_{FFN} = 2048$. We implement all models using wenet (Zhang et al., 2022).

During the training of the ASR model, we set the batch size to a maximum of 40,000 frames per card. We use inverse square root for lr scheduling, with warm-up steps set to 10,000 and peak lr set at $5e-4$. Adam is utilized as the optimizer. The model is trained on 4 V100 GPUs for 50 epochs, and the parameters for the last 4 epochs are averaged. To improve accuracy, all audio inputs are augmented with spectral augmentation and normalized with utterance cepstral mean and variance normalization.

MT For our experiments using the MT model, we utilize the Transformer deep model architecture. The configuration of the MT model is as follows: $n_{encoder\ layers} = 25$, $n_{decoder\ layers} = 6$, $n_{heads} = 16$, $d_{hidden} = 1024$, $d_{FFN} = 4096$, $pre\_ln = True$.

We utilize the open-source Fairseq (Ott et al., 2019) for training, with the following main parameters: each model is trained using 8 GPUs, with a batch size of 2048, a parameter update frequency of 32, and a learning rate of $5e-4$. Additionally, a label smoothing value of 0.1 was used, with 4000 warmup steps and a dropout of 0.1. The Adam optimizer is also employed, with $\beta 1 = 0.9$ and $\beta 2 = 0.98$. During the inference phase, a beam size of 8 is used. The length penalties are set to 1.0.

TTS For EN-DE direction, we utilize the open-source Espnet (Watanabe et al., 2018) for inference. For EN-JA/ZH, we use the pretrained models in huggingface. The pretrained models are VITS (Kim et al., 2021) architecture, which adopts variational inference augmented with normalizing flows and an adversarial training process.

4.3 Results

A detailed analysis of the results presented in Table 1 indicates that the TTS transcription results in Japanese have the smallest gap compared to the results obtained from the S2T system, with a difference of approximately 3 BLEU. However, in the German direction, the TTS system generates the worst results among all the evaluated systems. Further research is needed to understand the underlying reasons for this discrepancy and identify potential strategies to improve TTS performance in this language pair.

4.4 Ablation Study on Deblanking strategies

Language Pair	Training strategies	BLEU
EN-DE	Baseline	10.45
	- Context-aware wait	10.32
	- Unknown Filtering	10.27
EN-JA	Baseline	14.53
	- Context-aware wait	13.37
	- Unknown Filtering	13.08
EN-ZH	Baseline	20.19
	- Context-aware wait	18.64
	- Unknown Filtering	16.73

Table 2: Ablation Study on Deblanking strategies

The results presented in Table 2 provide strong evidence that our proposed strategies are effective in reducing the gap between offline and streaming TTS.

5 Conclusion

This paper details our involvement in the IWSLT 2023 simultaneous speech-to-speech translation evaluation. Our team presents an onlinization strategy that can be utilized by cascaded systems, which we have proven to be effective in three different language directions. Additionally, we introduce two strategies that address the disparity between offline and streaming TTS. Our approach is both simple and efficient. Moving forward, we aim to delve further into end-to-end systems.

References

Milind Agarwal, Sweta Agrawal, Antonios Anastasopoulos, Ondřej Bojar, Claudia Borg, Marine Carpuat, Roldano Cattoni, Mauro Cettolo, Mingda Chen, William Chen, Khalid Choukri, Alexandra Chronopoulou, Anna Currey, Thierry Declerck, Qianqian Dong, Yannick Estève, Kevin Duh, Marcello Federico, Souhir Gahbiche, Barry Haddow, Benjamin Hsu, Phu Mon Htut, Hirofumi Inaguma, Dávid Javorský, John Judge, Yasumasa Kano, Tom Ko, Rishu Kumar, Pengwei Li, Xutail Ma, Prashant Mathur, Evgeny Matusov, Paul McNamee, John P. McCrae, Kenton Murray, Maria Nadejde, Satoshi Nakamura, Matteo Negri, Ha Nguyen, Jan Niehues, Xing Niu, Atul Ojha Kr., John E. Ortega, Proyag Pal, Juan Pino, Lonneke van der Plas, Peter Polák, Elijah Rippeth, Elizabeth Salesky, Jiatong Shi, Matthias Sperber, Sebastian Stüker, Katsuhito Sudoh, Yun Tang, Brian Thompson, Kevin Tran, Marco Turchi, Alex Waibel, Mingxuan Wang, Shinji Watanabe, and Rodolfo Zevallos. 2023. Findings of the IWSLT 2023 Evaluation Campaign. In Proceedings of the 20th International Conference on Spoken Language Translation (IWSLT 2023). Association for Computational Linguistics.

Mattia Antonino Di Gangi, Roldano Cattoni, Luisa Bentivogli, Matteo Negri, and Marco Turchi. 2019. Must-c: a multilingual speech translation corpus. In Proceedings of the 2019 Conference of the North American Chapter of the Association for Computational Linguistics: Human Language Technologies, NAACL-HLT 2019, Minneapolis, MN, USA, June 2-7, 2019, Volume 1 (Long and Short Papers), pages 2012–2017. Association for Computational Linguistics.

Jiaxin Guo, Minghan Wang, Daimeng Wei, Hengchao Shang, Yuxia Wang, Zongyao Li, Zhengzhe Yu, Zhanglin Wu, Yimeng Chen, Chang Su, Min Zhang, Lizhi Lei, Shimin Tao, and Hao Yang. 2021. Self-distillation mixup training for non-autoregressive neural machine translation. CoRR, abs/2112.11640.

Melvin Johnson, Mike Schuster, Quoc V. Le, Maxim Krikun, Yonghui Wu, Zhifeng Chen, Nikhil Thorat, Fernanda B. Viégas, Martin Wattenberg, Greg Corrado, Macduff Hughes, and Jeffrey Dean. 2017. Google's multilingual neural machine translation system: Enabling zero-shot translation. Trans. Assoc. Comput. Linguistics, 5:339–351.

Jaehyeon Kim, Jungil Kong, and Juhee Son. 2021. Conditional variational autoencoder with adversarial learning for end-to-end text-to-speech. In Proceedings of the 38th International Conference on Machine Learning, ICML 2021, 18-24 July 2021, Virtual Event, volume 139 of Proceedings of Machine Learning Research, pages 5530–5540. PMLR.

Danni Liu, Gerasimos Spanakis, and Jan Niehues. 2020. Low-latency sequence-to-sequence speech recognition and translation by partial hypothesis selection. In Interspeech 2020, 21st Annual Conference of the International Speech Communication Association, Virtual Event, Shanghai, China, 25-29 October 2020, pages 3620–3624. ISCA.

Thai-Son Nguyen, Sebastian Stüker, and Alex Waibel. 2021. Super-human performance in online low-latency recognition of conversational speech. In Interspeech 2021, 22nd Annual Conference of the International Speech Communication Association, Brno, Czechia, 30 August - 3 September 2021, pages 1762–1766. ISCA.

Myle Ott, Sergey Edunov, Alexei Baevski, Angela Fan, Sam Gross, Nathan Ng, David Grangier, and Michael Auli. 2019. fairseq: A fast, extensible toolkit for sequence modeling. CoRR, abs/1904.01038.

Peter Polák, Ngoc-Quan Pham, Tuan-Nam Nguyen, Danni Liu, Carlos Mullov, Jan Niehues, Ondrej Bojar, and Alexander Waibel. 2022. CUNI-KIT system for simultaneous speech translation task at IWSLT 2022. In Proceedings of the 19th International Conference on Spoken Language Translation, IWSLT@ACL 2022, Dublin, Ireland (in-person and online), May 26-27, 2022, pages 277–285. Association for Computational Linguistics.

Ashish Vaswani, Noam Shazeer, Niki Parmar, Jakob Uszkoreit, Llion Jones, Aidan N. Gomez, Lukasz Kaiser, and Illia Polosukhin. 2017. Attention is all you need. In Advances in Neural Information Processing Systems 30: Annual Conference on Neural Information Processing Systems 2017, December 4-9, 2017, Long Beach, CA, USA, pages 5998–6008.

Shinji Watanabe, Takaaki Hori, Shigeki Karita, Tomoki Hayashi, Jiro Nishitoba, Yuya Unno, Nelson Enrique Yalta Soplin, Jahn Heymann, Matthew Wiesner, Nanxin Chen, Adithya Renduchintala, and Tsubasa Ochiai. 2018. Espnet: End-to-end speech processing toolkit. CoRR, abs/1804.00015.

Daimeng Wei, Zongyao Li, Zhanglin Wu, Zhengzhe Yu, Xiaoyu Chen, Hengchao Shang, Jiaxin Guo, Minghan Wang, Lizhi Lei, Min Zhang, Hao Yang, and Ying Qin. 2021. Hw-tsc's participation in the WMT 2021 news translation shared task. In Proceedings of the Sixth Conference on Machine Translation, WMT@EMNLP 2021, Online Event, November 10-11, 2021, pages 225–231. Association for Computational Linguistics.

Di Wu, Binbin Zhang, Chao Yang, Zhendong Peng, Wenjing Xia, Xiaoyu Chen, and Xin Lei. 2021. U2++: unified two-pass bidirectional end-to-end model for speech recognition. CoRR, abs/2106.05642.

Lijun Wu, Yiren Wang, Yingce Xia, Tao Qin, Jianhuang Lai, and Tie-Yan Liu. 2019. Exploiting monolingual data at scale for neural machine translation. In Proceedings of the 2019 Conference on Empirical Methods in Natural Language Processing and the 9th International Joint Conference on Natural Language Processing, EMNLP-IJCNLP 2019, Hong Kong, China, November 3-7, 2019, pages 4205–4215. Association for Computational Linguistics.

Binbin Zhang, Di Wu, Zhendong Peng, Xingchen Song, Zhuoyuan Yao, Hang Lv, Lei Xie, Chao Yang, Fuping Pan, and Jianwei Niu. 2022. Wenet 2.0: More productive end-to-end speech recognition toolkit. In Interspeech 2022, 23rd Annual Conference of the International Speech Communication Association, Incheon, Korea, 18-22 September 2022, pages 1661–1665. ISCA.

Towards Efficient Simultaneous Speech Translation: CUNI-KIT System for Simultaneous Track at IWSLT 2023

Peter Polák[1] and **Danni Liu**[2] and **Ngoc-Quan Ngoc**[2]

Jan Niehues[2] and **Alexander Waibel**[2,3] and **Ondřej Bojar**[1]

polak@ufal.mff.cuni.cz

[1] Charles University [2] Karlsruhe Institute of Technology

[3] Carnegie Mellon University

Abstract

In this paper, we describe our submission to the Simultaneous Track at IWSLT 2023. This year, we continue with the successful setup from the last year, however, we adopt the latest methods that further improve the translation quality. Additionally, we propose a novel online policy for attentional encoder-decoder models. The policy prevents the model to generate translation beyond the current speech input by using an auxiliary CTC output layer. We show that the proposed simultaneous policy can be applied to both streaming blockwise models and offline encoder-decoder models. We observe significant improvements in quality (up to 1.1 BLEU) and the computational footprint (up to 45 % relative RTF).

1 Introduction

Simultaneous speech translation (SST) is the task of translating speech into text in a different language before the utterance is finished. The goal of SST is to produce a high-quality translation in real-time while maintaining low latency. However, these two objectives are conflicting. If we decrease the latency, the translation quality also drops. Last year's IWSLT evaluation campaign (Anastasopoulos et al., 2022) showed that current methods for simultaneous speech translation can approach the translation quality of human interpreters (Polák et al., 2022). The disadvantage is a higher computation footprint that might make a widespread application prohibitive.

This paper describes the CUNI-KIT submission to the Simultaneous translation track at IWSLT 2023 (Agarwal et al., 2023). Following our last year's submission (Polák et al., 2022), we continue in our effort to onlinize the robust offline speech translation models. However, the main goal of this submission is to improve the computational footprint. To this end, we propose a novel online policy based on CTC. As we experimentally document, the online CTC policy can be used to onlinize the offline models achieving a 45 % improvement in real time factor (RTF) as well as to improve the quality of the streaming blockwise models (Tsunoo et al., 2021). Aside from improving the online policy, we also adopt the novel improved streaming beam search (Polák et al., 2023) that further improves the translation quality.

Our contributions are as follows:

- We adopt the latest online decoding algorithm that improves the translation quality of robust offline models in the simultaneous regime,
- We propose a novel online policy that significantly
  - lowers the computational complexity of the online decoding with robust offline models while maintaining the same or only slightly worse translation quality,
  - improves the translation quality of the streaming blockwise models while maintaining the same latency,
- We demonstrate that our systems can run on hardware accessible to a wide audience.

2 Methods

In our submission, we use two different model architectures — a traditional offline ST architecture and a blockwise simultaneous ST architecture (Tsunoo et al., 2021). In this section, we describe the methods applied to achieve simultaneous ST using these architectures.

2.1 Incremental Blockwise Beam Search with Controllable Quality-Latency Tradeoff

To use the traditional offline ST model in a simultaneous regime, Liu et al. (2020) proposed chunking, i.e., splitting the audio source utterance into small constant-length chunks that are then incrementally

Proceedings of the 20th International Conference on Spoken Language Translation (IWSLT 2023), pages 389–396
July 13-14, 2023 ©2023 Association for Computational Linguistics

fed into the model. As translation quality tends to diminish toward the end of the unfinished source, an online policy is employed to control the latency-quality tradeoff in the generated output. Popular online policies include wait-k (Ma et al., 2019), shared prefix (Nguyen et al., 2020), hold-n and local agreement (Liu et al., 2020). In Polák et al. (2022), we showed that the tradeoff could be controlled by varying the chunk length.

To generate the translation, a standard beam search is typically applied (Sutskever et al., 2014). While this decoding algorithm enables the model to generate a complete translation for the current input, it also suffers from overgeneration (i.e., hallucinating tokens beyond sounds present in the input segment) and low-quality translations towards the end of the source context (Dong et al., 2020; Polák et al., 2022).

To tackle this issue, we adopt an improved incremental blockwise beam search (Polák et al., 2023). We outline the algorithm in Algorithm 1 and highlight the main differences from the original approach used in Polák et al. (2022) with red.

Algorithm 1: Incremental blockwise streaming beam search algorithm for incremental ST

```
   Input  : A list of blocks, an ST model
   Output : A set of hypotheses and scores
1  Seen ← ∅;
2  for each block do
3      Encode block using the ST model;
4      Stopped ← ∅;
5      minScore ← −∞;
6      while #active beams > 0 and not max. length do
7          Extend beams and compute scores;
8          for each active beam b do
9              if b ends with <eos> or (score ≤ minScore
                 and b ∉ Seen) then
10                 minScore ← max(minScore, score);
11                 Stopped ← Stopped ∪ b;
12                 Remove b from the beam search;
13             end
14         end
15     end
16     Seen ← Seen ∪ Stopped;
17     Sort Stopped by length-normalized score;
18     Set the best hypothesis from Stopped as active beam;
19     Apply the incremental policy;
20     Remove the last two tokens from the active beam;
21 end
```

In Algorithm 1, the overgeneration problem is addressed by stopping unreliable beams (see Line 9). The unreliable beam is defined as a beam ending with <eos> token or having a score lower or equal to any other unreliable beam detected so far. This means, that we stop any beam that has a score lower than any beam ending with <eos> token. Since there might be a hypothesis that would always score lower than some hypothesis ending with the <eos> token, the algorithm allows generating a hypothesis with a score lower than the unreliable score if it was seen during the decoding of previous blocks.

Finally, the algorithm removes two instead of one token in the current beam (see Line 20). Removing the last two tokens mitigates the issue of low-quality translation toward the end of the context.[1]

2.2 Rethinking Online Policies for Attention-based ST Models

While the improved incremental blockwise beam search improves the performance, it still requires a strong online policy such as hold-n or local agreement (Liu et al., 2020). A common property of these online policies is that they require multiple re-generations of the output translation. For example, the local agreement policy must generate each token at least twice to show it to the user, as each token must be independently generated by two consecutive contexts to be considered stable. Depending on the model architecture, the generation might be the most expensive operation. Additionally, the sequence-to-sequence models tend to suffer from exposure bias (i.e., the model is not exposed to its own errors during the training) (Ranzato et al., 2015; Wiseman and Rush, 2016). The exposure bias then causes a lower translation quality, and sometimes leads to hallucinations (i.e., generation of coherent output not present in the source) (Lee et al., 2018; Müller et al., 2019; Dong et al., 2020). Finally, attentional encoder-decoder models are suspected to suffer from label bias (Hannun, 2020).

A good candidate to address these problems is CTC (Graves et al., 2006). For each input frame, CTC predicts either a blank token (i.e., no output) or one output token independently from its previous predictions, which better matches the streaming translation and reduces the risk of hallucinations. Because the CTC's predictions for each frame are conditionally independent, CTC does not suffer from the label bias problem (Hannun, 2020). Although, the direct use of CTC in either machine or speech translation is possible, yet, its quality lags behind autoregressive attentional modeling (Libovický and Helcl, 2018; Chuang et al., 2021).

[1]Initial experiments showed that removing more than two tokens leads to higher latency without any quality improvement.

Another way, how to utilize the CTC is joint decoding (Watanabe et al., 2017; Deng et al., 2022). In the joint decoding setup, the model has two decoders: the non-autoregressive CTC (usually a single linear layer after the encoder) and the attentional autoregressive decoder. The joint decoding is typically guided by the attentional decoder, while the CTC output is used for re-scoring. Since the CTC predicts hard alignment, the rescoring is not straightforward. To this end, Watanabe et al. (2017) proposed to use the CTC prefix probability (Graves, 2008) defined as a cumulative probability of all label sequences that have the current hypothesis h as their prefix:

$$p_{\text{ctc}}(h, ...) = \sum_{\nu \in \mathcal{V}^+} p_{\text{ctc}}(h \oplus \nu | X), \quad (1)$$

where $\mathcal{V}$ is output vocabulary (including the `<eos>` symbol), $\oplus$ is string concatenation, and X is the input speech. To calculate this probability effectively, Watanabe et al. (2017) introduce variables $\gamma_t^{(b)}(h)$ and $\gamma_t^{(n)}(h)$ that represent forward probabilities of h at time t, where the superscript denotes whether the CTC paths end with a blank or non-blank CTC symbol. If the hypothesis h is a complete hypothesis (i.e., ends with the `<eos>` token), then the CTC probability of $h = g \oplus$ `<eos>` is:

$$p_{\text{ctc}}(h|X) = \gamma_T^{(b)}(g) + \gamma_T^{(n)}(g), \quad (2)$$

where T is the final time stamp.

If $h = g \oplus c$ is not final, i.e., $c \neq$ `<eos>`, then the probability is:

$$p_{\text{ctc}}(h|X) = \sum_{t=1}^{T} \Phi_t(g) \cdot p(z_t = c|X), \quad (3)$$

where

$$\Phi_t(g) = \gamma_{t-1}^{(b)}(g) + \begin{cases} 0 & \text{last}(g) = c \\ \gamma_{t-1}^{(n)}(g) & \textit{otherwise}. \end{cases}$$

2.3 CTC Online Policy

Based on the the definition of $p_{\text{ctc}}(h|X)$ in Equations (2) and (3), we can define the odds of g being at the end of context T:

$$\text{Odds}_{\text{end}}(g) = \frac{p_{\text{ctc}}(g \oplus \texttt{<eos>}|X)}{\sum_{c \in \mathcal{V}/\{\texttt{<eos>}\}} p_{\text{ctc}}(g \oplus c|X)}. \quad (4)$$

The disadvantage of this definition is that $p_{\text{ctc}}(\ldots|X)$ must be computed for every vocabulary entry separately and one evaluation costs $\mathcal{O}(T)$, i.e., $\mathcal{O}(|\mathcal{V}| \cdot T)$ in total. Contemporary ST systems use vocabularies in orders of thousands items making this definition prohibitively expensive. Since the CTC is used together with the label-synchronous decoder, we can approximate the denominator with a single vocabulary entry c_{att} predicted by the attentional decoder p_{att}:

$$\text{Odds}_{\text{end}}(g) \approx \frac{p_{\text{ctc}}(g \oplus \texttt{<eos>}|X)}{p_{\text{ctc}}(g \oplus c_{\text{att}}|X)}, \quad (5)$$

where $c_{\text{att}} = \text{argmax}_{c \in \mathcal{V}/\{\texttt{<eos>}\}} p_{\text{att}}(g \oplus c|X)$. Now the evaluation of $\text{Odds}_{\text{end}}(g)$ is $\mathcal{O}(T)$. If we consider that the baseline model already uses CTC rescoring, then evaluating $\text{Odds}_{\text{end}}(g)$ amounts to a constant number of extra operations to evaluate $p_{\text{ctc}}(g \oplus \texttt{<eos>}|X)$.

Finally, to control the latency of the online decoding, we compare the logarithm of $\text{Odds}_{\text{end}}(g)$ with a tunable constant C_{end}. If $\log \text{Odds}_{\text{end}}(g) > C_{\text{end}}$, we stop the beam search and discard the last token from g. We found values of C_{end} between -2 and 2 to work well across all models and language pairs.

3 Experiments and Results

3.1 Models

Our offline multilingual ST models are based on attentional encoder-decoder architecture. Specifically, the encoder is based on WavLM (Chen et al., 2022), and the decoder is based on multilingual BART (Lewis et al., 2019) or mBART for short. The model is implemented in the NMTGMinor library.[2] For details on the offline model see KIT submission to IWSLT 2023 Multilingual track (Liu et al., 2023).

The small simultaneous speech translation models for English-to-German and English-to-Chinese language pairs follow the blockwise streaming Transformer architecture (Tsunoo et al., 2021) implemented in ESPnet-ST-v2 (Yan et al., 2023). Specifically, the encoder is a blockwise Conformer (Gulati et al., 2020) with a block size of 40 and look-ahead of 16, with 18 layers, and a hidden dimension of 256. The decoder is a 6-layer Transformer decoder (Vaswani et al., 2017). To improve the training speed, we initialize the encoder with

[2] `https://github.com/quanpn90/NMTGMinor`

weights pretrained on the ASR task. Further, we employ ST CTC (Deng et al., 2022; Yan et al., 2022) after the encoder with weight 0.3 during the training. During the decoding, we use 0.3 for English to German, and 0.4 for English to Chinese. We preprocess the audio with 80-dimensional filter banks. As output vocabulary, we use unigram models (Kudo, 2018) of size 4000 for English to German, and 8000 for English to Chinese.

3.2 Evaluation

In all our experiments with the offline models, we use beam search of size 8 except for the CTC policy experiments where we use greedy search. For experiments with the blockwise models, we use the beam search of 6. For experiments with the improved blockwise beam search, we follow Polák et al. (2023) and remove the repetition detection in the underlying offline models, while we keep the repetition detection on for all experiments with the blockwise models.

For evaluation, we use Simuleval (Ma et al., 2020) toolkit and `tst-COMMON` test set of MuST-C (Cattoni et al., 2021). To estimate translation quality, we report detokenized case-sensitive BLEU (Post, 2018), and for latency, we report average lagging (Ma et al., 2019). To realistically assess the inference speed, we run all our experiments on a computer with Intel i7-10700 CPU and NVIDIA GeForce GTX 1080 with 8 GB graphic memory.

3.3 Incremental Blockwise Beam Search with Controllable Quality-Latency Tradeoff

In Table 1, we compare the performance of the onlinized version of the baseline blockwise beam search (BWBS) with the improved blockwise beam search (IBWBS; Polák et al., 2023). As we can see in the table, the improved beam search achieves higher or equal BLEU scores than the baseline beam search across all language pairs. We can observe the highest improvement in English-to-German (1.1 BLEU), while we see an advantage of 0.1 BLEU for English-to-Japanese. and no improvement in English-to-Chinese.

In Table 1, we also report the real-time factor (RTF), and the computation-aware average lagging (AL_{CA}). Interestingly, we observe a higher computational footprint of the IBWBS compared to the baseline beam search by 13, 28, and 17 % on En→{De, Ja, Zh}, resp., when measured with RTF. This might be due to the fact that we recompute the decoder states after each source increment. Since the IBWBS sometimes waits for more source chunks to output more tokens, the unnecessary decoder state recomputations might increase the computational complexity.

Lang	Decoding	AL↓	AL_{CA}↓	RTF↓	BLEU↑
En-De	BWBS	1922	**3121**	**0.46**	30.6
	IBWBS	1977	3277	0.52	**31.7**
En-Ja	BWBS	1992	**3076**	**0.50**	15.5
	IBWBS	1935	3264	0.64	**15.6**
En-Zh	BWBS	1948	**2855**	**0.41**	**26.5**
	IBWBS	1945	3031	0.48	**26.5**

Table 1: Incremental SST with the original BWBS and IBWBS. Better scores in bold.

3.4 CTC Online Policy

In Figure 1, we compare the improved blockwise beam search (IBWBS) with the proposed CTC policy using the blockwise streaming models. The tradeoff curves for English-to-German (see Figure 1a) and English-to-Chinese (see Figure 1b) show that the proposed CTC policy improves the quality (up to 1.1 BLEU for En→De, and 0.8 BLEU for En→Zh), while it is able to achieve the same latencies.

3.5 CTC Online Policy for Large Offline Models

We were also interested in whether the CTC policy can be applied to large offline models. Unfortunately, due to limited resources, we were not able to train a large offline model with the CTC output. Hence, we decided to utilize the CTC outputs of the online blockwise models and used them to guide the large offline model. Since the models have very different vocabularies,[3] we decided to execute the CTC policy after a whole word is generated by the offline model (rather than after every sub-word token). For the very same reason, we do not use CTC for rescoring.

We report the results in Table 2. Unlike in the blockwise models (see Section 3.4), the CTC policy does not improve the quality in En→De, and has a slightly worse quality (by 0.7 BLEU) in En→Zh. This is most probably due to the delayed CTC-attention synchronization that is not present for the blockwise models (as both decoders there share the

[3]The blockwise models have a vocabulary size of 4000 for En→De and 8000 for En→Zh, and the offline model has 250k.

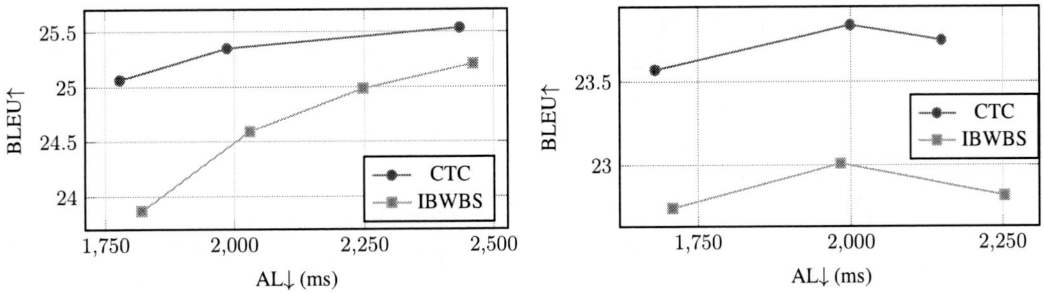

(a) English to German

(b) English to Chinese

Figure 1: Comparison of the improved blockwise beam search (IBWBS) and the proposed CTC policy using blockwise streaming models.

same vocabulary and the models compute the CTC policy after each token rather than word). However, we still observe a significant reduction in computational latency, namely by 45 and 34 % relative RTF for En→De and En→Zh, respectively.

Lang	Decoding	AL↓	AL_{CA}↓	RTF↓	BLEU↑
En-De	BWBS	1922	3121	0.46	30.6
	IBWBS	1977	3277	0.52	**31.7**
	CTC	1946	**2518**	**0.21**	30.6
En-Zh	BWBS	1948	2855	0.41	**26.5**
	IBWBS	1945	3031	0.48	**26.5**
	CTC	1981	**2515**	**0.28**	25.8

Table 2: Comparison of onlinization of the large offline model using chunking with the local agreement policy (LA-2) and with the proposed CTC policy.

4 Submission

In this section, we summarize our submission to the Simultaneous track at IWSLT 2023. In total, we submit 10 systems for all three language pairs.

4.1 Onlinized Offline Models

Following our last year's submission, we onlinize two large offline models (our models for IWSLT 2022 Offline ST track and IWSLT 2023 Multilingual track). This year, however, we utilize the improved blockwise beam search to yield higher BLEU scores. We submit systems for all language pairs based on the last year's model, and our new model. We summarize the submitted models and their performance in Table 3. As we can observe in Table 3, the 2023 model appears to perform worse. However, we learned during the writing of this paper that there was some overlap between the training and test data for the 2022 model[4], making the BLEU scores for the 2022 model unreliable.

Lang	Model	AL↓	AL_{CA}↓	BLEU↑
En-De	2022	1991	3138	31.8
	2023	1955	3072	31.4
En-Ja	2022	1906	3000	15.5
	2023	1982	3489	15.3
En-Zh	2022	1984	3289	26.8
	2023	1987	3508	26.6

Table 3: Submitted onlinized large offline models.

We also submit the system based on the large model onlinized using the CTC policy. The systems are summarized in Table 4. Unfortunately, we were not aware of the training and test data overlap during the evaluation period, so we decided to use our 2022 model also this year.

Lang	Model	AL↓	AL_{CA}↓	BLEU↑
En-De	2022	1959	2721	31.4
En-Zh	2022	1990	2466	26.3

Table 4: Submitted large offline models onlinized using the proposed CTC policy.

4.2 Blockwise Online Models

Finally, we submit small blockwise models. Their advantage is that they are able to run on a CPU faster than real time (more than 5× faster). We report their performance in Table 5.

Lang	AL↓	AL_{CA}↓	RTF↓	BLEU↑
En-De	1986	2425	0.19	25.4
En-Zh	1999	2386	0.19	23.8

Table 5: Submitted small blockwise models using the proposed CTC online policy.

[4](Zhang and Ao, 2022) found an overlap between ST-TED training corpus and tst-COMMON set of MuST-C dataset.

5 Conclusion and Future Work

In this paper, we present the CUNI-KIT submission to the Simultaneous track at IWSLT 2023. We experimented with the latest decoding methods and proposed a novel CTC online policy. We experimentally showed that the proposed CTC online policy significantly improves the translation quality of the blockwise streaming models. Additionally, the proposed CTC policy significantly lowers the computational footprint of the onlinized large offline models. Unaware of a data overlap issue in 2022, we eventually chose to use our last years' models in the official evaluation also this year.

Acknowledgments

This work has received support from the project "Grant Schemes at CU" (reg. no. CZ.02.2.69/0.0/0.0/19_073/0016935), the grant 19-26934X (NEUREM3) of the Czech Science Foundation, and by Charles University, project GA UK No 244523.

References

Milind Agarwal, Sweta Agrawal, Antonios Anastasopoulos, Ondřej Bojar, Claudia Borg, Marine Carpuat, Roldano Cattoni, Mauro Cettolo, Mingda Chen, William Chen, Khalid Choukri, Alexandra Chronopoulou, Anna Currey, Thierry Declerck, Qianqian Dong, Yannick Estève, Kevin Duh, Marcello Federico, Souhir Gahbiche, Barry Haddow, Benjamin Hsu, Phu Mon Htut, Hirofumi Inaguma, Dávid Javorský, John Judge, Yasumasa Kano, Tom Ko, Rishu Kumar, Pengwei Li, Xutail Ma, Prashant Mathur, Evgeny Matusov, Paul McNamee, John P. McCrae, Kenton Murray, Maria Nadejde, Satoshi Nakamura, Matteo Negri, Ha Nguyen, Jan Niehues, Xing Niu, Atul Ojha Kr., John E. Ortega, Proyag Pal, Juan Pino, Lonneke van der Plas, Peter Polák, Elijah Rippeth, Elizabeth Salesky, Jiatong Shi, Matthias Sperber, Sebastian Stüker, Katsuhito Sudoh, Yun Tang, Brian Thompson, Kevin Tran, Marco Turchi, Alex Waibel, Mingxuan Wang, Shinji Watanabe, and Rodolfo Zevallos. 2023. Findings of the IWSLT 2023 Evaluation Campaign. In *Proceedings of the 20th International Conference on Spoken Language Translation (IWSLT 2023)*. Association for Computational Linguistics.

Antonios Anastasopoulos, Loïc Barrault, Luisa Bentivogli, Marcely Zanon Boito, Ondřej Bojar, Roldano Cattoni, Anna Currey, Georgiana Dinu, Kevin Duh, Maha Elbayad, Clara Emmanuel, Yannick Estève, Marcello Federico, Christian Federmann, Souhir Gahbiche, Hongyu Gong, Roman Grundkiewicz, Barry Haddow, Benjamin Hsu, Dávid Javorský, Věra Kloudová, Surafel Lakew, Xutai Ma, Prashant Mathur, Paul McNamee, Kenton Murray, Maria Nădejde, Satoshi Nakamura, Matteo Negri, Jan Niehues, Xing Niu, John Ortega, Juan Pino, Elizabeth Salesky, Jiatong Shi, Matthias Sperber, Sebastian Stüker, Katsuhito Sudoh, Marco Turchi, Yogesh Virkar, Alexander Waibel, Changhan Wang, and Shinji Watanabe. 2022. Findings of the IWSLT 2022 evaluation campaign. In *Proceedings of the 19th International Conference on Spoken Language Translation (IWSLT 2022)*, pages 98–157, Dublin, Ireland (in-person and online). Association for Computational Linguistics.

Roldano Cattoni, Mattia Antonino Di Gangi, Luisa Bentivogli, Matteo Negri, and Marco Turchi. 2021. Must-c: A multilingual corpus for end-to-end speech translation. *Computer Speech & Language*, 66:101155.

Sanyuan Chen, Chengyi Wang, Zhengyang Chen, Yu Wu, Shujie Liu, Zhuo Chen, Jinyu Li, Naoyuki Kanda, Takuya Yoshioka, Xiong Xiao, et al. 2022. Wavlm: Large-scale self-supervised pre-training for full stack speech processing. *IEEE Journal of Selected Topics in Signal Processing*, 16(6):1505–1518.

Shun-Po Chuang, Yung-Sung Chuang, Chih-Chiang Chang, and Hung-yi Lee. 2021. Investigating the reordering capability in CTC-based non-autoregressive end-to-end speech translation. In *Findings of the Association for Computational Linguistics: ACL-IJCNLP 2021*, pages 1068–1077, Online. Association for Computational Linguistics.

Keqi Deng, Shinji Watanabe, Jiatong Shi, and Siddhant Arora. 2022. Blockwise Streaming Transformer for Spoken Language Understanding and Simultaneous Speech Translation. In *Proc. Interspeech 2022*, pages 1746–1750.

Linhao Dong, Cheng Yi, Jianzong Wang, Shiyu Zhou, Shuang Xu, Xueli Jia, and Bo Xu. 2020. A comparison of label-synchronous and frame-synchronous end-to-end models for speech recognition. *arXiv preprint arXiv:2005.10113*.

Alex Graves. 2008. *Supervised sequence labelling with recurrent neural networks*. Ph.D. thesis, Technical University Munich.

Alex Graves, Santiago Fernández, Faustino Gomez, and Jürgen Schmidhuber. 2006. Connectionist temporal classification: labelling unsegmented sequence data with recurrent neural networks. In *Proceedings of the 23rd international conference on Machine learning*, pages 369–376.

Anmol Gulati, James Qin, Chung-Cheng Chiu, Niki Parmar, Yu Zhang, Jiahui Yu, Wei Han, Shibo Wang, Zhengdong Zhang, Yonghui Wu, and Ruoming Pang. 2020. Conformer: Convolution-augmented Transformer for Speech Recognition. In *Proc. Interspeech 2020*, pages 5036–5040.

Awni Hannun. 2020. The label bias problem.

Taku Kudo. 2018. Subword regularization: Improving neural network translation models with multiple subword candidates. In *Proceedings of the 56th Annual Meeting of the Association for Computational Linguistics (Volume 1: Long Papers)*, pages 66–75, Melbourne, Australia. Association for Computational Linguistics.

Katherine Lee, Orhan Firat, Ashish Agarwal, Clara Fannjiang, and David Sussillo. 2018. Hallucinations in neural machine translation.

Mike Lewis, Yinhan Liu, Naman Goyal, Marjan Ghazvininejad, Abdelrahman Mohamed, Omer Levy, Ves Stoyanov, and Luke Zettlemoyer. 2019. Bart: Denoising sequence-to-sequence pre-training for natural language generation, translation, and comprehension. *arXiv preprint arXiv:1910.13461*.

Jindřich Libovický and Jindřich Helcl. 2018. End-to-end non-autoregressive neural machine translation with connectionist temporal classification. In *Proceedings of the 2018 Conference on Empirical Methods in Natural Language Processing*, pages 3016–3021, Brussels, Belgium. Association for Computational Linguistics.

Danni Liu, Ngoc-Quan Pham, Tuan Nam Nguyen, Thai-Binh Nguyen, Danni Liu, Carlos Mullov, Jan Niehues, and Alexander Waibel. 2023. KIT submission to multilingual track at IWSLT 2023. In *Proceedings of the 20th International Conference on Spoken Language Translation (IWSLT 2023)*. Association for Computational Linguistics.

Danni Liu, Gerasimos Spanakis, and Jan Niehues. 2020. Low-Latency Sequence-to-Sequence Speech Recognition and Translation by Partial Hypothesis Selection. In *Proc. Interspeech 2020*, pages 3620–3624.

Mingbo Ma, Liang Huang, Hao Xiong, Renjie Zheng, Kaibo Liu, Baigong Zheng, Chuanqiang Zhang, Zhongjun He, Hairong Liu, Xing Li, Hua Wu, and Haifeng Wang. 2019. STACL: Simultaneous translation with implicit anticipation and controllable latency using prefix-to-prefix framework. In *Proceedings of the 57th Annual Meeting of the Association for Computational Linguistics*, pages 3025–3036, Florence, Italy. Association for Computational Linguistics.

Xutai Ma, Mohammad Javad Dousti, Changhan Wang, Jiatao Gu, and Juan Pino. 2020. SIMULEVAL: An evaluation toolkit for simultaneous translation. In *Proceedings of the 2020 Conference on Empirical Methods in Natural Language Processing: System Demonstrations*, pages 144–150, Online. Association for Computational Linguistics.

Mathias Müller, Annette Rios, and Rico Sennrich. 2019. Domain robustness in neural machine translation. *arXiv preprint arXiv:1911.03109*.

Thai-Son Nguyen, Sebastian Stüker, and Alex Waibel. 2020. Super-human performance in online low-latency recognition of conversational speech. *arXiv preprint arXiv:2010.03449*.

Peter Polák, Ngoc-Quan Pham, Tuan Nam Nguyen, Danni Liu, Carlos Mullov, Jan Niehues, Ondřej Bojar, and Alexander Waibel. 2022. CUNI-KIT system for simultaneous speech translation task at IWSLT 2022. In *Proceedings of the 19th International Conference on Spoken Language Translation (IWSLT 2022)*, pages 277–285, Dublin, Ireland (in-person and online). Association for Computational Linguistics.

Peter Polák, Brian Yan, Shinji Watanabe, Alexander Waibel, and Ondrej Bojar. 2023. Incremental Blockwise Beam Search for Simultaneous Speech Translation with Controllable Quality-Latency Tradeoff. In *Proc. Interspeech 2023*.

Matt Post. 2018. A call for clarity in reporting BLEU scores. In *Proceedings of the Third Conference on Machine Translation: Research Papers*, pages 186–191, Brussels, Belgium. Association for Computational Linguistics.

Marc'Aurelio Ranzato, Sumit Chopra, Michael Auli, and Wojciech Zaremba. 2015. Sequence level training with recurrent neural networks. *arXiv preprint arXiv:1511.06732*.

Ilya Sutskever, Oriol Vinyals, and Quoc V Le. 2014. Sequence to sequence learning with neural networks. *Advances in neural information processing systems*, 27.

Emiru Tsunoo, Yosuke Kashiwagi, and Shinji Watanabe. 2021. Streaming transformer asr with blockwise synchronous beam search. In *2021 IEEE Spoken Language Technology Workshop (SLT)*, pages 22–29. IEEE.

Ashish Vaswani, Noam Shazeer, Niki Parmar, Jakob Uszkoreit, Llion Jones, Aidan N Gomez, Łukasz Kaiser, and Illia Polosukhin. 2017. Attention is all you need. *Advances in neural information processing systems*, 30.

Shinji Watanabe, Takaaki Hori, Suyoun Kim, John R Hershey, and Tomoki Hayashi. 2017. Hybrid ctc/attention architecture for end-to-end speech recognition. *IEEE Journal of Selected Topics in Signal Processing*, 11(8):1240–1253.

Sam Wiseman and Alexander M Rush. 2016. Sequence-to-sequence learning as beam-search optimization. In *Proceedings of the 2016 Conference on Empirical Methods in Natural Language Processing*, pages 1296–1306.

Brian Yan, Siddharth Dalmia, Yosuke Higuchi, Graham Neubig, Florian Metze, Alan W Black, and Shinji Watanabe. 2022. Ctc alignments improve autoregressive translation. *arXiv preprint arXiv:2210.05200*.

Brian Yan, Jiatong Shi, Yun Tang, Hirofumi Inaguma, Yifan Peng, Siddharth Dalmia, Peter Polák, Patrick Fernandes, Dan Berrebbi, Tomoki Hayashi, et al. 2023. Espnet-st-v2: Multipurpose spoken language translation toolkit. *arXiv preprint arXiv:2304.04596*.

Ziqiang Zhang and Junyi Ao. 2022. The YiTrans speech translation system for IWSLT 2022 offline shared task. In *Proceedings of the 19th International Conference on Spoken Language Translation (IWSLT 2022)*, pages 158–168, Dublin, Ireland (in-person and online). Association for Computational Linguistics.

Speech Translation with Foundation Models and Optimal Transport: UPC at IWSLT23

Ioannis Tsiamas, Gerard I. Gállego, José A. R. Fonollosa
Universitat Politècnica de Catalunya, Barcelona
{ioannis.tsiamas,gerard.ion.gallego,jose.fonollosa}@upc.edu

Marta R. Costa-jussà
Meta AI, Paris
costajussa@meta.com

Abstract

This paper describes the submission of the UPC Machine Translation group to the IWSLT 2023 Offline Speech Translation task. Our Speech Translation systems utilize foundation models for speech (wav2vec 2.0) and text (mBART50). We incorporate a Siamese pretraining step of the speech and text encoders with CTC and Optimal Transport, to adapt the speech representations to the space of the text model, thus maximizing transfer learning from MT. After this pretraining, we fine-tune our system end-to-end on ST, with Cross Entropy and Knowledge Distillation. Apart from the available ST corpora, we create synthetic data with SegAugment to better adapt our models to the custom segmentations of the IWSLT test sets. Our best single model obtains 31.2 BLEU points on MuST-C tst-COMMON, 29.8 points on IWLST.tst2020 and 33.4 points on the newly released IWSLT.ACLdev2023.

1 Introduction

In the past decade, the field of Speech Translation (ST) has seen significant advancements, mainly due to end-to-end models that directly translate speech, offering a more efficient method compared to traditional cascade systems (Sperber and Paulik, 2020). Despite data availability challenges, recent progress has diminished the performance disparity between these approaches (Bentivogli et al., 2021; Potapczyk and Przybysz, 2020; Inaguma et al., 2021; Ansari et al., 2020). Critical to the advancements in end-to-end models is the exploitation of ASR and MT data through pretraining strategies (Berard et al., 2018; Pino et al., 2019; Di Gangi et al., 2019; Gangi et al., 2019; Wang et al., 2020a; Zhang et al., 2020; Bansal et al., 2019).

Recently, Le et al. (2023) proposed a method to effectively utilize both ASR and MT pretraining to enhance ST. This approach involves pretraining an encoder-decoder MT system with available text data, followed by pretraining a speech encoder to generate representations similar to the MT system's encoder (*Siamese pretraining*) using Connectionist Temporal Classification (CTC) supervision (Graves et al., 2006) and Optimal Transport (Peyré and Cuturi, 2019). The resulting speech encoder and text decoder can be fine-tuned with ST data.

Another way of incorporating ASR and MT is to leverage large pretrained speech and text models as a foundation for end-to-end ST systems (Li et al., 2021; Gállego et al., 2021; Han et al., 2021; Zhang and Ao, 2022; Pham et al., 2022; Tsiamas et al., 2022b). However, these systems encounter representation discrepancy issues, which can hinder the full exploitation of pretrained foundation models. Gállego et al. (2021); Zhao et al. (2022) aimed to address this by adding *coupling modules* after the pretrained encoder, while other focus on solving the length discrepancies (Zhang et al., 2020; Xu et al., 2021a; Gaido et al., 2021). Han et al. (2021) tackled the issue by projecting speech and text features to a common semantic space using attention mechanisms and semantic memories.

In our work, we tackle the issue of misaligned speech and text encoder representations by adopting the approach proposed by Le et al. (2023). Our system uses a speech foundation model fine-tuned on English ASR, wav2vec 2.0 (Baevski et al., 2020), and an MT foundation model fine-tuned on multilingual MT (En-Xx), mBART50 (Tang et al., 2020), as described in Section 2.1. Building on prior research (Xu et al., 2021a; Han et al., 2021), we employ two encoders: an acoustic encoder from wav2vec 2.0 and a semantic encoder from mBART50. Coupling modules link these encoders to address length discrepancy. We extend Le et al. (2023) by applying CTC and OT losses to the outputs of the acoustic and semantic encoders, respectively, add a second auxiliary OT loss for the inputs of the semantic encoder, and keep the text encoder frozen to keep the MT space intact. This method aligns the speech encoder's represen-

Proceedings of the 20th International Conference on Spoken Language Translation (IWSLT 2023), pages 397–410
July 13-14, 2023 ©2023 Association for Computational Linguistics

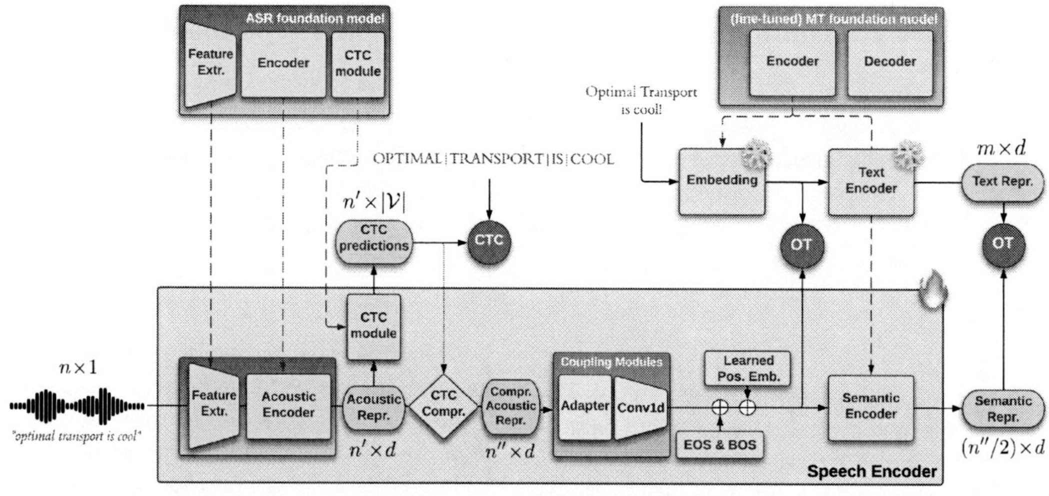

Figure 1: Extended Siamese pretraining

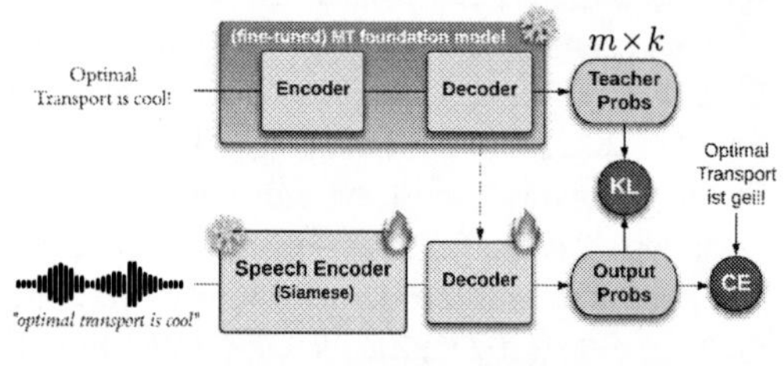

Figure 2: Speech Translation fine-tuning

tations with the MT foundation model, effectively improving the final ST system's performance by mitigating representation mismatch.

In summary, we participate in the IWSLT 2023 Offline Speech Translation task, focusing on translating spoken English to written German, by employing an end-to-end system. We leverage ASR and MT foundation models with the Siamese pretraining approach, to effectively bring their encoder's representations closer. We furthermore decouple acoustic and semantic modeling in our speech encoder, adjust for the length miss-match between speech and text with several coupling modules, and apply *knowledge distillation* (Hinton et al., 2015) from MT (Liu et al., 2019; Gaido et al., 2020), using mBART50.

2 Methodology

Our system, an encoder-decoder transformer, leverages ASR and MT foundation models (§2.1). We initially train the speech encoder with an Extended Siamese pretraining (§2.2), and then fine-tune it with the MT decoder for end-to-end ST (§2.3).

2.1 System architecture

As depicted in Figures 1 and 2, the encoder of our system is composed of several interconnected modules, while the decoder is adopted directly from the MT foundation model. The speech encoder is designed to generate representations closely resembling those of the MT foundation model, ensuring better compatibility between them. The following paragraphs provide a detailed overview of its key components and their functions.

Acoustic Modeling The speech waveform $x \in \mathbb{R}^n$ is first processed by a feature extractor, which consists of several strided convolutional layers, downsampling the input to a length of n'. Following, a Transformer encoder with dimensionality d is responsible for the acoustic modeling. Both these modules are initialized from an ASR foundation model.

CTC Compression The obtained acoustic representation $h \in \mathbb{R}^{n' \times d}$ is passed through a linear layer (initialized from the ASR model) and a softmax to generate the ASR vocabulary predictions $p^{(ctc)} \in \mathbb{R}^{n' \times |\mathcal{V}|}$, where $\mathcal{V}$ is the size of the vocabulary. We apply CTC compression (Gaido et al., 2021) to the acoustic representation, averaging the representations corresponding to repeating predictions on $p^{(ctc)}$ and removing those associated with the blank token. This process results in a new compressed representation $h^{(compr)} \in \mathbb{R}^{n'' \times d}$, where n'' denotes the compressed length of the sequence. This compression helps to reduce the length discrepancy between speech and text representations, which, in turn, facilitates the alignment process during Siamese pretraining (§2.2).

Coupling Modules Next, we apply an *adapter* (Houlsby et al., 2019), consisting of a linear projection to $8d$, a non-linear activation, a linear projection back to d. This module serves to (1) process the collapsed representations resulting from the compression and (2) provide sufficient parameters between the CTC and first OT loss to decouple their influence (§2.2). After the adapter we apply a strided 1D Convolution that subsamples the sequence by a factor of 2, which can help transform it closer to a sub-word level representation, rather than a character-level one, and subsequently aid in the Optimal Transport training with the sub-word level representation from the text encoder (§2.2).

Semantic Modeling At this point, we modify the representation to better match the input expected by the MT encoder. This is achieved by prepending and appending special tokens that correspond to the BOS and EOS tokens used in MT. We also re-introduce positional information to the representation with learned positional embeddings. Both the special tokens $t^{bos}, t^{eos} \in \mathbb{R}^d$ and the positional embeddings $E^{pos} \in \mathbb{R}^{(M+2)\times d}$ (with M representing the maximum sequence length) are learnable parameters initialized from the MT foundation model. The motivation is to bring the representation closer to the text embedding from the MT model, facilitating OT loss convergence (§2.2). Finally, the representation is processed by several more transformer encoder layers, which are initialized from the MT model and are responsible for semantic modeling.

2.2 Siamese pretraining

Our approach builds upon the Siamese pretraining proposed by Le et al. (2023), which exploits both ASR and MT pretraining to improve ST performance. This approach involves pretraining the encoder of an ST system jointly with Connectionist Temporal Classification (CTC) and Optimal Transport (OT), bringing its representations close to those of an MT encoder. This pretraining strategy has demonstrated superior results compared to traditional ASR pretraining with encoder-decoder and Cross-Entropy (Le et al., 2023). In this work, we build upon the method of Le et al. (2023) in several ways. First, we decouple the CTC and OT losses to correspond to the acoustic and semantic representations. Second, we add an extra auxiliary OT loss to better adapt the input to the semantic encoder. Next, we also employ CTC-based compression and coupling modules to better align the length of speech features with corresponding sub-word text representations. Finally, we opt to freeze the text encoder to not modify the MT decoder's representation space. The extended Siamese pretraining scheme is illustrated in Figure 1. For brevity, we refer to it simply as "Siamese" throughout the rest of the paper.

The Siamese pretraining is supervised by a combination of loss functions, each serving a distinct purpose. The CTC loss ensures the performance of the acoustic modeling by applying to the predictions of the CTC module. Meanwhile, the two OT losses target the input and output of the semantic encoder, and aim to align them with the text encoder representations. We calculate the OT loss as the Wasserstein distance (Frogner et al., 2015) between the text and speech representations, using an upper bound approximation, which is efficiently evaluated by the Sinkhorn algorithm (Knopp and Sinkhorn, 1967). Since the Wasserstein distance is position invariant, we follow (Le et al., 2023), and apply positional encodings, to make it applicable to sequences. The combined loss function for the Siamese pretraining stage is given by:

$$\mathcal{L}^{siamese} = \alpha\,\mathcal{L}^{CTC} + \beta\,\mathcal{L}^{OT_1} + \gamma\,\mathcal{L}^{OT_2} \quad (1)$$

Where α, β, and γ are hyperparameters that control the relative importance of each loss component in the combined pretraining loss.

2.3 Speech Translation fine-tuning

Upon obtaining the encoder from §2.2, we utilize it to initialize our ST system's encoder, while using the MT foundation model to initialize the decoder (Fig. 2). In addition to the Cross Entropy loss, we optionally provide guidance for the ST training through Knowledge Distillation (KD) (Tan et al., 2019), using the MT foundation model as a teacher. Specifically, we only use the top-k predictions rather than the entire distribution, and soften them using a temperature T (Gaido et al., 2020).

Since CTC supervision is not employed at this stage, we freeze the Feature Extractor, Acoustic Encoder, and CTC module from our encoder. During training, we optimize the parameters of the ST system's encoder and decoder with respect to the combined loss function, which is the sum of the Cross Entropy loss and the optional KD loss:

$$\mathcal{L}^{ST} = \lambda \, \mathcal{L}^{CE} + (1 - \lambda) \, \mathcal{L}^{KL} \quad (2)$$

Where $\mathcal{L}^{CE}$ is the Cross Entropy loss, $\mathcal{L}^{KL}$ is the Kullback–Leibler divergence between the MT and ST output distributions, and $0 \leq \lambda \leq 1$ is a hyperparameter that controls the relative importance of each loss component in the combined ST loss.

3 Data

3.1 Datasets

To train our ST models we used data from three speech translation datasets, MuST-C v3 (Cattoni et al., 2021), Europarl-ST (Iranzo-Sánchez et al., 2020) and CoVoST-2 (Wang et al., 2020b). MuST-C is based on TED talks, Europarl-ST on the European Parliament proceedings, and CoVoST is derived from the Common Voice dataset (Ardila et al., 2020). Their statistics are available in the first part of Table 1. We use as development data the IWSLT test sets of 2019 and 2020 (Niehues et al., 2019; Ansari et al., 2020), which are based on TED talks, and the ACL development set of 2023, which contains 5 presentations from ACL 2022. All development data are unsegmented, meaning that they are long and continuous speeches. We apply SHAS segmentation (§5) before translating them. For the Siamese pretraining, we used the English ASR data from MuST-C v3 and Europarl-ST, as well as CommonVoice v11 (Ardila et al., 2020) (Table 1).

3.2 Data Augmentation

We employ data augmentation, to create more ST data for training our models (Table 1). We use the MT foundation model, to translate the transcript of English CommonVoice v11 (Ardila et al., 2020). Since CommonVoice data contains various accents, we expect the synthetic data will be helpful for translating the ACL talks domain, which has predominantly non-native English accents. We additionally utilize SegAugment (Tsiamas et al., 2022a), which creates alternative versions of the training data by segmenting them differently with SHAS (Tsiamas et al., 2022c). We apply SegAugment to MuST-C v3, with three different length parameterizations: *medium (m)* (3 to 10 seconds), *long (l)* (10 to 20 seconds), and *extra-long (xl)* (20 to 30 seconds). We expect that SegAugment will be beneficial for translating the SHAS-segmented test sets, due to the similar segmentations of the training data it provides, as shown in Tsiamas et al. (2022a).

	Original	**Siamese**	**ST**
ST datasets			
MuST-C v3	427	417	421
↪ SegAugment	$1,364^\dagger$	–	$1,007^\dagger$
Europarl-ST	77	64	75
CoVoST 2	362	–	344
ASR datasets			
CommonVoice v11	1,503	1,361	$1,082^\dagger$
Total	–	1,842	2,929

Table 1: Filtered training data (in hours) for Siamese and ST training stages. Synthetic data is denoted with †.

3.3 Data Filtering

Siamese pretraining We remove speaker names, as well as events like "Laughter" and "Applause", we convert numbers to their spelled-out forms,[1] convert all text to lowercase, and finally remove all characters that are not included in the vocabulary of the ASR foundation model. Furthermore, we apply a step of ASR-based filtering, to filter out noisy examples stemming from wrong audio-text alignments, where we remove examples with high word-error-rate (WER). We adjust the threshold for each dataset dynamically, ensuring that the resulting data has a WER of 0.11. Thus, the thresholds are 0.5 for MuST-C, 0.28 for Europarl-ST, and 0.4 for CommonVoice, which indicates that Europarl-ST has a significant number of misalignments, a conclusion supported by manual inspection. Removing them allowed for faster convergence during Siamese pretraining.

ST fine-tuning We apply text normalization to the original ST data, remove speaker names and event-related tags from the MuST-C dataset, discard examples with extreme source-to-target text length ratios (Gaido et al., 2022), and finally remove audio-transcription misaligned examples with ASR-based filtering, using a fixed WER threshold of 0.5. For the synthetic CommonVoice data, we remove the ones already present in CoVoST. We also filter the synthetic examples of SegAugment, as the SHAS segmentation frequently resembles the original segmentation, thus resulting in highly similar examples. We retain only the ones that are sufficiently dissimilar from

[1]`https://github.com/savoirfairelinux/num2words`

the original ones, based on text similarity measures, using TF-IDF features from the translations. More concretely, for each talk id, we compute the similarity matrix of its original translations and the new candidates from SegAugment, find the most similar original example for each new candidate, and add it to the filtered data only if its similarity score is below 0.8. We apply this approach also between the different SegAugment versions (*m, l, xl*).

4 Experiments

Here we describe the experiments we carried out in this work. The implementation details are available in §A.1.

IWSLT '22 System For the IWSLT 2022 offline task, our submission employed a HuBERT encoder (Hsu et al., 2021a) and an mBART50 (En-Xx) decoder, which were efficiently fine-tuned to ST with the LNA strategy (Li et al., 2021) and parallel adapters (He et al., 2022), using datasets such as MuST-C v2, Europarl-ST and CoVoST. The architecture included three 1D convolutional layers between the encoder and decoder, resulting in a subsampling of the encoder representation by a factor of 8. The final ensemble also comprised models utilizing Knowledge Distillation and a wav2vec 2.0 encoder (Tsiamas et al., 2022b).

Baseline Our baseline has four main differences compared our last year's best system. We did an initial exploratory analysis of various encoders (§A.3), including different versions of wav2vec 2.0, and HuBERT. Upon observing no significant differences, we opted to utilize wav2vec 2.0 fine-tuned with pseudo-labels (Xu et al., 2021b), a more prevalent choice within the research community. Despite the strong performance demonstrated by efficient fine-tuning with LNA and parallel adapters, we chose to switch to standard ST fine-tuning in order to optimize performance. Moreover, we employ a semantic encoder initialized from the MT model. Lastly, we also pre-train the foundation models, wav2vec 2.0 with CTC on the ASR data of MuST-C, and mBART50 on the parallel text of MuST-C. It is important to note that only MuST-C data was utilized for the baseline.

Siamese Pre-training Instead of pre-training the speech encoder with CTC only, we follow the Siamese pre-training method (§2.2), with the encoder architecture described in §2.1, to align the encoder representations with the MT model's representation space. The system, instead of using three layers of 1D convolutions, now incorporates also CTC-based compression, a large adapter, and finally a single layer of 1D convolutions. Following the Siamese pre-training on MuST-C's ASR data, we jointly fine-tune the model and the MT decoder on the MuST-C ST data. Similar to the baseline, the MT model is also fine-tuned on the parallel text of MuST-C beforehand.

More Data We extend the previously described process by incorporating additional data. Initially, we fine-tune mBART50 using all the MT data (Table 6). Subsequently, we perform the Siamese pre-training and ST fine-tuning employing all the available speech data (Table 1). By incorporating a larger dataset, we aim to enhance the system's generalization capabilities and overall performance.

Data Augmentation We employ two data augmentation techniques to increase the performance of our system during ST fine-tuning (§3.2), while no modifications are made to the Siamese pre-training. First, we investigate the use of SegAugment (Tsiamas et al., 2022a), which we apply to MuST-C v3. Secondly, we generate synthetic data from Common Voice (Ardila et al., 2020), by leveraging the fine-tuned mBART50 (§A.2).

KD We use knowledge distillation with the fine-tuned mBART50 as the teacher (§A.2). The loss for training the ST model is the average of the standard cross entropy and the Kullback-Leibler (KL) divergence between the MT and ST output probability distributions. We utilize all available ST data in this experiment, including both real and synthetic data.

5 Audio Segmentation

To segment the audio of the IWSLT test sets, we use SHAS (Tsiamas et al., 2022c). The tst2023 test set, unlike previous years, contains another two domains apart from TED talks, which are ACL presentations and Press conferences. We tune the parameters of SHAS separately for each domain, but since no development set is available for the press conferences, we decided to treat it as the ACL domain. For fine-tuning the segmentation parameters, we used the ST model that was trained with synthetic data from CommonVoice and SegAugment and initialized from Siamese pre-training (Table 2, 2d). We evaluate the performance of the

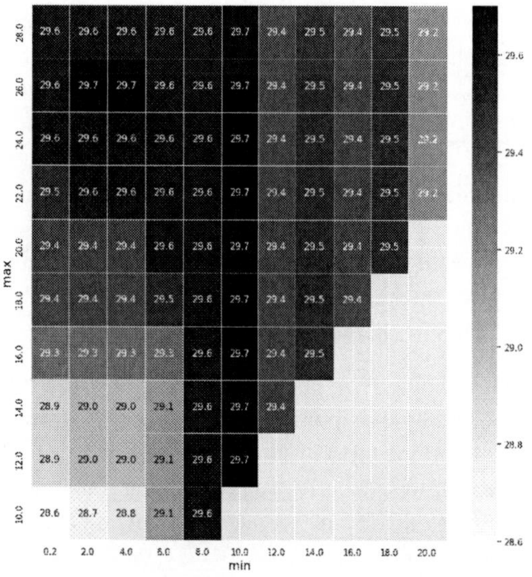

Figure 3: BLEU scores on IWSLT.tst2020 for different combinations of min and max segment length parameters of SHAS.

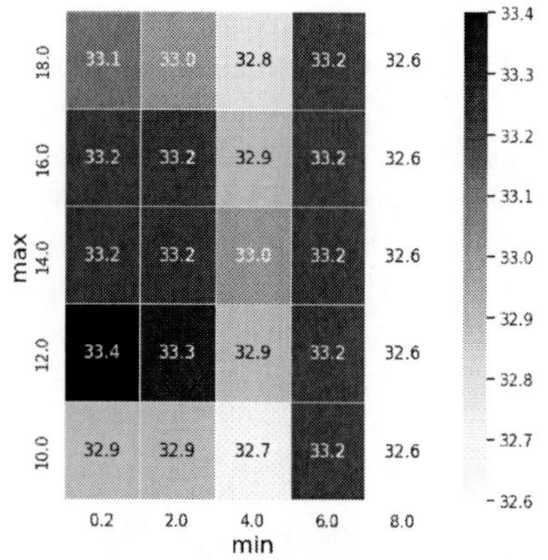

Figure 4: BLEU scores on IWSLT.ACLdev2023 for different combinations of min and max segment length parameters of SHAS.

ST model on many different combinations of the min and max segment length parameters, between 0.2-30 seconds on IWSLT.tst2019 and 0.2-18 on ACLdev2023. In Figure 3, we observe that the minimum segment length of 10 seconds is consistently reaching the best BLEU of 29.7 points. We decided to choose the combination of 10-26 seconds, since the max of 26, seemed to be slightly better compared to other neighboring values. As depicted in Figure 4, smaller segments are better for the ACL domain, with the best BLEU score obtained for min of 0.2 and max of 12. We hypothesize that the differences in the optimal segmentation between the IWSLT and ACL sets is because the ACL data are essentially out-of-domain for our ST models. In turn, the ST models are not confident in their predictions to handle long segments, and thus it is better to translate short segments instead.

6 Results

In Table 2 we provide the BLEU scores on MuST-C tst-COMMON and the IWLST test sets of tst2019 and tst2020 (TED domain), and acl2023 (ACL domain). We are using the original segmentation for MuST-C and apply SHAS with the optimal parameters (§5) of 10-26 secs for the TED domain, and 0.2-12 secs for the ACL one. We also provide the results from our submission to IWSLT '22.

In the first part of Table 2, we observe that this year's baseline (1a) improves results from last year best single model in both MuST-C and IWSLT test sets, although it only uses data from MuST-C. The reasons behind these improvements are the proper fine-tuning of learning rate and regularization parameters, as well as the choice of the speech encoder (§A.3). For the next exepriment (1b), by using the Siamese pretraining (§2.2), instead of just using CTC for the pretraining, we obtain substantial improvements in MuST-C v2, tst2020, and acl2023, indicating the efficacy of our pretraining method when applied on top of foundation models.

Adding more data in all parts of the training (2a), including the MT fine-tuning, Siamese pre-training and ST fine-tuning, did not bring any meaningful improvements to MuST-C and IWSLT.tst2019/20, but it dramatically improved the results on the acl2023 development set. We hypothesize that the CommonVoice and CoVoST data play an important role due to the large representation of foreign accents, similar to those in acl2023. Following, with the inclusion of SegAugment in the ST fine-tuning (2b) we observe an increase in all test sets, with larger ones in the IWSLT test sets, since SegAugment data have the same segmentation. Then, also using synthetic data from CommonVoice (2c) has minor improvements in MuST-C and a slight decrease in IWSLT. Despite that, we included synthetic data in subsequent experiments, since they were running in parallel. Applying Knowledge Distillation with the fine-tuned mBART50 as a teacher (2d), brings moderate gains of 0.1-0.4 BLEU in the IWSLT sets, and finally an increase in the learning rate (2e) from 5e-5 to 7.5e-5 provide a model that scored the best in tst2020 and acl2023.

		Dataset	MuST-C		IWSLT		
		split	v2	v3	tst2019	tst2020	acl2023
UPC '22 (Tsiamas et al., 2022b)							
0	a	Best Single	29.4	-	24.9	26.8	-
	b	Best Ensemble	30.8	-	25.4	27.8	-
Only MuST-C							
1	a	Baseline	29.8	29.9	25.7	27.3	25.1
	b	1a + Siamese Pretraining	30.8	30.1	25.9	28.5	26.4
Extended Data Conditions							
	a	1b + More Data	30.8	30.7	26.0	28.0	31.6
	b	2a + SegAugment	31.3	30.9	26.6	29.4	32.4
2	c	2b + synthCV	**31.4**	**31.0**	26.5	29.4	32.3
	d	2c + Knowledge Distillation	30.9	30.7	**26.8**	29.5	32.7
	e	2c + higher LR	31.2	30.8	26.4	**29.8**	**33.4**
Ensembles							
	a	Ensemble (2d, 2e)	31.4	31.1	26.9	29.7	32.8
3	b	Ensemble (2c, 2d, 2e)	31.4	31.1	**27.0**	**29.9**	32.7
	c	Ensemble (2b, 2c, 2d, 2e)	**31.5**	**31.2**	**27.0**	29.8	33.1

Table 2: BLEU scores for En-De MuST-C and IWSLT sets. In **bold** are the best scores by single models, and in **underlined bold** are the best scores overall.

Ensembling multiple models provided small increases in all sets. We believe that there is very little variation in our best models (2b-2e), since they are initialized from the same Siamese pre-training (2b), thus resulting in ineffective ensembles. In general, and in terms of single models, we improve our results from last year by 1.6 BLEU in tst2019 and 2.1 BLEU in tst2020, while the difference is larger in terms of single models.

7 Conclusions

We described the submission of the UPC Machine Translation group for the IWSLT 2023 Offline ST task. Our system leverages ASR and MT foundation models and a Siamese pretraining step to maximize the transfer learning from MT. We show that Siamese pretraining can bring significant improvements to our ST models, while fine-tuning with KD can also be helpful. We furthermore show that synthetic data are crucial at improving performance in the IWSLT test sets. In future work, we plan to investigate the zero-shot capabilities of optimal transport in the context of foundation models.

8 Submission Results

In Tables 3, 4 and 5, we present the official submission results for IWSLT 2023 with our best system, which is the Ensemble 3c of Table 2. Systems are evaluated on the three test sets (TED, ACL, Sub) with three metrics; BLEU (Papineni et al., 2002), chrF (Popović, 2017), and COMET (Rei et al., 2020). The TED test set also has two available references.

Metric	BLEU			chrF		COMET	
Reference	1	2	both	1	2	1	2
System 3c	25.5	29.8	36.6	0.56	0.58	0.7985	0.8098

Table 3: Official Results for the TED test set 2023.

Metric	BLEU	chrF	COMET
System 3c	32.1	0.6	0.7473

Table 4: Official Results for the ACL test set 2023.

Metric	BLEU	chrF	COMET
System 3c	15.6	0.47	0.3746

Table 5: Official Results for the Sub test set 2023.

Acknowledgements

The work done by Ioannis Tsiamas and Gerard I. Gállego was supported by the ADAVOICE project, PID2019-107579RB-I00 / AEI / 10.13039/501100011033

References

Ebrahim Ansari, Amittai Axelrod, Nguyen Bach, Ondrej Bojar, Roldano Cattoni, Fahim Dalvi, Nadir Durrani, Marcello Federico, Christian Federmann, Jiatao Gu, Fei Huang, Kevin Knight, Xutai Ma, Ajay Nagesh, Matteo Negri, Jan Niehues, Juan Pino, Elizabeth Salesky, Xing Shi, Sebastian Stüker, Marco Turchi, Alexander H. Waibel, and Changhan Wang. 2020. FINDINGS OF THE IWSLT 2020 EVALUATION CAMPAIGN. In *Proceedings of the 17th International Conference on Spoken Language Translation, IWSLT 2020, Online, July 9 - 10, 2020*, pages 1–34. Association for Computational Linguistics.

R. Ardila, M. Branson, K. Davis, M. Henretty, M. Kohler, J. Meyer, R. Morais, L. Saunders, F. M. Tyers, and G. Weber. 2020. Common voice: A massively-multilingual speech corpus. In *Proceedings of the 12th Conference on Language Resources and Evaluation (LREC 2020)*, pages 4211–4215.

Alexei Baevski, Yuhao Zhou, Abdelrahman Mohamed, and Michael Auli. 2020. wav2vec 2.0: A framework for self-supervised learning of speech representations. In *Advances in Neural Information Processing Systems*, volume 33, pages 12449–12460. Curran Associates, Inc.

Sameer Bansal, Herman Kamper, Karen Livescu, Adam Lopez, and Sharon Goldwater. 2019. Pre-training on high-resource speech recognition improves low-resource speech-to-text translation. In *Proceedings of the 2019 Conference of the North American Chapter of the Association for Computational Linguistics: Human Language Technologies*, pages 58–68, Minneapolis, Minnesota. Association for Computational Linguistics.

Luisa Bentivogli, Mauro Cettolo, Marco Gaido, Alina Karakanta, Alberto Martinelli, Matteo Negri, and Marco Turchi. 2021. Cascade versus direct speech translation: Do the differences still make a difference? In *Proceedings of the 59th Annual Meeting of the Association for Computational Linguistics and the 11th International Joint Conference on Natural Language Processing (Volume 1: Long Papers)*, pages 2873–2887, Online. Association for Computational Linguistics.

Alexandre Berard, Laurent Besacier, Ali Can Kocabiyikoglu, and Olivier Pietquin. 2018. End-to-End Automatic Speech Translation of Audiobooks. In *2018 IEEE International Conference on Acoustics, Speech and Signal Processing (ICASSP)*, pages 6224–6228, Calgary, AB. IEEE.

Roldano Cattoni, Mattia Antonino Di Gangi, Luisa Bentivogli, Matteo Negri, and Marco Turchi. 2021. Must-c: A multilingual corpus for end-to-end speech translation. *Computer Speech & Language*, 66:101155.

Alexis Conneau, Alexei Baevski, Ronan Collobert, Abdelrahman Mohamed, and Michael Auli. 2021. Unsupervised Cross-Lingual Representation Learning for Speech Recognition. In *Proc. Interspeech 2021*, pages 2426–2430.

Mattia A. Di Gangi, Matteo Negri, Viet Nhat Nguyen, Amirhossein Tebbifakhr, and Marco Turchi. 2019. Data Augmentation for End-to-End Speech Translation: FBK@IWSLT '19. In *Proceedings of the 16th International Workshop on Spoken Language Translation*, Hong Kong. Publisher: Zenodo.

Charlie Frogner, Chiyuan Zhang, Hossein Mobahi, Mauricio Araya-Polo, and Tomaso Poggio. 2015. Learning with a wasserstein loss. In *Proceedings of the 28th International Conference on Neural Information Processing Systems - Volume 2*, NIPS'15, page 2053–2061, Cambridge, MA, USA. MIT Press.

Marco Gaido, Mauro Cettolo, Matteo Negri, and Marco Turchi. 2021. CTC-based compression for direct speech translation. In *Proceedings of the 16th Conference of the European Chapter of the Association for Computational Linguistics: Main Volume*, pages 690–696, Online. Association for Computational Linguistics.

Marco Gaido, Mattia A. Di Gangi, Matteo Negri, and Marco Turchi. 2020. End-to-end speech-translation with knowledge distillation: FBK@IWSLT2020. In *Proceedings of the 17th International Conference on Spoken Language Translation*, pages 80–88, Online. Association for Computational Linguistics.

Marco Gaido, Sara Papi, Dennis Fucci, Giuseppe Fiameni, Matteo Negri, and Marco Turchi. 2022. Efficient yet competitive speech translation: FBK@IWSLT2022. In *Proceedings of the 19th International Conference on Spoken Language Translation (IWSLT 2022)*, pages 177–189, Dublin, Ireland (in-person and online). Association for Computational Linguistics.

Gerard I. Gállego, Ioannis Tsiamas, Carlos Escolano, José A. R. Fonollosa, and Marta R. Costa-jussà. 2021. End-to-end speech translation with pre-trained models and adapters: UPC at IWSLT 2021. In *Proceedings of the 18th International Conference on Spoken Language Translation (IWSLT 2021)*, pages 110–119, Bangkok, Thailand (online). Association for Computational Linguistics.

Mattia A. Di Gangi, Matteo Negri, and Marco Turchi. 2019. Adapting Transformer to End-to-End Spoken Language Translation. In *Proc. Interspeech 2019*, pages 1133–1137.

Alex Graves, Santiago Fernández, Faustino Gomez, and Jürgen Schmidhuber. 2006. Connectionist temporal classification: Labelling unsegmented sequence data with recurrent neural networks. In *Proceedings of the 23rd International Conference on Machine Learning*, ICML '06, page 369–376, New York, NY, USA. Association for Computing Machinery.

Chi Han, Mingxuan Wang, Heng Ji, and Lei Li. 2021. Learning shared semantic space for speech-to-text translation. In *Findings of the Association for Computational Linguistics: ACL-IJCNLP 2021*, pages 2214–2225, Online. Association for Computational Linguistics.

Junxian He, Chunting Zhou, Xuezhe Ma, Taylor Berg-Kirkpatrick, and Graham Neubig. 2022. Towards a unified view of parameter-efficient transfer learning. In *International Conference on Learning Representations*.

Dan Hendrycks and Kevin Gimpel. 2020. Gaussian error linear units (gelus).

Geoffrey E. Hinton, Oriol Vinyals, and Jeffrey Dean. 2015. Distilling the knowledge in a neural network. *ArXiv*, abs/1503.02531.

Neil Houlsby, Andrei Giurgiu, Stanislaw Jastrzebski, Bruna Morrone, Quentin De Laroussilhe, Andrea Gesmundo, Mona Attariyan, and Sylvain Gelly. 2019. Parameter-efficient transfer learning for NLP. In *Proceedings of the 36th International Conference on Machine Learning*, volume 97 of *Proceedings of Machine Learning Research*, pages 2790–2799. PMLR.

Wei-Ning Hsu, Benjamin Bolte, Yao-Hung Hubert Tsai, Kushal Lakhotia, Ruslan Salakhutdinov, and Abdelrahman Mohamed. 2021a. Hubert: Self-supervised speech representation learning by masked prediction of hidden units. *IEEE/ACM Transactions on Audio, Speech, and Language Processing*, 29:3451–3460.

Wei-Ning Hsu, Anuroop Sriram, Alexei Baevski, Tatiana Likhomanenko, Qiantong Xu, Vineel Pratap, Jacob Kahn, Ann Lee, Ronan Collobert, Gabriel Synnaeve, and Michael Auli. 2021b. Robust wav2vec 2.0: Analyzing Domain Shift in Self-Supervised Pre-Training. In *Proc. Interspeech 2021*, pages 721–725.

Hirofumi Inaguma, Brian Yan, Siddharth Dalmia, Pengcheng Guo, Jiatong Shi, Kevin Duh, and Shinji Watanabe. 2021. ESPnet-ST IWSLT 2021 offline speech translation system. In *Proceedings of the 18th International Conference on Spoken Language Translation (IWSLT 2021)*, pages 100–109, Bangkok, Thailand (online). Association for Computational Linguistics.

Javier Iranzo-Sánchez, Joan Albert Silvestre-Cerdà, Javier Jorge, Nahuel Roselló, Adrià Giménez, Albert Sanchis, Jorge Civera, and Alfons Juan. 2020. Europarl-st: A multilingual corpus for speech translation of parliamentary debates.

J. Kahn, M. Rivière, W. Zheng, E. Kharitonov, Q. Xu, P. E. Mazaré, J. Karadayi, V. Liptchinsky, R. Collobert, C. Fuegen, T. Likhomanenko, G. Synnaeve, A. Joulin, A. Mohamed, and E. Dupoux. 2020. Libri-light: A benchmark for asr with limited or no supervision. In *ICASSP 2020 - 2020 IEEE International Conference on Acoustics, Speech and Signal Processing (ICASSP)*, pages 7669–7673. `https://github.com/facebookresearch/libri-light`.

Eugene Kharitonov, Morgane Rivière, Gabriel Synnaeve, Lior Wolf, Pierre-Emmanuel Mazaré, Matthijs Douze, and Emmanuel Dupoux. 2021. Data augmenting contrastive learning of speech representations in the time domain. In *2021 IEEE Spoken Language Technology Workshop (SLT)*, pages 215–222.

Diederik P. Kingma and Jimmy Ba. 2014. Adam: A method for stochastic optimization.

Paul Knopp and Richard Sinkhorn. 1967. Concerning nonnegative matrices and doubly stochastic matrices. *Pacific Journal of Mathematics*, 21(2):343 – 348.

Philipp Koehn. 2004. Statistical significance tests for machine translation evaluation. In *Proceedings of the 2004 Conference on Empirical Methods in Natural Language Processing*, pages 388–395, Barcelona, Spain. Association for Computational Linguistics.

Philipp Koehn. 2005. Europarl: A parallel corpus for statistical machine translation. In *Proceedings of Machine Translation Summit X: Papers*, pages 79–86, Phuket, Thailand.

Phuong-Hang Le, Hongyu Gong, Changhan Wang, Juan Pino, Benjamin Lecouteux, and Didier Schwab. 2023. Pre-training for speech translation: Ctc meets optimal transport.

Xian Li, Changhan Wang, Yun Tang, Chau Tran, Yuqing Tang, Juan Pino, Alexei Baevski, Alexis Conneau, and Michael Auli. 2021. Multilingual speech translation from efficient finetuning of pretrained models. In *Proceedings of the 59th Annual Meeting of the Association for Computational Linguistics and the 11th International Joint Conference on Natural Language Processing (Volume 1: Long Papers)*, pages 827–838.

Yuchen Liu, Hao Xiong, Jiajun Zhang, Zhongjun He, Hua Wu, Haifeng Wang, and Chengqing Zong. 2019. End-to-End Speech Translation with Knowledge Distillation. In *Proc. Interspeech 2019*, pages 1128–1132.

J. Niehues, R. Cattoni, S. Stüker, M. Negri, M. Turchi, Elizabeth Salesky, Ramon Sanabria, Loïc Barrault, Lucia Specia, and Marcello Federico. 2019. The iwslt 2019 evaluation campaign. In *Proceedings of the 16th International Workshop on Spoken Language Translation*.

Myle Ott, Sergey Edunov, Alexei Baevski, Angela Fan, Sam Gross, Nathan Ng, David Grangier, and Michael Auli. 2019. fairseq: A fast, extensible toolkit for sequence modeling. In *Proceedings of NAACL-HLT 2019: Demonstrations*.

Vassil Panayotov, Guoguo Chen, Daniel Povey, and Sanjeev Khudanpur. 2015. Librispeech: An asr corpus based on public domain audio books. In *2015 IEEE International Conference on Acoustics, Speech and Signal Processing (ICASSP)*, pages 5206–5210.

Kishore Papineni, Salim Roukos, Todd Ward, and Wei-Jing Zhu. 2002. Bleu: a method for automatic evaluation of machine translation. In *Proceedings of the 40th Annual Meeting of the Association for Computational Linguistics*, pages 311–318, Philadelphia, Pennsylvania, USA. Association for Computational Linguistics.

Gabriel Peyré and Marco Cuturi. 2019. Computational optimal transport: With applications to data science.

Ngoc-Quan Pham, Tuan Nam Nguyen, Thai-Binh Nguyen, Danni Liu, Carlos Mullov, Jan Niehues, and Alexander Waibel. 2022. Effective combination of pretrained models - KIT@IWSLT2022. In *Proceedings of the 19th International Conference on Spoken Language Translation (IWSLT 2022)*, pages 190–197, Dublin, Ireland (in-person and online). Association for Computational Linguistics.

Juan Pino, Liezl Puzon, Jiatao Gu, Xutai Ma, Arya D. McCarthy, and Deepak Gopinath. 2019. Harnessing Indirect Training Data for End-to-End Automatic Speech Translation: Tricks of the Trade. In *Proceedings of the 16th International Workshop on Spoken Language Translation*, Hong Kong. Publisher: Zenodo.

Maja Popović. 2017. chrF++: words helping character n-grams. In *Proceedings of the Second Conference on Machine Translation*, pages 612–618, Copenhagen, Denmark. Association for Computational Linguistics.

Matt Post. 2018. A call for clarity in reporting BLEU scores. In *Proceedings of the Third Conference on Machine Translation: Research Papers*, pages 186–191, Belgium, Brussels. Association for Computational Linguistics.

Tomasz Potapczyk and Pawel Przybysz. 2020. SR-POL's System for the IWSLT 2020 End-to-End Speech Translation Task. In *Proceedings of the 17th International Conference on Spoken Language Translation*, pages 89–94, Online. Association for Computational Linguistics.

Ricardo Rei, Craig Stewart, Ana C Farinha, and Alon Lavie. 2020. COMET: A neural framework for MT evaluation. In *Proceedings of the 2020 Conference on Empirical Methods in Natural Language Processing (EMNLP)*, pages 2685–2702, Online. Association for Computational Linguistics.

Matthias Sperber and Matthias Paulik. 2020. Speech translation and the end-to-end promise: Taking stock of where we are. In *Proceedings of the 58th Annual Meeting of the Association for Computational Linguistics*, pages 7409–7421, Online. Association for Computational Linguistics.

Xu Tan, Yi Ren, Di He, Tao Qin, and Tie-Yan Liu. 2019. Multilingual neural machine translation with knowledge distillation. In *International Conference on Learning Representations*.

Yuqing Tang, Chau Tran, Xian Li, Peng-Jen Chen, Naman Goyal, Vishrav Chaudhary, Jiatao Gu, and Angela Fan. 2020. Multilingual translation with extensible multilingual pretraining and finetuning. *arXiv preprint arXiv:2008.00401*.

Ioannis Tsiamas, José A. R. Fonollosa, and Marta R. Costa-jussà. 2022a. SegAugment: Maximizing the Utility of Speech Translation Data with Segmentation-based Augmentations.

Ioannis Tsiamas, Gerard I. Gállego, Carlos Escolano, José Fonollosa, and Marta R. Costa-jussà. 2022b. Pretrained speech encoders and efficient fine-tuning methods for speech translation: UPC at IWSLT 2022. In *Proceedings of the 19th International Conference on Spoken Language Translation (IWSLT 2022)*, pages 265–276, Dublin, Ireland (in-person and online). Association for Computational Linguistics.

Ioannis Tsiamas, Gerard I. Gállego, José A. R. Fonollosa, and Marta R. Costa-jussà. 2022c. Shas: Approaching optimal segmentation for end-to-end speech translation.

Changhan Wang, Yun Tang, Xutai Ma, Anne Wu, Dmytro Okhonko, and Juan Pino. 2020a. Fairseq S2T: Fast speech-to-text modeling with fairseq. In *Proceedings of the 1st Conference of the Asia-Pacific Chapter of the Association for Computational Linguistics and the 10th International Joint Conference on Natural Language Processing: System Demonstrations*, pages 33–39, Suzhou, China. Association for Computational Linguistics.

Changhan Wang, Anne Wu, and Juan Pino. 2020b. Covost 2: A massively multilingual speech-to-text translation corpus. *arXiv preprint arXiv:2007.10310*.

Ruibin Xiong, Yunchang Yang, Di He, Kai Zheng, Shuxin Zheng, Chen Xing, Huishuai Zhang, Yanyan Lan, Liwei Wang, and Tie-Yan Liu. 2020. On layer normalization in the transformer architecture. In *Proceedings of the 37th International Conference on Machine Learning*, ICML'20. JMLR.org.

Chen Xu, Bojie Hu, Yanyang Li, Yuhao Zhang, Shen Huang, Qi Ju, Tong Xiao, and Jingbo Zhu. 2021a. Stacked acoustic-and-textual encoding: Integrating the pre-trained models into speech translation encoders. In *Proceedings of the 59th Annual Meeting of the Association for Computational Linguistics and the 11th International Joint Conference on Natural Language Processing (Volume 1: Long Papers)*, pages 2619–2630, Online. Association for Computational Linguistics.

Qiantong Xu, Alexei Baevski, Tatiana Likhomanenko, Paden Tomasello, Alexis Conneau, Ronan Collobert, Gabriel Synnaeve, and Michael Auli. 2021b. Self-training and pre-training are complementary for speech recognition. In *ICASSP 2021 - 2021 IEEE International Conference on Acoustics, Speech and Signal Processing (ICASSP)*, pages 3030–3034.

Biao Zhang, Ivan Titov, Barry Haddow, and Rico Sennrich. 2020. Adaptive feature selection for end-to-end speech translation. In *Findings of the Association for Computational Linguistics: EMNLP 2020*, pages 2533–2544, Online. Association for Computational Linguistics.

Ziqiang Zhang and Junyi Ao. 2022. The YiTrans speech translation system for IWSLT 2022 offline shared task. In *Proceedings of the 19th International Conference on Spoken Language Translation (IWSLT 2022)*, pages 158–168, Dublin, Ireland (in-person and online). Association for Computational Linguistics.

Ziqiang Zhang, Sanyuan Chen, Long Zhou, Yu Wu, Shuo Ren, Shujie Liu, Zhuoyuan Yao, Xun Gong, Lirong Dai, Jinyu Li, et al. 2022. Speechlm: Enhanced speech pre-training with unpaired textual data. *arXiv preprint arXiv:2209.15329*.

Jinming Zhao, Hao Yang, Gholamreza Haffari, and Ehsan Shareghi. 2022. M-Adapter: Modality Adaptation for End-to-End Speech-to-Text Translation. In *Proc. Interspeech 2022*, pages 111–115.

A Appendix

A.1 Implementation Details

This section presents the implementation details of our proposed model architecture.

As an ASR model, we are using wav2vec 2.0[2] which is composed of a 7-layer convolutional feature extractor and 24-layer Transformer encoder. It is pretrained with 60k hours of non-transcribed speech from Libri-Light (Kahn et al., 2020), and fine-tuned for ASR with 960 hours of labeled data from Librispeech (Panayotov et al., 2015). The wav2vec 2.0 version we use was also fine-tuned with pseudo-labels (Xu et al., 2021b).

As an MT model, we are using mBART50 (Tang et al., 2020), which is already fine-tuned on En-Xx multilingual machine translation[3]. We further pretrain it for two reasons. Firstly, we are only interested in the En-De direction, and thus we would like a more specialized model on that direction. Secondly, due to the 2nd step of encoder matching, we would like the text encoder to have a very good representation of our data. For MT fine-tuning, we use the original parameters of mBART50 (Tang et al., 2020), and the datasets listed in Table 6.

The acoustic encoder has 24 Transformer layers, while the semantic encoder and the decoder have 12 layers each. All layers have an embedding dimensionality of 1024, a feed-forward dimensionality of 4098, GELU activations (Hendrycks and Gimpel, 2020), 16 attention heads, and pre-layer normalization (Xiong et al., 2020). The vocabulary for the CTC has a size of 32 characters, while the one for the ST model has a size of 250,000.

The model takes waveforms with a 16kHz sampling rate as input, which are normalized to zero mean and unit variance. The models are trained using the data presented in Table 1, with maximum source length of 400,000 and target length of 1024 tokens. Gradient accumulation and data parallelism are employed to achieve an effective batch size of approximately 32 million tokens.

For the Siamese pre-training we use Adam (Kingma and Ba, 2014) with a base learning rate of $2 \cdot 10^{-4}$, a warm-up of 1,000 steps and an inverse square root scheduler. We follow a reduced regularization approach, as compared to the original configuration of wav2vec 2.0 and mBART50, which we found to work the best in our preliminary experiments. Thus, we use 0.1 activation dropout in the acoustic encoder, as well as time masking with probability of 0.2 and channel masking with probability of 0.1. For the context encoder, we use 0.1 dropout and 0.1 attention dropout. All other dropouts are inactive. All the weights in the loss function were set to 1.0 (Eq. 1). We train until the $\mathcal{L}^{OT_2}$ term of the loss does not improve for 5,000 steps, and then average the 10 best checkpoints according to the same loss term.

For ST fine-tuning, we use Adam with a base learning rate of $5 \cdot 10^{-5}$, fixed for the 20% of the training before decaying to $5 \cdot 10^{-7}$ for the rest. In the semantic encoder, we apply a dropout of 0.1 and an attention dropout of 0.1, while for the decoder we use a dropout of 0.3 and an attention dropout of 0.1. Neither dropout nor masking is applied in the frozen acoustic encoder. The loss is the cross-entropy with label smoothing of 0.2.

For the experiments incorporating Knowledge Distillation (KD) during ST fine-tuning, the loss is calculated as a weighted sum of the standard cross-entropy (no label smoothing) and the KL divergence between the teacher and student distributions, controlled by a hyperparameter λ, set to 0.5. The teacher distribution for each step is obtained offline using the fine-tuned mBART50, where we keep the top-8 indices, and both the teacher and student distributions are additionally modified with

[2]https://dl.fbaipublicfiles.com/fairseq/wav2vec/wav2vec2_vox_960h_new.pt

[3]https://dl.fbaipublicfiles.com/fairseq/models/mbart50/mbart50.ft.1n.tar.gz

temperature $T = 1.3$ (Gaido et al., 2020).

After ST fine-tuning, we pick the 10 best checkpoints according to the BLEU (Papineni et al., 2002) computed with sacreBLEU (Post, 2018) on the development set of MuST-C and average them. For generation, we use a beam search of 5. All models are implemented in FAIRSEQ (Ott et al., 2019), and experiments were run on a cluster of 8 NVIDIA GeForce RTX 3090. Our code is available at a public repository[4].

A.2 MT fine-tuning

For the MT fine-tuning, we use the parallel text of the ST datasets, as well as Europarl v10 En-De (Koehn, 2005) (Table 6). We perform text normalization and remove pairs with extremely short text segments (fewer than 4 characters) or extreme source-to-target length ratio (less than 0.5 or larger than 2).

	Original	**Filtered**
ST datasets		
MuST-C v3	270	235
Europarl-ST	33	26
CoVoST 2	231	203
MT datasets		
Europarl v10	1,829	1,566
Total	2,363	2,030

Table 6: Filtered training data (thousands of sentences) for MT fine-tuning stage.

	MuST-C v2	**MuST-C v3**	**Europarl-ST**	**CoVoST2**
Off-the-shelf				
mBART50	31.4	30.9	35.0	33.6
Fine-tuned				
MuST-C v2	35.3	34.4	34.6	35.3
All (§3.1)	34.9	34.2	40.3	39.9

Table 7: BLEU scores on MT test sets.

A.3 Preliminary experiments

Before starting the primary experiments for the IWSLT evaluation campaign, we conducted an array of preliminary tests, building on top of previous years' submissions (Gállego et al., 2021; Tsiamas et al., 2022b). These explorations were intended to examine the impact of system configuration variations on the performance metrics on the MuST-C v2 dev set, such as BLEU (Papineni et al., 2002), chrF2 (Popović, 2017), and COMET (Rei et al., 2020). To ensure the robustness of our findings, we estimated statistical significance using the bootstrap resampling method (Koehn, 2004).

In our initial experiment, we examined the impact of various fine-tuning strategies used in our last years' participations, specifically *LNA* (Li et al., 2021) and *LNA-Adapters* (Tsiamas et al., 2022b), in comparison to full fine-tuning. The goal was to verify whether these approaches inadvertently hurt the system's performance. As demonstrated in Table 8, these strategies indeed had a detrimental effect, leading to reductions of 1.9 BLEU points when applied to both the encoder and the decoder. Consequently, we opted to adopt a conventional full fine-tuning strategy for subsequent experiments.

Following this, we conducted a comparative analysis of various speech encoders, including different variations of *wav2vec 2.0* (Baevski et al., 2020; Xu et al., 2021b; Hsu et al., 2021b; Conneau et al., 2021), *HuBERT* (Hsu et al., 2021a), and *SpeechLM* (Zhang et al., 2022) (Table 9). Our baseline was the wav2vec 2.0 fine-tuned with pseudo-labels (Xu et al., 2021b), and intriguingly, most encoders exhibited a comparable level of performance. A marginal decrease was observed with the wav2vec 2.0 pretrained on a large pool of datasets (LV-60 + CV + SWBD + FSH) (Hsu et al., 2021b), and the multilingual version of wav2vec 2.0, XLSR (Conneau et al., 2021). The SpeechLM results were noticeably below expectations, leading us to suspect a bug in our implementation.

Upon noting that the hyperparameters were optimized for a specific speech encoder, we hypothesized that a reduction in the learning rate might boost HuBERT's performance. However, as demonstrated in Table 11, the performance was adversely affected, prompting us to retain the original wav2vec 2.0 as the primary speech encoder due to the lack of substantial improvements offered by other alternatives.

Our focus then shifted towards examining the influence of varying regularization and data augmentation strategies on system performance (Table 10). We explored a range, from our traditionally used setup (*base*), to the one employed in the *original* foundation model fine-tuning, and a *reduced* version. Implementing the *original* regularization within the speech encoder, as opposed to the *base* variant, significantly boosted performance, leading

[4] https://github.com/mt-upc/iwslt-2023

Encoder	Decoder	BLEU	chrF2	COMET
-	-	29.0	54.7	0.8001
LNA	-	28.0 *	54.1 *	0.7949 *
-	LNA	27.9 *	54.0 *	0.7882 *
LNA	LNA	27.1 *	53.2 *	0.7800 *
LNA-Adapt	-	28.2 *	54.3 *	0.7960 *
-	LNA-Adapt	27.6 *	53.6 *	0.7889 *
LNA-Adapt	LNA-Adapt	27.1 *	53.5 *	0.7847 *

Table 8: Performance comparison of fine-tuning strategies w.r.t. to full fine-tuning, evaluated on the MuST-C v2 dev set (en-de). *LNA* and *LNA-Adapters* represent the strategies proposed by (Li et al., 2021) and (Tsiamas et al., 2022b) respectively. $*$ indicates significance w.r.t. baseline (full fine-tuning).

us to select this configuration. We also explored the effectiveness of WavAugment (Kharitonov et al., 2021), ultimately finding that, despite its training speed slowdown, it did not enhance the results. Consequently, we opted to stop using it.

Lastly, we evaluated the potential benefits of employing the new MuST-C v3 training data on system performance (Table 12). Unexpectedly, no significant improvements were observed upon transitioning from MuST-C v2 to v3. Despite this, we decided to utilize v3, since it's specifically prepared for the IWSLT evaluation campaign.

These preliminary investigations have not only provided a more profound understanding of the role of each system's component and setting, but also have yielded us with a better starting point for the subsequent experiments of our work.

Learning Rate	BLEU	chrF2	COMET
$5 \cdot 10^{-4}$	30.3	56.1	0.8099
$2 \cdot 10^{-4}$	30.3	56.0	0.8069
$1 \cdot 10^{-4}$	30.2	55.9	0.8085
$5 \cdot 10^{-5}$	29.5*	55.3*	0.8047

Table 11: Learning rate search for HuBERT encoder, with MuST-C v2 dev set (en-de). ∗ indicates significance w.r.t. baseline (1st row).

Training Data	BLEU	chrF2	COMET
MuST-C v2	30.7	56.4	0.8127
MuST-C v3	30.5	56.6	0.8118

Table 12: Performance of the systems trained with different versions of MuST-C, evaluated with MuST-C v2 dev set (en-de). No significant improvements found.

System	ASR FT	BLEU	chrF2	COMET
Wav2Vec 2.0 Large (LV-60) + Self Training	✓	30.2	56.1	0.8087
Wav2Vec 2.0 Large (LV-60)	✓	30.1	55.9	0.8098
Wav2Vec 2.0 Large (LV-60)	✗	30.3	55.9	–
Wav2Vec 2.0 Large (LV-60 + CV + SWBD + FSH)	✓	29.7*	55.7*	0.8083
Wav2Vec 2.0 Large (LV-60 + CV + SWBD + FSH)	✗	30.0	55.9	–
Wav2Vec 2.0 Large conformer - rope (LV-60) †	✓	29.8	55.4*	–
XLSR-53	✗	28.9*	55.0*	–
HuBERT Large	✓	30.3	56.1	0.8099
HuBERT Large	✗	30.3	56.2	0.8110
SpeechLM-P Large ‡	✗	23.6*	50.2*	–

Table 9: Speech encoders exploration with MuST-C v2 dev set (en-de). ∗ indicates significance w.r.t. baseline (1st row). † uses *LNA-Adapters* (Tsiamas et al., 2022b). ‡ indicates a possible bug in our implementation.

Encoder Reg.	Decoder Reg.	WavAugm.	BLEU	chrF2	COMET
base	base	✓	30.2	56.1	0.8087
base	original	✓	30.5	56.4*	0.8149*
base	original	✗	30.7	56.4*	0.8127*
base	reduced	✓	30.1	55.9	0.8078
original	base	✓	29.8	55.8	0.8100
reduced	base	✓	30.1	55.9	0.8108
original	original	✓	30.4	56.2	0.8138*
reduced	reduced	✓	30.1	56.0	0.8122*

Table 10: Variations of the regularization and data augmentation strategies, with MuST-C v2 dev set (en-de). ∗ indicates significance w.r.t. baseline (1st row).

The Xiaomi AI Lab's Speech Translation Systems for IWSLT 2023 Offline Task, Simultaneous Task and Speech-to-Speech Task

Wuwei Huang[1*†] **Mengge Liu**[2*‡] **Xiang Li**[1] **Yanzhi Tian**[2‡] **Fengyu Yang**[1]
Wen Zhang[1] **Yuhang Guo**[2] **Jinsong Su**[3] **Jian Luan**[1] **Bin Wang**[1]
[1]Xiaomi AI Lab, Beijing, China
[2]Beijing Institute of Technology, Beijing, China
[3]Xiamen University, Xiamen, Fujian, China.
{huangwuwei,lixiang21,yangfengyu1,zhangwen17,luanjian,wangbin11}@xiaomi.com
{liumengge,tianyanzhi,guoyuhang}@bit.edu.cn jssu@xmu.edu.cn

Abstract

This system description paper introduces the systems submitted by Xiaomi AI Lab to the three tracks of the IWSLT 2023 Evaluation Campaign, namely the offline speech translation (Offline-ST) track, the offline speech-to-speech translation (Offline-S2ST) track, and the simultaneous speech translation (Simul-ST) track. All our submissions for these three tracks only involve the English-Chinese language direction. Our English-Chinese speech translation systems are constructed using large-scale pre-trained models as the foundation. Specifically, we fine-tune these models' corresponding components for various downstream speech translation tasks. Moreover, we implement several popular techniques, such as data filtering, data augmentation, speech segmentation, and model ensemble, to improve the system's overall performance. Extensive experiments show that our systems achieve a significant improvement over the strong baseline systems in terms of the automatic evaluation metric.

1 Introduction

We submit an end-to-end offline speech translation system, a cascaded offline speech-to-speech translation system, and an end-to-end simultaneous interpretation system to the Offline-ST track, Offline-S2ST track, and Simul-ST track, respectively. This paper provides a detailed description of the three systems we submit.

There are two commonly used solutions for speech translation models: the end-to-end approach and the cascaded approach. The cascaded system uses a pipeline where an automatic speech recognition (ASR) system is followed by a machine translation (MT) system. The ASR system first transcribes the speech utterances in the source language into text in the same language, and then the MT model translates the ASR output into text in the target language. In contrast, the end-to-end ST system directly translates speech utterances in the source language into text in the target language.

The scarcity of training data makes end-to-end systems still slightly inferior in translation quality to cascaded systems, which suffer from error propagation and information loss (Sperber and Paulik, 2020). Cascaded systems continue to dominate the systems submitted at IWSLT in previous years (Anastasopoulos et al., 2022, 2021; Ansari et al., 2020). However, with the rapid development of pre-training technology, a large number of large-scale pre-training models suitable for various modalities, such as speech (Baevski et al., 2020; Hsu et al., 2021; Tang et al., 2022) and text (Liu et al., 2020), have emerged. Therefore, end-to-end ST systems have gradually attracted attention from both the academic and industrial communities in recent years. In our submission, we have opted for an end-to-end approach to establish the ST system.

We briefly introduce the submitted systems:

Offline Speech Translation System. Our submitted end-to-end offline speech-to-text translation system is based on two pre-trained models: HuBERT (Hsu et al., 2021) and mBART (Liu et al., 2020). It has been proven that these two models have strong capabilities on ST and MT tasks, respectively. Our offline ST model consists of a *speech encoder*, a *text encoder*, and a *text decoder*, with all parameters initialized using the pre-trained HuBERT and mBART models.

Offline Speech-to-Speech Translation System. Speech-to-speech translation has great application value in various scenarios, such as international online lectures and multinational meetings. Lee et al. (2022) trained a sequence-to-sequence speech-to-unit translation (S2UT) model to directly predict the discrete representations of the target speech. Drawing on the method of Lee et al. (2022), we

*Equal contribution.

†Crossponding Author.

‡The work was done during the author's internship at Xiaomi.

Proceedings of the 20th International Conference on Spoken Language Translation (IWSLT 2023), pages 411–419
July 13-14, 2023 ©2023 Association for Computational Linguistics

implement a cascaded speech-to-speech translation system. Specifically, an end-to-end speech-to-text translation model is trained, followed by a text-to-speech (TTS) synthesis model.

To implement a cascaded speech-to-speech translation system, we first train an end-to-end speech-to-text translation model, followed by a text-to-speech (TTS) synthesis model that we train.

Simultaneous Speech Translation System. Apart from the above two offline systems, we also submit an end-to-end system for the English-Chinese language direction in the Simul-ST track. Simultaneous speech translation involves the challenge of striking a balance between translation quality and latency, as the system starts to translate the input audio even before the entire speech input is received. The Information-Transport-based Simultaneous Translation (ITST) (Zhang and Feng, 2022) architecture is adopted to build our end-to-end Simul-ST system, and we initialize its corresponding components using the HuBERT and mBART pre-trained models. When the AL value is less than 2000, our submitted end-to-end simultaneous ST system achieves a significant improvement of +3.2 BLEU scores over last year's best end-to-end simultaneous ST system. We also explore a streaming simultaneous interpretation approach by training an offline model and applying a wait-k decoding strategy, which even yields better performance.

The rest of this paper is organized as follows: Section 2 describes the data preparation, including data filtering, data augmentation, speech segmentation, etc. Section 3 elaborates on the models and strategies used in our systems. We present our experiment settings, results, and analyses in Section 4. Finally, Section 5 provides the conclusion.

2 Data Preparation

2.1 Statistics

Our English-Chinese (abbreviated as En⇒Zh) ST systems are developed under constrained conditions using two allowed ST corpora: MuST-C v2.0[1] and CoVoST[2]. The only text translation dataset available is OpenSubtitles2018[3]. To construct the English ASR corpus, we gather data from various sources, such as LibriSpeech[4], CommonVoice[5], TED LIUM[6], and Vox Populi[7]. In addition to this, we also utilize the audio-transcription pairs from English-German (En⇒De) ST data, including ST-TED, Europarl-ST, and MuST-C (indicated with a star in Table 1). Furthermore, AISHELL-3[8] and GigaS2S[9] datasets are used to train the TTS model. We filter out those samples in the MuST-C En⇒De training set whose source sentences are included in the MuST-C En⇒Zh training set. Table 1 presents the statistical results of the training samples for different tasks.

Corpora		Duration	#Spl.
ST	**MuST-C v2.0**	596h	359K
	CoVoST	1119h	870K
	GigaST	10000h	7.6M
MT	**OpenSubtitles**	-	11.2M
ASR	**LibriSpeech**	960h	273K
	Common Voice	2320h	1.62M
	TED LIUM (v3)	452h	268K
	Vox Populi	543h	181K
	ST-TED*	273h	171K
	Europal-ST*	~80h	30K
	MuST-C*	~100h	78K
TTS	**AISHELL-3**	85h	88K
	GigaS2S	10000h	7.6M
Unlabeled Audio	**Vox Populi**	24100h	-

Table 1: The statistical results of all available training corpora in the En⇒Zh translation direction for the offline speech translation track, the offline speech-to-speech translation track, and the simultaneous speech translation track. The tilde symbol (~) indicates a rough estimation. #Spl. indicates the number of samples.

2.2 Offline-ST and Simul-ST Corpus

For both the En⇒Zh offline speech translation and En⇒Zh simultaneous speech translation tracks, we use the same training corpus, the same data filtering and data augmentation methods.

2.2.1 Data Filtering

All text data involved in MT, ST, and TTS tasks are tokenized using `SentencePiece`[10]. For the MT data, we adopt heuristic rules to filter out noisy data

[1]https://ict.fbk.eu/must-c/

[2]https://github.com/facebookresearch/covost

[3]https://opus.nlpl.eu/OpenSubtitles2018.php

[4]http://www.openslr.org/12/

[5]https://commonvoice.mozilla.org/en/datasets

[6]https://lium.univ-lemans.fr/en/ted-lium3/

[7]https://github.com/facebookresearch/voxpopuli

[8]https://www.aishelltech.com/aishell_3

[9]https://github.com/SpeechTranslation/GigaS2S

[10]https://github.com/google/sentencepiece

in the training set similar to the rules used in (Guo et al., 2022), following these steps:

- A series of hand-crafted rules are adopted to filter out noisy sentences from the training set. In particular, we discard sentences that contain less than 50% linguistic words. For Chinese sentences, Chinese characters are considered linguistic words; for English sentences, words containing only alphabet characters are considered linguistic words;
- We utilize `fast_align`[11] open source tool to exclude sentence pairs with a score lower than −8. We also apply the language identification (LangID) tool[12] to filter out sentence pairs that are neither in Chinese nor English;
- Duplicate sentence pairs are discarded, and any pairs with a length ratio greater than 3.0 or sentences with a length exceeding 200 are also filtered out.

To filter out noise data in the ST training set, we apply the following steps:

- Pairs that have an audio duration exceeding 60 seconds or a text length exceeding 200 tokens are excluded;
- We calculate the ratio of the number of speech frames to tokens in each sample, and remove samples whose ratio exceeds three times the average ratio.

2.2.2 Data Augmentation

To effectively train an end-to-end speech translation model, it is impractical to rely solely on hand-annotated training data, due to the scarcity of hand-annotated data. To mitigate this issue, we utilize a well-trained MT model to translate the transcriptions from ASR data and synthesize a large amount of pseudo-data, which has been widely used in the previous years' competitions (Ding and Tao, 2021; Zhang and Ao, 2022; Zhang et al., 2022b; Li et al., 2022; Zhu et al., 2022).

We initially gather all available English-Chinese bilingual parallel sentence pairs from ST and MT tasks, as listed in Table 1. We then filter the data using the method mentioned in Section 2.2.1, generating 9M sentence pairs. These 9M sentence pairs are used to fine-tune the pre-trained one-to-many mBART50 model for 30 epochs. We further fine-tune mBART50 for another 30 epochs using

Models	BLEU
mBART50 (one-to-many)	25.81
+ domain fine-tuning on 9M corpus	28.41
+ domain fine-tuning on MuST-C	29.50

Table 2: The BLEU scores of MT models obtained by fine-tuning one-to-many mBART50 model using various bilingual datasets on the tst-COMMON test set.

MuST-C datasets to improve the domain adaptability of the model. The results are shown in Table 2.

In the Librispeech and TED-LIUM datasets, English sentences do not have punctuation or case information. We fine-tune the mBART50 model to add punctuation and restore case information to English sentences. Furthermore, samples already included in the CoVoST corpus are removed from the CommonVoice dataset. The transcriptions of the ASR data are then translated using the best fine-tuned mBART50 model and filtered using the same rules as the ST data in Section 2.2.1, resulting in a total of 1.6 million synthesized speech-to-text translation pairs.

Finally, for constrained data, we combine the hand-annotated ST corpus with the synthesized ST corpus to produce the final training corpus for the Offline-ST and Simul-ST models, yielding a total of 2.9 million speech-to-text translation pairs. In the case of unconstrained training on the offline track, we augment our training corpus with the GigaST corpus, resulting in 9 million speech-to-text translation pairs.

2.3 Cascaded S2ST Corpus

In the En⇒Zh speech-to-speech translation track, we leverage all available constrained data from the offline speech translation track as well as the GigaST corpus[13] to train our offline speech translation model. This model is then followed by a TTS model that is trained on the AISHELL-3 and GigaS2S datasets.

2.4 Speech Segmentation

Since the speech in the evaluation set is not pre-segmented, we apply SHAS (Tsiamas et al., 2022) to segment the full speech into shorter segments. However, we observe two issues. Firstly, some segments have incomplete final words, which could negatively impact the performance of the ST model. To alleviate this problem, we add a few extra frames

[11] `https://github.com/clab/fast_align`

[12] `https://github.com/saffsd/langid.py`

[13] `https://st-benchmark.github.io/resources/GigaST.html`

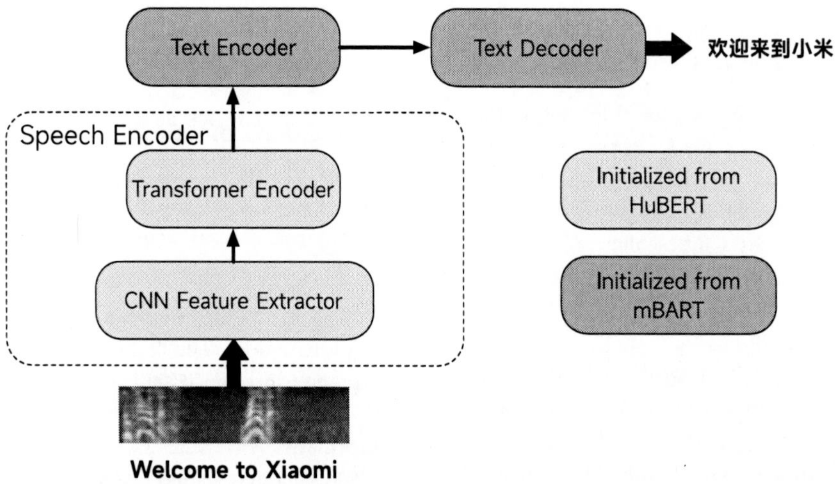

Figure 1: The architecture of our end-to-end offline speech translation model consists of three components: *speech encoder*, *text encoder*, and *text decoder*. The speech encoder is composed of a *CNN feature extractor* and a 24-layer *Transformer encoder* with a CNN positional encoder. Both the text encoder and the text decoder are 12-layer standard Transformer structures. Note that the speech encoder is initialized with the pre-trained HuBERT model, and both the text encoder and text decoder are initialized with the pre-trained mBART model.

at the end of each segment to ensure that the final word is fully pronounced. Secondly, the speaking rate varies among different speakers or types of speeches, resulting in different amounts of words being spoken within a given time period. Excessive words in a speech segment may result in missing translations. We choose different hyperparameters for different speakers or different types of speeches.

3 Methods

We build our Offline-ST system in an end-to-end manner (End-to-End Offline-ST) based on the HuBERT and mBART pre-trained models. Our simultaneous speech translation system (End-to-End Simul-ST) utilizes the same model architecture as the Offline-ST system and adopts wait-k and ITST strategies. The cascaded S2ST system involves an end-to-end speech-to-text translation model followed by a TTS model.

3.1 End-to-End Offline-ST System

The speech translation corpus typically consists of triples (x, z, y) that contain speech, transcription, and translation data, where x = $(x_1, \cdots, x_{|x|})$ represents a sequence of acoustic features, while z = $(z_1, \cdots, z_{|z|})$ and y = $(y_1, \cdots, y_{|y|})$ denote the corresponding transcription in the source language and translation in the target language, respectively.

Our end-to-end Offline-ST system is based on an encoder-decoder architecture from the pre-trained HuBERT and mBART models. Figure 1 illustrates the architecture of our model, which consists of a *speech encoder*, a *text encoder*, and a *text decoder*. More specifically, the speech encoder is composed of a feature extractor based on convolutional neural networks (CNN), named *CNN feature extractor* and a 24-layer *Transformer encoder*. The CNN feature extractor is used to extract speech features from waveform, with 7 layers each containing 512 channels and kernel widths of $[10, 3, 3, 3, 3, 2, 2]$ and strides of $[5, 2, 2, 2, 2, 2, 2]$. The Transformer encoder is derived from the standard Transformer (Vaswani et al., 2017) encoder, except for using CNN as the position encoder. The text encoder is a 12-layer standard Transformer encoder, and the text decoder is a 12-layer standard Transformer decoder. The training objective of our speech translation model can be formulated as:

$$\mathcal{L}(\mathbf{x}, \mathbf{y}; \boldsymbol{\theta}_e, \boldsymbol{\theta}_d) = \sum_{t=1}^{|\mathbf{y}|} -\log p\left(\mathbf{y}_t | \mathbf{y}_{<t}, \mathbf{x}; \boldsymbol{\theta}_e, \boldsymbol{\theta}_d\right) \quad (1)$$

where $\boldsymbol{\theta}_e$ and $\boldsymbol{\theta}_d$ represent the parameters of the encoder and the decoder, respectively.

3.2 Cascaded S2ST System

In the cascaded S2ST system, we reuse the offline speech translation model discussed in Section 3.1 as the ST model. For the TTS model, we first train a base TTS model and vocoder using the AISHELL-3 dataset with the Tacotron2 (Shen et al., 2018) open source framework. The final TTS model is obtained by fine-tuning the base model on the GigaS2S dataset.

3.3 End-to-End Simul-ST System

In order to take full advantage of the powerful capabilities of large pre-trained models, we develop an end-to-end Simul-ST system based on the HuBERT and mBART models. Furthermore, we employ two strategies, namely wait-k and ITST.

3.3.1 Wait-k

Ma et al. (2020b) adapts methods originally proposed for simultaneous machine translation to develop an end-to-end Simul-ST system. To achieve this, they employ the wait-k (Ma et al., 2019) strategy and a fixed pre-decision module. Under this approach, the system first reads k speech segments, each of which contains a fixed number (q, a hyper-parameter in the pre-decision module) of speech frames. When k speech segments have been read, the decoder generates one token in the target language. Similarly, we also apply the wait-k strategy in the decoding process of our end-to-end offline-ST system, as it strikes a good balance between translation quality and latency without requiring any streaming strategy during training (Papi et al., 2022; Polák et al., 2022). During inference, once a speech segment is accepted, the decoder takes the following action:

$$\textbf{Action} = \begin{cases} \text{continue to read} & |\mathbf{x}| - |\mathbf{y}| < k \\ \text{output } \mathbf{y}_t & |\mathbf{x}| - |\mathbf{y}| \geq k \end{cases} \quad (2)$$

where $\mathbf{y}_t$ denotes the t-th token of the target language, while $|\mathbf{x}|$ and $|\mathbf{y}|$ refer to the number of source speech segments and target tokens, respectively.

3.3.2 ITST

The Information-Transport-based Simultaneous Translation (ITST) architecture has achieved state-of-the-art performance in end-to-end simultaneous speech translation. To implement this strategy, we initialize the corresponding parameters by using the pre-trained HuBERT and mBART models, and randomly initialize additional parameters for computing the information transport matrix. We then optimize the quality and latency objectives using the ITST criterion, varying the δ value to control the latency in streaming inference.

Our end-to-end speech translation system is built based on the ITST architecture, equipped with a wait-k streaming decoding strategy, and finally evaluated using the SimulEval (Ma et al., 2020a) toolkit. To ensure accurate translations, we enforce a constraint that the model should not produce the final translation until it has fully processed the speech in the source language.

3.4 Self-Training

Self-training is a simple semi-supervised learning method that involves using unlabeled data to augment labeled data (Pino et al., 2020; Sun et al., 2021; Wang et al., 2021; Popuri et al., 2022). To leverage the large-scale unlabeled audio introduced in Section 2.1, we employ self-training in our approach. In particular, we first train the end-to-end speech translation model on both manually annotated data and augmentation data, as described in Section 2. Next, we use the model to generate Chinese translation text, which we merge with the original training data and unlabeled audio. We then continue training the end-to-end speech translation model on this merged dataset.

3.5 Contrastive Learning

The objective of contrastive learning (Chen et al., 2020; Gao et al., 2021; Ye et al., 2022; Zhang et al., 2023) is to learn an encoder that produces similar representations for similar instances, while producing dissimilar representations for dissimilar instances, as measured by their cosine similarity. In our approach, we assume that the same utterance, regardless of whether it is in speech or text modality, will have similar hidden representations. Therefore, we aim to minimize the cosine distance between the hidden representations of the two modalities for the same utterance, while increasing the cosine distance between the hidden representations of different utterances. Specifically, we minimize the cosine distance between the speech encoder output and the corresponding word embedding for the same utterance, while maximizing the distance between the representations of different utterances. The training objective is as follows:

$$\mathcal{L}_{CTR} = \sum_{t=1}^{N} \text{-}\log p \frac{\exp(sim(u, v)/T)}{\sum^{X} \exp(sim(u, v(x_j))/T)} \quad (3)$$

where u is the average state of the speech encoder output along the sequence length, v is the average word embedding, and T is the temperature hyper-parameter. More specifically, $\mathcal{L}_{CTR}$ quantifies the negative logarithm of the probability that the similarity between u and v is greater than the similarity between u and other candidate word embeddings $v(x_j)$. The probabilities are normalized using a softmax function over all candidate embeddings. In addition to contrastive learning, we also conduct multitask learning using labeled ASR and MT training data, which results in the final optimization objective:

$$\mathcal{L} = \mathcal{L}_{ST} + \mathcal{L}_{ASR} + \mathcal{L}_{MT} + \mathcal{L}_{CTR} \quad (4)$$

where $\mathcal{L}_{ST}$, $\mathcal{L}_{ASR}$, $\mathcal{L}_{MT}$, and $\mathcal{L}_{CTR}$ denote the losses for speech-to-text translation, ASR, MT, and contrastive learning, respectively.

4 Experiments

4.1 Experiment Settings

The `fairseq` toolkit[14] is used to train our speech-to-text models. During training, the models take the original waveform sampled at 16kHz as the input. The Adam optimizer (Kingma and Ba, 2015) with a fixed learning rate of 5e-5 is used to train the models. Each model is trained for 200k steps, and we save the model every 2.5k steps using an early stopping mechanism. In detail, if the BLEU score on the development set does not improve for 10 consecutive checkpoints, the training will be terminated. During the fine-tuning stage, we set the maximum number of updates to 50k and the learning rate to 2e-5. Our TTS model is implemented using the Tacotron2 toolkit[15].

4.2 Evaluation

As the official automatic evaluation criterion, the BLEU score (Papineni et al., 2002) is used to evaluate the translation quality of all our systems. For the Simul-ST system, we employ the average lag (AL) (Ma et al., 2019, 2020b) metric to measure the translation latency, which is a standard metric for simultaneous speech translation. The SimulEval open-source toolkit[16] is utilized to calculate both the BLEU and AL metrics for the Simul-ST system. All BLEU scores are calculated with the SacreBLEU[17] (Post, 2018) toolkit at the character level.

[14] https://github.com/pytorch/fairseq

[15] https://github.com/NVIDIA/tacotron2

[16] https://github.com/facebookresearch/SimulEval

[17] https://github.com/mjpost/sacrebleu

	Models	BLEU
0	wav2vec2.0 (small)	23.84
1	HuBERT + mBART50 (one-to-many)	27.74
2	+ fine-tuning on MuST-C	27.90
3	+ Self-Training	27.69
4	+ Contrastive Learning	28.11
5	+ fine-tuning on MuST-C	27.94
6	data2vec + mBART50 (one-to-many)	27.66
7	+ fine-tuning on MuST-C	27.59
8	Ensemble (2, 5)	27.79
9	Ensemble (2, 7)	27.61
10	Ensemble (2, 5, 7)	27.94

Table 3: The BLEU scores of ST models on the tst-COMMON test set.

4.3 Main Results

Offline En⇒Zh Speech Translation

We evaluate our offline-ST models on the tst-COMMON test set by reporting the BLEU score in accordance with the official evaluation criteria. To establish a baseline for comparison, we use the widely-used standard wav2vec2.0 model for speech translation tasks. Table 3 shows the comparison results among all models. Our end-to-end models exhibit a significant improvement of approximately 4 BLEU points over the wav2vec2.0 baseline, which demonstrates the effectiveness of our methods. Additionally, we also conduct experiments using data2vec (Baevski et al., 2022) pre-trained model and obtain comparable results on the tst-COMMON test set.

By analyzing our experimental results, we observe that domain fine-tuning does not significantly improve the performance of the model. Nevertheless, we believe domain fine-tuning will be beneficial for final human evaluation on the TED[18] test set. Our final submission is an ensemble of the models listed in rows 2, 5, and 7 of Table 3.

It is worth mentioning that we encounter some challenges when training our model. When the HuBERT model is used to initialize our model, instabilities are observed during training, with sudden gradient explosions leading to training collapse. After careful analysis, we determine that the problem is that the gradients of the CNN layers are relatively large during the entire training process. We address this issue by scaling down the gradients of the CNN layers.

[18] https://www.ted.com/

	Models	BLEU
1	Offline-ST	30.10
2	Offline-ST + GigaST	31.56
3	Ensemble $(1,2)$	31.81

Table 4: BLEU scores of our ST models on the development set of the S2ST track in IWSLT 2023. Offline-ST is trained on all manually annotated data and the augmented data described in Section 2.2.2. In addition to the data used by the offline-ST model, the Offline-ST + GigaST model incorporates additional GigaST data.

	Models	ASR-BLEU
1	Offline-ST	28.88
2	Offline-ST + GigaST	30.10
3	Ensemble $(1,2)$	30.18

Table 5: ASR-BLEU scores of our ST models on the development set of the S2ST track in IWSLT 2023. The models are identical to those presented in Table 4.

Offline En⇒Zh Speech-to-Speech Translation

We evaluate the performance of our end-to-end speech-to-text translation system and cascaded speech-to-speech system on the development set of the S2ST track in IWSLT 2023, comprising $5,000$ utterances. The results of the speech-to-text translation models and speech-to-speech translation models are demonstrated in Table 4 and 5, respectively. For the speech-to-text translation model, we adopt the ensemble of models corresponding to rows 1 and 2 in Table 4. To build the speech-to-speech translation system, we then leverage our trained Chinese TTS model to synthesize Chinese speech and generate the corresponding Chinese transcript with the Conformer model [19] trained on the WenetSpeech dataset (Zhang et al., 2022a). Finally, the generated Chinese transcript and reference are used to calculate the ASR-BLEU score.

Simultaneous En⇒Zh Speech Translation

We use the SimulEval toolkit to evaluate the quality and latency of our simultaneous speech translation model on the tst-COMMON set. In order to achieve a better balance between quality and latency, when the prediction probability is lower than 20%, the READ action is performed; when the delay exceeds 6000ms, the model performs a WRITE action to predict the next target token.

	Strategies	Models	BLEU	AL
1	Wait-k	HuBERT+mBART	25.99	1980
2	Wait-k	+ ST & CL	26.59	1966
3	ITST	HuBERT+mBART	26.25	1906

Table 6: The evaluation results of Simul-ST models on tst-COMMON. ST and CL denote self-training and contrastive learning for the Offline-ST model.

We evaluate the wait-k strategy using models 1 and 4 in Table 3, and train the ITST model with the same configuration as model 1 in Table 3. The results of the Simul-ST models are presented in Table 6. Although ITST shows better performance than wait-k in the same setting, the wait-k strategy combined with self-training and contrastive learning can achieve better results. Therefore, we finally submit the system corresponding to the second row in Table 6.

5 Conclusion

In this paper, we present our submissions for the IWSLT 2023 shared tasks. We participate in three tracks, namely the offline speech translation track, the offline speech-to-speech translation track, and the simultaneous speech translation track. All of our submissions use large-scale pre-trained models, and we further improve these models using various effective techniques, such as data augmentation, contrastive learning, and model ensembles. Extensive experiments validate the effectiveness of our proposed method and demonstrate that our submitted systems are comparable to state-of-the-art baseline systems in terms of performance.

Acknowledgements

Mengge Liu, Yanzhi Tian and Yuhang Guo have been supported in part by the National Key R&D Program of China (No. 2020AAA0106600). Jinsong Su has been supported by Youth Innovation Fund of Xiamen (No. 3502Z20206059).

[19] https://wenet-1256283475.cos.ap-shanghai.myqcloud.com/models/wenetspeech/wenetspeech_u2pp_conformer_exp.tar.gz

References

Antonios Anastasopoulos, Loïc Barrault, Luisa Bentivogli, Marcely Zanon Boito, Ondřej Bojar, Roldano Cattoni, Anna Currey, Georgiana Dinu, Kevin Duh, Maha Elbayad, Clara Emmanuel, Yannick Estève, Marcello Federico, Christian Federmann, Souhir Gahbiche, Hongyu Gong, Roman Grundkiewicz, Barry Haddow, Benjamin Hsu, Dávid Javorský, Věra Kloudová, Surafel Lakew, Xutai Ma, Prashant Mathur, Paul McNamee, Kenton Murray, Maria Nădejde, Satoshi Nakamura, Matteo Negri, Jan Niehues, Xing Niu, John Ortega, Juan Pino, Elizabeth Salesky, Jiatong Shi, Matthias Sperber, Sebastian Stüker, Katsuhito Sudoh, Marco Turchi, Yogesh Virkar, Alexander Waibel, Changhan Wang, and Shinji Watanabe. 2022. Findings of the IWSLT 2022 evaluation campaign. In *Proc. of IWSLT*.

Antonios Anastasopoulos, Ondřej Bojar, Jacob Bremerman, Roldano Cattoni, Maha Elbayad, Marcello Federico, Xutai Ma, Satoshi Nakamura, Matteo Negri, Jan Niehues, Juan Pino, Elizabeth Salesky, Sebastian Stüker, Katsuhito Sudoh, Marco Turchi, Alexander Waibel, Changhan Wang, and Matthew Wiesner. 2021. FINDINGS OF THE IWSLT 2021 EVALUATION CAMPAIGN. In *Proc. of IWSLT*.

Ebrahim Ansari, Amittai Axelrod, Nguyen Bach, Ondřej Bojar, Roldano Cattoni, Fahim Dalvi, Nadir Durrani, Marcello Federico, Christian Federmann, Jiatao Gu, Fei Huang, Kevin Knight, Xutai Ma, Ajay Nagesh, Matteo Negri, Jan Niehues, Juan Pino, Elizabeth Salesky, Xing Shi, Sebastian Stüker, Marco Turchi, Alexander Waibel, and Changhan Wang. 2020. FINDINGS OF THE IWSLT 2020 EVALUATION CAMPAIGN. In *Proc. of IWSLT*.

Alexei Baevski, Wei-Ning Hsu, Qiantong Xu, Arun Babu, Jiatao Gu, and Michael Auli. 2022. data2vec: A general framework for self-supervised learning in speech, vision and language. In *Proc. of ICML*.

Alexei Baevski, Henry Zhou, Abdelrahman Mohamed, and Michael Auli. 2020. wav2vec 2.0: A framework for self-supervised learning of speech representations. In *Proc. of NIPS*.

Ting Chen, Simon Kornblith, Mohammad Norouzi, and Geoffrey Hinton. 2020. A simple framework for contrastive learning of visual representations. In *Proc. of ICML*.

Liang Ding and Dacheng Tao. 2021. The USYD-JD speech translation system for IWSLT2021. In *Proc. of IWSLT*.

Tianyu Gao, Xingcheng Yao, and Danqi Chen. 2021. SimCSE: Simple contrastive learning of sentence embeddings. In *Proc. of EMNLP*.

Bao Guo, Mengge Liu, Wen Zhang, Hexuan Chen, Chang Mu, Xiang Li, Jianwei Cui, Bin Wang, and Yuhang Guo. 2022. The Xiaomi text-to-text simultaneous speech translation system for IWSLT 2022. In *Proc. of IWSLT*.

Wei-Ning Hsu, Benjamin Bolte, Yao-Hung Hubert Tsai, Kushal Lakhotia, Ruslan Salakhutdinov, and Abdelrahman Mohamed. 2021. HuBERT: Self-supervised speech representation learning by masked prediction of hidden units. In *Proc. of TALSP*.

Diederik P. Kingma and Jimmy Ba. 2015. Adam: A method for stochastic optimization. In *Proc. of ICLR*.

Ann Lee, Peng-Jen Chen, Changhan Wang, Jiatao Gu, Sravya Popuri, Xutai Ma, Adam Polyak, Yossi Adi, Qing He, Yun Tang, Juan Pino, and Wei-Ning Hsu. 2022. Direct speech-to-speech translation with discrete units. In *Proc. of ACL*.

Yinglu Li, Minghan Wang, Jiaxin Guo, Xiaosong Qiao, Yuxia Wang, Daimeng Wei, Chang Su, Yimeng Chen, Min Zhang, Shimin Tao, Hao Yang, and Ying Qin. 2022. The HW-TSC's offline speech translation system for IWSLT 2022 evaluation. In *Proc. of IWSLT*.

Yinhan Liu, Jiatao Gu, Naman Goyal, Xian Li, Sergey Edunov, Marjan Ghazvininejad, Mike Lewis, and Luke Zettlemoyer. 2020. Multilingual denoising pretraining for neural machine translation. In *Proc. of TACL*.

Mingbo Ma, Liang Huang, Hao Xiong, Renjie Zheng, Kaibo Liu, Baigong Zheng, Chuanqiang Zhang, Zhongjun He, Hairong Liu, Xing Li, Hua Wu, and Haifeng Wang. 2019. STACL: Simultaneous translation with implicit anticipation and controllable latency using prefix-to-prefix framework. In *Proc. of ACL*.

Xutai Ma, Mohammad Javad Dousti, Changhan Wang, Jiatao Gu, and Juan Pino. 2020a. SIMULEVAL: An evaluation toolkit for simultaneous translation. In *Proc. of EMNLP*.

Xutai Ma, Juan Pino, and Philipp Koehn. 2020b. SimulMT to SimulST: Adapting simultaneous text translation to end-to-end simultaneous speech translation. In *Proc. of AACL/IJCN*.

Sara Papi, Marco Gaido, Matteo Negri, and Marco Turchi. 2022. Does simultaneous speech translation need simultaneous models? In *Findings of the Association for Computational Linguistics: EMNLP 2022, Abu Dhabi, United Arab Emirates, December 7-11, 2022*, pages 141–153. Association for Computational Linguistics.

Kishore Papineni, Salim Roukos, Todd Ward, and Wei-Jing Zhu. 2002. Bleu: a method for automatic evaluation of machine translation. In *Proc. of ACL*.

Juan Pino, Qiantong Xu, Xutai Ma, Mohammad Javad Dousti, and Yun Tang. 2020. Self-training for end-to-end speech translation. In *Proc. of Interspeech*.

Peter Polák, Ngoc-Quan Pham, Tuan-Nam Nguyen, Danni Liu, Carlos Mullov, Jan Niehues, Ondrej Bojar, and Alexander Waibel. 2022. CUNI-KIT system for simultaneous speech translation task at IWSLT 2022.

In *Proceedings of the 19th International Conference on Spoken Language Translation, IWSLT@ACL 2022, Dublin, Ireland (in-person and online), May 26-27, 2022*, pages 277–285. Association for Computational Linguistics.

Sravya Popuri, Peng-Jen Chen, Changhan Wang, Juan Pino, Yossi Adi, Jiatao Gu, Wei-Ning Hsu, and Ann Lee. 2022. Enhanced direct speech-to-speech translation using self-supervised pre-training and data augmentation. In *Proc. of Interspeech*.

Matt Post. 2018. A call for clarity in reporting BLEU scores. In *Proc. of WMT*.

Jonathan Shen, Ruoming Pang, Ron J. Weiss, Mike Schuster, Navdeep Jaitly, Zongheng Yang, Zhifeng Chen, Yu Zhang, Yuxuan Wang, R. J. Skerry-Ryan, Rif A. Saurous, Yannis Agiomyrgiannakis, and Yonghui Wu. 2018. Natural TTS synthesis by conditioning wavenet on mel spectrogram predictions. In *Proc. of ICASSP*.

Matthias Sperber and Matthias Paulik. 2020. Speech translation and the end-to-end promise: Taking stock of where we are. In *Proc. of ACL*.

Haipeng Sun, Rui Wang, Kehai Chen, Masao Utiyama, Eiichiro Sumita, and Tiejun Zhao. 2021. Self-training for unsupervised neural machine translation in unbalanced training data scenarios. In *Proc. of NAACL*.

Yun Tang, Hongyu Gong, Ning Dong, Changhan Wang, Wei-Ning Hsu, Jiatao Gu, Alexei Baevski, Xian Li, Abdelrahman Mohamed, Michael Auli, and Juan Pino. 2022. Unified speech-text pre-training for speech translation and recognition. In *Proc. of ACL*.

Ioannis Tsiamas, Gerard I. Gállego, José A. R. Fonollosa, and Marta R. Costa-jussà. 2022. SHAS: approaching optimal segmentation for end-to-end speech translation. In *Proc. of Interspeech*.

Ashish Vaswani, Noam Shazeer, Niki Parmar, Jakob Uszkoreit, Llion Jones, Aidan N Gomez, Ł ukasz Kaiser, and Illia Polosukhin. 2017. Attention is all you need. In *Proc. of NIPS*.

Changhan Wang, Anne Wu, Juan Pino, Alexei Baevski, Michael Auli, and Alexis Conneau. 2021. Large-scale self- and semi-supervised learning for speech translation. In *Proc. of Interspeech*.

Rong Ye, Mingxuan Wang, and Lei Li. 2022. Cross-modal contrastive learning for speech translation. In *Proc. of NAACL*.

Binbin Zhang, Hang Lv, Pengcheng Guo, Qijie Shao, Chao Yang, Lei Xie, Xin Xu, Hui Bu, Xiaoyu Chen, Chenchen Zeng, Di Wu, and Zhendong Peng. 2022a. Wenetspeech: A 10000+ hours multi-domain mandarin corpus for speech recognition. In *Proc. of ICASSP*.

Hao Zhang, Nianwen Si, Yaqi Chen, Wenlin Zhang, Xukui Yang, Dan Qu, and Wei-Qiang Zhang. 2023. Improving speech translation by cross-modal multi-grained contrastive learning. *IEEE/ACM Transactions on Audio, Speech, and Language Processing*.

Shaolei Zhang and Yang Feng. 2022. Information-transport-based policy for simultaneous translation. In *Proc. of EMNLP*.

Weitai Zhang, Zhongyi Ye, Haitao Tang, Xiaoxi Li, Xinyuan Zhou, Jing Yang, Jianwei Cui, Pan Deng, Mohan Shi, Yifan Song, Dan Liu, Junhua Liu, and Lirong Dai. 2022b. The USTC-NELSLIP offline speech translation systems for IWSLT 2022. In *Proc. of IWSLT*.

Ziqiang Zhang and Junyi Ao. 2022. The YiTrans speech translation system for IWSLT 2022 offline shared task. In *Proc. of IWSLT*.

Qinpei Zhu, Renshou Wu, Guangfeng Liu, Xinyu Zhu, Xingyu Chen, Yang Zhou, Qingliang Miao, Rui Wang, and Kai Yu. 2022. The AISP-SJTU simultaneous translation system for IWSLT 2022. In *Proc. of IWSLT*.

Improving Formality-Sensitive Machine Translation using Data-Centric Approaches and Prompt Engineering

Seungjun Lee[1], Hyeonseok Moon[1], Chanjun Park[1,2], Heuiseok Lim[1*]
[1]Korea University, South Korea
[2]Upstage, South Korea
{dzzy6505, glee889, bcj1210, limhseok}@korea.ac.kr
chanjun.park@upstage.ai

Abstract

In this paper, we present the KU x Upstage team's submission for the Special Task on Formality Control on Spoken Language Translation, which involves translating English into four languages with diverse grammatical formality markers. Our methodology comprises two primary components: 1) a language-specific data-driven approach, and 2) the generation of synthetic data through the employment of large-scale language models and empirically-grounded prompt engineering. By adapting methodologies and models to accommodate the unique linguistic properties of each language, we observe a notable enhancement in performance relative to the baseline, substantiating the heightened efficacy of data-driven approaches. Moreover, our devised prompt engineering strategy yields superior synthetic translation instances.

1 Introduction

Neural machine translation (NMT) models have achieved remarkable progress in recent years, as evidenced by their high BLEU scores (Britz et al., 2017; Stahlberg, 2020). Nonetheless, these models generally rely on generic parallel corpora and assume a single target translation for a given source sentence, often overlooking the significance of style and pragmatic aspects in translation, such as formality or politeness (Li et al., 2022). To address this issue, formality-sensitive machine translation (FSMT) has emerged as a research area, aiming to control grammatical formality in translated text across languages (Niu et al., 2017).

The Special Task on Formality Control on Spoken Language Translation introduces a new benchmark with high-quality training datasets for diverse languages, encompassing both supervised and zero-shot language pairs. Despite these new datasets (Nădejde et al., 2022), controlling formality in MT remains a challenging problem due to the absence of gold translations with alternate formality levels and the extensive variation in grammatical formality markers across languages.

Source: **It did**, many people **liked** his show so yeah, **do** **you** **like** Chris Pratt?
Korean Formal: **그랬어요**, 많은 사람들이 그의 쇼를 **좋아했죠**. 그래서 **당신** 크리스 프랫 **좋아해요**?
Korean Informal: **그랬어**, 많은 사람들이 그의 쇼를 **좋아했지**. 그래서 **너** 크리스 프랫 **좋아해**?

Table 1: Contrastive translations in formal and informal styles into Korean are presented. Grammatical formality markers, which are bolded, can be aligned through colors.

In the 2023 shared task, an English source segment is paired with two references that are minimally contrastive in grammatical formality, representing both formal and informal levels as shown in Table 1. Training and test samples are provided in the domains of "telephony data" and "topical chat" (Gopalakrishnan et al., 2019) for two supervised language pairs, English-Korean (EN-KO) and English-Vietnamese (EN-VI), and two zero-shot language pairs, English-Portuguese (EN-PT) and English-Russian (EN-RU). Grammatical formality markers differ across these languages. Personal pronouns and verb agreement signal formality in many Indo-European languages (e.g., PT, RU), while in Korean, formality control is notably challenging due to the widespread use of morphological markers to convey polite, respectful, and humble speech, making it an intriguing test case for FSMT.

In this paper, we present our approach to FSMT, focusing on the supervised setting for the English-Korean (EN-KO) and English-Vietnamese (EN-VI) language pairs and evaluating our methods on the zero-shot English-Portuguese (EN-PT) and English-Russian (EN-RU) pairs. Our method consists of two main strategies: 1) a language-specific data-driven approach, and 2) synthetic data gener-

Proceedings of the 20th International Conference on Spoken Language Translation (IWSLT 2023), pages 420–432
July 13-14, 2023

ation using large-scale language models and empirical prompt engineering. We apply techniques and models tailored to the linguistic features of each language. For Korean, we utilize a morpheme-centric subword tokenization method, while for Vietnamese, we employ a pre-trained EnViT5 model with high-quality Vietnamese parallel corpora. Additionally, we generate synthetic translation datasets for Portuguese and Russian using prompt engineering and refine these datasets using formality classifiers for fine-tuning our models. Furthermore, we founded significant performance improvements in EN-KO and EN-VI and conducted an ablation study to utilize high-quality synthetic examples.

2 Proposed Method

2.1 Task Definition

In this submission, we focus on the supervised and zero-shot settings on unconstrained formality control machine translation task. Formally, provided with a source segment $\boldsymbol{X} = \{x_1, x_2, \ldots, x_m\}$ and a formality level $l \in \{\text{formal, informal}\}$, the objective is to identify a model defined by parameters Θ that produces the most probable translation $\boldsymbol{Y} = \{y_1, y_2, \ldots, y_n\}$ in accordance with the formality level:

$$\boldsymbol{Y} = \underset{Y_l}{\arg\max} P(\boldsymbol{X}, l; \boldsymbol{\Theta})$$

In simpler terms, the goal is to find the optimal model parameters Θ that produce the most likely translation $\boldsymbol{Y}$, given the source segment $\boldsymbol{X}$ and the desired formality level l (either formal or informal). This is achieved by maximizing the probability $P(\boldsymbol{X}, l; \boldsymbol{\Theta})$ of obtaining the translation $\boldsymbol{Y}$ at the specified formality level.

2.2 Language Specialized Data-Centric Approach

In this work, we employ a language specialized data-centric approach by integrating transfer learning techniques from Zoph et al. (2016) and language-specific subword methods, such as Unigram (Kudo, 2018) or byte-pair encoding (BPE) (Sennrich et al., 2015b). This combination effectively captures the unique morphological and syntactic structures of the target language, resulting in substantial improvements in translation performance, especially for low-resource languages (Zoph et al., 2016; Bojanowski et al., 2017; Park et al., 2020, 2021). Finally, we fine-tuned the pre-trained model (PLM) on the supervised train set each language pair.

EN-KO We discuss our approach to improve the English-Korean (EN-KO) translation performance by pre-training a Transformer using a high-quality dataset and leveraging morpheme-aware subword tokenization to better capture the linguistic characteristics of the Korean language such as agglutinative nature and structure.

We adopted a data-centric approach by pre-training a Transformer for EN-KO translation. To do so, we used a high-quality dataset from the AI Hub (Park et al., 2022)[1] data platform, which is operated by the Korean government. This comprehensive dataset includes various parallel corpora encompassing diverse domains such as technical and scientific fields, daily life and colloquial expressions, news articles, government and local government websites, publications, administrative regulations, Korean culture, and formal and informal language. By using a dataset specifically tailored for English-Korean translation, we aimed to capture finer nuances in both languages and enhance the translation quality by incorporating domain-specific knowledge and addressing the linguistic variations in different contexts.

Furthermore, we addressed the linguistic characteristics of the Korean language by applying a morpheme-aware subword tokenization method, which combines a segmentation strategy based on linguistic features with subwords. This approach has been shown to be effective in various Korean NLP tasks (Park et al., 2020). We utilized MeCab-ko [2], a widely-used morphological analyzer for the Korean language, for morpheme analysis. After obtaining the morphemes, we applied the Unigram subword tokenization method, which allowed our model to capture linguistic patterns specific to the Korean language, ultimately improving the overall translation performance.

EN-VI For the EN-VI language pair, we employed the EnViT5 (Ngo et al., 2022), a Text-to-Text Transfer Transformer (T5) model proposed by Raffel et al. (2020). We aimed to improve the fine-tuning translation performance of EN-VI in a low-resource setting by applying this data-centric approach to the multi-domain pre-trained EnViT5

[1] https://aihub.or.kr/

[2] https://bitbucket.org/eunjeon/mecab-ko-dic

model, which has been specifically designed for Vietnamese language tasks. Notably, EnViT5 models outperformed existing multilingual models such as mBART and M2M-100 while maintaining a significantly smaller parameter size, making them scalable and promising for both academic and industry applications (Ngo et al., 2022).

EnViT5 was pre-trained with the CC100 Dataset (Wenzek et al., 2020) which comprises monolingual data for over 100 languages. Subsequently, EnViT5 was fine-tuned on the MTet (Ngo et al., 2022) and PhoMT (Doan et al., 2021) datasets. MTet is a multi-domain EN-VI machine translation dataset encompassing a diverse range of domains, including educational videos, software user interfaces, COVID-related news articles, religious texts, subtitles, Wikipedia, and TED Talks (Reimers and Gurevych, 2020). Ultimately, when combined with PhoMT and IWSLT'15 (Cettolo et al., 2015), the final MTet dataset expands the training set size to 6 million examples, covering previously neglected areas such as law and biomedical data, which contains monolingual data for over 100 languages.

2.3 Synthetic Data Generation via Prompt Engineering

Leveraging synthetic examples in machine translation is crucial for improving translation quality, especially in low-resource settings (Edunov et al., 2018; Sennrich et al., 2015a). ChatGPT with GPT-4 engine (OpenAI, 2023), in particular, exhibits translation performance comparable to state-of-the-art WMT system and demonstrate good quality of generation conditioned translation generation in both few-shot and zero-shot settings (Hendy et al., 2023). To generate synthetic data, we employ ChatGPT to condition on formality and translate the IWSLT'22 Formality Track (Salesky et al., 2022) for all language pairs with English as the source language. Furthermore, we use a formality classifier (Rippeth et al., 2022) to filter synthetic examples, ensuring that both formal and informal examples are accurately translated for each language.

Supervised Setting We follow the prompt template depicted in Appendix A, which is based on the approach proposed by Hendy et al. (2023). To provide context for the model, we utilize n randomly selected shots from the English training set of other language pairs in the IWSLT 23 Formality Track (Agarwal et al., 2023). The few-shot examples are sourced from the target language's training set and include both informal and formal levels. ChatGPT is then tasked with translating the input text into either an informal or formal target language, depending on the specified prompt. For the input text, we use English source sentences from the IWSLT 22 Formality Track's other language pairs. After filtering the translated examples using a formality classifier, we fine-tuned the respective PLMs for EN-KO and EN-VI by incorporating synthetic examples into the training sets for each language pair. To verify the effectiveness of data augmentation through prompt engineering, we conduct experiments comparing the results with and without the augmented data.

Language	Size	
	Train	Test
EN-KO	400	600
EN-VI	400	600
EN-PT	0	600
EN-RU	0	600

Table 2: Data statistics in train and test sets of Formality Dataset

Zero-shot Setting In the EN-PT and EN-RU zero-shot settings, we generate synthetic examples for fine-tuning using the IWSLT'22 train set. We translate the source into both formal and informal target language levels, employing suitable prompts and filtering with a formality classifier to ensure conditioned formality. The template, shown in Appendix A, is adapted from the OpenAI Playground's default sentence-level translation task[3]. The model is instructed to translate English input into either informal or formal target language, guided by n random shots from the training set. Generated examples are then filtered using a formality classifier before fine-tuning the pre-trained multilingual translation model.

This zero-shot approach enables effective conditioned task performance with limited exposure to specific language pairs and formality levels. By generating synthetic translation data for fine-tuning, we capitalize on the model's generalization ability across languages and formality levels, enhancing translation performance in zero-shot settings. This highlights the potential of synthetic data in extending pre-trained language models' capabilities, even

[3]https://platform.openai.com/examples/default-translate

with novel language pair and formality combinations.

3 Experiment Settings

3.1 Dataset Details

The IWSLT shared task provides Formality Dataset which contains English source segments, each accompanied by two contrasting reference translations representing informal and formal formality levels. This is available for two language pairs, EN-{KO, VI}, in the supervised setting and two additional language pairs, EN-{PT, RU}, in the zero-shot setting. The statistics for the train and test sets of the dataset are shown in Table 2

For training and testing purposes, we randomly sampled 50 pairs of examples across each domain from the train set of Formality Dataset, and set them aside as validation sets (TASK DEV) for each supervised language. The remaining samples were utilized for training (TASK TRAIN).

Additionally, we utilized external datasets in conjunction with the data provided in the shared task. For EN-KO, we employed a parallel corpus comprising Formal/Informal, Social Science, Technology Science, and News domains from AI Hub for the pretraining of the PLM. For EN-VI, we utilized EnViT5, which was fine-tuned using the MTet (Ngo et al., 2022) and PhoMT (Doan et al., 2021) datasets.

In our research, we leverage ChatGPT for the augmentation of the EN-KO and EN-VI and the generation of synthetic examples for fine-tuning on EN-PT and EN-RU. This was done by using the source data from all available English-other language pairs (EN-XX) in the IWSLT'22 Formality Track (Anastasopoulos et al., 2022). To secure the quality and uniqueness of our training set, we implemented a preprocessing step that excludes duplicate sentences. Furthermore, to determine the optimal hyperparameters, we conducted a case study utilizing TASK DEV (details can be found in Section 4.3). The hyperparameters that led to the highest Matched-Accuracy (M-Acc) were selected for use. For all language pairs, we utilized a temperature of 0.9; specifically, we implemented 4-shot learning for EN-KO and 2-shot learning for EN-VI. For EN-PT and EN-RU, we proceeded with a zero-shot setting. More detailed information regarding the datasets and the preprocessing steps are presented in Table 3.

Language	Size	Source
EN-KO	6M	AI Hub (Formal/Informal + Tech/Sci + Social/Sci + News)
EN-VI	6.2M	MTet (Ngo et al., 2022) + PhoMT (Doan et al., 2021)
EN-{PT, RU}	1.6K	EN source from IWSLT'22 (Anastasopoulos et al., 2022)

Table 3: Additional external datasets used for the formality track in various language pairs.

3.2 Training Details

In the training details for the EN-KO language pair, we applied a morpheme-aware tokenization method to the translation dataset. To achieve this, we followed the training methods proposed by Park et al. (2020) and Gowda and May (2020), using `MeCab-ko` and Unigram to construct a vocabulary of 48K tokens. We then pre-trained the Transformer model (Vaswani et al., 2017). We used the `fairseq` library with 12 encoder and 12 decoder layers, each having 16 attention heads. Both encoder and decoder had an embedding dimension of 1024 and a feed-forward network (FFN) dimension of 4096. During pre-training, we trained for 20 epochs with a learning rate of 5e-4 and 4000 warmup updates. For fine-tuning, we trained for 200 epochs using a learning rate of 4e-5 and 100 warmup updates. We fine-tuned using the TASK TRAIN for all language pairs.

For EN-{VI, PT, RU} pairs, we fine-tuned using the `huggingface` library. For EN-VI, we used the `VietAI/envit5-translation` as the PLM. Fine-tuning was performed for 200 epochs with a learning rate of 4e-5, 200 warmup steps, and a batch size of 64. For EN-{PT,RU} pairs, we used `facebook/mbart-large-50` and trained for 200 epochs with a learning rate of 3e-5, 100 warmup steps, and a batch size of 16. All models were trained using four RTX A6000 GPUs. Detailed hyperparameters and training information can be found in the Appendix B.

3.3 Evaluation Details

In our experimental setting, we used the official test set from Formality Dataset (IWSLT'23) to evaluate our translation model's performance. The evaluation was conducted across two dimensions: overall translation quality and formality control. To assess the overall translation quality, we employed BLEU (Papineni et al., 2002) and COMET (Rei et al., 2020) (`eamt22-cometinho-da`) as au-

	Method	EN-KO BLEU	EN-KO COMET	EN-KO %M-Acc	EN-KO %C-F	EN-VI BLEU	EN-VI COMET	EN-VI %M-Acc	EN-VI %C-F
Formal	Official Baseline	4.91	0.211	78.3	98.6	26.71	0.363	96.0	99.7
	ChatGPT	5.65	0.524	83.3	**100.0**	27.07	0.510	**100.0**	98.0
	Ours	**26.60**	**0.727**	**87.0**	**100.0**	**47.00**	**0.669**	99.4	**100.0**
	Ours + Augmentation	17.09	0.667	79.4	99.5	41.57	0.653	99.4	99.7
Informal	Official Baseline	4.85	0.170	97.6	99.5	25.28	0.345	96.0	98.2
	ChatGPT	5.60	0.564	**100.0**	**100.0**	25.83	0.482	**100.0**	**100.0**
	Ours	**27.10**	**0.715**	98.0	95.0	**45.60**	**0.637**	98.8	**100.0**
	Ours + Augmentation	20.35	0.621	98.5	98.8	40.46	0.484	98.7	**100.0**

Table 4: Results on the test set of Formality Dataset for formal and informal supervised settings, obtained via our language specialized data-centric approach.

	Method	EN-PT BLEU	EN-PT COMET	EN-PT %M-Acc	EN-PT %C-F	EN-RU BLEU	EN-RU COMET	EN-RU %M-Acc	EN-RU %C-F
Formal	Official Baseline	27.29	0.448	96.3	97.7	21.96	0.349	96.2	92.0
	ChatGPT	**31.25**	**0.655**	92.0	96.0	**31.25**	0.655	92.0	96.0
	Ours	31.00	0.525	**100.0**	**100.0**	25.80	0.445	**100.0**	**100.0**
Informal	Official Baseline	**30.93**	0.416	**93.2**	**90.8**	21.63	0.348	84.1	85.2
	ChatGPT	27.38	**0.512**	48.4	46.0	**31.25**	**0.655**	92.0	**100.0**
	Ours	19.90	0.249	68.0	90.0	26.30	0.418	**100.0**	**100.0**

Table 5: Results on the test set of Formality Dataset for formal and informal zero-shot settings, achieved through our approach of synthetic data generation via prompt engineering.

tomatic evaluation metrics. We use 13A tokenizer to report SACREBLEU (Post, 2018) scores for all languages.

For formality control, we utilized Matched-Accuracy (M-Acc), a reference-based corpus-level metric that leverages phrase-level formality markers from the references to classify system-generated hypotheses as formal or informal. The corpus-level score is the percentage of system outputs that match the desired formality level.

Additionally, we used a reference-free variant of M-Acc (C-F) [4], which relies on a multilingual formality classifier to label system-generated hypotheses as formal or informal, with the corpus-level score representing the percentage of system outputs matching the desired formality level.

3.4 Prompt Design

We conducted experiments using ChatGPT with GPT-4 engine with `langchain`[5]. For EN-KO and EN-VI language pairs, we used a supervised setting, while for EN-PT and EN-RU pairs, we employed a zero-shot setting. In the supervised setting, we extracted arbitrary n-shot samples using the TASK TRAIN. We designed prompts by leveraging langchain's prompt guide and prompt examples from Hendy et al. (2023). Detailed examples and explanations of the prompts can be found in Appendix A.

4 Result & Findings

4.1 Results for Supervised Setting

Table 4 presents our experimental results in the supervised setting. As demonstrated by our results, our model, trained with the high-quality human-annotated Formality Dataset, exhibited outstanding performance. In particular, with respect to the C-F metric, our model shows almost perfect formality control performance (100% accuracy) for most of the tasks, except for the EN-KO informal task. Additionally, our model shows superior performance for the conventional NMT metrics (*i.e.* BLEU, COMET), outperforming ChatGPT with a 21.50 BLEU score for the EN-KO informal task. The EN-VI pair also exhibits high NMT metric

[4] https://github.com/amazon-science/contrastive-controlled-mt/tree/main/IWSLT2023

[5] https://python.langchain.com/

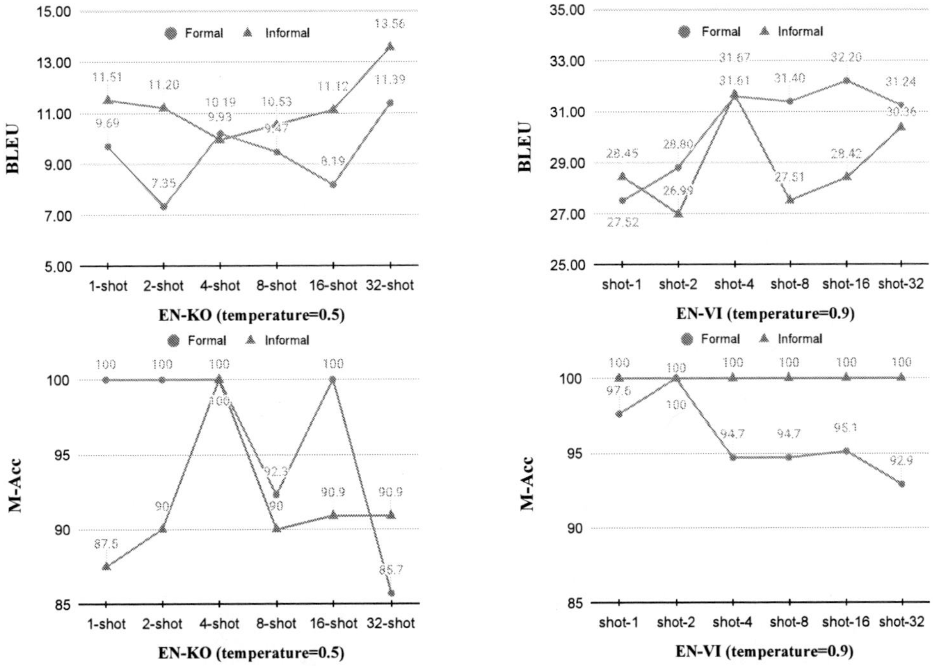

Figure 1: BLEU and M-Acc scores for ChatGPT based on superviesed setting, evaluated on TASK DEV.

scores, M-Acc, and C-F scores compared to the baseline. These results suggest that our language-specific data-centric approach is effective.

Through our experiments, we observed a significant degradation in the quality for supervised settings EN-{KO, VI}. This phenomenon can be attributed to the limitations of synthetic data produced by ChatGPT. While the data generated through ChatGPT exhibits considerable quality, it was not up to par with the sentences derived from our data-centric approach. We found that the integration of ChatGPT-augmented data inadvertently introduced noise into the system, leading to a decrease in overall performance. Despite the exceptional capabilities of ChatGPT, it appears that in this context, the quality of data augmented by conventional NMT methods is still superior. This observation further emphasizes the critical role of data quality over quantity in supervised learning environments, and highlights the potential benefits of more sophisticated prompting techniques that consider formality control, such as stylistic or sentence endings, for improving overall performance.

4.2 Results for Zero-shot Setting

The experimental results for the zero-shot setting are shown in Table 5. As can be seen from the experimental results, our model significantly outperforms the official baseline on all tasks except the EN-PT informal task. Notably, our model demonstrates consistently higher performance in terms of C-F metric compared to ChatGPT, achieving 100% M-ACC and C-F in the majority of tasks.

Exceptionally for EN-PT informal task, the performance of our model is markedly subpar, and ChatGPT even fails to exceed the official baseline. We find this result is highly noteworthy, as it suggest that ChatGPT may generate semantically accurate and plausible data, while the formality can hardly be controlled, especially for the EN-PT language pair. In our experiments, we utilized the same prompt for both EN-PT and EN-RU language pairs, differing only in language specification. The disparity in results between these two language pair suggests that specialized techniques for controlling formality are required for each language pair. This issue can be partially attributed to a data bias in ChatGPT, indicating a potential training data bias concerning formality.

4.3 Case Study

Impact of In-context Shots In this section, we examine the changes in performance based on the number of few-shot samples used for in-context learning, particularly when employing prompt engineering for translation. Previous research sug-

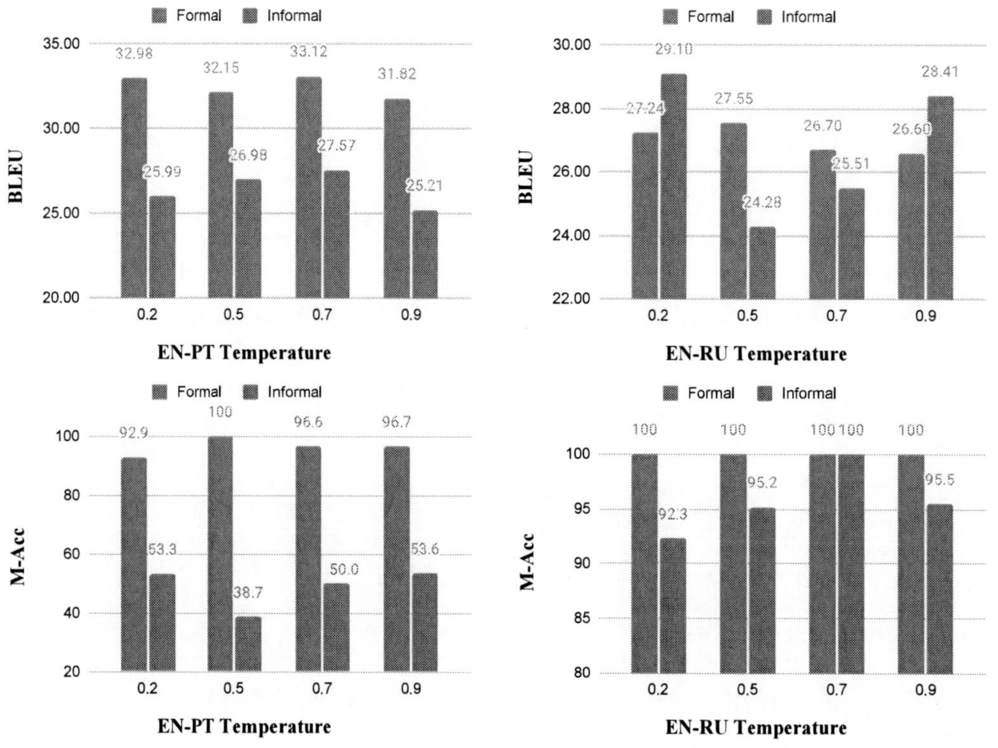

Figure 2: BLEU and M-Acc scores for ChatGPT based on zero-shot setting, evaluated on test set of Formality Dataset.

gests that increasing the number of shots beyond 10 does not significantly impact translation performance when using large language models (Zhang et al., 2023). However, we argue that applying the same perspective to formality control tasks proves challenging. This complexity arises as formality introduces a unique element required for these tasks. Additionally, previous research did not consider unintended consequences arising from this factor.

In pursuit of this, we conducted experiments where the number of shots was incrementally increased from 1 to 32, in powers of 2, using TASK DEV. The aim was to verify the differences in performance resulting from these changes. This process involved translating data via ChatGPT with an increasing number of shots and then evaluating the resulting translation data for its appropriateness. The experimental results are depicted in Figure 1. For this particular experiment, we selected one temperature (from the options of 0.2, 0.5, 0.7, 0.9) that demonstrated the highest performance and evaluated the changes in performance based on the number of shots.

As observed in our experimental results, increasing the number of shots for in-context learning led to an improvement in the general translation performance metric, BLEU. However, the scores of M-Acc and C-F, we found that the best performance was achieved with a smaller number of shots. This suggests that the nature of formality as a feature makes the "formality control" task distinct from conventional NMT, and it may be challenging to directly apply perspectives from conventional NMT to this task. We propose two hypotheses based on these results: (i) there exists a trade-off between translation performance and formality control as the number of shots increases, and (ii) increasing the number of shots while applying random sample selection may have caused confusion in performing formality control. We leave the analysis and validation of these hypotheses for future work.

Impact of Temperature Temperature is an important parameter to make ChatGPT generates varied responses to human queries (Peng et al., 2023). Basically, higher temperatures leads to the higher linguistic variety, while the lower one generates grammatically correct and deterministic text (Ippolito et al., 2019). Previous work suggested that for machine translation, a diverse generation may impede its translation quality with a high degree of certainty(*i.e.* high temperature) (Peng et al., 2023). In this sense, we experiment with different temperature setting and find the optimal temperature for the formality control data augmentation. In our experiments, we select the most appropriate one among seven shot-candidates (1, 2, 4, 8, 16, 32) for each language pair.

Experimental results reveal that varying temperature can lead to significant performance fluctuations. It is particularly noteworthy that the performance disparity due to temperature changes is exceptionally high for the informal tasks. For formal tasks, the impact of temperature is relatively minor, with the variation in BLEU score is at most 0.95 (EN-RU). However, for informal tasks, the performance shift can reach up to 4.82 points (EN-RU) as temperature changes. Additionally, we find that in informal task, the performance variation depending on the temperature shows distinct trend for each language pair. This is evident from the fact that a moderate temperature(0.7) yielded the highest BLEU performance in the EN-PT informal task, while a similarly moderate temperature(0.5) resulted in the lowest performance. Our findings suggest that handling ChatGPT in informal task necessitates more elaborate control compared to dealing with formal data.

5 Background

In this work, we focus on data-centric approaches to improve Neural Machine Translation (NMT) performance. Several studies have investigated different strategies to address the challenges of low-resource languages and enhance translation quality. Kudo (2018) proposed subword regularization to improve NMT models using multiple subword candidates, effectively increasing data diversity and robustness. Gu et al. (2018) introduced a universal NMT model for extremely low-resource languages, leveraging multilingual knowledge from high-resource languages to assist in translation. Zoph et al. (2016) explored transfer learning for low-resource NMT, utilizing pre-trained models on related high-resource languages to improve the performance on the target low-resource language. Additionally, Sennrich et al. (2015a) proposed a method of improving NMT models by generating synthetic parallel data through back-translation, which has proven successful in various translation tasks. These studies highlight the diverse data-centric approaches in NMT, aiming to improve translation quality and overcome the limitations of low-resource languages.

6 Conclusion

In this paper, we presented the KU x UpStage team's submission for four languages, employing two main strategies: 1) a language-specific data-driven approach, and 2) synthetic data generation using large-scale language models and empirical prompt engineering. While our data-driven approach excelled, particularly in EN-KO and EN-VI, the quality of synthetic data generation was called into question. In light of this feedback, we propose to enhance the quality of synthetic data by integrating Quality Estimation (QE) techniques as an additional filter in the generation process. This step aims to further refine our synthetic examples, potentially improving the overall system performance. We also plan to explore the use of translation models with larger parameters and conduct a thorough analysis through more shot examples and linguistically-grounded data augmentation techniques. Finally, we aim to extend our understanding of factors influencing FSMT performance, such as the impact of formal register versus grammatical formality in training data and a detailed examination of zero-shot transfer.

Acknowledgments

This work was generously supported by multiple grants. The Core Research Institute Basic Science Research Program, funded by the Ministry of Education through the National Research Foundation of Korea (NRF) (Grant NRF-2021R1A6A1A03045425), provided valuable support. Additionally, this research received backing from the Information Technology Research Center (ITRC) support program (IITP-2023-2018-0-01405), which is supervised by the Institute for Information & Communications Technology Planning & Evaluation (IITP) and funded by the Ministry of Science and ICT (MSIT), Korea. Finally, the Korea government's MSIT also funded a grant through the IITP (No. 2020-0-00368) dedicated to "A Neural-Symbolic Model for Knowledge Acquisition and Inference Techniques." We extend our gratitude for this comprehensive support.

Limitations

Due to the random sampling of shots, the results of the experiment may vary between repeated trials. However, we did not conduct repeated experiments under identical conditions, and thus we acknowledge the potential inconsistency of our experimental results.

Ethics Statement

This research study did not involve any human or animal subjects, and no personal data or sensitive information was used in this research. Therefore, no ethical issues were encountered in this study. The authors confirm that the research was conducted in accordance with the relevant ethical guidelines and principles.

References

Milind Agarwal, Sweta Agrawal, Antonios Anastasopoulos, Claudia Borg, Marine Carpuat, Roldano Cattoni, Mauro Cettolo, William Chen, Khalid Choukri, Alexandra Chronopoulou, Thierry Declerck, Qianqian Dong, Yannick Estève, Kevin Duh, Marcello Federico, Souhir Gahbiche, Benjamin Hsu, John Judge, Tom Ko, Rishu Kumar, Xutail Ma, Prashant Mathur, Evgeny Matusov, Paul McNamee, John P. McCrae, Kenton Murray, Matteo Negri, Jan Niehues, Xing Niu, Atul Ojha Kr., John E. Ortega, Proyag Pal, Juan Pino, Lonneke van der Plas, Elijah Rippeth, Elizabeth Salesky, Matthias Sperber, Sebastian Stüker, Katsuhito Sudoh, Brian Thompson, Marco Turchi, Alex Waibel, Mingxuan Wang, and Rodolfo Zevallos. 2023. Findings of the IWSLT 2023 Evaluation Campaign. In *Proceedings of the 20th International Conference on Spoken Language Translation (IWSLT 2023)*. Association for Computational Linguistics.

Antonios Anastasopoulos, Loïc Barrault, Luisa Bentivogli, Marcely Zanon Boito, Ondřej Bojar, Roldano Cattoni, Anna Currey, Georgiana Dinu, Kevin Duh, Maha Elbayad, Clara Emmanuel, Yannick Estève, Marcello Federico, Christian Federmann, Souhir Gahbiche, Hongyu Gong, Roman Grundkiewicz, Barry Haddow, Benjamin Hsu, Dávid Javorský, Věra Kloudová, Surafel Lakew, Xutai Ma, Prashant Mathur, Paul McNamee, Kenton Murray, Maria Nădejde, Satoshi Nakamura, Matteo Negri, Jan Niehues, Xing Niu, John Ortega, Juan Pino, Elizabeth Salesky, Jiatong Shi, Matthias Sperber, Sebastian Stüker, Katsuhito Sudoh, Marco Turchi, Yogesh Virkar, Alexander Waibel, Changhan Wang, and Shinji Watanabe. 2022. Findings of the IWSLT 2022 evaluation campaign. In *Proceedings of the 19th International Conference on Spoken Language Translation (IWSLT 2022)*, pages 98–157, Dublin, Ireland (in-person and online). Association for Computational Linguistics.

Piotr Bojanowski, Edouard Grave, Armand Joulin, and Tomas Mikolov. 2017. Enriching word vectors with subword information. *Transactions of the association for computational linguistics*, 5:135–146.

Denny Britz, Anna Goldie, Minh-Thang Luong, and Quoc Le. 2017. Massive exploration of neural machine translation architectures. *arXiv preprint arXiv:1703.03906*.

Mauro Cettolo, Jan Niehues, Sebastian Stüker, Luisa Bentivogli, Roldano Cattoni, and Marcello Federico. 2015. The IWSLT 2015 evaluation campaign. In *Proceedings of the 12th International Workshop on Spoken Language Translation: Evaluation Campaign*, pages 2–14, Da Nang, Vietnam.

Long Doan, Linh The Nguyen, Nguyen Luong Tran, Thai Hoang, and Dat Quoc Nguyen. 2021. PhoMT: A high-quality and large-scale benchmark dataset for Vietnamese-English machine translation. In *Proceedings of the 2021 Conference on Empirical Methods in Natural Language Processing*, pages 4495–4503, Online and Punta Cana, Dominican Republic. Association for Computational Linguistics.

Sergey Edunov, Myle Ott, Michael Auli, and David Grangier. 2018. Understanding back-translation at scale. *arXiv preprint arXiv:1808.09381*.

Karthik Gopalakrishnan, Behnam Hedayatnia, Qinlang Chen, Anna Gottardi, Sanjeev Kwatra, Anushree Venkatesh, Raefer Gabriel, and Dilek Hakkani-Tür. 2019. Topical-chat: Towards knowledge-grounded open-domain conversations.

Thamme Gowda and Jonathan May. 2020. Finding the optimal vocabulary size for neural machine translation. *arXiv preprint arXiv:2004.02334*.

Jiatao Gu, Hany Hassan, Jacob Devlin, and Victor OK Li. 2018. Universal neural machine translation for extremely low resource languages. *arXiv preprint arXiv:1802.05368*.

Amr Hendy, Mohamed Abdelrehim, Amr Sharaf, Vikas Raunak, Mohamed Gabr, Hitokazu Matsushita, Young Jin Kim, Mohamed Afify, and Hany Hassan Awadalla. 2023. How good are gpt models at machine translation? a comprehensive evaluation. *arXiv preprint arXiv:2302.09210*.

Daphne Ippolito, Reno Kriz, Maria Kustikova, João Sedoc, and Chris Callison-Burch. 2019. Comparison of diverse decoding methods from conditional language models. *arXiv preprint arXiv:1906.06362*.

Taku Kudo. 2018. Subword regularization: Improving neural network translation models with multiple subword candidates. *arXiv preprint arXiv:1804.10959*.

Can Li, Wenbo Wang, Bitty Balducci, Lingshu Hu, Matthew Gordon, Detelina Marinova, and Yi Shang. 2022. Deep formality: Sentence formality prediction with deep learning. In *2022 IEEE 23rd International Conference on Information Reuse and Integration for Data Science (IRI)*, pages 1–5. IEEE.

Maria Nădejde, Anna Currey, Benjamin Hsu, Xing Niu, Marcello Federico, and Georgiana Dinu. 2022. Cocoa-mt: A dataset and benchmark for contrastive controlled mt with application to formality. *arXiv preprint arXiv:2205.04022*.

Chinh Ngo, Trieu H Trinh, Long Phan, Hieu Tran, Tai Dang, Hieu Nguyen, Minh Nguyen, and Minh-Thang Luong. 2022. Mtet: Multi-domain translation for english and vietnamese. *arXiv preprint arXiv:2210.05610*.

Xing Niu, Marianna Martindale, and Marine Carpuat. 2017. A study of style in machine translation: Controlling the formality of machine translation output. In *Proceedings of the 2017 Conference on Empirical Methods in Natural Language Processing*, pages 2814–2819, Copenhagen, Denmark. Association for Computational Linguistics.

OpenAI. 2023. Gpt-4 technical report.

Kishore Papineni, Salim Roukos, Todd Ward, and Wei-Jing Zhu. 2002. Bleu: a method for automatic evaluation of machine translation. In *Proceedings of the 40th Annual Meeting of the Association for Computational Linguistics*, pages 311–318, Philadelphia, Pennsylvania, USA. Association for Computational Linguistics.

Chanjun Park, Sugyeong Eo, Hyeonseok Moon, and Heui-Seok Lim. 2021. Should we find another model?: Improving neural machine translation performance with one-piece tokenization method without model modification. In *Proceedings of the 2021 Conference of the North American Chapter of the Association for Computational Linguistics: Human Language Technologies: Industry Papers*, pages 97–104.

Chanjun Park, Midan Shim, Sugyeong Eo, Seolhwa Lee, Jaehyung Seo, Hyeonseok Moon, and Heuiseok Lim. 2022. Empirical analysis of parallel corpora and in-depth analysis using liwc. *Applied Sciences*, 12(11):5545.

Kyubyong Park, Joohong Lee, Seongbo Jang, and Dawoon Jung. 2020. An empirical study of tokenization strategies for various korean nlp tasks. *arXiv preprint arXiv:2010.02534*.

Keqin Peng, Liang Ding, Qihuang Zhong, Li Shen, Xuebo Liu, Min Zhang, Yuanxin Ouyang, and Dacheng Tao. 2023. Towards making the most of chatgpt for machine translation. *arXiv preprint arXiv:2303.13780*.

Matt Post. 2018. A call for clarity in reporting BLEU scores. In *Proceedings of the Third Conference on Machine Translation: Research Papers*, pages 186–191, Brussels, Belgium. Association for Computational Linguistics.

Colin Raffel, Noam Shazeer, Adam Roberts, Katherine Lee, Sharan Narang, Michael Matena, Yanqi Zhou, Wei Li, and Peter J Liu. 2020. Exploring the limits of transfer learning with a unified text-to-text transformer. *The Journal of Machine Learning Research*, 21(1):5485–5551.

Ricardo Rei, Craig Stewart, Ana C Farinha, and Alon Lavie. 2020. Comet: A neural framework for mt evaluation. *arXiv preprint arXiv:2009.09025*.

Nils Reimers and Iryna Gurevych. 2020. Making monolingual sentence embeddings multilingual using knowledge distillation. *arXiv preprint arXiv:2004.09813*.

Elijah Rippeth, Sweta Agrawal, and Marine Carpuat. 2022. Controlling translation formality using pre-trained multilingual language models. *arXiv preprint arXiv:2205.06644*.

Elizabeth Salesky, Marcello Federico, and Marta Costa-jussà, editors. 2022. *Proceedings of the 19th International Conference on Spoken Language Translation (IWSLT 2022)*. Association for Computational Linguistics, Dublin, Ireland (in-person and online).

Rico Sennrich, Barry Haddow, and Alexandra Birch. 2015a. Improving neural machine translation models with monolingual data. *arXiv preprint arXiv:1511.06709*.

Rico Sennrich, Barry Haddow, and Alexandra Birch. 2015b. Neural machine translation of rare words with subword units. *arXiv preprint arXiv:1508.07909*.

Felix Stahlberg. 2020. Neural machine translation: A review. *Journal of Artificial Intelligence Research*, 69:343–418.

Ashish Vaswani, Noam Shazeer, Niki Parmar, Jakob Uszkoreit, Llion Jones, Aidan N Gomez, Łukasz Kaiser, and Illia Polosukhin. 2017. Attention is all you need. *Advances in neural information processing systems*, 30.

Guillaume Wenzek, Marie-Anne Lachaux, Alexis Conneau, Vishrav Chaudhary, Francisco Guzmán, Armand Joulin, and Edouard Grave. 2020. CCNet: Extracting high quality monolingual datasets from web crawl data. In *Proceedings of the Twelfth Language Resources and Evaluation Conference*, pages 4003–4012, Marseille, France. European Language Resources Association.

Biao Zhang, Barry Haddow, and Alexandra Birch. 2023. Prompting large language model for machine translation: A case study. *arXiv preprint arXiv:2301.07069*.

Barret Zoph, Deniz Yuret, Jonathan May, and Kevin Knight. 2016. Transfer learning for low-resource neural machine translation. *arXiv preprint arXiv:1604.02201*.

A Prompt Template

A.1 Superviesd Setting

```
You are a helpful assistant that translates English to:
1. Informal [target language] or 2. Formal [target language]

####

[shot 1 source]

[shot 2 source]

[shot n source]

1. Informal [target language]: [shot 1 reference]

2. Formal [target language]: [shot 1 reference]

1. Informal [target language]: [shot 2 reference]

2. Formal [target language]: [shot 2 reference]

1. Informal [target language]: [shot n reference]

2. Formal [target language]: [shot n reference]

####

Translate this into only [1. Informal | 2. Formal] [target language]: [input]
```

Figure 3: Prompt template for supervised setting based on Hendy et al. (2023). We utilize n randomly selected shots from the English training set of other language pairs in the IWSLT 23 Formality Track as input for our model, with few-shot examples derived from the target language's training set.

A.2 Zero-shot Setting

```
You are a helpful assistant that translates English to:
1. Informal [target language] or 2. Formal [target language]

[shot n source]

Translate this into only [1. Informal | 2. Formal] [target language]: [input]
```

Figure 4: Prompt template for zero-shot setting, following the recommended instruction and format for the default sentence-level translation task in OpenAI playground[6]. This consistency enables us to maximize the benefits of the instruction finetuning protocol. We use n random shots from the training set.

B Experimental Setup

B.1 EN-KO

In the experimental setup for the EN-KO language pair, we employed a Transformer architecture with shared decoder input-output embeddings. The model's parameters included 1024-dimensional embeddings for both encoder and decoder, 16 attention heads for each, and 12 layers for both encoder and decoder. We used the Adam optimizer with beta values (0.9, 0.98) and a learning rate of 5e-4 scheduled by an inverse square root scheduler with a 4000-step warm-up. To prevent overfitting, we applied a dropout rate of 0.3 and weight decay of 0.0001. Our translation task utilized a label-smoothed cross-entropy criterion with a label smoothing factor of 0.1. The training process was performed with a maximum token limit of 4096 per batch and an update frequency of 4. Model performance was evaluated using BLEU scores with a beam size of 1 and detokenization using the Moses tokenizer. The training process was executed for a maximum of 20 epochs with a log interval of 200 and without epoch checkpoints, while sharing all embeddings.

Parameters for pre-training:

```
fairseq-train \
    --fp16 \
    --fp16-init-scale 4096 \
    --arch transformer --share-decoder-input-output-embed \
    --encoder-embed-dim 1024 --decoder-embed-dim 1024 \
    --encoder-attention-heads 16 --decoder-attention-heads 16 \
    --encoder-ffn-embed-dim 4096 --decoder-ffn-embed-dim 4096 \
    --encoder-normalize-before --decoder-normalize-before \
    --encoder-layers 12 --decoder-layers 12 \
    --optimizer adam --adam-betas '(0.9, 0.98)' --clip-norm 0.0 \
    --lr 5e-4 --lr-scheduler inverse_sqrt --warmup-updates 4000 \
    --dropout 0.3 --weight-decay 0.0001 \
    --task translation \
    --criterion label_smoothed_cross_entropy --label-smoothing 0.1 \
    --max-tokens 4096 \
    --update-freq 4 \
    --eval-bleu \
    --eval-bleu-args '{"beam": 1, "max_len_a": 1.2, "max_len_b": 10}' \
    --eval-bleu-detok moses \
    --eval-bleu-remove-bpe \
    --best-checkpoint-metric bleu --maximize-best-checkpoint-metric \
    --log-interval 200 \
    --max-epoch 20 \
    --skip-invalid-size-inputs-valid-test \
    --no-epoch-checkpoints \
    --share-all-embeddings
```

Parameters for fine-tuning:

```
fairseq-train \
    --batch-size 32 \
    --lr 4e-5  --warmup-updates 200 \
    --max-epoch 200 \
    --restore-file $MODELDIR/checkpoint_best.pt \
    --reset-optimizer --reset-meters --reset-dataloader --reset-lr-scheduler
```

B.2 EN-VI

We fine-tuned our model using the Hugging Face library and the code available at their repository[7]. The fine-tuning was performed with a learning rate of 4e-5, Adam optimizer with beta1 and beta2 values set to 0.9 and 0.98, respectively, and a weight decay of 0.0001. We also used mixed precision training (fp16) to accelerate the process. The learning rate scheduler was set to inverse square root with a warm-up of 200 steps. The training was conducted for 200 epochs with a maximum gradient norm of 0.0, label smoothing factor of 0.1, and a batch size of 64 for both training and evaluation. The model was saved and evaluated at the end of each epoch, and the logging was performed after each training step.

[7]https://github.com/huggingface/transformers/tree/main/examples/pytorch/translation

Parameters for fine-tuning:

```
python train_mt_trainer.py \
    --fp16 \
    --model_name_or_path VietAI/envit5-translation \
    --do_train \
    --do_eval \
    --do_predict \
    --source_lang en \
    --target_lang vi \
    --source_prefix "translate English to Vietnamese: " \
    --learning_rate 4e-5 \
    --adam_beta1 0.9 \
    --adam_beta2 0.98 \
    --max_grad_norm 0.0 \
    --num_train_epochs 200 \
    --lr_scheduler_type inverse_sqrt \
    --warmup_steps 200 \
    --weight_decay 0.0001 \
    --label_smoothing_factor 0.1 \
    --save_strategy epoch \
    --logging_steps 1 \
    --evaluation_strategy epoch \
    --per_device_train_batch_size=64 \
    --per_device_eval_batch_size=64
```

B.3 EN-{PT, RU}

We utilized the same training code as for the EN-VI task and employed the `facebook/mbart-large-50` model.

Parameters for fine-tuning:

```
export langs=ar_AR,cs_CZ,de_DE,en_XX,es_XX,et_EE,fi_FI,fr_XX,gu_IN,hi_IN,
it_IT,ja_XX,kk_KZ,ko_KR,lt_LT,lv_LV,my_MM,ne_NP,nl_XX,ro_RO,ru_RU,si_LK,
tr_TR,vi_VN,zh_CN

python train_mt_trainer.py \
    --fp16 \
    --model_name_or_path facebook/mbart-large-50 \
    --do_train \
    --do_eval \
    --do_predict \
    --source_lang en_XX \
    --target_lang pt_XX \
    --learning_rate 3e-5 \
    --adam_beta1 0.9 \
    --adam_beta2 0.98 \
    --max_grad_norm 0.0 \
    --num_train_epochs 200 \
    --lr_scheduler_type inverse_sqrt \
    --warmup_steps 100 \
    --weight_decay 0.0001 \
    --label_smoothing_factor 0.1 \
    --save_strategy epoch \
    --logging_steps 1 \
    --evaluation_strategy epoch \
    --per_device_train_batch_size=16 \
    --per_device_eval_batch_size=16
```

UM-DFKI Maltese Speech Translation

Aiden Williams* **Kurt Abela*** **Rishu Kumar**[◇] **Martin Bär***

Hannah Billinghurst* **Kurt Micallef*** **Ahnaf Mozib Samin***

Andrea De Marco* **Lonneke van der Plas**[†] **Claudia Borg***

*University of Malta, [◇]DFKI, [†]IDIAP

aiden.williams.19@um.edu.mt, kurt.abela@um.edu.mt, rishu.Kumar@dfki.de,martin.bar.22@um.edu.mt, hannah.billinghurst.22@um.edu.mt, kurt.micallef@um.edu.mt, ahnaf.samin.22@um.edu.mt, andrea.demarco@um.edu.mt, lonneke.vanderplas@idiap.ch, claudia.borg@um.edu.mt

Abstract

For the 2023 IWSLT (Agarwal et al., 2023) Maltese Speech Translation Task, UM-DFKI jointly presents a cascade solution which achieves 0.6 BLEU. While this is the first time that a Maltese speech translation task has been released by IWSLT, this paper explores previous solutions for other speech translation tasks, focusing primarily on low-resource scenarios. Moreover, we present our method of fine-tuning XLS-R models for Maltese ASR using a collection of multi-lingual speech corpora as well as the fine-tuning of the mBART model for Maltese to English machine translation.

1 Introduction

Speech Translation (ST), or speech-to-text translation, involves converting speech in a source language into written text in a target language. With the rise of deep learning, steep progress has been made in this field and many other areas that fall under the Natural Language Processing (NLP) umbrella (Khurana et al., 2023; Qiu et al., 2020). However, development for low-resource languages has continued to present difficulties and obstacles due to a variety of factors, including the lack of sufficient training data, language experts and other resources (Magueresse et al., 2020; Hedderich et al., 2021).

The International Workshop on Spoken Language Translation (IWSLT) shared task is an annual competition that aims to foster research in the field of speech translation. With its low-resource track, it also contributes to advanced research for speech translation in low-resource scenarios. In this paper, we present our submission to the low resource track: a pipeline system for English-Maltese speech-to-text translation.

We begin by discussing the state of the art in speech translation and describe the two main approaches, cascade and end-to-end. Afterwards, we briefly summarise the challenges posed by low-resource languages and possible mitigation strategies. We then describe our system, a pipeline approach containing an internal Automatic Speech Recognition (ASR) component and the outward facing Machine Translation (MT) component. The ASR component can use one of five fine-tuned XLS-R (Babu et al., 2021) models, whereas the MT stage always uses an mBART-50 model.

2 Literature Review

The following literature review aims to provide an overview of previous IWSLT ST submissions, with a particular focus on low-resource scenarios. The review is divided into two sections; where the first explores the general approaches and challenges associated with low-resource ST, and the second section discusses previous approaches to low-resource ST as applied to IWSLT.

2.1 Previous IWSLT Approaches for Low-Resource Languages

The IWSLT (Anastasopoulos et al., 2022) set the task in 2022 to attempt to solve "the problem of developing speech transcription and translation tools for under-resourced languages". This problem involved translating Tamasheq into English and Tunisian Arabic into French. Three different teams attempted to solve the problem of the Tamasheq-English ST; Taltech publish an encoder-decoder ST model that used a pre-trained XLS-R that they fine-tuned on unlabelled Tamasheq as the encoder and mBART-50 as the decoder, GMU used the Fairseq s2t extension with its transformer archi-

Proceedings of the 20th International Conference on Spoken Language Translation (IWSLT 2023), pages 433–441
July 13-14, 2023

tecture in which they fine-tuned the pre-trained XLS-R 300M encoder on French and Arabic and then trained the whole model on the provided data from the task; finally, ON-TRAC had a primary submission which used a pre-trained Wav2Vec 2.0 base model trained on Tamasheq and a contrastive model which was comprised of a partial Wav2Vec 2.0 model, a linear layer used for down projecting the output of the Wav2Vec and a transformer decoder. All three submissions decided to focus on using large pre-trained models when approaching the task, which is the approach taken for our models as well. The results from the submissions showed that using powerful speech feature extractors such as Wav2Vec 2.0 and massive multilingual decoders such as mBART-50 does not stop low-resource ST from being a major challenge. Of the three submissions, training self-supervised models on the target data and producing artificial supervision seemed to be the most effective approach to solving the problem (Zanon Boito et al., 2022).

Previous, well-performing systems submitted to the IWLST offline and low-resource speech translation tracks made use of various methods to improve the performance of their cascade system. For the ASR component, many submissions used a combination of transformer and conformer models (Zhang et al., 2022; Li et al., 2022; Nguyen et al., 2021) or fine-tuned existing models (Zhang and Ao, 2022; Zanon Boito et al., 2022; Denisov et al., 2021). They managed to increase ASR performance by voice activity detection for segmentation (Zhang et al., 2022; Ding and Tao, 2021), training the ASR on synthetic data with added punctuation, noise-filtering and domain-specific fine-tuning (Zhang and Ao, 2022; Li et al., 2022) or adding an intermediate model that cleans the ASR output in terms of casing and punctuation (Nguyen et al., 2021). The MT components were mostly transformer-based (Zhang et al., 2022; Nguyen et al., 2021; Bahar et al., 2021) or fine-tuned on pre-existing models (Zhang and Ao, 2022). Additional methods used to improve MT performance were multi-task learning (Denisov et al., 2021), back-translation (Ding and Tao, 2021; Zhang et al., 2022; Zhang and Ao, 2022), domain adaption (Nguyen et al., 2021; Zhang et al., 2022), knowledge distillation (Zhang et al., 2022), making the MT component robust by training it on noisy ASR output data (Nguyen et al., 2021; Zhang et al., 2022; Zhang and Ao, 2022), re-ranking and de-noising techniques (Ding and Tao, 2021). Bahar et al. (2021) trained their ASR and MT components jointly by passing the ASR output to the MT component as a probability vector instead of a one-hot vector to attenuate error propagation and avoid information loss of the otherwise purely textual output.

2.2 Wav2Vec 2.0 XLS-R For Maltese ASR

One of the latest developments for the Wav2Vec system is the introduction of multilingual pre-training. Due to the robust architectural design of Wav2Vec 2.0, models are able to learn cross-lingual speech representations (XLSR) while pre-training on massive amounts of data. This is put in practice with the XLSR models, which are pre-trained on up to 53 different languages from the Mozilla Commonvoice (v. Nov. 2019), BABEL (Gales et al., 2014) and Multilingual LibriSpeech (Pratap et al., 2020) speech corpora, with the largest model, pre-trained on a total of 56 thousand hours of speech data (Conneau et al., 2021). To test out the XLSR approach, several Wav2Vec BASE models are pre-trained either monolingually or multilingually. Monolingual models follow the process previously taken, i.e. they are pre-trained using the same language on which they are fine-tuned. This process is changed slightly for multilingual models, which are pre-trained on ten languages; then at the fine-tuning stage, a model is fine-tuned for each language. The experiment also included the pre-training of the Wav2Vec LARGE XLSR-53 model, which was pre-trained on the entire dataset of unannotated data, and just like the multilingual models, a separate model is then created for each language it was evaluated on during fine-tuning. The performance of different approaches, evaluated on four languages; Assamese, Tagalog, Swahili, and Georgian, is shown in Table 1. In these languages, the multilingual models, XLSR even more so, outperform the monolingual model.

The work on the XLSR approach continues in (Babu et al., 2021) with the release of the XLS-R model, which saw an increase in both the size of the unannotated data and the languages included. BABEL, Multilingual LibriSpeech, and CommonVoice (v. Dec. 2020) are joined by the VoxPopoli (Wang et al., 2021) and VoxLingua107 (Valk and Alumäe, 2021) corpora for a total of 436 thousand unannotated hours.

Table 1: XLSR Wav2Vec 2.0 performance on low-resource settings when evaluated using WER. Assamese (AS), Tagalog (TL), Swahili (SW), and Georgian (KA) are the languages presented.

Language	AS	TL	SW	KA
Annotated Data (h)	55	76	30	46
XLSR-10	44.9	37.3	35.5	-
XLSR-53	44.1	33.2	36.5	31.1
XLS-R (0.3B)	42.9	33.2	24.3	28.0
XLS-R (1B)	40.4	30.6	21.2	25.1
XLS-R (2B)	39.0	29.3	21.0	24.3

2.3 mBART For Maltese to English Translation

According to (Liu et al., 2020), using mBART-25 as the pre-trained model has been shown to improve translations over a randomly initialized baseline in low/medium resource language. mBART-25 is a transformer model trained on the BART (Lewis et al., 2019) objective. It is trained on 25 different languages. mBART-25 was later extended to include 25 more languages and was called mBART-50 (Tang et al., 2020). However, neither model included Maltese - in fact, translation experiments on Maltese are very limited. In our experiments, in Section 3.2, we checked whether these performance gains expand to the Maltese language, and this claim appears to hold.

3 Methodology

For this task, we decided to use a cascade system where the ASR and MT components were trained separately but evaluated jointly. In this section, a detailed description of both components is given. First, the training data is described, followed by the pre-processing steps applied to said data. Next, the models are introduced, and lastly training, the training procedure is outlined.

3.1 Automatic Speech Recognition

The ASR component in this submission continues the previous work done in (Williams, 2022), and so the same annotated dataset consisting of 50 hours of Maltese speech is used for this task. We opted not to use data released for this task for two reasons. First was the additional annotation work that was required, mainly segmentation, for which we experienced issues attempting to do in a timely manner. Secondly, this submission includes models fine-tuned with non-Maltese data. Making use of the dataset in (Williams, 2022) as a base has made comparisons with previous experiments possible.

As described in Table 2, the Maltese speech corpus is made up of several segments from two main Maltese speech corpora, MASRI (Hernandez Mena et al., 2020), CommonVoice (CV) (Ardila et al., 2020) and an annotated set from publicly available parliamentary sittings. Previous research in ASR for Maltese has used English speech data with varying degrees of success (Mena et al., 2021). However, when applied in fine-tuning an XLS-R model, the effect was detrimental. To further observe the effect non-Maltese data would have on the translation task, we used three other subsets from the CommonVoice speech corpus. Selecting 50 hours of validated each from the Italian, French and Arabic sets.

Individually these speech corpora each amount to 50 hours, from which four models are trained. One with just the Maltese data and the other three trained on the extra language combined with the Maltese set. A fifth model is also trained with all the data included. Further combinations were not tried due to time concerns.

Table 2: Each corpus is listed along with its total length, sample count and average sample length.

Dataset	Length (h,m)	Samples	Average Length (s)
HEADSET	6, 40	4979	4.81
MEP	1, 20	656	7.11
Tube	13, 20	8954	5.34
MERLIN	19, 4	9720	6.14
Parlament	2, 30	1672	5.35
CV Validated	4, 57	3790	12.68
CV Other	5, 4	3833	4.71
CV French	50	-	-
CV Italian	50	-	-
CV Arabic	50	-	-
Validation	2, 32	1912	4.89
Test MASRI	1	668	5.39
Test CV	0, 54	670	4.74

The XLS-R model comes in three pre-trained variants; the small model with 300 million parameters, the medium model with a billion parameters and the large model with two billion parameters. Size on disk scales with size with the small model being roughly 1GB in size and the large model being roughly 8GB. All three of them have been pre-trained on roughly 500 thousand hours of un-

Table 3: ASR Models and the data used for fine-tuning.

Model	Corpora used
MT Only	All Maltese corpora
MT+All	All corpora presented
MT+AR	All Maltese corpora + Arabic subset
MT+FR	All Maltese corpora + French subset
MT+IT	All Maltese corpora + Italian subset

labelled, multilingual speech. Previous research (Williams, 2022), has shown that both the small and large models fare well when fine-tuned for the downstream Maltese ASR task. With this in mind, the small 300M XLS-R variant model was chosen for this task. The main reason was due to its smaller size, a larger batch size could be used which expedited the fine-tuning process, while the performance loss was expected to be minimal.

This submission follows the same training procedure as outlined in (Williams, 2022). Where the procedure was conducted utilising the Huggingface Trainer object with the following hyper-parameters. Each model is trained for 30 epochs, using the AdamW criterion with a starting learning rate of $3e-4$. To stabilise the training process, the first 500 training steps were used as warm-up steps. Gradient accumulation was also used to effectively quadruple the batch size. The batch size was dependent on the training set used, where due to some differences in sample lengths, different batch sizes had to be used. We fine-tune 5 XLS-R 300m models as presented in Table 3.

3.2 Machine Translation

The dataset used to train the machine translation systems comes from publicly available sources. The original data sources include datasets from Arab-Acquis (Habash et al., 2017), the European Vaccination Portal[1],the Publications Office of the EU on the medical domain[2], the European Medicines Agency[3], the COVID-19 ANTIBIOTIC dataset[4], the COVID-19 EC-EUROPA dataset[5], the COVID-19 EU press corner V2 dataset[6], the COVID-19 EUROPARL v2 dataset[7], the Digital Corpus of the European Parliament (Hajlaoui et al., 2014), the DGT-Acquis (Steinberger et al., 2014), ELRC[8], the Tatoeba corpus[9], OPUS (Tiedemann, 2012), EUIPO - Trade mark Guidelines[10], Malta Government Gazette[11], MaCoCu (Bañón et al., 2022), as well as data extracted from the Laws of Malta[12].

The different datasets were compiled into a single one. The total number of parallel sentences amounts to 3,671,287. The development and test set was kept the exact same as the OPUS dataset (Tiedemann, 2012), which amount to 2000 sentences each, and the rest of the data was placed in the training set, which amounts to 3,667,287 parallel sentences.

Before training the system, the data has to be further pre-processed. Firstly, a BPE tokenizer is trained on the training set only. The MosesDecoder[13] package is used to pre-process the dataset, by normalising punctuation and training a true case on the training set and applying it to the whole dataset. In the case of Maltese data, a tokenizer specifically designed for Maltese was used because the regular English tokenizer does not tokenize everything correctly. For this, the tokenizer from MLRS[14] was used, which utilises regular expressions to tokenize linguistic expressions that are specific to Maltese, such as certain prefixes and articles. The dataset is then encoded using the previously trained BPE encoder.

The machine translation model is built and trained using Fairseq (Ott et al., 2019). Fairseq is a library that allows for easy implementation of a machine translation system through CLI commands, meaning minimal code is needed to create a fully working machine translation system.

For this system, a pre-trained mBART-50 model (Tang et al., 2020) was used and fine-tuned on our

[1]https://bit.ly/3dLbGX9
[2]https://bit.ly/3R2G5OH
[3]https://bit.ly/3QWIjPM

[4]https://bit.ly/3pBCg7u
[5]https://bit.ly/3AcjIzR
[6]https://bit.ly/3wmCyTD
[7]https://bit.ly/3wl3brZ
[8]https://www.lr-coordination.eu/node/2
[9]https://bit.ly/3cejoIU
[10]https://bit.ly/3AB01Tr
[11]https://bit.ly/3QDXmla
[12]https://legislation.mt/
[13]https://www.statmt.org/moses/
[14]https://mlrs.research.um.edu.mt/

data. An mBART-25 (Liu et al., 2020) model, as well as a randomly initialised baseline Transformer model, were also experimented with, however after training a system using a subset of the dataset, it was apparent that the mBART-50 model outperforms them both. Due to limited resource constraints, only one MT model was trained on the full dataset.

The maximum number of steps was set out to be 1,000,000, yet the validation was performed every 10,000 steps with a patience value of 10. This means that if the BLEU score on the validation set does not improve after ten validation steps, then the model stops training. After multiple experiments using a smaller subset of the dataset, it was seen that increasing max-tokens tended to result in higher overall performance. However, due to resource constraints, the maximum number of tokens per batch was set to 1024. The learning rate is set to $1e^{-3}$, but the initial learning rate is smaller at $1e^{-7}$ and increases using an inverse square root learning rate scheduler to linearly increase the rate after 10,000 steps. For inference, a beam size of five is used to generate predictions.

The total number of updates using mBART-50 was 990,000, with an early stop since the validation didn't improve in the last 10 validation epochs. This amounts to exactly three full epochs on the whole training set.

3.3 Completed Pipeline

To create a speech-to-text translation system, a Huggingface pipeline is set up to accept an audio file that is passed to the ASR system. The test set provided for this task is a single file of over one hour. Due to its size, the file needs to be segmented for inference and evaluation due to its size. The XLS-R model automatically returns a timestamp for each output word. These timestamps are used to create segments that align with the segments file provided with the test set.

This means that the ASR component returns a list of text strings. Each segment is an item in the list of strings. Each string is passed to the MT system. Before passing through the MT component, the resultant strings are pre-processed. The aforementioned MosesDecoder package is used to transform the strings using the same rules that have been applied to the MT training data. This means that the strings have their punctuation normalised, then true cased and finally tokenized. The processed strings are then passed to the mBART model to be inferred and the BPE model to encode the inputs. The beam size is set to five. The resulting tokens are then detokenized and saved.

4 Evaluation and Results

Table 4 contains the official results for our submission for the Maltese → English spoken language translation track. While we observed better scores during training and validation, our models struggled with the official test set. In this section, we note our few observations and qualitative analysis of results to highlight the errors.

The test set proved to be difficult for both the ASR and MT systems to get right due to the type of language used as well as the speed of the speech in general. Table 5 shows the reference transcription of the beginning of the file, accompanied by the MT Only and MT+All ASR transcription, and lastly, the machine translation of the mt-50 model. The monolingually fine-tuned MT Only model was our primary submission from the five submitted ASR models, with BLEU scores of 0.6.

The mt-50 output is relatively similar to the reference sentence, except for a few minor errors, including the misspelling of the name "Mark". However, this should still be a good sentence to input into the machine translation system. In stark contrast to the MT+All system outputs.

The main issue here is that this system does not output Maltese characters and completely omits them, which presents an issue for the downstream translation task since the meaning of the word is lost in these cases.

Machine translation also had similar issues. The training set contained data coming from legal texts, so the data is very formal, making it very difficult to evaluate since the input text is very informal and unlike the legal text data seen.

Unfortunately, most of this is unrelated to what

Table 4: Official Results for our models for Maltese → English SLT task

Submission Name	BLEU Score
MT Only	0.6
MT+All	0.7
MT+AR	0.4
MT+FR	0.3
MT+IT	0.4

Table 5: Reference transcription sample from the IWSLT 2023 test set along with the MT Only and MT+All automatic transcription and the machine translation of the MT Only output.

Reference	*merħba' għal- podcast ieħor din id- darba ma bniedem kemxejn polemikuż mhux għax jien għandi wisq xi ngħid però Mark Camilleri huwa il- mexxejj kemxejn kontroversjali tal- kunsill nazzjonali tal- ktieb*
MT Only	merba' l- pot kast ieħor din id- darba ma bniedem kemxejn polemikuż mhux għax jien għandi wisq xi ngħid però mar Camilleri huwa il- mexxejj kemxejn kontroversjali tal- kunsill nazzjonali tal- ktieb
MT+All	meba l Pold cast ieor din id-darba ma bniedem kemmxejn polemiku mhux gax jien Gandi wisq xi ngid per mar kamileri huwai - mexxejk emxejh kontroversjali tal- kunsill nazzjonali tal-ktieb
Translation MT Only	four of the other potential this time does not work very slightly at all , but not at all , the same time , it is the slightly cross- sectoral leader of the national when the book is also of humane

was actually said. Looking into the translations deeper, one can see the reasoning behind certain translations. For example, the dataset does not contain a lot of conversational data, so general greetings like "merħba" may not be present. This case is represented by the translation of the token "merba", which was translated to "four". Here the token "merba" (welcome) was mistaken for "erba" (four). Other mistakes include those that are phonetically plausible but grammatically incorrect output, such as the transcription for "podcast" which was transcribed as "pot kast". Certain expressions like "din id-darba" were correctly translated to "this time", however rarer words such as "polemikuż" and "kontroversjali", both of which have the same meaning as "controversial", seemed to not appear in the translation.

Continuing the trend observed in (Williams, 2022), the use of additional languages when fine-tuning an XLS-R model proved to be detrimental towards the final output. As observed in Section 4, some models trained with additional data lost the ability to transcribe Maltese-specific alphabetic characters. So far, the character-to-sound pair was always made with the source language in mind. For example, the French 'Ç' is transformed into the 'C' character, which itself is only present in the Maltese alphabet when English words are loaned and used directly. It's important to note that code-switching to English is very common in Maltese speech. Future work should explore these character-to-sound pairs.

5 Conclusion and Future Work

This paper showcased the results of a speech-to-text translation system in the direction of Maltese to English. A cascade system is chosen, where ASR and MT models are pipelined together.

The automatic speech recognition system chosen is based on XLS-R and is fine-tuned on data from different languages. The best-performing model was the XLS-R 300M model fine-tuned on 50 hours of Maltese speech. The machine translation system chosen is based on mBART-50, and it was fine-tuned on parallel Maltese - English data. Aside from fine-tuning, no modifications were made to the pre-trained models.

For future work, we have various potential avenues for improvement. For machine translation, since mBART-50 was not pre-trained on Maltese data, extending the vocabulary to include Maltese-specific tokens would improve the representation and potentially the downstream performance as well. Moreover, our approach solely relied on parallel data and did not investigate techniques which leverage monolingual data, such as back-translation. Monolingual corpora, such as Korpus Malti v4 (Micallef et al., 2022), not only provide significantly more data but also have more diversity in terms of domains. Apart from this, it might be beneficial to perform more quality checks on the parallel dataset since some portions of the publicly available datasets are automatically crawled and, in some cases, contain noise.

Regarding ASR improvement, other systems, such as Whisper and, most recently Meta's Massively Multilingual Speech (MMS) project should be tried and evaluated. The research made in multilingual fine-tuning needs to be more focused. One idea we can explore is the transliteration of foreign alphabetic characters into Maltese characters, e.g. 'h' in English would be transliterated as 'ħ'. It is also the case that no language model is used to correct the ASR output mistakes; this is currently our next milestone.

Acknowledgements

We acknowledge LT-Bridge Project (GA 952194). Rishu Kumar was supported financially by the EMLCT[15] programme during this entire work.

References

Milind Agarwal, Sweta Agrawal, Antonios Anastasopoulos, Ondřej Bojar, Claudia Borg, Marine Carpuat, Roldano Cattoni, Mauro Cettolo, Mingda Chen, William Chen, Khalid Choukri, Alexandra Chronopoulou, Anna Currey, Thierry Declerck, Qianqian Dong, Yannick Estève, Kevin Duh, Marcello Federico, Souhir Gahbiche, Barry Haddow, Benjamin Hsu, Phu Mon Htut, Hirofumi Inaguma, Dávid Javorský, John Judge, Yasumasa Kano, Tom Ko, Rishu Kumar, Pengwei Li, Xutail Ma, Prashant Mathur, Evgeny Matusov, Paul McNamee, John P. McCrae, Kenton Murray, Maria Nadejde, Satoshi Nakamura, Matteo Negri, Ha Nguyen, Jan Niehues, Xing Niu, Atul Ojha Kr., John E. Ortega, Proyag Pal, Juan Pino, Lonneke van der Plas, Peter Polák, Elijah Rippeth, Elizabeth Salesky, Jiatong Shi, Matthias Sperber, Sebastian Stüker, Katsuhito Sudoh, Yun Tang, Brian Thompson, Kevin Tran, Marco Turchi, Alex Waibel, Mingxuan Wang, Shinji Watanabe, and Rodolfo Zevallos. 2023. Findings of the IWSLT 2023 Evaluation Campaign. In *Proceedings of the 20th International Conference on Spoken Language Translation (IWSLT 2023)*. Association for Computational Linguistics.

Antonios Anastasopoulos, Loïc Barrault, Luisa Bentivogli, Marcely Zanon Boito, Ondřej Bojar, Roldano Cattoni, Anna Currey, Georgiana Dinu, Kevin Duh, Maha Elbayad, Clara Emmanuel, Yannick Estève, Marcello Federico, Christian Federmann, Souhir Gahbiche, Hongyu Gong, Roman Grundkiewicz, Barry Haddow, Benjamin Hsu, Dávid Javorský, Věra Kloudová, Surafel Lakew, Xutai Ma, Prashant Mathur, Paul McNamee, Kenton Murray, Maria Nădejde, Satoshi Nakamura, Matteo Negri, Jan Niehues, Xing Niu, John Ortega, Juan Pino, Elizabeth Salesky, Jiatong Shi, Matthias Sperber, Sebastian Stüker, Katsuhito Sudoh, Marco Turchi, Yogesh Virkar, Alexander Waibel, Changhan Wang, and Shinji Watanabe. 2022. Findings of the IWSLT 2022 Evaluation Campaign. In *Proceedings of the 19th International Conference on Spoken Language Translation (IWSLT 2022)*, pages 98–157, Dublin, Ireland (in-person and online). Association for Computational Linguistics.

[15]https://mundus-web.coli.uni-saarland.de/

Rosana Ardila, Megan Branson, Kelly Davis, Michael Kohler, Josh Meyer, Michael Henretty, Reuben Morais, Lindsay Saunders, Francis Tyers, and Gregor Weber. 2020. Common voice: A massively-multilingual speech corpus. In *Proceedings of the 12th Language Resources and Evaluation Conference*, pages 4218–4222, Marseille, France. European Language Resources Association.

Arun Babu, Changhan Wang, Andros Tjandra, Kushal Lakhotia, Qiantong Xu, Naman Goyal, Kritika Singh, Patrick von Platen, Yatharth Saraf, Juan Pino, Alexei Baevski, Alexis Conneau, and Michael Auli. 2021. XLS-R: self-supervised cross-lingual speech representation learning at scale. *CoRR*, abs/2111.09296.

Parnia Bahar, Patrick Wilken, Mattia A. Di Gangi, and Evgeny Matusov. 2021. Without Further Ado: Direct and Simultaneous Speech Translation by AppTek in 2021. In *Proceedings of the 18th International Conference on Spoken Language Translation (IWSLT 2021)*, pages 52–63, Bangkok, Thailand (online). Association for Computational Linguistics.

Marta Bañón, Miquel Esplà-Gomis, Mikel L. Forcada, Cristian García-Romero, Taja Kuzman, Nikola Ljubešić, Rik van Noord, Leopoldo Pla Sempere, Gema Ramírez-Sánchez, Peter Rupnik, Vít Suchomel, Antonio Toral, Tobias van der Werff, and Jaume Zaragoza. 2022. MaCoCu: Massive collection and curation of monolingual and bilingual data: focus on under-resourced languages. In *Proceedings of the 23rd Annual Conference of the European Association for Machine Translation*, pages 303–304, Ghent, Belgium. European Association for Machine Translation.

Alexis Conneau, Alexei Baevski, Ronan Collobert, Abdelrahman Mohamed, and Michael Auli. 2021. Unsupervised Cross-Lingual Representation Learning for Speech Recognition. In *Proc. Interspeech 2021*, pages 2426–2430.

Pavel Denisov, Manuel Mager, and Ngoc Thang Vu. 2021. IMS' Systems for the IWSLT 2021 Low-Resource Speech Translation Task. In *Proceedings of the 18th International Conference on Spoken Language Translation (IWSLT 2021)*, pages 175–181, Bangkok, Thailand (online). Association for Computational Linguistics.

Liang Ding and Dacheng Tao. 2021. The USYD-JD Speech Translation System for IWSLT2021. In *Proceedings of the 18th International Conference on Spoken Language Translation (IWSLT 2021)*, pages 182–191, Bangkok, Thailand (online). Association for Computational Linguistics.

Mark JF Gales, Kate M Knill, Anton Ragni, and Shakti P Rath. 2014. Speech recognition and keyword spotting for low-resource languages: Babel project research at cued. In *Fourth International workshop on spoken language technologies for under-resourced languages (SLTU-2014)*, pages 16–23. International Speech Communication Association (ISCA).

Nizar Habash, Nasser Zalmout, Dima Taji, Hieu Hoang, and Maverick Alzate. 2017. A parallel corpus for evaluating machine translation between arabic and european languages. In *Proceedings of the 15th Conference of the European Chapter of the Association for Computational Linguistics: Volume 2, Short Papers*, pages 235–241.

Najeh Hajlaoui, David Kolovratnik, Jaakko Väyrynen, Ralf Steinberger, and Daniel Varga. 2014. Dcep-digital corpus of the european parliament. In *Proceedings of the Ninth International Conference on Language Resources and Evaluation (LREC'14)*.

Michael A. Hedderich, Lukas Lange, Heike Adel, Jannik Strötgen, and Dietrich Klakow. 2021. A Survey on Recent Approaches for Natural Language Processing in Low-Resource Scenarios. In *Proceedings of the 2021 Conference of the North American Chapter of the Association for Computational Linguistics: Human Language Technologies*, pages 2545–2568, Online. Association for Computational Linguistics.

Carlos Daniel Hernandez Mena, Albert Gatt, Andrea DeMarco, Claudia Borg, Lonneke van der Plas, Amanda Muscat, and Ian Padovani. 2020. MASRI-HEADSET: A Maltese corpus for speech recognition. In *Proceedings of the 12th Language Resources and Evaluation Conference*, pages 6381–6388, Marseille, France. European Language Resources Association.

Diksha Khurana, Aditya Koli, Kiran Khatter, and Sukhdev Singh. 2023. Natural language processing: State of the art, current trends and challenges. *Multimedia tools and applications*, 82(3):3713–3744.

Mike Lewis, Yinhan Liu, Naman Goyal, Marjan Ghazvininejad, Abdelrahman Mohamed, Omer Levy, Ves Stoyanov, and Luke Zettlemoyer. 2019. Bart: Denoising sequence-to-sequence pre-training for natural language generation, translation, and comprehension. *arXiv preprint arXiv:1910.13461*.

Yinglu Li, Minghan Wang, Jiaxin Guo, Xiaosong Qiao, Yuxia Wang, Daimeng Wei, Chang Su, Yimeng Chen, Min Zhang, Shimin Tao, Hao Yang, and Ying Qin. 2022. The HW-TSC's Offline Speech Translation System for IWSLT 2022 Evaluation. In *Proceedings of the 19th International Conference on Spoken Language Translation (IWSLT 2022)*, pages 239–246, Dublin, Ireland (in-person and online). Association for Computational Linguistics.

Yinhan Liu, Jiatao Gu, Naman Goyal, Xian Li, Sergey Edunov, Marjan Ghazvininejad, Mike Lewis, and Luke Zettlemoyer. 2020. Multilingual denoising pre-training for neural machine translation.

Alexandre Magueresse, Vincent Carles, and Evan Heetderks. 2020. Low-resource languages: A review of past work and future challenges. *arXiv preprint arXiv:2006.07264*.

Carlos Daniel Hernandez Mena, Andrea DeMarco, Claudia Borg, Lonneke van der Plas, and Albert Gatt. 2021. Data augmentation for speech recognition in maltese: A low-resource perspective. *CoRR*, abs/2111.07793.

Kurt Micallef, Albert Gatt, Marc Tanti, Lonneke van der Plas, and Claudia Borg. 2022. Pre-training data quality and quantity for a low-resource language: New corpus and BERT models for Maltese. In *Proceedings of the Third Workshop on Deep Learning for Low-Resource Natural Language Processing*, pages 90–101, Hybrid. Association for Computational Linguistics.

Tuan Nam Nguyen, Thai Son Nguyen, Christian Huber, Ngoc-Quan Pham, Thanh-Le Ha, Felix Schneider, and Sebastian Stüker. 2021. KIT's IWSLT 2021 Offline Speech Translation System. In *Proceedings of the 18th International Conference on Spoken Language Translation (IWSLT 2021)*, pages 125–130, Bangkok, Thailand (online). Association for Computational Linguistics.

Myle Ott, Sergey Edunov, Alexei Baevski, Angela Fan, Sam Gross, Nathan Ng, David Grangier, and Michael Auli. 2019. fairseq: A fast, extensible toolkit for sequence modeling. In *Proceedings of NAACL-HLT 2019: Demonstrations*.

Vineel Pratap, Qiantong Xu, Anuroop Sriram, Gabriel Synnaeve, and Ronan Collobert. 2020. MLS: A Large-Scale Multilingual Dataset for Speech Research. In *Proc. Interspeech 2020*, pages 2757–2761.

Xipeng Qiu, Tianxiang Sun, Yige Xu, Yunfan Shao, Ning Dai, and Xuanjing Huang. 2020. Pre-trained models for natural language processing: A survey. *Science China Technological Sciences*, 63(10):1872–1897.

Ralf Steinberger, Mohamed Ebrahim, Alexandros Poulis, Manuel Carrasco-Benitez, Patrick Schlüter, Marek Przybyszewski, and Signe Gilbro. 2014. An overview of the european union's highly multilingual parallel corpora. *Language resources and evaluation*, 48(4):679–707.

Yuqing Tang, Chau Tran, Xian Li, Peng-Jen Chen, Naman Goyal, Vishrav Chaudhary, Jiatao Gu, and Angela Fan. 2020. Multilingual translation with extensible multilingual pretraining and finetuning. *arXiv preprint arXiv:2008.00401*.

Jörg Tiedemann. 2012. Parallel data, tools and interfaces in opus. In *Proceedings of the Eight International Conference on Language Resources and Evaluation (LREC'12)*, Istanbul, Turkey. European Language Resources Association (ELRA).

Jörgen Valk and Tanel Alumäe. 2021. Voxlingua107: A dataset for spoken language recognition. In *2021 IEEE Spoken Language Technology Workshop (SLT)*, pages 652–658.

Changhan Wang, Morgane Riviere, Ann Lee, Anne Wu, Chaitanya Talnikar, Daniel Haziza, Mary Williamson,

Juan Pino, and Emmanuel Dupoux. 2021. VoxPopuli: A large-scale multilingual speech corpus for representation learning, semi-supervised learning and interpretation. In *Proceedings of the 59th Annual Meeting of the Association for Computational Linguistics and the 11th International Joint Conference on Natural Language Processing (Volume 1: Long Papers)*, pages 993–1003, Online. Association for Computational Linguistics.

Aiden Williams. 2022. The applicability of Wav2Vec 2.0 for low-resource Maltese ASR. B.S. thesis, University of Malta.

Marcely Zanon Boito, John Ortega, Hugo Riguidel, Antoine Laurent, Loïc Barrault, Fethi Bougares, Firas Chaabani, Ha Nguyen, Florentin Barbier, Souhir Gahbiche, and Yannick Estève. 2022. ON-TRAC Consortium Systems for the IWSLT 2022 Dialect and Low-resource Speech Translation Tasks. In *Proceedings of the 19th International Conference on Spoken Language Translation (IWSLT 2022)*, pages 308–318, Dublin, Ireland (in-person and online). Association for Computational Linguistics.

Weitai Zhang, Zhongyi Ye, Haitao Tang, Xiaoxi Li, Xinyuan Zhou, Jing Yang, Jianwei Cui, Pan Deng, Mohan Shi, Yifan Song, Dan Liu, Junhua Liu, and Lirong Dai. 2022. The USTC-NELSLIP Offline Speech Translation Systems for IWSLT 2022. In *Proceedings of the 19th International Conference on Spoken Language Translation (IWSLT 2022)*, pages 198–207, Dublin, Ireland (in-person and online). Association for Computational Linguistics.

Ziqiang Zhang and Junyi Ao. 2022. The YiTrans Speech Translation System for IWSLT 2022 Offline Shared Task. In *Proceedings of the 19th International Conference on Spoken Language Translation (IWSLT 2022)*, pages 158–168, Dublin, Ireland (in-person and online). Association for Computational Linguistics.

NVIDIA NeMo Offline Speech Translation Systems for IWSLT 2023

Oleksii Hrinchuk[*1], **Vladimir Bataev**[1,2], **Evelina Bakhturina**[1], **Boris Ginsburg**[1]
[1]NVIDIA, Santa Clara, CA [2]University of London, London, UK

Abstract

This paper provides an overview of NVIDIA NeMo's speech translation systems for the IWSLT 2023 Offline Speech Translation Task. This year, we focused on end-to-end system which capitalizes on pre-trained models and synthetic data to mitigate the problem of direct speech translation data scarcity. When trained on IWSLT 2022 constrained data, our best En→De end-to-end model achieves the average score of 31 BLEU on 7 test sets from IWSLT 2010-2020 which improves over our last year cascade (28.4) and end-to-end (25.7) submissions. When trained on IWSLT 2023 constrained data, the average score drops to 29.5 BLEU.

1 Introduction

We participate in the IWSLT 2023 Offline Speech Translation Task (Agarwal et al., 2023) for English→German, English→Chinese, and English→Japanese. This year, we focus on an end-to-end model, which directly translates English audio into text in other languages.

In contrast to automatic speech recognition (ASR) and text-to-text neural machine translation (NMT), the data for direct speech translation (ST) is scarce and expensive. Thus, to train a high-quality end-to-end ST model, we heavily rely on a number of auxiliary models for which the amount of available data is enough. Specifically, we train the following models:

- ASR model with FastConformer-RNNT (Rekesh et al., 2023) architecture trained on all allowed data.
- NMT model with Transformer encoder-decoder architecture trained on all allowed bitext and in-domain fine-tuned on TED talks.
- Text-to-speech (TTS) model with FastPitch (Łańcucki, 2021) architecture trained on the English transcripts of TED talks.
- Supervised Hybrid Audio Segmentation (SHAS) model (Tsiamas et al., 2022) trained on TED talks.

Our constrained end-to-end ST model consists of a FastConformer encoder and a Transformer decoder. We initialize the encoder with the corresponding component from ASR and train our ST model on a mix of speech-to-text and text-to-text data. We replace all ground truth translations (wherever available) with synthetic ones generated with the NMT model and voice the English portion of parallel text corpora with TTS.

Our systems will be open-sourced as part of NVIDIA NeMo[1] framework (Kuchaiev et al., 2019).

2 Data

In this section, we describe the datasets used for training (Table 1). For evaluation, we used the development sets of Must-C v2 (Cattoni et al., 2021), as well as the test sets from past IWSLT competitions. We noticed that development data had a large overlap with training data, mostly because of the usage of the same TED talks in different datasets. Thus, we discarded all samples with overlapping transcripts and talk ids.

TED talks In the list of allowed data, there are several datasets comprised of TED talks, namely Must-C v1-v3, ST-TED (Jan et al., 2018), and TED-LIUM v3 (Hernandez et al., 2018) which have significant data overlap. After combining them together and doing deduplication, we ended up with the dataset of 370K unique samples (611 hours of English audio) we used for in-domain fine-tuning of various models. Further in the text, we refer to

*Correspondence to: ohrinchuk@nvidia.com

[1]https://github.com/NVIDIA/NeMo

Proceedings of the 20th International Conference on Spoken Language Translation (IWSLT 2023), pages 442–448
July 13-14, 2023 ©2023 Association for Computational Linguistics

Table 1: Statistics of different datasets used for training our models in a `constrained` regime.

Model	Segments (millions)	Time (hours)
ASR	2.7	4800
NMT En→De	11	–
NMT En→Zh	7.5	–
NMT En→Ja	21	–
TTS	0.37	611

this dataset and its subsets with available translations to De/Zh/Ja as **TED talks**. See Table 2 for the detailed statistics of this dataset.

ASR For training our ASR model, we used LibriSpeech (Panayotov et al., 2015), Mozilla Common Voice v11.0 (Ardila et al., 2019), TED-LIUM v3 (Hernandez et al., 2018), VoxPopuli v2 (Wang et al., 2021), all available speech-to-English data from Must-C v1-v3 (Cattoni et al., 2021) En-De/Zh/Ja datasets, ST-TED (Jan et al., 2018), and Europarl-ST (Iranzo-Sánchez et al., 2020).

We converted all audio data to mono-channel 16kHz wav format. Of all the datasets allowed under the constrained submission, LibriSpeech and TED-LIUM v3 were the only datasets that provided transcripts with neither punctuation nor capitalization (P&C). For LibriSpeech, we managed to restore P&C from the dataset metadata available at their website[2]. For TED-LIUM v3, we applied P&C restoration model trained on the English portion of allowed bitext. Finally, we discarded all samples shorter than 0.2s and longer than 22s and all samples with transcripts present in the evaluation dataset. As a result, our training dataset contained 2.7M audio segments with a total duration of 4.8k hours.

MT For training our NMT models, we used all available bitext allowed for IWSLT 2023 constrained submission. After training, we additionally fine-tuned our models on bitexts from TED talks for each language.

We applied `langid` and `bicleaner` filtering following Subramanian et al. (2021) and discarded all sentences longer than 128 tokens and sentences with the length ratio between source and target exceeding 3. We also applied Moses tokenization for En/De, jieba tokenization for Zh, and ja-mecab tokenization for Ja.

[2]https://www.openslr.org/12

Table 2: Statistics of TED talks dataset.

Model	Segments (thousands)	Time (hours)
En audio → En text	370	611
En audio → De text	280	459
En audio → Zh text	350	580
En audio → Ja text	321	528

TTS For training our TTS model, we used TED talks with English transcripts. The combination of Must-C v1-v3 and ST-TED contained 3696 speakers, however, some of them were not unique. Capitalizing on the huge overlap with TED-LIUM v3 and the speaker names from there, we managed to attribute several talks to a single speaker reducing the number of unique speakers to 3361. We also removed capitalization from English transcripts in TED talks.

ST For training our end-to-end ST models, we used the combination of 1) ASR data with the ground truth transcripts replaced by synthetic translations; 2) NMT data with TTS-generated English audios on source side (Table 1).

3 System

In this section, we describe the essential components of our end-to-end submission.

ASR We trained 17-layer large conformer-transducer (Gulati et al., 2020) with FastConformer (Rekesh et al., 2023) encoder and RNN-T loss and decoder (Graves, 2012). The prediction network consisted of a single layer of LSTM (Hochreiter and Schmidhuber, 1997), and the joint network is an MLP. All the hidden sizes in the decoder were set to 640. Unigram SentencePiece (Kudo and Richardson, 2018) with 1024 tokens was used for tokenization.

The ASR models were trained for 45 epochs, starting with a checkpoint pre-trained on LibriSpeech. We used AdamW (Loshchilov and Hutter, 2017) optimizer and Noam Annealing (Vaswani et al., 2017) with 10K warmup steps and a maximum learning rate of 1.15. Weight decay of 0.001 on all parameters was used for regularization. The effective batch size was set to 1200, and we could fit larger batch sizes via batch splitting for the RNN-T loss. Time-Adaptive SpecAugment (Park et al., 2020) with 2 freq masks ($F = 27$) and 10 time masks ($T = 5\%$) was used as the augmentation scheme. We also used dropout of 0.1 for both the attention scores and intermediate activations.

NMT We trained our NMT models (Transformer, 12×6 layers, $d_{\text{model}} = 1024$, $d_{\text{inner}} = 4096$, $n_{\text{heads}} = 16$) with Adam optimizer (Kingma and Ba, 2014) and inverse square root annealing (Vaswani et al., 2017) with 7.5K warmup steps and a maximum learning rate of 10^{-3}. The models were trained for a maximum of 75K steps with a dropout of 0.1 on intermediate activations and label smoothing with $\alpha = 0.1$. Our En→De models used joint BPE vocabulary of 16384 tokens and En→Zh/Ja used separate vocabularies with the same number of tokens per language.

After training, we did checkpoint averaging and fine-tuned all our base NMT models on TED talks for 3 epochs with an initial learning rate of 2×10^{-5}, inverse square root annealing, and a warmup of 10% steps. Finally, we ensembled 2 models trained with different initializations for each language direction.

TTS Our TTS model was multi-speaker FastPitch (Łańcucki, 2021) text-to-mel-spectrogram generator. Training vocoder was not necessary for our setup as the parameters of spectrograms matched ones for ST models following the approach described in (Bataev et al., 2023). TTS-generated spectrograms were fed directly into the FastConformer encoder when training the ST model. Our TTS model was trained for 200 epochs on TED talks with restored speakers from TED-LIUM v3 (Hernandez et al., 2018).

Segmentation We used Supervised Hybrid Audio Segmentation (SHAS) approach following Tsiamas et al. (2022). As using speech representation pre-trained wav2vec 2.0 (Baevski et al., 2020) goes beyond the scope of `constrained` submission, we replaced it with Conformer ASR encoder, pre-trained on LibriSpeech.

ST Our end-to-end model consisted of FastConformer encoder followed by Transformer trained on pairs of English audio and transcripts in other languages (17-layer FastConformer encoder, 6×6 Transformer, both with $d_{\text{model}} = 512$, $d_{\text{inner}} = 2048$, $n_{\text{heads}} = 8$). We used the vocabulary of 16384 YouTokenToMe[3] byte-pair-encodings, trained jointly for En→De and separately for En→Zh/Ja. All models were trained for 30k steps with ASR-initialized encoder and randomly initialized decoder.

Table 3: Word error rate (WER) of the English ASR model evaluated on TED talks from Must-C v2 and past test sets from IWSLT. All predictions and ground truths transcripts were normalized for WER computation.

Model	tst-COM		IWSLT.tst		
	De	Zh/Ja	2018	2019	2020
norm	5.9	5.8	9.8	5.6	8.0
punct	5.7	5.4	9.4	4.9	7.0
punct+capit	5.7	5.5	9.5	5.7	8.5

To speed up training and improve GPU utilization, we bucketed our ASR and NMT datasets on sequence length so each batch contained a similar number of tokens. On each iteration, we pick one batch from ASR and one batch which resulted in approximately 3:2 ratio between segments from ASR and NMT for En→De. TTS mel spectrograms were generated on-the-fly for a randomly selected speaker for each sample.

After pretraining on the ASR task, we fused BatchNorm in FastConformer layers as proposed in (Bataev et al., 2023) to avoid a mismatch between statistics for natural and generated mel spectrograms. The batch normalization layer was replaced with a trainable projection initialized from the original parameters. We observed meaningful improvements when using such an approach compared to retaining the original batch normalization.

4 Experiments

4.1 Results

ASR Table 3 shows word error rate (WER) of our ASR models on different evaluation datasets. We trained 3 models which differed by the format of transcripts: normalized (`norm`), with punctuation only (`punct`), with punctuation and capitalization (`punct+capit`).

All models exhibited similar results, with `punct` being slightly better on all evaluation datasets. However, in our further experiments of training end-to-end ST with an ASR-initialized en-

[3]https://github.com/VKCOM/YouTokenToMe

Table 4: En→De BLEU scores calculated on IWSLT test sets from different years by using automatic re-segmentation of the hypothesis based on the reference translation by `mwerSegmenter` implemented in SLTev (Ansari et al., 2021). Avg Δ computes the improvement over the cascade baseline averaged over 7 test sets.

Model description	2010	2013	2014	2015	2018	2019	2020	Avg
				Text-to-text NMT models				
Transformer 12 × 6 `constrained`	32.9	36.7	32.7	34.2	30.5	29.4	33.0	32.8
+ checkpoint averaging	33.1	37.4	32.8	35.1	30.3	29.8	33.5	33.1
+ TED talks fine-tuning	34.5	39.1	34.1	35.3	30.8	30.3	33.8	34.0
+ x2 ensembling	35.2	40.2	34.9	36.0	32.5	31.6	35.4	35.1
NeMo IWSLT'22 NMT model	35.7	41.2	36.2	38.1	34.7	31.7	35.0	36.1
				End-to-end ST models				
Conformer (17) + Transformer (6 × 6)	29.8	33.8	30.2	27.1	26.2	26.8	29.1	29.0
+ better WebRTC VAD parameters	31.2	35.4	31.8	28.6	27.3	27.6	29.7	30.2
+ SHAS segmentation	32.1	36.1	32.6	29.0	28.4	27.9	30.9	31.0
NeMo IWSLT 2023 `constrained`	31.0	34.9	30.7	28.6	27.4	27.7	30.3	29.5
NeMo IWSLT 2022 (end-to-end)	24.5	30.0	25.2	25.3	24.9	24.1	26.2	25.7
NeMo IWSLT 2022 (cascade)	26.6	32.2	26.8	28.3	28.1	27.3	29.7	28.4
KIT IWSLT 2022	–	–	–	27.9	–	27.6	30.0	–
USTC-NELSLIP IWSLT 2022	–	–	–	–	29.9	28.2	30.6	–
YiTrans IWSLT 2022	–	–	–	–	–	31.6	34.1	–

coder, we did not notice a significant difference in the corresponding BLEU scores.

ST En→De Table 4 shows the performance of our baseline En→De system and its ablations on 7 different IWSLT test sets over the years. All ablation experiments used the last year's constrained setup that included more NMT data from WMT to be comparable with the last year submissions. The systems we submit were retrained on the allowed data to comply with `constrained` restrictions.

We improve the average BLEU score by 5.3 over our last year end-to-end submission. We believe that such gain is attributed to several factors, most importantly, switching to synthetic transcripts, including TTS-generated data, and a better segmentation model. On some of the evaluation datasets, we approached the BLEU scores of top contestants from last year.

Retraining our model in accordance with this year `constrained` setup resulted in the average degradation of 1.5 BLEU. Most of this performance drop was attributed to worse NMT models trained on limited amount of data which did not include large bitexts from WMT.

ST En→Zh/Ja To train English-Chinese and English-Japanese ST systems, we followed a similar recipe to the English-German system. Specifically, we re-trained NMT components and used them to generate synthetic translations of audio segments. With other auxiliary models intact, we replaced bitexts used for TTS augmentations and trained En→Zh (Table 5) and En→Ja (Table 6) ST end-to-end models in a `constrained` setup.

The only difference in our submission was that the English-Chinese model used `punct+capit` ASR, while the English-Japanese model used `norm` ASR. This choice was based on a slightly higher (less than 0.5) BLEU score on Must-C v2 dev dataset.

4.2 Discarded alternatives

When designing our submission, we explored a number of alternatives that did not lead to a clear improvement in preliminary experiments and, thus, were not included in the final submission.

ASR We tried to replace BatchNorm with LayerNorm in the FastConformer backbone to mitigate the statistics mismatch between natural and TTS-generated mel-spectrograms. The resulting model

Table 5: En→Zh BLEU scores calculated on Must-C `dev` and `tst-COMMON` with official segmentation.

Model description	dev	tst-COM
Text-to-text NMT models		
Transformer 12 × 6	22.9	26.4
+ ckpt avg	23.0	26.4
+ TED talks fine-tuning	24.7	28.0
+ x2 ensembling	25.5	28.9
End-to-end ST models		
NeMo IWSLT 2023	23.9	27.5
USTC-NELSLIP IWSLT'22	–	28.7
YiTrans IWSLT'22	–	29.3

Table 6: En→Ja BLEU scores calculated on Must-C `dev` and `tst-COMMON` with official segmentation.

Model description	dev	tst-COM
Text-to-text NMT models		
Transformer 12 × 6	12.8	15.5
+ ckpt avg	13.3	16.2
+ TED talks fine-tuning	14.7	18.5
+ x2 ensembling	15.0	19.2
End-to-end ST models		
NeMo IWSLT 2023	14.5	18.3
USTC-NELSLIP IWSLT'22	–	18.2
YiTrans IWSLT'22	–	19.1

required more epochs to converge and resulted in slightly higher WER.

NMT We experimented with larger models of up to 12 × 8 layers, larger vocabularies of up to 32k tokens, and label smoothing of up to 0.2 but did not notice any improvements to BLEU scores. We also saw diminishing returns when using more than 2 models in the ensemble. Thus, we decided to stick to the ensemble of two 12 × 6 models with 16k vocab to speed up synthetic data generation.

TTS While debugging the code, we noticed that TTS model generating mel-spectrograms used the same single speaker and had dropout enabled. Surprisingly, it did not lead to performance degradation. We hypothesize that this was caused by using well converged pre-trained ASR encoder, which was not altered significantly by the low-quality signal. We also experimented with improving generated spectrograms with GAN enhancer following Bataev et al. (2023), which led to similar results at the cost of significant computation overhead.

Segmentation We experimented with voice activity detection implemented in `WebRTC`[4] toolkit, however, the BLEU scores on IWSLT test sets were lower even after extensive hyperparameter search.

ST Given the effectiveness of ensembling in last year's competition, we evaluated the performance of an ensemble of up to 3 models with different ASR encoder initializations. Unlike NMT, we did not observe any improvement in using the best model from the ensemble.

[4]https://github.com/wiseman/py-webrtcvad

We experimented with using RNN-T instead of the Transformer decoder. Despite its remarkable performance in ASR, RNN-T converged much slower and underperformed our Transformer decoder by more than 2 BLEU in our ST model.

5 Conclusion

We present NVIDIA NeMo group's offline speech translation systems for En→De, En→Zh, and En→Ja IWSLT 2023 Tasks.

Our *primary* end-to-end models that translate English speech directly into German, Chinese, and Japanese texts, consist of FastConformer encoder and Transformer decoder. To alleviate the problem of direct ST data scarcity, we capitalized on a number of auxiliary ASR, TTS, and NMT models, and their ability to generate hiqh-quality audio and translations. The resulting models achieve competitive performance without using any amount of direct ST data.

Although we participated in `constrained` scenario, our pipeline can be easily scaled to arbitrarily large amounts of ASR and NMT data.

Acknowledgments

The authors would like to thank Somshubra Majumdar for many useful discussions over the course of this project and Nithin Koluguri for help with training ASR models.

References

Milind Agarwal, Sweta Agrawal, Antonios Anastasopoulos, Ondřej Bojar, Claudia Borg, Marine Carpuat, Roldano Cattoni, Mauro Cettolo, Mingda

Chen, William Chen, Khalid Choukri, Alexandra Chronopoulou, Anna Currey, Thierry Declerck, Qianqian Dong, Yannick Estève, Kevin Duh, Marcello Federico, Souhir Gahbiche, Barry Haddow, Benjamin Hsu, Phu Mon Htut, Hirofumi Inaguma, Dávid Javorský, John Judge, Yasumasa Kano, Tom Ko, Rishu Kumar, Pengwei Li, Xutail Ma, Prashant Mathur, Evgeny Matusov, Paul McNamee, John P. McCrae, Kenton Murray, Maria Nadejde, Satoshi Nakamura, Matteo Negri, Ha Nguyen, Jan Niehues, Xing Niu, Atul Ojha Kr., John E. Ortega, Proyag Pal, Juan Pino, Lonneke van der Plas, Peter Polák, Elijah Rippeth, Elizabeth Salesky, Jiatong Shi, Matthias Sperber, Sebastian Stüker, Katsuhito Sudoh, Yun Tang, Brian Thompson, Kevin Tran, Marco Turchi, Alex Waibel, Mingxuan Wang, Shinji Watanabe, and Rodolfo Zevallos. 2023. Findings of the IWSLT 2023 Evaluation Campaign. In *Proceedings of the 20th International Conference on Spoken Language Translation (IWSLT 2023)*. Association for Computational Linguistics.

Ebrahim Ansari, Ondřej Bojar, Barry Haddow, and Mohammad Mahmoudi. 2021. SLTEV: Comprehensive evaluation of spoken language translation. In *Proceedings of the 16th Conference of the European Chapter of the Association for Computational Linguistics: System Demonstrations*, pages 71–79, Online. Association for Computational Linguistics.

Rosana Ardila, Megan Branson, Kelly Davis, Michael Henretty, Michael Kohler, Josh Meyer, Reuben Morais, Lindsay Saunders, Francis M Tyers, and Gregor Weber. 2019. Common voice: A massively-multilingual speech corpus. *arXiv preprint arXiv:1912.06670*.

Alexei Baevski, Yuhao Zhou, Abdelrahman Mohamed, and Michael Auli. 2020. wav2vec 2.0: A framework for self-supervised learning of speech representations. *Advances in neural information processing systems*, 33:12449–12460.

Vladimir Bataev, Roman Korostik, Evgeny Shabalin, Vitaly Lavrukhin, and Boris Ginsburg. 2023. Text-only domain adaptation for end-to-end asr using integrated text-to-mel-spectrogram generator. *ArXiv*, abs/2302.14036.

Roldano Cattoni, Mattia Antonino Di Gangi, Luisa Bentivogli, Matteo Negri, and Marco Turchi. 2021. Must-c: A multilingual corpus for end-to-end speech translation. *Computer Speech & Language*, 66:101155.

Alex Graves. 2012. Sequence transduction with recurrent neural networks. *arXiv preprint arXiv:1211.3711*.

Anmol Gulati, James Qin, Chung-Cheng Chiu, Niki Parmar, Yu Zhang, Jiahui Yu, Wei Han, Shibo Wang, Zhengdong Zhang, Yonghui Wu, and Ruoming Pang. 2020. Conformer: Convolution-augmented Transformer for speech recognition. In *Proceedings of Interspeech*, pages 5036–5040.

François Hernandez, Vincent Nguyen, Sahar Ghannay, Natalia Tomashenko, and Yannick Esteve. 2018. Tedlium 3: twice as much data and corpus repartition for experiments on speaker adaptation. In *International conference on speech and computer*, pages 198–208. Springer.

Sepp Hochreiter and Jürgen Schmidhuber. 1997. Long short-term memory. *Neural computation*, 9(8):1735–1780.

Javier Iranzo-Sánchez, Joan Albert Silvestre-Cerda, Javier Jorge, Nahuel Roselló, Adria Giménez, Albert Sanchis, Jorge Civera, and Alfons Juan. 2020. Europarl-st: A multilingual corpus for speech translation of parliamentary debates. In *ICASSP 2020-2020 IEEE International Conference on Acoustics, Speech and Signal Processing (ICASSP)*, pages 8229–8233. IEEE.

Niehues Jan, Roldano Cattoni, Stüker Sebastian, Mauro Cettolo, Marco Turchi, and Marcello Federico. 2018. The iwslt 2018 evaluation campaign. In *Proceedings of IWSLT*, pages 2–6.

Diederik Kingma and Jimmy Ba. 2014. Adam: A method for stochastic optimization. *arXiv preprint arXiv:1412.6980*.

Oleksii Kuchaiev, Jason Li, Huyen Nguyen, Oleksii Hrinchuk, Ryan Leary, Boris Ginsburg, Samuel Kriman, Stanislav Beliaev, Vitaly Lavrukhin, Jack Cook, et al. 2019. Nemo: a toolkit for building ai applications using neural modules. *arXiv preprint arXiv:1909.09577*.

Taku Kudo and John Richardson. 2018. Sentencepiece: A simple and language independent subword tokenizer and detokenizer for neural text processing. *arXiv preprint arXiv:1808.06226*.

Adrian Łańcucki. 2021. FastPitch: Parallel text-to-speech with pitch prediction. In *ICASSP*.

Ilya Loshchilov and Frank Hutter. 2017. Decoupled weight decay regularization. *arXiv preprint arXiv:1711.05101*.

Vassil Panayotov, Guoguo Chen, Daniel Povey, and Sanjeev Khudanpur. 2015. Librispeech: an ASR corpus based on public domain audio books. In *Proceedings of ICASSP*, pages 5206–5210. IEEE.

Daniel S Park, Yu Zhang, Chung-Cheng Chiu, Youzheng Chen, Bo Li, William Chan, Quoc V Le, and Yonghui Wu. 2020. Specaugment on large scale datasets. In *ICASSP 2020-2020 IEEE International Conference on Acoustics, Speech and Signal Processing (ICASSP)*, pages 6879–6883. IEEE.

Dima Rekesh, Samuel Kriman, Somshubra Majumdar, Vahid Noroozi, He Juang, Oleksii Hrinchuk, Ankur Kumar, and Boris Ginsburg. 2023. Fast conformer with linearly scalable attention for efficient speech recognition. *arXiv preprint arXiv:2305.05084*.

Sandeep Subramanian, Oleksii Hrinchuk, Virginia Adams, and Oleksii Kuchaiev. 2021. Nvidia nemo neural machine translation systems for english-german and english-russian news and biomedical tasks at wmt21. *arXiv preprint arXiv:2111.08634*.

Ioannis Tsiamas, Gerard I Gállego, José AR Fonollosa, and Marta R Costa-jussà. 2022. Shas: Approaching optimal segmentation for end-to-end speech translation. *arXiv preprint arXiv:2202.04774*.

Ashish Vaswani, Noam Shazeer, Niki Parmar, Jakob Uszkoreit, Llion Jones, Aidan N Gomez, Łukasz Kaiser, and Illia Polosukhin. 2017. Attention is all you need. In *Proceedings of NeurIPS*, pages 5998–6008.

Changhan Wang, Morgane Riviere, Ann Lee, Anne Wu, Chaitanya Talnikar, Daniel Haziza, Mary Williamson, Juan Pino, and Emmanuel Dupoux. 2021. Voxpopuli: A large-scale multilingual speech corpus for representation learning, semi-supervised learning and interpretation. *arXiv preprint arXiv:2101.00390*.

SRI-B's systems for IWSLT 2023 Dialectal and Low-resource track: Marathi-Hindi Speech Translation

Balaji Radhakrishnan, Saurabh Agrawal, Raj Prakash Gohil, Kiran Praveen, Advait Vinay Dhopeshwarkar, Abhishek Pandey
Samsung R&D Institute,Bangalore
{balaji.r, saurabh.a, raj.gohil, k.praveen.t, a.dhopeshwar, abhi3.pandey}@samsung.com

Abstract

This paper describes the speech translation systems SRI-B developed for the IWSLT 2023 Evaluation Campaign Dialectal and Low-resource track: Marathi-Hindi Speech Translation. We propose systems for both the constrained (systems are trained only on the datasets provided by the organizers) and the unconstrained conditions (systems can be trained with any resource). For both the conditions, we build end-to-end speech translation networks comprising of a conformer encoder and a transformer decoder. Under both the conditions, we leverage Marathi Automatic Speech Recognition (ASR) data to pre-train the encoder and subsequently train the entire model on the speech translation data. Our results demonstrate that pre-training the encoder with ASR data is a key step in significantly improving the speech translation performance. We also show that conformer encoders are inherently superior to its transformer counterparts for speech translation tasks. Our primary submissions achieved a BLEU% score of 31.2 on the constrained condition and 32.4 on the unconstrained condition. We secured the top position in the constrained condition and second position in the unconstrained condition.

1 Introduction

Speech translation (ST) is the task of automatically translating a speech signal in a given language into text in another language. While rapid strides have been made in speech translation in recent times, this progress has been restricted to a small number of high resource languages. This progress excludes sizable sections of people who speak languages that have very little speech data available. So, for these speech systems to be beneficial and impactful in the real world, they have to be developed and shown to work on low-resource languages as well.

In order to mitigate these issues and encourage research on low-resource languages, IWSLT propose a dialectal and low-resource speech translation track (Agarwal et al., 2023) as a part of their 2023 shared tasks evaluation campaign. While this track includes various low resource languages, we focus our efforts on the Marathi-Hindi language pair. The goal of this task is to translate Marathi speech to it's corresponding Hindi text. Marathi and Hindi are both Indo-Aryan languages used in India. Even though there were 83 million people across India speaking Marathi as per the 2011 census of India, it lacks sufficient speech data to support modern speech translation systems.

This paper discusses our work and submissions on the Marathi-Hindi low-resource speech translation task. Our experiments in this paper focus only on end-to-end architectures. We begin our experiments with a simple end-to-end Transformer and build on this approach with the following key contributions that significantly better our final performance:

- Encoder pre-training with Marathi ASR data.
- Replacing the Transformer encoder blocks with Conformer encoder blocks.
- Utilizing the dev split during speech translation training for the final submissions.

2 Related work

Traditionally, speech translation was performed using cascaded systems (Ney, 1999) (Casacuberta et al., 2008) (Post et al., 2013) (Kumar et al., 2014) of ASR and Machine Translation (MT) models. In this approach, speech was first transcribed using an ASR model and then the transcriptions were translated to text in the target language with the help of a MT model. This approach however possessed several key drawbacks like error propagation, increased latency, and architectural complexity due to multiple models.

The first attempt towards building an end-to-end speech translation system was by (Bérard et al., 2016), where they built a system that eliminated

Proceedings of the 20th International Conference on Spoken Language Translation (IWSLT 2023), pages 449–454
July 13-14, 2023 ©2023 Association for Computational Linguistics

Type	#Utterances	Hours
train	7990	15.53
dev	2103	3.39
test	2164	4.26

Table 1: Details of speech translation (ST) data.

the need for source language transcriptions. Similarly, (Weiss et al., 2017) proposed an attention based encoder-decoder architecture for end-to-end speech translation that exhibited improved performance over cascaded systems. (Bentivogli et al., 2021) perform a detailed comparison between the paradigms of cascaded and end-to-end speech translation.

Developing speech translation systems for low-resource scenarios are especially challenging given the scarcity of training data. Speech translation systems submitted in IWSLT 2019 (Niehues et al., 2019) tended to prefer cascaded approaches for low-resource tracks. The cascaded approach which was favoured in (Le et al., 2021), used a hybrid ASR system with wav2vec features followed by a MT model for two low-resource language pairs. Recently, as system trained with joint optimization of ASR, MT and ST (Anastasopoulos et al., 2022) exhibited good performance. Also, usage of self-supervised learning based pre-trained models such as XLR-S (Babu et al., 2021) and mBART (Tang et al., 2020) have been shown to be effective, especially for low-resource scenarios.

3 Data description

The challenge data consists of Marathi speech to Hindi text translation data from the news domain for the model training and development which we shall henceforth refer to as ST (speech translation) data. The details of this dataset has been mentioned in Table 1. This dataset was directly shared with all the participants involved. Development *(dev)* and test *(test)* sets were also provided for assessing the model performance. Hindi text labels for the test set were kept blind for all the participants.

The organizers shared additional Marathi audio data along with its transcripts which can be used for the constrained condition, the details of which have been mentioned in Table 2. Common Voice (Ardila et al., 2019) is a publicly available multi-language dataset prepared using crowd-sourcing. OpenSLR (He et al., 2020) is a multi-speaker speech corpora intended for text-to-speech (TTS) applications. Indian Language Corpora (Abraham et al., 2020) consists of crowd-sourcing recordings of low-income workers. From all three datasets, only the Marathi language subsets were utilized for training purposes.

For the unconstrained condition, in addition to the aforementioned datasets, IIIT-H Voices (Prahallad et al., 2012) (Prahallad et al., 2013) and IITM Indic TTS (Baby et al., 2016) were also utilized, both of which were designed for building TTS systems.

4 System Description

All the models we trained for this challenge are end-to-end speech translation (ST) systems. For the purposes of this challenge, we tried two architectures: Listen, attend and spell (LAS) (Chan et al., 2016) style Transformer (Vaswani et al., 2017) and the same model with its encoder replaced with Conformer (Gulati et al., 2020) layers. Both the models were implemented using the Fairseq S2T toolkit (Ott et al., 2019).

The Conformer model consists of a 16-layer Conformer encoder paired with a 6-layer Transformer decoder. The Transformer model comprises of a 12-layer Transformer encoder and a 6-layer Transformer decoder. In all the cases where pre-training is involved, the encoder blocks are pre-trained (Bahar et al., 2019) using Marathi ASR data mentioned in *Table 2*. Then, the model is trained on the Marathi-Hindi ST data with the encoder initialized from the previous ASR pre-training stage. Relative positional encoding was used in the case of the Conformer model.

For speech inputs, 80-channel log mel-filter bank features (25ms window size and 10ms shift) were extracted with utterance-level CMVN (Cepstral Mean and Variance Normalization) applied. SpecAugment (Park et al., 2019) is applied on top of this feature set. We experimented with character vocabulary and a 1000 BPE (Byte Pair Encoding) vocabulary and found that the former performs better for our task.

Adam (Kingma and Ba, 2014) with a learning rate of 2×10^{-3} was the optimizer of choice for all the experiments. Inverse square-root scheduling available in the toolkit was used with a warm-up of 1000 steps. Label-smoothed-cross-entropy with 0.1 as label smoothing was used as the criterion across all the experiments. We set dropout (Srivastava et al., 2014) to 0.15 during ASR pre-training and

Dataset	Condition	Hours
Indian Language Corpora	Constrained	109
Common Voice	Constrained	3.7
OpenSLR	Constrained	3
IIIT-H Voices	Unconstrained	40
IITM Indic TTS	Unconstrained	20

Table 2: Details of Marathi ASR datasets used for pre-training.

0.1 during ST training. We pre-train on the ASR data for 6000 steps and then train on the ST data for 2250 steps. After ST training, we average the last 10 checkpoints to create the final model. We used a beam size of 10 for decoding.

4.1 Constrained condition

For the constrained condition, we are only permitted to use the data provided by the organizers. For the constrained models, wherever pre-training is involved, we only utilize the 3 constrained datasets from *Table 2*. For this condition, we train the following models:

- The Transformer model trained with only the train split from the ST data.
- The Conformer model trained with only the train split from the ST data.
- The Transformer model encoder pre-trained with constrained ASR data mentioned in *Table 2* and then trained with only the train split from the ST data.
- The Conformer model encoder pre-trained with constrained ASR data mentioned in *Table 2* and then trained with only the train split from the ST data. This served as our constrained contrastive model for the final submission.
- The Conformer model encoder pre-trained with constrained ASR data mentioned in *Table 2* and then trained with both the train and the dev splits from the ST data. This served as our constrained primary model for the final submission.

4.2 Unconstrained condition

For the unconstrained condition, wherever pre-training is involved, we utlize all of the datasets mentioned in *Table 2*, both constrained and unconstrained. Since the Conformer models outperform the Transformer ones as can be gleaned from *Table 3*, we chose to use only Conformer models for the unconstrained condition. We train the following models for the unconstrained condition:

- The Conformer model encoder pre-trained with constrained and unconstrained ASR data mentioned in *Table 2* and then trained with only the train split from the ST data.This served as our unconstrained contrastive model for the final submission.
- The Conformer model encoder pre-trained with constrained and unconstrained ASR data mentioned in *Table 2* and then trained with both the train and the dev splits from the ST data. This served as our unconstrained primary model for the final submission.

5 Results

The results for all the models we trained can be seen in *Table 3*. The first striking result is that, irrespective of the scenario, the Conformer encoder strongly outperforms the Transformer encoder. Replacing the Transformer encoder blocks with it's Conformer counterpart results in the dev split BLEU score increasing by 3.2 points. Conformers are already state of the art when it comes to speech recognition, so it would make inherent sense that this advantage would carry over to speech translation as well.

Encoder pre-training with Marathi ASR data also results in a significant improvement in speech translation performance.This is a commonly used strategy while training speech translation models and allows us to increase the BLEU score on the dev split by 8.5 and 11.8 points on the Transformer and Conformer models respectively. Two additional Marathi ASR datasets were added for pre-training the encoder in the unconstrained condition. This resulted in the BLEU score increasing by 4.1 points on both the dev and test splits.

Condition	Model	Pretraining	Training Data		Dev	Test	
			ASR	ST	BLEU(%)	BLEU(%)	CHRF2(%)
Constrained	Transformer	✗	–	train	1.02	–	–
Constrained	Conformer	✗	–	train	4.26	–	–
Constrained	Transformer	✓	constrained	train	9.55	–	–
Constrained	Conformer	✓	constrained	train	16.09	25.7	49.4
Constrained	Conformer	✓	constrained	train+dev	–	31.2	54.8
Unconstrained	Conformer	✓	all	train	20.22	29.8	53.2
Unconstrained	Conformer	✓	all	train+dev	–	32.4	55.5

Table 3: Results for all our trained models on dev & test splits. Here *all* indicates that both constrained and unconstrained datasets were used for ASR pretraining.

Finally, since the dev and test splits come from a similar distribution, including the dev split in speech translation training boosted our BLEU scores on the test split by 5.5 and 2.6 points in the cases of constrained and unconstrained conditions respectively. Utilizing the dev split for speech translation training also narrowed down the gap in performance between the unconstrained and constrained models on the test split.

6 Conclusion

In this paper we present our approaches to the IWSLT 2023 Evaluation Campaign Dialectal and Low-resource track: Marathi-Hindi Speech Translation which secured the first and second places in the constrained and unconstrained conditions respectively. We start off with a simple end-to-end approach with Transformers and then apply a gamut of ideas like replacing the encoder blocks with Conformers, encoder pre-training, etc., to drastically improve our dev BLEU score from 1.02 to 20.22. Through our results, we also quantitatively demonstrate how much of an impact each of our ideas bring forth and sincerely hope that some of these ideas might be useful for researchers and practitioners alike working on low-resource speech translation problems.

References

Basil Abraham, Danish Goel, Divya Siddarth, Kalika Bali, Manu Chopra, Monojit Choudhury, Pratik Joshi, Preethi Jyothi, Sunayana Sitaram, and Vivek Seshadri. 2020. Crowdsourcing speech data for low-resource languages from low-income workers. In *Proceedings of the 12th Conference on Language Resources and Evaluation (LREC)*, pages 2819–2826.

Milind Agarwal, Sweta Agrawal, Antonios Anastasopoulos, Ondřej Bojar, Claudia Borg, Marine Carpuat, Roldano Cattoni, Mauro Cettolo, Mingda Chen, William Chen, Khalid Choukri, Alexandra Chronopoulou, Anna Currey, Thierry Declerck, Qianqian Dong, Yannick Estève, Kevin Duh, Marcello Federico, Souhir Gahbiche, Barry Haddow, Benjamin Hsu, Phu Mon Htut, Hirofumi Inaguma, Dávid Javorský, John Judge, Yasumasa Kano, Tom Ko, Rishu Kumar, Pengwei Li, Xutail Ma, Prashant Mathur, Evgeny Matusov, Paul McNamee, John P. McCrae, Kenton Murray, Maria Nadejde, Satoshi Nakamura, Matteo Negri, Ha Nguyen, Jan Niehues, Xing Niu, Atul Ojha Kr., John E. Ortega, Proyag Pal, Juan Pino, Lonneke van der Plas, Peter Polák, Elijah Rippeth, Elizabeth Salesky, Jiatong Shi, Matthias Sperber, Sebastian Stüker, Katsuhito Sudoh, Yun Tang, Brian Thompson, Kevin Tran, Marco Turchi, Alex Waibel, Mingxuan Wang, Shinji Watanabe, and Rodolfo Zevallos. 2023. Findings of the IWSLT 2023 Evaluation Campaign. In *Proceedings of the 20th International Conference on Spoken Language Translation (IWSLT 2023)*. Association for Computational Linguistics.

Antonios Anastasopoulos, Loïc Barrault, Luisa Bentivogli, Marcely Zanon Boito, Ondřej Bojar, Roldano Cattoni, Anna Currey, Georgiana Dinu, Kevin Duh, Maha Elbayad, Clara Emmanuel, Yannick Estève, Marcello Federico, Christian Federmann, Souhir Gahbiche, Hongyu Gong, Roman Grundkiewicz, Barry Haddow, Benjamin Hsu, Dávid Javorský, Věra Kloudová, Surafel Lakew, Xutai Ma, Prashant Mathur, Paul McNamee, Kenton Murray, Maria Nădejde, Satoshi Nakamura, Matteo Negri, Jan Niehues, Xing Niu, John Ortega, Juan Pino, Elizabeth Salesky, Jiatong Shi, Matthias Sperber, Sebastian Stüker, Katsuhito Sudoh, Marco Turchi, Yogesh Virkar, Alexander Waibel, Changhan Wang, and Shinji Watanabe. 2022. Findings of the IWSLT 2022 evaluation campaign. In *Proceedings of the 19th International Conference on Spoken Language Translation (IWSLT 2022)*, pages 98–157, Dublin, Ireland (in-person and online). Association for Computational Linguistics.

Rosana Ardila, Megan Branson, Kelly Davis, Michael Henretty, Michael Kohler, Josh Meyer, Reuben Morais, Lindsay Saunders, Francis M Tyers, and Gregor Weber. 2019. Common voice: A massively-multilingual speech corpus. *arXiv preprint arXiv:1912.06670*.

Arun Babu, Changhan Wang, Andros Tjandra, Kushal Lakhotia, Qiantong Xu, Naman Goyal, Kritika Singh, Patrick von Platen, Yatharth Saraf, Juan Pino, et al.

2021. Xls-r: Self-supervised cross-lingual speech representation learning at scale. *arXiv preprint arXiv:2111.09296.*

Arun Baby, Anju Leela Thomas, N. L. Nishanthi, and TTS Consortium. 2016. Resources for Indian languages. In *CBBLR – Community-Based Building of Language Resources*, pages 37–43, Brno, Czech Republic. Tribun EU.

Parnia Bahar, Tobias Bieschke, and Hermann Ney. 2019. A comparative study on end-to-end speech to text translation. In *2019 IEEE Automatic Speech Recognition and Understanding Workshop (ASRU)*, pages 792–799. IEEE.

Luisa Bentivogli, Mauro Cettolo, Marco Gaido, Alina Karakanta, Alberto Martinelli, Matteo Negri, and Marco Turchi. 2021. Cascade versus direct speech translation: Do the differences still make a difference? *arXiv preprint arXiv:2106.01045.*

Alexandre Bérard, Olivier Pietquin, Christophe Servan, and Laurent Besacier. 2016. Listen and translate: A proof of concept for end-to-end speech-to-text translation. *arXiv preprint arXiv:1612.01744.*

Francisco Casacuberta, Marcello Federico, Hermann Ney, and Enrique Vidal. 2008. Recent efforts in spoken language translation. *IEEE Signal Processing Magazine*, 25(3):80–88.

William Chan, Navdeep Jaitley, Quoc Le, and Oriol Vinyals. 2016. Listen, attend and spell: A neural network for large vocabulary conversational speech recognition. *IEEE International Conference on Acoustics, Speech and Signal Processing (ICASSP).*

Anmol Gulati, James Qin, Chung-Cheng Chiu, Niki Parmar, Yu Zhang, Jiahui Yu, Wei Han, Shibo Wang, Zhengdong Zhang, Yonghui Wu, et al. 2020. Conformer: Convolution-augmented transformer for speech recognition. *arXiv preprint arXiv:2005.08100.*

Fei He, Shan-Hui Cathy Chu, Oddur Kjartansson, Clara Rivera, Anna Katanova, Alexander Gutkin, Isin Demirsahin, Cibu Johny, Martin Jansche, Supheakmungkol Sarin, and Knot Pipatsrisawat. 2020. Open-source multi-speaker speech corpora for building Gujarati, Kannada, Malayalam, Marathi, Tamil and Telugu speech synthesis systems. In *Proceedings of the Twelfth Language Resources and Evaluation Conference*, pages 6494–6503, Marseille, France. European Language Resources Association.

Diederik P Kingma and Jimmy Ba. 2014. Adam: A method for stochastic optimization. *arXiv preprint arXiv:1412.6980.*

Gaurav Kumar, Matt Post, Daniel Povey, and Sanjeev Khudanpur. 2014. Some insights from translating conversational telephone speech. In *2014 IEEE International Conference on Acoustics, Speech and Signal Processing (ICASSP)*, pages 3231–3235.

Hang Le, Florentin Barbier, Ha Nguyen, Natalia Tomashenko, Salima Mdhaffar, Souhir Gahbiche, Bougares Fethi, Benjamin Lecouteux, Didier Schwab, and Yannick Estève. 2021. On-trac'systems for the iwslt 2021 low-resource speech translation and multilingual speech translation shared tasks. In *International Conference on Spoken Language Translation (IWSLT).*

H. Ney. 1999. Speech translation: coupling of recognition and translation. In *1999 IEEE International Conference on Acoustics, Speech, and Signal Processing. Proceedings. ICASSP99 (Cat. No.99CH36258)*, volume 1, pages 517–520 vol.1.

Jan Niehues, Rolando Cattoni, Sebastian Stüker, Matteo Negri, Marco Turchi, Thanh-Le Ha, Elizabeth Salesky, Ramon Sanabria, Loic Barrault, Lucia Specia, and Marcello Federico. 2019. The IWSLT 2019 evaluation campaign. In *Proceedings of the 16th International Conference on Spoken Language Translation*, Hong Kong. Association for Computational Linguistics.

Myle Ott, Sergey Edunov, Alexei Baevski, Angela Fan, Sam Gross, Nathan Ng, David Grangier, and Michael Auli. 2019. fairseq: A fast, extensible toolkit for sequence modeling. In *Proceedings of NAACL-HLT 2019: Demonstrations.*

Daniel S Park, William Chan, Yu Zhang, Chung-Cheng Chiu, Barret Zoph, Ekin D Cubuk, and Quoc V Le. 2019. Specaugment: A simple data augmentation method for automatic speech recognition. *arXiv preprint arXiv:1904.08779.*

Matt Post, Gaurav Kumar, Adam Lopez, Damianos Karakos, Chris Callison-Burch, and Sanjeev Khudanpur. 2013. Improved speech-to-text translation with the fisher and callhome Spanish-English speech translation corpus. In *Proceedings of the 10th International Workshop on Spoken Language Translation: Papers*, Heidelberg, Germany.

Kishore Prahallad, E Naresh Kumar, Venkatesh Keri, S Rajendran, and Alan W Black. 2012. The iiit-h indic speech databases. In *Thirteenth annual conference of the international speech communication association.*

Kishore Prahallad, Anandaswarup Vadapalli, Naresh Elluru, Gautam Mantena, Bhargav Pulugundla, Peri Bhaskararao, Hema A Murthy, Simon King, Vasilis Karaiskos, and Alan W Black. 2013. The blizzard challenge 2013–indian language task. In *Blizzard challenge workshop*, volume 2013.

Nitish Srivastava, Geoffrey Hinton, Alex Krizhevsky, Ilya Sutskever, and Ruslan Salakhutdinov. 2014. Dropout: a simple way to prevent neural networks from overfitting. *The journal of machine learning research*, 15(1):1929–1958.

Yuqing Tang, Chau Tran, Xian Li, Peng-Jen Chen, Naman Goyal, Vishrav Chaudhary, Jiatao Gu, and Angela Fan. 2020. Multilingual translation with extensible multilingual pretraining and finetuning. *arXiv preprint arXiv:2008.00401*.

Ashish Vaswani, Noam Shazeer, Niki Parmar, Jakob Uszkoreit, Llion Jones, Aidan N Gomez, Łukasz Kaiser, and Illia Polosukhin. 2017. Attention is all you need. *Advances in neural information processing systems*, 30.

Ron J Weiss, Jan Chorowski, Navdeep Jaitly, Yonghui Wu, and Zhifeng Chen. 2017. Sequence-to-sequence models can directly translate foreign speech. *arXiv preprint arXiv:1703.08581*.

BIT's System for Multilingual Track

Zhipeng Wang
Beijing Institute of Technology
wzp3139725181@163.com

Yuhang Guo*
Beijing Institute of Technology
guoyuhang@bit.edu.cn

Shuoying Chen
Beijing Institute of Technology
chensy@bit.edu.cn

Abstract

This paper describes the system we submitted to the IWSLT 2023 multilingual speech translation track, with the input is speech from one language, and the output is text from 10 target languages. Our system consists of CNN and Transformer, convolutional neural networks downsample speech features and extract local information, while transformer extract global features and output the final results. In our system, we use speech recognition tasks to pre-train encoder parameters, and then use speech translation corpus to train the multilingual speech translation model. We have also adopted other methods to optimize the model, such as data augmentation, model ensemble, etc. Our system can obtain satisfactory results on test sets of 10 languages in the MUST-C corpus.

1 Introduction

Speech translation refers to the technology of translating source language speech into target language text (or speech). This task has a very broad application space in real life, such as in international conferences, lectures, and overseas tourism; Adding speech translation to short videos or real-time subtitles in some foreign language videos can provide users with a better experience. Early speech translation is the combination of speech recognition and machine translation. Firstly, the speech recognition model recognizes source language speech as source language transcribed text, and then the machine translation model translates the recognized source language text into the target language text, which is also called cascade method. The advantage of cascade model is that it can use a large amount of data in speech recognition and machine translation to train the model, and it is relatively simple to implement. However, the disadvantages of cascade model are also obvious: errors in speech recognition results will be transferred to the next machine translation task. So researchers have focused on end-to-end speech translation. At present, bilingual end-to-end speech translation has achieved very good results, but using a single model to complete multiple language translations has always been a goal pursued by researchers, that is multilingual speech translation. Compared to bilingual speech translation, the advantages of multilingual speech translation include: (1) completing multilingual translation with fewer parameters; (2) low resource languages can learn knowledge from high resource languages. In this paper, we conducted one-to-many multilingual speech translation, and submitted our system to the IWSLT 2023(Agarwal et al., 2023) multilingual speech translation track. Here is an introduction to our submitted system:

We first use convolutional neural networks to downsample the input features, then input them into the Transformer model for further processing, and finally output the translation results at the output layer. The encoder for speech translation needs to complete both acoustic feature extraction and semantic feature extraction tasks. In order to reduce the encoding pressure of the model, we use speech recognition task to pre-train the parameters of the encoder. Before inputting the data into the model, we applied the SpecAugment(Park et al., 2019) method for data augmentation, which increased data diversity and resulted in better results for the model. After training the multilingual speech translation model, we calculated the average value of the model parameters obtained for the last 10 epochs to generate the model we used during testing, the model with the obtained average parameters can have better results.

The target language includes Arabic, Chinese, Dutch, French, German, Japanese, Farsi, Portuguese, Russian, and Turkish. The training data for these languages can be found in the commonly used corpus for speech translation – MUST-C(Di Gangi et al., 2019). We downloaded the

*Corresponding author

Proceedings of the 20th International Conference on Spoken Language Translation (IWSLT 2023), pages 455–460
July 13-14, 2023 ©2023 Association for Computational Linguistics

Table 1: Training Set Information

Tgt	talks	sentences	time	words src	words tgt
ar	2412	212k	463h	4520k	4000k
de	2043	229k	400h	4196k	3869k
fa	1911	181k	347h	3548k	4559k
fr	2460	275k	484h	5067k	5163k
ja	3258	328k	540h	5712k	69k
nl	2219	248k	434h	4548k	4251k
pt	2001	206k	376h	3887k	3621k
ru	2448	265k	481h	5007k	4192k
tr	2307	236k	445h	4600k	3388k
zh	3583	358k	596h	6251k	97k

data for the relevant languages from MUST-C v1.0, MUST-C v1.2, and MUST-C v2.0, merged them, and preprocessed them to obtain our training dataset. We used the Fairseq(Ott et al., 2019) toolkit to conduct our experiment, and after the training was completed, we scored the translation quality using the sacrebleu metric. Our model achieved our expected results on 10 target languages.

2 Data Preparation

As shown in the Table 1, we collected training data for relevant languages from the MUST-C corpus and provided their information. It can be seen from this that there are significant differences between different languages. There are differences in the number of source language words and target language words among different languages. For example, the number of source language words in the Arabic language corpus is greater than the number of target language words, while the number of source language words in the Farsi language corpus is less than the number of target language words. This indicates that the difficulty of length conversion required by the model when dealing with different languages varies to some extent.

Due to our task of one-to-many multilingual speech translation, the input received by the model is all English speech data, which enables us to perform the same preprocessing operation on all data. The original speech is in wav format, and most of it is long audio. We need to segment and extract features before inputting it into the model. So we segment the speech data based on the start time and duration of each segment given in MUST-C. The preprocessing stage includes extracting MFCC features, training the sentencepeice(Kudo and Richardson, 2018) model, generating a vocabulary, and finally generating a training set. The processed MFCC feature dimension is 80, and SpecAugment is applied for data augmentation. The relevant configurations used in the experiment regarding SpecAugment are shown in Table 2:

Table 2: Parameter settings for SpecAugment

Parameters	Values
freq_mask_F	27
freq_mask_N	2
time_mask_N	2
time_mask_T	100
time_mask_p	1.0
time_wrap_W	0

The SpecAugment method uses three different data augmentation methods: Time warping, Frequency masking, and Time masking. Time warping selects an area from the time dimension for warping. Frequency masking selects an area from the frequency dimension for masking, in our experimental configuration, the length of the masked part is 27, which is the parameter freq_mask_F, and the parameter freq_mask_N refers to the number of masked areas. Time masking selects an area from the time dimension for masking, the parameter time_mask_T we set is 100, and the number of masked areas is 2. SpecAugment increases the diversity of training data, making the trained model more robust.

3 Method

3.1 Speech Recognition

We use speech recognition tasks to pre train encoder parameters. After experimental verification, using speech recognition for pre training parameters is much better than not using pre-training. Due to the need to initialize the parameters of the speech translation model using the encoder of the speech recognition model, we use the same structure to train the speech recognition model. Although extracting MFCC features from the original audio can reduce the sequence length, the processed MFCC features still have a long time dimension and require further downsampling. In speech translation related works, a common practice is to use CNN or Shrink modules(Liu et al., 2020) to compress feature sequences. We use convolutional neural networks to downsample the extracted MFCC feature sequence, the input MFCC features are first extracted through a two-layer convolutional neural network to extract shallow features and downsampling, and then input into the Transformer model to complete the speech recognition task. The model structure is shown in the Figure 1. The reason why Transformer has strong modeling information ability is due to its self attention mechanism, the multi-head attention calculation in transformer is shown in the Figure 2. Perform different linear calculations on the input to obtain Q, K, and V. compute the matrix of outputs as:

$$Attention(Q,K,V) = softmax(\frac{QK^T}{\sqrt{d_k}})V \quad (1)$$

Each module in Transformer has its specific role, and the following is an analysis of its main modules:

Multi-head attention module. Self attention refers to calculating the attention of the current token to other tokens in the sequence, and using the calculated attention score as a weight to weight and sum the feature sequence, thus modeling global information. The final output of the multi-head self attention module is obtained by concatenating the results obtained from all the attention heads and then performing a linear mapping.

Feed forward module. In the feed forward module, the extracted global features are linearly combined, which includes two linear mappings: mapping feature sequences to high dimensions and mapping features from high dimensions back to their original dimensions, the calculation in the feed forward module is as follows:

$$FFN(x) = max(0, xW_1 + b_1)W_2 + b_2 \quad (2)$$

Positional Encoding. The transformer uses position encoding to indicate the relative position between tokens, and the calculation method is as follows:

$$PE_{(pos,2i)} = \sin(pos/10000^{2i/d_{model}}) \quad (3)$$

$$PE_{(pos,2i+1)} = \cos(pos/10000^{2i/d_{model}}) \quad (4)$$

After extracting shallow features from speech using convolutional neural networks, transformer combines the extracted information. Convolutional neural networks are good at extracting local features, while transformer have a stronger ability to model global features. This structure enables the model to perform well in several speech processing tasks.

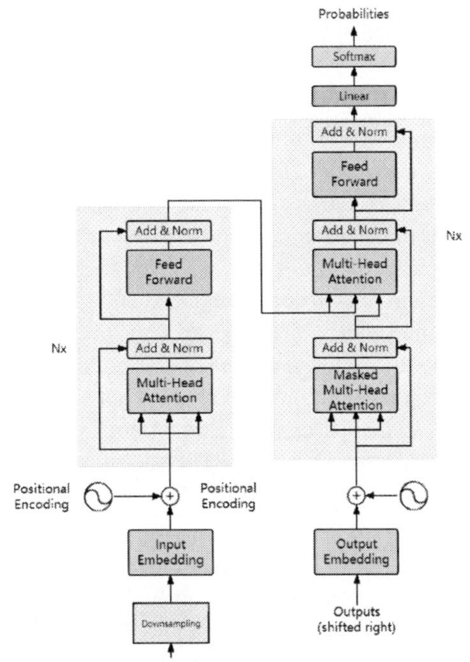

Figure 1: Model structure

3.2 Multilingual Speech Translation

The multilingual speech translation model also adopts the structure shown in the Figure 1, replacing the speech recognition vocabulary with the multilingual speech translation vocabulary, and training

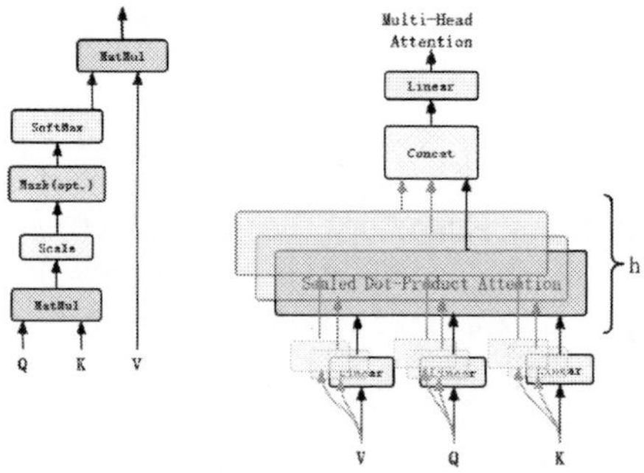

Figure 2: Multi-head Attention

the model using the speech translation training set. Unlike speech recognition task, the vocabulary in multilingual speech translation task contains language labels, and the sub words in the dictionary come from all target language texts. Before training the speech translation model, use the encoder of the trained speech recognition model to initialize the encoder parameters of the speech translation model, and optimize all model parameters during training.

We only use the encoder of the speech recognition model to initialize the multilingual speech translation model because the tasks completed by the two encoders are similar, that is, the shallow layer of the encoder needs to extract acoustic feature information. However, there are task differences between speech recognition and speech translation decoders. The speech translation decoder needs to complete language conversion, and the speech recognition decoder does not involve this task, so the speech recognition decoder is not used to initialize parameters. The speech recognition model will no longer be used in subsequent operations.

The decoder adopts an auto-regressive approach to output the translation sequence, and in this experiment, language labels are used to indicate the current translation direction. For example, <lang: de> indicates that the target language of the current translation task is German.

We conducted parameter fusion on the trained model. After the model was trained to converge, the last 10 checkpoint points were fused and the test set was scored by the fused model. The specific approach is to find variables with the same name from all the models read, calculate the average value, and save it in the new model.

4 Experiments

4.1 Implemention

The downsampling module contains two layers of convolutional neural networks, with convolutional kernel sizes of 5 and step sizes of 2. After the feature sequence passes through the downsampling layer, the sequence length becomes one quarter of the original, The dimension of the output feature is 1024.

The encoder of the model contains 12 transformer blocks, with each layer having an output feature dimension of 512. In order to fully model speech features, 8 attention heads were used to model information in speech from different perspectives. The feedforward neural network module contains two linear maps to reorganize the features. First, the feature dimension is mapped to 2048, and then it is mapped back to 512.

The decoder of the model consists of 6 Transformer blocks, which also use 8 attention heads.

In addition, we use the dropout of the attention matrix to prevent overfitting. The dropout rate of attention is set to 0.1. In speech recognition tasks, we set the vocabulary size to 8000; In the speech translation task, we set the vocabulary size to 10000. Because the speech recognition task only involves English text, while the speech translation task involves translated text from 10 target languages, a larger vocabulary needs to be used. At the time of model output, the probability of speech recognition task computing on 8000 sub words and the probability of speech translation task computing on 10000 sub words.

Adam optimizer and cross entropy loss function are used in model training. We use max tokens to dynamically control the number of samples included in a batch. In our experiment, the max tokens used for both speech recognition and speech translation tasks were 20000. The number of steps for optimizing speech recognition tasks is 100k, and the number of steps for optimizing speech translation tasks is 350k, based on the difficulty of these two tasks. Among them, perform warmup in the first 10k steps. The learning rate is 1e-3, and the label smoothing is 0.1. We trained our model using two NVIDIA TITAN RTX.

4.2 Main Results

We trained a speech recognition model with good performance, and the WER of the model on each language is shown in the Table 3.

Table 3: The WER of the ASR model on data in each language.

	ar	de	fa	fr	ja	nl	pt	ru	tr	zh
WER	16.01	10.64	11.65	10.74	8.79	10.43	10.76	10.71	11.10	8.80

Table 4: BLEU scores on the MUST-C test set.

	ar	de	fa	fr	ja	nl	pt	ru	tr	zh
BLEU	12.35	23.30	12.15	32.59	12.93	27.46	28.57	14.66	11.33	22.07

After training the model on the MUST-C training set, we used its tst-COMMON test set to verify the model's effectiveness. The experimental results are shown in the Table 4.

From the Table 4, it can be seen that our system can complete translations in these 10 target languages, and the BLEU score exceeds 20 in all 5 languages of them. Although using the same model for translation tasks, the difficulty of translation varies among different languages. As shown in the table, the BLEU scores of ar, fa, ja, ru, and tr are lower compared to other languages, but they use a similar amount of data. On the one hand, there are significant differences in grammar rules between these target languages and the source language, making it more difficult for the model to complete language conversion; On the other hand, the differences between target languages make it difficult to share information between them consistently.

In the current work of multilingual speech translation, many methods have modified the model architecture and optimization methods, and our system uses a simple convolutional neural network combined with the Transformer structure to achieve a relatively good effect. Compared to those complex systems that modify models, our system has the following advantages: On the one hand, our system's training method is relatively simple and requires fewer model parameters. On the other hand, this simple structure can also effectively complete multilingual speech translation tasks. Our system can be applied to devices with strict memory requirements, and can achieve relatively satisfactory results with a small number of parameters.

5 Conclusion

This paper introduces our system submitted on the IWSLT 2023 multilingual speech translation track. We used convolutional neural networks combined with Transformer models to complete the task of English speech to 10 target language texts. Our system is characterized by its simplicity and efficiency, effectively modeling local and global features in speech, and completing modal and language transformations within the model. Our system has achieved satisfactory results on the test set of 10 languages in MUST-C corpus.

References

Milind Agarwal, Sweta Agrawal, Antonios Anastasopoulos, Ondřej Bojar, Claudia Borg, Marine Carpuat, Roldano Cattoni, Mauro Cettolo, Mingda Chen, William Chen, Khalid Choukri, Alexandra Chronopoulou, Anna Currey, Thierry Declerck, Qianqian Dong, Yannick Estève, Kevin Duh, Marcello Federico, Souhir Gahbiche, Barry Haddow, Benjamin Hsu, Phu Mon Htut, Hirofumi Inaguma, Dávid Javorský, John Judge, Yasumasa Kano, Tom Ko, Rishu Kumar, Pengwei Li, Xutail Ma, Prashant Mathur, Evgeny Matusov, Paul McNamee, John P. McCrae, Kenton Murray, Maria Nadejde, Satoshi Nakamura, Matteo Negri, Ha Nguyen, Jan Niehues, Xing Niu, Atul Ojha Kr., John E. Ortega, Proyag Pal, Juan Pino, Lonneke van der Plas, Peter Polák, Elijah Rippeth, Elizabeth Salesky, Jiatong Shi, Matthias Sperber, Sebastian Stüker, Katsuhito Sudoh, Yun Tang, Brian Thompson, Kevin Tran, Marco Turchi, Alex Waibel, Mingxuan Wang, Shinji Watanabe, and Rodolfo Zevallos. 2023. Findings of the IWSLT 2023 Evaluation Campaign. In *Proceedings of the 20th International Conference on Spoken Language Translation (IWSLT 2023)*. Association for Computational Linguistics.

Mattia A Di Gangi, Roldano Cattoni, Luisa Bentivogli, Matteo Negri, and Marco Turchi. 2019. Must-c: a multilingual speech translation corpus. In *Proceedings of the 2019 Conference of the North American Chapter of the Association for Computational Linguistics: Human Language Technologies, Volume 1 (Long and Short Papers)*, pages 2012–2017. Association for Computational Linguistics.

Taku Kudo and John Richardson. 2018. Sentencepiece: A simple and language independent subword tokenizer and detokenizer for neural text processing. *arXiv preprint arXiv:1808.06226*.

Yuchen Liu, Junnan Zhu, Jiajun Zhang, and Chengqing Zong. 2020. Bridging the modality gap for speech-to-text translation. *arXiv preprint arXiv:2010.14920*.

Myle Ott, Sergey Edunov, Alexei Baevski, Angela Fan, Sam Gross, Nathan Ng, David Grangier, and Michael Auli. 2019. fairseq: A fast, extensible toolkit for sequence modeling. *arXiv preprint arXiv:1904.01038*.

Daniel S Park, William Chan, Yu Zhang, Chung-Cheng Chiu, Barret Zoph, Ekin D Cubuk, and Quoc V Le. 2019. Specaugment: A simple data augmentation method for automatic speech recognition. *arXiv preprint arXiv:1904.08779*.

Matesub: the Translated Subtitling Tool at the IWSLT2023 Subtitling task

Simone G. Perone
Translated srl
via Indonesia 23
00144 Rome - Italy
simone@translated.com

Abstract

This paper briefly describes Matesub, the subtitling tool Translated used to participate in the Subtitling shared task at IWSLT 2023. Matesub is a professional web-based tool that combines state-of-the-art AI with a WYSIWYG editor. The automatic generation of subtitles in Matesub is based on a cascade architecture, composed of ASR, text segmenter and MT neural models, which allows covering any pair from about 60 languages and their variants.

1 Matesub

Matesub[1] is a web-based tool released by Translated[2] that combines state-of-the-art AI with a WYSIWYG (What You See Is What You Get) editor for supporting professionals in the creation of subtitles for audio visual documents. Matesub generates subtitling suggestions through a processing pipeline which was used to participate in the Subtitling shared task at IWSLT 2023. This paper first describes the pipeline, and then presents and discusses the scores of the submission.

1.1 The subtitling pipeline

In Matesub, subtitles are automatically generated by a pipeline (Figure 1) which concatenates two main modules, based on neural models: an automatic speech recognition (ASR) system and a module providing the Captions & Subtitles Service. They are described in the following.

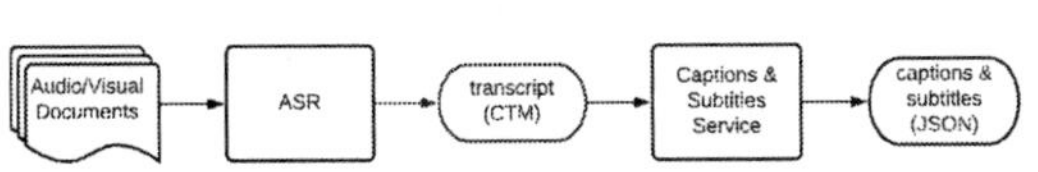

Figure 1: Architecture of the subtitling pipeline.

[1] https://matesub.com/
[2] https://translated.com/

1.1.1 Automatic speech recognition

The ASR is in charge of the transcription of the speech content of an audio signal. In Matesub, this processing stage is provided either by an in-house ASR model or by a 3rd party commercial ASR service, according to the availability of the internal solution and its relative quality. In both cases, the word hypotheses are expected to be given in conversation time mark (CTM) format. This text file consists of records each having 5 fields, e.g.:

23.66	0.29	human	0.00998	False
23.96	0.40	beings.	0.01000	True
24.48	0.13	We	0.33000	False

whose meaning is given in Table 1.

field	meaning
1	start time (sec)
2	duration (sec)
3	token (i.e. word)
4	confidence
5	end of sentence (boolean)

Table 1: Fields in the CTM format.

Note that the transcription is punctuated and cased; moreover, the flag indicating the *end of sentence* is typically set *on* for acoustic reasons, like the presence of the pause between the tokens *begin.* and *We*, but - less frequently - also for "linguistic" evidence (learned by the ASR from training data).

1.1.2 Captioning and subtitling

The Captions and Subtitles Service is in charge of building, starting from a given CTM file, the SubRip Subtitle (SRT) files of the transcription contained in the CTM file and its translation; the two SRTs are finally merged in a single JSON file. As shown in Figure 2, this module consists of two main components, a text segmenter and a neural machine translation (NMT) system, in addition to a number of secondary sub-components.

The two main components are built using the same sequence-to-sequence neural modeling tech-

Proceedings of the 20th International Conference on Spoken Language Translation (IWSLT 2023), pages 461–464
July 13-14, 2023

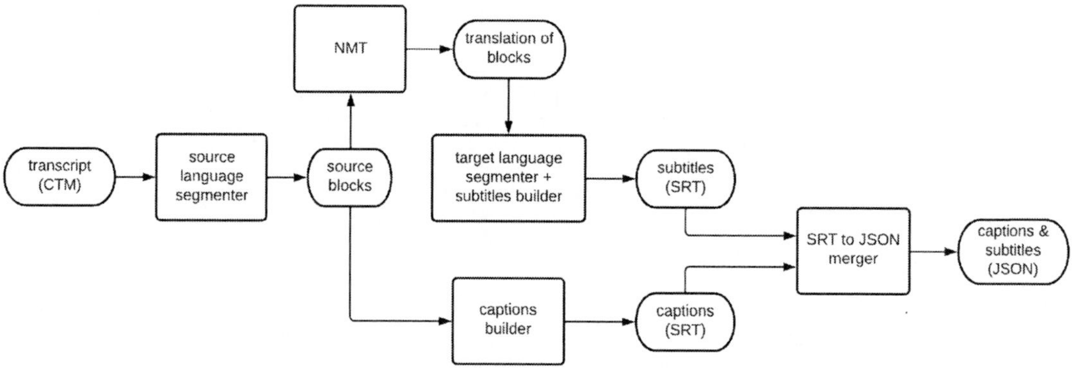

Figure 2: Captions and subtitles service.

nique. The segmenter, implemented as proposed in (Karakanta et al., 2020; Papi et al., 2022), inserts in an unsegmented input text - either in the source or in the target language - markers of segment boundaries. It is trained on pairs of unsegmented-segmented text, where segment boundaries are marked by means of two special symbols: *<eob>* to mark the end of block (caption or subtitle), and *<eol>* to mark the end of line. Figure 3 shows an example of a sentence after inserting the markers from the corresponding fragment of the SRT file.

164
00:08:57,020–>00:08:58,476
I wanted to challenge the idea

165
00:08:58,500–>00:09:02,060
that design is but a tool
to create function and beauty.

I wanted to challenge the idea <eob> that design is but a tool <eol> to create function and beauty. <eob>

Figure 3: Subtitle file (top) and the full sentence annotated with the subtitle breaks (bottom). Figure taken from (Karakanta et al., 2020).

The neural machine translation engine performs the translation of the text from the source language (English, in the IWSLT 2023 context) into the corresponding text in the target language (here German and Spanish). Other processing modules are in charge of (i) generating captions/subtitles in SRT format (starting from transcripts, word timestamps, translations and segmentations), and (ii) merging the SRTs of captions and subtitles into a single JSON file. The main processing steps are:

1. Segmentation of the transcription on the basis of acoustic cues (*audio blocks*)
2. Segmentation of audio blocks into *caption blocks* (and lines) by means of the source language segmenter
3. Automatic translation of each caption block into the target language(s) (*subtitle blocks*)
4. Segmentation of subtitle blocks into lines by means of the target language segmenter
5. Timing projection from the CTM to the caption/subtitle blocks
6. Packaging of SRT and JSON files.

Note that the translation of each block in step 3 is done without looking at the context, i.e. at the surrounding blocks. On the one hand, this worsens the quality of the translation a little, but, on the other, it facilitates the satisfaction of the reading speed requirement through the n-best mechanism, sketched in the next section.

1.1.3 Machine translation

Neural machine translation is provided by ModernMT[3] (Bertoldi et al., 2021) through a REST API connection. ModernMT implements the Transformer (Vaswani et al., 2017) architecture; generic *big* models (about 200M parameters each), trained on both public and proprietary data, cover hundred of languages[4] in any direction, through a seamless integration of the pivot based approach, where the pivot language is English. Matesub requests ModernMT to provide the 16 best translations of

[3]https://www.modernmt.com/
[4]https://www.modernmt.com/api/#languages

each block (step 3 mentioned in the previous section); between them, the hypothesis with the highest probability and whose length permits to satisfy the reading speed constraint (given the duration of the block) is selected. If no such hypothesis exists, the shortest is chosen.

1.2 The editor

Matesub provides a WYSIWYG editor, which allows the user to review and correct the subtitles automatically generated and synced in the chosen target language by the back-end subtitling pipeline. Figure 4 shows a screenshot of the Matesub editor.

The editor permits the user to easily fix both translation and segmentation errors, thanks to the rich catalogue of functions and user-friendliness. Once the editing is over, subtitles can be embedded in the video or exported in production-ready SRT files or any other supported subtitles format.

2 Submission and Results

Translated participated in the Subtitling shared task at IWSLT 2023 with the back-end subtitling pipeline of Matesub. No adaptation of the general purpose pipeline was carried out, therefore the quality of subtitles generated for the audio-visual documents proposed in the shared task is that typically expected by the in-production system before the post-editing stage. Since neural models of Matesub (ASR, text segmenter and MT) were trained on more resources than those allowed for the constrained condition, we labelled our submission as *unconstrained*; it was also our unique submission, and as such it is the *primary* run.

Table 2 shows scores of our test set subtitles as computed by the organizers (Agarwal et al., 2023). They are in line with those we obtained on the dev sets.

Without knowing the results of the other submissions, it is hard to judge the results obtained. However, some considerations can be made:

- As expected, from the pure speech translation perspective, the TED domain is the easiest one by far
- Surprisingly, at least when German is the target language, the EPTV domain is as much challenging as ITV and PELOTON, which we expected to be the most difficult ones
- Assuming that BLEURT and ChrF are more reliable than BLEU and TER (according to (Kocmi et al., 2021), for example), it seems that the quality of TED and of Spanish EPTV subtitles is high, while subtitles of ITV, PELOTON and German EPTV documents would need major post-editing
- Since SubER is based on TER and Sigma on BLEU, their values match the scores of those metrics rather than BLEURT, ChrF and the subtitle compliance as measured by CPS/CPL/LPB, possibly affecting the final ranking of Matesub
- The compliance of subtitles is language independent
- Despite the fact that Matesub does not implement any hard rule, relying only on machine learning methods, CPL and CPL are (almost) perfect
- The reading speed (CPS) is under the max threshold of 21 characters per second in about 85% of subtitles; more in detail, the average is about 18.5 and only in 5% of cases it exceeds 30 characters per second, values that we consider satisfactory.

Acknowledgements

Matesub received funding from the European Institute of Innovation and Technology (EIT), a body of the European Union, through the MateDub (2020) and MateDub++ (2021) projects. Within them, the Matesub subtitling chain was developed in collaboration with the FBK's MT research unit. We especially thank Mauro Cettolo for his invaluable contribution to the success of this product and the support he gave us in the participation to the Subtitling track at IWSLT 2023.

References

Milind Agarwal, Sweta Agrawal, Antonios Anastasopoulos, Claudia Borg, Marine Carpuat, Roldano Cattoni, Mauro Cettolo, William Chen, Khalid Choukri, Alexandra Chronopoulou, Thierry Declerck, Qianqian Dong, Yannick Estève, Kevin Duh, Marcello Federico, Souhir Gahbiche, Benjamin Hsu, John Judge, Tom Ko, Rishu Kumar, Xutail Ma, Prashant Mathur, Evgeny Matusov, Paul McNamee, John P. McCrae, Kenton Murray, Matteo Negri, Jan Niehues, Xing Niu, Atul Ojha Kr., John E. Ortega, Proyag Pal, Juan Pino, Lonneke van der Plas, Elijah Rippeth, Elizabeth Salesky, Matthias Sperber, Sebastian Stüker, Katsuhito Sudoh, Brian Thompson, Marco Turchi, Alex Waibel, Mingxuan Wang, and Rodolfo Zevallos. 2023. Findings of the IWSLT 2023 Evaluation Campaign. In Proc. of IWSLT, Toronto, Canada.

		Subtitle quality		Translation quality				Subtitle compliance		
en-	domain	SubER↓	Sigma↑	BLEU↑	ChrF↑	TER↓	BLEURT↑	CPS↑	CPL↑	LPB↑
-de	EPTV	87.04	57.73	12.08	43.59	85.53	.4705	88.59	99.20	100.00
	TED	67.70	62.01	20.37	50.05	65.55	.5500	90.55	98.61	100.00
	ITV	73.11	67.04	14.92	37.13	71.27	.4501	80.21	99.47	100.00
	PELOTON	79.72	68.27	10.06	34.46	78.25	.4264	89.17	99.29	100.00
	ALL	75.41	65.22	14.81	39.50	73.60	.4591	84.97	99.25	100.00
-es	EPTV	74.47	59.59	21.06	54.11	72.08	.5728	90.15	99.44	100.00
	TED	45.94	66.85	40.36	65.72	43.81	.7047	92.62	99.48	100.00
	ITV	71.25	71.06	18.50	41.07	69.57	.4592	81.93	99.51	100.00
	PELOTON	74.87	70.99	15.96	41.86	73.88	.4666	88.27	99.60	100.00
	ALL	68.11	68.37	22.34	47.38	66.66	.5059	86.07	99.52	100.00

Table 2: Results of the Matesub submission.

Figure 4: Screenshot of Matesub Editor

Nicola Bertoldi, Davide Caroselli, M. Amin Farajian, Marcello Federico, Matteo Negri, Marco Trombetti, and Marco Turchi. 2021. Translation system and method. US Patent 11036940.

Alina Karakanta, Matteo Negri, and Marco Turchi. 2020. MuST-cinema: a speech-to-subtitles corpus. In Proc. of LREC, pages 3727–3734, Marseille, France.

Tom Kocmi, Christian Federmann, Roman Grundkiewicz, Marcin Junczys-Dowmunt, Hitokazu Matsushita, and Arul Menezes. 2021. To ship or not to ship: An extensive evaluation of automatic metrics for machine translation. In Proc. of WMT, pages 478–494.

Sara Papi, Alina Karakanta, Matteo Negri, and Marco Turchi. 2022. Dodging the data bottleneck: Automatic subtitling with automatically segmented st corpora. In Proc. of AACL-IJCNLP, pages 480–487.

Ashish Vaswani, Noam Shazeer, Niki Parmar, Jakob Uszkoreit, Llion Jones, Aidan N. Gomez, Lukasz Kaiser, and Illia Polosukhin. 2017. Attention is all you need. In Proc. of NIPS, pages 5998—-6008.

Augmentation Invariant Discrete Representation for Generative Spoken Language Modeling

Itai Gat[◇], **Felix Kreuk**[◇], **Tu Anh Nguyen**[◇], **Ann Lee**[◇], **Jade Copet**[◇], **Gabriel Synnaeve**[◇], **Emmanuel Dupoux**[♠,◇], **Yossi Adi**[♡,◇]

[◇]FAIR Team, Meta AI Research

[♠]ENS, INRIA, INSERM, UPEC, PSL Research University

[♡]The Hebrew University of Jerusalem

Abstract

Generative Spoken Language Modeling research focuses on optimizing speech Language Models (LMs) using raw audio recordings without accessing any textual supervision. Such speech LMs usually operate over discrete units obtained from quantizing internal representations of self-supervised models. Although such units show impressive modeling results, their robustness capabilities have not been extensively investigated. This work focuses on improving the invariance of discrete input representations to non-spoken augmentations for generative spoken language modeling. First, we formally define how to measure the robustness of such representations to various signal variations that do not alter the spoken information (e.g., time-stretch). Next, we empirically demonstrate how current state-of-the-art representation models lack robustness to such variations. To overcome this, we propose an effective and efficient method to learn invariant discrete speech representation for generative spoken language modeling. The proposed approach is based on applying a set of signal transformations to the speech signal and optimizing the model using an iterative pseudo-labeling scheme. Our method significantly improves over the evaluated baselines when considering encoding and modeling metrics. We additionally evaluate our method on the speech-to-speech translation task, considering Spanish-English and French-English translations, and show the proposed approach outperforms the evaluated baselines.

1 Introduction

Self-supervised speech models were shown to learn effective representations for various downstream tasks (Hsu et al., 2021; Chen et al., 2022; Baevski et al., 2020). These models were mainly evaluated on discriminative tasks, such as automatic speech recognition, speaker verification, intent classification, etc. (Yang et al., 2021). Recently, Lakhotia et al. (2021) demonstrated that such self-supervised learning (SSL) representations can be used for Generative Spoken Language Modeling.

Generative Spoken Language Modeling (GSLM) is the task of learning the acoustic and linguistic characteristics of a language from raw audio. In other words, a discrete representation of the audio signal is being learned. A common practice is to extract continuous representation using an SSL model, then apply vector quantization, usually using the k-means algorithm (Lakhotia et al., 2021; Kharitonov et al., 2021a; Borsos et al., 2022). Then a speech-language model is trained on top of the obtained representation. Finally, a neural vocoder converts the output units to raw audio. As the discrete speech representation often operates over units extracted over relatively short windows (e.g., 20ms), sequences can be long and contain repetitions, e.g., `10 11 11 11 21 32 32 32 21`. Preliminary studies have found that removing sequential repetitions of units improves performance, hence applying it universally (Lakhotia et al., 2021). For example, a pseudo-text `10 11 11 11 21 32 32 32 21` becomes `10 11 21 32 21`. This framework was shown to be effective in modeling multiple levels of the speech utterance, namely prosody, and content (Lakhotia et al., 2021; Kharitonov et al., 2021a; Borsos et al., 2022), speech codec (Polyak et al., 2021), speech emotion conversion (Kreuk et al., 2021), spoken dialogue (Nguyen et al., 2022), and speech-to-speech translation (Lee et al., 2021; Popuri et al., 2022; Lee et al., 2022).

An essential prerequisite for such an audio representation to be used in real-world conditions is robustness to various signal corruptions. Although the aforementioned audio representation models have shown effectiveness in many tasks, they were mainly evaluated on academic benchmarks.

In this work, we evaluate current state-of-the-art self-supervised speech representation models on what are arguably the most basic signal vari-

Proceedings of the 20th International Conference on Spoken Language Translation (IWSLT 2023), pages 465–477

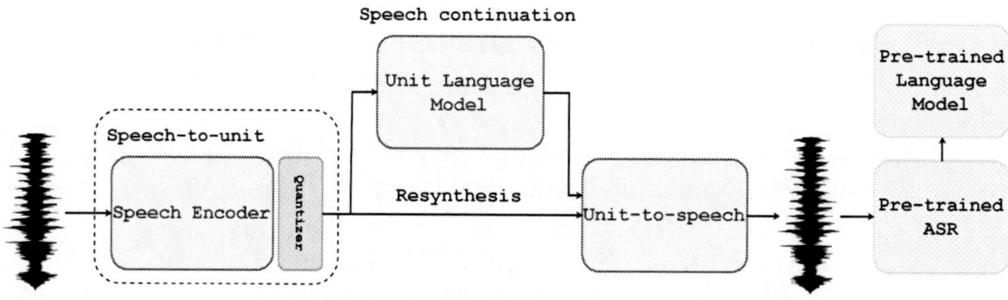

Figure 1: Generative Spoken Language Modeling is composed of three components: (i) Speech-to-unit, (ii) Unit language model, and (iii) Unit-to-speech. Pre-trained ASR and language models are used for evaluation.

ations, namely time-stretch, pitch-shift, additive-noise, and reverberation. Our premise is that while these variations modify the signal, its' underlying content remains the same, especially under the units repetition removal process. Therefore, a robust representation should be affected by such variations to a minimal extent.

As a first step, we propose a set of metrics for evaluating the model's robustness. Then, we point to the lack of robustness of these models with respect to the aforementioned variations. Next, we design a simple and effective method for learning augmentation-invariant discrete representation on top of any speech SSL model. We demonstrate how such a method greatly improves robustness. Then, we empirically show that performance improves on several tasks for various SSL models. Specifically, we evaluate the newly proposed speech encoders when considering zero-shot evaluation tasks considering encoding and modeling, i.e., ABX, sWUGGY, and sBLIMP (Nguyen et al., 2020), together with a high-level downstream task in the form of speech-to-speech translation.

2 Background

The general Generative Spoken Language Modeling (GSLM) pipeline is comprised of three main modules: (i) Speech-to-unit, (ii) Unit language model, and (iii) Unit-to-speech, where each of these modules is trained separately. Speech resynthesis can be achieved while ignoring the language model and directly feeding the quantized units into the unit-to-speech module (Polyak et al., 2021) (See Figure 1 for a visual description). In the following paragraphs, we give detailed background for each of the three components mentioned above, including the standard evaluation methods.

Speech-to-unit module encodes the raw speech signal into a discrete representation. The common approach is first to encode the speech into a continuous representation and then quantize the representation to achieve a sequence of discrete units (Lakhotia et al., 2021; Polyak et al., 2021; Popuri et al., 2022; Lee et al., 2021; Kharitonov et al., 2021a; Kreuk et al., 2021; Kharitonov et al., 2022; Nguyen et al., 2022; Borsos et al., 2022; Tjandra et al., 2019, 2020).

Formally, denote the domain of audio samples by $\mathcal{X} \subset \mathbb{R}$. The representation for a raw signal is therefore a sequence of samples $x = (x_1, \ldots, x_T)$, where $x_t \in \mathcal{X}$ for all $1 \leq t \leq T$.

Consider an encoder network, f, that gets as input the speech utterance and outputs a sequence of spectral representations sampled at a low frequency as follows $f(x) = (v_1, \ldots, v_{T'})$. Note that we do not assume anything about the structure of the encoder network f. Lakhotia et al. (2021), evaluated several speech encoders, namely, Mel-spectrogram, Contrastive Predictive Coding (Oord et al., 2018, CPC), wav2vec2 (Baevski et al., 2020), and HuBERT (Hsu et al., 2021).

Since the representations learned by such models are usually continuous, a k-means algorithm is applied over the models' outputs to generate discrete units, denoted as $z = (z_1, \ldots, z_{T'})$. Each element z_i in z is a positive integer, $z_i \in \{1, .., K\}$ for $1 \leq i \leq T'$, where K is the number of discrete units. We denote the quantization model with E.

Unit Language Model is trained on the extracted discrete units, z. Such a language model learns a probability distribution of the learned unit sequences, which enables direct modeling of speech data without textual supervision.

The language model can be used to generate speech conditionally or unconditionally, replicating what toddlers achieve before learning to read. Moreover, such a modeling framework allows for capturing and modeling prosodic features (Kharitonov et al., 2021a), as well as speaker identity (Borsos et al., 2022), or even natural dialogues (Nguyen et al., 2022). This is in contrast to using textual features, as they do not encode such information.

Unit-to-speech module converts the speech discrete units to a raw waveform. Lakhotia et al. (2021) used a Tacotron2.0 (Shen et al., 2018) based model followed by WaveGlow (Prenger et al., 2019) vocoder. Later, Polyak et al. (2021) proposed a unit-based vocoder based on the HiFi-GAN architecture to convert units to speech directly. Such a paradigm seems to provide high-quality generations with better efficiency as it uses only one model rather than two. Kreuk et al. (2021) and Lee et al. (2021) additionally improved the unit based vocoder to include emotional tokens for speech emotion conversion tasks, and duration modeling for direct speech-to-speech translation.

Zero-shot Evaluation. Evaluating such a complex pipeline comprised of several components is a challenging task. Lakhotia et al. (2021) proposed a set of zero-shot evaluation tasks aiming for each of the modules. Overall the proposed tasks can be divided into four main groups: (i) acoustic encoding using ABX, bitrat, (ii) language encoding using sWUGGY, sBLIMP (Nguyen et al., 2020; Lakhotia et al., 2021), (iii) resynthesis using Phoneme/Word Error Rate; (iv) speech generation using VERT (Lakhotia et al., 2021), Meaningfulness Mean Opinion Score.

3 Robustness of Speech-to-Unit Models

The first step toward developing an effective spoken language model is to develop a robust representation. The focus of a robust representation should be on the spoken information rather than unrelated signals, such as prosodic features in the form on duration and F0, background noise, or reverberations. In the following section, we propose a metric for quantifying the degree to which augmentations change the resulting encoding.

3.1 Unit Edit Distance

A spoken language model is built on top of a discrete representation of a continuous encoder. We examine the robustness of the discrete space to augmentations that do not change the spoken content. Therefore, we are interested in a sequential distance metric between two discrete representations. It is essential to note that augmentations can alter the spatial dimension of the signal. For example, stretching a signal results in more frames, yielding a longer representation sequence. Similar phenomenon will happen when convolving with different room impulse response to simulate reverberation. Hence, the metric should be able to measure the distance between two sequences of different lengths. Ideally, it will consider the number of deletions, insertions, and substitutions that occur due to augmenting the input data. For this purpose, we find the Levenshtein distance a good fit (Levenshtein, 1966). The Levenshtein distance measures the minimum changes one should make to modify one sequence to another. It has two essential properties: the first is that the score is non-negative, and when the sequences are equal, the metric equals zero. The second property is that the maximum value it can get equals the longer sequence length between the two sequences. We provide a detailed explanation of the Levenshtein distance in the Appendix material.

We aggregate the distance values over the evaluation set while considering the sequence length. This is desirable since we want to normalize scores for sequences in different lengths, and the Levenshtein distance's maximum value is the original sequence's length. Another essential property of a spatial metric is repetitions. Consider time stretch as an example, it changes the number of the input frames, but one would expect the deduplicated quantized signal to be the same as before the augmentation. Hypothetically, one can maximize the score by stretching the signal infinitely. To eliminate such dependencies, we compute the score on a deduplicated quantized representation. Formally, our final metric is:

Definition 3.1 (Unit Edit Distance). Given a continuous encoder $f : \mathbb{R}^T \to \mathbb{R}^{T'}$, a quantizer $E : \mathbb{R}^{T'} \to \{1, .., K\}^{T'}$, and an input augmentation $g : \mathbb{R}^{T'} \to \mathbb{R}^{\widehat{T'}}$. The deduplicated unit edit distance $\text{UED}_{\mathcal{D}}(E, f, g)$ on the evaluation set $\mathcal{D}$ is:

$$\sum_{x \in \mathcal{D}} \frac{1}{T'_x} \text{LEV}\left((E \circ f)(x), (E \circ f \circ g)(x)\right), \quad (1)$$

where T'_x is the number of frames of a sample x.

Ideally, a perfect spoken language quantizer obtains a zero distance after deduplication. Next, we study state-of-the-art spoken language representations using our proposed metric in different settings.

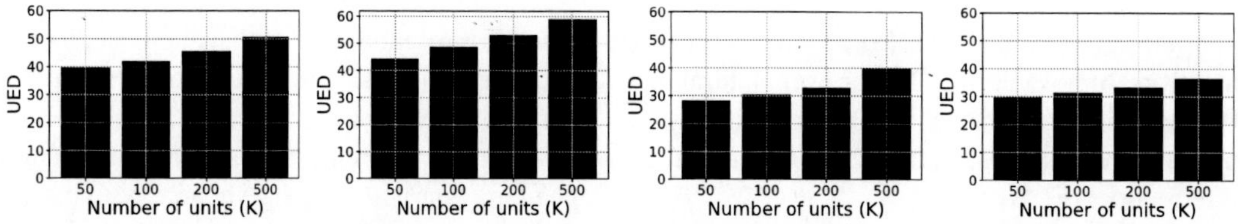

(a) Time stretch (b) Pitch shift (c) Reverberation (d) Noise

Figure 2: UED scores for various augmentations and number of clusters. We note that the UED is relatively high (the distance is normalized). We also note that the UED monotonically increases with the number of units used. We multiply the scores by a hundred.

3.2 Evaluation

In the following, we study current state-of-the-art representations for generative spoken language modeling using the proposed metric. The current popular quantization technique is a k-means model trained on top of a pre-trained encoder (Lakhotia et al., 2021). In our evaluation setup, we use a different number of clusters and encoder architectures. Our ablation study include quantizers with 50, 100, 200, and 500 clusters. We further investigate our metric on top of HuBERT (Hsu et al., 2021), wav2vec2 (Baevski et al., 2020), and WavLM (Chen et al., 2022). For readability, throughout the paper, we report results for the HuBERT model while leaving the rest of the results in the Appendix material.

3.2.1 Augmentations

This work focus on four simple signal modifications which mimic real-world signal variations:

Time stretch. We use the Phase Vocoder method (Karrer et al., 2006) to stretch or shrink the time domain signal with a rate of τ without changing the pitch. For example, $\tau = 1.2$ speeds up the signal by 20%. In this work, for each sample, we sample uniformly a value in the range $[0.8, 1.2]$.

Pitch shift. We change the original pitch of the speech signal by a given number of semitones using the resampling method over the time-stretched signal (Karrer et al., 2006). In this paper, we shift the pitch by up to four semitones.

Reverberation. We follow a similar setting of Chazan et al. (2021), in which we consider an Acoustic Transfer Function (ATF) to be simulated using the pyroomacoustics (Scheibler et al., 2018) audio room simulations package. We randomly sample room dimensions, microphone location, and source location, then convolve the ATF with the speech signal.

Noise injection. We mix a given speech signal with non-stationary additive noise, using a randomly sampled Signal-to-Noise Ratio (SNR) in the range of $[5, 15]$. Background noises are sampled from the Deep Noise Suppression (DNS) challenge (Reddy et al., 2020) which includes a diverse set of noise types from AudioSet (Gemmeke et al., 2017), Freesound, [1] and Demand (Thiemann et al., 2013).

3.2.2 Results

In Figure 2, we use our metric to study the robustness of k-means trained on top of HuBERT with various augmentations and values of K. This evaluation points to the lack of robustness of the current state-of-the-art representation of simple, non-spoken augmentations. For example, for time stretch augmentation, the UED score is between 39 and 51. Considering that UED is computed on deduplicated signals, those numbers are high. Moreover, this number increases as a function of K. The high numbers and the monotonicity of the UED as a function of K are consistent for all values of K, augmentations, and models we experimented with (HuBERT, wav2vec2, and WavLM). Next, we propose a method that improves the robustness of such representations.

4 Invariant Discrete Representation

Our findings in Section 3 suggest that current state-of-the-art representations may be too sensitive to augmentations that do not alter spoken information. Preliminary invariance research focused primarily on noise augmentation. This is convenient since the signal length is not affected by such augmentations. In practice, real-world augmentations may modify the signal length. In order to work with various types of augmentations, we must align the original and augmented sequences. The following section

[1] https://freesound.org/

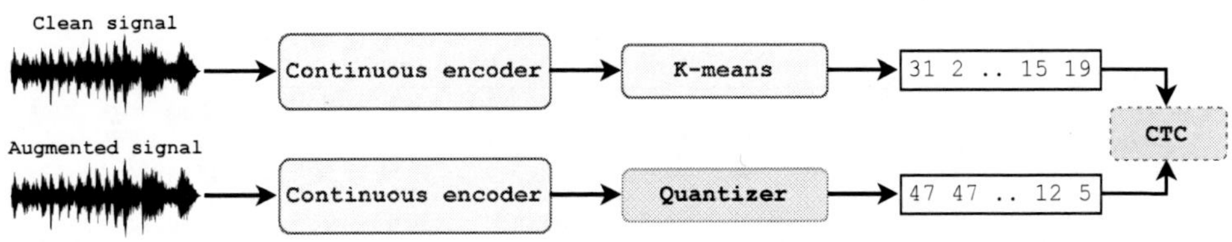

Figure 3: Illustration of our method: We forward a clean signal through an encoder followed by a pre-trained quantizer (k-means). Next, we forward an augmented signal through the same encoder, followed by a new quantizer (green). The CTC loss between the deduplicated output of the clean signal and the output of the augmented signal is used to learn the parameters of the new quantizer. In the iterative approach, post the convergence of the learned quantizer E_0, we freeze it and learn a new quantizer E_1 that distills information from E_0.

presents a pseudo-labeling, alignment-based approach to learning an augmentation-invariant quantizer.

4.1 Pseudo-labeling

The GSLM encoding framework comprises a raw audio signal forwarded through an encoder, then a quantizer. The quantizer is learned on top of a trained encoder, e.g., k-means trained on each embedding vector extracted from HuBERT.

As discussed above, we do not want to limit the invariance process to a family of augmentations that do not change the signal's length. To align and use augmentations that may modify the signal's length, we use the Connectionist Temporal Classification (CTC) loss (Graves et al., 2006). The CTC operation computes the probability of an alignment based on the predicted and target sequences. Finally, the CTC loss considers the negative log-likelihood produced by the CTC operation.

We forward a clean signal through an encoder f followed by a pre-trained quantizer E_0. Parallelly, we forward an augmented signal through the same encoder f and train a non-linear multi-layer-perceptron E_1. Using the CTC loss, which accounts for the alignment between the outputs, we learn the parameters of E_1. Formally, the probability given by the CTC loss $\ell(E_0, E_1, x, g)$ for a single data point x follows

$$-p\left((E_0 \circ f)(x) | (E_1 \circ f \circ g)(x)\right), \quad (2)$$

which can be decomposed to a sum over the set of all alignments $\mathcal{A}_x$

$$-\sum_{\mathcal{A} \in \mathcal{A}_x} \prod_{t=1}^{r} p_t(a_t | (E_1 \circ f \circ g)(x)). \quad (3)$$

Finally, for a training set $\mathcal{D}$, a set of augmentations $\mathcal{G}$, a pre-trained quantizer E_0, and a learned quantizer E_1, our loss function is as follows:

$$\mathcal{L}_{\mathcal{D}}(E_0, E_1, \mathcal{G}) \triangleq \mathbb{E}_{x \sim \mathcal{D}, g \sim \mathcal{U}(\mathcal{G})} \left[\ell(E_0, E_1, x, g)\right].$$

Note that the alignment between the predicted and target sequences is many-to-one. Thus, one or more output units can be aligned to a single target unit. Hence, to work with augmentations that stretch the signal, we are required to deduplicate the target sequence. Intuitively, this process distills quantization knowledge from the pre-trained quantizer into the new quantizer while injecting E_1 knowledge about the contextual similarity between the original and augmented signals.

A significant advantage of our method is that it is highly efficient. Our method requires training only a relatively small amount of parameters. In contrast to previous methods that train HuBERT from scratch, which takes up to seven days on 32 GPUs, our method converges in a few hours on a single GPU. In fact, our experiments show that learning the parameters of the encoder performs worse than freezing them. While the UED is boosted, but the ABX are negatively affected. The freezing of the upstream model thus serves as a regularizer.

4.2 Iterative Pseudo-labeling

In the previous section, we presented a pseudo-labeling approach that relies on a converged quantizer E_0, e.g., k-means on top of HuBERT. This raises the question of whether it is possible to enhance the invariance of the learned quantizer E_1 by iteratively replacing the pre-trained quantizer with the converged quantizer and learning another MLP on top of it. It turns out that such a process can further improve the model's invariance.

The iterative process begins with a pre-trained quantizer E_0, then, as in Section 4.1 we learn an invariant quantizer E_1. Upon E_1 convergence, we replace E_0 with E_1 and use it as the pre-trained quantizer. Then, we learn a new MLP E_2 on top of

# units	Method	Augmentation			
		Time	Pitch shift	Reverberation	Noise
50	k-means	39.61±0.37	44.33±0.92	28.25±0.61	29.74 ±0.31
	Ours	27.91±0.42	30.74±0.71	20.16±0.60	25.33±0.36
	Ours (Iterative)	**26.89**±0.33	**30.22**±0.79	**19.89**±0.54	**24.67**±0.29
100	k-means	41.97±0.42	48.68±0.96	30.42±0.69	31.38±0.33
	Ours	31.05±0.39	34.77±0.92	22.21±0.63	28.05±0.31
	Ours (Iterative)	**29.72**±0.41	**32.84**±0.91	**21.31**±0.71	**25.06**±0.31
200	k-means	45.59±0.39	53.14±1.01	32.89±0.72	33.34 ±0.38
	Ours	34.40±0.46	38.51±1.09	24.10±0.66	30.19±0.37
	Ours (Iterative)	**32.99**±0.42	**36.45**±1.03	**22.94**±0.67	**26.76** ±0.31
500	k-means	50.60±0.42	58.92±0.98	39.71±0.81	36.47±0.44
	Ours	38.04±0.44	43.48±1.03	28.43±0.73	29.99±0.45
	Ours (Iterative)	**36.50**±0.49	**40.82**±1.02	**25.78**±0.74	**27.51**±0.49

Table 1: Unit edit distance study: Using our metric, we assess the robustness of various quantization methods on top of a HuBERT representation. This study uses four different augmentations: time stretching, pitch shifting, reverberation, and noise injection. The non-iterative (Section 4.1) and iterative (Section 4.2) methods significantly and consistently improve the robustness of k-means. Pseudo-labeling accounts for most of the improvement. By applying our method iteratively, we can improve it further. For readability, we multiply the scores by a hundred.

the converged E_1. We repeat this process K times. This process needs more careful training. We note that it is essential to replace the quantizers only post-convergence.

5 Experiments

In the following, we assess the efficacy of our method using state-of-the-art self-supervised representations and popular discriminative and generative evaluation tasks. It is important to note that a single metric cannot tell the whole story. For example, similarly to perplexity, all representations can be assigned to the same cluster, which achieves a perfect unit edit distance but a poor representation. We first examine our proposed method using the unit edit distance along with other discriminative and generative performance metrics. Then, we show that our method improves downstream tasks.

In Section 5.1 we use our proposed metric from Section 3 to analyze the robustness of our method. In Section 5.2 we study the discriminative capabilities of our method using the ABX test (Schatz et al., 2013). Then, we evaluate our methods using generative zero-shot evaluation tasks such as sWUGGY and sBLIMP (Nguyen et al., 2020; Lakhotia et al., 2021). Finally, we demonstrate the effect of using our invariant quantizer's units in speech-to-speech translation.

Experimental Setup. We study our method using the base versions of HuBERT, wav2vec2, and WavLM. For readability, we report results for HuBERT in the main paper. The results for wav2vec2 and WavLM are in Appendix C. To match the current k-means training set, we use the Librispeech-100h to learn our quantizer (Panayotov et al., 2015). We analyze our metric using the 'clean' and 'other' development sets from Librispeech. A detailed setup is provided in Appendix B.

5.1 Analysis

In Section 3, we presented an evaluation metric that assesses the robustness of a quantized speech representation to augmentations. The metric is insensitive to changes in the length of the signal. Using it, we investigated the current state-of-the-art representations. In the following, we study our invariant quantization method.

Table 1 presents the unit edit distance metric using our robustness method with and without the iterative approach. Compared with the k-means method, which is currently in use, our non-iterative method consistently outperforms it by a large margin (relative improvement of at least 30%). We also note that different augmentations affect the representation differently. Our iterative method provides a slight but consistent improvement over the non-iterative method. It is noticeable that the UED is increasing (i.e., worse performing) with the number of units used.

5.2 Zero-shot Evaluation

We evaluate the proposed method using the standard GSLM setup, i.e., ABX, sWUGGY, sBLIMP. The ABX task examines the discriminative phonetic abilities of the representation. Versteegh et al.

# units	Method	ABX (clean) ↓		ABX (other)↓		sWUGGY ↑	sBLIMP ↑
		Within	Across	Within	Across		
50	k-means	7.52	8.90	9.84	13.5	66.12	54.91
	Ours	6.76	7.72	**9.03**	**11.78**	**67.59**	55.76
	Ours (Iterative)	**6.63**	**7.55**	9.53	12.14	67.42	**57.04**
100	k-means	6.37	7.72	8.4	12.29	67.70	56.16
	Ours	5.50	**6.21**	**7.24**	**10.11**	67.79	**57.01**
	Ours (Iterative)	**5.39**	6.22	7.46	10.20	**68.20**	56.99
200	k-means	5.99	7.14	8.23	11.51	66.51	54.64
	Ours	5.29	**6.01**	7.22	9.78	70.51	56.19
	Ours (Iterative)	**5.19**	**6.00**	**7.18**	**9.70**	**70.68**	**56.26**
500	k-means	5.98	6.98	7.89	11.43	66.92	55.97
	Ours	5.16	6.03	7.06	9.76	**70.13**	55.19
	Ours (Iterative)	**4.96**	**5.73**	**6.93**	**9.63**	69.33	**56.93**

Table 2: Zero-shot discriminative and generative evaluation tasks: We evaluate the ABX score on the 'clean' and 'other' development sets from Librispeech. Our method improves the scores scores in all setups.

(2015) show that the ABX result is a good proxy to signal content (i.e., Phoneme Error Rate). The input to the ABX is a pair of words with a phoneme modification and a reference word containing the same phoneme as one of the pair's words. Next, the ABX measures the distance of the test phoneme representation to both the correct and incorrect representations. Finally, the distance between the test and the correct representation is expected to be lower than the distance to the incorrect representation. The ABX task is conducted in two setups: 'within' and 'across.' 'Within' is evaluated on input data from the same speaker, while 'across' is evaluated on input data from different speakers.

Table 2 shows the ABX results for both Librispeech 'clean' and 'other'. In our experiments, we found that the ABX score consistently and significantly improved on all the setups we tested. In this case, the iterative approach improves more than the non-iterative one, but the improvement is inconsistent. For a small number of units and the 'other' split, the ABX score is lower than the iterative model's score. Note that the 'other' split is challenging as it is characterized by recordings that contain background noise and various accents.

The spot-the-word task (sWUGGY) requires detecting the real word from a pair of short utterances such as 'brick' vs. 'blick.' The detection is done by comparing the probabilities given by a language model for each word. This allows comparing representations by training language models on top of them. Differently, the acceptability judgment test (sBLIMP) requires detecting the syntactically correct sentence from a pair of sentences, one of which is syntactically correct and the other is wrong. The detection is based on the perplexity of the language model. As presented in Table 2, our method enables improvement in all the investigated setups for both the spot-the-word and acceptability judgment tests. This is especially noticeable for a larger number of units. For instance, when considering 200 or 500 units, the absolute improvement of the sWUGGY score is 4.17 and 3.21, respectively.

5.3 Speech-to-speech Translation

Lastly, we evaluate the proposed method considering the speech-to-speech translation task. To better assess the effectiveness of the proposed augmentation-invariant discrete representation we follow the same setup as in Lee et al. (2022) while changing the discrete speech representation only.

Lee et al. (2022) propose a textless speech-to-speech translation method by forwarding a source speech signal and predicting its target's discrete representation. The authors use a k-means model trained on top of a multilingual HuBERT (mHuBERT) for speech representation. Additionally, the authors show that solving an auxiliary task enhances performance. We investigate the impact of using our augmentation-invariant quantizer as an alternative to the k-means used by Lee et al. (2022). Differently, we use HuBERT (instead of mHuBERT). Besides that, we follow the same setup in terms of model, computation resources, and data. To evaluate the quality of the translation the sentence BLEU score (SacreBLEU) (Post, 2018) was used.

Table 3 presents the results for the Spanish-English and French-English setups on the Europarl-ST development and test sets (Iranzo-Sánchez et al., 2020). It also shows the original result from Lee et al. (2022). The proposed method improves over

	# units	Method	S-E	F-E
Dev	500	Invariant	17.3	16.4
	1000	k-means	15.4	16.0
	1000	Invariant	**18.2**	**17.5**
Test	500	Invariant	14.4	15.75
	1000	k-means	13.1	15.4
	1000	Invariant	**15.9**	**17.1**

Table 3: Speech-to-Speech Translation results: We report BLEU scores for the proposed method (Invariant) and compare it against the k-means used in Lee et al. (2022). We report both development and test sets results for Spanish(S)-English(E) and French(F)-English(E).

Lee et al. (2022) under all the evaluated setups. Note, these results are especially interesting as the proposed method was trained on significantly less data (ours was trained on 1k hours while Lee et al. (2022) was trained on 100k hours).

6 Related work

This work investigates the robustness of self-supervised representations for language modeling. This is related to the advancements in speech self-supervised learning, their robustness, and modern generative spoken language modeling. In the following, we review all three areas.

Self-supervised Learning. The field of deep learning research has significantly benefited from self-supervised learning. Commonly, it involves encoding the input data and performing a task that enforces the representation to learn contextual embeddings. Speech self-supervised learning can be divided into two lines of research.

The first is discriminative, Oord et al. (2018) introduced Contrastive Predictive Coding (CPC), which trains a convolutional encoder and a predictor for future embeddings of the encoder using a contrastive loss. On top of it, Kharitonov et al. (2021b) propose to use time domain augmentations to improve the CPC model further. Wav2vec2 (Schneider et al., 2019) suggest using a contrastive loss that requires distinguishing between true and false future audio samples. Later, wav2vec2 (Baevski et al., 2020) learn quantized units using Gumbel softmax and predict masked spans of the latent speech representation. HuBERT (Hsu et al., 2021) employ a frame-based masked prediction task. First, it quantizes input frames and then predicts masked frames.

The second line of work is generative. An early generative self-supervised work is Autoregresstive Predictive Coding (Chung et al., 2019), which predicts the spectrum of a future frame. Later, Liu et al. (2020) introduced Mockingjay, which learns its representation by predicting non-causal context. TERA (Liu et al., 2021) alters time, frequency, and magnitude. Then it is required to reconstruct acoustic frames from altered versions.

Robustness. A desired property of a spoken language representation is robustness to augmentations that do not change the spoken information. The spoken information should not differ significantly when male and female speakers say the same content. There is an interesting trade-off between training a robust representation and the quality of the input data. It is possible, for example, to use the same speaker for all data points in the training set. The model would not be able to learn any speaker bias, but this constraint prevents scaling.

Recently, the robustness of self-supervised speech representations has gained attention from the community. WavLM (Chen et al., 2022) proposes adopting the well-known HuBERT model (Hsu et al., 2021) and training it with an additional denoising process. The authors apply a noising process to the training data and then predict the clean units from it. ContentVec (Qian et al., 2022) is focused on the disentanglement of a speaker from self-supervised speech representation. The authors propose to use three disentanglement components. First, the student network is disentangled through two transformations. Then the representations are forwarded through a speaker condition component. Finally, voice-converted input data points are used to generate teacher labels.

7 Conclusions

In this work, we first propose a metric for evaluating the robustness of self-supervised speech representations applied for spoken language modeling tasks. Equipped with the aforementioned metric, we point out the lack of robustness in current state-of-the-art speech encoders with respect to simple signal variations that do not alter the spoken information. We then propose a simple and effective method to augmentation-invariant discrete representation that boosts the robustness of the current approaches and demonstrate it on three state-of-the-art self-supervised speech representation models. We empirically show the efficacy of the proposed approach when considering encoding methods together with a textless speech-to-speech translation.

Broader Impact

As for broader impacts, this work is the first (to the best of our knowledge) which analyzes self-supervised speech representation models, considering basic signal variations. We hope that with the provided analysis and evaluation, researchers working on spoken language modeling and self-supervised speech representation learning will consider reporting the proposed metric setup along with evaluation of down stream tasks.

Limitations

The proposed method has several limitations that should be taken into consideration when employing it. First, the method relies on an existing model, e.g., k-means, which creates a dependency between the performance of the initial and the robust models. Second, the flow is not trained end-to-end, which can also limit its performance as end-to-end training allows improvement of the robustness of the whole representation. Lastly, to fully assess the effectiveness of the method, multiple metrics need to be examined. This can be a limitation as interpreting the results from multiple metrics may not be straightforward. However, it gives a more complete picture of the model's performance.

References

Alexei Baevski, Yuhao Zhou, Abdelrahman Mohamed, and Michael Auli. 2020. wav2vec 2.0: A framework for self-supervised learning of speech representations. *NeurIPS*.

Zalán Borsos, Raphaël Marinier, Damien Vincent, Eugene Kharitonov, Olivier Pietquin, Matt Sharifi, Olivier Teboul, David Grangier, Marco Tagliasacchi, and Neil Zeghidour. 2022. Audiolm: a language modeling approach to audio generation. *arXiv preprint arXiv:2209.03143*.

Shlomo E Chazan, Lior Wolf, Eliya Nachmani, and Yossi Adi. 2021. Single channel voice separation for unknown number of speakers under reverberant and noisy settings. In *ICASSP*.

Sanyuan Chen, Chengyi Wang, Zhengyang Chen, Yu Wu, Shujie Liu, Zhuo Chen, Jinyu Li, Naoyuki Kanda, Takuya Yoshioka, Xiong Xiao, et al. 2022. Wavlm: Large-scale self-supervised pre-training for full stack speech processing. *IEEE Journal of Selected Topics in Signal Processing*.

Yu-An Chung, Wei-Ning Hsu, Hao Tang, and James Glass. 2019. An unsupervised autoregressive model for speech representation learning. In *INTERSPEECH*.

Jort F Gemmeke, Daniel PW Ellis, Dylan Freedman, Aren Jansen, Wade Lawrence, R Channing Moore, Manoj Plakal, and Marvin Ritter. 2017. Audio set: An ontology and human-labeled dataset for audio events. In *ICASSP*.

Alex Graves, Santiago Fernández, Faustino Gomez, and Jürgen Schmidhuber. 2006. Connectionist temporal classification: labelling unsegmented sequence data with recurrent neural networks. In *ICLR*.

Wei-Ning Hsu, Benjamin Bolte, Yao-Hung Hubert Tsai, Kushal Lakhotia, Ruslan Salakhutdinov, and Abdelrahman Mohamed. 2021. Hubert: Self-supervised speech representation learning by masked prediction of hidden units. *IEEE/ACM Transactions on Audio, Speech, and Language Processing*.

Javier Iranzo-Sánchez, Joan Albert Silvestre-Cerdà, Javier Jorge, Nahuel Roselló, Adrià Giménez, Albert Sanchis, Jorge Civera, and Alfons Juan. 2020. Europarl-st: A multilingual corpus for speech translation of parliamentary debates. In *ICASSP*.

Thorsten Karrer, Eric Lee, and Jan O Borchers. 2006. Phavorit: A phase vocoder for real-time interactive time-stretching. In *ICMC*.

Eugene Kharitonov, Jade Copet, Kushal Lakhotia, Tu Anh Nguyen, Paden Tomasello, Ann Lee, Ali Elkahky, Wei-Ning Hsu, Abdelrahman Mohamed, Emmanuel Dupoux, et al. 2022. textless-lib: a library for textless spoken language processing. *arXiv preprint arXiv:2202.07359*.

Eugene Kharitonov, Ann Lee, Adam Polyak, Yossi Adi, Jade Copet, Kushal Lakhotia, Tu-Anh Nguyen, Morgane Rivière, Abdelrahman Mohamed, Emmanuel Dupoux, et al. 2021a. Text-free prosody-aware generative spoken language modeling. *arXiv preprint arXiv:2109.03264*.

Eugene Kharitonov, Morgane Rivière, Gabriel Synnaeve, Lior Wolf, Pierre-Emmanuel Mazaré, Matthijs Douze, and Emmanuel Dupoux. 2021b. Data augmenting contrastive learning of speech representations in the time domain. In *SLT*.

Diederik P Kingma and Jimmy Ba. 2014. Adam: A method for stochastic optimization. *arXiv preprint arXiv:1412.6980*.

Felix Kreuk, Adam Polyak, Jade Copet, Eugene Kharitonov, Tu-Anh Nguyen, Morgane Rivière, Wei-Ning Hsu, Abdelrahman Mohamed, Emmanuel Dupoux, and Yossi Adi. 2021. Textless speech emotion conversion using decomposed and discrete representations. *arXiv preprint arXiv:2111.07402*.

Kushal Lakhotia, Eugene Kharitonov, Wei-Ning Hsu, Yossi Adi, Adam Polyak, Benjamin Bolte, Tu-Anh Nguyen, Jade Copet, Alexei Baevski, Abdelrahman Mohamed, and Emmanuel Dupoux. 2021. On Generative Spoken Language Modeling from Raw Audio. *TACL*.

Ann Lee, Peng-Jen Chen, Changhan Wang, Jiatao Gu, Xutai Ma, Adam Polyak, Yossi Adi, Qing He, Yun Tang, Juan Pino, et al. 2021. Direct speech-to-speech translation with discrete units. *arXiv preprint arXiv:2107.05604*.

Ann Lee, Hongyu Gong, Paul-Ambroise Duquenne, Holger Schwenk, Peng-Jen Chen, Changhan Wang, Sravya Popuri, Yossi Adi, Juan Pino, Jiatao Gu, and Wei-Ning Hsu. 2022. Textless speech-to-speech translation on real data. In *NAACL*.

Vladimir Levenshtein. 1966. Binary codes capable of correcting deletions, insertions, and reversals. In *Soviet physics doklady*.

Andy T Liu, Shang-Wen Li, and Hung-yi Lee. 2021. Tera: Self-supervised learning of transformer encoder representation for speech. *IEEE/ACM Transactions on Audio, Speech, and Language Processing*.

Andy T Liu, Shu-wen Yang, Po-Han Chi, Po-chun Hsu, and Hung-yi Lee. 2020. Mockingjay: Unsupervised speech representation learning with deep bidirectional transformer encoders. In *ICASSP*.

Tu Anh Nguyen, Maureen de Seyssel, Patricia Rozé, Morgane Rivière, Evgeny Kharitonov, Alexei Baevski, Ewan Dunbar, and Emmanuel Dupoux. 2020. The zero resource speech benchmark 2021: Metrics and baselines for unsupervised spoken language modeling. In *NeurIPS – Self-Supervised Learning for Speech and Audio Processing Workshop*.

Tu Anh Nguyen, Eugene Kharitonov, Jade Copet, Yossi Adi, Wei-Ning Hsu, Ali Elkahky, Paden Tomasello, Robin Algayres, Benoit Sagot, Abdelrahman Mohamed, et al. 2022. Generative spoken dialogue language modeling. *arXiv preprint arXiv:2203.16502*.

Aaron van den Oord, Yazhe Li, and Oriol Vinyals. 2018. Representation learning with contrastive predictive coding. *arXiv preprint arXiv:1807.03748*.

Vassil Panayotov, Guoguo Chen, Daniel Povey, and Sanjeev Khudanpur. 2015. Librispeech: an asr corpus based on public domain audio books. In *ICASSP*.

Adam Polyak, Yossi Adi, Jade Copet, Eugene Kharitonov, Kushal Lakhotia, Wei-Ning Hsu, Abdelrahman Mohamed, and Emmanuel Dupoux. 2021. Speech resynthesis from discrete disentangled self-supervised representations. *arXiv preprint arXiv:2104.00355*.

Sravya Popuri, Peng-Jen Chen, Changhan Wang, Juan Pino, Yossi Adi, Jiatao Gu, Wei-Ning Hsu, and Ann Lee. 2022. Enhanced direct speech-to-speech translation using self-supervised pre-training and data augmentation. *arXiv preprint arXiv:2204.02967*.

Matt Post. 2018. A call for clarity in reporting BLEU scores. In *EMNLP*.

Ryan Prenger, Rafael Valle, and Bryan Catanzaro. 2019. Waveglow: A flow-based generative network for speech synthesis. In *ICASSP*.

Kaizhi Qian, Yang Zhang, Heting Gao, Junrui Ni, Cheng-I Lai, David Cox, Mark Hasegawa-Johnson, and Shiyu Chang. 2022. Contentvec: An improved self-supervised speech representation by disentangling speakers. In *ICML*.

Chandan KA Reddy, Vishak Gopal, Ross Cutler, Ebrahim Beyrami, Roger Cheng, Harishchandra Dubey, Sergiy Matusevych, Robert Aichner, Ashkan Aazami, Sebastian Braun, et al. 2020. The interspeech 2020 deep noise suppression challenge: Datasets, subjective testing framework, and challenge results. *arXiv preprint arXiv:2005.13981*.

Thomas Schatz, Vijayaditya Peddinti, Francis Bach, Aren Jansen, Hynek Hermansky, and Emmanuel Dupoux. 2013. Evaluating speech features with the minimal-pair abx task: Analysis of the classical mfc/plp pipeline. In *INTERSPEECH*.

Robin Scheibler, Eric Bezzam, and Ivan Dokmanić. 2018. Pyroomacoustics: A python package for audio room simulation and array processing algorithms. In *ICASSP*.

Steffen Schneider, Alexei Baevski, Ronan Collobert, and Michael Auli. 2019. wav2vec: Unsupervised pre-training for speech recognition. In *INTERSPEECH*.

Jonathan Shen, Ruoming Pang, Ron J Weiss, Mike Schuster, Navdeep Jaitly, Zongheng Yang, Zhifeng Chen, Yu Zhang, Yuxuan Wang, Rj Skerrv-Ryan, et al. 2018. Natural tts synthesis by conditioning wavenet on mel spectrogram predictions. In *ICASSP*.

Joachim Thiemann, Nobutaka Ito, and Emmanuel Vincent. 2013. Demand: a collection of multi-channel recordings of acoustic noise in diverse environments. In *Proc. Meetings Acoust.*

Andros Tjandra, Sakriani Sakti, and Satoshi Nakamura. 2020. Transformer vq-vae for unsupervised unit discovery and speech synthesis: Zerospeech 2020 challenge. In *Interspeech*.

Andros Tjandra, Berrak Sisman, Mingyang Zhang, Sakriani Sakti, Haizhou Li, and Satoshi Nakamura. 2019. Vqvae unsupervised unit discovery and multi-scale code2spec inverter for zerospeech challenge 2019. In *Interspeech*.

Maarten Versteegh, Roland Thiolliere, Thomas Schatz, Xuan Nga Cao, Xavier Anguera, Aren Jansen, and Emmanuel Dupoux. 2015. The zero resource speech challenge 2015. In *Sixteenth annual conference of the international speech communication association*.

Shu-wen Yang, Po-Han Chi, Yung-Sung Chuang, Cheng-I Jeff Lai, Kushal Lakhotia, Yist Y Lin, Andy T Liu, Jiatong Shi, Xuankai Chang, Guan-Ting Lin, et al. 2021. Superb: Speech processing universal performance benchmark. *arXiv preprint arXiv:2105.01051*.

A Levenshtein Distance

Throughout the paper, we use a version of the Levenshtein distance. In this section, we detail the Levenshtein distance between two sequences. Let $x \in \{1, .., K\}^{T_x}$ and $y \in \{1, .., K\}^{T_y}$ be two discrete vectors, not necessary in the same size. Let us also denote the operator $\text{tail}(x)$ to return a copy of the vector x without its first element. Then, the Levenshtein distance is defined recursively by $\text{Lev}(x, y) =$

$$\begin{cases} |x|, & \text{if } |y| = 0 \\ |y|, & \text{if } |x| = 0 \\ 1 + \min \begin{cases} \text{Lev}(\text{tail}(x), y) \\ \text{Lev}(x, \text{tail}(y)) \\ \text{Lev}(\text{tail}(x), \text{tail}(y)) \end{cases}, & \text{otherwise} \end{cases}$$

where $|x|, |y|$ are the lengths of the vectors x and y respectively. Note, in our implementation, we use deduplicated sequences.

B Extended Experimental Setup

Models. We study our method using the base versions of HuBERT, wav2vec2, and WavLM. Similar to prior work, for HuBERT and WavLM, we use the ninth and sixth layers for wav2vec2. For readability, we report results for HuBERT in the main paper. The results for wav2vec2 and WavLM are presented in Appendix C. In our quantizer learning process, we use a learning rate of 0.0001, a batch size of 32, and Adam optimizer (Kingma and Ba, 2014). Our quantizer is composed of three fully connected layers with LeakyReLU activation between them. The dimensions of those layers are determined by the division floor of the difference between the upstream dimension to the number of units. We train our quantizer using a single NVIDIA V100 GPU.

Datasets. To match the current k-means popular training set, we use the Librispeech-100h to learn our quantizer (Panayotov et al., 2015). We analyze our metric using the 'clean' and 'other' development sets from Librispeech. The augmentations in all setups include time stretch, pitch shift, reverberation, and noise injection (exact parameters are detailed in Section 3.2.1). For the sWUGGY and sBLIMP evaluations, we use the 'big' transformer language model from Lakhotia et al. (2021).

This appendix begins with a detailed explanation on the Levenshtein distance (Section A). Then, in Section C, we present additional results. We report results on two additional state-of-the-art self-supervised speech representations. We show that our method is indeed effective for those representations as well as shown in the main paper.

C Additional Results

In the following, we provide additional results on the state-of-arts representations "wav2vec2" and "WavLM" (Baevski et al., 2020; Chen et al., 2022).

Tables 4 and 5 present the UED scores for both the wav2vec2 and WavLM models. Using our method, we observe robustness improvements for both of the models. However, it is notable that the WavLM model is more robust than the wav2vec2 model. It is reasonable since the WavLM trained to be a more robust model using noisy training samples.

Tables 6 and 7 present the discriminative and generative metrics for both wav2vec2 and WavLM. We observe a consistent improvement using our robust quantizer as in the robustness metrics. However, for the WavLM, the improvements are sometimes marginal (except for $k = 50$ where k-means outperforms our method). The WavLM model is trained with a HuBERT architecture, with more data and noisy samples. Interestingly, while presenting better performance on various downstream tasks than HuBERT, their ABX, sWUGGY, and sBLIMP scores are lower.

# units	Method	Augmentation			
		Time	Pitch shift	Reverberation	Noise
50	k-means	50.81±0.41	58.66±1.16	43.71±0.77	32.17±0.61
	Ours	38.74±0.45	42.33±0.97	33.69±0.73	25.36±0.49
	Ours (Iterative)	**36.68**±0.39	**40.29**±1.04	**33.28**±0.74	**23.99**±0.51
100	k-means	55.30±0.61	65.23±0.91	48.41±0.72	33.97±0.46
	Ours	42.32±0.46	47.07±0.88	36.83±0.71	27.15±0.75
	Ours (Iterative)	**40.43**±0.57	**45.73**±0.90	**36.34**±0.77	**26.22**±0.59
200	k-means	59.85±0.39	70.80±1.31	53.13±0.67	36.64±0.62
	Ours	46.84±0.42	51.60±1.21	**40.54**±0.66	32.61±0.67
	Ours (Iterative)	**44.90**±0.35	**49.59**±1.25	**40.58**±0.62	**29.49** ±0.57
500	k-means	66.12±0.48	77.01±0.98	59.69±1.01	37.22±0.65
	Ours	51.65±0.49	**55.40**±1.03	45.85±0.93	33.17±0.62
	Ours (Iterative)	**50.50**±0.53	57.12±1.02	**44.67**±0.98	**31.92**±0.69

Table 4: Wav2vec2 unit edit distance

# units	Method	Augmentation			
		Time	Pitch shift	Reverberation	Noise
50	k-means	47.66±0.49	52.93±1.02	33.45±0.62	28.46±0.61
	Ours	39.12±0.43	44.25±1.06	31.58±0.62	25.32±0.67
	Ours (Iterative)	**36.79**±0.46	**40.16**±1.05	**25.73**±0.64	**25.01**±0.66
100	k-means	52.61±0.51	58.44±0.72	36.27±0.45	29.44±0.64
	Ours	43.55±0.53	49.03±0.75	30.54±0.44	25.93±0.67
	Ours (Iterative)	**42.11**±0.50	**46.08**±0.74	**28.88**±0.47	**25.47**±0.59
200	k-means	58.50±0.42	64.75±1.02	41.05±0.54	30.93±0.62
	Ours	49.57±0.41	53.48±1.09	34.29±0.53	26.66±0.65
	Ours (Iterative)	**47.82**±0.46	**52.47**±1.01	**32.88**±0.55	**26.09** ±0.62
500	k-means	64.25±0.67	70.55±0.75	45.63±0.83	33.17±0.71
	Ours	55.41±0.64	59.79±0.87	42.85±0.78	28.46±0.79
	Ours (Iterative)	**52.92**±0.69	**57.840**±0.81	**40.46**±0.81	**27.09**±0.72

Table 5: WavLM unit edit distance

# units	Method	ABX (clean) ↓		ABX (other)↓		sWUGGY ↑	sBLIMP ↑
		Within	Across	Within	Across		
50	k-means	12.03	15.31	13.61	19.07	**49.76**	53.92
	Ours	11.18	13.82	13.34	18.39	-	-
	Ours (Iterative)	**10.35**	**12.75**	**12.64**	**17.29**	49.65	**55.29**
100	k-means	11.27	13.99	13.06	17.11	51.63	53.87
	Ours	9.86	11.81	11.44	16.63	-	
	Ours (Iterative)	**9.24**	**11.30**	**11.37**	**16.14**	**51.90**	**54.95**
200	k-means	11.13	14.42	12.37	18.02	51.29	54.99
	Ours	10.19	12.41	11.85	17.52	-	-
	Ours (Iterative)	**9.00**	**11.11**	**11.49**	**16.53**	**51.99**	**55.67**
500	k-means	12.06	15.61	13.77	19.94	52.21	54.32
	Ours	10.76	13.83	13.52	19.60	-	-
	Ours (Iterative)	**10.16**	**12.42**	**12.56**	**18.24**	**52.93**	**55.17**

Table 6: Wav2vec2 discriminative and generative evaluation metrics.

# units	Method	ABX (clean) ↓		ABX (other)↓		sWUGGY ↑	sBLIMP ↑
		Within	Across	Within	Across		
50	k-means	7.60	9.06	**9.22**	12.99	63.91	55.29
	Ours	7.41	8.68	9.51	**11.78**	-	-
	Ours (Iterative)	**7.19**	**8.25**	9.41	11.87	**64.87**	**55.81**
100	k-means	6.91	8.06	8.95	11.86	63.61	54.59
	Ours	**6.02**	7.13	8.36	**10.95**	-	-
	Ours (Iterative)	6.39	**7.02**	**8.17**	11.21	**63.99**	**54.97**
200	k-means	6.74	8.12	8.76	12.09	65.97	55.59
	Ours	**6.40**	**7.45**	**8.61**	**11.49**	-	-
	Ours (Iterative)	6.51	7.73	8.93	11.94	**66.90**	**55.89**
500	k-means	7.14	8.10	9.09	11.70	64.56	55.91
	Ours	**7.03**	**7.91**	**8.99**	**11.21**	-	-
	Ours (Iterative)	7.08	7.87	9.03	11.54	**65.81**	**56.09**

Table 7: WavLM discriminative and generative evaluation metrics.

DePA: Improving Non-autoregressive Machine Translation with Dependency-Aware Decoder

Jiaao Zhan[1], **Qian Chen, Boxing Chen, Wen Wang, Yu Bai**[1], **Yang Gao**[1*]
[1]School of Computer Science and Technology,
Beijing Institute of Technology, Beijing, China
jiaao_zhan@163.com
{lukechan1231,chenboxing,wwang.969803}@gmail.com
{yubai,gyang}@bit.edu.cn

Abstract

Non-autoregressive machine translation (NAT) models have lower translation quality than autoregressive translation (AT) models because NAT decoders do not depend on previous target tokens in the decoder input. We propose a novel and general **Dependency-Aware Decoder (DePA)** to enhance target dependency modeling in the decoder of fully NAT models from two perspectives: decoder self-attention and decoder input. First, we propose an autoregressive forward-backward pre-training phase before NAT training, which enables the NAT decoder to gradually learn bidirectional target dependencies for the final NAT training. Second, we transform the decoder input from the source language representation space to the target language representation space through a novel attentive transformation process, which enables the decoder to better capture target dependencies. DePA can be applied to any fully NAT models. Extensive experiments show that DePA consistently improves highly competitive and state-of-the-art fully NAT models on widely used WMT and IWSLT benchmarks by up to **1.88** BLEU gain, while maintaining the inference latency comparable to other fully NAT models.[1]

1 Introduction

Autoregressive translation (AT) systems achieve state-of-the-art (SOTA) performance for neural machine translation (NMT) and Transformer (Vaswani et al., 2017) encoder-decoder is the prevalent architecture. In AT systems, each generation step depends on previously generated tokens, resulting in high inference latency when output is long. Non-autoregressive translation (NAT) models (Gu et al., 2018) significantly accelerate inference by generating all target tokens independently and simultaneously. However, this independence assumption leads to degradation in accuracy compared to AT models, as NAT models cannot properly learn target dependencies. *Dependency* in prior works and our work takes its standard definition in NLP, i.e., syntactic relations between words in a sentence.

The mainstream NAT models fall into two categories: iterative NAT models and fully NAT models. Iterative NAT models (Gu et al., 2019; Ghazvininejad et al., 2019; Lee et al., 2018) improve translation accuracy by iteratively refining translations at the expense of slower decoding speed. In contrast, fully NAT models (Gu et al., 2018; Bao et al., 2022) have great latency advantage over AT models by making parallel predictions with a single decoding round, but they suffer from lower translation accuracy. In this paper, we aim at improving the translation accuracy of **fully NAT models** while preserving their latency advantage.

Previous research (Gu and Kong, 2021) argues that reducing dependencies is crucial for training a fully NAT model effectively, as it allows the model to more easily capture target dependencies. However, dependency reduction limits the performance upper bound of fully NAT models, since models may struggle to generate complex sentences. Previous studies show that multi-modality (Ran et al., 2020) is the main problem that NAT models suffer from (Huang et al., 2021; Bao et al., 2022), i.e., the target tokens may be generated based on different possible translations, often causing over-translation (token repetitions), under-translation (source words not translated), and wrong lexical choice for polysemous words. Table 1 Row3 shows all three multimodality error types from the highly competitive fully NAT model GLAT (Qian et al., 2021) with modeling only forward dependency (F-NAT) in our experiments. We observe that **lack of complete dependency modeling could cause multi-modality errors**. For example, for the source text (in German) "*Woher komme ich?*" in the last column of Table 1, "*Woher*" means both "*where*" and "*how*".

*Corresponding Author

[1]We released our code at: https://github.com/zhanjiaao/NAT_DePA.

Proceedings of the 20th International Conference on Spoken Language Translation (IWSLT 2023), pages 478–490
July 13-14, 2023 ©2023 Association for Computational Linguistics

	Under-Translation	Over-Translation	Wrong Lexical Choice
Source	Wir haben es **weltweit** in 300 Gemeinden gemacht.	Einige leute wollten ihn einfach König nennen	Woher komme ich ? Wer bin ich ?
Target Reference	We 've done it in 300 communities around the world.	Some people just wanted to call him King .	Where am I from ? Who am I ?
F-NAT	We did it the world in 300 communities.	Some people just wanted to call him him king.	How do I come from ? Who am I ?
FB-NAT	We 've done it in 300 communities around the world.	Some people just wanted to call him king.	Where do I come from? Who am I ?

Table 1: Case studies of our proposed **FBD** approach on the highly competitive fully NAT model GLAT (Qian et al., 2021) for alleviating three types of multi-modality errors on the IWSLT16 DE-EN validation set. Repetitive tokens are in red. Source words that are not semantically translated are in bold and underlined. Wrong lexical choices (for polysemous words) and redundant words are in blue. **F-NAT** denotes only modeling forward dependencies while **FB-NAT** denotes modeling both forward and backward dependencies, the same as the models in Table 5. Case studies of our proposed **IT** approach are in Appendix.

The NAT model modeling only forward dependency (F-NAT) incorrectly translates "*woher*" into "*how*" and outputs "*How do I come from?*"; whereas the model modeling both forward and backward dependency (**FB-NAT**) translates it correctly into "*Where do I come from?*". Therefore, instead of dependency reduction, we propose a novel and general Dependency-Aware Decoder (**DePA**), which enhances the learning capacity of fully NAT models and enables them to learn *complete* and *complex* forward and backward target dependencies in order to alleviate the multi-modality issue.

Firstly, we enhance the NAT decoder to learn complete target dependencies by exploring decoder self-attention. We believe that previous works (Guo et al., 2020a) incorporating only forward dependency modeled by AT models into NAT models are inadequate to address multi-modality. Therefore, we propose an effective forward-backward dependency modeling approach, denoted by **FBD**, as an auto-aggressive forward-backward pre-training phase before NAT training, using curriculum learning. The FBD approach implements *triangular attention masks* and takes different decoder inputs and targets *in a unified framework* to train the model to attend to previous or future tokens and learn both forward or backward dependencies.

Secondly, we enhance target dependency modeling within the NAT decoder from the perspective of the decoder input. Most prior NAT models (Gu et al., 2018; Wang et al., 2019; Wei et al., 2019) use a copy of the source text embedding as the decoder input, which is independent from the target representation space and hence makes target dependency modeling difficult. We transform the initial decoder input from the source language representation space to the target language representation space through a novel attentive transformation process, denoted by **IT**. Previous works on transforming the decoder input cannot guarantee that the decoder input is in the exact target representation space, resulting in differences from the true target-side distribution. Our proposed IT ensures that the decoder input is in the *exact* target representation space hence enables the model to better capture target dependencies.

Our contributions can be summarized as follows: (1) We propose a novel and general **Dependency-Aware Decoder (DePA)** for fully NAT models. For DePA, we propose a novel approach **FBD** for learning both forward and backward dependencies in NAT decoder, through which the target dependencies can be better modeled. **To the best of our knowledge, our work is the first to successfully model both forward and backward target-side dependencies *explicitly* for fully NAT models.** We also propose a novel decoder input transformation approach (**IT**). IT could ease target-side dependency modeling and enhance the effectiveness of FBD. DePA is **model-agnostic** and can be applied to any fully NAT models. (2) Extensive experiments on WMT and IWSLT benchmarks demonstrate that our DePA consistently improves the representative vanilla NAT model (Gu et al., 2018), the highly competitive fully NAT model GLAT (Qian et al., 2021) and the current SOTA of fully NAT models, CTC w/ DSLP & Mixed Training (denoted by **CTC-DSLP-MT**) (Huang et al., 2021) (**DSLP** denotes Deep Supervision and Layer-wise Prediction), by up to **+0.85** BLEU on the SOTA CTC-DSLP-MT, **+1.88** BLEU on GLAT, and **+2.2** BLEU on vanilla NAT, while reserving inference latency as other fully NAT models, about **15**$\times$ speed-up over AT models. Experiments show that DePA achieves greater BLEU gains with less speed-up loss than DSLP when applied to various fully NAT models.

2 Related Work

Forward and Backward Dependencies Prior works explore bidirectional decoding to improve modeling of both forward and backward dependencies in phrase-based statistical MT (Finch and Sumita, 2009) and RNN-based MT (Zhang et al., 2018). For NAT, Guo et al. (2020a) and Wei et al. (2019) use forward auto-regressive models to guide NAT training. Liu et al. (2020) introduces an intermediate semi-autoregressive translation task to smooth the shift from AT training to NAT training. However, backward dependencies are rarely investigated in NAT.

Decoder Input of Fully NAT Models The decoder input of AT models consists of previously generated tokens. However, selecting appropriate decoder input for fully NAT models could be challenging. Most prior NAT models (Gu et al., 2018; Wang et al., 2019; Wei et al., 2019) use uniform copy (Gu et al., 2018) or soft copy (Wei et al., 2019) of the source text embedding as the decoder input, which is independent of the target representation space hence hinders target dependency modeling. Methods such as GLAT (Qian et al., 2021) and (Guo et al., 2020a,b) attempt to make the NAT decoder input similar to the target representation space by substituting certain positions in the decoder input with the corresponding target embedding. However, this creates a mismatch between training and inference. Guo et al. (2019) uses phrase-table lookup and linear mapping to make the decoder input closer to the target embedding, but this method still causes difference between the decoder input and the real target-side distribution.

Fully NAT Models To address multi-modality for fully NAT models, various approaches are proposed. Gu et al. (2018) uses knowledge distillation (KD) (Kim and Rush, 2016) to reduce dataset complexity. Libovickỳ and Helcl (2018) and Saharia et al. (2020) use connectionist temporal classification (CTC) (Graves et al., 2006) for latent alignment. Sun et al. (2019) utilizes CRFs to model target positional contexts. Kaiser et al. (2018), Ma et al. (2019) and Shu et al. (2020) incorporate latent variables to guide generation, similar to VAEs (Kingma and Welling, 2013). Guo et al. (2020c) initializes NAT decoders with pretrained language models. Huang et al. (2021) proposes CTC with Deep Supervision and Layer-wise Prediction and Mixed Training (**CTC-DSLP-MT**), setting new SOTA for fully NAT models on WMT benchmarks. DA-Transformer (Huang et al., 2022) represents hidden states in a directed acyclic graph to capture dependencies between tokens and generate multiple possible translations. In contrast, our DePA utilizes forward-backward pre-training and a novel attentive transformation of decoder input to enhance target dependency modeling. Under same settings and with KD, DA-Transformer performs only comparably to CTC-DSLP-MT; however, performance of DA-Transformer benefits notably from *Transformer-big* for KD while CTC-DSLP-MT uses *Transformer-base* for KD. DDRS w/ NMLA (Shao and Feng, 2022) benefits greatly from using diverse KD references while CTC-DSLP-MT uses only a single KD reference. Hence, **CTC-DSLP-MT is still the current SOTA for fully NAT models on WMT benchmarks**.

Non-autoregressive Models Besides fully NAT models, iterative NAT models are proposed such as iterative refinement of target sentences (Lee et al., 2018), masking and repredicting words with low probabilities (Ghazvininejad et al., 2019), edit-based methods to iteratively modify decoder output (Stern et al., 2019; Gu et al., 2019), and parallel refinement of every token (Kasai et al., 2020). Iterative NAT models improve translation accuracy at the cost of slower speed. Non-autoregressive models are practically important due to high efficiency. Other than MT, they are applied to various tasks such as image captioning (Gao et al., 2019), automatic speech recognition (Chen et al., 2019), and text-to-speech synthesis (Oord et al., 2018).

3 Methodology

3.1 Problem Formulation

NMT can be formulated as a sequence-to-sequence generation problem. Given a sequence $X = \{x_1, ..., x_N\}$ in the source language, a sequence $Y = \{y_1, ..., y_T\}$ in the target language is generated following the conditional probability $P(Y|X)$. NAT models are proposed to speed up generation by decoding all the target tokens in parallel, using conditional independent factorization as:

$$P_{NA}(Y|X) = P_L(T|x_{1:N}) \cdot \prod_{t=1}^{T} P(y_t|x_{1:N};\theta) \quad (1)$$

where the target sequence length T is modeled by the conditional distribution P_L, and dependence on previous target tokens is removed. Compared to AT models, NAT models speed up inference significantly at the expense of translation quality, because the conditional independence assumption

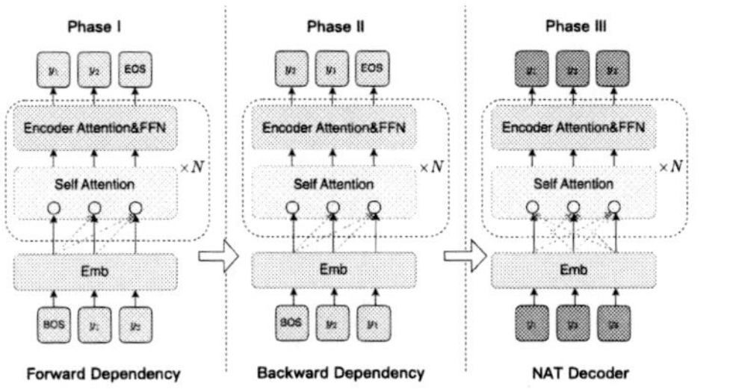

Figure 1: The proposed forward-backward dependency modeling (**FBD**) with triangular attention masks in a unified framework. The red dashed lines indicate the attention masks. We use different colors to highlight the difference of inputs and targets in each phase.

in Eq.1 enables parallel processing but lacks explicit modeling of dependency between target tokens. To enhance target dependency modeling, we propose two innovations as incorporating both forward and backward dependency modeling into the training process (Section 3.2) and transforming the decoder input into the target representation space (Section 3.3).

3.2 Target Dependency Modeling with Curriculum Learning (FBD)

Prior work (Guo et al., 2020a) utilizes forward dependency in AT models to initialize model parameters for NAT. However, as discussed in Section 1, for fully NAT models, only modeling forward dependency is inadequate for addressing the multi-modality problem (Finch and Sumita, 2009; Zhang et al., 2018) (the Row for F-NAT in Table 1). Our innovations include incorporating both forward and backward dependency modeling into NAT models, via *triangular attention masks* in a *unified framework* through *curriculum learning* (Figure 1), and investigating efficacy of different curricula. In Figure 1, the **NAT decoder** phase denotes standard NAT training of any NAT decoder Dec. The **Forward Dependency** and **Backward Dependency** phases serve pre-training for NAT training, learning left-to-right and right-to-left dependencies to initialize NAT models with better dependencies. Forward Dependency and Backward Dependency training phases apply *the same upper triangle attention mask* on Dec. We use KD data from AT models for each phase but the inputs and the targets are different. The Forward Dependency training phase uses y_1 to predict y_2 and so on. The Backward Dependency training phase reverses the target sequence and uses y_2 to predict y_1 and so on. The NAT Training phase uses features of each word to predict the word itself. We make the following hypotheses: (1) Considering the nature of languages, learning forward dependency in Phase 1 is easier for the model for language generation. (2) Modeling backward dependency relies on learned forward dependency knowledge, hence it should be in the second phase. In fact, we observe the interesting finding that **the best curriculum remains forward-backward-forward-NAT (FBF-NAT) for both left-branching and right-branching languages**, proving our hypotheses. We speculate that NAT training may benefit from another forward dependency modeling in Phase 3 because the order of left-to-right is more consistent with characteristics of natural languages, hence adding the second forward dependency modeling after FB (i.e., FBF) smooths the transition to the final NAT training. Detailed discussions are in Section 4.3.

3.3 Decoder Input Transformation (IT) for Target Dependency Modeling

Given the initial decoder input z as a copy of source text embedding, we propose to directly select relevant representations from target embedding to form a new decoder input z' (Figure 2). z is used as the query and the selection is implemented as a learnable attention module. The learnable parameters bridge the gap between training and inference while the selection guarantees consistency between the decoder input matrix and the target representation space (i.e., the output embedding matrix of the decoder). This way, the decoder input is in the *exact* target-side embedding space and more conducive to modeling target dependencies for NAT models than previous approaches using source text embedding or transformed decoder input.

Decoder Input Transformation To transform z into the target representation space, we apply attention mechanism between z and the output embedding matrix $Emb \in \mathbb{R}^{d \times v}$, where d and v denote sizes of hidden states and the target vocabulary. Since NAT models usually have embedding matrix Emb including both source and target vocabularies, first, we conduct a filtering process to remove source vocabulary (mostly not used by the decoder) from the decoder output embedding matrix (the linear layer before decoder softmax). We build a dictionary that contains only target-side tokens in the training set. We then use this dictionary to filter Emb and obtain the new output embedding matrix

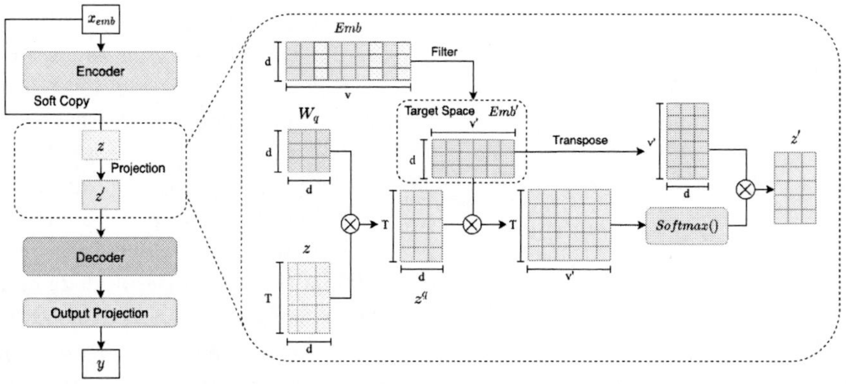

Figure 2: The proposed Decoder Input Transformation **(IT)** from z to z', where $z \in \mathbb{R}^{T\times d}$ denotes the initial decoder input copied from the source text embedding x_{emb}, T and d denote the length of the target text y and the size of hidden states, respectively. $Emb \in \mathbb{R}^{d\times v}$ denotes the output embedding matrix of the decoder (the target representation space), where v denotes the size of the target vocabulary.

of the decoder $Emb' \in \mathbb{R}^{d\times v'}$, where v' denotes size of the filtered vocabulary. This filtering process guarantees that Emb' is strictly from the target representation space. The attention process starts with a linear transformation:

$$z^l = W_q \cdot z \tag{2}$$

Next, the dot-product attention is performed on z^l (as query) and Emb' (as key and value):

$$Sim = \text{softmax}(z^l \cdot Emb') \tag{3}$$

Sim represents similarity between each z_i^l and each embedding in the target vocabulary. Finally, we compute a weighted sum z' of target embedding based on their similarity values:

$$z' = Sim \cdot Emb'^T \tag{4}$$

Since z' is a linear combination of Emb' which is strictly in the target representation space, z' is also strictly in the target representation space, hence using z' as the decoder input provides a more solid basis for target dependency modeling.

Target-side Embedding Compression To reduce the computational cost of IT, we propose a target-side embedding compression approach to compress the large target embedding matrix. We process Emb' through a linear layer to obtain a new target embedding $Emb^* \in \mathbb{R}^{d\times v^*}$:

$$Emb^* = (W_c \cdot Emb'^T)^T \tag{5}$$

where $W_c \in \mathbb{R}^{v^*\times v'}$ is trainable and the size of compressed vocabulary v^* is set manually. The result Emb^* is still in the target representation space. Since we can manually set v^* as a relatively small number (e.g., 1000, 2000), the computational cost of the attention mechanism can be greatly reduced. We hypothesize that target-side embedding compression may also alleviate over-fitting on small datasets and confirm this hypothesis in Section 4.3.

4 Experiments

4.1 Experimental Setup

Datasets We compare our methods with prior works on widely used MT benchmarks for evaluating NAT models: WMT14 EN↔DE (4.5M pairs), WMT16 EN↔RO (610K pairs). Also, we use IWSLT16 DE-EN (196K pairs), IWSLT14 DE-EN (153K pairs), and SP EN-JA[2] (50K pairs) for further analysis. For WMT16 EN↔RO and IWSLT16 DE-EN, we adopt the processed data from (Lee et al., 2018). For WMT14 EN↔DE, we apply the same preprocessing and learn subwords as Gu and Kong (2021). For IWSLT14 DE-EN, we follow preprocessing in (Guo et al., 2019). For SP EN-JA, we use sentencepiece[3] to tokenize the text into subword units following Chousa et al. (2019). Following prior works, we share the source and target vocabulary and embeddings in each language pair in Emb, except EN-JA. Also following prior works (Gu et al., 2018; Qian et al., 2021), all NAT models in our experiments are trained on data generated from **pre-trained AT Transformer-base** with *sequence-level knowledge distillation (KD)* for all datasets except EN-JA.

[2] https://github.com/odashi/small_parallel_enja
[3] https://github.com/google/sentencepiece

Baselines and Training We implement the baseline models based on their released codebases. We implement the representative vanilla NAT (Gu et al., 2018; Qian et al., 2021; Huang et al., 2021)[4], the highly competitive fully NAT model GLAT (Qian et al., 2021)[5], and **current fully NAT SOTA CTC w/ DSLP & Mixed Training (CTC-DSLP-MT)** (Huang et al., 2021)[6] and apply our methods to them. Following Qian et al. (2021), we use base-Transformer (d_{model}=512, n_{head}=8, n_{layer}=6) for WMT datasets and small-Transformer (d_{model}=256, n_{head}=4, n_{layer}=5) for IWSLT and SP EN-JA datasets. We use the same training setup for training the three models, Vanilla NAT , GLAT, and CTC-DSLP-MT as in their original papers cited above. We train models with batches of 64K tokens for WMT datasets, and 8K tokens for IWSLT and SP EN-JA datasets, using NVIDIA V100 GPUs. For GLAT, we use Adam optimizer (Kingma and Ba, 2015) with β = (0.9, 0.999) and set dropout rate to 0.1. For Vanilla NAT and CTC-DSLP-MT, we use Adam optimizer (Kingma and Ba, 2015) with β = (0.9, 0.98). For WMT datasets, the learning rate warms up to 5e-4 in 4K steps and gradually decays according to inverse square root schedule (Vaswani et al., 2017). As for IWSLT and SP EN-JA datasets, we adopt linear annealing (from 3e-4 to 1e-5) as in Lee et al. (2018). We choose the model with the best performance on the validation set as the final model and evaluate the final model on the test sets. For experiments using our method FBD (Section 3.2), we use the **FBF-NAT configuration** (as in Section 4.3) and train the same number of steps at each phase (including NAT training phase), with 300K steps for each phase for WMT datasets and 100K steps for each phase for IWSLT datasets and SP EN-JA. IT by default is **without Target-side Embedding Compression** (Section 3.3).

Evaluation To evaluate the translation accuracy, we use **SacreBLEU** (Post, 2018) for all experiments and ChrF (Popovic, 2015) (also using the SacreBLEU tool) additionally for ablation study on IWSLT benchmark. To evaluate the inference latency, following Gu and Kong (2021), we measure the wall-clock time for translating the entire WMT14 EN-DE test set with batch_size=1 on a single NVIDIA V100 GPU, then compute the average time per sentence. We report **Speed-up** based on the inference latency of *Transformer-base AT (teacher)* and fully NAT models.

4.2 Main Results

Table 2 shows the main results on the WMT benchmarks. For EN↔RO, we report the mean of BLEU from 3 runs with different random seeds for Row 12-13, all with quite small standard deviations (≤ 0.16) [7]. We apply our proposed DePA, which includes IT and FBD, to vanilla NAT, GLAT, and the current fully NAT SOTA CTC-DSLP-MT, on WMT, IWSLT, and EN-JA benchmarks. We use the same hyperparameters and random seeds to fairly compare two models. **It is crucial to point out that accuracies of vanilla NAT, GLAT, and CTC-DSLP-MT models have plateaued out after 300K training steps on WMT datasets hence original papers of these three models set max training steps to 300K**. We verify this observation in our own experiments as we also see no gains on these models after 300K training steps on the WMT datasets. Hence, although our DePA trains $300K \times 4 = 1200K$ steps on WMT datasets due to **FBF** pre-training as in Section 4.3, **all comparisons between baselines w/ DePA and w/o DePA are fair comparisons**. Table 2 shows that DePA consistently improves the translation accuracy for both vanilla NAT and GLAT on each benchmark, achieving **mean=+1.37 and max=+1.88** BLEU gain on GLAT and **mean=+2.34 and max=+2.46** BLEU gain on vanilla NAT. DePA also improves the SOTA CTC-DSLP-MT by **mean=+0.42 and max=+0.49** BLEU gain on the WMT test sets (Table 2), **+0.85** BLEU gain on the IWSLT16 DE-EN validation set and **+1.43** BLEU gain on the EN-JA test set (Table 3). All gains from DePA on vanilla NAT, GLAT, and CTC-DSLP-MT are **statistically significant** ($p < 0.05$) based on a paired bootstrap resampling test conducted using 1K resampling trials and the SacreBLEU tool.

Table 2 also shows that on each benchmark, the average improvement from DePA on three models (vanilla NAT, GLAT, and CTC-DSLP-MT) is within **[0.90,1.56]** (Row15), always larger than the average improvement from w/DSLP on

[4] https://github.com/facebookresearch/fairseq/tree/main/examples/nonautoregressive_translation

[5] https://github.com/FLC777/GLAT

[6] https://github.com/chenyangh/DSLP

[7] WMT14 EN↔DE is much larger than WMT16 EN↔RO. Since standard deviations of BLEU from multiple runs with different random seeds on WMT14 EN↔DE are very small, ≤ 0.08 (Huang et al., 2022), following prior works, we report single-run BLEU on WMT14 EN↔DE to save energy.

Row#	Models	Speed-up ↑	WMT'14 EN-DE	WMT'14 DE-EN	WMT'16 EN-RO	WMT'16 RO-EN
1	Transformer-*base* (teacher)	1.0×	**27.48**	**31.39**	**33.70**	**34.05**
2	+ KD	2.5×	27.34	30.95	33.52	34.01
3	Vanilla NAT	15.6×	20.36	24.81	28.47	29.43
4	w/ DSLP*	14.8×	22.72	25.83	30.48	31.46
5	w/ DePA (**Ours**)	15.4×	**23.15**	**26.59**	**30.78**	**31.89**
6	GLAT	15.3×	25.21	29.84	31.19	32.04
7	w/ DSLP*	14.9×	25.69	29.90	32.36	33.06
8	w/ DePA (**Ours**)	15.1×	**26.43**	**30.42**	**33.07**	**33.82**
10	CTC*	15.5×	25.72	29.89	32.89	33.79
11	w/ DSLP*	14.8×	26.85	31.16	33.85	34.24
12	w/ DSLP & Mixed Training	14.8×	27.02	31.61	33.99	34.42
13	w/ DSLP & Mixed Training & w/ DePA (**Ours**)	14.7×	**27.51**	**31.96**	**34.48**	**34.77**
14	Average improvement from DSLP	-	1.32	0.78	1.38	1.17
15	**Average improvement from DePA (Ours)**	-	**1.50**	**0.90**	**1.56**	**1.53**

Table 2: BLEU and Speed-up from our **DePA** and existing methods on WMT benchmark test sets. **Speed-up** is measured on WMT14 EN-DE test set. BLEUs without rescoring are reported, with the best BLEU scores in bold for each group. * denotes the results are copied from previous work (Huang et al., 2021), other results are obtained by our implementation. Average improvements of DSLP are re-calculated using our results, which are slightly different from Table 1 in (Huang et al., 2021).

them, **[0.78,1.38]** (Row14). DePA brings consistent improvement over SOTA CTC-DSLP-MT on all benchmarks (Table 2 Row13-over-Row12, Table 3), hence we expect DePA to also improve DA-Transformer (Huang et al., 2022) and DDRS w/ NMLA (Shao and Feng, 2022) and will verify this w/ and w/o KD in future work. **Applying DePA to fully NAT models retains the inference speed-up advantages of fully NAT models.** Applying DePA to vanilla NAT, GLAT, and SOTA CTC-DSLP-MT obtain **15.4**×, **15.1**×, and **14.7**× speed-up over the autoregressive Transformer-base (teacher) (Row1). Overall Table 2 shows that **DePA achieves greater BLEU gains with less speed-up loss than DSLP on all baselines.** These results demonstrate superiority of DePA over DSLP on improving other fully NAT models.

4.3 Analysis

Ablation Study We analyze the respective efficacy of IT and FBD in DePA on the IWSLT16 DE-EN validation and the WMT and SP EN-JA test sets. Table 3 shows that FBD and IT improve GLAT by **+1.26 BLEU/+1.5 ChrF** and **+0.34 BLEU/+1.0 ChrF** on IWSLT16 DE-EN validation set, respectively. Considering that GLAT w/FBD has more training steps than GLAT, we also train GLAT (400K steps) which has the same training steps as GLAT w/FBD for fair comparison. **Similar to findings on WMT datasets, we observe plateaus of accuracy on IWSLT and EN-JA datasets from more training steps than the original 100K**. Just training more steps hardly improves the baseline (only +0.07 BLEU gain) on IWSLT16 DE-EN, whereas GLAT w/FBD brings **+1.19 BLEU/+1.2 ChrF** gains over GLAT (400K steps).

Table 4 shows our IT outperforms Linear Mapping (Guo et al., 2019) by **+2.31** BLEU gain on IWSLT14 DE-EN test set. IT has the same number of extra parameters as Linear Mapping. Hence, the large gain proves that improvements from IT are not just from additional layers. The number of extra parameters of IT, as from W_q in Eq.2, is quite small: 512*512=262144 for Transformer-base on WMT datasets and 256*256=65536 for Transformer-small on IWSLT datasets. The large BLEU gain **+3.18** from applying IT to vanilla NAT proves vanilla transformer decoder cannot achieve similar transformation effectiveness as IT. Table 3 shows that for language pairs with different levels of source-target vocabulary sharing, such as WMT EN-DE and DE-EN, IWSLT DE-EN, EN-RO, and EN-JA, our IT method can achieve consistent improvements over GLAT and CTC-DSLP-MT. Applying IT consistently improves GLAT and CTC-DSLP-MT although these gains are smaller than gain on vanilla NAT. This is because decoder input of vanilla NAT only replicates source embedding, whereas GLAT and CTC-DSLP-MT already transform decoder input by replacing selected positions in decoder input with target embedding, hence reducing improvements of IT. Still, gains from w/IT+FBD over w/FBD confirms our hypothesis that IT can enhance effectiveness of FBD. On GLAT, IT+FBD yields **+1.4 BLEU/+2.7 ChrF** gains on IWSLT16 DE-EN and **+1.43 BLEU**

Models	IWSLT16 DE-EN BLEU	IWSLT16 DE-EN ChrF	WMT'14 EN-DE BLEU	WMT'14 DE-EN BLEU	WMT'16 EN-RO BLEU	WMT'16 RO-EN BLEU
CTC-DSLP-MT	31.04	56.7	27.02	31.61	34.17	34.60
CTC-DSLP-MT w/ IT	31.29	57.1	27.21	31.78	34.32	34.71
CTC-DSLP-MT w/ FBD	31.73	57.5	27.44	31.90	34.60	34.92
CTC-DSLP-MT w/ IT+FBD	**31.89**	**57.8**	**27.51**	**31.96**	**34.68**	**34.98**

Models	IWSLT16 DE-EN BLEU	IWSLT16 DE-EN ChrF	EN-JA BLEU
GLAT	29.61	51.8	27.67
GLAT (400K step)	29.68	52.1	–
GLAT w/ IT	29.95	52.8	27.95
GLAT w/ FBD	30.87	53.3	28.87
GLAT w/ IT+FBD	**31.01**	**54.5**	**29.10**

Table 3: Effect of **IT** and **FBD** and IT+FBD (i.e., **DePA**) on the IWSLT16 DE-EN validation set, the WMT and SP EN-JA test sets. We report **mean of BLEU/ChrF** from 3 runs with different random seeds. BLEU gains from DePA on SOTA CTC-DSLP-MT on each set, **[0.85, 0.49, 0.51]**, are larger than std (≤ 0.17).

Models	BLEU
Vanilla NAT (Guo et al., 2019)	22.95
Vanilla NAT w/ Linear Mapping (Guo et al., 2019)	24.13
Vanilla NAT (our implementation)	23.26
Vanilla NAT w/ IT	**26.44**

Table 4: Compare **IT** and Linear Mapping (Guo et al., 2019) on vanilla NT on the IWSLT14 DE-EN test set.

on EN-JA and on SOTA CTC-DSLP-MT, **+0.85 BLEU/+1.1 ChrF** gain on IWSLT16 DE-EN.

To further analyze IT, we compare cosine similarity between the target embedding against the original decoder input and the transformed decoder input, respectively. For each sample in the IWSLT16 DE-EN validation set, we average all its token embeddings as the decoder input representation and the same for the target representation and then compute cosine similarity. We average similarities of all samples as the final similarity. We find that **IT significantly improves similarity between the decoder input and the target representation**, $0.04951 \rightarrow 0.14521$ for GLAT and $0.04837 \rightarrow 0.14314$ for vanilla NAT.

Impact of Different Dependency Curricula in FBD Table 5 presents results from applying different forward-backward dependency modeling curricula (Figure 1) on GLAT on the IWSLT16 DE-EN validation and the SP EN-JA test sets. Compared with modeling backward dependency in Phase 1 (B-NAT and BF-NAT), modeling forward dependency in Phase 1 (F-NAT , FB-NAT, and FBF-NAT) performs notably better. FB-NAT outperforms BF-NAT by **+3.04** BLEU on IWSLT16 DE-EN and **+2.08** BLEU on EN-JA. It seems that forward dependency modeling achieves good initialization for subsequent training phases, while backward dependency modeling cannot. We observe the best curriculum as **FBF-NAT**, i.e., first learn forward dependency, next learn backward dependency, then another round of forward dependency training before NAT training. Table 5 shows the same trend of curricula on SP EN-JA as on IWSLT16 DE-EN, with FBF-NAT performing best, demonstrating that this trend of forward-backward dependency modeling curricula is consistent for both right-branching (English) and left-branching (Japanese) target languages. All these observations confirm our hypotheses in Section 3.2. Our FBF-NAT consistently outperforms baseline GLAT (denoted by NAT in Table 5) by **+1.58** on IWSLT16 DE-EN and **+1.56** on SP EN-JA and outperforms prior works modeling forward dependency only (Guo et al., 2020a) on GLAT (denoted by F-NAT in Table 5) by **+1.15** on DE-EN and **+1.08** on EN-JA.

DePA on Raw Data We evaluate DePA on raw data by training models on the original training set without KD (Section 4.1). DePA improves GLAT on the IWSLT16 DE-EN validation set by **+1.57** BLEU ($26.57 \rightarrow 28.14$), proving that DePA effectively enhances the dependency modeling ability of fully NAT models hence **reduces dependence of NAT training on AT models**.

Effectiveness of Target-side Embedding Compression We propose a linear compression module to reduce the selection candidates of the target

IWSLT16 DE-EN validation set				SP EN-JA test set			
Models	**BLEU**	**Models**	**BLEU**	**Models**	**BLEU**	**Models**	**BLEU**
NAT	29.61	BF-NAT	27.83	NAT	27.67	BF-NAT	26.79
F-NAT	30.04	FB-NAT	30.87	F-NAT	28.15	FB-NAT	28.87
B-NAT	27.05	FBF-NAT	**31.19**	B-NAT	25.83	FBF-NAT	**29.23**

Table 5: BLEU from different dependency modeling curricula on GLAT. Best results for each set are in bold. **NAT** denotes GLAT baseline. **F** and **B** denote forward dependency and backward dependency phase respectively (Figure 1). For example, F-NAT denotes forward dependency training then NAT training.

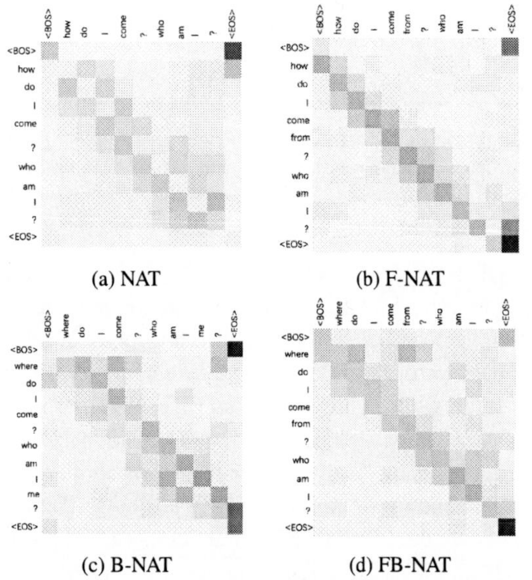

(a) NAT (b) F-NAT (c) B-NAT (d) FB-NAT

Figure 3: Visualization of the decoder self-attention distribution in NAT models on IWSLT16 DE-EN validation set. Definitions of model names are the same as in Table 5.

Compressed Dimension	w/o IT	1000	1200	1400	1600	1800	2000
BLEU	29.61	29.45	29.56	29.77	29.85	**30.39**	29.14

Table 6: BLEU from GLAT w/ IT on the IWSLT16 DE-EN validation set with Target-side Embedding Compression described in Section 3.3.

embedding for IT (Section 3.3). We use the dichotomy to determine the compression dimension interval $[1000, 2000]$ and evaluate GLAT w/ IT using different dimensions with step size 200 in this interval for IT on the IWSLT16 DE-EN validation set. As shown in Table 6, applying IT on GLAT improves BLEU up to **+0.78** (29.61→ 30.39) with compressed dimension 1800. We also experiment with target-side embedding compression on a larger model on WMT16 EN-RO but find no gains. We assume that for relatively small models and data, this approach helps filter out some redundant target information, hence refines the target representation space and improves the translation accuracy.

4.4 Case Study and Visualization

Table 1 presents case studies of GLAT w/ FBD ("FB-NAT") and with only forward modeling ("F-NAT") on IWLST16 DE-EN validation set. Some typical multi-modality errors in F-NAT predictions are corrected by incorporating both forward and backward dependency modeling through FBD.

For a more intuitive analysis of FBD, we present a visualization of the decoder self-attention distribution of different NAT models in Figure 3. All models are based on GLAT and model names conform to those in Table 5. In the baseline GLAT (Figure 3a), the self-attention distribution of each position is scattered in adjacent positions, indicating that the NAT model lacks dependency and has high confusion during decoding, causing multi-modality errors. In F-NAT and B-NAT models, significant forward and backward dependencies can be observed in Figure 3b and 3c, indicating that these two models can better use information in previous or future positions. Encouragingly, forward and backward dependencies are fused in the FB-NAT model (Figure 3d), which can focus on future information while modeling forward dependency, capable of alleviating problems shown in Table 1.

5 Conclusion

We propose a novel and general Dependency-Aware Decoder (DePA) to enhance target dependency modeling for fully NAT models, with forward-backward dependency modeling and decoder input transformation. Extensive experiments show that DePA improves the translation accuracy of highly competitive and SOTA fully NAT models while preserving their inference latency. In future work, we will evaluate DePA on iterative NAT models such as Imputer, CMLM, and Levenshtein Transformer and incorporate ranking approaches into DePA.

6 Limitations

Apart from all the advantages that our work achieves, some limitations still exist. Firstly, in this work, we investigate the efficacy of applying our proposed DePA approach on the representative vanilla NAT, the highly competitive fully NAT model GLAT and current SOTA CTC-DSLP-MT for fully NAT models, but we have yet to apply DePA to iterative NAT models, such as Imputer (Saharia et al., 2020), CMLM (Ghazvininejad et al., 2019), and Levenshtein Transformer (Gu et al., 2019). Hence, the effectiveness of DePA on iterative NAT models still needs to be verified. Secondly, we have not yet incorporated reranking approaches such as Noisy Parallel Decoding (NPD) (Gu et al., 2018) into DePA. Thirdly, our proposed method FBD requires multiple additional training phases before NAT training, resulting in longer training time and using more GPU resources. Reducing the computational cost of FBD training is one future work that will be beneficial for energy saving. Last but not least, NAT models have limitations on handling long text. They suffer from worse translation quality when translating relatively long text. We plan to investigate all these topics in future work.

References

Yu Bao, Hao Zhou, Shujian Huang, Dongqi Wang, Lihua Qian, Xinyu Dai, Jiajun Chen, and Lei Li. 2022. GLAT: glancing at latent variables for parallel text generation. In *Proceedings of the 60th Annual Meeting of the Association for Computational Linguistics (Volume 1: Long Papers), ACL 2022, Dublin, Ireland, May 22-27, 2022*, pages 8398–8409. Association for Computational Linguistics.

Nanxin Chen, Shinji Watanabe, Jesús Villalba, and Najim Dehak. 2019. Listen and fill in the missing letters: Non-autoregressive transformer for speech recognition. *arXiv preprint arXiv:1911.04908*.

Katsuki Chousa, Katsuhito Sudoh, and Satoshi Nakamura. 2019. Simultaneous neural machine translation using connectionist temporal classification. *arXiv preprint arXiv:1911.11933*.

Andrew M. Finch and Eiichiro Sumita. 2009. Bidirectional phrase-based statistical machine translation. In *Proceedings of the 2009 Conference on Empirical Methods in Natural Language Processing, EMNLP 2009, 6-7 August 2009, Singapore, A meeting of SIGDAT, a Special Interest Group of the ACL*, pages 1124–1132. ACL.

Junlong Gao, Xi Meng, Shiqi Wang, Xia Li, Shanshe Wang, Siwei Ma, and Wen Gao. 2019. Masked non-autoregressive image captioning. *arXiv preprint arXiv:1906.00717*.

Marjan Ghazvininejad, Omer Levy, Yinhan Liu, and Luke Zettlemoyer. 2019. Mask-predict: Parallel decoding of conditional masked language models. *arXiv preprint arXiv:1904.09324*.

Alex Graves, Santiago Fernández, Faustino J. Gomez, and Jürgen Schmidhuber. 2006. Connectionist temporal classification: labelling unsegmented sequence data with recurrent neural networks. In *Machine Learning, Proceedings of the Twenty-Third International Conference (ICML 2006), Pittsburgh, Pennsylvania, USA, June 25-29, 2006*, volume 148 of *ACM International Conference Proceeding Series*, pages 369–376. ACM.

Jiatao Gu, James Bradbury, Caiming Xiong, Victor OK Li, and Richard Socher. 2018. Non-autoregressive neural machine translation. In *International Conference on Learning Representations*.

Jiatao Gu and Xiang Kong. 2021. Fully non-autoregressive neural machine translation: Tricks of the trade. In *Findings of the Association for Computational Linguistics: ACL-IJCNLP 2021*, pages 120–133, Online. Association for Computational Linguistics.

Jiatao Gu, Changhan Wang, and Jake Zhao. 2019. Levenshtein transformer. *arXiv preprint arXiv:1905.11006*.

Junliang Guo, Xu Tan, Di He, Tao Qin, Linli Xu, and Tie-Yan Liu. 2019. Non-autoregressive neural machine translation with enhanced decoder input. In *Proceedings of the AAAI Conference on Artificial Intelligence*, volume 33, pages 3723–3730.

Junliang Guo, Xu Tan, Linli Xu, Tao Qin, Enhong Chen, and Tie-Yan Liu. 2020a. Fine-tuning by curriculum learning for non-autoregressive neural machine translation. In *Proceedings of the AAAI Conference on Artificial Intelligence*, volume 34, pages 7839–7846.

Junliang Guo, Linli Xu, and Enhong Chen. 2020b. Jointly masked sequence-to-sequence model for non-autoregressive neural machine translation. In *Proceedings of the 58th Annual Meeting of the Association for Computational Linguistics*, pages 376–385.

Junliang Guo, Zhirui Zhang, Linli Xu, Hao-Ran Wei, Boxing Chen, and Enhong Chen. 2020c. Incorporating bert into parallel sequence decoding with adapters. In *NeurIPS*.

Chenyang Huang, Hao Zhou, Osmar R Zaïane, Lili Mou, and Lei Li. 2021. Non-autoregressive translation with layer-wise prediction and deep supervision. *arXiv preprint arXiv:2110.07515*.

Fei Huang, Hao Zhou, Yang Liu, Hang Li, and Minlie Huang. 2022. Directed acyclic transformer for non-autoregressive machine translation. *CoRR*, abs/2205.07459.

Lukasz Kaiser, Samy Bengio, Aurko Roy, Ashish Vaswani, Niki Parmar, Jakob Uszkoreit, and Noam Shazeer. 2018. Fast decoding in sequence models using discrete latent variables. In *International Conference on Machine Learning*, pages 2390–2399. PMLR.

Jungo Kasai, James Cross, Marjan Ghazvininejad, and Jiatao Gu. 2020. Non-autoregressive machine translation with disentangled context transformer. In *International Conference on Machine Learning*, pages 5144–5155. PMLR.

Yoon Kim and Alexander M Rush. 2016. Sequence-level knowledge distillation. In *Proceedings of the 2016 Conference on Empirical Methods in Natural Language Processing*, pages 1317–1327.

Diederik P Kingma and Jimmy Ba. 2015. Adam: A method for stochastic optimization. In *ICLR (Poster)*.

Diederik P Kingma and Max Welling. 2013. Auto-encoding variational bayes. *arXiv preprint arXiv:1312.6114*.

Jason Lee, Elman Mansimov, and Kyunghyun Cho. 2018. Deterministic non-autoregressive neural sequence modeling by iterative refinement. In *Proceedings of the 2018 Conference on Empirical Methods in Natural Language Processing*, pages 1173–1182.

Jindřich Libovickỳ and Jindřich Helcl. 2018. End-to-end non-autoregressive neural machine translation with connectionist temporal classification. In *Proceedings of the 2018 Conference on Empirical Methods in Natural Language Processing*, pages 3016–3021.

Jinglin Liu, Yi Ren, Xu Tan, Chen Zhang, Tao Qin, Zhou Zhao, and Tie-Yan Liu. 2020. Task-level curriculum learning for non-autoregressive neural machine translation. In *Proceedings of the Twenty-Ninth International Joint Conference on Artificial Intelligence, IJCAI 2020*, pages 3861–3867. ijcai.org.

Xuezhe Ma, Chunting Zhou, Xian Li, Graham Neubig, and Eduard Hovy. 2019. Flowseq: Non-autoregressive conditional sequence generation with generative flow. In *Proceedings of the 2019 Conference on Empirical Methods in Natural Language Processing and the 9th International Joint Conference on Natural Language Processing (EMNLP-IJCNLP)*, pages 4282–4292.

Aaron Oord, Yazhe Li, Igor Babuschkin, Karen Simonyan, Oriol Vinyals, Koray Kavukcuoglu, George Driessche, Edward Lockhart, Luis Cobo, Florian Stimberg, et al. 2018. Parallel wavenet: Fast high-fidelity speech synthesis. In *International conference on machine learning*, pages 3918–3926. PMLR.

Maja Popovic. 2015. chrf: character n-gram f-score for automatic MT evaluation. In *Proceedings of the Tenth Workshop on Statistical Machine Translation, WMT@EMNLP 2015, 17-18 September 2015, Lisbon, Portugal*, pages 392–395. The Association for Computer Linguistics.

Matt Post. 2018. A call for clarity in reporting BLEU scores. In *Proceedings of the Third Conference on Machine Translation: Research Papers, WMT 2018, Belgium, Brussels, October 31 - November 1, 2018*, pages 186–191. Association for Computational Linguistics.

Lihua Qian, Hao Zhou, Yu Bao, Mingxuan Wang, Lin Qiu, Weinan Zhang, Yong Yu, and Lei Li. 2021. Glancing transformer for non-autoregressive neural machine translation. In *Proceedings of the 59th Annual Meeting of the Association for Computational Linguistics and the 11th International Joint Conference on Natural Language Processing (Volume 1: Long Papers)*, pages 1993–2003, Online. Association for Computational Linguistics.

Qiu Ran, Yankai Lin, Peng Li, and Jie Zhou. 2020. Learning to recover from multi-modality errors for non-autoregressive neural machine translation. In *Proceedings of the 58th Annual Meeting of the Association for Computational Linguistics*, pages 3059–3069.

Chitwan Saharia, William Chan, Saurabh Saxena, and Mohammad Norouzi. 2020. Non-autoregressive machine translation with latent alignments. In *Proceedings of the 2020 Conference on Empirical Methods in Natural Language Processing (EMNLP)*, pages 1098–1108.

Chenze Shao and Yang Feng. 2022. Non-monotonic latent alignments for ctc-based non-autoregressive machine translation. *arXiv preprint arXiv:2210.03953*.

Raphael Shu, Jason Lee, Hideki Nakayama, and Kyunghyun Cho. 2020. Latent-variable non-autoregressive neural machine translation with deterministic inference using a delta posterior. In *Proceedings of the AAAI Conference on Artificial Intelligence*, volume 34, pages 8846–8853.

Mitchell Stern, William Chan, Jamie Kiros, and Jakob Uszkoreit. 2019. Insertion transformer: Flexible sequence generation via insertion operations. In *International Conference on Machine Learning*, pages 5976–5985. PMLR.

Zhiqing Sun, Zhuohan Li, Haoqing Wang, Di He, Zi Lin, and Zhi-Hong Deng. 2019. Fast structured decoding for sequence models. In *NeurIPS*.

Ashish Vaswani, Noam Shazeer, Niki Parmar, Jakob Uszkoreit, Llion Jones, Aidan N Gomez, Łukasz Kaiser, and Illia Polosukhin. 2017. Attention is all you need. In *Advances in neural information processing systems*, pages 5998–6008.

Yiren Wang, Fei Tian, Di He, Tao Qin, ChengXiang Zhai, and Tie-Yan Liu. 2019. Non-autoregressive machine translation with auxiliary regularization. In *Proceedings of the AAAI Conference on Artificial Intelligence*, volume 33, pages 5377–5384.

Bingzhen Wei, Mingxuan Wang, Hao Zhou, Junyang Lin, and Xu Sun. 2019. Imitation learning for non-autoregressive neural machine translation. In *Proceedings of the 57th Annual Meeting of the Association for Computational Linguistics*, pages 1304–1312.

Xiangwen Zhang, Jinsong Su, Yue Qin, Yang Liu, Rongrong Ji, and Hongji Wang. 2018. Asynchronous bidirectional decoding for neural machine translation. In *Proceedings of the Thirty-Second AAAI Conference on Artificial Intelligence, (AAAI-18), the 30th innovative Applications of Artificial Intelligence (IAAI-18), and the 8th AAAI Symposium on Educational Advances in Artificial Intelligence (EAAI-18), New Orleans, Louisiana, USA, February 2-7, 2018*, pages 5698–5705. AAAI Press.

Case study for the proposed IT NAT models generally suffer from the multi-modality problem, which shows as *over-translation* (repetition), *under-translation* (missing information), and *wrong lexical choice* (incorrect translations caused by polysemy) (Ran et al., 2020). As shown in Table 7, Vanilla NAT and GLAT tend to generate repetitive tokens which are highlighted in red (over-translation). Additionally, Vanilla NAT omits the translation of "schließlich" which is in bold and underlined (under-translation). By applying our method IT, the decoder input is closer to the target representation space and the model has a better perception for the target-side information, so that the repetition and under-translation problems can be effectively alleviated. As for incorrect translations caused by polysemy, as shown in Case #1 in Table 7, "Drucks" means both "printing" and "pressure" in German. GLAT mistakenly translates "Drucks" into "printing", but our method can help the model correctly translate it into "pressure". Particularly, in Case #2, "Bauplan" means "blueprint" in German. Although both baseline models Vanilla NAT and GLAT generate the correct words, they also generate the redundant word "plan" which is also a subword of "Bauplan". These examples demonstrate that the baseline models may confuse the source representation space with the target representation space during generation, but our method IT effectively remedies this problem.

	Case #1	Case #2
Source	obwohl sie erwischt wurden , wurden sie **schließlich** freigelassen aufgrund immensen internationalen Drucks .	das ist ein Bauplan für Länder wie China und den Iran .
Target Reference	even though they were caught , they were eventually released after heavy international pressure .	this is a blueprint for countries like China and Iran .
Vanilla NAT	although they were caught , they were released released because because of huge drug .	this is a blueprint plan for countries like China and and Iran .
Vanilla NAT w/ IT	although they were caught , they were finally released because huge international pressure .	this is a blueprint for countries like China and Iran .
GLAT	although they were caught , they finally were released because of of international printing .	this is a blueprint plan for countries like China and Iran .
GLAT w/ IT	although they were caught , they were finally released after huge international pressure .	this is a blueprint for countries like China and Iran .

Table 7: Case studies of our method **IT** on the IWSLT16 DE-EN validation set by comparing the translations from the two baseline models Vanilla NAT and GLAT and from them after applying IT (models in bold). Repetitive tokens are in red. Source words that are not semantically translated are marked in bold and underlined (under-translation). Wrong lexical choice (incorrect translations caused by polysemy) and redundant words are in blue.

On the Copying Problem of Unsupervised NMT: A Training Schedule with a Language Discriminator Loss

Yihong Liu[*◇], **Alexandra Chronopoulou**[*◇], **Hinrich Schütze**[*◇], **and Alexander Fraser**[*◇]

[*]Center for Information and Language Processing, LMU Munich
[◇]Munich Center for Machine Learning (MCML)
{yihong, achron, fraser}@cis.lmu.de

Abstract

Although unsupervised neural machine translation (UNMT) has achieved success in many language pairs, the copying problem, i.e., directly copying some parts of the input sentence as the translation, is common among distant language pairs, especially when low-resource languages are involved. We find this issue is closely related to an unexpected copying behavior during online back-translation (BT). In this work, we propose a simple but effective training schedule that incorporates a language discriminator loss. The loss imposes constraints on the intermediate translation so that the translation is in the desired language. By conducting extensive experiments on different language pairs, including similar and distant, high and low-resource languages, we find that our method alleviates the copying problem, thus improving the translation performance on low-resource languages.

1 Introduction

UNMT (Lample et al., 2018; Artetxe et al., 2018) is a new and effective approach for tackling the scarcity of parallel data. Typically, a cross-lingual pretrained language model (PLM) (Peters et al., 2018; Devlin et al., 2019) is trained on two languages and then used to initialize the model for the UNMT task (Conneau and Lample, 2019; Song et al., 2019; Yang et al., 2020; Liu et al., 2020). However, when it comes to low-resource languages, especially when translating between distant language pairs, UNMT often yields very poor results (Neubig and Hu, 2018; Guzmán et al., 2019; Marchisio et al., 2020). One of the major problems that lead to low translation quality is the copying problem or off-target problem (Kim et al., 2020; Zhang et al., 2020). That is: the trained model does not translate but copies some words or even the whole sentence from the input as the translation.

We find the copying problem is closely related to an unexpected behavior in BT (Sennrich et al., 2016): the model does not translate into the correct intermediate language but simply copies tokens from the source language. To address this problem, this work proposes a simple but effective method that can be integrated into the standard UNMT training. We leverage a language discriminator to detect the language of the intermediate translation generated in BT and backpropagate the gradients to the main model. In this way, we can provide implicit supervision to the model. We find that by adding such a training objective, the copying problem can be largely alleviated, especially for low-resource languages. Noticeably, we do not introduce any language-specific architectures into the main model. To the best of our knowledge, this is the first work that introduces a language discriminator loss to force the intermediate translations in BT to be in the correct language. The contributions of our work are as follows:

(1) We explore the reasons behind the copying problem in UNMT and propose a training schedule with a language discriminator loss.
(2) We evaluate our method on many languages, including high- and low-resource, and similar and distant language pairs.
(3) We carry out an analysis, showing the proposed method can reduce the copying ratio, especially on small-size datasets and distant language pairs.
(4) We make our code publicly available. [1]

2 Problem Statement & Approach

2.1 Copying Problem

The copying problem is also known as an off-target translation issue in multilingual NMT especially zero-shot scenario (Gu et al., 2019; Yang et al., 2021; Chen et al., 2023). One important task in zero-shot NMT is to let the model translate into the correct language given so many target languages. Our motivation in UNMT is similar, while each

[1] https://github.com/yihongL1U/xlm_lang_dis

Proceedings of the 20th International Conference on Spoken Language Translation (IWSLT 2023), pages 491–502
July 13-14, 2023

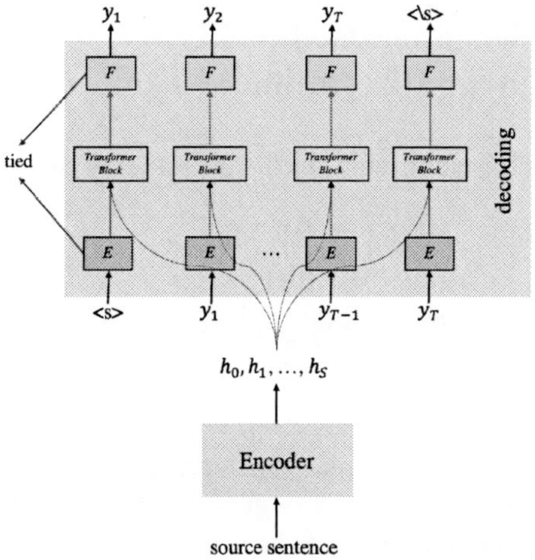

Figure 1: A view of the UNMT architecture. The weights of the final fully connected layer (block F) are tied with the weight of the embedding layer (block E).

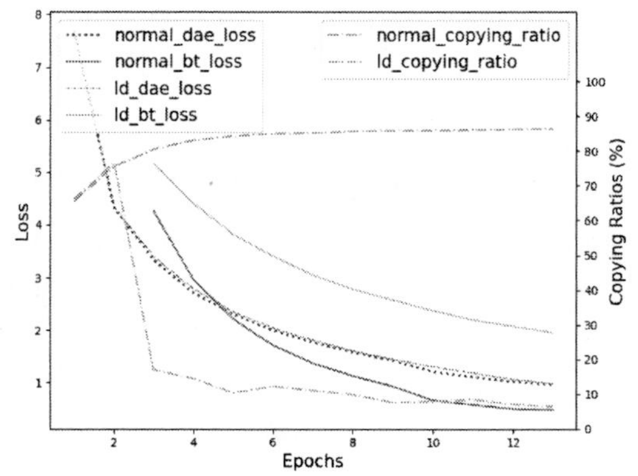

Figure 2: The losses (left ordinate) and copying ratios (right ordinate) of Multi30K English-French pair over epochs. The normal_dae_loss (resp. normal_bt_loss) and normal_copying_ratio are DAE loss (resp. BT loss) and copying ratio from the **vanilla** UNMT. The ld_dae_loss (resp. ld_bt_loss) and ld_copying_ratio are DAE loss (resp. BT loss) and the copying ratio from the UNMT incorporated with the **language discriminator**.

UNMT model often specifically deals with two languages, therefore only two translation directions are considered. Although adding language tags (Wu et al., 2021) is effective in addressing the copying problem in multilingual NMT, it is not a standard process in UNMT. This is because a language embedding is often added to each token embedding (Conneau and Lample, 2019; Song et al., 2019; Liu et al., 2022). Language embeddings have similar functions to language tags: providing information about the language of each token. Unfortunately, language embeddings turn out to be not very effective in addressing the copying problem, especially for low-resource or distant language pairs (Kim et al., 2020). Thus, in this work, we explore why the copying problem occurs and how we can alleviate it in UNMT. We analyze the problem from two perspectives:

Architecture perspective. In UNMT, the weight of the final fully connected layer (for obtaining the logits of each word in the vocabulary) is often tied to the weight of a cross-lingual embedding layer, as shown in Figure 1. That is, the representations of tokens from two languages are shared in the same space. Although this setting is arguably a better starting point for most modern NMT models, it unfortunately also allows the models to generate a token in an unexpected language at any time step. Furthermore, because of an autoregressive decoder, errors can easily accumulate, as the tokens initially generated by the model highly influence the generation of the subsequent tokens. In contrast to this setting, using separate word look-up tables or separate decoders for involved languages can address the problem (Lample et al., 2018; Liu et al., 2022). However, such a setting can be harmful for learning cross-lingual knowledge and largely increase the number of parameters. In this view, it is desired to keep the structure simple (no language-specific architecture) while preventing the model from decoding in a copying way.

Objective perspective. Typically, a UNMT model is trained by denoising autoencoding (DAE) (Vincent et al., 2008) and online back-translation (BT) (Sennrich et al., 2016) objectives. In DAE objective, even though the model is trained to denoise on two languages simultaneously, there is no guarantee that the model can transfer the cross-lingual information that might improve translation between the two languages. In fact, Song et al. (2019) empirically find that a pretrained encoder-decoder model with DAE objective can even perform worse than the model without it because DAE encourages the model to perform the copying. In comparison with DAE, BT is arguably more important, as it tries to directly optimize the translation. However, we find that BT can also "fail" during training. That is, the model can take the shortcut, i.e., copy the input sentence as the intermediate translation and then copy it again for the reconstruction. By taking such a shortcut, the loss of BT can quickly decrease while the copying ratio (Liu et al., 2021), a metric to measure the percentage of generated tokens that are copied from the input, keeps increasing and reaches a high-value plateau, as shown in Figure 2. This indicates that: because of no constraints on the intermediate translation, the model can always choose the easiest shortcut for BT, which finally corrupts the model's translation capability.

2.2 A Language Discriminator Loss

To avoid such an unexpected copying behavior in BT, our intuition suggests that forcing the intermediate generation to be in the correct language would be helpful. Instead of forcing all tokens, we could simply force the first token to be in the correct language, because the first generated token will influence the generation of all the subsequent tokens. Next, the problem is how to force the first generated token to be in the desired target language. An equivalent question would be: *how can we force the output vector of the decoder at the first time step to be closer to the embedding of a token in the target language?* The answer might be trivial. We could use a trained **language discriminator** (LD), which is a classifier, to classify the first-time-step output vectors of the decoder and then backpropagate the gradients to the main model (encoder and decoder). In this way, the model knows which intermediate language it should generate for the first-time-step token, therefore preventing the copying behavior.

For training LD, we could use the first-time-step outputs of the decoder in DAE steps. The LD is trained to predict the language of the first-time-step outputs by minimizing the cross entropy loss:

$$\mathcal{L}_{LD} = \mathbb{E}_{x \sim \mathcal{D}_l}[p(l|LD(\mathcal{O}_l)] \quad (1)$$

where LD is the language discriminator, $\mathcal{O}_l$ are the first-time-step outputs generated by $Dec(Enc(x, l), l)$ and l denotes the language (either *src* or *tgt*). Notably, $\mathcal{L}_{LD}$ only backpropagates to the language discriminator in the DAE step. In this way, the discriminator is able to distinguish representations from different languages.

In the BT process, the language discriminator is fixed and $\mathcal{L}_{LD}$ loss is only used to update the main model so it learns to differentiate representations from different languages. Taking *src-tgt-src* BT for example, the loss is as follows:

$$\mathcal{L}_{LD} = \mathbb{E}_{x \sim \mathcal{D}_{src}}[p(tgt|LD(\mathcal{O}_{tgt})] \quad (2)$$

where $\mathcal{O}_{tgt}$ are the first-time-step outputs generated in the *src*-to-*tgt* step, i.e., $Dec(Enc(x, src), tgt)$. The language discriminator does not have to be used for the next step in BT, i.e., *tgt*-to-*src* translation, because there are already ground-truth *src*-language sentences as supervision. All we need to do is to make sure the intermediate translation is in the correct language. We use a weight λ_{LD} to control the contribution of the LD loss to the final loss that is used to update the parameters of the main model. It is easy to note that the larger the weight, the model will be more focusing on the task of distinguishing representations from different languages.

This training schedule is similar to the adversarial loss (Goodfellow et al., 2014) used by Lample et al. (2018), where they trained a discriminator to make the **outputs of the encoder** language-agnostic, aiming to improve the cross-linguality of a shared encoder. Our aim, however, is different: we want to enable the **decoder** to generate distinguishable outputs which correctly correspond to the language that the model is expected to generate in the BT process. Algorithm 1 presents the training schedule in detail.

Algorithm 1: Training Schedule

Input: pretrained encoder Enc and decoder Dec, language discriminator LD, source and target monolingual data $\mathcal{D}_{src}$, $\mathcal{D}_{tgt}$, maximum finetuning steps T and coefficient λ_{LD} ;
Output: Finetuned encoder Enc and decoder Dec);

$t \leftarrow 0$;
while *not converged* or $t < T$ **do**
  // for *src* language do DAE and BT:
  $\mathcal{B}_{src} \leftarrow$ sample batch from $\mathcal{D}_{src}$;
  // DAE step (below)
  $\tilde{\mathcal{B}}_{src}, \mathcal{O}_{src} \leftarrow$ generate reconstructions and first-time-step outputs from $Dec(Enc(noise(\mathcal{B}_{src}), src), src)$;
  detach $\mathcal{O}_{src}$ from the compute graph ;
  $\boldsymbol{\theta}_{Enc}, \boldsymbol{\theta}_{Dec} \leftarrow \arg\min \mathcal{L}_{DAE}(\mathcal{B}_{src}, \tilde{\mathcal{B}}_{src})$;
  $\boldsymbol{\theta}_{LD} \leftarrow \arg\min \mathcal{L}_{LD}(\mathcal{O}_{src}, src)$;
  // BT step (below)
  freeze $\boldsymbol{\theta}_{LD}$;
  $\tilde{\mathcal{B}}_{tgt}, \mathcal{O}_{tgt} \leftarrow$ generate *tgt*-language translations and first-time-step outputs from $Dec(Enc(\mathcal{B}_{src}, src), tgt)$;
  $\tilde{\mathcal{B}}_{src} \leftarrow$ generate *src*-language back-translations from $Dec(Enc(\tilde{\mathcal{B}}_{tgt}, tgt), src)$;
  $\boldsymbol{\theta}_{Enc}, \boldsymbol{\theta}_{Dec} \leftarrow \arg\min \mathcal{L}_{BT}(\mathcal{B}_{src}, \tilde{\mathcal{B}}_{src}) + \lambda_{LD}\,\mathcal{L}_{LD}(\mathcal{O}_{tgt}, tgt)$;
  // for *tgt* language do the same as above
  $t \leftarrow t + 1$;
end
return Enc and Dec;

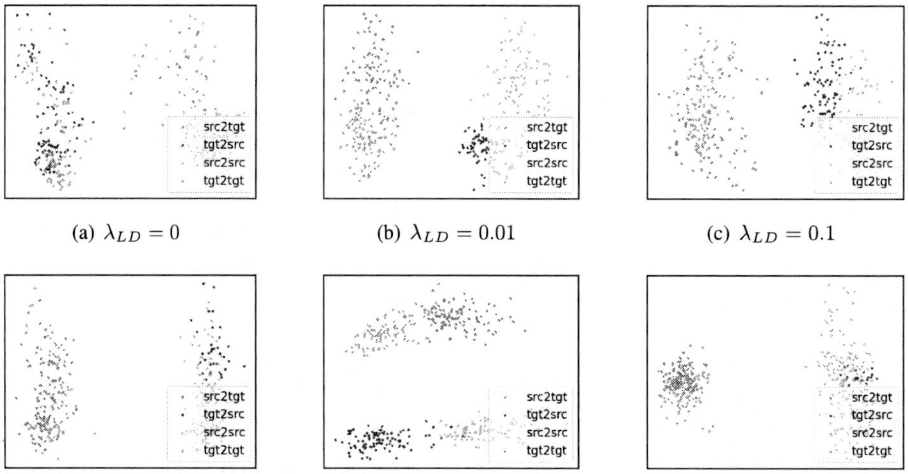

(a) $\lambda_{LD} = 0$ (b) $\lambda_{LD} = 0.01$ (c) $\lambda_{LD} = 0.1$

(d) $\lambda_{LD} = 1$ (e) $\lambda_{LD} = 10$ (f) $\lambda_{LD} = 100$

Figure 3: The visualizations of the first-time-step output vectors of the decoder in UNMT trained with different weights for the proposed language discriminator loss. The dimension of the outputs is originally 1024. Principal component analysis (PCA) is leveraged to project those outputs into a 2-dimensional subspace for convenience of visualization. src2src (resp. tgt2tgt) denotes the output in the English-to-English (resp. German-to-German) autoencoding task. src2tgt (resp. tgt2src) denotes the output in the English-to-German (resp. German-to-English) translation task. The sentences used for the visualizations are the same or the corresponding parallel translations.

3 Experiments

3.1 Setups

Multi30K (Elliott et al., 2016, 2017)[2]. The officially provided train, validation and test sets in English (**En**), German (**De**) and French (**Fr**) are used. Similar to Lample et al. (2018), we only use the caption of each image, and we split the train and validation sets into monolingual corpora by only using one-half of the data for a language.

WMT (Barrault et al., 2019). We select 50M sentences for high-resource languages: English (**En**), French (**Fr**), German (**De**), Russian (**Ru**) and Chinese (**Zh**) (14M available) and all available monolingual sentences for low-resource language: Gujarati (**Gu**) (3M), Kazakh (**Kk**) (4M). We report the results on *newtest2014* for En-Fr pair, *newtest2016* for En-De pair, *newtest2018* for En-Ru pair and *newtest2019* for the remaining language pairs.

Pretrained Models We use cross-lingual pretrained language model (*xlm-mlm-ende-1024* and *xlm-mlm-enfr-1024*) from HuggingFace[3] (Wolf et al., 2020) to initialize a shared encoder (parameters are fixed) in Multi30K experiments. In those experiments, we randomly initialize a shared decoder because Multi30k is so small that a randomly initialized decoder can work already very well based on our preliminary experiments. For WMT experiments, we pretrain our own cross-lingual language models using the code base of XLM[4] and use the pretrained models to initialize both the encoder and decoder for UNMT task.[5]

3.2 Analysis on Multi30K

To figure out how the LD loss could influence the performance, we use six different weights for it: 0, 0.01, 0.1, 1, 10 and 100. When the weight equals 0, the UNMT training will not consider the LD loss at all and this setting would then be exactly the same as the vanilla (i.e., DAE + BT) UNMT. The results are shown in Table 2. In addition to BLEU scores (Papineni et al., 2002), we also compute copying ratios (Liu et al., 2021) for each listed direction.

The general trend shows that: when $0 \leq \lambda_{LD} \leq 1$, the BLEU scores increase and the copying ratios decrease when increasing the weight, suggesting the copying problem is alleviated by introducing the LD loss. However, when $\lambda_{LD} > 1$, the BLEU

[2] `https://github.com/multi30k/dataset`

[3] `https://github.com/huggingface`

[4] `https://github.com/facebookresearch/XLM`

[5] Details of hyperparameters and relevant information of all the models are shown in Section A.2 in the Appendix.

Model	Source input	Model output	Reference output
$\lambda_{LD} = 0$	a man in an orange hat starring at something.	a man in an orange hat staring at something.	ein mann mit einem orangefarbenen hut, der etwas anstarrt.
$\lambda_{LD} = 0.01$		ein mann in an orange hat starring at something.	
$\lambda_{LD} = 0,1$		ein mann in an orange hat gerade etwas bei etwas.	
$\lambda_{LD} = 1$		ein mann in einem orangefarbenen hut spielt bei etwas.	
$\lambda_{LD} = 10$		ein mann in einem orangefarbenen hut spielt bei etwas.	
$\lambda_{LD} = 100$		eine frau in einem orangefarbenen hut spielt bei etwas.	
$\lambda_{LD} = 0$	a boston terrier is running on lush green grass in front of a white fence.	a boston dog is running on leafy grass in front of a white fence.	ein boston terrier läuft über saftig-grünes gras vor einem weißen zaun.
$\lambda_{LD} = 0.01$		ein boston terrier läuft auf einem gepflasterten grünen grass in front of a white fence.	
$\lambda_{LD} = 0.1$		ein boston terrier läuft auf einem grünen rasen vor einem weißen zaun.	
$\lambda_{LD} = 1$		ein boston terrier läuft auf einem grünen rasen vor einem weißen zaun.	
$\lambda_{LD} = 10$		ein boston terrier läuft auf einem grünen gras vor einem weißen zaun.	
$\lambda_{LD} = 100$		eine boston terrier läuft auf grünen gras vor einem weißen zaun.	

Table 1: Examples of translations from the model trained on Multi30K dataset (En-De pair) with different weights λ_{LD} for language discriminator loss. We do not use beam search to generate these translations.

Models	En→De	De→En	En→Fr	Fr→En
0	0.22 (87%)	0.19 (84%)	0.14 (89%)	0.10 (83%)
0.01	15.78 (42%)	22.04 (24%)	24.73 (24%)	22.15 (25%)
0.1	25.91 (14%)	28.46 (15%)	39.72 (6%)	37.50 (7%)
1	**27.96** (12%)	**30.05** (12%)	**42.74** (5%)	**39.02** (6%)
10	24.35 (14%)	25.60 (13%)	41.26 (5%)	37.61 (6%)
100	20.66 (12%)	26.74 (10%)	30.65 (5%)	32.10 (7%)

Table 2: BLEU scores and copying ratios (inside parentheses) of models trained with different weights λ_{LD} on Multi30K dataset. When the weight $\lambda_{LD} = 0$, the model degenerates to the vanilla UNMT model.

scores decrease while copying ratios remain at the same level with the increase of the weight. This indicates that the model is over-emphasizing distinguishing the outputs when the weights are large. Therefore, moderate weights, e.g., 1, might be optimal if we want to alleviate the copying problem while achieving good translation performance.

When $\lambda_{LD} = 0$, poor BLEU scores are obtained because of the copying problem. We see that all copying ratios in Table 2 are very high: more than 80% for all directions. Example translations from the translation model for En-De pair in Table 1 show that when $\lambda_{LD} = 0$, the MT system simply copies the input sentences. It is very clear that with the increase of the weight, it becomes less likely for the model to copy the words from the source input as the output translation. However, when the weight is too large, e.g., $\lambda_{LD} = 100$, there are obvious mistakes made by the translation model. For example, "man" in English is wrongly translated to "frau" (means woman) in German, "a" is wrongly translated into "eine" since boston terrier is a masculine instead of a feminine noun. Moderate weights, e.g., $\lambda_{LD} = 1$, achieves the best performance while obtaining fewer errors.

To figure out how the LD loss influences the representations, i.e., the first-time-step output vectors generated by the decoder, we visualize these vectors in 2D by using principal component analysis (PCA), as shown in Figure 3. The visualization verifies the relationship between the output and the occurrence of the copying problem. src2tgt and tgt2tgt first-time-step outputs should be close to each other in the subspace as they are both used to directly generate target-language sentences. However, in Fig. 3 (a), when $\lambda_{LD} = 0$, src2tgt and src2src are located together while tgt2src and tgt2tgt are together. In contrast, when LD loss is imposed, e.g., $\lambda_{LD} = 1$ (Fig. 3 (d)), the outputs are distributed as we expect: src2tgt and tgt2tgt are located together and tgt2src and src2src together.

Models	En → De	De → En	En → Fr	Fr → En	En → Ru	Ru → En	En → Zh	Zh → En
XLM baseline	**20.51**	**25.99**	**22.87**	25.88	**14.10**	**16.92**	6.36	4.28
XLM (+ LD)	20.40	25.85	21.22	**26.92**	13.49	16.12	**6.80**	**4.69**

Table 3: BLEU scores of the XLM baseline and the same model enhanced with the LD loss on high-resource language pairs. The scores of baseline are obtained by reproducing the published code (Conneau and Lample, 2019).

Models	En-De	En-Fr	En-Ru	En-Zh	En-Kk	En-Gu
baseline	18%	23%	11%	29%	57%	68%
(+ LD)	19%	25%	11%	24%	42%	52%
Δ	+1%	+2%	-0%	-5%	-15%	-14%

Table 4: The copying ratio for each language pair of XLM baselines and LD model. The average of the ratios of two directions for a language pair is reported. The translations used to compute the ratios are the same as translations for BLEU used in Table 3 and Table 5.

Models	En→Kk	Kk→En	En→Gu	Gu→En
XLM baseline (512)	0.80	**2.00**	0.60	0.60
XLM baseline (1024)	1.80	1.59	2.12	0.54
XLM (+ LD)	**2.03**	1.70	**3.55**	**0.64**

Table 5: BLEU scores of the XLM baseline and the same model enhanced with the LD loss on low-resource language pairs. The scores of baseline (512) are copied from (Kim et al., 2020). Same as the setting for high-resource languages, we reproduced XLM with 1024-dim embeddings to obtain the scores for baseline (1024).

3.3 Main Results on WMT

As the proposed LD is helpful to alleviate the copying problem in Multi30K experiments when the weight λ_{LD} is moderate, we further conduct experiments on WMT datasets, which are much larger than Multi30K. We use $\lambda_{LD} = 1$ as default.

High-resource language pairs. We report the results on Table 3 and average copying ratios for each language pair in Table 4. Firstly, we observe that there is a slight decrease in BLEU scores for En-De and En-Ru pair. Different from Table 2 where we see that the vanilla models suffer from the copying problem, the vanilla models in Table 3 perform fairly well on En-De and En-Ru. The copying ratios of each pair are also below 20%. We therefore speculate that **the size** and **complexity** of the training data can influence the effectiveness of the language discriminator, as it can easily distinguish the decoder outputs in Multi30K because the size is small and each sentence has a similar and simple structure. The copying problem does not severely impact the BLEU scores of these language pairs when training on WMT data, presumably because of the much larger dataset sizes. When the two languages are more distant, however, the copying problem can occur even if considerable training data is there: XLM baseline has a copying ratio of 29% on En-Zh pair. XLM (+LD) can improve results by 0.44 and 0.41 in En → Zh and Zh → En directions, and decrease the copying ratio by 5%, which indicates that the LD loss can improve the translation where the copying problem is obvious.

Low-resource language pairs. En-Kk and En-Gu represent two very distant pairs that include low-resource languages. We report the BLEU scores in Table 5 and average copying ratios in Table 4. From the results, we first see that the performance of all considered UNMT systems is rather poor. This is because they are all distant pairs and unsupervised training cannot learn enough cross-lingual information. We find the copying problem overwhelming, with 57% and 68% copying ratios on En-Kk and En-Gu pair respectively. By using the proposed LD loss, we see a consistent increase in BLEU scores and an evident decrease in average copying ratios (15% decrease on En-Kk and 14% on En-Gu pair respectively). This shows the incorporation of LD loss can significantly alleviate the copying problem. On the other hand, we attribute the weak translation quality to the already poor performance of the vanilla UNMT models, which cannot be largely improved simply by alleviating the copying problem. Decreasing copying ratios does not necessarily lead to a correct translation. Because of the unsupervised nature of the task, it can still be extremely hard for the model to learn enough cross-lingual information that is useful to perform good translation. Table 6 shows some examples, we notice that XLM (+ LD) generates sentences in the correct language, but the semantics of the output sentences is not that related to the original ones, indicating that lower copying ratios do not necessarily induce better translation quality.

Model	Source input	Model output	Reference output
XLM baseline	Негізі , менің қарсылығым жоқ .	Негізі , менің қарсылығым жоқ .	Actually , I have no objection .
XLM (+LD)		"Негізі , I have no idea .	
XLM baseline	Бұл сома алты еуроға тең .	The сома алты еуроға тең .	This amount equals to six euro .
XLM (+LD)		The price of six еуроға тең .	
XLM baseline	Олардың көпшілігі ауыл шаруашылығы саласында болып отыр .	Their көпшілігі family life has changed .	Most of them are in agricultural area .
XLM (+LD)		Their family members have been in the area for the past two years .	

Table 6: Examples of translations from Kazakh to English by XLM baseline (1024) and XLM (+LD) in Table 5. The examples show XLM (+LD) suffers fewer the copying problem but it can generate incorrect tokens that do not match the semantics of the input sentence.

Based on the high- and low-resource translation experiments, our insights are as follows: the UNMT models can (easily) learn a lot of cross-lingual information on similar and high-resource languages and thus the copying problem is less obvious. Under such a case, additionally using LD loss can divert the focus of the training. However, on distant pairs involving low-resource languages, models would struggle to learn enough cross-lingual information and therefore the copying problem is obvious. In such a case, although involving LD loss cannot provide additional cross-lingual knowledge, it can alleviate the copying problem thus improving the performance to a certain extent.

4 Discussion

From the Multi30K and WMT experiments, we verify the ability of the LD loss to alleviate the copying problem by showing consistently lower copying ratios. However, the performance in terms of BLEU scores on these two datasets shows slightly different trends: we improve translation quality on Multi30K a lot by reducing the copying ratios; whereas we do not see a prominent improvement on WMT even if copying ratios are largely reduced. This discrepancy can be explained as follows. Two main issues are preventing the model from achieving good performance: (1) lacking cross-lingual alignment information that is useful for learning translation (2) no clear guidance on which language to translate into. The experiments on the small dataset Multi30K indicate that issue (1) is not the major obstacle when two similar languages are considered, e.g., En and Fr. In such a case, it is the issue (2) that prevents the model from performing the actual translation. This is why large improvements are achieved by simply adding the LD loss when training a model on Multi30k (note that the language discriminator does not provide any additional cross-lingual information but only acts as an implicit supervision). In the case of distant language pairs including low-resource languages, e.g., En-Gu and En-Kk in our WMT experiments, both issues (1) and (2) prohibit the model from learning to translate accurately. Although the copying problem is alleviated, as shown in Table 6, this does not guarantee a correct or even good translation quality. We therefore expect future research could explore using a more powerful baseline model, e.g., including static cross-lingual embeddings to improve the cross-linguality (Chronopoulou et al., 2021), which might further improve the performance for distant language pairs including low-resource languages.

5 Conclusion

In this paper, we find that the copying problem in UNMT is closely related to the lack of constraints on the intermediate translation in the BT process. To address this issue, we propose an LD loss to give additional supervision to the first-time-step output vectors generated by the decoder in the BT process. We find that the method can alleviate the copying problem by correcting the wrong behavior in BT. In addition, through extensive experiments on different language pairs (including low-resource languages and distant pairs), we discover that the method can consistently improve the performance of distant language pairs.

6 Limitations and Risks

Our training schedule introduces a language discriminator loss to impose constraints on the intermediate translation in the back-translation period. The experimental results suggest that our method can alleviate the copying problem when the involved languages are distant language pairs or lack training data. However, for language pairs that are not distant, and especially high-resource languages, our model does not show improvement over the baseline. Due to time and resource limitations, we do not further explore whether the optimal weight for the language discriminator loss can have a connection with the size of the dataset and the involved language pairs. For example, for WMT En-De or En-Fr pairs, the languages are not distant language pairs and therefore we might obtain better results if the weights are slightly smaller. We believe that future research could explore this direction: to adapt the weight to different language pairs and the size of the training data. In addition, we do not conduct hyperparameter search for other hyperparameters, instead directly using suggested values.

In this work, we propose a novel training schedule that tries to address the copying problem, which is common among distant language pairs in UNMT. We experiment with high-resource languages English, German, French, Russian and Chinese, and low-resource languages including Gujarati and Kazakh. The training data we use is monolingual text extracted from online newspapers and released for the WMT series of shared tasks. As far as we know, all the monolingual corpora do not contain any metadata and therefore it would be unlikely that anyone can use the concerned data to attribute to specific individuals.

Acknowledgements

We would like to thank the anonymous reviewers. This work was funded by the European Research Council (grant #740516) and by the German Research Foundation (DFG, grant FR 2829/4-1).

References

Mikel Artetxe, Gorka Labaka, Eneko Agirre, and Kyunghyun Cho. 2018. Unsupervised neural machine translation. In *6th International Conference on Learning Representations, ICLR 2018, Vancouver, BC, Canada, April 30 - May 3, 2018, Conference Track Proceedings*.

Loïc Barrault, Ondřej Bojar, Marta R. Costa-jussà, Christian Federmann, Mark Fishel, Yvette Graham, Barry Haddow, Matthias Huck, Philipp Koehn, Shervin Malmasi, Christof Monz, Mathias Müller, Santanu Pal, Matt Post, and Marcos Zampieri. 2019. Findings of the 2019 conference on machine translation (WMT19). In *Proceedings of the Fourth Conference on Machine Translation (Volume 2: Shared Task Papers, Day 1)*, pages 1–61, Florence, Italy.

Liang Chen, Shuming Ma, Dongdong Zhang, Furu Wei, and Baobao Chang. 2023. On the off-target problem of zero-shot multilingual neural machine translation. *arXiv preprint arXiv:2305.10930*.

Alexandra Chronopoulou, Dario Stojanovski, and Alexander Fraser. 2021. Improving the lexical ability of pretrained language models for unsupervised neural machine translation. In *Proceedings of the 2021 Conference of the North American Chapter of the Association for Computational Linguistics: Human Language Technologies*, pages 173–180, Online.

Alexis Conneau and Guillaume Lample. 2019. Cross-lingual language model pretraining. In *Advances in Neural Information Processing Systems*, volume 32.

Jacob Devlin, Ming-Wei Chang, Kenton Lee, and Kristina Toutanova. 2019. BERT: Pre-training of deep bidirectional transformers for language understanding. In *Proceedings of the 2019 Conference of the North American Chapter of the Association for Computational Linguistics: Human Language Technologies, Volume 1 (Long and Short Papers)*, pages 4171–4186, Minneapolis, Minnesota.

Desmond Elliott, Stella Frank, Loïc Barrault, Fethi Bougares, and Lucia Specia. 2017. Findings of the second shared task on multimodal machine translation and multilingual image description. In *Proceedings of the Second Conference on Machine Translation*, pages 215–233, Copenhagen, Denmark.

Desmond Elliott, Stella Frank, Khalil Sima'an, and Lucia Specia. 2016. Multi30K: Multilingual English-German image descriptions. In *Proceedings of the 5th Workshop on Vision and Language*, pages 70–74, Berlin, Germany.

Ian Goodfellow, Jean Pouget-Abadie, Mehdi Mirza, Bing Xu, David Warde-Farley, Sherjil Ozair, Aaron Courville, and Yoshua Bengio. 2014. Generative adversarial nets. In *Advances in Neural Information Processing Systems*.

Jiatao Gu, Yong Wang, Kyunghyun Cho, and Victor O.K. Li. 2019. Improved zero-shot neural machine translation via ignoring spurious correlations. In *Proceedings of the 57th Annual Meeting of the Association for Computational Linguistics*, pages 1258–1268, Florence, Italy.

Francisco Guzmán, Peng-Jen Chen, Myle Ott, Juan Pino, Guillaume Lample, Philipp Koehn, Vishrav Chaudhary, and Marc'Aurelio Ranzato. 2019. The FLORES evaluation datasets for low-resource machine translation: Nepali–English and Sinhala–English. In *Proceedings of the 2019 Conference on Empirical Methods in Natural Language Processing and the 9th International Joint Conference on Natural Language Processing (EMNLP-IJCNLP)*, pages 6098–6111, Hong Kong, China.

Yunsu Kim, Miguel Graça, and Hermann Ney. 2020. When and why is unsupervised neural machine translation useless? In *Proceedings of the 22nd Annual Conference of the European Association for Machine Translation*, pages 35–44, Lisboa, Portugal.

Diederik P. Kingma and Jimmy Ba. 2015. Adam: A method for stochastic optimization. In *3rd International Conference on Learning Representations,*

ICLR 2015, San Diego, CA, USA, May 7-9, 2015, Conference Track Proceedings.

Philipp Koehn. 2004. Statistical significance tests for machine translation evaluation. In *Proceedings of the 2004 Conference on Empirical Methods in Natural Language Processing*, pages 388–395, Barcelona, Spain.

Guillaume Lample, Alexis Conneau, Ludovic Denoyer, and Marc'Aurelio Ranzato. 2018. Unsupervised machine translation using monolingual corpora only. In *6th International Conference on Learning Representations, ICLR 2018, Vancouver, BC, Canada, April 30 - May 3, 2018, Conference Track Proceedings*.

Xuebo Liu, Longyue Wang, Derek F. Wong, Liang Ding, Lidia S. Chao, Shuming Shi, and Zhaopeng Tu. 2021. On the copying behaviors of pre-training for neural machine translation. In *Findings of the Association for Computational Linguistics: ACL-IJCNLP 2021*, pages 4265–4275, Online.

Yihong Liu, Haris Jabbar, and Hinrich Schuetze. 2022. Flow-adapter architecture for unsupervised machine translation. In *Proceedings of the 60th Annual Meeting of the Association for Computational Linguistics (Volume 1: Long Papers)*, pages 1253–1266, Dublin, Ireland.

Yinhan Liu, Jiatao Gu, Naman Goyal, Xian Li, Sergey Edunov, Marjan Ghazvininejad, Mike Lewis, and Luke Zettlemoyer. 2020. Multilingual denoising pre-training for neural machine translation. *Transactions of the Association for Computational Linguistics*, 8:726–742.

Kelly Marchisio, Kevin Duh, and Philipp Koehn. 2020. When does unsupervised machine translation work? In *Proceedings of the Fifth Conference on Machine Translation*, pages 571–583, Online.

Graham Neubig and Junjie Hu. 2018. Rapid adaptation of neural machine translation to new languages. In *Proceedings of the 2018 Conference on Empirical Methods in Natural Language Processing*, pages 875–880, Brussels, Belgium.

Kishore Papineni, Salim Roukos, Todd Ward, and Wei-Jing Zhu. 2002. Bleu: a method for automatic evaluation of machine translation. In *Proceedings of the 40th Annual Meeting of the Association for Computational Linguistics*, pages 311–318, Philadelphia, Pennsylvania, USA.

Matthew E. Peters, Mark Neumann, Mohit Iyyer, Matt Gardner, Christopher Clark, Kenton Lee, and Luke Zettlemoyer. 2018. Deep contextualized word representations. In *Proceedings of the 2018 Conference of the North American Chapter of the Association for Computational Linguistics: Human Language Technologies, Volume 1 (Long Papers)*, pages 2227–2237, New Orleans, Louisiana.

Maja Popović. 2015. chrF: character n-gram F-score for automatic MT evaluation. In *Proceedings of the Tenth Workshop on Statistical Machine Translation*, pages 392–395, Lisbon, Portugal.

Ricardo Rei, Craig Stewart, Ana C Farinha, and Alon Lavie. 2020. COMET: A neural framework for MT evaluation. In *Proceedings of the 2020 Conference on Empirical Methods in Natural Language Processing (EMNLP)*, pages 2685–2702, Online.

Rico Sennrich, Barry Haddow, and Alexandra Birch. 2016. Improving neural machine translation models with monolingual data. In *Proceedings of the 54th Annual Meeting of the Association for Computational Linguistics (Volume 1: Long Papers)*, pages 86–96, Berlin, Germany.

Kaitao Song, Xu Tan, Tao Qin, Jianfeng Lu, and Tie-Yan Liu. 2019. MASS: masked sequence to sequence pre-training for language generation. In *Proceedings of the 36th International Conference on Machine Learning, ICML 2019, 9-15 June 2019, Long Beach, California, USA*, volume 97, pages 5926–5936.

Pascal Vincent, Hugo Larochelle, Yoshua Bengio, and Pierre-Antoine Manzagol. 2008. Extracting and composing robust features with denoising autoencoders. In *Proceedings of the 25th international conference on Machine learning*, pages 1096–1103.

Thomas Wolf, Lysandre Debut, Victor Sanh, Julien Chaumond, Clement Delangue, Anthony Moi, Pierric Cistac, Tim Rault, Remi Louf, Morgan Funtowicz, Joe Davison, Sam Shleifer, Patrick von Platen, Clara Ma, Yacine Jernite, Julien Plu, Canwen Xu, Teven Le Scao, Sylvain Gugger, Mariama Drame, Quentin Lhoest, and Alexander Rush. 2020. Transformers: State-of-the-art natural language processing. In *Proceedings of the 2020 Conference on Empirical Methods in Natural Language Processing: System Demonstrations*, pages 38–45, Online.

Liwei Wu, Shanbo Cheng, Mingxuan Wang, and Lei Li. 2021. Language tags matter for zero-shot neural machine translation. In *Findings of the Association for Computational Linguistics: ACL-IJCNLP 2021*, pages 3001–3007, Online.

Yilin Yang, Akiko Eriguchi, Alexandre Muzio, Prasad Tadepalli, Stefan Lee, and Hany Hassan. 2021. Improving multilingual translation by representation and gradient regularization. In *Proceedings of the 2021 Conference on Empirical Methods in Natural Language Processing*, pages 7266–7279, Online and Punta Cana, Dominican Republic.

Zhen Yang, Bojie Hu, Ambyera Han, Shen Huang, and Qi Ju. 2020. CSP:code-switching pre-training for neural machine translation. In *Proceedings of the 2020 Conference on Empirical Methods in Natural Language Processing (EMNLP)*, pages 2624–2636, Online.

Biao Zhang, Philip Williams, Ivan Titov, and Rico Sennrich. 2020. Improving massively multilingual neural machine translation and zero-shot translation. In *Proceedings of the 58th Annual Meeting of the Association for Computational Linguistics*, pages 1628–1639, Online.

A Appendix

A.1 Scores of Other Metrics

In addition to BLEU scores, we also compute other scores in other metrics, such as CHRF (Popović, 2015) in Table 9 and Table 7, COMET (Rei et al., 2020) in Table 10 and Table 8, and confidence interval of BLEU scores (Koehn, 2004) in Table 11, Table 12 and Table 13. The translations used for computing the scores are the same as the translations used to compute the BLEU scores in Table 3 and Table 5.

To quantify the copying problem, we use the copying ratio proposed by Liu et al. (2021), which is defined as follows:

$$\text{Ratio} = \frac{\sum_{i=1}^{I} \text{count(copying tokens)}}{\sum_{i=1}^{I} \text{count(tokens)}} \quad (3)$$

where I denotes the number of the total sentences in the test set, copying tokens are those tokens in the translation which are directly copied from the source language and the denominator is the total number of tokens in the generated translations. This metric will directly reflect the degree of the copying behavior of the translation model. The higher the copying ratio, the model tends to perform more copying instead translation. We report the average of the copying ratios of the two translation directions for each language pair in Table 4. We could see that the copying problem of the XLM baseline models is very obvious in low-resource language pairs, i.e., En-Kk and En-Gu. When the language discriminator loss is introduced, the copying ratios decrease by more than 10%. We also notice that XLM (+LD) has a less obvious copying problem than the baseline in En-Zh pair, a distant language pair. For other language pairs, the copying problem is not that severe and therefore introducing the language discriminator loss does not much change the ratios.

A.2 Model Details

In Section 3.2, we use the pretrained XLM models from HuggingFace[6] (Wolf et al., 2020) (*xlm-mlm-enfr-1024*, *xlm-mlm-ende-1024*) to initialize a shared encoder and randomly initialize a shared decoder. A single embedding layer (containing the words/subwords of both the source and target languages) from the pretrained encoder is used. The weight of the final fully connected layer is tied with the embedding layer. The parameters of the encoder are fixed except for this embedding layer which is also used by the decoder. The embedding size is 1024 and the hidden size of the decoder is 512. The decoder has 8 heads and 3 layers. We follow the denoising autoencoding hyperparameter settings used by Lample et al. (2018) and the training schedule of Liu et al. (2022), i.e., firstly fine-tuning the models with only DAE loss and LD loss for the language discriminator for the first 2 epochs, then fine-tuning the models with all losses (including the BT) for the rest of the epochs. We set the batch size to 32 and use Adam optimizer (Kingma and Ba, 2015) with an initial learning rate of 0.0001. We stop the training when the model does not improve the BLEU scores on the validation set for 5 epochs. We do not use beam search to generate translations for Multi30K.

In Section 3.3, we pretrain all our own cross-lingual language models of each language pair based on XLM code base[7] (Conneau and Lample, 2019). Then the encoder and decoder are both initialized with the same cross-lingual pretrained model. The recommended hyperparameters for the model architecture are used, i.e., 1024 for the embedding size, 4096 for the hidden size, 8 heads and 6 layers for the transformer blocks. We follow the recommended pretraining as well as UNMT fine-tuning hyperparameters from XLM. We only change the hyperparameter *tokens_per_batch* to 250 to adapt to small- or moderate memory GPUs. We generate the translations by using beam search of size 5. These translations are used to compute the scores in all the WMT-related experiments.

For the language discriminator, we simply use a feed-forward neural network (FFNN). The language discriminator has two hidden layers and each layer has the same dimension as the embedding, i.e., 1024, for both Multi30K and WMT-related experiments. The output dimension is two which corresponds to the number of language domains we want to classify into, as we have two languages involved in the training for each model.

[6]https://github.com/huggingface

[7]https://github.com/facebookresearch/XLM

Models	En→Kk	Kk→En	En→Gu	Gu→En
XLM baseline	8.85	7.61	7.95	4.76
XLM (+ LD)	**11.78**	**10.09**	**11.71**	**7.12**

Table 7: CHRF scores (Popović, 2015) of the XLM UNMT baseline as well as the XLM model with the language discriminator on low-resource language pairs (the translations used are the same as used in Table 5 for BLEU scores).

Models	En→Kk	Kk→En	En→Gu	Gu→En
XLM baseline	-1.41	-1.10	-1.40	-1.90
XLM (+ LD)	**-1.14**	**-1.04**	**-0.91**	**-1.68**

Table 8: COMET scores (Rei et al., 2020) of the XLM UNMT baseline as well as the XLM model with the language discriminator on low-resource language pairs (the translations used are the same as used in Table 5 for BLEU scores). We use *wmt20-comet-da* model to evaluate the translations.

Models	En→De	De→En	En→Fr	Fr→En	En→Ru	Ru→En	En→Zh	Zh→En
XLM baseline	**45.09**	**48.20**	**44.99**	49.93	**34.75**	**38.56**	16.11	19.08
XLM (+ LD)	44.42	**48.20**	42.94	**50.50**	34.39	36.56	**16.74**	**20.45**

Table 9: CHRF scores (Popović, 2015) of the XLM UNMT baseline as well as the XLM model with the language discriminator on high-resource language pairs (the translations used are the same as used in Table 3 for BLEU scores).

Models	En→De	De→En	En→Fr	Fr→En	En→Ru	Ru→En	En→Zh	Zh→En
XLM baseline	**-0.19**	**-0.22**	**-0.04**	0.19	**-0.34**	**-0.22**	-0.43	**-0.78**
XLM (+ LD)	-0.22	-0.23	**-0.04**	**0.21**	-0.37	-0.33	**-0.36**	-0.81

Table 10: COMET scores (Rei et al., 2020) of the XLM UNMT baseline as well as the XLM model with the language discriminator on high-resource language pairs (the translations used are the same as used in Table 3 for BLEU scores). We use *wmt20-comet-da* model to evaluate the translations.

Models	En→De	De→En	En→Fr	Fr→En
XLM baseline	20.53±0.59	25.96±0.66	**22.85±0.72**	**25.89±0.57**
XLM (+ LD)	20.42±0.61	25.84±0.63	**21.18±0.76**	**26.92±0.59**

Table 11: 95% confidence interval for the BLEU scores of the XLM UNMT baseline as well as the XLM model with the language discriminator on En-De and En-Fr pair (the translations used are the same as used in Table 3 for BLEU scores). Differences between bold results are statistically significant under $p = 0.05$. For the statistical test, we use paired bootstrap resampling (Koehn, 2004).

Models	En→Ru	Ru→En	En→Zh	Zh→En
XLM baseline	**14.08±0.48**	**16.93±0.51**	**6.34±0.34**	**4.28±0.28**
XLM (+ LD)	**13.48±0.45**	**16.11±0.51**	**6.80±0.37**	**4.69±0.31**

Table 12: 95% confidence interval for the BLEU scores of the XLM UNMT baseline as well as the XLM model with the language discriminator on En-Ru and En-Zh pair (the translations used are the same as used in Table 3 for BLEU scores). Differences between bold results are statistically significant under $p = 0.05$. For the statistical test, we use paired bootstrap resampling (Koehn, 2004).

Models	En→Kk	Kk→En	En→Gu	Gu→En
XLM baseline	1.80±0.37	1.58±0.48	**2.13±0.31**	0.54±0.17
XLM (+ LD)	2.04±0.45	1.69±0.49	**3.56±0.41**	0.64±0.20

Table 13: 95% confidence interval for the BLEU scores of the XLM UNMT baseline as well as the XLM model with the language discriminator on En-Kk and En-Gu pair (the translations used are the same as used in Table 3 for BLEU scores). Differences between bold results are statistically significant under $p = 0.05$. For the statistical test, we use paired bootstrap resampling (Koehn, 2004).

Author Index

Association for Computational Linguistics
209 N. Eighth Street
Stroudsburg, Pennsylvania 18360

ISBN 978-1-7138-8227-5

CURRAN ASSOCIATES INC.
proceedings.com